IMPORTANT:

HERE IS YOUR REGISTRATION CODE TO ACCESS
YOUR PREMIUM McGRAW-HILL ONLINE RESOURCES.

For key premium online resources you need THIS CODE to gain access. Once the code is entered, you will be able to use the Web resources for the length of your course.

If your course is using **WebCT** or **Blackboard**, you'll be able to use this code to access the McGraw-Hill content within your instructor's online course.

Access is provided if you have purchased a new book. If the registration code is missing from this book, the registration screen on our Website, and within your WebCT or Blackboard course, will tell you how to obtain your new code.

Registering for McGraw-Hill Online Resources

TO gain access to your McGraw-Hill web resources simply follow the steps below:

1. USE YOUR WEB BROWSER TO GO TO: **www.mhhe.com/santrockldt2**
2. CLICK ON **FIRST TIME USER**.
3. ENTER THE REGISTRATION CODE* PRINTED ON THE TEAR-OFF BOOKMARK ON THE RIGHT.
4. AFTER YOU HAVE ENTERED YOUR REGISTRATION CODE, CLICK **REGISTER**.
5. FOLLOW THE INSTRUCTIONS TO SET-UP YOUR PERSONAL UserID AND PASSWORD.
6. WRITE YOUR UserID AND PASSWORD DOWN FOR FUTURE REFERENCE. KEEP IT IN A SAFE PLACE.

TO GAIN ACCESS to the McGraw-Hill content in your instructor's **WebCT** or **Blackboard** course simply log in to the course with the UserID and Password provided by your instructor. Enter the registration code exactly as it appears in the box to the right when prompted by the system. You will only need to use the code the first time you click on McGraw-Hill content.

Thank you, and welcome to your McGraw-Hill online Resources!

* YOUR REGISTRATION CODE CAN BE USED ONLY ONCE TO ESTABLISH ACCESS. IT IS NOT TRANSFERABLE.

0-07-297652-7 T/A SANTROCK: A TOPICAL APPROACH TO LIFE-SPAN DEVELOPMENT, 2/E

REGISTRATION CODE

AS18-47ZP-G6DF-D0C4-OAH8

A Topical Approach to Life-Span Development

SECOND EDITION

John W. Santrock
University of Texas at Dallas

Boston   Burr Ridge, IL   Dubuque, IA   Madison, WI   New York   San Francisco   St. Louis
Bangkok   Bogotá   Caracas   Kuala Lumpur   Lisbon   London   Madrid   Mexico City
Milan   Montreal   New Delhi   Santiago   Seoul   Singapore   Sydney   Taipei   Toronto

Higher Education

A TOPICAL APPROACH TO LIFE-SPAN DEVELOPMENT
Published by McGraw-Hill, a business unit of The McGraw-Hill Companies, Inc., 1221 Avenue of
the Americas, New York, NY, 10020. Copyright 2005, 2002 by The McGraw-Hill Companies, Inc.
All rights reserved. No part of this publication may be reproduced or distributed
in any form or by any means, or stored in a database or retrieval system, without the prior
written consent of The McGraw-Hill Companies, Inc., including, but not limited to, in any network
or other electronic storage or transmission, or broadcast for distance learning.

Some ancillaries, including electronic and print components, may not be available to customers
outside the United States.

This book is printed on acid-free paper.

1 2 3 4 5 6 7 8 9 0 VNH/VNH 0 9 8 7 6 5 4

ISBN   0 07 288016 3

Publisher: *Stephen D. Rutter*
Executive editor: *Michael J. Sugarman*
Director of development and new media: *Judith Kromm*
Developmental editor I: *Mary Kate Ellenton*
Marketing manager: *Melissa S. Caughlin*
Media technology producer: *Ginger Bunn*
Senior project manager: *Jean Hamilton*
Senior production supervisor: *Carol A. Bielski*
Senior designer: *Gino Cieslik*
Associate media project manager: *Meghan Durko*
Photo research coordinator: *Alexandra Ambrose*
Art Manager: *Robin K. Mouat*
Photo researcher: *Alexandra Ambrose*
Art director: *Robin Mouat*
Permissions editor: *Marty Granahan*
Cover design: *© Corbis 2004*
Typeface: *9.5/12 Meridien*
Compositor: *GTS-Los Angeles, CA Campus*
Printer: *Von Hoffmann Corporation*

Library of Congress Control Number: 2004 101158

www.mhhe.com

With special appreciation to my wife
Mary Jo

About the Author

John W. Santrock

John Santrock received his Ph.D. from the University of Minnesota in 1973. He taught at the University of Charleston and the University of Georgia before joining the Program in Psychology and Human Development at the University of Texas at Dallas, where he currently teaches a number of undergraduate courses. In 1982, John created the life-span development course at UT-Dallas and has taught it every year since then.

John has been a member of the editorial boards of *Child Development* and *Development Psychology*. His research on father custody is widely cited and used in expert witness testimony to promote flexibility and alternative considerations in custody disputes. John also has authored these exceptional McGraw-Hill texts: *Psychology* (7th edition), *Child Development* (10th edition), *Children* (7th edition), *Adolescence* (10th edition), *Life-Span Development,* (9th edition), and *Educational Psychology* (2nd edition).

For many years, John was involved in tennis as a player, teaching professional, and coach of professional tennis players. He has been married for more than 35 years to his wife, Mary Jo, who is a Realtor. He has two daughters—Tracy, who is a technology specialist at Nortel in Raleigh, North Carolina, and Jennifer, who is a medical sales specialist for Medtronic in San Antonio. He has one granddaughter, Jordan, age 12. Tracy recently completed the Boston Marathon, and Jennifer was in the top 100 ranked players on the Women's Professional Tennis Tour. In the last decade, John also has spent time painting expressionist art.

Brief Contents

Contents

Preface

It is gratifying that the first edition of *A Topical Approach to Life-Span Development* was so well received. This is reflected in the positive comments of instructors who have adopted the book, reviewers, and students who have used the book.

Most textbooks on life-span development are chronologically organized. Why present life-span development topically? In a topical approach, students can see the processes involved in a particular aspect of development in a single chapter and often in a particular part of a chapter. In contrast, in a chronologically organized textbook, a topic such as the development of the brain appears in a number of chapters—typically early in the book in an infancy chapter, later in a childhood chapter, and then again toward the end of the book in a aging chapter. Examining life-span development topically allows developmental changes through the life span to be described in close proximity to one another, which let students make better connections between them.

A Topical Approach to Life-Span Development, second edition, is not just an age-stage chronological-within-a-topical-organization text. Where key chronological, sequential changes take place, they are emphasized. The focus, though, is mainly on the processes of development, how these processes function, and how they change developmentally throughout the life span.

In the first edition of the book, three main themes were emphasized: research, applications, and contexts. I believe it is important for students to have a firm grasp of the research foundation of the field. I also think that students benefit from knowing how information can be applied to people's lives. Further, I believe students benefit from learning about contextual variations in life-span development, especially those that involve culture, ethnicity, and gender. These themes are woven throughout the book and each chapter has three interludes that focus on an aspect of research, applications, and contexts related to a chapter topic. These three themes—research, applications, and contexts—continue as important themes in the second edition of *A Topical Approach to Life-Span Development.*

What is new in the second edition of the book? The revision focuses on these main areas that reviewers and adopters told me to emphasize more:

- Research and content
- Applications and contexts
- Accessibility and interest

First, I will describe the thrust of these changes in general terms and then provide a list of detailed chapter-by-chapter changes.

RESEARCH AND CONTENT

Above all, a topical life-span development text must have a solid research foundation. This new edition has a more extensive research orientation than the first edition and includes the latest, most contemporary research.

Research Citations

A Topical Approach to Life-Span Development, second edition, has more than 1,200 citations from 2000–2004, making it truly a twenty-first century rendition of the field of life-span development.

Research Presentation, Depth, and Figures

Reviewers recommended that I include more depth in research descriptions and more graphs of data to show how researchers visually present their data. I took this recommendation to heart. A number of research studies are described in greater depth to show students how research is conducted. The second edition has more than 60 new research figures, many of which illustrate the results of research studies. Special care was taken to make sure these illustrations were clearly designed so that students can interpret and understand them. An example of the increased emphasis on depth of research description and visual presentation of data is Alan Slater's research on habituation and dishabituation in chapter 7, "Information Processing." Another example is the research of Carol Ryff on age and well-being in chapter 11, "The Self, Identity, and Personality."

Content

Many new content areas have been added and many others updated and expanded. Among the content improvements are new material on evolutionary developmental psychology (Bjorklund & Pellegrini, 2002) (chapter 2), the collaborative gene (Gottlieb, 2002) (chapter 2), brain lateralization in older adults (chapter 3), developmental changes in attention (chapter 7), emotions in adolescence (Rosenblum & Lewis, 2003) (chapter 10), personal control (Heckhausen, 2002) (chapter 11), meaning in life (Baumeister & Voh, 2002) (chapter 13), stepfamilies (Hetherington & Stanley-Hagan, 2002) (chapter 14), gender and peer relations (Maccoby, 2002) (chapter 15), and work during adolescence (chapter 16).

Research in Life-Span Development Interludes

A Research in Life-Span Development interlude appears in each chapter. The research interludes provide an in-depth look at research on a topic related to the chapter's content. Among the new, revised, and updated Research in Life-Span Development interludes are Studying the Newborn's Perception (chapter 5), Object Permanence and Causality (chapter 6), and Family Environment and Young Children's Language Development (chapter 9).

Expert Research Consultants

Life-span development has become an enormous, complex field and no single author, or even several authors, can possibly be an expert in many different areas of life-span development. To solve this problem, I have sought the input of leading experts in many different research areas of life-span development. The experts provided me with detailed evaluations and recommendations for a chapter(s) in their area(s) of expertise. The expert research consultants for *A Topical Approach to Life-Span Development, second edition* are:

Pamela Balls Organista
University of San Francisco
Ethnicity and culture throughout the text

Gilbert Gottlieb
*University of North Carolina–
Chapel Hill*
Chapter 2: Biological Beginnings

Linda Mayes
Yale University
Chapter 2: Biological Beginnings

James Birren
UCLA
Chapter 3: Physical Development and Biological Aging and
Chapter 4: Health

Rachel Keen
University of Massachusetts
Chapter 5: Motor, Sensory, and Perceptual Development

Jonathan Tudge
University of North Carolina at Greensboro
Chapter 6: Cognitive Developmental Approaches

William Hoyer
Syracuse University
Chapter 7: Information Processing; and Chapter 8: Intelligence

Elena Grigorenko
Yale University
Chapter 8: Intelligence

Jay Belsky
University of London
Chapter 10: Emotional Development; and Chapter 14:
Families, Lifestyles, and Parenting

Daniel Mroczek
Fordham University
Chapter 10: Emotional Development

James Marcia
Simon Fraser University
Chapter 11: The Self, Identity, and Personality

Janet Shibley Hyde
University of Wisconsin
Chapter 12: Gender and Sexuality

James Garbarino
Boston College
Chapter 13: Moral Development, Values, and Religion

Linda George
Duke University
Chapter 15: Peers and the Sociocultural World

Allan Wigfield
University of Maryland
Chapter 16: Schools, Achievement, and Work

Robert Kastenbaum
Arizona State University
Chapter 17: Death and Grieving

The photographs and biographies of the expert consultants appear later in the Preface.

APPLICATIONS AND CONTEXTS

It is not only important to present the scientific foundations of life-span development to students, but also to describe real-world applications and the contexts of development.

Applications

There is increasing interest in the real-world applications of research and these are highlighted in this text. Every effort has been made to give applied examples of concepts and to give students a sense that the field of life-span development has personal meaning for them. Applications are woven throughout each of the book's chapters and also are emphasized in an Applications in Life-Span Development interlude that appears once in each chapter. The new material on applications includes research related to family policy (Gennetian & Miller, 2003) (chapter 1), groundbreaking research on the reduction of preterm births by administering progesterone to pregnant women (Meis, 2003) (chapter 2), physical fitness and mortality (chapter 4), training the attention and memory of older adults (chapter 6), intervention in improving children's intelligence (Brooks-Gunn, 2003) (chapter 7), latest results from the National Institute of Child Health and Development's longitudinal study of child care (NICHD, 2002, 2003) (chapter 10), Vaillant's (2002) longitudinal study which identifies the factors in the fifties that are linked with health, happiness, and mortality in the seventies (chapter 11), acquaintance rape (chapter 12), Fast Track intervention for preventing conduct problems (The Conduct Problems Prevention Research Group, 2002) (chapter 13), punishment and discipline (Gershoff, 2002) (chapter 14), bullying (chapter 15), and high school dropouts (chapter 16).

In addition to giving special attention to applications throughout the text, a Careers in Life-Span Development appendix appears at the end of the book. It describes a number of careers in education/research, clinical/counseling, medical/nursing/physical, and families/relationship categories. Numerous Web links provide students with opportunities to read about these careers in greater depth.

Contexts

Contextual variations in development are discussed throughout the text and in the Contexts of Life-Span Development interludes, which especially highlight cultural and ethnic aspects of development. The new material on contexts includes a new Contexts in Life-Span Development interlude, Living Longer in Okinawa (Wilcox, Wilcox, & Suzuki, 2002) (chapter 3), cross-cultural comparisons of intelligence (Grigorenko & others, 2001) (chapter 8), stereotype threat (Aronson, Fried, & Good, 2002) (chapter 8), a new Contexts in Life-Span Development interlude, Bilingual Education (chapter 9), gender, culture, and temperament (chapter 10), generation status and identity development in immigrants (Phinney, 2003) (chapter 11), ethnic variation in timing of sexual behaviors in U.S. adolescents (chapter 12), cross-cultural comparisons of punishment (chapter 14), socioeconomic status and parenting (Hoff, Laursen, & Tardiff, 2002) (chapter 15), acculturation and ethnic minority parenting (Coll & Pachter, 2002) (chapter 15), home environments of families from different ethnic groups (Bradley & others, 2001) (chapter 15), and cross-cultural comparisons of work in adolescence (chapter 16).

IMPROVED ACCESSIBILITY AND INTEREST

This new edition of this text should be more accessible to students because of the extensive rewriting, better organization, and improved learning system.

Writing and Organization

Every sentence, paragraph, section, and chapter of this book was carefully examined and when appropriate revised and rewritten. The result is a much clearer, better organized presentation of material in this new edition. Many new introductions to sections were written, numerous sections were moved, and a number of new examples of concepts were introduced—all in the interest of providing students with a more understandable, integrated book.

The Learning System

I strongly believe that students should not only be challenged to study hard and think more deeply and productively about life-span development, but should also be provided with an effective learning system. Instructors and students commented about how student-friendly the first edition was. However, I strive to keep making the learning system better and I am excited about the substantial improvements for this new edition.

Now more than ever, students struggle to find the main ideas in their courses, especially in courses like life-span development, which include so much material. The new learning system centers on learning goals that, together with the main text headings, keep the key ideas in front of the reader from the beginning to the end of the chapter. Each chapter has no more than six main headings and corresponding learning goals, which are presented side-by-side in the chapter-opening spread. At the end of each main section of a chapter, the learning goal is repeated in a feature called "Review and Reflect," which prompts students to review the key topics in the section and poses a question to encourage them to think critically about what they have read. At the end of the chapter, under the heading, "Reach Your Learning Goals," the learning goals guide students through the bulleted chapter review.

In addition to the verbal tools just described, maps that link up with the learning goals are presented at the beginning of each major section in the chapter. At the end of each chapter, the section maps are assembled into a complete map of the chapter that provides a visual review guide. The complete learning system, including many additional features not mentioned here, is presented later in the Preface in a section titled To the Student.

CHAPTER-BY-CHAPTER CHANGES

Numerous changes were made in each of the 17 chapters in *A Topical Approach to Life-Span Development, second edition.*

CHAPTER 1
Introduction

Extensively revised and improved discussion of issues in development (nature/nurture, stability/change, and continuity/discontinuity)
New research data presented in figure 1.5 on age and happiness
Revised, easier-to-understand presentation of Vygotsky's theory
Updated, revised Applications in Life-Span Development interlude, Family Policy, including recent research (Gennetian & Miller, 2003)
Revised, expanded Contexts in Life-Span Development interlude on individual, family, and extrafamilial contexts, including recent research on ethnicity, socioeconomic status, and families (Bradley & others, 2001)

Reorganization of main section on research into four parts: Methods for Collecting Data; Research Designs; Time Span of Research; and Ethics

New Research Designs section that focuses on descriptive, correlational, and experimental research

New discussion of naturalistic observational research study on parents' explanations of science to sons and daughters at a science museum, including new figure 1.14 that illustrates results of the study (Crowley & others, 2001)

New discussion of Erikson's case study analysis of Mahatma Ghandi's life

Expanded discussion of ethics in research

CHAPTER 2
Biological Beginnings

New section on evolutionary developmental psychology (Bjorklund & Pellegrini, 2002)

New section on genetic imprinting

Updated, very contemporary coverage of the Human Genome Project (Klug & Cummings, 2003)

New high interest figure 2.10, Your Genetic Future

Important new section on the collaborative gene, which describes the views of David Moore, Gilbert Gottlieb, and Barry Commoner, who believe there has been too much emphasis on genetic determinism

New section on the epigenetic view, including new figure 2.12

New coverage of phenylketonuria (PKU) in terms of the nature-nurture issue

New discussion of teratogens in terms of dose, time of exposure, and genetic susceptibility

Added recent review of research on prenatal exposure to cocaine (Frank & others, 2001; Lester & others, 2002)

Recent research on marijuana's effects during pregnancy (Richardson & others, 2002)

New section on incompatible blood types

Added recent research on age of mother and low birth weight delivery (Tough & others, 2002)

New discussion of labor and delivery across cultures

New coverage of low birth weight infants in terms of distinguishing low and very low birth weight; also new discussion of small for date infants

New discussion of cross-cultural comparisons of low birth weight infants and new figure 2.16 that illustrates low birth weight rates by country

Recent research showing outcomes for low birth weight infants in childhood and adolescence (Ment & others, 2003)

New research figure 2.17, showing the results of one of Tiffany Field's studies on massaged preterm infants

New coverage of recent groundbreaking study on the reduction of preterm births by administering progesterone to pregnant women (Meis, 2003)

CHAPTER 3
Physical Development and Biological Aging

Expanded, updated coverage of puberty, especially in terms of adrenarche, gonadarche, and hormonal changes (Susman, Dorn, & Schiefelbein, 2003)

New discussion of the role of leptin in weight and body weight during puberty

New discussion of recent research on parent-adolescent relationships and links between hormones and adolescent behavior (Booth & others, 2003)

New section on physiological changes in lung capacity during middle age and new figure 3.5 showing the relation of lung capacity to age and cigarette smoking

New figure 3.6 on changes in body composition of bone, muscle, and fat from 25 to 75 years of age

Substantially revised organization of the discussion of the brain with a much improved introduction of basic aspects of brain physiology to set the stage for improved understanding of developmental changes in the brain through the life span

Expanded coverage of early deprivation and brain activity, including new figure 3.11 of the brain scan of a Romanian orphan and a normal child

New discussion of the fascinating story of Michael Rehbein, who had the left hemisphere of his brain removed when he was 7 years old, including new figure 3.12 of brain scans showing how his right hemisphere took over some of the functioning previously carried out by his left hemisphere.

New research on brain changes during adolescence (Baird & others, 1999)

New section on neurotransmitters and aging, including recent research (Leventhal & others, 2003)

Expanded coverage of changes in neurons and aging, including new figure 3.16 that shows new nerve cells generated in adult mice (Kempermann, van Praag, & Gage, 2000)

Important new brain research on decreased brain lateralization in older adults, including new figure 3.17 showing brain scans that illustrate this concept

Updated research coverage of SIDS, including the reasons why sleeping in a prone position is linked with SIDS (Horne & others, 2002; Kahn & others, 2002)

New Contexts of Life-Span Development Interlude, Living Longer in Okinawa, with emphasis on diet, low-stress lifestyle, a caring community, activity, and spirituality; includes new figure 3.21 on the risks of dying from cancer in Okinawa, Japan, and the United States

Coverage of new theory of aging—the mitochondrial theory—that is receiving increased attention (Dillin & others, 2002; Pierson, 2003)

New discussion of increased myelination of neural pathways that connect the limbic system and the prefrontal cortex in the forties and fifties, which is likely linked with increased reflection in middle-aged adults (Fischer & Pruyne, 2003)

New section on the decrease in brain weight and volume with aging (O'Connor & Kaplan, 2003)

New analysis by Baltes and Smith showing the significant problems faced by individuals 85 and over and the increase in successful aging for those in their sixties and seventies

CHAPTER 4
Health

Added recent research on the failure of many adult males to adequately use the health-care system (Courtenay, McCreary, & Merighi, 2002)

New data on the percentage of older adults of different ages with a disability, including new figure 4.2

New data on the percentage of older adults of different ages in nursing homes, including new figure 4.4

New research figure 4.5 on the link between perceived control and mortality

Moved section on leading causes of death across the life span to chapter 17, "Death and Grieving," at the request of reviewers

At the request of reviewers, deleted section on stress and coping, especially because this research has lacked a developmental focus; the chapter now focuses more clearly on physical health, with a better-integrated presentation, reducing length and number of topics in chapter

Significant research updating of breastfeeding versus bottle-feeding (Oddy, 2002; Ryan, Wenjun, & Acosta, 2002), including new figure 4.6 on trends in breastfeeding; also new research on link between breastfeeding and lower risk of obesity (Dewey, 2003)

Significant updating of research on childhood obesity (Guo & others, 2002; Wisotsky & Swenioinis, 2003)

Very recent research on childhood obesity including new figure 4.7 on the percentage of overweight children who become overweight adults (Guo & others, 2002; Maynard & others, 2003)

New discussion of obesity and eating disorders in adolescence, including new figure 4.8 on the increase in obesity from 1968 to 2000 (National Center for Health Statistics, 2003)

Recent update on calorie restriction and longevity (Johannes, 2002)

New discussion of decrease in PE programs in U.S. schools (Health Management Resources, 2001)

New research figure 4.11 on the link between physical fitness and mortality

Addition of new review of research on aging and exercise (Slade & others, 2002)

Research update of trends in adolescent drug use (Johnston, O'Malley, & Bachman, 2003)

Recent research on binge drinking in college students (Wechsler & others, 2002)

New figure 4.13 on fatal lung cancer and years since quitting smoking

Recent longitudinal research on developmental change in drinking patterns from late adolescence to the early thirties (Bachman & others, 2002), including new figure 4.14

New section on substance abuse in older adults including recent national data on the decline in alcohol use in middle and late adulthood (National Center for Health Statistics, 2002), including new figure 4.15

CHAPTER 5
Motor, Sensory, and Perceptual Development

Many new examples of concepts, especially challenging concepts such as the dynamic systems view and the ecological view of perceptual development

Expanded and improved discussion of Karen Adolph's research on the role of experience in learning a new motor behavior, including new figure 5.2

New coverage of movement and aging, including new figure 5.3

Expanded coverage of fine motor development in older adults, including two explanations of the slowing of this activity: neural noise and strategy

Extensively revised and updated coverage of handedness

Much expanded and more detailed discussion of research techniques for studying infant perception in the Research in Life-Span Development interlude, including the visual preference method, habituation, and tracking; includes new figure 5.6 on Alan Slater's research on habituation

New figure 5.7 showing visual acuity during the first months of life

New figure 5.8 showing how 1- and 2-month-old infants scan the human face

Expanded coverage of perceptual constancy in infancy

New discussion of binocular vision and its emergence at 3 to 4 months of age, providing a powerful cue to depth

New figure 5.10 from Bruce Hood's laboratory showing a research study being conducted on toddlers' perception of ball being dropped in a tube and where they will search for it

New research on the importance of age of older adults in determining the degree of their decline in visual perception (Brabyn & others, 2001), including new figure 5.11

New discussion of the decline in depth perception in older adults

New discussion of speech perception and when infants become "native listeners" (Jusczyk, 2002)

Expanded coverage of hearing in infancy to include changes in the perception of loudness, pitch, and sound localization

CHAPTER 6
Cognitive Developmental Approaches

Revised and expanded coverage of Piaget's concept of schemes

New figure 6.1 that summarizes the main characteristics of Piaget's four stages

Expanded coverage in the Research on Life-Span Development interlude with discussion of the violations of expectations method and new figure 6.4 to show the procedures used in the study of object permanence

Provided extensive example of the concept of zone of proximal development

Expanded material on description of private speech with examples and research

Updated coverage of Barbara Rogoff's ideas on cognitive apprenticeship

New entry in figure comparing Piaget and Vygotsky on sociocultural contexts

Added criticisms of Vygtosky's approach

CHAPTER 7
Information Processing

Expanded coverage of the role of computers in the information-processing approach and new figure 7.1 showing the computer metaphor for human information processing

New figure 7.2 showing a simplified version of information processing to improve students' understanding of this approach

New coverage of the explanations for increased information-processing speed in childhood and decreased processing speed in aging adults

New figure 7.3, The Relation of Age to Reaction Time

Completely revised, updated coverage of developmental changes in attention in adulthood in terms of selective attention, divided attention, and sustained attention

Discussion of recent research by Pickrell & Loftus (2001) on implanted false memories at Disneyland

New figure 7.7 on developmental changes in memory span

Expanded coverage of working memory and new figure 7.8 showing Baddeley's working memory model

New discussion of research on imagery and memory of verbal information, including new research figure 7.9 on this topic

New research figure 7.10 on the role of expertise in memory

New section on memory reconstruction and schema theory

New section on memory development in adolescence and movement of memory and study strategies from main text to a new figure

New research figure 7.13 on memory for Spanish as function of age since Spanish was learned

New section on prospective memory

New coverage of source memory and aging (Hasher, 2003)

Expanded discussion of "use it or lose it" with recent research studies

New figure 7.14 on recent research involving training of attention and memory in older adults (Levy, Jennings, & Langer, 2001)

Expanded, updated research coverage of scientific thinking in children

Revised, updated, easier-to-understand coverage of theory of mind, including new figure 7.17 involving developmental changes in theory of mind

New discussion of research on time of day effects on the memory of younger and older adults (Hasher & others, 2002)

New discussion of research on the role of expectancy in the memory of older adults (Hess & others, 2002)

CHAPTER 8
Intelligence

Extensive rewriting and reorganization of the chapter for better student understanding

Brief discussion and definition of factor analysis added to help students understand the factor analytic approach to intelligence

New discussion of the Key School as reflective of Gardner's multiple intelligence theory

New section on the Sternberg Triarchic Abilities Test (STAT)

New section on emotional intelligence, including very recent material on the development of a measure to assess emotional intelligence (Mayer, Salovey, & Caruso, 2002)

New figure 8.3 that compares Gardner's, Sternberg's, and Salovey/Mayer's approaches

New discussion of whether people have a general intelligence with links between general intelligence and job success, as well as John Carroll's (1993) extensive examination of intellectual abilities

New figure 8.4 on the correlation between intelligence test scores and twin status (Grigorenko, 2000)

Much expanded coverage of the influence of heredity and environment on intelligence

New discussion of heritability

New figure 8.5 on the Flynn effect

New coverage of a leading expert's conclusions on what research indicates about the role of intervention in improving children's intelligence (Brooks-Gunn, 2003)

New section on controversies and group comparisons in intelligence, which includes new material on gender comparisons

Much expanded coverage of cross-cultural comparisons of intelligence, including recent research (Grigorenko & others, 2001; Sternberg & others, 2001)

New coverage of the concept of stereotype threat and the intelligence of ethnic minority individuals (Aronson, Fried, & Good, 2002; Steele & Aronson, 1995)

New figure 8.10 on classification of mental retardation based on IQ

New figure 8.11 on classification of mental retardation based on levels of support needed

New discussion of the role of practice in giftedness

New photo of Mihaly Csikszentmihalyi in the setting where he gets his most creative thoughts

Expanded discussion of Baltes' research on wisdom (Baltes & Kunzmann, 2003; Kunzmann & Baltes, 2003)

CHAPTER 9
Language Development

Extensive rewriting and reorganization of the chapter with the development of language now preceding the section on biological and environmental influences

New figure 9.1 on the rule systems of language with numerous examples

Updated material on change in language in early childhood and middle and late childhood

Considerable expansion and reorganization of material on the development of language in infancy with subsections on babbling and other vocalizations, recognizing language sounds, first words, two-word utterances, and language production and language comprehension

New figure 9.2 showing the research setting in Patricia Kuhl's studies of infants changing from being universal linguists to specializing in the speech of their native language

Deletion of the discussion of MLU at the request of reviewers and adopters

New Research in Life-Span Development interlude, Family Environment and Young Children's Language Development, including new figure 9.7

Considerably updated coverage of the best way to teach children to read, including the recommendations of the prestigious National Reading Panel (2000)

New figure 9.9 showing the results of a national assessment of reading achievement and its relation to how much children read daily

New section on preparing for literacy in early childhood (Pressley, 2003)

Expanded coverage of children's writing with new material on the importance of planning, drafting, and revising (Pressley, 2003)

New Contexts in Life-Span Development interlude on bilingual education that includes Kenji Hakuta and his colleagues' (2000) research on how long it takes to develop proficiency in a second language

CHAPTER 10
Emotional Development

New discussion of biological foundations of emotions and experience in emotions, including early development in the brain and cultural influences (Thompson, 2003)

New section on early developmental changes in emotions, including new figures 10.1 and 10.2 with a focus on the distinction between primary and self-conscious emotions (Lewis, 2002)

New section on infant fear, including new discussion of separation protest and new research figure 10.3 on separation protest in four cultures

New section on emotional regulation and coping in infancy (Kopp & Neufeld, 2002)

Expanded, revised, and updated discussion of emotion in adolescence (Rosenblum & Lewis, 2003)

New figure 10.6 on differences in the emotions of adolescents and their parents

Expanded coverage of developmental changes in positive and negative emotions across the adult years, including new figure 10.7 (Mroczek, 2001)

Based on recommendations of reviewers, moved material on suicide to chapter 17, "Death and Grieving," and deleted material on depression from this chapter to provide a more cohesive, integrated chapter

New discussion of Kagan's ideas on inhibition to the unfamiliar as an important temperament category and recent research showing that a substantial number of toddlers who are inhibited become less inhibited at 7 years of age (Pfeifer & others, 2002)

New section in temperament on the roles of biological foundations and experience

Expanded coverage of positive affect and approach, and effortful control, as temperament categories

New section in temperament on developmental contexts

New discussion of gender, culture, and temperament

New research figure 10.10 showing the dramatic effects of Harlow's contact comfort study

Expanded coverage of attachment and culture, including new figure 10.12 comparing the attachment patterns of U.S., German, and Japanese babies

Extensively updated coverage of the National Institute of Child Health and Human Development's longitudinal study of child care (NICHD Early Child Care Research Network, 2001, 2002, 2003) in the Research in Life-Span Development interlude

Expanded, updated material on adolescent dating and romantic relationships, including new research figure 10.13 on age patterns (Buhrmester, 2001)

CHAPTER 11
The Self, Identity, and Personality

New figure 11.1 illustrating the development of self-recognition in infancy

More streamlined, focused coverage of changes in self-understanding in adolescence

New figure 11.3 on changes in global self-esteem across the human life span (Robins & others, 2002)

New section on personal control that focuses on Jutta Heck-hausen's (1997, 2001, 2002) views on primary control striving and secondary control striving, including new figure 11.6

New discussion of the increase in identity certainty from the thirties through the fifties, including new figures 11.7 and 11.8

New discussion of Jean Phinney's (2003) recent ideas about generational status and identity in immigrants

Revision of material on the big five factors of personality, using the OCEAN acronym to help students to remember the big five

New figure 11.12 on emotional instability and age

New figure 11.13 on age and well-being

New section on generativity including recent research and new figures 11.15 and 11.16 (Stewart, Ostrove, & Helson, 2001)

New figure 11.17 showing age changes in openness to experience in early and middle adulthood

New section on George Vaillant's (2002) longitudinal studies, including new figure 11.18 on links between characteristics at age 50 and health and happiness at ages 75 to 80

Revised, updated discussion of conclusions about stability and change based on Avshalom Caspi and Brent Robert's (2001) views

Added Jean Phinney's (2003) recent views on generation status and identity development in immigrants

CHAPTER 12
Gender and Sexuality

Extensive revision, updating of discussion of hormonal influences and gender (Lippa, 2002)

Expanded, updated coverage of peer group influences on gender (Maccoby, 2002; Martin & Fabes, 2001)

New figures 12.1 and 12.2, summarizing different gender theories

Updated, expanded discussion of differences in the brains of males and females

New coverage of William Pollack's (1999) view on what he calls the "boy code" of showing little if any emotion as boys grow up

Updated coverage of AIDS (Centers for Disease Control and Prevention, 2002b)

Expanded, updated coverage of acquaintance rape, including new figure 12.7 (Fisher, Cullen, & Turner, 2000)

New discussion of research on ethnic variations in the timing of sexual behaviors in U.S. adolescents, including new figure 12.8

Expanded, updated coverage of developmental pathways in a sexual identity development in gay and lesbian individuals (Diamond, 2003)

Updated coverage of risk factors for sexual behavior, including recent research (Buhrmester, 2001; Miller, Benson, & Galbraith, 2001)

Recent research on cross-cultural comparisons of adolescent pregnancy, including figure 12.9

Change in labeling from sexually transmitted diseases (STDs) to sexually transmitted infections (STIs) in line with current terminology

CHAPTER 13
Moral Development, Values, and Religion

Substantial revision of organization of chapter with main headings now domains of moral development; contexts of moral development; prosocial and antisocial behavior; and values, religion, spirituality, and meaning in life

Added figure 13.2 showing typical responses of individuals at each of Kohlberg's stages to the Heinz and the Druggist story

Substantial updating of the social cognitive theory of moral development based on Bandura's (1999, 2002) recent views

New discussion of Kohlberg's contemplation of adding a seventh stage to his theory

Added material on Rest's Defining Issues Test and criticism of Kohlberg's approach to assessing moral reasoning, including new figure 13.4 on the moral dilemmas of interest to adolescents

Expanded discussion of how moral thoughts can be used to justify immoral behavior with examples from 9/11/01 and the war on terrorism (Bandura, 2002)

New discussion of research on guilt (Kochanska & others, 2002)

New research on the link between maternal warmth and children's empathy (Zhou & others, 2002)

New discussions of gender differences in altruism and volunteering (Eisenberg & Morris, 2004)

Added discussion of study of caring and prosocial behavior in a highly impoverished group of adolescents

Addition of new research showing a link between altruism and longevity (Brown, in press)

New coverage of the Pittsburgh Youth Study, a longitudinal study of the development of delinquency (Loeber & others, 2002; Stouthamer-Loeber & others, 2002)

New research on the role of siblings in delinquency

Expansion of material on the antecedents of delinquency to include cognitive distortions, authority conflict, and other factors

New discussion of Fast Track, an extensive delinquency prevention study (The Conduct Problems Prevention Research Group, 2002)

Recent research linking early problems in aggression with later delinquency for boys but not girls (Broidy & others, 2003)

Research update on the values of college students (Sax & others, 2002)

Reorganization of section on religion and adolescents, including new material on parenting/attachment and religious interest in adolescents (Ream & Savin-Williams, 2003)

New section on the positive role of religion in adolescents' lives

Discussion of link between happiness and having a meaningful faith (Diener, Lucas, & Oishi, 2002)

Coverage of recent study showing an increase in spirituality between late middle adulthood (mid-fifties/early sixties) and late adulthood (late sixties/mid-seventies) (Wink & Dillon, 2002), including new research figure 13.8

Much expanded coverage of meaning in life with description of Baumeister's (1991; Baumeister & Vohs, 2002) views on the four needs that guide how people try to make sense of their lives

Inclusion of recent research on the link between finding meaning in religion and life satisfaction in older adults (Krause, 2003)

Recent study of church attendance in older adults (Idler, Kasl, & Hays, 2001)

CHAPTER 14
Families, Lifestyles, and Parenting

Revised, new chapter title: Families, Lifestyles, and Parenting

Reorganization of chapter's main section for better flow

Added critique of family life cycle concept

New section on family processes that focuses on reciprocal socialization, the family system, and sociocultural and historical influences

At beginning of section on family processes, connection with Bronfenbrenner's ecological theory; connections with Bronfenbrenner's theory several other times in chapter as well

New figure 14.2 on Belsky's concept of direct and indirect effects in family processes

New discussion of research on links between marital relations and parenting (Grych, 2002)

Expanded coverage of cohabitation, including explanations of why cohabiting is linked with greater vulnerability to divorce

New coverage of Hetherington's six pathways that divorced adults follow (Hetherington & Kelly, 2002)

New discussion of recommended strategies for divorced adults

New discussion of anxiety that many childless highly successful women have (Hewlett, 2002)

Updated research on stepfamilies (Hetherington & Stanley-Hagan, 2002)

New section on the transition to parenting

Expanded, updated coverage of parenting styles including new material on why authoritative parenting is linked with positive developmental outcomes (Steinberg & Silk, 2002)

New section on punishment and discipline, including new figure 14.8 on attitudes toward corporal punishment in different countries, as well as recent theory and research on punishment (Gershoff, 2002)

Recent research on child maltreatment and problems in regulating emotion (Maughan & Cicchetti, 2002)

New section on coparenting, including recent research (McHale & others, 2002)

Updated, extensively revised discussion of working parents based on recent research (Gottfried, Gottfried, & Bathurst, 2002; Hill & others, 2001)

New figure 14.11 on the percentage of children with problems in intact and divorced families (Hetherington & Kelly, 2002)

Added comments about marital conflict having negative consequences in the contexts of marriage or divorce (Cummings, Braungart-Rieker, & Du Rocher-Schudlich, 2003)

New research on child-rearing antecedents of intergenerational relations (Belsky & others, 2001)

CHAPTER 15
Peers and the Sociocultural World

Reorganization of chapter with this order of topics: peer relations in childhood and adolescence, friendship, play and leisure, aging and the social world, and sociocultural influences

Reordering of "B" headings/sections under peer relations in childhood and adolescence to put peer statuses, bullying, and gender and peer relations in sequence

New figure 15.1, illustrating the development of communication skills and perspective taking

Recent research on rejected children (Buhs & Ladd, 2002)

Updated coverage of bullying and new figure 15.2 on bullying behaviors by U.S. youth based on a recent national study (Nansel & others, 2001)

New section on gender and peer relations, including new figure 15.3 (Maccoby, 1998, 2002)

Updated coverage of peer statuses to include average children

Extensive revision of section on cliques and crowds with improved distinctions between these two types of adolescent groups

New Contexts in Life-Span Development interlude on cross-cultural comparisons of peer relations

New figure 15.6 on developmental changes in self-disclosing conversations

New discussion of why friendship in adulthood may contribute more to psychological well-being than family relationships (Pruchno & Rosenbaum, 2003)

New sections on leisure in adolescence and in adulthood

Research updates on activity and social networks in late adulthood (Menec, 2003; Zunzunegui & others, 2003)

New description of research on how self-conceptions are linked to culture, including research study and new figure 15.9 comparing U.S. and Chinese college students

Updated, expanded coverage of socioeconomic status and parenting (Hoff, Laursen, & Tardif, 2002; Magnuson & Duncan, 2002)

Updated coverage of poverty rates in the United States, which have declined recently (Children's Defense Fund, 2001) and cross-cultural comparisons of poverty rates

New figure 15.10 on the percentages of youth under 18 who are living in distressed neighborhoods

Extensive updating on families and poverty with recent research (Gennetian & Miller, 2002; Huston & others, 2001; Mistry & others, 2002)

New figure 15.11 on the actual number of adolescents from different ethnic groups in the United States and the number projected in 2100

New Applications in Life-Span Development interlude, Acculturation and Ethnic Minority Parenting, based on the views of Cynthia Garcia Coll and Lee Pachter (2002)

Recent research on similarities and differences in the home environments of families from different ethnic groups, including new figure 15.12 (Bradley & others, 2001)

CHAPTER 16
Schools, Achievement, and Work

New section on accountability and testing in education

New discussion of updated *Turning Points 2000* (Jackson & Davis, 2002) recommendations for improving U.S. middle schools

New section on high schools that focuses on school dropouts and what needs to be done to improve U.S. high schools (National Commission on the High School Senior Year, 2001)

Updated coverage of the transition to college (Sax & others, 2002)

Much expanded and updated discussion of learning disabilities (Siegel, 2003)

Updated research on intervention with ADHD children (Swanson & others, 2001; Swanson & Volkow, 2002)

Extensively expanded, updated, and revised coverage of achievement

Expanded discussion of intrinsic and extrinsic motivation with new subsection on extrinsic rewards and intrinsic motivation (Cameron, 2001)

New section on mastery motivation

New figure 16.6 on mothers' beliefs about the factors responsible for children's math achievement in three countries

Updated coverage of the occupational outlook for various fields (*The Occupational Outlook Handbook, 2002–2003*)

Revised organization of section on work to give it a stronger developmental focus

New section on work in adolescence

New coverage of cross-cultural comparisons of work in adolescence

Updated, revised coverage of dual-career couples, including new figure 16.8 on historical changes in the percentage of traditional and dual-career couples in the United States (Barnett, 2001)

New figure 16.9 on developmental changes in job satisfaction

New research study on morale of individuals depending on how long they had been retired (Kim & Moen, 2001)

CHAPTER 17
Death and Grieving

New discussion of palliative care (Chochinov, 2002; Williams and Wheeler, 2001)

Update on Oregon's active euthanasia law through 2001

Increased coverage of end-of-life issues (Wilson & Truman, 2002)

New section on suicide, including recent U.S. data on suicide rates through the life span and new figure 17.2 (National Center for Health Statistics, 2002)

Recent research on meaning and purpose in life, as well as spirituality, in helping dying individuals to cope (McClain, Rosenfeld, & Breitbart, 2003; Smith, McCullough, & Poll, in press)

New coverage of three aspects of meaning-making coping: (1) personal, (2) family, and (3) community (Hayslip & Hansson, 2003)

Addition of new information about recent study on the economic consequences of widowhood on older women in the United States and Germany (Hungerford, 2001)

New discussion of recent study on the role of psychological and religious factors in the well-being of older adults following the loss of a spouse (Fry, 2001)

ACKNOWLEDGMENTS

I very much appreciate the support and guidance provided to me by many people at McGraw-Hill. Steve Debow, President, and Thalia Dorwick, Editor-in-Chief, have been truly outstanding in their administration of the social sciences area at McGraw-Hill. Steve Rutter, Publisher, has brought a wealth of publishing knowledge and vision to bear on improving this book. Rebecca Hope is a wonderful editor who has made very competent decisions and provided valuable recommendations about many aspects of the second edition of this book. Judith Kromm, senior developmental editor, has done a remarkable job of coordinating and managing the editorial and production phases of this project. I am indebted to Kathleen Field, whose editorial skill, insight, and effort have improved this book immeasurably. The new edition has considerably benefited from the enthusiasm and competence of Kate Russillo, Editorial Assistant. Melissa Caughlin, Marketing Manager, has contributed in numerous creative ways to this book. Marilyn Rothenberger was a superb project manager and Beatrice Sussman did outstanding work in copy-editing the book.

Thanks go to the many reviewers of both the second and first editions of this text. Their extensive contributions have made this a far better book.

REVIEWERS

Dr. Sheri Bauman, *University of Arizona*
Dr. Ann Calhoun-Sauls, *Belmont Abbey College*
Dr. Dan P. Fawaz, *Georgia Perimeter College*
Dr. Dan Flovell, *Eastern Kentucky University*
Dr. James Forbes, *Angelo State University*
Dr. Janet Gebelt, *University of Portland*
Dr. Carol H. Hoare, *George Washington University*
Dr. Fergus Hughes, *University of Wisconsin*
Dr. Mary P. Hughes Stone, *San Francisco State University*
Dr. Sue A. Kelley, *Lycoming College*
Dr. Kathleen Lawler, *University of Tennessee*
Dr. Salvador Macias, III, *University of South Carolina*
Dr. Carole Martin, *Colorado College*
Dr. Patricia A. Mills, *Miami University*
Dr. Bridget Murphy-Kelsey, *University of Oklahoma*
Dr. Scott Peterson, *Cameron University*
Dr. Warren Phillips, *Iowa State University*
Dr. Robert B. Stewart, Jr., *Oakland University*
Dr. Linda M. Woolf, *Webster University*

SUPPLEMENTS

This second edition of *A Topical Approach to Life-Span Development* is accompanied by a comprehensive and fully integrated array of supplemental materials that are written specifically for the instructors and students of life-span development. Please contact your McGraw-Hill representative for details concerning policies, prices, and availability. To locate your McGraw-Hill representative, please go to www.mhhe.com and select Rep Locator.

FOR THE INSTRUCTOR

Instructor's Manual

Prepared by Sue A. Kelley of Lycoming College, this thorough Instructor's Manual is a great resource for instructors. Its Total Teaching Package Outline in each chapter provides a detailed outline of the chapter with corresponding references and resources that will assist you in preparing lectures and assignments. The Instructor's Manual provides the following tools, all of which are tied to the Learning Goals as appropriate: key terms and people, lecture suggestions, classroom activities, personal applications, research projects, film and video lists, and website suggestions. The Instructor's Manual is available electronically on the Instructor's Resource CD-ROM and on the password-protected Instructor's Online Learning Center.

Test Bank

Prepared by Rita Zimmerman, this complete Test Bank includes a wide range of conceptual multiple-choice and essay questions.

Each question references the Learning Goal it covers. The Test Bank is available only on the Instructor's Resource CD-ROM as a Computerized Test Bank (Mac/IBM) and also in Word and Rich Text formats.

Online Learning Center

This site includes a secured Instructor Edition that stores your essential course materials to save you prep time before class. With just a couple clicks you can access the Instructor's Manual and presentation materials. The Instructor Edition also contains the text's PowerPoint presentation, selected video clips from the McGraw-Hill Visual Asset Database, and Taking it to the Net Exercises. You will also find PowerWeb content within the OLC to give you faster access to real-world material specific to your discipline. These resources and more can be found by logging on to the website at www.mhhe.com/santrockldt2.

McGraw-Hill's Visual Assets Database (VAD) for Lifespan Development

Jasna Jovanovic, University of Illinois, Urbana-Champaign McGraw-Hill's Visual Assets Database is a password protected online database of hundreds of multimedia resources for use in classroom presentations, including original video clips, audio clips, photographs, and illustrations—all designed to bring to life concepts in developmental psychology. In addition to offering ready-made multimedia presentations for every stage of the life span, the VAD's search engine and unique "My Modules" program allows instructors to select from the database's resources to create their own customized presentations, or "modules." These customized presentations are saved in an instructor's folder on the McGraw-Hill site, and the presentation is then run directly from the VAD to the internet-equipped classroom.

PowerWeb

PowerWeb offers you a great way to make coursepacks. Instead of searching through newspaper and magazines, you can point and click your way through PowerWeb for articles that complement your text. Print them out or direct your students to them electronically. Either way, you save prep time while bringing the very latest real-world coverage to your course. PowerWeb articles are recommended by professors like you, which means you won't get all the clutter that results from most Web searches.

FOR THE STUDENT

Multimedia Courseware for Life-Span Development CD-ROM

Packaged with your text is a set of interactive CD-ROMs created by Charlotte Patterson of the University of Virginia. These CDs cover the central phenomena and classic experiments in Child Development. Following Charlotte Patterson's model, Carolyn

Johnson from Pennsylvania State University gathered material and created exercises focusing on the studies and theories surrounding Adult Development. Together, these two sets of CDs make up Multimedia Courseware for *Life-Span Development*. Look for the CD icon that appears several times in the margins of each chapter. This will direct you to either the Child Development CD or the Adult Development CD to learn more about the experiments that have shaped life-span development.

These CDs include video footage of classic and contemporary experiments, detailed viewing guides, challenging previews, follow up and interactive feedback, graphics, graduated developmental charts, a variety of hands-on projects, related websites and navigation aids. Programmed in a modular format, the content focuses on integrating digital media to better explain physical, cognitive, social, and emotional development from early childhood through adult development.

Online Learning Center

As you study, you can refer to the site's Student Edition for learning objectives, video clips, an interactive glossary, and much more. You can also access PowerWeb content to see chapter topics illustrated in the real world. Before taking an exam, you can point and click your way through the chapter summary, take self-grading quizzes, and work through interactive exercises. These resources and more can be found by logging on to the website at www.mhhe.com/santrockldt2.

Expert Consultants

Pamela Balls Organista

Pamela Balls Organista, Professor of Psychology at the University of San Francisco, is one of the world's leading experts on ethnicity. She completed her bachelor's degree in Psychology and Black Studies at Washington University in St. Louis, doctorate in clinical psychology at Arizona State University, and clinical psychology post-doctorate in the Department of Psychiatry at the University of California—San Francisco. Prior to joining the faculty at USF, she was an Assistant Clinical Professor providing psychotherapy, consultation, and supervision in the Department of General Internal Medicine at UCSF. Her research interests include prevention interventions and ethnic minority health issues. Dr. Organista's publications include *Readings in Ethnic Psychology: African Americans, American Indians, Asian Americans, and Hispanics/Latinos* (1998), and *Acculturation: Advances in Theory, Measurement, and Applied Research* (2003), which she co-edited with Kevin Chun and Gerardo Marín. She also has published articles on migrant laborers and AIDS and on stress and coping in primary care patients. She is the founding and present faculty coordinator of the Ethnic Studies Program at the University of San Francisco and from 1998–2000 served as the Director of Academic Advising in the College of Arts and Sciences at the University of San Francisco.

Gilbert Gottlieb

Gilbert Gottlieb is one of the world's leading experts on early biological and environmental influences on development. He has been a Research Professor of Psychology in the Center for Developmental Science at the University of North Carolina at Chapel Hill since 1995. He served as an Excellence Foundation Professor of Psychology at UNC-Greensboro from 1982–1995, and as a Research Scientist at Dorothea Dix Hospital in Raleigh, NC, from 1961–1982. He received his Ph.D. from Duke University, where he participated in both the clinical and experimental psychology programs and was the first graduate from the joint Psychology-Zoology graduate training program in animal behavior. In 1973, he helped to revive interest in the field of behavioral embryology by editing a volume by that name, along with contributing theoretical reviews of the field to the *Quarterly Review of Biology* (1968) and the *Psychological Review* (1976). His interest in the developmental basis of evolution resulted in a 1992 book, *Individual Development and Evolution*. More recently, Professor Gottlieb summarized his career-long research and theoretical efforts in *Synthesizing Nature-Nurture* (1997), which won the 1998 Eleanor Maccoby Award of the Developmental Psychology Division of the American Psychological Association. In 1999 Clark University Press published his monograph, *Probabilistic Epigenesis and Evolution,* which is based upon the Heinz Werner Lectures he gave there. From 1962 through 2003, Professor Gottlieb has been a recipient of research grants from the National Institutes of Mental Health and from Child Health and Human Development, as well as from the National Science Foundation. He has been a guest of the Czechoslovak Academy of Science in Prague and the USSR Academy of Sciences in Moscow, and advisor to the German National Science Foundation. He is a past president of the International Society for Developmental Psychobiology and a recipient of the Distinguished Scientific Contributions to Child Development Award from the Society for Research in Child Development.

Linda Mayes

Linda Mayes is one of the world's leading experts on prenatal and infant development. Dr. Mayes is the Arnold Gesell Professor of Child Psychiatry, Pediatrics, and Psychology in the Yale Child Study Center, where she coordinates the early childhood programs. Trained as both a child and adult psychoanalyst and as a pediatrician, neonatologist, and child developmentalist, her work integrates perspectives from developmental psychology, neuroscience, and child psychiatry. Dr. Mayes' scientific papers and chapters are published in child psychiatric, developmental psychology, pediatric, and psychoanalytic journals. Her recent book for parents (written with Dr. Donald Cohen) is entitled *The Yale Child Study Center Guide to Understanding Your Child's Development* and is dedicated to helping parents understand the many ways children develop, to learn to observe their children's individual personality, and to reflect on their own development as a parent. Dr. Mayes's work at the Center is bringing the most informed and contemporary understanding of children's development into practical applications for families.

James E. Birren

James E. Birren is a pioneering figure in the field of life-span development and continues to be one of the world's leading experts on adult development and aging. He currently is Associate Director of the UCLA Center on Aging and is also Professor Emeritus of Gerontology and Psychology at the University of Southern California. Birren received his M.A. and Ph.D. from Northwestern University, and has been a Visiting Scientist at the University of Cambridge, England, and a Fellow at the Center for Advanced Study in the Behavioral Sciences at Stanford University. Birren's career includes serving as founding Executive Director and Dean of the Gerontology Center at the University of Southern California, as well as Past President of the Gerontological Society of America, the Western Gerontological Society, and the Division on Adult Development and Aging of the American Psychological Association. In addition, he has served as Chief of the Section on Aging of the National Institutes of Mental Health. His awards include the Brookdale Foundation Award for Gerontological Research; honorary doctorates from the University of Gothenberg, Sweden, Northwestern University, and St. Thomas University, Canada; the Gerontological Society Award for Meritorious Research; the Sandoz Prize for Gerontological Research; and the Canadian Association of Gerontology Award for Outstanding Contribution to Gerontology. Birren is Series Editor of the internationally recognized *Handbooks on Aging* and has published more than 250 academic journal articles and books.

Rachel Keen

Rachel Keen (formerly Rachel Keen Clifton) is one of the world's leading experts on perceptual-motor and cognitive development in infants. She received her doctorate from the Institute of Child Development at the University of Minnesota. After a postdoctoral fellowship at the University of Wisconsin and University of Iowa, she came to the University of Massachusetts-Amherst in 1968 where she is now a professor. Her research has been supported by the National Institutes of Health, the National Science Foundation, and the March of Dimes. She held a Research Scientist Award from the National Institute of Mental Health from 1981–2001, and currently has a MERIT award from the National Institute of Child Health and Human Development. She has served terms on three research review panels at these institutes and has been on the editorial board of *Developmental Psychology, Infant Behavior and Development,* and *Journal of Experimental Child Psychology.* Dr. Keen has served as Associate Editor of *Child Development* (1977–1997) and *Psychophysiology* (1972–1975), and as Editor of *SCRD Monographs* (1993–1999). She is a fellow of the American Psychological Association, the American Association for the Advancement of Science, the Acoustical Society of America, and the American Psychological Society. She was President of the International Society on Infant Studies in 1998–2000, received a Distinguished Alumna Award from her undergraduate college, Berea College in 1994, and was given the Distinguished Faculty Award in 1988 and the Samuel F. Conti Faculty Fellowship Award in 2002 from the University of Massachusetts.

Jonathan Tudge

Jonathan Tudge is an expert on children's social cognitive development and education, especially related to Vygotsky's sociocultural cognitive theory. He is currently a professor in the Department of Human Development and Family Studies at the University of North Carolina at Greensboro. He studies developmental issues that stress the mutual influences of the individual, relationships, culture, and history. His multidisciplinary background includes an undergraduate degree in history (Lancaster University, England), a master's degree in sociology (Oxford University, England), two diplomas in early childhood education (both from the University of London, England), a Ph.D. from the Department of Human Development and Family Sciences (Cornell University), and a postdoctorate in developmental psychology (University of Utah). Before becoming a professor, he taught young children in England, Russia, and the United States. Dr. Tudge's primary area of research examines the types of everyday activities and social relationships in which young children become involved in different parts of the world (the United States, Russia, Estonia, Finland, Korea, Kenya, and Brazil), and how these activities and relationships influence their transition to school.

William Hoyer

William Hoyer is one of the world's leading experts on cognitive processes in adult development and aging. He is currently Professor of Psychology at Syracuse University. He received his Ph.D. in experimental psychology from West Virginia University in 1972. Dr. Hoyer is Director of the Graduate Training Program in Experimental Psychology, and an associate of the Gerontology Center at Syracuse University. Dr. Hoyer has contributed over 100 articles, books, and book chapters to the professional literature. Currently, he is Principal Investigator of a five-year research grant from the National Institute on Aging on the aging of cognitive mechanisms. His research program has been continuously supported by the National Institute on Aging since 1981. Because of his expertise in the field of cognitive aging, Dr. Hoyer has served as a member of a number of grant review groups for NIH, NIMH, NSF, the John D. and Catherine T. McArthur Foundation, and other organizations. He is a past chair of the NIH Human Development and Aging study section, and has served as organizer and chair of a number of panels for federal agencies on health-related research in the behavioral and social sciences. He is a Fellow of the American Psychological Association, the American Psychological Society, and the Gerontological Society of America. He also has served on the editorial boards for a number of professional journals including *Journal of Gerontology: Psychological Sciences* and *Psychology and Aging,* and he is currently on the editorial board of three journals in the field of aging. The major focus of Dr. Hoyer's current research is to specify the mechanisms that account for age-related differences in learning, visual selective attention, and skilled performance. Dr. Hoyer's research contributes knowledge that bears on the understanding of the processes and mechanisms associated with effective cognitive functioning in healthy middle-aged and older individuals. One of the specific findings of Dr. Hoyer's research has been to describe the strategies and skills that enable older adults to perform competently in various task situations despite age-related and illness-related cognitive deficits.

Elena Grigorenko

Elena Grigorenko is one of the world's leading researchers in the areas of individual differences and exceptional children. She is currently a professor of psychology at Yale and Moscow State (Russia) Universities. She obtained her first Ph.D. (in general psychology) from Moscow State University (1990) and a second Ph.D. (in developmental psychology and genetics) from Yale (1996). Her professional experiences include conducting research, teaching psychology, and designing educational curricula. Dr. Grigorenko has published more than 100 books and articles. She is currently Associate Editor of *Contemporary Psychology.* Dr. Grigorenko has worked with and studied American, Russian, Indian, and African children. Her main interests are individual differences, child development and exceptional children.

Jay Belsky

Jay Belsky is one of the world's leading researchers on infant and early child socioemotional development. He is currently Director of the Institute for the Study of Children, Families and Social Issues and Professor of Psychology at Birkbeck University of London. Professor Belsky obtained his Ph.D. in 1978 in Human Development and Family Studies from Cornell University. Prior to joining the University of London in 1999, Professor Belsky served on the faculty at Penn State University for 21 years, rising to the rank of Distinguished Professor of Human Development. In 1983, he won the Boyd McCandless Award for Distinguished Early Contribution from the Developmental Psychology Division of the American Psychological Association. Dr. Belsky has served on the editorial boards of a number of research journals, including *Child Development, Developmental Psychology, Journal of Marriage and the Family, Development and Psychopathology,* and *Human Nature.* His areas of special expertise include child care, parent-child relations during the infancy and early childhood years, the transition to parenthood, child maltreatment, and the evolutionary basis of parent and child functioning. He is the author of more than 200 scientific articles and chapters and the author of several books. Dr. Belsky's research focuses on fathers as well as mothers, marriage as well as parent-child relations, and naturalistic home observations of family interaction patterns. Dr. Belsky's work has been funded, in the U.S., by grants from the National Science Foundation, the National Institute of Mental Health, the National Institute of Child Health and Human Development, the March of Dimes Foundation, and the Sara Scaife Family Foundation. In the U.K., he has received funding from The Welcome Trust and Department for Education and Skills.

Daniel K. Mroczek

Daniel K. Mroczek is an expert on socioemotional and personality development in adulthood and aging. He received his Ph.D. in psychology from Boston University and also was a postdoctoral fellow at the University of Michigan's Institute for Social Research. Dr. Mroczek is currently a professor at Fordham University in New York City. His research interests include stability and change in personality traits and psychological well-being across the life span, as well as personality predictors of physical health. His research on estimating trajectories of personality change has been funded by the National Institute on Aging. He has several statistical and methodological interests as well, including the use of mixed models, issues in longitudinal design and data analysis, and psychometrics.

James Marcia

James Marcia, Professor Emeritus at Simon Fraser University, is one of the world's leading experts on identity development. He obtained his Ph.D. in Clinical Psychology from Ohio State University. He was an Assistant and Associate Professor of Psychology at SUNY/Buffalo from 1965–1972 where he directed the Psychological Clinic. Dr. Marcia joined the Simon Fraser faculty in 1972, became a Full Professor there in 1976, and directed the Psychological Clinic from 1986–1988 and 1999–2001. He was also a Visiting Associate Professor at Harvard Medical School in 1981. His publications include two co-authored books on identity research as well as numerous journal articles, book chapters, and encyclopedia pieces dealing largely with construct validity of Erikson's psychosocial developmental theory. He served as a consulting editor for *The Journal of Youth and Adolescence* and *Journal of Applied Developmental Psychology*. Currently, he is on the editorial board of *The Narrative Study of Lives* and is a Senior Editor of *Identity: An International Journal of Theory and Research*. He has made many presentations at professional conferences, as well as invited addresses and keynote talks, including the Lansdowne Scholar lectures at the University of Victoria.

Janet Shibley Hyde

Janet Shibley Hyde is one of the world's leading experts on gender and sexuality. She currently is Professor of Psychology and Women's Studies at the University of Wisconsin–Madison. Dr. Hyde earned her Ph.D. (1972) in psychology from the University of California, Berkeley. Dr. Hyde has received the Outstanding Teaching Award from the Wisconsin Students Association and the Chancellor's Award for excellence in teaching at the University of Wisconsin. Dr. Hyde's publications include more than 100 scientific articles and chapters with most focusing on topics related to gender and sexuality. In addition, she is the author of two undergraduate textbooks, *Half the Human Experience: The Psychology of Women*, and *Understanding Human Sexuality*. She has received the Kinsey Award from the Society for the Scientific Study of Sexuality, for her contributions to sexuality research, and the Heritage Award from the Society for the Psychology of Women (Division 35 of the American Psychological Association), for her research on women and gender. Over the past 30 years, Dr. Hyde has held a variety of elected and appointed positions in her field, including editor of *Psychology of Women Quarterly* and associate editor of *The Journal of Sex Research*. She is a past-president of the Society for the Psychology of Women and the Society for the Scientific Study of Sexuality. She also has served on the Board of Directors of the National Council for Research on Women.

James Garbarino

James Garbarino is one of America's leading and most respected advocates for children. He has made outstanding research and conceptual contributions to a number of areas in child development. Dr. Garbarino obtained his Ph.D. from Cornell University and is currently Co-Director of the Family Life Development Center and Elizabeth Lee Vincent Professor of Human Development at Cornell. Prior to his current position, he served as President of the Erikson Institute for Advanced Study in Child Development (1985–1994). Dr. Garbarino has served as consultant or advisor to the National Committee to Prevent Child Abuse, the National Institute for Mental Health, the American Medical Association, the National Black Child Development Institute, the National Science Foundation, the National Resource Center for Children in Poverty, Childwatch International Research Network, the U.S. Advisory Board on Child Abuse and Neglect, and the FBI. In 1991 he undertook missions for UNICEF to assess the impact of the Gulf War upon children in Kuwait and Iraq, and has served as a consultant for programs serving Vietnamese, Bosnian, and Croatian children. Books he has authored or edited include: *And words can hurt forever: How to protect adolescents from bullying, harassment, and emotional violence (2002), Parents under siege (2001),* and *Lost boys(1999).* Dr. Garbarino serves as a consultant to television, magazine, and newspaper reports on children and families. The National Conference on Child Abuse and Neglect honored Dr. Garbarino in 1985 with its first C. Henry Kempe Award, in recognition of his efforts on behalf of abused and neglected children. He is a past President of the American Psychological Association's Division on Child, Youth, and Family Services, and has received the American Psychological Association's Award for Distinguished Professional Contributions to Public Service. In 2003, he was given the Outstanding Service to Children Award of the Chicago Association for the Education of Young Children.

Allan Wigfield

Allan Wigfield is one of the world's leading experts on children's and adolescents' motivation, achievement, and education. He is currently Professor of Human Development and Distinguished Scholar-Teacher at the University of Maryland, College Park. His research focuses on the development of children's motivation in different areas, including reading. Dr. Wigfield has authored more than 80 peer-reviewed journal articles and book chapters on children's motivation. He is associate editor of *Child Development* and a Fellow of Division 15 of the American Psychological Association. He currently is collaborating with John Guthrie on a National Science Foundation funded study of how two reading programs, Concept Oriented Reading Instruction and Strategy Instruction, influence elementary school-aged children's reading motivation and comprehension.

Robert Kastenbaum

Robert Kastenbaum, former Professor of Gerontology at Arizona State University, is widely recognized as one of the world's leading experts on death and dying. He is a psychologist with an interdisciplinary approach to life-course human development with particular emphasis on death-related situations and experiences. He has been active as therapist, researcher, program director, and educator since receiving his doctorate at the University of Southern California. Kastenbaum's books include *The Psychology of Death; Death, Society, and Human Experience;* and *On Our Way: The Final Passage through Life and Death.* Dr. Kastenbaum has served as director of a geriatric hospital and is cofounder of the National Caucus on Black Aging. He has been editor of the *International Journal of Aging and Human Development* and *Omega: Journal of Death and Dying.* He also explores themes of love and death in theater pieces such as the opera *Closing Time* and the musical play *Parlor Games.*

To the Student

This book provides you with important study tools to help you more effectively learn about life-span development. Especially important is the learning goals system that is integrated throughout each chapter. In the visual walk-through of features, pay special attention to how the learning goals system works.

THE LEARNING GOALS SYSTEM

Using the learning goals system will help you to learn the material more easily. Key aspects of the learning goals system are the learning goals, chapter maps, Review and Reflect, and Reach Your Learning Goals sections, which are all linked together.

At the beginning of each chapter, you will see a page that includes both a chapter outline and three to six learning goals that preview the chapter's main themes and underscore the most important ideas in the chapter. Then, at the beginning of each major section of a chapter, you will see a mini–chapter map that provides you with a visual organization of the key topics you are about to read in the section. At the end of each section is Review and Reflect, in which the learning goal for the section is restated, a series of review questions related to the mini–chapter map are asked, and a question that encourages you to think critically about a topic related to the section appears. At the end of the chapter, you will come to a section titled Reach Your Learning Goals. This includes an overall chapter map that visually organizes all of the main headings, a restatement of the chapter's learning goals, and a summary of the chapter's content that is directly linked to the chapter outline at the beginning of the chapter and the questions asked in the Review part of the Review and Reflect sections within the chapter. The Summary essentially answers the questions asked in the within-chapter Review and Reflect sections.

The Learning Goals System

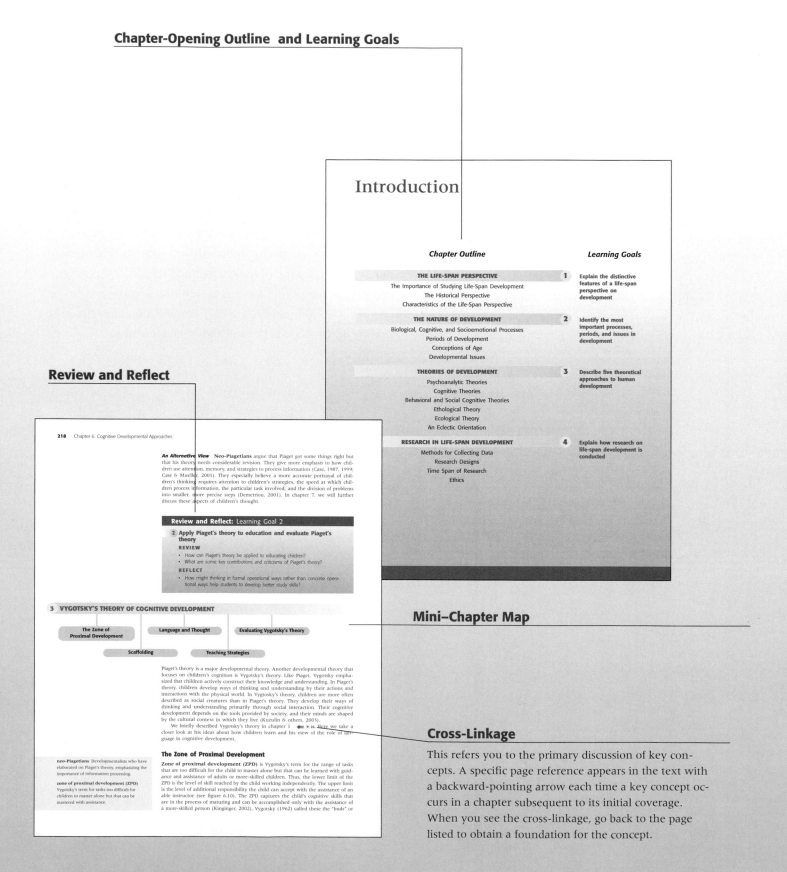

Chapter-Opening Outline and Learning Goals

Introduction

Chapter Outline | **Learning Goals**

THE LIFE-SPAN PERSPECTIVE
The Importance of Studying Life-Span Development
The Historical Perspective
Characteristics of the Life-Span Perspective

1 Explain the distinctive features of a life-span perspective on development

THE NATURE OF DEVELOPMENT
Biological, Cognitive, and Socioemotional Processes
Periods of Development
Conceptions of Age
Developmental Issues

2 Identify the most important processes, periods, and issues in development

THEORIES OF DEVELOPMENT
Psychoanalytic Theories
Cognitive Theories
Behavioral and Social Cognitive Theories
Ethological Theory
Ecological Theory
An Eclectic Orientation

3 Describe five theoretical approaches to human development

RESEARCH IN LIFE-SPAN DEVELOPMENT
Methods for Collecting Data
Research Designs
Time Span of Research
Ethics

4 Explain how research on life-span development is conducted

Review and Reflect

218 Chapter 6 Cognitive Developmental Approaches

An Alternative View Neo-Piagetians argue that Piaget got some things right but that his theory needs considerable revision. They give more emphasis to how children use attention, memory, and strategies to process information (Case, 1987, 1999; Case & Mueller, 2001). They especially believe a more accurate portrayal of children's thinking requires attention to children's strategies, the speed at which children process information, the particular task involved, and the division of problems into smaller, more precise steps (Demetriou, 2001). In chapter 7, we will further discuss these aspects of children's thought.

Review and Reflect: Learning Goal 2

2 Apply Piaget's theory to education and evaluate Piaget's theory

REVIEW
• How can Piaget's theory be applied to educating children?
• What are some key contributions and criticisms of Piaget's theory?

REFLECT
• How might thinking in formal operational ways rather than concrete operational ways help students to develop better study skills?

3 **VYGOTSKY'S THEORY OF COGNITIVE DEVELOPMENT**

The Zone of Proximal Development
Scaffolding
Language and Thought
Teaching Strategies
Evaluating Vygotsky's Theory

Mini–Chapter Map

Piaget's theory is a major developmental theory. Another developmental theory that focuses on children's cognition is Vygotsky's theory. Like Piaget, Vygotsky emphasized that children actively construct their knowledge and understanding. In Piaget's theory, children develop ways of thinking and understanding by their actions and interactions with the physical world. In Vygotsky's theory, children are more often described as social creatures than in Piaget's theory. They develop their ways of thinking and understanding primarily through social interaction. Their cognitive development depends on the tools provided by society, and their minds are shaped by the cultural context in which they live (Kuzulin & others, 2003).

We briefly described Vygotsky's theory in chapter 1 ◀ P. 23. Here we take a closer look at his ideas about how children learn and his view of the role of language in cognitive development.

The Zone of Proximal Development

Zone of proximal development (ZPD) is Vygotsky's term for the range of tasks that are too difficult for the child to master alone but that can be learned with guidance and assistance of adults or more-skilled children. Thus, the lower limit of the ZPD is the level of skill reached by the child working independently. The upper limit is the level of additional responsibility the child can accept with the assistance of an able instructor (see figure 6.10). The ZPD captures the child's cognitive skills that are in the process of maturing and can be accomplished only with the assistance of a more-skilled person (Kinginger, 2002). Vygotsky (1962) called these the "buds" or

neo-Piagetians Developmentalists who have elaborated on Piaget's theory, emphasizing the importance of information processing.

zone of proximal development (ZPD) Vygotsky's term for tasks too difficult for children to master alone but that can be mastered with assistance.

Cross-Linkage

This refers you to the primary discussion of key concepts. A specific page reference appears in the text with a backward-pointing arrow each time a key concept occurs in a chapter subsequent to its initial coverage. When you see the cross-linkage, go back to the page listed to obtain a foundation for the concept.

Critical Thinking and Content Questions in Photograph Captions

Most photographs have a caption that ends with a critical thinking or knowledge question in italics to stimulate further thought about a topic.

---

352 Chapter 10 Emotional Development

An insecurely attached infant, by contrast, avoids the mother or is ambivalent toward her, fears strangers, and is upset by minor, everyday separations.

If early attachment to a caregiver is important, it should relate to a child's social behavior later in development. For some children, early attachments seem to foreshadow later functioning (Egeland & Carlson, 2004; Sroufe, 2002). For other children, there is little continuity (Thompson, Easterbrooks, & Walker, 2003). For example, in one longitudinal study, attachment classification in infancy did not predict attachment classification at 18 years of age (Lewis, 1997). In this study, the best predictor of an insecure attachment classification at 18 was the occurrence of divorce in the intervening years. Consistency in caregiving over a number of years is likely an important factor in connecting early attachment and the child's functioning later in development.

Not all developmentalists believe that attachment in infancy is the only path to competence in life. Indeed, some developmentalists believe that too much emphasis has been placed on the attachment bond in infancy. Jerome Kagan (1987, 2000), for example, believes that infants are highly resilient and adaptive; he argues that they are evolutionarily equipped to stay on a positive developmental course, even in the face of wide variations in parenting. Kagan and others stress that genetic and temperament characteristics play more important roles in a child's social competence than the attachment theorists, such as Bowlby and Ainsworth, are willing to acknowledge (Chaudhuri & Williams, 1999; Young & Shahinfar, 1995). For example, infants may have inherited a low tolerance for stress. This, rather than an insecure attachment bond, may be responsible for their inability to get along with peers.

Another criticism of attachment theory is that it ignores the diversity of socializing agents and contexts that exists in an infant's world. In some cultures, infants show attachments to many people. Among the Hausa (who live in Nigeria), both grandmothers and siblings provide a significant amount of care for infants (Harkness & Super, 1995). Infants in agricultural societies tend to form attachments to older siblings, who are assigned a major responsibility for younger siblings' care.

Researchers recognize the importance of competent, nurturant caregivers in an infant's development (Maccoby, 1999; McHale & others, 2001; Parke, 2001). At issue, though, is whether or not secure attachment, especially to a single caregiver, is critical.

Despite such criticisms, there is ample evidence that security of attachment is important to development (Atkinson & Goldberg, 2004; Thompson, Easterbrooks, & Walker, 2003). Secure attachment in infancy is important because it reflects a positive parent-infant relationship and provides the foundation that supports healthy socioemotional development in the years that follow.

Caregiving Styles and Attachment Classification Is the style of caregiving linked with the quality of the infant's attachment? Securely attached babies have caregivers who are sensitive to their signals and are consistently available to respond to their infants' needs (Gao, Elliot, & Waters, 1999; Main, 2000). These caregivers often let their babies have an active part in determining the onset and pacing of interaction in the first year of life. One recent study found that maternal sensitivity in parenting was linked with secure attachment in infants in two different cultures: the United States and Colombia (Carbonell & others, 2002).

How do the caregivers of insecurely attached babies interact with them? Caregivers of avoidant babies tend to be unavailable or rejecting (Berlin & Cassidy, 2000). They often don't respond to their babies' signals and have little physical contact with them. When they do interact with their babies, they may behave in an angry and irritable way. Caregivers of resistant babies tend to be inconsistent; sometimes they respond to their babies' needs, and sometimes they don't. In general, they tend not to be very affectionate with their babies and show little synchrony when interact-

In the Hausa culture, siblings and grandmothers provide a significant amount of care for infants. *How might this practice affect attachment?*

Reach Your Learning Goals

Reach Your Learning Goals

Cognitive Developmental Approaches

1 PIAGET'S THEORY OF COGNITIVE DEVELOPMENT

- Processes of Development
- Preoperational Stage
- Formal Operational Stage
- Sensorimotor Stage
- Concrete Operational Stage

2 APPLYING AND EVALUATING PIAGET'S THEORY

- Piaget and Education
- Evaluating Piaget's Theory

3 VYGOTSKY'S THEORY OF COGNITIVE DEVELOPMENT

- The Zone of Proximal Development
- Language and Thought
- Evaluating Vygotsky's Theory
- Scaffolding
- Teaching Strategies

4 COGNITIVE CHANGES IN ADULTHOOD

- Piaget's View
- Reflective and Relativistic Thinking
- Realistic and Pragmatic Thinking
- Is There a Fifth, Postformal Stage?

226

Other Learning System Features

Contexts of Life-Span Development Interlude

Once in each chapter a Contexts of Life-Span Development interlude provides information about contextual influences—especially related to diversity and culture—linked to a chapter topic.

Research in Life-Span Development Interlude

One Research in Life-Span interlude appears in every chapter. The research interludes describe a research study or program and are designed to acquaint you with how research in life-span development is conducted.

sights, sounds, smells, touches, language, and eye contact help shape the brain's neural connections (Black, 2001).

The unfolding of developmental changes in the brain likely holds some important keys to understanding why individuals think and behave the way they do. But as the Research in Life-Span Development interlude indicates, studying the brains of babies is not an easy task.

Research in Life-Span Development
Studying Babies' Brains

Studying the brain's development in infancy is not easy. Even the latest brain-imaging technologies can't make out fine details—and they can't be used on babies. PET scans (in which the amount of specially treated glucose in various areas of the brain is measured and then analyzed by computer) pose a radiation risk, and infants wriggle too much for an MRI (in which a magnetic field is created around the body and radio waves are used to construct images of brain tissue and biochemical activity) (Marcus, Mulrine, & Wong, 1999).

However, one researcher who is making strides in finding out more about the brain's development in infancy is Charles Nelson (1999, 2000, 2001, 2003). In his research, he might attach up to 128 electrodes to a baby's scalp. He has found that even newborns produce distinctive brain waves that reveal they can distinguish their mother's voice from another woman's, even while they are asleep. Other research conducted by Nelson found that by 8 months of age babies can distinguish the picture of a wooden toy they were allowed to feel, but not see, from pictures of other toys. This achievement coincides with the development of neurons in the brain's hippocampus (an important structure in memory) that enable the infant to remember specific items and events.

In Charles Nelson's research, electrodes are attached to a baby's scalp to measure the brain's activity to determine its role in the development of an infant's memory. *Why is it so difficult to measure infants' brain activity?*

---

though Bugs is a Warner Brothers character who would never appear at a Disney theme park.

Many other studies have demonstrated that questions or suggestions of false information can distort memories. These findings have created great concern about finding ways to avoid implanting false memories among eyewitnesses and ways to determine the accuracy of the memories of eyewitnesses at trials.

In their study of memory, researchers have not extensively examined the roles that sociocultural factors might play (Park & Gutchess, 2002). In the Contexts of Life-Span Development interlude, we will explore how culture and gender might be linked with memory.

Contexts of Life-Span Development
Culture, Gender, and Memory

A culture sensitizes its members to certain objects, events, and strategies, which in turn can influence the nature of memory (Mistry & Rogoff, 1994). Sir Frederick Bartlett believed that a person's background, which is encoded in schemas, is revealed in the way the person reconstructs a story. This effect of cultural background on memory is called the *cultural specificity hypothesis*. It states that cultural experiences determine what is relevant in a person's life and, thus, what the person is likely to remember. For example, imagine that you live on a remote island in the Pacific Ocean and make your livelihood by fishing. Your memory about how weather affects fishing is likely to be highly developed. By contrast, a Pacific Islander might be hard-pressed to encode and recall the details of one hour of MTV. The culture specificity hypothesis also refers to subgroups within a culture. For example, many basketball fans in the U.S. can recount an impressive array of National Basketball Association (NBA) statistics. A devout gardener might know the informal and Latin names of plants ... ests in our culture and su ... schemas on any given topi ...

Scripts are schemas for ... and Mexico remembered ... Hensley, 1992). In line wit ... uals in the United States re ... no chaperone was present ... the information better whe ...

Gender is another asp ... attention in memory resea ... Researchers have found th ...

- Females are better at ... that include the time a ... 2001). Females are als ... memory for an emotio ...
- Males are better than ... spatial working memor ... which involves the ima ... would look like if it w ...

On many memory tasks, ... when they do occur, they ...

Applications in Life-Span Development
Project Spectrum

What is a Spectrum classroom like? Teachers do not try to evoke intelligences directly by using materials that are labeled "spatial" or "verbal." But the classroom has rich and engaging materials that can stimulate a range of intelligences. For example, in a naturalist corner there are biological specimens that students can explore and compare. This area stimulates students' sensory capacities and logical thinking skills. In a storytelling area, students create imaginative tales with stimulating props and design their own storyboards. This area encourages children to use their linguistic, dramatic, and imaginative skills. In a building corner, students can construct a model of their classroom and arrange small-scale photographs of the students and the teachers in their class using spatial and personal skills. In all, the Spectrum classroom has 12 such areas that are designed to bring out students' multiple intelligences.

The Spectrum classroom can identify skills that typically are not tapped in a regular classroom. In one first-grade Spectrum classroom, a boy who was a product of a highly conflicted broken home was at risk for school failure. However, when Project Spectrum was introduced the boy was identified as especially skilled in one area. He was the best student in the class at taking apart and putting together common objects, such as a doorknob and a food grinder. His teacher became encouraged when she found that he possessed this skill and his overall school performance began to improve.

In addition to identifying unexpected strengths in students, Project Spectrum also can pinpoint undetected weaknesses. Gregory, who was especially skilled in math computation and conceptual knowledge, was doing very well in the first grade. However, he performed poorly in a number of Spectrum areas. Gregory did well only in the areas in which he needed to give a correct answer and a person in authority gave it to him. As a result of the Spectrum Project, Gregory's teacher began to search for ways to encourage him to take risks on more open-ended tasks, to try different ways of doing things, and to realize that it is okay to make mistakes.

Student in a Spectrum classroom engaged in a science project. *What combinations of materials might you expect to find in other corners of a Spectrum classroom?*

Sternberg's Triarchic Theory Like Gardner, Robert J. Sternberg (1986, 1999, 2002, 2003) believes that traditional IQ tests fail to measure some important dimensions of intelligence. Sternberg proposes a **triarchic theory of intelligence** with three main types of intelligence: analytical, creative, and practical.

Analytical, Creative, and Practical Intelligence To understand what analytical, creative, and practical intelligence mean, let's look at examples of people who reflect these three types of intelligence:

- Consider Latisha, who scores high on traditional intelligence tests such as the Stanford-Binet and is a star analytical thinker. Sternberg calls Latisha's analytical thinking and abstract reasoning *analytical intelligence*. It is the closest to what has traditionally been called intelligence and what is commonly assessed by intelligence tests. In Sternberg's view of analytical intelligence, the basic unit of analytical intelligence is a *component*, which is a basic unit of information process-

triarchic theory of intelligence Sternberg's theory that intelligence consists of componential intelligence, experiential intelligence, and contextual intelligence.

Applications in Life-Span Development Interlude

Every chapter has one Applications in Life-Span Development interlude, which provides applied information about parenting, education, or health and well-being related to a topic in the chapter.

Key Terms and Glossary

Key terms appear in boldface. Their definitions appear in the margin near where they are introduced.

Cognitive developmental approaches place a special emphasis on how individuals actively construct their thinking. They also focus heavily on how thinking changes from one point in development to another. In this chapter, we will highlight the cognitive developmental approaches of Jean Piaget and Lev Vygotsky. We also will explore the possibility that adults think in a qualitatively more advanced way than adolescents do.

1 PIAGET'S THEORY OF COGNITIVE DEVELOPMENT

Processes of Development | Preoperational Stage | Formal Operational Stage | Sensorimotor Stage | Concrete Operational Stage

Piaget with his wife and three children; he often used his observations of his children to provide examples of his theory.

Piaget thought that, just as our physical bodies have structures that enable us to adapt to the world, we build mental structures that help us to adapt to the world. *Adaptation* involves adjusting to new environmental demands. Piaget also stressed that children actively construct their own cognitive worlds; information is not just poured into their minds from the environment. He sought to discover how children at different points in their development think about the world and how these systematic changes occur P. 22.

Processes of Development

Poet Nora Perry asked, "Who knows the thoughts of the child?" As much as anyone, Piaget knew. Through careful observations of his own three children—Laurent, Lucienne, and Jacqueline—and inquisitive interviews of other children, Piaget changed our perceptions of the way children think about the world.

What processes do children use as they construct their knowledge of the world? Piaget believed that these processes are especially important in this regard: schemes, assimilation, accommodation, organization, equilibrium, and equilibration.

Schemes Piaget (1954) said that as the child seeks to construct an understanding of the world, the developing brain creates **schemes.** These are actions or mental representations that organize knowledge. In Piaget's theory, behavioral schemes (physical activities) characterize infancy, and mental schemes (cognitive activities) develop in childhood. A baby's schemes involve simple actions that can be performed on objects such as sucking, looking, and grasping. Older chidren have schemes that include strategies and plans for solving problems. For example, a 5-year-old might have a scheme that involves the strategy of classifying objects by size, shape, or color. By the time we have reached adulthood, we have constructed an enormous number of diverse schemes, ranging from how to drive a car to balancing a budget to the concept of fairness.

Assimilation and Accommodation To explain how children use and adapt their schemes, Piaget offered two concepts: assimilation and accommodation. **Assimilation** occurs when children incorporate new information into their existing schemes. **Accommodation** occurs when children adjust their schemes to fit new information and experiences. Consider an 8-year-old girl who is given a hammer and nails to hang a picture on the wall. She has never used a hammer, but from experience and observation she realizes that a hammer is an object to be held, that it is swung by the handle to hit the nail, and that it is usually swung a number of times. Recognizing each of these things, she fits the current task into her existing scheme

schemes In Piaget's theory, actions or mental representations that organize knowledge.

assimilation Piagetian concept of the incorporation of new information into existing schemes.

accommodation Piagetian concept of adjusting schemes to fit new information and experiences.

200

Key terms also are listed and page-referenced at the end of each chapter.

transform the classroom and establish a meaningful context for instruction.

- Like Piaget, Vygotsky emphasized that children actively construct their understanding of the world. Unlike Piaget, he did not propose stages of cognitive development, and he emphasizes that children construct knowledge through social interaction. In Vygotsky's theory, children depend on tools provided by the culture, which determines which skills they will develop. Some critics say that Vygotsky overemphasized the role of language.

4 Describe cognitive changes in adulthood

- Piaget said that formal operational thought, entered at 11 to 15 years of age, is the final cognitive stage, although adults are more knowledgeable than adolescents.
- Some experts argue that the idealism of Piaget's formal operational stage declines in young adults, being replaced by more realistic, pragmatic thinking.
- Perry said that adolescents often engage in dualistic, absolutist thinking, whereas young adults are more likely to think reflectively and relativistically.
- Postformal thought is reflective, relativistic, and provisional; realistic; and open to emotions and subjective.

Key Terms

schemes 200
assimilation 200
accommodation 200
organization 201
equilibration 201
sensorimotor stage 202
object permanence 204
AB̄ error 207
preoperational stage 207
operations 207
symbolic function substage 208
egocentrism 208
animism 208
intuitive thought substage 209
centration 209
conservation 209
concrete operational stage 211
horizontal décalage 211
seriation 213
transitivity 213
formal operational stage 213
hypothetical-deductive reasoning 214
adolescent egocentrism 214
imaginary audience 214
personal fable 215
neo-Piagetians 218
zone of proximal development (ZPD) 218
scaffolding 219
social constructivist approach 222
postformal thought 225

Key People

Jean Piaget 200
Renée Baillargeon 205
Barbel Inhelder 208
Rochel Gelman 211
David Elkind 214
Lev Vygotsky 218
K. Warner Schaie 224
William Perry 224

Glossary

A

AB̄ error The Piagetian object-permanence concept in which an infant progressing into substage 4 makes frequent mistakes, selecting the familiar hiding place (A) rather than the new hiding place (B̄). 207

acceptance Kübler-Ross' fifth stage of dying, in which the dying person develops a sense of peace, an acceptance of her or his fate, and, in many cases, a desire to be left alone. 612

accommodation Piagetian concept of adjusting schemes to fit new information and experiences. 200

accommodation of the eye The eye's ability to focus and maintain an image on the retina. 185

active euthanasia Death induced deliberately, as by injecting a lethal dose of a drug. 603

active (niche-picking) genotype-environment correlations Correlations that exist when children seek out environments they find compatible and stimulating. 63

activity theory The theory that the more active and involved older adults are, the more likely they are to be satisfied with their lives. 339

addiction A pattern of behavior characterized by an overwhelming involvement with using a drug and securing its supply. 155

adolescent egocentrism The heightened self-consciousness of adolescents, which is reflected in adolescents' beliefs that others are as interested in them as they are in them selves, and in adolescents' sense of personal uniqueness and invincibility. 214

adoption study A study in which investigators seek to discover whether, in behavior and psychological characteristics, adopted children are more like their adoptive parents, who provided a home environment, or more like their biological parents, who contributed their heredity. Another form of the adoption study is to compare adoptive and biological siblings. 62

aerobic exercise Sustained activity that stimulates heart and lung functioning. 152

affectionate love Also called companionate love, this type of love occurs when individuals desire to have another person near and have a deep, caring affection for the person. 359

affordances Opportunities for interaction offered by objects that are necessary to perform activities. 178

ageism Prejudice against other people because of their age, especially prejudice against older adults. 539

AIDS A sexually transmitted infection caused by the human immunodeficiency virus (HIV), which destroys the body's immune system. 423

altruism An unselfish interest in helping another person. 458

Alzheimer's disease A progressive, irreversible brain disorder characterized by a gradual deterioration of memory, reasoning, language, and, eventually, physical function. 139

androgens A main class of sex hormones, an important one of which is testosterone, that promote the development of male genitals and secondary sex characteristics. 97

androgens The main class of male sex hormones. 402

androgyny The presence of a high degree of feminine and masculine characteristics in the same individual. 411

anger Kübler-Ross' second stage of dying, in which the dying person's denial gives way to anger, resentment, rage, and envy. 612

anger cry A cry similar to the basic cry but with more excess air forced through the vocal cords (associated with exasperation or rage). 336

animism A facet of preoperational thought—the belief that inanimate objects have "lifelike" qualities and are capable of action. 208

anorexia nervosa An eating disorder that involves the relentless pursuit of thinness through starvation. 147

Apgar Scale A widely used method to assess the health of newborns at 1 and 5 minutes after birth. The Apgar Scale evaluates infants' heart rate, respiratory effort, muscle tone, body color, and reflex irritability. 86

aphasia A language disorder resulting from brain damage that involves a loss of the ability to use words. 319

assimilation Piagetian concept of the incorporation of new information into existing schemes. 200

associative play Play that involves social interaction with little or no organization. 535

attachment A close emotional bond between two people. 348

attention Concentrating and focusing mental resources. 237

attention deficit hyperactivity disorder (ADHD) A disability in which children consistently show one or more of the following characteristics: (1) inattention, (2) hyperactivity, and (3) impulsivity. 574

attribution theory The theory that, in their effort to make sense out of their own behavior or performance, individuals are motivated to discover its underlying causes. Attributions are perceived causes of outcomes. 581

authoritarian parenting A restrictive, punitive style in which parents exhort the child to follow their directions and to respect their work and effort. Firm limits are placed on the child and little verbal exchange is allowed. 498

authoritative parenting A style that encourages children to be independent but still places limits and controls on children's actions; extensive verbal give-and-take is allowed and parents are warm and nurturant toward the child. 498

automaticity The ability to process information with little or no effort. 234

autonomous morality The second stage of moral development in Piaget's theory, displayed by older children (about 10 years of age and older). The child becomes aware that rules and laws are created by people and that, in judging an action, one should consider the actor's intentions as well as the consequences. 443

average children Children who receive an average number of both positive and negative nominations from their peers. 525

B

bargaining Kübler-Ross' third stage of dying, in which the dying person develops the hope that death can somehow be postponed. 612

basal metabolism rate (BMR) The minimal amount of energy a person uses in a resting state. 145

basic cry A rhythmic pattern usually consisting of a cry, a briefer silence, a shorter inspiratory whistle that is higher pitched than

G-1

Key terms are alphabetically listed, defined, and page-referenced in a Glossary at the end of the book.

Key People

The most important theorists and researchers in the chapter are listed and page-referenced at the end of each chapter.

Quotations

These appear occasionally in the margins to stimulate further thought about a topic.

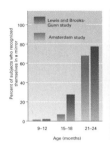

The Self **369**

FIGURE 11.1 The Development of Self-Recognition in Infancy
The graph shows the findings of two studies in which infants less than 1 year of age did not recognize themselves in the mirror. A slight increase in the percentage of infant self-recognition occurred around 15 to 18 months of age. By 2 years of age, a majority of children recognized themselves.

How do preschool children understand the self? Young children generally confuse self, mind, and body (Broughton, 1978). Most young children conceive of the self as part of the body, which usually means the head. For them, the self can be described along many material dimensions, such as size, shape, and color.

Preschool children think of themselves and define themselves in physical terms. "Physical" in this case includes physical actions as well as body image and material possessions. Young children distinguish themselves from others through many physical and material attributes. Says 4-year-old Sandra, "I'm different from Jennifer because I have brown hair and she has blond hair." Says 4-year-old Ralph, "I am different from Hank because I am taller, and I am different from my sister because I have a bicycle." The *active dimension* is a central component of the self in early childhood (Keller, Ford, & Meacham, 1978). For example, preschool children often describe themselves in terms of activities such as play. In sum, in early childhood, children often describe themselves in terms of a physical self or an active self.

Preschool children also develop an awareness of how their present selves are causally bound to previous states of the self (Povinelli & Simon, 1998). For example in one study, 2-, 3-, and 4-year-old children briefly saw video images of themselves (Povinelli, Perilloux, & Landau, 1996). The images showed the children playing an unusual game and revealed that one experimenter had covertly placed a large sticker on each child's head. Few 2- and 3-year-olds reached up to their heads to remove the sticker while a majority of the 4- and 5-year-olds did so immediately after the delayed tape revealed that the experimenter had placed it there.

Middle and Late Childhood In middle and late childhood, self-understanding increasingly shifts away from defining the self in terms of external characteristics. Children develop a more complex self-understanding with three key characteristics.

First, in middle and late childhood, children shift toward defining themselves in terms of internal characteristics. They now recognize the difference between inner and outer states, and they are also more likely than young children to include subjective inner states in their definition of self. For example, in one investigation, second-grade children were much more likely than younger children to name psychological characteristics (such as preferences or personality traits) in their self-definition and less likely to name physical characteristics (such as eye color or possessions) (Aboud & Skerry, 1983). Eight-year-old Todd says, "I am smart and I am popular." Ten-year-old Tina

> **K**now thyself, for once we know ourselves, we may learn how to care for ourselves, but otherwise we never shall.
> —SOCRATES
> *Greek Philosopher, 5th Century B.C.*

Concepts of Person and Self
Self-Development in Infancy

The Internet

Web icons appear a number of times in each chapter. They signal you to go to the book's website where you will find connecting links that provide additional information on the topic discussed in the text. The labels under the Web icon appear as Web links at the Santrock *A Topical Approach to Life-Span Development,* second edition, website, under that chapter for easy access.

E-Learning Tools

This feature appears at the end of each chapter and consists of three parts: *Taking It to the Net* Internet problem-solving exercises, *Self-Assessment,* which consists of one or more self-evaluations, and *Health and Well-Being, Parenting, and Education,* which provides an opportunity to practice decision-making skills related to health and well-being, parenting, and education. By going to the Online Learning Center for this book, you will find many learning activities to improve your knowledge and understanding of the chapter.

E-Learning Tools

Connect to **www.mhhe.com/santrockldt2** to research the answers and complete these exercises. In addition, you'll find a number of other resources and valuable study tools for chapter 11, "The Self, Identity, and Personality," on the Student CD-ROM that came with this book.

Taking It to the Net

1. Ted is the activities director at an adult retirement community. A friend who is a social worker suggested that Ted might want to develop a program in which the residents engage in the process of reminiscence and life review. What benefits might the residents gain from such an activity?

2. Janice, who has recently been appointed principal of a high school that has a large population of Middle Eastern, Asian, and Hispanic students, wants to conduct in-service training for the school's teachers to help them understand the challenges the ethnic students face as they strive to achieve their self-identity and ethnic identity. What challenges do the ethnic students face in resolving their identity crises, and how can the school assist them?

3. Eduardo is vice president for human resources at a 200-employee manufacturing plant. He wants to use a personality assessment for job selection and to help him plan interventions for employees who have job-related problems, such as poor motivation, personality problems with co-workers, and conflicts with supervisors. Would an assessment based on the five-factor model of personality be a good choice?

Self Assessment

To evaluate your self-esteem, identity, and personality, complete these self-assessments.

- *My Self-Esteem*
- *Exploring My Identity*
- *How Generative Am I?*
- *Am I Introverted or Extraverted?*

Health and Well-Being, Parenting, and Education

Build your decision-making skills by trying your hand at the health and well-being, parenting, and education "Scenarios."

Careers in Life-Span Development Appendix

A Careers in Life-Span Development appendix that describes a number of careers appears following chapter 17.

Appendix *Careers in Life-Span Development*

Some of you may be quite sure about what you plan to make your life's work. Others of you might not have decided on a major yet and might be uncertain about which career path you want to follow. Each of us wants to find a rewarding career and enjoy the work we do. The field of life-span development offers an amazing breadth of career options that can provide extremely satisfying work.

If you decide to pursue a career in life-span development, what career options are available to you? Many. College and university professors teach courses in many different areas of life-span development, education, family development, nursing, and medicine. Teachers impart knowledge, understanding, and skills to children and adolescents. Counselors, clinical psychologists, nurses, and physicians help people of different ages to cope more effectively with their lives and improve their well-being. Various professionals work with families to improve the quality of family functioning.

Although an advanced degree is not absolutely necessary in some areas of life-span development, you usually can considerably expand your opportunities (and income) by obtaining a graduate degree. Many careers in life-span development pay reasonably well. For example, psychologists earn well above the median salary in the United States. Also, by working in the field of life-span development, you can guide people in improving their lives, understand yourself and others better, possibly advance the state of knowledge in the field, and have an enjoyable time while you are doing these things.

If you are considering a career in life-span development, would you prefer to work with infants? children? adolescents? older adults? As you go through this term, try to spend some time with people of different ages. Observe their behavior. Talk with them about their lives. Think about whether you would like to work with people of this age in your life's work.

Another important aspect of exploring careers is to talk with people who work in various jobs. For example, if you have some interest in becoming a school counselor, call a school, ask to speak with a counselor, and set up an appointment to discuss the counselor's career and work. If you have an interest in becoming a nurse, think about whether you would rather work with babies, children, adolescents, or older adults. Call the nursing department at a hospital, ask to speak with the nursing department, and set up an appointment to speak with the nursing coordinator about a nursing career.

Something else that should benefit you is to work in one or more jobs related to your career interests while you are in college. Many colleges and universities have internships or work experiences for students who major in such fields as life-span development. Some of these opportunities are for course credit or pay; others are strictly on a volunteer basis. Take advantage of these opportunities. They can provide you with valuable experiences to help you decide if this is the right career area for you, and they can help you get into graduate school, if you decide you want to go.

In the upcoming sections, we will profile a number of careers in four areas: education/research; clinical/counseling; medical/nursing/physical; and families/relationships. These are not the only career options in life-span development, but they

A-1

The Life-Span Perspective

All the world's a stage. And all the men and women merely players. They have their exits and their entrances, and one man in his time plays many parts.

—WILLIAM SHAKESPEARE
English Playwright, 17th Century

This book is about human development—its universal features, its individual variations, its nature. Every life is distinct, a new biography in the world. Examining the shape of life-span development allows us to understand it better. *A Topical Approach to Life-Span Development* is about the rhythm and meaning of people's lives, about turning mystery into understanding, and about weaving a portrait of who each of us was, is, and will be. In Section 1, you will read "Introduction" (chapter 1).

Introduction

Chapter Outline	**Learning Goals**

THE LIFE-SPAN PERSPECTIVE 1

The Importance of Studying Life-Span Development

The Historical Perspective

Characteristics of the Life-Span Perspective

1 Explain the distinctive features of a life-span perspective on development

THE NATURE OF DEVELOPMENT 2

Biological, Cognitive, and Socioemotional Processes

Periods of Development

Conceptions of Age

Developmental Issues

2 Identify the most important processes, periods, and issues in development

THEORIES OF DEVELOPMENT 3

Psychoanalytic Theories

Cognitive Theories

Behavioral and Social Cognitive Theories

Ethological Theory

Ecological Theory

An Eclectic Orientation

3 Describe five theoretical approaches to human development

RESEARCH IN LIFE-SPAN DEVELOPMENT 4

Methods for Collecting Data

Research Designs

Time Span of Research

Ethics

4 Explain how research on life-span development is conducted

This book is a window into the journey of human development—your own and that of every other member of the human species. In this first chapter, we will explore what it means to take a life-span perspective on development, examine the nature of development, and outline how science helps us to understand it.

1 THE LIFE-SPAN PERSPECTIVE

| The Importance of Studying Life-Span Development | The Historical Perspective | Characteristics of the Life-Span Perspective |

Each of us develops partly like all other individuals, partly like some other individuals, and partly like no other individuals. Most of the time our attention is directed to an individual's uniqueness. But as humans, we all have traveled some common paths. Each of us—Leonardo Da Vinci, Joan of Arc, George Washington, Martin Luther King, Jr., and you—walked at about 1 year, engaged in fantasy play as a young child, and became more independent as youth. Each of us, if we live long enough, will experience hearing problems and the death of family members and friends. This is the general course of our **development,** the pattern of movement or change that begins at conception and continues through the human life span.

The Importance of Studying Life-Span Development

How might people benefit from examining life-span development? Perhaps you are, or will be, a parent or teacher. If so, responsibility for children is, or will be, a part of your everyday life. The more you learn about them, the better you can deal with them. Perhaps you hope to gain some insight about your own history—as an infant, a child, an adolescent, or a young adult. Perhaps you want to know more about what your life will be like as you grow through the adult years—as a middle-aged adult, or as an adult in old age, for example. Or perhaps you just stumbled onto this course, thinking that it sounded intriguing and that the study of the human life span might raise some provocative issues. Whatever your reasons, you will discover that the study of life-span development is intriguing and filled with information about who we are, how we came to be this way, and where our future will take us.

Most development involves growth, but it also includes decline (as in dying). In exploring development we will examine the life span from the point of conception until the time when life (at least, life as we know it) ends. You will see yourself as an infant, as a child, and as an adolescent, and be stimulated to think about how those years influenced the kind of individual you are today. And you will see yourself as a young adult, as a middle-aged adult, and as an adult in old age, and be motivated to think about how your experiences today will influence your development through the remainder of your adult years.

Researchers who study life-span development aim to describe, explain, and discover ways to optimize development. Consider these research findings:

- Massage therapy facilitates the growth and improves the immune system functioning of preterm infants (Field, 2001, 2002).
- When high school students take part in community service projects such as tutoring or helping in a hospital, their grades and self-esteem improve, and they have an increased sense of being able to make a difference for others (Santilli, Falbo, & Harris, 2002; Search Institute, 1999; Youniss & others, 2003).

> $\mathcal{W}$e reach backward to our parents and forward to our children and through their children to a future we will never see, but about which we need to care.
>
> —CARL JUNG
> *Swiss Psychoanalyst, 20th Century*

development The pattern of change that begins at conception and continues through the life span.

- Friendship is a critical aspect of marital success, even for individuals who rate sexual satisfaction as highly important in a marriage (Gottman & others, 2002).
- Scientists have demonstrated the ability to extend the life span of human cells in a test tube, which suggests that it might be possible to raise the upper boundary of the human life span (Ouellette & others, 2000).

These are but a few of the thousands of research findings we will examine in this text that can improve your understanding of the human life span.

The Historical Perspective

The maximum span of human life is approximately 120 years. This upper boundary has not changed since the beginning of recorded history. However, in other ways the life span has varied in striking ways over the centuries.

Child Development   Childhood has become such a distinct time of life that it is hard to imagine it was not always thought of as a special stage. In medieval Europe, for example, laws generally did not distinguish between childhood offenses and adult offenses. Historian Philippe Ariès (1962) examined European paintings and found that prior to 1600, the children were often dressed in small versions of adult clothing. To some extent, children were treated as miniature adults in medieval Europe.

Ideas about children have also varied. Throughout history, philosophers have speculated about the nature of children and how they should be reared. In the West, three influential philosophical views are based on the ideas of original sin, tabula rasa, and innate goodness:

Children learn to love when they are loved

- According to the Christian doctrine of **original sin,** children are born into the world corrupted, with an inclination toward evil. The goal of child rearing is to save children from sin.
- Toward the end of the seventeenth century, English philosopher John Locke proposed that at birth each child is a **tabula rasa**—a "blank tablet." Locke believed that people acquire their characteristics through experience and that childhood experiences are important in determining adult characteristics. He advised parents to spend time with their children and help them become contributing members of society.
- In the eighteenth century, the concept of **innate goodness** was presented by Swiss-born French philosopher Jean-Jacques Rousseau. He stressed that children are inherently good. As a result, Rousseau said that they should be permitted to grow naturally with little parental monitoring or constraint.

These conflicting views formed the historical backdrop for the study of childhood and for child-rearing practices. Today, we conceive of childhood as a highly eventful and unique period of life that lays an important foundation for the adult years and is highly differentiated from them (Graham, 2001; Pittman & Diversi, 2003). Most approaches to childhood identify distinct periods in which special skills are mastered and new life tasks are confronted. We now value childhood as a special time of growth and change, and we invest great resources in caring for and educating our children (Parke & Clarke-Stewart, 2003). That investment includes creating government provisions for helping them when ordinary family support systems fail or when families seriously endanger the child's well-being. The Applications in Life-Span Development interlude explores government programs for improving the lives of children.

www.mhhe.com/santrockld2

History of Childhood

Children's Issues

Children's Rights

UNICEF

original sin Based on Christian doctrine, the view that children are born into the world corrupted with an inclination toward evil.

tabula rasa Locke's view that children are born as "blank slates" and acquire their characteristics through experience.

innate goodness Rousseau's view that children are born inherently good.

Applications in Life-Span Development

Family Policy

No matter how our society values children in general, many children live in families that cannot or do not adequately care for them (Crouter & Booth, 2004; Zaslow, 2004). When other support systems fail or when families seriously endanger a child's well-being, what should happen? How a society answers that question is an important part of its *social policy*—the laws, regulations, and government programs that influence the welfare of its citizens.

In the United States, the national government, state governments, and city governments all play a role in influencing the well-being of children (Bogenschneide, 2002; Pittman & others, 2003). At the national and state levels, controversy has focused for decades on whether the government can promote children's well-being by giving money to parents who are very poor so that they can feed and house their children. If the government gives money to the parents, what should it expect in return? Should the government help parents living in poverty pay for someone to take care of their children so that the parents can work? If parents are homeless, what if anything should the government do for the parents or their children?

Answers to these questions are part of a government's family policy. Some experts argue that a successful family policy will not be shaped primarily by committees and lobbyists in Washington, D.C., but by parents themselves, when they come to understand their need for each other and the interconnectedness of families, schools, and communities (Louv, 1990).

The family policies of the United States are overwhelmingly treatment-oriented: only those families and individuals who already have problems are eligible. Few preventive programs are available on any widespread basis. For example, families in which the children are on the verge of being placed in foster care are eligible, and often required, to receive counseling; families in which problems are brewing but are not yet full-blown usually cannot qualify for public services. Most experts on family policy believe that more attention should be given to preventing family problems (Hawkins & Whitman, 2004).

Effective prevention programs focus not just on a reduction of problems but also on enhancing the competence of parents and children (Clampet-Lundquist & others, 2004; Kalil & DeLeire, 2004). For example, a comprehensive competence-enhancement program might attempt to help a child's parents find good jobs and health care, provide education for the child, and seek to improve the child's social skills. Skills such as self-control, stress management, problem solving, decision making, communication, peer resistance, and assertiveness have been found to reduce children's aggressive behavior and improve their adjustment and competence (Weisberg & Greenberg, 1998).

One recent study examined the influence of the Minnesota Family Investment Program (MFIP) on children (Gennetian & Miller, 2002). The MFIP was designed to primarily affect the employment behavior and economic self-sufficiency of adults. An important positive outcome was that increases in income for working poor parents were linked with their children's improved achievement in school and a reduction in behavioral problems.

How might improved social policy benefit homeless families?

life expectancy The number of years that a person is expected to live on average when born in a particular year.

Adult Development For much of human history, many families could not expect that their children would even survive into adulthood. **Life expectancy**—the number of years that an average person is expected to live when born in a particular year—was only 20 in ancient Greece. Because so many infants and children died, it took 5,000 years of human history to extend human life expectancy by 25 years (see figure 1.1). In contrast, in the twentieth century alone, life expectancy in the United States increased by 30 years. Improvements in sanitation, nutrition, and medical knowledge led to this amazing increase.

How much has the older population grown in the United States? Figure 1.2 reveals a dramatic increase in the over-65 age group since 1900 and projects continued increases through 2040. A significant increase will also occur in the number of individuals in the 85-and-over and in the 100-and-over age categories. Currently, fewer than 50,000 Americans are 100 years of age or older; the number in 2050 is projected to be more than 300,000. A woman born today has a 1 in 3 chance of living to be 100 years of age!

As the older population continues to increase in the twenty-first century, an increasing number of older adults will be without either a spouse or children (traditionally the main sources of support for older adults) (Berado, 2004). In recent decades, American adults were less likely to be married, more likely to be childless, and more likely to be living alone than earlier in the twentieth century. As these individuals become older, their need for social relationships, networks, and supports is increasing at the same time as their supply is dwindling (Nussbaum & Copeland, 2004).

These changing needs are but one illustration of the fact that human development is lifelong. For too long we believed that development was something that happened only to children. To be sure, growth and development are dramatic in the first two decades of life, but a great deal of change goes on in the next five or six decades of life, too. Consider this description of development after age 20:

> The next five or six decades are every bit as important, not only to those adults who are passing through them but to their children, who must live with and understand parents and grandparents. The changes in body, personality, and abilities through these later decades is great. Developmental tasks are imposed by marriage and parenthood, by the waxing and waning of physical prowess and of some intellectual capacities, by the children's flight from the nest, by the achievement of an occupational plateau, and by retirement and the prospect of final extinction. Parents have always been fascinated by their children's development, but it is high time adults began to look objectively at themselves, to examine the systematic changes in their own physical, mental, and emotional qualities as they pass through the life span, and to get acquainted with the limitations and assets they share with so many others of their age (Sears & Feldman, 1973, pp. v–vi).

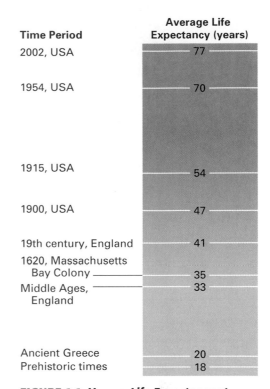

FIGURE 1.1 Human Life Expectancy at Birth from Prehistoric to Contemporary Times

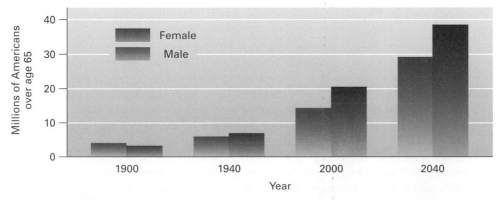

FIGURE 1.2 The Aging of America

This graph shows the millions of Americans over age 65 from 1900 to 2000 as well as the projected increase in the year 2040.

Development in childhood is important, but a complete view of development requires that we also consider developmental changes in the adult years (Overton, 2003). Although interest in children has a long and rich history, interest in adults began to develop seriously in the latter half of the twentieth century (Havighurst, 1973). The traditional approach to development emphasizes extreme change from birth to adolescence, little or no change in adulthood, and decline in old age. In contrast, the life-span approach emphasizes that developmental change occurs during adulthood as well as during childhood.

Characteristics of the Life-Span Perspective

The belief that development is lifelong is central to the life-span perspective, but according to leading theorist and researcher Paul Baltes (1987, 2000, 2003; Baltes & Smith, 2003), the life-span perspective includes several additional characteristics. Baltes describes the *life-span perspective* as one that sees human development as lifelong, multidimensional, multidirectional, plastic, contextual, and multidisciplinary, and as involving growth, maintenance, and regulation. Let's look at each of these concepts.

Development Is Lifelong   In the life-span perspective, early adulthood is not the endpoint of development; rather, no age period dominates development. Researchers increasingly study the experiences and psychological orientations of adults at different points in their development (Bertand & Lachman, 2003; Connell & Janevic, 2003).

Development Is Multidimensional   Development consists of biological, cognitive, and socioemotional dimensions. Each dimension has many components. For example, the cognitive dimension includes abstract intelligence, nonverbal intelligence, and social intelligence.

Development Is Multidirectional   Both growth and decline characterize development. Some dimensions or components of a dimension may expand and others shrink as individuals develop. In language development, for example, the capacity for acquiring second and third languages decreases later in development, especially after early childhood (Levelt, 1989). In socioemotional development, as heterosexual adolescents begin to establish intimate relationships with opposite-sex peers, their relationships with same-sex peers might decrease (Hartup, 2000). In cognitive development, older adults might become wiser by calling on experience to guide their decision making (Baltes, 2000, 2003; Baltes & Kunzmann, 2003). However, they perform more poorly on tasks that require speed in processing information (Madden, 2001; Salthouse, 2000).

*T*he strong interest in plasticity on the part of life-span developmentalists highlights the potentialities of development, including its lower and upper boundary conditions.

—PAUL BALTES
*Contemporary Psychologist,
Max Planck Institute, Berlin*

Development Is Plastic   If aging is associated with declines in certain intellectual abilities, are these declines irreversible, or can older adults develop strategies to prevent or reduce these declines (Singer, Lindenberger, & Baltes, 2003)? In one research study, the reasoning abilities of older adults were improved through retraining (Willis & Schaie, 1994). This is an example of *plasticity*, the potential for change. Chapter 3 discusses another example of plasticity: A young boy had a large part of the left side of his brain removed to stop severe seizures; the right side of his brain began to take over functions normally carried out by the left side of the brain.

Development Is Contextual   The individual continually responds to and acts on contexts, which include a person's biological makeup, physical environment, and cognitive processes, as well as historical, social, and cultural contexts. *Social* and *cultural contexts* have received the most attention in research on life-span development. These contexts are the environmental settings in which people live. They range from families to peer groups to schools to neighborhoods to entire cultures. For example, one contextual effect is that parents in the United States are more likely to rear their children to be independent than parents in Japan are (Rothbaum & others, 2000).

Contexts, like individuals, change. Thus, individuals are changing beings in a changing world. As a result of these changes, three types of influences are exerted by contexts (Baltes, 2000): (1) normative age-graded influences, (2) normative history-graded influences, and (3) nonnormative life events.

- **Normative age-graded influences** are similar for individuals in a particular age group. These influences include biological processes such as puberty and menopause. They also include sociocultural, environmental processes such as beginning formal education (usually at about age 6 in most cultures) and retirement (which takes place in the fifties and sixties in most cultures).
- **Normative history-graded influences** are common to people of a particular generation because of historical circumstances. Examples include economic changes (such as the Great Depression in the 1930s), war (such as World War II in the 1940s), the changing role of women, the current technology revolution, political upheaval (such as the decrease in hard-line communism in the 1990s), and the 9/11/2001 terrorist attacks and the changes they have produced (Modell & Elder, 2002).
- **Nonnormative life events** are unusual occurrences that have a major impact on the individual's life. Examples include the death of a parent when a child is young, pregnancy in early adolescence, a fire that destroys a home, winning the lottery, or getting an unexpected career opportunity with special privileges.

Considering development in context is so important that each chapter of this book includes a Contexts of Life-Span Development interlude, where we consider some aspects of contexts related to the discussion at hand.

The Study of Development Is Multidisciplinary   Because of the complexity of human development, the expertise necessary to understand it comes from many disciplines. To understand how intelligence develops, for example, researchers ask questions such as: What constraints on intelligence are set by the individual's heredity and health? Are changes in intelligence with age universal, or do they vary from one culture to another? How do variations in families and neighborhoods affect the development of intelligence? Help in answering these questions comes from work in neuroscience, genetics, anthropology, sociology, and other disciplines, as well as psychology.

Furthermore, the knowledge gained through the study of life-span development sheds light on questions in many other disciplines. Psychologists, anthropologists, neuroscientists, and medical researchers all study human development and share an interest in unlocking the mysteries of development through the life span (Alexpoulos & others, 2002; Toseland & others, 2002; Velez-Pardo, Lopera, & Del Rio, 2002).

Development Involves Growth, Maintenance, and Regulation   Baltes and his colleagues (Baltes, 2000, 2003; Baltes & Smith, 2003) believe that the mastery of life often involves conflicts and competition among three aspects of human development: growth, maintenance, and regulation. As individuals age into middle and late adulthood, the maintenance and regulation of their capacities takes center stage away from the growth that characterized development through childhood and early adulthood. Thus, for many middle-aged and older adults, the goal is not to seek growth in intellectual capacities (such as memory) or physical capacities (such as physical strength), but to maintain those skills or minimize their deterioration.

normative age-graded influences Biological and environmental influences that are similar for individuals in a particular age group.

normative history-graded influences Biological and environmental influences that are associated with history. These influences are common to people of a particular generation.

nonnormative life events Unusual occurrences that have a major impact on a person's life. The occurrence, pattern, and sequence of these events are not applicable to many individuals.

Review and Reflect: Learning Goal 1

1 **Explain the distinctive features of a life-span perspective on development**

REVIEW

- What is development? Why is the study of life-span development important?
- What is the historical background of the study of life-span development?
- What are the seven main characteristics of the life-span perspective? What are three aspects of the contextual characteristic?

REFLECT

- Imagine what your development would have been like in a culture that offered fewer or distinctly different choices than your own. How might your development have been different if your family had been significantly richer or poorer than it was?

2 THE NATURE OF DEVELOPMENT

- Biological, Cognitive, and Socioemotional Processes
- Conceptions of Age
- Periods of Development
- Developmental Issues

The life-span perspective on development, as we have just seen, assumes that development is multidimensional and lifelong. Let's further examine some key dimensions of development that explain what moves us along a particular developmental path and the major milestones along the way.

Biological, Cognitive, and Socioemotional Processes

At the beginning of this chapter, we defined *development* as the pattern of movement or change that begins at conception and continues through the life span. The pattern of movement is complex because it is the product of several processes—biological, cognitive, and socioemotional.

Biological processes involve changes in the individual's physical nature. Genes inherited from parents, the development of the brain, height and weight gains, change in motor skills, the hormonal changes of puberty, and cardiovascular decline all reflect the role of biological processes in development.

Cognitive processes involve changes in the individual's thought, intelligence, and language. Watching a colorful mobile swinging above the crib, putting together a two-word sentence, memorizing a poem, imagining what it would be like to be a movie star, and solving a crossword puzzle all reflect the role of cognitive processes in development.

Socioemotional processes involve changes in the individual's relationships with other people, changes in emotions, and changes in personality. An infant's smile in response to her mother's touch, a young boy's aggressive attack on a playmate, a girl's development of assertiveness, an adolescent's joy at the senior prom, and the affection of an older couple all reflect the role of the socioemotional processes in development.

Remember as you read about biological, cognitive, and socioemotional processes that they are intricately interwoven. Socioemotional processes shape cognitive processes, cognitive processes promote or restrict socioemotional processes, and biological processes influence cognitive processes. Although it is helpful to study the different processes in separate sections of the book, keep in mind that you are studying the development of an integrated individual with a mind and body that are interdependent (see figure 1.3).

Periods of Development

The interplay of biological, cognitive, and socioemotional processes produces a pattern of changes through the years so that a young child is obviously different from an infant and an adolescent is clearly different from an adult. As a result, people's lives are commonly thought of as being divided into stages or *periods* such as infancy. For purposes of organization and understanding, developmental psychologists most often divide the human life span into these developmental periods: prenatal period, infancy, early childhood, middle and late childhood, adolescence, early adulthood, middle adulthood, and late adulthood. No precise ages mark the beginning or end of each period, but approximate age ranges are associated with each.

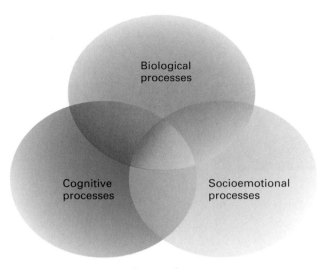

FIGURE 1.3 Processes in Development

Development is the product of the interaction of biological, cognitive, and socioemotional processes.

The *prenatal period* is the time from conception to birth. It involves tremendous growth—from a single cell to an organism complete with a brain and behavioral capabilities, produced in approximately nine months.

Infancy is the developmental period extending from birth through 18 to 24 months. Infancy is a time of extreme dependence on adults. Many psychological activities are just beginning—language, symbolic thought, sensorimotor coordination, and social learning, for example.

Early childhood extends from the end of infancy to about 6 years. This period is sometimes called the "preschool years." During this time, young children learn to become more self-sufficient and to care for themselves, develop school readiness skills (following instructions, identifying letters), and spend many hours in play with peers. First grade typically marks the end of early childhood.

Middle and late childhood extends from about 6 to 11 years of age, and it is sometimes called the "elementary school years." The fundamental skills of reading, writing, and arithmetic are mastered. The child is formally exposed to the larger world and its culture. Achievement becomes a more central theme of the child's world, and self-control increases.

Adolescence is the period of transition from childhood to early adulthood, starting at approximately 10 to 12 years of age and ending at about 18 to 22 years of age. Adolescence begins with rapid physical changes—dramatic gains in height and weight, changes in body contour, and the development of sexual characteristics such as enlargement of the breasts, development of pubic and facial hair, and deepening of the voice. At this point in development, the pursuit of independence and an identity are prominent. Thought is more logical, abstract, and idealistic. More time is spent outside of the family.

Early adulthood begins in the late teens and early twenties and lasts through the thirties. It is a time of establishing personal and economic independence, career development, and, for many, selecting a mate, learning to live with someone in an intimate way, starting a family, and rearing children.

Middle adulthood is the developmental period beginning at approximately 35 to 45 years of age and extending to the sixties. It is a time of expanding personal and social involvement and responsibility; of assisting the next generation in becoming competent, mature individuals; and of reaching and maintaining satisfaction in a career.

Late adulthood begins in the sixties or seventies and lasts until death. It is a time of adjustment to decreasing strength and health, life review, retirement, and adjustment to new social roles.

Periods of Development

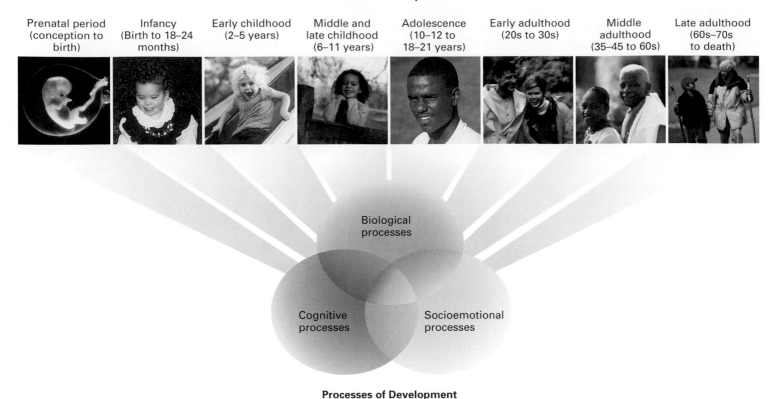

FIGURE 1.4 Processes and Periods of Development

The unfolding of life's periods of development is influenced by the interaction of biological, cognitive, and socioemotional processes.

Late adulthood has the longest span of any period of development. Life-span developmentalists increasingly distinguish between two age groups in late adulthood: the young old, or old age (65 to 74 years of age), and the old old, or late old age (75 years and older). Some also distinguish the oldest old (85 years and older) from younger older adults (Pearlin, 1994). Because of its lengthy span and the dramatic increase in the number of adults living to older ages, we will see increased attention to differentiating the late adulthood period (Baltes & Smith, 2003).

The periods of the human life span are shown in figure 1.4 along with the processes of development—biological, cognitive, and socioemotional. Every period of the life span has its stresses, pluses and minuses, hills and valleys. For example, although adolescents must cope with developing an identity, feelings of insecurity, mood swings, and peer pressure, most adolescents develop positive perceptions of themselves, feelings of competence about their skills, positive relationships with friends and family, and an optimistic view of their future. And while older adults face a life of reduced income, less energy, decreasing physical skills, and concerns about death, they are also less pressured to achieve and succeed, have more time for leisurely pursuits, and have accumulated many years of experience that help them adapt to their lives with a wisdom they might not have had in their younger years.

Might people be happier in one developmental period than in other periods? When individuals report how happy they are and how satisfied they are with their lives, no particular age group reports more happiness or satisfaction than any other age group (Diener, 2004; Diener, Lucas, & Oishi, 2002). In one study in eight Western European countries, there was no difference in the percentages of people who were satisfied with life at different ages: 78 percent of 15- to 24-year-olds, 78 percent of 35- to 44-year-olds, and 78 percent of those 65 years and older (Ingelhart & Rabier, 1986) (see figure 1.5). Similarly, slightly less than 20 percent of each of the age groups reported that they were "very happy." Growing older is a certain outcome of living, so we can derive considerable pleasure from knowing that we are likely to be just as happy as older adults as when we were younger.

Conceptions of Age

To what extent do the approximate age ranges associated with developmental periods matter? Life-span expert Bernice Neugarten (1988) believes we are rapidly becoming an age-irrelevant society. There are 28-year-old mayors, 35-year-old grandmothers, and 70-year-old students. Neugarten stresses that similar choices, dilemmas, and themes appear and reappear throughout life. The issues of intimacy and freedom, for example, can haunt couples throughout their relationship. Feeling the pressure of time, reformulating goals, and coping with success and failure are not the exclusive property of adults of a particular age.

Neugarten's ideas raise questions about how age should be conceptualized. Some of the ways in which age has been conceptualized are as chronological age, biological age, psychological age, and social age (Hoyer & Roodin, 2003):

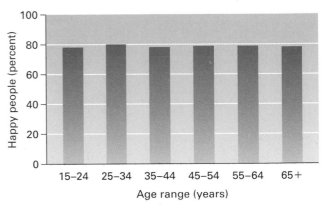

FIGURE 1.5 Age and Happiness

Analysis of surveys of nearly 170,000 people in 16 countries found no age differences in happiness from adolescence into the late adulthood years.

- **Chronological age** is the number of years that have elapsed since birth. Many people consider chronological age to be synonomous with the concept of age, but as this section on conceptions of age indicates, there are other dimensions to age.
- **Biological age** is a person's age in terms of biological health. Determining biological age involves knowing the functional capacities of a person's vital organs. One person's vital capacities may be better or worse than those of others of comparable age. The younger the person's biological age, the longer the person is expected to live, regardless of chronological age.
- **Psychological age** is an individual's adaptive capacities compared with those of other individuals of the same chronological age. Thus, older adults who continue to learn, are flexible, are motivated, control their emotions, and think clearly are engaging in more adaptive behaviors than their chronological age-mates who do not continue to learn, are rigid, are unmotivated, do not control their emotions, and do not think clearly.
- **Social age** refers to social roles and expectations related to a person's age. Consider the role of "mother" and the behaviors that accompany the role (Huyck & Hoyer, 1982). In predicting an adult woman's behavior, it may be more important to know that she is the mother of a 3-year-old child than to know whether she is 20 or 30 years old. We still have some expectations for when certain life events—such as getting married, having children, becoming a grandparent, and retiring—should occur. However, as Neugarten concluded, chronological age has become a less accurate predictor of these life events in our society.

Developmental Issues

Although age is the index people most often use to mark the journey through life, the fact that its meaning blurs when closely examined suggests the journey is complex. For example, is your journey through life marked out ahead of time, or can your experiences change your path? Are the experiences you have early in your journey more important than later ones? Is your journey more like taking an elevator up a skyscraper with distinct stops along the way or more like a cruise down a river with smoother ebbs and flows? These questions point to three issues about

chronological age The number of years that have elapsed since a person's birth; what is usually meant by "age."

biological age A person's age in terms of biological health.

psychological age An individual's adaptive capacities compared with those of other individuals of the same chronological age.

social age Social roles and expectations related to a person's age.

the nature of development: the roles played by nature and nurture, stability and change, and continuity and discontinuity.

Nature and Nurture The **nature-nurture issue** involves the debate about the extent to which development is influenced by nature and by nurture. *Nature* refers to an organism's biological inheritance, *nurture* to its environmental experiences.

According to those who emphasize the role of nature, just as a sunflower grows in an orderly way—unless flattened by an unfriendly environment—so does the human grow in an orderly way. An evolutionary and genetic blueprint produces commonalities in growth and development (Durrant & Ellis, 2003). We walk before we talk, speak one word before two words, grow rapidly in infancy and less so in early childhood, experience a rush of sex hormones in puberty, reach the peak of our physical strength in late adolescence and early adulthood, and then physically decline. Proponents of the importance of nature acknowledge that extreme environments—those that are psychologically barren or hostile—can depress development. However, they believe that basic growth tendencies are genetically wired into humans.

By contrast, other psychologists emphasize the importance of nurture, or environmental experiences, in development. Experiences run the gamut from the individual's biological environment (nutrition, medical care, drugs, and physical accidents) to the social environment (family, peers, schools, community, media, and culture). Consider the family experiences of adolescents. Researchers have revealed that when parents effectively monitor adolescents' lives, adolescents are less likely to take drugs or engage in delinquency (Collins & Laursen, 2004; Steinberg & Silk, 2002). Researchers have also found that when children are rejected by their peers, they often develop behavioral problems (Brown, 2004; Buhs & Ladd, 2002).

Stability and Change Is the shy child who hides behind the sofa when visitors arrive destined to become a wallflower at college dances, or might the child become a sociable, talkative individual? Will the fun-loving, carefree adolescent have difficulty holding down a 9-to-5 job as an adult or become a straitlaced conformist? These questions reflect the **stability-change issue,** which involves the degree to which early traits and characteristics persist through life or change.

Many developmentalists who emphasize stability in development argue that stability is the result of heredity and possibly early experiences in life. For example, many argue that if an individual is shy throughout life, heredity and possibly early experiences in which the infant or young child encountered considerable stress when interacting with people are the reasons for this stability.

Developmentalists who emphasize change take the more optimistic view that later experiences can produce change. Recall that in the life-span perspective, *plasticity,* the potential for change, exists throughout the life span. One reason why adult development was ignored by researchers until fairly recently was the belief that nothing much changes in adulthood. The major changes were thought to take place in childhood, especially during the first five years of life. Today, most developmentalists believe that some change is possible throughout the human life span, although they disagree, sometimes vehemently, about just how much change can take place, and how much stability there is. Experts such as Paul Baltes (2000, 2003) argue that older adults often show less capacity for change than younger adults.

The roles of early and later experience are an aspect of the stability-change issue that has long been hotly debated (Gottlieb, 2002). Some believe that unless infants experience warm, nurturant caregiving in the first year or so of life, their development will never be optimal (Waters & Cummings, 2000). Plato was sure that infants who were rocked frequently became better athletes. Nineteenth-century New England ministers told parents in Sunday sermons that the way they handled their infants would determine their children's future character. The emphasis on the

nature-nurture issue The debate about the extent to which development is influenced by nature and by nurture. Nature refers to an organism's biological inheritance, nurture to its environmental experiences.

stability-change issue The debate about the degree to which early traits and characteristics persist through life or change.

importance of early experience rests on the belief that each life is an unbroken trail on which a psychological quality can be traced back to its origin (Kagan, 1992, 2000, 2003).

The later-experience advocates argue that children are malleable throughout development and that later sensitive caregiving is just as important as earlier sensitive caregiving. A number of life-span developmentalists stress that too little attention has been given to later experiences in development (Baltes, 2000, 2003; Birren & Schaie, 2001). They argue that early experiences are important contributors to development, but no more important than later experiences. Jerome Kagan (2000, 2003) points out that even children who are shy and timid (qualities of an inhibited temperament, which is linked to heredity) have the capacity to change their behavior. In his research, almost one-third of a group of children who had an inhibited temperament at 2 years of age were not unusually shy or fearful when they were 4 years of age.

People in Western cultures have tended to support the idea that early experiences are more important than later experiences. But the majority of people in the world do not share this belief. For example, people in many Asian countries believe that experiences occurring after about 6 to 7 years of age are more important to development than earlier experiences. This stance stems from the long-standing belief in Eastern cultures that children's reasoning skills begin to develop in important ways in the middle childhood years.

Continuity and Discontinuity   When developmental change occurs, is it gradual or abrupt? Think about your own development for a moment. Did you become the person you are gradually, like the seedling that slowly, cumulatively grows into a giant oak? Or did you experience sudden, distinct changes in your growth, like the caterpillar that changes into a butterfly (see figure 1.6)? For the most part, developmentalists who emphasize nurture usually describe development as a gradual, continuous process. Those who emphasize nature often describe development as a series of distinct stages.

The **continuity-discontinuity issue** focuses on the extent to which development involves gradual, cumulative change (continuity) or distinct stages (discontinuity). In terms of continuity, as the oak grows from seedling to giant oak, it becomes *more* oak—its development is continuous. Similarly, a child's first word, though seemingly an abrupt, discontinuous event, is actually the result of weeks and months of growth and practice. Puberty might seem abrupt, but it is a gradual process that occurs over several years.

In terms of discontinuity, each person is described as passing through a sequence of stages in which change is qualitatively rather than quantitatively different. As the caterpillar changes to a butterfly, it is not just more caterpillar, it is a *different kind* of organism—its development is discontinuous. Similarly, at some point a child moves from not being able to think abstractly about the world to being able to. This is a qualitative, discontinuous change in development, not a quantitative, continuous change.

Evaluating the Developmental Issues   It is important to keep in mind that most life-span developmentalists do not take extreme positions on the three developmental issues. They acknowledge that development is not all nature or all nurture, not all stability or all change, and not all continuity or all discontinuity (Lerner, 2002; Lerner & Steinberg, 2004). Nature and nurture, stability and change, and continuity and discontinuity characterize development throughout the human life span. With respect to the nature-nurture issue, then, the key to development is the *interaction* of nature and nurture (Lippa, 2002; Rutter, 2002). For instance, an individual's cognitive development is the result of heredity-environment interaction, not heredity or environment alone. (Much more about heredity-environment interaction appears in chapter 2.)

FIGURE 1.6 Continuity and Discontinuity in Development

Is our development like that of a seedling gradually growing into a giant oak? Or is it more like that of a caterpillar suddenly becoming a butterfly?

continuity-discontinuity issue The debate about the extent to which development involves gradual, cumulative change (continuity) or distinct stages (discontinuity).

Although most developmentalists do not take extreme positions on these three important issues, there is spirited debate regarding how strongly development is influenced by each of these factors (Sroufe & others, 2001). Are girls less likely to do well in math because of their "feminine" nature, or because of what they learn as a result of society's masculine bias? How much, if at all, does our memory decline in old age? Can techniques be used to prevent or reduce the decline? Can enriched experiences in adolescence remove "deficits" resulting from childhood experiences of poverty, neglect by parents, and poor schooling? The answers depend on the relative importance of nature and nurture, stability and change, and continuity and discontinuity.

Review and Reflect: Learning Goal 2

2 Identify the most important processes, periods, and issues in development

REVIEW

- What are the three key developmental processes?
- What are eight main developmental periods?
- What are four ways age can be conceptualized?
- What are three important developmental issues?

REFLECT

- Do you think there is a best age to be? If so, what is it? Why?

---

3 THEORIES OF DEVELOPMENT

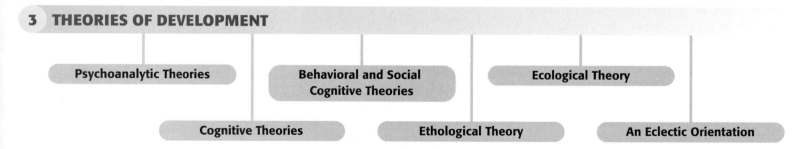

Psychoanalytic Theories	Behavioral and Social Cognitive Theories	Ecological Theory
Cognitive Theories	Ethological Theory	An Eclectic Orientation

How can we answer questions about the roles of nature and nurture, stability and change, and continuity and discontinuity in development? How can we determine, for example, whether memory declines in older adults can be prevented or whether special care can repair the harm inflicted by child neglect? The scientific method is the best tool we have to answer such questions (Wozniak, 2004).

The *scientific method* is essentially a four-step process:

1. Conceptualize a process or problem to be studied.
2. Collect research information (data).
3. Analyze data.
4. Draw conclusions.

In step 1, when researchers are formulating a problem to study, they often draw on *theories* and develop *hypotheses*. A **theory** is an interrelated, coherent set of ideas that helps to explain phenomena and make predictions. It may suggest **hypotheses,** which are specific assertions and predictions that can be tested. For example, a theory on mentoring might state that sustained support and guidance from an adult makes a difference in the lives of children from impoverished backgrounds because the mentor gives the children opportunities to observe and imitate the behavior and strategies of the mentor.

theory A coherent set of ideas that helps to explain data and to make predictions.

hypotheses Assertions or predictions, often derived from theories, that can be tested.

The diversity of theories makes understanding life-span development a challenging undertaking. Just when you think one theory has the correct explanation of life-span development, another theory crops up and makes you rethink your earlier conclusion. No single theory has been able to account for all aspects of life-span development. Each theory contributes an important piece to the life-span development puzzle. Although the theories sometimes disagree about certain aspects of life-span development, different theories contain many ideas that are complementary rather than contradictory. Together they let us see the total landscape of life-span development in all its richness.

We will briefly outline five major theoretical perspectives on development: psychoanalytic, cognitive, behavioral and social cognitive, ethological, and ecological. Each tends to focus on one or two of the major processes involved in development that we discussed earlier: biological, cognitive, and socioemotional. You will read more about these theories and processes at different points in later chapters in the book. We will begin our exploration of theories with the first of the theories proposed: Freud's psychoanalytic theory.

Sigmund Freud, the pioneering architect of psychoanalytic theory. *How did Freud believe each individual's personality is organized?*

Psychoanalytic Theories

According to **psychoanalytic theories,** development depends primarily on the unconscious mind and is heavily couched in emotion. Psychoanalytic theorists believe that behavior is merely a surface characteristic and that, to truly understand development, we have to analyze the symbolic meanings of behavior and the deep inner workings of the mind. Psychoanalytic theorists also stress that early experiences with parents extensively shape our development. These characteristics are highlighted in the main psychoanalytic theory, that of Sigmund Freud.

Freud's Theory Freud (1856–1939) developed his ideas about psychoanalytic theory from work with mental patients. He was a medical doctor who specialized in neurology. After spending most of his years in Vienna, he moved to London near the end of his career to flee Nazi anti-Semitism.

Freud (1917) believed that personality has three structures: the id, the ego, and the superego. The *id* is the Freudian structure of personality that consists of instincts, which are an individual's reservoir of psychic energy. In Freud's view, the id is totally unconscious; it has no contact with reality. As children experience the demands and constraints of reality, a new structure of personality emerges—the *ego*. It deals with the demands of reality and is called the "executive branch" of personality because it uses reasoning to make decisions. The id and the ego have no morality—they do not take into account whether something is right or wrong. The *superego* is the Freudian structure of personality that is the moral branch of personality, the part that considers whether something is right or wrong. Think of the superego as what we often refer to as our "conscience."

In Freud's view, the ego must resolve conflicts between the demands of reality, the wishes of the id, and the constraints of the superego. These conflicts cause anxiety. The anxiety alerts the ego to resolve the conflict by means of *defense mechanisms*, which are the ego's protective methods for reducing anxiety by unconsciously distorting reality.

Repression is the most powerful and pervasive defense mechanism, according to Freud. It pushes unacceptable id impulses (such as intense sexual and aggressive desires) beneath awareness and back into the unconscious mind. Early childhood, in Freud's view, often brings sexually laden experiences that are too threatening and stressful for us to deal with consciously. We reduce the anxiety of this conflict by repressing these experiences.

As Freud listened to, probed, and analyzed his patients, he became convinced that their problems were the result of experiences early in life. He thought that as children grow up, their focus of pleasure and sexual impulses shifts from the mouth

Freud's Theory

psychoanalytic theories Theories that hold that development depends primarily on the unconscious mind and is heavily couched in emotion, that behavior is merely a surface characteristic, that it is important to analyze the symbolic meanings of behavior, and that early experiences are important in development.

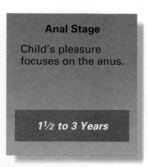
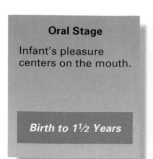

Oral Stage	Anal Stage	Phallic Stage	Latency Stage	Genital Stage
Infant's pleasure centers on the mouth.	Child's pleasure focuses on the anus.	Child's pleasure focuses on the genitals.	Child represses sexual interest and develops social and intellectual skills.	A time of sexual reawakening; source of sexual pleasure becomes someone outside the family.
Birth to 1½ Years	1½ to 3 Years	3 to 6 Years	6 Years to Puberty	Puberty Onward

FIGURE 1.7 Freudian Stages
According to Freud, people develop through five psychosexual stages in which the focus of pleasure changes.

Erik Erikson with his wife, Joan, who is an artist. Erikson generated one of the most important developmental theories of the twentieth century. *Which of Erikson's stages are you in? Does Erikson's description of this stage characterize you?*

Erikson's Theory

Erikson's theory A psychoanalytic theory in which eight stages of psychosocial development unfold throughout the human life span. Each stage consists of a unique developmental task that confronts individuals with a crisis that must be faced.

to the anus and eventually to the genitals. As a result, we go through five stages of *psychosexual development:* oral, anal, phallic, latency, and genital (see figure 1.7). Our adult personality, Freud claimed, is determined by the way we resolve conflicts between sources of pleasure at each stage and the demands of reality.

Freud's theory has been significantly revised by a number of psychoanalytic theorists. Many contemporary psychoanalytic theorists believe that Freud overemphasized sexual instincts; they place more emphasis on cultural experiences as determinants of an individual's development. Unconscious thought remains a central theme, but most contemporary psychoanalysts believe that conscious thought plays a greater role than Freud envisioned. Next, we will outline the ideas of an important revisionist of Freud's ideas—Erik Erikson.

Erikson's Theory Erik Erikson (1902–1994) recognized Freud's contributions but believed that Freud misjudged some important dimensions of human development. For one, Erikson (1950, 1968) said we develop in *psychosocial* stages, in contrast to Freud's psychosexual stages. For another, Freud and Erikson took different positions on the stability-change issue. Erikson emphasized developmental change throughout the human life span, whereas Freud argued that our basic personality is shaped in the first five years of life.

In **Erikson's theory,** eight psychosocial stages of development unfold as we go through the life span. Each stage consists of a unique developmental task that confronts individuals with a crisis that must be faced. According to Erikson, this crisis is not a catastrophe but a turning point, a time of increased vulnerability and enhanced potential. The more successfully we resolve the crises, the healthier our development will be (Hopkins, 2000).

Erikson's eight stages are trust versus mistrust, autonomy versus shame and doubt, initiative versus guilt, industry versus inferiority, identity versus identity confusion, intimacy versus isolation, generativity versus stagnation, and integrity versus despair. An overview of Erikson's eight stages is presented in figure 1.8. At each stage, if the positive pole of the crisis dominates, a foundation is built for healthy development. In the first stage, for example, the infants should learn not to trust all people under all circumstances but how to trust. At appropriate places in this book, we will discuss Erikson's theory and stages in more detail.

Evaluating the Psychoanalytic Theories The contributions of psychoanalytic theories include these themes:

- Early experiences play an important part in development.
- Family relationships are a central aspect of development.
- The mind is not all conscious; unconscious aspects of the mind need to be considered.

Erikson's Stages	Developmental period	Description
Trust versus mistrust	Infancy (Birth to 1½ years)	A sense of trust requires a feeling of physical comfort and minimal amount of fear about the future. Infants' basic needs are met by responsive, sensitive caregivers.
Autonomy versus shame and doubt	Toddlerhood (1½ to 3 years)	After gaining trust in their caregivers, infants start to discover that they have a will of their own. They assert their sense of autonomy, or independence. They realize their will. If infants are restrained too much or punished too harshly, they are likely to develop a sense of shame and doubt.
Initiative versus guilt	Early childhood (preschool years, ages 3–5)	As preschool children encounter a widening social world, they are challenged more and need to develop more purposeful behavior to cope with these challenges. Children are now asked to assume more responsibility. Uncomfortable guilt feelings may arise, though, if the children are irresponsible and are made to feel too anxious.
Industry versus inferiority	Middle and late childhood (elementary school years, 6 years–puberty)	At no other time are children more enthusiastic than at the end of early childhood's period of expansive imagination. As children move into the elementary school years, they direct their energy toward mastering knowledge and intellectual skills. The danger at this stage involves feeling incompetent and unproductive.
Identity versus identity confusion	Adolescence (10–20 years)	Individuals are faced with finding out who they are, what they are all about, and where they are going in life. An important dimension is the exploration of alternative solutions to roles. Career exploration is important.
Intimacy versus isolation	Early adulthood (20s, 30s)	Individuals face the developmental task of forming intimate relationships with others. Erikson described intimacy as finding oneself yet losing oneself in another person.
Generativity versus stagnation	Middle adulthood (40s, 50s)	A chief concern is to assist the younger generation in developing and leading useful lives.
Integrity versus despair	Late adulthood (60s–)	Individuals look back and evaluate what they have done with their lives. The retrospective glances can either be positive (integrity) or negative (despair).

FIGURE 1.8 Erikson's Eight Life-Span Stages

According to Erikson, people develop through eight psychosocial stages. Each stage is characterized by a particular task, such as developing intimate relationships during early adulthood.

- Changes take place in the adulthood as well as the childhood years in Erikson's theory.

Here are some criticisms of psychoanalytic theories:

- The main concepts of psychoanalytic theories have been difficult to test scientifically.
- Much of the data used to support psychoanalytic theories come from individuals' reconstructions of the past, often the distant past, and are of unknown accuracy.
- The sexual underpinnings of development are given too much importance, especially in Freud's theory.
- The unconscious mind is given too much credit for influencing development.
- Their images of human beings in psychoanalytic theories are too negative, especially in Freud's theory.
- They are culture- and gender-biased. For example, critics argue that Freud's theory has a masculine bias and does not adequately reflect the extensive cultural and gender changes that have taken place in the last century.

Jean Piaget, the famous Swiss developmental psychologist, changed the way we think about the development of children's minds. *What are some key ideas in Piaget's theory?*

Vygotsky's Theory

Piaget's theory The theory that children construct their understanding of the world and go through four stages of cognitive development.

Vygotsky's theory A sociocultural cognitive theory that emphasizes how culture and social interaction guide cognitive development.

Cognitive Theories

Whereas psychoanalytic theories mainly focus on socioemotional processes, cognitive theories emphasize thinking, reasoning, language, and other cognitive processes. The important cognitive theories are Piaget's cognitive developmental theory, Vygotsky's sociocultural cognitive theory, and the information-processing approach.

Piaget's Cognitive Developmental Theory Swiss psychologist Jean Piaget (1896–1980) developed a theory of cognitive development that revolutioned our way of thinking about children's minds. Piaget (1954) stressed that humans use cognition to adapt more effectively to their environment.

Piaget's theory states that children actively construct their understanding of the world as they go through four stages of cognitive development. Each of these stages is age-related and is *qualitatively* different from other stages. Each stage brings distinct ways of thinking. Remember, it is the *different* way of understanding the world that makes one stage more advanced than another. For example, according to Piaget, when children are in the second stage (preoperational), they use faulty logic and cannot distinguish their perspective from someone else's. However, in the third stage (concrete operational), they develop logical thinking and perspective-taking skills. Piaget's four stages of cognitive development are described in figure 1.9.

We will examine Piaget's theory, including the four stages of cognitive development, in greater detail in chapter 6, "Cognitive Developmental Approaches."

Vygotsky's Sociocultural Cognitive Theory Like Piaget, the Russian developmentalist Lev Vygotsky (1896–1934) believed that children actively construct their knowledge, but he did not describe their development as stagelike. Vygotsky gave social interaction and culture far more important roles in cognitive development than Piaget did. **Vygotksy's theory** is a sociocultural cognitive theory that emphasizes how culture and social interaction guide cognitive development. Both Piaget's and Vygotsky's (1962) ideas remained virtually unknown to American scholars until the 1960s.

Vygotsky portrayed the child's development as inseparable from social and cultural activities. He believed that the development of memory, attention, and reasoning involves learning to use the inventions of society, such as language, mathematical systems, and memory strategies. In one culture, this might consist of learning to count with the help of a computer. In another, it might consist of counting on one's fingers or using beads. Thus, knowledge is *collaborative* (John-Steiner & Mahn, 2003; Rogoff, 2001, 2003). It is not generated from within the individual but is constructed through interaction with other people and objects in the culture, such as books. This suggests that knowing can best be advanced through interaction with others in cooperative activities.

Vygotsky believed that children's social interaction with more-skilled adults and peers is indispensable in advancing cognitive development. It is through this interaction that less-skilled members of the culture learn to use the tools that will help them adapt and be successful in the culture. For example, when a skilled reader regularly helps a child learn how to read, this not only advances a child's reading skills but also communicates to the child that reading is an important activity in the culture. In chapter 6, "Cognitive Developmental Approaches," we will further explore Vygotsky's contributions to our understanding of development.

Information-Processing Approach Machines may be the best candidate for the title of "founding father" of the information-processing approach. Although a number of factors stimulated the growth of this approach, none was more important than the computer. Psychologists began to wonder if the logical operations carried out by computers might tell us something about how the human mind works. They drew analogies between a computer's hardware and the brain and

Sensorimotor Stage	Preoperational Stage	Concrete Operational Stage	Formal Operational Stage
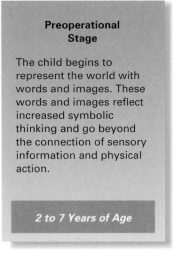 The infant constructs an understanding of the world by coordinating sensory experiences with physical actions. An infant progresses from reflexive, instinctual action at birth to the beginning of symbolic thought toward the end of the stage.	 The child begins to represent the world with words and images. These words and images reflect increased symbolic thinking and go beyond the connection of sensory information and physical action.	The child can now reason logically about concrete events and classify objects into different sets.	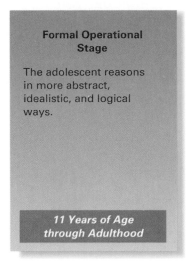 The adolescent reasons in more abstract, idealistic, and logical ways.
Birth to 2 Years of Age	*2 to 7 Years of Age*	*7 to 11 Years of Age*	*11 Years of Age through Adulthood*

FIGURE 1.9 Piaget's Four Stages of Cognitive Development
According to Piaget, distinct ways of thinking characterize children of different ages.

between computer software and cognition. The physical brain is said to be analogous to the computer's hardware, cognition is said to be analogous to its software.

This line of thinking helped to generate the **information-processing approach,** which emphasizes that individuals manipulate information, monitor it, and strategize about it. According to this approach, individuals develop a gradually increasing capacity for processing information, which allows them to acquire increasingly complex knowledge and skills (Mayer, 2003; Siegler, 2001). Unlike Piaget's theory but like Vygotsky's theory, the information-processing approach does not describe development as stagelike.

Robert Siegler (1998, 2003), a leading expert on children's information processing, believes that thinking is information processing. He says that when individuals perceive, encode, represent, store, and retrieve information, they are thinking. Siegler suggests that learning good strategies for processing information is especially important to cognitive development. For example, becoming a better reader might involve learning to monitor the key themes of the material being read (McCormick, 2003). We will explore information processing theory in depth in chapter 7.

Evaluating the Cognitive Theories Here are some contributions of cognitive theories:

- The cognitive theories emphasize the individual's active construction of understanding.
- The cognitive theories underscore the value of examining developmental changes in children's thinking.
- The information-processing approach offers detailed descriptions of cognitive processes.

Here are some criticisms of cognitive theories:

- There is skepticism about whether children develop cognitive skills at the time and in the way Piaget envisioned.
- The cognitive theories do not give adequate attention to individual variations in cognitive development.
- The information-processing approach does not provide an adequate description of developmental changes in cognition.
- Psychoanalytic theorists argue that the cognitive theories underrate the importance of unconscious thought.

There is considerable interest today in Lev Vygotsky's sociocultural cognitive theory of child development. *What were Vygotsky's basic claims about children's development?*

information-processing approach An approach that emphasizes that individuals manipulate information, monitor it, and strategize about it. The processes of memory and thinking are central.

Behavioral and Social Cognitive Theories

Behavioral and Social Cognitive Theories

At about the same time that Freud was interpreting patients' unconscious minds through their reports of early childhood experiences, Ivan Pavlov and John B. Watson were conducting detailed observations of behavior in the laboratory. Out of their work grew the *behavioral tradition,* which holds that behavior can be explained without considering what goes on in a person's mind. In the behavioral tradition, all that is needed to explain behavior is the link between the behavior and the environment.

The behavioral tradition was the foundation for the **behavioral and social cognitive theories,** which state that the environment and behavior play important roles in development. These theories emphasize the role of nurture and see development as the result of gradual, cumulative, and continuous change. The three versions of this approach that we will describe are Pavlov's classical conditioning, Skinner's operant conditioning, and social cognitive theory.

Pavlov's Classical Conditioning   In the early 1900s, Russian physiologist Ivan Pavlov (1927) knew that dogs innately salivate when they taste food. He became curious when he observed that dogs salivate to various sights and sounds before eating. For example, if a bell rang when the dog was given food, the dog subsequently salivated when the bell rang by itself. Pavlov had discovered the principle of *classical conditioning:* After a neutral stimulus (in our example, ringing a bell) has been paired with a stimulus (in our example, food) that automatically produces a response, that response will be elicited by the previously neutral stimulus on its own.

In the 1920s, John Watson applied classical conditioning to humans. He showed a little boy named Albert a white rat to see if he was afraid of it. He was not. As Albert played with the rat, Watson sounded a loud nose behind Albert's head. As you might imagine, the noise caused little Albert to cry. After only several pairings of the loud noise and the white rat, Albert began to fear the rat even when the noise was not sounded (Watson & Rayner, 1920).

Similarly, many of our fears can be learned through classical conditioning. For instance, we might learn fear of the dentist from a painful dental experience, fear of driving from being in an automobile accident, fear of heights from falling off a highchair when we were infants, and fear of dogs from being bitten. Classical conditioning explains how we develop many involuntary responses, such as these fears, but B. F. Skinner showed how many of our actions might be explained by a different type of learning known as operant conditioning.

Skinner's Operant Conditioning   In Skinner's (1938) *operant conditioning,* the consequences of a behavior produce changes in the probability of the behavior's occurrence. A behavior that is followed by a rewarding stimulus is more likely to recur, but a behavior that is followed by a punishing stimulus is less likely to recur. For example, a child is more likely to repeat a behavior if it is greeted with a smile than if it is met with a nasty look.

For Skinner, such rewards and punishments shape individuals' development. For example, according to Skinner, a child learns to be shy as a result of environmental experiences; rearranging the environment can help the boy to become more socially oriented.

Social Cognitive Theory   Some psychologists found that although classical and operant conditioning could explain some aspects of behavior, they also needed to consider how people think in order to account for behavior. **Social cognitive theory** holds that behavior, environment, and person/cognition are important factors in development. *Person/cognition* refers to characteristics of the person (for example, being introverted or extraverted) and cognitions (thinking and planning) that

behavioral and social cognitive theories Theories that hold that development can be best described in terms of the behaviors learned through interactions with the environment.

social cognitive theory The theory that behavior, environment, and person/cognitive factors are important in understanding development.

mediate connections between environment and behavior. American psychologists Albert Bandura (1986, 2000, 2001) and Walter Mischel (1973, 1995, 2004) are the main architects of contemporary social cognitive theory, which Mischel (1973) initially labeled cognitive social learning theory.

Bandura's early research focused heavily on *observational learning*—learning that occurs through observing what others do. Observational learning is also referred to as *imitation* or *modeling*. In observational learning, people cognitively represent the behavior of others and then sometimes adopt this behavior themselves. For example, a young boy who regularly observes his father's aggressive outbursts and hostile interchanges with people might also be very aggressive with his peers. A girl who adopts the dominating, sarcastic style of her teacher might say to her younger brother, "You are so slow! How can you do this work so slowly?" People acquire a wide range of such behaviors, thoughts, and feelings through observing others' behavior.

In his recent work, Bandura (2000, 2001) emphasizes reciprocal interactions among behavior, the person/cognition, and the environment, as shown in figure 1.10. Behavior can influence person/cognitive factors and vice versa. The person's cognitive activities can influence the environment, the environment can change the person's cognition, and so on.

Let's consider how Bandura's model might work in the case of a college student's achievement behavior. As the student diligently studies and gets good grades, her behavior produces positive thoughts about her abilities. As part of her effort to make good grades, she plans and develops strategies to make her studying more efficient. In these ways, her behavior has influenced her thought and her thought has influenced her behavior. At the beginning of the term, her college made a special effort to involve students in a study skills program. She decided to join. Because of her success, along with that of other students in the program, the college is expanding the program next semester. In these ways, environment influenced behavior, and behavior changed the environment. And the college administrators' expectations that the study skills program would work made the program possible in the first place. The program's success has spurred expectations that this type of program could work in other colleges. In these ways, cognition changed the environment and the environment changed cognition.

Evaluating the Behavioral and Social Cognitive Theories

Here are some contributions of the behavioral and social cognitive theories:

- They emphasize the importance of scientific research.
- They focus on the environmental determinants of behavior.
- Bandura underscores the importance of observational learning.
- Social cognitive theory emphasizes person and cognitive factors.

Here are criticisms of the behavioral and social cognitive theories:

- Skinner's theory places too little emphasis on cognition.
- The theories place too much emphasis on environmental determinants.
- They give inadequate attention to developmental changes.
- Their consideration of human spontaneity and creativity is too mechanical and inadequate.

Ethological Theory

In striking contrast to the behavioral and social cognitive theories, another approach to development grew out of ethology, a scientific discipline that studies animal behavior. The **ethological theory of development** holds that behavior is strongly influenced by biology and evolution (Hinde, 1992; Rosenzweig, 2000). It also emphasizes that our sensitivity to different kinds of experience varies during our life

Albert Bandura has been one of the leading architects of social cognitive theory. *What is the nature of his theory?*

Albert Bandura

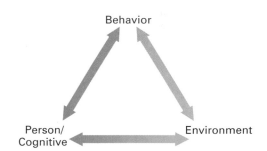

FIGURE 1.10 Bandura's Social Cognitive Model

The arrows illustrate how relations between behavior, person (cognitive), and environment are reciprocal rather than unidirectional.

ethological theory of development An approach that stresses that behavior is strongly influenced by biology, tied to evolution, and characterized by critical or sensitive periods.

span. In other words, there are critical or sensitive periods for some experiences. If we fail to have these experiences during this sensitive period, ethological theory argues that our development is not likely to be optimal.

Ethology emerged as an important contributor to theories of human development because of the work of European zoologists, especially Konrad Lorenz (1903–1989). Working mostly with greylag geese, Lorenz (1965) studied a behavior pattern that was thought to be programmed by the birds' genes. A newly hatched gosling seemed to be born with the instinct to follow its mother. Observations showed that the gosling was capable of such behavior as soon as it hatched. Lorenz proved that it was incorrect to assume that such behavior was programmed in the animal. In a remarkable set of experiments, Lorenz separated the eggs laid by one goose into two groups. One group he returned to the goose to be hatched by her. The other group was hatched in an incubator. The goslings in the first group performed as predicted. They followed their mother as soon as they hatched. However, those in the second group, which saw Lorenz when they first hatched, followed him everywhere, as though he were their mother.

Lorenz marked the goslings and then placed both groups under a box. Mother goose and "mother" Lorenz stood aside as the box lifted. Each group of goslings went directly to its "mother." Lorenz called this process *imprinting:* the rapid, innate learning within a limited critical period of time that involves attachment to the first moving object seen.

The ethological view of Lorenz and other European zoologists forced American developmental psychologists to recognize the importance of the biological basis of behavior. However, the research and theorizing of ethology still lacked some ingredients that would elevate it to the ranks of the other theories discussed so far in this chapter. In particular, there was little or nothing in the classical ethological view about the nature of social relationships across the human life span, something that any major theory of development must explain. Also, its concept of *critical period,* a fixed time period very early in development during which certain behaviors optimally emerge, seemed to be overdrawn. Classical ethological theory was weak in simulating studies with humans.

Recent expansion of the ethological view has improved its status as a viable developmental perspective. One way ethological theory has become more viable with humans is that rather than relying on a rigid, very narrow critical period, more emphasis has been given to a longer *sensitive period.*

One of the most important applications of ethological theory to human development involves John Bowlby's (1969, 1989) theory of attachment. Bowlby argues that attachment to a caregiver over the first year of life has important consequences

Konrad Lorenz, a pioneering student of animal behavior, is followed through the water by three imprinted greylag geese. Describe Lorenz's experiment with the geese. *Do you think his experiment would have the same results with human babies? Explain.*

throughout the life span. In his view, if this attachment is positive and secure, the individual will likely develop more positively in childhood and adulthood. If it is negative and insecure, life-span development will likely not be optimal. In chapter 10, "Emotional Development," we will explore the concept of infant attachment in much greater detail.

Exploring Ethology

Evaluating Ethological Theory   Here are some contributions of ethological theory:

- It increased the focus on the biological and evolutionary basis of development.
- It uses careful observations in naturalistic settings.
- It emphasizes sensitive periods of development.

Here are some criticisms of ethological theory:

- The concepts of critical period and sensitive period may still be too rigid.
- It places too much emphasis on biological foundations.
- It gives inadequate attention to cognition.
- The theory has been better at generating research with animals than with humans.

In addition to ethological theory, another theory that emphasizes the biological aspects of human development—evolutionary psychology—will be presented in chapter 2, "Biological Beginnings," along with views on the role of heredity in development. Also, we will examine a number of biological theories of aging in chapter 3, "Physical Development and Biological Aging."

Ecological Theory

Unlike ethological theory, which stresses biological factors, ecological theory emphasizes environmental contexts. One ecological theory that has important implications for understanding life-span development was created by Urie Bronfenbrenner (1917–).

Ecological theory is Bronfenbrenner's view that development is influenced by five environmental systems, ranging from the fine-grained contexts of direct interactions with people to the broad-based contexts of culture. The five systems in Bronfenbrenner's ecological theory are the microsystem, mesosystem, exosystem, macrosystem, and chronosystem (Bronfenbrenner, 1986, 1995, 2000; Bronfenbrenner & Morris, 1998) (see figure 1.11):

- The *microsystem* is the setting in which the individual lives. These contexts include the person's family, peers, school, and neighborhood. It is in the microsystem that the most direct interactions with social agents take place—with parents, peers, and teachers, for example.
- The *mesosystem* involves relationships between microsystems, or connections between contexts. Examples are the relation of family experiences to school experiences, school experiences to church experiences, and family experiences to peer experiences.
- The *exosystem* is involved when experiences in another social setting—in which the individual does not have an active role—influence what the individual experiences in an immediate context. For example, work experiences can affect a woman's relationship with her husband and their child. The mother might receive a promotion that requires more travel, which could increase marital conflict and change patterns of parent-child interaction.
- The *macrosystem* involves the culture in which individuals live. *Culture* refers to the behavior patterns, beliefs, and all other products of a group of people that are passed on from generation to generation.
- The *chronosystem* involves the patterning of environmental events and transitions over the life course, as well as sociohistorical circumstances. For example, in

Bronfenbrenner developed ecological theory, a perspective that is receiving increased attention. His theory emphasizes the importance of both micro and macro dimensions of the environment in which the child lives.

ecological theory Bronfenbrenner's view that development is influenced by five environmental systems—microsystem, mesosystem, exosystem, macrosystem, and chronosystem. These emphasize the role of social contexts in human development.

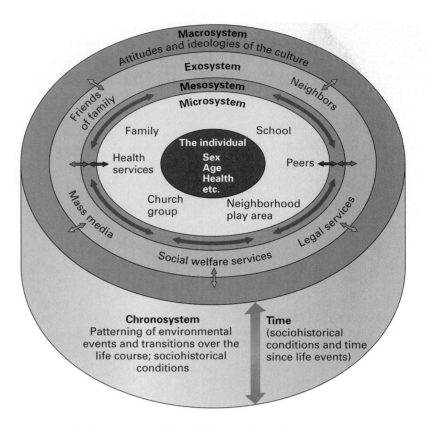

FIGURE 1.11 Bronfenbrenner's Ecological Theory of Development
Bronfenbrenner's ecological theory consists of five environmental systems: microsystem, mesosystem, exosystem, macrosystem, and chronosystem.

studying the effects of divorce on children, researchers have found that the negative effects often peak in the first year after the divorce (Hetherington, 1993, 2000). By two years after the divorce, family interaction is less chaotic and more stable. With regard to sociocultural circumstances, women today are much more likely to be encouraged to pursue a career than they were 20 or 30 years ago.

Bronfenbrenner (2000; Bronfenbrenner & Morris, 1998) recently added biological influences to his theory and now describes it as a *bioecological* theory. Nonetheless, ecological, environmental contexts still predominate in Bronfenbrenner's theory (Ceci, 2000).

Sociocultural Contexts The focus on contexts in Bronfenbrenner's ecological theory is echoed in the life-span perspective on human development. As we discussed earlier, this perspective views development as contextual, and life-span researchers have emphasized *sociocultural contexts*. Key dimensions of sociocultural contexts include culture, ethnicity, and gender.

A culture results from the interaction of people over many years. A culture can be as large as the United States or as small as an African hunter-gatherer group. Whatever its size, the group's culture influences the behavior of its members (Sarawathi & Mistry, 2003). **Cross-cultural studies** compare cultures. The comparison provides information about the degree to which development is similar across cultures or is culture-specific.

Ethnicity and race are sometimes misrepresented. *Race* is a controversial classification of people according to real or imagined biological characteristics such as skin color and blood group; ethnicity is a broader concept. **Ethnicity** refers to a range of characteristics rooted in cultural heritage, including nationality, race, religion, and language. Thus, you might describe a person's ethnicity by saying that the individual

Bronfenbrenner's Theory

Bronfenbrenner and a Multicultural Framework

cross-cultural studies Comparisons of one culture with one or more other cultures. These provide information about the degree to which children's development is similar, or universal, across cultures, and to the degree to which it is culture-specific.

ethnicity A range of characteristics rooted in cultural heritage, including nationality, race, religion, and language.

Two Korean-born children on the day they became United States citizens. Asian American and Latino children are the fastest-growing immigrant groups in the United States. *How diverse are the students in this class on life-span development that you now are taking? How are their experiences in growing up likely similar to or different from yours?*

is a non-Latino White and a fifth-generation Texan who is a Catholic and speaks English and Spanish fluently.

A related concept is the *ethnic group,* which refers to people who share a national background, such as Polish Americans, Italian Americans, and so on. It is easy to fall into the trap of stereotyping people by thinking that all members of an ethnic group are alike, but diversity characterizes any ethnic group (Chun & Akutsu, 2003; Cushner, 2003). Obviously, not all African Americans have low incomes; not all Latinos are Catholic (Nieman, 2004).

Yet another key aspect of the sociocultural context is **gender,** which refers to the psychological and sociocultural dimensions of being female or male. *Sex* refers to the biological aspects of being female or male; expectations about how female and males should behave and beliefs about their traits are aspects of gender. Few characteristics are more central to the development of our identity and social relationships than gender (Eagly, 2001; Hyde, 2004; Matlin, 2004).

Our society's attitudes about gender have been changing during the last thirty years. In fact, the whole tapestry of American culture has changed recently. Bronfenbrenner's theory suggests that the effects of these changes in context will be complicated, depending on interactions between a number of environmental systems. In the Contexts of Life-Span Development interlude, you can read more about how contexts influence development.

Contexts of Life-Span Development
Individual, Family, and Extrafamilial Contexts

Determining which aspects of sociocultural contexts make a difference for particular aspects of development is a challenging task. Consider a study that recently examined the home environments of children in four ethnic groups: European American, African American, Latino, and Asian American (Bradley & others, 2001). The researchers observed the children in their homes and interviewed the mothers

gender The psychological and sociocultural dimensions of being female or male.

Source	Characteristic
Individual	Good intellectual functioning
	Appealing, sociable, easygoing disposition
	Self-confidence, high self-esteem
	Talents
	Faith
Family	Close relationship to caring parent figure
	Authoritative parenting: warmth, structure, high expectations
	Socioeconomic advantages
	Connections to extended supportive family networks
Extrafamilial context	Bonds to caring adults outside the family
	Connections to positive organizations
	Attending effective schools

FIGURE 1.12 Characteristics of Resilient Children

five times in the children's lives from infancy through early adolescence. Although there were some differences among the ethnic groups, the most consistent differences occurred between families classified as poor or nonpoor. For example, regardless of their ethnic group, children growing up in nonpoor home environments were more likely than those in poor homes to have their speech responded to, be provided with toys or interesting activities, have ten or more books of their own, and see their father daily, and they were less likely to be slapped or spanked.

What can make children resilient when they face adverse contexts? Ann Masten (1999, 2001) analyzed the research literature on resilience and concluded that resilient children have a number of different kinds of positive characteristics and support in their lives—including positive individual traits (such as good intellectual functioning), family ties (close relationships in a caring family), and extrafamilial supports (connections with competent, caring adults outside the family). Figure 1.12 summarizes the sources of resilience that may come from individual, family, and extrafamilial contexts.

Evaluating Ecological Theory Here are some contributions of ecological theory:

- It systematically examines macro and micro dimensions of environmental systems.
- It pays attention to connections between environmental settings (mesosystem).
- It considers the sociohistorical influences on development (chronosystem).

Here are some criticisms of ecological theory:

- Even with the added discussion of biological influences in recent years, it still gives too little attention to biological foundations of development.
- It does not pay enough attention to cognitive processes.

An Eclectic Orientation

Figure 1.13 compares the main theoretical perspectives in terms of how they view the three developmental issues described earlier in the chapter. No single theory described in this chapter can entirely explain the rich complexity of life-span development. Each of the theories, however, has made important contributions to our understanding of development. Psychoanalytic theory best explains the unconscious

Theory	Issues		
	Nature/Nurture	**Stability/Change**	**Continuity/Discontinuity**
Psychoanalytic	In Freud's theory biological determinants interact with early family experiences. Erikson proposes more balance between biological and cultural factors.	Change in early childhood; stability after early childhood. Early experiences emphasized.	Emphasis on discontinuity between stages.
Cognitive	Piaget's theory emphasizes interaction and adaptation; environment provides the setting for cognitive structures to develop. Vygotsky's theory involves the interaction of nature and nurture with a strong emphasis on culture. The information-processing approach has not addressed this issue extensively but mainly emphasizes biological-environment interaction.	Change during childhood and adolescence in Piaget's theory; change during childhood in Vygotsky's theory. Stability in adulthood for both theories. Potential for change throughout the life span in the information-processing approach.	Discontinuity between stages in Piaget's theory; no stages in Vygotsky's theory or in the information-processing approach.
Behavioral and social cognitive	Environment is viewed as the main influence on development.	Stability or change depending on the experiences people have. With little change in experiences, stability will occur; with extensive variations in experience, change will take place.	Continuity with no stages.
Ethological	Strong emphasis on biological influences.	Early experience is very important, which can contribute to change early in development. After an early critical or sensitive period has passed, stability is likely.	Discontinuity because of early critical or sensitive periods; no stages.
Ecological	Strong emphasis on environmental influences.	Change is emphasized more than stability.	No stages, but the theory gives little attention to this issue.

FIGURE 1.13 A Comparison of Theories and Issues in Life-Span Development

mind. Erikson's theory best describes the changes that occur in adult development. Piaget's, Vygotsky's, and the information-processing views provide the most complete descriptions of cognitive development. The behavioral and social cognitive and ecological theories have been the most adept at examining the environmental determinants of development. The ethological theories have made us aware of biology's role and the importance of sensitive periods in development.

It is important to recognize that, although theories are helpful guides, it would probably be a mistake to rely on a single theory to explain development. An **eclectic orientation** does not follow any theoretical approach but rather selects and uses what is considered the best in each theory. This is the approach that will be maintained throughout the book. In this way, you can view the study of development as it exists—with different theorists making different assumptions, stressing different empirical problems, and using different strategies to discover information.

Review and Reflect: Learning Goal 3

3 Describe five theoretical approaches to human development

REVIEW

- What are the four steps in the scientific method? What is the relation between a theory and hypotheses? What are two main psychoanalytic theories? What are some strengths and weaknesses of the psychoanalytic theories?
- What are the three main cognitive theories? What are the strengths and weaknesses of the cognitive theories?

eclectic orientation An approach that selects and uses whatever is considered the best in many theories.

- What are the three main behavioral and social cognitive theories, and how can they be characterized? What are the strengths and weaknesses of the behavioral and social cognitive theories?
- What is the nature of the ethological theory of development? What are its strengths and weaknesses?
- What is the nature of ecological theory? What are its strengths and weaknesses?
- What is an eclectic orientation?

REFLECT

- Which of the life-span theories do you think best explains development? Why?

4 RESEARCH IN LIFE-SPAN DEVELOPMENT

Methods for Collecting Data

Time Span of Research

Research Designs

Ethics

If you take an eclectic approach, how do you decide what is "best" in different theories? Scientific research is the answer. All scientific knowledge stems from a rigorous, systematic method of research. Through research, theories are modified to reflect new data.

How are data about life-span development collected? What types of research designs are used to study life-span development? If researchers want to study people of different ages, what research designs can they use? What ethical considerations are involved in conducting research? These are the questions that we will examine next.

Methods for Collecting Data

Whether we are interested in studying attachment in infants, the cognitive skills of children, or marital relations in older adults, we can choose from several ways of collecting data. Here we outline the measures most often used, including their advantages and disadvantages, beginning with observation.

Observation Scientific observation requires an important set of skills (Nadelman, 2004). Unless we are trained observers and practice our skills regularly, we might not know what to look for, we might not remember what we saw, we might not realize that what we are looking for is changing from one moment to the next, and we might not communicate our observations effectively.

For observations to be effective, they have to be systematic (Elmes, Kantowitz, & Roedinger, 2003). We have to have some idea of what we are looking for. We have to know whom we are observing, when and where we will observe, and how the observations will be made. In what form they will be recorded: In writing? Tape recording? Video?

Where should we make our observations? We have two choices: (1) a **laboratory,** a controlled setting with many of the complex factors in the "real world" removed, and (2) the everyday world.

Making observations in a laboratory allows us to control certain factors that influence behavior but are not the focus of our inquiry (Crano & Brewer, 2002;

*S*cience refines everyday thinking.

—ALBERT EINSTEIN
German-born American Physicist, 20th Century

laboratory A controlled setting.

In this research study, mother-child interaction is being videotaped. Later, researchers will code the interaction using precise categories.

Hoyle & Judd, 2002). But laboratory research does have some drawbacks. First, it is almost impossible to conduct research without the participants' knowing they are being studied. Second, the laboratory setting is unnatural and therefore can cause the participants to behave unnaturally. Third, people who are willing and able to come to a university laboratory may not fairly represent the population we are interested in studying. Those who are unfamiliar with university settings, and with the idea of "helping science," may be intimidated by the setting. Finally, some aspects of life-span development are difficult if not impossible to examine in the laboratory.

Naturalistic observation provides insights that we sometimes cannot achieve in the laboratory (Billman, 2003; Langston, 2002). **Naturalistic observation** means observing behavior in real-world settings, making no effort to manipulate or control the situation. Life-span researchers conduct naturalistic observations at sporting events, day-care centers, work settings, malls, and other places people live in and frequent. Suppose that you wanted to study the level of civility on your campus. Most likely, you would want to include some naturalistic observation of how people treat one another in places like the cafeteria or the library reading room.

Figure 1.14 shows the results of another example of naturalistic observation. In this case, researchers observed how mothers and fathers interacted with their sons and daughters in a children's science museum (Crowley & others, 2001). Parents were three times as likely to engage boys than girls in explanatory talk while visiting different exhibits at the science museum, suggesting a gender bias that encourages boys more than girls in science.

Survey and Interview   Sometimes the best and quickest way to get information about people is to ask them for it. One technique is to *interview* them directly. A related method that is especially useful when information from many people is needed is the *survey*, sometimes referred to as a questionnaire. A standard set of questions is used to obtain people's self-reported attitudes or beliefs about a particular topic. In a good survey, the questions are clear and unbiased, allowing respondents to answer unambiguously (Beins, 2004).

Surveys and interviews can be used to study a wide range of topics from religious beliefs to sexual habits to attitudes about gun control to beliefs about how to improve schools. Surveys and interviews can be conducted in person or over the

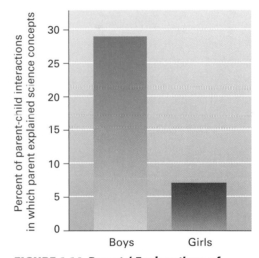

FIGURE 1.14 Parents' Explanations of Science to Sons and Daughters at a Science Museum

In a naturalistic observation study at a children's science museum, parents were three times more likely to explain science to boys than to girls (Crowley & others, 2001). The gender difference occurred regardless of whether the father, the mother, or both parents were with the child, although the gender difference was greatest for fathers' science explanations to sons and daughters.

naturalistic observation Observation that occurs in a real-world setting without an attempt to manipulate the situation.

"Would you say Attila is doing an excellent job, a good job, a fair job, or a poor job?"

© Charles Addams. Courtesy Tee and Charles Addams Foundation.

telephone. In addition, some surveys are now being conducted over the Internet.

Some survey and interview questions are unstructured and openended, such as "Could you elaborate on your optimistic tendencies?" or "How fulfilling would you say your marriage is?" They allow for unique responses from each person surveyed. Other survey and interview questions are more structured and specific. For example, one national poll on beliefs about what needs to be done to improve U.S. schools asked: "Of the following four possibilities, which one do you think offers the most promise for improving public schools in the community: a qualified, competent teacher in every classroom; free choice for parents among a number of private, church-related, and public schools; rigorous academic standards; the elimination of social promotion; or don't know? (Rose & Gallup, 2000). More than half of the respondents said that the most important way to improve schools is to have a qualified, competent teacher in every classroom.

One problem with surveys and interviews is the tendency of participants to answer questions in a way that they think is socially acceptable or desirable rather than telling what they truly think or feel (Best & Kahn, 2003). For example, on a survey or in an interview some individuals might say that they do not take drugs even though they do.

Standardized Test A **standardized test** has uniform procedures for administration and scoring. Many standardized tests allow a person's performance to be compared with the performance of other individuals (Aiken, 2003; Cohen & Swerdlik, 2002; Gregory, 2004). One example is the Stanford-Binet intelligence test, which is described in chapter 8, "Intelligence."

Scores on standardized tests are often stated in *percentiles*, which indicate how much higher or lower one person's score is than the scores of people who previously took the test. If you scored in the 92nd percentile on the SAT, 92 percent of a large group of individuals who previously took the test received scores lower than yours.

The main advantage of standardized tests is that they provide information about individual differences among people. One problem with standardized tests is that they do not always predict behavior in nontest situations. Another problem is that standardized tests are based on the belief that a person's behavior is consistent and stable, yet personality and intelligence—two primary targets of standardized testing—can vary with the situation. For example, a person may perform poorly on a standardized intelligence test in an office setting but score much higher at home, where he or she is less anxious. This criticism is especially relevant for members of minority groups, some of whom have been inaccurately classified as mentally retarded on the basis of their scores on intelligence tests.

In addition, cross-cultural psychologists caution that many psychological tests developed in Western cultures might not be appropriate in other cultures (Matsumoto, 2004). People in other cultures may have had experiences that cause them to interpret and respond to questions much differently from the people on whom the test was standardized.

Case Study A **case study** is an in-depth look at a single individual. Case studies are performed mainly by mental health professionals when, for either practical or ethical reasons, the unique aspects of an individual's life cannot be duplicated and tested in other individuals (Dattilio, 2001). A case study provides information about one person's fears, hopes, fantasies, traumatic experiences, upbringing, family relationships, health, or anything that helps the psychologist understand the person's mind and behavior.

standardized test A test that is given with uniform procedures for administration and scoring.

case study An in-depth examination of an individual.

An example of a case study is Erik Erikson's (1969) analysis of India's spiritual leader Mahatma Gandhi. Erikson studied Gandhi's life in great depth to discover insights about how his positive spiritual identity developed, especially during his youth. In putting the pieces of Gandhi's identity development together, Erikson described the contributions of culture, history, family, and various other factors that might affect the way other people develop an identity.

Case histories provide dramatic, in-depth portrayals of people's lives, but remember that we must be cautious when generalizing from this information. The subject of a case study is unique, with a genetic makeup and personal history that no one else shares. In addition, case studies involve judgments of unknown reliability. Psychologists who conduct case studies rarely check to see if other psychologists agree with their observations.

Mahatma Gandhi was the spiritual leader of India in the middle of the twentieth century. Erik Erikson conducted an extensive case study of his life to determine what contributed to his identity development. *What are some limitations of the case study approach?*

Life-History Record   **Life-history records** are records of information about a lifetime chronology of events and activities. They often involve a combination of data records on education, work, family, and residence. These records may be generated with information from public records, historical documents, or interviews, which might include obtaining a life calendar from the respondent. Life calendars record the age (year and month) at which life events and transitions occur in a variety of domains, thus portraying an unfolding life course. In compiling life-history records, researchers increasingly use a wide array of materials, including written and oral reports from the subject, vital records, observation, and public documents (Clausen, 1993). One advantage of the multiple-materials approach is that information from varied sources can be compared and discrepancies sometimes can be resolved, resulting in a more accurate life-history record.

Research Designs

Suppose you want to find out whether the children of permissive parents are more likely than other children to be rude and unruly. Life-history records are not likely to be very helpful. The data-collection method that researchers choose often depends on the goal of their research. The goal may be simply to describe a phenomenon, or it may be to describe relationships between phenomena, or to determine the causes or effects of a phenomenon.

Perhaps you decide that you need to observe both permissive and strict parents with their children and compare them. How would you do that? In addition to a method for collecting data, you would need a research design. There are three main types of research design: descriptive, correlational, and experimental.

Descriptive Research   All of the data-collection methods that we have discussed can be used in **descriptive research,** which aims to observe and record behavior. For example, a researcher might observe the extent to which people are altruistic or aggressive toward each other. By itself, descriptive research cannot prove what causes some phenomenon, but it can reveal important information about people's behavior.

Correlational Research   In contrast to descriptive research, correlational research goes beyond describing phenomena to provide information that will help us to predict how people will behave. In **correlational research,** the goal is to describe the strength of the relationship between two or more events or characteristics. The more strongly the two events are correlated (or related or associated), the more effectively we can predict one event from the other (Whitley, 2002).

For example, to study if children of permissive parents have less self-control than other children, you would need to carefully record observations of parents'

life-history records Information about events and activities over a lifetime.

descriptive research This type of research aims to observe and record behavior.

correlational research The goal is to describe the strength of the relation between two or more events or characteristics.

Observed correlation   **Possible explanations for this correlation**

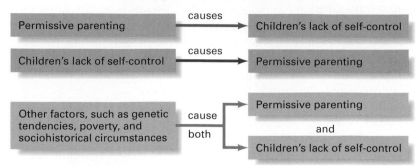

FIGURE 1.15 **Possible Explanations for Correlational Data**

An observed correlation between two events cannot be used to conclude that one event caused the other. Some possibilities are that the second event caused the first event or that a third, unknown event caused the correlation between the first two events.

permissiveness and their children's self-control. The data could then be analyzed statistically to yield a numerical measure, called a **correlation coefficient,** a number based on a statistical analysis that is used to describe the degree of association between two variables. The correlation coefficient ranges from +1.00 to −1.00. A negative number means an inverse relation. For example, researchers often find a *negative* correlation between permissive parenting and children's self-control. By contrast, they often find a *positive* correlation between parental monitoring of children and children's self-control.

The higher the correlation coefficient (whether positive or negative), the stronger the association between the two variables. A correlation of 0 means that there is no association between the variables. A correlation of −.40 is stronger than a correlation of +.20 because we disregard whether the correlation is positive or negative in determining the strength of the correlation.

A caution is in order, however. Correlation does not equal causation (Leary, 2004). The correlational finding just mentioned does not mean that permissive parenting necessarily causes low self-control in children. It could mean that, but it also could mean that a child's lack of self-control caused the parents to simply throw up their arms in despair and give up trying to control the child. It also could mean that other factors, such as heredity or poverty, caused the correlation between permissive parenting and low self-control in children. Figure 1.15 illustrates these possible interpretations of correlational data.

Throughout this book you will read about numerous correlational research studies. Keep in mind how easy it is to assume causality when two events or characteristics merely are correlated.

Correlational Research

Experimental Research

Experimental Research To study causality, researchers turn to experimental research (Christiansen, 2004). An **experiment** is a carefully regulated procedure in which one or more factors believed to influence the behavior being studied are manipulated while all other factors are held constant. If the behavior under study changes when a factor is manipulated, we say that the manipulated factor has caused the behavior to change. In other words, the experiment has demonstrated cause and effect. The cause is the factor that was manipulated. The effect is the behavior that changed because of the manipulation. Nonexperimental research methods (descriptive and correlational research) cannot establish cause and effect because they do not involve manipulating factors in a controlled way (Myers & Hansen, 2002).

Independent and Dependent Variables Experiments include two types of changeable factors, or *variables*: independent and dependent. An *independent variable* is a

correlation coefficient A number based on statistical analysis that is used to describe the degree of association between two variables.

experiment A carefully regulated procedure in which one or more of the factors believed to influence the behavior being studied is manipulated and all other factors are held constant. Experimental research permits the determination of cause.

manipulated, influential, experimental factor. It is a potential cause. The label *independent* is used because this variable can be manipulated independently of other factors to determine its effect. One experiment may include several independent variables.

A *dependent variable* is a factor that can change in an experiment, in response to changes in the independent variable. As researchers manipulate the independent variable, they measure the dependent variable for any resulting effect.

For example, suppose that you conducted a study to determine whether aerobic exercise by pregnant women changes the breathing and sleeping patterns of newborn babies. You might require one group of pregnant women to engage in a certain amount of exercise each week; the amount of exercise is thus the independent variable. When the infants are born, you would observe and measure their breathing and sleeping patterns. These patterns are the dependent variable, the factor that changes as the result of your manipulation.

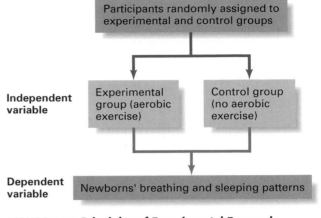

FIGURE 1.16 Principles of Experimental Research

Experimental and Control Groups   Experiments can involve one or more experimental groups and one or more control groups. An *experimental group* is a group whose experience is manipulated. A *control group* is a comparison group that is as much like the experimental group as possible and that is treated in every way like the experimental group except for the manipulated factor (independent variable). The control group serves as a baseline against which the effects of the manipulated condition can be compared.

Random assignment is an important principle for deciding whether each participant will be placed in the experimental group or in the control group. *Random assignment* means that researchers assign participants to experimental and control groups by chance. It reduces the likelihood that the experiment's results will be due to any preexisting differences between groups. In the example of the effects of aerobic exercise by pregnant women on the breathing and sleeping patterns of their newborns, you would randomly assign half of the pregnant women to engage in aerobic exercise over a period of weeks (the experimental group) and the other half to not exercise over the same number of weeks (the control group). Figure 1.16 illustrates the nature of experimental research.

Time Span of Research

Developmentalists must deal with some additional issues when they design research. Often, they want to focus on the relation of age to some other variable. The time span of a research investigation is a special concern to them. Researchers can study different individuals of different ages and compare them; they can study the same individuals as they age over time; or they can use some combination of these two approaches.

Cross-Sectional Approach   The **cross-sectional approach** is a research strategy in which individuals of different ages are compared at one time. A typical cross-sectional study might include a group of 5-year-olds, 8-year-olds, and 11-year-olds. Another might include a group of 15-year-olds, 25-year-olds, and 45-year-olds. The different groups can be compared with respect to a variety of dependent variables: IQ, memory, peer relations, attachment to parents, hormonal changes, and so on. All of this can be accomplished in a short time. In some studies data are collected in a single day. Even in large-scale cross-sectional studies with hundreds of subjects, data collection does not usually take longer than several months to complete.

The main advantage of the cross-sectional study is that the researcher does not have to wait for the individuals to grow up or become older. Despite its time efficiency, the cross-sectional approach has its drawbacks. It gives no information about

cross-sectional approach A research strategy in which individuals of different ages are compared at one time.

how individuals change or about the stability of their characteristics. The increases and decreases of development—the hills and valleys of growth and development—can become obscured in the cross-sectional approach. For example, in a cross-sectional study of life satisfaction, average increases and decreases might be revealed. But the study would not show how the life satisfaction of individual adults waxed and waned over the years. It also would not tell us whether adults who had positive or negative perceptions of life satisfaction as young adults maintained their relative degree of life satisfaction as middle-aged or older adults.

Longitudinal Approach   The **longitudinal approach** is a research strategy in which the same individuals are studied over a period of time, usually several years or more. For example, if a study of life satisfaction were conducted longitudinally, the same adults might be assessed periodically over a 70-year time span—at the ages of 20, 35, 45, 65, and 90, for example. Many longitudinal studies take place over much shorter time frames, even just a year or so.

Although longitudinal studies provide a wealth of information about such important issues as stability and change in development and the importance of early experience for later development, they are not without their problems (Raudenbush, 2001). They are expensive and time-consuming. The longer the study lasts, the more subjects drop out—they move, get sick, lose interest, and so forth. This can bias the outcome of a study, because those who remain may be dissimilar to those who drop out. Those individuals who remain in a longitudinal study over a number of years may be more compulsive and conformity-oriented, for example, or they might have more stable lives.

Sequential Approach   Sometimes developmentalists combine the cross-sectional and longitudinal approaches to learn about life-span development (Cavanaugh & Whitbourne, 2003; Schaie, 1993). The **sequential approach** is the combined cross-sectional, longitudinal design. In most instances, this approach starts with a cross-sectional study that includes individuals of different ages. A number of months after the initial assessment, the same individuals are tested again—this is the longitudinal aspect of the design. At this later time, a new group of participants is assessed at each age level. The new groups at each level are added at the later time to control for changes that might have taken place in the original group—some might have dropped out of the study, or retesting might have improved their performance, for example.

The sequential approach is complex, expensive, and time-consuming, but it does provide information that is impossible to obtain from cross-sectional or longitudinal approaches alone. The sequential approach has been especially helpful in examining cohort effects in life-span development, which we will discuss next.

Cohort Effects   A *cohort* is a group of people who are born at a similar point in history and share similar experiences as a result, such as living through the Great Depression of the 1930s or growing up in the same city around the same time. For example, those who were teenagers during the Great Depression are likely to differ from a cohort born in 1980 in characteristics such as years of education, child-rearing practices, health, attitudes toward sex, religious values, and economic status. In life-span development research, **cohort effects** are due to a person's time of birth or generation but not to actual age.

Cohort effects are important because they can powerfully affect the dependent measures in a study ostensibly concerned with age (Cavanaugh & Whitbourne, 2003). Researchers have shown it is especially important to be aware of cohort effects in the assessment of adult intelligence (Schaie, 1996). Individuals born at different points in time—such as 1920, 1940, and 1960—have had varying opportunities for education. Individuals born in the earlier years had less access to education.

Early Adulthood: The Harvard Men Study, 1938

longitudinal approach A research strategy in which the same individuals are studied over a period of time, usually several years or more.

sequential approach A combined cross-sectional, longitudinal design.

cohort effects Effects that are due to a subject's time of birth or generation but not age.

Cross-sectional studies can show how different cohorts respond, but they can confuse age changes and cohort effects. Longitudinal studies are effective in studying age changes but only within one cohort. With sequential studies, age changes in one cohort can be examined and compared with age changes in another cohort.

So far we have discussed many aspects of scientific research in life-span development. In the Research in Life-Span Development interlude, you can read about the research journals in which this research is published.

Research in Life-Span Development
Research Journals

Regardless of whether you pursue a career in life-span development, psychology, or some related scientific field, you can benefit by learning about the journal process. As a student you might be required to look up original research in journals. As a parent, teacher, or nurse you might want to consult journals to obtain information that will help you understand and work more effectively with people. And as an inquiring person, you might look up information in journals after you have heard or read something that piqued your curiosity.

A journal publishes scholarly and academic information, usually in a specific domain—like physics, math, sociology, or, our current interest, life-span development.

Research journals are the core of information in virtually every academic discipline. Those shown here are among the increasing number of research journals that publish information about life-span development. *What are the main parts of a research article that present findings from original research?*

Scholars in these fields publish most of their research in journals, which are the source of core information in virtually every academic discipline.

An increasing number of journals publish information about life-span development. Among the leading journals in life-span development are *Developmental Psychology, Child Development, Pediatrics, Pediatric Nursing, The Journals of Gerontology, Infant Behavior and Development, Journal of Research on Adolescence, Journal of Adult Development, Journal of Gerontological Nursing, Psychology and Aging, Human Development*, and many others. Also, a number of journals that do not focus solely on development include articles on various aspects of human development. These journals include *Journal of Educational Psychology, Sex Roles, Journal of Cross-Cultural Research, Journal of Marriage and the Family, and Journal of Consulting and Clinical Psychology.*

Every journal has a board of experts who evaluate articles submitted for publication. Each submitted paper is accepted or rejected on the basis of such factors as its contribution to the field, methodological excellence, and clarity of writing. Some of the most prestigious journals reject as many as 80 to 90 percent of the articles submitted.

Journal articles are usually written for other professionals in the specialized field of the journal's focus; therefore they often contain technical language and terms specific to the discipline that are difficult for nonprofessionals to understand. Their organization often takes this course: abstract, introduction, method, results, discussion, and references.

The *abstract* is a brief summary that appears at the beginning of the article. The abstract lets readers quickly determine whether the article is relevant to their interests. The *introduction* introduces the problem or issue that is being studied. It includes a concise review of research relevant to the topic, theoretical ties, and one or more hypotheses to be tested. The *method* section consists of a clear description of the subjects evaluated in the study, the measures used, and the procedures that were followed. The method section should be sufficiently clear and detailed so that by reading it another researcher could repeat or replicate the study. The *results* section reports the analysis of the data collected. In most cases, the results section includes statistical analyses that are difficult for nonprofessionals to understand. The *discussion* section describes the author's conclusions, inferences, and interpretation of what was found. Statements are usually made about whether the hypotheses presented in the introduction were supported, limitations of the study, and suggestions for future research. The last part of the journal article, called *references*, includes bibliographic information for each source cited in the article. The references section is often a good source for finding other articles relevant to the topic you are interested in.

Where do you find journals such as those we have described? Your college or university library likely has some of them, and some public libraries also carry journals.

Ethics

Safeguarding the rights of research participants is a challenge because the potential harm is not always obvious (Gall, Borg, & Gall, 2003). At first glance, you might not imagine that a questionnaire on dating relationships among college students would have any substantial impact or that an experiment involving treatment of memory loss in older adults would be anything but beneficial. But researchers increasingly recognize that lasting harm might come to the participants in a study of life-span development.

Today colleges and universities have review boards that evaluate the ethical nature of research conducted at their institutions. Proposed research plans must pass the scrutiny of a research ethics committee before the research can be initiated.

In addition, the American Psychological Association (APA) has developed ethics guidelines for its members. The code of ethics instructs psychologists to protect their participants from mental and physical harm. The participants' best interests need to be kept foremost in the researcher's mind (Rosnow, 1995). APA's guidelines address four important issues:

Psychologists' Ethical Principles

- **Informed Consent** All participants must know what their participation will involve and what risks might develop (Cavanaugh & Whitbourne, 2003). For example, participants in a study on dating should be told beforehand that a questionnaire might stimulate thoughts about issues in their relationship that they have not considered. Participants also should be informed that in some instances a discussion of the issues might improve their relationship, but in others might worsen the relationship and even end it. Even after informed consent is given, participants must retain the right to withdraw from the study at any time and for any reason. If participants are not old enough (typically 7 years or older), their parents' or guardians' consent must be obtained.
- **Confidentiality** Researchers are responsible for keeping all of the data they gather on individuals completely confidential and when possible, completely anonymous.
- **Debriefing** After the study has been completed, participants should be informed of its purpose and the methods that were used. In most cases, the experimenter also can inform participants in a general manner beforehand about the purpose of the research without altering the participants' behavior and affecting the results.
- **Deception** This is an ethical issue that psychologists debate extensively. In some circumstances, telling the participants beforehand what the research study is about substantially alters the participants' behavior and invalidates the data. In all cases of deception, however, the psychologist must ensure that the deception will not harm the participants and that the participants will be told the complete nature of the study as soon as possible after the study is completed.

Review and Reflect: Learning Goal 4

4 Explain how research on life-span development is conducted

REVIEW
- How are data on life-span development collected?
- What are the main research designs used in studying development?
- What are some ways that researchers study the effects of time on people's lives?
- What are researchers' ethical responsibilities to the people they study?

REFLECT
- You have learned that correlation does not equal causation. Develop an example of two variables (two sets of observations) that are correlated but that you believe certainly have no causal relationship.

In this chapter, we have studied many aspects of the importance of life-span development from a scientific and personal perspective. In chapter 2, we will turn our attention to the biological beginnings of life-span development.

Reach Your Learning Goals

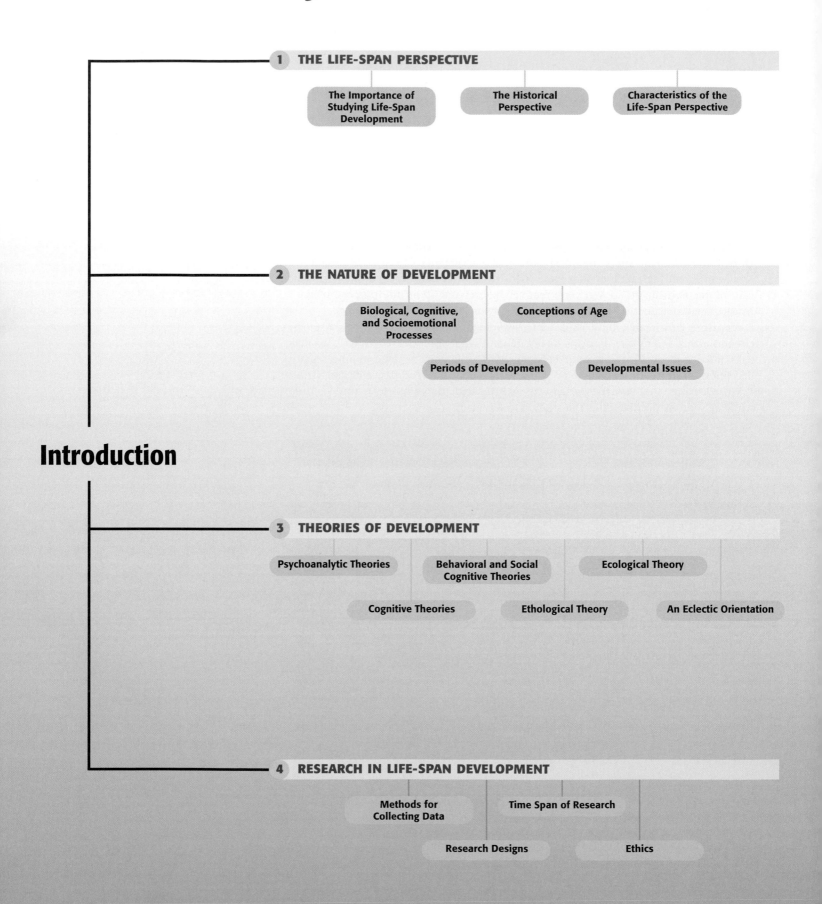

Introduction

1 THE LIFE-SPAN PERSPECTIVE

- The Importance of Studying Life-Span Development
- The Historical Perspective
- Characteristics of the Life-Span Perspective

2 THE NATURE OF DEVELOPMENT

- Biological, Cognitive, and Socioemotional Processes
- Conceptions of Age
- Periods of Development
- Developmental Issues

3 THEORIES OF DEVELOPMENT

- Psychoanalytic Theories
- Behavioral and Social Cognitive Theories
- Ecological Theory
- Cognitive Theories
- Ethological Theory
- An Eclectic Orientation

4 RESEARCH IN LIFE-SPAN DEVELOPMENT

- Methods for Collecting Data
- Time Span of Research
- Research Designs
- Ethics

Summary

1 Explain the distinctive features of a life-span perspective on development

- Development is the pattern of movement or change that begins at conception and continues through the human life span. Development includes growth and decline. Responsibility for children is or will be a part of the everyday lives of most of us. Studying development also gives us knowledge about what our lives will be like as adults.

- Interest in children has a long and rich history. Prior to the mid-nineteenth century, philosophical views of childhood were prominent, including the notions of original sin, tabula rasa, and innate goodness. The traditional approach to the study of development emphasizes extensive change in childhood but stability in adulthood; the life-span perspective emphasizes that change is possible throughout the life span.

- The life-span perspective includes these basic conceptions: Development is lifelong, multidimensional, multidirectional, plastic, multidisciplinary, and contextual, and it involves growth, maintenance, and regulation. Three important sources of contextual influences are (1) normative age-graded influences, (2) normative history-graded influences, and (3) nonnormative life events.

2 Identify the most important processes, periods, and issues in development

- Development is influenced by an interplay of biological, cognitive, and socioemotional processes.

- The life span is commonly divided into the following eight main periods of development: prenatal, infancy, early childhood, middle and late childhood, adolescence, early adulthood, middle adulthood, and late adulthood.

- We usually think of age in terms of chronological age, but Neugarten believes we are moving toward a society in which chronological age is a weaker predictor of development in adulthood. A full evaluation of age requires consideration of four dimensions of age: chronological, biological, psychological, and social.

- The nature-nurture issue focuses on the extent to which development is mainly influenced by nature (biological inheritance) or nurture (experience). The stability-change issue focuses on the degree to which early traits or characteristics persist through life or change. A special aspect of the stability-change issue is the extent to which development is determined by early versus later experiences. The continuity-discontinuity issue concerns the extent to which development is characterized by gradual, cumulative change or an abrupt series of stages. Most developmentalists recognize that extreme positions on the nature-nurture, stability-change, and continuity-discontinuity issues are unwise.

3 Describe five theoretical approaches to human development

- The scientific method involves four main steps: (1) conceptualize a problem, (2) collect data, (3) analyze data, and (4) draw conclusions. Theory is often involved in conceptualizing a problem. A theory is an interrelated, coherent set of ideas that helps to explain phenomena and to make predictions. Hypotheses are specific assertions and predictions, often derived from theory, that can be tested. According to psychoanalytic theories, development primarily depends on the unconscious mind and is heavily couched in emotion. Psychoanalytic theorists believe that behavior is merely a surface characteristic and that early experiences with parents shape development. Two main psychoanalytic theories were proposed by Freud and Erikson. Freud said that personality is made up of the id, ego, and superego. The conflicting demands of these structures produce anxiety. Freud also believed that individuals go through five psychosexual stages. Erikson's theory emphasizes eight psychosocial stages of development: trust vs. mistrust, autonomy vs. shame and doubt, initiative vs. guilt, industry vs. inferiority, identity vs. identity confusion, intimacy vs. isolation, generativity vs. stagnation, and integrity vs. despair. Contributions of psychoanalytic theories include an emphasis on a developmental framework, family relationships, and unconscious aspects of the mind. Criticisms include a lack of scientific support, too much emphasis on sexual underpinnings, and an image of people that is too negative.

- Cognitive theories emphasize thinking, reasoning, language, and other cognitive processes. Three main cognitive theories are Piaget's, Vygotsky's, and information processing. Piaget proposed a cognitive developmental theory in which children use their cognition to adapt to their world. In Piaget's theory, children go through four cognitive stages: sensorimotor, preoperational, concrete operational, and formal operational. Vygotsky's sociocultural cognitive theory emphasizes how culture and social interaction guide cognitive development. The information-processing approach emphasizes that individuals manipulate information, monitor it, and strategize about it. Contributions of cognitive theories include an emphasis on the active construction of understanding and developmental changes in thinking. Criticisms include giving too little attention to individual variations and underrating the unconscious aspects of thought.

- Three main behavioral and social cognitive theories are Pavlov's classical conditioning, Skinner's operant conditioning, and social cognitive theory. In Pavlov's classical conditioning, a neutral stimulus acquires the ability to produce a response originally produced by another stimulus. In Skinner's operant conditioning, the consequences of a behavior produce changes in the probability of the behavior's occurrence. In social cognitive theory, observational learning is a key aspect of life-span development. Bandura emphasizes reciprocal interactions among person/cognition, behavior, and environment. Contributions of the behavioral and social cognitive theories include an emphasis on scientific research, a focus on environmental factors, and the importance of social and cognitive factors in social cognitive theory. Criticisms include inadequate attention to developmental changes, too much emphasis on environmental determinism, and in Skinner's view, too little attention to cognition.

- Ethology stresses that behavior is strongly influenced by biology, is tied to evolution, and is characterized by critical or sensitive periods. Contributions of ethological theory include a focus on the biological and evolutionary basis of development. Criticisms include a belief that the concepts of critical and sensitive periods may be too rigid.

- Ecological theory is Bronfenbrenner's environmental systems view of development. It proposes five environmental systems: microsystem, mesosystem, exosystem, macrosystem, and chronosystem. Contributions of the theory include a systematic examination of macro and micro dimensions of environmental systems and consideration of sociohistorical influences. Criticisms include giving inadequate attention to biological factors, as well as a lack of emphasis on cognitive factors.

- An eclectic orientation does not follow any one theoretical approach but rather selects from each theory whatever is considered the best in it.

4 Explain how research on life-span development is conducted

- The main methods for collecting data about life-span development are observation (in a laboratory or a naturalistic setting), survey (questionnaire) or interview, standardized test, case study, and life-history record.

- Three main research designs are descriptive, correlational, and experimental. Descriptive research aims to observe and record behavior. In correlational research, the goal is to describe the strength of the relationship between two or more events or characteristics. Experimental research involves conducting an experiment, which can determine cause and effect. An independent variable is the manipulated, influential, experimental factor. A dependent variable is a factor that can change in an experiment, in response to changes in the independent variable. Experiments can involve one or more experimental groups and control groups. In random assignment, researchers assign participants to experimental and control groups by chance.

- To examine the effects of time and age, researchers can conduct cross-sectional, longitudinal, or sequential studies. Life-span researchers are especially concerned about cohort effects.

- Researchers' ethical responsibilities include seeking participants' informed consent, ensuring confidentiality, debriefing them about the purpose and potential personal consequences of participating, and avoiding unnecessary deception of participants.

Key Terms

Key People

E-Learning Tools

To help you master the material in this chapter, you will find a number of valuable study tools on the Student CD-ROM that accompanies this book. In addition, visit the Online Learning Center for *A Topical Approach to Life-Span Development*, second edition, where you will find these helpful resources for chapter 1, "Introduction."

Taking It to the Net

1. Charise and Tom are getting a divorce. Charise believes strongly that they ought to share custody of their children, Dalton, age 5, and Jasmine, 8. What evidence can Charise use to help convince Tom that this is best for both of their children?

2. Deanna wants to enroll her 7-year-old son, Victor, in a local university's clinical trials for treatment research in attention deficit hyperactivity disorder. Victor's father is overseas on business for two months. Is Victor's father's consent necessary for Victor to participate? Does the university need Victor's approval before accepting him as a research subject?

3. Carmen is completing her Ph.D. in clinical psychology. She is interested in geropsychology. What are some of the areas in which geropsychologists might conduct research and practice?

Connect to **www.mhhe.com/santrockld2** to research the answers and complete these exercises.

Self-Assessment

To evaluate yourself on topics related to this chapter, complete these self-assessments:

- *Evaluating My Interest in a Career in Life-Span Development*
- *Models and Mentors in My Life*

Health and Well-Being, Parenting, and Education

Build your decision-making skills by trying your hand at the health and well-being, parenting, and education "Scenarios."

Biological Processes, Physical Development, and Health

Babies are such a nice way to start people.
—Don Herold
American Writer, 20th Century

The rhythm and meaning of life involve biological foundations. How, from so simple a beginning, can endless forms develop and grow and mature? What was this organism, what is it, and what will it be? In Section 2 you will read and study four chapters: "Biological Beginnings" (chapter 2), "Physical Development and Biological Aging" (chapter 3), "Health" (chapter 4), and "Motor, Sensory, and Perceptual Development" (chapter 5).

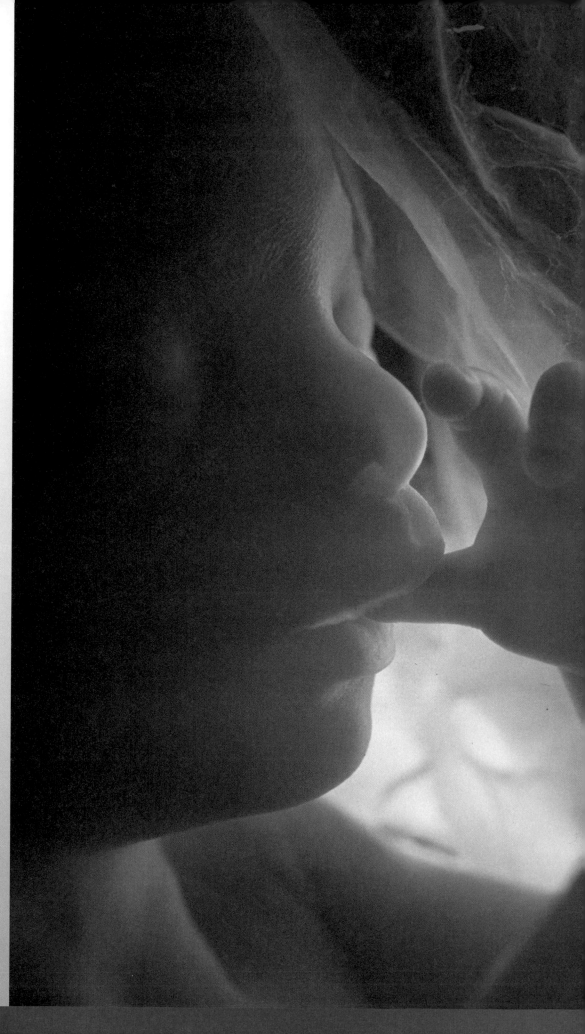

Biological Beginnings

Chapter Outline

Learning Goals

THE EVOLUTIONARY PERSPECTIVE

Natural Selection and Adaptive Behavior

Evolutionary Psychology

1 Discuss the evolutionary perspective on life-span development

GENETIC FOUNDATIONS

The Genetic Process

Genetic Principles

Chromosome and Gene-Linked Abnormalities

2 Describe what genes are and how they influence human development

HEREDITY, ENVIRONMENT, AND INDIVIDUAL DIFFERENCES

Behavior Genetics

Heredity-Environment Correlations

Shared and Nonshared Environmental Experiences

The Epigenetic View

Conclusions About Heredity-Environment Interaction

3 Explain some of the ways that heredity and environment interact to produce individual differences in development

PRENATAL DEVELOPMENT

The Course of Prenatal Development

Prenatal Diagnostic Tests

Teratogens and the Prenatal Environment

4 Characterize the course of prenatal development and its hazards

BIRTH

The Process of Birth

Strategies for Childbirth

Neonatal Health and Responsiveness

Bonding

5 Summarize how birth takes place

Organisms are not like billiard balls, moved by simple external forces to predictable positions on life's table. Environmental experiences and biological foundations work together to make us who we are. In this chapter, we will explore life's biological beginnings and experiences, charting growth from conception through the prenatal period and examining the birth process itself. We will begin our exploration of the biological foundations of development by exploring possible evolutionary influences.

1 THE EVOLUTIONARY PERSPECTIVE

Natural Selection and Adaptive Behavior

Evolutionary Psychology

In evolutionary time, humans are relative newcomers to Earth, yet we have established ourselves as the most successful and dominant species. If we consider evolutionary time as a calendar year, humans arrived here in the last moments of December (Sagan, 1977). As our earliest ancestors left the forest to feed on the savannahs, and then to form hunting societies on the open plains, their minds and behaviors changed. How did this evolution come about?

Natural Selection and Adaptive Behavior

Natural selection is the evolutionary process that favors individuals of a species that are best adapted to survive and reproduce. To understand natural selection, let's return to the middle of the nineteenth century, when the British naturalist Charles Darwin was traveling around the world, observing many different species of animals in their natural surroundings. Darwin, who published his observations and thoughts in *On the Origin of Species* (1859), noted that most organisms reproduce at rates that would cause enormous increases in the population of most species and yet populations remain nearly constant. He reasoned that an intense, constant struggle for food, water, and resources must occur among the many young born each generation, because many of the young do not survive. Those that do survive and reproduce pass on their characteristics to the next generation. Darwin believed that these survivors are probably superior in a number of ways to those who do not survive. In other words, the survivors are better *adapted* to their world than are the nonsurvivors (Raven & Johnson, 2002). The best-adapted individuals survive to leave the most offspring. Over the course of many generations, organisms with the characteristics needed for survival would make up an increased percentage of the population. Over many, many generations, this could produce a gradual modification of the whole population. If environmental conditions change, however, other characteristics might become favored by natural selection, moving the species in a different direction (Lewis & others, 2004).

All organisms must adapt to particular places, climates, food sources, and ways of life. An example of adaptation is an eagle's claws, which facilitate predation. *Adaptive behavior* is behavior that promotes an organism's survival in the natural habitat (Cosmides & others, 2003). For example, in the human realm, attachment between a caregiver and a baby ensures the infant's closeness to a caregiver for feeding and protection from danger, thus increasing the infant's chances of survival.

Evolutionary Psychology

Although Darwin introduced the theory of evolution by natural selection in 1859, his ideas only recently have become a popular framework for explaining behavior.

www.mhhe.com/santrockldt2

Evolution

Evolution and Behavior

Psychology's newest approach, **evolutionary psychology,** emphasizes the importance of adaptation, reproduction, and "survival of the fittest" in shaping behavior. In this view, the evolutionary process of natural selection has favored behaviors that increase our reproductive success, our ability to pass our genes to the next generation (Caporael, 2001; Cosmides & others, 2003; Durrant & Ellis, 2003; Kenrick, Li, & Butler, 2003; Moore, 2004).

David Buss (1995, 2000, 2004; Larsen & Buss, 2002) has been especially influential in stimulating interest in how evolution can explain human behavior. He believes that just as evolution shapes our physical features, such as body shape and height, it also pervasively influences how we make decisions, how aggressive we are, our fears, and our mating patterns. For example, assume that our ancestors were hunters and gatherers on the plains and that men did most of the hunting and women stayed close to home gathering seeds and plants for food. If you have to travel some distance from your home in an effort to find and slay a fleeing animal, you need not only certain physical skills but also skills for certain types of spatial thinking. Men with these skills would be more likely than men without them to survive, to bring home lots of food, and to be considered attractive mates—and thus to reproduce and pass on these characteristics to their children. Over many generations, men with good spatial thinking skills might become more numerous in the population. However, this skill would provide no reproductive advantage to the women.

Evolutionary Developmental Psychology   Much of the thinking about evolutionary psychology has not had a developmental focus. Recently, however, interest has grown in applying the concepts of evolutionary psychology to the changes that take place as people develop. Here are a few ideas proposed by evolutionary developmental psychologists (Bjorklund & Pellegrini, 2002):

- *An extended "juvenile" period evolved because humans need time to develop a large brain and learn the complexity of human social communities.* Humans take longer to become reproductively mature than any other mammal (see figure 2.1). During this time they develop a large brain and the experiences required for mastering the complexities of human society.
- *Many aspects of childhood function as preparations for adulthood and were selected over the course of evolution.* For example, through their play children learn much about their physical and social worlds that can help them adapt as adults. Beginning in the preschool years, boys in all cultures engage in more rough-and-tumble play than girls. Perhaps rough-and-tumble play is preparation for adult fighting and hunting by males. Girls engage in more play parenting (such as doll play) and less physical dominance than boys do. This, according to evolutionary psychologists, is an evolved tendency that prepares females for being the primary caregivers for their offspring.
- *Some characteristics of childhood were selected to be adaptive at specific points in development and not as preparation for adulthood.* For example, some aspects of play may function not as preparation for adulthood, but to help children adapt to their immediate circumstances, perhaps to learn about their current environment.
- *Many evolved psychological mechanisms are domain-specific—that is, they apply to a specific aspect of a person's psychological makeup.* According to evolutionary psychology, domain-specific information processing evolved as our ancestors dealt with certain recurring problems. In this view, the mind is not a general-purpose device that can be applied equally well to a vast array of problems. Rather, it consists of a set of specialized modules, such as a module for physical knowledge, a module for mathematical knowledge, and a module for language (Geary & Huffman,

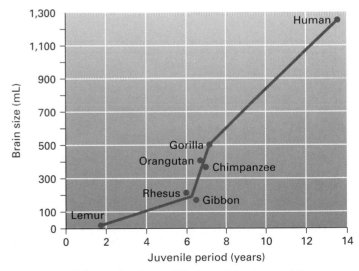

FIGURE 2.1 The Brain Sizes of Various Primates and Humans in Relation to the Length of the Juvenile Period

evolutionary psychology Emphasizes the importance of adaptation, reproduction, and "survival of the fittest" in shaping behavior.

Evolutionary Psychology
Handbook of Evolutionary Psychology
Evolutionary Psychology Resources

2002). Also in this view, infants enter the world prepared to learn some information more readily than others, and these preparations serve as a foundation for social and cognitive development across the childhood and adolescent years.

- *Evolved mechanisms are not always adaptive in contemporary society.* Some behaviors that were adaptive for our prehistoric ancestors may not serve us well today. For example, being physically aggressive was adaptive for survival for prehistoric males, but violent aggression might not be adaptive for males in the twenty-first century.

Evolution and Life-Span Development   In evolutionary theory, what matters is that individuals live long enough to reproduce and pass on their characteristics. So why do humans live so long after reproduction? Currently, there is a great deal of interest in evolutionary explanations of aging (Gavrilov & Gavrilova, 2002; Siegfried, 2002). Perhaps evolution favored a long life because having older people around improves the survival of babies. For example, an evolutionary advantage may have taken place because grandparents cared for the young while parents were out hunting and gathering food.

According to life-span developmentalist Paul Baltes (2000, 2003; Baltes & Smith, 2003), the benefits conferred by evolutionary selection decrease with age. Natural selection has not weeded out many harmful conditions and nonadaptive characteristics that appear among older adults. Why? Natural selection operates primarily on characteristics that are tied to reproductive fitness, which extends through the earlier part of adulthood. Thus, says Baltes, selection primarily operates during the first half of life. As an example, consider Alzheimer's disease, an irreversible brain disorder characterized by gradual deterioration. This disease typically does not appear until age 70 or later. If it were a disease that struck 20-year-olds, perhaps natural selection would have eliminated it eons ago.

Thus, unaided by evolutionary pressures against nonadaptive conditions, we suffer the aches, pains, and infirmities of aging. And as the benefits of evolutionary selection decrease with age, argues Baltes, the need for culture increases (see figure 2.2). That is, as older adults weaken biologically, they need culture-based resources such as cognitive skills, literacy, medical technology, and social support. For example, older adults may need help and training from other people to maintain their cognitive skills (Hoyer & Roodin, 2003).

Evaluating Evolutionary Psychology   Although the popular press gives a lot of attention to the ideas of evolutionary psychology, it remains just one theoretical approach. Like the theories described in chapter 1, it has limitations, weaknesses, and critics. Albert Bandura (1998), whose social cognitive theory was described in chapter 1, acknowledges the important influence of evolution on human adaptation. ◀⫴ **P. 24.** However, he rejects what he calls "one-sided evolutionism," which sees social behavior as the product of evolved biology. An alternative is a *bidirectional view*, in which environmental and biological conditions influence each other. For example, evolutionary pressures created changes in biological structures that allowed the use of tools, which enabled organisms to manipulate, alter, and construct new environmental conditions. In turn, environmental innovations produced new selection pressures for the evolution of specialized biological systems for consciousness, thought, and language.

In other words, evolution gave us bodily structures and biological potentialities; it does not dictate behavior. People have used their biological capacities to produce diverse cultures—aggressive, pacific, egalitarian, or autocratic. As American scientist Steven Jay Gould (1981) concluded, in most domains of human functioning, biology allows a broad range of cultural possibilities.

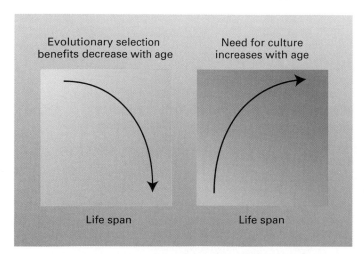

FIGURE 2.2 Baltes' View of Evolution and Culture Across the Life Span

Review and Reflect: Learning Goal 1

1 **Discuss the evolutionary perspective on life-span development**

REVIEW

- How can natural selection and adaptive behavior be defined?
- What is evolutionary psychology? What are some basic ideas about human development proposed by evolutionary psychologists? How can evolutionary psychology be evaluated?

REFLECT

- Which is more persuasive: the views of evolutionary psychologists or their critics? Why?

2 GENETIC FOUNDATIONS

| The Genetic Process | Genetic Principles | Chromosome and Gene-Linked Abnormalities |

Every species has a mechanism for transmitting characteristics from one generation to the next. This mechanism is explained by the principles of genetics. Each of us carries a "genetic code" that we inherited from our parents, and it is a distinctly human code. Because it carries this human code, a fertilized human egg cannot grow into an egret, eagle, or elephant.

The Genetic Process

Each of us began life as a single cell weighing about one twenty-millionth of an ounce! This tiny piece of matter housed our entire genetic code—instructions that orchestrated growth from that single cell to a person made of trillions of cells, each containing a replica of the original genetic code. That code is carried by our genes. What are they, and what do they do?

DNA: The Collaborative Gene The nucleus of each human cell contains **chromosomes,** which are threadlike structures that contain the remarkable substance deoxyribonucleic acid, or DNA. **DNA** is a complex molecule that contains genetic information. It has a double helix shape, like a spiral staircase. **Genes,** the units of hereditary information, are short segments of DNA, as you can see in figure 2.3. They direct cells to reproduce themselves and to assemble proteins. Proteins, in turn, are the building blocks of cells and direct the body's processes.

Each gene has its own function and each gene has its own location, its own designated place on a particular chromosome. Today, there is a great deal of enthusiasm about efforts to discover the specific locations of genes that are linked to certain functions (Plomin, 2003; Polychronakos, 2003; Trinklein & others, 2004; Venter, 2003; Zvara & others, 2003). An important step in this direction was accomplished when the Human Genome Project and the Celera Corporation completed a preliminary map of the human *genome*—the complete set of instructions for making an organism (U.S. Department of Energy, 2001).

One of the big surprises of the Human Genome Project was the finding that humans have only about 30,000 to 35,000 genes (U.S. Department of Energy, 2001). Biologists had thought that humans had as many as 100,000 or more genes. They

chromosomes Threadlike structures that contain the genetic substance DNA.

DNA A complex molecule that contains genetic information.

genes Units of hereditary information composed of DNA. Genes direct cells to reproduce themselves and manufacture the proteins that maintain life.

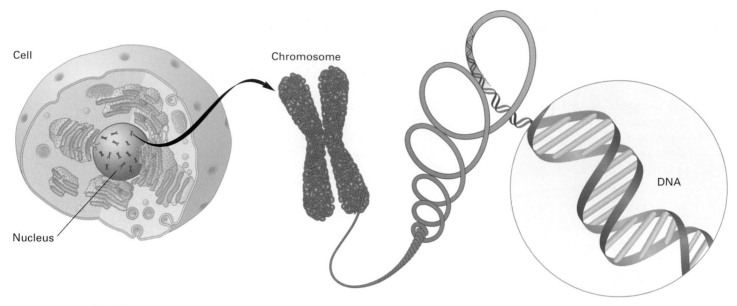

FIGURE 2.3 Cells, Chromosomes, Genes, and DNA

(Left) The body contains trillions of cells, which are the basic structural units of life. Each cell contains a central structure, the nucleus. *(Middle)* Chromosomes are located in the nucleus of the cell. Chromosomes are threadlike structures composed mainly of DNA. *(Right)* The structure of DNA resembles a spiral ladder. A gene is a segment of DNA that contains the hereditary code.

had also believed that each gene programmed just one protein. In fact, humans appear to have far more proteins than they have genes, so there cannot be a one-to-one correspondence between them (Commoner, 2002; Moore, 2001). Each segment of DNA is not translated, in automaton-like fashion, into one and only one protein. A gene does not act independently, as developmental psychologist David Moore (2001) emphasized by titling his recent book *The Dependent Gene.*

Instead, the DNA gene acts only in collaboration with many other molecules and processes in the cell. The collaboration operates at many points. Small pieces of DNA are mixed, matched, and linked by the cellular machinery. That machinery is sensitive to its context—that is, it is influenced by what is going on around it. Whether a gene is turned "on," working to assemble proteins, is also a matter of collaboration. The activity of genes (*genetic expression*) is affected by their environment (Gottlieb, 2000, 2002, 2004). For example, hormones that circulate in the blood make their way into the cell where they can turn genes "on" and "off." And the flow of hormones can be affected by environmental conditions, such as light, day length, nutrition, and behavior. Numerous studies have shown that external events outside of the cell and the person, and internal events inside of the cell, can excite or inhibit gene expression (Gottlieb, Wahlsten, & Lickliter, 1998; Mauro & others, 1994; Rusak & others, 1990).

In short, no single gene is the source of the protein's genetic information, much less of an inherited trait (Gottlieb, 2004; Moore, 2001). Rather than being an independent gene, DNA is a collaborative gene.

Genes and Chromosomes   Genes not only are collaborative; they are enduring. How do the genes manage to get passed from generation to generation and end up in all of the trillion cells in the body? Three processes tell the heart of the story: mitosis, meiosis, and fertilization.

Mitosis, Meiosis, and Fertilization   All cells in the body except the sperm and egg have 46 chromosomes arranged in 23 pairs. These cells reproduce by a process called **mitosis.** During mitosis, the cell's nucleus—including the chromosomes—duplicates

mitosis Cellular reproduction in which the cell's nucleus duplicates itself with two new cells being formed, each containing the same DNA as the parent cell, arranged in the same 23 pairs of chromosomes.

itself. Two new cells are formed, each containing the same DNA as the parent cell, arranged in the same 23 pairs of chromosomes.

However, a specialized form of cell division—**meiosis**—occurs to form eggs and sperm (or *gametes*). During meiosis, a cell of the testes or ovaries duplicates its chromosomes and then divides twice, forming four eggs or sperm, each of which has only half of the genetic material of the parent cell (Bean & others, 2004). In other words, each egg or sperm has 23 *unpaired* chromosomes.

In the process of **reproduction,** an egg is fertilized by a sperm (see figure 2.4). Fertilization creates a single cell, called a **zygote.** In the zygote, the two sets of unpaired chromosomes from the egg and sperm combine to form one set of paired chromosomes—one member of each pair from the mother's egg and the other member from the father's sperm. In this manner, each parent contributes half of the offspring's heredity.

Sources of Variability The chromosomes in the zygote, however, are not perfect copies of the chromosomes of the mother's ovaries and the father's testes. During the formation of the sperm and egg in meiosis, pieces of the parent's chromosomes are exchanged, creating a new combination of genes. Thus, when chromosomes from the mother's egg and the father's sperm are brought together in the zygote, the result is a truly unique combination of genes (Mader, 2004).

Figure 2.5 shows 23 paired chromosomes of a male and a female. The members of each pair of chromosomes are both similar and different: Each chromosome in the pair contains varying forms of the same genes, at the same location on the chromosomes. A gene for hair color, for example, is located on both members of one pair of chromosomes, in the same location on each. However, one of those chromosomes might carry the gene for blond hair; the other chromosome in the pair might carry the gene for brown hair.

What is the difference between the chromosomes of the male and the chromosomes of the female in figure 2.5? Just one pair of chromosomes makes the difference. Ordinarily, females have two chromosomes called *X chromosomes;* males have an X and a *Y chromosome.*

All of a person's genetic material makes up his or her **genotype.** However, not all of the genetic material is apparent in our observed and measurable characteristics. A **phenotype** consists of observable characteristics. Phenotypes include physical characteristics (such as height, weight, and hair color) and

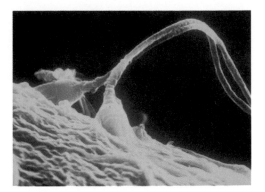

FIGURE 2.4 Union of Sperm and Egg

Human Genome Project
Landmarks in the History of Genetics
Heredity Resources
Genetic Journals and News

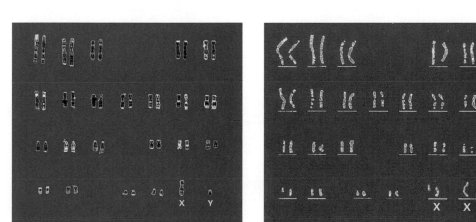

FIGURE 2.5 The Genetic Difference Between Males and Females
The chromosome structures of a male *(left)* and female *(right)*. The 23rd pair is shown at bottom right. Notice that the male's Y chromosome is smaller than his X chromosome. To obtain pictures of chromosomes, a cell is removed from a person's body, usually from inside the mouth, and the chromosomes are photographed under magnification.

meiosis A specialized form of cell division that occurs to form eggs and sperm (or gametes).

reproduction The process that, in humans, begins when a female gamete (ovum) is fertilized by a male gamete (sperm).

zygote A single cell formed through fertilization.

genotype A person's genetic heritage; the actual genetic material.

phenotype The way an individual's genotype is expressed in observed and measurable characteristics.

psychological characteristics (such as personality and intelligence). For each genotype, a range of phenotypes can be expressed. An individual can inherit the genetic potential to grow very large, but good nutrition will also be important to achieving that potential.

Genetic Principles

What determines the phenotype that is expressed? Much is unknown about the answer to this question (Lewis, 2003). However, a number of genetic principles have been discovered, among them those of dominant-recessive genes, sex-linked genes, genetic imprinting, polygenically determined characteristics, and reaction range.

Dominant-Recessive Genes Principle   According to the *dominant-recessive genes principle*, if one gene of a pair is dominant and one is recessive, the dominant gene exerts its effect, overriding the potential influence of the other, recessive gene. A recessive gene exerts its influence only if the two genes of a pair are both recessive. If you inherit a recessive gene for a trait from each of your parents, you will show the trait. If you inherit a recessive gene from only one parent, you may never know you carry the gene. Brown hair, farsightedness, and dimples rule over blond hair, nearsightedness, and freckles in the world of dominant-recessive genes.

Can two brown-haired parents have a blond-haired child? Yes, they can. Suppose that in each parent the gene pair that governs hair color includes a dominant gene for brown hair and a recessive gene for blond hair. Since dominant genes override recessive genes, the parents have brown hair, but both are carriers of blondness and pass on their recessive genes for blond hair. With no dominant gene to override them, the recessive genes can make the child's hair blond. Figure 2.6 illustrates the dominant-recessive genes principle.

Sex-Linked Genes   *X-linked inheritance* is the term used to describe the inheritance of an altered (*mutated*) gene that is carried on the X chromosome (Trappe & others, 2001). Males have only one X chromosome. When there is an alteration of the X chromosome, males have no "backup" copy and therefore may carry an X-linked disease. However, females have a second X chromosome, which is likely to be

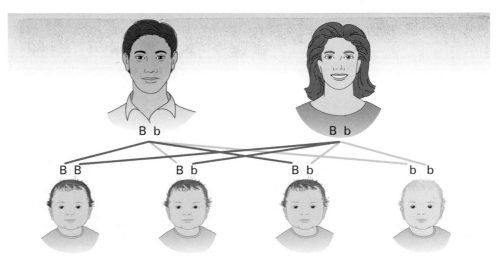

B = Gene for brown hair   b = Gene for blond hair

FIGURE 2.6 How Brown-Haired Parents Can Have a Blond-Haired Child

Although both parents have brown hair, each parent can have a recessive gene for blond hair. In this example, both parents have brown hair, but each parent carries the recessive gene for blond hair. Therefore, the odds of their child having blond hair are one in four—the probability the child will receive a recessive gene *(b)* from each parent.

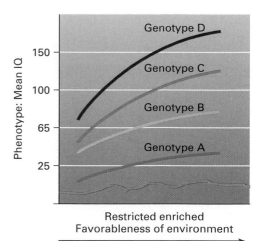

FIGURE 2.7 Hypothetical Reaction Ranges
Although each genotype responds favorably to improved environments, some are more responsive than others to environmental deprivation and enrichment.

unchanged. As a result, they are not likely to have the X-linked disease. Thus, most individuals who have X-linked diseases are males. Females who have one changed copy of the X gene are known as "carriers," and they usually do not show any signs of the X-linked disease. Hemophilia and fragile-X syndrome, which we will discuss later in the chapter, are examples of X-linked inheritance (Gonzales-del Angel & others, 2000).

Genetic Imprinting   *Genetic imprinting* occurs when genes have differing effects depending on whether they are inherited from the mother or the father (Jirtle, Sander, & Barret, 2000). An imprinted gene dominates one that has not been imprinted. For example, individuals who inherit Huntington disease from their fathers show symptoms of the disease at an earlier age than when they inherit from their mother (Navarrette, Martinez, & Salamanca, 1994). (We describe Huntington disease later in this chapter.)

Polygenetic Inheritance   *Genetic transmission* is usually more complex than the simple examples we have examined thus far (Hartwell & others, 2004; Lewis, 2003). *Polygenic inheritance* occurs when many genes interact to influence a characteristic. Few psychological characteristics are the result of single pairs. Most are determined by the interaction of many different genes; they are said to be *polygenically determined*. There are about 30,000 to 35,000 human genes, so you can imagine that possible combinations are staggering in number.

Reaction Range   Imagine that we could identify all of the genes that influence whether a person is introverted or extraverted. Would measured introversion-extraversion be predictable from knowledge of the specific genes? The answer is no, because, even if our genetic model was adequate, introversion-extraversion is shaped by experience throughout life. For example, parents may push an introverted child into social situations and encourage the child to become more gregarious.

Think about a series of genetic codes that predispose the child to develop in a particular way, and imagine environments that are responsive or unresponsive to this development. For instance, one person may be genetically predisposed to be introverted, yet in an environment that encourages social interaction and outgoingness, that person may become more extraverted. However, it is unlikely that an individual predisposed to introversion would become a strong extravert.

The **reaction range** is the range of possible phenotypes for each genotype. This concept suggests the importance of an environment's restrictiveness or richness (see figure 2.7). Sandra Scarr (1984) explains reaction range this way. Each of us has a range of potential. For example, an individual with "medium-tall" genes for height who grows up in a poor environment may be shorter than average; however, in an excellent nutritional environment, the individual may grow up taller than average. No matter how well fed the person is, though, someone with "short" genes will never be taller than average.

reaction range The range of possible phenotypes for each genotype, suggesting the importance of an environment's restrictiveness or richness.

Name	Description	Treatment	Incidence
Down syndrome	An extra chromosome causes mild to severe retardation and physical abnormalities.	Surgery, early intervention, infant stimulation, and special learning programs	1 in 1,900 births at age 20 1 in 300 births at age 35 1 in 30 births at age 45
Klinefelter syndrome	An extra X chromosome causes physical abnormalities.	Hormone therapy can be effective	1 in 800 males
Fragile X syndrome	An abnormality in the X chromosome can cause mental retardation, learning disabilities, or short attention span.	Special education, speech and language therapy	More common in males than in females
Turner syndrome	A missing X chromosome in females can cause mental retardation and sexual underdevelopment.	Hormone therapy in childhood and puberty	1 in 2,500 female births
XYY syndrome	An extra Y chromosome can cause above-average height.	No special treatment required	1 in 1,000 male births

FIGURE 2.8 Some Chromosome Abnormalities

Note: Treatment does not necessarily erase the problem but may improve the individual's adaptive behavior and quality of life.

Prenatal Testing and Down Syndrome

canalization The process by which characteristics are restricted to a narrow developmental course, apparently protecting a person from environmental extremes.

Down syndrome A chromosomally transmitted form of mental retardation caused by the presence of an extra (47th) chromosome.

Scarr believes that characteristics such as intelligence and introversion work the same way. That is, there is a range within which the environment can modify intelligence, but intelligence is not completely malleable. Reaction range gives us an estimate of how modifiable intelligence is.

Although some traits have a wide reaction range, others are somewhat immune to extensive changes in the environment. These characteristics seem to stay on a particular developmental course, regardless of environmental assaults (Waddington, 1957). For example, Jerome Kagan (1984) studied Guatemalan infants who had experienced extreme malnutrition as infants yet showed normal social and cognitive development later in childhood.

Canalization is the term used to describe the narrow path, or developmental course, that certain characteristics take. Apparently, preservative forces help to protect, or buffer, a person from environmental extremes (Stearns, 2002).

Chromosome and Gene-Linked Abnormalities

In some cases, abnormalities characterize the genetic process (Plomin & McGuffin, 2003). Some of these abnormalities involve chromosomes, others are produced by harmful genes.

Chromosome Abnormalities Sometimes, when a gamete is formed, the sperm or ovum does not have its normal set of 23 chromosomes. The most notable examples involve Down syndrome and abnormalities of the sex chromosomes (see figure 2.8).

Down Syndrome An individual with **Down syndrome** has a round face, a flattened skull, an extra fold of skin over the eyelids, a protruding tongue, short limbs, and retardation of motor and mental abilities. The syndrome is caused by the presence of an extra (47th) chromosome. It is not known why the extra chromosome is present, but the health of the male sperm or female ovum may be involved (Davison, Gardiner, & Costa, 2001; MacLean, 2000). Women between the ages of 18 and 38 are less likely to give birth to a child with Down syndrome than are younger or older women (Morris & others, 2003). Down syndrome appears approximately once in every 700 live births. African American children are rarely born with Down syndrome.

Sex-Linked Chromosome Abnormalities   Recall that a newborn normally has either an X and a Y chromosome, or two X chromosomes. However, approximately 1 in every 500 infants either is missing a second X chromosome, or has an X chromosome that is combined with two more sex chromosomes. These abnormalities produce the sex-linked chromosomal disorders known as Klinefelter syndrome, Turner syndrome, and XYY syndrome (Baum, 2000).

Klinefelter syndrome is a genetic disorder in which males have an extra X chromosome, making them XXY instead of XY (Lowe & others, 2001; O'Donnell & Warren, 2003). Males with this disorder have undeveloped testes, and they usually have enlarged breasts and become tall. Klinefelter syndrome occurs approximately once in every 800 live male births.

Turner syndrome is a chromosomal disorder in females in which either an X chromosome is missing, making the person XO instead of XX, or the second chromosome is partially deleted (Frias & Davenport, 2003). These females are short in stature and have a webbed neck. They might be infertile and have difficulty in mathematics, but their verbal ability is often quite good. Turner syndrome occurs in approximately 1 of every 2,500 live females births.

The **XYY syndrome** is a chromosomal disorder in which the male has an extra Y chromosome (Parmar, Muranjan, & Swami, 2003). Early interest in this syndrome focused on the belief that the extra Y chromosome found in some males contributed to aggression and violence. However, researchers subsequently found that XYY males are no more likely to commit crimes than are XY males (Witkin & others, 1976).

A fourth sex-linked chromosomal disorder is **fragile X syndrome;** it results from an abnormality in the X chromosome, which becomes constricted and often breaks. Mental deficiency often is an outcome; it may take the form of mental retardation, a learning disability, or a short attention span (Lewis, 2003). This disorder occurs more frequently in males than in females, possibly because the second X chromosome in females negates the disorder's negative effects (O'Donnell & Warren, 2003).

These athletes, many of whom have Down syndrome, are participating in a Special Olympics competition. Notice the distinctive facial features of the individuals with Down syndrome, such as a round face and a flattened skull. *What causes Down syndrome?*

Gene-Linked Abnormalities

Genetic disorders can be produced not only by abnormal chromosomes but also by harmful genes (Croyle, 2000). More than 7,000 such genetic disorders have been identified, although most of them are rare.

Phenylketonuria (PKU) is a genetic disorder in which the individual cannot properly metabolize an amino acid. Phenylketonuria is now easily detected, but, if it is left untreated, mental retardation and hyperactivity result. The disorder is treated by diet to prevent an excess accumulation of phenylalanine, an amino acid (Bendelius, 2003; Schulpis & others, 2003). Phenylketonuria involves a recessive gene and occurs about once in every 10,000 to 20,000 live births. Phenylketonuria accounts for about 1 percent of institutionalized mentally retarded individuals, and it occurs primarily in Whites.

The story of phenylketonuria has important implications for the nature-nurture issue. Although phenylketonuria is a genetic disorder (nature), how or whether a gene's influence in phenylketonuria is played out can depend on environmental influences since the disorder can be treated (nurture) (Luciana, Sullivan, & Nelson, 2001; Merrick, Aspler, & Schwartz, 2001).

Sickle-cell anemia is a genetic disorder that impairs the body's red blood cells. A red blood cell is usually shaped like a disk, but in sickle-cell anemia, a change in a recessive gene modifies its shape to a hook-shaped "sickle." These cells die quickly, causing anemia and early death of the individual because of their failure to carry oxygen to the body's cells (Fixler & Styles, 2002; Luffy & Grove, 2003). In the United

Klinefelter syndrome A chromosomal disorder in which males have an extra X chromosome, making them XXY instead of XY.

Turner syndrome A chromosomal disorder in females in which either an X chromosome is missing, making the person XO instead of XX, or the second X chromosome is partially deleted.

XYY syndrome A chromosomal disorder in which males have an extra Y chromosome.

fragile X syndrome A genetic disorder involving an abnormality in the X chromosome, which becomes constricted and often breaks.

phenylketonuria (PKU) A genetic disorder in which an individual cannot properly metabolize an amino acid. PKU is now easily detected but, if left untreated, results in mental retardation and hyperactivity.

sickle-cell anemia A genetic disorder that affects the red blood cells and occurs most often in people of African descent.

During a physical examination for a college football tryout, Jerry Hubbard, 32, learned that he carried the gene for sickle-cell anemia. Daughter Sara is healthy but daughter Avery (in the flowered dress) has sickle-cell anemia. *If you were a genetic counselor, would you recommend that this family have more children? Explain.*

States sickle-cell anemia occurs most often in African Americans. About 1 in 400 African American babies is affected. One in 10 African Americans is a carrier, as is 1 in 20 Latin Americans.

Other disorders that can result from harmful genes include cystic fibrosis, diabetes, hemophilia, Huntington disease, spina bifida, and Tay-Sachs disease. Figure 2.9 provides further information about these conditions. The work of the Human Genome Project and similar research holds out the promise that someday scientists may identify why these and other genetic abnormalities occur and discover how to cure them. The Human Genome Project has already linked specific DNA variations with increased risk of a number of diseases and conditions, including Huntington disease (in which the central nervous system deteriorates), some forms of cancer, asthma, diabetes, hypertension, and Alzheimer's disease (Davies, 2001; Goodstadt & Point, 2001).

Every individual carries DNA variations that might predispose that person to serious physical disease or mental disorder. Identifying the flaws could enable doctors to predict an individual's disease risks, recommend healthy lifestyle regimens, and prescribe the safest and most effective drugs. A decade or two from now, parents of a newborn baby may be able to leave the hospital with a full genome analysis of their offspring that reveals disease risks.

However, this knowledge might bring important costs as well as benefits. Who would have access to a person's genetic profile? An individual's ability to land and hold jobs or obtain insurance

Name	Description	Treatment	Incidence
Cystic fibrosis	Glandular dysfunction that interferes with mucus production; breathing and digestion are hampered, resulting in a shortened life span.	Physical and oxygen therapy, synthetic enzymes, and antibiotics; most individuals live to middle age.	1 in 2,000 births
Diabetes	Body does not produce enough insulin, which causes abnormal metabolism of sugar.	Early onset can be fatal unless treated with insulin.	1 in 2,500 births
Hemophilia	Delayed blood clotting causes internal and external bleeding.	Blood transfusions/injections can reduce or prevent damage due to internal bleeding.	1 in 10,000 males
Huntington disease	Central nervous system deteriorates, producing problems in muscle coordination and mental deterioration.	Doesn't usually appear until age 35 or older; death likely 10 to 20 years after symptoms appear.	1 in 20,000 births
Phenylketonuria (PKU)	Metabolic disorder that, left untreated, causes mental retardation.	Special diet can result in average intelligence and normal life span.	1 in 14,000 births
Sickle-cell anemia	Blood disorder that limits the body's oxygen supply; it can cause joint swelling, as well as heart and kidney failure.	Penicillin, medication for pain, antibiotics, and blood transfusions groups.	1 in 400 African American children (lower among other groups)
Spina bifida	Neural tube disorder that causes brain and spine abnormalities.	Corrective surgery at birth, orthopedic devices, and physical/medical therapy.	2 in 1,000 births
Tay-Sachs disease	Deceleration of mental and physical development caused by an accumulation of lipids in the nervous system.	Medication and special diet are used, but death is likely by 5 years of age.	One in 30 American Jews is a carrier.

FIGURE 2.9 Some Gene-Linked Abnormalities

	Yes	No	Undecided
1. Would you want you or your loved one to be tested for a gene that increases your risk for a disease, but does not determine whether you will actually develop the disease?	☐	☐	☐
2. Would you want you and your mate to be tested before having offspring to determine your risk for having a child who is likely to contract various diseases?	☐	☐	☐
3. Should testing of unborn children be restricted to traits that are commonly considered to have negative outcomes, such as disease?	☐	☐	☐
4. Should altering a newly conceived person's genes to improve qualities such as intelligence, appearance, and strength be allowed?	☐	☐	☐
5. Should employers be permitted access to your genetic information?	☐	☐	☐
6. Should life insurance companies have access to your genetic information?	☐	☐	☐

FIGURE 2.10 Exploring Your Genetic Future

might be threatened if it is known that a person is considered at risk for some disease. For example, should an airline pilot or a neurosurgeon who is predisposed to develop a disorder that makes one's hands shake be required to leave that job early? To think further about such issues, see figure 2.10.

Review and Reflect: Learning Goal 2

2 **Describe what genes are and how they influence human development**

REVIEW

- How does the genetic process work?
- What are some important genetic principles?
- What are some chromosome and gene-linked abnormalities?

REFLECT

- What are some possible ethical issues regarding genetics and development that might arise in the future?

3 **HEREDITY, ENVIRONMENT, AND INDIVIDUAL DIFFERENCES**

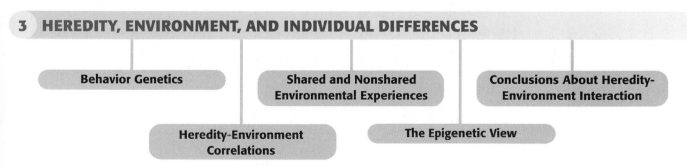

Behavior Genetics

Shared and Nonshared Environmental Experiences

Conclusions About Heredity-Environment Interaction

Heredity-Environment Correlations

The Epigenetic View

So far, we have described genes and how they work, and one theme is apparent: Heredity and environment interact to produce development. Whether we are studying how genes produce proteins, their influence on how tall a person is, or how

Behavior Genetics

Twin Research

**Early Adulthood: Swedish
Twin Performance Studies**

behavior genetics The field that seeks to discover the influence of heredity and environment on individual differences in human traits and development.

twin study A study in which the behavioral similarity of identical twins is compared with the behavioral similarity of fraternal twins.

adoption study A study in which investigators seek to discover whether, in behavior and psychological characteristics, adopted children are more like their adoptive parents, who provided a home environment, or more like their biological parents, who contributed their heredity. Another form of the adoption study is to compare adoptive and biological siblings.

passive genotype-environment correlations Correlations that occur because the biological parents, who are genetically related to the child, provide a rearing environment for the child.

PKU might affect an individual, we end up discussing heredity-environment interactions. Is it possible, though, to untangle the influence of heredity from that of environment and discover the role of each in producing individual differences in development? When heredity and environment interact, how does heredity influence the environment, and vice versa?

Behavior Genetics

Behavior genetics is the field that seeks to discover the influence of heredity and environment on individual differences in human traits and development (Eaves & Silberg, 2003; Maxson, 2003; Rowe, 2001). If you think about all of the people you know, you have probably realized that people differ in terms of their level of introversion/extraversion. What behavior geneticists try to do is to figure out what is responsible for those differences—that is, to what extent do people differ because of differences in genes, environment, or a combination of these (Haig, 2003)?

To study the influence of heredity on behavior, behavior geneticists often use either twins or adoption situations. In the most common **twin study,** the behavioral similarity of identical twins is compared with the behavioral similarity of fraternal twins. *Identical twins* (called monozygotic twins) develop from a single fertilized egg that splits into two genetically identical replicas, each of which becomes a person. *Fraternal twins* (called dizygotic twins) develop from separate eggs and separate sperm, making them genetically no more similar than ordinary siblings. Although fraternal twins share the same womb, they are no more alike genetically than are nontwin brothers and sisters, and they may be of different sexes.

By comparing groups of identical and fraternal twins, behavior geneticists capitalize on the basic knowledge that identical twins are more similar genetically than are fraternal twins (Jacob & others, 2001; Rietveld & others, 2003). In one twin study, the extraversion and neuroticism (psychological instability) of 7,000 pairs of Finnish identical and fraternal twins were compared (Rose & others, 1988). On both of these personality traits, the identical twins were much more similar than the fraternal twins were, suggesting an important role for heredity in both traits. However, several issues complicate interpretation of twin studies. For example, perhaps the environments of identical twins are more similar than the environments of fraternal twins. Adults might stress the similarities of identical twins more than those of fraternal twins, and identical twins might perceive themselves as a "set" and play together more than fraternal twins do. If so, observed similarities in identical twins could be more strongly influenced by the environment than the results suggested.

In an **adoption study,** investigators seek to discover whether the behavior and psychological characteristics of adopted children are more like those of their adoptive parents, who have provided a home environment, or more like those of their biological parents, who have contributed their heredity. Another form of the adoption study involves comparing adoptive and biological siblings.

Heredity-Environment Correlations

The difficulties that researchers encounter when they interpet the results of twin studies and adoption studies reflect the complexities of heredity-environment interactions. Some of these interactions are *heredity-environment correlations*, which means that individuals' genes influence the types of environments to which they are exposed. In a sense, individuals "inherit" environments that are related or linked to genetic propensities (Plomin & others, 2001, 2003).

Behavior geneticist Sandra Scarr (1993) described three ways that heredity and environment are correlated (see figure 2.11):

- **Passive genotype-environment correlations** occur because biological parents, who are genetically related to the child, provide a rearing environment for the child. For example, the parents might have a genetic predisposition to be

Heredity-Environment Correlation	Description	Examples
Passive	Children inherit genetic tendencies from their parents and parents also provide an environment that matches their own genetic tendencies.	Musically inclined parents usually have musically inclined children and they are likely to provide an environment rich in music for their children.
Evocative	The child's genetic tendencies elicit stimulation from the environment that supports a particular trait. Thus genes evoke environmental support.	A happy, outgoing child elicits smiles and friendly responses from others.
Active (niche-picking)	Children actively seek out "niches" in their environment that reflect their own interests and talents and are thus in accord with their genotype.	Libraries, sports fields, and a store with musical instruments are examples of environmental niches children might seek out if they have intellectual interests in books, talent in sports, or musical talents, respectively.

FIGURE 2.11 Exploring Heredity-Environment Correlations

intelligent and read skillfully. Because they read well and enjoy reading, they provide their children with books to read. The likely outcome is that their children, given their own inherited predispositions from their parents, will become skilled readers.

- **Evocative genotype-environment correlations** occur because a child's genetically shaped characteristics elicit certain types of physical and social environments. For example, active, smiling children receive more social stimulation than passive, quiet children do. Cooperative, attentive adolescents evoke more pleasant and instructional responses from the adults around them than uncooperative, distractible adolescents do. Athletically inclined youth tend to elicit encouragement to engage in school sports. As a consequence, these adolescents tend to be the ones who try out for sport teams and go on to participate in athletically oriented activities.

- **Active (niche-picking) genotype-environment correlations** occur when children seek out environments that they find compatible and stimulating. *Niche-picking* refers to finding a setting that is suited to one's abilities. Adolescents select from their surrounding environment some aspects that they respond to, learn about, or ignore. Their active selections of environments are related to their genotypes. For example, attractive adolescents tend to seek out attractive peers. Adolescents who are musically inclined are likely to select musical environments in which they can successfully perform their skills.

Scarr believes that the relative importance of the three genotype-environment correlations changes as children develop from infancy through adolescence. In infancy, much of the environment that children experience is provided by adults. Thus, passive genotype-environment correlations are more common in the lives of infants and young children than they are for older children and adolescents who can extend their experiences beyond the family's influence and create their environments to a greater degree.

Shared and Nonshared Environmental Experiences

Another way of analyzing the environment's role in heredity-environment interaction considers experiences that children share with other children living in the same home, as well as experiences that are not shared (Feinberg & Hetherington, 2001; Plomin, Ashbury, & Dunn, 2001). **Shared environmental experiences** are siblings' common experiences, such as their parents' personalities or intellectual orientation, the family's socioeconomic status, and the neighborhood in which they live. By contrast, **nonshared environmental experiences** are a child's experiences, both within the family and outside the family, that are not shared with a sibling. Even experiences

evocative genotype-environment correlations Correlations that exist when the child's genotype elicits certain types of physical and social environments.

active (niche-picking) genotype-environment correlations Correlations that exist when children seek out environments they find compatible and stimulating.

shared environmental experiences Siblings' common experiences, such as their parents' personalities and intellectual orientation, the family's socioeconomic status, and the neighborhood in which they live.

nonshared environmental experiences The child's own experiences, both within the family and outside the family, that are not shared by another sibling. Thus, experiences occurring within the family can be part of the "nonshared environment."

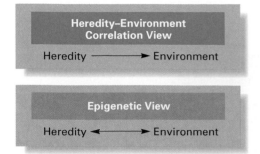

FIGURE 2.12 Comparison of the Heredity-Environment Correlation and Epigenetic Views of Development

*T*he interaction of heredity and environment is so extensive that to ask which is more important, nature or nurture, is like asking which is more important to a rectangle, height or width.

—WILLIAM GREENOUGH
Contemporary Developmental Psychologist, University of Illinois at Urbana

epigenetic view Emphasizes that development is the result of an ongoing, bidirectional interchange between heredity and environment.

occurring within the family can be part of the "nonshared environment." For example, parents often interact differently with each sibling, and siblings interact differently with parents (Hetherington, Reiss, & Plomin, 1994; Reiss & others, 2000). Siblings often have different peer groups, different friends, and different teachers.

Behavior geneticist Robert Plomin (1993) has found that common rearing, or shared environment, accounts for little of the variation in children's personality or interests. In other words, even though two children live under the same roof with the same parents, their personalities are often very different. Further, behavior geneticists argue that heredity influences the nonshared environments of siblings through heredity-environment correlations (Plomin & others, 2001). For example, a child who has inherited a genetic tendency to be athletic is likely to spend more time in environments related to sports while a child who has inherited a tendency to be musically inclined is more likely to spend time in environments related to music.

The Epigenetic View

The heredity-environment correlation view emphasizes how heredity directs the kind of environmental experiences individuals have. Critics argue that the concept of heredity-environment correlation gives heredity too much influence in determining development (Gottlieb, 2002). Recall from earlier in the chapter that DNA is collaborative; it does not function independently but through interactions with its environment. In line with the concept of a collaborative gene, the **epigenetic view** emphasizes that development is the result of an ongoing, bidirectional interchange between heredity and the environment (Gottlieb, 1998, 2003, 2004). Figure 2.12 compares the heredity-environment correlation and epigenetic views of development.

Let's look at an example that reflects the epigenetic view. A baby inherits genes from both parents at conception (the genotype). During prenatal development, toxins, nutrition, and stress can influence some genes to stop functioning while others become stronger or weaker. During infancy, environmental experiences such as toxins, nutrition, stress, learning, and encouragement continue to modify genetic activity.

Conclusions About Heredity-Environment Interaction

Heredity and environment operate together—or cooperate—to produce a person's intelligence, temperament, height, weight, ability to pitch a baseball, ability to read, and so on (Gottlieb, 2004; Gottlieb, Wahlsten, & Lickliter, 1998; Wahlsten, 2003). If an attractive, popular, intelligent girl is elected president of her senior class in high school, is her success due to heredity or to environment? Of course, the answer is both.

The relative contributions of heredity and environment are not additive. That is, we can't say that such-and-such a percentage of nature and such-and-such a percentage of experience make us who we are. Nor is it accurate to say that full genetic expression happens once, around conception or birth, after which we carry our genetic legacy into the world to see how far it takes us. Genes produce proteins throughout the life span, in many different environments. Or they don't produce these proteins, depending in part on how harsh or nourishing those environments are.

The emerging view is that many complex behaviors likely have some *genetic loading* that gives people a propensity for a particular developmental trajectory (Plomin & others, 2001). However, the actual development requires more: an environment. And that environment is complex, just like the mixture of genes we inherit (Sternberg & Grigorenko, 2001). Environmental influences range from the things we lump together under "nurture" (such as parenting, family dynamics, schooling, and neighborhood quality) to biological encounters (such as viruses, birth complications, and even biological events in cells) (Greenough, 1997, 1999; Greenough & others, 2001).

Imagine for a moment that there is a cluster of genes somehow associated with youth violence (this example is hypothetical because we don't know of any such combination). The adolescent who carries this genetic mixture might experience a world of loving parents, regular nutritious meals, lots of books, and a series of masterful teachers. Or the adolescent's world might include parental neglect, a neighborhood in which gunshots and crime are everyday occurrences, and inadequate schooling. In which of these environments are the adolescent's genes likely to manufacture the biological underpinnings of criminality?

The most recent nature-nurture controversy erupted when Judith Harris (1998) published *The Nurture Assumption.* In this provocative book, she argued that what parents do does not make a difference in their children's and adolescents' behavior. Yell at them. Hug them. Read to them. Ignore them. Harris says it won't influence how they turn out. She argues that genes and peers are far more important than parents in children's and adolescents' development.

Genes and peers do matter, but Harris' descriptions of peer influences do not take into account the complexity of peer contexts and developmental trajectories (Hartup, 1999). In addition, Harris is wrong in saying that parents don't matter. For example, in the early child years parents play an important role in selecting children's peers and indirectly influencing children's development (Baumrind, 1999). A huge parenting literature with many research studies documents the importance of parents in children's development (Collins & others, 2000, 2001; Maccoby, 2002). We will discuss parents' important roles throughout this book.

Review and Reflect: Learning Goal 3

3 **Explain some of the ways that heredity and environment interact to produce individual differences in development**

REVIEW

- What is behavior genetics?
- What are three types of heredity-environment correlations?
- What is meant by the concepts of shared and nonshared environmental experiences? What stance do many behavior geneticists take on this topic?
- What is the epigenetic view of development? How does it compare to Scarr's view?
- What conclusions can be reached about heredity-environment interaction?

REFLECT

- Someone tells you that he or she has analyzed their genetic background and environmental experiences and reached the conclusion that environment definitely has had little influence on their intelligence. What would you say to this person about their ability to make this self-diagnosis?

4 PRENATAL DEVELOPMENT

| The Course of Prenatal Development | Prenatal Diagnostic Tests | Teratogens and the Prenatal Environment |

Imagine how you came to be. Out of hundreds of eggs and millions of sperm, one egg and one sperm united to produce you. Union of a different sperm and egg would have produced someone very different. Conception occurs when a single sperm cell from the male unites with an ovum (egg) in the female's fallopian tube in a process called *fertilization,* forming a zygote. What happens next?

Beginnings: Prenatal Development

*T*he history of man for nine months preceding his birth would, probably, be far more interesting, and contain events of greater moment than all three score and ten years that follow it.

—Samuel Taylor Coleridge
English Poet, Essayist, 19th Century

germinal period The period of prenatal development that takes place in the first two weeks after conception. It includes the creation of the zygote, continued cell division, and the attachment of the zygote to the uterine wall.

embryonic period The period of prenatal development that occurs two to eight weeks after conception. During the embryonic period, the rate of cell differentiation intensifies, support systems for the cells form, and organs appear.

The Course of Prenatal Development

Prenatal development is divided into three periods: germinal, embryonic, and fetal.

The Germinal Period   The **germinal period** is the period of prenatal development that takes place in the first two weeks after conception. It includes the creation of the zygote, continued cell division, and the attachment of the zygote to the wall of the uterus.

The germinal period begins with rapid cell division of the zygote. By approximately 1 week after conception, the zygote is composed of 100 to 150 cells. The *differentiation* of cells—their specialization for different tasks—has begun, as inner and outer layers of the organism are formed. The *blastocyst* is the inner layer of cells. These cells later develop into the embryo. The *trophoblast* is the outer layer of cells. They later develop into the systems that provide nutrition and support for the embryo. The germinal period ends with *implantation,* the attachment of the zygote to the uterine wall, which takes place about 10 days after conception.

The Embryonic Period   The **embryonic period** is the period of prenatal development that occurs from two to eight weeks after conception. During the embryonic period, the rate of cell differentiation intensifies, support systems for cells form, and organs appear.

This period begins as the zygote attaches to the uterine wall and forms additional layers of cells. At this stage, the developing organism is called an *embryo*. The embryo's *endoderm* is the inner layer of cells, which will develop into the digestive and respiratory systems. The outer layer of cells divides into two parts. The *ectoderm* is the outermost layer, which will become the nervous system, sensory receptors (ears, nose, and eyes, for example), and skin parts (hair and nails, for example). The *mesoderm* is the middle layer, which will become the circulatory system, bones, muscles, excretory system, and reproductive system. Every body part eventually develops from these three layers.

As the embryo's three layers form, life-support systems for the embryo develop rapidly, mostly from the trophoblast. These life-support systems include the amnion, the placenta, and the umbilical cord. The *amnion* is a sac that contains a clear fluid in which the developing embryo floats. This fluid, known as *amniotic fluid,* provides an environment that is temperature- and humidity-controlled, as well as shockproof. The *placenta* is a life-support system that consists of a disk-shaped group of tissues in which small blood vessels from the mother and the offspring intertwine but do not join. Figure 2.13 provides an illustration of the placenta, the umbilical cord, and the nature of blood flow in the expectant mother and developing child. The *umbilical cord* contains two arteries and one vein that connect the baby to the placenta.

Mechanisms that govern the transfer of substances between the mother and the embryo are still not entirely understood (Garcia-Bournissen, Feig, & Koren, 2003; Rosenblith, 1992). But we do know that very small molecules—oxygen, water, salt, food from the mother's blood, as well as carbon dioxide and digestive wastes from the embryo's blood—pass back and forth. Large molecules cannot pass through the placental wall; these include red blood cells and harmful substances, such as most bacteria, maternal wastes, and hormones.

Before most women even know they are pregnant, every major organ has begun to form. This is know as *organogenesis,* the process of organ formation. In the third week, the neural tube that eventually becomes the spinal cord forms. At about 21 days, eyes begin to appear, and at 24 days the cells for the heart begin to differentiate. During the fourth week, the urogenital system is apparent, and arm and leg buds emerge. Four chambers of the heart take shape, and blood vessels surface. From the fifth to the eighth week, arms and legs differentiate further; at this time, the face starts to form but still is not very recognizable. The intestinal tract develops and the facial structures fuse. At 8 weeks, the developing organism weighs about 1/30 ounce and is just over 1 inch long.

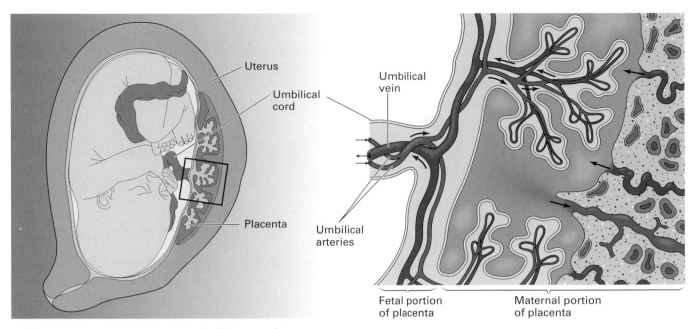

FIGURE 2.13 The Placenta and the Umbilical Cord
Maternal blood flows through the uterine arteries to the spaces housing the placenta, and it returns through the uterine veins to the maternal circulation. Fetal blood flows through the umbilical arteries into the capillaries of the placenta and returns through the umbilical veins to the fetal circulation. The exchange of materials takes place across the layer separating the maternal and fetal blood supplies, so the bloods never come into contact. *Note:* The area bound by the square is enlarged in the right half of the illustration. Arrows indicate the direction of blood flow.

The Fetal Period   The **fetal period** is the prenatal period of development that begins two months after conception and lasts for seven months, on the average. Growth and development continue their dramatic course during this time. Three months after conception, the fetus is about 3 inches long and weighs about 1 ounce. It has become active, moving its arms and legs, opening and closing its mouth, and moving its head. The face, forehead, eyelids, nose, and chin are distinguishable, as are the upper arms, lower arms, hands, and lower limbs. The genitals can be identified as male or female.

All of the development we have discussed so far—the germinal period, the embryonic period, and the beginning of the fetal period—occurs during the first *trimester* of pregnancy (in other words, the first three months). Rapid growth characterizes the second trimester—the fourth through the sixth months of pregnancy. By the end of the fourth month the fetus has grown to 6 inches in length and weighs 4 to 7 ounces. At this time, a growth spurt occurs in the body's lower parts. Prenatal reflexes are stronger; arm and leg movements can be felt for the first time by the mother.

By the end of the fifth month, the fetus is about 12 inches long and weighs close to a pound. Structures of the skin have formed—toenails and fingernails, for example. The fetus is more active, showing a preference for a particular position in the womb. By the end of the sixth month, the fetus is about 14 inches long and has gained another half pound to a pound. The eyes and eyelids are completely formed, and a fine layer of hair covers the head. A grasping reflex is present and irregular breathing movements occur.

The first time the fetus has a chance of surviving outside of the womb comes in the third trimester at about 7 months. Even when infants are born in the seventh month, they usually need assistance in breathing. By the end of the seventh month, the fetus is about 16 inches long and has gained another pound, now weighing about 3 pounds. During the eighth and ninth months, the fetus grows longer and gains substantial weight—about another 4 pounds. In these last two months, fatty tissues develop, and the functioning of various organ systems—heart and kidneys, for example—steps up. At birth, the average American baby weighs 7½ pounds and is about 20 inches long.

The Visible Embryo

fetal period The prenatal period of development that begins two months after conception and lasts for seven months, on the average.

An overview of some of the main developments we have discussed and some more specific changes in prenatal development are presented in figure 2.14. Of course, the expectant mother is experiencing changes during these fateful months, and her behavior can help or harm the fetus. The Contexts of Life-Span Development interlude discusses some effects of cultural beliefs on behavior during pregnancy.

Contexts of Life-Span Development
Cultural Beliefs About Pregnancy

All cultures have beliefs and rituals that surround life's major events, including pregnancy. Some cultures treat pregnancy simply as a natural occurrence; others see it as a medical condition. Obtaining medical care during pregnancy may not seem important to a woman whose culture defines pregnancy as a natural condition. How expectant mothers behave during pregnancy may depend in part on the prevalence of traditional home-care remedies and folk beliefs, the importance of indigenous healers, and the influence of health-care professionals in their culture. For example, some Filipinos will not take any medication during pregnancy. Many Mexican-American women seek advice about their pregnancy from their mothers and from older women in the community. They may also call on an indigenous healer known as a *curandero*. In various cultures pregnant women may turn to herbalists, faith healers, root doctors, or spiritualists for help.

When health-care professionals work with expectant mothers, cultural assessment should be an important component of their care. In other words, they should identify beliefs, values, and behaviors related to childbearing. In particular, ethnic background, degree of affiliation with the ethnic group, patterns of decision making, religious preference, language, communication style, and etiquette may all affect a woman's attitudes about the care needed during pregnancy. Health-care workers should assess whether a woman's beliefs or practices pose a threat to her or the fetus. If they do, health-care professionals should consider a culturally sensitive way to handle the problem.

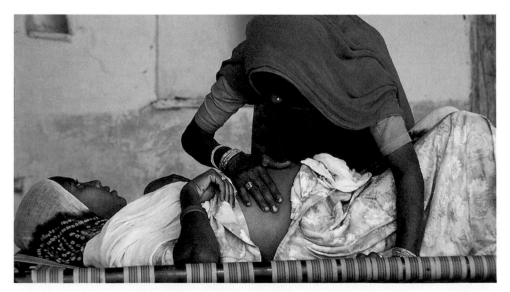

In India, a midwife checks on the size, position, and heartbeat of a fetus. Midwives deliver babies in many cultures around the world. *What are some cultural variations in prenatal care?*

First trimester (first 3 months)

Prenatal growth	Conception to 4 weeks	8 weeks	12 weeks	
	• Is less than ¹/₁₀ inch long	• Slightly more than 1 inch long	• Is about 3 inches long and weighs about 1 ounce	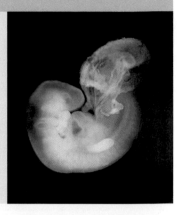
	• Beginning development of spinal cord, nervous system, gastrointestinal system, heart, and lungs	• Face is forming with rudimentary eyes, ears, mouth, and tooth buds	• Can move arms, legs, fingers, and toes	
	• Amniotic sac envelopes the preliminary tissues of entire body	• Arms and legs are moving	• Fingerprints are present	
		• Brain is forming	• Can smile, frown, suck, and swallow	
	• Is called a "zygote"	• Fetal heartbeat is detectable with ultrasound	• Sex is distinguishable	
		• Is called an "embryo"	• Can urinate	
			• Is called a "fetus"	

Second trimester (middle 3 months)

Prenatal growth	16 weeks	20 weeks	24 weeks	
	• Is about 5¹/₂ inches long and weighs about 4 ounces	• Is 10 to 12 inches long and weighs ¹/₂ to 1 pound	• Is 11 to 14 inches long and weighs 1 to 1¹/₂ pounds	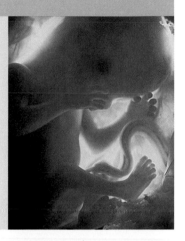
	• Heartbeat is strong	• Heartbeat is audible with ordinary stethoscope	• Skin is wrinkled and covered with protective coating (vernix caseosa)	
	• Skin is thin, transparent	• Sucks thumb	• Eyes are open	
	• Downy hair (lanugo) covers body	• Hiccups	• Waste matter is collected in bowel	
	• Fingernails and toenails are forming	• Hair, eyelashes, eyebrows are present	• Has strong grip	
	• Has coordinated movements; is able to roll over in amniotic fluid			

Third trimester (last 3 months)

Prenatal growth	28 weeks	32 weeks	36 to 38 weeks	
	• Is 14 to 17 inches long and weighs 2¹/₂ to 3 pounds	• Is 16¹/₂ to 18 inches long and weighs 4 to 5 pounds	• Is 19 inches long and weighs 6 pounds	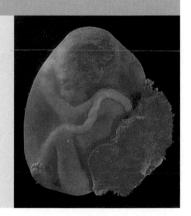
	• Is adding body fat	• Has periods of sleep and wakefulness	• Skin is less wrinkled	
	• Is very active	• Responds to sounds	• Vernix caseosa is thick	
	• Rudimentary breathing movements are present	• May assume the birth position	• Lanugo is mostly gone	
		• Bones of head are soft and flexible	• Is less active	
		• Iron is being stored in liver	• Is gaining immunities from mother	

FIGURE 2.14 The Three Trimesters of Prenatal Development

Prenatal Diagnostic Tests

In the mainstream U.S. culture, obtaining medical tests to determine whether a fetus is developing normally has become an accepted practice. But people disagree sharply about whether an abortion should be obtained if the test suggests that the fetus is likely to be born with a birth defect.

Amniocentesis and ultrasound sonography are two well-known tests for assessing the fetus. *Amniocentesis* is a prenatal medical procedure in which a sample of amniotic fluid is withdrawn by syringe and tested to discover if the fetus is suffering from any chromosomal or metabolic disorders (Tercyak & others, 2001; Welch,

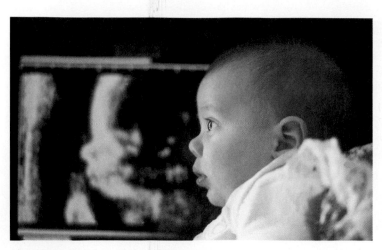

A 6-month-old infant poses with the ultrasound sonography record taken 4 months into the baby's prenatal development. *What is ultrasound sonography?*

Obstetric Ultrasound

Genetic Counseling

Blessed, & Lacoste, 2003). Amniocentesis is performed between the 12th and 16th weeks of pregnancy. The later amniocentesis is performed, the better its diagnostic potential. The earlier it is performed, the more useful it is in deciding whether a pregnancy should be terminated (Pinette & others, 2004). Amniocentesis brings a small risk of miscarriage; about 1 woman in every 200 to 300 miscarries after amniocentesis.

Ultrasound sonography is a prenatal medical procedure in which high-frequency sound waves are directed into the pregnant woman's abdomen (Bahado-Singh & others, 2003). The echo from the sounds is transformed into a visual representation of the fetus' inner structures. This technique can reveal such disorders as *microencephaly,* a form of mental retardation involving an abnormally small brain. Ultrasound sonography is often used in conjunction with amniocentesis to determine the precise location of the fetus in the mother's abdomen. When ultrasound sonography is used five or more times, the risk of low birth weight may be increased.

Another test can detect conditions very early in pregnancy. *Chorionic villi sampling* is a prenatal medical procedure in which a small sample of the placenta is removed at some point between the 8th and 11th weeks of pregnancy (Zoppi & others, 2001). Diagnosis takes approximately 10 days. Chorionic villi sampling allows a decision about abortion to be made near the end of the first trimester of pregnancy, a point when abortion is safer and less traumatic than after amniocentesis in the second trimester (Papp & Papp, 2003). Chorionic villi sampling creates a slightly higher risk of miscarriage than amniocentesis and is linked with a slight risk of limb deformities.

The *maternal blood test (alpha-fetoprotein—AFP)* is a prenatal diagnostic technique that is used to assess blood alphaprotein level, which is associated with neural-tube defects (Erdem & others, 2002). This test is administered to women 14 to 20 weeks into pregnancy only when they are at risk for bearing a child with defects in the formation of the brain and spinal cord.

Teratogens and the Prenatal Environment

Although living in a protected, comfortable environment, the fetus is not totally immune to the larger world surrounding the mother. The environment can affect the child in many well-documented ways. Thousands of babies are born deformed or mentally retarded every year as the result of events in the mother's life. Factors related to the father also can influence the health of the fetus.

Some General Principles Any agent that causes a birth defect is known as a **teratogen.** (The word comes from the Greek word *tera* meaning "monster.") The field of study that investigates the causes of birth defects is called *teratology.* So many teratogens exist that practically every fetus is exposed to at least some teratogens. For this reason, it is difficult to determine which teratogen causes which birth defect. In addition, it may take a long time for the effects of a teratogen to show up (Iannucci, 2000). Only about half of all potential effects appear at birth.

A specific teratogen (such as a drug) usually does not cause a specific birth defect (such as malformation of the legs). The dose, genetic susceptibility, and the time of exposure to a particular agent influence the severity of the damage and the type of defect that occurs:

- *Dose* The greater the dose of an agent, such as a drug, the greater the effect.
- *Genetic Susceptibility* The type and severity of abnormalities caused by a teratogen are linked to the genotype of the pregnant woman and the genotype of the fetus. For example, the pregnant woman's genotype may create variations in metabolism,

teratogen Any agent that causes a birth defect. The field of study that investigates the causes of birth defects is called teratology.

placental membranes, and placental transport that can influence the degree to which a drug's effects are transmitted to the fetus. The genotype of the fetus may also influence vulnerability to a particular teratogen.

- *Time of Exposure* Teratogens do more damage when they occur at some points in development than others (Brent & Fawcett, 2000). When organs are being formed, they are especially vulnerable to environmental changes. In general, the embryonic period of the first trimester is a more vulnerable time than the second and third trimesters.

Figure 2.15 summarizes additional information about the effect of the time of exposure. The probability of a structural defect is greatest earliest in the embryonic period because this is when organs are being formed. The vulnerability of the brain is greatest at 15 to 25 days after conception, the eyes at 24 to 40 days, the heart at 20 to 40 days, and the legs at 24 to 36 days. Thus, as shown in figure 2.15, each body structure has its own critical period of formation. Recall from chapter 1 that a *critical period* is a fixed time period very early in development during which certain experiences or events can have a long-lasting effect on development.

After organogenesis is complete, teratogens are less likely to cause anatomical defects. Exposure later, during the fetal period, is more likely to stunt growth or to create problems in the way organs function.

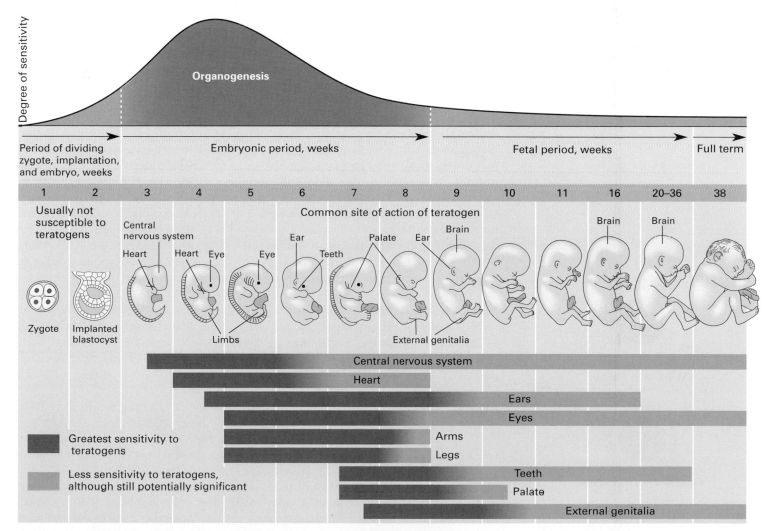

FIGURE 2.15 Teratogens and the Timing of Their Effects on Prenatal Development

The danger of structural defects caused by teratogens is greatest early in embryonic development, during the period of organogenesis (red color). Later assaults by teratogens (blue-green color) are more likely to stunt growth or cause problems of organ function instead of causing structural damage.

What are these agents that can harm the unborn child? Major types of teratogens include certain medicines and other drugs, radiation and various pollutants, and infectious diseases in the mother.

Prescription and Nonprescription Drugs   Occasionally, the damage that prescription and nonprescription drugs can create is discovered only after a cluster of deformed babies is born. This happened in 1961 after many doctors prescribed the tranquilizer thalidomide for pregnant women to alleviate their morning sickness. In adults, the effects of thalidomide are mild; in embryos, however, they are devastating. Not all infants were affected in the same way. If the mother took thalidomide on day 26 (probably before she knew she was pregnant), an arm might not grow. If she took the drug two days later, the arm might not grow past the elbow. The thalidomide tragedy shocked the medical community and taught a valuable lesson: taking the wrong drug at the wrong time is enough to physically handicap the offspring for life.

Because of the devastating effects of thalidomide on embryos, its use in the United States and some other countries was banned. However, thalidomide is once again being used to treat a number of diseases, including cancer and leprosy (Chaudhry & others, 2002; Jin & others, 2002; Thompson & Hansen, 2003). The renewed availability of thalidomide is controversial because of the fear that it may be misused and once again harm embryos.

Prescription drugs that can function as teratogens include antibiotics, such as streptomycin and tetracycline; some antidepressants; certain hormones, such as progestin and synthetic estrogen; and Accutane (which often is prescribed for acne) (Committee on Drugs, 2000).

Nonprescription drugs that can be harmful include diet pills, aspirin, and caffeine. Let's explore the research on caffeine. A review of studies on caffeine consumption during pregnancy concluded that a small increase in the risks for spontaneous abortion and low birth weight occurs for pregnant women who consumed more than 150 milligrams of caffeine (approximately two cups of brewed coffee or two to three 12-ounce cans of cola) per day (Fernandez & others, 1998). (We will discuss the implications of low birth weight later in the chapter.) For example, in one study, pregnant women who drank caffeinated coffee were more likely to have preterm deliveries and newborns with a lower birth weight compared with their counterparts who did not drink caffeinated coffee (Eskenazi & others, 1999). Decaffeinated coffee had no effects. Taking into account such results, the Food and Drug Administration recommends that pregnant women either not consume caffeine or consume it only sparingly.

Psychoactive Drugs   *Psychoactive drugs* are drugs that act on the nervous system to alter states of consciousness, modify perceptions, and change moods. A number of psychoactive drugs—including alcohol, nicotine, cocaine, marijuana, and heroin—have been studied to determine their links to prenatal and child development (Caulfield, 2001; Fogel, 2001).

Alcohol   Heavy drinking by pregnant women can be devastating to offspring (Barr & Streissguth, 2001; Committee on Substance Abuse, 2000; Enoch & Goldman, 2002; O'Leary, 2004). **Fetal alcohol syndrome (FAS)** is a cluster of abnormalities that appears in the offspring of mothers who drink alcohol heavily during pregnancy (Archibald & others, 2001). The abnormalities include facial deformities and defective limbs, face, and heart. Most of these children are below average in intelligence, and some are mentally retarded (Bookstein & others, 2002; Olson, 2000). According to one study, having fetal alcohol syndrome increases the chances that an adult will have a mental disorder, such as depression or anxiety (Famy, Streissguth, & Unis, 1998). Although many mothers of FAS infants are heavy drinkers, many mothers who are heavy drinkers do not have children with FAS or have one child with FAS and other children who do not have it.

Beginnings: Effects of Prenatal Exposure to Alcohol

Fetal Alcohol Syndrome

fetal alcohol syndrome (FAS) A cluster of abnormalities that appears in the offspring of mothers who drink alcohol heavily during pregnancy.

Is moderate drinking by pregnant women also harmful? In one study, children whose mothers drank moderately (one to two drinks a day) during pregnancy were less attentive and alert, even at 4 years of age (Streissguth & others, 1984). Also, in a longitudinal study, the more alcohol mothers drank in the first trimester of pregnancy, the more 14-year-olds fell behind on growth markers such as weight, height, and head size (Day & others, 2002).

What are some guidelines for alcohol use during pregnancy? Moderate drinking of one or two servings of beer or wine or one serving of hard liquor a few days a week can have negative effects on the fetus, although it is generally agreed that this level of alcohol use will not cause fetal alcohol syndrome (Parazzini & others, 2003; Riley & others, 2003). The U.S. Surgeon General recommends that *no* alcohol be consumed during pregnancy.

A child with fetal alcohol syndrome (FAS). Notice the wide-set eyes, flat bones, and thin upper lip.

Nicotine   Cigarette smoking by pregnant women can also adversely influence prenatal development, birth, and postnatal development. Fetal and neonatal deaths, preterm births, low birth weights, respiratory problems, and sudden infant death syndrome (also known as crib death) are all more common among the offspring of smoking than nonsmoking mothers (Bush & others, 2001; Stocks & Dezateaux, 2003; Wang & others, 2002). One study also linked prenatal exposure to cigarette smoking to poorer language and cognitive skills at 4 years of age (Fried & Watkinson, 1990). Intervention programs that help pregnant women to stop smoking can reduce some of smoking's effects, especially by raising birth weights (Klesges & others, 2001; Lightwood, Phibbs, & Glantz, 1999).

The father's smoking during the mother's pregnancy also can cause problems for the offspring. In one investigation, the newborns of fathers who smoked during their wives' pregnancy were 4 ounces lighter at birth for each pack of cigarettes smoked per day than were the newborns whose fathers did not smoke during their wives' pregnancy (Rubin & others, 1986). In another study, in China, the longer the fathers smoked, the stronger the risk for their children to develop cancer (Ji & others, 1997). Also, in an analysis of seven studies, it was recently concluded that an association exists between paternal smoking and the development of brain tumors in children (Huncharek, Kupelnick, & Klassen, 2002). In such studies, it is difficult to tease apart prenatal and postnatal effects. The negative influence of paternal smoking on fetal development is likely due to environmental tobacco smoke exposure. Thus, if the father does not smoke around the pregnant woman, there will likely be no harmful effects on the fetus.

Cocaine   Does cocaine use during pregnancy harm the developing embryo and fetus? The most consistent finding is that cocaine exposure during prenatal development is associated with reduced birth weight, length, and head circumference (Smith & others, 2001). Also, in one study, prenatal cocaine exposure was associated with impaired motor development at 2 years of age (Arendt & others, 1999). Other studies link fetal cocaine exposure with impaired information processing (Singer & others, 1999). In one study, for example, prenatal cocaine exposure was moderately related to poor attentional skills through 5 years of age (Bandstra & others, 2000). In another study, prenatal exposure to cocaine was related to impaired processing of auditory information after birth (Potter & others, 2000).

A cautious interpretation of these findings has been emphasized (Chavkin, 2001; Frank & others, 2001; Vidaeff & Mastrobattista, 2003). Why? Because other factors (such as poverty, malnutrition, and other substance abuse) in the lives of pregnant women who use cocaine often cannot be ruled out as possible contributors to the problems found in their children

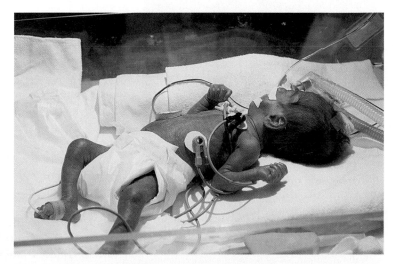

What do we know about the effects of cocaine on children's development?

(Kaugers & others, 2000). For example, cocaine users are more likely than nonusers to smoke cigarettes, use marijuana, drink alcohol, and take amphetamines.

However, despite these cautions, the weight of recent research evidence indicates that children born to cocaine-using mothers are likely to have neurological and cognitive deficits (Mayes, 2003). For example, in a recent study that controlled for the use of other drugs, prenatal cocaine exposure was related to lower arousal, less effective self-regulation, higher excitability, and lower quality of reflexes when the infant was 1 month old (Lester & others, 2002). Because of the potential harmful effect of cocaine to the pregnant mother, and to the fetus, its use is not recommended.

Marijuana   In spite of marijuana being used by a number of women of reproductive age, there has not been extensive research on its effects on the offspring. In a recent review of research, it was concluded that marijuana use during pregnancy is not linked to the offspring's general intelligence but that the child's attention may be impaired (Fried & Smith, 2001). Also, the National Institute of Drug Abuse's (2001) review of marijuana effects concludes that babies born to mothers who used marijuana during pregnancy are smaller than babies born to mothers who did not use the drug. Further, in a longitudinal study, prenatal marijuana exposure was related to learning and memory difficulties at age 11 (Richardson & others, 2002). However, because of the small numbers of studies, it is difficult to reach conclusions about the effects of marijuana use by mothers during pregnancy on the child's development. Nonetheless, marijuana use by pregnant women is not recommended.

Heroin   It is well documented that infants whose mothers are addicted to heroin show behavioral difficulties (Hulse & others, 2001). These infants have tremors and display irritability, abnormal crying, disturbed sleep, and impaired motor control—all symptoms of withdrawal from heroin. Many still have behavioral problems at 1 year of age and some show attention deficits later in development. Newborns whose mothers received the most common treatment for heroin addiction, methadone, may also display severe withdrawal symptoms.

Environmental Hazards   The medicines and other drugs discussed so far are teratogens that a pregnant woman can avoid in order to protect her offspring. But many other teratogens come from the environment and are beyond a mother's or a father's control. For example, men's exposure to lead, radiation, certain pesticides, and petrochemicals may cause abnormalities in sperm that can lead to miscarriage or diseases, such as childhood cancer (Lindbohm, 1991; Trasler, 2000). Radiation, many chemicals, and other features of our modern world are potential hazards to the embryo or fetus (Grigorenko, 2001).

Exposure to radiation of various sorts can cause gene mutations (abrupt, permanent changes in genetic material). Chromosomal abnormalities are higher among the offspring of fathers exposed to high levels of radiation in their occupations (Schrag & Dixon, 1985). Radiation from X rays also can affect the developing embryo and fetus, with the most dangerous time being the first several weeks after conception, when women do not yet know they are pregnant (Barnett & Maulik, 2001). It is important for women and their physicians to weigh the risk of an X ray when an actual or potential pregnancy is involved (Shaw, 2001). Computer monitors also emit radiation, but researchers have not found exposure to computer monitors to be related to miscarriage (Schnorr & others, 1991).

Environmental pollutants and toxic wastes are also sources of danger to unborn children. Among the dangerous pollutants are carbon monoxide, lead, and mercury. People may be exposed to lead because they live in houses in which lead-based paint flakes off the walls, or near busy highways where there are heavy automobile emissions from leaded gasoline. Researchers believe that early exposure to lead affects children's mental development (Markowitz, 2000). For example, in one study, 2-year-olds who prenatally had high levels of lead in their umbilical-cord blood performed poorly on a test of mental development (Bellinger & others, 1987).

An explosion at the Chernobyl nuclear power plant in the Ukraine produced radioactive contamination that spread to surrounding areas. Thousands of infants were born with health problems and deformities as a result of the nuclear contamination, including this boy whose arm did not form. *Other than radioactive contamination, what are some other types of environmental hazards to prenatal development?*

Some fish contain high levels of mercury, which is released into the air both naturally and by industrial pollution. When mercury falls into the water it can become toxic and accumulates in large fish, such as shark, swordfish, king mackerel, and some species of large tuna. Because mercury is easily transferred across the placenta, the embryo is highly sensitive to birth defects involving the developing brain and nervous system (Castoldi, Coccini, & Manzo, 2003; Grandjean & others, 2003; University of Louisville Birth Defects Center, 2001). The U.S. Food and Drug Administration (2001) recommends that pregnant women avoid eating these fish and further recommends that mothers who are nursing or trying to conceive, and young children, should also avoid eating these fish.

Manufacturing chemicals known as PCBs are also harmful to prenatal development (Vreugdenhil & others, 2002). Although banned in the 1970s in the United States, PCBs continue to be present in landfills, sediments, and wildlife. One study kept track of the extent to which pregnant women ate PCB-polluted fish from Lake Michigan and subsequently observed their children as newborns, young children, and at 11 years of age (Jacobson & others, 1984; Jacobson & Jacobson, 2002). The women who had eaten more PCB-polluted fish were more likely to have smaller, preterm infants who were more likely to react slowly to stimuli. As preschool children, their exposure to PCBs was linked with less effective short-term memory, and at age 11 with lower verbal intelligence and reading comprehension.

Infectious Diseases   Some maternal diseases and infections can produce defects in the mother's offspring by crossing the placental barrier, or they can cause damage during the birth itself (Iannucci, 2000). Rubella and certain sexually transmitted infections are the most common examples.

Rubella (German measles) is a maternal disease that can cause prenatal defects. A rubella outbreak in 1964–1965 resulted in 30,000 prenatal and neonatal (newborn) deaths, and more than 20,000 affected infants were born with malformations, including mental retardation, blindness, deafness, and heart problems. The greatest damage occurs when mothers contract rubella in the third and fourth weeks of pregnancy, although infection during the second month is also damaging. Elaborate preventive efforts ensure that rubella will never again have the disastrous effects it had in the mid 1960s. A vaccine that prevents German measles is now routinely administered to children, and women who plan to have children should have a blood test before they become pregnant to determine if they are immune to the disease (Signore, 2001; Ward, Lambert, & Lester, 2001).

Syphilis (a sexually transmitted infection) is more damaging later in prenatal development—four months or more after conception. Rather than affecting organogenesis, as rubella does, syphilis damages organs after they have formed. Damage includes eye lesions, which can cause blindness, and skin lesions. When syphilis is present at birth, other problems, involving the central nervous system and gastrointestinal tract, can develop. Most states require that pregnant women be given a blood test to detect the presence of syphilis.

Another infection that has received widespread attention recently is genital herpes. Newborns contract this virus when they are delivered through the birth canal of a mother with genital herpes (Qutub & others, 2001). About one-third of babies delivered through an infected birth canal die; another one-fourth become brain damaged. If an active case of genital herpes is detected in a pregnant woman close to her delivery date, a cesarean section can be performed (in which the infant is delivered through an incision in the mother's abdomen) to keep the virus from infecting the newborn (Watts & others, 2003).

AIDS is a sexually transmitted infection that is caused by the human immunodeficiency virus (HIV), which destroys the body's immune system. Mothers infected with HIV may transmit the virus to their offspring in three ways: (1) during gestation across the placenta, (2) during delivery through contact with maternal blood or fluids, and (3) postpartum (after birth) through breastfeeding. Babies born to HIV-infected mothers can be (1) infected and symptomatic (show AIDS symptoms), (2) infected but *asymptomatic* (not show AIDS symptoms), or (3) not infected at all. An infant who is infected and asymptomatic may still develop HIV symptoms up until 15 months of age.

In the early 1990s, before preventive treatments were available, 1,000 to 2,000 infants were born with HIV infection each year in the United States. This number has been dramatically reduced by giving zidovudine (AZT) to infected women during pregnancy and delivery and to the infants after birth (Capparelli & others, 2003; Gerrard & Chudasama, 2003; Centers for Disease Control and Prevention, 2000). In many poor countries, however, treatment with AZT is limited and HIV infection of infants remains a major problem (Sullivan, 2003).

Incompatible Blood Types The incompatibility of the mother's and the father's blood types is another risk to prenatal development. Variations in blood cells create not only the blood groups (A, B, O, AB) but also blood that is said to be either Rh positive or Rh negative (depending on whether Rh factor is present). A woman is at risk during pregnancy when she is Rh negative and her partner is Rh positive. This combination can produce a fetus whose blood is Rh positive. When the fetus' blood is Rh positive and the mother's is Rh negative, antibodies in the mother may attack the fetus. This can result in any number of problems, including miscarriage or stillbirth, anemia, jaundice, heart defects, brain damage, or death soon after birth (Narang & Jain, 2001).

In most instances, the first Rh-positive baby of an Rh-negative mother is not affected, but with each pregnancy the risk becomes greater. A vaccine (RhoGAM) may be given to the mother within three days after the child's birth that will prevent her body from making antibodies that will attack future Rh-positive fetuses. Also, babies affected by Rh incompatibility can be given blood transfusions, in some cases before birth.

Other Parental Factors So far we have discussed a number of drugs, environmental hazards, and maternal diseases that can harm the embryo or fetus. Here we will explore other characteristics of the mother and father that can affect prenatal and child development: nutrition, age, and emotional states and stress.

Nutrition A developing fetus depends completely on its mother for nutrition, which comes from the mother's blood. The nutritional status of the fetus is determined by the mother's total caloric intake and levels of proteins, vitamins, and minerals. Children born to malnourished mothers are more likely to be malformed (Wong & others, 2003).

One aspect of maternal nutrition of particular interest is folic acid (Callender, Rickard, & Rinsky-Eng, 2001; Stepanuk & others, 2002). The U.S. Public Health Service recommends that pregnant women consume a minimum of 400 micrograms of folic acid per day (that is about twice the amount the average woman gets in one day). What is important about folic acid? A lack of folic acid is linked with neural-tube defects in offspring, such as spina bifida (Honein & others, 2001). Orange juice and spinach are examples of folic-acid-rich foods. Researchers have found that neural-tube defects are more likely to be prevented through the consumption of foods rich in folic acid than through supplements (Langley-Evans & Langley-Evans, 2002).

Being overweight before and during pregnancy can also affect the fetus (Castro & Avila, 2002). In two recent studies, obese women had a significant risk of late fetal death although the risk of preterm delivery was reduced in these women (Cnattinugis & others, 1998; Kumari, 2001).

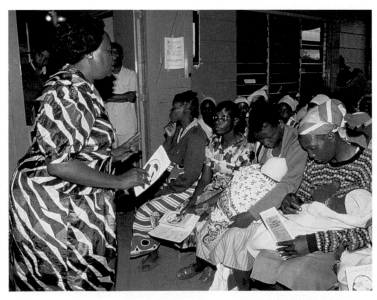

Because the fetus depends entirely on its mother for nutrition, it is important for the pregnant woman to have good nutritional habits. In Kenya, this government clinic provides pregnant women with information about how their diet can influence the health of their fetus and offspring. *What might the information about diet be like?*

Age When possible harmful effects on the fetus and infant are considered, two maternal ages are of special interest: adolescence and the thirties and beyond (Abel, Kruger, & Burd, 2002; Tough & others, 2002). Approximately one of every five births in the United States is to an adolescent; in some urban areas, the figure reaches as high as one in every two births. Infants born to adolescents are often premature (Ekwo & Moawad, 2000). The mortality rate of infants born to adolescent mothers is double that of infants born to mothers in their twenties. Although this high rate probably reflects the immaturity of the mother's reproductive system, poor nutrition, lack of prenatal care, and low socio-economic status may also play a role (Lenders, McElrath, & Scholl, 2000). Prenatal care decreases the probability that a child born to an adolescent girl will have physical problems. However, adolescents are the least likely of women in all age groups to obtain prenatal assistance from clinics, pediatricians, and health services.

When the mother is older than 30, key dangers to the fetus include the increased risk for low birth weight and for Down syndrome. One recent study found that low birth weight deliveries increased 11 percent and preterm deliveries increased 14 percent in women 35 years and older (Tough & others, 2002). As we discussed earlier in the chapter, the risk for Down syndrome is related to the mother's age (Holding, 2002). A baby with Down syndrome rarely is born to a mother under the age of 30, but the risk increases after the mother reaches 30. By age 40, the probability is slightly over 1 in 100, and by age 50 it is almost 1 in 10. The risk also is higher before age 18.

The father's age also makes a difference. When fathers are older, their offspring face increased risk for certain birth defects, including Down syndrome (about 5 percent of these children have older fathers), dwarfism, and Marfan's syndrome, which involves head and limb deformities.

There are also risks to offspring when both the mother and father are older. In one recent study, the risk of an adverse pregnancy outcome, such as miscarriage, was much greater when the woman was 35 years or older and the man was 40 years or older (de la Rochebrochard & Thonneau, 2002).

We still have much to learn about the role of the mother's age in pregnancy and childbirth. As women remain active, exercise regularly, and are careful about their nutrition, their reproductive systems may remain healthier at older ages than was thought possible in the past (Blickstein, 2003).

What are some of the risks for infants born to adolescent mothers?

Emotional States and Stress   Tales abound about how a pregnant woman's emotional state affects the fetus. For centuries it was thought that frightening experiences—such as a severe thunderstorm or a family member's death—leave birthmarks on the child or affect the child in more serious ways. In fact, a mother's stress can be transmitted to the fetus, and we now have a better grasp of how this takes place (Monk & others, 2000; Relier, 2001). When a pregnant woman experiences intense fears, anxieties, and other emotions, physiological changes occur that may also affect her fetus. For example, producing adrenaline in response to fear restricts blood flow to the uterine area and can deprive the fetus of adequate oxygen.

Researchers have been uncovering links between fetal health and various states in the mother, although the mechanisms that link the two are still far from certain. Women under stress are about four times more likely than their low-stress counterparts to deliver babies prematurely (Dunkel-Schetter, 1998; Dunkel-Schetter & others, 2001). Why? Maternal stress may increase the level of corticotrophin-releasing hormone (CRH) early in pregnancy (Hobel & others, 1999). CRH, in turn, has been linked to premature delivery. A mother's stress may also influence the fetus indirectly by increasing the likelihood that the mother will engage in unhealthy behaviors, such as taking drugs and engaging in poor prenatal care.

The mother's emotional state during pregnancy can influence the birth process, too. An emotionaly distraught mother might have irregular contractions and a more difficult labor, which can cause irregularities in the supply of oxygen to the fetus or other problems after birth. Babies born after extended labor also may adjust more slowly to their world and be more irritable.

www.mhhe.com/santrockld2

Reproductive Health Links

Exploring Pregnancy

Childbirth Classes

Prenatal Care

Health-Care Providers

Positive emotional states also appear to make a difference to the fetus. Pregnant women who are optimistic thinkers have less adverse outcomes than pregnant women who are pessimistic thinkers (Loebel & others, 2002). Optimists are more likely to believe that they have control over the outcomes of their pregnancies.

In fact, although much of our discussion has focused on what can go wrong with prenatal development, most pregnancies do not go awry. In most pregnancies, development follows along the positive path we described earlier. Positive prenatal development can often be enhanced by good prenatal care and classes, as the Applications in Life-Span Development interlude describes.

Applications in Life-Span Development

Prenatal Care and Classes

Prenatal care varies enormously but usually involves a package of medical care services in a defined schedule of visits. This medical care usually includes screening that can reveal manageable conditions or treatable diseases in the baby and the pregnant mother (Cosey & Bechtel, 2001). In addition to medical care, prenatal programs often include comprehensive educational, social, and nutritional services (Shiono & Behrman, 1995).

Early prenatal classes may include couples in both early pregnancy and prepregnancy (Nichols & Humenick, 2000). The classes often focus on topics such as changes in the development of the embryo and the fetus, environmental dangers for the fetus, sexuality during pregnancy, birth setting and types of care providers, nutrition, rest, and exercise during pregnancy, common discomforts and relief measures, psychological changes in both the expectant mother and her partner, and factors that increase risk of preterm labor.

Prenatal education classes also may include information on the advantages and disadvantages of breastfeeding and bottlefeeding. Most expectant mothers (50 to 80 percent) make this infant feeding decision prior to the sixth month of pregnancy. When the expectant mother is in the second or third trimester of pregnancy, classes focus on preparation for the birth, infant care and feeding, postpartum self-care, and choices related to the birth.

The education the mother receives in these classes can be extremely valuable especially for first-time mothers. Prenatal care is also very important for women in poverty because it links them with other social services (Howell, 2001). The legacy of prenatal care continues after the birth because women who experience this type of care are more likely to get preventive care for their infants (Bates & others, 1994).

Women sometimes receive inadequate prenatal care for reasons related to the health-care system, provider practices,

Early prenatal education classes focus on such topics as changes in the development of the fetus. Later classes focus on preparation for the birth and care of the newborn. *To what extent should fathers, as well as mothers, participate in these classes?*

and their own characteristics (McCormick, 2001). In one national study, 71 percent of low-income women experienced a problem in getting prenatal care (U.S. General Accounting Office, 1987). They cited finances, transportation, and child care as barriers. Motivating positive attitudes toward pregnancy is also important. Women who do not want to be pregnant, who have negative attitudes about being pregnant, or who unintentionally become pregnant are more likely to delay prenatal care or to miss appointments (Joseph, 1989).

Review and Reflect: Learning Goal 4

4 **Characterize the course of prenatal development and its hazards**

REVIEW

- What are the three periods of prenatal development?
- What are some of the main diagnostic tests that are used to determine whether prenatal development is proceeding normally?
- What is teratology? What are some of the main hazards to prenatal development?

REFLECT

- What needs to be done to get women who are pregnant not to smoke or drink? Consider the role of health-care providers, the role of insurance companies, and specific programs targeted at women who are pregnant.

---

5 BIRTH

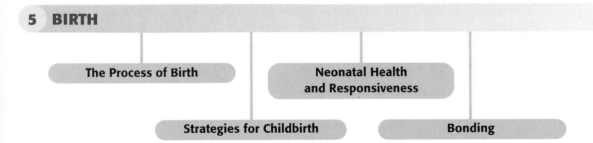

Many changes take place during the birth of a baby (Verklan, 2002). Nature sets the general course of these changes, but parents do have some important choices to make about the conditions surrounding the birth. Do their decisions make a difference? And what happens during the newborn's first hours? Do they have special significance? Let's begin by examining the birth process itself.

The Process of Birth

Despite all the aid that technology can provide, birth remains a fateful step, one still filled with stress and hazards for newborns.

Stages of Birth The birth process occurs in three stages. For a woman having her first child, the first stage lasts an average of 12 to 24 hours; it is the longest of the three stages. In the first stage, uterine contractions are 15 to 20 minutes apart at the beginning and last up to a minute. These contractions cause the woman's cervix to stretch and open. As the first stage progresses, the contractions come closer together, appearing every 2 to 5 minutes. Their intensity increases too. By the end of the first birth stage, contractions dilate the cervix to an opening of about 4 inches, so that the baby can move from the uterus to the birth canal.

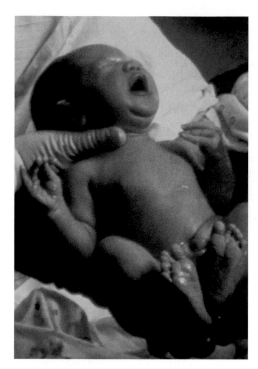

After the long journey of prenatal development, birth takes place. During birth the baby is on a threshold between two worlds. *What is the fetus/newborn transition like?*

The second birth stage begins when the baby's head starts to move through the cervix and the birth canal. It terminates when the baby completely emerges from the mother's body. This stage lasts approximately 1½ hours. With each contraction, the mother bears down hard to push the baby out of her body. By the time the baby's head is out of the mother's body, the contractions come almost every minute and last for about a minute. At the time of birth, the baby is covered with *vernix caseosa,* a protective skin grease. This vernix consists of fatty secretions and dead cells, thought to help protect the baby's skin against heat loss before and during birth.

Afterbirth is the third stage, at which time the placenta, umbilical cord, and other membranes are detached and expelled. This final stage is the shortest of the three birth stages, lasting only minutes.

The Transition from Fetus to Newborn   Being born involves considerable stress for the baby. During each contraction, when the placenta and umbilical cord are compressed as the uterine muscles draw together, the supply of oxygen to the fetus is decreased. If the delivery takes too long, anoxia can develop (Mohan, Golding, & Paterson, 2001). *Anoxia* is the condition in which the fetus or newborn has an insufficient supply of oxygen. Anoxia can cause brain damage.

The baby has considerable capacity to withstand the stress of birth. Large quantities of the hormones adrenaline and noradrenaline are secreted, protecting the fetus in the event of oxygen deficiency. These hormones increase the heart's pumping, speed up heart rate, channel blood flow to the brain, and raise the blood-sugar level. Never again in life will such large amounts of these hormones be secreted. This fact underscores both how stressful it is to be born and how adapted the fetus is for birth (Committee on Fetus and Newborn, 2000; Van Beveren, 2002).

The umbilical cord is cut immediately after birth, and the baby is on its own. Until now, oxygen came from the mother via the umbilical cord, but now the baby has to be self-sufficient and breathe on its own. Now 25 million little air sacs in the lungs must be filled with air. These air sacs have held fluid, but this fluid is rapidly expelled. The first breaths may be the hardest ones at any point in life.

Strategies for Childbirth

Expectant parents have several decisions to make about the birth: What will the setting be, who will attend the birth, and which childbirth technique will be used?

Childbirth Setting and Attendants   In the United States, 99 percent of births take place in hospitals, and more than 90 percent are attended by physicians (Ventura & others, 1997). Many hospitals now offer birthing centers, in which fathers or birth coaches may remain with the mother during labor and delivery. Some people believe these centers offer a good compromise between a technological, depersonalized hospital birth (which cannot offer the emotional experience of a home birth) and a birth at home (which cannot offer the medical backup of a hospital). A birthing room approximates a home setting as much as possible. The birthing room allows for a full range of birth experiences, from a totally unmedicated, natural birth to the most complex, medically intensive care.

Some women with good medical histories and low risk for problems choose a home delivery or a delivery in a freestanding birthing center, which is usually staffed by nurse-midwives (Wong, Perry, & Hockenberry, 2001). Approximately 6 percent of women who deliver a baby in the United States are attended by a midwife (Ventura & others, 1997). Most midwives are nurses who have been specially trained in delivering babies (Moyo, 2003).

One study found that risk of *neonatal mortality* (an infant death occurring in the first 28 days of life) was 33 percent lower and the risk of low birth weight was 31 percent lower for births attended by a certified midwife than for births attended by physicians (MacDorman & Singh, 1998). Compared with physicians, certified nurse-midwives

*W*e must respect this instant of birth, this fragile moment. The baby is between two worlds, on a threshold, hesitating . . .

—FREDERICK LEBOYER
French Obstetrician, 20th Century

generally spend more time with patients during prenatal visits, place more emphasis on patient counseling and education, provide more emotional support, and are more likely to be with the patient one-on-one throughout labor and delivery, which may explain the more positive outcomes for babies delivered by certified nurse-midwives.

Support seems to the theme of many childbirth practices around the world. In many cultures, a knowledgeable woman helps a mother in labor. In some cultures, childbirth is a community affair. For example, in the Pukapukan culture in the Pacific Islands, women give birth in a shelter that is open for villagers to observe. In the Nigoni culture of East Africa, when a woman is ready to give birth, female relatives move into the woman's hut. The husband, however, leaves, taking his belongings with him. He is not permitted to return until after the baby is born. In fact, Nigoni women conceal their pregnancies from their husbands as long as possible.

In many countries around the world, births at home are more common than they are in the United States. For example, in Holland, 35 percent of the babies are born at home, and more than 40 percent are delivered by midwives rather than doctors (Treffers & others, 1990). In many countries, a doula attends a childbearing woman. *Doula* is a Greek word meaning "a woman who helps." A doula is a caregiver who provides continuous physical, emotional, and educational support for the mother before, during, and after childbirth (Gilliland, 2002). The doula remains with the mother throughout labor, assessing and responding to her needs. In one study, mothers who received doula support reported less labor pain than mothers who did not receive doula support (Klaus, Kennell, & Klaus, 1993).

A woman in the African !Kung culture giving birth in a sitting position. Notice the help and support being given by another woman. *What are some cultural variations in childbirth?*

Methods of Delivery   Even after the setting for birth is determined, some choices remain regarding the method of delivery. Of course, circumstances may end up forcing changes in these decisions. One important choice is the medication to be used, if any.

Medication   The American Academy of Pediatrics recommends the least possible medication during delivery (Hotchner, 1997). Three basic kinds of drugs are used for labor: analgesia, anesthesia, and oxytocics.

Analgesia is used to relieve pain. Analgesics include tranquilizers, barbiturates, and narcotics (such as Demerol).

Anesthesia is used in late first-stage labor and during expulsion of the baby to block sensation in an area of the body or to block consciousness. There is a trend toward avoiding general anesthesia in normal births because it can be transmitted through the placenta to the fetus. However, an epidural anesthesia does not cross the placenta. An *epidural block* is regional anesthesia that numbs the woman's body from the waist down. Even this drug, thought to be relatively safe, has come under recent criticism because it is associated with fever, extended labor, and increased risk for cesarean delivery (Ransjo-Arvidson & others, 2001).

Oxytocics are synthetic hormones that are used to stimulate contractions. Pitocin is the most commonly used oxytocic (Carbonne, Tsatsarius, & Goffinet, 2001; Gard & others, 2002; Oboro & Tabowei, 2003).

Predicting how a particular drug will affect an individual pregnant woman and the fetus is difficult. A drug might have only a minimal effect on one fetus yet have a much stronger effect on another fetus. The drug's dosage also is a factor. Stronger doses of tranquilizers and narcotics given to decrease the mother's pain have a potentially more negative effect on the fetus than mild doses. It is important for the mother to assess her level of pain and be an important voice in the decision of whether she should receive medication (Young, 2001).

Natural and Prepared Childbirth   Not long ago the idea of giving birth without any medication gained favor among U.S. women as part of an effort to take control over their experience of childbirth. Through education about childbirth and the use of special techniques, they reduced the need to rely on medicines for pain and on doctors for directions. Two approaches were popular: natural childbirth and prepared childbirth.

Today, the idea of avoiding all medication has declined in popularity, but interest in some aspects of natural and prepared childbirth remains strong.

Natural childbirth was developed in 1914 by an English obstetrician, Grantley Dick-Read. It attempts to reduce the mother's pain by decreasing her fear through education about childbirth and by teaching her to use breathing methods and relaxation techniques during delivery. Dick-Read also believed that the doctor's relationship with the mother can help reduce her perception of pain. He said the doctor should be present during her active labor prior to delivery and should provide reassurance.

Prepared childbirth was developed by French obstetrician Ferdinand Lamaze. The *Lamaze method* is similar to natural childbirth but includes a special breathing technique to control pushing in the final stages of labor and a detailed course in anatomy and physiology. The pregnant woman's husband or a friend usually serves as a coach, who attends childbirth classes with her and helps her with her breathing and relaxation during delivery.

Many other prepared childbirth techniques have been developed (Samuels & Samuels, 1996). For instance, the Bradley method emphasizes the father's role as a labor coach. Virtually all of the prepared childbirth methods emphasize some degree of education, relaxation and breathing exercises, and support. Recently, guided mental imagery, massage, and meditation have been used to teach relaxation. In sum, the current belief in prepared childbirth is that, when information and support are provided, women *know* how to give birth.

Cesarean Delivery In a *cesarean delivery*, the baby is removed from the mother's uterus through an incision made in her abdomen. This is sometimes called a *cesarean section*. A cesarean section is usually performed if the baby is in a *breech position*, which causes the baby's buttocks to be the first part to emerge from the vagina. Normally, the crown of the baby's head comes through the vagina first, but in 1 of every 25 babies, the head does not come through first. Breech babies' heads are still in the uterus while the rest of their bodies are out, which can cause respiratory problems.

Cesarean sections have saved the lives of many babies. They are safer than breech deliveries. Cesarean deliveries may also be life-saving if the baby is lying crosswise in the uterus, if the baby's head is too large to pass through the mother's pelvis, if the baby develops complications, or if the mother is bleeding vaginally. But cesarian deliveries also bring risks. They involve a higher infection rate than vaginal delivery, longer hospital stay, and the increased expense and stress that accompany any surgery.

The benefits and risks of cesarean sections continue to be debated (Alexander, McIntire, & Leveno, 2001; Morrison & MacKenzie, 2003; Peskin & Reine, 2002). Some critics believe that in the United States too many babies are delivered by cesarean section. The cesarean delivery rate jumped 7 percent from 2000 to 2001 in the United States to 24.4 percent of all births, the highest level reported since these data began being reported on birth certificates in 1989 (MacDorman & others, 2002). Indeed, more cesarean sections are performed in the United States than in any other country in the world.

Neonatal Health and Responsiveness

After the baby and mother have met and become acquainted, the newborn is cleaned, examined, weighed, and evaluated. A surprisingly large number of babies are born with problems because of what may look like a trivial fact: Their birth weight is low.

Low Birth Weight Infants **Low birth weight infants** weigh less than 5½ pounds at birth. *Very low birth weight* newborns weigh under 3 pounds and *extremely low birth weight* newborns under 2 pounds. Another way of classifying newborns involves whether they are preterm or small for date.

Preterm infants are those born three weeks or more before the pregnancy has reached its full term—in other words, 35 or fewer weeks after conception. A short gestation period does not necessarily harm an infant. The neurological development

Childbirth Strategies
Childbirth Setting and Attendants
Midwifery
Doula
Fathers and Childbirth
Siblings and Childbirth

natural childbirth Developed in 1914 by Dick-Read, this method attempts to reduce the mother's pain by decreasing her fear through education about childbirth and relaxation techniques during delivery.

prepared childbirth Developed by French obstetrician Ferdinand Lamaze, this childbirth strategy is similar to natural childbirth but includes a special breathing technique to control pushing in the final stages of labor and a more detailed anatomy and physiology course.

low birth weight infant An infant who weighs less than 5½ pounds at birth.

preterm infant An infant born three weeks or more before the pregnancy has reached its full term.

of the preterm baby continues after birth on approximately the same timetable as if the infant were still in the womb. For example, consider a preterm baby born 30 weeks after conception. At 38 weeks, approximately two months after birth, this infant shows the same level of brain development as a 38-week fetus who is yet to be born. But most preterm babies are also low birth weight babies. In one recent study, weekly injections of the hormone progesterone, which is naturally produced by the ovaries, lowered the rate of preterm births by one-third (Meis, 2003). Researchers are recommending that further research be conducted to determine the safest and most effective way to administer the drug.

Small for date infants (also called *small for gestational age infants*) are those whose birth weight is below normal when the length of the pregnancy is considered. They weigh less than 90 percent of all babies of the same gestational age. Small for date infants may be preterm or full term.

The incidence of low birth weight varies considerably from country to country. In the United States, there has been an increase in low birth weight infants in the last two decades, and the U.S. low birth weight rate of 7.6 percent is considerably higher than that of many other developed countries (UNICEF, 2001) (see figure 2.16). In the developing world, low birth weight stems mainly from the mother's poor health and nutrition. Diseases such as diarrhea and malaria, which are common in developing countries, can impair fetal growth if the mother becomes infected while she is pregnant. In developed countries, cigarette smoking during pregnancy is the leading cause of low birth weight (UNICEF, 2001). In both developed and

Neonatal Research
Preterm Infants

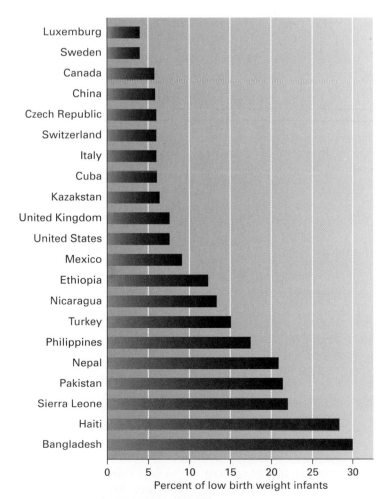

FIGURE 2.16 Low Birth Weight Rates by Country

The graph shows the percentage of children born with low birth weight in a wide range for countries around the world (UNICEF, 2001).

small for date infant Also called small for gestational age infant, this infant's birth weight is below normal when the length of pregnancy is considered. A small for date infant may be preterm or full term.

A "kilogram kid," weighing less than 2.3 pounds at birth. *What are some long-term outcomes for weighing so little at birth?*

Touch Research Institute

developing countries, adolescents who give birth when their bodies have not fully matured are at risk for having low birth weight babies. In the United States, the increase in the number of low birth weight infants is thought to be due to the increasing number of adolescents having babies, the use of drugs, and poor nutrition (Chan, Keane, & Robinson, 2001; England & others, 2001).

Consequences of Low Birth Weight Although most low birth weight infants are normal and healthy, as a group they have more health and developmental problems than normal birth weight infants (Herbst & others, 2003; Rickards & others, 2001; Sweet & others, 2003; Tang & others, 2004). The number and severity of these problems increase as birth weight decreases (Kilbride, Thorstad, & Daily, 2000). Survival rates for infants who are born very early and very small have risen, but this improvement has brought increases in rates of severe brain damage (Yu, 2000). The lower the brain weight, the greater the likelihood of brain injury (Watenberg & others, 2002). Approximately 7 percent of moderately low birth weight infants (3 pounds 5 ounces to 5 pounds 8 ounces) have brain injuries. This figure increases to 20 percent for the smallest newborns (1 pound 2 ounces to 3 pounds 5 ounces). Low birth weight infants are also more likely than normal birth weight infants to have lung or liver diseases.

At school age, children who were born low in birth weight are more likely than their normal birth weight counterparts to have a learning disability, attention deficit hyperactivity disorder, or breathing problems such as asthma (Saigal & others, 2003; Taylor, Klein, & Hack, 1994). Very low birth weight children have more learning problems and lower levels of achievement in reading and math than moderately low birth weight children. Approximately 50 percent of all low birth weight children are enrolled in special education programs.

Not all of these adverse consequences can be attributed solely to being born low in birth weight. Some of the less severe but more common developmental and physical delays occur because many low birth weight children come from disadvantaged environments (Fang, Madhaven, & Alderman, 1999).

Some of the devastating effects of being born low in birth weight can be reversed (Blair & Ramey, 1996; Maulik, 2003; Thompson & others, 2003). Intensive enrichment programs that provide medical and educational services for both the parents and children can improve short-term outcomes for low birth weight children. Federal laws mandate that services for school-age children be expanded to include family-based care for infants. At present, these services are aimed at children born with severe disabilities. The availability of services for moderately low birth weight children who do not have severe physical problems varies, but most states do not provide these services. The Research in Life-Span Development interlude describes one promising type of intervention for at-risk babies.

Research in Life-Span Development
Tiffany Field's Research on Massage Therapy

Interest in using touch and massage to improve the growth, health, and well-being of infants has been stimulated by the research of Tiffany Field (1998, 2001, 2003), director of the Touch Research Institute at the University of Miami School of Medicine. In her first study in this area, massage therapy consisting of firm stroking with the palms of the hands was given three times per day for 15-minute periods to preterm infants (Field & others, 1986). The massage therapy led to 47 percent greater weight gain than standard medical treatment (see figure 2.17). The massaged infants also were more active and alert than preterm infants who were not massaged, and they performed better on developmental tests.

In later studies, Field demonstrated the benefits of massage therapy for infants who faced a variety of problems. For example, in one study, Field (1992) gave massage to preterm infants who were exposed to cocaine in utero. These infants gained weight and improved their scores on developmental tests. In another investigation, newborns born to HIV-positive mothers were randomly assigned to a massage therapy group or to a control group that did not receive the therapy (Scafidi & Field, 1996). Infants in the massage therapy group received three 15-minute massages daily for 10 days. The massaged infants showed superior performance on a wide range of assessments, including daily weight gain. Another study investigated 1- to 3-month-old infants born to depressed adolescent mothers (Field & others, 1996). The infants of depressed mothers who received massage therapy had lower stress—as well as improved emotionality, sociability, and soothability—compared with the nonmassaged infants of depressed mothers.

In other studies by Field and her colleagues, infants are not the only ones who may benefit from massage therapy. They have demonstrated the benefits of massage therapy with women in reducing labor pain (Field, Hernandez-Rief, Taylor, & others, 1997), with children who have arthritis (Field, Hernandez-Rief, Seligman, & others, 1997), with children who have asthma (Field, Henteleff, & others, 1998), with autistic children's attentiveness (Field, Lasko, & others, 1997), and with adolescents who have attention deficit hyperactivity disorder (Field, Quintino, & others, 1998). Field and her colleagues (Cigales & others, 1996) also are studying the amount of touch a child normally receives in early childhood education programs. They hope that positive forms of touch will return to school systems, where touching has been outlawed because of the fear of sexual abuse lawsuits.

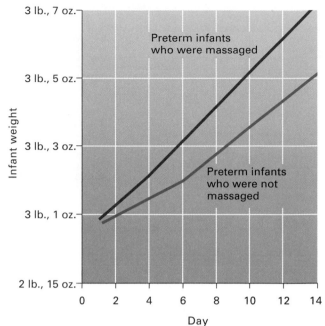

FIGURE 2.17 Weight Gain Comparison of Preterm Infants Who Were Massaged or Not Massaged

The graph shows that the mean daily gain of preterm infants who were massaged was greater than that of preterm infants who were not massaged.

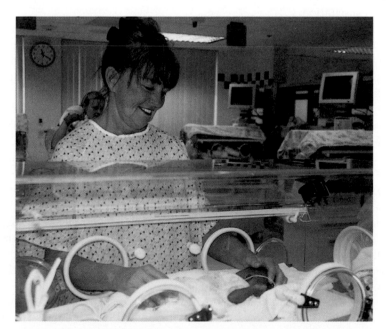

Tiffany Field massages a newborn infant. Her research has demonstrated the power of massage in improving the developmental outcome of at-risk infants. Under her direction, the Touch Research Institute in Miami, Florida, investigates the role of touch in a number of domains of health and well-being.

Score	0	1	2
Heart rate	Absent	Slow—less than 100 beats per minute	Fast—100–140 beats per minute
Respiratory effort	No breathing for more than one minute	Irregular and slow	Good breathing with normal crying
Muscle tone	Limp and flaccid	Weak, inactive, but some flexion of extremities	Strong, active motion
Body color	Blue and pale	Body pink, but extremities blue	Entire body pink
Reflex irritability	No response	Grimace	Coughing, sneezing and crying

FIGURE 2.18 The Apgar Scale

Beginnings: Childbirth

Apgar Scale A widely used method to assess the health of newborns at 1 and 5 minutes after birth. The Apgar Scale evaluates infants' heart rate, respiratory effort, muscle tone, body color, and reflex irritability.

Brazelton Neonatal Behavioral Assessment Scale A test given shortly after birth to assess newborns' neurological development, reflexes, and reactions to people.

Assessing the Newborn In addition to weight, other characteristics of the newborn are also evaluated at birth so that infants at risk for various problems can be quickly identified. The **Apgar Scale** is widely used to assess the health of newborns at 1 and 5 minutes after birth. The Apgar Scale evaluates infants' heart rate, respiratory effort, muscle tone, body color, and reflex irritability. An obstetrician or a nurse does the evaluation and gives the newborn a score, or reading, of 0, 1, or 2 on each of these five health signs (see figure 2.18). A total score of 7 to 10 indicates that the newborn's condition is good. A score of 5 indicates there may be developmental difficulties. A score of 3 or below signals an emergency and indicates that the baby might not survive. The Apgar Scale is especially good at assessing the newborn's ability to respond to the stress of delivery and the new environment (Casey, McIntire, & Leveno, 2001). The Apgar Scale also identifies high-risk infants who need resuscitation.

To evaluate the newborn more thoroughly, the **Brazelton Neonatal Behavioral Assessment Scale** is performed within 24 to 36 hours after birth. It assesses the newborn's neurological development, reflexes, and reactions to people. The newborn is an active participant, and the score is based on the newborn's best performance. Sixteen reflexes, such as sneezing, blinking, and rooting, are assessed, along with reactions to circumstances, such as the infant's reaction to a rattle. (We will have more to say about reflexes in chapter 5.) The examiner makes detailed ratings of the newborn on each of 27 items. Consider item 15: "cuddliness." Nine categories are involved in assessing this item, and scoring is done on a continuum that ranges from the infant's being very resistant to being held to the infant's being extremely cuddly and clinging.

The Brazelton scale is used not only as a sensitive index of neurological competence in the week after birth but also as a measure in many research studies on infant development (Ohgi & others, 2003). In scoring the Brazelton scale, T. Berry Brazelton and his colleagues (Brazelton, Nugent, & Lester, 1987) categorize the 27 items into four categories—physiological, motoric, state, and interaction. They also classify the baby in global terms, such as "worrisome," "normal," or "superior," based on these categories (Nugent & Brazelton, 2000).

A very low Brazelton score can indicate brain damage, or it can reflect stress to the brain that may heal in time. If an infant merely seems sluggish, parents are encouraged to give the infant attention and become more sensitive to the infant's needs. Parents are shown how the newborn can respond to people and how to stimulate such responses. Researchers have found that the interaction skills of both high-risk infants and healthy, responsive infants can be improved through such communication with parents (Worobey & Belsky, 1982).

Bonding

A special component of the parent-infant relationship is **bonding,** the formation of a connection, between parents and the newborn in the period shortly after birth. Sometimes, the practices of hospitals seem designed to prevent this bonding. Drugs given to the mother to make delivery less painful can make the mother drowsy, thus interfering with her ability to respond to and stimulate her newborn. Mothers and newborns are often separated after delivery, and preterm infants are isolated from their mothers even more than full-term infants. Do these practices do any harm?

Some physicians believe that during the period shortly after birth, the parents and child need to form an emotional attachment in order to build a foundation for optimal development in years to come (Kennell & McGrath, 1999). Is there evidence that such close contact between mothers and newborns is critical? Although some research supports the bonding hypothesis (Klaus & Kennell, 1976), a body of research challenges the significance of the first few days of life as a critical period (Bakeman & Brown, 1980; Rode & others, 1981). Indeed, the extreme form of the bonding hypothesis—that the newborn must have close contact with the mother in the first few days of life to develop optimally—simply is not true.

Nonetheless, the weakness of the maternal-infant bonding research should not be used as an excuse to keep motivated mothers from interacting with their infants in the postpartum period. Such contact brings pleasure to many mothers. In some mother-infant pairs—especially preterm infants, adolescent mothers, or mothers from disadvantaged circumstances—the early close contact may establish a climate for healthy interaction after the mother and infant leave the hospital.

In recognition of the belief that bonding may get the parental-infant relationship off to a good start, many hospitals now offer a *rooming-in* arrangement, in which the baby remains in the mother's room most of the time during its hospital stay. However, if parents choose not to use this rooming-in arrangement, the weight of the research evidence suggests that this decision will not harm the infant emotionally (Lamb, 1994).

bonding The formation of a connection, especially a physical bond, between parents and the newborn in the period shortly after birth.

Review and Reflect: Learning Goal 5

5 Summarize how birth takes place

REVIEW

- What are the three main stages of birth?
- What are some different birth strategies?
- What effects does a low birth weight have on development? What are two measures of neonatal health and responsiveness?
- How critical is bonding for development?

REFLECT

- If you are a female, which birth strategy do you prefer? Why? If you are a male, how involved would you want to be in helping with pregnancy and the birth of your baby?

Reach Your Learning Goals

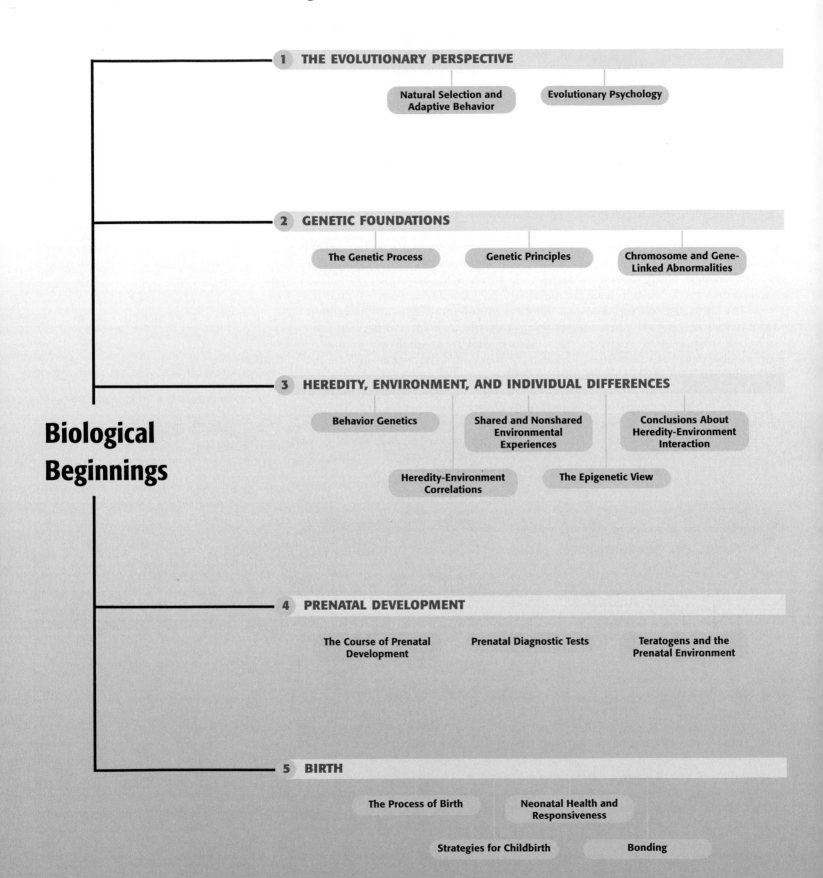

Biological Beginnings

1 THE EVOLUTIONARY PERSPECTIVE

- Natural Selection and Adaptive Behavior
- Evolutionary Psychology

2 GENETIC FOUNDATIONS

- The Genetic Process
- Genetic Principles
- Chromosome and Gene-Linked Abnormalities

3 HEREDITY, ENVIRONMENT, AND INDIVIDUAL DIFFERENCES

- Behavior Genetics
- Shared and Nonshared Environmental Experiences
- Conclusions About Heredity-Environment Interaction
- Heredity-Environment Correlations
- The Epigenetic View

4 PRENATAL DEVELOPMENT

- The Course of Prenatal Development
- Prenatal Diagnostic Tests
- Teratogens and the Prenatal Environment

5 BIRTH

- The Process of Birth
- Neonatal Health and Responsiveness
- Strategies for Childbirth
- Bonding

Summary

1 Discuss the evolutionary perspective on life-span development

- Natural selection is the process that favors the individuals of a species that are best adapted to survive and reproduce. The process of natural selection was originally proposed by Charles Darwin. In evolutionary theory, adaptive behavior is behavior that promotes the organism's survival in a natural habitat.
- Evolutionary psychology holds that adaptation, reproduction, and "survival of the fittest" are important in shaping behavior. Ideas proposed by evolutionary developmental psychology include the view that an extended "juvenile" period is needed to develop a large brain and learn the complexity of human social communities. According to Baltes, the benefits conferred by evolutionary selection decrease with age while our needs for culture-based resources increase. Bandura argues for a bidirectional link between biology and environment. Biology allows for a broad range of cultural possibilities.

2 Describe what genes are and how they influence human development

- The nucleus of each human cell contains chromosomes, which are composed of DNA. Genes are short segments of DNA that direct cells to reproduce and manufacture proteins. DNA does not act independently but collaboratively. In the process of reproduction, an egg is fertilized by sperm, producing a zygote, which has 23 pairs of chromosomes. The zygote's chromosomes, however, are not simply a copy of the mother's and father's chromosomes. When the sperm and eggs are formed (through meiosis), pieces of the parent chromosomes are exchanged, creating chromosomes with a new combination of genes. Thus when sperm and egg unite, the chromosomes of the resulting zygote have a unique combination of genes. Variability also results from the fact that for each genotype, a range of phenotypes can be expressed.
- Genetic principles include those involving dominant-recessive genes, sex-linked genes, genetic imprinting, polygenic inheritance, and reaction range.
- Chromosome abnormalities occur when chromosomes do not divide evenly. Down syndrome is the result of a chromosomal abnormality caused by the presence of a 47th chromosome. Sex-linked chromosomal abnormalities include Klinefelter syndrome, Turner syndrome, XYY syndrome, and fragile X syndrome. Gene-linked abnormalities involve harmful genes. Gene-linked disorders include phenylketonuria (PKU) and sickle-cell anemia.

3 Explain some of the ways that heredity and environment interact to produce individual differences in development

- Behavior genetics is the field concerned with the degree and nature of behavior's hereditary basis. Methods used by behavior geneticists include twin studies and adoption studies.
- Scarr describes three heredity-environment correlations: passive, evocative, and active (niche-picking). Scarr believes that the relative importance of these three genotype-environment correlations changes as children develop.
- Shared environmental experiences refer to siblings common experiences, such as their parents' personalities and intellectual orientation. Nonshared environmental experiences are experiences that are not shared with a sibling, both within a family and outside a family. Many behavior geneticists argue that differences in the development of siblings are due to nonshared environmental experiences (and heredity) rather than shared environmental experiences.
- In Scarr's heredity-environment correlations view, heredity directs the types of environments that children experience. In contrast, the epigenetic view emphasizes that development is the result of an ongoing, bidirectional interchange between heredity and environment.
- Many complex behaviors have some genetic loading that gives people a propensity for a particular developmental trajectory. However, actual development also requires an environment and that environment is complex. The interaction of heredity and environment is extensive. Much remains to be discovered about the specific ways that heredity and environment interact to influence development.

4 Characterize the course of prenatal development and its hazards

- Prenatal development is divided into three periods: germinal (first two weeks after conception), which ends when the zygote (a fertilized egg) attaches to the uterine wall; embryonic (two to eight weeks after conception), during which the embryo differentiates into three layers, life-support systems develop, and organ systems form (organogenesis); and fetal (two months after conception until about nine months, or when the infant is born), a time when organ systems mature.
- Amniocentesis, ultrasound sonography, chorionic villi sampling, and the maternal blood test are used to determine the presence of defects once pregnancy has begun.
- Teratology is the field that investigates the causes of congenital (birth) defects. Any agent that causes birth defects is called a teratogen. Dose, genetic susceptibility, and time of exposure influence the severity of the damage to an unborn child and the type of defect that occurs. Prescription drugs that can be harmful include antibiotics. Nonprescription drugs that can be harmful include diet pills, aspirin, and caffeine. Fetal alcohol syndrome is a cluster of abnormalities that appear in offspring of mothers who drink heavily during pregnancy. Even when pregnant women drink moderately (one to two drinks a day), negative effects on their offspring have been found. Cigarette smoking by pregnant women has serious adverse effects on prenatal and child development (such as low birth weight). Illegal drugs that are

potentially harmful to offspring include marijuana, cocaine, and heroin. Potential environmental hazards include radiation, environmental pollutants, and toxic wastes. Rubella (German measles) syphilis, genital herpes, and AIDS are other teratogens. Incompatibility of the mother's and the father's blood types can also be harmful to the fetus. A developing fetus depends entirely on its mother for nutrition. One nutrient that is especially important very early in development is folic acid. Maternal age can negatively affect the offspring's development if the mother is an adolescent or over 30. High stress in the mother is linked with less than optimal prenatal and birth outcomes. Most of the time pregnancy and prenatal development go well. Avoiding teratogens helps ensure a positive outcome.

5 Summarize how birth takes place

- Childbirth occurs in three stages. In the first stage, the cervix dilates to about 4 inches. The second stage begins when the baby's head moves through the cervix and ends with the baby's complete emergence. The third stage is afterbirth. Being born involves considerable stress for the baby, but the baby is well prepared and adapted to handle the stress. Anoxia—insufficient oxygen supply to the fetus or newborn—is a potential hazard.

- Childbirth strategies include the choice of setting and attendants. In many countries, a doula attends a childbearing woman. Methods of delivery include medicated, natural and prepared, and cesarean.

- Low birth weight infants weigh less than $5\frac{1}{2}$ pounds. They may be preterm (born three weeks or more before the pregnancy has reached full term) or small for date (also called small for gestational age, which refers to infants whose birth weight is below normal when the length of pregnancy is considered). Small for date infants may be preterm or full term. Although most low birth weight infants are normal and healthy, as a group they have more health and developmental problems than normal birth weight infants. For many years, the Apgar Scale has been used to assess the newborn's health. The Brazelton Neonatal Behavioral Assessment Scale examines the newborn's neurological development, reflexes, and reactions to people.

- Bonding has not been found to be critical in the development of a competent infant but it may benefit some mothers, such as those in poverty and adolescent mothers.

Key Terms

evolutionary psychology 51
chromosomes 53
DNA 53
genes 53
mitosis 54
meiosis 55
reproduction 55
zygote 55
genotype 55
phenotype 55
reaction range 57
canalization 58
Down syndrome 58

Klinefelter syndrome 59
Turner syndrome 59
XYY syndrome 59
fragile X syndrome 59
phenylketonuria (PKU) 59
sickle-cell anemia 59
behavior genetics 62
twin study 62
adoption study 62
passive genotype-environment correlations 62
evocative genotype-environment correlations 63

active (niche-picking) genotype-environment correlations 63
shared environmental experiences 63
nonshared environmental experiences 63
epigenetic view 64
germinal period 66
embryonic period 66
fetal period 67
teratogen 70

fetal alcohol syndrome (FAS) 72
natural childbirth 82
prepared childbirth 82
low birth weight infant 82
preterm infant 82
small for date infants 83
Apgar Scale 86
Brazelton Neonatal Behavioral Assessment Scale 86
bonding 87

Key People

Charles Darwin 50
David Buss 51
Paul Baltes 52

Albert Bandura 52
Steven Jay Gould 52
Sandra Scarr 57, 62

Robert Plomin 64
Judith Harris 65
Grantley Dick-Read 82

Ferdinand Lamaze 82
Tiffany Field 84
T. Berry Brazelton 86

E-Learning Tools

Connect to **www.mhhe.com/santrockldt2** to research the answers and complete the following exercises. In addition, you'll find a number of other resources and valuable study tools for chapter 2, "Biological Beginnings," on the Student CD-ROM that came with this book.

Taking It to the Net

1. Ahmahl, a biochemistry major, is writing a psychology paper on the potential dilemmas that society and scientists may face as a result of the decoding of the human genome. What are some of the main issues or concerns that Ahmahl should address in his class paper?

2. Brandon and Katie are thrilled to learn that they are expecting their first child. They are curious about the genetic makeup of their unborn child and want to know (a) what disorders might be identified through prenatal genetic testing, and (b) which tests, if any, Katie should undergo to help determine this information.

3. Greg and Courtenay have three boys. They would love to have a girl. Courtenay read that there is a clinic in Virginia where you can pick the sex of your child. How successful are such efforts? Would you want to have this choice available to you?

Connect to **www.mhhe.com/santrockldt2** to research the answers and complete these exercises.

Self-Assessment

To evaluate your genetic history and prenatal issues, complete these self-assessments:

- *Prenatal Genetic Screening Questionnaire*
- *My Family Health Tree*

Health and Well-Being, Parenting, and Education

Build your decision-making skills by trying your hand at the health and well-being, parenting, and education "Scenarios."

Physical Development and Biological Aging

Think about how much you have changed physically and will continue to change as you age. We come into this life as small beings but grow very rapidly in infancy, more slowly in childhood, and once again more rapidly during puberty, and then another slowdown takes place. Eventually we decline, but many older adults are still physically robust. In this chapter, we will explore changes in body growth, the brain, and sleep across the life span. We also will examine longevity and evaluate some fascinating ideas about why we age.

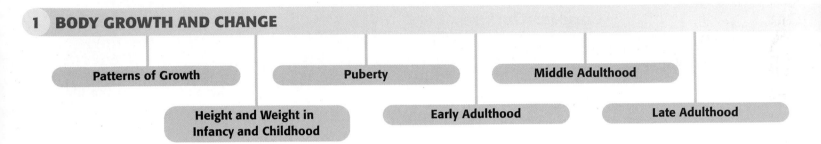

In life's long journey, we go through many bodily changes. We grow up, we grow out, we shrink. The very visible changes in height and weight are accompanied by less visible ones in bones, lungs, and every other organ of the body. These changes will help shape how we think about ourselves, how other people think about us, and what we are capable of thinking, doing, and feeling. Are there strict timelines for these changes? Are they set in our genes? Let's begin by studying some basic patterns of growth and then turn to bodily changes from the time we are infants through the time we are older adults.

Patterns of Growth

The **cephalocaudal pattern** is the sequence in which the fastest growth always occurs at the top—the head—with physical growth in size, weight, and feature differentiation gradually working its way down from the top to the bottom (for example, neck, shoulders, middle trunk, and so on). This same pattern occurs in the head area, because the top parts of the head—the eyes and brain—grow faster than the lower parts, such as the jaw. During prenatal development and early infancy, the head constitutes an extraordinarily large proportion of the total body (see figure 3.1).

Sensory and motor development proceed according to the cephalocaudal principle. For example, infants see objects before they can control their torso, and they can use their hands long before they can crawl or walk. We will have much more to say about sensory and motor development in chapter 5.

The **proximodistal pattern** is the growth sequence that starts at the center of the body and moves toward the extremities. An example is the early maturation of muscular control of the trunk and arms, as compared with that of the hands and fingers. Further, infants use the whole hand as a unit before they can control several fingers.

Height and Weight in Infancy and Childhood

Height and weight increase rapidly in infancy. Then, they take a slower course during the childhood years.

Infancy The average North American newborn is 20 inches long and weighs 7½ pounds. Ninety-five percent of full-term newborns are 18 to 22 inches long and weigh between 5½ and 10 pounds.

In the first several days of life, most newborns lose 5 to 7 percent of their body weight. Once infants adjust to sucking, swallowing, and digesting, they grow rapidly,

cephalocaudal pattern The sequence in which the fastest growth occurs at the top—the head—with physical growth in size, weight, and feature differentiation gradually working from top to bottom.

proximodistal pattern The sequence in which growth starts at the center of the body and moves toward the extremities.

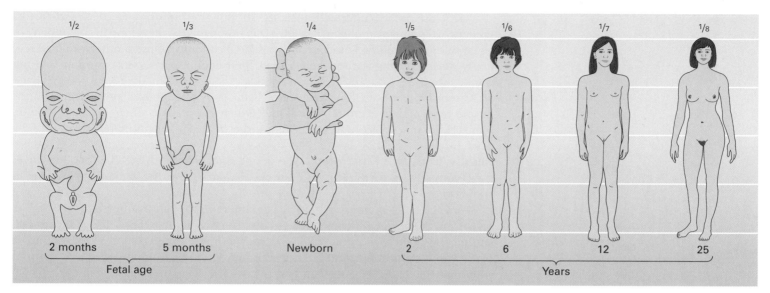

| 1/2 | 1/3 | 1/4 | 1/5 | 1/6 | 1/7 | 1/8 |

2 months 5 months Newborn 2 6 12 25

Fetal age Years

FIGURE 3.1 Changes in Proportions of the Human Body During Growth

As individuals develop from infancy through adulthood, one of the most noticeable physical changes is that the head becomes smaller in relation to the rest of the body. The fractions listed refer to head size as a proportion of total body length at different ages.

gaining an average of 5 to 6 ounces per week during the first month. They have doubled their birth weight by the age of 4 months and have nearly tripled it by their first birthday. Infants grow about 1 inch per month during the first year, reaching approximately 1½ times their birth length by their first birthday.

Infants' rate of growth is considerably slower in the second year of life. By 2 years of age, infants weigh approximately 26 to 32 pounds, having gained a quarter to half a pound per month during the second year; now they have reached about one-fifth of their adult weight. The average 2-year-old is 32 to 35 inches tall, which is nearly one-half of adult height.

Early Childhood As the preschool child grows older, the percentage of increase in height and weight decreases with each additional year. Girls are only slightly smaller and lighter than boys during these years. Both boys and girls slim down as the trunks of their bodies lengthen. Although their heads are still somewhat large for their bodies, by the end of the preschool years most children have lost their top-heavy look. Body fat also shows a slow, steady decline during the preschool years. Girls have more fatty tissue than boys; boys have more muscle tissue.

Growth patterns vary individually. Think back to your preschool years. This was probably the first time you noticed that some children were taller than you, some shorter; some were fatter, some thinner; some were stronger, some weaker. Much of the variation is due to heredity, but environmental experiences are also involved. A review of the height and weight of children around the world concluded that two important contributors to height differences are ethnic origin and nutrition (Meredith, 1978). Also, urban, middle-socioeconomic-status, and firstborn children were taller than rural, lower-socioeconomic-status, and later-born children. The children whose mothers smoked during pregnancy were half an inch shorter than the children whose mothers did not smoke during pregnancy. In the United States, African American children are taller than White children.

The bodies of 5-year-olds and 2-year-olds are different. The 5-year-old not only is taller and heavier, but also has a longer trunk and legs than the 2-year-old. *What might be some other physical differences between 2- and 5-year-olds?*

Why are some children unusually short? The culprits are *congenital* factors (genetic or prenatal problems), a physical problem that develops in childhood, or an emotional difficulty. For example, preschool children whose mothers smoked regularly during pregnancy are shorter than their counterparts whose mothers did not smoke, children who are chronically sick are shorter than their counterparts who are rarely sick, and children who have been physically abused or neglected might not secrete adequate growth hormone, which can restrict their physical growth. Many children with growth problems can be treated with hormones.

Middle and Late Childhood The period of middle and late childhood involves slow, consistent growth. This is a period of calm before the rapid growth spurt of adolescence.

During the elementary school years, children grow an average of 2 to 3 inches a year. At the age of 8 the average girl and the average boy are 4 feet 2 inches tall. During the middle and late childhood years, children gain about 5 to 7 pounds a year. The average 8-year-old girl and the average 8-year-old boy weigh 56 pounds (National Center for Health Statistics, 2000). The weight increase is due mainly to increases in the size of the skeletal and muscular systems, as well as the size of some body organs. Muscle mass and strength gradually increase as "baby fat" decreases in middle and late childhood.

The loose movements and knock-knees of early childhood give way to improved muscle tone in middle and late childhood. The increase in muscular strength is due to heredity and to exercise. Children also double their strength capabilities during these years. Because of their greater number of muscle cells, boys tend to be stronger than girls.

Changes in proportions are among the most pronounced physical changes in middle and late childhood. Head circumference, waist circumference, and leg length decrease in relation to body height. A less noticeable physical change is that bones continue to harden during middle and late childhood but yield to pressure and pull more than mature bones.

Puberty

Puberty is a period of rapid physical maturation involving hormonal and bodily changes that take place in early adolescence. We will begin our exploration of puberty by focusing on its determinants, then turn to some of the most important physical changes associated with puberty, and finally discuss its psychological accompaniments.

Determinants of Puberty Puberty can be distinguished from adolescence. For virtually everyone, puberty ends long before adolescence is exited. Puberty is often thought of as the most important marker for the beginning of adolescence. Among the key factors involved in puberty are heredity, hormones, and weight and body fat.

Heredity Puberty is not an environmental accident. Programmed into the genes of every human being is a timing for the emergence of puberty. Puberty does not take place at 2 or 3 years of age, and it does not occur in the twenties. Nonetheless, within the boundaries of about 9 to 16 years of age, environmental factors can influence the onset and duration of puberty.

Hormones Behind the first whisker in boys and the widening of hips in girls is a flood of hormones. Let's explore the nature of these hormonal changes.

Hormones are powerful chemical substances secreted by the endocrine glands and carried through the body by the bloodstream. The endocrine system's role in puberty involves the interaction of the hypothalamus, the pituitary gland, and the gonads (sex glands). The *hypothalamus* is a structure in the brain that monitors

Middle and Later Childhood: Physical Changes in Middle and Later Childhood

puberty A period of rapid physical maturation involving hormonal and bodily changes during early adolescence.

hormones Powerful chemical substances secreted by the endocrine glands and carried through the body by the bloodstream.

From Penguin Dreams and Stranger Things by Berkeley Breathed. Copyright © 1985 by The Washington Post Company. By Permission of Little, Brown and Company (Inc.).

Biological Changes

eating, drinking, and sex. The *pituitary gland* is an important endocrine gland that controls growth and regulates other glands. The *gonads* are the sex glands—the testes in males, the ovaries in females.

How does this hormonal system work? The pituitary gland sends a signal via *gonadotropins* (hormones that stimulate the testes and ovaries) to the appropriate gland to manufacture the hormone. Then the pituitary gland, through interaction with the hypothalamus, detects when the optimal level of hormones is reached and responds by adjusting gonadotropin secretion.

Two classes of hormones have significantly different concentrations in males and females. **Androgens** are the main class of male sex hormones. **Estrogens** are the main class of female hormones.

Testosterone is an androgen that plays an important role in male pubertal development. Throughout puberty, a rising testosterone level is associated with a number of physical changes in boys—development of external genitals, increase in height, and voice changes (Hiort, 2002). *Estradiol* is an estrogen that plays an important role in female pubertal development. As estradiol level rises, breast development, uterine development, and skeletal changes occur. In one study, testosterone levels increased eighteenfold in boys but only twofold in girls across puberty; estradiol levels increased eightfold in girls but only twofold in boys across puberty (Nottleman & others, 1987) (see figure 3.2).

Not only does the pituitary gland release gonadotropins that stimulate the testes and ovaries, but through interaction with the hypothalamus the pituitary gland also secretes hormones that either directly lead to growth and skeletal maturation or produce growth effects through interaction with the *thyroid gland,* located in the neck region. Initially, growth hormones are secreted at night during puberty, later they are also secreted during the day, although daytime levels are usually very low (Susman, Dorn, & Schiefelbein, 2003). Growth can also be influenced by other endocrine factors, such as *cortisol* which is secreted by the adrenal cortex. Testosterone and estrogen also facilitate growth during puberty (Guercio & others, 2003).

Puberty has two phases that are linked with hormonal changes: adrenarche and gonadarche (Susman, Dorn, & Schiefelbein, 2003; Susman & Rogol, 2004). *Adrenarche* involves hormonal changes in the adrenal glands, which are located just above the kidneys. These changes occur surprisingly early, from about 6 to 9 years of age and before what we generally consider to be the beginning of puberty. Adrenal androgens are secreted by the adrenal glands during adrenarche and continuing on through puberty.

Gonadarche is what most people think of as puberty, and it involves sexual maturation and the development of reproductive maturity. Gonadarche begins at approximately 9 to 10 years of age in non-Latino White girls, and 8 to 9 years of age in African American girls in the United States (Grumbach & Styne, 1992).

androgens The main class of male sex hormones.

estrogens The main class of female sex hormones.

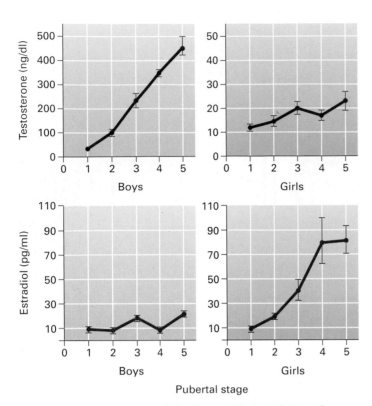

FIGURE 3.2 Hormone Levels by Sex and Pubertal Stage for Testosterone and Estradiol

The five stages range from the early beginning of puberty (stage 1) to the most advanced stage of puberty (stage 5). Notice the significant increase in testosterone in boys and the significant increase in estradiol in girls.

Gonadarche begins at about 10 to 11 years of age in boys. The culmination of gonadarche in girls is **menarche,** a girls' first menstruation, and in boys **spermarche,** a boy's first ejaculation of semen.

Are there links between concentrations of hormones and adolescent behavior? Findings are inconsistent. Some studies have found higher levels of testosterone to be related to aggressive behaviors, other studies have not (Susman & others, 1998). Links between high levels of adrenal androgens and antisocial behavior have been found (van Goozen & others, 1998). Few studies have focused on estrogens, but there is some indication that increased levels of estrogens are linked with depression in adolescent girls (Angold, Costello, & Worthman, 1998; Steiner, Dunn, & Born, 2003).

In any event, hormonal factors alone are not responsible for adolescent behavior. For example, one study found that social factors accounted for two to four times as much variance as hormonal factors in depression and anger among young adolescent girls (Brooks-Gunn & Warren, 1989). Another study found little direct connection between adolescent male and female testosterone levels and risky behavior or depression (Booth & others, 2003). Instead, a link between testosterone levels and behavior depended on the quality of parent-adolescent relations. When relationship quality decreased, testosterone-linked risk-taking behavior and symptoms of depression increased. Hormones do not act independently; hormonal activity and its consequences are influenced by many environmental factors, including parent-adolescent relationships. Stress, eating patterns, sexual activity, and depression can also activate or suppress various aspects of the hormone system (Archibald, Graber, & Brooks-Gunn, 2003; Graber & Brooks-Gunn, 2002).

Weight and Body Fat One recent study found that higher weight was strongly associated with having reached menarche (Anderson, Dallal, & Must, 2003). Some researchers have even proposed that a body weight of approximately 106 ± 3 pounds triggers menarche and the end of the pubertal growth spurt. For menarche to begin and continue, fat must make up 17 percent of the girl's body weight. Both anorexic adolescents whose weight drops dramatically and females in certain sports (such as gymnastics) may become *amenorrheic* (having an absence or suppression of menstrual discharge) (Fujii & Demura, 2003). Undernutrition also can delay puberty in boys (Susman, Dorn, & Schiefelbein, 2003).

The hormone *leptin* might be a signal of the beginning and progression of puberty (Mantzoros, 2000; Rogol, Roemmich, & Clark, 2002). Leptin may be one of the messengers that signals the adequacy of fat stores for reproduction and maintenance of pregnancy at puberty. Leptin concentrations are higher in girls than in boys. They also are related to the amount of fat in girls and androgen concentrations in boys (Roemmich & others, 1998). Changes in leptin have not yet been studied in relation to adolescent behavior.

In sum, the determinants of puberty include heredity, hormones, and weight and body fat. Next, we will turn our attention to the key changes that characterize puberty, beginning with the growth spurt.

menarche A girl's first menstrual period.

spermarche A boy's first ejaculation of semen.

Growth Spurt Growth slows throughout childhood, and puberty ushers in the most rapid increases in growth since infancy. As indicated in figure 3.3, the growth spurt associated with puberty occurs approximately two years earlier for girls than for boys. The mean beginning of the growth spurt in the United States today is 9 years of age for girls and 11 years of age for boys. Pubertal change peaks at an average of 11.5 years for girls and 13.5 years for boys. During their growth spurt, girls increase in height about 3.5 inches per year, boys about 4 inches.

Boys and girls who are shorter or taller than their peers before adolescence are likely to remain so during adolescence. At the beginning of adolescence, girls tend to be as tall as or taller than boys their age, but by the end of the middle school years most boys have caught up with, or in many cases even surpassed, girls in height. And even though height in elementary school is a good predictor of height later in adolescence, as much as 30 percent of the height of individuals in late adolescence is unexplained by height in the elementary school years.

The rate at which adolescents gain weight follows approximately the same timetable as the rate at which they gain height. Marked weight gains coincide with the onset of puberty. Fifty percent of adult body weight is gained during adolescence (Rogol & others, 1998). At the peak of weight gain during puberty, girls gain an average of 18 pounds in 1 year at about 12 years of age (approximately 6 months after their peak height increase). Boys' peak weight gain per year (20 pounds in 1 year) occurs at about the same time as their peak increase in height (about 13 to 14 years of age). During early adolescence, girls tend to outweigh boys; but just as with height, by about 14 years of age, boys begin to surpass girls in weight.

In addition to increases in height and weight, body shape changes. Adolescent girls experience a spurt in hip width, and boys undergo an increase in shoulder width. In girls, increased hip width is linked with an increase in estrogens; in boys, increased shoulder width is associated with an increase in testosterone.

The later growth spurt of boys also produces greater leg length in boys than girls. Also, in many cases boys' facial structure becomes more angular during puberty, and girls' facial structure becomes more round and soft.

Sexual Maturation Think back to the onset of your puberty. Of the striking changes that were taking place in your body, what was the first change that occurred? Researchers have found that male pubertal characteristics develop in this order: increase in penis and testicle size, appearance of straight pubic hair, minor voice change, first ejaculation (spermarche—this usually occurs through masturbation or a wet dream), appearance of pubic hair, onset of maximum body growth, growth of hair in armpits, more detectable voice changes, and growth of facial hair. Three of the most noticeable areas of sexual maturation in boys are penis elongation, testes development, and growth of pubic hair. The normal range and average age of development for these sexual characteristics, along with height spurt, are shown in figure 3.4.

What is the order of appearance of physical changes in females? First either the breasts enlarge or pubic hair appears. These are two of the most noticeable aspects

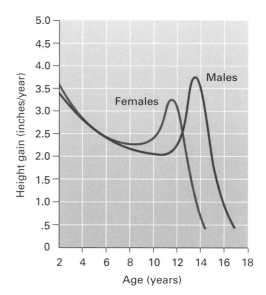

FIGURE 3.3 Pubertal Growth Spurt

On the average, the peak of the growth spurt that characterizes pubertal change occurs two years earlier for girls (10½) than for boys (12½).

Biological Changes

ZITS By Jerry Scott and Jim Borgman

IT WAS ALL NATURAL, RIGHT? / ALL NATURAL.

NO MEDICATIONS? / NOPE.

AND YOU LIVED THROUGH IT. / OBVIOUSLY.

WOW.

I KNOW! I STILL CAN'T BELIEVE I GAVE BIRTH TO SOMETHING THIS BIG!

ZITS Partnership. Reprinted with special permission of King Features Syndicate.

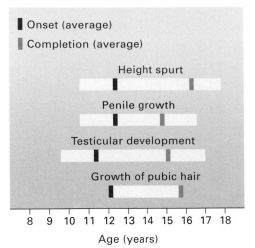

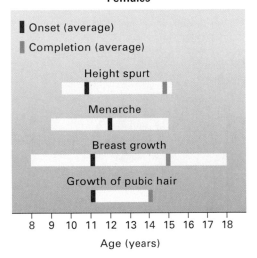

FIGURE 3.4 Normal Range and Average Development of Sexual Characteristics in Males and Females

of female pubertal development. Later, hair appears in the armpits. As these changes occur, the female grows in height, and her hips become wider than her shoulders. Her first menstruation (menarche) occurs rather late in the pubertal cycle. Initially, her menstrual cycles may be highly irregular. For the first several years, she might not ovulate during every menstrual cycle. Some girls do not become fertile until two years after their periods begin. Pubertal females do not experience voice changes comparable to those in pubertal males. By the end of puberty, the female's breasts have become more fully rounded.

It is important to understand that there can be wide individual variations in the onset and progression of puberty. The pubertal sequence might begin as early as 10 years of age or as late as 13½ for boys. It might end as early as 13 years or as late as 17. The normal range is wide enough that, given two boys of the same chronological age, one might complete the pubertal sequence before the other one has begun it. For girls, the age range of menarche is even wider. It is considered within a normal range when it occurs between 9 and 15 years of age.

Secular Trends in Puberty   The term *secular trends* refers to temporal, generational changes. Imagine a toddler displaying all the features of puberty—a 3-year-old girl with fully developed breasts or a boy just slightly older with a deep male voice. That is what toddlers would be like by the year 2250 if the age at which puberty arrives were to continue decreasing as it did for much of the twentieth century. For example, in Norway, menarche now occurs at just over 13 years of age, compared to 17 years of age in the 1840s (Petersen, 1979). In the United States, in the 1840s menarche occurred at an average of 15 years of age, compared to about 12½ years today. The earlier onset of puberty likely is the result of improved health and nutrition.

In one large-scale study of pubertal development in 17,000 American girls (Herman-Giddens & others, 1997), non-Latina White girls began puberty at an average of 10 years of age and African American girls began puberty between 8 and 9 years of age. The authors concluded that puberty is coming much earlier for American girls. However, some reports suggest that we need more research to conclude that puberty is coming as early as this study suggested (Rosenfield & others, 2000). Other researchers report that in the last decade we have begun to see a slowdown in the earlier onset of puberty (Archibald, Graber, & Brooks-Gunn, 2003).

Body Image   One psychological aspect of physical change in puberty is certain: Adolescents are preoccupied with their bodies and develop individual images of what their bodies are like (McCabe & Ricciardelli, 2003). Perhaps you looked in the mirror on a daily, and sometimes even hourly, basis to see if you could detect anything different about your changing body. Preoccupation with one's body image is strong throughout adolescence, but it is especially acute during puberty, a time when adolescents are more dissatisfied with their bodies than in late adolescence (Wright, 1989).

There also are gender differences in adolescents' perceptions of their bodies. In general, girls are less happy with their bodies and have more negative body images, compared with boys, throughout puberty (Brooks-Gunn & Paikoff, 1993). Also, as puberty proceeds, girls often become more dissatisfied with their bodies, probably because their body fat increases, whereas boys become more satisfied as they move through puberty, probably because their muscle mass increases (Gross, 1984).

Early and Late Maturation   Did you enter puberty early, late, or on time? When adolescents mature earlier or later than their peers, might they perceive themselves differently? In the Berkeley Longitudinal Study conducted some years ago, early-maturing boys perceived themselves more positively and had more successful peer relations than did late-maturing boys (Jones, 1965). The findings for early-maturing girls were similar but not as strong as for boys. When the late-maturing boys were in their thirties, however, they had developed a more positive identity than the early-maturing boys had (Peskin, 1967). Perhaps the late-maturing boys had had more time to explore life's options, or perhaps the early-maturing boys continued to focus on their physical status instead of paying attention to career development and achievement.

More recent research confirms that at least during adolescence it is advantageous to be an early-maturing rather than a late-maturing boy (Simmons & Blyth, 1987). However, early maturation increases girls' vulnerability to a number of problems (Brooks-Gunn & Paikoff, 1993). Compared with other girls, early-maturing girls are more likely to smoke, drink, be depressed, have an eating disorder, request earlier independence from their parents, and have older friends. Their bodies are likely to elicit responses from males that lead to earlier dating and earlier sexual experiences. In one study, early-maturing girls had lower educational and occupational attainment in adulthood than late-maturing girls (Statin & Magnusson, 1990). Apparently as a result of their social and cognitive immaturity, combined with early physical development, early-maturing girls are easily lured into problem behaviors (Petersen, 1993; Sarigiani & Petersen, 2000). As you will read in the Applications in Life-Span Development interlude, early and late pubertal timing can also involve health problems.

Applications in Life-Span Development

Pubertal Timing and Health Care

Many adolescents whose development is extremely early or extremely late—such as a boy who has not had a spurt in height by the age of 16 or a girl who has not menstruated by the age of 15—are likely to come to the attention of a physician. Girls and boys who are early or late maturers but are well within the normal range are less likely to be taken to a physician because of their maturational status. Nonetheless, these boys and girls might have fears and doubts about being normal that they do not express unless a physician, counselor, or other health-care provider takes the initiative. A brief discussion outlining the sequence and timing of events and the large individual variations in them could be all that is required to reassure many adolescents who are maturing very early or very late.

Health-care providers may want to discuss the adolescent's off-time development with the adolescent's parents as well. Information about the peer pressures of off-time development can be beneficial. Especially helpful to early-maturing girls is a discussion of peer pressures to date and to engage in adultlike behavior at an early age. The transition to middle school, junior high school, or high school can be more stressful for girls and boys who are in the midst of puberty than for those who are not (Brooks-Gunn, 1988).

If pubertal development is extremely late, a physician might recommend hormonal treatment. This approach may or may not be helpful (Lee, 2003; Yanovski & others, 2003). In one study of extended pubertal delay in boys, hormonal treatment increased the height, dating interest, and peer relations in several boys but resulted in little or no improvement in other boys (Lewis, Money, & Bobrow, 1977).

In sum, most early- and late-maturing individuals weather puberty's challenges and stresses competently. For those who do not, discussions with sensitive and knowledgeable health-care providers and parents can improve coping abilities.

Early Adulthood

After the dramatic physical changes of puberty, the years of early adulthood seem an uneventful time in the body's history. Physical changes during these years may be subtle, but they do continue.

Famous actor Sean Connery as a young adult in his twenties (left) and as a middle-aged adult in his fifties (right). *What are some of the most outwardly noticeable signs of aging in the middle adulthood years?*

$\mathcal{M}$iddle age is when your age starts to show around your middle.

—BOB HOPE
American Comedian, 20th Century

Middle Adulthood: Senescence

Height remains rather constant during the early adulthood years. Peak functioning of the body's joints also usually occurs in the twenties. Many individuals also reach a peak of muscle tone and strength in their late teens and twenties. However, these may begin to decline in the thirties. Sagging chins and protruding abdomens may also appear for the first time. Muscles start to have less elasticity, and aches may begin to show in places not felt before. Said one 30-year-old tennis player, "I played tennis last night and my knees are sore. Last month, it was my lower back that hurt. Several years ago it wasn't that way. I could play all day and not be sore the next morning."

Middle Adulthood

Like the changes of early adulthood, midlife physical changes are usually gradual (Merrill & Verbrugge, 1999). Although everyone experiences some physical change due to aging in the middle adulthood years, the rates of aging vary considerably from one individual to another. Genetic makeup and lifestyle factors play important roles in whether and when chronic disease will appear. (In chapter 4, "Health," we will explore these diseases.)

Physical Appearance   Middle-aged individuals lose height, and many gain weight. Adults lose about a half inch of height per decade beginning in their forties (Memmler & others, 1995). On the average, body fat accounted for about 10 percent of body weight in adolescence; it makes up 20 percent or more in middle age.

Noticeable signs of aging usually are apparent by the forties or fifties. The skin begins to wrinkle and sag because of a loss of fat and collagen in underlying tissues. Small, localized areas of pigmentation in the skin produce aging spots, especially in areas that are exposed to sunlight, such as the hands and face. The hair thins and grays due to a lower replacement rate and a decline in melanin production. Fingernails and toenails develop ridges and become thicker and more brittle.

American culture exalts youth, so many individuals whose hair is graying, whose skin is wrinkling, whose bodies are sagging, and whose teeth are yellowing strive to make themselves look younger. Undergoing cosmetic surgery, dyeing hair, purchasing wigs, enrolling in weight reduction programs, participating in exercise regimens, and taking heavy doses of vitamins are common practices among middle-aged Americans. One study found that middle-aged women focus more attention on facial attractiveness than do older or younger women (Nowak, 1977). In this same study, middle-aged women were more likely than middle-aged men to perceive the signs of aging as diminishing their physical attractiveness. In our culture, some aspects of aging in middle adulthood are considered attractive in men but not in women. For instance, facial wrinkles and gray hair might be taken to symbolize strength and maturity in men but might be perceived as unattractive in women.

Strength, Joints, and Bones   Muscle strength decreases noticeably by the mid forties, especially in the back and legs. It is estimated that about 10 to 15 percent of maximum strength is lost from age 35 to 60. The cushions for the movement of bones (such as tendons and ligaments) become less efficient in the middle adulthood years, a time when many individuals experience joint stiffness and more difficulty in movement.

Maximum bone density occurs by the mid to late thirties. From this point on, there is a progressive loss of bone. The rate of bone loss begins slowly but accelerates in the fifties (Burke & others, 2003). Women experience about twice the rate of bone loss as men. By the end of midlife, bones break more easily and heal more slowly.

Cardiovascular System and Lungs   The level of cholesterol in the blood increases through the adult years. By age 60, cholesterol begins to accumulate on the artery walls, which are also thickening. The result: Arteries are more likely to become clogged. This increases the pressure on the arterial walls, which in turn pushes the heart to work harder to pump blood, thus making a stroke or heart attack more likely.

Blood pressure, too, usually rises in the forties and fifties (Siegler & others, 1999). At menopause, a woman's blood pressure rises sharply and usually remains above that of a man through life's later years.

There is little change in lung capacity through most of middle adulthood. However, at about the age of 55, the proteins in lung tissue become less elastic. This change, combined with a gradual stiffening of the chest wall, decreases the lungs' capacity to shuttle oxygen from the air people breathe to the blood in their veins.

For smokers, however, the picture is different and bleaker. As shown in figure 3.5, the lung capacity of individuals who are smokers drops precipitously in middle age. However, if the individuals quit smoking their lung capacity improves, although not to the level of individuals who have never smoked (Williams, 1995).

Sexuality   **Climacteric** is a term that is used to describe the midlife transition in which fertility declines. **Menopause** is the time in middle age, usually in the late forties or early fifties, when a woman's menstrual periods cease. The average age at which women have their last period is 52. A small percentage of women—10 percent—go through menopause before 40. Just as puberty has been coming earlier, menopause has been coming later (Birren, 2002). Specific causes of the later incidence of menopause have not been documented, but improved nutrition and lower incidence of infectious diseases may be the reasons.

Menopause involves a dramatic decline in the production of estrogen by the ovaries. This decline may produce "hot flashes," nausea, fatigue, and rapid heartbeat, for example. Cross-cultural studies reveal wide variations in the menopause experience. For example, "hot flashes" are uncommon in Mayan women (Beyene, 1986). Asian women report fewer hot flashes than women in Western societies (Payer, 1991). It is difficult to determine whether these cross-cultural variations are due to genetic, dietary, reproductive, or cultural factors.

Menopause is not the negative experience for most women that it was once thought to be. However, the loss of fertility is an important marker for women.

Do men go through anything like the menopause that women experience? That is, is there a male menopause? During middle adulthood, most men do not lose their capacity to father children, although there usually is a modest decline in their sexual hormone level and activity (Sommner, 2001). Testosterone production begins to decline about 1 percent a year during middle adulthood, which can reduce sexual drive. Sperm count usually shows a slow decline, but men do not lose their fertility. We will have more to say about the climacteric and the sexual attitudes and behaviors of middle-aged men in chapter 12, "Gender and Sexuality."

Late Adulthood

Late adulthood brings an increased risk of physical disability, but there is considerable variability in rates of decline in functioning (Birren, 1996). What factors are involved in the successful maintenance of functional abilities? One analysis involved the MacArthur Research Network on Successful Aging Study, a three-site longitudinal study of successful aging in women and men aged 70 to 79 years of age. In this study, physical performance (such as walking efficiency, maintaining balance, and repeatedly standing up and sitting down) did decline with age, but there was considerable individual variation (Seeman & others, 1995). The physical performance of older adults in poor health from low-income backgrounds was inferior to that of their higher-income, healthy counterparts. A majority of the older adults

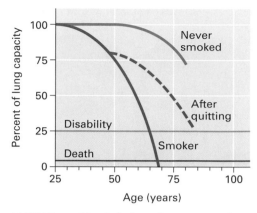

FIGURE 3.5 The Relation of Lung Capacity to Age and Cigarette Smoking

Lung capacity shows little change through middle age for individuals who have not smoked. However, smoking is linked with reduced lung capacity in middle-aged and older adults. When individuals stop smoking, their lung capacity becomes greater than those who continue to smoke, but not as great as the lung capacity of individuals who have never smoked.

climacteric The midlife transition in which fertility declines.

menopause The time in middle age, usually in the late forties or early fifties, when a woman's menstrual periods cease.

Percentage of total weight

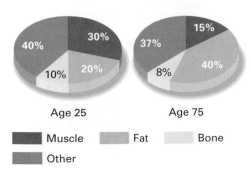

Age 25   Age 75

■ Muscle   ■ Fat   □ Bone

■ Other

FIGURE 3.6 Changes in Body Composition of Bone, Muscle, and Fat from 25 to 75 Years of Age

Notice the decrease in bone and muscle and the increase in fat from 25 to 75 years of age.

maintained their physical performance over a 3-year period in their seventies, and some even improved their performance during this time.

Physical Appearance   The changes in physical appearance that take place in middle adulthood become more pronounced in late adulthood. Most noticeable are facial wrinkles and age spots.

We also get shorter when we get older. From 30 to 50 years of age, men lose about a half inch in height, then might lose another three-fourths inch from 50 to 70 years of age. The height loss for women can be as much as 2 inches from 25 to 75 years of age (Hoyer & Roodin, 2003).

Our weight usually drops after we reach 60 years of age. This likely occurs because we lose muscle, which also gives our bodies a more "sagging" look. Figure 3.6 shows the decline in percentage of muscle and bone from age 25 to age 75, and the corresponding increase in the percentage of fat. The good news is that exercise and weight lifting can help slow the decrease in muscle mass and improve the older adult's body appearance.

Circulatory System   Significant changes also take place in the circulatory system of older adults. Lifestyle plays a key role in these changes. Blood pressure can rise with age because of illness, obesity, anxiety, stiffening of blood vessels, or lack of exercise. The longer any of these factors persist, the worse the individual's blood pressure gets (Rowe & Kahn, 1998).

In the past, a 60-year-old with a blood pressure reading of 160/90 and above would have been told, "For your age, that is normal." Now medication, exercise, or a healthier diet might be prescribed to lower blood pressure. Most experts on aging recommend that consistent blood pressures at 160/90 and above should be treated to reduce the risk of heart attack, stroke, or kidney disease (Lakatta, 1992).

Review and Reflect: Learning Goal 1

1 Discuss major changes in the body through the life span

REVIEW

- What are cephalocaudal and proximodistal patterns?
- How do height and weight change in infancy and childhood?
- What changes characterize puberty?
- What physical changes occur in early adulthood?
- How do people develop physically during middle adulthood?
- What is the nature of physical changes in late adulthood?

REFLECT

- Did you experience puberty early, late, or on time? How do you think this affected your social relationships and development?

2 THE BRAIN

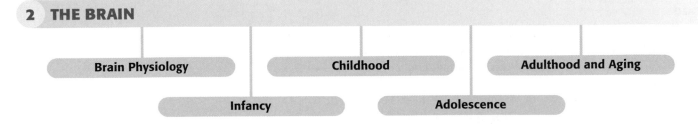

Brain Physiology   Childhood   Adulthood and Aging

Infancy   Adolescence

Until recently little was known for certain about how the brain changes as we grow and age. Today, dramatic progress is being made in understanding these changes. The study of age-related changes in the brain truly is one of the most exciting frontiers in science.

In every change of the body we have described so far, the brain is involved in some way. Structures of the brain help to regulate not only behavior but also metabolism, blood pressure, the release of hormones, and other aspects of the body's physiology. As the rest of the body is changing, what is happening in the brain?

Not long ago, scientists thought that our genes determined how our brains were "wired" and that unlike most cells, the cells in the brain responsible for processing information stopped dividing at some point early in childhood. Whatever brain your heredity dealt you, you were essentially stuck with it. This view, however, turned out to be wrong. Instead, principles of the life-span perspective discussed in chapter 1 apply to the brain. For example, it changes throughout life, in both positive and negative ways. It has "plasticity," and its development depends on context. What you do and how you live can change the development of your brain.

The old view of the brain in part reflected the fact that scientists did not have the technology that could detect and map sensitive changes in the brain as it develops. The creation of sophisticated brain-scanning techniques has allowed better detection of these changes. Before exploring these changes, let's examine some key structures of the brain and how they function.

Brain Physiology

The brain includes a number of major structures. The key components of these structures are **neurons,** which are nerve cells that handle information processing.

Structure and Function   Looked at from above, the brain has two halves, or *hemispheres* (see figure 3.7). The top portion of the brain, farthest from the spinal cord, is known as the *forebrain.* Its outer layer of cells, the *cerebral cortex,* covers it like a cap. The cerebral cortex is responsible for about 80 percent of the brain's volume and is critical in perception, thinking, language, and other important functions.

Each hemisphere of the cortex has four major areas, called *lobes.* Although the lobes usually work together, each has a somewhat different primary function (see figure 3.8):

- *Frontal lobes* are involved in voluntary movement, thinking, personality, and intentionality or purpose.
- *Occipital lobes* function in vision.
- *Temporal lobes* have an active role in hearing, language processing, and memory.
- *Parietal lobes* play important roles in registering spatial location, attention, and motor control.

Deeper in the brain, beneath the cortex, lie other key structures. These include the hypothalamus and the pituitary gland as well as the *amygdala,* which plays an important role in emotions, and the *hippocampus,* which is especially important in memory and emotion.

Neurons   How do these structures work? As we indicated, the *neurons* process information. Figure 3.9 shows some important parts of the neuron, including the *axon* and *dendrites.* Basically, an axon sends electrical signals away from the central part of the neuron. At tiny gaps called *synapses* the axon communicates with the dendrites of other neurons, which then pass the signals on. The communication in the synapse occurs through the release of chemical substances known as *neurotransmitters.*

As figure 3.9 shows, most axons are covered by a *myelin sheath,* which is a layer of fat cells. The sheath helps impulses travel faster along the axon, increasing the speed with which information travels from neuron to neuron.

Which neurons get which information? Clusters of neurons known as *neural circuits* work together to handle particular types of information. The brain is organized in many neural circuits. For example, one neural circuit is important in attention

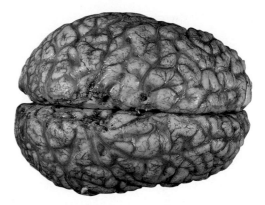

FIGURE 3.7 The Human Brain's Hemispheres

The two halves (hemispheres) of the human brain can be seen clearly in this photograph.

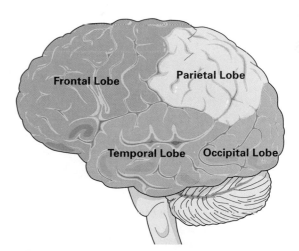

FIGURE 3.8 The Brain's Four Lobes

Shown here are the locations of the brain's four lobes: frontal, occipital, temporal, and parietal.

neuron Nerve cell that handles information processing.

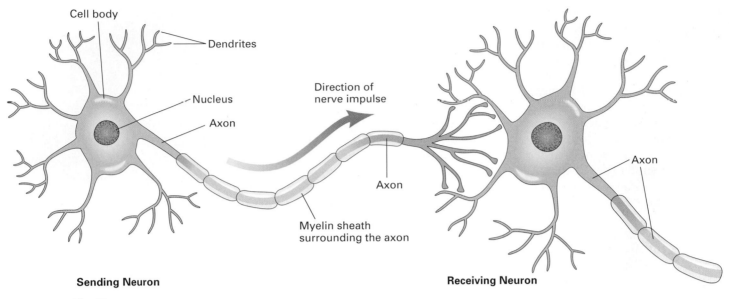

Cell body

Dendrites

Nucleus

Axon

Direction of nerve impulse

Axon

Myelin sheath surrounding the axon

Axon

Sending Neuron

Receiving Neuron

FIGURE 3.9 The Neuron

The drawing shows the parts of a neuron and the connection between one neuron and another. Note the cell body, branching of dendrites, and the axon with a myelin sheath.

Neural Processes

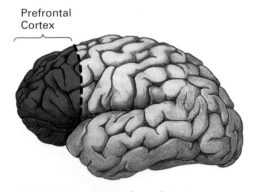

Prefrontal Cortex

FIGURE 3.10 The Prefrontal Cortex

This evolutionarily-advanced portion (shaded in purple) of the brain shows extensive development from 3 to 6 years of age and is believed to play important roles in attention and working memory.

lateralization Specialization of function in one hemisphere of the cerebral cortex.

and *working memory* (the type of memory that holds information for a brief time and is like a "mental workbench" as we perform a task) (Krimel & Goldman-Rakic, 2001). This neural circuit uses the neurotransmitter *dopamine* and lies in the *prefrontal cortex* (see figure 3.10).

To some extent, the type of information handled by neurons depends on whether they are in the left or right hemisphere of the cortex. Speech and grammar, for example, depend on activity in the left hemisphere in most people; humor and the use of metaphors depends on activity in the right hemisphere. This specialization of function in one hemisphere of the cerebral cortex or the other is called **lateralization.** However, most neuroscientists agree that complex functions such as reading or performing music involve both hemispheres. Labeling people as "left-brained" because they are logical thinkers and "right-brained" because they are creative thinkers does not correspond to the way the brain's hemispheres work. Complex thinking in normal people is the outcome of communication between both hemispheres of the brain (Knect & others, 2003).

The degree of lateralization may change as people develop through the human life span. Let's now explore a number of age-related changes in the brain.

Infancy

As an infant walks, talks, runs, shakes a rattle, smiles, and frowns, changes in its brain are occurring. Consider that the infant began life as a single cell and 9 months later was born with a brain and nervous system that contained approximately 100 billion nerve cells, or neurons. What determines how those neurons are connected to communicate with each other?

Early Experience and the Brain Until the middle of the twentieth century, scientists believed that the brain's development was determined almost exclusively by genetic factors. Researcher Mark Rosenzweig (1969) was curious about whether early experiences change the brain's development. He conducted a number of experiments with rats and other animals to investigate this possibility. Animals were randomly assigned to grow up in different environments. Animals in an enriched early environment lived in cages with stimulating features, such as wheels to rotate, steps

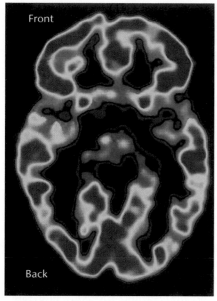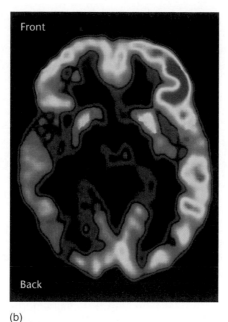

Front

Back

(a)

Front

Back

(b)

Development of the Brain

Early Experience and the Brain

FIGURE 3.11 Early Deprivation and Brain Activity

These two photographs are PET (positron-emission tomography) scans (which use radioactive tracers to image and analyze blood flow and metabolic activity in the body's organs) of the brains of *(a)* a normal child and *(b)* an institutionalized Romanian orphan who experienced substantial deprivation since birth. In PET scans, the highest to lowest brain activity is reflected in the colors of red, yellow, green, blue, and black, respectively. As can be seen, red and yellow show up to a much greater degree in the PET scan of the normal child than the deprived Romanian orphan.

to climb, levers to press, and toys to manipulate. In contrast, other animals had the early experience of growing up in standard cages or in barren, isolated conditions.

The results were stunning. The brains of the animals growing up in the enriched environment developed better than the brains of the animals reared in standard or isolated conditions. The brains of the "enriched" animals weighed more, had thicker layers, had more neuronal connections, and had higher levels of neurochemical activity. Similar findings occurred when older animals were reared in vastly different environments, although the results were not as strong as for the younger animals.

Children who grow up in a deprived environment may also have depressed brain activity (Cicchetti, 2001). As shown in figure 3.11, a child who grew up in the unresponsive and unstimulating environment of a Romanian orphanage showed considerably depressed brain activity compared with a normal child (Begley, 1997).

Are the effects of deprived environments irreversible? There is reason to think the answer is no. The brain demonstrates both flexibility and resilience. Consider 14-year-old Michael Rehbein. At age 7, he began to experience uncontrollable seizures—as many as 400 a day. Doctors said the only solution was to remove the left hemisphere of his brain where the seizures were occurring. Recovery was slow, but his right hemisphere began to reorganize and take over functions that normally occur in the brain's left hemisphere, including speech (see figure 3.12).

Neuroscientists believe that what wires the brain—or rewires it, in the case of Michael Rehbein—is repeated experience (Nash, 1997). Each time a baby tries to touch an attractive object or gazes intently at a face, tiny bursts of electricity shoot through the brain, knitting together neurons into circuits. The results are some of the behavioral milestones we discuss in this and other chapters.

In sum, the infant's brain is waiting for experiences to determine how connections are made (Greenough, 2000, 2001; Johnson, 2000, 2001). Before birth, it appears that genes mainly direct basic wiring patterns. Neurons grow and travel to distant places awaiting further instructions. After birth, the inflowing stream of

(a)

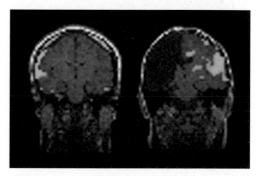

(b)

FIGURE 3.12 Plasticity in the Brain's Hemispheres

(a) Michael Rehbein at 14 years of age. *(b)* Michael's right hemisphere *(right)* has reorganized to take over the language functions normally carried out by corresponding areas in the left hemisphere of an intact brain *(left).* However, the right hemisphere is not as efficient as the left, and more areas of the brain are recruited to process speech.

sights, sounds, smells, touches, language, and eye contact help shape the brain's neural connections (Black, 2001).

The unfolding of developmental changes in the brain likely holds some important keys to understanding why individuals think and behave the way they do. But as the Research in Life-Span Development interlude indicates, studying the brains of babies is not an easy task.

Research in Life-Span Development
Studying Babies' Brains

Studying the brain's development in infancy is not easy. Even the latest brain-imaging technologies can't make out fine details—and they can't be used on babies. PET scans (in which the amount of specially treated glucose in various areas of the brain is measured and then analyzed by computer) pose a radiation risk, and infants wriggle too much for an MRI (in which a magnetic field is created around the body and radio waves are used to construct images of brain tissue and biochemical activity) (Marcus, Mulrine, & Wong, 1999).

However, one researcher who is making strides in finding out more about the brain's development in infancy is Charles Nelson (1999, 2000, 2001, 2003). In his research, he might attach up to 128 electrodes to a baby's scalp. He has found that even newborns produce distinctive brain waves that reveal they can distinguish their mother's voice from another woman's, even while they are asleep. Other research conducted by Nelson found that by 8 months of age babies can distinguish the picture of a wooden toy they were allowed to feel, but not see, from pictures of other toys. This achievement coincides with the development of neurons in the brain's hippocampus (an important structure in memory) that enable the infant to remember specific items and events.

In Charles Nelson's research, electrodes are attached to a baby's scalp to measure the brain's activity to determine its role in the development of an infant's memory. *Why is it so difficult to measure infants' brain activity?*

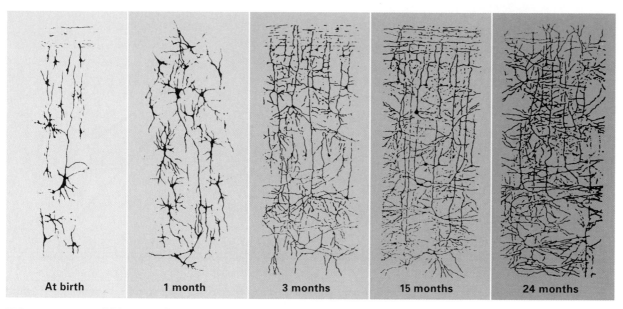

FIGURE 3.13 Dendritic Spreading

Note the increase in connections among neurons over the course of the first 2 years of life.

Changing Neurons   At birth, the newborn's brain is about 25 percent of its adult weight. By the second birthday, the brain is about 75 percent of its adult weight. Two key developments during these first two years involve the myelin sheath (the layer of fat cells that speeds up the electrical impulse along the axon) and connections between dendrites.

Myelination, the process of encasing axons with a myelin sheath, begins prenatally and continues after birth. Myelination for visual pathways occurs rapidly after birth, being completed in the first 6 months. Auditory myelination is not completed until 4 or 5 years of age. Some aspects of myelination continue even into adolescence.

Dramatic increases in dendrites and synapses (the tiny gaps between neurons across which neurotransmitters carry information) also characterize the development of the brain in the first two years of life (see figure 3.13). Nearly twice as many of these connections are made as will ever be used (Huttenlocher & others, 1991; Huttenlocher & Dabholkar, 1997). The connections that are used become strengthened and survive while the unused ones are replaced by other pathways or disappear (Casey, Durston, & Fossella, 2001; Muller & Nikonenko, 2003). That is, connections are "pruned." Figure 3.14 vividly illustrates the growth and later pruning of synapses in the visual, auditory, and prefrontal cortex areas of the brain (Huttenlocher & Dabholker, 1997).

As shown in figure 3.14, "blooming and pruning" vary considerably by brain region in humans (Thompson & Nelson, 2001). For example, the peak synaptic overproduction in the area concerned with vision occurs about the fourth postnatal month, followed by a gradual pruning until the middle to end of the preschool years (Huttenlocher & Dabholker, 1997). In areas of the brain involved in hearing and language, a similar, though somewhat later, course is detected. However, in the *prefrontal cortex* (the area of the brain where higher-level thinking and self-regulation occur), the peak of overproduction occurs at just after 3 years of age. Both heredity and environment are thought to influence synaptic overproduction and subsequent pruning.

Using the *electroencephalogram (EEG),* which measures the brain's electrical activity, researchers have found that a spurt in EEG activity occurs from about 1½ to 2 years of age (Fischer & Bidell, 1998). This spurt of brain activity is likely associated with an increase in conceptual and language development.

**Infancy and Toddlerhood: Infant
Brain Development**

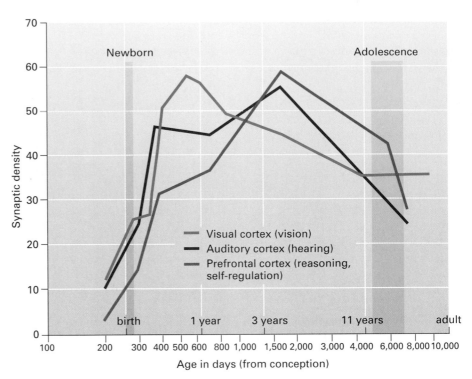

FIGURE 3.14 Synaptic Density in the Human Brain from Infancy to Adulthood

The graph shows the dramatic increase in synaptic density, and then pruning, in three regions of the brain: visual cortex, auditory cortex, and prefrontal cortex. Synaptic density is believed to be an important indication of the extent of connectivity between neurons.

Changing Structures At birth, the hemispheres already have started to specialize: Newborns show greater electrical activity in the left hemisphere than in the right hemisphere when they are listening to speech sounds (Hahn, 1987).

The areas of the brain do not mature uniformly. The frontal lobe is immature in the newborn. As neurons in the frontal lobe become myelinated and interconnected during the first year of life, infants develop an ability to regulate their physiological states (such as sleep) and gain more control over their reflexes. Cognitive skills that require deliberate thinking don't emerge until later (Bell & Fox, 1992).

At about two months of age, the motor control centers of the brain develop to the point at which infants can suddenly reach out and grab a nearby object. At about 4 months, the neural connections necessary for depth perception begin to form. And at about 12 months the brain's speech centers are poised to produce one of infancy's magical moments: when the infant utters its first word.

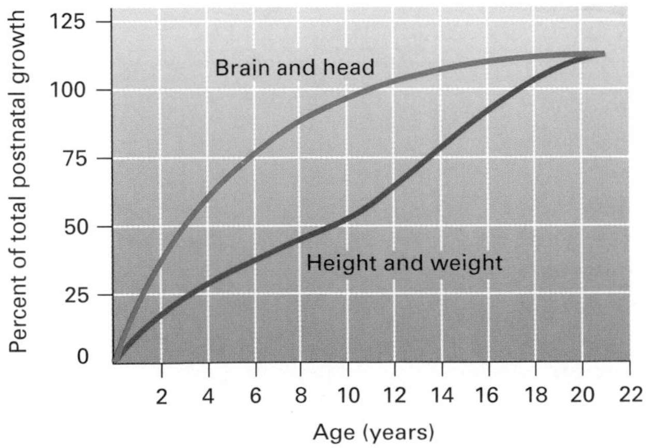

Childhood

The brain and other parts of the nervous system continue developing through childhood and adolescence (Byrnes, 2001, 2003). These changes enable children to plan their actions, to attend to stimuli more effectively, and to make considerable strides in language development.

During early childhood, the brain and head grow more rapidly than any other part of the body. Figure 3.15 shows how the growth curve for the head and brain advances more rapidly than the growth curve for height and weight. Some of the brain's increase in size is due to myelination and some is due to an increase in the number and size of dendrites, which continue to grow at least until adolescence.

FIGURE 3.15 Growth Curves for the Head and Brain and for Height and Weight

The more rapid growth of the brain and head can easily be seen. Height and weight advance more gradually over the first two decades of life.

Still, the brain in early childhood is not growing as rapidly as in infancy. However, the anatomical changes in the child's brain between the ages of 3 and 15 are dramatic. By repeatedly obtaining brain scans of the same children for up to four years, scientists have found that children's brains experience rapid, distinct bursts of growth (Thompson & others, 2000). The amount of brain material in some areas can nearly double in as little as one year, followed by a drastic loss of tissue as unneeded cells are purged and the brain continues to reorganize itself. The overall size of the brain does not increase dramatically from 3 to 15. What does dramatically change are local patterns within the brain (Thompson & others, 2000). From 3 to 6 years of age, the most rapid growth occurs in the frontal lobe areas involved in planning and organizing new actions and in maintaining attention to tasks. From age 6 through puberty, the most dramatic growth takes place in the temporal and parietal lobes, especially in areas that play major roles in language and spatial relations.

The development of the brain and opportunities to experience a widening world contribute to children's emerging cognitive abilities. Scientists are beginning to chart connections between children's cognitive development, their changing brain structures, and the transmission of information at the level of the neuron. For example, we mentioned earlier that a neural circuit for attention and working memory is located in the prefrontal cortex and uses the neurotransmitter dopamine. The concentration of dopamine in a child's brain typically increases considerably from 3 to 6 years of age (Diamond, 2001). Perhaps this change, as well as rapid growth in the frontal lobe during this same period, is tied to the child's growing cognitive skills. As advances in technology allow scientists to see inside the brain and observe its activity, we will likely understand more precisely how the brain functions in cognitive development (Gaillard & others, 2003).

Adolescence

As advances in technology take place, significant strides will also likely be made in charting developmental changes in the adolescent brain. What do we know now?

Spurts in EEG activity seem to occur at about 9, 12, 15, and 18 to 20 years of age. These may signal changes in cognitive development. During puberty, neural activity using the neurotransmitter dopamine increases while activity using the neurotransmitter serotonin decreases (Walker, 2002). What does this mean? Scientists do not know, but it has been speculated that the increased risk for some mental disorders, such as schizophrenia, during adolescence and early adulthood may be due to elevation of dopamine activity.

Also, as indicated in figure 3.14, the pruning of synapses continues into late adolescence (Huttenlocher & Dabholkar, 1997). Activity in the frontal lobe also continues to increase in adolescence (Casey, Giedd, & Thomas, 2000; Rubia & others, 2000). This increased activity is believed to contribute to advances in higher-level cognitive processes, such as abstract reasoning (Walker, 2002).

Other changes in the brain may hold clues to emotional development during adolescence. Whereas the frontal lobe is the focus of higher-level reasoning and thinking, the amygdala and hippocampus are highly involved in emotion (LeDoux, 2000, 2002). Both the amygdala and the hippocampus increase in volume during adolescence (Giedd & others, 1999; Sowell & Jernigan, 1998).

In one study, researchers used magnetic resonance imaging (MRI) to discover if the brain activity of adolescents (10- to 18-year-olds) differed from that of adults (20- to 40-years-olds) during the processing of emotional information (Baird & others, 1999). Participants viewed pictures of faces displaying fearful expressions while undergoing an MRI. When adolescents (especially the younger ones) processed emotional information, brain activity in the amygdala was more pronounced than in the frontal lobe, but the reverse occurred in adults. The researchers interpreted these findings to suggest that adolescents might be more likely to respond with "gut" reactions to emotional stimuli whereas adults might be more likely to respond with rational, reasoned responses. They also concluded that these changes are linked with growth in the frontal lobe of the brain from adolescence to adulthood. However, more research is needed to clarify these findings on possible developmental changes in brain activity during the processing of emotional stimuli.

Leading researcher Charles Nelson (2003) points out that while adolescents are capable of very strong emotions, their prefrontal cortex hasn't adequately developed to the point at which they can control these passions. It is as if their brains don't have the brakes to slow down their emotions.

Adulthood and Aging

Changes in the brain continue during adulthood. Most of the research on the brains of adults, however, has focused on the aging brain of older adults. What are some of the general findings about the aging brain? How much plasticity and adaptiveness does it retain?

Late Adulthood: Greenough's Aging Brain Experiments

The Shrinking, Slowing Brain   On average, the brain loses 5 to 10 percent of its weight between the ages of 20 and 90. Brain volume also decreases. Scientists are not sure why these changes occur but believe these might result from the decrease in dendrites, damage to the myelin sheath that covers axons, or simply the death of brain cells.

Some areas shrink more than others. The prefrontal cortex is one area that shrinks with aging, and recent research has found that this shrinkage is linked with a decrease in working memory in older adults (O'Connor & Kaplan, 2003; Salat, Kaye, & Janowski, 2002).

A general slowing of function in the brain and spinal cord begins in middle adulthood and accelerates in late adulthood (Birren, 2002). Both physical coordination and intellectual performance are affected. For example, after age 70, many adults no longer show a knee jerk, and by age 90 most reflexes are much slower. The slowing of the brain can impair the performance of older adults on intelligence tests, especially timed tests (Birren, Woods, & Williams, 1980).

Changes in the supply of neurotransmitters also characterize the aging brain. Among the neurotransmitters that have been studied in the aging process are acetylcholine, dopamine, and GABA.

- Some researchers believe that a small reduction in acetylcholine may be responsible for the decline of memory associated with normal functioning and that a major reduction in acetylcholine causes the severe memory loss associated with Alzheimer's disease (Small & Fodero, 2002).
- Normal age-related reductions in dopamine may cause problems in planning and carrying out motor activities. Age-related diseases characterized by a loss of motor control, such as Parkinson's disease, are linked with a severe reduction in the production of dopamine (Kaasinen & Rinne, 2002; Piccini, Pavese, & Brooks, 2003).
- GABA (gamma aminobutyric acid) helps to control the preciseness of the signal carried from one neuron to the next. Its production decreases with aging (Mhatre, Fernandez, & Ticku, 1991). One recent study found that injecting GABA in the brains of aging monkeys helped them to focus their vision and thinking by silencing interfering static from other neurons in their brains (Leventhal & others, 2003).

If the brain were a computer, this description of the aging brain might lead you to think that it could not do much of anything. However, unlike a computer, the brain has a remarkable ability to adapt. Even in late adulthood, the brain loses only a portion of its ability to function.

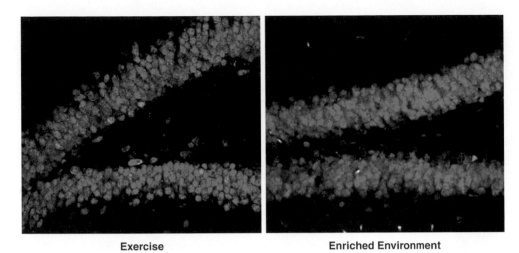

Exercise   Enriched Environment

FIGURE 3.16 Generating New Nerve Cells in Adult Mice

Researchers have found that exercise (running) and an enriched environment (a larger cage and many toys) can cause brain cells to divide and form new brain cells (Kempermann, van Praag, & Gage, 2000). Cells were labeled with a chemical marker that becomes integrated into the DNA of dividing cells (red). Four weeks later, they were also labeled to mark neurons (nerve cells). As shown here, both the running mice and the mice in an enriched environment had many cells that were still dividing (red) and others that had differentiated into new nerve cells (orange).

The Adapting Brain As the adult brain ages, it adapts in several ways. First, humans can grow new brain cells throughout their lives (Gould & others, 1999; Nelson, 2003; Nottebohm, 2002). The extent to which we do so, however, may depend in part on environmental stimulation (Churchill & others, 2002; Fabel & others, 2003; Prickaerts & others, 2004; Zitnik & Martin, 2002). Figure 3.16 shows the results of one study in which adult mice that ran and adult mice that were placed in an enriched environment generated new brain cells.

A second type of adaptation was demonstrated in a study that compared the brains of adults at various ages (Coleman, 1986). From the forties through the seventies, the growth of dendrites increased. However, in people in their nineties, dendritic growth no longer occurred. Thus, dendritic growth might compensate for the possible loss of neurons through the seventies but not in the nineties. Lack of dendritic growth in older adults could be due to a lack of environmental stimulation and activity.

Stanley Rapaport (1994), chief of the neurosciences laboratory at the National Institute on Aging, demonstrated another way in which the aging brain can adapt. He compared the brains of younger and older people engaged in the same tasks. The older brains had rewired themselves to compensate for losses. If one neuron was not up to the job, neighboring neurons helped to pick up the slack. Rapaport concluded that as brains age, they can shift responsibilities for a given task from one region to another.

Another way the brain adapts as people grow older is that myelination connecting the prefrontal cortex to the limbic system increases in the forties and fifties (Fischer & Pruyne, 2003). This type of myelination likely increases the integration of the emotional responses of the limbic system with the reasoning skills of the prefrontal cortex. This integration of cognition and emotion likely facilitates reflection, which characterizes many middle-aged adults.

Changes in lateralization may provide another type of adaptation in aging adults. Recall that *lateralization* is the specialization of function in one hemisphere of the brain or the other. Using neuroimaging techniques, researchers recently found that brain activity in the prefrontal cortex is lateralized less in older adults than in younger adults when they are engaging in cognitive tasks (Cabeza, 2002; Dixit & others, 2000). For example, figure 3.17 shows that when

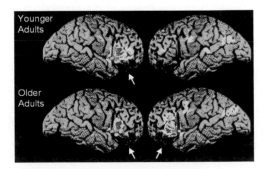

FIGURE 3.17 The Decrease in Brain Lateralization in Older Adults

Younger adults primarily used the right prefrontal region of the brain (top left photo) during a recall memory task, while older adults used both the left and right prefrontal regions (bottom two photos).

FIGURE 3.18 The Brains of the Mankato Nuns

Top: Sister Marcella Zachman *(left)* finally stopped teaching at age 97. Now, at 99, she helps ailing nuns exercise their brains by quizzing them on vocabulary or playing a card game called Skip-Bo, at which she deliberately loses. Sister Mary Esther Boor *(right),* also 99 years of age, is a former teacher who stays alert by doing puzzles and volunteering to work the front desk. *Bottom:* A technician holds the brain of a deceased Mankato nun. The nuns donate their brains for research that explores the effects of stimulation on brain growth.

younger adults are given the task of recognizing words they have previously seen, they process the information primarily in the right hemisphere; older adults are more likely to use both hemispheres (Madden & others, 1999).

The decrease in lateralization in older adults might play a compensatory role in the aging brain. That is, using both hemispheres may improve the cognitive functioning of older adults. Support for this view comes from another study in which older adults who used both brain hemispheres were faster at completing a working memory task than their counterparts who primarily used only one hemisphere (Reuter-Lorenz & others, 2000). However, the decrease in lateralization may be a mere by-product of aging; it may reflect an age-related decline in the brain's ability to specialize functions. In this view, during childhood the brain becomes increasingly differentiated in terms of its functions; as adults become older, this process may reverse. Support for the dedifferentiation view is found in the higher intercorrelations of performance on cognitive tasks in older adults than in younger adults (Baltes & Lindenberger, 1997).

Preventing and Treating Brain Diseases One intriguing ongoing investigation of the brain involves nearly 700 nuns, many of whom are from a convent in Mankato, Minnesota (Danner, Snowdon, & Frieden, 2001; Kemper & others, 2001; Mortimer, Snowdon, & Markesbery, 2003; Riley, Snowdon, & Markesbery, 2002; Snowdon, 1995, 1997, 2002, 2003) (see figure 3.18). The nuns are the largest group of brain donors in the world. Examination of the nuns' donated brains, as well as others, has led neuroscientists to believe that the brain has a remarkable capacity to change and grow, even in old age. The Sisters of Notre Dame in Mankato lead an intellectually challenging life, and brain researchers believe this contributes to their quality of life as older adults and possibly to their longevity. Findings from the nuns study so far include:

- Positive emotions early in adulthood were linked to their longevity (Danner, Snowdon, & Friesen, 2001). Handwritten autobiographies from 180 nuns, composed when they were 22 years of age, were scored for emotional content. The nuns whose early writings had higher scores for positive emotional content were more likely to still be alive at 75 to 95 years of age than their counterparts whose early writings were characterized by negative emotional content.
- Sisters who had taught for most of their lives showed more moderate declines in intellectual skills than those who had spent most of their lives in service-based tasks, which supports the notion that stimulating the brain with intellectual activity keeps neurons healthy and alive (Snowdon, 2002).
- Sisters with high levels of folic acid showed little evidence of Alzheimer's-like damage to their brain after death (Snowdon & others, 2000). Possibly the substantial folic acid in the blood means less chance of having a stroke and possibly helps to protect the brain from decline.

This and other research provides hope that scientists will discover ways to tap into the brain's capacity to adapt in order to prevent and treat brain diseases. For example, scientists might learn more effective ways to help older adults recover from strokes. Even when areas of the brain are permanently damaged by stroke, new message routes can be created to get around the blockage or to resume the function of that area.

Review and Reflect: Learning Goal 2

2 Describe how the brain changes through the life span

REVIEW

- What are the major areas of the brain, and how does it process information?
- How does the brain change in infancy?
- What characterizes the development of the brain in childhood?
- How can the changes in the brain during adolescence be summarized?
- What is the aging brain like?

REFLECT

- If you could interview the Mankato nuns, what would you want to ask them?

3 SLEEP

```
                Infancy              Adolescence

                      Childhood            Adulthood and Aging
```

Sleep restores, replenishes, and rebuilds our brains and bodies. Some neuroscientists believe that sleep gives neurons that are used while we are awake a chance to shut down and repair themselves (National Institute of Neurological Disorders and Stroke, 2003). How do our sleeping patterns change across the life span?

Infancy

How much do infants sleep? Are there any special problems that can develop regarding infants' sleep?

The Sleep/Wake Cycle   When we were infants, sleep consumed more of our time than it does now (Ingersoll & Thoman, 1999). Newborns sleep 16 to 17 hours a day, although some sleep more and others less—the range is from a low of about 10 hours to a high of about 21 hours, although the longest period of sleep is not always between 11 P.M. and 7 A.M. Although total sleep remains somewhat consistent for young infants, their sleep during the day does not always follow a rhythmic pattern. An infant might change from sleeping several long bouts of 7 or 8 hours to three or four shorter sessions only several hours in duration. By about 1 month of age, most infants have begun to sleep longer at night, and by about 4 months of age, they usually have moved closer to adultlike sleep patterns, spending their longest span of sleep at night and their longest span of waking during the day (Daws, 2000).

There are cultural variations in infant sleeping patterns. For example, in the Kipsigis culture in the African country of Kenya, infants sleep with their mothers at night and are permitted to nurse on demand (Super & Harkness, 1997). During the day they are strapped to their mothers' backs, accompanying them on their daily rounds of chores and social activities. As a result, Kipsigis infants do not sleep through the night until much later than American infants. During their first 8 months, Kipsigis infants rarely sleep longer than 3 hours at a stretch, even at night. This contrasts with many American infants, who generally begin to sleep up to 8 hours a night by 8 months of age.

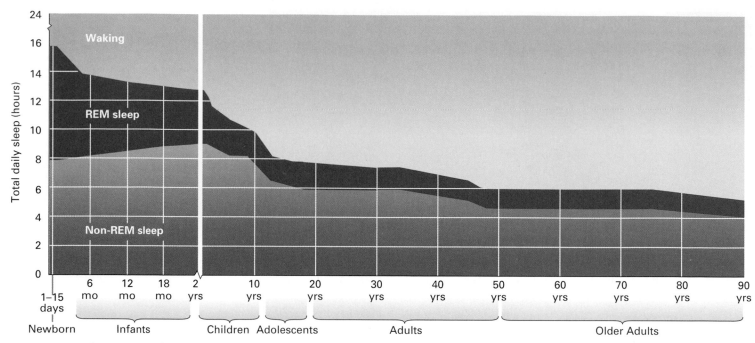

FIGURE 3.19 Sleep Across the Human Life Span

REM Sleep Researchers are intrigued by the various forms of infant sleep. They are especially interested in *REM (rapid eye movement) sleep*. Most adults spend about one-fifth of their night in REM sleep, and REM sleep usually appears about 1 hour after non-REM sleep. We know that for adults dreaming mainly occurs during REM sleep (Hobson, 2000). Figure 3.19 illustrates the average number of total hours spent in sleep and the amount of time spent in REM sleep across the human life span.

About one-half of an infant's sleep is REM sleep—more than at any other time in life—and infants often begin their sleep cycle with REM sleep rather than non-REM sleep. By the time infants reach 3 months of age, the percentage of time they spend in REM sleep falls to about 40 percent, and REM sleep no longer begins their sleep cycle. The large amount of REM sleep might provide infants with added self-stimulation, because they spend less time awake than older children do. REM sleep also might promote the brain's development in infancy.

Shared Sleeping Some child experts believe there are benefits to shared sleeping (as when an infant sleeps in the same bed with its mother). It can promote breastfeeding, and it can enable the mother to respond more quickly to the baby's cries and detect breathing pauses in the baby that might be dangerous (McKenna, Moski, & Richard, 1997). However, shared sleeping remains a controversial issue, with some experts recommending it, others arguing against it. The American Academy of Pediatrics Task Force on Infant Positioning and SIDS (1997; Cohen, 2000) recommends against shared sleeping. They argue that in some instances bed sharing might lead to sudden infant death syndrome (SIDS), as could be the case if a sleeping mother rolls over on her baby. One recent study found that bed sharing was significantly linked with the incidence of SIDS (Unger & others, 2003).

SIDS

sudden infant death syndrome (SIDS) A condition that occurs when an infant stops breathing, usually during the night, and suddenly dies without an apparent cause.

SIDS **Sudden infant death syndrome (SIDS)** occurs when infants stop breathing, usually during the night, and suddenly die without an apparent cause. SIDS remains the highest cause of infant death in the United States with nearly 3,000 infant deaths due to SIDS. Risk of SIDS is highest at 4 to 6 weeks of age (National Center for Health Statistics, 2002).

Researchers have found that SIDS decreases when infants sleep on their backs rather than on their stomachs or sides (Hunt & others, 2003; Li & others, 2003; Smith & Hattersley, 2000). Among the reasons given for prone sleeping being a high risk factor for SIDS are that it impairs arousal from sleep and restricts the ability to swallow effectively (Horne & others, 2002; Kahn & others, 2002). Other risk factors for SIDS include the following (American Academy of Pediatrics Task Force on Infant Sleep Position and SIDS, 2000; Goldwater, 2001):

- Low birth weight infants are 5 to 10 times more likely to die of SIDS than are their normal-weight counterparts (Horne & others, 2002; Sowter & others, 1999).
- Infants whose siblings have died of SIDS are two to four times as likely to die of it (Lenoir, Mallet, & Calenda, 2000).
- Six percent of infants with *sleep apnea,* a temporary cessation of breathing in which the airway is completely blocked, usually 10 seconds or longer, die of SIDS (McNamara & Sullivan, 2000).
- African American and Eskimo infants are two to six times as likely as all others to die of SIDS (Hauck & others, 2002; Unger & others, 2003). One recent study found that prone sleeping was linked to SIDS in African American infants, suggesting the importance of educational outreach to African American families regarding the importance of placing infants on their backs while sleeping (Hauck & others, 2002).
- SIDS is more common in lower socioeconomic groups (Mitchell & others, 2000).
- SIDS is more common in infants who are exposed to cigarette smoke (Chan-Yeung & Dimich-Ward, 2003; Pollack & Frohna, 2001; Tutka, Wielosz, & Zatonski, 2003).
- Soft bedding is not recommended (Flick & others, 2001).

Childhood

Most young children sleep through the night and have one daytime nap. Sometimes, though, it is difficult to get young children to go to sleep because they drag out their bedtime routine. Helping the child slow down before bedtime often helps reduce their resistance to going to bed. Reading the child a story, playing quietly with the child in the bath, or letting the child sit on the caregiver's lap while listening to music are quieting activities.

One recent study examined the sleep patterns of children in second, fourth, and sixth grade (Sadeh, Raviv, & Gruber, 2000). The children were evaluated with activity monitors, and the children and their parents completed sleep questionnaires and daily reports. Sixth-grade children went to sleep at night about 1 hour later (just after 10:30 P.M. versus just after 9:30 P.M.) and reported more daytime sleepiness than the second-grade children. Girls spent more time in sleep than boys. Also, family stress was linked with poor sleep, such as nightly wakings, in children.

Among the sleep problems that children can develop are nightmares and night terrors (Gaylor, Anders, & Goodlin Jones, 1999). *Nightmares* are frightening dreams that awaken the sleeper, more often toward the morning than just after the child has gone to bed at night. Almost every child has occasional nightmares, but persistent nightmares might indicate that the child is feeling too much stress during waking hours.

Night terrors are characterized by sudden arousal from sleep and an intense fear, usually accompanied by a number of physiological reactions, such as rapid heart rate and breathing, loud screams, heavy perspiration, and physical movement. In most instances, the child has little or no memory of what happened during the night terror. Night terrors are less common than nightmares and occur more often in deep sleep than do nightmares. Many children who experience night terrors return to sleep rather quickly. These sleep disruptions are not believed to reflect any emotional problems in children.

What are some developmental changes in sleep patterns during adolescence? How might this influence alertness at school?

Adolescence

There has recently been a surge of interest in adolescent sleep patterns (Pollak & Bright, 2003). This interest focuses on the belief that many adolescents are not getting enough sleep, that there are physiological underpinnings to the desire of adolescents, especially older ones, to stay up later at night and sleep longer in the morning, and that these findings have implications for understanding when adolescents learn most effectively in school (Dahl & Lewin, 2002).

Mary Carskadon and her colleagues (Carskadon & others, 1998; Carskadon & others, 1999; Carskdadon, Acebo, & Seifer, 2001) have conducted a number of research studies on adolescent sleep patterns. They found that adolescents sleep an average of 9 hours and 25 minutes when given the opportunity to sleep as long as they like. Most adolescents get considerably less sleep than this, especially during the week. This creates a *sleep debt,* which adolescents often try to make up on the weekend. The researchers also found that older adolescents are often more sleepy during the day than younger adolescents. They concluded that this was not because of factors such as academic work and social pressures. Rather, their research suggests that adolescents' biological clocks undergo a hormonal phase shift as they get older. This pushes the time of wakefulness to an hour later than when they were young adolescents. The researchers found that this shift was caused by a delay in the nightly presence of the hormone *melatonin,* which is produced by the brain's pineal gland in preparation for the body to sleep. Melatonin is secreted at about 9:30 P.M. in younger adolescents but is produced approximately an hour later in older adolescents, which delays the onset of sleep.

Carskadon determined that early school starting times can result in grogginess and lack of attention in class and poor performance on tests. Based on this research, schools in Edina, Minnesota, made the decision to start classes at 8:30 A.M. instead of 7:25 A.M. Discipline problems and the number of students who report an illness or depression have dropped. Test scores in Edina have improved for high school students, but not for middle school students, which supports Carskadon's idea that older adolescents are more affected by earlier school start times than younger adolescents are.

Adulthood and Aging

It is not only many adolescents who are getting inadequate sleep. Many adults don't get enough either. The average American adult gets just under 7 hours of sleep a night (National Commission on Sleep Disorders, 1993). How much sleep do adults need to function optimally the next day? An increasing number of experts believe that 8 hours of sleep or more per night are necessary to be at your best the next day (Maas, 1998; Dement & Vaughn, 2000). These experts argue that many adults have become sleep deprived. Work pressures, school pressures, family obligations, and social obligations often lead to long hours of wakefulness and irregular sleep/wake schedules.

Some aspects of sleep become more problematic in middle age (Floyd, 2002). The total number of hours slept usually remains the same as in early adulthood, but beginning in the forties, wakeful periods are more frequent and there is less of the deepest type of sleep (Floyd, 2003). The amount of time spent lying awake in bed at night begins to increase in middle age, which can produce a feeling of being less rested in the mornings (Katchadourian, 1987).

Beginning in middle adulthood and continuing through late adulthood, the timing of sleep also changes (Abbott, 2003; Huang & others, 2002; Humm, 2001). Many older adults go to bed earlier at night and wake up earlier in the morning. Many older adults also take a nap in the afternoon (Hoffman, 2003).

Insomnia increases in late adulthood, with almost one-half of older adults reporting that they experience some degree of insomnia (Avidan, 2002; Bachman,

1992). Here are some strategies to help older adults sleep better at night (Maas, 1998): Avoid caffeine. Avoid over-the-counter sleep remedies. Stay physically active during the day. Stay mentally active. Limit naps.

Review and Reflect: Learning Goal 3

3 **Summarize how sleep patterns change as people develop**

REVIEW

• How can sleep be characterized in infancy?
• What changes occur in sleep during childhood?
• How does adolescence affect sleep?
• What changes in sleep take place during adulthood and aging?

REFLECT

• How much sleep do you get on the average each night? Do you get enough sleep to function optimally the next day? Explain.

---

*S*leep that knits up the ravelled sleave of care . . . Balm of hurt minds, nature's second course Chief nourisher in life's feast.

—WILLIAM SHAKESPEARE
English Playwright, 17th Century

---

4   LONGEVITY

Life Expectancy and Life Span

The Young-Old, the Old-Old, and the Oldest-Old

Biological Theories of Aging

In his eighties, American Nobel Prize winner Linus Pauling argued that vitamin C slows the aging process. Aging researcher Roy Walford fasts two days a week because he believes undernutrition (not malnutrition) also slows the aging process. What do we really know about longevity? How long do most people live, and what distinguishes people who live a very long time? What is life likely to be like for those who live to a very ripe old age, and why do we age in the first place?

Life Expectancy and Life Span

We are no longer a youthful society. As more individuals live to older ages, the proportion of individuals at different ages has become increasingly similar. Indeed, the concept of a period called "late adulthood" is a recent one—until the twentieth century most individuals died before they reached 65.

Recall from chapter 1 that a much greater percentage of persons live to an older age P. 9. However, the life span has remained virtually unchanged since the beginning of recorded history. **Life span** is the upper boundary of life, the maximum number of years an individual can live. The maximum life span of human beings is approximately 120 years of age. Life expectancy is the number of years that will probably be lived by the average person born in a particular year. Improvements in medicine, nutrition, exercise, and lifestyle have increased our life expectancy an average of 30 additional years since 1900.

The average life expectancy of individuals born today in the United States is 77 years (80 for women, 74 for men). There is still a gap (7 years) between the life expectancy of non-Latino Whites (77) and African Americans (70) in the United States, but the gap is narrowing. In 1970 the gap was 8 years (National Center for Health Statistics, 2001).

How does the United States fare in life expectancy, compared with other countries around the world? We do considerably better than some, a little worse than some others. For example, Australia has the highest life expectancy at birth today

life span The upper boundary of life, the maximum number of years an individual can live. The maximum life span of human beings is about 120 years of age.

Frenchwoman Jeanne Louise Calment recently died at age 122. It has been claimed that some people have lived longer, but scientists say the maximum human life span is about 120 years.

To me old age is always fifteen years older than I am.
—BERNARD BARUCH
American Statesman, 20th Century

(80 years). Differences in life expectancies across countries are due to such factors as health conditions and medical care throughout the life span.

Is there a sex difference in how long people live? Today, the life expectancy for females is 80 years of age, while for males it is 74. Beginning at age 25, females outnumber males; this gap widens during the remainder of the adult years. By the time adults are 75 years of age, more than 61 percent of the population is female; for those 85 and over, the figure is almost 70 percent female. Why? Social factors such as health attitudes, habits, lifestyles, and occupation are probably important. For example, men are more likely than women to die from the leading causes of death in the United States, such as cancer of the respiratory system, motor vehicle accidents, suicide, cirrhosis of the liver, emphysema, and coronary heart disease. These causes of death are associated with lifestyle. For example, the sex difference in deaths due to lung cancer and emphysema occurs because men are heavier smokers than women.

If life expectancy is influenced strongly by stress in the workplace, the sex difference should be narrowing, because so many more women have entered the labor force. Yet in the last 40 years, just the opposite has occurred: the gap is widening. Perhaps working outside the home brings women benefits such as improved self-esteem and work satisfaction that outweigh whatever additional stress might come from being in the workforce.

The sex difference in longevity is also influenced by biological factors. In virtually all species, females outlive males. Women have more resistance to infections and degenerative diseases. For example, the female's estrogen production helps to protect her from arteriosclerosis (hardening of the arteries). And the additional X chromosome that women carry in comparison to men may be associated with the production of more antibodies to fight off disease.

Centenarians Remember that the life expectancy figures we have cited indicate the years that a person born in a particular year could expect to live. How much longer can 65-year-olds in the United States expect to live? Today, they can expect to live an average of 18 more years (20 for females, 16 for males) (National Center for Health Statistics, 2001). What about yourself? What is the likelihood that you will live to be 100? To evaluate this possibility, see figure 3.20.

In 1980, there were only 15,000 centenarians (individuals 100 years and older) in the United States. In 2000, there were 77,000, and it is projected that this number will be 834,000 in 2050. Many people expect that "the older you get, the sicker you get." However, researchers are finding that is not true for some centenarians. One recent study found that 32 percent of the male and 15 percent of more than 400 centenarians had never been diagnosed with common age-associated diseases such as heart disease, cancer, and stroke (Evert & others, 2003).

Genes play an important role in surviving to an extreme old age (Martin & Buckwalter, 2001; Perls, Lauerman, & Silver, 1999). But there are also other factors at work. A disproportionate number of centenarians are women who have never been married. In the ongoing New England Centenarian study, a majority of the centenarians have had difficult lives, such as surviving the Holocaust and living in extreme poverty as an immigrant to the United States (Perls, Lauerman, & Silver, 1999). What has contributed to their survival is their ability to cope successfully with stress.

In one study, 1,200 centenarians were interviewed about many aspects of their lives (Segerberg, 1982). Through their eyes, life looks like this:

- Mary Butler said that finding something to laugh about every day is important. She believes a good laugh is better than a dose of medicine anytime.
- Elza Wynn concluded that he has been able to live so long because he made up his mind to live. He was thinking about dying when he was 77, but decided he would wait a while.

This survey gives you a rough guide for predicting your longevity. The basic life expectancy for males is age 73, and for females is 80. Write down your basic life expectancy. If you are in your fifties or sixties, you should add ten years to the basic figure because you have already proved yourself to be a durable individual. If you are over age sixty and active, you can even add another two years.

Life Expectancy

Decide how each item applies to you and add or subtract the appropriate number of years from your basic life expectancy.

1. Family history
___ Add five years if two or more of your grandparents lived to 80 or beyond.
___ Subtract four years if any parent, grandparent, sister, or brother died of a heart attack or stroke before 50.
___ Subtract two years if anyone died from these diseases before 60.
___ Subtract three years for each case of diabetes, thyroid disorder, breast cancer, cancer of the digestive system, asthma, or chronic bronchitis among parents or grandparents.

2. Marital status
___ If you are married, add four years.
___ If you are over twenty-five and not married, subtract one year for every unmarried decade.

3. Economic status
___ Add two years if your family income is over $60,000 per year.
___ Subtract three years if you have been poor for the greater part of your life.

4. Physique
___ Subtract one year for every ten pounds you are overweight.
___ For each inch your girth measurement exceeds your chest measurement deduct two years.
___ Add three years if you are over forty and not overweight.

5. Exercise
___ Add three years if you exercise regularly and moderately (jogging three times a week).
___ Add five years if you exercise regularly and vigorously (long-distance running three times a week).
___ Subtract three years if your job is sedentary.
___ Add three years if your job is active.

6. Alcohol
___ Add two years if you are a light drinker (one to three drinks a day).
___ Subtract five to ten years if you are a heavy drinker (more than four drinks per day).
___ Subtract one year if you are a teetotaler.

7. Smoking
___ Subtract eight years if you smoke two or more packs of cigarettes per day.
___ Subtract two years if you smoke one to two packs per day.
___ Subtract two years if you smoke less than one pack.
___ Subtract two years if your regularly smoke a pipe or cigars.

8. Disposition
___ Add two years if you are a reasoned, practical person.
___ Subtract two years if you are aggressive, intense, and competitive.
___ Add one to five years if you are basically happy and content with life.
___ Subtract one to five years if you are often unhappy, worried, and often feel guilty.

9. Education
___ Subtract two years if you have less than a high school education.
___ Add one year if you attended four years of school beyond high school.
___ Add three years if you attended five or more years beyond high school.

10. Environment
___ Add four years if you have lived most of your life in a rural environment.
      Subtract two years if you have lived most of your life in an urban environment.

11. Sleep
___ Subtract five years if you sleep more than nine hours a day.

12. Temperature
___ Add two years if your home's thermostat is set at no more than 68° F.

13. Health care
___ Add three years if you have regular medical checkups and regular dental care.
___ Subtract two years if you are frequently ill.
___ **Your Life Expectancy Total**

FIGURE 3.20 Can You Live to Be 100?

- Anna Marie Robertson ("Grandma") Moses commented that she felt older at 16 than at any time since then. Even when she became very old, she said that she never thought about being old.
- Billy Red Fox believes that being active and not worrying are important keys to living to be 100. At 95, he switched jobs to become a public relations representative. Even at 100, Billy travels 11 months of the year making public appearances and talking to civic clubs.
- Duran Baez remarried at 50 and went on to have fifteen more children. At 100 years of age, he was asked, "Do you have any ambition you have not yet realized?" Duran replied, "No." He said that he had lived the kind of life he expected, raising a good family, never doing any harm to anybody, staying honest all his life, and finding out that people really do like him. Duran says, "That's enough for the time being."

Aging Links
New England
Centenarian Study

What chance do you have of living to be 100? According to the items in figure 3.20, among the most important factors in longevity are heredity and family history, health (weight, diet, smoking, and exercise), education, personality, and lifestyle. To further examine the factors that are involved in living to a very old age, read the following Contexts in Life-Span Development interlude.

Contexts of Life-Span Development
Living Longer in Okinawa

Individuals live longer on the Japanese island of Okinawa in the East China Sea than anywhere else in the world. In Okinawa, there are 34.7 centenarians for every 100,000 inhabitants, the highest ratio in the world. In comparison, the United States has about 10 centenarians for every 100,000 residents. The life expectancy in Okinawa is 81.2 years (86 for women, 78 for men), also highest in the world.

What is responsible for such longevity in Okinawa? Some possible explanations include (Willcox, Willcox, & Suzuki, 2002):

- *Diet.* Okinawans eat very healthy food, heavy on grains, fish, and vegetables, light on meat, eggs, and dairy products. The risk of dying of cancer is far lower among Okinawans than among Japanese and Americans (see figure 3.21). About 100,000 Okinawans moved to Brazil and quickly adopted the eating regimen of their new home, one heavy on red meat. The result: The life expectancy of the Brazilian Okinawans is now 17 years lower than Okinawa's 81 years!
- *Low-Stress Lifestyle.* The easygoing lifestyle in Okinawa more closely resembles that of a laid-back South Sea island than that of the high-stress world on the Japanese mainland.
- *Caring Community.* Okinawans look out for each other and do not isolate or ignore their older adults. If older adults need help, they don't hesitate to ask a neighbor. Such support and caring is likely responsible for Okinawa having the

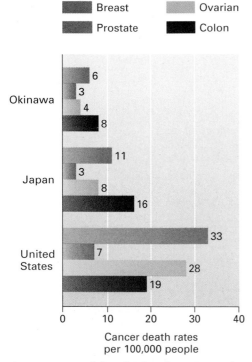

FIGURE 3.21 Risks of Dying from Cancer in Okinawa, Japan, and the United States

The risk of dying from different forms of cancer is lower in Okinawa than in the United States and Japan (Willcox, Willcox, & Suzuki, 2002). Okinawans eat lots of tofu and soy products, which are rich in flavonoids (believed to lower the risk of breast and prostate cancer). They also consume large amounts of fish, especially tuna, mackerel, and salmon, which reduce the risk of breast cancer.

Toshiko Taira, 80, weaves cloth from the fibers of banana trees on a loom in Okinawa. She, like many Okinawans, believes that such sense of purpose helps people to live longer.

lowest suicide rate among older women in East Asia, an area noted for its high suicide rate among older women.

- *Activity.* Many older adults in Okinawa are active, engaging in such activities as taking walks and working in their gardens. Many older Okinawans also continue working at their jobs.
- *Spirituality.* Many older adults in Okinawa find a sense of purpose in spiritual matters. Prayer is commonplace and believed to ease the mind of stress and problems.

The Young-Old, the Old-Old, and the Oldest-Old

Do you want to live to be 100, or 90? As we discussed in chapter 1, these ages are part of late adulthood, which begins in the sixties and extends to approximately 120 years of age. Some developmentalists distinguish between the *young-old* or *old age* (65 to 74 years of age) and the *old-old* or *old age* (75 years and older) (Charness & Bosman, 1992). Yet others distinguish the *oldest-old* (85 years and older) from younger older adults (Pearlin, 1994).

Many experts on aging prefer to talk about such categories as the young-old, old-old, and oldest-old in terms of *function* rather than age. Remember from chapter 1 that we described age not only in terms of chronological age, but also in terms of biological age, psychological age, and social age ◀║║ **P. 15.** In terms of *functional age*—the person's actual ability to function—an 85-year-old might well be more biologically and psychologically fit than a 65-year-old.

Still, there are some significant differences between those still in their sixties or seventies and the 85-and-older age group (Baltes & Smith, 2003; Suzman & others, 1992).

Paul Baltes (Baltes, 2000; Baltes & Smith, 2003) argues that the oldest-old (85 and over) face a number of problems, including sizeable losses in cognitive potential and ability to learn; an increase in chronic stress; a sizeable prevalence of physical and mental disabilities; high levels of frailty; increased loneliness; and the difficulty of dying at older ages with dignity. Baltes contrasts the problems of the oldest-old with the increase in successful aging of older adults in their sixties and seventies: a substantial potential for fitness, physically and cognitively; high levels of emotional well-being; and effective strategies for mastering the gains and losses of old age.

The oldest-old today are mostly female. The majority of these women are widowed and live alone, if not institutionalized; the majority are hospitalized at some time in the last years of life; and the majority die alone in a hospital or institution (Baltes & Smith, 2003). Their needs, capacities, and resources are often different from those of older adults in their sixties and seventies.

But even the oldest-old are a heterogeneous, diversified group (Roberts, Dunkle, & Haug, 1994). Many of the oldest-old have outlived their social and financial supports and depend on society for their daily living, but this is not true of all. A significant number have cognitive impairments, but many do not. Almost one-fourth of the oldest-old are institutionalized, and many report some limitation of activity or difficulties in caring for themselves. However, more than three-fourths are not institutionalized. The majority of older adults aged 80 and over continue to live in the community. More than one-third of older adults 80 and over who live in the community report that their health is excellent or good; 40 percent say that they have no activity limitation (Suzman & others, 1992).

Biological Theories of Aging

Even if we stay remarkably healthy through our adult lives, we begin to age at some point. Life-span experts even argue that biological aging begins at birth (Schaie, 1997). What are the biological explanations of aging? Intriguing explanations of why

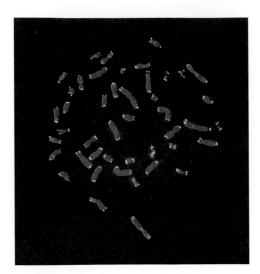

FIGURE 3.22 Telomeres and Aging
The above photograph shows telomeres lighting up the tips of chromosomes.

Telomeres Research
Theories of Biological Aging

we age are provided by four biological theories: cellular clock theory, free-radical theory, mitochondrial theory, and hormonal stress theory.

Cellular Clock Theory   **Cellular clock theory** is Leonard Hayflick's (1977) theory that cells can divide a maximum of about 75 to 80 times and that, as we age, our cells become less capable of dividing. Hayflick found that cells extracted from older adults, in their fifties to seventies, divided fewer than 75 to 80 times. Based on the ways cells divide, Hayflick places the upper limit of the human life-span potential at about 120 to 125 years of age.

In the last decade, scientists have tried to fill in a gap in cellular clock theory (Cherif & others, 2003; Hultdin & others, 2003; Meeker & De Marzo, 2004). Hayflick did not know why cells die. Recently, scientists have found that the answer might lie at the tips of chromosomes (Shay & Wright, 1999, 2000, 2002).

Telomeres are DNA sequences that cap chromosomes. Each time a cell divides, the telomeres become shorter and shorter (see figure 3.22). After about 70 or 80 replications, the telomeres are dramatically reduced, and the cell no longer can reproduce. Researchers also have found that injecting the enzyme *telomerase* into human cells grown in the laboratory can substantially extend the life of the cells beyond the approximately 70 to 80 normal cell divisions (Shay & Wright, 1999). In one study, age-related telomere erosion was linked with an impaired ability to recover from stress and an increased rate of cancer (Rudolf & others, 1999).

Free-Radical Theory   A second microbiological theory of aging is **free-radical theory,** which states that people age because when their cells metabolize energy, they generate waste that includes unstable oxygen molecules known as *free radicals*. These molecules ricochet around the cells, damaging DNA and other cellular structures (Berr, 2002; Hasnis & Rezick, 2003). This damage can lead to a range of disorders, including cancer and arthritis (Hauck & Bartke, 2001; Mahakunakorn & others, 2004; Troen, 2003). Overeating is linked with an increase in free radicals, and researchers recently have found that *undernutriton*—a diet restricted in calories although adequate in proteins, vitamins, and minerals—reduces the damage created by free radicals (Yu, Lim, & Sugano, 2002). We will further discuss possible links between undernutrition and aging in chapter 4.

Mitochondrial Theory   There is increasing interest in the role that *mitochondria*—tiny cellular bodies that supply energy for function, growth, and repair—might play in aging (Bossy-Wetzel & others, 2003; Dillin & others, 2002). The **mitochondrial theory** of aging states that aging is due to the decay of mitochondria. It appears that the decay of mitochondria is primarily due to oxidative damage and loss of critical micronutrients supplied by the cell (Mattson & Liu, 2002; Pierson, 2003).

Among the by-products of mitochondrial energy production are the free radicals we just described. According to the mitochondrial theory, the damage caused by free radicals initiates a self-perpetuating cycle in which oxidative damage impairs mitochondrial function, which results in the generation of even greater amounts of free radicals. The result is that over time, the affected mitochondria become so inefficient that they cannot generate enough energy to meet cellular needs (Kang & Hamanski, 2003).

In support of mitochondrial theory, researchers have found that the mitochondria of older adults are less efficient than those of younger adults (Wanagat, Lopez, & Aiken, 2001). Defects in mitochondria are linked with cardiovascular disease, neurodegenerative diseases such as dementia, and decline in liver functioning (Anantharaju, Feller, & Chedid, 2002; Floyd & Hensley, 2002). However, it is not known whether these defects in mitochondria cause aging or are merely accompaniments of the aging process (DiMauro & others, 2002).

cellular clock theory Leonard Hayflick's theory that the maximum number of times that human cells can divide is about 75 to 80. As we age, our cells have less capability to divide.

free-radical theory A microbiological theory of aging that states that people age when their cells metabolize energy, they generate waste that includes unstable oxygen molecules known as free radicals that damage DNA and other cellular structures.

mitochondrial theory The theory that aging is caused by the decay of mitochondria, tiny cellular bodies that supply energy for function, growth, and repair.

Hormonal Stress Theory   The three theories of aging that we have discussed so far—cellular clock, free radical, and mitochondrial—attempt to explain aging at the cellular level. In contrast, **hormonal stress theory** argues that aging in the body's hormonal system can lower resistance to stress and increase the likelihood of disease (Finch & Seeman, 1999).

According to this theory, the *hypothalamic-pituitary-adrenal (HPA) axis* plays a key role in aging. It is one of the body's main systems for responding to external stress and maintaining the body's internal equilibrium. (Note that *hypothalamic* refers to the hypothalamus of the brain, *pituitary* to the body's master gland located near the hypothalamus, and *adrenal* to the two adrenal glands that sit just above the kidneys.) As people age, the hormones stimulated by stress remain elevated longer than when people were younger (Parsons, 2003). These prolonged, elevated levels of stress-related hormones are associated with increased risks for many diseases, including cardiovascular disease, cancer, diabetes, and hypertension.

Which of these biological theories best explains aging? That question has not been answered yet. It might turn out that all of these biological processes are involved in aging.

> **hormonal stress theory** The theory that aging in the body's hormonal system can lower resistance to stress and increase the likelihood of disease.

Late Adulthood: Hayflick Limit
Late Adulthood: Progeria

Review and Reflect: Learning Goal 4

4 Explain longevity and the biological aspects of aging

REVIEW

- What is the difference between life span and life expectancy? What sex differences exist in longevity? What characterizes centenarians?
- How can the differences between the young-old, old-old, and oldest-old be summarized?
- What are the four main biological theories of aging?

REFLECT

- If we could increase the maximum human life span, would this be beneficial? If so, to whom?

In this chapter, we have studied many aspects of physical development across the life span. We touched on some health issues, such as the role of early maturation in the problems of adolescent females, the relation of lung capacity to cigarette smoking, sudden infant death syndrome (SIDS), the inadequate sleep that characterizes many individuals, and the likely connection between nutritional habits and risk of dying from cancer in Okinawa and the United States. In the next chapter, we will focus exclusively on the health of individuals at different points in the life span, including further exploration of nutrition and eating behavior.

Reach Your Learning Goals

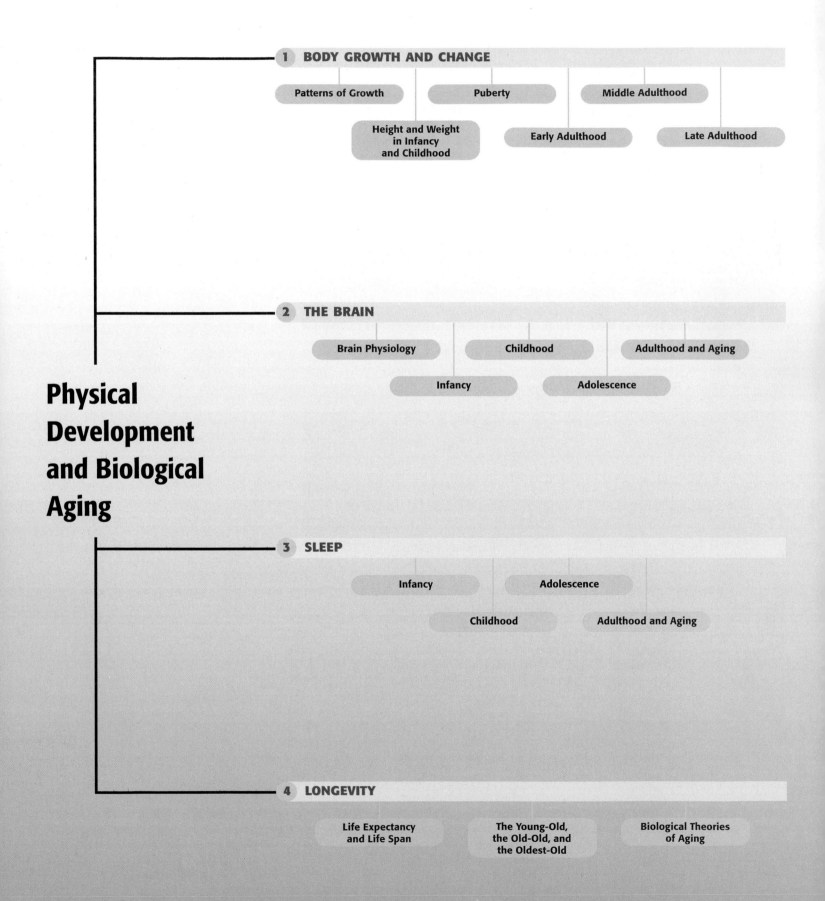

Physical Development and Biological Aging

1 **BODY GROWTH AND CHANGE**

- Patterns of Growth
- Height and Weight in Infancy and Childhood
- Puberty
- Early Adulthood
- Middle Adulthood
- Late Adulthood

2 **THE BRAIN**

- Brain Physiology
- Infancy
- Childhood
- Adolescence
- Adulthood and Aging

3 **SLEEP**

- Infancy
- Childhood
- Adolescence
- Adulthood and Aging

4 **LONGEVITY**

- Life Expectancy and Life Span
- The Young-Old, the Old-Old, and the Oldest-Old
- Biological Theories of Aging

Summary

1 Discuss major changes in the body through the life span

- Human growth follows cephalocaudal (fastest growth occurs at the top) and proximodistal patterns (growth starts at the center of the body and moves toward the extremities).
- Height and weight increase rapidly in infancy and then take a slower course during childhood.
- Puberty is a period of rapid maturation involving hormonal and body changes that occur primarily in early adolescence. Pubertal growth occurs on the average about two years sooner for girls than for boys. Early maturation favors boys during adolescence, but in adulthood late-maturing boys have a more successful identity. Early-maturing girls are vulnerable to a number of problems.
- In early adulthood, height remains rather constant. Many individuals reach their peak of muscle tone and strength in their twenties; however, these can decline in the thirties.
- In middle adulthood, changes often are gradual. Visible signs of aging, such as the wrinkling of skin, appear in the forties and fifties. Middle-aged individuals also tend to lose height and gain weight. Strength, joints, and bones show declines in middle age. The cardiovascular system declines in functioning, and at about 55 years of age lung capacity begins to decline, more so in smokers than nonsmokers. The climacteric is a term used to describe the midlife transition in which fertility declines. Menopause is the time in middle age, usually in the later forties or early fifties, when a woman's menstrual periods cease.
- In late adulthood, outwardly noticeable physical changes become more prominent, individuals get shorter, and weight often decreases because of muscle loss. The circulatory system declines further.

2 Describe how the brain changes through the life span

- The brain has two hemispheres, each of which has four lobes (frontal, occipital, temporal, and parietal). Throughout the brain, nerve cells called neurons process information. Communication among neurons involves the axon, dendrites, synapses, neurotransmitters, and the myelin sheath. Clusters of neurons, known as neural circuits, work together to handle particular types of information.
- Researchers have found that early experience influences the brain's development. Myelination begins prenatally and continues after birth. In infancy, one of the most impressive changes in the brain is the enormous increase in dendrites and synapses. These connections between neurons are overproduced and pruned. Specialization of functioning does occur in the brain's hemispheres, as in language, but for the most part both hemispheres are at work in most complex functions.
- During early childhood, the brain and head grow more rapidly than any other part of the body. Recently, researchers have found that changes in brain patterns occur from 3 to 15 years of age, often involving spurts of brain activity.
- Spurts in EEG activity seem to occur at about 9, 12, 15, and 18 to 20 years of age. The pruning of synapses continues into late adolescence. Activity in the frontal lobe continues to increase in adolescence. The amygdala and hippocampus, which are involved in emotion, continue to increase in volume during adolescence.
- On average, the brain loses 5 to 10 percent of its weight between the ages of 20 and 90. Brain volume also decreases with aging. Shrinking occurs in some areas of the brain, such as the prefrontal cortex, more than in other areas. A general slowing of function characterizes the central nervous system beginning in middle adulthood and increasing in late adulthood. A decline in the production of some neurotransmitters is related to aging. Adults can grow new brain cells, and growth of dendrites can occur in older adults. The brain has the capacity to virtually rewire itself to compensate for loss in older adults. One way the brain adapts is the increased myelination of the pathways that connect the limbic system and the prefrontal cortex during the forties and fifties, which likely is linked with increased reflection in middle-aged adults. Another change is a decrease in brain lateralization in older adults.

3 Summarize how sleep patterns change as people develop

- By about 4 months, most infants have sleep patterns similar to those of adults. REM sleep occurs more in infancy than in childhood and adulthood. Sleeping arrangements vary across cultures.
- Most young children sleep through the night and have one daytime nap.
- Many adolescents stay up later than when they were children.
- An increasing concern is that adults do not get enough sleep. In middle age, wakeful periods may interrupt nightly sleep more often. Many older adults go to bed earlier and wake up earlier the next morning. Almost one-half of older adults report having some insomnia.

4 Explain longevity and the biological aspects of aging

- Life expectancy is the number of years an individual is expected to live when he or she is born. Life span is the maximum number of years any member of a species has been known to live. On the average, females live about six years longer than males do. The sex difference is likely due to biological and social factors. An increasing number of individuals live to be 100 or older.
- In terms of chronological age, the young-old have been described as being 65 to 74 years of age, the old-old as 75 years and older, and the oldest-old as 85 years and older. Many experts on aging prefer to describe the young-old,

old-old, and oldest-old in terms of functional age rather than chronological age. This view accounts for the fact that some 85-year-olds are more biologically and psychologically fit than some 65-year-olds. However, those 85 and older face significant problems while those in their sixties and seventies are experiencing an increase in successful aging.

- Four biological theories are cellular clock theory, free-radical theory, mitochondrial theory, and hormonal stress theory. Hayflick proposed the cellular clock theory, which states that cells can divide a maximum of about 75 to 80 times and that as we age, our cells become less capable of dividing. Telomeres are likely involved in explaining why cells lose their capacity to divide. According to free-radical theory, people age because unstable oxygen molecules called free radicals are produced in the cells. According to mitochondrial theory, aging is due to the decay of mitochondria, tiny cellular bodies that supply energy. According to hormonal stress theory, aging in the body's hormonal system can lower resilience to stress and increase the likelihood of disease.

Key Terms

Key People

E-Learning Tools

Connect to **www.mhhe.com/santrockldt2** to research the answers and complete the following exercises. In addition, you'll find a number of other resources and valuable study tools for chapter 3, "Physical Development and Biological Aging," on the Student CD-ROM that came with this book.

Taking It to the Net

1. June's only child, 12-year-old Suzanne, is starting to show all of the signs of puberty. What behavioral changes in Suzanne should June expect as a result of puberty?

2. Tanika, a grandmother from Tanzania, is visiting her American-born granddaughter, Nicola, who just gave birth. As Tanika prepares to wrap the baby in blankets according to the Tanzanian custom of swaddling, the hospital nurse urges her to stop, telling her that swaddling a baby may cause it to die from SIDS. Is the nurse correct?

3. Doris is pregnant for the first time at the age of 45. She half-jokingly bemoans to her husband, John, that she won't live long enough to know her grandchildren. "Of course you will," John said. "I just read that women who have children after the age of 40 live longer than mothers who had children in their twenties or thirties." What's the evidence and explanation for this?

Connect to **www.mhhe.com/santrockldt2** to research the answers and complete these exercises.

Self-Assessment

To evaluate yourself in regard to your sleep, complete this self-assessment:

- *Do You Get Enough Sleep?*

Health and Well-Being, Parenting, and Education

Build your decision-making skills by trying your hand at the health and well-being, parenting, and education "Scenarios."

Health

Chapter Outline

Learning Goals

1 Describe the bio-psycho-social health model and developmental changes in health

2 Characterize developmental changes in nutrition and eating behavior

3 Summarize the roles of exercise in child and adult health

4 Evaluate substance use in adolescence and adulthood

Life is more than just living. It is important to live healthily. In this chapter, we will explore many aspects of health, including illness and disease, nutrition and eating behavior, exercise, and substance use and addiction.

1 HEALTH, ILLNESS, AND DISEASE

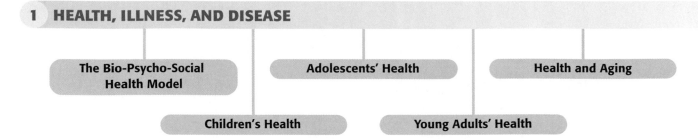

Changing patterns of illness have fueled an interest in searching not just for biological causes of health, illness, and disease, but for psychological and sociocultural causes as well. First, we will describe the bio-psycho-social model of health and then turn to developmental changes in health through the human life span.

The Bio-Psycho-Social Health Model

Asian physicians, around 2600 B.C., and later Greek physicians, around 500 B.C., recognized that good habits are essential for good health. They did not blame the gods for illness and think that magic would cure illness. They realized that people had control over their health. Today, we are returning to this ancient view that the ultimate responsibility for influencing health rests with individuals themselves (Baum, Revenson, & Singer, 2001; Marks, Sykes, & McKinley, 2003). Of course, this applies mainly to adults because children's health depends a great deal on the extent to which parents and the community provide adequate health care for them and model positive health attitudes and behavior.

Except in ancient Asia and Greece, throughout most of history physical illness has been viewed purely in biological terms—that is, as involving only bodily factors, not mental factors. The contemporary view is that body *and* mind can exert important influences on health. Indeed, the **bio-psycho-social health model,** which states that health is best understood in terms of a combination of biological, psychological, and social factors, is currently endorsed by health psychologists (Stowell & others, 2003; Taylor, 2003).

Biological Factors A biological approach to health views the functioning of the individual's body as the cause of illness. Today, scientists who adopt a biological approach often focus on the brain and genetic factors as causes of health problems. For example, some people have a genetic predisposition for developing high cholesterol, which is a risk factor for cardiovascular disease. In the biological approach, drug therapy is frequently used to treat health problems. For example, if a person has high cholesterol, a cholesterol-lowering drug is typically prescribed.

Psychological Factors Among the psychological factors that have been proposed as causes of health problems are lack of self-control, emotional turmoil, and negative thinking. Here are some research findings that illustrate the importance of these psychological factors in cardiovascular disease:

- Individuals who develop coronary problems are more likely than other people to be outwardly hostile or to turn anger inward (Pickering, 2001). People can reduce their risk of coronary problems by learning to control their anger (Williams, 2001).
- Chronic emotional stress is linked with cardiovascular disease (O'Callahan, Andrews, & Krantz, 2003; Fogoros, 2001). Apparently, the surge in adrenaline

*N*othing can be changed until it is faced.

—JAMES BALDWIN
American Novelist, 20th Century

Middle Adulthood: Stress and Glucocorticoids

bio-psycho-social health model The approach in which health is viewed in terms of a combination of biological, psychological, and social factors.

caused by emotional stress causes the blood to clot more rapidly, and blood clotting is a key contributor to heart attacks.

- Positive thinking is linked to some aspects of health (Manne, 2003). In one study, older men and older women who expressed a positive outlook toward life were less likely to suffer heart attacks than those who expressed a negative outlook (Danner, Snowdon, & Friesen, 2001).

Social Factors Most health problems are universal, but the frequency and intensity of the problems vary across cultures. The variations are linked to social, economic, technological, and religious aspects of cultures (Tanaka-Matsumi, 2001; Whitfield & others, 2003). Social factors that influence health problems include socioeconomic status and poverty. For example, people living in poverty encounter more health problems, such as cardiovascular disease, and have less access to health-care professionals than their higher-income counterparts. Recent research has found that Chinese Americans and Vietnamese Americans wanted to discuss the use of non-Western medical practices with their providers but encountered considerable barriers (Ngo-Metzger & others, 2003).

Children's Health

Prevention and poverty are important factors in children's health.

Prevention To a pediatrician who stopped practicing medicine 50 years ago, a description of children's health and illness today might seem to be science fiction. The story of children's health in the past 50 years is a shift toward prevention and outpatient care (Melamed, Roth, & Fogel, 2001). In recent decades, vaccines have nearly eradicated disabling bacterial meningitis and prevented measles, rubella, mumps, and chicken pox. Although the dangers of many diseases for children have greatly diminished, it is still important for parents to keep their children on a timely immunization schedule. Many immunizations can be given to individuals of any age, but the recommended schedule begins in infancy (AAP, 2001). The recommended ages for various immunizations are shown in figure 4.1.

In addition to immunization, another important aspect of preventing health problems in children is to avoid accidents, which are the leading cause of death in children (Barakat, Kunin-Batson, & Kazak, 2003). Infants need close monitoring as they gain locomotor and manipulative skills, along with a strong curiosity to explore the environment (Karns, 2001). Falls are most common after 4 months of age, when infants have learned to roll over. Also, once locomotion begins, danger from poisoning is present almost everywhere in the infant's environment. There are more than 500 toxic substances in the typical home, and about one-third of infant poisonings occur in the kitchen.

The status of children's motor, cognitive, and socioemotional development makes their health-care needs unique (Bolen, Bland, & Sacks, 1999). For example, think about how the infant's and young child's motor skills are inadequate to ensure their personal safety while riding in an automobile. Adults must take preventive measures to restrain infants and young children in car seats. Young children also lack the cognitive skills, including reading ability, to discriminate between safe and unsafe household substances. And they may lack the impulse control to keep from running out into a busy street while chasing a ball or toy.

Caregivers play an important role in children's health. For example, one study found that if the mother smoked, her children were twice as likely to have respiratory

Members of the Masai tribe in Kenya, Africa, can stay on a treadmill for a long time because of their very active life. Heart disease is extremely low in the Masai tribe, which also can be attributed to their energetic lifestyle. *What are some ways that biological, psychological, and social factors might be involved in health and illness?*

Age	Immunization
2 months	Diphtheria Polio Influenza
4 months	Diphtheria Polio Influenza
6 months	Diphtheria Influenza
1 year	TB test
15 months	Measles Mumps Rubella Influenza
18 months	Diphtheria Polio
4 to 6 years	Diphtheria Polio
11 to 12 years	Measles Mumps Rubella
14 to 16 years	Tetanus-diphtheria

FIGURE 4.1 Recommended Immunization Schedule for Normal Infants and Children

ailments (Etzel, 1988). By driving at safe speeds, decreasing or eliminating drinking—especially before driving—and not smoking around children, caregivers enhance their children's health.

Poverty Of special concern in the United States is the poor health of many young children from low-income families. Approximately 16 percent of children in the United States live in poverty conditions (National Center for Health Statistics, 2002), a much higher rate than that in other industrialized nations. For example, Canada has a poverty rate of 9 percent and Sweden has a poverty rate of 2 percent. An estimated 7 percent of U.S. children have no usual source of health care. Approximately 11 million preschool children in the United States are malnourished. Their malnutrition places their health at risk. Many have poor resistance to diseases—including minor ones, such as colds, and major ones, such as influenza.

What is the best way to improve the health of children who live in poverty? Some experts argue that offering medical care is not enough. If you give an antibiotic to a child with a sore throat who then returns to a home where she will be cold and hungry, have you provided good health care? One approach to children's health aims to treat not only medical problems of the individual child but the conditions of the entire family. In fact, some programs seek to identify children who are at risk for problems and then try to alter the risk factors in an effort to prevent illness and disease. The Contexts of Life-Span Development interlude describes one program that takes this ambitious approach.

Contexts of Life-Span Development
A Healthy Start

The Hawaii Family Support/Healthy Start Program began in 1985 (Allen, Brown, & Finlay, 1992). It was designed by the Hawaii Family Stress Center in Honolulu, which already had been making home visits to improve family functioning and reduce child abuse for more than a decade. Participation is voluntary. Families of newborns are screened for family risk factors, including unstable housing, histories of substance abuse, depression, parents' abuse as a child, late or no prenatal care, fewer than 12 years of schooling, poverty, and unemployment. Healthy Start workers screen and interview new mothers in the hospital. They also screen families referred by physicians, nurses, and others. Because the demand for services outstrips available resources, only families with a substantial number of risk factors can participate.

Each new participating family receives a weekly visit from a family support worker. Each of the program's eight home visitors works with approximately 25 families at a time. The worker helps the family cope with any immediate crises, such as unemployment or substance abuse. The family also is linked directly with a pediatrician to ensure that the children receive regular health care. Infants are screened for developmental delays and are immunized on schedule. Pediatricians are notified when a child is enrolled in Healthy Start and when a family at risk stops participating.

The Family Support/Healthy Start Program recently hired a child development specialist to work with families of children with special needs. And, in some instances, the program's male family support worker visits a father to talk about his role in the

The Hawaii Family Support/Healthy Start Program provides overburdened families of newborns and young children many home-visitor services. This program has been very successful in reducing abuse and neglect in families. *What are some examples of the home-visitor services in the program?*

family. The support workers encourage parents to participate in group activities held each week at the program center located in a neighborhood shopping center.

Over time, parents are encouraged to assume more responsibility for their family's health and well-being. Families can participate in Healthy Start until the child is 5 and enters public school.

Adolescents' Health

How important is adolescence in the development of health habits? How much do adolescents use health services?

A Critical Juncture in Health   Adolescence is a critical juncture in the adoption of behaviors relevant to health (Phillips, 2003; Roth & Brooks-Gunn, 2000; Spear & Kulbock, 2001). Many of the factors linked to poor health habits and early death in the adult years begin during adolescence.

The early formation of healthy behavioral patterns, such as eating foods low in fat and cholesterol and engaging in regular exercise, not only has immediate health benefits, but also contributes to the delay or prevention of the major causes of premature disability and mortality in adulthood—heart disease, stroke, diabetes, and cancer (Jessor, Turbin, & Costa, 1998).

A recent comparison of adolescent health behavior in 28 countries found that U.S. adolescents exercised less than their counterparts in most other countries (World Health Organization, 2000). Just two-thirds of U.S. adolescents exercised at least twice a week, compared with 80 percent or more adolescents in Ireland, Austria, Germany, and the Slovak Republic. U.S. adolescents' eating choices were similar to those of adolescents in England. U.S. 11-year-olds were as likely as European 11-year-olds to smoke, but at age 15, U.S. adolescents were less likely to smoke.

Social contexts, including families, peers, and schools, influence adolescent health (Roth & Brooks-Gunn, 2000). Parents and older siblings can be important models of health-enhancing behaviors. In the National Longitudinal Study of Health, based on data collected from more than 12,000 seventh- through twelfth-graders, youth who did not eat dinner with a parent five or more days a week had

Adolescent Health

**Adolescent Health Attitudes
and Behavior**

**National Longitudinal Study
of Adolescent Health**

*I*dentifying adolescents'
unmet needs and setting goals
for health promotion are
important steps to take in
maximizing adolescent
development.

—SUSAN MILLSTEIN
*Contemporary Psychologist,
University of California–
San Francisco*

dramatically higher rates of smoking cigarettes, using marijuana, getting into fights, and initiating sexual activity (Council of Economic Advisors, 2000). Parental caring and monitoring often combine to produce less risk-taking in youth.

Peers also can influence adolescents' health. Adolescents who have a limited capacity to resist dares often engage in risk-taking at the urging of their peers. Peer pressure can instigate such health-compromising behaviors as cigarette smoking, substance abuse, early sexual activity, and violence (Bearman & Bruckner, 1999).

Because adolescents spend so much time in school, it is not surprising that what goes on there can influence their health behavior. Teachers, just like parents, can serve as important health role models. For example, one study found that adolescents smoked less when teachers were not allowed to smoke in front of students (Perry, Kelder, & Komro, 1993).

Health experts increasingly recognize that whether adolescents will develop a health problem or be healthy depends primarily on their own behavior. Improving adolescent health involves (1) reducing adolescents' health-compromising behaviors, such as drug abuse, violence, unprotected sexual intercourse, and dangerous driving; and (2) increasing health-enhancing behaviors, such as eating nutritiously, exercising, and wearing seat belts.

Health Services Adolescents have a greater number of acute health conditions than adults do, but they use private physician services at a lower rate than any other age group does (Edelman, 1996). And adolescents often underutilize other health-care systems as well (Millstein, 1993). Health services are especially unlikely to meet the health needs of younger adolescents, ethnic minority adolescents, and adolescents living in poverty. Among the chief barriers to better health services for adolescents are high cost, poor organization, and unavailability of health services, as well as lack of confidentiality of care. Also, few health-care providers receive any special training for working with adolescents. As a result, many feel unprepared to provide services such as contraceptive counseling and accurate evaluation of what constitutes abnormal behavior in adolescence (Irwin, 1993). Health-care providers might transmit to their adolescent patients their discomfort in discussing such topics as sexuality, which can lead to adolescents' unwillingness to discuss sensitive issues with them.

Young Adults' Health

Young adults have few chronic health problems, and they have fewer colds and respiratory problems than when they were children. Most college students know what it takes to prevent illness and promote health. In one study, college students' ranking of health-protective activities—nutrition, sleep, exercise, watching one's weight, and so on—virtually matched that of licensed nurses (Turk, Rudy, & Salovey, 1984).

Although most college students know what it takes to prevent illness and promote health, they don't fare very well when it comes to applying this information to themselves. In one study, college students reported that they probably would never have a heart attack or drinking problem, but that other college students would (Weinstein, 1984). The college students also said there was no relation between their risk of heart attack and how much they exercise, smoke, or eat meat or other high-cholesterol food such as eggs, even though they correctly recognized that factors such as family history influence risk. Many college students, it seems, have unrealistic, overly optimistic beliefs about their future health risks.

In early adulthood, few individuals stop to think about how their personal lifestyles will affect their health later in their adult lives. As young adults, many of us develop a pattern of not eating breakfast, not eating regular meals, and relying on snacks as our main food source during the day, eating excessively to the point where we exceed the normal weight for our age, smoking moderately or excessively, drinking moderately or excessively, failing to exercise, and getting by with only a few hours of sleep at night. These lifestyles are associated with poor health (Belloc & Breslow, 1972). In the Berkeley Longitudinal Study—in which individuals were evaluated over a period of 40 years—physical health at age 30 predicted life satisfaction at age 70, more so for men than for women (Mussen, Honzik, & Eichorn, 1982).

There are some hidden dangers in the peaks of performance and health in early adulthood. Young adults can draw on physical resources for a great deal of pleasure, often bouncing back easily from physical stress and abuse. However, this can lead them to push their bodies too far. The negative effects of abusing one's body might not show up in the first part of early adulthood, but they probably will surface later in early adulthood or in middle adulthood (Csikszentmihalyi & Rathunde, 1998).

When adults turn to the health-care system for help, women and men are likely to experience the system differently. We explore this topic in the Applications in Life-Span Development interlude.

Applications in Life-Span Development

Gender, Health, and the Health-Care System

Women and men experience health and the health-care system differently (Geller, Graf, & Dyson-Washington, 2003; Paludi, 2002; Pinn, 2003). Special concerns about women's health today focus on unintended and unwanted childbirth, abuse and violence, AIDS, the role of poverty in women's health, eating disorders, drug abuse, breast diseases, reproductive health, and the discrimination of the medical establishment against women.

During the 1960s and 1970s, the women's health movement in the United States worked to ensure that women would have more control over their health care. In consciousness-raising and self-help groups throughout the country, women educated themselves about their bodies, reproductive rights, nutrition, and health care. One possible outcome of the women's health movement is that recent research shows that female patients, especially young women, are more demanding in interactions with health-care professionals than male patients are (Foss & Sundby, 2003).

Despite a growing number of female physicians, medicine continues to be a male-dominated profession. All too often in this male-dominated world, women's physical complaints are devalued, interpreted as "emotional" rather than physical in origin, and dismissed as trivial. In one study, physicians described their men and women patients differently. The men were characterized as very direct, very logical, good decision makers, and rarely emotional. In contrast, the women were characterized as very excitable in minor crises, more easily influenced, less adventurous, less independent, very illogical, and even very sneaky (Broverman & others, 1972).

Gender bias has also affected medical research studies (Rabinowitz & Sechzur, 1994). Most medical research has been conducted with men, and frequently the results are generalized to women without apparent justification. For example, in a large-scale study involving 22,000 physicians that demonstrated the beneficial effect of an aspirin every other day on coronary heart disease, not a single woman was included in the study. Women's health advocates continue to press for greater inclusion of women in medical studies to reduce the bias that has characterized research on health. They also hope that the medical establishment will give increased attention to women's health concerns and treat women in less prejudiced and biased ways (Strickland, 1988).

There are also concerns about the failure of many males to adequately use the health-care system. For example, male college students are less likely than female college students to consult a physician or health-care provider when they have unfamiliar physical symptoms, less likely to go to scheduled health checkups, and more likely to be substance abusers (Courtenay, McCreary, & Merighi, 2002). In many instances, this sex difference continues through the adult years, with males being less likely to go to a medical doctor when they have an illness.

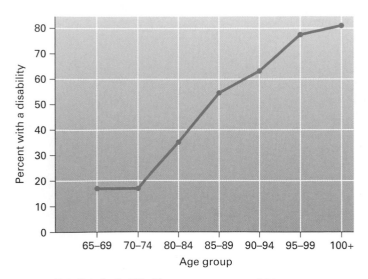

Note: Data for the 75 to 79 age group were unavailable.

FIGURE 4.2 Percentage of U.S. Older Adults of Different Ages Who Have a Disability

Most Americans who are younger than 85 do not have a disability.

chronic disorders Disorders characterized by slow onset and long duration.

osteoporosis A disorder of aging that involves an extensive loss of bone tissue and is the main reason many older adults walk with a marked stoop. Women are especially vulnerable to osteoporosis.

dementia A global term for any neurological disorder in which the primary symptoms involve a deterioration of mental functioning.

Health and Aging

Aging can bring on new health problems, such as Alzheimer's disease. Keep in mind, though, that many older adults are healthy. For example, only 17 percent of U.S. adults from 65 to 74 years of age have a disability. As shown in figure 4.2, the percentage of Americans without a disability continues above 50 percent until they reach 85 years and older.

Chronic Disorders Chronic disorders are characterized by a slow onset and long duration. Chronic disorders are rare in early adulthood, increase in middle adulthood, and become common in late adulthood.

The most common chronic disorders in middle age differ for females and males. The most common chronic disorders in middle adulthood for U.S. women, in order, are arthritis, hypertension, and sinus problems; the most common ones for U.S. men are hypertension, arthritis, hearing impairments, and heart disease. Men have a higher incidence of fatal chronic conditions (such as coronary heart disease, cancer, and stroke); women have a higher incidence of nonfatal ones (such as arthritis, varicose veins, and bursitis). Older women have higher incidences of arthritis and hypertension, and are more likely to have visual problems, but are less likely to have hearing problems than older men are.

Even when adults over the age of 65 have a physical impairment, many of them can still carry on their everyday activities or work. Chronic conditions associated with the greatest limitation on work are heart conditions (52 percent), diabetes (34 percent), asthma (27 percent), and arthritis (27 percent).

Low income is also strongly related to health problems in late adulthood. Approximately three times as many poor as nonpoor older adults report that their activities are limited by chronic disorders.

Normal aging involves some loss of bone tissue from the skeleton. However, in some instances loss of bone tissue can become severe. **Osteoporosis** involves an extensive loss of bone tissue. Osteoporosis is the main reason many older adults walk with a marked stoop. Women are especially vulnerable to osteoporosis, the leading cause of broken bones in women. Approximately 80 percent of osteoporosis cases in the United States occur in females, 20 percent in males. Almost two-thirds of all women over the age of 60 are affected by osteoporosis. This aging disorder is more common in non-Latina White, thin, and small-framed women.

Osteoporosis is related to deficiencies in calcium, vitamin D, estrogen, and exercise (De Villers, 2003; Hauselmann & Rizzoli, 2003). To prevent osteoporosis, young and middle-aged women should eat foods rich in calcium, get more exercise, and avoid smoking. Calcium-rich foods include dairy products (low-fat milk and low-fat yogurt, for example) and certain vegetables (such as broccoli, turnip greens, and kale). Drugs such as Fosimax can be used to reduce the risk of osteoporosis. Aging women should also get bone density checks (Burke & others, 2003).

A program of regular exercise has the potential to reduce osteoporosis (Fitzpatrick, 2003; Nies & others, 2003). In one study, women aged 50 to 70 lifted weights twice a week (Nelson & others, 1994). Their risk of osteoporosis (and resulting broken bones) was sharply reduced, while their balance and muscular strength improved. The weight-lifting program included three sets of eight repetitions on machines to strengthen muscles in the abdomen, back, thighs, and buttocks.

Health problems that accompany aging not only can involve bones, muscles, and the cardiovascular system. They also can involve neurological disorders.

Alzheimer's Disease Dementia is a global term for any neurological disorder in which the primary symptom is deterioration of mental functioning. Individuals with dementia often lose the ability to care for themselves and can lose the ability to recognize familiar surroundings and people (including family members) (Warner & Butler, 2002; Yamada & others, 2003). One form of dementia is **Alzheimer's disease**—a progressive, irreversible brain disorder that is characterized by a gradual deterioration of memory, reasoning, language, and eventually, physical function.

Alzheimer's disease was first diagnosed in 1906 by the German doctor Alois Alzheimer, but serious research on the disease did not begin until the 1950s, as Alzheimer's became more clearly distinguished from other types of dementia. There is a predictable, progressive decline in physical, cognitive, and social functioning in individuals with Alzheimer's disease (Morris & others, 2001; Mungas & others, 2002). Most Alzheimer's patients, once diagnosed, live approximately eight years and progress from early problems of memory loss and declining intellectual functioning to later stages in which hospitalization in a near vegetative state ensues (Weatherford, 1999).

As Alzheimer's disease progresses, the brain deteriorates and shrinks. Figure 4.3 compares the brain of a normally aging individual and the brain of an individual with Alzheimer's disease. Among the main characteristics of Alzheimer's disease are the increasing number of *neural tangles* (tied bundles of protein that impair the functioning of neurons) and *plaques* (deposits that accumulate in the brain's blood vessels) in the brain. The formation of tangles and plaques is a normal part of aging. However, in Alzheimer's disease these are much more pervasive (Galvin & others, 2002; Velez-Pardo, Lopera, & Del Rio, 2002).

Early Detection Special brain scans, such as MRI (magnetic resonance imaging), can detect changes in the brain that are fairly typical of early Alzheimer's disease even before symptoms develop (Li & others, 2002; Weatherford, 1999). In addition, certain spinal fluids give reasonably good early signals of Alzheimer's disease. Recently a sophisticated urine test called the *neural thread protein test* has predicted the occurrence of Alzheimer's in some individuals two years before the symptoms (such as memory loss) appear. When positive, the urine test allows preventive measures to be initiated that delay the cognitive decline of Alzheimer's disease.

Causes and Treatments Alzheimer's disease is currently perceived as a puzzle with many pieces (Hodges, 2000). In the 1970s, it was discovered that Alzheimer's involves a deficiency in the important neurotransmitter acetylcholine, which plays an important role in memory (Camps & Munoz-Torrero, 2002; Ikonomovic & others, 2003). But efforts to identify the cause of Alzheimer's have not yet been successful. Scientists now believe that Alzheimer's disease is a complex unraveling of neural structure and function that likely involves many different molecular and cellular dimensions. Today some scientists argue that the best strategy might be not to search for a single cause of Alzheimer's but to discover how to put all of the pieces of the puzzle together.

At present, there is no cure for Alzheimer's disease and no way to slow the progress of the disease. For some individuals in the early or middle stages of the disease, medications such as tacrine may alleviate some of the cognitive symptoms (National Institutes of Health, 2003). Tacrine (the trade name of the drug is Cognex) works by blocking chemicals that ordinarily cut acetylcholine apart. Some medications may help to control behavioral symptoms such as sleeplessness, agitation, wandering, anxiety, and depression. These treatments are aimed at making the patient more comfortable.

Caring for Individuals with Alzheimer's Disease A special concern is caring for Alzheimer's patients (Bordaty & others, 2003). Psychologists believe that the family can be an important support system for the Alzheimer's patient. However, this support can have costs for the family, which can become emotionally and physically drained by the extensive care required for a person with Alzheimer's (Toseland & others, 2002; Zarit & Downs, 1999). For example, depression has been reported in 50 percent of family caregivers for Alzheimer's patients (Redinbaugh, MacCallum, & Kiecolt-Glaser, 1995). Respite care has been developed to help people who have to

*H*ow many of us older persons have really been prepared for the second half of life, for old age, and eternity?
—CARL JUNG
Swiss Psychoanalyst, 20th Century

Dementia Web
Exploring Dementia
Alzheimer's.com
Alzheimer's Resources

Late Adulthood: Alzheimer's Disease

Alzheimer's disease A progressive, irreversible brain disorder characterized by a gradual deterioration of memory, reasoning, language, and, eventually, physical function.

meet the day-to-day needs of Alzheimer's patients. This type of care provides an important break away from the burden of providing chronic care.

The Robust Oldest-Old   Our image of the oldest-old (eighties and older) is predominantly of being disabled and frail, an image that is fueled by the media. The implications of the projected rapid growth of the oldest-old population have often been pessimistic—an expensive burden in which the oldest-old often require the everyday help of other persons. However, as we discussed in chapter 3, the oldest-old are a heterogeneous group. For example, less than 60 percent of U.S. 85- to 89-year-olds have a disability.

Because so much attention has been given to chronic disabilities of the oldest-old, those who have aged successfully have gone virtually unnoticed and unstudied. An increased interest in successful aging is producing a more optimistic portrayal of the oldest-old (Freund & Riedeger, 2003). For example, cataract surgery and a variety of rehabilitation strategies can improve the functioning of the oldest old. In one study, 8 weeks of leg-strength training markedly improved the walking ability of nursing home residents who averaged 90 years of age (Fiatarone & others, 1990).

In sum, earlier portraits of the oldest-old have been stereotypes. A substantial subgroup of the oldest-old are robust and active. And there is cause for optimism in the development of new regimens of prevention and intervention.

Health Treatment for Older Adults   About 3 percent of adults 65 to 69 years of age in the United States reside in a nursing home at any point in time. However, as older adults age, their probability of being in a nursing home or other extended-care facility increases (see figure 4.4). Twenty-three percent of adults 85 years of age and older live in nursing homes or other extended-care facilities. What is the quality of nursing homes and extended-care facilities for older adults? What is the relationship between older adults and health-care providers?

The quality of nursing homes and other extended-care facilities for older adults varies enormously and is a source of continuing national concern. More than one-third are seriously deficient. They fail federally mandated inspections because they do not meet the minimum standards for physicians, pharmacists, and various rehabilitation specialists (occupational and physical therapists). Further concerns focus on the patient's right to privacy, access to medical information, safety, and lifestyle freedom within the individual's range of mental and physical capabilities.

Because of the inadequate quality of many nursing homes and the escalating costs for nursing home care, many specialists in the health problems of the aged believe

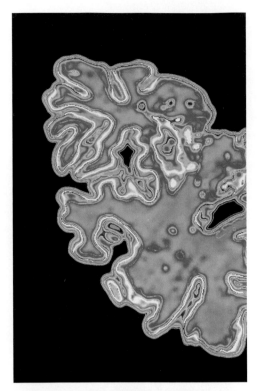

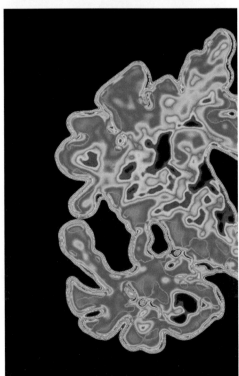

FIGURE 4.3 Two Brains: Normal Aging and Alzheimer's Disease

The top computer graphic shows a slice of a normal aging brain, the bottom photograph a slice of a brain ravaged by Alzheimer's disease. Notice the deterioration and shrinking in the Alzheimer's disease brain.

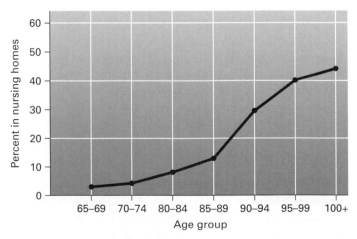

Note: Data for the 75 to 79 age group were unavailable.

FIGURE 4.4 Percentage of U.S. Older Adults of Different Ages in Nursing Homes

that home health care, elder-care centers, and preventive medicine clinics are good alternatives (Castle, 2001). They are potentially less expensive than hospitals and nursing homes. They also are less likely to engender the feelings of depersonalization and dependency that occur so often in residents of institutions (Greene & others, 1995). To read about the importance of personal control in health and well-being, read this Research in Life-Span Development interlude on older adults in nursing homes.

Research in Life-Span Development
Giving Options for Control and Teaching Coping Skills

In a classic study, Judith Rodin and Ellen Langer (1977) found that an important factor related to health, and even survival, in a nursing home is the patient's feelings of control and self-determination. A group of elderly nursing home residents were encouraged to make more day-to-day choices and thus feel they had more responsibility for control over their lives. They began to decide such matters as what they ate, when their visitors could come, what movies they saw, and who could come to their rooms. A similar group in the same nursing home was told by the administrator how caring the nursing home was and how much the staff wanted to help, but these elderly nursing home residents were given no opportunities to take more control over their lives. Eighteen months later, the residents given responsibility and control were more alert and active, and said they were happier, than the residents who were only encouraged to feel that the staff would try to satisfy their needs. And the "responsible" or "self-control" group had significantly better improvement in their health than did the "dependent" group. Even more important was the finding that after 18 months only half as many nursing home residents in the "responsibility" group had died as in the "dependent" group (see figure 4.5). Perceived control over one's environment, then, can literally be a matter of life or death.

In another research study, Rodin (1983) measured stress-related hormones in several groups of nursing home residents. Then she taught the residents coping skills to help them deal better with day-to-day problems. They were taught how to say no when they did not want something, without worrying whether they would offend someone. They were given assertiveness training, and learned time-management skills.

Ellen Langer *(left)* and Judith Rodin conducted a classic study of perceived control in nursing homes. They found that perceived control over their environment literally was a matter of life or death for the elderly nursing home residents. *What made their study an experimental rather than a correlational study?*

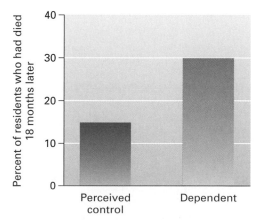

FIGURE 4.5 Perceived Control and Mortality

In the study by Rodin and Langer (1977), nursing home residents who were encouraged to feel more in control of their lives were more likely to be alive 18 months later than those who were treated to feel more dependent on the nursing home staff.

After the training, the nursing home residents had greatly reduced levels of cortisol (a hormone closely related to stress that has been implicated in a number of diseases). The cortisol levels of the assertiveness-training residents remained lower, even after 18 months. Further, these nursing home residents were healthier and had a reduced need for medication, compared with residents who had not been taught the coping skills. Rodin's research shows that simply giving nursing home residents options for control and teaching them coping skills can change their behavior and improve their health.

Late Adulthood: Depression and the Elderly

The attitudes of both the health-care provider and the older adult are important aspects of the older adult's health care (Ahmad & Lachs, 2002). Unfortunately, health-care providers too often share society's stereotypes and negative attitudes toward older adults. In a health-care setting, these attitudes can take the form of avoidance, dislike, and begrudged tolerance rather than positive, hopeful treatment. Health-care personnel are more likely to be interested in treating younger persons, who more often have acute problems with a higher prognosis for successful recovery. They often are less motivated to treat older persons, who are more likely to have chronic problems with a lower prognosis for successful recovery.

Not only are physicians less responsive to older patients, but older patients often take a less active role in medical encounters with health-care personnel than do younger patients (Woodward & Wallston, 1987). Older adults should be encouraged to take a more active role in their own health care.

Review and Reflect: Learning Goal 1

1 **Describe the bio-psycho-social health model and developmental changes in health**

REVIEW

- How can the bio-psycho-social health model be summarized?
- How can children's health be characterized?
- What is the nature of adolescents' health?
- What is young adults' health like?
- How extensively does health decline in old age?

REFLECT

- What changes in your lifestyle right now might help you to age more successfully when you get older?

---

2 NUTRITION AND EATING BEHAVIOR

Infancy   Adolescence   Childhood   Adult Development and Aging

Nutritional needs, eating behavior, and related issues vary to some extent across the life span. Let's begin by exploring what takes place with infants.

Infancy

For the infant, the importance of receiving adequate energy and nutrients in a loving and supportive environment cannot be overstated (More, 2003; Samour, Helm, &

Lang, 2000). From birth to 1 year of age, human infants triple their weight and increase their length by 50 percent. Because infants vary in their nutrient reserves, body composition, growth rates, and activity patterns, their nutrient needs vary as well. However, because parents need guidelines, nutritionists recommend that infants consume approximately 50 calories per day for each pound they weigh—more than twice an adult's requirement per pound.

Breastfeeding Versus Bottlefeeding Human milk, or alternative formula, is the baby's source of nutrients and energy for the first 4 to 6 months of life. In the United States, "formula" became the conventional choice for a while, but breastfeeding is increasing, as figure 4.6 shows, and is better for the infant's health (Cronin, 2003; Kramer, 2003). The American Pediatric Association strongly endorses breastfeeding throughout the first year of life (AAP Work Group on Breastfeeding, 1997). Increasingly, mothers who return to work during the infant's first year use a breast pump to extract breast milk that can be stored and later fed to the infant in a bottle when the mother is not present.

What are some of the benefits of breastfeeding? During the first two years of life and later, they include (AAP Work Group on Breastfeeding, 1997; Eiger & Olds, 1999; Hanson & others, 2002; London & others, 2000; Oddy, 2002):

- Appropriate weight gain and lowered risk of childhood obesity (Bergmann & others, 2003). A recent review of 11 studies found that breastfeeding reduces the risk of childhood obesity to a moderate extent (Dewey, 2003). One candidate for explaining this lowered risk is early metabolic programming.
- Fewer allergies (Arshad, 2001; Hoppu & others, 2001; Miyake, Yura, & Iki, 2003; Prescott, 2003).
- Prevention or reduction of diarrhea, respiratory infections (such as pneumonia and bronchitis), bacterial and urinary tract infections, and otitis media (a middle ear infection) (AAP Work Group on Breastfeeding, 1997; Hanson & Korotkova, 2002; Hanson & others, 2003; Kramer & others, 2001; Noguera-Obenza & others, 2003).
- Denser bones in childhood and adulthood (Gibson & others, 2000; Jones, Riley, & Dwyer, 2000).
- Reduced childhood cancer and reduced incidence of breast cancer in mothers and their female offspring (Bernier & others, 2000; Eisinger & Burke, 2003; Lee & others, 2003).
- Lower incidence of sudden infant death syndrome (SIDS)—in one study, for every month of exclusive breastfeeding, the rate of SIDS was cut in half (Fredrickson, 1993).
- Neurological and cognitive development (Brody, 1994).
- Visual acuity (Makrides & others, 1995).

Does breastfeeding also bring psychological benefits? Some researchers have found no psychological differences between breastfed and bottlefed infants (Ferguson, Harwood, & Shannon, 1987; Young, 1990).

Are there circumstances when mothers should not breastfeed? Yes, they are (1) when the mother is infected with AIDS, which can be transmitted through her milk, or has another infectious disease; (2) if she has active tuberculosis; or (3) if she is taking any drug that might not be safe for the infant (AAP Work Group on Breastfeeding, 1997; Brown, 2003; Ito & Lee, 2003; Richardson & Hughes, 2003).

Some women cannot breastfeed their infants because of physical difficulties. Also, if they are not constantly at home,

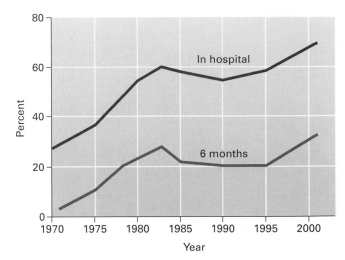

Breastfeeding

Feeding Infants

FIGURE 4.6 Trends in Breastfeeding in the United States: 1970–2001

The prevalence of initiating breastfeeding in the hospital and breastfeeding at six months after birth in the United States reached 69.5 percent and 32.5 percent, respectively, in 2001 (Ryan, Wenjun, & Acosta, 2002).

Human milk, or an alternative formula, is a baby's source of nutrients for the first 4 to 6 months. The growing consensus is that breastfeeding is better for the baby's health. *Why is breastfeeding strongly recommended by pediatricians?*

This Honduran child has kwashiorkor. Notice the tell-tale sign of kwashiorkor—a greatly expanded abdomen without the appearance of such expansion in other body areas, such as arms and legs. *What are some other characteristics of kwashiorkor?*

www.mhhe.com/santrockldt2

Malnutrition in Infancy

marasmus A wasting away of body tissues in the infant's first year, caused by insufficient caloric intake.

kwashiorkor A condition caused by a deficiency in protein in which the child's face, legs, and abdomen swell with water.

some women may be deterred from breastfeeding because they are uncomfortable breastfeeding in public places. Yet other women may feel guilty if they terminate breastfeeding early (Mozingo & others, 2000).

Which women are least likely to breastfeed? They include mothers who work full time outside of the home, mothers under age 25, mothers without a high school education, African American mothers, and mothers in low-income circumstances (Ryan, 1997). In one study of low-income mothers in Georgia, interventions (such as counseling focused on the benefits of breastfeeding and the free loan of a breast pump) increased the incidence of breastfeeding (Ahluwalia & others, 2000).

In poor countries in particular, breastfeeding may be the only way a mother can feed her infant adequately. In many of the world's developing countries, mothers used to breastfeed their infants for at least two years. To become more modern, some stopped breastfeeding or abandoned it earlier in the infant's life. Sometimes the substitute for breastfed milk is an unsuitable and unsanitary cow's milk formula; sometimes it is a form of tapioca or rice. The result may be malnutrition. Studies in countries such as Afghanistan, Haiti, Ghana, and Chile found that the death rate of bottlefed infants is as much as five times that of breastfed infants (Grant, 1997).

Malnutrition in Infancy When they are severely malnourished, infants fail to grow adequately and they are listless. Very severe malnutrition usually takes the form of marasmus or kwashiorkor. **Marasmus** is severe malnutrition due to insufficient caloric intake. Infants with marasmus have a shrunken wasted, elderly appearance. **Kwashiorkor** is severe malnutrition caused by a deficiency in protein. The child's abdomen and feet swell with water. Otherwise, children with kwashiorkor may look well-fed. In fact, their vital organs are collecting whatever nutrients are present, depriving other parts of the body. The disease usually appears between 1 to 3 years of age. Marasmus and kwashiorkor are serious problems in developing countries, with as many as 50 percent of deaths under the age of 5 in these countries due to such severe protein-energy malnutrition (UNICEF, 2003).

The incidence of marasmus and kwashiorkor in the United States is rare, although there still is concern about some specific aspects of energy and nutrient intakes in infants from low-income families. One recent study found low intakes of vitamin D, zinc, and iron, especially at 12 and 18 months, in U.S. infants (Nolan & others, 2002). In this study, high protein intake was noted at all of the ages the infants were assessed: 3, 6, 9, 12, 18, and 24 months. Iron and zinc deficiency also are prevalent during infancy in developing countries. One recent study found that supplements of these minerals benefited the motor development of infants in Bangladesh (Black & others, 2003).

The effects of nutrition in infancy may extend at least into early childhood. One study linked the diets of rural Guatemalan infants with their social development when they entered elementary school (Barrett, Radke-Yarrow, & Klein, 1982). Researchers compared children whose mothers had been given nutritional supplements during pregnancy and who themselves had been given more nutritious, high-calorie foods in their first two years of life with children who had not received nutritional supplements. When they entered elementary school, the children who had received the supplements were more active, more involved, more helpful with their peers, less anxious, and happier.

Nutritional supplements for infants can also improve their cognitive development. In a longitudinal investigation conducted over two decades in rural Guatemala, Ernesto Pollitt and his colleagues (1993) found that giving malnourished infants or children protein supplements and increased calories had long-term effects on cognitive development. Both the socioeconomic status of the children and the period during which the nutritional supplements were given influenced the effects of the supplements. For example, the children in the lowest socioeconomic groups benefited more than the children in the higher socioeconomic groups. Also, when supplements were given only after the children were 2 years old, they still had a positive influence, but the effect on cognitive development was less powerful.

Childhood

Malnutrition continues to be a major threat to millions during the childhood years (Chopra, 2003). Malnutrition and starvation are a daily fact of life for children in many developing countries (UNICEF, 2003). Even in the United States, as was mentioned earlier, millions of children are malnourished. For most children in the United States and other developed nations, however, insufficient food is often not the key problem. Instead, poor nutrition as a result of unhealthy eating habits and being overweight threaten their present and future health.

Healthy and Unhealthy Eating   One recent national study found that from the late 1970s through the late 1990s, key dietary shifts took place in U.S. children: greater away-from-home consumption, large increases in total energy from salty snacks, soft drinks, and pizza; and large decreases in energy from low- and medium-fat milk and medium- and high-fat beef and pork (Nielsen, Siega-Riz, & Popkin, 2002). In this study, children's total energy intake increased from the late 1970s to late 1990s. These dietary changes occurred for children as young as 2 years of age through the adult years.

Another recent national assessment found that most children's diets need improvement (Federal Interagency Forum on Child and Family Statistics, 2002). In this assessment, only 27 percent of 2- to 5-year-old children were categorized as having good diets. Their diets worsened as they became older—only 13 percent of 6- to 9-year-old children had healthy diets.

What children eat affects their skeletal growth, body shape, and susceptibility to disease (Tershakovec & others, 2003). How much children should eat depends on their energy needs. These needs can be different even for children of the same age, sex, and size. Their energy requirements depend mostly on their physical activity and their **basal metabolism rate (BMR),** which is the minimum amount of energy a person uses in a resting state.

What children eat also has a long-term effect on their eating habits because eating habits become ingrained early in life (Poulton & Sexton, 1996). The context in which children eat can influence their eating habits and weight. In one recent study, children who ate with their families were more likely to eat low-fat foods (such as low-fat milk and salad dressing and lean meats) and vegetables, and they drank fewer sodas than children who ate alone (Cullen, 2001). In this study, overweight children ate 50 percent of their meals in front of a TV, compared with only 35 percent of normal-weight children.

Unfortunately, eating fast food may be the key habit that U.S. children are learning today. Many children start eating fast foods in their preschool years (Poulton & Sexton, 1996). The habit of eating on the run and picking up fast-food meals clashes with caregivers' concerns about the appropriate amount of fat content in children's diets (Troiano & Flegal, 1998). Most fast-food meals are high in protein, but the average American child does not need to be concerned about getting enough protein. What must be of concern is the vast number of children being raised on fast foods that are high in fat. The American Heart Association recommends that no more than 35 percent of daily calories should come from fat.

American culture provides substantial opportunities and encouragement for both adults and children to overeat. Food is everywhere you go and easy to get. Both portion size and the quantity of food that U.S. adults and children eat have grown. Fast-food restaurants give people the opportunity to "super-size" a meal at a relatively low additional cost. These trends are producing increasing numbers of overweight children and adults, and being overweight can be a serious problem (Freeman-Fobbs, 2003; Kohn & Golden, 2001; Regan & Anderson, 2003; Treuth & others, 2003).

Obesity   Fifteen percent of U.S. children 6 to 11 years of age are overweight (Ogden & others, 2002). Girls are more likely than boys to be obese. Obesity is less common in African American than in White children during childhood, but during

basal metabolism rate (BMR) The minimal amount of energy a person uses in a resting state.

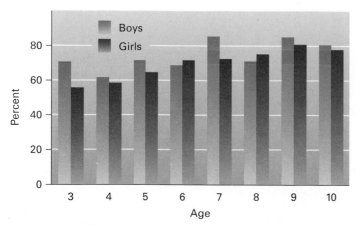

FIGURE 4.7 Relation to Being Overweight in Childhood with Being Overweight in Adulthood

Note: Data show the chance that children who are in the 95th percentile among their peers in terms of weight are likely to be overweight when they are 35.

Helping an Overweight Child

Heart Smart

adolescence this reverses. The percentage of U.S. children who are overweight has more than doubled since 1980 and almost quadrupled since 1965 (National Center for Health Statistics, 2002). And a high percentage of children who are in the 95th percentile among their peers in terms of weight are still likely to be overweight when they are in their thirties (Guo & others, 2002) (see figure 4.7). Researchers also recently found that one-third of the mothers of overweight children believed their children were of normal weight (Maynard & others, 2003).

Consequences of Obesity Obesity increases a child's risk of developing many medical and psychological problems (Etelson & others, 2003; Lumeng & others, 2003). Obese children can develop pulmonary problems, such as sleep apnea (which involves upper airway obstruction) (Li & others, 2003). Hip problems also are common in obese children. Obese children are more likely than nonobese children to develop diabetes (Kiess & others, 2001). Obese children also are prone to have high blood pressure and elevated blood cholesterol levels (Daniels, 2001; Ribero & others, 2003). Once considered rare, hypertension in children has become increasingly common in association with obesity (Sorof & Daniels, 2002). Obese children are three times more likely to develop hypertension than nonobese children (Sorof & Daniels, 2002). Obese children often are excluded from peer groups. Low self-esteem and depression also are common outgrowths of obesity (Lumeng & others, 2003). Furthermore, obesity at 6 years of age results in approximately a 25 percent probability that the child will be obese as an adult; obesity at age 12 results in approximately a 75 percent chance that the adolescent will be obese as an adult.

Treatment of Obesity One recent study found that obese children spent 51 percent more time in sedentary activity than nonobese children (Yu & others, 2002). Thus, exercise is believed to be an extremely important component of a successful weight-loss program for overweight children (Amisola & Jacobson, 2003; Hodges, 2003; Yu & others, 2002). Exercise increases the child's lean body mass, which increases the child's resting metabolic rate. This results in more calories being burned in the resting state. Many experts on childhood obesity recommend a treatment that involves a combination of diet, exercise, and behavior modification (Campbell & others, 2001; Schwartz & Puhl, 2003; Wisotsky & Swencionis, 2003). Diets only moderately deficient in calories are more successful over the long term than are those involving extreme deprivation of calories.

Adolescence

Nutrition and being overweight are also key problems among adolescents (Schimmer, Burwinkle, & Varni, 2003). A comparison of adolescents in 28 countries found that U.S. adolescents ate more junk food than teenagers in most other countries (World Health Organization, 2000). They were also more likely to eat fried food and less likely to eat fruits and vegetables. Not surprisingly, the percentage of overweight adolescents has been increasing, as figure 4.8 shows.

Are there ethnic variations in being overweight during adolescence? A recent survey by the National Center for Health Statistics (2002) found that African American girls and Latino boys have especially high risks of being overweight during adolescence (see figure 4.9).

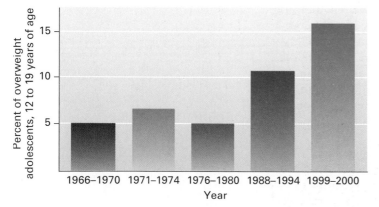

FIGURE 4.8 The Increase in Being Overweight in Adolescence from 1968 to 2000 in the United States

In this study, being overweight was determined by body mass index (BMI), which is computed by a formula that takes into account height and weight (National Center for Health Statistics, 2003). Only adolescents above the 95th percentile in the overweight category were included in the study. There was a substantial increase in the percentage of adolescents who were overweight from 1968 to 2000.

Another problem related to eating habits becomes prominent during adolescence, especially among non-Latino White girls. Intense concern about their appearance and especially their weight may lead to unhealthy eating and excessive dieting.

A number of studies document that adolescent girls have a strong desire to weigh less (Graber & Brooks-Gunn, 2001). Girls who are motivated to try to look like the girls and women they see in the media are especially likely to become very concerned about their weight (Field & others, 2001). Relationships with parents are also linked to adolescent girls' eating behavior. One study found that over a one-year period, poor relationships with parents were linked with increased dieting by adolescent girls (Archibad, Graber, & Brooks-Gunn, 1999).

Eating disorders have become an increasing problem among U.S. adolescents (Fairburn & Harrison, 2003; McVey & others, 2002; Polivy & others, 2003). Research on adolescent eating disorders reveals that:

- Girls who felt negatively about their bodies in early adolescence were more likely to have developed eating disorders when they were assessed two years later than were girls who did not feel negatively about their bodies (Attie & Brooks-Gunn, 1989).
- Girls who were both sexually active with their boyfriends and in pubertal transition were the most likely to be dieting or engaged in disordered eating patterns (Caufmann, 1994).

Let's examine two eating disorders that may appear in adolescence: anorexia nervosa and bulimia nervosa.

Anorexia Nervosa **Anorexia nervosa** is an eating disorder that involves the relentless pursuit of thinness through starvation. Anorexia nervosa is a serious disorder that can lead to death. Three main characteristics of anorexia nervosa are (Davison & Neale, 2001):

- Weighing less than 85 percent of what is considered normal for their age and height.
- Having an intense fear of gaining weight. The fear does not decrease with weight loss.
- Having a distorted image of their body shape (Polivy & others, 2003). Even when they are extremely thin, they see themselves as too fat. They never think they are thin enough, especially in the abdomen, buttocks, and thighs. They usually weigh themselves frequently, often take their body measurements, and gaze critically at themselves in mirrors.

Anorexia nervosa typically begins in the early to middle teenage years, often following an episode of dieting and some type of life stress. It is about 10 times more likely to characterize females than males. Although most U.S. adolescent girls have been on a diet at some point, slightly less than 1 percent ever develop anorexia nervosa (Walters & Kendler, 1994). When anorexia nervosa does occur in males, the symptoms and other characteristics (such as family conflict) are usually similar to those reported by females who have the disorder (Olivardia & others, 1995).

Most anorexics are White adolescent or young adult females from well-educated, middle- and upper-income families that are competitive and high-achieving (Schmidt, 2003). They set high standards, become stressed about not being able to reach the standards, and are intensely concerned about how others perceive them (Striegel-Moore, Silberstein, & Rodin, 1993). Unable to meet these high expectations, they turn to something they can control: their weight.

The fashion image in the American culture which emphasizes that "thin is beautiful" contributes to the incidence of anorexia nervosa (Andrist, 2003; Polivy & others, 2003). This image is reflected in the saying, "You never can be too rich or too thin." The media portrays thin as beautiful in their choice of fashion models, which many adolescent girls want to emulate.

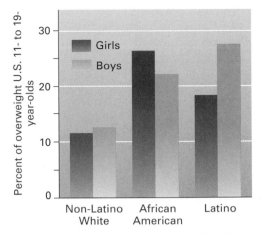

FIGURE 4.9 Percentage of Overweight U.S. Adolescent Boys and Girls in Different Ethnic Groups

Anorexia nervosa has become an increasing problem for adolescent girls and young adult women. *What are some possible causes of anorexia nervosa?*

anorexia nervosa An eating disorder that involves the relentless pursuit of thinness through starvation.

Adolescence: Adolescent Eating Disorders

Bulimia Nervosa While anorexics control their eating by restricting it, most bulimics cannot. **Bulimia nervosa** is an eating disorder in which the individual consistently follows a binge-and-purge eating pattern. The bulimic goes on an eating binge and then purges by self-inducing vomiting or using a laxative. Although many people binge and purge occasionally and some experiment with it, a person is considered to have a serious bulimic disorder only if the episodes occur at least twice a week for three months

As with anorexics, most bulimics are preoccupied with food, have a strong fear of becoming overweight, and are depressed or anxious (Davison & Neale, 2001; Quadflieg & Fichter, 2003). Unlike anorexics, people who binge-and-purge typically fall within a normal weight range, which makes bulimia more difficult to detect (Hay & Bacaltchuk, 2003; Orbanic, 2001).

Bulimia nervosa typically begins in late adolescence or early adulthood. About 90 percent of the cases are women. Approximately 1 to 2 percent of women are estimated to develop bulimia nervosa (Gotesdam & Agras, 1995). Many women who develop bulimia nervosa were somewhat overweight before the onset of the disorder, and the binge eating often began during an episode of dieting. One recent study of adolescent girls found that increased dieting, pressure to be thin, exaggerated importance of appearance, body dissatisfaction, depression symptoms, low self-esteem, and low social support predicted binge eating two years later (Stice, Presnell, & Spangler, 2002). As with anorexia nervosa, about 70 percent of individuals who develop bulimia nervosa eventually recover from the disorder.

Adult Development and Aging

Nutrition and eating behavior continue to play important roles in adult physical development and health. Among the topics we will discuss are obesity, dieting, and links among aging, weight, and nutrition.

Obesity Obesity is not only a problem for many children, it is also a serious and pervasive problem for many adults (Corsica & Perry, 2003; Steiger, Bruce, & Israel, 2003: Wing & Polley, 2001). The prevalence of obesity in U.S. adults increased from 19 percent in 1997 to 25 percent in 2002 (National Center for Health Statistics, 2003). Obesity is linked with increased risk of hypertension, diabetes, and cardiovascular disease in adults (Stunkard, 2000). For individuals who are 30 percent overweight, the probability of dying in middle adulthood increases by about 40 percent.

What causes obesity? Some individuals do inherit a tendency to be overweight. Only 10 percent of children who do not have obese parents become obese themselves, whereas 40 percent of children who become obese have one obese parent. Further, 70 percent of children who become obese have two obese parents. Researchers also have documented that animals can be inbred to have a propensity for obesity (Blundell, 1984). And identical human twins have similar weights, even when they are reared apart.

Evolutionary psychology offers some insight into our problems with obesity. The human gustatory system and taste preferences developed at a time when reliable food sources were scarce. Our earliest ancestors probably developed a preference for sweets, because ripe fruit, which is a concentrated source of sugar (and calories), was so accessible. Today many people still have a "sweet tooth," but unlike our ancestors' ripe fruit that contained sugar plus vitamins and minerals, the soft drinks and candy bars we snack on today often fill us with empty calories.

Strong evidence of the environment's influence on weight is the doubling of the rate of obesity in the United States since 1900. This dramatic increase in obesity likely is due to greater availability of food (especially food high in fat), energy-saving devices, and declining physical activity.

Dieting As recent cohorts of Americans have become increasingly overweight and obese, their interest in dieting has dramatically increased. Many groups now clash

Anorexia Nervosa

Obesity

Heredity and Obesity

Why People Are Getting Fatter

bulimia nervosa An eating disorder in which the individual consistently follows a binge-purge eating pattern.

in debates about the benefits and costs of dieting and the effectiveness of particular diets. These include the public, health professionals, policymakers, the media, and the powerful diet and food industries. On one side, societal norms that promote a lean body are supported by the $30 billion spent annually on diet books, programs, videos, foods, and pills. On the other side, health professionals and a growing minority of the press are frustrated by high relapse rates and the obsession with excessive thinness, which can lead to chronic dieting and serious health risks (Brownell, 2000; Brownell & Rodin, 1994).

Restrained Eating   Too many people live their lives as one long diet, interrupted by occasional hot fudge sundaes or chocolate chip cookies. **Restrained eaters** are individuals who chronically restrict their food intake to control their weight. Restrained eaters are often on diets, are very conscious of what they eat, and tend to feel guilty after splurging on sweets. When they stop dieting, restrained eaters tend to binge eat—that is, eat large quantities of food in a short time (McFarlane, Polivy, & Herman, 1998; Roemmich, Wright, & Epstein, 2002).

Dieting: Harm or Benefit?   Although many Americans regularly embark on a diet, few are successful in keeping weight off long-term. Some critics argue that all diets fail (Wooley & Garner, 1991). However, the evidence is that some individuals who go on diets do lose weight and maintain the loss (Brownell & Cohen, 1995). When overweight people diet and maintain their weight loss, they do become less depressed and reduce their risk for a number of health-impairing disorders (Christensen, 1996).

How often dieting works and whether some diet programs work better than others are still open questions. What we do know about losing weight is that the most effective programs include exercise (Anderson & others, 2002; Nicklas & others, 2003). Exercise not only burns off calories, but continues to elevate the person's metabolic rate for several hours after the exercise. Also, exercise lowers a person's *set point* for weight, which makes it easier to maintain a lower weight (Bennett & Gurin, 1982).

Many people who are on diets, however, should not be. A 10 percent reduction in body weight might produce striking benefits for an older, obese, hypertensive man but be unhealthy for a female college student who is not overweight. The pressure to be thin, and thus to diet, is greatest among young women, yet they do not have the highest risk of obesity.

Even when diets do produce weight loss, they can place the dieter at risk for other health problems. One main concern focuses on *weight cycling* (commonly called "yo-yo dieting"), in which the person goes through recurring cycles of dieting and weight gain (Wadden & others, 1996). Researchers have found a link between frequent changes in weight and chronic disease (Brownell & Rodin, 1994). Also, liquid diets and other very-low-calorie strategies are related to gallbladder damage.

As with children and adolescents, a combination of moderate calorie reduction and regular exercise is the best recipe for losing weight, especially over the long term (Jakicic & Gallagher, 2003). One recent study found that women who want to lose weight benefit from regular exercise and cutting calories (Jakicic & others, 2003). Researchers studied 184 sedentary women 21 to 45 years of age who weighed an average of 200 pounds. Women who walked briskly 50 to 60 minutes a day and consumed about 1,500 calories a day for one year lost and kept off 12 to 14 percent of their starting weight, or about 25 to 30 pounds.

Food Restriction and Longevity   In one large-scale study of middle-aged individuals, 7 of 10 said that they were overweight (Brim, 1999). Nearly half of the individuals over 45 years of age said they were less fit than they were five years ago. Might a decrease in the intake of food increase longevity or even extend the human life span?

Scientists have accumulated considerable evidence that food restriction in laboratory animals (in most cases rats) can increase the animals' life span (Goto & others, 2002; Hadley & others, 2001; Kirk, 2001). Animals fed diets restricted in calories—

𝒰nfortunately, for too many women one deviation in diet can spell the difference between confidence and despair.

—JUDITH RODIN
Contemporary Psychologist, University of Pennsylvania

restrained eaters Individuals who chronically restrict their food intake to control their weight. Restrained eaters are often on diets, are very conscious of what they eat, and tend to feel guilty after splurging on sweets.

Roy Walford's Views

Middle Adulthood: Reducing Caloric Intake

although adequate in protein, vitamins, and minerals—live as much as 40 percent longer than animals given unlimited access to food. And chronic problems such as kidney disease appear only at a later age. Diet restriction also delays biochemical alterations such as the age-related rise in cholesterol observed in both humans and animals (Mattson & others, 2002).

Whether similar very low-calorie diets (in some instances the animals eat 40 percent less than normal) can stretch the human life span is not known (Roth & others, 2002). Most nutritional experts do not recommend very low-calorie diets for older adults; rather, they recommend a well-balanced, low-fat diet that includes the nutritional factors needed to maintain good health.

No one knows for certain how calorie restriction works to increased the life span of animals (Hu & others, 2003) **P. 124.** Some scientists believe it might lower the level of free radicals (discussed in chapter 3) or potentially toxic particles created by the breakdown of food. Others believe calorie restriction might trigger a state of emergency called *survival mode* in which the body eliminates all unnecessary functions to focus only on staying alive. Encouraged by the research on animals, the National Institute of Health is planning calorie restriction studies on humans (Johannes, 2002). Calorie restriction of 30 percent in humans would translate into about 1,120 calories a day for the average woman and 1,540 for the average man.

Leaner men do live longer, healthier lives. In one study of 19,297 Harvard alumni, those weighing the least were less likely to die over the past three decades (Lee & others, 1993). The men were divided into five categories according to *body mass index* (a complex formula that takes into account weight and height). As body mass increased, so did risk of death. The most overweight men had a 67 percent higher risk of dying than the thinnest men. For example, the heaviest men (such as 181 pounds or more for a 5-foot-10-inch man) also had 2½ times the risk of death from cardiovascular disease. Currently, these researchers are studying the relation of body mass index to longevity in women.

The Vitamin-and-Aging Controversy For years, most experts on aging and health argued that a balanced diet is all that is needed for successful aging; vitamin supplements were not recommended. However, recent research suggests the possibility that some vitamin supplements—mainly antioxidants, which include vitamin C, vitamin E, and beta-carotene—help slow the aging process and improve the health of older adults.

The theory is that antioxidants counteract the cell damage caused by free radicals, which are produced both by the body's own metabolism and by environmental factors such as smoking, pollution, and bad chemicals in the diet **P. 124.** When free radicals cause damage (oxidation) in one cell, a chain reaction of damage follows. Antioxidants act much like a fire extinguisher, helping to neutralize free-radical activity.

One leading expert on nutrition and aging at the National Institute of Aging, Hubert Warner (2002), recently concluded that most scientists agree that oxidative damage has something to do with aging. As people get older, their bodies aren't as good at mopping up free radicals. However, the degree to which oxidative damage plays a role in aging and whether antioxidant vitamins can slow the age process have not yet been determined. Studies are mixed on whether vitamin E and vitamin C can prevent heart disease (Huang & others, 2002; Ianuzzi & others, 2002). There is some evidence that vitamin E might help protect against prostate cancer, but the protective effect may be limited to smokers (tobacco smoke fires up the production of free radicals) (Fairfield & Fletcher, 2002). Also, vitamin C and vitamin E might provide some protection against Alzheimer's disease (Engelhart & others, 2002).

Researchers are continuing to study whether vitamins can slow aging (Irshad & Chaudhuri, 2003; Khodr & others, 2003; Nelson & others, 2003). Perhaps certain combinations of vitamins are beneficial, and the form of the vitamin may make a difference. For example, a diet rich in foods that naturally contain antioxidants may protect better against disease than pill supplements.

Review and Reflect: Learning Goal 2

2 **Characterize developmental changes in nutrition and eating behavior**

REVIEW

- What are some important aspects of nutrition and eating behavior in infancy?
- What are some key nutritional problems in American children?
- How can eating behavior and disorders in adolescence be characterized?
- What are some controversies and issues in nutrition and eating behavior in the adult years?

REFLECT

- How good are you at eating nutritiously and healthily? Has your lifestyle and behavior in this area affected your health? Might they affect your health in the future?

3 EXERCISE

| Childhood and Adolescence | Adulthood | Aging and Longevity |

We have just seen the important role exercise plays in losing weight. Exercise is linked with many aspects of being physically and mentally healthy. Let's explore exercise throughout the life span.

Childhood and Adolescence

Are children getting enough exercise? A 1997 national poll found that only 22 percent of U.S. children in grades 4 through 12 were physically active for 30 minutes every day of the week (Harris, 1997). Their parents said their children were too busy watching TV, spending time on the computer, or playing video games to exercise much. Boys were more physically active at all ages than girls. In one historical comparison, the percentage of children involved in daily P.E. programs in schools decreased from 80 percent in 1969 to 20 percent in 1999 (Health Management Resources, 2001).

Researchers have found that individuals become less active as they reach and progress through adolescence (Amisola & Jacobson, 2003). In one recent study, activity habits of more than 1,000 African American and more than 1,000 non-Latino White girls were examined annually from 9 to 10 years of age to 18 to 19 years of age (Kimm & others, 2002). The study did not examine boys because it was designed to determine why more African American women than non-Latino White women become obese. At 9 to 10 years of age, most girls reported that they were engaging in some physical activity outside of school. However, by 16 to 17 years of age, 56 percent of African American girls and 31 percent of non-Latino White girls were not engaging in any regular physical activity in their spare time. By 18 to 19 years of age, the figures were 70 percent and 29 percent, respectively. In sum, substantial declines in physical activity occur during adolescence in girls and are greater in African American than non-Latino White girls (Frenn & others, 2003; Kimm & Obarzanek, 2002).

Some ways to get children and adolescents to exercise more are:

- Improving physical fitness classes in schools.
- Offering more physical activity programs run by volunteers at school facilities.
- Having children plan community and school exercise activities that really interest them.

FIGURE 4.10 The Jogging Hog Experiment

Jogging hogs reveal the dramatic effects of exercise on health. In one investigation, a group of hogs was trained to run approximately 100 miles per week (Bloor & White, 1983). Then, the researchers narrowed the arteries that supplied blood to the hogs' hearts. The hearts of the jogging hogs developed extensive alternate pathways for blood supply, and 42 percent of the threatened heart tissue was salvaged compared to only 17 percent in a control group of nonjogging hogs.

Aerobic Institute

aerobic exercise Sustained activity that stimulates heart and lung functioning.

- Encouraging families to focus on physical activity and encouraging parents to exercise more.

An exciting possibility is that physical exercise might buffer adolescents' stress. In one investigation of 364 females in grades 7 through 11 in Los Angeles, the negative impact of stressful events on health declined as exercise levels increased (Brown & Siegel, 1988). Another investigation found that adolescents who exercised regularly coped more effectively with stress and had more positive identities than did adolescents who engaged in little exercise (Grimes & Mattimore, 1989).

Adulthood

The benefits of exercise continue in adulthood. Both moderate and intense exercise may produce important physical and psychological gains (Thayer & others, 1996; Powers & Howley, 2004). The enjoyment and pleasure we derive from exercise added to its physical benefits make exercise one of life's most important activities.

One of the primary health benefits of exercise is prevention of heart disease (Williams, 2001). Some people get the benefits of vigorous exercise on the job. For example, longshoremen who are on their feet all day and lift, push, and carry heavy cargo, have about half the risk of fatal heart attacks as co-workers like crane drivers and clerks, who have physically less demanding jobs. Even in jogging hogs, exercise helps the heart, as figure 4.10 discusses.

Although exercise designed to strengthen muscles and bones or to improve flexibility is important to fitness, many health experts stress aerobic exercise. **Aerobic exercise** is sustained activity—jogging, swimming, or cycling, for example—that stimulates heart and lung functioning. Elaborate studies of 17,000 male alumni of Harvard University found that those who exercised strenuously on a regular basis had a lower risk of heart disease and were more likely to be alive in their middle adulthood years than their more sedentary counterparts (Lee, Hsieh, & Paffenbarger, 1995; Paffenbarger & others, 1993).

Some health experts conclude that, regardless of other risk factors (smoking, high blood pressure, overweight, heredity), if you exercise enough to burn more than 2,000 calories a week, you can cut your risk of heart attack by an impressive two-thirds (Sherwood, Light, & Blumenthal, 1989). But burning up 2,000 calories a week through exercise requires a lot of effort, far more than most of us are willing to expend. To burn 300 calories a day through exercise, you would have to do one of the following: swim or run for about 25 minutes, walk for 45 minutes at about 4 miles an hour, or participate in aerobic dancing for 30 minutes.

As a more realistic goal, many health experts recommend that adults engage in 30 minutes or more of moderate physical activity on most, preferably all, days of the week. Most recommend that you should try to raise your heart rate to at least 60 percent of your maximum heart rate. However, only about one-fifth of adults are active at these recommended levels of physical activity.

Exercise benefits not only physical health, but mental health as well (Leith, 1998; Phillips, Kiernan, & King, 2001). In particular, exercise improves self-concept and reduces anxiety and depression (Moses & others, 1989).

Some helpful strategies for building exercise into your life are:

- *Reducing TV time.* Heavy TV viewing by college students is linked to their poor health (Astin, 1993). Replace some of your TV time with exercise time.
- *Charting your progress.* Systematically recording your exercise workouts will help you to chart your progress. This strategy is especially helpful in maintaining an exercise program over an extended period.
- *Getting rid of excuses.* People make up all kinds of excuses for not exercising. A typical excuse is "I just don't have enough time." You probably do have the time to make exercise a priority.
- *Imagining the alternative.* Ask yourself whether you are too busy to take care of your own health. What will your life be like if your lose your health?

- *Learning more about exercise.* The more you know about exercise, the more you are likely to start an exercise program and continue it.

Aging and Longevity

Regular exercise can lead to a healthier life as a middle-aged and older adult, and increase longevity. In one study, exercise meant a difference in life or death for middle-aged and older adults (Blair, 1990). More than 10,000 men and women were divided into categories of low fitness, medium fitness, and high fitness (Blair & others, 1989). Then they were studied over a period of eight years. As shown in figure 4.11, sedentary participants (low fitness) were more than twice as likely to die during the eight-year time span of the study than those who were moderately fit and more than three times as likely to die as those who were highly fit. The positive effects of being physically fit occurred for both men and women in this study. In another study, changes in level of physical activity and cigarette smoking were associated with risk of death during the middle and late adulthood years (Paffenbarger & others, 1993). Beginning moderately vigorous sports activity from the forties through the eighties was associated with a 23 percent lower risk of death, quitting cigarette smoking with a 41 percent lower death risk.

Gerontologists recommend strength training in addition to aerobic activity and stretching for older adults (Pennix & others, 2002; Rubenstein & others, 2000). The average person's lean body mass declines with age—about 6.6 pounds of lean muscle are lost each decade during the adult years. The rate of loss accelerates after age 45. Also, the average percentage ratio of muscle to fat for a 60- to 70-year-old woman is 44 percent fat. In a 20-year-old woman the ratio is 23 to 24 percent. Weight lifting can preserve and possibly increase muscle mass in older adults (Slade & others, 2002). In one study, it also reduced depression in the elderly (Singh, Clements, & Fiatarone, 1997).

Everything we know about older adults suggests they are healthier and happier the more active they are. Researchers continue to document the positive effects of exercise in older adults (Dunn & Blair, 2002). Exercise helps people to live independent lives with dignity in late adulthood. At 80, 90, and even 100 years of age, exercise can help prevent elderly adults from falling down or even being institutionalized. Being physically fit means being able to do the things you want to do, whether you are young or old.

A recent review of research on exercise and aging reached these conclusions (Singh, 2002):

- *Exercise can minimize the physiological changes associated with aging and contribute to health and well-being.* Changes that can be modified by exercise include brain tissue, motor coordination, cardiovascular function, metabolism (of cholesterol, for example), and attention span. One recent study using magnetic resonance imaging revealed that aerobic exercise was linked with less brain tissue loss in the frontal, parietal, and temporal lobes (Colcombe & others, 2003).
- *Exercise can optimize body composition as aging occurs.* Exercise can increase muscle mass and bone mass, as well as decrease bone fragility (Slade & others, 2002).
- *Exercise is related to prevention of common chronic diseases.* Exercise can reduce the risk of cardiovascular disease, type 2 diabetes, osteoporosis, stroke, and breast cancer (Miller & others, 2000).
- *Exercise is associated with improvement in the treatment of many diseases.* When exercise is used as part of the treatment, individuals with these diseases show improvement in symptoms: arthritis, pulmonary disease, congestive heart failure, coronary artery disease, hypertension, type 2 diabetes, and obesity (Jadelis & others, 2001; Wallace, Mills, & Browning, 1997).
- *Exercise is related to the prevention of disability and can be used effectively in the treatment of disability.* One study of more than 5,000 individuals found that physical activity was associated with slower progression of functional limitations and disability (Miller & others, 2000). Specifically, older adults who walked a mile at

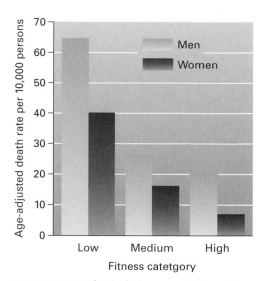

FIGURE 4.11 Physical Fitness and Mortality

In this study of middle-aged and older adults, being moderately fit or highly fit meant that individuals were less likely to die over a period of eight years than their low-fitness (sedentary) counterparts (Blair & others, 1989).

Moderate or intense exercise benefits physical and mental health. *How would you characterize your exercise habits?*

least once per week were less likely than their sedentary counterparts to face functional limitations over the six years of the study.

- *Exercise can be used to counteract the side effects of standard medical care and thus improve disease outcomes and quality-of-life.* For example, depression is sometimes an unintended side effect of drugs used to treat hypertension and exercise may reduce the depression (Singh, 2002).
- *Exercise is linked to increased longevity.* Energy expenditure during exercise of at least 1,000 kcal per week reduces mortality by about 30 percent, while 2,000 kcal per week reduces mortality by about 50 percent (Lee & Skerrett, 2001).

Review and Reflect: Learning Goal 3

3 **Summarize the roles of exercise in child and adult health**

REVIEW

- How extensively do U.S. children and adolescents exercise?
- What roles does exercise play in adult health?
- How does exercise influence development in aging adults?

REFLECT

- Suppose a middle-aged person asked this question: "What would give me the greatest advantage: Exercising more or eating less?" What would your answer be?

---

4 SUBSTANCE USE AND ADDICTION

Drugs, Health, and Addiction   **Substance Abuse in Adolescence**   **Substance Abuse in Adulthood**

Beside exercising, another important healthy practice is to avoid using substances such as alcohol, cigarettes, and other psychoactive drugs. For example, in longitudinal study, individuals who exercised when they were 50 years of age were more likely to be alive and healthy when they were 75 to 80 years old than their counterparts who did not exercise (Vaillant, 2002). In this same study, not abusing alcohol at age 50 was also linked with still being alive and healthy at 75 to 80 years of age.

In chapter 2, we described the negative effects on the fetus and developing child that can result from drug use by the pregnant mother. Here we will examine how drug use affects adolescents and adults. What are some of the main dangers of drug use? How extensively do U.S. adolescents and adults use drugs?

Drugs, Health, and Addiction

Around the world, people use a long menu of psychoactive drugs. Different cultures chew or smoke a variety of plants and roots in order to reduce tension, change their mood, or somehow alter their psychological state. How people use—or do not use—substances to alter their psychological state depends on their cultural context.

Consider the use of alcohol. There are differences in alcohol use by religion, gender, and nationality around the world (Koenig, 2001; Melinder & Anderson, 2001). Some religions, such as Islam, prohibit the use of alcohol. However, Catholics, Reform Jews, and liberal Protestants all consume alcohol at a fairly high level. Alcohol use is high in Russia but low in China. Europeans, especially the French, drink alcohol at high rates. Across cultures, men drink more alcohol than women.

The cultural acceptability of substance abuse is no measure of its safety, as the mainstream acceptance of alcohol illustrates (Insel & Roth, 2004). Among the many drugs used by adolescents and adults, we focus on alcohol and cigarettes because their use is so widespread. They pose serious dangers to health and development.

Alcohol, Cigarettes, and Health   Estimates are that about 30 percent of French adults have impaired health related to alcohol consumption. More than 13 million people in the United States are classified as alcoholics. Each year, approximately 25,000 people are killed and 1.5 million injured by drunk drivers. In 65 percent of the aggressive male acts against females, the offender is under the influence of alcohol (Goodman & others, 1986).

Smoking cigarettes, or even being around those who smoke, also can produce serious health problems (Pomerleau, 2000). For example, smoking is linked to 30 percent of cancer deaths, 21 percent of heart disease deaths, and 82 percent of chronic pulmonary disease deaths in the United States. Secondhand smoke is implicated in as many as 9,000 cancer deaths a year (Sandler & others, 1989). Children of smokers are at special risk for respiratory and middle-ear infections.

Addiction   Beyond the risks to physical health and safety, alcohol and cigarettes also endanger development (Fields, 2004). They can distort a person's experience of life and opportunities by creating psychological dependence, physical dependence, or both. *Psychological dependence* exists when a person is preoccupied with obtaining a drug for emotional reasons, such as the reduction of stress. *Physical dependence* exists when discontinuing use of a drug creates unpleasant, significant changes in physical functioning and behavior. These changes are called *withdrawal symptoms*. Depending on the drug, withdrawal symptoms include insomnia, tremors, nausea, vomiting, cramps, elevation of heart rate and blood pressure, convulsions, anxiety, and depression.

The result of this dependence is known as **addiction,** a pattern of behavior characterized by overwhelming involvement with using a drug and securing its supply. Thus, experts on drug abuse use the term *addiction* to refer to physical or psychological dependence, or both.

Cigarette smoking can easily become an addiction. Nicotine, the active drug in cigarettes, is a stimulant that increases the smoker's energy and alertness, a pleasurable and reinforcing experience. Nicotine also stimulates neurotransmitters that have a calming or pain-reducing effect.

Quitting smoking is not easy. Use of nicotine substitutes, such as nicotine gum and the nicotine patch, work on the principle that supplying small amounts of nicotine diminishes the intensity of withdrawal. Another technique that helps smokers quit is stimulus control. For example, if the smoker associates a morning cup of coffee with smoking, the smoker avoids this stimulus cue for smoking and learns to substitute other behaviors for smoking. Some smokers just quit, but this strategy is more successful with light rather than heavy smokers.

Whether addictions are diseases is a matter of controversy. The **disease model of addiction** describes addictions as biologically based, lifelong diseases that involve a loss of control over behavior and require medical and/or spiritual treatment for recovery. In the disease model, addiction is either inherited or taught to the person early in life. Current or recent problems or relationships are not believed to be causes of the disease. Once you have the disease, you can never completely rid yourself of it, according to this model. The disease model has been strongly promoted and supported by the medical profession and Alcoholics Anonymous (AA) (Humphreys, 2000).

In contrast to the disease model of addiction, which focuses on biological mechanisms, some psychologists believe that understanding addiction requires that it be placed in the context of people's lives, their personalities, their relationships, their environments, and their perspectives. In this **life-process model of addiction,** addiction is not a disease but a habitual response that can be understood only in the context of social relationships and experiences.

Alcoholism

addiction A pattern of behavior characterized by an overwhelming involvement with using a drug and securing its supply.

disease model of addiction The view that addictions are biologically based, lifelong diseases that involve a loss of control over behavior and require medical and/or spiritual treatment for recovery.

life-process model of addiction The view that addiction is not a disease but a habitual response and a source of gratification and security that can be understood only in the context of social relationships and experiences.

Adolescent Substance Use

Substance Abuse in Adolescence

Cigarette smoking begins primarily in childhood and adolescence, and many alcoholics established their drinking habits during secondary school or college (Wood, Vinson, & Sher, 2001). In fact, most adolescents use drugs at some point, whether limited to alcohol, caffeine, and cigarettes or extended to marijuana, cocaine, and other so-called "hard" drugs. However, drug use poses a special hazard to development when adolescents use drugs as a way of coping with stress. This practice can interfere with the development of coping skills and responsible decision making. Drug use in childhood or early adolescence has more detrimental long-term effects on the development of responsible, competent behavior than drug use in late adolescence (Newcomb & Bentler, 1988).

Trends in Drug Use   Each year since 1975, Lloyd Johnston, Patrick O'Malley, and Gerald Bachman, working at the Institute of Social Research at the University of Michigan, have carefully monitored the drug use of America's high school seniors in a wide range of public and private high schools. Since 1991, they also have surveyed drug use by eighth- and tenth-graders. The University of Michigan study is called the Monitoring the Future Study. In 2002, the study surveyed approximately 44,000 students in nearly 400 secondary schools.

According to this study, the use of drugs among U.S. secondary school students declined in the 1980s but began to increase in the early 1990s (Johnston, O'Malley, & Bachman, 2001). In the late 1990s and the first two years of the twenty-first century, the proportions of tenth- and twelfth-grade students' use of any illicit drug had been holding fairly steady, while eighth-graders were showing a slight decline in use (Johnston, O'Malley, & Bachman, 2003). In 2002, the proportion of students reporting the use of any illicit drug in the past 30 days declined at all three grade levels, significantly so in grades 8 and 10. Figure 4.12 shows the trends in illegal drug use by U.S. high school seniors since 1975 and by U.S. eighth- and tenth-graders since 1991.

Nonetheless, even with the recent leveling off in use, the United States still has the highest rate of adolescent drug use of any industrialized nation. Also, the University of Michigan survey likely underestimates the percentage of adolescents who take drugs because it does not include high school dropouts, who have a higher rate of drug use than do students who are still in school. Johnston, O'Malley, and Bachman (2003) believe that "generational forgetting" contributed to the rise of adolescent drug use in the 1990s, with adolescents' beliefs about the dangers of drugs eroding considerably. The recent downturn in drug use by U.S. adolescents has been

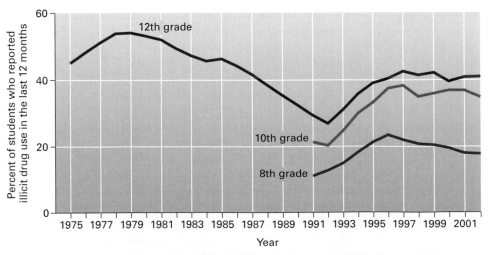

FIGURE 4.12 Trends in Drug Use by U.S. Eighth-, Tenth-, and Twelfth-Grade Students

This graph shows the percentage of U.S. eighth-, tenth-, and twelfth-grade students who reported having taken an illicit drug in the last 12 months from 1975 through 2002 for twelfth-graders and from 1975 through 2002 for eighth- and tenth-graders (Johnson, O'Malley, & Bachman, 2003).

attributed to such factors as an increase in the perceived dangers of drug use and the tragedy of the terrorist attacks of 9/11/01 having a sobering effect on youth (Johnston, O'Malley, & Bachman, 2003).

Alcohol and Cigarettes   How extensive is alcohol use by U.S. adolescents? Sizeable declines have occurred in recent years (Johnston, O'Malley, & Bachman, 2003). The percentage of U.S. eighth-graders saying that they had any alcohol to drink in the past 30 days has fallen from a 1996 high of 26 percent to 20 percent in 2002. From 2001 to 2002, 30-day prevalence among tenth-graders fell from 39 to 35 percent. Monthly prevalence among high school seniors was 72 percent in 1980 but had declined to 49 percent in 2002. Binge drinking (defined in the University of Michigan surveys as having five or more drinks in a row in the last two weeks) fell from 41 percent to 30 percent in 2002. Binge drinking by eighth- and tenth-graders also dropped in 2002 (7 percent of eighth-graders, 18 percent of tenth-graders). While still high, these rates are down from 1 to 4 percent from 2001. A consistent sex difference occurs in binge drinking, with males engaging in this more than females. In 1997, 39 percent of male high school seniors said they had been drunk in the last two weeks, compared with 29 percent of their female counterparts.

Cigarette smoking is also decreasing among adolescents. Cigarette smoking peaked in 1996 and 1997 and then gradually declined. In the national survey by the Institute of Social Research, the percentage of U.S. adolescents who are current cigarette smokers continued to decline in 2002 (Johnston, O'Malley, & Bachman, 2003). The percentage of eighth-, tenth-, and twelfth-graders who said they had ever smoked cigarettes dropped by 4 to 5 percentage points in 2002—more than any recent year. Following peak use in 1996, smoking rates for U.S. eighth-graders have fallen by 50 percent. Percentage declines in upper grades have been smaller, although the picture for older adolescents should improve in the next few years as a result of the current eighth-graders becoming older.

There are a number of explanations for the decline in cigarette use by U.S. youth. These include increasing prices, less tobacco advertising reaching adolescents, more antismoking advertisements, and an increase in negative publicity about the tobacco industry. Since the mid-1990s, an increasing percentage of adolescents have reported that they perceive cigarette smoking as dangerous, that they disapprove of it, that they are less accepting of being around smokers, and that they prefer to date nonsmokers (Johnston, O'Malley, & Bachman, 2003).

The devastating effects of early smoking were brought home in a research study that found that smoking in the adolescent years causes permanent genetic changes in the lungs and forever increases the risk of lung cancer, even if the smoker quits (Weincke & others, 1999). The damage was much less likely among smokers in the study who started in their twenties. One of the remarkable findings in the study was that the early age of onset of smoking was more important in predicting genetic damage than how much the individuals smoked.

The Roles of Parents and Peers   Parents and peers play important roles in preventing adolescent drug abuse (Dishion, 2001; Reifman, 2001; Windle & Windle, 2003). Positive relationships with parents and others are important in reducing adolescents' drug use (Brody & Ge, 2001). In one recent study, low parental involvement, peer pressure, and associating with problem-behaving friends were linked with high use of drugs by adolescents (Simons-Morton & others, 2001). Also, in a recent national survey, parents who were more involved in setting limits (such as where adolescents went after school and what they were exposed to on TV and the Internet) were more likely to have adolescents who did not use drugs (National Center for Addiction and Substance Abuse, 2001). One longitudinal study linked early substance abuse with certain characteristics during early childhood (Kaplow, Curran, & Dodge, 2002). Risk factors at kindergarten for substance use at 10 to 12 years of age included being male, having a parent who abused substances, a low level of verbal reasoning by parents, and low social problem-solving skills.

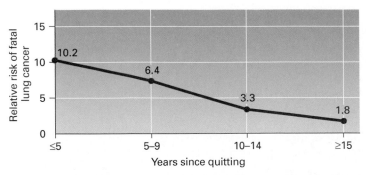

FIGURE 4.13 Fatal Lung Cancer and Years Since Quitting Smoking
One study compared more than 43,000 former male smokers with almost 60,000 males who had never smoked (Enstrom, 1999). For comparison purposes, a zero level was assigned as the risk of fatal lung cancer for men who had never smoked. Over time, the relative risk for smokers who had quit declined, but even after 15 years it was still above that of nonsmokers.

Substance Abuse in Adulthood

How pervasive is cigarette smoking in adults? Fewer smoke today than in the past and almost half of all living adults who ever smoked have quit. Figure 4.13 shows that when individuals quit smoking, over time their risk of lung cancer declines. The prevalence of smoking among U.S. men has dropped from over 50 percent in 1965 to about 25 percent today. However, more than 50 million Americans still smoke cigarettes, and recently cigar smoking, with risks similar to cigarette smoking, has increased (Ray & Ksir, 2004).

Drinking in College and Early Adulthood Unlike cigarette smoking, drinking alcohol remains an accepted part of mainstream U.S. culture. Almost half of U.S. college students say they drink heavily (Johnston, O'Malley, & Bachman, 1996). The effects of heavy drinking take a toll. In a national survey of drinking patterns on 140 campuses, almost half of the binge drinkers reported problems that included (Wechsler & others, 1994)

- missing classes,
- physical injuries,
- troubles with police, and
- having unprotected sex.

This survey also found that binge-drinking college students were 11 times more likely to drive after drinking, and twice as likely to have unprotected sex, than college students who did not binge drink. In another study, first-year college students who met the criteria of alcohol dependence were more likely to have failing grades than their counterparts who did not meet the criteria (Aertgeerts & Buntix, 2002).

More than 40,000 full-time U.S. college students were asked about their drinking habits in 1993, 1997, 1999, and 2001 (Wechsler & others, 2002). Binge-drinking rates (men who drank five or more drinks in a row and women who drank four or more drinks at least once in the two weeks prior to the questionnaire) remained remarkably consistent—at about 44 percent—over the eight years. Further, almost 75 percent of underage students living in fraternities or sororities were binge drinkers and 70 percent of traditional-age college students who lived away from home were binge drinkers. The lowest rate of binge drinking—25 percent—occurred for students living at home with their parents.

A special concern is the increase in binge drinking by females during emerging adulthood. One study found a 125 percent increase in binge drinking at all-women colleges from 1993 through 2001 (Wechsler & others, 2002).

Fortunately, by the time individuals reach their mid-twenties, many have reduced their use of alcohol and drugs. That is the conclusion reached by Gerald Bachman and his colleagues (2002) in a longitudinal analysis of more than 38,000 individuals (see figure 4.14). They were evaluated from the time they were high school seniors through their twenties. Some of the main findings in the study were:

- College students drink more than youths who end their education after high school.
- Those who don't go to college smoke more than those who do.
- Singles use marijuana more than married individuals.
- Drinking is heaviest among singles and divorced individuals. Becoming engaged, married, or even remarried quickly brings down alcohol use. Thus, living arrangements and marital status are key factors in alcohol and drug use rates during the twenties.
- Individuals who considered religion to be very important in their lives and who frequently attended religious services were less likely to take drugs than their less religious counterparts.

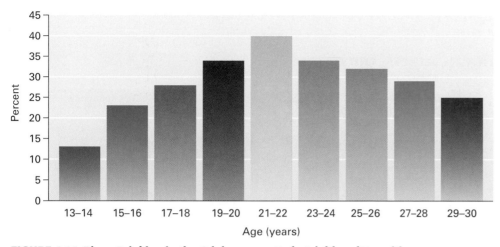

FIGURE 4.14 Binge Drinking in the Adolescence–Early Adulthood Transition

Note that the percentage of individuals engaging in binge drinking peaked at 21 to 22 years of age and then began to gradually decline through the remainder of the twenties. Binge drinking was defined as having five or more alcoholic drinks in a row in the past two weeks.

Substance Abuse in Older Adults How extensive is substance abuse in older adults? A recent national survey found that binge drinking (having five or more drinks on at least one day) declines through the late adulthood years (National Center for Health Statistics, 2002) (see figure 4.15). Indeed, a majority (58 percent) of U.S. adults 65 years and older completely abstain from alcohol, an increase from 38 percent of 45- to 64-year-olds. The reasons for these declines are usually attributed to an increase in illness and disease.

Despite these declines in alcohol use, the Substance Abuse and Mental Health Services Administration (2002) has identified substance abuse among older adults as the "invisible epidemic" in the United States. The belief is that substance abuse often goes undetected in older adults, and there is concern about older adults who abuse not only illicit drugs but prescription drugs as well (Scott & Popovich, 2001). The consequences of abuse—such as depression, inadequate nutrition, congestive heart failure, and frequent falls—may erroneously be attributed to other medical or psychological conditions (Hoyer & Roodin, 2003). As the number of older adults rises, substance abuse is likely to characterize an increasing number of older adults (Atkinson, Ryan, & Turner, 2001). For older adults who are taking multiple medications, the dangers of substance abuse rise. For example, when combined with tranquilizers or sedatives, alcohol use can impair breathing, produce excessive sedation, and be fatal.

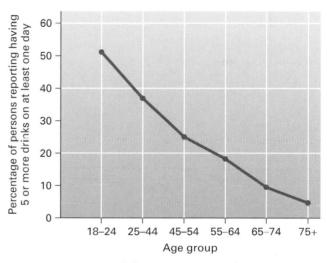

FIGURE 4.15 Age and the Consumption of Five or More Drinks on at Least One Day in the United States

The graph shows the considerable decline in having five or more drinks on at least one day as people get older (National Center for Health Statistics, 2002).

Review and Reflect: Learning Goal 4

4 Evaluate substance use in adolescence and adulthood

REVIEW

- What characterizes addiction? What are two models for understanding addiction?
- How extensively do adolescents take drugs?
- What is the nature of substance use in college students and young adults? How can substance abuse in older adults be described?

REFLECT

- Do you know someone who has a drug problem? If so, describe the nature of the problem. Is he or she willing to admit to having a problem?

www.mhhe.com/santrockldt2

Clearinghouse for Drug Information

Smoking/Tobacco Control

Smoking Cessation

Reach Your Learning Goals

CHAPTER 4

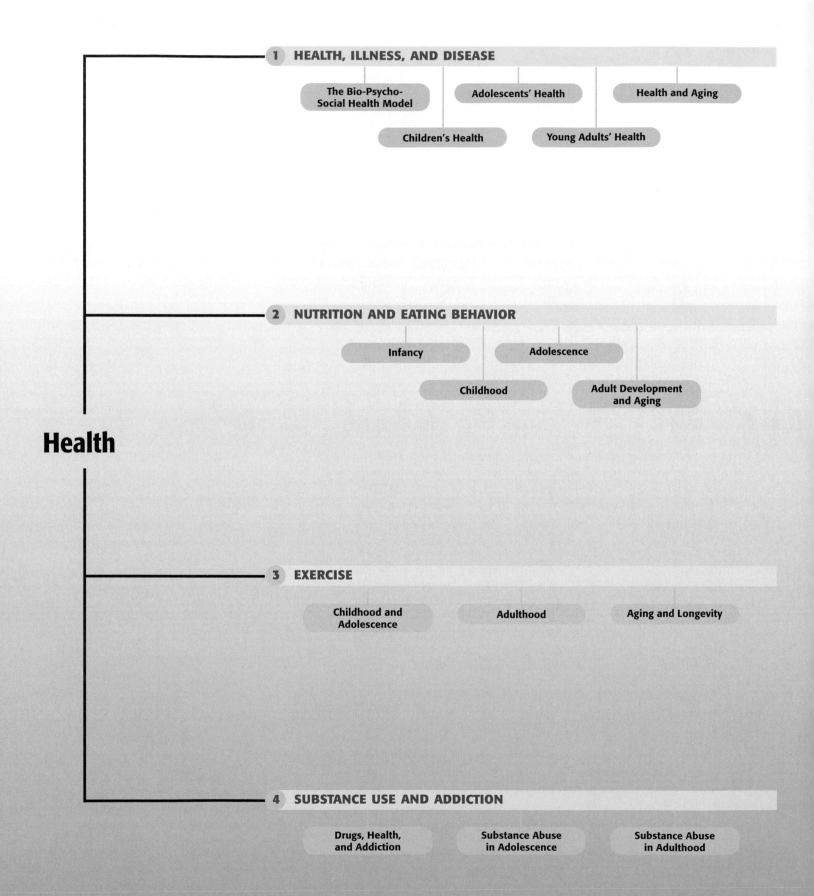

Health

1 HEALTH, ILLNESS, AND DISEASE

- The Bio-Psycho-Social Health Model
- Children's Health
- Adolescents' Health
- Young Adults' Health
- Health and Aging

2 NUTRITION AND EATING BEHAVIOR

- Infancy
- Childhood
- Adolescence
- Adult Development and Aging

3 EXERCISE

- Childhood and Adolescence
- Adulthood
- Aging and Longevity

4 SUBSTANCE USE AND ADDICTION

- Drugs, Health, and Addiction
- Substance Abuse in Adolescence
- Substance Abuse in Adulthood

Summary

1 Describe the bio-psycho-social health model and developmental changes in health

- Health is best understood as a combination of biological, psychological, and social factors. In the biological approach, health problems are caused by the function of the individual's body. Among the psychological factors that have been proposed as causes of health problems are a lack of self-control, emotional turmoil, and negative thinking. Social factors include cross-cultural variations, socioeconomic factors, and poverty.
- Prevention and poverty are important factors in children's health. Children need timely immunizations. Accident prevention is a key aspect of children's health. Of special concern are children living in poverty, who often are malnourished.
- Adolescence is a critical juncture in health because many health habits—good or bad—still are being formed. Adolescents use health services at a lower rate than any other age group.
- Few young adults have health problems. Many young adults don't stop to think about how their personal lifestyles will affect their health later in their lives.
- Chronic disorders are rare in young adults, increase in middle-aged adults, and are common in older adults. Osteoporosis is a concern, especially among older women. Dementias, especially Alzheimer's disease, are a major health problem. A sizeable portion of older adults do not have a disability, and are more physically robust than previously thought. Special concerns are the quality of nursing homes for older adults and the treatment of older adults by the medical community.

2 Characterize developmental changes in nutrition and eating behavior

- The importance of adequate energy intake consumed in a loving and supportive environment in infancy cannot be overstated. Breastfeeding is usually recommended over bottlefeeding. Marasmus and kwashiorkor are diseases caused by severe malnutrition.
- Concerns about nutrition in childhood focus on fat content in diet and obesity. Fifteen percent of U.S. children are overweight. Obesity increases a child's risk of developing many medical and psychological problems.
- Nutrition and being overweight are also key problems among adolescents. Anorexia nervosa and bulimia nervosa can develop in adolescence.
- Obesity is a major concern in adulthood, and dieting is pervasive. Food restriction is associated with longevity, but a balanced diet is usually recommended for older adults. Controversy surrounds whether antioxidant vitamins can reduce the risk for disease.

3 Summarize the roles of exercise in child and adult health

- Most children and adolescents are not getting nearly enough exercise.
- Exercise produces both physical and psychological advantages, such as lowered risk of heart disease and lowered anxiety.
- Regular exercise can lead to a healthier life as a middle-aged and older adult, and increase longevity.

4 Evaluate substance use in adolescence and adulthood

- Addiction is a pattern of behavior characterized by overwhelming involvement with using a drug and securing its supply. Addiction can refer to physical or psychological dependence, or both. Two views of addiction are the disease model and the life-process model.
- The United States has the highest rate of adolescent drug use of any industrialized nation. Alcohol and cigarette smoking are special concerns. Parents and peers play important roles in preventing drug abuse in adolescents.
- Although cigarette smoking has decreased in U.S. adults, it still is a major health hazard. Almost half of U.S. college students say they drink heavily. By the mid-twenties, substance abuse decreases. Alcohol use and abuse decline in older adults, although abuse is more difficult to detect in older adults than younger adults.

Key Terms

bio-psycho-social health model 132
chronic disorders 138
osteoporosis 138
dementia 138

Alzheimer's disease 139
marasmus 144
kwashiorkor 144
basal metabolism rate (BMR) 145

anorexia nervosa 147
bulimia nervosa 148
restrained eaters 149
aerobic exercise 152

addiction 155
disease model of addiction 155
life-process model of addiction 155

Key People

Judith Rodin and Ellen Lange 141
Ernesto Pollitt 144

Lloyd Johnston, Patrick O'Malley, and Gerald Bachman 156

E-Learning Tools

Connect to **www.mhhe.com/santrockldt2** to research the answers and complete the following exercises. In addition, you'll find a number of other resources and valuable study tools for chapter 4, "Health," on the Student CD-ROM that came with this book.

Taking It to the Net

1. Eric's 72-year-old mother, Janie, has been diagnosed with Alzheimer's disease. Eric plans to move Janie from her apartment to his home, where he will take care of her as long as he can. What things should he do to make his home safe for Janie?

2. Darren and Angie are concerned to learn from their pediatrician that Heather, their 7-year-old daughter, is considered obese. Darren and Angie are both big eaters and self-described "couch potatoes." What can they do to help Heather lose weight and develop healthy nutrition and exercise habits for themselves at the same time?

3. Forty-four-year-old Donald started smoking at 15; he has been smoking a pack of cigarettes a day for at least 20 years. He wants to quit, but he has decided that he needs some form of nicotine replacement for a while. What are the pros and cons of the nicotine patch versus nicotine gum?

Connect to **www.mhhe.com/santrockldt2** to research the answers and complete these exercises.

Self-Assessments

To evaluate yourself on topics related to health, complete these self-assessments:

- *Is Your Lifestyle Good for Your Health?*
- *My Health Habits*
- *Do I Abuse Drugs?*

Health and Well-Being, Parenting, and Education

Build your decision-making skills by trying your hand at the health and well-being, parenting, and education "Scenarios."

Motor, Sensory, and Perceptual Development

Think about what is required for people to find their way around their environment, to play sports, or to create art. These activities require both active perception and precisely timed motor actions. Neither innate, automatic movements nor simple sensations are enough to let us do the things we take for granted every day. How do we develop perceptual and motor abilities, and what happens to them as we age? In this chapter, we will focus first on the development of motor skills, then on sensory and perceptual development, and on the coupling of perceptual-motor skills.

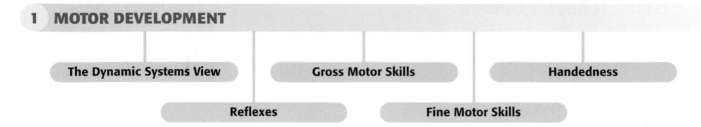

1 MOTOR DEVELOPMENT

The Dynamic Systems View   **Gross Motor Skills**   **Handedness**

Reflexes   **Fine Motor Skills**

Most adults are capable of coordinated, purposive actions of considerable skill, including driving a car, playing golf, and typing effectively on a computer keyboard. Some adults have extraordinary motor skills, such as those involved in winning an Olympic pole vault competition, painting a masterpiece, or performing heart surgery. Look all you want at a newborn infant, and you will observe nothing even remotely approaching these skilled actions. How, then, do the motor behaviors of adults come about?

The Dynamic Systems View

Developmentalist Arnold Gesell (1934) thought his painstaking observations had revealed how people develop their motor skills. He had discovered that infants and children develop motor skills in a fixed order and within specific time frames. Most babies go through a series of developmental milestones such as learning to crawl and learning to walk in a fixed sequence. These observations, said Gesell, show that motor development comes about through the unfolding of a genetic plan, or *maturation*.

Later studies, however, demonstrated that motor development is not the consequence of nature or nurture alone. In the 1990s, the study of motor development experienced a renaissance as psychologists developed new insights into *how* motor skills develop (Thelen & Smith, 1998). One increasingly influential theory is dynamic systems theory, proposed by Esther Thelen.

According to **dynamic systems theory**, infants assemble motor skills for perceiving and acting. Perception and action are coupled in this theory (Thelen, 1995, 2000, 2001; Thelen & Smith, 1998). For example, in order to develop motor skills, infants must perceive something in the environment that motivates them to act, and they must use their perceptions to fine-tune their movements. Motor skills represent solutions to the infant's goals.

How is a motor skill developed according to this theory? When infants are motivated to do something, they might create a new motor behavior. The new behavior is the result of many converging factors: the development of the nervous system, the body's physical properties and its possibilities for movement, the goal the child is motivated to reach, and the environmental support for the skill. For example, babies learn to walk only when maturation of the nervous system allows them to control certain leg muscles, when their legs have grown enough to support their weight, and when they want to move.

Mastering a motor skill requires the infant's active efforts to coordinate several components of the skill (Spencer & others, 2000). Infants explore and select possible

dynamic systems theory A theory, proposed by Esther Thelen, that seeks to explain how motor behaviors are assembled for perceiving and acting.

solutions to the demands of a new task; they assemble adaptive patterns by modifying their current movement patterns. The first step occurs when the infant is motivated by a new challenge—such as the desire to cross a room—and gets into the "ball park" of the task demands by taking a couple of stumbling steps. Then the infant "tunes" these movements to make them smoother and more effective. The tuning is achieved through repeated cycles of action and perception of the consequences of that action. According to the dynamic systems view, even universal milestones, such as crawling, reaching, and walking, are learned through this process of adaptation: Infants modulate their movement patterns to fit a new task by exploring and selecting possible configurations (Adolph, Weise, & Marin, 2003; Smith & Samuelson, 2003).

Thus, according to dynamic systems theory, motor development is not a passive process in which genes dictate the unfolding of a sequence of skills over time. Rather, the infant actively puts together a skill in order to achieve a goal within the constraints set by the infant's body and environment. Nature and nurture, the infant and the environment, perception and action, are all working together as part of an ever-changing system.

As we examine the course of motor development, we will describe how dynamic systems theory applies to some specific skills. To begin, though, we describe how the story of motor development starts with reflexes.

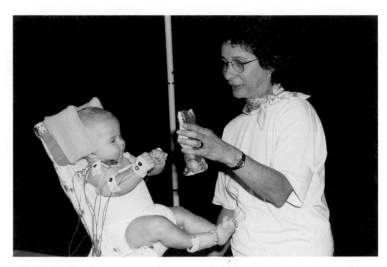

Esther Thelen is shown conducting an experiment to discover how infants learn to control their arms to reach and grasp for objects. A computer device is used to monitor the infant's arm movements and to track muscle patterns. Thelen's research is conducted from a dynamic systems perspective. *What is the nature of this perspective?*

Reflexes

The newborn is not a completely helpless organism. Among other things, it has some basic reflexes, which are genetically carried survival mechanisms. For example, the newborn naturally holds its breath and contracts its throat to keep water out. *Reflexes* are built-in reactions to stimuli; they govern the newborn's movements, which are automatic and beyond the newborn's control. They allow infants to respond adaptively to their environment before they have had the opportunity to learn.

For example, the sucking and rooting reflexes have survival value for newborn mammals, who must find a mother's breast to obtain nourishment. The **sucking reflex** occurs when newborns automatically suck an object placed in their mouth. This reflex enables newborns to get nourishment before they have associated a nipple with food. The **rooting reflex** occurs when the infant's cheek is stroked or the side of the mouth is touched. In response, the infant turns its head toward the side that was touched in an apparent effort to find something to suck. The sucking and rooting reflexes both disappear when the infant is 3 to 4 months old. They are replaced by the infant's voluntary eating.

The **Moro reflex** is a neonatal response that occurs in response to a sudden, intense noise or movement. When startled, the newborn arches its back, throws back its head, and flings out its arms and legs. Then the newborn rapidly closes its arms and legs to the center of its body. Steady pressure on any part of the infant's body calms the infant after it has been startled. The Moro reflex is believed to be a way of grabbing for support while falling; it would have had survival value for our primate ancestors. This reflex, which is normal in all newborns, also tends to disappear at 3 to 4 months of age.

An overview of reflexes is given in figure 5.1. Some reflexes present in the newborn—coughing, blinking, and yawning, for example—persist throughout life. They are as important for the adult as they are for the infant. Other reflexes, though, disappear several months following birth, as the infant's brain matures, and voluntary control over many behaviors develops. The movements of some reflexes eventually become incorporated into more complex, voluntary actions. One important

Esther Thelen's Research

sucking reflex A newborn's built-in reaction of automatically sucking an object placed in its mouth. The sucking reflex enables the infant to get nourishment before it has associated a nipple with food.

rooting reflex A newborn's built-in reaction that occurs when the infant's cheek is stroked or the side of the mouth is touched. In response, the infant turns its head toward the side that was touched, in an apparent effort to find something to suck.

Moro reflex A neonatal startle response that occurs in reaction to a sudden, intense noise or movement. When startled, the newborn arches its back, throws its head back, and flings out its arms and legs. Then the newborn rapidly closes its arms and legs to the center of the body.

Reflex	Stimulation	Infant's Response	Developmental Pattern
Blinking	Flash of light, puff of air	Closes both eyes	Permanent
Babinski	Sole of foot stroked	Fans out toes, twists foot in	Disappears after 9 months to 1 year
Grasping	Palms touched	Grasps tightly	Weakens after 3 months, disappears after 1 year
Moro (startle)	Sudden stimulation, such as hearing loud noise or being dropped	Startles, arches back, throws head back, flings out arms and legs and then rapidly closes them to center of body	Disappears after 3 to 4 months
Rooting	Cheek stroked or side of mouth touched	Turns head, opens mouth, begins sucking	Disappears after 3 to 4 months
Stepping	Infant held above surface and feet lowered to touch surface	Moves feet as if to walk	Disappears after 3 to 4 months
Sucking	Object touching mouth	Sucks automatically	Disappears after 3 to 4 months
Swimming	Infant put face down in water	Makes coordinated swimming movements	Disappears after 6 to 7 months
Tonic neck	Infant placed on back	Forms fists with both hands and usually turns head to the right (sometimes called the "fencer's pose" because the infant looks like it is assuming a fencer's position)	Disappears after 2 months

FIGURE 5.1 Infant Reflexes

Beginnings: Behavior of the Newborn

example is the **grasping reflex,** which occurs when something touches the infant's palms. The infant responds by grasping tightly. By the end of the third month, the grasping reflex diminishes, and the infant shows a more voluntary grasp, which is often produced by visual stimuli. For example, when an infant sees a mobile whirling above her crib, she may reach out and try to grasp it. As its motor development becomes smoother, the infant will grasp objects, carefully manipulate them, and explore their qualities.

Sucking is especially important: It serves as the infant's route to nourishment. The sucking capabilities of newborns vary considerably. Some newborns are efficient at forceful sucking and obtaining milk; others are not as adept and get tired before they are full. Most infants take several weeks to establish a sucking style that is coordinated with the way the mother is holding the infant, the way milk is coming out of the bottle or breast, and the infant's sucking speed and temperament.

Pediatrician T. Berry Brazelton (1956) observed infants for more than a year to determine the incidence of their sucking when they were nursing and how their sucking changed as they grew older. Over 85 percent of the infants engaged in considerable sucking behavior unrelated to feeding. They sucked their finger, their fists, and pacifiers. By the age of 1 year, most had stopped the sucking behavior. However, as many as 40 percent of children continue to suck their thumbs after they have started school (Kessen Haith, & Salapatek, 1970). Most developmentalists do not attach a great deal of significance to this behavior and are not aware of parenting strategies that might contribute to it. Individual differences in children's biological makeup may be involved to some degree in the continuation of sucking behavior.

Gross Motor Skills

grasping reflex A neonatal reflex that occurs when something touches the infant's palms. The infant responds by grasping tightly.

Ask any parents about their baby, and sooner or later you are likely to hear about one or more motor milestone, such as "Cassandra just learned to crawl," "Jesse is finally sitting alone," or "Angela took her first step last week." It is no wonder that parents proudly announce such milestones. They reflect the transformation of babies from being unable to lift their heads to being able to grab things off the grocery store shelf, to chase a cat, and to participate actively in the family's social life (Thelen, 1995, 2000). These milestones are examples of gross motor skills. **Gross motor skills** involve large-muscle activities, such as moving one's arms and walking. How do gross motor skills develop through the life span?

The Development of Posture   Gross motor skills, as well as many other activities, require postural control (Thelen, 1995, 2000). Infants need to control their heads to stabilize their gaze and to track moving objects. They also must have strength and balance in their legs to walk.

Newborn infants cannot voluntarily control their posture. Within a few weeks, though, they can hold their heads erect, and soon they can lift their heads while prone. By 2 months of age, babies can sit while supported on a lap or an infant seat, but sitting independently is not accomplished until 6 or 7 months of age. Standing also develops gradually across the first year of life. By about 8 months of age, infants usually learn to pull themselves up and hold on to a chair, and they often can stand alone by about 10 to 12 months of age.

In Thelen's (1995, 2000) view, posture is more than just holding still and straight though. Posture, like other movements, is a dynamic process that is linked with several sensory modalities: proprioception from the skin, joints, and muscles; vestibular organs in the inner ear that regulate balance and equilibrium; and cues from vision and hearing (Spencer & others, 2000).

Learning to Walk   Locomotion and postural control are closely linked, especially in walking upright (Adolph, 2002; Adolph & Eppler, 2002). Walking upright requires being able both to balance on one leg as the other is swung forward and to shift the weight from one leg to the other (Thelen, 2000).

Although infants usually learn to walk about their first birthday, the neural pathways that control the leg alternation component of walking are in place from a very early age, possibly even at birth or before. Infants engage in frequent alternating kicking movements throughout the first six months of life when they are lying on their backs. Also when 1- to 2-month-olds are given support with their feet in contact with a motorized treadmill, they show well-coordinated, alternating steps.

If infants can produce forward stepping movements so early, why does it take them so long to learn to walk? The key skills in learning to walk appear to be stabilizing balance on one leg long enough to swing the other forward and shifting the weight without falling. This is a difficult biomechanical problem to solve, and it takes infants about a year to do it.

In learning to locomote, infants learn what kinds of places and surfaces afford safe locomotion (Adolph, Vereijken, & Shrout, 2003; Berger & Adolph, 2003). Karen Adolph's research (1997) investigated how experienced and inexperienced crawling infants and walking infants go down steep slopes (see figure 5.2). Newly crawling infants, who averaged about 8½ months in age, rather indiscriminately went down the steep slopes, often falling in the process (with their mothers next to the slope to catch them). However, with further weeks of practice, the crawling babies became more adept at judging which slopes were too steep to crawl down and which ones they could navigate safely. Newly walking infants also could not judge the safety of the various slopes, but infants who were experienced walkers accurately matched locomotor skills with the steepness of the slopes. They rarely fell downhill, either refusing to go down the steep slopes or going down backward in a cautious manner. Experienced walkers perceptually assessed the situation—looking, swaying, touching, and thinking before they moved down the slope. With experience, both the crawlers and the walkers learned to avoid the risky slopes where they would fall, integrating perceptual information with the development of a new motor behavior. In this research, we again see the importance of perceptual-motor coupling in the development of motor skills (Adolph, Weise, & Marin, 2003).

Karen Adolph's Research

gross motor skills Motor skills that involve large-muscle activities, such as walking.

Newly crawling infant

Experienced walker

FIGURE 5.2 The Role of Experience in Crawling and Walking Infants' Judgments of Whether to Go Down a Slope

Karen Adolph (1997) found that locomotor experience rather than age was the primary predictor of adaptive responding on slopes of varying steepness. Newly crawling and walking infants could not judge the safety of the various slopes. With experience, they learned to avoid slopes where they would fall. When expert crawlers began to walk, they again made mistakes and fell, even though they had judged the same slope accurately when crawling. Adolph referred to this as the *specificity of learning* because it does not transfer across crawling and walking.

A baby is an angel whose wings decrease as his legs increase.

—FRENCH PROVERB

www.mhhe.com/santrockld2

Developmental Milestones

Figure 5.3 summarizes important accomplishments in gross motor skills during the first year, culminating in the ability to walk easily. The timing of these milestones varies by as much as two to four months, especially among older infants. What remains fairly uniform, however, is the sequence of accomplishments. These motor accomplishments bring increasing independence. Older infants can explore their environment more extensively and initiate interaction with caregivers and peers more readily than when they were younger.

Development in the Second Year In the second year of life, toddlers become more motorically skilled and mobile. They are no longer content with being in a playpen and want to move all over the place. Child development experts believe that motor activity during the second year is vital to the child's competent development and that few restrictions, except for safety, should be placed on their motoric adventures.

By 13 to 18 months, toddlers can pull a toy attached to a string and use their hands and legs to climb up a number of steps. By 18 to 24 months, toddlers can walk quickly or run stiffly for a short distance, balance on their feet in a squat position while playing with objects on the floor, walk backward without losing their balance, stand and kick a ball without falling, stand and throw a ball, and jump in place.

Can parents give their babies a head start on becoming physically fit and physically talented through structured exercise classes? Physical fitness classes for babies range from passive fare—with adults putting infants through the paces—to programs called "aerobic" because they demand crawling, tumbling, and ball skills. However, pediatricians point out that when an adult is stretching and moving an infant's limbs, it is easy for them to go beyond the infant's physical limits without knowing it. Pediatricians also recommend that exercise for infants should not be of the intense, aerobic variety. Babies cannot adequately stretch their bodies to achieve aerobic benefits.

In short, most infancy experts recommend against structured exercise classes for babies. But there are other ways of guiding infants' motor development. As discussed in the Contexts of Life-Span Development interlude, caregivers in some cultures do handle babies vigorously, and this might advance motor development.

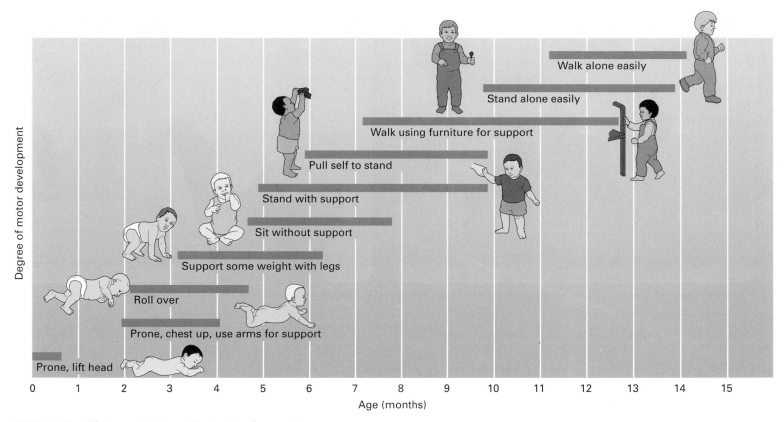

FIGURE 5.3 **Milestones in Gross Motor Development**

Contexts of Life-Span Development

Cultural Variations in Guiding Infants' Motor Development

Mothers in developing countries tend to stimulate their infants' motor skills more than mothers in industrialized cultures (Hopkins, 1991). For example, Jamaican mothers regularly massage their infants and stretch their arms and legs (Hopkins, 1991). Mothers in the Gusii culture of Kenya also encourage vigorous movement in their babies (Hopkins & Westra, 1988). We can only speculate about the reasons for this cultural difference. Perhaps this stimulation in developing countries improves the infants' chances of survival or perhaps caregivers recognize that motor skills are required for important jobs in the culture.

Do these cultural variations make a difference in the infant's motor development? When caregivers provide babies with physical guidance by physically handling them in special ways (such as stroking, massaging, or stretching) or by giving them opportunities for exercise, the infants often attain motor milestones earlier than infants whose caregivers have not provided these physical activities. For example, Jamaican mothers expect their infants to sit and walk alone two to three months earlier than English mothers do (Hopkins & Westra, 1990).

Nonetheless, regardless of how much practice and stretching takes place, infants around the world still reach these motor milestones within a close age range. For example, Algonquin infants in Quebec, Canada, spend much of their first year strapped to a cradle board. Despite their inactivity, these infants still sit up, crawl, and walk within an age range similar to infants in cultures who have had much greater opportunity for activity.

 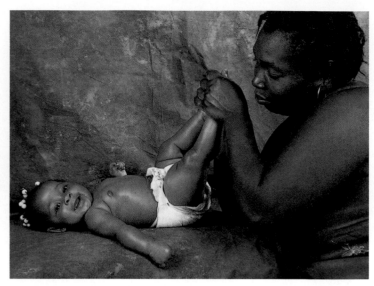

(Left) In the Algonquin culture in Quebec, Canada, babies are strapped to a cradle board for much of their infancy. *(Right)* In Jamaica, mothers massage and stretch their infants' arms and legs. *To what extent do cultural variations in their activity influence the time at which infants reach motor milestones?*

In sum, there are variations in the ages at which infants reach motor milestones in different cultures that likely depend on their activity opportunities. However, the variations are not large and milestones are reached within normal age ranges.

Childhood The preschool child no longer has to make an effort to stay upright and to move around. As children move their legs with more confidence and carry themselves more purposefully, moving around in the environment becomes more automatic.

At 3 years of age, children enjoy simple movements, such as hopping, jumping, and running back and forth, just for the sheer delight of performing these activities. They take considerable pride in showing how they can run across a room and jump all of 6 inches. The run-and-jump will win no Olympic gold medals, but for the 3-year-old the activity is a source of considerable pride and accomplishment.

At 4 years of age, children are still enjoying the same kind of activities, but they have become more adventurous. They scramble over low jungle gyms as they display their athletic prowess. Although they have been able to climb stairs with one foot on each step for some time, they are just beginning to be able to come down the same way.

At 5 years of age, children are even more adventuresome than they were at 4. It is not unusual for self-assured 5-year-olds to perform hair-raising stunts on practically any climbing object. They run hard and enjoy races with each other and their parents.

During middle and late childhood, children's motor development becomes much smoother and more coordinated than it was in early childhood. For example, only one child in a thousand can hit a tennis ball over the net at the age of 3, yet by the age of 10 or 11 most children can learn to play the sport. Running, climbing, skipping rope, swimming, bicycle riding, and skating are just a few of the many physical skills elementary school children can master. And, when mastered, these physical skills are a source of great pleasure and accomplishment. In gross motor skills involving large-muscle activity, boys usually outperform girls.

As children move through the elementary school years, they gain greater control over their bodies and can sit and pay attention for longer periods of time. However, elementary school children are far from being physically mature, and they need to be active. Elementary school children become more fatigued by long periods of sitting than by running, jumping, or bicycling. Physical action is essential for these children to refine their developing skills, such as batting a ball, skipping rope, or balancing on a beam. Elementary school children should be engaged in active, rather than passive, activities.

Organized sports are one way of encouraging children to be active and to develop their motor skills. Schools and community agencies offer programs for children that involve baseball, soccer, football, basketball, swimming, gymnastics, and other sports. For children who participate in them, these programs may play a central role in their lives. The Applications in Life-Span Development interlude examines the role of parents in children's sports.

Applications in Life-Span Development

Parents and Children's Sports

Participation in sports can have both positive and negative consequences for children (Kuchenbecker, 2000). Children's participation in sports can provide exercise, opportunities to learn how to compete, self-esteem, and a setting for developing peer relations and friendships. However, sports also can have negative outcomes for children: the pressure to achieve and win, physical injuries, a distraction from academic work, and unrealistic expectations for success as an athlete (Emery, 2003; Demorest & Landry, 2003). Few people challenge the value of sports for children when conducted as part of a school's physical education or intramural program. However, some critics question the appropriateness of children's sports activities that emphasize a highly competitive, win-at-all-costs atmosphere.

There is a special concern about children in high-pressure sports that involve championship play under the media spotlight. Some clinicians and child developmentalists believe such activities put undue stress on children and teach them the wrong values—namely, a win-at-all-costs philosophy. Overly ambitious parents, coaches, and community boosters can unintentionally create a highly stressful atmosphere in children's sports. When the prestige of parents, an institution, or a community becomes the focus of the child's participation in sports, the danger of exploitation is clearly present. Programs oriented toward such purposes often require arduous training over many months and years, frequently leading to sports specialization at too early an age. In such circumstances, adults often communicate the distorted view that the sport is the most important aspect of the child's life (Pratt, Patel, & Greydanus, 2003).

If parents do not become overinvolved, they can help children build their physical skills and help them emotionally—for example, by discussing how to deal with a difficult coach, how to cope with a tough loss, and how to put a poorly played game in perspective (Goodman, 2000). Parents should monitor their children as they participate in sports for signs of developing stress. If the problems appear to be beyond the intuitive skills of a volunteer coach or parent, consultation with a counselor or clinician may be needed. Also, the parent should be sensitive to whether a particular sport is the best one for the child and whether the child can handle its competitive pressures (Pratt, Patel, & Greydanus, 2003).

Here are some guidelines that can benefit both parents and coaches of all children in sports (Women's Sports Foundation, 2001):

The Dos

• Make sports fun; the more children enjoy sports, the more they will want to play.

- Remember that it is okay for children to make mistakes; it means they are trying.
- Allow children to ask questions about the sport and discuss the sport in a calm, supportive manner.
- Show respect for the child's sports participation.
- Be positive and convince the child that he or she is making a good effort.
- Be a positive role model for the child in sports.

The Don'ts

- Don't yell or scream at the child.
- Don't condemn the child for poor play or continue to bring up failures long after they happen.
- Don't point out the child's errors in front of others.
- Don't expect the child to learn something immediately.
- Don't expect the child to become a pro.
- Don't ridicule the child.
- Don't compare the child to siblings or to more talented children.
- Don't make sports all work and no fun.

Adolescence and Adulthood Gross motor skills typically improve during adolescence. Most of us reach our peak physical performance before the age of 30, often between the ages of 19 and 26. This peak occurs both for the average young adult and for outstanding athletes. Even though athletes keep getting better than their predecessors—running faster, jumping higher, and lifting more weight—the age at which they reach their peak performance has remained virtually the same (Schultz & Curnow, 1988). Most swimmers and gymnasts reach their peak in their late teens. Many athletes, including track performers in sprint races (100-, 200-yard dashes), peak in their early to mid-twenties. Golfers and marathon runners tend to peak in their late twenties or even early thirties.

After an individual reaches the age of 30, most biological functions begin to decline, although the decline of specific organs can vary considerably (Gabbard, 2000). The decrement in general biological functioning that begins at about age 30 occurs at a rate of about 0.75 to 1 percent a year. Decrements often occur in cardiovascular functioning, muscle strength, bone tissue (especially for females), neural function, balance, and flexibility.

People slow down in late adulthood. Older adults move slower than young adults. This difference occurs across a wide range of movement difficulty (see figure 5.4). General slowing of movement in older adults has been found in everyday tasks such as moving from one place to another and continuous movement (Ketchman & Stelmach, 2001).

No matter how well individuals take care of themselves, aging eventually produces declines in biological functions. But as discussed in chapter 1, chronological age (an individual's age since birth) does differ from biological age (an individual's biological health). Aging individuals who are active and biologically healthy perform motor skills at a higher level than their less active, less healthy aging counterparts. As we saw in chapter 4, "Health," physical activity can have positive effects on motor skills in older adults. For example, in one study of nursing home residents in their nineties, weight training led to significant gains in mobility (Fiatarone & others, 1990).

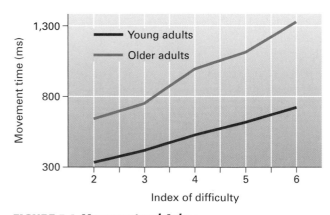

FIGURE 5.4 Movement and Aging

Older adults take longer to move than young adults and this occurs across a range of movement difficulty (Ketcham & Stelmach, 2001).

Fine Motor Skills

fine motor skills Motor skills that involve finely tuned movements, such as any activity that requires finger dexterity.

Whereas gross motor skills involve large-muscle activity, **fine motor skills** involve finely tuned movements. Buttoning a shirt, typing, or anything that requires finger dexterity demonstrates fine motor skills.

Motor skills decline less in older adults who are active and biologically healthy. *What is the difference between chronological age and biological age?*

Infancy Infants have hardly any control over fine motor skills at birth, but they have many components of what will become finely coordinated arm, hand, and finger movements (Rosenblith, 1992). A significant achievement in their interactions with their surroundings comes with the onset of reaching and grasping (McCarty & Ashmead, 1999).

For many years it was believed that when infants reach for an object, they must continuously have sight of the hand and the target (White, Castle, & Held, 1964). However, Rachel Clifton and her colleagues (1993) demonstrated that infants do not have to see their own hands in order to reach for an object. They concluded that proprioceptive cues from muscles, tendons, and joints, not sight of the limb, guide reaching by 4-month-old infants.

The development of reaching and grasping becomes more refined during the first two years of life. Initially, infants move their shoulders and elbows crudely, but later they move their wrists, rotate their hands, and coordinate their thumb and forefinger.

The infant's grasping system is very flexible. Infants vary their grip on an object depending on its size and shape, as well as the size of their own hands relative to the object's size. Infants grip small objects with their thumb and forefinger (and sometimes their middle finger too), whereas they grip large objects with all of the fingers of one hand or both hands.

Perceptual-motor coupling is necessary for the infant to coordinate grasping. Studies have found age differences in regard to which perceptual system is most likely to be used in coordinating grasping. Four-month-old infants rely greatly on touch to determine how they will grip an object; 8-month-olds are more likely to use vision as a guide (Newell & others, 1989). This developmental change is efficient because vision lets infants preshape their hands as they reach for an object.

Childhood and Adolescence At 3 years of age, children have had the ability to pick up the tiniest objects between their thumb and forefinger for some time, but they are still somewhat clumsy at it. Three-year-olds can build surprisingly high block towers, each block placed with intense concentration but often not in a completely straight line. When 3-year-olds play with a form board or a simple puzzle, they are rather rough in placing the pieces. Even when they recognize the hole that a piece fits into, they are not very precise in positioning the piece. They often try to force the piece in the hole or pat it vigorously.

By 4 years of age, children's fine motor coordination has become much more precise. Sometimes 4-year-old children have trouble building high towers with blocks because, in their desire to place each of the blocks perfectly, they may upset

Early Childhood: Motor Skills and Birth-Order During Early Childhood

those already stacked. By age 5, children's fine motor coordination has improved further. Hand, arm, and fingers all move together under better command of the eye. Mere towers no longer interest the 5-year-old, who now wants to build a house or a church, complete with steeple, though adults may still need to be told what each finished project is meant to be.

Increased myelination of the central nervous system is reflected in the improvement of fine motor skills during middle and late childhood. (Recall from chapter 3 that *myelination* involves the covering of the axon with a myelin sheath, a process that increases the speed with which information travels from neuron to neuron.) Children use their hands more adroitly as tools. Six-year-olds can hammer, paste, tie shoes, and fasten clothes. By 7 years of age, children's hands have become steadier. At this age, children prefer a pencil to a crayon for printing, and reversal of letters is less common. Printing becomes smaller. At 8 to 10 years of age, children can use their hands independently with more ease and precision; children can now write rather than print words. Letter size becomes smaller and more even. At 10 to 12 years of age, children begin to show manipulative skills similar to the abilities of adults. The complex, intricate, and rapid movements needed to produce fine-quality crafts or to play a difficult piece on a musical instrument can be mastered. Girls usually outperform boys in fine motor skills.

Adult Development Fine motor skills may undergo some decline in middle and late adulthood as dexterity decreases, although for most healthy individuals, fine motor skills, such as reaching and grasping, continue to be performed in functional ways. However, pathological conditions may result in weakness or paralysis of an individual's hands, in which case performance of fine motor skills may be impossible.

Slowed movement is one way in which fine motor skills may decline. For example, older adults are slower in their handwriting than younger adults are, although many older adults continue to perform handwriting competently (Dixon & others, 1993). Two explanations of the slower motor behavior of older adults are (1) neural noise and (2) strategy (Ketcham & Stelmach, 2001).

Neural noise refers to an increase in irregular neural activity in the central nervous system, which could affect a wide range of sensorimotor activities (Welford, 1984). Older adults are thought to have higher neural noise than younger adults (Walker, Philbin, & Fisk, 1997). An increase in neural noise disturbs the processing of incoming signals, delaying their interpretation and implementation. The consequences are slower and more variable movement performance by older adults.

Aging adults also may engage in *strategies* to compensate for declines in their gross and fine motor skills (Ketcham & Stelmach, 2001). Many older adults are strongly motivated to perform a task as accurately as possible (Salthouse, 1988). When they try to perform motor activities (such as handwriting or typing on a computer) too fast, older adults are prone to make more errors than younger adults, so they may slow their movements to execute a task more accurately.

Older adults are capable of learning new motor tasks just as younger adults are, although older adults typically do this at a slower rate of improvement (Ketcham & Stelmach, 2001). Thus, practice and training programs may minimize declines in motor function.

Handedness

One interesting aspect of motor development is *handedness*, a preference for using one hand rather than the other. For centuries, left-handers have suffered unfair discrimination in a world designed for right-handers. For many years, teachers forced all children to write with their right hand, even if they had a left-hand tendency. Fortunately, today most teachers let children write with the hand they favor.

Origin and Development of Handedness   What is the origin of hand prefer-ence? Genetic inheritance seems to be a strong influence (Yetkin, 2002). In one study, the handedness of adopted children was not related to the handedness of their adopted parents, but it was related to the handedness of their biological parents (Carter-Saltzman, 1980).

Right-handedness is dominant in all cultures (it appears in a ratio of about nine right-handers to one left-hander), and it appears before culture can influence the child (Cavill & Bryden, 2003). For example, in ultrasound observations of fetal thumb sucking, 9 of 10 fetuses were more likely to be sucking their right hand's thumb (Hepper, Shahidullah, & White, 1990). A study of newborns found that 65 percent turned their head to the right when they were lying on their back in a crib (Michel, 1981). Fifteen percent preferred to face toward the left and the remaining 20 percent showed no preference. These preferences for the right or the left were linked with handedness later in development.

Handedness and Other Characteristics   Approximately 85 to 95 percent of right-handed individuals primarily process speech in the brain's left hemisphere (Khedr & others, 2002; Springer & Deutsch, 1985). However, left-handed individu-als show more variation (Knecht & others, 2000; Szaflarski & others, 2002). Almost 75 percent of left-handers process speech in their left hemisphere, just like right-handers (Khedr & others, 2002). However, about 10 percent of left-handers process speech in their right hemisphere and approximately 15 percent of left-handers process speech equally in both hemispheres (Khedr & others, 2002).

Are there other differences between left- and right-handers? Left-handers are more likely to have reading problems (Geschwind & Behan, 1984; Natsopoulos & others, 1998, 2002). But left-handers also tend to have unusually good visual spa-tial skills and the ability to imagine spatial layouts (Holtzen, 2000). A higher per-centage of mathematicians, musicians, architects, and artists than would be expected are left-handers (For example, Michelangelo, Leonardo da Vinci, and Picasso were all left-handed) (Schacter & Ransil, 1996). In one study of more than 100,000 stu-dents taking the Scholastic Aptitude Test (SAT), 20 percent of the top-scoring group was left-handed, twice the rate of left-handedness found in the general population (10 percent) (Bower, 1985).

In sum, while a large majority of people are right-handed, both right-handers and left-handers have a number of strengths. Despite sometimes having to compen-sate for living in a right-handed world where it may be difficult to write on right-handed desks and cut with right-handed scissors, overall, being left-handed does not seem to handicap individuals to any significant degree (Porac & Searleman, 2002; Teasdale & Owen, 2001).

Today, most teachers let children write with the hand they favor. *What are the main reasons chil-dren become left- or right-handed?*

Handedness

Review and Reflect: Learning Goal 1

1 Describe how motor skills develop

REVIEW

- What is the dynamic systems view of motor development?
- What are reflexes? What are some reflexes of infants?
- What are gross motor skills and how do they develop?
- What are fine motor skills? How do fine motor skills develop?
- How does handedness develop?

REFLECT

- How would you evaluate the benefits and drawbacks of allowing an eight-year-old to play Little League baseball?

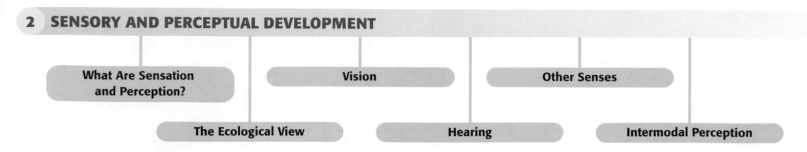

2   **SENSORY AND PERCEPTUAL DEVELOPMENT**

What Are Sensation and Perception?	Vision	Other Senses

| The Ecological View | Hearing | Intermodal Perception |

Right now, I am looking at my computer screen to make sure the words are being printed accurately as I am typing them. My perceptual and motor skills are working together. Recall that even control of posture uses information from the senses. And when people grasp an object, they use perceptual information about the object to adjust their motions.

How do these sensations and perceptions develop? Can a newborn see? If so, what can it perceive? What about the other senses—hearing, smell, taste, touch, and pain? What are they like in the newborn, and how do they develop? Can an infant put together information from two modalities, such as sight and sound? These are among the intriguing questions that we will explore in this section.

What Are Sensation and Perception?

How does a newborn know that her mother's skin is soft rather than rough? How does a 5-year-old know what color his hair is? How does a 10-year-old know that a firecracker is louder than a cat's meow? Infants and children "know" these things because of information that comes through the senses. Without vision, hearing, touch, taste, smell, and other senses, we would be isolated from the world; we would live in dark silence, a tasteless, colorless, feelingless void.

Sensation occurs when information interacts with sensory *receptors*—the eyes, ears, tongue, nostrils, and skin. The sensation of hearing occurs when waves of pulsating air are collected by the outer ear and transmitted through the bones of the inner ear to the auditory nerve. The sensation of vision occurs as rays of light contact the eyes, become focused on the retina, and are transmitted by the optic nerve to the visual centers of the brain.

Perception is the interpretation of what is sensed. The air waves that contact the ears might be interpreted as noise or as musical sounds, for example. The physical energy transmitted to the retina of the eye might be interpreted as a particular color, pattern, or shape.

The Ecological View

For the past several decades, much of the research on perceptual development in infancy has been guided by the ecological view of Eleanor and James J. Gibson (E. Gibson, 1969, 1989, 2001; J. Gibson, 1966, 1979). They argue that we do not have to take bits and pieces of data from sensations and build up representations of the world in our minds. The environment itself is rich with information; our perceptual system selects from that rich output.

According to the Gibsons' **ecological view,** we directly perceive information that exists in the world around us. Perception brings us into contact with the environment in order to interact with and adapt to it. Perception is designed for action. Perception gives people such information as when to duck, when to turn their bodies through a narrow passageway, and when to put their hands up to catch something.

In the Gibsons' view, all objects have **affordances,** which are opportunities for interaction offered by objects that are necessary to perform activities. A pot may afford you something to cook with, and it may afford a toddler something to bang. Adults immediately know when a chair is appropriate for sitting, when a surface is

Newborns' Senses
Richard Aslin's Research
International Society on Infant Studies

sensation Reaction that occurs when information contacts sensory receptors—the eyes, ears, tongue, nostrils, and skin.

perception The interpretation of sensation.

ecological view The view, proposed by the Gibsons, that people directly perceive information in the world around them. Perception brings people in contact with the environment in order to interact with it and adapt to it.

affordances Opportunities for interaction offered by objects that are necessary to perform activities.

safe for walking, or when an object is within reach. We directly and accurately perceive these affordances by sensing information from the environment—the light or sound reflecting from the surfaces of the world—and from our own bodies through muscle receptors, joint receptors, and skin receptors, for example.

Through perceptual development, children become more efficient at discovering and using affordances. An important developmental question is, What affordances can infants or children detect and use? In one study, for example, when babies who could walk were faced with a squishy waterbed, they stopped and explored it, then chose to crawl rather than walk across it (Gibson & others, 1987). They combined perception and action to adapt to the demands of the task.

Similarly, as we described earlier in the section on motor development, infants who were just learning to crawl or just learning to walk were less cautious when confronted with a steep slope than experienced crawlers or walkers were (Adolph, 1997; Adolph & Avolio, 2000) ◀▥ **P. 169.** The more experienced crawlers and walkers perceived that a slope *affords* the possibility not only for faster locomotion but also for falling. Again, infants coupled perception and action to make a decision about what to do in their environment.

Studying the infant's perception has not been an easy task. The Research in Life-Span Development interlude describes some of the ingenious ways researchers study the newborn's perception.

> *T*he infant is by no means as helpless as it looks and is quite capable of some very complex and important actions.
>
> —HERB PICK
> *Contemporary Developmental Psychologist, University of Minnesota*

Research in Life-Span Development
Studying The Newborn's Perception

The creature has poor motor coordination and can move itself only with great difficulty. Although it cries when uncomfortable, it uses few other vocalizations. In fact, it sleeps most of the time, about 16 to 17 hours a day. You are curious about this creature and want to know more about what it can do. You think to yourself, "I wonder if it can see. How could I find out?"

You obviously have a communication problem with the creature. You must devise a way that will allow the creature to "tell" you that it can see. While examining the creature one day, you make an interesting discovery. When you move a large object toward it, it moves its head backward, as if to avoid a collision with the object. The creature's head movement suggests that it has at least some vision.

In case you haven't already guessed, the creature you have been reading about is the human infant, and the role you played is that of a researcher interested in devising techniques to learn about the infant's visual perception. After years of work, scientists have developed research methods and tools sophisticated enough to examine the subtle abilities of infants and to interpret their complex actions (Bendersky & Sullivan, 2002; Kellman & Banks, 1998).

Visual Preference Method

Robert Fantz (1963) was a pioneer in this effort. Fantz made an important discovery that advanced the ability of researchers to investigate infants' visual perception: Infants look at different things for different lengths of time. Fantz placed infants in a "looking chamber," which had two visual displays on the ceiling above the infant's head. An experimenter viewed the infant's eyes by looking through a peephole. If the infant was fixating on one of the displays, the experimenter could see the display's reflection in the infant's eyes. This allowed the experimenter to determine how long the infant looked at each display. Fantz (1963) found that infants only 2 days old look longer at patterned stimuli, such as faces and concentric circles, than at red, white, or yellow discs. Infants 2 to 3 months old preferred to look at patterns—a

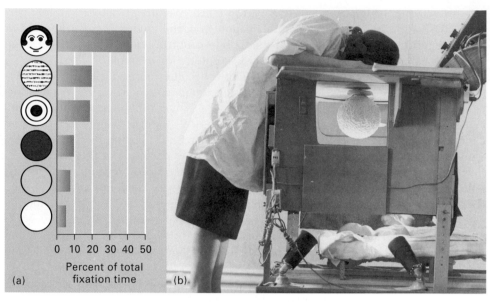

FIGURE 5.5 Fantz's Experiment on Infants' Visual Perception

(a) Infants 2 to 3 months old preferred to look at some stimuli more than others. In Fantz's experiment, infants preferred to look at patterns rather than at color or brightness. For example, they looked longer at a face, a piece of printed matter, or a bull's-eye than at red, yellow, or white discs. *(b)* Fantz used a "looking chamber" to study infants' perception of stimuli.

face, a piece of printed matter, or a bull's-eye—longer than at red, yellow, or white discs (see figure 5.5). Fantz' research method—studying whether infants can distinguish one stimulus from another by measuring the length of time they attend to different stimuli—is referred to as the **visual preference method.**

Habituation and Dishabituation

Another way that researchers have studied infant perception is to present a stimulus (such as a sight or a sound) a number of times. If the infant reduces its attention to the stimulus after a number of presentations, it indicates that the infant is no longer interested in the stimulus. **Habituation** is decreased responsiveness to a stimulus after repeated presentations of the stimulus. **Dishabituation** is the recovery of a habituated response after a change in stimulation. Among the measures researchers use to study whether habituation is occurring are sucking behavior (sucking behavior stops when the young infant attends to a novel object), heart and respiration rates, and the length of time the infant looks at an object. Newborn infants can habituate to repeated sights, sounds, smells, or touches (Rovee-Collier, 2001). Figure 5.6 shows the results of one study of habituation and dishabituation with newborns (Slater, Morison, & Somers, 1988).

Tracking

Another valuable technique to determine what an infant can see or hear is called *tracking* (Bendersky & Sullivan, 2002). Newborns typically turn their eyes and heads in the direction of an interesting sound or sight, especially the human voice and face. For example, newborns as well as older infants show reactions to sounds that are out of view. A startle is a typical reaction to a loud noise. A reduction in movement and head turning may suggest the ability to hear softer sounds.

Equipment

Videotape equipment allows researchers to investigate elusive behaviors. High-speed computers make it possible to perform complex data analysis in minutes. Other

visual preference method A method developed by Fantz to determine whether infants can distinguish one stimulus from another by measuring the length of time they attend to different stimuli.

habituation Decreased responsiveness to a stimulus after repeated presentations of the stimulus.

dishabituation The recovery of a habituated response after a change in stimulation.

Habituation

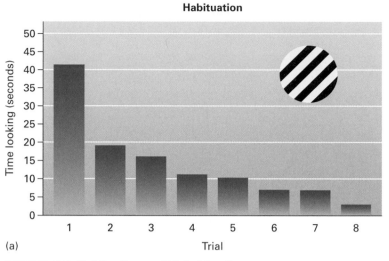

(a)

Dishabituation

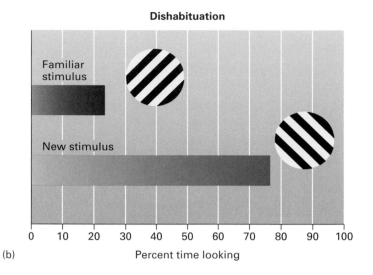

(b)

FIGURE 5.6 Habituation and Dishabituation

In the first part of one study, 7-hour-old newborns were shown the stimulus in *(a)*. As indicated, the newborns looked at it an average of 41 seconds when it was first presented to them (Slater, Morison, & Somers, 1988). Over seven more presentations of the stimulus, they looked at it less and less. In the second part of study, infants were presented with both the familiar stimulus to which they had just become habituated *(a)* and a new stimulus (shown in *b,* which was rotated 90 degrees). The newborns looked at the new stimulus three times as much as the familiar stimulus.

equipment records respiration, heart rate, body movement, visual fixation, and sucking behavior, which provide clues to what the infant is perceiving. For example, some researchers use equipment that detects if infants' respiration changes after a change in the pitch of a sound. If so, it suggests that the infants heard the pitch change. Thus, scientists have become ingenious at assessing the development of infants, discovering ways to "interview" them even though they cannot yet talk.

Vision

Some important changes in visual perception with age can be traced to differences in how the eye itself functions over time. These changes in the eye's functioning influence, for example, how clearly we can see an object, whether we can differentiate its colors, at what distance, and in what light. But the differences between what the newborn sees and what a toddler or adult sees go far beyond those that can be explained by changes in the eye's functioning, as we discuss in this section.

Infancy   What do newborns see? Psychologist William James (1890/1950) called the newborn's perceptual world a "blooming, buzzing confusion." A century later, we can safely say that he was wrong (Slater, 2001). Even the newborn perceives a world with some order. That world, however, is far different from the one perceived by the toddler or the adult.

Visual Acuity and Color   Just how well can infants see? Newborns cannot see small things that are far away. The newborn's vision is estimated to be 20/600 on the well-known Snellen chart, with which you are tested when you have your eyes examined (Banks & Salapatek, 1983). In other words, an object 20 feet away is only as clear to the newborn as it would be if it were 600 feet away from an adult with normal vision (20/20). By 6 months of age, though, vision is 20/100 or better, and, by about the first birthday, the infant's vision approximates that of an adult (Banks & Salapatek, 1983). Figure 5.7 shows a computer estimation of what a picture of a face looks like to an infant at different ages from a distance of about 6 inches.

 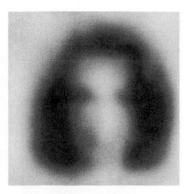  

FIGURE 5.7 Visual Acuity During the First Months of Life

The four photographs represent a computer estimation of what a picture of a face looks like to a 1-month-old, 2-month-old, 3-month-old, and 1-year-old (which approximates the visual acuity of an adult).

The infant's color vision also improves. At birth, babies can distinguish between green and red (Adams, 1989). Adultlike functioning of all of the eye's color-sensitive receptors *(cones)* is present by 2 months of age.

Perceiving Patterns What does the world look like to infants? Do they recognize patterns? As we saw in the Research on Life-Span Development interlude, using his "looking chamber," Robert Fantz (1963) revealed that infants look at different things for different lengths of time. Even 2- to 3-month-old infants prefer to look at patterned displays rather than nonpatterned displays. For example, they prefer to look at a normal human face rather than one with scrambled features, and prefer to look at a bull's-eye target or black-and-white stripes rather than a plain circle.

Even very young infants soon change the way they gather information from the visual world. By using a special mirror arrangement, researchers projected an image of human faces in front of infants' eyes so that the infants' eye movements could be photographed (Maurer & Salapatek, 1976). Figure 5.8 shows the plotting of eye fixations of a 1-month-old and a 2-month-old infant. Notice that the 2-month-old scanned a much wider area of the face than the 1-month-old. The older infant also spent more time examining the internal details of the face, whereas the younger infant concentrated on the outer contours of the face.

Perceptual Constancy Some changes in the infant's visual abilities are especially intriguing because they indicate that the infant's view of the world is better than it should be based on sensory information alone (Bower, 2002; Slater, Field, & Hernandez, 2002). This is the case in *perceptual constancy,* in which sensory stimulation is changing but perception of the physical world remains constant. Two types of perceptual constancy are size constancy and shape constancy.

Size constancy is the recognition that an object remains the same even though the retinal image of the object changes. The size of an object on the retina is not sufficient to determine its actual size. The farther away from us an object is, the smaller its image is on our eyes. For example, a bicycle standing right in front of a child appears smaller than the car parked across the street, even though the bicycle casts a larger image on the child's eyes than the car does.

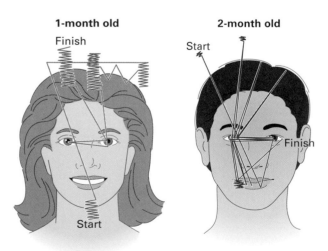

FIGURE 5.8 How 1- and 2-Month-Old Infants Scan the Human Face

size constancy Recognition that an object remains the same even though the retinal image of the object changes.

But what about babies? Do they have size constancy? Researchers have found that babies as young as 3 months of age show size constancy (Bower, 1966; Day & McKenzie, 1973). However, at 3 months of age, this ability is not full-blown and continues to develop. Infants' ability to perceive size constancy improves between 4 and 5 months of age as their binocular vision develops (Aslin, 1987). (*Binocular vision* involves the fact that we have two eyes separated by several inches that give us slightly different views of the world; the brain combines these images so that we see one rather than two views of the world.) Further progress in perceiving size constancy continues until 10 or 11 years of age (Kellman & Banks, 1998).

Shape constancy is the recognition that an object remains the same shape even though its orientation to us changes. Look around the room you are in right now. You likely see objects of varying shapes, such as tables and chairs. If you get up and walk around the room, you will see these objects from different sides and angles. Even though your retinal image of the objects changes as you walk and look, you will still perceive the objects as the same shape.

Do babies have shape constancy? As with size constancy, researchers have found that babies as young as 3 months of age have shape constancy (Bower, 1966; Day & McKenzie, 1973). Three-month-old infants, however, do not have shape constancy for irregularly shaped objects, such as tilted planes (Cook & Birch, 1984).

Why is it important for infants to develop perceptual constancy early in their lives? If infants did not develop perceptual constancy, each time they saw an object at a different distance or in a different orientation, they would perceive it as a different object. Thus, the development of perceptual constancy allows the infant to perceive its world as stable.

FIGURE 5.9 Examining Infants' Depth Perception on the Visual Cliff
Eleanor Gibson and Richard Walk (1960) found that most infants would not walk out on the glass over the dropoff, which indicated that they had depth perception.

Depth Perception   How early can infants perceive depth? To investigate this question, Eleanor Gibson and Richard Walk (1960) conducted a classic experiment. They constructed a miniature cliff with a drop-off covered by glass. The motivation for this experiment arose when Gibson was eating a picnic lunch on the edge of the Grand Canyon. She wondered whether an infant looking over the canyon's rim would perceive the dangerous dropoff and back up. She also was worried that her two young children would play too close to the canyon's edge and fall off. In their laboratory, Gibson and Walk placed infants on the edge of a visual cliff and had their mothers coax them to crawl onto the glass (see figure 5.9). Most infants would not crawl out on the glass, choosing instead to remain on the shallow side, an indication that they could perceive depth. However, because the 6- to 14-month-old infants had extensive visual experience, this research did not answer the question of whether depth perception is innate.

Exactly how early in life does depth perception develop? Because younger infants do not crawl, this question is difficult to answer. Research with 2- to 4-month-old infants shows differences in heart rate when they are placed directly on the deep side of the visual cliff instead of on the shallow side (Campos, Langer, & Krowitz, 1970). However, an alternative interpretation is that young infants respond to differences in some visual characteristics of the deep and shallow cliffs, with no actual knowledge of depth.

Interestingly, human infants begin to avoid the visual cliff at about the same time as they begin to crawl—at about 7 to 8 months of age. Compared with age-matched noncrawlers, infants who have begun to crawl independently show more wariness when placed on the deep side of the visual cliff (Campos & others, 2000). Also, when infants who have not yet crawled or walked are given experience moving in a walker, they are more wary of the visual cliff than infants with no such experience (Campos, Kermoian, & Zumbahlen, 1992). Again, we see the coupling of perception with motor development in determining what an infant will do in a particular situation.

An important contributor to depth perception is binocular vision. Newborns do not have binocular vision; it develops at about 3 to 4 months of age and it provides a powerful cue to depth (Slater, Field, & Hernandez-Reif, 2002).

shape constancy Recognition that an object remains the same even though its orientation to us changes.

Visual Expectations Infants not only see forms and figures at an early age but also develop expectations about future events in their world by the time they are 3 months of age (Adler & Haith, 2003). Marshall Haith and his colleagues (Canfield & Haith, 1991; Haith, Hazen, & Goodman, 1988) studied whether babies would form expectations about where an interesting picture would appear. The pictures were presented to the infants in either a regular alternating sequence (such as left, right, left, right) or an unpredictable sequence (such as right, right, left, right). When the sequence was predictable, the 3-month-old infants began to anticipate the location of the picture, looking at the side on which it was expected to appear. The young infants formed this visual expectation in less than 1 minute. However, younger infants did not develop expectations about where a picture would be presented.

Elizabeth Spelke (1991, 2000; Spelke & Hespos, 2001) also has demonstrated that young infants form visual expectations. She placed babies before a puppet stage and showed them a series of unexpected actions—for example, one ball seemed to roll through a solid barrier, another seemed to leap between two platforms, and a third appeared to hang in midair (Spelke, 1979). Spelke measured the babies' looking times and recorded longer intervals for unexpected than expected actions. She concluded that, by 4 months of age—even though infants do not yet have the ability to talk about objects, move around objects, manipulate objects, or even see objects with high resolution—they can recognize the solidity of objects and the continuity of objects. However, she has found that at 4 months of age, infants do not expect an object to obey gravitational constraints (Spelke & others, 1992).

By 6 to 8 months, infants have learned to perceive gravity and support—for example, that an object hanging on the end of a table should fall, that ball-bearings will travel farther when rolled down a longer rather than a shorter ramp, and that cup handles will not fall when attached to a cup (Slater, Field, & Hernandez-Reif, 2002). As infants develop, their experiences and actions on objects help them to understand physical laws.

Childhood Children become increasingly efficient at detecting the boundaries between colors (such as red and orange) at 3 to 4 years of age (Gibson, 1969). When they are about 4 or 5 years old, most children's eye muscles are adequately developed so that they can move their eyes efficiently across a series of letters. Many preschool children are *farsighted*, unable to see close up as well as they can see far away. By the time they enter the first grade, though, most children can focus their eyes and sustain their attention effectively on close-up objects.

What are the signs of vision problems in children? They include rubbing the eyes, excessive blinking, squinting, appearing irritable when playing games that require good distance vision, shutting or covering one eye, and tilting the head or thrusting it forward when looking at something. A child who shows any of these behaviors should be examined by an ophthalmologist.

After infancy, children's visual expectations about the physical world continue to develop. In one study, 2- to 4½-year-old children were given a task in which the goal was to find a toy ball that had been dropped through an opaque tube (Hood, 1995). As shown in figure 5.10, if the ball is dropped into the tube at the top right, it will land in the box at the bottom left. However, in this task, most of the 2-year-olds, and even some of the 4-year-olds, persisted in searching in the box immediately beneath the dropping point. For them, gravity ruled and they had failed to perceive the end location of the curved tube.

How do children learn to deal with situations like that in figure 5.10, and how do they come to understand other laws of the physical world? These questions are addressed by studies of cognitive development, which we will discuss in chapters 6 and 7.

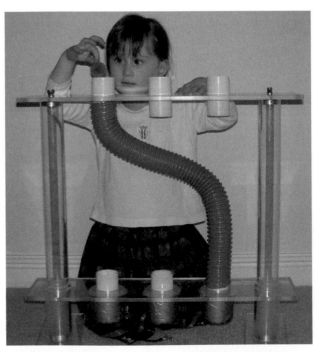

FIGURE 5.10 Visual Expectations About the Physical World

Even when toddlers see a ball dropped into the tube they will search for it immediately below the dropping point.

Adulthood   Vision is believed to change little after childhood until the effects of aging emerge (Bornstein & Arterberry, 1999). With aging, declines in visual acuity, color vision, and depth perception occur. Several diseases of the eye also may emerge in aging adults.

Visual Acuity   **Accommodation of the eye**—the eye's ability to focus and maintain an image on the retina—declines most sharply between 40 and 59 years of age. This loss of accommodation is what is commonly known as *presbyopia*. In particular, middle-aged individuals begin to have difficulty viewing close objects. The eye's blood supply also diminishes, although usually not until the fifties or sixties. The reduced blood supply may decrease the visual field's size and account for an increase in the eye's *blind spot*, the location where the retina does not register any light. And there is some evidence that the retina becomes less sensitive to low levels of illumination (Hughes, 1978). As a result, middle-aged adults begin to have difficulty reading or working in dim light. Presbyopia is correctable with bifocals and reading glasses.

In late adulthood, the decline in vision that began for most adults in early or middle adulthood becomes more pronounced (Fozard, 2000; Kosnick & others, 1989). Night driving is especially difficult, to some extent because tolerance for glare diminishes. *Dark adaptation* is slower, meaning that older individuals take longer to recover their vision when going from a well-lighted room to semidarkness. The area of the visual field becomes smaller, suggesting that the intensity of a stimulus in the peripheral area of the visual field needs to be increased if the stimulus is to be seen. Events taking place away from the center of the visual field might not be detected (Fozard & Gordon-Salant, 2001).

This visual decline often can be traced to a reduction in the quality or intensity of light reaching the retina. In extreme old age, these changes might be accompanied by degenerative changes in the retina, causing severe difficulty in seeing (Bonnel, Mohand-Said, & Sahel, 2003). Large-print books and magnifiers might be needed in such cases.

One recent extensive study of visual changes in adults found that the age of older adults was a significant factor in how extensively they differed in visual functioning from younger adults (Brabyn & others, 2001). Beyond 75, and more so beyond age 85, older adults showed significantly worse performance on a number of visual tasks than young adults and adults in their sixties and early seventies. The greatest decline in visual perception beyond 75, and especially beyond 85, involved glare (see figure 5.11). For example, whereas young adults recover vision following glare in less than 10 seconds, 50 percent of 90-year-olds have not recovered vision after 1.5 minutes.

Color Vision   Color vision also may decline with age in older adults as a result of the yellowing of the lens of the eye (Weale, 1992). This change in color vision is most likely to occur in the green-blue-violet part of the color spectrum. As a result, it may be more difficult to accurately match up closely related colors such as navy socks and black socks.

Depth Perception   As with many other areas of perception, there are few changes in depth perception following infancy until adults become older. Depth perception typically declines in late adulthood, which can make it difficult for the older adult to determine how close or far away or how high or low something is (Brabyn & others, 2001; Zarof, Knutelska, & Frumkes, 2003). A decline in depth perception can make steps or street curbs difficult to manage.

A decrease in contrast sensitivity is one factor that diminishes the older adult's ability to perceive depth. Light-dark contrast is produced by the amount of light

Aging and Sensory Changes
Aging and Vision Problems

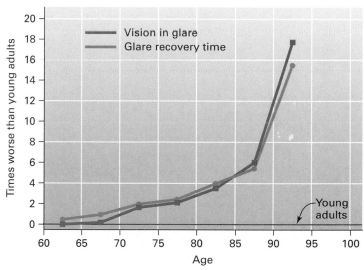

FIGURE 5.11 Rates of Decline in Visual Functioning Related to Glare in Adults of Different Ages.

Older adults, especially those 85 and older, fare much worse than younger adults in being able to see clearly when glare is present, and their recovery from glare is much slower. These data were collected from a random sample of community-dwelling older adults living in Marin County, California. For each age, the factor by which the group's median performance was worse than normative values for young adults is shown.

accommodation of the eye The eye's ability to focus and maintain an image on the retina.

Infancy and Toddlerhood: Visual Cliff Studies

reflected by surfaces (a light object is brighter than a dark object). Compared with younger adults, older adults need sharper contrasts and sharper edges around the object to differentiate the object from its background.

Diseases of the Eye Three diseases that can impair the vision of older adults are cataracts, glaucoma, and macular degeneration:

- **Cataracts** involve a thickening of the lens of the eye that causes vision to become cloudy, opaque, and distorted. By age 70, approximately 30 percent of individuals experience a partial loss of vision due to cataracts. Initially, cataracts can be treated by glasses; if they worsen, a simple surgical procedure can remove them (Hylton & others, 2003).
- **Glaucoma** involves damage to the optic nerve because of the pressure created by a buildup of fluid in the eye (Babaloa & others, 2003; Veach, 2003). Approximately 1 percent of individuals in their seventies and 10 percent of those in their nineties have glaucoma, which can be treated with eye drops, but if left untreated can ultimately destroy a person's vision.
- **Macular degeneration** is disease that involves deterioration of the retina. It affects 1 in 25 individuals from 66 to 74 years of age and 1 in 6 of those 75 years old and older. If the disease is detected early, it can be treated with laser surgery (Howe, 2003). However, macular degeneration is difficult to treat and thus a leading cause of blindness in older adults (Chopdar, Chakravarthy, & Verma, 2003; Sarks, 2002).

These and other changes in sensory functioning can make a big difference to competence in everyday activities (Drum, 2003). In one study of more than 500 adults 70 to 102 years of age, sensory acuity, especially in vision, was related to whether and how well older adults bathed and groomed themselves, completed household chores, engaged in intellectual activities, and watched TV (Marsiske, Klumb, & Baltes, 1997).

Hearing

Can the fetus hear? What kind of changes in hearing take place in infancy? When does hearing begin to decline in adulthood?

The Fetus, Infant, and Child During the last two months of pregnancy, the fetus can hear sounds as it nestles in its mother's womb: It hears the mother's voice, music, and so on (Kisilevsky, 1995; Smith, Muir, & Kisilevsky, 2001). Two psychologists wanted to find out if a fetus that heard Dr. Seuss' classic story *The Cat in the Hat* while still in the mother's womb would prefer hearing the story after birth (DeCasper & Spence, 1986). During the last months of pregnancy, sixteen women read *The Cat in the Hat* to their fetuses. Then shortly after they were born, the mothers read to them either *The Cat in the Hat* or a story with a different rhyme and pace, *The King, the Mice and the Cheese* (which was not read to them during prenatal development). The infants sucked on a nipple in a different way when the mothers read the two stories, suggesting that the infants recognized the pattern and tone of *The Cat in the Hat* (see figure 5.12). This study illustrates that an infant's brain has a remarkable ability to learn even before birth.

Immediately after birth, infants cannot hear soft sounds quite as well as adults can; a stimulus must be louder to be heard by a newborn than by an adult (Trehub & others, 1991). For example, an adult can hear a whisper from about 4 to 5 feet away, but a newborn requires that sounds be closer to a normal conversational level to be heard at that distance.

Infants are also less sensitive to the pitch of a sound than adults are. *Pitch* is the perception of the frequency of a sound. A soprano voice sounds high pitched, a bass voice low pitched. Infants are less sensitive to low-pitched sounds and are more likely to hear high-pitched sounds (Aslin & others, 1998). By 2 years of age, infants have considerably improved their ability to distinguish sounds with different pitches.

cataracts A thickening of the lens of the eye that causes vision to become cloudy, opaque, and distorted.

glaucoma Damage to the optic nerve because of the pressure created by a buildup of fluid in the eye.

macular degeneration A vision problem in the elderly that involves deterioration of the retina.

(a)

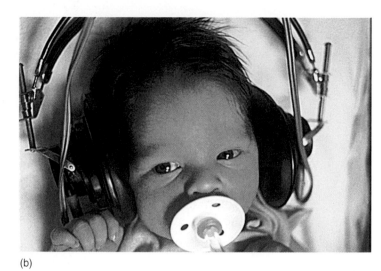

(b)

FIGURE 5.12 Hearing in the Womb

(a) Pregnant mothers read *The Cat in the Hat* to their fetuses during the last few months of pregnancy. *(b)* When they were born, the babies preferred listening to a recording of their mothers reading *The Cat in the Hat,* as evidenced by their sucking on a nipple rather than another story, *The King, the Mice and the Cheese.*

Changes also occur in the ability to *localize* sounds, detecting their origins. Even newborns can determine the general location from where a sound is coming, but by 6 months of age, they are more proficient at localizing sounds, and this ability continues to improve in the second year (Litovsky & Ashmead, 1997; Morrongiello, Fenwick, & Chance, 1990).

Even newborns display auditory preferences. They will suck more rapidly on a nipple in order to listen to some sounds rather than others. Their sucking behavior indicates that they prefer a recording of their mother's voice to the voice of an unfamiliar woman, their mother's native language to a foreign language, and the classical music of Beethoven to the rock music of Aerosmith (Flohr & others, 2001; Mehler & others, 1988; Spence & DeCasper, 1987).

Newborns are especially sensitive to the sounds of human speech. Our sensory-perceptual system seems built to give a special place to the sounds of language. Babies are born into the world prepared to respond to the sounds of any human language. Even young infants can discriminate subtle phonetic differences, such as those between the speech sounds of *ba* and *ga*. Experience with the native language, however, has an effect on speech perception. In the second half of the first year of life, infants become "native listeners," especially attuned to the sounds of their native language (Jusczyk, 2002). In chapter 9, "Language Development," we will further discuss the development of infants' ability to distinguish the sounds they need for speech.

Most children's hearing is adequate. However, about 1 in 1,000 newborns are deaf (Mason & Hermann, 1998). Hearing aids or surgery can improve hearing for many of them.

Otitis media is a middle-ear infection that can impair hearing temporarily. If it continues too long, it can interfere with language development and socialization (O'Neil, 2002). As many as one-third of all U.S. children from birth to 3 years of age have three or more episodes. In some cases, the infection can develop into a more chronic condition in which the middle ear becomes filled with fluid, and this can seriously impair hearing. Treatments for otitis media include antibiotics and placement of a tube in the inner ear to drain fluid (Cruz, Kasse, & Leonhart, 2003; Steinman, Landefeld, & Gonzales, 2003).

Adolescence Most adolescents' hearing is excellent. However, anyone who listens to loud sounds for sustained periods of time runs the risk of developing hearing problems. H.E.A.R (Hearing Education and Awareness for Rockers) was founded by rock musicians whose hearing has been damaged by their exposure to high-volume rock music. Increasingly, rock musicians, such as the group Metallica, wear earplugs when they are playing their music.

Aging and Hearing Problems

Adulthood Few changes in hearing are believed to take place during the adult years until middle adulthood. Hearing can start to decline by the age of 40. Sensitivity to high pitches usually declines first. The ability to hear low-pitched sounds does not seem to decline much in middle adulthood, though. Men usually lose their sensitivity to high-pitched sounds sooner than women do, but this sex difference might be due to men's greater exposure to noise in occupations such as mining and automobile work (Olsho, Harkins, & Lenhardt, 1985).

Hearing impairment usually does not become much of an impediment until late adulthood (Fozard, 2000; Fozard & Gordon-Salant, 2001; Gratton & Vazquez, 2003). Even then, some, but not all, hearing problems can be corrected by hearing aids. Only 19 percent of individuals from 45 to 54 years of age experience some type of hearing problem, but for those 75 to 79, the figure reaches 75 percent (Harris, 1975). It has been estimated that 15 percent of the population over the age of 65 is legally deaf, usually due to degeneration of the *cochlea,* the primary neural receptor for hearing in the inner ear (Olsho, Harkins, & Lenhardt, 1985). Wearing two hearing aids that are balanced to correct each ear separately can sometimes help hearing-impaired adults.

Earlier, in our discussion of vision, we described research on the importance of the age of older adults in determining the degree of their visual decline. Age also is a factor in the degree of hearing decline in older adults. As indicated in figure 5.13, the decline in vision and hearing is much greater in individuals 75 years and older than in individuals 65 to 74 years of age (Charness & Bosman, 1992).

Other Senses

As we develop, we not only obtain information about the world from our eyes and our ears. We also gather information about the world through sensory receptors in our skin, nose, and tongue.

Touch and Pain Do newborns respond to touch? Can they feel pain? How does the perception of touch and pain change with age?

Infancy Newborns do respond to touch. A touch to the cheek produces a turning of the head; a touch to the lips produces sucking movements.

An important perceptual ability is the capacity to connect information about vision with information about touch. One-year-olds clearly can do this, and it appears that 6-month-olds can, too (Acredolo & Hake, 1982). Whether still-younger infants can coordinate vision and touch is yet to be determined.

AGE

Perceptual System	65 to 74 years	75 years and o lder
Vision	There is a loss of acuity even with corrective lenses. Less transmission of light occurs through the retina (half as much as in young adults).	There is a significant loss of visual acuity and a decrease in the size of the perceived visual field. The ability to see effectively when glare is present decreases as does the recovery of vision after experiencing glare. Visual dysfunction from cataracts and glaucoma increases.
Hearing	There is a significant loss of hearing at high frequencies and some loss at middle frequencies. These losses can be helped by a hearing aid. There is greater susceptibility to masking of what	There is a significant loss at high and middle frequencies. A hearing aid is more likely to be needed than in young-old age.

FIGURE 5.13 Vision and Hearing Decline in Old Age and Late Old Age

If and when you have a son and need to consider whether he should be circumcised, the issue of an infant's pain perception probably will become important to you. Circumcision is usually performed on young boys about the third day after birth. Will your young son experience pain if he is circumcised when he is 3 days old? Megan Gunnar and her colleagues (1987) found that newborn infant males cried intensely during circumcision. Circumcised infants also display amazing resiliency. Within several minutes after the surgery, they can nurse and interact in a normal manner with their mothers. And, if allowed to, the newly circumcised newborn drifts into a deep sleep, which seems to serve as a coping mechanism.

For many years, doctors performed operations on newborns without anesthesia. This practice was accepted because of the dangers of anesthesia and because of the supposition that newborns do not feel pain. As researchers have demonstrated that newborns can feel pain, the practice of operating on newborns without anesthesia is being challenged. Anesthesia now is used in some circumcisions.

Adulthood There has been little research on developmental changes in touch and pain after infancy until the middle and late adulthood years. Changes in touch are associated with aging (Gescheider, 1997). One study found that older adults could detect touch much less in the lower extremities (ankles, knees, and so on) than in the upper extremities (wrists, shoulders, and so on) (Corso, 1997). For most older adults, though, a decline in touch sensitivity is not problematic.

Older adults are less sensitive to pain and suffer from it less than younger adults do (Harkins, Price, & Martinelli, 1986). Although decreased sensitivity to pain can help older adults cope with disease and injury, it can be harmful if it masks injury or illness that needs to be treated.

Smell As with the other senses, most research on developmental changes in smell focuses on early infancy and aging. Newborns can differentiate odors. The expressions on their faces seem to indicate that they like the way vanilla and strawberry smell but do not like the way rotten eggs and fish smell (Steiner, 1979). In one investigation, 6-day-old infants who were breastfed showed a clear preference for smelling their mother's breast pad (compared with a clean breast pad), (MacFarlane, 1975) (see figure 5.14). However, when they were 2 days old, they did not show this preference, indicating that they require several days of experience to recognize this odor.

Most older adults lose some of their sense of smell, often at around 60 years of age (Schiffman, 1996). This decline can reduce older adults' enjoyment of food and their life satisfaction. The decline in the sense of smell also brings reduced ability to detect smoke from a fire.

Taste Sensitivity to taste might be present even before birth. When saccharin was added to the amniotic fluid of a near-term fetus, swallowing increased (Windle, 1940). In one study, even at only 2 hours of age, babies made different facial expressions when they tasted sweet, sour, and bitter solutions (Rosenstein & Oster, 1988) (see figure 5.15). At about 4 months of age, infants begin to prefer salty tastes, which as newborns they had found to be aversive (Harris, Thomas, & Booth, 1990).

Declines in taste often begin to occur in the sixties (Schiffman, 1996). As with smell, there is less decline in taste in healthy older adults than in unhealthy older adults. Many older adults prefer highly seasoned foods (sweeter, spicier, saltier) to compensate for their diminished taste and smell (Hoyer & Roodin, 2003). This can lead to increased eating of nonnutritious, highly seasoned "junk food."

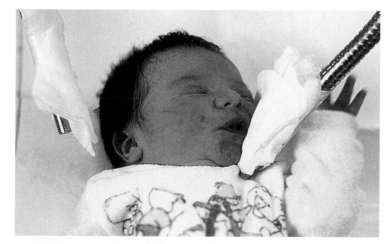

FIGURE 5.14 Newborns' Preference for the Smell of Their Mother's Breast Pad

In the experiment by MacFarlane (1975), 6-day-old infants preferred to smell their mother's breast pad rather than a clean one that had never been used, but 2-day-old infants did not show the preference, indicating that this odor preference requires several days of experience to develop.

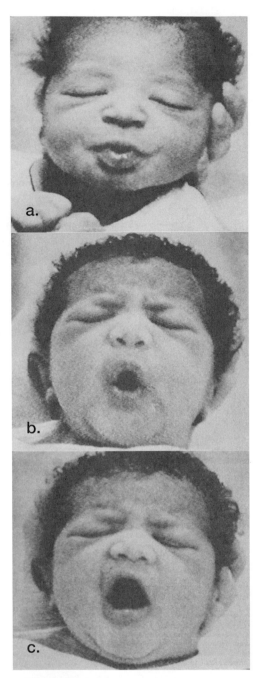

FIGURE 5.15 Newborns' Facial Responses to Basic Tastes

Facial expressions elicited by (*a*) a sweet solution, (*b*) a sour solution, and (*c*) a bitter solution.

www.mhhe.com/santrockld2

Elizabeth Spelke's Research

intermodal perception The ability to integrate information about two or more sensory modalities, such as vision and hearing.

Intermodal Perception

Imagine yourself playing basketball or tennis. You are experiencing many visual inputs: the ball coming and going, other players moving around, and so on. However, you are experiencing many auditory inputs as well: the sound of the ball bouncing or being hit, the grunts and groans, and so on. There is good correspondence between much of the visual and auditory information: When you see the ball bounce, you hear a bouncing sound; when a player stretches to hit a ball, you hear a groan.

We live in a world of objects and events that can be seen, heard, and felt. When mature observers simultaneously look at and listen to an event, they experience a unitary episode. All of this is so commonplace that it scarcely seems worth mentioning. But consider the task of very young infants with little practice at perceiving. Can they put vision and sound together as precisely as adults do?

Intermodal perception involves integrating information from two or more sensory modalities, such as vision and hearing. To test intermodal perception, Elizabeth Spelke (1979) showed 4-month-old infants two films simultaneously. In each film, a puppet jumped up and down, but in one of the films the soundtrack matched the puppet's dancing movements; in the other film, it did not. By measuring the infant's gaze, Spelke found that the infants looked more at the puppet whose actions were synchronized with the sound track, suggesting that they recognized the visual-sound correspondence. Young infants can also coordinate visual-auditory information involving people. In one study, as early as at 3½ months old, infants looked more at their mother when they also heard her voice and longer at their father when they also heard his voice (Spelke & Owsley, 1979).

Might auditory-visual relations be coordinated even in newborns? Newborns do turn their eyes and their head toward the sound of a voice or rattle when the sound is maintained for several seconds (Clifton & others, 1981), but the newborn can localize a sound and look at an object only in a crude way (Bechtold, Bushnell, & Salapatek, 1979). Improved accuracy at auditory-visual coordination likely requires experience with visual and auditory stimuli.

In sum, crude exploratory forms of intermodal perception exist in newborns. These exploratory forms of intermodal perception become sharpened with experience in the first year of life. In the first six months, infants have difficulty connecting sensory input from different modes, but in the second half of the first year they show an increased ability to make this connection mentally. Thus, babies are born into the world with some innate abilities to perceive relations among sensory modalities, but their intermodal abilities improve considerably through experience. As with all aspects of development, in perceptual development, nature and nurture interact and cooperate (Condry, Smith, & Spelke, 2001; Lickliter & Bahrick, 2000).

Review and Reflect: Learning Goal 2

2 Outline the course of sensory and perceptual development

REVIEW
- What are sensation and perception?
- What is the ecological view of perception? What are some research methods used to study infant perception?
- How does vision develop?
- How does hearing develop?
- How do touch and pain develop? How does smell develop? How does taste develop?
- What is intermodal perception and how does it develop?

REFLECT
- What would you do to stimulate the hearing of a 1-year-old infant?

3 PERCEPTUAL-MOTOR COUPLING

As we come to end of this chapter, we return to the important theme of perceptual-motor coupling ◄▐▐▐ **P. 166.** The distinction between perceiving and doing has been a time-honored tradition in psychology. However, a number of experts on perceptual and motor development question whether this distinction makes sense (Bertenthal & Clifton, 1998; Bornstein & Arterberry, 1999; Gibson, 2001; Lochman, 2000; Pick, 1997; Thelen, 1995, 2000, 2001). The main thrust of research in Esther Thelen's dynamic systems approach is to explore how people assemble motor behaviors for perceiving and acting. The main theme of the ecological approach of Eleanor and James J. Gibson is to discover how perception guides action. Action can guide perception and perception can guide action. Only by moving one's eyes, head, hands, and arms and by moving from one location to another can an individual fully experience his or her environment and learn how to adapt to it. Perception and action are coupled.

Babies, for example, continually coordinate their movements with perceptual information to learn how to maintain balance, reach for objects in space, and move across various surfaces and terrains (Thelen, 2000). They are motivated to move by what they perceive. Consider the sight of an attractive toy across the room. In this situation, infants must perceive the current state of their bodies and learn how to use their limbs to reach the toy. Although their movements at first are awkward and uncoordinated, babies soon learn to select patterns that are appropriate for reaching their goals.

Equally important is the other part of the perception-action coupling (Smith & Samuelson, 2003). That is, action educates perception. For example, watching an object while exploring it manually helps infants to discriminate its properties of texture, size, and hardness. Locomoting in the environment teaches babies about how objects and people look from different perspectives, or whether surfaces will support their weight. Individuals perceive in order to move and move in order to perceive. Perceptual and motor development do not occur in isolation from one another but instead are coupled (Thelen, 1995, 2000).

Driving a car illustrates the coupling of perceptual and motor skills. The decline in perceptual-motor skills in late adulthood makes driving a car difficult for many older adults. Drivers over the age of 65 are involved in more accidents than middle-aged adults because of such mistakes as improper turns, not yielding the right of way, and not obeying traffic signs, than their younger counterparts (who are more likely to have accidents because they are speeding) (Sterns, Barrett, & Alexander, 1985). Older adults can compensate for declines in perceptual-motor skills by driving shorter distances, choosing less congested routes, and driving only in daylight.

Review and Reflect: Learning Goal 3

3 Discuss the connection of perception and action

REVIEW

- How are perception and motor actions coupled in development?

REFLECT

- Describe two examples not given in the text in which perception guides action. Then describe two examples not given in the text in which action guides perception.

Reach Your Learning Goals

CHAPTER 5

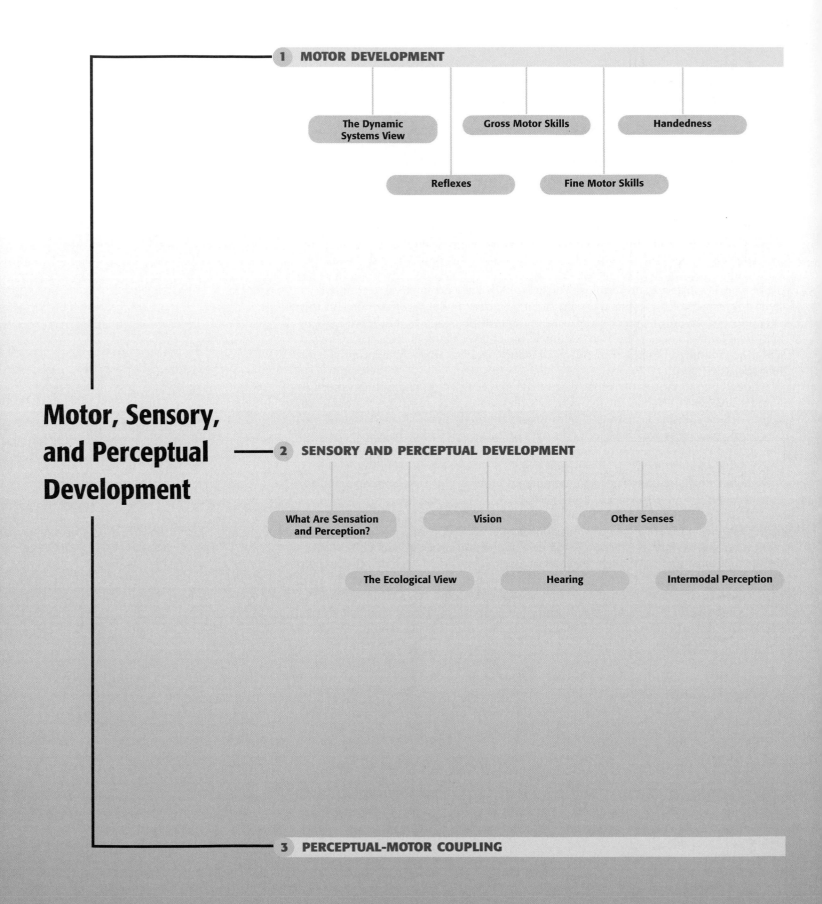

Motor, Sensory, and Perceptual Development

1 MOTOR DEVELOPMENT

- The Dynamic Systems View
- Reflexes
- Gross Motor Skills
- Fine Motor Skills
- Handedness

2 SENSORY AND PERCEPTUAL DEVELOPMENT

- What Are Sensation and Perception?
- The Ecological View
- Vision
- Hearing
- Other Senses
- Intermodal Perception

3 PERCEPTUAL-MOTOR COUPLING

Summary

1 Describe how motor skills develop

- Thelen's dynamic systems theory seeks to explain how motor behaviors are assembled for perceiving and acting. Perception and action are coupled. According to this theory, motor skills are the result of many converging factors, such as the development of the nervous system, the body's physical properties and its movement possibilities, the goal the child is motivated to reach, and environmental support for the skill. In the dynamic systems view, motor development is far more complex than the result of a genetic blueprint.
- Reflexes—automatic movements—govern the newborn's behavior. They include the sucking, rooting, and Moro reflexes—all of which typically disappear after three to four months.
- Gross motor skills involve large motor activities. Key skills developed during infancy include control of posture and walking. Gross motor skills improve dramatically in the childhood years. The peak of gross motor skills often occurs from 19 to 26 years of age. In general, older adults show a slowing of movement.
- Fine motor skills are finely tuned motor actions. The onset of reaching and grasping marks a significant accomplishment. Fine motor skills continue to develop through the childhood years and then experience some decline with aging. Neural noise and strategy have been proposed as possible explanations for the slowing of motor skills in older adults.
- Handedness likely has a genetic link. About 90 percent of children are right-handed, 10 percent left-handed. Left-handers are more likely to process speech in the right hemisphere of the brain than right-handers, and left-handers have more reading problems. Left-handers often show up in higher than expected numbers as mathematicians, musicians, architects, and artists. Left-handers tend to have unusually good visuospatial skills.

2 Outline the course of sensory and perceptual development

- Sensation occurs when information interacts with sensory receptors. Perception is the interpretation of sensation.
- Created by the Gibsons, the ecological view states that people directly perceive information that exists in the world. Perception brings people in contact with the environment in order to interact and adapt to it. Affordances provide opportunities for interaction offered by objects that are necessary to perform activities. Researchers have developed a number of methods to assess the infant's perception, including the visual preference method (which Fantz used to determine young infants' interest in looking at patterned over non-patterned displays), habituation and dishabituation, and tracking.
- The infant's visual acuity increases dramatically in the first year of life. Newborns can distinguish green and red; all three of the color-sensitive receptors function in adultlike ways by 2 months of age. Young infants systematically scan human faces. By 3 months of age, infants show size and shape constancy. As visual perception develops, infants develop visual expectations. In Gibson and Walk's classic study, infants as young as 6 months of age had depth perception. During the preschool years, children become better at differentiating colors and scanning the visual world. After the early adult years, visual acuity declines. Eye accommodation decreases the most from 40 to 59 years of age. In older adults, the yellowing of the eye's lens reduces color differentiation, and the ability to see the periphery of a visual field declines. Significant declines in visual functioning related to glare characterize adults 75 years and older and even more so those 85 years and older. Three diseases that can impair the vision of older adults are cataracts, glaucoma, and macular degeneration.
- The fetus can hear several weeks prior to birth. Immediately after birth newborns can hear, but their sensory threshold is higher than that of adults. Developmental changes in the perception of loudness, pitch, and localization of sound occur during infancy. Most children's hearing is adequate, but one special concern is otitis media. A concern in adolescence is listening to loud rock music for prolonged periods of time, which can damage hearing. Hearing can start to decline by the age of 40, especially sensitivity to high-pitched sounds. However, hearing impairment usually doesn't become much of an impediment until late adulthood. Hearing aids can diminish hearing problems for many older adults.
- Newborns can respond to touch and feel pain. Sensitivity to pain decreases in late adulthood. Newborns can differentiate odors, and sensitivity to taste may be present before birth. Smell and taste may decline in late adulthood, although in healthy individuals the decline is minimal.
- Crude, exploratory forms of intermodal perception—the ability to relate and integrate information from two or more sensory modalities—are present in newborns and become sharpened over the first year of life.

3 Discuss the connection of perception and action

- Perception and action often are not isolated but rather are coupled. Individuals perceive in order to move and move in order to perceive.

Key Terms

Key People

E-Learning Tools

Connect to **www.mhhe.com/santrockldt2** to research the answers and complete these exercises. In addition, you'll find a number of other resources and valuable study tools for chapter 5, "Motor, Sensory, and Perceptual Development," on the Student CD-ROM that came with this book.

Taking It to the Net

1. Ten-year-old Kristin is a new member of her soccer league's select team. Kristin's parents are reluctant to allow Kristin to participate in what has a reputation for being a high-pressure, intensely competitive atmosphere. If they allow her to participate, what can they do to make it a healthy experience for themselves and for Kristin?

2. Frank and Elise just got back the sonogram results—it's a boy. Frank wants them to plan to circumcise their son. Elise does not want their baby to undergo this painful procedure. Frank was circumcised and assures Elise that he has no memory of the pain—if there was any. Is circumcision medically neces-sary? If Frank and Elise decide on circumcision, can their baby have some form of anesthesia?

3. Patty's 85-year-old mother, who lives with her and her family, has begun eating less and less. She tells Patty, "Eating is no fun anymore. I can't taste anything." What can Patty do to make meals more appealing for her mother?

Self-Assessment

To think further about how you think parents should interact with their babies to effectively promote their physical development, complete this self-assessment:

- *My Beliefs About Nurturing a Baby's Physical Development.*

Health and Well-Being, Parenting, and Education

Build your decision-making skills by trying your hand at the health and well-being, parenting, and education "Scenarios."

Cognitive
Processes and
Development

SECTION 3

Learning is an ornament in prosperity, a refuge in adversity.

—ARISTOTLE
Greek Philosopher, 4th Century B.C.

Children thirst to know and understand. They construct their own ideas about the world around them and are remarkable for their curiosity, intelligence, and language. And it is always in season for the old to learn. In Section 3, you will read four chapters: "Cognitive Developmental Approaches" (chapter 6), "Information Processing" (chapter 7), "Intelligence" (chapter 8), and "Language Development" (chapter 9).

Cognitive Developmental Approaches

Learning Goals

1 Discuss the key processes and four stages in Piaget's theory

2 Apply Piaget's theory to education and evaluate Piaget's theory

3 Identify the main concepts in Vygotsky's theory and compare it with Piaget's theory

4 Describe cognitive changes in adulthood

Cognitive developmental approaches place a special emphasis on how individuals actively construct their thinking. They also focus heavily on how thinking changes from one point in development to another. In this chapter, we will highlight the cognitive developmental approaches of Jean Piaget and Lev Vygotsky. We also will explore the possibility that adults think in a qualitatively more advanced way than adolescents do.

1 PIAGET'S THEORY OF COGNITIVE DEVELOPMENT

Processes of Development		Preoperational Stage		Formal Operational Stage
	Sensorimotor Stage		Concrete Operational Stage	

Piaget thought that, just as our physical bodies have structures that enable us to adapt to the world, we build mental structures that help us to adapt to the world. *Adaptation* involves adjusting to new environmental demands. Piaget also stressed that children actively construct their own cognitive worlds; information is not just poured into their minds from the environment. He sought to discover how children at different points in their development think about the world and how these systematic changes occur ◀‖‖ **P. 22.**

Processes of Development

Poet Nora Perry asked, "Who knows the thoughts of the child?" As much as anyone, Piaget knew. Through careful observations of his own three children—Laurent, Lucienne, and Jacqueline—and inquisitive interviews of other children, Piaget changed our perceptions of the way children think about the world.

What processes do children use as they construct their knowledge of the world? Piaget believed that these processes are especially important in this regard: schemes, assimilation, accommodation, organization, equilibrium, and equilibration.

Schemes Piaget (1954) said that as the child seeks to construct an understanding of the world, the developing brain creates **schemes.** These are actions or mental representations that organize knowledge. In Piaget's theory, behavioral schemes (physical activities) characterize infancy, and mental schemes (cognitive activities) develop in childhood. A baby's schemes involve simple actions that can be performed on objects such as sucking, looking, and grasping. Older children have schemes that include strategies and plans for solving problems. For example, a 5-year-old might have a scheme that involves the strategy of classifying objects by size, shape, or color. By the time we have reached adulthood, we have constructed an enormous number of diverse schemes, ranging from how to drive a car to balancing a budget to the concept of fairness.

Assimilation and Accommodation To explain how children use and adapt their schemes, Piaget offered two concepts: assimilation and accommodation. **Assimilation** occurs when children incorporate new information into their existing schemes. **Accommodation** occurs when children adjust their schemes to fit new information and experiences. Consider an 8-year-old girl who is given a hammer and nails to hang a picture on the wall. She has never used a hammer, but from experience and observation she realizes that a hammer is an object to be held, that it is swung by the handle to hit the nail, and that it is usually swung a number of times. Recognizing each of these things, she fits the current task into her existing scheme

Piaget with his wife and three children; he often used his observations of his children to provide examples of his theory.

schemes In Piaget's theory, actions or mental representations that organize knowledge.

assimilation Piagetian concept of the incorporation of new information into existing schemes.

accommodation Piagetian concept of adjusting schemes to fit new information and experiences.

(assimilation). However, the hammer is heavy, so she holds it near the top. She swings too hard and the nail bends, so she adjusts the pressure of her strikes. These adjustments reveal her ability to alter her scheme (accommodation).

As another example of assimilation and accommodation, think about a toddler who has learned the word *car* to identify the family's car. The toddler might call all moving vehicles on roads "cars," including motorcycles and trucks; the child has assimilated these objects into his or her existing scheme. But the child soon learns that motorcycles and trucks are not cars and fine-tunes the category to exclude motorcycles and trucks, accommodating the scheme.

Assimilation and accommodation operate even in very young infants. Newborns reflexively suck everything that touches their lips; they assimilate all sorts of objects into their sucking scheme. By sucking different objects, they learn about their taste, texture, shape, and so on. After several months of experience, though, they construct their understanding of the world differently. Some objects, such as fingers and the mother's breast, can be sucked, and others, such as fuzzy blankets, should not be sucked. In other words, they accommodate their sucking scheme.

Organization To make sense out of their world, said Piaget, children cognitively organize their experiences. **Organization** is Piaget's concept of grouping isolated behaviors into a higher-order system. Items are grouped into categories. Every level of thought is organized. Continual refinement of this organization is an inherent part of development. A boy who has only a vague idea about how to use a hammer may also have a vague idea about how to use other tools. After learning how to use each one, he must relate these uses, or organize his knowledge, if he is to become skilled in using tools. In the same way, children continually integrate and coordinate the many other branches of knowledge that often develop independently.

Equilibrium and Equilibration **Equilibration** is a mechanism that Piaget proposed to explain how children shift from one stage of thought to the next. The shift occurs as children experience cognitive conflict, or disequilibrium, in trying to understand the world. Eventually, they resolve the conflict and reach a balance, or equilibrium, of thought. Piaget believed there is considerable movement between states of cognitive equilibrium and disequilibrium as assimilation and accommodation work in concert to produce cognitive change. For example, if a child believes that the amount of a liquid changes simply because the liquid is poured into a container with a different shape—for instance, from a container that is short and wide into a container that is tall and narrow—she might be puzzled by such issues as where the "extra" liquid came from and whether there is actually more liquid to drink. The child will eventually resolve these puzzles as her thought becomes more advanced. In the everyday world, the child is constantly faced with such counterexamples and inconsistencies.

Stages of Development Piaget's theory is a general, unifying story of how biology and experience sculpt the infant's cognitive development: Assimilation and accommodation always take the child to a higher ground. For Piaget, the motivation for change is an internal search for equilibrium. As a result of this change toward becoming more cognitively competent, Piaget theorized that individuals go through four stages of development. A different way of understanding the world makes one stage more advanced than another. Cognition is *qualitatively* different in one stage compared with another. In other words, the way children reason at one stage is different from the way they reason at another stage. This contrasts with the *quantitative* assessments of intelligence made through the use of standardized intelligence tests, which we will discuss in chapter 8. In these tests, the focus is on *what* the child knows, or how many questions the child can answer correctly.

Each of Piaget's stages is age-related and consists of distinct ways of thinking. Piaget believed that there are four stages of cognitive development: sensorimotor, preoperational, concrete operational, and formal operational (see figure 6.1).

organization Piaget's concept of grouping isolated behaviors into a higher-order, more smoothly functioning cognitive system; the grouping or arranging of items into categories.

equilibration A mechanism that Piaget proposed to explain how children shift from one stage of thought to the next. The shift occurs as children experience cognitive conflict, or disequilibrium, in trying to understand the world. Eventually, they resolve the conflict and reach a balance, or equilibrium, of thought.

Stage	Age Range	Description
Sensorimotor	**0 to 2 Years**	Infants gain knowledge the world from the physical actions they perform on it. Infants coordinate sensory experiences with these physical actions. An infant progresses from reflexive, instinctual action at birth to the beginning of symbolic thought toward the end of the stage.
Preoperational	**2 to 7 Years**	The child begins to use mental representations to understand the world. Symbolic thinking, reflected in the use of words and images, is used in this mental representation, which goes beyond the connection of sensory information with physical action. However, there are some constraints on the child's thinking at this stage, such as egocentrism and centration.
Concrete Operational	**7 to 11 Years**	The child can now reason logically about concrete events, understands the concept of conservation, organizes objects into hierarchical classes (classification), and places objects in ordered series (seriation).
Formal Operational	**11 Years Through Adulthood**	The adolescent reasons in more abstract, idealistic, and logical (hypothetical-deductive) ways.

FIGURE 6.1 Piaget's Four Stages of Cognitive Development

Sensorimotor Stage

The **sensorimotor stage** lasts from birth to about 2 years of age. In this stage, infants construct an understanding of the world by coordinating sensory experiences (such as seeing and hearing) with physical, motoric actions—hence the term "sensorimotor." At the beginning of this stage, newborns have little more than reflexive patterns with which to work. At the end of the stage, 2-year-olds have complex sensorimotor patterns and are beginning to operate with primitive symbols. We first will summarize Piaget's descriptions of how infants develop. Later we will consider criticisms of his view.

Substages Piaget divided the sensorimotor stage into six substages: (1) simple reflexes; (2) first habits and primary circular reactions; (3) secondary circular reactions; (4) coordination of secondary circular reactions; (5) tertiary circular reactions, novelty, and curiosity; and (6) internalization of schemes.

Simple reflexes, the first sensorimotor substage, corresponds to the first month after birth. In this substage, sensation and action are coordinated primarily through reflexive behaviors. These include the rooting and sucking reflexes, which the infant has at birth. In this substage, the infant develops an ability to produce behaviors that resemble reflexes in the absence of the usual stimulus for the reflex. For example, when the baby was just born, a bottle or nipple would produce sucking only when it was placed directly in the baby's mouth or touched to the lips. But soon the infant might suck when a bottle or nipple is only nearby. Reflexlike actions in the absence of a triggering stimulus demonstrate that the infant is initiating action and is actively structuring experiences in the first month of life.

First habits and primary circular reactions is the second sensorimotor substage, which develops between 1 and 4 months of age. In this substage, the infant learns

sensorimotor stage The first of Piaget's stages, which lasts from birth to about 2 years of age; infants construct an understanding of the world by coordinating sensory experiences (such as seeing and hearing) with motoric actions.

to coordinate sensation and two types of schemes: habits and primary circular reactions. A *habit* is a scheme based on a reflex that has become completely separated from its eliciting stimulus. For example, infants in substage 1 might suck when bottles are put to their lips or when they see a bottle. Infants in substage 2 might suck even when no bottle is present. A *circular reaction* is a repetitive or stereotyped action.

A *primary circular reaction* is a scheme based on the attempt to reproduce an event that initially occurred by chance. For example, suppose an infant accidentally sucks his fingers when they are placed near his mouth. Later, he searches for his fingers to suck them again, but the fingers do not cooperate because the infant cannot coordinate visual and manual actions.

Habits and circular reactions are stereotyped: That is, the infant repeats them the same way each time. During this substage, the infant's own body remains the infant's center of attention. There is no outward pull by environmental events.

Secondary circular reactions is the third sensorimotor substage, which develops between 4 and 8 months of age. In this substage, the infant becomes more object-oriented, moving beyond preoccupation with the self. By chance, an infant might shake a rattle. The infant repeats this action for the sake of experiencing fascination. The infant also imitates some simple actions, such as the baby talk or burbling of adults, and some physical gestures. However, the baby imitates only actions that he or she is already able to produce. Although directed toward objects in the world, the infant's schemes lack an intentional, goal-directed quality.

Coordination of secondary circular reactions is Piaget's fourth sensorimotor substage, which develops between 8 and 12 months of age. The critical requirement for the infant to progress into this substage is the coordination of vision and the sense of touch, or hand-eye coordination. Actions become more outwardly directed. Significant changes in this substage involve the coordination of schemes and intentionality. Infants readily combine and recombine previously learned schemes in a coordinated way. They might look at an object and grasp it simultaneously, or they might visually inspect a toy, such as a rattle, and finger it simultaneously, in obvious tactile exploration. Related to this coordination is the second achievement—the presence of intentionality. For example, infants might manipulate a stick in order to bring a desired toy within reach or they might knock over one block to reach and play with another one.

Tertiary circular reactions, novelty, and curiosity is Piaget's fifth sensorimotor substage, which develops between 12 and 18 months of age. In this substage, infants become intrigued by the many properties of objects and by the many things that they can make happen to objects. A block can be made to fall, spin, hit another object, and slide across the ground. *Tertiary circular reactions* are schemes in which the infant purposely explores new possibilities with objects, continually doing new things to them and exploring the results. Piaget says that this stage marks the starting point for human curiosity and interest in novelty.

Internalization of schemes is Piaget's sixth and final sensorimotor substage, which develops between 18 and 24 months of age. In this substage, the infant develops the ability to use primitive symbols. For Piaget, a *symbol* is an internalized sensory image or word that represents an event. Primitive symbols permit the infant to think about concrete events without directly acting them out or perceiving them. Moreover, symbols allow the infant to manipulate and transform the represented events in simple ways. In a favorite Piagetian example, Piaget's young daughter saw a matchbox being opened and closed. Later, she mimicked the event by opening and closing her mouth. This was an obvious expression of her image of the event.

Object Permanence   Imagine what your life would be like if you could not distinguish between yourself and your world. It would be chaotic and unpredictable.

I wish I could travel by the road that crosses the baby's mind, and out beyond all bounds; where messengers run errands for no cause between the kingdoms of kings of no history; where reason makes kites of her laws and flies them, and truth sets facts free from its fetters.

—RABINDRANATH TAGORE
*Bengali Poet and Essayist,
20th Century*

**Piaget's Theory
Piaget's Stages
The Jean Piaget Society**

Sensorimotor Stage	Behavior
Substage 1	There is no apparent object permanence. When a spot of light moves across the visual field, an infant follows it but quickly ignores its disappearance.
Substage 2	A primitive form of object permanence develops. Given the same experience, the infant looks briefly at the spot where the light disappeared, with an expression of passive expectancy.
Substage 3	The infant's sense of object permanence undergoes further development. With the newfound ability to coordinate simple schemes, the infant shows clear patterns of searching for a missing object, with sustained visual and manual examination of the spot where the object apparently disappeared.
Substage 4	The infant actively searches for a missing object in the spot where it disappeared, with new actions to achieve the goal of searching effectively. For example, if an attractive toy has been hidden behind a screen, the infant may look at the screen and try to push it away with a hand. If the screen is too heavy to move or is permanently fixed, the infant readily substitutes a secondary scheme—for example, crawling around it or kicking it. These new actions signal that the infant's belief in the continued existence of the missing object is strengthening.
Substage 5	The infant now is able to track an object that disappears and reappears in several locations in rapid succession. For example, a toy may be hidden under different boxes in succession in front of the infant, who succeeds in finding it. The infant is apparently able to hold an image of the missing object in mind longer than before.
Substage 6	The infant can search for a missing object that disappeared and reappeared in several locations in succession, as before. In addition, the infant searches in the appropriate place even when the object has been hidden from view as it is being moved. This activity indicates that the infant is able to "imagine" the missing object and to follow the image from one location to the next.

FIGURE 6.2 The Six Substages of Object Permanence

This is what the life of a newborn must be like, according to Piaget. There is no differentiation between the self and world; objects have no separate, permanent existence.

By the end of the sensorimotor period, however, both are present. **Object permanence** is the understanding that objects and events continue to exist even when they cannot be seen, heard, or touched. Acquiring the sense of object permanence is one of the infant's most important accomplishments. According to Piaget, infants develop object permanence in a series of substages that correspond to the six substages of sensorimotor development. Figure 6.2 shows how the six substages of object permanence reflect Piaget's substages of sensorimotor development.

How could Piaget or other developmentalists know whether an infant had a sense of object permanence? The principal way that object permanence is studied is by watching an infant's reaction when an interesting object disappears (see figure 6.3). If infants search for the object, it is assumed that they believe it continues to exist.

Object permanence is just one of the basic concepts about the physical world developed by babies. To Piaget, children, even infants, are much like little scientists, examining the world to see how it works. The Research in Life-Span Development interlude describes some of the ways in which adult scientists try to discover what these "baby scientists" are finding out about the world.

object permanence The Piagetian term for one of an infant's most important accomplishments: understanding that objects and events continue to exist even when they cannot directly be seen, heard, or touched.

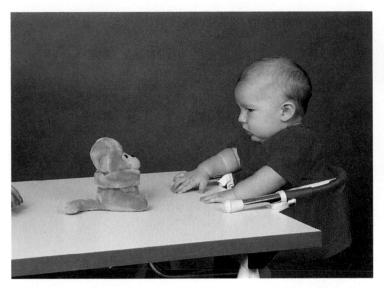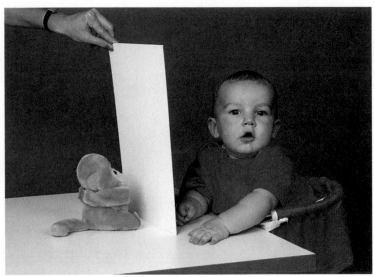

FIGURE 6.3 Object Permanence

Piaget thought that object permanence is one of infancy's landmark cognitive accomplishments. For this 5-month-old boy, "out-of-sight" is literally out of mind. The infant looks at the toy monkey *(left),* but, when his view of the toy is blocked *(right),* he does not search for it. Several months later, he will search for the hidden toy monkey, reflecting the presence of object permanence.

Research in Life-Span Development

Object Permanence and Causality

**Infancy and Toddlerhood: Baillargeon
Object Permanence Studies**

Two accomplishments of infants that Piaget examined were the development of object permanence and the child's understanding of causality. Let's examine two research studies that address these topics. In both studies, Renée Baillargeon and her colleagues used a research method that involves *violation of expectations*. In this method, infants see an event happen as it normally would. Then, the event is changed in a way that violates what the infant expects to see. When infants look longer at the event that violates their expectations, it indicates they are surprised by it.

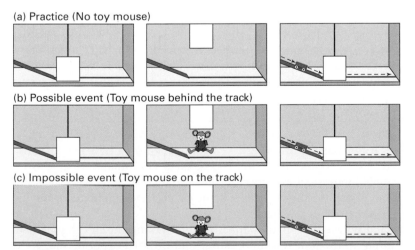

(a) Practice (No toy mouse)

(b) Possible event (Toy mouse behind the track)

(c) Impossible event (Toy mouse on the track)

**FIGURE 6.4 Using the Violation of Expectations Method to Study Object
Permanence in Infants**

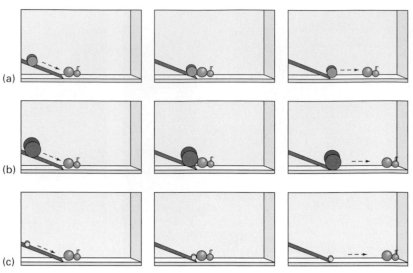

FIGURE 6.5 Infants' Understanding of Causality

After young infants saw how far the medium-sized cylinder *(a)* pushed a toy bug, they showed more surprise at the event in *(c)* that showed a very small cylinder pushing the toy bug as far as the large cylinder *(b)*. Their surprise, indicated by looking at *(c)* longer than *(b)*, indicated that they understood the size of a cylinder was a causal factor in determining how far the toy bug would be pushed when it was hit by the cylinder.

Causal Cognition

In one study focused on object permanence, researchers showed infants a toy car that moved down an inclined track, disappeared behind a screen, and then reemerged at the other end, still on the track (Baillargeon & DeVos, 1991) (see figure 6.4a). After this sequence was repeated several times, the infants then saw something different take place. In a "possible event" a toy mouse was placed *behind* the tracks but was hidden by the screen while the car rolled by (b). Then, in an "impossible event," the toy mouse was placed *on* the tracks but was secretly removed after the screen was lowered so that the car seemed to go through the mouse (c). In this study, infants as young as 3½ months of age looked longer at the impossible event than at the possible event indicating that they were surprised by it. Their surprised look suggested they remembered not only that the toy mouse still existed (object permanence) but its location.

Another study focused on the infant's understanding of causality. Researchers found that even young infants comprehend that the size of a moving object determines how far it will move a stationary object that it collides with (Kotovsky & Baillargeon, 1994) (see figure 6.5). In this research, a cylinder rolls down a ramp and hits a toy bug at the bottom of the ramp. By 5½ and 6½ months of age, infants understand that the bug will roll farther if it is hit by a large cylinder than if it is hit by a small cylinder after they have observed how far it will be pushed by a medium-sized cylinder. Thus, by the middle of the first year of life these infants understood that the size of the cylinder was a causal factor in determining how far the bug would move if it was hit by the cylinder.

Evaluating Piaget's Sensorimotor Stage   Piaget opened up a new way of looking at infants with his view that their main task is to coordinate their sensory impressions with their motor activity. However, the infant's cognitive world is not as neatly packaged as Piaget portrayed it, and some of Piaget's explanations for the cause of change are debated.

Piaget constructed his view of infancy mainly by observing the development of his own three children. In the past several decades, sophisticated experimental techniques have been devised to study infants, and there have been a large number of research studies on infant development. Much of the new research suggests that Piaget's view of sensorimotor development needs to be modified.

A number of theorists, such as Eleanor Gibson (1989) and Elizabeth Spelke (1991; Spelke & Newport, 1998), believe that infants' perceptual abilities are highly developed very early in development. For example, in chapter 5 we discussed Spelke's research that demonstrated the presence of *intermodal perception*—the ability to coordinate information from two more sensory modalities, such as vision and hearing. Research by Renée Baillargeon (1995, 2002) and her colleagues (Aguiar & Baillargeon, 2002) documents that infants as young as 3 to 4 months expect objects to be *substantial* (in the sense that other objects cannot move through them) and *permanent* (in the sense that objects continue to exist when they are hidden).

In sum, researchers believe that infants see objects as bounded, unitary, solid, and separate from their background, possibly at birth or shortly thereafter, but definitely by 3 to 4 months of age, much earlier than Piaget envisioned. Young infants still have much to learn about objects, but the world appears both stable and orderly to them and, thus, capable of being conceptualized. Infants are continually trying to structure and make sense of their world (Meltzoff & Gopnik, 1997).

Piaget claimed that certain processes are crucial in stage transitions, but the data do not always support his explanations. For example, in Piaget's theory, an important feature in the progression into substage 4, coordination of secondary circular reactions, is an infant's inclination to search for a hidden object in a familiar location rather than to look for the object in a new location. **AB̄ error** is the term used to describe infants who make the mistake of selecting the familiar hiding place (A) rather than the new hiding place (B̄) as they progress into substage 4. Researchers have found, however, that the AB̄ error does not show up consistently (Corrigan, 1981; Sophian, 1985). The evidence indicates that AB̄ errors are sensitive to the delay between hiding the object at B and the infant's attempt to find it (Diamond, 1985). Thus, the AB̄ error might be due to a failure in memory.

Many of today's researchers believe that Piaget wasn't specific enough about how infants learn about their world and that infants are more competent than Piaget thought (Mandler, 2003; Meltzoff, 2000). As they have examined the specific ways that infants learn, the field of infant cognition has become very specialized. There are many researchers working on different questions, with no general theory emerging that can connect all of the different findings (Nelson, 1999). Their theories are local theories, focused on specific research questions, rather than grand theories like Piaget's (Kuhn, 1998). If there is a unifying theme, it is that investigators in infant development struggle with how developmental changes in cognition take place and the big issue of nature and nurture.

Challenges to Piaget

*I*nfants know that objects are substantial and permanent at an earlier age than Piaget envisioned.

—RENÉE BAILLARGEON
*Contemporary Psychologist,
University of Illinois*

Preoperational Stage

The cognitive world of the preschool child is creative, free, and fanciful. The imagination of preschool children works overtime, and their mental grasp of the world improves. Piaget described the preschool child's cognition as *preoperational*. What did he mean?

The **preoperational stage,** which lasts from approximately 2 to 7 years of age, is the second Piagetian stage. In this stage, children begin to represent the world with words, images, and drawings. Symbolic thought goes beyond simple connections of sensory information and physical action. Stable concepts are formed, mental reasoning emerges, egocentrism is present, and magical beliefs are constructed.

Because Piaget called this stage preoperational, it might sound unimportant. Not so. Preoperational thought is anything but a convenient waiting period for the next stage, concrete operational thought. However, the label *preoperational* emphasizes that the child does not yet perform **operations,** which are internalized actions that allow children to do mentally what before they could do only physically. Operations are reversible mental actions. Mentally adding and subtracting numbers are examples of operations.

Thought in the preoperational stage is flawed and not well organized. Preoperational thought is the beginning of the ability to reconstruct in thought what has

AB̄ error The Piagetian object-permanence concept in which an infant progressing into substage 4 makes frequent mistakes, selecting the familiar hiding place (A) rather than the new hiding place (B̄).

preoperational stage The second Piagetian developmental stage, which lasts from about 2 to 7 years of age; children begin to represent the world with words, images, and drawings.

operations Internalized sets of actions that allow children to do mentally what before they had done physically. Operations also are reversible mental actions.

been established in behavior. It also involves a transition from primitive to more sophisticated use of symbols. Preoperational thought can be divided into substages: the symbolic function substage and the intuitive thought substage.

The Symbolic Function Substage   The **symbolic function substage** is the first substage of preoperational thought, occurring roughly between the ages of 2 and 4. In this substage, the young child gains the ability to mentally represent an object that is not present. This ability vastly expands the child's mental world (DeLoache, 2001). Young children use scribble designs to represent people, houses, cars, clouds, and so on. Other examples of symbolism in early childhood are language and pretend play. However, although young children make distinct progress during this substage, their thought still has several important limitations, two of which are egocentrism and animism.

Egocentrism is the inability to distinguish between one's own perspective and someone else's perspective. The following telephone conversation between 4-year-old Mary, who is at home, and her father, who is at work, typifies Mary's egocentric thought:

> **Father:** Mary, is Mommy there?
> **Mary:** (Silently nods)
> **Father:** Mary, may I speak to Mommy?
> **Mary:** (Nods again silently)

Mary's response is egocentric in that she fails to consider her father's perspective before replying. A nonegocentric thinker would have responded verbally.

Piaget and Barbel Inhelder (1969) initially studied young children's egocentrism by devising the three mountains task (see figure 6.6). The child walks around the model of the mountains and becomes familiar with what the mountains look like from different perspectives, and she can see that there are different objects on the mountains. The child is then seated on one side of the table on which the mountains are placed. The experimenter moves a doll to different locations around the table, at each location asking the child to select from a series of photos the one photo that most accurately reflects the view the doll is seeing. Children in the preoperational stage often pick their own view rather than the doll's view. Preschool children frequently show perspective skills on some tasks but not others.

Animism, another limitation of preoperational thought, is the belief that inanimate objects have lifelike qualities and are capable of action (Gelman & Offer, 2002). A young child might show animism by saying, "That tree pushed the leaf

Symbolic Thinking

symbolic function substage The first substage of preoperational thought, occurring roughly between the ages of 2 and 4. In this substage, the young child gains the ability to represent mentally an object that is not present.

egocentrism An important feature of preoperational thought—the inability to distinguish between one's own and someone else's perspective.

animism A facet of preoperational thought—the belief that inanimate objects have "lifelike" qualities and are capable of action.

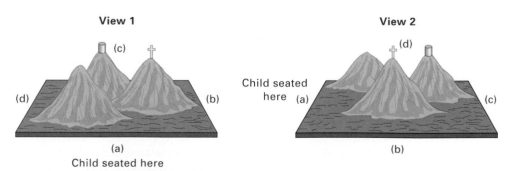

FIGURE 6.6 The Three Mountains Task

View 1 shows the child's perspective from where he or she is sitting. View 2 is an example of the photograph the child would be shown, mixed in with others from different perspectives. To correctly identify this view, the child has to take the perspective of a person sitting at spot *(b)*. Invariably, a preschool child who thinks in a preoperational way cannot perform this task. When asked what a view of the mountains looks like from position *(b)*, the child selects a photograph taken from location *(a)*, the child's view at the time.

off, and it fell down," or "The sidewalk made me mad; it made me fall down." A young child who uses animism fails to distinguish the appropriate occasions for using human and nonhuman perspectives.

Possibly because young children are not very concerned about reality, their drawings are fanciful and inventive. Suns are blue, skies are yellow, and cars float on clouds in their symbolic, imaginative world. One 3½-year-old looked at a scribble he had just drawn and described it as a pelican kissing a seal. The symbolism is simple but strong, like abstractions found in some modern art. Twentieth-century Spanish artist Pablo Picasso commented, "I used to draw like Raphael but it has taken me a lifetime to draw like young children." In the elementary school years, a child's drawings become more realistic, neat, and precise. Suns are yellow, skies are blue, and cars travel on roads (Winner, 1986).

The Intuitive Thought Substage   Tommy is 4 years old. Although he is starting to develop his own ideas about the world he lives in, his ideas are still simple, and he is not very good at thinking things out. He has difficulty understanding events that he knows are taking place but which he cannot see. His fantasized thoughts bear little resemblance to reality. He cannot yet answer the question "What if?" in any reliable way. For example, he has only a vague idea of what would happen if a car were to hit him. He also has difficulty negotiating traffic because he cannot do the mental calculations necessary to estimate whether an approaching car will hit him when he crosses the road.

The **intuitive thought substage** is the second substage of preoperational thought, occurring between approximately 4 and 7 years of age. In this substage, children begin to use primitive reasoning and want to know the answers to all sorts of questions. By the age of 5 children have just about exhausted the adults around them with "why" questions. The child's questions signal the emergence of interest in reasoning and in figuring out why things are the way they are. Here are some samples of the questions children ask during the questioning period of 4 to 6 years of age (Elkind, 1976):

> "What makes you grow up?"
> "What makes you stop growing?"
> "Why does a lady have to be married to have a baby?"
> "Who was the mother when everybody was a baby?"
> "Why do leaves fall?"
> "Why does the sun shine?"

Piaget called this substage *intuitive* because young children seem so sure about their knowledge and understanding yet are unaware of how they know what they know. That is, they know something but know it without the use of rational thinking.

One characteristic of preoperational thought is **centration,** a centering of attention on one characteristic to the exclusion of all others. Centration is most clearly evidenced in young children's lack of **conservation,** the awareness that altering an object's or a substance's appearance does not change its basic properties. To adults, it is obvious that a certain amount of liquid stays the same, regardless of a container's shape. But this is not at all obvious to young children. Instead, they are struck by the height of the liquid in the container; they focus on that characteristic to the exclusion of others. In the conservation task—Piaget's most famous task— a child is presented with two identical beakers, each filled to the same level with liquid (see figure 6.7). The child is asked if these beakers have the same amount of liquid, and she usually says yes. Then the liquid from one beaker is poured into a third beaker, which is taller and thinner than the first two. The child is then asked if the amount of liquid in the tall, thin beaker is equal to that which remains in one of the original beakers. Children who are less than 7 or 8 years old usually say

"I still don't have all the answers, but I'm beginning to ask the right questions."

intuitive thought substage The second substage of preoperational thought, occurring between approximately 4 and 7 years of age. Children begin to use primitive reasoning and want to know the answers to all sorts of questions.

centration The focusing of attention on one characteristic to the exclusion of all others.

conservation The idea that an amount stays the same regardless of how its container changes.

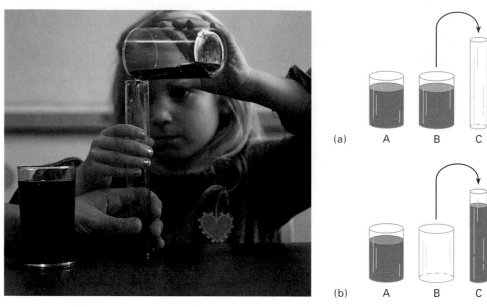

FIGURE 6.7 Piaget's Conservation Task

The beaker test is a well-known Piagetian test to determine whether a child can think operationally—that is, can mentally reverse actions and show conservation of the substance. *(a)* Two identical beakers are presented to the child. Then, the experimenter pours the liquid from B into C, which is taller and thinner than A or B. *(b)* The child is asked if these beakers (A and C) have the same amount of liquid. The preoperational child says no. When asked to point to the beaker that has more liquid, the preoperational child points to the tall, thin beaker.

no and justify their answers in terms of the differing height or width of the beakers. Older children usually answer yes and justify their answers appropriately ("If you poured the water back, the amount would still be the same").

In Piaget's theory, failing the conservation-of-liquid task is a sign that children are at the preoperational stage of cognitive development. The preoperational child fails to show conservation not only of liquid but also of number, matter, length, volume, and area. Figure 6.8 portrays several of these.

Type of Conservation	Initial Presentation	Manipulation	Preoperational Child's Answer
Number	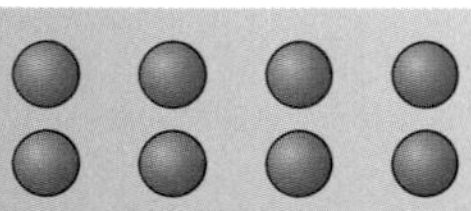 Two identical rows of objects are shown to the child, who agrees they have the same number.	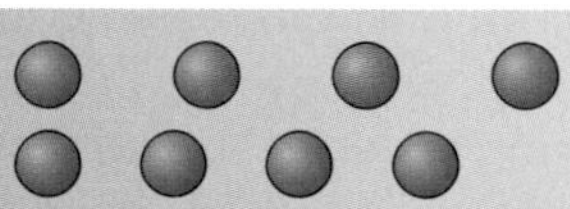 One row is lengthened and the child is asked whether one row now has more objects.	Yes, the longer row.
Matter	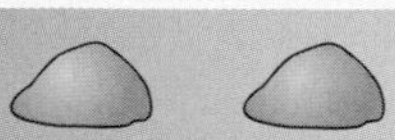 Two identical balls of clay are shown to the child. The child agrees that they are equal.	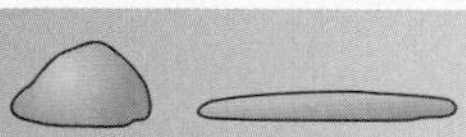 The experimenter changes the shape of one of the balls and asks the child whether they still contain equal amounts of clay.	No, the longer one has more.
Length	 Two sticks are aligned in front of the child. The child agrees that they are the same length.	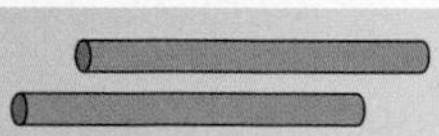 The experimenter moves one stick to the right, then asks the child if they are equal in length.	No, the one on the top is longer.

FIGURE 6.8 Some Dimensions of Conservation: Number, Matter, and Length

Concrete Operational Stage

The **concrete operational stage,** which lasts approximately from 7 to 11 years of age, is the third Piagetian stage. In this stage, children can perform concrete operations (operations that involve concrete objects) and logical reasoning replaces intuitive reasoning as long as the reasoning can be applied to specific or concrete examples. For instance, concrete operational thinkers cannot imagine the steps necessary to complete an algebraic equation, which is too abstract for thinking at this stage of development.

Conservation   The conservation tasks demonstrate a child's ability to perform concrete operations. In the test of reversibility of thought involving conservation of matter (shown in figure 6.8), a child is presented with two identical balls of clay. An experimenter rolls one ball into a long, thin shape; the other remains in its original ball shape. The child is then asked if there is more clay in the ball or in the long, thin piece of clay. By the time children reach the age 7 or 8, most answer that the amount of clay is the same. To answer this problem correctly, children have to imagine the clay ball rolling back into a ball after it has been changed into a long, thin shape. Thus, a *concrete operation* is a reversible mental action on real, concrete objects.

Concrete operations allow children to coordinate several characteristics rather than focus on a single property of an object. In the clay example, a preoperational child is likely to focus on height or width; a concrete operational child coordinates information about both dimensions. Conservation involves recognition that the length, number, mass, quantity, area, weight, and volume of objects and substances are not changed by transformations that merely alter their appearance.

Children do not conserve all quantities or on all tasks simultaneously. The order of their mastery is number, length, liquid quantity, mass, weight, and volume. **Horizontal décalage** is Piaget's concept that similar abilities do not appear at the same time within a stage of development. During the concrete operational stage, conservation of number usually appears first and conservation of volume last. Also, an 8-year-old child may know that a long stick of clay can be rolled back into a ball but not understand that the ball and the stick weigh the same. At about 9 years of age, the child recognizes that they weigh the same, and eventually, at about 11 to 12 years of age, the child understands that the clay's volume is unchanged by rearranging it. Children initially master tasks in which the dimensions are more salient and visible, only later mastering those not as visually apparent, such as volume.

Evaluating Piaget's Conservation Tasks   Some developmentalists do not believe that Piaget was entirely correct in his estimate of when children's conservation skills emerge. For example, Rochel Gelman (1969) showed that when the child's attention to relevant aspects of the conservation task is improved, the child is more likely to conserve. Gelman has also demonstrated that attentional training on one dimension, such as number, improves the preschool child's performance on another dimension, such as mass. Thus, Gelman believes that conservation appears earlier than Piaget thought and that attention is especially important in explaining conservation.

Gelman and other developmentalists also believe that many of the tasks used to assess cognitive development are not sensitive to the child's cognitive abilities (Gelman & Williams, 1998). Thus, rather than revealing limitations in a child's cognitive development, the tasks might merely reveal limitations in the methods used to assess children's cognitive development.

Similar questions about assessments come up when researchers explore another issue related to Piaget's theory: Are his stages of cognitive development universal? Does the cultural context alter the child's development? In the Contexts in Life-Span Development interlude, we explore the age at which children develop conservation skills in different cultures.

Early Childhood: Piaget's Conservation Tasks

concrete operational stage Piaget's third stage, which lasts from approximately 7 to 11 years of age; children can perform concrete operations, and logical reasoning replaces intuitive reasoning as long as the reasoning can be applied to specific, concrete examples.

horizontal décalage Piaget's concept that similar abilities do not appear at the same time within a stage of development.

Contexts of Life-Span Development

Conservation Skills Around the World

Psychologist Patricia Greenfield (1966) conducted a series of studies among Wolof children in the West African nation of Senegal to see if Piaget's theory of concrete operational thought is universal. Using Piaget's beaker tasks, she found that only 50 percent of the 10- to 13-year-olds understood the principle of conservation. Comparable studies among cultures in central Australia, New Guinea (an island north of Australia), the Amazon jungle region of Brazil, and rural Sardinia (an island off the coast of Italy) yielded strongly similar results (Dasen, 1977). These findings suggested that adults in some cultures do not reach the stage of concrete operational thought. However, if this were so, such adults would be severely handicapped in everyday life. Like preschool children, they would be unable to think through the implications of their actions and would be unable to coordinate various kinds of information about objects. They also would be incapable of going beyond an egocentric perspective to understand another person's point of view.

Some researchers believe that the failure to find concrete operational thought in various cultures is due to inadequate communication between the experimenter and the children. For example, one study involved two cultural groups from Cape Breton, Nova Scotia—one English-speaking European, the other Micmac Indian. No difference in conservation abilities appeared between the groups of 10- to 11-year-olds when they were interviewed in their native languages (Nyiti, 1982). The Micmac children all spoke their ancestral tongue at home but had also spoken English since the first grade. When the Micmac children were interviewed in English, they understood the concept of conservation only half as well as the English-speaking children of European descent did. This study illustrates the importance of communication between the experimenter and the research participants in cross-cultural studies.

Researchers have also investigated whether a child's ability to use the concept of conservation can improve if the child comes from a culture in which conservation is not widely practiced (Greenfield & Suzuki, 1998). In one study, rural aboriginal Australian children performed some exercises similar to Piaget's beaker task (Dasen, Ngini, & Lavalée, 1979). This "training" improved their performance on the beaker task. Even so, their grasp of the conservation concept lagged behind that of children from the Australian city of Canberra by approximately three years. These findings suggest that the aboriginal culture does not provide practice that is relevant to the conservation concept.

In sum, the age at which individuals acquire conservation skills is associated with the degree to which their culture provides relevant practice. However, such cross-cultural differences tend to disappear when the studies are conducted by experimenters who are familiar with the language of the people being studied or when the participants receive special training (Cole & Cole, 2001).

The age at which children acquire conservation skills is related to the extent to which the culture provides practice relevant to the concept of conservation. The children shown here live in Nepal, and they have extensive experience as potters. They gain an understanding of the concept of conservation of quantity earlier than children the same age who do not have experience manipulating a material like clay.

Classification Many of the concrete operations identified by Piaget involve the ways children reason about the properties of objects. One important skill that characterizes concrete operational children is the ability to classify things and to consider their relationships. An example of concrete operational classification skills involves a family tree of four generations (Furth & Wachs, 1975) (see figure 6.9). This family tree suggests that the grandfather (A) has three children (B, C, and D), each of whom has two children (E through J), and that one of these children (J) has three children (K, L, and M). The concrete operational child understands that person J can, at the same time, be father, brother, and grandson. A child who comprehends this classification system can move up and down a level (vertically), across a level (horizontally), and up and down and across (obliquely) within the system.

Another example of the ability of concrete operational children to reason about relations is **seriation,** which involves stimuli along a quantitative dimension (such as length). To see if children can serialize, a teacher might haphazardly place eight sticks of different lengths on a table. The teacher then asks the children to order the sticks by length. Many young children put the sticks into two or three small groups of "big" sticks or "little" sticks, rather than a correct ordering of all eight sticks. Or they line up the tops of the sticks but ignore the bottoms. The concrete operational thinker simultaneously understands that each stick must be longer than the one that precedes it and shorter than the one that follows it.

Another aspect of reasoning about the relations between classes is **transitivity:** If a relation holds between a first object and a second object, and also holds between the second object and a third object, then it also holds between the first and third objects. For example, consider three sticks (A, B, and C) of differing lengths. A is the longest, B is intermediate in length, and C is the shortest. Does the child understand that if A is longer than B, and B is longer than C, then A is longer than C? In Piaget's theory, concrete operational thinkers do; preoperational thinkers do not.

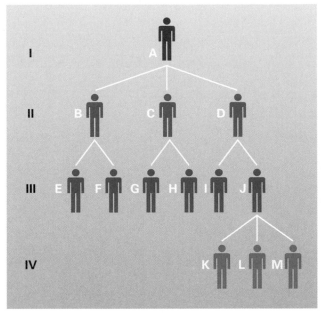

FIGURE 6.9 Classification: An Important Ability in Concrete Operational Thought

A family tree of four generations *(I to IV):* The preoperational child has trouble classifying the members of the four generations; the concrete operational child can classify the members vertically, horizontally, and obliquely (up and down and across). For example, the concrete operational child understands that a family member can be a son, a brother, and a father, all at the same time.

Formal Operational Stage

So far we have studied the first three of Piaget's stages of cognitive development: sensorimotor, preoperational, and concrete operational. What are the characteristics of the fourth and final stage?

The **formal operational stage,** which appears between 11 and 15 years of age, is the fourth and final Piagetian stage. In this stage, individuals move beyond concrete experiences and think in abstract and more logical ways. As part of thinking more abstractly, adolescents develop images of ideal circumstances. They might think about what an ideal parent is like and compare their parents to their ideal standards. They begin to entertain possibilities for the future and are fascinated with what they can be. In solving problems, formal operational thinkers are more systematic and use logical reasoning.

Abstract, Idealistic, and Logical Thinking   The abstract quality of the adolescent's thought at the formal operational level is evident in the adolescent's verbal problem-solving ability. Whereas the concrete operational thinker needs to see the concrete elements A, B, and C to be able to make the logical inference that if A = B and B = C, then A = C, the formal operational thinker can solve this problem merely through verbal presentation.

Another indication of the abstract quality of adolescents' thought is their increased tendency to think about thought itself. One adolescent commented, "I began thinking about why I was thinking about what I was. Then I began thinking about why I was thinking about what I was thinking about what I was." If this

seriation The concrete operation that involves ordering stimuli along a quantitative dimension (such as length).

transitivity If a relation holds between a first object and a second object, and holds between the second object and a third object, then it holds between the first object and the third object. Piaget believed that an understanding of transitivity is characteristic of concrete operational thought.

formal operational stage Piaget's fourth and final stage, which occurs between the ages of 11 and 15; individuals move beyond concrete experiences and think in more abstract and logical ways.

sounds abstract, it is, and it characterizes the adolescent's enhanced focus on thought and its abstract qualities.

Accompanying the abstract nature of formal operational thought in adolescence is thought full of idealism and possibilities. While children frequently think in concrete ways, or in terms of what is real and limited, adolescents begin to engage in extended speculation about ideal characteristics—qualities they desire in themselves and in others. Such thoughts often lead adolescents to compare themselves with others in regard to such ideal standards. And the thoughts of adolescents are often fantasy flights into future possibilities. It is not unusual for the adolescent to become impatient with these newfound ideal standards and to become perplexed over which of many ideal standards to adopt.

As adolescents are learning to think more abstractly and idealistically, they are also learning to think more logically. Children are more likely to solve problems in a trial-and-error fashion. Adolescents begin to think more as a scientist thinks, devising plans to solve problems and systematically testing solutions. They use **hypothetical-deductive reasoning,** which means that they develop hypotheses, or best guesses, and systematically deduce, or conclude, which is the best path to follow in solving the problem.

One example of hypothetical-deductive reasoning involves a modification of the familiar game Twenty Questions. Individuals are shown a set of 42 color pictures, displayed in a rectangular array (six rows of seven pictures each) and are asked to determine which picture the experimenter has in mind (that is, which is "correct"). The individuals are allowed to ask only questions to which the experimenter can answer yes or no. The object of the game is to select the correct picture by asking as few questions as possible. Adolescents who are deductive hypothesis testers formulate a plan and test a series of hypotheses, which considerably narrows the field of choices. The most effective plan is a "halving" strategy (Q: Is the picture in the right half of the array?).

Assimilation (incorporating new information into existing knowledge) dominates the initial development of formal operational thought, and these thinkers perceive the world subjectively and idealistically. Later in adolescence, as intellectual balance is restored, these individuals accommodate to the cognitive upheaval that has occurred (they adjust to the new information).

Some of Piaget's ideas on formal operational thought are being challenged (Byrnes, 2001, 2003; Eccles, Wigfield, & Byrnes, 2003; Overton & Byrnes, 1991). There is much more individual variation in formal operational thought than Piaget envisioned (Kuhn, 2000). Only about one in three young adolescents is a formal operational thinker. Many American adults never become formal operational thinkers, and neither do many adults in other cultures.

Adolescent Egocentrism

In addition to thinking more logically, abstractly, and idealistically—characteristics of Piaget's formal operational thought stage—in what other ways do adolescents change cognitively? David Elkind (1978) has described how adolescent egocentrism governs the way that adolescents think about social matters. **Adolescent egocentrism** is the heightened self-consciousness of adolescents, which is reflected in their belief that others are as interested in them as they are themselves, and in their sense of personal uniqueness and invincibility. Elkind believes that adolescent egocentrism can be dissected into two types of social thinking—imaginary audience and personal fable.

The **imaginary audience** refers to the aspect of adolescent egocentrism that involves attention-getting behavior—the attempt to be noticed, visible, and "on stage." An adolescent might think that others are as aware of a few hairs that are out of place as he is. An adolescent girl walks into her classroom and thinks that all eyes are riveted on her complexion. Adolescents especially sense that they are "on stage" in early adolescence, believing they are the main actors and all others are the audience.

hypothetical-deductive reasoning Piaget's formal operational concept that adolescents have the cognitive ability to develop hypotheses about ways to solve problems and can systematically deduce which is the best path to follow in solving the problem.

adolescent egocentrism The heightened self-consciousness of adolescents, which is reflected in adolescents' beliefs that others are as interested in them as they are in themselves, and in adolescents' sense of personal uniqueness and invincibility.

imaginary audience The aspect of adolescent egocentrism that involves attention-getting behavior motivated by a desire to be noticed, visible, and "on stage."

According to Elkind, the **personal fable** is the part of adolescent egocentrism that involves an adolescent's sense of personal uniqueness and invincibility. Adolescents' sense of personal uniqueness makes them feel that no one can understand how they really feel. For example, an adolescent girl thinks that her mother cannot possibly sense the hurt she feels because her boyfriend has broken up with her. As part of their effort to retain a sense of personal uniqueness, adolescents might craft stories about themselves that are filled with fantasy, immersing themselves in a world that is far removed from reality. Personal fables frequently show up in adolescent diaries.

Adolescents also often show a sense of invincibility—feeling that although others might be vulnerable to tragedies, such as a terrible car wreck, these things won't happen to them. Some developmentalists believe that the sense of uniqueness and invincibility that egocentrism generates is responsible for some of the seemingly reckless behavior of adolescents, including drag racing, drug use, suicide, and failure to use contraceptives during intercourse (Dolcini & others, 1989). For example, one study found that eleventh- and twelfth-grade females who were high in adolescent egocentrism were more likely to say they would not get pregnant from engaging in sex without contraception than were their counterparts who were low in adolescent egocentrism (Arnett, 1990).

Many adolescent girls spend long hours in front of the mirror, depleting cans of hair spray, tubes of lipstick, and jars of cosmetics. *How might this behavior be related to changes in adolescent cognitive and physical development?*

Review and Reflect: Learning Goal 1

1 Discuss the key processes and four stages in Piaget's theory

REVIEW

- What are the key processes in Piaget's theory of cognitive development? What are Piaget's four stages of cognitive development?
- What are the main characteristics of the sensorimotor stage?
- What are the main characteristics of the preoperational stage?
- What are the main characteristics of the concrete operational stage?
- What are the main characteristics of the formal operational stage?

REFLECT

- Do you consider yourself to be a formal operational thinker? Do you still sometimes feel like a concrete operational thinker? Give examples.

I check my look in the mirror. I wanna change my clothes, my hair, my face.

—BRUCE SPRINGSTEEN
Contemporary American Rock Star

2 APPLYING AND EVALUATING PIAGET'S THEORY

Piaget and Education   **Evaluating Piaget's Theory**

What are some applications of Piaget's theory to education? What are the main contributions and criticisms of Piaget's theory?

Piaget and Education

Piaget was not an educator but he provided a sound conceptual framework for viewing learning and education. Here are some ideas in Piaget's theory that can be applied to teaching children (Elkind, 1976; Heuwinkel, 1996):

personal fable The part of adolescent egocentrism that involves an adolescent's sense of uniqueness and invincibility.

1. *Take a constructivist approach.* Piaget emphasized that children learn best when they are active and seek solutions for themselves. Piaget opposed teaching methods that treat children as passive receptacles. The educational implication of Piaget's view is that, in all subjects, students learn best by making discoveries, reflecting on them, and discussing them, rather than blindly imitating the teacher or doing things by rote.

2. *Facilitate, rather than direct, learning.* Effective teachers design situations that allow students to learn by doing. These situations promote students' thinking and discovery. Teachers listen, watch, and question students, to help them gain better understanding. Don't just examine what students think and the product of their learning. Rather, carefully observe them and find out how they think. Ask relevant questions to stimulate their thinking, and ask them to explain their answers.

3. *Consider the child's knowledge and level of thinking.* Students do not come to class with empty minds. They have many ideas about the physical and natural world. They have concepts of space, time, quantity, and causality. These ideas differ from the ideas of adults. Teachers need to interpret what a student is saying and respond in a way that is not too far from the student's level. Also, Piaget suggested that it is important to examine children's mistakes in thinking, not just what they get correct, to help guide them to a higher level of understanding.

4. *Use ongoing assessment.* Individually constructed meanings cannot be measured by standardized tests. Math and language portfolios (which contain work in progress as well as finished products), individual conferences in which students discuss their thinking strategies, and students' written and verbal explanations of their reasoning can be used to evaluate progress.

5. *Promote the student's intellectual health.* When Piaget came to lecture in the United States, he was asked, "What can I do to get my child to a higher cognitive stage sooner?" He was asked this question so often here compared with other countries that he called it the American question. For Piaget, children's learning should occur naturally. Children should not be pushed and pressured into achieving too much too early in their development, before they are maturationally ready. Some parents spend long hours every day holding up large flash cards with words on them to improve their baby's vocabulary. In the Piagetian view, this is not the best way for infants to learn. It places too much emphasis on speeding up intellectual development, involves passive learning, and will not work.

6. *Turn the classroom into a setting of exploration and discovery.* What do actual classrooms look like when the teachers adopt Piaget's views? Several first- and second-grade math classrooms provide some good examples (Kamii, 1985, 1989). The teachers emphasize students' own exploration and discovery. The classrooms are less structured than what we think of as a typical classroom. Workbooks and predetermined assignments are not used. Rather, the teachers observe the students' interests and natural participation in activities to determine what the course of learning will be. For example, a math lesson might be constructed around counting the day's lunch money or dividing supplies among students. Often, games are prominently used in the classroom to stimulate mathematical thinking. For example, a version of dominoes teaches children about even-numbered combinations. A variation on tic-tac-toe involves replacing *X*s and *O*s with numbers. Teachers encourage peer interaction during the lessons and games because students' different viewpoints can contribute to advances in thinking.

Evaluating Piaget's Theory

What were Piaget's main contributions? Has his theory withstood the test of time?

Contributions   Piaget was a giant in the field of developmental psychology, the founder of the present field of children's cognitive development. Psychologists owe him a long list of masterful concepts of enduring power and fascination: assimilation, accommodation, object permanence, egocentrism, conservation, and others. Psychologists also owe him the current vision of children as active, constructive thinkers (Vidal, 2000). And they have a debt to him for creating a theory that generated a huge volume of research on children's cognitive development.

Piaget also was a genius when it came to observing children. His careful observations showed us inventive ways to discover how children act on and adapt to their world. Piaget showed us some important things to look for in cognitive development, such as the shift from preoperational to concrete operational thinking. He also showed us how children need to make their experiences fit their schemes (cognitive frameworks) yet simultaneously adapt their schemes to experience. Piaget also revealed how cognitive change is likely to occur if the context is structured to allow gradual movement to the next higher level. Concepts do not emerge suddenly, full-blown, but instead develop through a series of partial accomplishments that lead to increasingly comprehensive understanding (Haith & Benson, 1998).

Criticisms   Piaget's theory has not gone unchallenged (Byrnes, 2001, 2003). Questions are raised about estimates of children's competence at different developmental levels, stages, the training of children to reason at higher levels, and culture and education.

Estimates of Children's Competence   Some cognitive abilities emerge earlier than Piaget thought (Flavell, Miller, & Miller, 2002; Mandler, 2003). For example, as previously noted, some aspects of object permanence emerge earlier than he believed. Even 2-year-olds are nonegocentric in some contexts. When they realize that another person will not see an object, they investigate whether the person is blindfolded or looking in a different direction. Some understanding of the conservation of number has been demonstrated as early as age 3, although Piaget did not think it emerged until 7. Young children are not as uniformly "pre" this and "pre" that (precausal, preoperational) as Piaget thought.

Other cognitive abilities also can emerge later than Piaget thought. Many adolescents still think in concrete operational ways or are just beginning to master formal operations. Even many adults are not formal operational thinkers. In sum, recent theoretical revisions highlight more cognitive competencies of infants and young children and more cognitive shortcomings of adolescents and adults (Flavell, Miller, & Miller, 2002).

Stages   Piaget conceived of stages as unitary structures of thought. Thus, his theory assumes developmental synchrony—that is, various aspects of a stage should emerge at the same time. However, some concrete operational concepts do not appear in synchrony. For example, children do not learn to conserve at the same time they learn to cross-classify. Thus, most contemporary developmentalists agree that children's cognitive development is not as stagelike as Piaget thought (Kuhn, 2000).

Effects of Training   Some children who are at one cognitive stage (such as preoperational) can be trained to reason at a higher cognitive stage (such as concrete operational). This poses a problem for Piaget's theory. He argued that such training is only superficial and ineffective, unless the child is at a maturational transition point between the stages (Gelman & Williams, 1998).

Culture and Education   Culture and education exert stronger influences on children's development than Piaget believed (Greenfield, 2000). For example, the age at which children acquire conservation skills is related to how much practice their culture provides in these skills. An outstanding teacher and education in the logic of math and science can promote concrete and formal operational thought.

> We owe to Piaget the present field of cognitive development with its image of the developing child, who through its own active and creative commerce with its environment, builds an orderly succession of cognitive structures enroute to intellectual maturity.
>
> —JOHN FLAVELL
> *Contemporary Psychologist,*
> *Stanford University*

An Alternative View Neo-Piagetians argue that Piaget got some things right but that his theory needs considerable revision. They give more emphasis to how children use attention, memory, and strategies to process information (Case, 1987, 1999; Case & Mueller, 2001). They especially believe a more accurate portrayal of children's thinking requires attention to children's strategies, the speed at which children process information, the particular task involved, and the division of problems into smaller, more precise steps (Demetriou, 2001). In chapter 7, we will further discuss these aspects of children's thought.

Review and Reflect: Learning Goal 2

2 Apply Piaget's theory to education and evaluate Piaget's theory

REVIEW

- How can Piaget's theory be applied to educating children?
- What are some key contributions and criticisms of Piaget's theory?

REFLECT

- How might thinking in formal operational ways rather than concrete operational ways help students to develop better study skills?

---

3 VYGOTSKY'S THEORY OF COGNITIVE DEVELOPMENT

The Zone of Proximal Development	Language and Thought	Evaluating Vygotsky's Theory
Scaffolding	Teaching Strategies	

Piaget's theory is a major developmental theory. Another developmental theory that focuses on children's cognition is Vygotsky's theory. Like Piaget, Vygotsky emphasized that children actively construct their knowledge and understanding. In Piaget's theory, children develop ways of thinking and understanding by their actions and interactions with the physical world. In Vygtosky's theory, children are more often described as social creatures than in Piaget's theory. They develop their ways of thinking and understanding primarily through social interaction. Their cognitive development depends on the tools provided by society, and their minds are shaped by the cultural context in which they live (Kuzulin & others, 2003).

We briefly described Vygotsky's theory in chapter 1 ◀▏▏▏ P. 22. Here we take a closer look at his ideas about how children learn and his view of the role of language in cognitive development.

The Zone of Proximal Development

Zone of proximal development (ZPD) is Vygotsky's term for the range of tasks that are too difficult for the child to master alone but that can be learned with guidance and assistance of adults or more-skilled children. Thus, the lower limit of the ZPD is the level of skill reached by the child working independently. The upper limit is the level of additional responsibility the child can accept with the assistance of an able instructor (see figure 6.10). The ZPD captures the child's cognitive skills that are in the process of maturing and can be accomplished only with the assistance of a more-skilled person (Kinginger, 2002). Vygotsky (1962) called these the "buds" or

neo-Piagetians Developmentalists who have elaborated on Piaget's theory, emphasizing the importance of information processing.

zone of proximal development (ZPD) Vygotsky's term for tasks too difficult for children to master alone but that can be mastered with assistance.

"flowers" of development, to distinguish them from the "fruits" of development, which the child already can accomplish independently. Vygotsky's emphasis on the ZPD underscores his belief in the importance of social influences, especially instruction, on children's cognitive development.

Let's consider an example that reflects the zone of proximal development (Frede, 1995). A five-year-old child is pushing a small shopping cart through the house area of his preschool. His teacher notices that he is putting fruit in the small basket and all other groceries in the larger section of the cart. She has watched him sort objects over the last several weeks and thinks that he may now be able to classify along two dimensions at the same time, with some help from her. She goes to the cash register and says, "We need to be careful how we divide your groceries into bags. We want to use one bag for things that go in the refrigerator and other bags for things that will go in the cabinet." Together they devise a system with one bag for each of the following categories: food in cartons that will go into the refrigerator, loose vegetables and fruits for the refrigerator, food cartons that go in the cabinet, and food cans that go in the cabinet. In this example, the child's unassisted level of classification was simple: fruit versus nonfruit. With the teacher's help, he was able to apply a more sophisticated form of classification.

Scaffolding

Closely linked to the idea of the ZPD is the concept of scaffolding. **Scaffolding** means changing the level of support. Over the course of a teaching session, a more-skilled person (a teacher or advanced peer) adjusts the amount of guidance to fit the child's current performance (Donovan & Smolkin, 2002; John-Steiner & Mahn, 2003; Many, 2002). When the student is learning a new task, the skilled person may use direct instruction. As the student's competence increases, less guidance is given.

Dialogue is an important tool of scaffolding in the zone of proximal development (Tappan, 1998). Vygotsky viewed children as having rich but unsystematic,

Upper limit

Level of additional responsibility child can accept with assistance of an able instructor

Zone of proximal development (ZPD)

Lower limit

Level of problem solving reached on these tasks by child working alone

FIGURE 6.10 Vygotsky's Zone of Proximal Development

Vygotsky's zone of proximal development has a lower limit and an upper limit. Tasks in the ZPD are too difficult for the child to perform alone. They require assistance from an adult or a skilled child. As children experience the verbal instruction or demonstration, they organize the information in their existing mental structures, so they can eventually perform the skill or task alone.

Lev Vygotsky (1896–1934), shown here with his daughter, believed that children's cognitive development is advanced through social interaction with skilled individuals embedded in a sociocultural backdrop.

scaffolding In cognitive development, Vygotsky used this term to describe the changing support over the course of a teaching session, with the more-skilled person adjusting guidance to fit the child's current performance level.

Vygotsky's Theory

Vygotsky Resources

Vygotsky Links

Scaffolding

disorganized, and spontaneous concepts. In a dialogue, these concepts meet with the skilled helper's more systematic, logical, and rational concepts. As a result, the child's concepts become more systematic, logical, and rational. For example, a dialogue might take place between a teacher and a child when the teacher uses scaffolding to help a child understand a concept like "transportation."

Language and Thought

The use of dialogue as a tool for scaffolding is only one example of the important role of language in a child's development. According to Vygotsky, children use speech not only for social communication, but also to help them solve tasks. Vygotsky (1962) further believed that young children use language to plan, guide, and monitor their behavior. This use of language for self-regulation is called *private speech*. For Piaget private speech is egocentric and immature, but for Vygotsky it is an important tool of thought during the early childhood years.

Vygotsky said that language and thought initially develop independently of each other and then merge. He emphasized that all mental functions have external, or social, origins. Children must use language to communicate with others before they can focus inward on their own thoughts. Children also must communicate externally and use language for a long period of time before they can make the transition from external to internal speech. This transition period occurs between 3 and 7 years of age and involves talking to oneself. After a while, the self-talk becomes second nature to children, and they can act without verbalizing. When this occurs, children have internalized their egocentric speech in the form of *inner speech*, which becomes their thoughts.

Vygotsky believed that children who use a lot of private speech are more socially competent than those who don't (Santiago-Delefosse & Delefosse, 2002). He argued that *private speech* represents an early transition in becoming more socially communicative. For Vygotsky, when young children talk to themselves, they are using language to govern their behavior and guide themselves. For example, a child working on a puzzle might say to herself, "Which pieces should I put together first? I'll try those green ones first. Now I need some blue ones. No, that blue one doesn't fit there. I'll try it over here."

Researchers have found support for Vygotsky's view that private speech plays a positive role in children's development (Winsler, Diaz, & Montero, 1997; Winsler, Carlton, & Barry, 2000). Researchers have found that children use private speech more when tasks are difficult, following errors, and when they are not sure how to proceed (Berk, 1994). They also have revealed that children who use private speech are more attentive and improve their performance more than children who do not use private speech (Berk & Spuhl, 1995).

Teaching Strategies

Vygotsky's theory already has been embraced by many teachers and has been successfully applied to education (Bearison & Dorvall, 2002; Bodrova & Leong, 2003; Rogoff, 2003; Rowe & Wertsch, 2002; Tudge & Scrimsher, 2003; Winsler & others, 2002). Here are some ways Vygotsky's theory can be incorporated in classrooms:

1. *Use the child's zone of proximal development in teaching.* Teaching should begin toward the zone's upper limit, so that the child can reach the goal with help and move to a higher level of skill and knowledge. Offer just enough assistance. You might ask, "What can I do to help you?" Or simply observe the child's intentions and attempts, smoothly providing support when needed. When the child hesitates, offer encouragement. And encourage the child to practice the skill. You may watch and appreciate the child's practice or offer support when the child forgets what to do.

2. *Use more-skilled peers as teachers.* Remember that it is not just adults that Vygotsky believed are important in helping children learn important skills. Children

also benefit from the support and guidance of more-skilled children (John-Steiner & Mahn, 2003).

3. *Monitor and encourage children's use of private speech.* Be aware of the developmental change from externally talking to oneself when solving a problem during the preschool years to privately talking to oneself in the early elementary school years. In the elementary school years, encourage children to internalize and self-regulate their talk to themselves.

4. *Effectively assess the child's ZPD.* Like Piaget, Vygotsky did not believe that formal, standardized tests are the best way to assess children's learning. Rather, Vygotsky argued that assessment should focus on determining the child's zone of proximal development (Meijer & Elshout, 2001). The skilled helper presents the child with tasks of varying difficulty to determine the best level at which to begin instruction.

5. *Place instruction in a meaningful context.* In education today, there is an increased emphasis on moving away from abstract presentations of material to providing students with opportunities to experience learning in meaningful, real-world settings. Thus, instead of just teaching children to memorize math formulas, students work on math problems with real-world implications (Santrock, 2004).

6. *Transform the classroom with Vygotskian ideas.* What does a Vygotskian classroom look like? The Kamehameha Elementary Education Program (KEEP) is based on Vygotsky's theory (Tharp, 1994). The zone of proximal development is the key element of instruction in this program. Children might read a story and then interpret its meaning. Many of the learning activities take place in small groups. All children spend at least 20 minutes each morning in a setting called "Center One." In this context, scaffolding is used to improve children's literary skills. The instructor asks questions, responds to students' queries, and builds on the ideas that students generate. Thousands of children from low-income families have attended KEEP public schools—in Hawaii, on an Arizona Navajo Indian reservation, and in Los Angeles. Compared with a control group of non-KEEP children, the KEEP children participated more actively in classroom discussion, were more attentive in class, and had higher reading achievement (Tharp & Gallimore, 1988). The Applications in Life-Span Development interlude further explores the education of children.

Barbara Rogoff's Views
The Collaborative Classroom

Applications in Life-Span Development
Apprenticeship Thinking

Drawing heavily on Vygotsky's theory, Barbara Rogoff (1990, 2001, 2003; Rogoff, Turkanis, & Bartlett, 2001) argues that children serve a sort of apprenticeship in thinking through participation in social activity, guided by companions who stretch and support children's understanding of the "tools" of the culture and their skills in using these tools. Important tools for handling information include (1) language that organizes categories of reality and structures ways of approaching situations; (2) practices for recording and transforming information; (3) mathematical systems; and (4) memory strategies. Some of these tools have material supports, such as pencil and paper, word-processing programs, knots on ropes, and so on. These tools provide mechanisms for transmitting information from one generation to the next.

Rogoff says that guided participation is widely used around the world. Cultures may differ, though, in the goals of development—what lessons are to be learned—and the means for providing guided participation (Rogoff, 2003; Rogoff & Morelli, 1989). Around the world, caregivers and children arrange children's activities and revise children's responsibilities as they gain skill and knowledge. With guidance,

Cognitive development occurs as new generations collaborate with older generations in varying forms of interpersonal engagement and institutional practices.

—BARBARA ROGOFF
Contemporary Psychologist,
University of California—
Santa Cruz

At about 7 years of age, Mayan girls in Guatemala are assisted in beginning to learn to weave a simple belt, with the loom already set up for them. The young girl shown here is American developmental psychologist Barbara Rogoff's daughter, being taught to weave by a Mayan woman. *How is Rogoff's idea of a cognitive apprenticeship compatible with Vygotsky's theory?*

children participate in cultural activities that socialize them into skilled activities. For example, Mayan mothers in Guatemala help their daughters learn to weave through guided participation. In the United States and in many other nations, creative thinkers interact with a knowledgeable person rather than by only studying books or by attending classes and exhibits.

Children begin to practice the skills for using cultural tools, such as literacy, even before they have contact with the technology. American parents read stories to their young children at bedtime as part of their daily routine. Most middle-socioeconomic-status American parents embed their children in a way of life in which reading and writing are integral parts of communication, recreation, and livelihood (Rogoff, 1990, 1998).

Evaluating Vygotsky's Theory

Even though their theories were proposed at about the same time, most of the world learned about Vygotsky's theory later than they learned about Piaget's theory, so Vygotsky's theory has not yet been evaluated as thoroughly. Vygotsky's view of the importance of sociocultural influences on children's development fits with the current belief that it is important to evaluate the contextual factors in learning (Kozulin, 2000).

We already have mentioned several comparisons of Vygotsky's and Piaget's theories, such as Vygotsky's emphasis on the importance of inner speech in development and Piaget's view that such speech is immature. Although both theories are constructivist, Vygotsky's is a **social constructivist approach,** which emphasizes the social contexts of learning and the construction of knowledge through social interaction.

In moving from Piaget to Vygotsky, the conceptual shift is from the individual to collaboration, social interaction, and sociocultural activity (Rogoff, 1998, 2003). The endpoint of cognitive development for Piaget is formal operational thought. For Vygotsky, the endpoint can differ depending on which skills are considered to be the most important in a particular culture. For Piaget, children construct knowledge by transforming, organizing, and reorganizing previous knowledge. For Vygotsky, children construct knowledge through social interaction (Hogan & Tudge, 1999). The

social constructivist approach An emphasis on the social contexts of learning and the construction of knowledge through social interaction. Vygotsky's theory reflects this approach.

	VYGOTSKY	PIAGET
Sociocultural Context	Strong Emphasis	Little Emphasis
Constructivism	Social constructivist	Cognitive constructivist
Stages	No general stages of development proposed	Strong emphasis on stages (sensorimotor, preoperational, concrete operational, and formal operational)
Key Processes	Zone of proximal development, language, dialogue, tools of the culture	Schema, assimilation, accommodation, operations, conservation, classification, hypothetical-deductive reasoning
Role of Language	A major role; language plays a powerful role in shaping thought	Language has a minimal role; cognition primarily directs language
View on Education	Education plays a central role, helping children learn the tools of the culture.	Education merely refines the child's cognitive skills that have already emerged.
Teaching Implications	Teacher is a facilitator and guide, not a director; establish many opportunities for children to learn with the teacher and more-skilled peers	Also views teacher as a facilitator and guide, not a director; provide support for children to explore their world and discover knowledge

FIGURE 6.11 Comparison of Vygotsky's and Piaget's Theories

implication of Piaget's theory for teaching is that children need support to explore their world and discover knowledge. The main implication of Vygotsky's theory for teaching is that students need many opportunities to learn with the teacher and more-skilled peers. In both Piaget's and Vygotsky's theories, teachers serve as facilitators and guides, rather than as directors and molders of learning. Figure 6.11 compares Vgotsky's and Piaget's theories.

Criticisms of Vygotsky's theory also have surfaced. Some critics say he overemphasized the role of language in thinking. Also, his emphasis on collaboration and guidance has potential pitfalls. Might facilitators be too helpful in some cases, as when a parent becomes too overbearing and controlling? Further, some children might become lazy and expect help when they might have done something on their own.

Review and Reflect: Learning Goal 3

3 **Identify the main concepts in Vygotsky's theory and compare it with Piaget's theory**

REVIEW
- What is the zone of proximal development?
- What is scaffolding?
- How did Vygotsky view language and thought?
- How can Vygotsky's theory be applied to education?
- What are some similarities and differences between Vygotsky's and Piaget's theories?

REFLECT
- Which theory—Piaget's or Vygotsky's—do you like the best? Why?

Early Childhood: Piaget vs. Vygotsky— Who Was Right?

4 COGNITIVE CHANGES IN ADULTHOOD

Piaget's View	Reflective and Relativistic Thinking

Realistic and Pragmatic Thinking	Is There a Fifth, Postformal Stage?

We have described the theories that Piaget and Vygotsky proposed to account for how the cognitive development of children proceeds. Neither had much to say about cognitive development in adulthood. What do developmentalists know about changes in the way that adults think?

Piaget's View

Recall that, according to Piaget, the formal operational stage of thought begins at 11 to 15 years of age. During this stage, the final one in Piaget's theory, thinking becomes more abstract, idealistic, and logical than the concrete operational thinking of 7- to 11-year-olds. Of course, young adults have more knowledge than adolescents. But according to Piaget, adults and adolescents use the same type of reasoning. Adolescents and adults think in *qualitatively* the same way.

Many individuals don't reach the highest level of their formal operational thinking until adulthood. That is, though many individuals begin to plan and hypothesize about intellectual problems as adolescents, they become more systematic and sophisticated at this as young adults. Also, many adults do not think in formal operational ways (Keating, 1990).

Realistic and Pragmatic Thinking

Some developmentalists propose that as young adults move into the world of work, their way of thinking does change. One idea is that as they face the constraints of reality, which work promotes, their idealism decreases (Labouvie-Vief, 1986).

A related change in thinking was proposed by K. Warner Schaie (1977). He concluded that it is unlikely that adults go beyond the powerful methods of scientific thinking characteristic of the formal operational stage. However, Schaie argued that adults do progress beyond adolescents in their use of intellect. For example, in early adulthood individuals often switch from acquiring knowledge to applying knowledge as they pursue success in their work.

Reflective and Relativistic Thinking

William Perry (1970) also described changes in cognition that take place in early adulthood. He said that adolescents often view the world in terms of polarities—right/wrong, we/they, or good/bad. As youth age into adulthood, they gradually move away from this type of absolutist thinking as they become aware of the diverse opinions and multiple perspectives of others. Thus, in Perry's view, the absolutist, dualistic thinking of adolescence gives way to the reflective, relativistic thinking of adulthood. Other developmentalists also believe that reflective thinking is an important indicator of cognitive change in young adults (Fischer & Pruyne, 2003).

What are some possible ways that young adults and adolescents might think differently?

Is There a Fifth, Postformal Stage?

Late Adulthood: Postformal Thought

Late Adulthood: Dialectical Thought

Some theorists have pieced together these descriptions of adult thinking and proposed that young adults move into a new qualitative stage of cognitive development, postformal thought (Sinnott, 2003). **Postformal thought** is:

- *Reflective, relativistic, and contextual.* As young adults engage in solving problems, they might think deeply about many aspects of work, politics, relationships, and other areas of life (Labouvie-Vief, 1996). They find that what might be the best solution to a problem at work (with a boss or co-worker) might not be the best solution at home (with a romantic partner). Thus, postformal thought holds that the correct answer to a problem requires reflective thinking and may vary from one situation to another. Some psychologists argue that reflective thinking continues to increase in the forties and fifties (Fischer & Pruyne, 2003).
- *Provisional.* Many young adults also become more skeptical about the truth and seem unwilling to accept an answer as final. Thus, they come to see the search for truth as an ongoing and perhaps never-ending process.
- *Realistic.* Young adults understand that thinking can't always be abstract. In many instances it must be realistic and pragmatic.
- *Open to emotions and subjective.* Many young adults accept that emotion and subjective factors can influence thinking (Kitchener & King, 1981; Kramer, Kahlbaugh, & Goldston, 1992). For example, as young adults, they understand that a person thinks more clearly in a calm rather than an angry state.

How strong is the evidence for a fifth, postformal stage of cognitive development? Researchers have found that young adults are more likely to engage in this postformal thinking than adolescents are (Commons & Richards, 2003; Commons & others, 1989). But critics argue that research has yet to document that postformal thought is a qualitatively more advanced stage than formal operational thought.

There has been little discussion about whether specific cognitive stages might characterize middle and late adulthood. One candidate for a possible stage is "wisdom," which we will discuss in chapter 8. In addition, researchers have documented many ways in which particular aspects of cognition change during adulthood, and we will discuss those in chapter 7.

Review and Reflect: Learning Goal 4

4 Describe cognitive changes in adulthood

REVIEW

- What is Piaget's view of adult cognitive development?
- Do young adults retain the idealism of the formal operational stage?
- What is Perry's view of cognitive changes from adolescence to adulthood?
- What characteristics have been proposed for a fifth, postformal stage of cognitive development?

REFLECT

- What do you think are the most important cognitive changes that take place in young adults?

postformal thought Thinking that is reflective, relative, and contextual; provisional; realistic; and open to emotions and subjective.

Reach Your Learning Goals

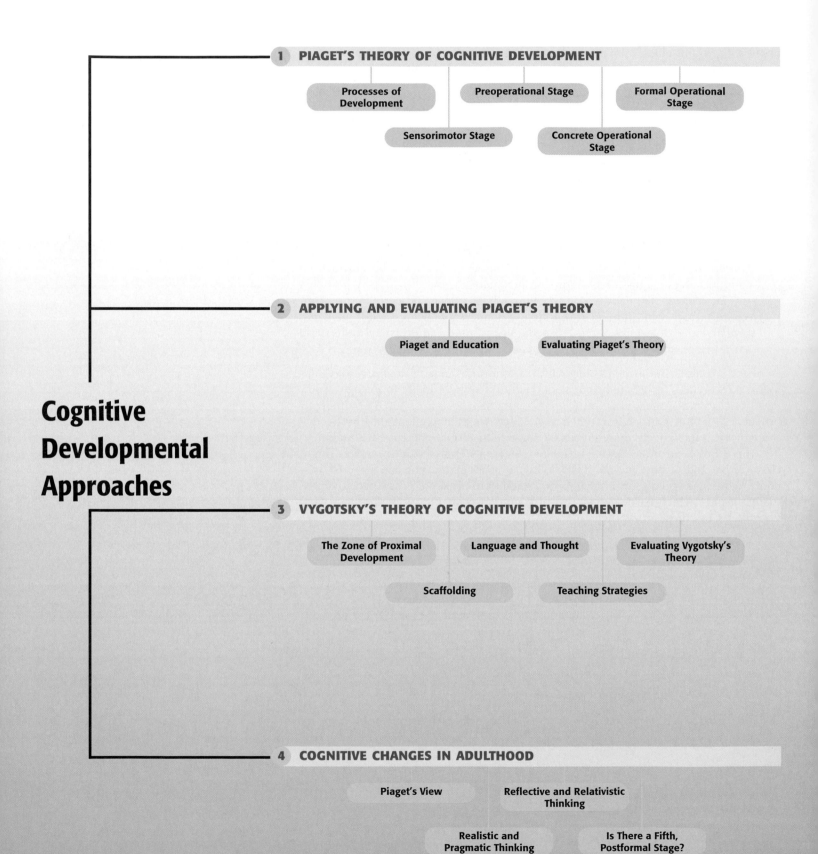

Cognitive Developmental Approaches

1 PIAGET'S THEORY OF COGNITIVE DEVELOPMENT

- Processes of Development
- Sensorimotor Stage
- Preoperational Stage
- Concrete Operational Stage
- Formal Operational Stage

2 APPLYING AND EVALUATING PIAGET'S THEORY

- Piaget and Education
- Evaluating Piaget's Theory

3 VYGOTSKY'S THEORY OF COGNITIVE DEVELOPMENT

- The Zone of Proximal Development
- Scaffolding
- Language and Thought
- Teaching Strategies
- Evaluating Vygotsky's Theory

4 COGNITIVE CHANGES IN ADULTHOOD

- Piaget's View
- Realistic and Pragmatic Thinking
- Reflective and Relativistic Thinking
- Is There a Fifth, Postformal Stage?

Summary

1 Discuss the key processes and four stages in Piaget's theory

- In Piaget's theory, children construct their own cognitive worlds, building mental structures to adapt to their world. Schemes are actions or mental representations that organize knowledge. Behavioral schemes (physical activities) characterize infancy while mental schemes (cognitive activities) develop in childhood. Adaptation involves assimilation and accommodation. Assimilation occurs when children incorporate new information into existing knowledge. Accommodation refers to children's adjustment to new information. Through organization, children group isolated behaviors into a higher-order, more smoothly functioning cognitive system. Equilibration is a mechanism Piaget proposed to explain how children shift from one cognitive stage to the next. As children experience cognitive conflict in trying to understand the world, they seek equilibrium. The result is equilibration, which brings the child to a new stage of thought. According to Piaget, there are four qualitatively different stages of thought: sensorimotor, preoperational, concrete operational, and formal operational.

- In sensorimotor thought, the first of Piaget's four stages, the infant organizes and coordinates sensations with physical movements. The stage lasts from birth to about 2 years of age and is nonsymbolic throughout, according to Piaget. Sensorimotor thought has six substages: simple reflexes; first habits and primary circular reactions; secondary circular reactions; coordination of secondary circular reactions; tertiary circular reactions, novelty, and curiosity; and internalization of schemes. One key aspect of this stage is object permanence, the ability to understand that objects continue to exist even though the infant is no longer observing them. Another aspect involves infants' understanding of cause and effect. In the past two decades, revisions of Piaget's view have been proposed based on research. For example, researchers have found that a stable and differentiated perceptual world is established earlier than Piaget envisioned.

- Preoperational thought is the beginning of the ability to reconstruct at the level of thought what has been established in behavior. It involves a transition from a primitive to a more sophisticated use of symbols. In preoperational thought, the child does not yet think in an operational way. The symbolic function substage occurs roughly from 2 to 4 years of age and is characterized by symbolic thought, egocentrism, and animism. The intuitive thought substage stretches from 4 to 7 years of age. It is called intuitive because children seem so sure about their knowledge yet they are unaware of how they know what they know. The preoperational child lacks conservation and asks a barrage of questions.

- Concrete operational thought occurs roughly from 7 to 11 years of age. During this stage, children can perform concrete operations, think logically about concrete objects, classify things, and reason about relationships among classes of things. Concrete thought is not as abstract as formal operational thought.

- Formal operational thought appears between 11 and 15 years of age. Formal operational thought is more abstract, idealistic, and logical than concrete operational thought. Piaget believes that adolescents become capable of engaging in hypothetical-deductive reasoning. But Piaget did not give adequate attention to individual variation in adolescent thinking. Many young adolescents do not think in hypothetical-deductive ways but rather are consolidating their concrete operational thinking. In addition, adolescents develop a special kind of egocentrism that involves an imaginary audience and a personal fable about being unique and invulnerable.

2 Apply Piaget's theory to education and evaluate Piaget's theory

- Piaget was not an educator, but his constructivist views have been applied to teaching. These applications include an emphasis on facilitating rather than directing learning, considering the child's level of knowledge, using ongoing assessment, promoting the student's intellectual health, and turning the classroom into a setting of exploration and discovery.

- We owe to Piaget the field of cognitive development. He was a genius at observing children, and he gave us a number of masterful concepts. Critics question his estimates of competence at different developmental levels, his stage concept, and other ideas. Neo-Piagetians emphasize the importance of information processing.

3 Identify the main concepts in Vygotsky's theory and compare it with Piaget's theory

- Zone of proximal development (ZPD) is Vygotsky's term for the range of tasks that are too difficult for children to master alone but that can be learned with the guidance and assistance of more-skilled adults and peers.

- Scaffolding is a teaching technique in which a more-skilled person adjusts the level of guidance to fit the child's current performance level. Dialogue is an important aspect of scaffolding.

- Vygotsky believed that language plays a key role in cognition. Language and thought initially develop independently, but then children internalize their egocentric speech in the form of inner speech, which becomes their thoughts. This transition to inner speech occurs from 3 to 7 years of age. Vygotsky's view contrasts with Piaget's view that young children's speech is immature and egocentric.

- Applications of Vygotsky's ideas to education include using the child's zone of proximal development and scaffolding, using skilled peers as teachers, monitoring and encouraging children's use of private speech, and accurately assessing the zone of proximal development. These practices can transform the classroom and establish a meaningful context for instruction.

- Like Piaget, Vygotsky emphasized that children actively construct their understanding of the world. Unlike Piaget, he did not propose stages of cognitive development, and he emphasizes that children construct knowledge through social interaction. In Vygotsky's theory, children depend on tools provided by the culture, which determines which skills they will develop. Some critics say that Vygotsky overemphasized the role of language.

4 Describe cognitive changes in adulthood

- Piaget said that formal operational thought, entered at 11 to 15 years of age, is the final cognitive stage, although adults are more knowledgeable than adolescents.
- Some experts argue that the idealism of Piaget's formal operational stage declines in young adults, being replaced by more realistic, pragmatic thinking.
- Perry said that adolescents often engage in dualistic, absolutist thinking, whereas young adults are more likely to think reflectively and relativistically.
- Postformal thought is reflective, relativistic, and provisional; realistic; and open to emotions and subjective.

Key Terms

schemes 200
assimilation 200
accommodation 200
organization 201
equilibration 201
sensorimotor stage 202
object permanence 204
AB̄ error 207
preoperational stage 207

operations 207
symbolic function
   substage 208
egocentrism 208
animism 208
intuitive thought substage 209
centration 209
conservation 209
concrete operational stage 211

horizontal décalage 211
seriation 213
transitivity 213
formal operational stage 213
hypothetical-deductive
   reasoning 214
adolescent egocentrism 214
imaginary audience 214
personal fable 215

neo-Piagetians 218
zone of proximal development
   (ZPD) 218
scaffolding 219
social constructivist
   approach 222
postformal thought 225

Key People

Jean Piaget 200
Renée Baillargeon 205

Barbel Inhelder 208
Rochel Gelman 211

David Elkind 214
Lev Vygotsky 218

K. Warner Schaie 224
William Perry 224

E-Learning Tools

Connect to **www.mhhe.com/santrockldt2** to research the answers and complete these exercises. In addition, you'll find a number of other resources and valuable study tools for chapter 6, "Cognitive Developmental Approaches," on the Student CD-ROM that came with this book.

Taking It to the Net

1. Irene, who will soon receive her master's degree in elementary education from the University of Virginia, is participating in a debate within the School of Education about Virginia's new mandatory testing requirements for all public schoolchildren based upon state-mandated Standards of Learning (SOLs). She will argue that SOLs and testing are contrary to Piaget's and Vygotsky's theories about the nature of education and how learning should be assessed. What are some of the arguments she can use?

2. Oliver is applying for the position of principal of a high school in a small district that needs skilled laborers. The school board is committed to utilizing vocational education to meet the needs of the local economy. Oliver has read about cognitive apprenticeships in other cultures, and he wonders if this model would be applicable to vocational education. How might the high school benefit from a vocational education?

3. Alex is preparing to teach in a community college program designed for adults returning to school to prepare for new careers. How can Alex plan his curriculum to take into account his adult students' cognitive development and learning styles?

Self-Assessment

Complete these self-assessments to explore your views on how parents should interact with a baby to effectively promote the baby's cognitive development and to examine how the way you think may change from adolescence to adulthood.

- *My Beliefs about Nurturing a Baby's Mind*
- *Exploring Changes in My Thinking from Adolescence to Adulthood*

Health and Well-Being, Parenting, and Education

Build your decision-making skills by trying your hand at the health and well-being, parenting, and education "Scenarios."

Information Processing

Learning Goals

1 Explain the information-processing approach

2 Define attention and outline its developmental changes

3 Describe what memory is and how it changes through the life span

4 Characterize thinking and its developmental changes

5 Define metacognition and summarize its developmental changes

What do people notice in the environment? What do they remember? And how do they think about it? Questions like these characterize the information-processing approach. Using this approach, which we discuss in this chapter, researchers usually do not describe individuals as being in one stage of cognitive development or another. But they do describe and analyze how the speed of processing information, attention, memory, thinking, and metacognition change over time.

1 THE INFORMATION-PROCESSING APPROACH

What Is the Information-Processing Approach?	The Information-Processing Approach to Development	Speed of Processing Information

What are some of the basic ideas of the information-processing approach? How is it similar to and different from the cognitive developmental approaches we described in chapter 6?

What Is the Information-Processing Approach?

The information-processing approach shares some characteristics with the theories of cognitive development that were discussed in chapter 6 ◀||||| **P. 201**. Both those theories and the information-processing approach rejected the behavioral approach that dominated psychology during the first half of the twentieth century. As we discussed in chapter 1, the behaviorists argued that to explain behavior it is important to examine associations between stimuli and behavior ◀||||| **P. 24**. In contrast, the theories of Piaget and Vygotsky, which were presented in chapter 6, and the information-processing approach focus on how people think.

In fact, in the 1950s and 1960s, many psychologists began to acknowledge the limitations of behaviorism (Gardner, 1985). *Cognitive psychology* became the term used to describe attempts to explain behavior by examining mental processes such as memory and thinking. To a great extent, computers inspired those cognitive psychologists who took an information-processing approach. The first modern computer, developed by John von Neumann in the 1940s, showed that machines could perform logical operations. This achievement suggested an important question: If computers can perform operations that are like mental operations performed by people, might people's minds work like computers when they perform mental operations?

If the computer is an analogy for the mind, the physical brain is like the computer's hardware, cognition like its software (see figure 7.1). In this analogy, the sensory and perceptual systems provide an "input channel," similar to the way data are entered into a computer. As input comes into the mind, mental processes, or operations, act on it, just as the computer's software acts on data. The transformed input generates information that remains in memory much the way a computer stores what it has worked on. Finally, the information is retrieved from memory and "printed out" or "displayed" as an overt, observable response.

In short, the **information-processing approach** analyzes how individuals manipulate information, monitor it, and create strategies for handling it (Siegler, 2001). Effective information processing involves attention, memory, and thinking (Mayer, 2003). To see how these processes work, let's examine a student solving an algebraic equation. An event or stimulus (S) occurs in the environment. Suppose the event involves a teacher writing an algebraic equation on the chalkboard in a mathematics class with the accompanying instruction: "$2x + 10 = 34$. Solve for x." The student looks up and focuses on what the teacher has written on the board (*attention*). This "something" is determined to be a series of numbers, letters, and signs, and—at a higher level of identification—two simple statements: (1) $2x + 10 = 34$ and (2)

information-processing approach An approach that focuses on the ways children process information about their world—how they manipulate information, monitor it, and create strategies to deal with it.

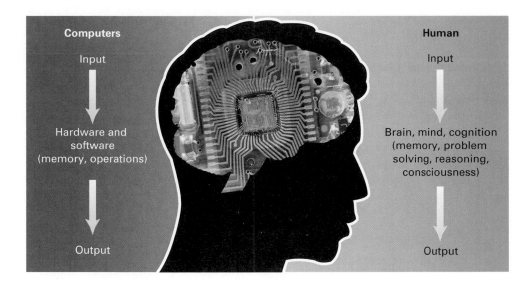

FIGURE 7.1 Computers and Human Information Processing

An analogy is commonly drawn between human information processing and the way computers work. The physical brain is analogous to a computer's hardware, and cognition is analogous to a computer's software.

Solve for x. The student must preserve the results of this attention by *encoding* the information in memory and storing it over a period of time (*memory*), even if only for the brief time needed to write the problem on a worksheet. Then the student begins manipulating and transforming the information (*thinking*). The student might think, "Okay, first I have to collect the information on one side of the equation and the known values on the other side. To do this, I'll leave the $2x$ where it is—on the left. This leaves $2x = 24$. Now I have to express the equation as '$x =$ something,' and it's solved. How do I do this? I'll divide each side by 2 and that will leave $1x = 12$. That's the answer." The student writes down the answer (*response*). A summary of the basic processes used in solving the algebraic equation are shown in figure 7.2.

Figure 7.2 is a basic, simplified representation of how information processing works; it omits a great deal and does not indicate the many routes that the flow of information takes. For example, the processes may overlap and not always go in the left-to-right direction indicated. A number of different processes may be involved in the way memory functions in processing information. The purpose of the model is to get you to begin thinking in a general way about how people process information. In subsequent sections, we will fill in more of the details about the way people process information and how information processing changes as they develop.

The Information-Processing Approach to Development

Another aspect of the computer metaphor can be used to illustrate how the information-processing approach can be applied to development. A computer's information processing is *limited* by its hardware and software. The hardware limitations include the computer's basic capacity for processing information and how efficiently it executes operations. The software limitations include the strategies and knowledge available for specific tasks. In the information-processing approach, children's cognitive development results from their ability to overcome processing limitations by increasingly executing basic operations, expanding information-processing capacity, and acquiring new knowledge and strategies. Robert Siegler (1998) believes

FIGURE 7.2 A Basic, Simplified Model of Information Processing

that *mechanisms of change* are especially important in the advances children make in cognitive development.

Mechanisms of Change According to Siegler, three mechanisms work together to create changes in children's cognitive skills: encoding, automatization, and strategy construction.

Encoding is the process by which information gets into memory. Changes in children's cognitive skills depend on increased skill at encoding relevant information and ignoring irrelevant information. For example, to a 4-year-old, an *s* in cursive writing is a shape very different from an *s* that is printed. But a 10-year-old has learned to encode the relevant fact that both are the letter *s* and to ignore the irrelevant differences in their shape.

Automaticity refers to the ability to process information with little or no effort. Practice allows children to encode increasing amounts of information automatically. For example, once children have learned to read well, they do not think about each letter in a word as a letter; instead, they encode whole words. Once a task is automatic, it does not require conscious effort. As a result, as information processing becomes more automatic, we can complete tasks more quickly and handle more than one task at a time. If you did not encode words automatically but instead read this page by focusing your attention on each letter in each word, imagine how long it would take you to read it.

Strategy construction is the creation of new procedures for processing information. For example, children's reading benefits when they develop the strategy of stopping periodically to take stock of what they have read so far (Pressley, 2003).

In addition, Siegler (1998) argues that children's information processing is characterized by *self-modification*. That is, children learn to use what they have learned in previous circumstances to adapt their responses to a new situation. Part of this self-modification draws on **metacognition,** which means "knowing about knowing" (Flavell, 1999; Flavell, Miller, & Miller, 2002). One example of metacognition is what children know about the best ways to remember what they have read. Do they know that they will remember what they have read better if they can relate it to their own lives in some way? Thus, in Siegler's application of the information processing to development, children play an active role in their cognitive development.

Comparisons with Piaget's Theory How does the information-processing approach compare with Piaget's theory? According to Piaget, as we discussed in chapter 6, children actively construct their knowledge and understanding of the world P. 202. Their thinking develops in distinct stages. At each stage, the child develops qualitatively different types of mental structures (or schemes) that allow the child to think about the world in new ways.

Like Piaget's theory, some versions of the information-processing approach are constructivist; they see children as directing their own cognitive development. And like Piaget, information-processing psychologists identify cognitive capabilities and limitations at various points in development. They describe ways in which individuals do and do not understand important concepts at different points in life and try to explain how more advanced understanding grows out of a less advanced one. They emphasize the impact that existing understanding has on the ability to acquire a new understanding of something.

Unlike Piaget, however, developmentalists who take an information-processing approach do not see development as occurring abruptly in distinct stages with a brief transition period from one stage to the next. Instead, according to the information-processing approach, individuals develop a gradually increasing capacity for processing information, which allows them to acquire increasingly complex knowledge and skills (Siegler, 2001; Mayer, 2003). The information-processing approach also focuses on more precise analysis of change than Piaget and on the

Robert Siegler's Research

encoding The mechanism by which information gets into memory.

automaticity The ability to process information with little or no effort.

strategy construction Discovering a new procedure for processing information.

metacognition Cognition about cognition, or "knowing about knowing."

contributions of ongoing cognitive activity—such as encoding and strategies—to that change.

Speed of Processing Information

One of the important limitations on processing is speed of processing. How fast we process information often influences what we can do with that information. If you are trying to add up in your mind the cost of items you are buying at the grocery store, you need to be able to compute the sum before you have forgotten the price of the individual items. If someone gives you a phone message, you want to be able to write it down before the person hangs up or before you have forgotten what the person said.

Many everyday tasks are constrained by the time that is available. For example, a child may be told to finish writing a letter in 5 minutes so the family can leave. A teacher might give children 10 minutes to complete a series of arithmetic problems. In these cases, if the children do not complete the tasks in the time allowed, the cause is uncertain. For example, perhaps they are simply slow at the physical act of writing, or possibly they are slow in the mental operation of deciding what to say or at spelling words or at doing arithmetic.

Researchers have devised a number of ways for assessing processing speed. For example, processing speed can be assessed using a *reaction-time task* in which individuals are asked to push a button as soon as they see a stimulus such as a light. Or individuals might be asked to match letters or match numbers with symbols on a computer screen.

Changes in Processing Speed with Age   There is abundant evidence that the speed with which such tasks are completed improves dramatically across the childhood years. (Kail, 1988, 2000; Stigler, Nusbaum, & Chalip, 1988). Processing speed continues to improve in early adolescence. For example, in one study, 10-year-olds were approximately 1.8 times slower at processing information than young adults on such tasks as reaction time, letter matching, mental rotation, and abstract matching (Hale, 1990). Twelve-year-olds were approximately 1.5 times slower than young adults, but 15-year-olds processed information on the tasks as fast as the young adults.

There is controversy about whether the increase in processing speed is due to experience or biological maturation (Case, 1992; Chi, 1981). Experience clearly plays an important role. Think how much faster you could process the answer to a simple arithmetic problem as an adolescent than as a child. Also think about how much faster you can process information in your native language than in a second language. The role of biological maturation likely involves *myelination*. As we discussed in chapter 3, in myelination a myelin sheath covers the axon and increases the speed of electrical impulses in the brain. Myelination continues developing through childhood and adolescence.

In K. Warner Schaie's Seattle Longitudinal Study (Schaie, 1994, 1996), processing speed began declining in early adulthood and continued to decline further in middle adulthood. For example, when asked to push a button when a light appears, young adults are faster than middle-aged adults. However, the decline is not dramatic—under 1 second in most studies. For unknown reasons the reaction time decline is stronger for women than for men (Salthouse, 1994). As figure 7.3 shows, the slowdown in processing speed continues into late adulthood (Salthouse, 1996, 2000).

The decline in processing speed in older adults is likely due to a decline in functioning of the brain and central nervous system (Groth, Gilmore, & Thomas, 2003; Hoyer & Touron, 2003; Madden, 2001). Health and exercise may influence how much decline in processing speed occurs (Gerritsen & others, 2003). One study found that following six months of aerobic exercise older adults showed improvement on reaction time tasks (Kramer & others, 1999).

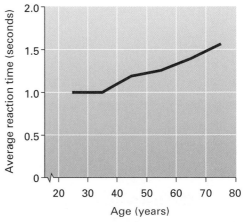

FIGURE 7.3 The Relation of Age to Reaction Time

In one study, the average reaction time began to slow in the forties and this decline accelerated in the sixties and seventies (Salthouse, 1994). The task used to assess reaction time required individuals to match numbers with symbols on a computer screen.

Does Processing Speed Matter? How fast children can process information is linked with their competence in thinking (Bjorklund & Rosenblum, 2000; Demetriou & others, 2002). For example, how fast children can articulate a series of words affects how many words they can store and remember.

For many tasks in everyday life, the speed of processing information may become unimportant. The strategies that people learn through experience may compensate for any decline in processing speed with age. For example, in an experiment that studied the reaction time and typing skills of typists of varying ages, older typists usually had slower reactions, but they actually typed just as fast as the younger typists (Salthouse, 1994). A variation in the experiment showed how the older typists compensated for their slower reaction times. When a limit was placed on how many characters ahead the typists could look, the older typists slowed considerably; the restriction had less effect on the younger typists. The older typists had been looking farther ahead, allowing them to type as fast as their younger counterparts. The older, experienced typists had a very efficient strategy for processing the information they were typing, which compensated for their slower reaction times.

In sum, processing speed is an important aspect of processing information. Generally, when individuals are able to process information faster, it is linked with their ability to perform well on cognitive tasks. However, some compensation for slower processing speed can be achieved by developing effective strategies. We will discuss other aspects of processing speed as we consider various aspects of information processing over the life span, such as attention, memory, and thinking.

Review and Reflect: Learning Goal 1

1 Explain the information-processing approach

REVIEW

- What is the information-processing approach?
- How can the information-processing approach be applied to development? How can the information-processing approach be compared with Piaget's theory?
- How does processing speed change developmentally?

REFLECT

- In terms of ability to learn, are there ways that people process information similar to the way that a computer does? What might be some differences in the way that people and computers process information?

---

2 ATTENTION

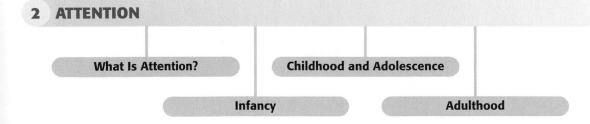

| What Is Attention? | Childhood and Adolescence |
| Infancy | Adulthood |

The world holds a lot of information to perceive. Right now, you are perceiving the letters and words that make up this sentence. Now look around the setting where you are and pick out something to look at other than this book. After that, curl up the toes on your right foot. In each of these circumstances you engaged in the process of paying attention. What is attention and what effect does it have? How does it change with age?

What Is Attention?

Attention is the focusing of mental resources. Attention improves cognitive processing for many tasks. At any one time, though, people can pay attention to only a limited amount of information.

Individuals can allocate their attention in different ways. Psychologists have labeled these types of allocation as sustained attention, selective attention, and divided attention.

- **Sustained attention** is the state of readiness to detect and respond to small changes occurring at random times in the environment. Sustained attention is also called *vigilance*.
- **Selective attention** is focusing on a specific aspect of experience that is relevant while ignoring others that are irrelevant. Focusing on one voice among many in a crowded room or a noisy restaurant is an example of selective attention. When you switched your attention to the toes on your right foot, you were engaging in selective attention.
- **Divided attention** involves concentrating on more than one activity at the same time. If you are listening to music or the television while you are reading this, you are engaging in divided attention.

Infancy

How effectively can infants attend to something? Even newborns can detect a contour in a visual pattern and fixate on it. Older infants scan patterns more thoroughly. Infants as young as 4 months can selectively attend to an object.

Closely linked with attention are the processes of habituation and dishabituation that we discussed in chapter 5, "Motor, Sensory, and Perceptual Development" ◀‖‖ **P. 180**. Recall that if a stimulus—a sight or sound—is presented to infants several times in a row, they usually pay less attention to it each time. This suggests they are bored with it. This is the process of *habituation*—decreased responsiveness to a stimulus after repeated presentations of the stimulus. *Dishabituation* is the recovery of a habituated response after a change in stimulation.

Researchers study habituation to determine the extent to which infants can see, hear, smell, taste, and experience touch (Slater, 2002). Studies of habituation can also indicate whether infants recognize something they have previously experienced.

Habituation provides a measure of an infant's maturity and well-being. Infants who have brain damage do not habituate well.

Parents can use knowledge of habituation and dishabituation to improve interaction with their infant. If parents keep repeating the same form of stimulation, the infant will stop responding. It is important for parents to do novel things and to repeat them often until the infant stops responding. Wise parents sense when the infant shows interest and know that many repetitions of the stimulus may be necessary for the infant to process the information. The parents stop or change their behavior when the infant redirects attention (Rosenblith, 1992).

Childhood and Adolescence

The toddler wanders around, shifts attention from one activity to another, and seems to spend little time focused on any one object or event. In contrast, the preschool child might watch television for half an hour at a time (Giavecchio, 2001). One study that observed 99 families in their homes for 4,672 hours found that visual attention to television dramatically increased in the preschool years (Anderson & others, 1986).

attention Concentrating and focusing mental resources.

sustained attention The state of readiness to detect and respond to small changes occurring at random times in the environment; also called vigilance.

selective attention Focusing on a specific aspect of experience that is relevant while ignoring others that are irrelevant.

divided attention Concentrating on more than one activity at a time.

Control over attention shows important changes during childhood (Ruff & Capozzoli, 2003). External stimuli are likely to determine the target of the preschooler's attention; what is *salient* grabs the preschooler's attention. For example, suppose a flashy, attractive clown presents the directions for solving a problem. Preschool children are likely to pay attention to the clown and ignore the directions. They are influenced strongly by the features of the task that stand out. After the age of 6 or 7, children attend more efficiently to the dimensions of the task that are relevant to performing a task or solving a problem, such as the directions. This change reflects a shift to *cognitive control* of attention, so that children act less impulsively and reflect more.

Attention to relevant information increases steadily through the elementary and secondary school years (Davidson, 1996). Processing of irrelevant information decreases in adolescence.

Another important aspect of attention is the ability to shift it from one activity to another as needed. For example, writing a good story requires shifting attention among the competing tasks of forming letters, composing grammar, structuring paragraphs, and conveying the story as a whole. Older children and adolescents are better than younger children at tasks that require shifts of attention.

In one investigation, 12-year-olds were markedly better than 8-year-olds and slightly worse than 20-year-olds at allocating their attention in a situation involving two tasks (divided attention) (Manis, Keating, & Morrison, 1980). These improvements in divided attention might be due to having more resources available (through increased processing speed, capacity, and automaticity), or to being more skilled at directing these resources.

Adulthood

What happens to attention in adulthood? Attentional skills are often excellent in early adulthood. However, older adults may not be able to focus on relevant information as effectively as younger adults (Hogan, 2003; McDowd & others, 2003).

Older adults perform as well as middle-aged and younger adults on measures of sustained attention (Berardi, Parasuraman, & Haxby, 2001). However, older adults tend to be less adept at selective attention—focusing on a specific aspect of experience while ignoring others—than younger adults are (Rogers & Fisk, 2001). These age differences are minimal if the task involves a simple search (such as determining whether a target item is present on a computer screen) or if individuals have practiced the task (Humphrey & Kramer, 1997).

As the demands on attention increase, the performance of older adults declines. As long as two competing tasks are reasonably easy, age differences among adults are minimal or nonexistent. However, as competing tasks become more difficult, older adults divide attention less effectively than younger adults (Maciokas & Crognale, 2003; Stine-Morrow & Soederberg Miller, 1999; Wood,

2002). In one study, the ability to engage in a conversation while simultaneously driving a simulator through highway traffic (in an experimental laboratory) was examined in 17- to 25-, 26- to 49-, and 50- to 80-year-olds (McKnight & McKnight, 1993). A nondistraction control condition also was included. Overall, the participants performed more poorly in the divided attention condition than in the nondistraction control condition. Also, the older adults (50 to 80 years old) performed worse in the divided attention condition than the younger two groups but not in the control condition. Thus, placing more demands on the attention of the older adults led them to perform more poorly on the driving task.

Review and Reflect: Learning Goal 2

2 **Define attention and outline its developmental changes**

REVIEW

- What is attention? What are three ways that people allocate their attention?
- How does attention develop in infancy?
- How does attention develop in childhood and adolescence?
- How does attention change during the adult years?

REFLECT

- Imagine that you are an elementary school teacher. Devise some strategies to help children pay attention in class.

---

3   MEMORY

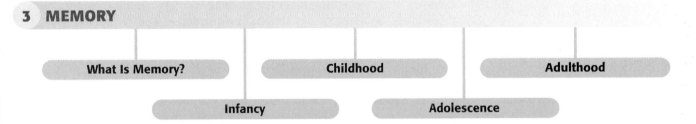

| What Is Memory? | Childhood | Adulthood |
| Infancy | Adolescence | |

Twentieth-century American playwright Tennessee Williams once commented that life is all memory except for that one present moment that goes by so quickly that you can hardly catch it going. But just what is memory?

What Is Memory?

Memory is the retention of information over time. Without memory you would not be able to connect what happened to you yesterday with what is going on in your life today. Human memory is truly remarkable when you think of how much information we put into our memories and how much we must retrieve to perform all of life's activities. However, human memory has its imperfections, as we will discuss shortly.

Processes of Memory   Researchers study how information is initially placed or encoded into memory, how it is retained or stored after being encoded, and how it is found or retrieved for a certain purpose later (see figure 7.4). Encoding, storage, and retrieval are the basic processes required for memory. Failures can occur in any of these processes.

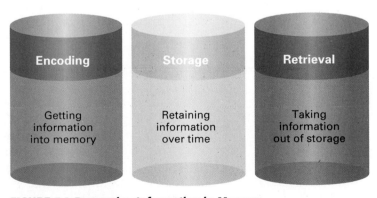

FIGURE 7.4 Processing Information in Memory

As you read about the many aspects of memory in this chapter, think about the organization of memory in terms of these three main activities.

memory Retention of information over time.

One night two young men from Egulac went down to the river to hunt seals, and while they were there it became foggy and calm. Then they heard war cries, and they thought: "Maybe this is a war party." They escaped to the shore, and hid behind a log. Now canoes came up, and they heard the noise of paddles, and they saw one canoe coming up to them. There were five men in the canoe and they said:

"What do you think? We wish to take you along. We are going up the river to make war on the people."

One of the young men said: "I have no arrows."

"Arrows are in the canoe," they said.

"I will not go along, I might be killed. My relatives do not know where I have gone. But you," he said, turning to the other, "may go with them."

So one of the young men went, but the other returned home.

And the warriors went up the river to a town on the other side of Kalama. The people came down to the water, and they began to fight, and many were killed. But presently the young man heard one of the warriors say: "Quick, let us go home: that Indian has been hit." Now he thought: "Oh, they are ghosts." He did not feel sick, but they said he had been shot.

So the canoes went back to Egulac and the young man went ashore to his house, and made a fire. And he told everybody and said: "Behold I accompanied the ghosts, and we went to fight. Many of our fellows were killed, and many of those who attacked us were killed. They said I was hit, and I did not feel sick."

He told it all, and then he became quiet. When the sun rose he fell down. Something black came out of his mouth. His face became contorted. The people jumped up and cried.

He was dead.

FIGURE 7.5 The War of the Ghosts

When Sir Frederick Bartlett (1932) asked individuals to recall this story, they tended to change details.

schema theory States people mold memories to fit information that already exists in their minds.

schemas Mental frameworks that organize concepts and information.

Some part of an event might not be encoded, the mental representation of the event might not be stored, or even if the memory exists, you might not be able to retrieve it.

Constructing Memories Memories may also be inaccurate for a number of reasons (Terry, 2003). Memory is not like a tape recorder or a camera or even like computer memory. People construct and reconstruct their memories. According to **schema theory,** people mold memories to fit information that already exists in their minds (Terry, 2003). This process is guided by **schemas,** which are mental frameworks that organize concepts and information. Schemas influence the way people encode, make inferences about, and retrieve information. Often when we retrieve information, we fill in the gaps.

The schema theory of memory began with Sir Frederick Bartlett's (1932) studies of how a person's background (which is encoded in schemas) would reveal itself in a person's reconstruction of stories. For example, one of Bartlett's stories, "War of the Ghosts," was a translation of a Native American folktale (see figure 7.5). The story relates events that were completely foreign to the experiences of the British participants in Bartlett's study. They read the story twice and then, after 15 minutes, wrote down the tale as best as they could remember it.

The British participants used their general schemas, schemas of daily experiences, and their schemas for adventurous ghost stories in particular to reconstruct "War of the Ghosts." Familiar details from the story that fit into a participant's schemas were successfully recalled. But details that departed from a person's schemas were often greatly distorted. For example, the "something black" that came from the Indian's mouth in the original became "blook" in one reconstruction and "condensed air" in another. One person said that the two young men were hunting beavers, rather than seals. Another person said that the death at the end was due to a fever (that wasn't in the story).

We have schemas for all sorts of information. If a teacher tells your class a story about two men and two women who were involved in a train crash in France, students won't remember every detail of the story and will reconstruct the story with their own particular stamp on it. One student might reconstruct the story by saying they died in a plane crash, another might describe three men and three women, another might say the crash was in Germany, and so on. Such reconstruction and distortion are nowhere more apparent than in clashing testimony given by eyewitnesses at trials.

In sum, schema theory accurately predicts that people don't store and retrieve bits of data in computer-like fashion (Schacter, 2001). We reconstruct the past rather than take an exact photograph of it, and the mind can distort an event as it encodes and stores impressions of it (Mayer, 2003).

False Memories New information can also alter memories. Consider a recent study of individuals who had visited Disneyland (Pickrell & Loftus, 2001). Four groups of participants read ads and answered questionnaires about a trip to Disneyland. One group saw an ad that mentioned no cartoon characters; the second read the same ad and saw a four-foot-tall cardboard figure of Bugs Bunny; the third read a fake ad for Disneyland with Bugs Bunny on it; and the fourth saw the same fake ad along with cardboard Bugs. Participants were asked whether they had ever met Bugs Bunny at Disneyland. Less than 10 percent who saw the first two groups reported having met Bugs Bunny on a trip to Disneyland, but approximately 30 to 40 percent of the third and fourth groups erroneously remembered Bugs at Disneyland. People were persuaded they had met Bugs Bunny at Disneyland even though Bugs is a Warner Brothers character who would never appear at a Disney theme park.

Many other studies have demonstrated that questions or suggestions of false information can distort memories. These findings have created great concern about finding ways to avoid implanting false memories among eyewitnesses and ways to determine the accuracy of the memories of eyewitnesses at trials.

In their study of memory, researchers have not extensively examined the roles that sociocultural factors might play (Park & Gutchess, 2002). In the Contexts of Life-Span Development interlude, we will explore how culture and gender might be linked with memory.

Contexts of Life-Span Development
Culture, Gender, and Memory

A culture sensitizes its members to certain objects, events, and strategies, which in turn can influence the nature of memory (Mistry & Rogoff, 1994). Sir Frederick Bartlett believed that a person's background, which is encoded in schemas, is revealed in the way the person reconstructs a story. This effect of cultural background on memory is called the *cultural specificity hypothesis*. It states that cultural experiences determine what is relevant in a person's life and, thus, what the person is likely to remember. For example, imagine that you live on a remote island in the Pacific Ocean and make your livelihood by fishing. Your memory about how weather affects fishing is likely to be highly developed. By contrast, a Pacific Islander might be hard-pressed to encode and recall the details of one hour of MTV. The culture specificity hypothesis also refers to subgroups within a culture. For example, many basketball fans in the U.S. can recount an impressive array of National Basketball Association (NBA) statistics. A devout gardener might know the informal and Latin names of all plants seen on a garden tour. Our specific interests in our culture and subculture shape the richness of our memory stores and schemas on any given topic.

Scripts are schemas for an event. In one study, individuals in the United States and Mexico remembered according to script-based knowledge (Harris, Schoen, & Hensley, 1992). In line with common practices in their respective cultures, individuals in the United States remembered information about a dating script better when no chaperone was present on a date, whereas individuals in Mexico remembered the information better when a chaperone was present.

Gender is another aspect of sociocultural diversity that has been given little attention in memory research until recently (Aarsten, Martin, & Zimprich, 2003). Researchers have found these gender differences in memory:

* Females are better at episodic memory, which is memory for personal events that include the time and place the event occurred (Andersson, 2001; Halpern, 2001). Females are also better than males at emotion-linked memory, such as memory for an emotional film (Cahill & others, 2001).
* Males are better than females on tasks that require transformations in visual-spatial working memory (Halpern, 2001). These tasks include mental rotation, which involves the imagined motion of stationary objects (such as what a shape would look like if it were rotated in space).

On many memory tasks, though, researchers do not find gender differences, or when they do occur, they are small.

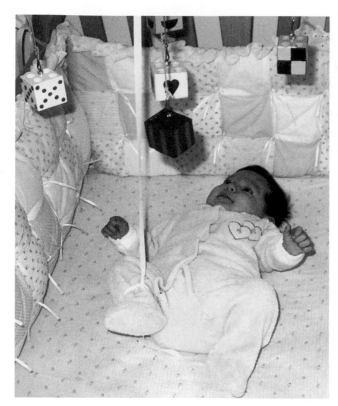

FIGURE 7.6 The Technique Used in Rovee-Collier's Investigation of Infant Memory

In Rovee-Collier's experiment, operant conditioning was used to demonstrate that infants as young as 2½ months of age can retain information from the experience of being conditioned.

Memory Links

Infant Memory Research

implicit memory Memory without conscious recollection: memory of skills and routine procedures that are performed automatically.

explicit memory Conscious memory of facts and experiences.

Infancy

Popular child-rearing expert Penelope Leach (1990) told parents that 6- to 8-month-old babies cannot hold a picture of their mother or father in their mind. And historically psychologists believed that infants cannot store memories until they have language skills. Recently, though, child development researchers have revealed that infants as young as 3 months of age show a limited type of memory.

First Memories Carolyn Rovee-Collier (1987, 2002) has conducted research that demonstrates infants can remember perceptual-motor information. In a characteristic experiment, she places a baby in a crib underneath an elaborate mobile and ties one end of a ribbon to the baby's ankle and the other end to the mobile. The baby kicks and makes the mobile move (see figure 7.6). Weeks later, the baby is returned to the crib, but its foot is not tied to the mobile. The baby kicks, apparently trying to make the mobile move. However, if the mobile's makeup is changed even slightly, the baby doesn't kick. If the mobile is then restored to being exactly as it was when the baby's ankle was originally tied to it, the baby will begin kicking again. According to Rovee-Collier, even by 2½ months the baby's memory is incredibly detailed.

How well can infants remember? Some researchers such as Rovee-Collier have concluded that infants as young as 2 to 6 months of age can remember some experiences through 1½ to 2 years of age (Rovee-Collier, 2002). However, critics such as Jean Mandler (2000), a leading expert on infant cognition, argue that the infants in Rovee-Collier's experiments are displaying only implicit memory. **Implicit memory** refers to memory without conscious recollection—memories of skills and routine procedures that are performed automatically. In contrast, **explicit memory** refers to the conscious memory of facts and experiences.

When people think about memory, they are usually referring to explicit memory. Most researchers find that babies do not show explicit memory until the second half of the first year (Mandler & McDonough, 1995). Then, explicit memory improves substantially during the second year of life (Bauer, 2002; Bauer & others, 2003; Carver & Bauer, 2001). In one longitudinal study, infants were assessed several times during their second year (Bauer & others, 2000). Older infants showed more accurate memory and required fewer prompts to demonstrate their memory than younger infants. In sum, most of infants' conscious memories are fragile and short-lived, except for memory of perceptual-motor actions, which can be substantial (Mandler, 2000).

Infantile Amnesia Do you remember your third birthday party? Probably not. Most adults can remember little if anything from the first three years of their life. This is called *infantile* or *childhood amnesia*. The few reported adult memories of life at age 2 or 3 are at best very sketchy (Eacotte & Crawley, 1998; Newcombe & others, 2000). Elementary school children also do not remember much of their early child years. In one study, about three years after leaving preschool, children were much poorer at remembering their former classmates than their teacher was (Lie & Newcombe, 1999). In another study, 10-year-olds were shown pictures of their preschool classmates and they recognized only about 20 percent of them (Newcombe & Fox, 1994).

What is the cause of infantile amnesia? One reason for the difficulty older children and adults have in recalling events from their infant and early child years is the immaturity of the prefrontal lobes of the brain, which are believed to play an important role in memory for events (Boyer & Diamond, 1992).

Childhood

Children's memory improves considerably after infancy. What are some of the significant strides in memory as children grow older? The progress includes improvements in short-term and long-term memory, as well as the use of strategies.

Short-Term and Working Memory   When people talk about memory, they are usually referring to **long-term memory,** which is relatively permanent and unlimited. When you remember the type of games you enjoyed playing as a child, your first date, or characteristics of the life-span perspective (which we discussed in chapter 1), you are drawing on your long-term memory. But when you remember the word you just read, you are using short-term memory. **Short-term memory** involves the retention of information for up to 15 to 30 seconds, without rehearsal of the information. Using rehearsal, individuals can keep the information in short-term memory longer.

Memory Span   Unlike long-term memory, short-term memory has a very limited capacity. One method of assessing that capacity is the *memory-span task.* You simply hear a short list of stimuli—usually digits—presented at a rapid pace (one per second, for example). Then you are asked to repeat the digits.

Research with the memory-span task suggests that short-term memory increases during childhood. For example, in one investigation, memory span increased from about 2 digits in 2- to 3-year-old children to about 5 digits in 7-year-old children. Between 7 and 13 years of age, memory span increased only by 1½ digits (Dempster, 1981) (see figure 7.7). Keep in mind, though, that individuals have different memory spans.

Why does memory span change with age? Rehearsal of information is important; older children rehearse the digits more than younger children. Speed of processing information is important, too, especially the speed with which memory items can be identified. For example, one study tested children on their speed at repeating words presented orally (Case, Kurland, & Goldberg, 1982). Speed of repetition was a powerful predictor of memory span. Indeed, when the speed of repetition was controlled, the 6-year-olds' memory spans were equal to those of young adults.

Working Memory   Short-term memory is like a passive storehouse with shelves to store information until it is moved to long-term memory. **Working memory** is a kind of mental "workbench" where individuals manipulate and assemble information when they make decisions, solve problems, and comprehend written and spoken language (Baddeley, 1990, 1998, 2001) (see figure 7.8). Working memory is described as more active and powerful in modifying information than short-term memory.

Working memory is linked to many aspects of children's development. For example, children who have better working memory are more advanced in reading comprehension and problem solving than their counterparts with less effective working memory (Bjorklund, 2000; Demetriou & others, 2002).

Children's Long-Term Memory   Sometimes the long-term memories of preschoolers seem to be erratic, but young children can remember a great deal of information if they are given appropriate cues and prompts. One area in which children's long-term memory is being examined extensively relates to whether young children should be allowed to testify in court. Increasingly, young children are being allowed to testify, especially if they are the only witnesses to abuse, a crime, and so forth. Here are

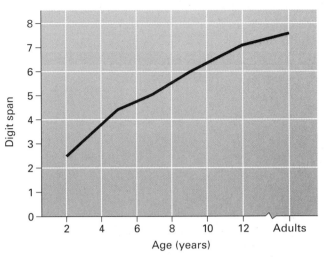

FIGURE 7.7 Developmental Changes in Memory Span

In one study, memory span increased about 3 digits from 2 years of age to 5 digits at 7 years of age (Dempster, 1981). By 12 years of age, memory span had increased on average another 1½ digits to 7 digits.

Infancy and Toddlerhood: Rovee-Collier Studies of Infant Cognition

Baddeley's Research
Explore Working Memory

long-term memory A relatively permanent and unlimited type of memory.

short-term memory Retention of information for up to 15 to 30 seconds, without rehearsal of the information. Using rehearsal, individuals can keep the information in short-term memory longer.

working memory A mental "workbench" where individuals manipulate and assemble information when making decisions, solving problems, and comprehending written and spoken language.

Working Memory

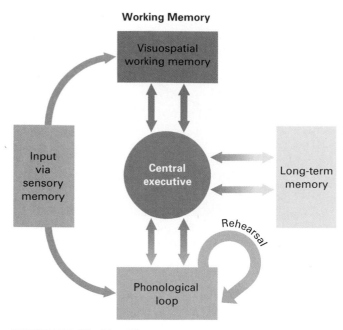

FIGURE 7.8 Working Memory

In Baddeley's working memory model, working memory is like a mental workbench where a great deal of information processing is carried out. Working memory consists of three main components: The phonological loop and visuospatial working memory serve as assistants, helping the central executive do its work. Input from sensory memory goes to the phonological loop, where information about speech is stored and rehearsal takes place, and visuospatial working memory, where visual and spatial information, including imagery, are stored. Working memory is a limited-capacity system, and information is stored there for only a brief time. Working memory interacts with long-term memory, using information from long-term memory in its work and transmitting information to long-term memory for longer storage.

Four-year-old Jennifer Royal was the only eyewitness to one of her playmates' being shot to death. She was allowed to testify in open court and the clarity of her statements helped to convict the gunman. *What are some issues in whether young children should be allowed to testify in court?*

the conclusions that have been reached about children as eyewitnesses (Bruck & Ceci, 1999):

- *There are age differences in children's susceptibility to suggestion.* Preschoolers are the most suggestible age group in comparison with older children and adults (Ceci & Bruck, 1993; McAuliff, Kovera, & Viswesvaran, 1998). For example, preschool children are more susceptible to misleading or incorrect postevent information. Despite these age differences, there is still concern about older children when they are subjected to suggestive interviews (Poole & Lindsay, 1996).

- *There are individual differences in susceptibility.* Some preschoolers are highly resistant to interviewers' suggestions, whereas others immediately succumb to the slightest suggestion. Among the factors related to individual differences in susceptibility are children's knowledge base, self-esteem, and conformity orientation (Bruck & Ceci, 1997).

- *Interviewing techniques can produce substantial distortions in children's reports about highly salient events.* Children are suggestible not just about peripheral details but also about the central aspects of an event (Bruck, Ceci, & Hembrooke, 1998). In some cases, children's false reports can be tinged with sexual connotations. In laboratory research studies, young children have made false claims about "silly events" that involved body contact (such as "Did the nurse lick your knee?" or "Did she blow in your ear?"). And these false claims have been found to persist for at least three months (Ornstein, Gordon, & Larus, 1992). A significant number of preschool children have falsely reported that someone touched their private parts, kissed them, and hugged them, when these events clearly did not happen in the research. Nonetheless, despite this extensive evidence about young children's suggestibility, they are capable of recalling much that is relevant about an event (Fivush, 1993; Goodman, Batterman-Faunce, & Kenney, 1992). When children do accurately recall information about an event, the interviewer often has a neutral tone, there is limited use of misleading questions, and there is an absence of any motivation for the child to make a false report (Bruck & Ceci, 1999).

In sum, whether a young child's eyewitness testimony is accurate or not may depend on a number of factors such as the type, number, and intensity of the suggestive techniques the child has experienced (Loftus, 2002; Ornstein & Haden, 2001). It appears that the reliability of young children's reports has as much or more to do with the skills and motivation of the interviewer as with any natural limitations on young children's memory. Because of the possibility that they can be led into saying something falsely, young children should be interviewed by a neutral professional (Hyman & Loftus, 2001).

Children's long-term memory improves even more as they move into the middle and late childhood years. This is especially true when they use the strategies that we describe next.

Strategies *Strategies* involve the use of mental activities to improve the processing of information. For memory, rehearsing information and organizing are two typical strategies that older children (and adults) use to remember information more effectively. Rehearsal—repetition—works better for short-term memory. Strategies like organization, elaborating on the information to be remembered, and making it personally relevant make long-term memory more effective. Preschool children usually do not use strategies like rehearsal and organization to remember (Flavell, Miller, & Miller, 2002).

Imagery   Creating mental images is another strategy for improving memory. However, using imagery to remember verbal information works better for older children than for younger children (Schneider & Pressley, 1997). In one study, 20 sentences were presented to first- through sixth-grade children to remember—such as "The angry bird shouted at the white dog" and "The policeman painted the circus tent on a windy day" (Pressley & others, 1987). Children were randomly assigned to an imagery condition (in which they were told to make a picture in their head for each sentence) and a control condition (in which they were told just to try hard). Figure 7.9 shows that the imagery instructions helped older elementary school children (grades 4 through 6) but did not help the younger elementary school children (grades 1 through 3). However, mental imagery can help young school children to remember pictures (Schneider & Pressley, 1997).

Elaboration   One important strategy is **elaboration,** which involves engaging in more extensive processing of information. When individuals engage in elaboration, their memory benefits (Terry, 2003). Thinking of examples and self-reference are effective ways to elaborate information. Thinking about personal associations with information makes the information more meaningful and helps children to remember it.

The use of elaboration changes developmentally (Pressley, 2003; Schneider & Pressley, 1997). Adolescents are more likely to use elaboration spontaneously than children. Elementary school children can be taught to use elaboration strategies on a learning task, but they will be less likely than adolescents to use the strategies on other learning tasks in the future. Nonetheless, verbal elaboration can be an effective strategy even for young elementary school children.

Knowledge   An especially important influence on memory is the knowledge that individuals possess about a particular topic or skill (National Research Council, 1999). Knowledge influences what people notice and how they organize, represent, and interpret information. This, in turn, affects their ability to remember, reason, and solve problems.

One study found that 10- and 11-year-olds who were experienced chess players were able to remember more information about chess pieces than college students who were not chess players (Chi, 1978) (see figure 7.10) In contrast, the college students were able to remember other stimuli better than the children were. Thus, the children's expertise in chess gave them superior memories, but only in chess.

Adolescence

One way that memory changes in adolescence involves an increase in working memory capacity. In a series of experiments, third-grade, sixth-grade, ninth-grade, and college students were given analogies (which involve detecting a correspondence in some respects between two dissimilar things) to solve (Sternberg, 1997; Sternberg & Nigro, 1980; Sternberg & Rifkin, 1979). Solving analogies requires individuals to make continued comparisons between newly encoded and previously

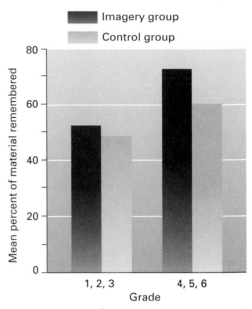

FIGURE 7.9 Imagery and Memory of Verbal Information

Imagery improved older elementary school children's memory for sentences more than younger elementary school children's memory for sentences.

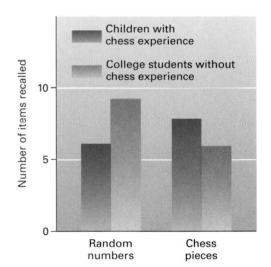

FIGURE 7.10 The Role of Expertise in Memory

Notice that when 10- to 11-year-old children and college students were asked to remember a string of random numbers that had been presented to them, the college students fared better. However, the 10- to 11-year-olds who had experience playing chess ("experts") had better memory for the location of chess pieces on a chess board than college students with no chess experience ("novices") (Chi, 1978).

elaboration Engaging in more extensive processing of information which benefits memory.

encoded information. The main differences in solving the analogies occurred between the younger (third- and sixth-grade) and older (ninth-grade and college) students. The older students were more likely to complete the information processing required to solve the analogy. The children, by contrast, often stopped their processing of information before they had considered all of the necessary steps required to solve the problems. The information processing may have been incomplete because the children's working memory capacity was overloaded. Adolescents probably have more storage space in their working memory, which results in fewer errors on problems like analogies.

As individuals move through adolescence and into the early adulthood years, they are faced with many educational and work tasks that require effective memory and study strategies. To read about a number of these strategies, see figure 7.11.

Adulthood

Memory changes during the adult years, but not all memory changes with age in the same way (Balota, Dolani, & Ducheck, 2000; Baxter, 2003). Let's look first at working memory and processing speed.

Working Memory and Processing Speed   Two important cognitive resources that are linked with aging are working memory and processing speed. Remember that working memory is like a mental "workbench" that allows us to manipulate and assemble information (Baddeley, 2001) ◀▥ **P. 243.** One study examined working memory from 6 to 57 years of age (Swanson, 1999). Working memory performance generally increased across childhood, adolescence, and early adulthood, peaked at 45 years of age, and declined at 57 years of age. The increase and decrease in working memory were related to both remembering new information and maintaining the memory of old information. In this study, working memory performance was also linked with reading and math achievement. Researchers also have found declines in working memory during the late adulthood years (Leonards, Ibanez, & Giannakopoulos, 2002; Light, 2000; Park & others, 2002; Salthouse, 1994, 2000).

Also recall from earlier in the chapter that processing speed declines in middle and late adulthood. Further, the decline in processing speed is linked with a decline in working memory (Salthouse, 2000; Salthouse & Miles, 2002).

Explicit and Implicit Memory   Long-term memory systems include explicit and implicit memory (see figure 7.12). Recall that *explicit memory* refers to the conscious memory of facts and experiences. Explicit memory is also sometimes called *declarative memory.* Examples of explicit memory include being at a grocery store and remembering that you want to buy something or remembering the events of a movie you have seen.

Explicit memory can be subdivided into episodic memory and semantic memory. **Episodic memory** is the retention of information about the where and when of life's happenings (Tulving, 2000). For example, what was it like when your younger sister or brother was born? What happened to you on your first date? What were you doing when you heard that the Persian Gulf War had begun? What did you eat for breakfast this morning?

Semantic memory is a person's knowledge about the world. It includes a person's fields of expertise (such as knowledge of chess, for a skilled chess player); general academic knowledge of the sort learned in school (such as knowledge of geometry); and "everyday knowledge" about meanings of words, famous individuals, important places, and common things (such as who Nelson Mandela and Mahatma Gandhi are). Semantic memory appears to be independent of an individual's personal identity with the past. For example, you can access a fact—such

episodic memory Retention of information about the where and when of life's happenings.

semantic memory A person's knowledge about the world, including fields of expertise, general academic knowledge, and "everyday knowledge" about meaning of words, famous individuals, important places, and common things.

FIGURE 7.11 **Memory and Study Strategies**

Pay attention and minimize distraction

Paying attention helps you remember something. Monitor how well you pay attention. If you find yourself becoming distracted, cue yourself aloud with a word or phrase like "Focus" or "Zero in."

Understand the material rather than memorize

Rehearsal works well for encoding information into short-term memory, but if you need to remember information over a long term, give the information meaning, elaborate on it, and personalize it.

Organize what you put into memory

You will remember information better if you organize it hierarchically. Arrange information, rework material, and give it a structure to help you remember it.

Use Mnemonics

Mnemonics are specific aids for remembering a list of items or specific facts. These aids may use words or images. Here are three types of mnemonics:

- The *method of loci* is a strategy in which you develop images of items to be remembered and imagine each item stored in familiar locations (which is what *loci* means). For example, if you need to remember a list of concepts, you can mentally place each in the rooms of a house that you are familiar with, such as entry foyer, living room, dining room, kitchen, and so on. When you need to retrieve the information, you imagine the house, mentally go through the rooms, and retrieve the concepts.

- *Acronyms* are words created from the first letters of items to be remembered. For example, *HOMES* can be used for remembering the Great Lakes: *H*uron, *O*ntario, *M*ichigan, *E*rie, and *S*uperior.

- The *keyword method* attaches vivid imagery to important words. For example, if you need to remember Annapolis is the capital of Maryland, you might create the image of two apples getting married. The strategy is to help you associate *apple* with Annapolis and *marry* with Maryland.

Ask yourself questions

When you ask yourself questions about what you have read or an activity, you expand the number of associations you make with the information, which makes the information easier to retrieve. As you read, periodically ask yourself questions, such as "What is the meaning of what I just read?", "Why is this important?", and "What is an example of this concept?"

Spread out and consolidate your learning

Distribute your learning over a long period rather than cramming at the last minute. Cramming tends to produce short-term memory that is not deeply processed. Regularly review what you learn—then give yourself a final, concentrated pretest tuneup.

Cognitively monitor your progress

Cognitive monitoring involves taking stock of your progress. For example, summarize what you have read and restudy those parts that were unclear. In this book, the Review and Reflect questions after major sections of each chapter provide guides for cognitive monitoring.

Be a good time manager and planner

Managing time effectively and planning for lots of time to study will be necessary to do well academically. How many hours do you need to study for each hour you are in class? Study skills experts report that students who make high grades typically spend a minimum of 2, and in some cases 3, hours studying outside of class for every hour they spend in class (Santrock and Halonen, 2004). That means if you are in class 15 hours a week, you likely will need to manage your time to study 30 to 45 hours outside of class each week if you want to make high grades.

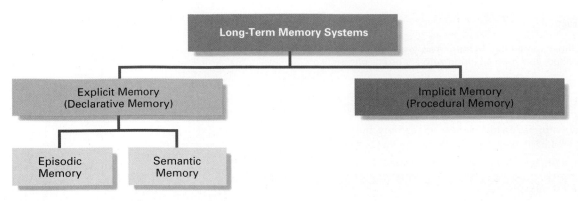

FIGURE 7.12 Systems of Long-Term Memory

Cognitive Psychology Laboratory

Timothy Salthouse's Research

Fredda Blanchard-Field's Research

as "Lima is the capital of Peru"—and not have the foggiest idea of when and where you learned it.

Recall that *implicit memory* refers to memory of skills and routine procedures that are performed automatically. (Implicit memory is sometimes referred to as procedural memory.) Examples of implicit memory include unconsciously remembering how to drive a car, swing a golf club, or type on a computer keyboard.

Aging and Explicit Memory Younger adults have better episodic memory than older adults (Piolino & others, 2002; Wingfield & Kahana, 2002). Older adults remember older events better than more recent events, typically reporting that they can remember what happened to them years ago but can't remember what they did yesterday. However, researchers consistently have found that, contrary to such self-reports, in older adults the older the memory, the less accurate it is. This has been documented in studies of memory for high school classmates, foreign language learned in school over the life span, names of grade school teachers, and autobiographical facts kept in diaries (Kausler, 1994).

Does semantic memory decline with age? Older adults do often take longer to retrieve semantic information, but usually they can ultimately retrieve it. In one study, even after almost five decades, adults picked out their high school classmates with better than 70 percent accuracy (Bahrick, Bahrick, & Wittlinger, 1975). In the Research in Life-Span Development interlude, we focus on another study that examined the developmental aspects of semantic memory.

Research in Life-Span Development

How Well Do Adults Remember What They Learned in High School and College Spanish?

When older adults are assessed for what they learned in high school or college, researchers find neither great durability in memory nor huge deterioration (Salthouse, 1991). In one study, non-Latino adults of various ages in the United States were studied to determine how much Spanish they remembered from classes they had taken in high school or college (Bahrick, 1984). The individuals chosen for the study had used Spanish very little since they initially learned it in high school or college. Not surprisingly, young adults who had taken Spanish classes within the last three years remembered their Spanish best. After that, the deterioration in memory was very gradual (see figure 7.13). For example, older adults who had studied Spanish 50 years earlier remembered about 80 percent of what young adults did who had studied it in the last three years! The most important factor in the adults' memory of Spanish was not how long ago they studied it but how well they initially learned it—those who got an A in Spanish 50 years earlier remembered more Spanish than adults who got a C when taking Spanish only one year earlier.

FIGURE 7.13 Memory for Spanish as a Function of Age Since Spanish Was Learned

An initial steep drop over about a three-year period in remembering the vocabulary learned in Spanish classes occurred. However, there was little dropoff in memory for Spanish vocabulary from three years after taking Spanish classes to 50 years after taking them. Even 50 years after taking Spanish classes, individuals still remembered almost 50 percent of the vocabulary.

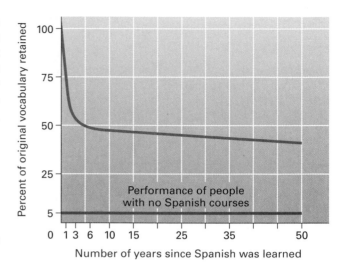

Aging and Implicit Memory Implicit memory is less likely to be adversely affected by aging than explicit memory (Schugens & others, 1997; Tulving, 2000). Thus, older adults are more likely to forget which items they wanted to buy at the grocery store (unless they wrote them down on a list and took it with them) than they are to forget how to drive a car. Their processing speed may be slower when driving the car, but they can remember how to do it.

Source Memory **Source memory** is the ability to remember where one learned something. Failures of source memory increase with age in the adult years, and they can be quite awkward as when an older adult forgets who told a joke and retells it to the source (Hedden & Park, 2003; Hellmuth, 2003).

One recent study found that awareness of character can compensate for the age decline in source memory (Rahhal, May, & Hasher, 2002). In a typical source memory study, before playing a tape, participants listen to a series of statements spoken by either a male or a female voice. At the end, participants read the statements and say which voice spoke to them. The researchers added this twist to their study: Before playing the tape, some of the older adults were told that one voice belonged to a saintly person who never told a lie and that the other person was a dishonest cad. As in past studies, the older adults had difficulty in remembering which voice spoke which given line. However, those who were told about the trustworthiness of the speakers more accurately judged whether a given statement was likely to be true or false, suggesting that older adults can remember information about a source when it is important to them.

Lynn Hasher (2003), one of the researchers who conducted the source memory study just described, argues that age differences are robust when researchers ask for a piece of information that doesn't matter much, but when older adults are asked about information that is important to them, they do as well as young adults. She believes that young adults have mental resources "to burn," but as people get older they become more selective in how they use their resources.

Prospective Memory **Prospective memory** involves remembering to do something in the future, such as remembering to take your medicine or remembering to do an errand. Although some researchers have found a decline in prospective memory with age, a number of studies show that whether there is a decline is complex and depends on such factors as the nature of the task and what is being assessed (Cherry & LeCompte, 1999; Einstein & others, 2000; Kliegel, McDaniel, & Einstein,

source memory The ability to remember where something is learned.

prospective memory Involves remembering to do something in the future.

2000; Vogels & others, 2002; West & Craik, 2001). For example, age-related deficits occur more often in time-based tasks (such as remembering to call someone next Friday) than in event-based tasks (remembering to tell your friend to read a particular book the next time you see her).

Influences on the Memory of Older Adults   We have described how some, but not all, aspects of memory decline in older adults. The decline occurs primarily in working memory, processing speed, and episodic memory, with less decline in semantic memory and implicit memory. What are some factors that might be linked to these declines?

Physiological Factors and Health   The declines in physiological functioning and the brain that we described in chapter 3 are likely involved in the decline of memory skills in older adults ◀▥ P. 93. So is the health of older adults, which we discussed in chapter 4 ◀▥ P. 131. Although such noncognitive factors as good health are associated with less memory decline in older adults, they do not eliminate memory decline.

Beliefs, Expectations, and Feelings   An increasing number of studies are finding that people's beliefs and expectancies about memory play a role in their actual memory (Cavanaugh, 2000): It matters what people tell themselves about their ability to remember. Positive or negative beliefs or expectancies about one's memory skills are related to actual memory performance (Kwon, 1999). In one study, older adults were randomly assigned to read one of two mock newspaper articles at the beginning of a testing situation (Hess & others, 2003). One described the declines in memory that characterize aging; the other emphasized research on the preservation of memory skills in older adults. The older adults who read the pessimistic account of memory and aging remembered 20 to 30 percent fewer words than people who read about the ability to maintain memory in old age. Despite such findings, some experts argue that beliefs about memory are not robust (Schaie, 2000).

Attitudes and feelings also matter. One study found that individuals with low anxiety about their memory skills and high self-efficacy regarding their use of memory in everyday contexts had better memory performance than their high-anxiety/ low-self-efficacy counterparts (McDougall & others, 1999).

Education, Memory Tasks, and Assessment   Education and experience with the tasks used to assess memory can also influence an older adult's performance on memory tasks. One criticism of research on memory and aging is that it has relied primarily on laboratory tests of memory. The argument is that such tasks are contrived and do not represent the everyday cognitive tasks performed by older adults. If researchers used more everyday life memory tasks, would memory decline be found in older adults?

A number of researchers have found that using more familiar tasks reduces age decrements in memory but does not eliminate them. Younger adults are better than older adults at remembering faces, routes through town, grocery items, and performed activities. In one study, young adults (20 to 40 years old) remembered news content in print, audio, and TV format better than old adults (60 to 80 years old) (Frieske & Park, 1999). In another study, older adults showed a keen memory for retirement-home search but not for their first job experience (Hess & others, 2003).

The time of day when memory is assessed is related to the memory performance of adults of different ages. To isolate the relation of age to memory performance, researchers try to make assessment conditions as identical as possible between participants of different ages. Participants come to the same laboratory and take the same memory tasks, for example. However, researchers have recently discovered that the optimum assessment conditions are not the same for younger and older adults. Most researchers assess participants in the afternoon, a convenient time for researchers and undergraduate volunteers. However, estimates suggest that about 75 percent of older adults are morning people while a majority of traditional-age college students perform at their best in the afternoon (Helmuth, 2003).

Lynn Hasher and her colleagues (2001) tested the memory of college students 18 to 32 years of age and community volunteers 58 to 78 years of age in the late afternoon (about 4 to 5 p.m.) and in the morning (about 8 to 9 a.m.). Regardless of the time of day, the younger college students performed better than the older adults on the memory tests, which involved recognizing sentences from a story and memorizing a list of words. However, when the participants took the memory tests in the morning rather than in the late afternoon, the age difference in performance was cut in half (see Figure 7.14).

Memory Training   Training and using mnemonics can improve older adults' memory ◀▦ **P. 247**. For example, in one study the *method of loci,* which we discussed earlier, was used to improve the memory of older adults (Kliegl & Baltes, 1987). The older adults were also trained to use *chunking*—organizing items into meaningful or manageable units. For example, if you need to remember the account number 283651492, you might remember it as three chunks: the number of days in February, the number of days in a year, and the year Columbus discovered America. Chunking can be used to remember telephone numbers, Social Security numbers, license plate numbers, and many other items encountered every day.

Using the method of loci and chunking, the older adults could recall more than 32 of 40 Berlin landmarks. Later they were able to apply what they had learned from their training to recall long lists of digits. One 69-year-old woman correctly recalled 120 digits presented in intervals of eights.

Such results suggest that healthy, mentally fit older adults retain substantial memory capacity. In another study, the method of loci was again effective in improving the memory of older adults (Kliegl, Smith, & Baltes, 1990). In yet another study, older adults benefited from mnemonic instruction, but not as much as younger adults (Verhaeghen & Marcoen, 1996).

The memory of older adults can also be improved by increasing their attention. In one study, instructing older adults to notice distinctions in pictures improved their memory of the pictures (Levy, Jennings, & Langer, 2001).

In short, older adults can improve memory if they use successful strategies. Successful aging, however, does not mean eliminating memory decline, but reducing it and adapting to it (Nyberg & others, 2003).

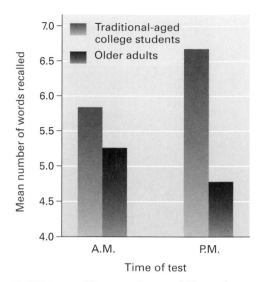

FIGURE 7.14 Memory, Age, and Time of Day Tested (A.M. or P.M.)

The traditional-aged college students performed better than older adults both in the a.m. and the p.m. However, note that the memory of the older adults was better when they were tested in the morning than in the afternoon while the memory of the traditional-aged college students was not as good in the morning as it was in the afternoon.

Review and Reflect: Learning Goal 3

3 Describe what memory is and how it changes through the life span

REVIEW

- What is memory? What are memory's processes? What is involved in constructing memory? Can new information alter memories?
- How does memory develop in infancy?
- How does memory change in childhood?
- How does memory change during adolescence?
- What are some changes in memory during the adult years?

REFLECT

- What is your earliest memory? Why do you think you can remember this particular situation?

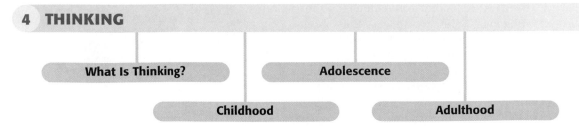

4 THINKING

What Is Thinking?   Adolescence   Childhood   Adulthood

Attention and memory are often steps toward another level of information processing—thinking. What is thinking? How does it change developmentally? What is children's scientific thinking like? Let's explore these questions.

What Is Thinking?

Thinking involves manipulating and transforming information in memory. We can think about the concrete (such as a vacation at the beach or how to win at a video game), or we can think in more abstract ways (such as pondering the meaning of freedom or identity). We can think about the past (what happened to us last month) and the future (what our life will be like in the year 2020). We can think about reality (such as how to do better on the next test) and fantasy (what it would be like to meet Elvis Presley or land a spacecraft on Mars). We think in order to reason, reflect, evaluate ideas, solve problems, and make decisions.

Childhood

To explore thinking in childhood, we will examine these questions: What is critical thinking? How can critical thinking be encouraged in schools? What is children's scientific thinking like? How do children solve problems?

Critical Thinking   Currently, there is considerable interest among psychologists and educators in critical thinking, although it is not an entirely new idea (Gardner, 1999; Runco, 1999). The famous educator John Dewey (1933) proposed a similar idea when he talked about the importance of getting students to think reflectively. The well-known psychologist Max Wertheimer (1945) talked about the importance of thinking productively rather than guessing at a correct answer. **Critical thinking** involves thinking reflectively and productively, and evaluating evidence.

If you think critically, you will do the following:

- Ask not only what happened but how and why.
- Examine supposed "facts" to determine whether there is evidence to support them.
- Argue in a reasoned way rather than through emotions.
- Recognize that there is sometimes more than one good answer or explanation.
- Compare various answers and judge which is the best answer.
- Evaluate what other people say rather than immediately accepting it as the truth.
- Ask questions and speculate beyond what is known to create new ideas and new information.

According to critics such as Jacqueline and Martin Brooks (1993, 2001), few schools teach students to think critically. Schools spend too much time on getting students to give a single correct answer rather than encouraging students to come up with new ideas and rethink conclusions. Too often teachers ask students to recite, define, describe, state, and list rather than to analyze, infer, connect, synthesize, criticize, create, evaluate, think, and rethink. As a result, many schools graduate students

"For God's sake, think!
Why is he being so nice to you?"

thinking Manipulating and transforming information in memory, usually to form concepts, reason, think critically, and solve problems.

critical thinking Thinking reflectively and productively, and evaluating the evidence.

who think superficially, staying on the surface of problems rather than becoming deeply engaged in meaningful thinking.

Daniel Perkins and Sarah Tishman (1997) work with teachers to incorporate critical thinking into classrooms. Here are some of the critical-thinking skills that they encourage teachers to help their students develop:

- *Open-mindedness.* Encourage students to avoid narrow thinking and to explore options. For example, when teaching literature, teachers might ask students to generate multiple critiques of Aldous Huxley's *Brave New World.*
- *Intellectual curiosity.* Encourage students to wonder, probe, and question. Recognize inconsistencies. In history class, this might mean reading British or Native American views on the American Revolution.
- *Planning and strategy.* Work with students to help them develop plans, set goals, find direction, and seek outcomes. In physical education, this might involve determining the best strategy to win a basketball or softball game.
- *Intellectual carefulness.* Encourage students to check for inaccuracies and errors, to be precise, and to be organized. For example, when students write a paper, they learn to structure the content and check the facts that they include.

The Applications in Life-Span Development interlude describes an educational program designed to encourage children to think critically.

Critical Thinking Resources
Schools for Thought

Applications in Life-Span Development

Fostering a Community of Learners

An innovative program that encourages critical thinking, Fostering a Community of Learners (FCL), was created by Anne Brown and Joe Campione (1996; Brown, 1997, 1998). The program focuses on literacy and biology. As currently established, it is set in inner-city elementary schools and is appropriate for 6- to 12-year-old children. Reflection and discussion are key dimensions of the program. Constructive commentary, questioning, and criticism are the norm rather than the exception. Three strategies used by FCL that encourage reflection and discussion are (1) having children teach children, (2) implementing online computer consultation, and (3) using adults as role models.

Children Teaching Children

Cross-age teaching, in which older students teach younger students, occurs both face-to-face and via e-mail in FCL. Older students often serve as discussion leaders. Cross-age teaching provides students with invaluable opportunities to talk about learning, gives students responsibility and purpose, and fosters collaboration among peers.

Reciprocal teaching, in which individuals take turns leading a small-group discussion, is another strategy used in FCL. It requires students to discuss complex passages, collaborate, and share their individual expertise and perspectives.

FCL also uses a modified version of the "jigsaw classroom" (students cooperate by doing different parts of a project to reach a common goal). As students create preliminary drafts of reports, they participate in "cross-talk" sessions—whole-class activities in which groups periodically summarize the status of their activity and receive input from the other groups. If group members can't understand what someone is saying or writing, the students revise their product and present it again later. Students are then grouped into reciprocal teaching seminars in which each

reciprocal teaching Individuals take turns leading small-group discussions.

student teaches one subtopic to the others and also participates in constructing test questions based on the subunit.

Online Computer Consultation

Face-to-face communication is not the only way to build community and expertise. FCL classrooms also used e-mail. Through e-mail, experts provide coaching and advice, as well as commentary about what it means to learn and understand. Online experts function as role models of thinking. They wonder, query, and make inferences based on incomplete knowledge.

Adults as Role Models

Visiting experts and classroom teachers introduce the big ideas and difficult principles at the beginning of a unit. The adult models how to think and reflect. The adults continually ask students to justify their opinions and then support them with evidence, to think of counterexamples to rules, and so on.

One example of a teaching theme used in FCL is "changing populations." Outside experts or teachers introduce this lesson and ask students to generate as many questions about it as possible. It is not unusual for students to come up with more than a hundred questions. The teacher and the students categorize the questions into subtopics according to the type of population they refer to, such as extinct, endangered, artificial, and urbanized populations. About six students make up a learning group, and each group takes responsibility for one subtopic.

A culture of learning, negotiating, sharing, and producing work that is displayed to others is at the heart of FCL. The educational experience involves an interpretive community that encourages active exchange and reciprocity. This approach has much in common with what Jerome Bruner (1996) recommended for improving the culture of education. Research evaluation of FCL suggests that it benefits students' thinking skills (Brown, 1998).

Scientific Thinking Some aspects of thinking are specific to a particular domain, such as mathematics, science, or reading. We will explore reading in chapter 9, "Language Development." Here we will examine scientific thinking by children.

Like scientists, children ask fundamental questions about reality and seek answers to problems that seem utterly trivial or unanswerable to other people (such as "Why is the sky blue?"). Do children generate hypotheses, perform experiments, and reach conclusions about their data in ways resembling those of scientists (Clinchy, Mansfield, & Schott, 1995; Dunbar, 2001; Schunn & Anderson, 2001)?

Scientific reasoning often is aimed at identifying causal relations. Like scientists, children place a great deal of emphasis on causal mechanisms (Frye & others, 1996). Their understanding of how events are caused weighs more heavily in their causal inferences than even such strong influences as whether the cause happened immediately before the effect.

There also are important differences between the reasoning of children and the reasoning of scientists. Children are more influenced by happenstance events than by an overall pattern (Kuhn, Amsel, & O'Laughlin, 1988). Often, children maintain their old theories regardless of the evidence (Kuhn, Schauble, & Garcia-Mila, 1992). Children might go through mental gymnastics trying to reconcile seemingly contradictory new information with their existing beliefs. For example, after learning about the solar system, children sometimes conclude that there are two Earths, the seemingly flat world in which they live and the round ball floating in space that their teacher described.

Children also have difficulty designing experiments that can distinguish among alternative causes. Instead, they tend to bias the experiments in favor of whatever hypothesis they began with. Sometimes they see the results as supporting their original hypothesis even when the results directly contradict it (Schauble, 1996).

Researchers have stepped up their efforts to discover ways to help children learn science (Carey, 2000; Cocking, Mestre, & Brown, 2000; Lehrer, Schauble, & Petrosino, 2001). Good teachers diagnose and understand a child's underlying concepts, then use the concepts as a scaffold for learning. Effective science teaching helps children distinguish between fruitful errors and misconceptions—between errors that are on the right path, but stem from incomplete understanding, and plainly wrong ideas that need to be replaced by more accurate conceptions.

Key skills typically used by scientists are not routinely taught in U.S. schools. These include making careful observations; collecting, organizing, and analyzing data; measuring, graphing, and understanding spatial relations; paying attention to and regulating one's own thinking; and knowing when and how to apply one's knowledge to solve problems. Scientists and educators believe that schools need to guide students in learning these skills (Cocking, Mestre, & Brown, 2000).

Solving Problems   Children face many problems that they must solve in order to adapt effectively, both in school and out of school. *Problem solving* involves finding an appropriate way to attain a goal. What are some ways children solve problems?

Using Strategies to Solve Problems   In Michael Pressley's view (Pressley, 1983, 2003; McCormick & Pressley, 1997), the key to education is helping students learn a rich repertoire of strategies for solving problems. Good thinkers routinely use strategies and effective planning to solve problems (McCormick, 2003). Pressley argues that when children are given instruction about effective strategies, they often can apply strategies that they had not used on their own. Pressley emphasizes that children benefit when the teacher models the appropriate strategy, verbalizes the steps in the strategy, and then guides the children to practice the strategy. Their practice is supported by the teacher's feedback until the children can effectively execute the strategy autonomously.

When instructing children about employing the strategy, it also is a good idea to explain how using the strategy will benefit them. Children need to be motivated to learn and to use the strategies. Just having children learn a new strategy is usually not enough for them to continue to use it and to transfer the strategy to new situations. For effective maintenance and transfer, children should be encouraged to monitor the effectiveness of the new strategy by comparing their performance on tests and other assessments.

Learning to use strategies effectively often takes time. Initially, it takes time to execute the strategies and to practice them. "Practice" means that children use the effective strategy over and over again until they perform it automatically. To execute the strategies effectively, they need to have the strategies in long-term memory, and extensive practice makes this possible.

Let's examine an example of effective strategy instruction. Good readers extract the main ideas from text and summarize them. In contrast, novice readers (for example, most children) usually don't store the main ideas of what they read. One intervention based on what is known about the summarizing strategies of good readers consisted of instructing children to (1) skim over trivial information, (2) ignore redundant information, (3) replace less inclusive terms with more inclusive ones, (4) use a more inclusive action term to combine a series of events, (5) choose a topic sentence, and (6) create a topic sentence if none is given (Brown & Day, 1983). Instructing elementary school students to use these summarizing strategies improves their reading performance (Rinehart, Stahl, & Erickson, 1986).

Do children use one strategy or multiple strategies in memory and problem solving? They often use more than one strategy (Siegler, 1998). Most children benefit from generating a variety of alternative strategies and experimenting with different approaches to a problem, discovering what works well, when, and where. This is especially true for children from the middle elementary school grades on,

www.mhhe.com/santrockld2

Science Resources for Teachers
Science Learning Network

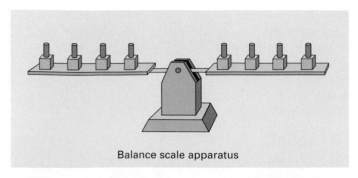

FIGURE 7.15 The Type of Balance Scale Used by Siegler (1976)
Weights could be placed on pegs on each side of the fulcrum; the torque (the weight on each side times the distance of that weight from the fulcrum) determined which side would go down.

although some cognitive psychologists believe that even young children should be encouraged to practice varying strategies (Siegler, 1998).

Using Rules to Solve Problems One aspect of information-processing research on problem solving aims to identify the rules children use to solve problems. The balance scale problem is useful for illustrating this research. The type of balance scale that has been used to examine children's understanding is shown in figure 7.15. The scale includes a fulcrum and an arm that can rotate around it. The arm can tip left or right or remain level, depending on how weights (metal disks with holes in the center) are arranged on the pegs on each side of the fulcrum. The child's task is to look at the configuration of weights on the pegs for each problem and then predict whether the left side will go down, the right side will go down, or the arm will balance.

Robert Siegler (1976) hypothesized that children would use one of the four rules depicted in figure 7.16:

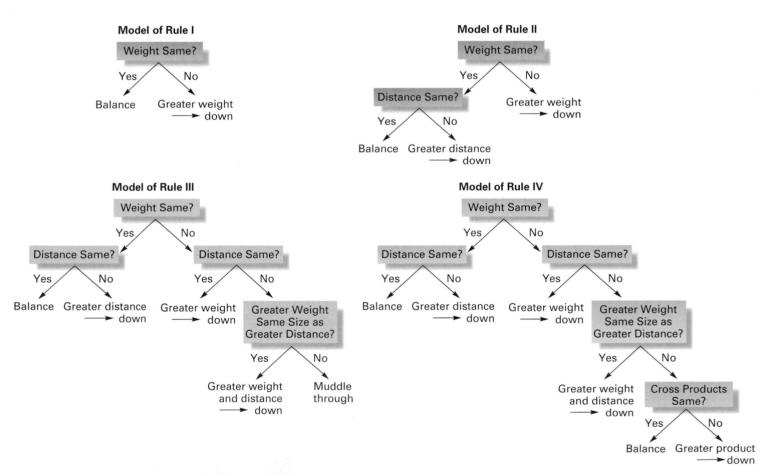

FIGURE 7.16 Four Rules for Solving the Balance Scale Task
Children following Rule I would always pick the side with more weight as the one that would go down, and would say that the scale would balance whenever the two sides had the same amount of weight. Children using Rule II would do the same, except that if the two sides had the same amount of weight, they would base their judgments on the distance of the weights from the fulcrum. Children using Rule III would always consider both weight and distance, and would respond correctly if one or both were equal. However, they would muddle through or guess if one side had more weight and the other had its weight farther from the fulcrum. Finally, children using Rule IV would act the same as those using Rule III, except that they would compute torques when one side had more weight and the other had its weight farther from the fulcrum.

Rule I. If the weight is the same on both sides, predict that the scale will balance. If the weight differs, predict that the side with more weight will go down.

Rule II. If the weight is greater on one side, say that that side will go down. If the weights on the two sides are equal, choose the side on which the weight is farther from the fulcrum.

Rule III. Act as in Rule II, except that if one side has more weight and the weight on the other side is farther from the fulcrum, then guess.

Rule IV. Proceed as in Rule III, unless one side has more weight and the other more distance. In that case, calculate torques by multiplying weight times distance on each side. Then predict that the side with the greater torque will go down.

But how could it be determined which rule, if any, a given child was using? Siegler reasoned that presenting problems on which different rules would generate different outcomes would allow assessment of each child's rules. For example, suppose there were four weights on the third peg to the left of the fulcrum and three weights on the fourth peg to the right of the fulcrum. A child using Rule I or Rule II would say that the left side will go down, because it has more weight; a child using Rule III would guess and therefore sometimes say one answer and sometimes another; and a child using Rule IV would compute torques and realize that the two sides would balance. Through a child's pattern of correct answers and errors on a set of such problems, that child's underlying rule could be inferred.

This *rule assessment approach* demonstrated that almost 90 percent of children aged 5 to 17 years used one of the four rules. Almost all 5-year-olds used Rule I, almost all 9-year-olds used either Rule II or Rule III, and both 13-year-olds and 17-year-olds generally used Rule III.

Interestingly, despite the 17-year-olds' having studied balance scales in their physics course, almost none of them used the only rule that generated consistently correct answers, Rule IV. Discussions with their teachers revealed why; the balance scale the students had studied was a pan balance, on which small pans could be hung from various locations along the arm, rather than an arm balance, with pegs extending upward. Retesting the children showed that most could consistently solve the problems when the familiar pan balance was used. This example illustrates a set of lessons that frequently has emerged from studies of problem solving: Learning is often quite narrow; generalization beyond one's existing knowledge is difficult; and even analogies that seem straightforward are often missed.

Using Analogies to Solve Problems Recall from an earlier discussion in this chapter that an *analogy* involves correspondence in some respects between things that are dissimilar. The development of *analogical problem solving* resembles that of scientific reasoning. Even very young children can draw reasonable analogies under some circumstances and use them to solve problems (Freeman & Gehl, 1995). Under other circumstances, even college students fail to draw seemingly obvious analogies (as in the earlier example of the high school students' difficulty in extrapolating from the familiar pan balance to the unfamiliar arm balance). This resemblance is not coincidental, since scientific reasoning often depends on drawing useful analogies.

Ann Brown and her collaborators (Brown, 1990; Brown, Kane, & Echols, 1986) have demonstrated some of the types of analogical reasoning that occur even as early as 1 and 2 years of age. When 1- and 2-year-olds are shown that a curved stick can be used as a tool to pull in a toy that is too far away to be reached unaided, they draw the correct analogy in choosing which stick to use the next time. They do not choose sticks on the basis of their being the same color as the stick they used before. They also do not just choose objects that look exactly like the tool they saw demonstrated to be effective (such as a curved cane); instead they identify the essential property and will choose whichever objects have it (they will choose a straight

Judy DeLoache (left) has conducted research that focuses on young children's developing cognitive abilities. She has demonstrated that children's symbolic representation between 2½ and 3 years of age enables them to find a toy in a real room that is a much bigger version of the scale model.

rake as well as the curved cane). The 2-year-olds were more likely than the 1-year-olds to learn the initial task without any help, but once they learned the task, both 1- and 2-year-olds drew the right analogy to new problems.

Successful analogical problem solving often involves tools more abstract than curved sticks for hauling in objects that are beyond one's reach. Maps and verbal descriptions of routes, for example, often help us to figure out how to get where we want to go (DeLoache, Miller, & Pierroutakos, 1998). Recent studies of toddlers' abilities to use scale models to guide their problem-solving activities show that dramatic developments occur in such tool use quite early in development.

Judy DeLoache (1989) created a situation in which 2½- and 3-year-olds were shown a small toy hidden within a scale model of a room. The child was then asked to find the toy in a real room that was a bigger version of the scale model. If the toy was hidden under the armchair in the scale model, it was also hidden under the armchair in the real room. Considerable development occurred between 2½ and 3 years of age on this task. Thirty-month-old children rarely could solve the problem; by 36 months they generally could.

What was the source of the 2½-year-olds' difficulty on the task? It was not inability to understand how any type of symbol could represent another situation. Shown line drawings or photographs of the larger room, 2½-year-olds had no difficulty finding the object. Instead, the difficulty seemed to come from the toddlers' simultaneously viewing the scale model as a symbol of the larger room and as an object in itself. Surprising consequences followed from this insight. Allowing children to play with the scale model before using it as a symbol worsened their performance, presumably because playing with it made them think of it more as an object in itself. Conversely, putting the scale model in a glass case, where the children could not handle it at all, resulted in children more often being able to use it successfully to find the object hidden in the larger room. The general lesson is that young children can use a variety of tools to draw analogies, but they easily can forget that an object is being used as a symbol of something else and instead take it as being of interest as an object in its own right.

Adolescence

How does critical thinking change in adolescence? How do adolescents make decisions?

Critical Thinking If a solid basis of fundamental skills (such as literacy and math skills) is not developed during childhood, critical-thinking skills are unlikely to mature in adolescence. For the subset of adolescents who lack fundamental skills, potential gains in adolescent thinking are not likely. For other adolescents, this time is an important transitional period in the development of critical thinking (Keating, 1990, 2003, 2004). Some of the cognitive changes that allow improved critical thinking in adolescence are these:

- Increased speed, automaticity, and capacity of information processing, which frees cognitive resources for other purposes
- More knowledge in a variety of domains
- An increased ability to construct new combinations of knowledge

- A greater range and more spontaneous use of strategies or procedures such as planning, considering alternatives, and cognitive monitoring

In one study of fifth-, eighth-, and eleventh-graders, critical thinking increased with age but still only occurred in 43 percent of even the eleventh-graders. Many adolescents showed self-serving biases in their reasoning (Klaczynski & Narasimham, 1998).

Decision Making Adolescence is a time of increased decision making—about the future, which friends to choose, whether to go to college, which person to date, whether to have sex, whether to buy a car, and so on (Byrnes, 1997, 2003; Galloti & Kozberg, 1996). How competent are adolescents at making decisions?

Older adolescents appear to be more competent decision makers than younger adolescents, who, in turn, are more competent than children (Keating, 1990). Compared with children, young adolescents are more likely to generate options, to examine the situation from a variety of perspectives, to anticipate the consequences of decisions, and to consider the credibility of sources.

Being able to make competent decisions does not guarantee that one will make them in everyday life, where breadth of experience often comes into play (Jacobs & Kalczynski, 2002; Jacobs & Potenza, 1990; Keating, 1990). For example, driver-training courses improve adolescents' cognitive and motor skills to levels equal to, or sometimes superior to, those of adults. However, driver training has not reduced adolescents' high rate of traffic accidents (Potvin, Champagne, & Laberge-Nadeau, 1988). An important research agenda is to study the ways adolescents make decisions in actual situations.

Adulthood

Earlier in the chapter, we examined the changes that take place in speed of processing information, attention, and memory during adulthood. Here we will focus on some gains in thinking during the middle adulthood years and the challenges that older adults face.

Practical Problem Solving and Expertise The years of early and middle adulthood bring some important advances in memory for many individuals. Practical problem solving increases. Nancy Denney (1986, 1990) observed circumstances such as how young and middle-aged adults handled a landlord who would not fix their stove and what they did if a bank failed to deposit a check. She found that the ability to solve such practical problems improved through the forties and fifties as individuals accumulated practical experience.

Experience as well as years of learning and effort may also bring the rewards of **expertise,** or extensive, highly organized knowledge and understanding of a particular domain. Because it takes so long to attain, expertise often shows up more among middle-aged or older adults than younger adults (Clancy & Hoyer, 1994; Hoyer & Roodin, 2003). Individuals may be experts in areas as diverse as physics, art, or knowledge of wine.

Whatever their area of expertise, within that domain experts tend to process information differently than novices (Hardin, 2003). Here are some of the characteristics that distinguish experts from novices:

- Experts are more likely to rely on their accumulated experience to solve problems.
- Experts often process information automatically and analyze it more efficiently when solving a problem in their domain than a novice does.
- Experts have better strategies and short-cuts to solving problems in their domain than novices do.

Stephen J. Hawking is a world-renowned expert in physics. Hawking authored the best-selling book, *A Brief History of Time*. Hawking has a neurological disorder that prevents him from being able to walk or talk. He communicates with the aid of a voice-equipped computer. *What distinguishes experts from novices?*

expertise Having extensive, highly organized knowledge and understanding of a particular domain.

*E*ngaging in regular cognitive activity helps to stave off cognitive decline in older adults.

—SHERRY WILLIS
Contemporary Psychologist,
Pennsylvania State University

- Experts are more creative and flexible in solving problems in their domain than novices are (Csikszentmihalyi, 1997).

Use It or Lose It   The adage "Use it or lose it" applies to cognitive skills among older adults. Activities such as reading books, doing crossword puzzles, and going to lectures and concerts can help older adults maintain cognitive skills. These studies support this idea:

- In both the Victoria Longitudinal Study and another longitudinal study over 45 years, participating in intellectually engaging activities buffered middle-aged and older adults against cognitive decline (Arbuckle & others, 1998; Hultsch & others, 1999).
- In a 4½-year longitudinal study of 801 Catholic priests 65 years and older, those who regularly read books, did crossword puzzles, or otherwise exercised their minds were 47 percent less likely to develop Alzheimer's disease than the priests who rarely engaged in these activities (Wilson & others, 2002).
- In a study of chess players from 20 to 80 years of age, success in chess tournaments was more closely linked with the amount of time they engaged in deliberate practice than with their age (Charness, Krampe, & Mayr, 1996).

Cognitive Training   If an older adult is losing cognitive skills, can those skills be retrained? Two key conclusions can be derived from research: (1) Training can improve the cognitive skills of many older adults, but (2) there is some loss in plasticity in late adulthood (Baltes, 1995).

Evidence of plasticity and the effectiveness of cognitive training comes from the research of Sherry Willis and K. Warner Schaie (1986), who studied approximately 400 adults, most of whom were older adults. Using individualized training, they improved the spatial orientation and reasoning skills of two-thirds of the adults. Nearly 40 percent of those whose abilities had declined returned to a level they had reached 14 years earlier. Further, the effects of training on reasoning lasted up to seven years after training (Saczynksi, & Willis, 2001).

What activities are part of successful cognitive training? A seven-year longitudinal study by Sherry Willis and Carolyn Nesselroade (1990) used cognitive training to help adults maintain fluid intelligence (the ability to reason abstractly) with advancing age. The older adults were taught strategies for identifying the rule or pattern required to solve problems. The trainer modeled correct strategies for solving problems. Individuals practiced on training items, received feedback about the correct solutions to practice problems, and participated in group discussion. After this cognitive training, adults in their seventies and eighties performed at a higher level than they had in their late sixties.

Researchers are also finding that improving the physical fitness of older adults can improve their cognitive functioning (Kramer & Willis, 2002). A recent review of studies revealed that aerobic fitness training improved the planning, scheduling, working memory, resistance to distraction, and processing involving multiple tasks in older adults (Colcombe & Kramer, in press).

In sum, the cognitive vitality of older adults can be improved through cognitive and fitness training (Kramer & Willis, 2002). However, benefits have not been observed in all studies (Salthouse, 1990). Further research is needed to determine more precisely which cognitive improvements occur in older adults (Dixon & Cohen, 2003).

Sherry Willis (right) assessing the cognitive skills of aging adults. Willis has shown that older adults can be trained to improve their reasoning ability. She especially believes it is important for adults to use their cognitive abilities and believes that maintaining an active mental life is important.

Review and Reflect: Learning Goal 4

4 **Characterize thinking and its developmental changes**

REVIEW

- What is thinking?
- What is critical thinking? Do children and scientists think in the same ways? What are three important aspects of problem solving?
- What are some changes in thinking during adolescence?
- What are some changes in thinking in adulthood?

REFLECT

- Choose an area in which you consider yourself at least somewhat of an expert. Compare your ability to learn in this field with the ability of a novice.

5 METACOGNITION

What Is Metacognition?   Metamemory in Children

The Young Child's   Metacognition in
Theory of Mind   Adolescence and Adulthood

As you read at the beginning of this chapter, *metacognition* is cognition about cognition, or "knowing about knowing" (Flavell, 1999; Flavell, Flavell, & Miller, 2002).

What Is Metacognition?

Metacognition can take many forms. It includes knowledge about when and where to use particular strategies for learning or for solving problems. **Metamemory,** individuals' knowledge about memory, is an especially important form of metacogntion ◀▦ **P. 234.** Metamemory includes general knowledge about memory, such as knowing that recognition tests (such as multiple-choice questions) are easier than recall tests (such as essay questions). It also encompasses knowledge about one's own memory, such as knowing whether you have studied enough for an upcoming test.

Metacognition helps people to perform many cognitive tasks more effectively (McCormick, 2003). In one study, students were taught metacognitive skills to help them solve math problems (Cardelle-Elawar, 1992). In each of thirty daily lessons involving math story problems, a teacher guided low-achieving students to recognize when they did not know the meaning of a word, did not have all of the information necessary to solve a problem, did not know how to subdivide the problem into specific steps, or did not know how to carry out a computation. After the thirty daily lessons, the students who were given this metacognitive training had better math achievement and attitudes toward math.

The Young Child's Theory of Mind

Theory of mind refers to awareness of one's own mental processes and the mental processes of others. Even young children are curious about the nature of the human mind (Flavell, 1999; Wellman, 1997, 2000, 2002). Their theory of mind changes as they go through the childhood years (Flavell, Miller, & Miller, 2002):

Metacognition
Metacognition Links

metamemory Knowledge about memory.

theory of mind Thoughts about how mental processes work, such as a child's becoming aware that the mind exists and understanding cognitive connections to the physical world.

*T*he developing cognitive competencies that are the most relevant to critical thinking are metacognitive competencies.

—DEANNA KUHN
*Contemporary Psychologist,
Columbia University*

- When they are 2 to 3 years old, children begin to understand three mental states:
  Perceptions. Children realize that other people see what is in front of their eyes and not necessarily what is in front of the children's eyes.
  Desires. Children understand that if someone wants something, he or she will try to get it. A child might say, "I want my mommy."
  Emotions. Children can distinguish between positive (for example, "happy") and negative (for example, "sad") emotions. A child might say, "Tommy feels bad."
    Despite these advances, children who are 2 to 3 years of age have only a minimal understanding of how mental life can be linked to behavior. They think that people are at the mercy of their desires and don't understand how beliefs influence behavior.
- When they are 4 to 5 years of age, children begin to understand that the mind can represent objects and events accurately or inaccurately. The realization that people have *false beliefs*—beliefs that are not true—develops in a majority of children by the time they are 5 years old (Wellman, Cross, & Watson, 2001) (see figure 7.17). For example, in one study children were shown a Band-Aids box and asked what was inside (Jenkins & Astington, 1996). To the children's surprise, the box contained pencils. When asked what a child who had never seen the box would think was inside, 3-year-olds typically responded "pencils." The 4- and 5-year-olds, grinning in anticipation of other children's false beliefs, were more likely to say "Band-Aids."

Metamemory in Children

By 5 or 6 years of age, children usually know that familiar items are easier to learn than unfamiliar ones, that short lists are easier than long ones, that recognition is easier than recall, and that forgetting becomes more likely over time (Lyon & Flavell, 1993). However, in other ways young children's metamemory is limited. They don't understand that related items are easier to remember than unrelated ones or that remembering the gist of a story is easier than remembering information verbatim (Kreutzer, Leonard, & Flavell, 1975). By fifth grade, students understand that gist recall is easier than verbatim recall.

Preschool children also have an inflated opinion of their memory abilities. For example, in one study, a majority of preschool children predicted that they would be able to recall all ten items of a list of ten items. When tested, none of the young children managed this feat (Flavell, Friedrichs, & Hoyt, 1970). As they move through the elementary school years, children give more realistic evaluations of their memory skills (Schneider & Pressley, 1997).

Preschool children also have little appreciation for the importance of cues for memory, such as "It helps when you can think of an example of it." By 7 or 8 years of age, children better appreciate the importance of cueing for memory.

In general, children's understanding of their memory abilities and their skill in evaluating their performance on memory tasks is relatively poor at the beginning of the elementary school years but improves considerably by 11 to 12 years of age (Bjorklund & Rosenbaum, 2000).

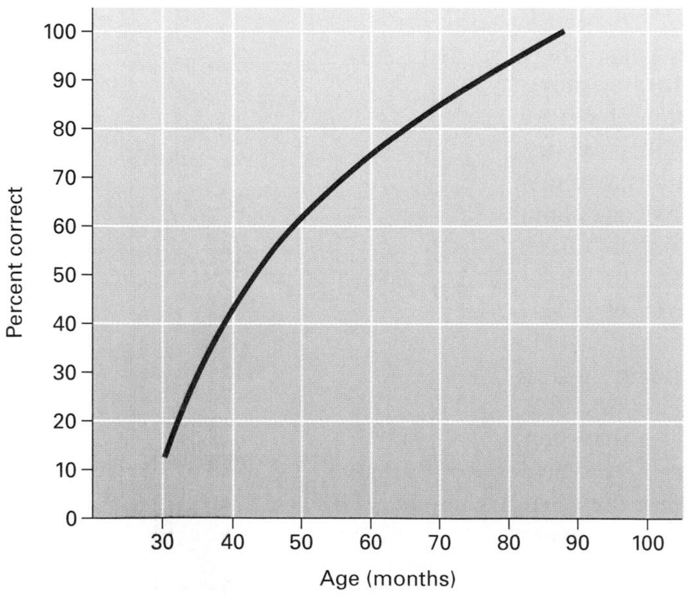

Metacognition in Adolescence and Adulthood

Adolescents are more likely than children to manage and monitor their thinking. Adolescents are also more introspective than children, turning inward to examine their thoughts and emotions. This improving metacognition helps adolescents to evaluate and monitor

FIGURE 7.17 Developmental Changes in False-Belief Performance

False-belief performance dramatically increases from 2½ years of age through the middle of the elementary school years. In a summary of the results of many studies, 2½-year-olds gave incorrect responses about 80 percent of the time (Wellman, Cross, & Watson, 2001). At 3 years, 8 months, they were correct about 50 percent of the time, and after that, gave increasingly correct responses.

their academic learning. For example, they are better than children at estimating how long it will take them to complete an assignment and are more aware of the need to plan and monitor such work.

By middle age, adults have accumulated a great deal of metacognitive knowledge. They can draw on this metacognitive knowledge to help them combat a decline in memory skills. For example, they are likely to understand that they need to have good organizational skills and reminders to help combat the decline in memory skills they face.

Older adults tend to overestimate the memory problems they experience on a daily basis. They seem to be more aware of their memory failures than younger adults and become more anxious about minor forgetfulness than younger adults (Hoyer & Roodin, 2003).

Review and Reflect: Learning Goal 5

5 Define metacognition and summarize its developmental changes

REVIEW

- What is metacognition?
- How does the child's theory of mind change during the preschool years?
- How does metamemory typically change during childhood?
- How does metacognition change in adolescence and adulthood?

REFLECT

- How might metacognition be involved in the ability of college students to have better study skills than children?

Reach Your Learning Goals

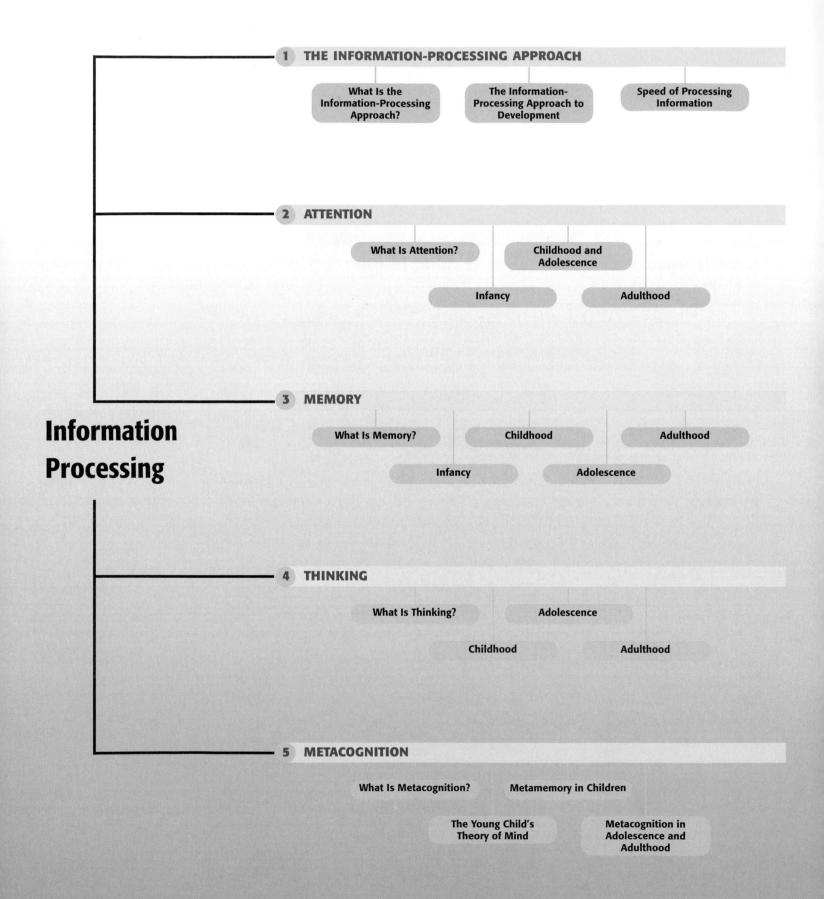

Information Processing

1 THE INFORMATION-PROCESSING APPROACH

- What Is the Information-Processing Approach?
- The Information-Processing Approach to Development
- Speed of Processing Information

2 ATTENTION

- What Is Attention?
- Childhood and Adolescence
- Infancy
- Adulthood

3 MEMORY

- What Is Memory?
- Childhood
- Adulthood
- Infancy
- Adolescence

4 THINKING

- What Is Thinking?
- Adolescence
- Childhood
- Adulthood

5 METACOGNITION

- What Is Metacognition?
- Metamemory in Children
- The Young Child's Theory of Mind
- Metacognition in Adolescence and Adulthood

Summary

1 Explain the information-processing approach

- The information-processing approach analyzes how individuals manipulate information, monitor it, and create strategies for handling it. Attention, memory, and thinking are involved in effective information processing. The computer has served as a model for how humans process information.
- In the information-processing approach, children's cognitive development results from their ability to overcome processing limitations by increasingly executing basic operations, expanding information-processing capacity, and acquiring new knowledge and strategies. According to Siegler, three important mechanisms of change are encoding (how information gets into memory), automaticity (ability to process information with little or no effort), and strategy construction (creation of new procedures for processing information). Children's information processing is characterized by self-modification and an important aspect of this self-modification involves metacognition—that is, knowing about knowing. Unlike Piaget, the information-processing approach does not see development as occurring in distinct stages. Instead, this approach holds that individuals develop a gradually increasing capacity for processing information, which allows them to develop increasingly complex knowledge and skills.
- Processing speed increases across childhood and adolescence and in early adulthood. Processing speed slows as individuals go through their later adulthood years.

2 Define attention and outline its developmental changes

- Attention is the focusing of mental resources. Three ways that people can allocate their attention are sustained attention (the state of readiness to detect and respond to small changes occurring at random times in the environment; also referred to as vigilance), selective attention (focusing on a specific aspect of experience that is relevant while ignoring others that are irrelevant), and divided attention (concentrating on more than one activity at the same time).
- Even newborns can fixate on a contour, but as they get older they scan a pattern more thoroughly. Attention in infancy is often studied through habituation and dishabituation.
- Salient stimuli tend to capture the attention of the preschooler. After 6 or 7 years of age, there is a shift to more cognitive control of attention. Selective attention improves through childhood and adolescence.
- Attentional skills often are excellent in early adulthood. Older adults are generally less adept than younger adults at selective and divided attention.

3 Describe what memory is and how it changes through the life span

- Memory is the retention of information over time. Psychologists study the processes of memory: how information is initially placed or encoded into memory, how it is retained or stored, and how it is found or retrieved for a certain purpose later. People construct and reconstruct their memories. Schema theory states that people mold memories to fit the information that already exists in their minds. Researchers also study false memories and how new information can alter memories.
- Infants as young as 2 to 3 months of age display implicit memory, which is memory without conscious recollection as in memory of perceptual-motor skills. However, many experts believe that explicit memory, which is the conscious memory of facts and experiences, does not emerge until the second half of the first year of life. Older children and adults remember little if anything from the first three years of their lives.
- One method of assessing short-term memory (the retention of information for up to 15 to 30 seconds, assuming there is no rehearsal of the information) is with a memory span task, on which there are substantial developmental changes through the childhood years. Working memory (a kind of "mental workbench" where individuals manipulate and assemble information when they make decisions, solve problems, and comprehend language) is linked to children's reading comprehension and problem solving. Young children can remember a great deal of information if they are given appropriate cues and prompts. Strategies can improve children's memory, and older children are more likely to use these than younger children. Imagery and elaboration are two important strategies. Knowledge is an important influence on memory.
- Working memory capacity likely increases in adolescence and is linked to improved problem solving. It is important to develop a number of effective memory and study strategies during adolescence and into early adulthood.
- Younger adults have better episodic memory than older adults. Older adults have more difficulty retrieving semantic information. Working memory and processing speed decrease in older adults. Explicit memory is more likely to decline in older adults than implicit memory. Source memory—remembering where one learned something—declines with age in adulthood. However, when the information is important to older adults, the accuracy of their source memory improves. Controversy characterizes whether prospective memory, which is remembering to do something in the future, declines as adults age. Among the factors that may be linked with memory changes in older adults are physiological functioning; the brain and health; people's beliefs, expectancies, and feelings about memory; education; types of tasks used to assess memory; time of day when memory is assessed; and training to improve memory skills.

4 Characterize thinking and its developmental changes

- Thinking involves manipulating and transforming information in memory.

- Critical thinking involves thinking reflectively and productively, and evaluating the evidence. A lack of emphasis on critical thinking in schools is a special concern. Children and scientists think alike in some ways, but not alike in others. Three important aspects of solving problems involve using strategies, using rules, and using analogies.
- Adolescence is an important transitional period in critical thinking. Decision making increases in adolescence.
- Practical problem solving and expertise often increases in the middle adulthood years. Using cognitive skills helps older adults retain a higher level of cognitive functioning. Cognitive training and physical fitness training can help remediate cognitive decline.

5 **Define metacognition and summarize its developmental changes**

- Metacognition is cognition about cognition, or "knowing about knowing."

- Young children are curious about the human mind, and this has been studied under the topic of theory of mind. At 2 to 3 years of age, children begin to understand three mental states: perceptions, desires, and emotions. At 4 to 5 years of age, they begin to recognize that the mind can represent objects accurately and inaccurately.
- By 5 to 6 years of age, children usually know that familiar items are easier to learn than unfamiliar ones and that short lists are easier than long ones. By 7 to 8 years of age, children better appreciate the importance of cues for memory.
- Adolescents are more likely than children to manage and monitor their thinking. Metacognition continues to improve in early adulthood, and many middle-aged individuals have accumulated considerable metacognitive knowledge. Older adults tend to overestimate their everyday memory problems.

Key Terms

information-processing approach 232
encoding 234
automaticity 234
strategy construction 234
metacognition 234
attention 237
sustained attention 237

selective attention 237
divided attention 237
memory 239
schema theory 240
schemas 240
implicit memory 242
explicit memory 242
long-term memory 243

short-term memory 243
working memory 243
elaboration 245
episodic memory 246
semantic memory 246
source memory 249
prospective memory 249
thinking 252

critical thinking 252
reciprocal teaching 253
expertise 259
metamemory 261
theory of mind 261

Key People

Robert Siegler 233
K. Warner Schaie 235
Carolyn Rovee-Collier 242
Daniel Perkins and Sarah Tishman 253

Anne Brown and Joe Campione 253
Michael Pressley 255

Judy DeLoache 258
Nancy Denney 259

Sherry Willis and Carolyn Nesselroade 260

E-Learning Tools

Connect to **www.mhhe.com/santrockldt2** to research the answers and complete these exercises. In addition, you'll find a number of other resources and valuable study tools for chapter 7, "Information Processing," on the Student CD-ROM that came with this book.

Taking It to the Net

1. Six-year-old Matthew is in the habit of asking his parents to repeat every comment or question. They know he does not have a hearing problem—they think he just doesn't pay attention. How can they teach Matthew to pay attention and listen?

2. Fourteen-year-old Nancy, who lives with her grandparents, already has a history of sexual acting-out, substance abuse, and arrests for petty crimes. Her grandmother knows that Nancy's parents physically and sexually abused Nancy before she came to live with her at the age of 5. Might Nancy recall or otherwise be affected by those early traumatic experiences?

3. In the past year, 58-year-old Alan has experienced some lapses in memory. He sometimes forgets where he put his car keys, it can take him a few minutes to recall the name of someone he met on the golf course last week, and it takes him longer to balance his checkbook than it used to. Is Alan showing signs of dementia or normal age-related forgetfulness?

Self-Assessment

In our discussion of memory in adulthood, we discussed a number of study and memory strategies. To evaluate your study skills, complete this self-assessment:

- *My Study Skills*

Health and Well-Being, Parenting, and Education

Build your decision-making skills by trying your hand at the health and well-being, parenting, and education "Scenarios."

CHAPTER

8

Intelligence

The concept of intelligence has generated many controversies, including whether intelligence is more strongly influenced by heredity or by environment, whether there is cultural bias in intelligence testing, and whether intelligence tests are misused. We will explore these controversies, as well as these topics: the extent to which we have a single intelligence or multiple intelligences, the development of intelligence across the life span, and the extremes of intelligence and creativity.

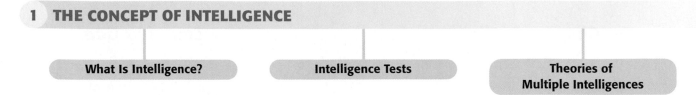

1 THE CONCEPT OF INTELLIGENCE

What Is Intelligence? Intelligence Tests Theories of Multiple Intelligences

Intelligence is one of our most prized possessions. However, intelligence is a concept that even the most intelligent people have not been able to agree on how to define and how to measure.

What Is Intelligence?

What does the term *intelligence* mean to psychologists? Some experts describe intelligence as the ability to solve problems. Others describe it as the capacity to adapt and learn from experience. Still others argue that intelligence includes characteristics such as creativity and interpersonal skills.

The problem with intelligence is that, unlike height, weight, and age, intelligence cannot be directly measured. We can't peel back a person's scalp and see how much intelligence he or she has. We can evaluate intelligence only *indirectly* by studying and comparing the intelligent acts that people perform.

The primary components of intelligence are similar to the cognitive processes of thinking and memory that we discussed in chapter 7 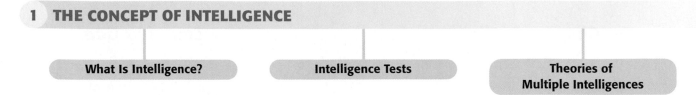 P. 231. The differences in how we described these cognitive processes in chapter 7, and how we will discuss intelligence, lie in the concepts of individual differences and assessment. *Individual differences* are the stable, consistent ways in which people are different from one another. Individual differences in intelligence generally have been measured by intelligence tests designed to tell us whether a person can reason better than others who have taken the test.

Intelligence and personality are the two areas of psychology in which individual differences have mainly been emphasized. As you will see shortly, though, the use of intelligence tests to assess intelligence is controversial. However, we'll temporarily set aside the contentions of psychologists who believe that the conventional intelligence tests are inadequate measures of intelligence and use as our definition of **intelligence** the ability to solve problems and to adapt and learn from experiences.

Intelligence Tests

Robert Sternberg (1997) had considerable childhood anxieties about intelligence tests. Because he got so stressed out about taking the tests, he did very poorly on them. Fortunately, a fourth-grade teacher worked with Robert and helped instill the confidence in him to overcome his anxieties. He not only began performing better on them, but when he was 13, he devised his own intelligence test and began using it to assess classmates—until the school principal found out and scolded him. Sternberg became so fascinated by intelligence that he made its study a lifelong pursuit. Later in this chapter, we will discuss his theory of intelligence.

Individual Tests Early psychologists ignored the "higher mental processes," such as thinking and problem solving, that we equate with intelligence today. Sir Frances

intelligence Thinking skills and the ability to adapt to and learn from life's everyday experiences.

Galton, an English psychologist who is considered the father of mental tests, believed that sensory, perceptual, and motor processes were the key dimensions of intelligence. In the late nineteenth century, he set out to demonstrate that there are systematic individual differences in these processes. Although his research provided few conclusive results, Galton raised many important questions about intelligence—how it should be measured, what its components are, and the degree to which it is inherited—that we continue to study today.

The Binet Tests In 1904 the French Ministry of Education asked psychologist Alfred Binet to devise a method to determine which students would not profit from typical school instruction. Binet and his student Theophile Simon developed an intelligence test to meet this request. The test consisted of 30 items ranging from the ability to touch one's nose or ear when asked to the ability to draw designs from memory and to define abstract concepts.

The Binet tests represented a major advance over earlier efforts to measure intelligence. Binet stressed that the core of intelligence consists of complex cognitive processes, such as memory, imagery, comprehension, and judgment. In addition, he believed that a developmental approach was crucial for understanding intelligence. He proposed that a child's intellectual ability increases with age. Therefore, he tested potential items and determined that age at which a typical child could answer them correctly. Thus, Binet developed the concept of **mental age (MA),** which is an individual's level of mental development relative to others. For an average child, MA scores correspond to *chronological age (CA)*, which is age from birth. A bright child has an MA considerably above CA; a dull child has an MA considerably below CA.

The Binet test has been revised many times to incorporate advances in the understanding of intelligence and intelligence testing. Many revisions were carried out by Lewis Terman, who developed extensive norms and provided detailed, clear instructions for each problem on the test. Terman also applied a concept introduced by William Stern. In 1812, Stern coined the term **intelligence quotient (IQ)** to refer to an individual's mental age divided by chronological age multiplied by 100:

$$IQ = \frac{MA}{CA} \times 100$$

If a child's mental age, as measured by the Binet test, was the same as the child's chronological age, then the child's IQ score would be 100. If the measured mental age was above chronological age, then the IQ score was more than 100. If mental age was below chronological age, the IQ score was less than 100. Although this scoring system is no longer used, the term *IQ* is often still used to refer to a score on a standardized intelligence test.

In 1985, the test, now called the Stanford-Binet (Stanford University is where the revisions were done), was revised to analyze an individual's responses in four content areas: verbal reasoning, quantitative reasoning, abstract/visual reasoning, and short-term memory. A general composite score also is obtained. Today the test is scored by comparing how the test-taker performs compared with other people of the same age. The average score is set at 100.

The current Stanford-Binet is given to individuals from the age of 2 through adulthood. It includes a wide variety of items, some requiring verbal responses, others nonverbal responses. For example, a 6-year-old is expected to complete the verbal task of defining at least six words, such as *orange* and *envelope,* and the nonverbal task of tracing a path through a maze. An adult with average intelligence is expected to define such words as *disproportionate* and *regard,* explain a proverb, and compare the concepts of idleness and laziness.

Over the years, the Stanford-Binet test has been given to thousands of children and adults of different ages. By administering the test to large numbers of individuals selected at random from different parts of the United States, it has been found

Alfred Binet constructed the first intelligence test after being asked to create a measure to determine which children would benefit from instruction in France's schools.

mental age (MA) An individual's level of mental development relative to others.

intelligence quotient (IQ) An individual's mental age divided by chronological age multiplied by 100; devised in 1912 by William Stern.

FIGURE 8.1 The Normal Curve and Stanford-Binet IQ Scores

The distribution of IQ scores approximates a normal curve. Most of the population falls in the middle range of scores, between 84 and 116. Notice that extremely high and extremely low scores are rare. Only about 1 in 50 individuals has an IQ of more than 132 or less than 68.

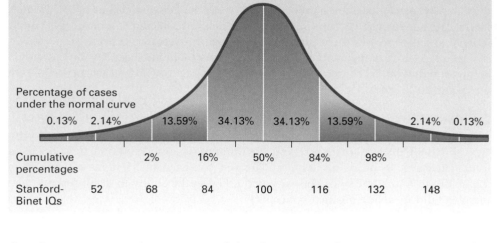

Percentage of cases under the normal curve								
0.13%	2.14%		13.59%	34.13%	34.13%	13.59%		2.14%	0.13%

Cumulative percentages		2%	16%	50%	84%	98%	

Stanford-Binet IQs	52	68	84	100	116	132	148

that the scores approximate a normal distribution (see figure 8.1). A **normal distribution** is a symmetrical, bell-shaped curve with a majority of the cases falling in the middle of the range of possible scores and few scores appearing toward the extremes of the range. The Stanford-Binet continues to be one of the most widely used individual tests of intelligence.

The Wechsler Scales   Besides the Stanford-Binet, the other most widely used intelligence tests are the Wechsler scales, developed by David Wechsler. In 1939, Wechsler introduced the first of his scales, designed for use with adults (Wechsler, 1939). Now in its third edition, the Wechsler Adult Intelligence Scale–III (WAIS-III), was followed by the Wechsler Intelligence Scale for Children–III (WISC-III) for children between the ages of 6 and 16, and the Wechsler Preschool and Primary Scale of Intelligence (WPPSI) for children from the ages of 4 to 6½.

The Wechsler scales not only provide an overall IQ score but also scores on six verbal and five nonverbal measures. This allows the examiner to separate verbal and nonverbal IQ scores and to see quickly the areas in which the individual is below average, average, or above average. The inclusion of a number of nonverbal subscales makes the Wechsler test more representative of verbal and nonverbal intelligence; the Binet test includes some nonverbal items, but not as many as the Wechsler scales. Several of the Wechsler subscales are shown in figure 8.2.

Group Tests   The Stanford-Binet and Wechsler tests are individually administered intelligence tests. The psychologist has an opportunity to sample the behavior of the individual being tested. During testing the psychologist observes the ease with which rapport is established, the energy and enthusiasm of the individual, and the tolerance of frustration and persistence that the individual shows in performing difficult tasks. Each of these observations helps the psychologist understand the individual.

On some occasions, it is necessary to administer group intelligence tests, which are more convenient and economical than individual tests. But group tests have some significant disadvantages. When a test is given to a large group, the examiner cannot establish rapport, determine the level of anxiety, and so on.

Most testing experts recommend that, when important decisions are to be made about an individual, a group intelligence test should be supplemented by other information about the individual's abilities. For example, if a decision is to be made about placing a child in a special education class, it is a legal requirement that the decision not be based on a group intelligence test. The psychologist must administer an individual intelligence test, such as the Stanford-Binet or Wechsler, and obtain extensive information about the child's abilities outside the testing situation.

www.mhhe.com/santrockldt2

David Wechsler

normal distribution A symmetrical distribution with a majority of the cases falling in the middle of the possible range of scores and few scores appearing toward the extremes of the range.

Verbal Subscales

Similarities

A child must think logically and abstractly to answer a number of questions about how things might be similar.

Example: "In what way are a lion and a tiger alike?"

Comprehension

This subscale is designed to measure an individual's judgment and common sense.

Example: "What is the advantage of keeping money in a bank?"

Nonverbal Subscales

Block Design

An child must assemble a set of multicolored blocks to match designs that the examiner shows. Visual-motor coordination, perceptual organization, and the ability to visualize spatially are assessed.

Example: "Use the four blocks on the left to make the pattern on the right."

The Wechsler includes 11 subscales, 6 verbal and 5 nonverbal. Three of the subscales are shown here.

FIGURE 8.2 Sample Subscales of the Wechsler Intelligence Scale for Children (WISC-III)

Simulated items similar to those in the Wechsler Intelligence Scale for Children, Third Edition. Copyright © 1981 by The Psychological Corporation, a Harcourt Assessment Company. Reproduced by permission. All rights reserved. "Wechsler Intelligence Scale for Children" and "WISC-R" are trademarks of The Psychological Corporation registered in the United States of America and/or other jurisdictions.

The Use and Misuse of Intelligence Tests Psychological tests are tools. Like all tools, their effectiveness depends on the knowledge, skill, and integrity of the user. A hammer can be used to build a beautiful kitchen cabinet or it can be used as a weapon of assault. Like a hammer, psychological tests can be used for positive purposes or they can be abused.

Intelligence tests have real-world applications as predictors of school and job success (Brody, 2000). For example, scores on tests of general intelligence are substantially correlated with school grades and achievement test performance, both at the time of the test and years later (Brody, 2000). IQ in the sixth grade correlates about .60 with the number of years of education the individual will eventually obtain (Jencks, 1979).

Intelligence tests are moderately correlated with work performance (Lubinski, 2000). Individuals with higher scores on tests designed to measure general intelligence tend to get higher-paying, more prestigious jobs (Wagner, 1997). However, general IQ tests predict only about one-fourth of the variation in job success, with the majority of job success due to motivation, education, and other factors (Wagner & Sternberg, 1986). Further, the correlations between IQ and achievement decrease the longer people work at a job, presumably because as they gain more job experience they perform better (Hunt, 1995).

Thus, although there are correlations between IQ scores and academic achievement and occupational success, many other factors contribute to success in school and work. These include the motivation to succeed, physical and mental health, and social skills (Sternberg, 2003).

The single number provided by many IQ tests can easily lead to false expectations about an individual (Rosnow & Rosenthal, 1996). Sweeping generalizations are too often made on the basis of an IQ score. For example, imagine that you are a teacher in the teacher's lounge the day after school has started in the fall. You mention a student—Johnny Jones—and a fellow teacher remarks that she had Johnny in class last year; she comments that he was a real dunce and points out that his IQ is 78. You cannot help but remember this information, and it might lead to thoughts that Johnny Jones is not very bright so it is useless to spend much time teaching him. In this way, IQ scores are misused and can become self-fulfilling prophecies (Rosenthal & Jacobsen, 1968).

Intelligence tests can help teachers group children who function at roughly the same level in such subject areas as math or reading so they can be taught the same concepts together. However, extreme caution is necessary when test scores are used to place children in tracks, such as "advanced," "intermediate," and "low." Periodic assessment is required. Intelligence tests measure *current* performance, and maturational changes or enriched experiences may advance a child's intelligence, indicating that he or she should be moved to a higher-level group.

Even though they have limitations, tests of intelligence are among psychology's most widely used tools. To be effective, they should be used in conjunction with other information about an individual. For example, an intelligence test alone should not determine whether a child is placed in a special education or gifted class. The child's developmental history, medical background, performance in school, social competencies, and family experiences should be taken into account too.

Despite their limitations, when used judiciously, intelligence tests provide valuable information. There are not many alternatives to these tests. Subjective judgments about individuals simply reintroduce the bias that the tests were designed to eliminate.

Theories of Multiple Intelligences

The use of a single score to describe how people perform on intelligence tests suggests intelligence is a general ability, a single trait. Wechsler scales provide scores for a number of intellectual skills, as well as an overall score. Do people have some general mental ability that determines how they perform on all of these tests? Or is intelligence a label for a combination of several distinct abilities? And do conventional intelligence tests measure everything that should be considered part of intelligence? Psychologists disagree about the answers to these questions.

Wechsler was not the first psychologist to break down intelligence into a number of abilities. Nor was he the last. A number of contemporary psychologists continue to search for specific components that make up intelligence. Some do not rely on traditional intelligence tests in their conceptualization of intelligence. Let's explore several key alternative conceptions of intelligence, beginning with Wechsler's predecessor, Charles Spearman.

Factor Approaches   Some time before Wechsler analyzed intelligence in terms of general and specific abilities, Charles Spearman (1927) proposed that intelligence has two factors. **Two-factor theory** is Spearman's theory that individuals have both general intelligence, which he called *g,* and a number of specific abilities, or *s.* Spearman believed that these two factors account for a person's performance on an intelligence test. Spearman developed his theory by applying a technique called **factor analysis** to a number of intelligence tests. Factor analysis is a statistical procedure that correlates test scores to identify underlying clusters, or factors.

L. L. Thurstone (1938) also used factor analysis in analyzing a number of intelligence tests, but he concluded that the tests measure only a number of specific factors, and not general intelligence. **Multiple-factor theory** is Thurstone's theory that intelligence consists of seven primary mental abilities: verbal comprehension, number ability, word fluency, spatial visualization, associative memory, reasoning, and perceptual speed.

Gardner's Theory of Multiple Intelligences   Both Spearman and Thurstone relied on traditional types of intelligence tests in their attempts to clarify the nature of intelligence. In contrast, Howard Gardner argues that these tests are far too narrow. Imagine someone who has great musical skills but does not do well in math

two-factor theory Spearman's theory that individuals have both general intelligence, which he called *g,* and a number of specific intelligences, referred to as *s.*

factor analysis A statistical procedure that correlates test scores to identify underlying clusters, or factors.

multiple-factor theory L. L. Thurstone's theory that intelligence consists of seven primary mental abilities: verbal comprehension, number ability, word fluency, spatial visualization, associative memory, reasoning, and perceptual speed.

or English. The famous composer, Ludwig van Beethoven, was just such a person. Would you call Beethoven "unintelligent?" Unlikely!

According to Gardner, people have multiple intelligences, and IQ tests measure only a few of these. These intelligences are independent of each other. For evidence of the existence of multiple intelligences, Gardner uses information about the ways in which certain cognitive abilities survive particular types of brain damage. He also points to child prodigies and to some individuals who are retarded or autistic but have an extraordinary skill in a particular domain. An example was portrayed by Dustin Hoffman in the movie *Rain Man*. Hoffman's character was autistic but had a remarkable computing ability. In one scene, he helped his brother successfully gamble in Las Vegas by keeping track of all the cards that had been played.

From Verbal Intelligence to Naturalist Intelligence   Gardner (1983, 1993, 2001, 2002) has proposed eight types of intelligence. They are described here along with examples of the occupations in which they are reflected as strengths (Campbell, Campbell, & Dickson, 2003):

- *Verbal Skills:* The ability to think in words and use language to express meaning.
  Occupations: Authors, journalists, speakers.
- *Mathematical Skills:* The ability to carry out mathematical operations.
  Occupations: Scientists, engineers, accountants.
- *Spatial Skills:* The ability to think three-dimensionally.
  Occupations: Architects, artists, sailors.
- *Bodily-Kinesthetic Skills:* The ability to manipulate objects and be physically adept.
  Occupations: Surgeons, craftspeople, dancers, athletes.
- *Musical Skills:* A sensitivity to pitch, melody, rhythm, and tone.
  Occupations: Composers, musicians, and sensitive listeners.
- *Interpersonal Skills:* The ability to understand and effectively interact with others.
  Occupations: Successful teachers, mental health professionals.
- *Intrapersonal Skills:* The ability to understand oneself.
  Occupations: Theologians, psychologists.
- *Naturalist Skills:* The ability to observe patterns in nature and understand natural and human-made systems.
  Occupations: Farmers, botanists, ecologists, landscapers.

Gardner believes that each of the eight intelligences can be destroyed by brain damage, that each involves unique cognitive skills, and that each shows up in exaggerated fashion in the gifted and in individuals who have mental retardation or autism. According to Gardner, everyone has all of these intelligences but to varying degrees. As a result, we prefer to learn and process information in different ways. People learn best when they can apply their strong intelligences to the task.

Multiple Intelligences in the Classroom   Currently there is considerable interest in applying Gardner's theory of multiple intelligences to children's education (Kornhaber, Fierros, & Veenema, 2004). The goal is to allow students to discover and then explore the domains in which they have natural curiosity and talent. According to Gardner, if teachers give students opportunities to use their bodies, imaginations, and different senses, almost every student finds that she or he is good at something. Even students who are not outstanding in any single area will find that they have relative strengths. Thus, at the Key School in Indianapolis, each day every student is exposed to materials that are designed to stimulate a range of human abilities, including art, music, language skills, math skills, and physical games. In addition, attention is given to understanding oneself and others. Another Gardner-based program is Project Spectrum (Gardner, 1993). To read about Project Spectrum, see the Applications in Life-Span Development interlude.

If by 2013 [the 30th anniversary of the publication of Gardner's Frames of Mind] there is a wider acceptance of the notion that intelligence deserves to be pluralized, I will be pleased.

—HOWARD GARDNER
Contemporary Psychologist, Harvard University

Multiple Intelligences
Multiple Intelligences Links

Applications in Life-Span Development

Project Spectrum

What is a Spectrum classroom like? Teachers do not try to evoke intelligences directly by using materials that are labeled "spatial" or "verbal." But the classroom has rich and engaging materials that can stimulate a range of intelligences. For example, in a naturalist corner there are biological specimens that students can explore and compare. This area stimulates students' sensory capacities and logical thinking skills. In a storytelling area, students create imaginative tales with stimulating props and design their own storyboards. This area encourages children to use their linguistic, dramatic, and imaginative skills. In a building corner, students can construct a model of their classroom and arrange small-scale photographs of the students and the teachers in their class using spatial and personal skills. In all, the Spectrum classroom has 12 such areas that are designed to bring out students' multiple intelligences.

The Spectrum classroom can identify skills that typically are not tapped in a regular classroom. In one first-grade Spectrum classroom, a boy who was a product of a highly conflicted broken home was at risk for school failure. However, when Project Spectrum was introduced the boy was identified as especially skilled in one area. He was the best student in the class at taking apart and putting together common objects, such as a doorknob and a food grinder. His teacher became encouraged when she found that he possessed this skill and his overall school performance began to improve.

In addition to identifying unexpected strengths in students, Project Spectrum also can pinpoint undetected weaknesses. Gregory, who was especially skilled in math computation and conceptual knowledge, was doing very well in the first grade. However, he performed poorly in a number of Spectrum areas. Gregory did well only in the areas in which he needed to give a correct answer and a person in authority gave it to him. As a result of the Spectrum Project, Gregory's teacher began to search for ways to encourage him to take risks on more open-ended tasks, to try different ways of doing things, and to realize that it is okay to make mistakes.

Student in a Spectrum classroom engaged in a science project. *What combinations of materials might you expect to find in other corners of a Spectrum classroom?*

Sternberg's Triarchic Theory Like Gardner, Robert J. Sternberg (1986, 1999, 2002, 2003) believes that traditional IQ tests fail to measure some important dimensions of intelligence. Sternberg proposes a **triarchic theory of intelligence** with three main types of intelligence: analytical, creative, and practical.

Analytical, Creative, and Practical Intelligence To understand what analytical, creative, and practical intelligence mean, let's look at examples of people who reflect these three types of intelligence:

- Consider Latisha, who scores high on traditional intelligence tests such as the Stanford-Binet and is a star analytical thinker. Sternberg calls Latisha's analytical thinking and abstract reasoning *analytical intelligence*. It is the closest to what has traditionally been called intelligence and what is commonly assessed by intelligence tests. In Sternberg's view of analytical intelligence, the basic unit of analytical intelligence is a *component*, which is a basic unit of information process-

triarchic theory of intelligence Sternberg's theory that intelligence consists of compotential intelligence, experiential intelligence, and contextual intelligence.

ing. Sternberg's components include the ability to acquire or store information; to retain or retrieve information; to transfer information; to plan, make decisions, and solve problems; and to translate thoughts into performance.

- Todd does not have the best test scores but has an insightful and creative mind. The type of thinking at which Todd excels is called *creative intelligence* by Sternberg. According to Sternberg, creative people like Todd have the ability to solve new problems quickly, but they also learn how to solve familiar problems in an automatic way so their minds are free to handle other problems that require insight and creativity.

- Finally, consider Emanuel, a person whose scores on traditional IQ tests are low but who quickly grasps real-life problems. He easily picks up knowledge about how the world works. Emanuel's "street smarts" and practical know-how indicate that he has what Sternberg calls *practical intelligence.* Practical intelligence includes the ability to get out of trouble and a knack for getting along with people. Sternberg describes practical intelligence as all of the important information about getting along in the world that you are not taught in school.

"You're wise, but you lack tree smarts."

Assessing Triarchic Intelligence   Sternberg (1993) developed the Sternberg Triarchic Abilities Test (STAT) that assesses analytical, creative, and practical intelligence. The three kinds of abilities are examined in four different ways: (1) verbal, (2) quantitative, (3) figural multiple-choice items, and (4) essays. The goal is to obtain a more complete assessment of intelligence than is possible with a conventional test.

The memory-analytical section is much like a conventional test with individuals required to provide the meanings of words, complete number series, and complete matrices. The creative and practical sections are much different than conventional tests. For example, in the creative section, individuals are required to write an essay on designing an ideal school. The practical section requires individuals to solve practical everyday problems that involve such matters as planning routes and purchasing tickets to an event.

An increasing number of studies are investigating the effectives of the STAT in predicting such important aspects of life as success in school. For example, in one recent study of 800 college students, scores on the STAT were effective in predicting college grade point average (Sternberg & others, 2001a). However, more research is needed to determine the validity and reliability of the STAT.

Triarchic Theory in the Classroom   Sternberg (1997) says that students with different triarchic patterns look different in school. Students with high analytic ability tend to be favored in conventional schools. They often do well in classes in which the teacher lectures and gives objective tests. They often are considered smart students, typically get good grades, do well on traditional IQ tests and the SAT, and later gain admission to competitive colleges.

Students who are high in creative intelligence often are not in the top rung of their class. Creatively intelligent students might not conform to the expectations that teachers have about how assignments should be done. They give unique answers, for which they might get reprimanded or marked down.

Like students high in creative intelligence, students who are practically intelligent often do not relate well to the demands of school. However, these students frequently do well outside the classroom's walls. Their social skills and common sense may allow them to become successful managers, entrepreneurs, or politicians, despite undistinguished school records.

Sternberg's Theory

Middle and Later Childhood; Young Brazilian Street Vendor's Math Skills

Gardner	Sternberg	Salovey/Mayer
Verbal Mathematical	Analytical	
Spatial Movement Musical	Creative	
Interpersonal Intrapersonal	Practical	Emotional
Naturalistic		

FIGURE 8.3 Comparing Gardner's, Sternberg's, and Salovey/Mayer's Intelligences

Sternberg (1999) believes that few tasks are purely analytic, creative, or practical. Most tasks require some combination of these skills. For example, when students write a book report, they might (1) analyze the book's main themes, (2) generate new ideas about how the book could have been written better, and (3) think about how the book's themes can be applied to people's lives. Sternberg argues that it is important for classroom instruction to give students opportunities to learn through all three types of intelligence.

Emotional Intelligence   Both Gardner's and Sternberg's theories include one or more categories related to social intelligence. In Gardner's theory, the categories are interpersonal intelligence and intrapersonal intelligence; in Sternberg's theory, practical intelligence. Another theory that emphasizes interpersonal, intrapersonal, and practical aspects of intelligence is called **emotional intelligence,** which has been popularized by Daniel Goleman (1995) in his book *Emotional Intelligence.* The concept of emotional intelligence was initially developed by Peter Salovey and John Mayer (1990), who define it as the ability to perceive and express emotion accurately and adaptively (such as taking the perspective of others), to understand emotion and emotional knowledge (such as understanding the roles that emotions play in friendship and marriage), to use feelings to facilitate thought (such as being in a positive mood, which is linked to creative thinking), and to manage emotions in oneself and others (such as being able to control one's anger).

Recently, the Mayer-Salovey-Caruso Emotional Intelligence Test (MSCEIT) was developed to measure the four aspects of emotional intelligence just described: perceiving emotions, understanding emotions, facilitating thought, and managing emotions (Mayer, Salovey, & Caruso, 2002). The test consists of 141 items, can be given to individuals 17 years of age and older, and takes about 30 to 45 minutes to administer. Because the MSCEIT has only been available since 2001, there are few studies that have been conducted to examine its ability to predict outcomes (Salovey & Pizarro, 2003). One recent study that used the MSCEIT found that youths with higher emotional intelligence were less likely to have smoked cigarettes or to have used alcohol (Trinidad & Johnson, 2002).

Do People Have One Intelligence or Many Intelligences?   Figure 8.3 provides a comparison of Gardner's, Sternberg's, and Mayer/Salovey's views. Notice that Gardner includes a number of types of intelligence that are not addressed by the other views and that Sternberg is unique in emphasizing creative intelligence. These theories of multiple intelligence have much to offer. They have stimulated us to think more broadly about what makes up people's intelligence and competence. And they have motivated educators to develop programs that instruct students in different domains.

Theories of multiple intelligences also have many critics. Many argue that the research base to support these theories has not yet developed. In particular, some critics say that Gardner's classification seems arbitrary. For example, if musical skills represent a type of intelligence, why don't we also refer to chess intelligence, prizefighter intelligence, and so on?

A number of psychologists still support Spearman's concept of *g* (general intelligence). For example, one expert on intelligence, Nathan Brody (2000) argues that people who excel at one type of intellectual task are likely to excel in other intellectual tasks. Thus, individuals who do well at memorizing lists of digits are also likely to be good at solving verbal problems and spatial layout problems. This general intelligence includes abstract reasoning or thinking, the capacity to acquire knowledge, and problem-solving ability (Brody, 2000; Carroll, 1993).

emotional intelligence The ability to perceive and express emotions accurately and adaptively, to understand emotion and emotional knowledge, to use feelings to facilitate thought, and to manage emotions in oneself and others.

Some experts who argue for the existence of general intelligence believe that individuals also have specific intellectual abilities (Brody, 2000). In one study, John Carroll (1993) conducted an extensive examination of intellectual abilities and concluded that all intellectual abilities are related to each other, which supports the concept of general intelligence, but that there are many specialized abilities as well. Some of these specialized abilities, such as spatial abilities and mechanical abilities, are not adequately reflected in the curriculum of most schools.

Review and Reflect: Learning Goal 1

1 **Explain the nature of intelligence**

REVIEW

- What is intelligence?
- What are the main individual tests of intelligence? What are some issues in the use of group tests of intelligence?
- What theories of multiple intelligence have been developed? Do people have one intelligence or many intelligences? What are some criticisms of the multiple intelligences concept?

REFLECT

- A CD-ROM is being sold to parents for testing their child's IQ. What are some potential problems with parents giving their child an IQ test and interpreting the results?

---

2 CONTROVERSIES AND GROUP COMPARISONS

The Influence of Heredity and Environment

Group Comparisons and Issues

We have seen that intelligence is a slippery concept with competing definitions, tests, and theories. It is not surprising, therefore, that attempts to understand the concept of intelligence are filled with controversy. In some cases, the controversies involve comparisons of the intelligence of different groups, such as people from different cultures or ethnic groups.

The Influence of Heredity and Environment

One of the hottest areas in the study of intelligence centers on the extent to which intelligence is influenced by genetics and the extent to which it is influenced by environment. In chapter 2, we indicated how difficult it is to tease apart these influences, but that has not kept psychologists from trying to unravel them.

Genetic Influences The issue with respect to genetics and intelligence is the degree to which our genes make us smart (Petrill, 2003). At one end of the debate, Arthur Jensen (1969) argued that intelligence is primarily inherited and that environment plays only a minimal role in intelligence. Jensen reviewed the research on intelligence, much of which involved comparisons of identical and fraternal twins, and which also used IQ as the indicator of intelligence. Identical twins have exactly the same genetic makeup; if intelligence is genetically determined, Jensen reasoned, identical twins' IQs should be more similar than the intelligence of fraternal twins.

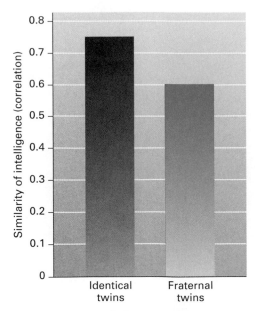

FIGURE 8.4 Correlation Between Intelligence Test Scores and Twin Status
The graph represents a summary of research findings that have compared the intelligence test scores of identical and fraternal twins. An approximate .15 difference has been found, with a higher correlation (.75) for identical twins and a lower correlation (.60) for fraternal twins.

The studies on intelligence in identical twins that Jensen examined showed an average correlation of .82, a very high positive association. Investigations of fraternal twins, however, produced an average correlation of .50, a moderately high positive correlation. A difference of .32 is substantial. However, a more recent research review that included many studies conducted since Jenson's original review found that the difference in intelligence between identical and fraternal twins was .15, substantially less than what Jensen found (Grigorenko, 2000) (see figure 8.4).

Jensen also compared the correlation of IQ scores for identical twins reared together with those reared apart. The correlation for those reared together was .89, and for those reared apart was .78, a difference of .11. Jensen argued that if environmental factors were more important than genetic factors, the difference should have been greater.

Adoption studies have been inconclusive about the relative importance of heredity in intelligence. In most *adoption studies,* researchers determine whether the behavior of adopted children is more like that of their biological parents or their adopted parents. In one study, the educational levels attained by biological parents were better predictors of children's IQ scores than were the IQs of the children's adopted parents (Scarr & Weinberg, 1983). Because of the stronger genetic link between the adopted children and their biological parents, the implication is that heredity is more important than environment. Environmental effects also have been found in studies of adoption. For example, moving children into an adopted family with a better environment than the child had in the past increased the children's IQs by an average of 12 points (Lucurto, 1990).

How strong is the effect of heredity on intelligence? The concept of heritability attempts to tease apart the effects of heredity and environment in a population. **Heritability** is the fraction of the variance in a population that is attributed to genetics. The heritability index is computed using correlational techniques. Thus, the highest degree of heritabilty is 1.00 and correlations of .70 and above suggest a strong genetic influence. A committee of respected researchers convened by the American Psychological Association concluded that by late adolescence, the heritability of intelligence is about .75, which reflects a strong genetic influence (Neisser & others, 1996).

An important point to keep in mind about heritability is that it refers to a specific group (population), *not* to individuals. Researchers use the concept of heritability to try to describe why people differ. Heritability says nothing about why a single individual, like yourself, has a certain intelligence; nor does it say anything about differences *between* groups.

Most research on heredity and environment does not include environments that differ radically. Thus, it is not surprising that many genetic studies show environment to be a fairly weak influence on intelligence (Fraser, 1995).

Interestingly, researchers have found that the heritability of intelligence increases from as low as .45 in infancy to as high as .80 in late adulthood (McGue & others, 1993; Petrill, 2003; Plomin & others, 1997). Why might hereditary influences on intelligence increase with age? Possibly as we grow older, our interactions with the environment are shaped less by the influence of others and the environment on us and more by our ability to choose our environments to allow the expression of genetic tendencies (Neisser & others, 1996). For example, sometimes children's parents push them into environments that are not compatible with their genetic inheritance (wanting to be a doctor or an engineer, for example), but as adults these individuals may select their own career environments.

The heritability index has several flaws. It is only as good as the data that are entered into its analysis and the interpretations made from it. The data are virtually all from traditional IQ tests, which some experts believe are not always the best indicator of intelligence (Gardner, 2002; Sternberg, 2002). Also, the heritability index assumes that we can treat genetic and environmental influences as factors that can be separated, with each part contributing a distinct amount of influence.

heritability The fraction of the variance in a population that is attributed to genetics.

As we discussed in chapter 2, genes and the environment always work together. Genes always exist in an environment, and the environment shapes their activity.

Environmental Influences   Today, most researchers agree that heredity does not determine intelligence to the extent Jensen claimed (Ceci, 1996; Grigorenko, 2000). For most people, this means modifications in environment can change their IQ scores considerably (Campbell & others, 2001). Although genetic endowment may always influence a person's intellectual ability, the environmental influences and opportunities we provide children and adults do make a difference.

In one study, researchers went into homes and observed how extensively parents from welfare and middle-income professional families talked and communicated with their young children (Hart & Risley, 1995). They found that the middle-income professional parents were much more likely to communicate with their young children than the welfare parents were. And how much the parents communicated with their children in the first three years of their lives was correlated with the children's Stanford-Binet IQ scores at age 3. The more parents communicated with their children, the higher the children's IQs were. Other studies also have found substantial socioeconomic status differences in intelligence (Seifer, 2001).

Schooling also influences intelligence (Ceci & Gilstrap, 2000; Christian, Bachnan, & Morrison, 2001). The biggest effects have been found when large groups of children have been deprived of formal education for an extended period, resulting in lower intelligence. One study examined the intellectual functioning of Indian children in South Africa whose schooling was delayed for four years because of the unavailability of teachers (Ramphal, 1962). Compared with children in nearby villages who had teachers, the Indian children whose entry into school was delayed by four years experienced a decrement of 5 IQ points for every year of delay.

Another possible effect of education can be seen in rapidly increasing IQ test scores around the world (Flynn, 1999). IQ scores have been increasing so fast that a high percentage of people regarded as having average intelligence at the turn of the last century would be considered below average in intelligence today (Howard, 2001) (see figure 8.5). If a representative sample of people today took the Stanford-Binet test used in 1932, about one-fourth would be defined as having very superior intelligence, a label usually accorded to fewer than 3 percent of the population (Horton, 2001). Because the increase has taken place in a relatively short time, it can't be due to heredity, but rather may be due to increasing levels of education attained by a much greater percentage of the world's population or to other environmental factors such as the explosion of information to which people are exposed. The worldwide

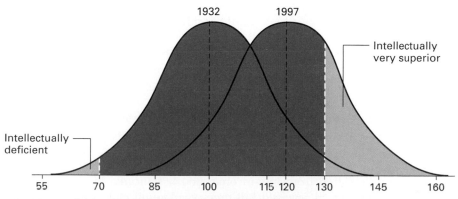

FIGURE 8.5 The Increase in IQ Scores from 1932 to 1997

As measured by the Stanford-Binet intelligence test, American children seem to be getting smarter. Scores of a group tested in 1932 fell along a bell-shaped curve with half below 100 and half above. Studies show that if children took that same test today, half would score above 120 on the 1932 scale. Very few of them would score in the "intellectually deficient" end, on the left side, and about one-fourth would rank in the "very superior" range.

increase in intelligence test scores that has occurred over a short time frame has been called the *Flynn effect,* after the researcher who discovered it—James Flynn.

Keep in mind that environmental influences are complex (Neisser & others, 1996; Sternberg, 2001) ◀◀◀ P. 64. Growing up with all the "advantages," for example, does not guarantee success. Children from wealthy families may have easy access to excellent schools, books, travel, and tutoring, but they may take such opportunities for granted and fail to develop the motivation to learn and to achieve. In the same way, "poor" or "disadvantaged" does not automatically equal "doomed."

Researchers increasingly are interested in manipulating the early environment of children who are at risk for impoverished intelligence (Ramey, Ramey, & Lanzi, 2001; Sternberg & Grigorenko, 2001). The emphasis is on prevention rather than remediation. Many low-income parents have difficulty providing an intellectually stimulating environment for their children. Programs that educate parents to be more sensitive caregivers and better teachers, as well as support services such as quality child-care programs, can make a difference in a child's intellectual development.

A recent review of the research on early interventions concluded that (1) high-quality center-based interventions (such as the Abcedarian Project) improve children's intelligence and school achievement; (2) the effects are strongest for poor children and for children whose parents have little education; (3) the positive benefits continue into the late middle and late childhood, and adolescence, although the effects are smaller than in early childhood or the beginning of elementary school; and (4) the programs that are continued into elementary school have the most sustained long-term effects (Brooks-Gunn, 2003). To read further about environmental influences on intelligence, see the Research in Life-Span Development interlude.

Research in Life-Span Development
The Abecedarian Project

> *T*he highest-risk children often benefit the most cognitively when they experience early interventions.
>
> —CRAIG RAMEY
> *Contemporary Psychologist,*
> *University of Alabama–Birmingham*

Each morning a young mother waited with her child for the bus that would take the child to school. The child was only 2 months old, and "school" was an experimental program at the University of North Carolina at Chapel Hill. There the child experienced a number of interventions designed to improve her intellectual development—everything from bright objects dangled in front of her eyes while she was a baby to language instruction and counting activities when she was a toddler (Wickelgren, 1999). The child's mother had an IQ of 40 and could not read signs or determine how much change she should receive from a cashier. Her grandmother had a similarly low IQ.

Today, at age 20, the child's IQ measures 80 points higher than her mother's did when the child was 2 months old. Not everyone agrees that IQ can be affected this extensively, but environment can make a substantial difference in a child's intelligence. As behavior geneticist Robert Plomin (1999) says, even something that is highly heritable (like intelligence) may be malleable through interventions.

The child we just described was part of the Abecedarian Intervention program at the University of North Carolina at Chapel Hill conducted by Craig Ramey and his associates (Ramey & Campbell, 1984; Ramey & Ramey, 1998). They randomly assigned 111 young children from low-income, poorly educated families to either an intervention group, which received full-time, year-round child care along with medical and social work services, or a control group, which received medical and social benefits but no child care. The child-care program included gamelike learning activities aimed at improving language, motor, social, and cognitive skills.

The success of the program in improving IQ was evident by the time the children were 3 years of age. At that age, the experimental group showed normal IQs averaging 101, a 17-point advantage over the control group. Recent follow-up results suggest that the effects are long-lasting. More than a decade later, at 15, children from the intervention group still maintained an IQ advantage of 5 points over the control-group children (97.7 to 92.6) (Campbell & others, 2001; Ramey, Ramey, & Lanzi, 2001). They also did better on standardized tests of reading and math, and were less likely to be held back a year in school. Also, the greatest IQ gains were made by the children whose mothers had especially low IQs—below 70. At age 15, these children showed a 10-point IQ advantage over a group of children whose mothers' IQs were below 70 but did not experience the child-care intervention.

Group Comparisons and Issues

Among the ways that group comparisons in intelligence can be made involve cultures, ethnic groups, and gender.

Cross-Cultural Comparisons

Cultures vary in the way they describe what it means to be intelligent (Benson, 2003; Greenfield, Keller, & Fulgini, 2003). People in Western cultures tend to view intelligence in terms of reasoning and thinking skills while people in Eastern cultures see intelligence as a way for members of a community to successfully engage in social roles (Nisbett, 2003). One study found that Taiwanese-Chinese conceptions of intelligence emphasize understanding and relating to others, including when to show and when not to show one's intelligence (Yang & Sternberg, 1997).

Robert Serpell (1974, 1982, 2000) has studied concepts of intelligence in rural African communities since the 1970s. He has found that people in rural African communities, especially those in which Western schooling is not common, tend to blur the distinction between being intelligent and being socially competent. In rural Zambia, for example, the concept of intelligence involves being both clever and responsible. Elena Grigorenko and her colleagues (2001) have also studied the concept of intelligence among rural Africans. They found that people in the Luo culture of rural Kenya view intelligence as consisting of four domains: (1) academic intelligence; (2) social qualities such as respect, responsibility, and consideration; (3) practical thinking; and (4) comprehension. In another study in the same culture, children who scored highly on a test of knowledge about medicinal herbs—a measure of practical intelligence—tended to score poorly on tests of academic intelligence (Sternberg & others, 2001b). These results indicated that practical and academic intelligence can develop independently and may even conflict with each other. They also suggest that the values of a culture may influence the direction in which a child develops. In a cross-cultural context, then, intelligence depends a great deal on environment.

Cultural Bias in Testing

Many of the early intelligence tests were culturally biased, favoring people who were from urban rather than rural environments, middle-socioeconomic status rather than low-socioeconomic status, and White rather than African American (Miller-Jones, 1989; Provenzo, 2002; Watras, 2002). For example, one question on an early test asked what you should do if you find a 3-year-old child in the street. The correct answer was "call the police." But children from inner-city families who perceive the police as adversaries are unlikely to choose this answer. Similarly, children from rural areas might not choose this answer if there is no police force nearby. Such questions clearly do not measure the knowledge necessary to adapt to one's environment or to be "intelligent" in an

"You can't build a hut, you don't know how to find edible roots and you know nothing about predicting the weather. In other words, you do terribly on our I.Q. test."

© 1992 by Sidney Harris. Reprinted with permission.

inner-city neighborhood or in rural America (Scarr, 1984). Also, members of minority groups who do not speak English or who speak nonstandard English are at a disadvantage in trying to understand questions framed in standard English (Gibbs & Huang, 1989). The Contexts of Life-Span Development interlude examines some of the ways intelligence testing can be culturally biased.

Contexts of Life-Span Development

Larry P.: Intelligent, But Not on Intelligence Tests

Larry P. is African American and poor. When he was 6 years old, he was placed in a class for the "educable mentally retarded" (EMR), which to school psychologists means that Larry learned much more slowly than average children. The primary reason Larry was placed in the EMR class was his very low score of 64 on an intelligence test.

Is there a possibility that the intelligence test Larry was given was culturally biased? Psychologists still debate this issue. A major class-action suit challenged the use of standardized IQ tests to place African American elementary school students in EMR classes. The initial lawsuit, filed on behalf of Larry P., claimed that the IQ test he took underestimated his true learning ability. The lawyers for Larry P. argued that IQ tests place too much emphasis on verbal skills and fail to account for the backgrounds of African American children. Therefore, it was argued, Larry was incorrectly labeled mentally retarded and might forever be saddled with that stigma.

As part of the lengthy court battle involving Larry P., six African American EMR students were independently retested by members of the Bay Association of Black Psychologists in California. The psychologists made sure they established good rapport with the students and made special efforts to overcome the students' defeatism and distraction. For example, items were rewarded in terms more consistent with the children's social background, and recognition was given to nonstandard answers that showed a logical, intelligent approach to problems. This testing approach produced scores of 79 to 104—17 to 38 points higher than the scores the students received when initially tested by school psychologists. In every case, the retest scores were above the ceiling for placement in an EMR class.

What was the state's argument for using intelligence tests as one criterion for placing children in EMR classes? Testimony by intelligence testing experts supported the *predictive validity* (using a measure, such as an intelligence test, to predict performance on another measure, such as grades in school) of IQ for different ethnic groups. In Larry's case, the judge ruled that IQ tests are biased and that their use discriminates against ethnic minorities. IQ tests cannot be used now in California to place children in EMR classes. The decision in favor of Larry P. was upheld by an appeals panel. However, in another court case, *Pace v. Hannon* in Illinois, a judge ruled that IQ tests are not culturally biased.

A specific case illustrating how cultural bias in intelligence tests can affect people is that of Gregory Ochoa. When Gregory was a high school student, he and his classmates took an IQ test. Gregory understood only a few words on the test because he did not speak English very well and spoke Spanish at home. Several weeks later, Gregory was placed in a special class for mentally retarded students. Many of the students in the class, it turns out, had last names such as Ramirez and Gonzales. Gregory lost interest in school, dropped out, and eventually joined the Navy. In the

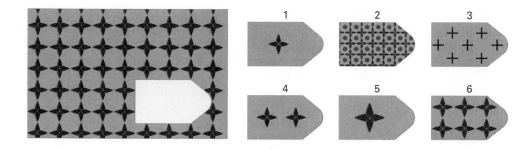

FIGURE 8.6 Sample Item from the Raven Progressive Matrices Test
Individuals are presented with a matrix arrangement of symbols, such as the one at the left of this figure, and must then complete the matrix by selecting the appropriate missing symbol from a group of symbols.

Navy, Gregory took high school courses and earned enough credits to attend college later. He graduated from San Jose City College as an honor student, continued his education, and became a professor of social work at the University of Washington in Seattle.

As a result of cases like Gregory Ochoa's, researchers have developed **culture-fair tests,** which are intelligence tests that are intended not to be culturally biased. Two types of culture-fair tests have been developed. The first includes questions that are familiar to people from all socioeconomic and ethnic backgrounds. For example, a child might be asked how a bird and a dog are different, on the assumption that virtually all children are familiar with birds and dogs. The second type of culture-fair test contains no verbal questions. Figure 8.6 shows a sample question from the Raven Progressive Matrices Test. Even though tests such as the Raven Progressive Matrices are designed to be culture-fair, people with more education still score higher than those with less education do (Greenfield, 2003).

Why is it so hard to create culture-fair tests? Most tests tend to reflect what the dominant culture thinks is important (Aiken, 2003; Greenfield & others, 2003). If tests have time limits, that will bias the test against groups not concerned with time. If languages differ, the same words might have different meanings for different language groups. Even pictures can produce bias because some cultures have less experience than others with drawings and photographs (Anastasi & Urbina, 1996). Within the same culture, different groups could have different attitudes, values, and motivation, and this could affect their performance on intelligence tests. Items that ask why buildings should be made of brick are biased against children who have little or no experience with brick houses. Questions about railroads, furnaces, seasons of the year, distances between cities, and so on can be biased against groups who have less experience than others with these contexts.

Cultural Bias and Testing

Ethnic Comparisons Comparisons of the IQ scores of ethnic groups were at the heart of the controversy that erupted in response to the book *The Bell Curve: Intelligence and Class Structure in American Life* (1994) by Richard Herrnstein and Charles Murray. Recall that the bell curve is the shape of a normal distribution graph, which represents large numbers of people who are sorted according to some shared characteristic, such as weight, taste in clothes, or IQ. Herrnstein and Murray note that predictions about any individual based exclusively on the person's IQ are virtually useless. Weak correlations between IQ and job success have predictive value only when they are applied to large groups of people. But within large groups, say Herrnstein and Murray, the pervasive influence of IQ on human society becomes apparent. The authors argued that America is developing a huge underclass of intellectually deprived individuals whose cognitive abilities will never match the future needs of most employers. They believe that this underclass, a large proportion of which is African American, may be doomed by their shortcomings to welfare dependency, poverty, and crime.

Significant criticisms have been leveled at *The Bell Curve*. The average score of African Americans is lower than the average score of Whites on IQ tests. On the average, African American schoolchildren score 10 to 15 points lower on standardized

culture-fair tests Intelligence tests that are intended to not be culturally biased.

intelligence tests than White American schoolchildren do (Brody, 2000; Lynn, 1996). These are *average scores*, however. About 15 to 25 percent of African American schoolchildren score higher than half of White schoolchildren do, and many Whites score lower than most African Americans. The reason is that the distribution of scores for African Americans and Whites overlap.

As African Americans have gained social, economic, and educational opportunities, the gap between African Americans and Whites on standardized intelligence tests has begun to narrow (Ogbu & Stern, 2001; Onwuegbuzi & Daley, 2001). This gap especially narrows in college, where African American and White students often experience more similar environments than in the elementary and high school years (Myerson & others, 1998). Also, when children from disadvantaged African American families are adopted into more-advantaged middle-socioeconomic status families, their scores on intelligence tests more closely resemble national averages for middle-socioeconomic status children than for lower-socioeconomic status children (Scarr & Weinberg, 1983).

Furthermore, as we have discussed, many experts raise serious questions about the ability of IQ tests to accurately measure a person's intelligence. One potential influence on intelligence test performance is **stereotype threat,** the anxiety that one's behavior might confirm a negative stereotype about one's group. For example, when African Americans take an intelligence test, they may experience anxiety about confirming the old stereotype that Blacks are "intellectually inferior." In one study, the verbal part of the Graduate Record Exam was given individually to African American and White students at Stanford University (Steele & Aronson, 1995). Half the students of each ethnic group were told that the researchers were interested in assessing their intellectual ability. The other half were told that the researchers were trying to develop a test and that it might not be reliable and valid (therefore, it would not mean anything in relation to their intellectual ability). The White students did equally well on the test in both conditions. However, the African American students did more poorly when they thought the test was assessing their intellectual ability. When they thought the test was just in the development stage and might not be reliable or valid, the African American students performed as well as the White students.

Other studies have confirmed the existence of stereotype threat. African American students do more poorly on standardized tests if they believe they are being evaluated. If they believe the test doesn't count, they perform as well as White students (Aronson, 2002; Aronson & others, 1999; Aronson, Fried, & Good, 2002). However, some critics believe the extent to which stereotype threat explains the testing gap has been exaggerated (Sackett, 2003).

Gender Comparisons The average scores of males and females do not differ on intelligence tests, but variability in their scores does differ (Brody, 2000). For example, males are more likely than females to have extremely high or extremely low scores.

There also are gender differences in specific intellectual abilities (Brody, 2000). Males score better than females in some nonverbal areas, such as spatial reasoning, and females score better than males in some verbal areas, such as the ability to find synonyms for words. However, there often is extensive overlap in the scores of females and males in these areas, and there is debate about just how strong the differences are (Brabeck & Shore, 2003; Hyde & Mezulis, 2001).

stereotype threat The anxiety that one's behavior might confirm a negative stereotype about one's group.

Review and Reflect: Learning Goal 2

2 Outline key controversies about differences in IQ scores

REVIEW

- What evidence suggests that genetics influences IQ scores? What evidence suggests that the environment influences IQ scores?

- What do IQ tests tell us about intelligence among people in different cultures and ethnic groups? What do IQ tests tell us about the intelligence of males and females?

REFLECT

- Do you think your performance on standardized tests has provided an accurate reflection of your intelligence?

3 THE DEVELOPMENT OF INTELLIGENCE

| Tests of Infant Intelligence | Stability and Change in Intelligence Through Adolescence | Intelligence in Adulthood |

How can the intelligence of infants be assessed? Is intelligence stable through childhood? Does intelligence decline in older adults and, if so, how much and when? These are some of the questions we will explore as we examine the development of intelligence.

Tests of Infant Intelligence

The infant-testing movement grew out of the tradition of IQ testing. However, tests that assess infants are necessarily less verbal than IQ tests for older children. Tests for infants contain far more items related to perceptual-motor development. They also include measures of social interaction.

The most important early contributor to the testing of infants was Arnold Gesell (1934). He developed a measure that helped sort out potentially normal babies from abnormal ones. This was especially useful to adoption agencies, which had large numbers of babies awaiting placement. Gesell's examination was used widely for many years and still is frequently employed by pediatricians to distinguish normal and abnormal infants. The current version of the Gesell test has four categories of behavior: motor, language, adaptive, and personal-social. The **developmental quotient (DQ)** combines subscores in these categories to provide an overall score.

The **Bayley Scales of Infant Development** are widely used in assessing infant development. They have three components: a mental scale, a motor scale, and the infant behavior profile. Initially created by Nancy Bayley (1969), the second edition of the Bayley Scales was recently developed (Black & Matula, 1999). What do they measure? On the Bayley mental scale, for example, the 6-month-old infant should be able to vocalize pleasure and displeasure, persistently search for objects that are just out of immediate reach, and approach a mirror that is placed in front of the infant. By 12 months of age, the infant should be able to inhibit behavior when commanded to do so, imitate words the examiner says (such as *Mama*), and respond to simple requests (such as "Take a drink").

Among the uses of the Bayley scales are the diagnosis of developmental delays and the planning of intervention strategies. The Bayley scales can be used to assess infants from 1 to 42 months of age.

Overall scores on such tests as the Gesell and the Bayley scales do not correlate highly with IQ scores obtained later in childhood. In one study conducted by Nancy Bayley, no relation was found between the Bayley scales and intelligence as measured by the Stanford-Binet at the ages of 6 and 7 (Bayley, 1943). This is not surprising: Remember that the components tested in infancy are not the same as the components tested by IQ tests.

www.mhhe.com/santrockldt2

Bayley Scales of Infant Development (2nd ed.)

developmental quotient (DQ) An overall developmental score that combines subscores on motor, language, adaptive, and personal-social domains in the Gesell assessment of infants.

Bayley Scales of Infant Development Developed by Nancy Bayley, these scales are widely used in assessing infant development. The current version has three parts: a Mental Scale, a Motor Scale, and the Infant Behavior Profile.

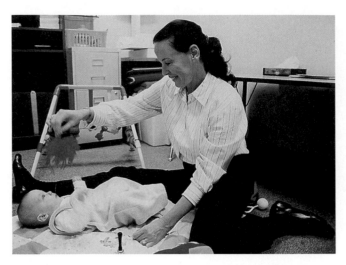

Toosje Thyssen Van Beveren, conducting an infant assessment. Van Beveren is a developmental psychologist at the University of Texas Medical Center in Dallas. Her main current work involves a program called "New Connections," a 12-week program for infants who have been affected by substance abuse prenatally and for their caregivers. Van Beveren conducts assessments of infants' developmental status and progress, identifying delays and deficits.

The explosion of interest in infant development has produced many new measures, especially tasks that evaluate the ways infants process information (Rose, Feldman, & Wallace, 1992). The Fagan Test of Infant Intelligence is increasingly being used (Fagan, 1992). This test focuses on the infant's ability to process information in such ways as encoding the attributes of objects, detecting similarities and differences between objects, forming mental representations, and retrieving these representations. For example, it uses the amount of time babies look at a new object compared with the amount of time they spend looking at a familiar object to estimate their intelligence.

The Fagan Test of Infant Intelligence elicits similar performances from infants in different cultures and, unlike the Gesell and Bayley scales, is correlated with measures of intelligence in older children. In fact, evidence is accumulating that measures of habituation and dishabituation predict intelligence in childhood (Bornstein & Sigman, 1986; DiLalla, 2000; Sigman, Cohen, & Beckwith, 2000). Recall from our discussion in chapter 7 that *habituation* is reduced responsiveness to a stimulus after repeated presentations of the stimuli and *dishabituation* is recovery of a habituated response after a change in stimulation P. 237. Quicker habituation and greater amounts of looking in dishabituation reflect more efficient information processing. When measured in the first six months of infancy, both are related to higher IQ scores on tests given at various times between infancy and adolescence.

Stability and Change in Intelligence Through Adolescence

One study examined correlations between the IQs of children at a number of different ages (Honzik, MacFarlane, & Allen, 1948). There was a strong relation between IQ scores obtained at the ages of 6, 8, and 9 and IQ scores obtained at the age of 10. For example, the correlation between IQ at the age of 8 and IQ at the age of 10 was .88. The correlation between IQ at the age of 9 and IQ at the age of 10 was .90. These figures show a very high relation between IQ scores obtained in these years. The correlation between IQ in the preadolescent years and IQ at the age of 18 was slightly less but still statistically significant. For example, the correlation between IQ at the age of 10 and IQ at the age of 18 was .70.

What has been said so far about the stability of intelligence has been based on measures of *groups* of individuals. The stability of intelligence also can be evaluated through studies of individuals. Robert McCall and his associates (McCall, Applebaum, & Hogarty, 1973) studied 140 children between the ages of 2½ and 17. They found that the average range of IQ scores was more than 28 points. The scores of one out of three children changed by as much as 40 points.

What can we conclude about the stability and change of intelligence in childhood? Intelligence test scores can fluctuate dramatically across the childhood years. Intelligence is not as stable as the original intelligence theorists envisioned. Children are adaptive beings. They have the capacity for intellectual change but they do not become entirely new intelligent beings. In a sense, children's intelligence changes but has connections to early points in development.

Intelligence in Adulthood

Does intelligence increase or decrease in adulthood? Might older adults have greater wisdom than younger adults? These are among the questions that we will explore in this section.

Early Adulthood: Fluid and Crystallized Intelligence

Fluid and Crystallized Intelligence John Horn believes that some abilities increase throughout the life span while others steadily decline from middle adulthood on (Horn & Donaldson, 1980). Horn argues that **crystallized intelligence,** an individual's accumulated information and verbal skills, continues to increase throughout the life span. However, he believes that **fluid intelligence,** the ability to reason abstractly, begins to decline in middle adulthood (see figure 8.7).

Horn's data were collected in a cross-sectional manner. Remember from chapter 1 that a *cross-sectional study* assesses individuals of different ages at the same point in time ◀▥ **P. 37.** For example, a cross-sectional study might assess the intelligence of groups of 40-, 50-, and 60-year-olds in one evaluation, such as in 1990. The average 40-year-old and the average 60-year-old were born in different eras, which offered different economic and educational opportunities. For example, as the 60-year-olds grew up they likely had fewer educational opportunities, which probably influenced their scores on intelligence tests. Thus, if we find differences between 40- and 60-year-olds on intelligence tests when they are assessed cross-sectionally, these differences might be due to *cohort effects* (due to an individual's time of birth or generation but not to age) related to educational differences rather than to age.

In contrast, in a *longitudinal study*, the same individuals are studied over a period of time. Thus, a longitudinal study of intelligence in middle adulthood might consist of giving the same intelligence test to the same individuals when they are 40, when they are 50, and when they are 60 years of age. Whether data are collected cross-sectionally or longitudinally makes a difference in what is found about intellectual decline.

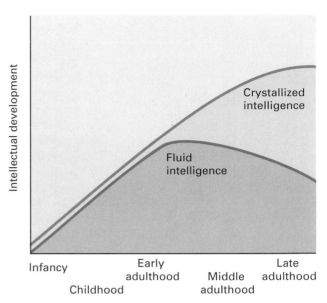

FIGURE 8.7 Fluid and Crystallized Intellectual Development Across the Life Span

According to Horn, crystallized intelligence (based on cumulative learning experiences) increases throughout the life span, but fluid intelligence (the ability to perceive and manipulate information) steadily declines from middle adulthood.

The Seattle Longitudinal Study K. Warner Schaie (1983, 1996, 2000) is conducting an extensive study of intellectual abilities in the adulthood years. Five hundred individuals initially were tested in 1956. New waves of participants are added periodically. The main mental abilities tested in the Seattle Longitudinal Study are:

- *Vocabulary* (ability to understand ideas expressed in words)
- *Verbal memory* (ability to encode and recall meaningful language units, such as a list of words)
- *Number* (ability to perform simple mathematical computations such as addition, subtraction, and multiplication)
- *Spatial orientation* (ability to visualize and mentally rotate stimuli in two- and three-dimensional space)
- *Inductive reasoning* (ability to recognize and understand patterns and relationships in a problem and use this understanding to solve other instances of the problem)
- *Perceptual speed* (ability to quickly and accurately make simple discriminations in visual stimuli)

As shown in figure 8.8, the highest level of functioning for four of the six intellectual abilities occurred in the middle adulthood years (Willis & Schaie, 1999). For both women and men, performance on vocabulary, verbal memory, inductive reasoning, and spatial orientation peaked in middle age. Only two of the six abilities—numerical ability and perceptual speed—declined in middle age. Perceptual speed showed the earliest decline, with this beginning in early adulthood.

When Schaie (1994) assessed intellectual abilities both cross-sectionally and longitudinally, he found decline more likely to occur in the cross-sectional than in the longitudinal assessments. For example, as shown in figure 8.9, when assessed longitudinally, inductive reasoning increased until toward the end of middle adulthood, when it began to show a slight decline. In contrast, when assessed cross-sectionally, inductive reasoning showed a consistent decline in the middle

*T*he peaking of some important mental abilities in mental age suggests that substantial improvement in these abilities has occurred since early adulthood.

—K. WARNER SCHAIE
*Contemporary Psychologist,
Pennsylvania State University*

**K. Warner Schaie
Midlife Baby-Boomer Characteristics**

crystallized intelligence Accumulated information and verbal skills, which increase with age, according to Horn.

fluid intelligence The ability to reason abstractly, which steadily declines from middle adulthood on, according to Horn.

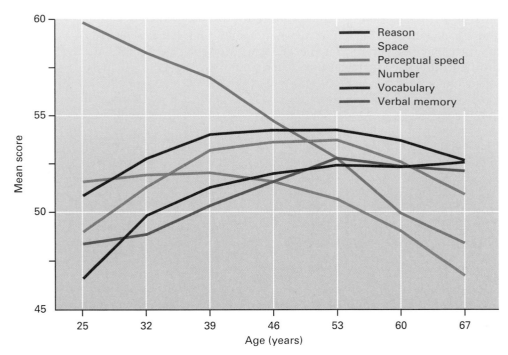

FIGURE 8.8 Longitudinal Changes in Six Intellectual Abilities from Age 25 to Age 67

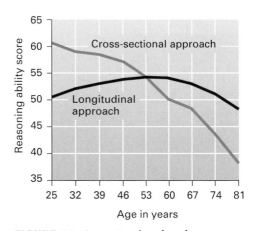

FIGURE 8.9 Cross-Sectional and Longitudinal Comparisons of Reasoning Ability Across the Adulthood Years

In Schaie's most recent research, the cross-sectional approach revealed declining scores with age; the longitudinal approach showed a slight rise of scores in middle adulthood and only a slight decline beginning in the early part of late adulthood.

wisdom Expert knowledge about the practical aspects of life that permits excellent judgment about important matters.

adulthood years. Interestingly, for the participants in the Seattle Longitudinal Study, middle age was a time of peak performance for both some aspects of crystallized intelligence (vocabulary) and fluid intelligence (spatial orientation and inductive reasoning).

Wisdom Some experts believe that an important aspect of intelligence in adulthood is wisdom (Kramer, 2003; Shedlock & Cornelius, 2003). Much of the interest in research on wisdom has been generated by Paul Baltes and his colleagues (Baltes, 1993, 2000; Baltes, Glück, & Kunzmann, 2002; Baltes & Kunzmann, 2003; Baltes, Staudinger, & Lindenberger, 1999; Kunzmann & Baltes, 2003). Does wisdom, like good wine, improve with age? What is this thing we call "wisdom"?

Wisdom is expert knowledge about the practical aspects of life that permits excellent judgment about important matters. This practical knowledge involves exceptional insight about human development and life matters, good judgment, and understanding how to cope with difficult life problems. Thus, wisdom, more than standard conceptions of intelligence, focuses on life's pragmatic concerns and human conditions (Baltes, Staudinger, & Lindenberger, 1999).

In regard to wisdom, research by Baltes and his colleagues (Baltes, Glück, & Kunzmann, 2002; Baltes & Kunzmann, 2003) has found that:

- High levels of wisdom are rare. Few people, including older adults, attain a high level of wisdom (Baltes & Smith, 1990). That only a small percentage of adults show wisdom supports the contention that it requires experience, practice, or complex skills (Kramer, 2003).
- The time frame of late adolescence and early adulthood is the main age window for wisdom to emerge. No further advances in wisdom have been found for middle-aged and older adults beyond the level they attained as young adults.
- Factors other than age are critical for wisdom to develop to a high level. For example, certain life experiences, such as being trained and working in a field concerned with difficult life problems and having wisdom-enhancing mentors, contribute to higher levels of wisdom. Also, people higher in wisdom have

values that are more likely to consider the welfare of others rather than their own happiness.

- Personality-related factors, such as openness to experience, generativity, and creativity, are better predictors of wisdom than cognitive factors such as intelligence.

Older adults might not be as quick with their thoughts or behavior as younger adults, but are they likely to be wiser than younger adults? This elderly woman shares the wisdom of her experiences with a classroom of children.

Review and Reflect: Learning Goal 3

3 Discuss the development of intelligence across the human life span

REVIEW

- How is intelligence assessed during infancy?
- How much does intelligence change through childhood and adolescence?
- To what extent does intelligence change as adults age? What is wisdom and how can it be characterized?

REFLECT

- What do you think are the most important cohort effects that can influence the development of intelligence in middle and late adulthood? How are these likely to change in the future?

4 THE EXTREMES OF INTELLIGENCE AND CREATIVITY

| Mental Retardation | Giftedness | Creativity |

Mental retardation and intellectual giftedness are the extremes of intelligence. Often intelligence tests are used to identify exceptional individuals. Let's explore the nature of mental retardation and giftedness. Then we'll explore how creativity differs from intelligence.

Mental Retardation

The most distinctive feature of mental retardation is inadequate intellectual functioning. Long before formal tests were developed to assess intelligence, individuals with mental retardation were identified by a lack of age-appropriate skills in learning and caring for themselves. Once intelligence tests were developed, they were used to identify degrees of mental retardation. But of two individuals with mental retardation who have the same low IQ, one might be married, employed, and involved in the community and the other require constant supervision in an institution. Such differences in social competence led psychologists to include deficits in adaptive behavior in their definition of mental retardation.

Mental retardation is a condition of limited mental ability in which the individual (1) has a low IQ, usually below 70 on a traditional intelligence test; (2) has difficulty adapting to everyday life; and (3) first exhibits these characteristics by age 18. The age limit is included in the definition of mental retardation because, for example, we don't usually think of a college student who suffers massive brain damage in a car accident, resulting in an IQ of 60, as being "mentally retarded." The low IQ and low adaptiveness should be evident in childhood, not after normal functioning is interrupted by damage of some form. About 5 million Americans fit this definition of mental retardation.

There are several ways of classifying degrees of mental retardation (Hallahan & Kaufmann, 2003). Most school systems use the classifications shown in figure 8.10. It uses IQ scores to categorize retardation as mild, moderate, severe, or profound.

www.mhhe.com/santrockldt2

Mental Retardation

Type of Mental Retardation	IQ Range	Percentage of Mentally Retarded Individuals
Mild	55 to 70	89
Moderate	40 to 54	6
Severe	25 to 39	4
Profound	Below 25	1

FIGURE 8.10 Classification of Mental Retardation Based on IQ

mental retardation A condition of limited mental ability in which the individual (1) has a low IQ, usually below 70 on a traditional intelligence test; (2) has difficulty adapting to everyday life; and (3) has an onset of these characteristics by age 18.

FIGURE 8.11 Classification of Mental Retardation Based on Levels of Support Needed

Intermittent	Supports are provided "as needed." The individual may need episodic or short-term support during life-span transitions (such as job loss or acute medical crisis). Intermittent supports may be low or high intensity when provided.
Limited	Supports are intense and relatively consistent over time. They are time-limited but not intermittent. Require fewer staff members and cost less than more intense supports. These supports likely will be needed for adaptation to the changes involved in the school-to-adult period.
Extensive	Supports are characterized by regular involvement (for example, daily) in at least some setting (such as home or work) and are not time-limited (for example, extended home-living support).
Pervasive	Supports are constant, very intense, and are provided across settings. They may be of a life-sustaining nature. These supports typically involve more staff members and intrusiveness than the other support categories.

A child with Down syndrome. *What causes Down syndrome?*

gifted Having high intelligence (an IQ of 130 or higher) or superior talent for something.

Note that a large majority of individuals diagnosed with mental retardation fit into the mild category. However, these categories are not perfect predictors of functioning. The American Association of Mental Retardation (1992) developed a different classification based on the degree of support required for a person with mental retardation to function at the highest level. As shown in figure 8.11, these categories of support are intermittent, limited, extensive, and pervasive.

Some cases of mental retardation have an organic cause. *Organic retardation* is mental retardation caused by a genetic disorder or by brain damage. Down syndrome is one form of organic mental retardation and it occurs when an extra chromosome is present ◀▥ P. 58. Other causes of organic retardation include fragile X syndrome, an abnormality in the X chromosome that was discussed in chapter 2; prenatal malformation; metabolic disorders; and diseases that affect the brain. Most people who suffer from organic retardation have IQs between 0 and 50.

When no evidence of organic brain damage can be found, cases of mental retardation are labeled *cultural-familial retardation*. Individuals with this type of retardation have IQs between 55 and 70. Psychologists suspect that these mental deficits often result from growing up in a below-average intellectual environment. Children who are familially retarded can be identified in schools, where they often fail, need tangible rewards (candy rather than praise), and are highly sensitive to what others expect of them. However, as adults, the familially retarded are usually invisible, perhaps because adult settings don't tax their cognitive skills as sorely. It may also be that the familially retarded increase their intelligence as they move toward adulthood.

Giftedness

There have always been people whose abilities and accomplishments outshine others'—the whiz kid in class, the star athlete, the natural musician. People who are **gifted** have high intelligence (an IQ of 130 or higher) or superior talent for something. Programs for the gifted in most school systems select children who have intellectual superiority and academic aptitude. They tend to overlook children who are talented in the arts or athletics or who have other special aptitudes (Olszewski-Kublius, 2003).

Until recently, giftedness and emotional distress were thought to go hand in hand. English novelist Virginia Woolf, Sir Isaac Newton, Vincent van Gogh, Ann Sexton, Socrates, and Sylvia Plath all had emotional problems. However, these individuals are the exception rather than the rule. In general, no relation between giftedness and mental disorder has been found. Recent studies support the conclusion that gifted people tend to be more mature and have fewer emotional problems than others, and to grow up in a positive family climate (Feldhusen, 1999; Feldman, 1997).

Characteristics of Children Who Are Gifted   What about children who are gifted? Aside from their abilities, do they have distinctive characteristics? Lewis Terman (1925) conducted an extensive study of 1,500 children whose Stanford-Binet IQs averaged 150. Contrary to the popular myth that children who are gifted are maladjusted, Terman found that they were socially well adjusted.

Ellen Winner (1996) described three criteria that characterize gifted children, whether in art, music, or academic domains:

1. *Precocity.* Gifted children are precocious. They begin to master an area earlier than their peers. Learning in their domain is more effortless for them than for ordinary children. In most instances, these gifted children are precocious because they have an inborn high ability.
2. *Marching to their own drummer.* Gifted children learn in a qualitatively different way than ordinary children. For one thing, they need minimal help from adults to learn. In many cases, they resist explicit instruction. They also often make discoveries on their own and solve problems in unique ways.
3. *A passion to master.* Gifted children are driven to understand the domain in which they have high ability. They display an intense, obsessive interest and an ability to focus. They do not need to be pushed by their parents. They motivate themselves, says Winner.

Art prodigy Alexandra Nechita. *What are some characteristics of gifted children?*

Life Course of the Gifted   As a 10-year-old, Alexandra Nechita was described as a child prodigy. She paints quickly and impulsively on large canvases, some as large as 5 feet by 9 feet. It is not unusual for her to complete several of these large paintings in a week's time. Her paintings sell for up to $80,000 apiece. When she was only 2 years of age, Alexandra colored in coloring books for hours. She had no interest in dolls or friends. Once she started school, she would start painting as soon as she got home. And she continues to paint—relentlessly and passionately. It is, she says, what she loves to do.

Is giftedness, like Alexandria Nechita's artistic talent, a product of heredity or environment? Likely both. Individuals who are gifted recall that they had signs of high ability in a particular area at a very young age, prior to or at the beginning of formal training (Howe & others, 1995). This suggests the importance of innate ability in giftedness. However, researchers also have found that individuals with world-class status in the arts, mathematics, science, and sports all report strong family support and years of training and practice (Bloom, 1985). Deliberate practice is an important characteristic of individuals who become experts in a particular domain. For example, in one study, the best musicians engaged in twice as much deliberate practice over their lives as the least successful ones did (Ericsson, Krampe, & Tesch, 1993).

Do gifted children become gifted and highly creative adults? In Terman's research on children with superior IQs, the children typically became experts in a well-established domain, such as medicine, law, or business. However, they did not become major creators (Winner, 2000). That is, they did not create a new domain or revolutionize an old domain.

One reason that some gifted children do not become gifted adults is that they have been pushed too hard by overzealous parents and teachers. As a result, they lose their intrinsic (internal) motivation (Winner, 1996). As adolescents, they may ask themselves, "Who am I doing this for?" If the answer is not for one's self, they may not want to do it anymore.

Children Who Are Gifted
National Association of Gifted Children

Creativity

We brought up the term "creative" on several occasions in our discussion of giftedness. What does it mean to be creative? **Creativity** is the ability to think about something in novel and unusual ways and come up with unique solutions to problems.

creativity The ability to think in novel and unusual ways and come up with unique solutions to problems.

Intelligence and creativity are not the same thing (Lubart, 2003; Sternberg, 2002). Most creative people are quite intelligent, but the reverse is not necessarily true. Many highly intelligent people (as measured by high scores on conventional tests of intelligence) are not very creative (Sternberg & O'Hara, 2000). Many highly intelligent people produce large numbers of products but they are not necessarily novel.

Why don't IQ scores predict creativity? Creativity requires divergent thinking (Guilford, 1967). **Divergent thinking** produces many answers to the same question. In contrast, conventional intelligence tests require **convergent thinking.** For example, a typical item on a conventional intelligence test is, "How many quarters will you get in return for 60 dimes?" There is only one correct answer to this question. In contrast, a question such as, What image comes to mind when you hear the phrase "sitting alone in a dark room?" has many possible answers; it calls for divergent thinking.

Steps in the Creative Process   The creative process has often been described as a five-step sequence:

1. *Preparation.* You become immersed in a problem or an issue that interests you and arouses your curiosity.
2. *Incubation.* You churn ideas around in your head. This is the point at which you are likely to make some unusual connections in your thinking.
3. *Insight.* You experience the "Aha!" moment when all pieces of the puzzle seem to fit together.
4. *Evaluation.* Now you must decide whether the idea is valuable and worth pursuing. Is the idea really novel or is it obvious?
5. *Elaboration.* This final step often covers the longest span of time and the hardest work. This is what the famous twentieth-century American inventor Thomas Edison was talking about when he said that creativity is 1 percent inspiration and 99 percent perspiration. Elaboration may require a great deal of perspiration.

Mihaly Csikszentmihalyi (pronounced ME-high CHICK-sent-me-high-ee) (1996) believes that this five-step sequence provides a helpful framework for thinking about how creative ideas are developed. However, he argues that creative people don't always go through the steps in a linear sequence. For example, elaboration is often interrupted by periods of incubation. Fresh insights may appear during incubation, evaluation, and elaboration. And insight might take years or only a few hours. Sometimes the creative idea consists of one deep insight. Other times it's a series of small ones.

Characteristics of Creative Thinkers   Creative thinkers tend to have these characteristics (Perkins, 1994):

- *Flexibility and playful thinking.* Creative thinkers are flexible and play with problems, which gives rise to a paradox. Although creativity takes hard work, the work goes more smoothly if you take it lightly. In a way, humor greases the wheels of creativity (Goleman, Kaufmann, & Ray, 1993). When you are joking around, you are more likely to consider any possibility. Having fun helps to disarm your inner censor, which can condemn your ideas as off-base. *Brainstorming* is a technique in which members of a group are encouraged to come up with as many ideas as possible, play off each other's ideas, and say practically whatever comes to mind. Individuals usually are told to avoid criticizing others' ideas until the end of the brainstorming session.
- *Inner motivation.* Creative people often are motivated by the joy of creating. They tend to be less inspired by grades, money, or favorable feedback from others. Thus, creative people are motivated more internally than externally (Runco, 2004).

divergent thinking Thinking that produces many answers to the same question; characteristic of creativity.

convergent thinking Thinking that produces one correct answer; characteristic of the kind of thinking required on conventional intelligence tests.

Mark Strand, former U.S. poet laureate, says that in his most creative moments he loses a sense of time and becomes absorbed in what he is doing. In this state, he feels he is dismantling meaning and remaking it. Strand comments that he can't stay in this absorbed frame of mind for an entire day. It comes and goes: His attention coils and uncoils; his focus sharpens and softens. When an idea clicks, he focuses intensely, transforming the idea into a vivid verbal image that will communicate its essence to the reader.

Nina Holton, a leading contemporary sculptor, turns playfully wild germs of ideas into stunning sculptures. She says that sculpture is a combination of wonderful, unique ideas and a lot of hard work. She comments that when she is introduced to people they often say. "It must be so exciting and wonderful being a sculptor." Holton loves her work but says that most people see only its creative side, not the hard work.

Jonas Salk, who invented the polio vaccine, says his best ideas come to him when he suddenly wakes up. After a few minutes of visualizing problems he had thought about the day before, he begins to see an unfolding, as if a painting or story is taking form. Salk also believes that many creative ideas are generated in conversations with others who have open, curious minds and positive attitudes. Salk's penchant for seeing emergent possibilities often brought him in conflict with people who had orthodox opinions.

- *Willingness to risk.* Creative people make more mistakes than their less imaginative counterparts. It's not that they are less proficient, but that they come up with more ideas, more possibilities (Lubart, 2003). They win some, they lose some. For example, the twentieth-century Spanish artist Pablo Picasso created more than 20,000 paintings. Not all of them were masterpieces. Creative thinkers learn to cope with unsuccessful projects and see failure as an opportunity to learn.
- *Objective evaluation of work.* Contrary to the stereotype that creative people are eccentric and highly subjective, most creative thinkers strive to evaluate their work objectively. They may use established criteria to make this judgment or rely on the judgments of people they respect. In this manner, they can determine whether further creative thinking will improve their work.

Changes During Adulthood At the age of 30, Thomas Edison invented the phonograph, Hans Christian Andersen wrote his first volume of fairy tales, and Mozart composed *The Marriage of Figaro*. One early study of creativity found that individuals' most creative products were generated in their thirties and that 80 percent of the most important creative contributions were completed by age 50 (Lehman, 1960). More recently, researchers have found that creativity often peaks in the forties before declining (Simonton, 1996). However, any generalization about a relationship between age and creative accomplishments must be qualified

Leading creativity theorist Mihaly Csikszentmihalyi, in the setting where he gets his most creative ideas.

> *A* genuinely creative accomplishment is almost never the result of a sudden insight, a lightbulb flashing in the dark, but comes after years of hard work.
>
> —MIHALY CSIKSZENTMIHALYI
> *Contemporary Psychologist,*
> *University of Chicago*

by consideration of (1) the size of the decline and (2) differences across domains (Simonton, 1996).

Even though a decline in creative contributions is often found in the fifties and later, the decline is often not great. An impressive array of creative accomplishments have occurred in late adulthood (Tahir & Gruber, 2003). Benjamin Franklin invented the bifocal lens when he was 78 years old; Goethe completed *Faust* when he was in his eighties. After a distinguished career as a physicist, Henri Chevreul switched fields in his nineties to become a pioneer in gerontological research. He published his last research paper just a year prior to his death at the age of 103!

Furthermore, the age at which creativity typically declines varies with the domain involved. In philosophy and history, for example, older adults often show as much creativity as when they were in their thirties and forties. In contrast, in lyric poetry, abstract mathematics, and theoretical physics, the peak of creativity is often reached in the twenties or thirties.

Living a More Creative Life Csikszentmihalyi (1996) interviewed 90 leading figures in art, business, government, education, and science to learn how creativity works. He discovered that creative people regularly engage in challenges that absorb them. Based on his interviews with some of the most creative people in the world, he concluded that the first step toward a more creative life is to cultivate your curiosity and interest. Here are his recommendations for doing this:

- *Try to be surprised by something every day.* Maybe it is something you see, hear, or read about. Become absorbed in a lecture or a book. Be open to what the world is telling you. Life is a stream of experiences. Swim widely and deeply in it, and your life will be richer.
- *Try to surprise at least one person every day.* In a lot of things you do, you have to be predictable and patterned. Do something different for a change. Ask a question you normally would not ask. Invite someone to go to a show or a museum you never have visited.
- *Write down each day what surprised you and how you surprised others.* Most creative people keep a diary, notes, or lab records to ensure that their experience is not forgotten. Start with a specific task. Each evening record the most surprising event that occurred that day and your most surprising action. After a few days, reread your notes and reflect on your experiences. After a few weeks, you might see a pattern emerging, one that suggests an area you can explore in greater depth.
- *When something sparks your interest, follow it.* Usually when something captures your attention, it is short-lived—an idea, a song, a flower. Too often we are too busy to explore the idea, song, or flower further. Or we think these areas are none of our business because we are not experts about them. Yet the world is our business. We can't know which part of it is best suited to our interests until we make a serious effort to learn as much about as many aspects of it as possible.
- *Wake up in the morning with a specific goal to look forward to.* Creative people wake up eager to start the day. Why? Not necessarily because they are cheerful, enthusiastic types but because they know that there is something meaningful to accomplish each day, and they can't wait to get started.
- *Take charge of your schedule.* Figure out which time of the day is your most creative time. Some of us are more creative late at night, others early in the morning. Carve out some time for yourself when your creative energy is at its best.
- *Spend time in settings that stimulate your creativity.* In Csikszentmihalyi's (1996) research, he gave people an electronic pager and beeped them randomly at different times of the day. When he asked them how they felt, they reported the highest levels of creativity when walking, driving, or swimming. "I do my most creative thinking when I'm jogging." These activities are semiautomatic in that

they take a certain amount of attention while leaving some time free to make connections among ideas. Another setting in which highly creative people report coming up with novel ideas is the half-asleep, half-awake state we are in when we are deeply relaxed or barely awake.

Review and Reflect: Learning Goal 4

4 Describe the characteristics of mental retardation, giftedness, and creativity

REVIEW

- What is mental retardation and what are its causes?
- What makes people gifted?
- What makes people creative?

REFLECT

- How many of the tips in the section on "Living a More Creative Life" do you practice? How might you benefit from these suggestions, in addition to becoming more creative?

Reach Your Learning Goals

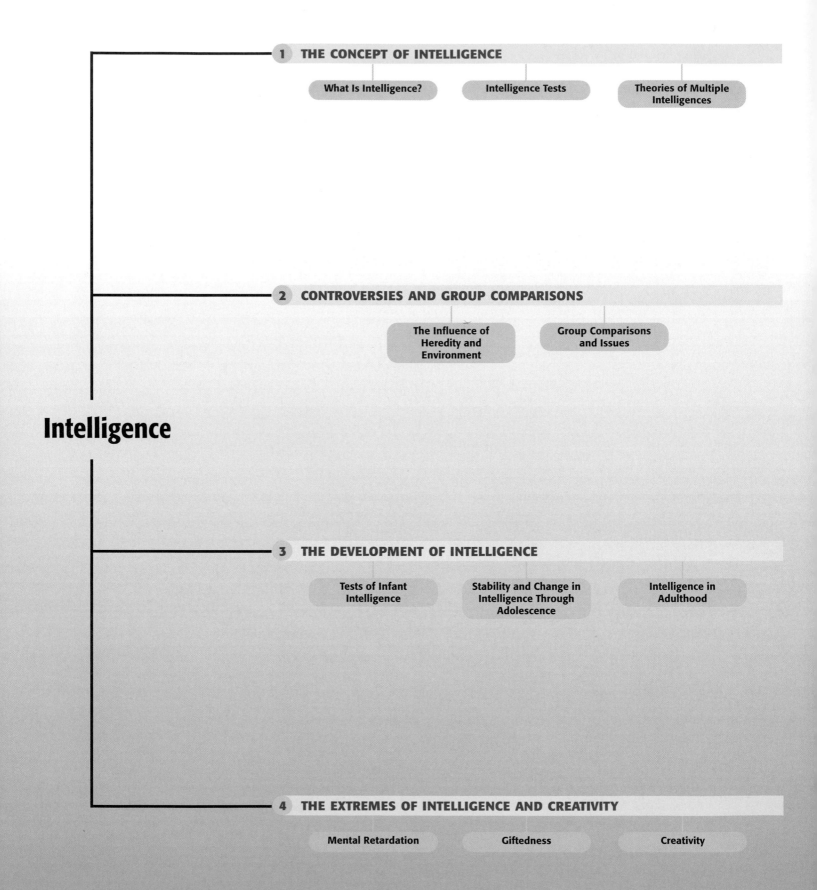

Intelligence

1   THE CONCEPT OF INTELLIGENCE

- What Is Intelligence?
- Intelligence Tests
- Theories of Multiple Intelligences

2   CONTROVERSIES AND GROUP COMPARISONS

- The Influence of Heredity and Environment
- Group Comparisons and Issues

3   THE DEVELOPMENT OF INTELLIGENCE

- Tests of Infant Intelligence
- Stability and Change in Intelligence Through Adolescence
- Intelligence in Adulthood

4   THE EXTREMES OF INTELLIGENCE AND CREATIVITY

- Mental Retardation
- Giftedness
- Creativity

Summary

1 Explain the nature of intelligence

- Intelligence consists of the ability to solve problems and to adapt and learn from everyday experiences. A key aspect of intelligence focuses on its individual variations. Traditionally, intelligence has been measured by tests designed to compare people's performance on cognitive tasks.

- Sir Frances Galton is the father of mental tests. Alfred Binet developed the first intelligence test and created the concept of mental age. William Stern developed the concept of IQ for use with the Binet test. Revisions of the Binet test are called the Stanford-Binet. The test scores on the Stanford-Binet approximate a normal distribution. The Wechsler scales, created by David Wechsler, are the other main intelligence assessment tool. These tests provide an overall IQ, verbal and performance IQs, and information about 11 subtests. Group intelligence tests are convenient and economical, but they do not allow an examiner to monitor the testing closely. When used by a judicious examiner, tests can be valuable tools for determining individual differences in intelligence. Test scores should be only one type of information used to evaluate an individual. IQ scores can produce unfortunate stereotypes and expectations. Ability tests can help divide children into homogeneous groups but periodic testing should be done to ensure that the groupings are appropriate.

- Factor analysis is a statistical procedure that compares various items or measures and identifies underlying factors that are correlated with each other. Spearman (two-factor theory of *g* and *s*) and Thurstone (multiple-factor theory) used factor analysis in developing their views of intelligence. Gardner believes there are eight types of intelligence: verbal skills, mathematical skills, spatial skills, bodily-kinesthetic skills, musical skills, interpersonal skills, intrapersonal skills, and naturalist skills. Sternberg's triarchic theory states that there are three main types of intelligence: analytical, creative, and practical. Sternberg created the Sternberg Triarchic Abilities Test to assess these three types of intelligence and has described applications of triarchic theory to children's education. Emotional intelligence is the ability to perceive and express emotion accurately and adaptively, to understand emotion and emotional knowledge, to use feelings to facilitate thought, and to manage emotions in oneself and others. The multiple intelligences approaches have broadened the definition of intelligence and motivated educators to develop programs that instruct students in different domains. Critics maintain that the multiple intelligence theories include factors that really aren't part of intelligence, such as musical skills and creativity. Critics also say that there isn't enough research to support the concept of multiple intelligences.

2 Outline key controversies about differences in IQ scores

- Genetic similarity might explain why identical twins show stronger correlations on intelligence tests than fraternal twins do. Some studies indicate that the IQs of adopted children are more similar to the IQs of their biological parents than to those of their adoptive parents. Many studies show that intelligence has a reasonably strong heritability component. Criticisms of the heritability concept have been made. Intelligence test scores have risen considerably around the world in recent decades—called the Flynn effect—and this supports the role of environment in intelligence. Researchers have found that how much parents talk with their children in the first three years of life is correlated with the children's IQs and that being deprived of formal education lowers IQ scores. Ramey's research revealed the positive effects of educational child care on intelligence.

- Cultures vary in the way they define intelligence. Early intelligence tests favored White, middle-socioeconomic status urban individuals. Tests may be biased against certain groups because they are not familiar with a standard form of English, with the content tested, or with the testing situation. Tests are likely to reflect the values and experience of the dominant culture. In the United States, children from African American and Latino families score below children from White families on standardized intelligence tests. Males are more likely than females to have extremely high or extremely low IQ scores. There also are gender differences in specific intellectual abilities.

3 Discuss the development of intelligence across the human life span

- Tests designed to assess infant intelligence include the widely used Bayley scales and a test developed by Gesell was an important early contributor to the developmental testing of infants. The Fagan Test of Infant Intelligence, which assesses how effectively infants process information, is increasingly being used. Infant information-processing tasks that involve attention—especially habituation and dishabituation—are related to standardized scores of intelligence in childhood.

- Although intelligence is more stable across the childhood and adolescent years than are many other attributes, many children's and adolescents' scores on intelligence tests fluctuate considerably.

- Horn argued that crystallized intelligence continues to increase in middle adulthood, while fluid intelligence declines. Schaie found that when assessed longitudinally, intellectual abilities are less likely to decline and more likely to even improve than when assessed cross-sectionally in middle adulthood. The highest level of four intellectual abilities (vocabulary, verbal memory, inductive reasoning, and spatial ability) occur in middle adulthood. Wisdom is expert knowledge about the practical aspects of life that permits excellent judgment about important matters. Baltes and his colleagues have found that high levels of wisdom are rare, the time frame of late adolescence and early adolescence is the main window for the wisdom to emerge, factors other than age are critical for wisdom to develop, and personality-related factors are better predictors of wisdom than cognitive factors such as intelligence.

4 Discuss the characteristics of mental retardation, giftedness, and creativity

- Mental retardation is a condition of limited mental ability in which the individual (1) has a low IQ, usually below 70; (2) has difficulty adapting to everyday life; and (3) has an onset of these characteristics by age 18. Most affected individuals have an IQ in the 55 to 70 range (mild retardation). Mental retardation can have an organic cause (called organic retardation) or be social and cultural in origin if there is no evidence of organic brain damage (called cultural-familial retardation).
- People who are gifted have high intelligence (an IQ of 130 or higher) or superior talent for something. Three characteristics of gifted children are precocity, marching to their own drum-

mer, and a passion to master in their domain. Giftedness is likely a consequence of both heredity and environment.
- Creativity is the ability to think about something in novel and unusual ways and come up with unique solutions to problems. Although most creative people are intelligent, individuals with high IQs are not necessarily creative. Creative people tend to be divergent thinkers; traditional intelligence tests measure convergent thinking. Creativity has often been described as occurring in a five-step process: preparation, incubation, insight, evaluation, and elaboration. Characteristics of creative thinkers include flexibility and playful thinking, inner motivation, a willingness to take risks, and interest in objective evaluation. Creativity often peaks in the forties and then declines, but the decline may be slight and the peak age varies across domains. Csikszentmihalyi believes that cultivating curiosity and interest is the first step toward a more creative life.

Key Terms

intelligence 270
mental age (MA) 271
intelligence quotient (IQ) 271
normal distribution 272
two-factor theory 274
factor analysis 274
multiple-factor theory 274

triarchic theory of
   intelligence 276
emotional intelligence 278
heritability 280
culture-fair tests 285
stereotype threat 286

developmental quotient
   (DQ) 287
Bayley Scales of Infant
   Development 287
crystallized intelligence 289
fluid intelligence 289

wisdom 290
mental retardation 291
gifted 292
creativity 293
divergent thinking 294
convergent thinking 294

Key People

Alfred Binet 271
Theophile Simon 271
Lewis Terman 271
David Wechsler 272
Charles Spearman 274
L. L. Thurstone 274
Howard Gardner 274

Robert J. Sternberg 276
Daniel Goleman 278
Peter Salovey and John
   Mayer 278
Arthur Jensen 279
James Flynn 282
Robert Plomin 282

Craig Ramey 282
Robert Serpell 283
Elena Grigorenko 283
Richard Herrnstein and Charles
   Murray 285
Arnold Gesell 287
Nancy Bayley 287

Robert McCall 288
John Horn 288
K. Warner Schaie 289
Paul Baltes 290
Lewis Terman 293
Ellen Winner 293
Mihaly Csikszentmihalyi 294

E-Learning Tools

Connect to **www.mhhe.com/santrockldt2** to research the answers and complete these exercises. In addition, you'll find a number of other resources and valuable study tools for chapter 8, "Intelligence," on the Student CD-ROM that came with this book.

Taking It to the Net

1. Penny teaches fifth grade in a school that has received a grant to pilot a Creative Classrooms Project. The principal has asked Penny to create one month of lesson plans utilizing the project's model of creative teaching. What are some main aspects of teaching with this method?

2. Crystal, age 25, is having a discussion with her 60-year-old grandmother, Jean, about which of them would make the better contestant on *Jeopardy!* and *Who Wants to Be a Millionaire.* Crystal says that she would naturally be a better contestant because she is quicker to understand the question and come up with an answer. Jean counters that she might be slower, but she knows more of the answers. Who is right?

3. Juan and Carmen's 7-year-old gifted son, Nicholas, is in a school without a gifted program, but one where teachers try to create challenging learning situations within the normal classroom. Nicholas' teacher wants to meet with Juan and Carmen to discuss Nicholas' classroom behavior problems. What types of behavioral challenges do gifted children present in the classroom?

Self-Assessment

To evaluate yourself on various aspects of intelligence and creativity, complete these self-assessments:

- *Evaluating Myself on Gardner's Eight Types of Intelligence*
- *How Emotionally Intelligent Am I?*
- *Examining My Creative Thinking*

Health and Well-Being, Parenting, and Education

Build your decision-making skills by trying your hand at the health and well-being, parenting, and education "Scenarios."

Language Development

Chapter Outline

Learning Goals

1 Define language and describe its rule systems

2 Describe how language develops through the life span

3 Discuss the biological and environmental contributions to language skills

In this chapter, we will tell the remarkable story of language and how it develops. The questions we will explore include these: What is language? What is the course of language development across the life span? What does biology contribute to language? How does experience influence language?

1 WHAT IS LANGUAGE?

Defining Language

Language's Rule Systems

In 1799, a nude boy was observed running through the woods in France. The boy was captured when he was 11 years old. He was called the Wild Boy of Aveyron and was believed to have lived in the woods alone for 6 years (Lane, 1976). When found, he made no effort to communicate. He never learned to communicate effectively. Sadly, a modern-day wild child named Genie was discovered in Los Angeles in 1970. Despite intensive intervention, Genie has never acquired more than a primitive form of language. We will discuss Genie's development in greater detail later in the chapter. Both cases—the Wild Boy of Aveyron and Genie—raise questions about the biological and environmental determinants of language, topics that we also will examine later in the chapter. First, though, we need to define language.

Defining Language

Language is a form of communication—whether spoken, written, or signed—that is based on a system of symbols. Language consists of the words used by a community and the rules for varying and combining them.

Think how important language is in our everyday lives. We need language to speak with others, listen to others, read, and write. Our language enables us to describe past events in detail and to plan for the future. Language lets us pass down information from one generation to the next and create a rich cultural heritage.

All human languages have some common characteristics. These include infinite generativity and organizational rules. **Infinite generativity** is the ability to produce an endless number of meaningful sentences using a finite set of words and rules. Let's further explore what these rules involve.

Language's Rule Systems

When nineteenth-century American writer Ralph Waldo Emerson said, "The world was built in order and the atoms march in tune," he must have had language in mind. Language is highly ordered and organized (Berko Gleason, 2000). The organization involves five systems of rules: phonology, morphology, syntax, semantics, and pragmatics.

Phonology   Every language is made up of basic sounds. The **phonology** of a language consists of rules regarding how sounds are perceived as different and which sound sequences may occur in the language. For example, in English *sp*, *ba*, and *ar* may occur. But *zx* and *qp* do not.

The basic unit of sound in a language is a *phoneme*; it is the smallest unit of sound that affects meaning. A good example of a phoneme in English is /k/, the sound represented by the letter *k* in the word *ski* and the letter *c* in the word *cat*. The /k/ sound is slightly different in these two words. But this variation is not distinguished in English, and the /k/ sound is therefore a single phoneme. In some languages, such as Arabic, this variation represents separate phonemes.

Phonology provides a basis for constructing a large and expandable set of words out of two or three dozen phonemes. Imagine what language would be like if there

language A form of communication, whether spoken, written, or signed, that is based on a system of symbols.

infinite generativity The ability to produce an endless number of meaningful sentences using a finite set of words and rules.

phonology Rules regarding how sounds are perceived as different and which sound sequences may occur in the language.

were no phonology. Each word in the language would have to be represented by a signal—a sound, for example—that differed from the signals of all other words. The obvious consequence is that the number of words could be no larger than the number of signals that an individual could efficiently produce and perceive. We do not know precisely what that number is, but we do know that it is very small, in contrast to the hundreds of thousands of words that commonly constitute a language.

Morphology   **Morphology** refers to the units of meaning involved in word formation. A *morpheme* is a unit of sound that conveys a specific meaning. Every word in the English language is made up of one or more morphemes. Some words consist of a single morpheme (for example, *help*), whereas others are made up of more than one morpheme (for example, *helper*, which has two morphemes, *help + er*, with the morpheme *-er* meaning "one who," in this case "one who helps"). Thus, not all morphemes are words by themselves (for example, *pre-, -tion,* and *-ing*).

Just as the rules that govern phonemes determine which sound sequences occur in a language, the rules that govern morphemes ensure that certain strings of sounds occur in meaningful sequences. Morphemes have many jobs in grammar, such as marking tense (for example, she walks versus she walked) and number (she walks versus they walk).

Syntax   **Syntax** involves the ways words are combined to form acceptable phrases and sentences. If someone says to you, "Bob slugged Tom" or "Bob was slugged by Tom," you know who did the slugging and who was slugged in each case because you have a syntactic understanding of these sentence structures. You also understand that the sentence "You didn't stay, did you?" is a grammatical sentence but that "You didn't stay, didn't you?" is unacceptable and ambiguous.

If you learn another language, English syntax will not get you very far. For example, in English an adjective usually precedes a noun *(as in blue sky)*, whereas in Spanish the adjective usually follows the noun *(cielo azul)*. Despite the differences in their syntactic structures, however, the world's languages have much in common. For example, consider these short sentences:

The cat killed the mouse.
The mouse ate the cheese.
The farmer chased the cat.

In many languages it is possible to combine these sentences into more complex sentences. For example:

The farmer chased the cat that killed the mouse.
The mouse the cat killed ate the cheese.

However, no language in the world permits sentences like this one:

The mouse the cat the farmer chased killed ate the cheese.

Can you make sense of this sentence? If you can, you probably can do it only after wrestling with it for several minutes. You likely could not understand it at all if someone uttered it during a conversation. It appears that language users cannot

Frank and Ernest reprinted by permission of Newspaper Enterprise Association, Inc.

morphology Units of meaning involved in word formation.

syntax The ways words are combined to form acceptable phrases and sentences.

> *Words not only affect us temporarily; they change us, they socialize us, and they unsocialize us.*
>
> —David Riesman
> *American Social Scientist,
> 20th Century*

Pragmatics

semantics The meanings of words and sentences.

pragmatics The appropriate use of language in context.

process subjects and objects arranged in too complex a fashion in a sentence. That is good news for language learners, because it means that all syntactic systems adhere to some common ground. Such findings are also considered important by researchers who are interested in the universal properties of syntax (Maratsos, 1998).

Semantics **Semantics** refers to the meaning of words and sentences. Every word has a set of semantic features, or required attributes related to meaning. *Girl* and *woman*, for example, share many semantic features but they differ semantically in regard to age.

Words have semantic restrictions on how they can be used in sentences. The sentence *The bicycle talked the boy into buying a candy bar* is syntactically correct but semantically incorrect. The sentence violates our semantic knowledge that bicycles do not talk.

Pragmatics A final set of language rules involves **pragmatics,** the appropriate use of language in context. The domain of pragmatics is broad. When you take turns speaking in a discussion or use a question to convey a command ("Why is it so noisy in here? What is this, Grand Central Station?"), you are demonstrating knowledge of pragmatics. You also apply the pragmatics of English when you use *the* and *a* in a way that enhances understanding ("I read *a* book last night. *The* plot was boring"), use polite language in appropriate situations (for example, when talking to one's teacher), or tell stories that are interesting, jokes that are funny, and lies that convince.

Pragmatic rules can be complex and differ from one culture to another. If you were to study the Japanese language, you would come face-to-face with countless pragmatic rules about conversing with individuals of various social levels and with various relationships to you. Some of these pragmatic rules concern the ways of saying thank you. Indeed, the pragmatics of saying thank you are complex even in our own culture. Preschoolers' use of the phrase *thank you* varies with sex, socioeconomic status, and the age of the individual they are addressing.

At this point, we have discussed five important rule systems involved in language. An overview of these rule systems is presented in figure 9.1.

Rule System	Description	Examples
Phonology	The sound system of a language. A phoneme is the smallest sound unit in a language.	The word *chat* has three phonemes: /ch/ /a/ /t/. An example of phonological rule in the English language is that while the phoneme /r/ can follow the phonemes /t/ or /d/ in an English consonant cluster (such as *track* or *drab*), the phoneme /l/ cannot follow these letters.
Morphology	The system of meaningful units involved in word formation.	The smallest sound units that have a meaning are called morphemes or meaning units. The word *girl* is one morpheme or meaning unit; it cannot be broken down any further and still have meaning. When the suffix *s* is added, the word becomes *girls* and has two morphemes because the *s* changed the meaning of the word, indicating that there is more than one girl.
Syntax	The system that involves the way words are combined to form acceptable phrases and sentences.	Word order is very important in determining meaning in the English language. For example, the sentence, "Sebastian pushed the bike" has a different meaning than "The bike pushed Sebastian."
Semantics	The system that involves the meaning of words and sentences.	Knowing the meaning of individual words—that is, vocabulary. For example, semantics includes knowing the meaning of such words as *orange*, *transportation*, and *intelligent*.
Pragmatics	The system of using appropriate conversation and knowledge of how to effectively use language in context.	An example is using polite language in appropriate situations, such as being mannerly when talking with one's teacher. Taking turns in a conversation involves pragmatics.

FIGURE 9.1 The Rule Systems of Language

2 HOW LANGUAGE DEVELOPS

Infancy	Middle and Late Childhood	Adulthood

Early Childhood	Adolescence

In the thirteenth century, the Holy Roman Emperor Frederick II had a cruel idea. He wanted to know what language children would speak if no one talked to them. He selected several newborns and threatened their caregivers with death if they ever talked to the infants. Frederick never found out what language the children spoke because they all died. As we move forward in the twenty-first century, we are still curious about infants' development of language, although our experiments and observations are, to say the least, far more humane than the evil Frederick's.

Infancy

Whatever language they learn, infants all over the world follow a similar path in language development. What are some key milestones in this development?

Babbling and Other Vocalizations   Babies actively produce sounds from birth onward. These early communications attract attention from their caregivers and other people (Locke, 2002). Babies' sounds and gestures go through this sequence during their first year:

- *Crying.* Babies cry even at birth and crying can signal distress. However, as we will discuss in chapter 10, there are different types of cries that signal different things.
- *Cooing.* Babies first coo at about 1 to 2 months. These are *oo* sounds such as *coo* or *goo.* They usually occur during interaction with the caregiver.
- *Babbling.* This first occurs in the middle of the first year and includes strings of consonant-vowel combinations, such as "ba, ba, ba, ba."
- *Gestures.* Infants start using gestures, such as showing and pointing, at about 8 to 12 months of age. They may wave bye-bye, nod to mean "yes," show an empty cup to ask for more milk, and point to a dog to draw attention to it.

Deaf infants with deaf parents who use sign language babble with their hands and fingers at about the same age as hearing children babble vocally (Bloom, 1998). Such similarities in timing and structure between manual and vocal babbling indicate that a unified language capacity underlies signed and spoken language.

Infancy and Toddlerhood: Early Language

Recognizing Language Sounds Long before they begin to learn words, infants can sort through spoken sounds in search of the ones that have meaning. Patricia Kuhl's (1993, 2000) research has demonstrated that from birth up to about 6 months of age, infants are "citizens of the world," recognizing when sounds change most of the time no matter what language the syllables come from. But over the next six months, infants get even better at perceiving the changes in sounds from their "own" language, the one their parents speak, and gradually lose the ability to recognize changes in sounds that don't exist in their native tongue.

In Kuhl's research, syllables that consist of phonemes from languages all over the world are piped through a speaker for infants to hear (see figure 9.2). A string of identical syllables is played and then the sound changes. A box with a toy bear in it is placed where the infant can see it. If the infant turns its head when the sounds of the syllables change, the darkened box lights up and the bear briefly dances and drums. That is, if the infant turns its head to look at the box as soon as it notices the sound changing, the infant is rewarded by getting to see the bear's performance.

An example involves the English *r* and *l* sounds, which distinguish sounds such as *rake* and *lake* (Iverson & Kuhl, 1996; Iverson & others, 2003). In the United States, infants from English-speaking homes detect the changes from *ra* to *la* when they are 6 months old and get better at it by 12 months of age. However, in Japanese there is no such *r* or *l*. In Japan, 6-month-old infants perform as well as their American counterparts in recognizing the *r* and *l* distinction, but by 12 months of age they lose this ability.

An important task for infants is to fish out individual words from the nonstop stream of sound that makes up ordinary speech (Brownlee, 1998; Jusczyk, 2000). To do so, they must find the boundaries between words, which is very difficult for infants because adults don't pause between words when they speak. Still, infants begin to detect word boundaries by 8 months of age. For example, in one study, 8-month-old infants listened to recorded stories that contained unusual words, such as *hornbill* and *python* (Jusczyk & Hohne, 1997). Two weeks later, the researchers tested the infants with two lists of words, one made up of words in the stories, the other of new, unusual words that did not appear in the stories. The infants listened to the familiar words for a second longer, on average, than to new words.

First Words At about 8 to 12 months of age, infants often indicate their first understanding of words. On average, infants understand about 50 words at about 13 months, but they can't say this many words until about 18 months (Menyuk, Liebergott, & Schultz, 1995). Thus, in infancy, *receptive vocabulary* (words the child understands) considerably exceeds *spoken vocabulary* (words the child uses).

The infant's first word is a milestone eagerly anticipated by every parent. This event usually occurs at about 10 to 15 months of age, and on average at about 13 months. However, as we have seen, long before babies say their first words, they have been communicating with their parents, often by gesturing and using their own special sounds. The appearance of first words is a continuation of this communication process (Berko Gleason, 2002).

A child's first words include those that name important people (*dada*), familiar animals (*kitty*), vehicles (*car*), toys (*ball*), food (*milk*), body parts (*eye*), clothes (*hat*), household items (*clock*), and greeting terms (*bye*). These were the first words of babies 50 years ago. They are the first words of babies today. Children often express various intentions with their single words, so that "cookie" might mean "That's a cookie" or "I want a cookie."

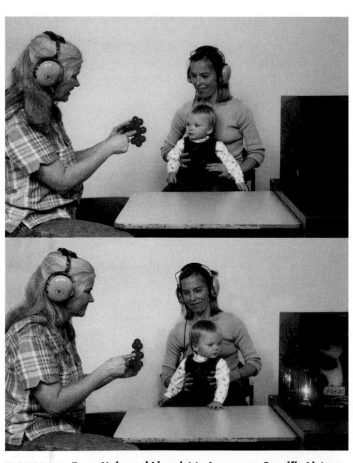

FIGURE 9.2 From Universal Linguist to Language-Specific Listener
A baby is shown in Patricia Kuhl's research laboratory. In this research, babies listen to tape-recorded voices that repeat syllables. When the sounds of the syllables change, the babies quickly learn to look at the bear. Using this technique, Kuhl has demonstrated that babies are universal linguists until about 6 months of age, but in the next six months become language-specific listeners.

The infant's spoken vocabulary rapidly increases once the first word is spoken. The average 18-month-old can speak about 50 words, but by the age of 2 years can speak about 200 words. This rapid increase in vocabulary that begins at approximately 18 months is called the *vocabulary spurt* (Bloom, Lifter, & Broughton, 1985).

The timing of a child's first word and vocabulary spurt varies (Bloom, 1998). Figure 9.3 shows the range for these language milestones for 14 children. On average, these children said their first word at 13 months and had a vocabulary spurt at 19 months. However, the ages for the first word of individual children ranged from 10 to 17 months and for their vocabulary spurt from 13 to 25 months.

Children sometimes overextend or underextend the meanings of the words they use (Woodward & Markman, 1998). *Overextension* is the tendency to apply a word to objects that are not related to, or are inappropriate for, the word's meaning. For example, when children learn to say *dada* for "father," they often also apply the word to other men, strangers, or boys. With time, overextensions decrease and eventually disappear. *Underextension* is the tendency to apply a word too narrowly; it occurs when children fail to use a word to name a relevant event or object. For example, a child might use the word *boy* to describe a 5-year-old neighbor but not apply the word to a male infant or to a 9-year-old male.

Two-Word Utterances   By the time children are 18 to 24 months of age, they usually utter two-word statements. To convey meaning with just two words, the child relies heavily on gesture, tone, and context. The wealth of meaning children can communicate with a two-word utterance includes these (Slobin, 1972):

- Identification: "See doggie."
- Location: "Book there."
- Repetition: "More milk."
- Nonexistence: "Allgone thing."
- Negation: "Not wolf."
- Possession: "My candy."
- Attribution: "Big car."
- Agent-action: "Mama walk."
- Action-direct object: "Hit you."
- Action-indirect object: "Give Papa."
- Action-instrument: "Cut knife."
- Question: "Where ball?"

These examples are from children whose first language is English, German, Russian, Finnish, Turkish, or Samoan.

Notice that the two-word sentences omit many parts of speech and are remarkably succinct. In fact, in every language, a child's first combinations of words have this economical quality; they are telegraphic. **Telegraphic speech** is the use of short and precise words without grammatical markers such as articles, auxiliary verbs, and other connectives. Telegraphic speech is not limited to two-word phrases. "Mommy give ice cream" and "Mommy give Tommy ice cream" also are examples of telegraphic speech.

We have discussed a number of language milestones in infancy. Figure 9.4 summarizes the time at which infants typically reach these milestones.

Early Childhood

As children leave the two-word stage, they move rather quickly into three-, four-, and five-word combinations. The transition from simple sentences expressing a single

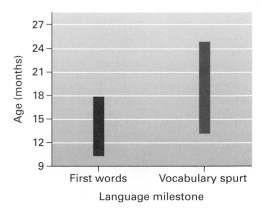

FIGURE 9.3 **Variation in Language Milestones**

Language Milestones
The Naming Explosion

Around the world, young children learn to speak in two-word utterances, in most cases at about 18 to 24 months of age. *What implications does this have for the biological basis of language?*

telegraphic speech The use of short and precise words without grammatical markers such as articles, auxiliary verbs, and other connectives.

Age	Language Milestones
Birth	Crying
1 to 2 months	Cooing begins
6 months	Babbling begins
6 to 12 months	Change from universal linguist to language-specific listener
8 to 12 months	Use gestures, such as showing and pointing Comprehension of words appears
13 months	First word spoken
18 months	Vocabulary spurt starts
18 to 24 months	Uses two-word utterances Rapid expansion of understanding of words

FIGURE 9.4 Some Language Milestones in Infancy

Language Development in Early Childhood

This is a wug.

Now there is another one. There are two of them. There are two _____.

FIGURE 9.5 Stimuli in Berko's Classic Study of Children's Understanding of Morphological Rules

In Jean Berko's study, young children were presented cards such as this one with a "wug" on it. Then the children were asked to supply the missing word and say it correctly.

proposition to complex sentences begins between 2 and 3 years of age and continues into the elementary school years (Bloom, 1998).

Young children's understanding sometimes gets way ahead of their speech. One 3-year-old, laughing with delight as an abrupt summer breeze stirred his hair and tickled his skin, commented, "I got breezed!" Many of the oddities of young children's language sound like mistakes to adult listeners. However, from the children's point of view, they are not mistakes. They represent the way young children perceive and understand their world at that point in their development. As children go through their early childhood years, their grasp of the rule systems that govern language increase.

Understanding Phonology and Morphology   During the preschool years, most children gradually become sensitive to the sounds of spoken words (National Research Council, 1999). They notice rhymes, enjoy poems, make up silly names for things by substituting one sound for another (such as *bubblegum, bubblebum, bubbleyum*), and clap along with each syllable in a phrase.

As they move beyond two-word utterances, there is clear evidence that children know morphological rules. Children begin using the plural and possessive forms of nouns (*dogs* and *dog's*); putting appropriate endings on verbs (*-s* when the subject is third-person singular, *-ed* for the past tense, and *-ing* for the present progressive tense); and using prepositions (*in* and *on*), articles (*a* and *the*), and various forms of the verb *to be* ("I *was going* to the store"). In fact, they *overgeneralize* these rules, applying them to words that do not follow the rules. For example, a preschool child might say "foots" instead of "feet" or "goed" instead of "went."

Children's understanding of morphological rules was the subject of a classic experiment by children's language researcher Jean Berko (1958). Berko presented preschool and first-grade children with cards such as the one shown in figure 9.5. Children were asked to look at the card while the experimenter read the words on it aloud. Then the children were asked to supply the missing word. This might sound easy, but Berko was interested not just in the children's ability to recall the right word but also in their ability to say it "correctly" with the ending that was dictated by morphological rules. *Wugs* is the correct response for the card in figure 9.5. Although the children were not perfectly accurate, they were much better than chance would dictate. Moreover, they demonstrated their knowledge of morphological rules not only with the plural forms of nouns ("There are two wugs") but also with the possessive forms of nouns and with the third-person singular and past-tense forms of verbs.

Berko's study demonstrated not only that the children relied on rules, but also that they had *abstracted* the rules from what they had heard and could apply them to novel situations. What makes Berko's study impressive is that all of the words were *fictional;* they were created especially for the experiment. Thus, the children could not base their responses on remembering past instances of hearing the words. Instead, they were forced to rely on *rules.* Their performance suggested that they did so successfully.

Understanding Syntax   Preschool children also learn and apply rules of syntax (Budwig, 1993). After advancing beyond two-word utterances, the child shows a growing mastery of complex rules for how words should be ordered. Consider the case of *wh-* questions, such as "Where is Daddy going?" or "What is that boy doing?" To ask these questions properly, the child must know two important differences between *wh-* questions and affirmative statements (for instance, "Daddy is going to work" and "That boy is waiting on the school bus"). First, a *wh-* word must be added at the beginning of the sentence. Second, the auxiliary verb must be inverted—that is, exchanged with the subject of the sentence. Young children learn quite early where to put the *wh-* word, but they take much longer to learn the auxiliary-inversion rule. Thus, it is common to hear preschool children asking such questions as "Where Daddy is going?" and "What that boy is doing?"

As children move into the elementary school years, they become skilled at using syntactical rules to construct lengthy and complex sentences. Utterances such as "The man who fixed the house went home" and "I don't want you to use my bike" are impressive demonstrations of how the child can use syntax to combine ideas into a single sentence. Just how young children master such complex rules—and may at the same time be struggling with relatively simple arithmetic rules—is a mystery.

Advances in Semantics   As children move beyond the two-word stage, their knowledge of meanings also rapidly advances (Bloom, 2002). The speaking vocabulary of a 6-year-old child ranges from 8,000 to 14,000 words (Carey, 1977; Clark, 2000). Assuming that word learning began when the child was 12 months old, this translates into a rate of learning 5 to 8 new word meanings a day between the ages of 1 and 6. The 6-year-old child does not slow down. According to some estimates, the average 6-year-old is moving along at the awe-inspiring rate of learning 22 words a day (Miller, 1981). How would you fare if you were given the task of learning 22 new words every day?

Children who enter elementary school with a small vocabulary are at risk for developing reading problems (Berko Gleason, 2002). Researchers have found that the quantity of talk that parents direct to their children is linked with the children's vocabulary growth and the socioeconomic status of families. To read about this link, see the Research in Life-Span Development Interlude.

Research in Life-Span Development

Family Environment and Young Children's Language Development

In one study, Janellen Huttenlocher and her colleagues (1991) observed mothers' speech when interacting with their infants. As indicated in figure 9.6, infants whose mothers spoke more often to them had markedly higher vocabularies. By the second birthday, vocabulary differences were substantial.

In another study, extensive conversations between 22 toddlers and their mothers were taped during the children's typical daily activities (Huttenlocher, Levine, & Vevea, 1998). Tapings were carried out every two to four months when the children were 16 to 26 months of age. The researchers found a remarkable link between the size of a child's vocabulary and the talkativeness of his or her mother. The mothers varied as much as tenfold in how much they talked. The toddlers of the most talkative mother had a vocabulary more than four times the size of the vocabulary of the child with the quietest mother. This link might be due at least partly to genetics. However, Huttenlocher believes that is not the case, because the mothers did not vary much in their verbal IQs. Also, the children clearly were picking up what their mothers were saying, because the words each child used the most often mirrored those favored by the mother.

Young children's vocabularies are linked to the socioeconomic status of their families. Betty Hart and Todd Risley (1995) observed the language environments of children whose parents were professionals and children whose parents were on welfare. Compared with the professional parents, the welfare parents talked much less to their young children, talked less about past events, and provided less elaboration. All of the children learned to talk and acquired all of the forms of English. However, as indicated in figure 9.7, the children of the professional parents had a much larger vocabulary at 36 months of age than the children of the welfare parents.

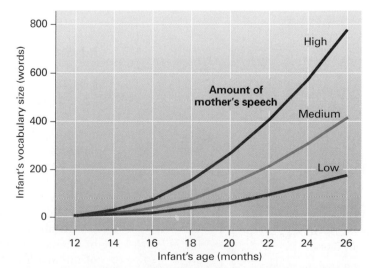

FIGURE 9.6 Amount of Maternal Speech and Infant Vocabulary

The amount of the mother's speech consisted of all utterances directed at the infant.

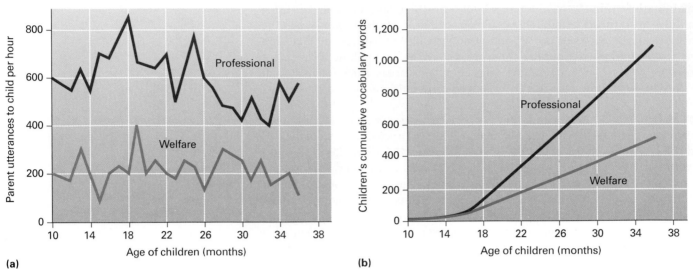

FIGURE 9.7 Language Input in Professional and Welfare Families and Young Children's Vocabulary Development

(a) Parents from professional families talked more with their young children than parents from welfare families. (b) Children from professional families developed vocabularies that were twice as large as those from welfare families. Thus, by the time children go to preschool, they already have experienced considerable differences in language input in their families and developed different levels of vocabulary that are linked with the socioeconomic status in which they have lived.

Other studies have linked home language environment to other aspects of the child's language beyond vocabulary. In one study, home language environment was linked to the child's syntax (Huttenlocher & Cymerman, 1999). The speech of 34 parents and their 4-year-old children was taped to determine the proportion of complex, multiclause sentences (such as "I am going to go to the store because we need to get some food") versus that of simple, single-clause ones (such as "Go to your room"). A significant relation was found between the proportion of complex sentences spoken by the parents and proportion of such sentences spoken by the children (both at home and at school). Such research demonstrates the important effect that early speech input can have on the development of a child's language skills.

Advances in Pragmatics Changes in pragmatics also characterize young children's language development. A 6-year-old is simply a much better conversationalist than a 2-year-old is. What are some of the improvements in pragmatics that are made in the preschool years?

At about 3 years of age, children improve their ability to talk about things that are not physically present—that is, they improve their command of an aspect of language known as *displacement*. Displacement is revealed in games of pretend. Although a 2-year-old might know the word *table*, he is unlikely to use this word to refer to an imaginary table that he pretends is standing in front of him. A child over 3 years of age is more likely to do so. There are large individual differences in preschoolers' talk about imaginary people and things.

At about 4 years of age, children develop a remarkable sensitivity to the needs of others in conversation. One way in which they show such sensitivity is their use of the articles *the* and *an* (or *a*). When adults tell a story or describe an event, they generally use *an* (or *a*) when they first refer to an animal or an object, and then use *the* when referring to it later. (For example, "Two boys were walking through the jungle when *a* fierce lion appeared. *The* lion lunged at one boy while the other ran for cover.") Even 3-year-olds follow part of this rule; they consistently use the word *the* when referring to previously mentioned things. However, the use of the word *a* when something is initially mentioned develops more slowly. Although 5-year-old children follow this rule on some occasions, they fail to follow it on others.

Around 4 to 5 years of age children learn to change their speech style to suit the situation. For example, even 4-year-old children speak differently to a 2-year-old than to a same-aged peer; they use shorter sentences with the 2-year-old. They also speak differently to an adult than to a same-aged peer, using more polite and formal language with the adult (Shatz & Gelman, 1973).

Preparing for Literacy   The preschool years set the stage for literacy. During these years children may have many *print-related interactions*—such as having books read to them, looking through books and magazines, and learning to print their names. For children who participate in print-related interactions as preschoolers, literacy often comes quickly in school. However, many children who have not had print-related interactions in the preschool years will take longer to develop literacy (Hiebert & Raphael, 1996; Pressley, 2003).

A child's literacy is influenced by more than what goes on in school. As we have seen, the family environment is linked with differences in children's language and literacy skills. The National Center for Educational Statistics (2000) recently reported the results of a national survey of America's kindergarten class of 1998–1999. The mother's education level was positively correlated with the number of books in the home. Single-parent families had fewer books than families with both parents present in the home and welfare parents had fewer books in their homes than more affluent families. Further, parents who read to their kindergarten children three or more times a week had children with better language skills than parents who read to their children less than three times a week.

The International Reading Association and the National Association for the Education of Young Children (NAEYC, the leading organization of childhood educators) (1998) believe that it is extremely important for young children to have literacy experiences. Here are some recommendations for parents and teachers:

- Create a supportive environment in which children can generate a positive perception of themselves and develop a positive approach toward reading and writing (Pianta, 2003).
- Take time to read to children from a wide variety of poetry, fiction, and nonfiction. Reading aloud to children is one of the most important literacy activities in early childhood (Bus, van IJzendoorn, & Pellegrini, 1995).
- Present models for children to emulate by using language appropriately, listening and responding to children's talk, and reading and writing oneself.
- Limit the amount of time children spend watching telvision. Recently, the American Academy of Pediatrics (2001) recommended that children under 2 years of age should watch zero hours of television. Why zero? Because children under 2 years of age who watch TV are not likely to spend time in print-related interactions with caregivers.
- Develop a positive school-home partnership so that teachers can involve parents in helping children to improve their literacy skills.

Middle and Late Childhood

During middle and late childhood, children make advances in their vocabulary and grammar. As children enter elementary school, they gain skills that make it possible for them to read and write. Reading and writing assume a prominent role in their language world.

Stage	Age range/Grade level	Descripton
0	Birth to first grade	Children master several prerequisites for reading. Many learn the left-to-right progression and order of reading, how to identify letters of the alphabet, and how to write their names. Some learn to read words that appear on signs. As a result of TV shows like *Sesame Street* and attending preschool and kindergarten programs, many young children today develop greater knowledge about reading earlier than in the past.
1	First and second grades	Many children learn to read at this time. In doing so, they acquire the ability to sound out words (that is, translate letters into sounds and blend sounds into words). They also complete their learning of letter names and sounds.
2	Second and third grades	Children become more fluent at retrieving individual words and other reading skills. However, at this stage reading is still not used much for learning. The demands of reading are so taxing for children at this stage that they have few resources left over to process the content.
3	Fourth through eighth grades	In fourth through eighth grade, children become increasingly able to obtain new information from print. In other words, they read to learn. They still have difficulty understanding information presented from multiple perspectives within the same story. When children don't learn to read, a downward spiral unfolds that leads to serious difficulties in many academic subjects.
4	High school	Many students become fully competent readers. They develop the ability to understand material told from many perspectives. This allows them to engage in sometimes more sophisticated discussions of literature, history, economics, and politics.

FIGURE 9.8 A Model of Developmental Stages in Reading

Vocabulary and Grammar During middle and late childhood, a change occurs in the way children think about words. They become less tied to the actions and perceptions associated with words, and they become more analytical in their approach to words.

This analytical approach is apparent if children are asked to say the first thing that comes to mind when they hear a word. Preschool children typically respond with a word that often follows the stimulus word in a sentence. For example, when asked to respond to *dog,* the young child may say *barks;* to the word *eat, lunch.* But at about 7 years of age, children may begin to respond with a word that is the same part of speech as the stimulus word. For example, a child may now respond to the word *dog* with *cat* or *horse.* To *eat,* the 7-year-old might say *drink.* This is evidence that children now have begun to categorize their vocabulary by parts of speech (Berko Gleason, 2002).

Children make similar advances in grammar. The elementary school child's improvement in logical reasoning and analytical skills helps in the understanding of such constructions as the appropriate use of comparatives (*shorter, deeper*) and subjunctives ("*If* I *were* president . . .").

Reading One model describes the development of reading skills as occurring in five stages (Chall, 1979) (see figure 9.8). The age boundaries are approximate and do not apply to every child but the stages convey a sense of the developmental changes involved in learning to read.

Before learning to read, children learn to use language to talk about things that are not present; they learn what a word is; and they learn how to recognize and talk about sounds (Berko Gleason, 2002). They also learn the *alphabetic principle*—that letters represent sounds in the language.

How should children be taught to read? Currently, debate focuses on the whole-language approach versus the basic-skills-and-phonetics approach (O'Donnell & Wood, 2004).

The **whole-language approach** stresses that reading instruction should parallel children's natural language learning. Reading materials should be whole and

whole-language approach An approach that stresses that reading instruction should parallel children's natural language learning. Reading materials should be whole and meaningful.

meaningful. That is, children should be given material in its complete form, such as stories and poems, so that they learn to understand language's communicative function. Reading should be connected with listening and writing skills. Although there are variations in whole-language programs, most share the premise that reading should be integrated with other skills and subjects, such as science and social studies, and that it should focus on real-world material. Thus, a class might read newspapers, magazines, or books, and then write about and discuss them.

In contrast, the **basic-skills-and-phonetics approach** emphasizes that reading instruction should teach phonetics and its basic rules for translating written symbols into sounds. Early reading instruction should involve simplified materials. Only after they have learned phonological rules should children be given complex reading materials, such as books and poems (Lane & Pullen, 2004; Smith, 2004).

Which approach is better? Children can benefit from both approaches. Researchers have found strong evidence that the basic-skills-and-phonetics approach should be used in teaching children to read but that students also benefit from the whole-language approach (Durkin, 2004; Fox & Hull, 2002; Silva & Martins, 2003; Wilson & others, 2001). These were the conclusions of the National Reading Panel (2000), which conducted a comprehensive review of research on reading.

The most effective phonological awareness training involves two main skills:

- *Blending*, which involves listening to a series of separate spoken sounds and blending them, such as /g/ /o/ = go
- *Segmentation*, which consists of tapping out or counting out the sounds in a word, such as /g/ /o/ = go, which is two sounds

In addition, researchers have found that training for phonological awareness is best when it is integrated with reading and writing, is simple, and is conducted in small groups rather than with a whole class (Stahl, 2002).

Other conclusions reached by the National Reading Panel (2000) suggest that children benefit from *guided oral* reading—that is, from reading aloud with guidance and feedback. Learning strategies for reading comprehension—such as monitoring one's own reading progress and summarizing—also helps children (Pressley, 2003).

Reading, like other important skills, takes time and effort (Graves, Juel, & Graves, 2004). In a national assessment, children in the fourth grade had higher scores on a national reading test when they read 11 or more pages daily for school and homework (National Assessment of Reading Progress, 2000) (see figure 9.9). Teachers who required students to read a great deal on a daily basis had students who were more proficient at reading than teachers who required little reading by their students.

Writing   Children's writing emerges out of their early scribbles, which appear at around 2 to 3 years of age. In early childhood, children's motor skills usually develop to the point that they can begin printing letters. Most 4-year-olds can print their first name. Five-year-olds can reproduce letters and copy several short words. They gradually learn to distinguish the distinctive characteristics of letters, such as whether the lines are curved or straight, open or closed. Through the early elementary grades, many children continue to reverse letters such as *b* and *d* and *p* and *q* (Temple & others, 1993). At this age, if other aspects of the child's development are normal, letter reversals do not predict literacy problems.

As they begin to write, children often invent spellings. Usually they base these spellings on the sounds of words they hear (Spandel, 2004).

Parents and teachers should encourage children's early writing but not be overly concerned about the formation of letters or spelling (McGee & Richgels, 2004; Wasik, 2004). I once had a conference with my youngest daughter's first-grade teacher when she brought home papers with her printing all marked up and sad faces drawn on the paper. Fortunately, the teacher agreed to reduce her criticism of Jennifer's print skills. Printing errors are a natural part of the child's growth. Corrections of spelling

> *C*hildren most at risk for reading difficulties in the first grade are those who began school with less verbal skill, less phonological awareness, less letter knowledge, and less familiarity with the basic purposes and mechanisms of reading.
>
> —CATHERINE SNOW
> *Harvard University*

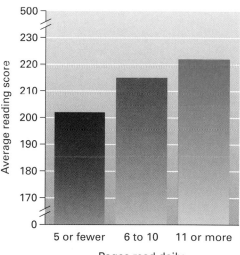

FIGURE 9.9 The Relation of Reading Achievement to Number of Pages Read Daily

In the recent analysis of reading in the fourth grade in the National Assessment of Educational Progress (2000), reading more pages daily in school and as part of homework assignments was related to higher scores on a reading test in which scores ranged from 0 to 500.

basic-skills-and-phonetics approach An approach that emphasizes that reading instruction should teach phonetics and its basic rules for translating written symbols into sounds.

The devl and the babe goste

A DEVL NAPD iN The BRITe SUNLITE he SeD iT iS HOLOWENE I HAV to GeT uP AND GeT. reDE to SCeR The littL CHILJRIN WeN THAEGO to CHRICOR CHRETE FRST He MADE A JACAL ETRN He PUT 2 CEDIS iN it to RELE SCeR THEM THN He MADE A COL JRIN to CAST SPELS ON The CHIL JRIN.

Anna Mudd is the 6-year-old author of "The Devl and the Babe Goste." Anna has been writing stories for at least two years. Her story includes poetic images, sophisticated syntax, and vocabulary that reflect advances in language development.

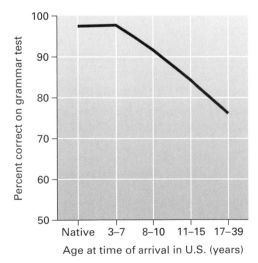

FIGURE 9.10 Grammar Proficiency and Age at Arrival in the United States

In one study, ten years after arriving in the United States, individuals from China and Korea took a grammar test (Johnson & Newport, 1991). People who arrived before the age of 8 had a better grasp of grammar than those who arrived later.

and printing should be selective and made in positive ways that do not discourage the child's writing and spontaneity.

Like becoming a good reader, becoming a good writer takes many years and lots of practice. Children should be given many writing opportunities. As their language and cognitive skills improve with good instruction, so will their writing skills. For example, developing a more sophisticated understanding of syntax and grammar serves as an underpinning for better writing. So do such cognitive skills as organization and logical reasoning. Through the course of the school years, students develop increasingly sophisticated methods of organizing their ideas. In early elementary school, they narrate and describe or write short poems. In late elementary and middle school, they can combine narration with reflection and analysis in projects such as book reports.

Effective writing instruction provides guidance about planning, drafting, and revising, not only in elementary school but through college (Graham, 1997; Pressley, 2003). One strategy for stimulating writing focuses on prompts for each part of a story to be written by students: Who is the main character? Who else is in the story? When does the story take place? Where does the story take place? What does the main character do or want to do? What do other characters do? And so on (Harris & Graham, 1996).

Bilingualism Learning a second language is easier for children than for adolescents or adults. Adults make faster initial progress, but their eventual success in the second language is not as great as children's. For example, in one study, Chinese and Korean adults who immigrated to the United States at different ages were given a test of grammatical knowledge (Johnson & Newport, 1991). Those who began learning English when they were 3 to 7 years old scored as well as native speakers on the test, but those who arrived in the United States (and started learning English) in later childhood or adolescence had lower test scores (see figure 9.10). Children's ability to pronounce a second language with the correct accent also decreases with age, with an especially sharp drop occurring after the age of about 10 to 12 (Asher & Garcia, 1969). In sum, researchers have found that early bilingual exposure is optimal and ensures the least amount of damage to the home language and to the new language (Lesaux & Siegel, 2003; Petitto, Kovelman, & Harasymowycz, 2003).

Students in the United States are far behind their counterparts in many developed countries in learning a second language. For example, in Russia, schools have 10 grades, called *forms*, which roughly correspond to the 12 grades in American schools. Children begin school at age 7 in Russia and begin learning English in the third form. Because of this emphasis on teaching English, most Russian citizens under the age of 40 today are able to speak at least some English.

U.S. students may be missing more than the chance to acquire a skill by not learning to speak a second language. *Bilingualism*—the ability to speak two languages—has a positive effect on children's cognitive development. Children who are fluent in two languages perform better than their single-language counterparts on tests of control of attention, concept formation, analytical reasoning, cognitive flexibility, and cognitive complexity (Bialystok, 1999, 2001). They also are more conscious of the structure of spoken and written language and better at noticing errors of grammar and meaning, skills that benefit their reading ability (Bialystok, 1997).

A current controversy related to bilingualism involves the most effective way of teaching children whose primary language is not English (Diaz-Rico, 2004; Echevarria, Voght, & Short, 2004). For a discussion of the debate about bilingual education, see the Contexts of Life-Span Development interlude.

Contexts of Life-Span Development
Bilingual Education

As many as 10 million children in the United States come from homes in which English is not the primary language. What is the best way to teach these children?

For the last two decades, the preferred strategy has been *bilingual education*, which teaches academic subjects to immigrant children in their native language while slowly teaching English (Garcia & Willis, 2001; Peregoy & Boyle, 2001). Advocates of bilingual education programs argue that if children who do not know English are taught only in English, they will fall behind in academic subjects. How, they ask, can 7-year-olds learn arithmetic or history taught only in English when they do not speak the language? Critics of bilingual education argue that as a result of these programs, the children of immigrants are not learning English, which puts them at a permanent disadvantage in U.S. society. Some states have eliminated their bilingual education programs.

What have researchers found regarding outcomes of bilingual education programs? The results generally support bilingual education in that (1) children have difficulty in a subject when it is taught in a language they do not understand, and (2) when both languages are integrated in the classroom, children learn the second language more readily and participate more actively (Hakuta, 2000, 2001; Pérez, 2004; Soltero, 2004).

Some critics argue that too often it is believed that immigrant children need only one year of bilingual education. However, researchers have found that in general it takes immigrant children approximately three to five years to develop speaking proficiency and seven years to develop reading proficiency in English (Hakuta, Butler, & Witt, 2000). Also, it is important to recognize that individual variations characterize the ability of immigrant children to learn English. Children who come from lower socioeconomic backgrounds have more difficulty than those from higher socioeconomic backgrounds (Hakuta, 2001). Thus, especially for immigrant children from low socioeconomic backgrounds, more years of bilingual education may be needed than they currently are receiving.

Bilingual Education
Bilingualism and Bilingual Education
Multilingual Multicultural Research
Improving Schooling for Language-Minority Children: A Research Agenda

Adolescence

Language development during adolescence includes increased sophistication in the use of words (Fischer & Lazerson, 1984). With an increase in abstract thinking, adolescents are much better than children at analyzing the function a word plays in a sentence.

Adolescents also develop more subtle abilities with words. They make strides in understanding **metaphor,** which is an implied comparison between unlike things. For example, individuals "draw a line in the sand" to indicate a nonnegotiable position; a political campaign is said to be a marathon, not a sprint; a person's faith is shattered. And adolescents become better able to understand and to use **satire,** which is the use of irony, derision, or wit to expose folly or wickedness. Caricatures are an example of satire. More advanced logical thinking also allows adolescents, from about 15 to 20 years of age, to understand complex literary works.

Most adolescents are also much better writers than children are. They are better at organizing ideas before they write, at distinguishing between general and specific points as they write, at stringing together sentences that make sense, and at organizing their writing into an introduction, body, and concluding remarks.

Everyday speech may also change during adolescence. Young adolescents often speak a dialect with their peers that is characterized by jargon and slang (Cave, 2002). A **dialect** is a variety of language that is distinguished by its vocabulary, grammar, or pronunciation. For example, when meeting a friend, instead of saying hello, a young adolescent might say, "Give me five." Nicknames that are satirical

metaphor An implied comparison between two unlike things.

satire The use of irony, derision, or wit to expose folly or wickedness.

dialect A variety of language that is distinguished by its vocabulary, grammar, or pronunciation.

and derisive ("Stilt," "Refrigerator," "Spaz") also characterize the dialect of young adolescents. Such labels might be used to show that one belongs to the group and to reduce the seriousness of a situation (Cave, 2002).

Adulthood

Most research on language development has focused on infancy and childhood. It is generally believed that for most of adulthood individuals maintain their language skills. The vocabulary of individuals often continues to increase throughout most of the adult years, at least until late adulthood (Schaie, 1996).

In late adulthood, however, some decrements in language may appear. For example, if older adults develop hearing problems, they may have difficulty distinguishing speech sounds. Because of a decline in memory skills, older adults may have difficulty in retrieving words from long-term memory (MacKay & Abrams, 1996). This often involves the *tip-of-the-tongue phenomenon*, in which individuals are confident that they can remember something but just can't quite seem to retrieve it from memory. To compensate for this decline, older adults may use words that they are very familiar with and shorten the length of their sentences. In general, though, most language skills decline little among older adults if they are healthy (Stine, Soederberg, & Morrow, 1996).

Language does change among individuals with Alzheimer's disease (Bates & others, 1995). (Recall our discussion of Alzheimer's disease in chapter 4, "Health.") Word-finding difficulties are one of the earliest symptoms of Alzheimer's disease, but most individuals with Alzheimer's disease retain much of their ability to produce well-formed sentences until the late stages of the disease. Nonetheless, they do make more grammatical errors than older adults without Alzheimer's disease.

Review and Reflect: Learning Goal 2

2 **Describe how language develops through the life span**

REVIEW
- What are some key milestones of language development during infancy?
- How do language skills change during early childhood?
- How does language develop in middle and late childhood?
- How does language develop in adolescence?
- How do language skills change during adulthood?

REFLECT
- Should children in the United States be required to learn more than one language?

---

3 BIOLOGICAL AND ENVIRONMENTAL INFLUENCES

Biological Influences	Behavioral and Environmental Influences	An Interactionist View of Language

We have described how language develops, but we have not explained what makes this amazing development possible. Everyone who uses language in some way "knows" its rules and has the ability to create an infinite number of words and sentences. Where does this knowledge come from? Is it the product of biology? Or is language learned and influenced by experiences?

Biological Influences

Some language scholars view the remarkable similarities in how children acquire language all over the world, despite the vast variation in language input they receive, as strong evidence that language has a biological basis. What role did evolution play in the biological foundations of language?

Evolution and the Brain's Role in Language The ability to speak and understand language requires a certain vocal apparatus as well as a nervous system with certain capabilities. The nervous system and vocal apparatus of humanity's predecessors changed over hundreds of thousands of years. Once equipped with these physical requirements for speaking, *Homo sapiens* went beyond grunting and shrieking to develop speech. Although estimates vary, many experts believe that humans acquired language about 100,000 years ago. In evolutionary time, then, language is a very recent acquisition. It clearly gave humans an enormous edge over other animals and increased the chances of human survival (Pinker, 1994).

There is evidence that particular regions of the brain are predisposed to be used for language (Gazzaniga, Ivy, & Magnum, 2002). Two regions involved in language were first discovered in studies of brain-damaged individuals. In 1861, a patient of Paul Broca, a French surgeon and anthropologist, received an injury to the left side of his brain. The patient became known as Tan, because that was the only word he could speak after his brain injury. Tan suffered from **aphasia,** a language disorder resulting from brain damage that involves a loss of the ability to use words. Tan died several days after Broca evaluated him, and an autopsy revealed the location of the injury. Today, we refer to the part of the brain in which Broca's patient was injured as **Broca's area,** an area of the left frontal lobe of the brain that directs the muscle movements involved in speech production (see figure 9.11).

Another place in the brain where an injury can seriously impair language is **Wernicke's area,** a region of the brain's left hemisphere involved in language comprehension (see figure 9.11). Individuals with damage to Wernicke's area often babble words in a meaningless way.

Note that both Broca's area and Wernicke's area are in the brain's left hemisphere. Evidence suggests that language processing primarily occurs in the left hemisphere (Gazzaniga, 1986; Gazzaniga, Ivy, and Magnum, 2002; Shapiro & Caramazza, 2003). But keep in mind that in most activities there is an interplay between the brain's two hemispheres (Grodzinsky, 2001; Nocentini & others, 2001). For example, in reading, most people rely on activity in areas of the left hemisphere for comprehending syntax, but most people rely on activity in the right hemisphere to understand intonation and emotion.

Language Acquisition Device

Linguist Noam Chomsky (1957) believes that humans are biologically prewired to learn language at a certain time and in a certain way. He said that children are born into the world with a **language acquisition device (LAD),** a biological endowment that enables the child to detect the features and rules of language, including phonology, syntax, and semantics. Children are prepared by nature with the ability to detect the sounds of language, for example, and to detect and follow rules such as how to form plurals and ask questions.

Chomsky's LAD is a theoretical construct, not a physical part of the brain. Is there evidence for the existence of an LAD? Supporters of the LAD concept cite the uniformity of language milestones across languages and cultures, evidence that children create language even in the absence of well-formed input, and biological substrates of language.

In the wild, chimps communicate through calls, gestures, and expressions, which evolutionary psychologists believe might be the roots of true language. *How strong is biology's role in language?*

Brain and Language Development

aphasia A language disorder resulting from brain damage that involves a loss of the ability to use words.

Broca's area An area of the brain's left frontal lobe that directs the muscle movements involved in speech production.

Wernicke's area An area of the brain's left hemisphere that is involved in language comprehension.

language acquisition device (LAD) Chomsky's term that describes a biological endowment that enables the child to detect the features and rules of language, including phonology, syntax, and semantics.

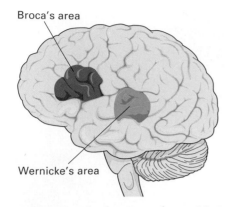

FIGURE 9.11 Broca's Area and Wernicke's Area

Broca's area is located in the brain's left hemisphere, and it is involved in the control of speech. Individuals with damage to Broca's area have problems saying words correctly. Also shown is Wernicke's area, a portion of the left hemisphere that is involved in understanding language. Individuals with damage to this area cannot comprehend words; that is, they hear the words but don't know what they mean.

MIT linguist Noam Chomsky was one of the early architects of the view that children's language development cannot be explained by environmental input. In Chomsky's view, language has strong biological underpinnings, with children biologically prewired to learn language at a certain time and in a certain way.

Is There a Critical Period for Learning Language? Most babies learn a language by a certain age if they are to learn to speak at all. Recall from chapter 1 that a *critical period* is a fixed time period in which certain experiences can have a long-lasting effect on development. It is a time of readiness for learning, after which learning is difficult or impossible. For example, baby white-crowned sparrows learn their song quite well if they are exposed to it during a specific time as a chick. After this time, they can never develop a fully formed song pattern; thus, for these sparrows there seems to be a critical period for learning their song.

Whether the notion of a critical period can be extended to human learning is much less certain. Almost all children learn one or more languages during their early years, so it is difficult to determine whether there is a critical period for language development (Obler, 1993). In the 1960s, Eric Lenneberg (1967) proposed that language depends on maturation and that there is a critical period between about 18 months and puberty during which a first language must be acquired. Lenneberg especially thought that the preschool years were an important time frame because this is when language develops rapidly and with ease.

The case study of Genie, a modern-day "wild child" with stunted language development, addresses the issue of a critical period in language development. In 1970, a California social worker made a routine visit to the home of a partially blind woman who had applied for public assistance. The social worker discovered that the woman and her husband had kept their 13-year-old daughter, Genie, locked away in almost total isolation during her childhood. Genie could not speak or stand erect. She had spent every day bound naked to a child's potty seat. She could move only her hands and feet. At night she was placed in a kind of straightjacket and caged in a crib with wire mesh sides and a cover. Whenever Genie made a noise, her father beat her. He never communicated with her in words; he growled and barked at her instead (Rymer, 1992).

After she was rescued from her parents, Genie spent a number of years in extensive rehabilitation programs, including speech and physical therapy (Curtiss, 1977). She eventually learned to walk, although with a jerky motion, and to use the toilet. Genie also learned to recognize many words and to speak in rudimentary sentences. Eventually, she was able to string together two-word combinations, such as "Big teeth," "Little marble," and "Two hand," then three-word combinations such as "Small two cup." As far as we know, unlike normal children, Genie did not learn to ask questions and did not develop a language system that allowed her to understand English grammar. Four years after she began stringing words together, Genie's speech still sounded like a garbled telegram. As an adult, she speaks in short, mangled sentences, such as "Father hit leg," "Big wood," and "Genie hurt."

Children like Genie, who are abandoned, abused, and not exposed to language for many years, rarely speak normally. Although some language experts have argued that cases such as Genie support the existence of a critical period for language development, because these children also suffer severe emotional trauma and possible neurological deficits, the issue is still far from clear.

Are the preschool years a critical period for language acquisition? Evidence for this notion comes from studies of brain development in young children, and from the amount of language learned by preschool children. However, other evidence suggests that we do not have a critical period for language learning. In particular, although much language learning takes place during the preschool years, learning continues well into the later school years and adulthood (Hakuta, Bialystok, & Wiley, 2003). In other words, young children's proficiency in language does not seem to involve a biologically critical period that older children and adults have passed.

Behavioral and Environmental Influences

As we said earlier, some language scholars view the similarities in children's language acquisition all over the world as strong evidence that language has a biological foundation. Other language experts emphasize that experiences of the child, the particular language to be learned, and the context in which learning takes place can strongly influence language acquisition (Marchman, 2003).

The Behavioral View   According to behaviorists, language is a complex learned skill, much like playing the piano or dancing. Behaviorists argued that language represents chains of responses acquired through reinforcement (Skinner, 1957). A baby happens to babble "Ma-ma"; Mama rewards the baby with hugs and smiles; the baby says "Mama" more and more. Bit by bit, the baby's language is built up. This view of language acquisition has several problems.

First, the behaviorist view does not explain how people create novel sentences—sentences that people have never heard or spoken before. For example, the child hears the sentence, "The plate fell on the floor" and then after dropping a mirror on a blanket says, "My mirror fell on the blanket."

Second, the evidence indicates that children learn the syntax of their native language even if they are not reinforced for doing so. Social psychologist Roger Brown (1973) spent long hours observing parents and their young children. He found that parents did not pay attention to the grammatical form of their children's utterances. They were just as likely to reinforce the ungrammatical utterances of the child as the grammatical ones.

A third problem with the behavioral view is that it fails to explain the extensive orderliness of language. Because each child has a unique history of reinforcement, the behaviorist view predicts that vast individual differences should appear in children's speech development. When children learn a certain aspect of a language, according to the behaviorist view, should depend on whether their parents or someone else has rewarded or punished them for something they have said. But as we have seen, a compelling fact about language is its orderly development. For example, all toddlers produce one-word utterances before two-word utterances.

Environmental Influences   Although the behaviorist view is no longer considered to be a viable explanation of language, the environment contributes in important ways to the development of children's language skills. Our overview of how language develops through the life span described some of the ways this occurs. Recall, for example, Janellen Huttenlocher's research that linked the mother's language to her child's vocabulary development. Also remember Betty Hart and Todd Risley's research, which found that professional parents talked to their children more than welfare parents did and that this talk was linked with their children's vocabulary growth.

One intriguing component of the young child's linguistic environment is **child-directed speech,** language spoken in a higher pitch than normal with simple words and sentences. Child-directed speech has the important function of capturing the infant's attention and maintaining communication. It is hard to use child-directed speech when not in the presence of a baby. As soon as you start talking to a baby, though, you shift into child-directed speech. Much of this is automatic and something most parents are not aware they are doing. Older children also modify their speech when talking to babies and younger children who are learning language. Even 4-year-olds speak in simpler ways to 2-year-olds than to their 4-year-old friends.

Are there strategies other than child-directed speech that adults use to enhance the child's acquisition of language? Three candidates are recasting, expanding, and labeling:

- **Recasting** is rephrasing something the child has said, perhaps turning it into a question. For example, if the child says, "The dog was barking," the adult can respond by asking, "When was the dog barking?" Effective use of recasting involves letting the child indicate an interest and then elaborating on that interest.
- **Expanding** is restating, in a linguistically sophisticated form, what a child has said.
- **Labeling** is identifying the names of objects. Young children are forever being asked to identify the names of objects. Roger Brown (1973) called this the "the great word game" and claimed that much of a child's early vocabulary is motivated by this adult pressure to identify the words associated with objects.

GENIE
What were Genie's experiences like? What implications do they have for language acquisition?

child-directed speech Language spoken in a higher pitch than normal with simple words and sentences.

recasting Rephrasing a statement that a child has said, perhaps turning it into a question.

expanding Restating, in a linguistically sophisticated form, what a child has said.

labeling Identifying the names of objects.

Communicating with Babies

*T*he linguistics problems children have to solve are always embedded in personal and interpersonal contexts.

—LOIS BLOOM
Contemporary Psychologist, Columbia University

These strategies are used naturally and in meaningful conversations. Parents do not (and should not) use any deliberate method to teach their children to talk, even for children who are slow in learning language. Children usually benefit when parents guide their children's discovery of language rather than overloading them with language; "following in order to lead" helps a child learn language. If children are not ready to take in some information, they are likely to tell you (as by turning away). Thus, giving the child more information is not always better.

Children vary in their ability to acquire language and this variation cannot be readily explained by differences in environmental input alone. For children who are slow in developing language skills, however, opportunities to talk and be talked with are important. Children whose parents provide them with a rich verbal environment show many positive benefits. Parents who pay attention to what their children are trying to say, expand their children's utterances, read to them, and label things in the environment are providing valuable, if unintentional, benefits (Berko Gleason, 2002).

Remember, though, that the encouragement of language development, not drill and practice, is the key. Language development is not a simple matter of imitation and reinforcement. To read further about ways that parents can facilitate children's language development, see the Applications in Life-Span Development interlude.

Applications in Life-Span Development

How Parents Can Facilitate Infants' and Toddlers' Language Development

In *Growing Up with Language,* linguist Naomi Baron (1992) provided ideas to help parents facilitate their child's language development. A summary of her ideas is presented here:

Infants

- *Be an active conversational partner.* Initiate conversation with the infant. If the infant is in a daylong child-care program, ensure that the baby receives adequate language stimulation from adults.
- *Talk as if the infant understands what you are saying.* Parents can generate self-fulfilling prophecies by addressing their young children as if they understand what is being said. The process may take four to five years, but children gradually rise to match the language model presented to them.
- *Use a language style with which you feel comfortable.* Don't worry about how you sound to other adults when you talk with your child. Your affect, not your content, is more important when talking with an infant. Use whatever type of baby talk with which you feel comfortable.

Toddlers

- *Continue to be an active conversational partner.* Engaging toddlers in conversation, even one-sided conversation, is the most important thing a parent can do to nourish a child linguistically.
- *Remember to listen.* Since toddlers' speech is often slow and laborious, parents are often tempted to supply words and thoughts for them. Be patient and let toddlers express themselves, no matter how painstaking the process is or how great a hurry you are in.

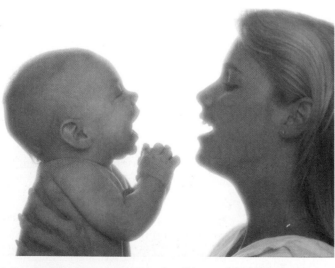

It is a good idea for parents to begin talking to their babies at the start. The best language teaching occurs when the talking is begun before the infant becomes capable of its first intelligible speech. *Why is such early talking important?*

- *Use a language style with which you are comfortable, but consider ways of expanding your child's language abilities and horizons.* For example, using long sentences need not be problematic. Don't be afraid to use ungrammatical language to imitate the toddler's novel forms (such as "No eat"). Use rhymes. Ask questions that encourage answers other than "Yes" and "No." Actively repeat, expand, and recast the child's utterances. Introduce new topics. And use humor in your conversation.
- *Adjust to your child's idiosyncrasies instead of working against them.* Many toddlers have difficulty pronouncing words and making themselves understood. Whenever possible, make toddlers feel that they are being understood.
- *Avoid sexual stereotypes.* Don't let the toddler's sex determine your amount or style of conversation. Many American mothers are more linguistically supportive of girls than of boys, and many fathers talk less with their children than mothers do. Cognitively enriching initiatives from both mothers and fathers benefit both boys and girls.
- *Resist making normative comparisons.* Be aware of the ages at which your child reaches specific milestones (first word, first 50 words, first grammatical combination). However, be careful not to measure this development rigidly against children of neighbors or friends. Such social comparisons can bring about unnecessary anxiety.

An Interactionist View of Language

If language acquisition depended only on biology, then Genie and the Wild Boy of Aveyron (discussed in the chapter's opening) should have talked without difficulty. Children do not learn language in a social vacuum. The child's experiences influence language acquisition. But we have seen that language does have strong biological foundations. No matter how much you converse with a dog, it won't learn to talk. In contrast, children are biologically prepared to learn language. Children all over the world acquire language milestones at about the same time and in about the same order. An *interactionist view* emphasizes that both biology and experience contribute to language development.

American psychologist Jerome Bruner (1983, 1996) proposed that the sociocultural context is extremely important in understanding children's language development. His view has some similarities with the ideas of Lev Vygotsky that were described in chapter 6. Bruner stresses the role of parents and teachers in constructing what he called *language acquisition support system (LASS).* The LASS resembles Vygotsky's concept of a zone of proximal development ◀◀||| **P. 218.**

Today, most language acquisition researchers believe that children from a wide variety of cultural contexts acquire their native language without explicit teaching. In some cases, they do so even without encouragement. Thus, very few aids are necessary for learning language. However, caregivers greatly facilitate a child's language learning.

Review and Reflect: Learning Goal 3

3 Discuss the biological and environmental contributions to language skills

REVIEW
- What are the biological foundations of language?
- What are the behavioral and environmental aspects of language?
- How does an interactionist view describe language?

REFLECT
- How should parents respond to children's grammatical mistakes in conversation? Should parents allow the mistakes to continue and assume their young children will grow out of them, or should they closely monitor their children's grammar and correct mistakes whenever they hear them?

Reach Your Learning Goals

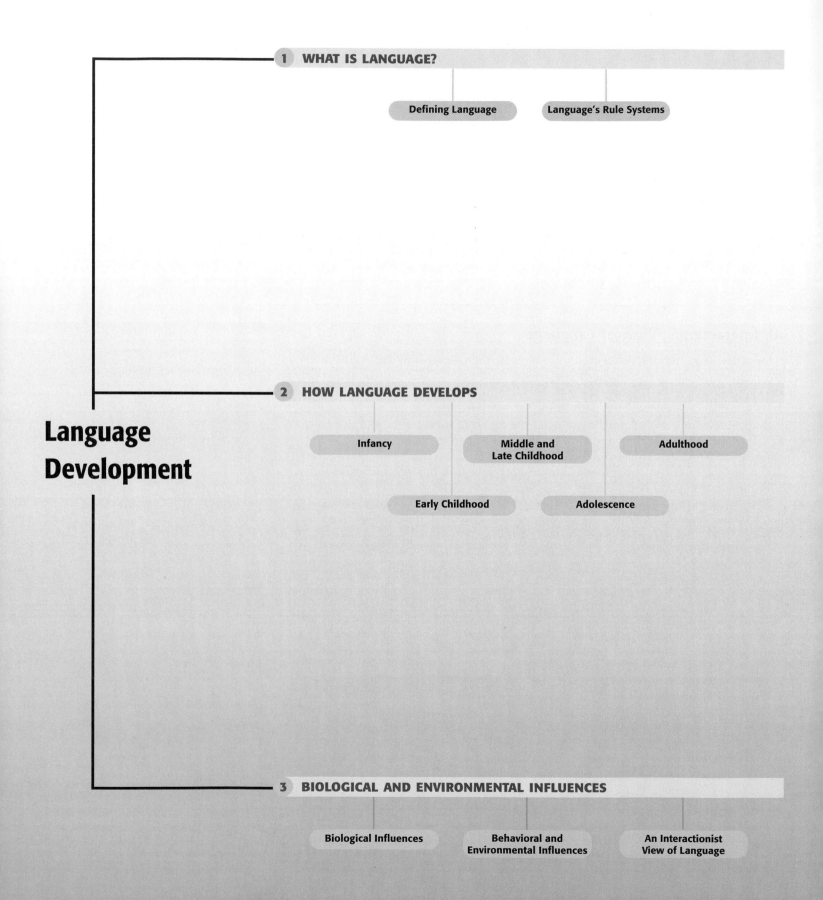

Language Development

1 WHAT IS LANGUAGE?

Defining Language

Language's Rule Systems

2 HOW LANGUAGE DEVELOPS

Infancy

Middle and
Late Childhood

Adulthood

Early Childhood

Adolescence

3 BIOLOGICAL AND ENVIRONMENTAL INFLUENCES

Biological Influences

Behavioral and
Environmental Influences

An Interactionist
View of Language

Summary

1 Define language and describe its rule systems

- Language is a form of communication, whether spontaneous, written, or signed, that is based on a system of symbols. Language consists of all the words used by a community and the rules for varying and combining them. Infinite generativity is the ability to produce an endless number of meaningful sentences using a finite set of words and rules.
- The main rule systems of language are phonology, morphology, syntax, semantics, and pragmatics. Phonology consists of rules regarding how sounds are perceived as different and which sound sequences may occur in the language. Morphology refers to word formation. Syntax is the way words are combined to form acceptable phrases and sentences. Semantics involves the meaning of words and sentences. Pragmatics is the appropriate use of language in context.

2 Describe how language develops through the life span

- Among the milestones in infant language development are crying (birth), cooing (1 to 2 months), babbling (6 months), making the transition from universal linguist to language-specific listener (6 to 12 months), using gestures (8 to 12 months), comprehension of words (8 to 12 months), first word spoken (13 months), vocabulary spurt (18 months), rapid expansion of understanding words (18 to 24 months), and two-word utterances (18 to 24 months).
- Advances in phonology, morphology, syntax, semantics, and pragmatics continue in early childhood. The transition to complex sentences begins at 2 or 3 years and continues through the elementary school years. Literacy involves learning to read and write; this should occur in a supportive atmosphere. The foundations of literacy in early childhood involve not only schooling experiences but the language environment of the home.
- In middle and late childhood, children become more analytical and logical in their approach to words and grammar. Chall's model proposes five stages in reading, ranging from birth/first grade to high school. Current debate involving how to teach children to read focuses on the whole-language approach versus the basic-skills-and-phonetics approach. Many experts recommend a balance of these two approaches. Children's writing emerges out of scribbling. Advances in children's language and cognitive development provide the underpinnings for improved writing. Bilingual education aims to teach academic subjects to immigrant children in their native languages while gradually adding English instruction. Researchers have found that bilingualism does not interfere with performance in either language. Success in learning a second language is greater in childhood than in adolescence.
- In adolescence, language changes include more effective use of words; improvements in the ability to understand metaphor and adult literary works; and improvements in writing.
- For most of adulthood, language competencies remain strong. Vocabulary growth continues through most of the adult years. In late adulthood, some decline in language skills may occur as a consequence of declines in hearing or memory, or as a result of disease.

3 Discuss the biological and environmental contributions to language skills

- In evolution, language clearly gave humans an enormous edge over other animals and increased their chance of survival. A substantial portion of language processing occurs in the brain's left hemisphere, with Broca's area and Wernicke's area being important left-hemisphere locations. Chomsky argues that children are born with the ability to detect basic features and rules of language. In other words, they are biologically prepared to learn language with a prewired language acquisition devise (LAD). The idea that there is a critical period in language development is still controversial.
- The behavioral view—that children acquire language as a result of reinforcement—has not been supported. Adults help children acquire language through child-directed speech, recasting, expanding, and labeling. Environmental influences are demonstrated by differences in the language development of children as a consequence of being exposed to different language environments in the home. Parents should talk extensively with an infant, especially about what the baby is attending to.
- An interactionist view emphasizes the contributions of both biology and experience in language. One interactionist view is that both Chomsky's LAD and Bruner's LASS are involved in language acquisition.

Key Terms

Key People

E-Learning Tools

Connect to **www.mhhe.com/santrockldt2** to research the answers and complete these exercises. In addition, you'll find a number of other resources and valuable study tools for chapter 9, "Language Development," on the Student CD-ROM that came with this book.

Taking It to the Net

1. Clarissa wants to be a speech therapist. In her child development class, she learned that Vygotsky believed that linguistic and cognitive development go hand in hand after a certain age. She wants to know more about his theory, because it might give her insight into children's language problems.
2. Todd is working in a child-care center after school. He notices that there is a wide range in the children's use of language, even within age groups. He wonders if there are guidelines that can indicate whether a child is delayed in language development.

3. Jared is concerned because his 7-year-old son, Damion, does not like to read. Damion's second-grade teacher says he is about average for his age, but she has to prod him to do his reading assignments at school. What can Jared do to help Damion become a better reader?

Self-Assessment

Reading and writing skills are two important aspects of language, not only in childhood but also in adulthood. To evaluate your reading and writing skills, complete these self-assessments:

- *Evaluating My Writing Skills*
- *A Checklist for Written Work*

Health and Well-Being, Parenting, and Education

Build your decision-making skills by trying your hand at the health and well-being, parenting, and education "Scenarios."

Socioemotional Processes and Development

Generations will depend on the ability of all procreating individuals to face their children.

—ERIK ERIKSON
Danish-Born American Psychoanalyst, 20th Century

As children develop, they need "the meeting eyes of love." They split the universe into two halves: "me and not me." They juggle the need to curb their will with becoming what they can freely. Children and youth want to fly but discover that first they have to learn to stand and walk and climb and dance. Adolescents try on one face after another, searching for a face of their own. As adults age, they seek satisfaction in their emotional lives and search for the meaning of life. Section 4 contains four chapters: "Emotional Development" (chapter 10), "The Self, Identity, and Personality" (chapter 11), "Gender and Sexuality" (chapter 12), and "Moral Development, Values, and Religion" (chapter 13).

Emotional Development

Chapter Outline		*Learning Goals*
EXPLORING EMOTION	**1**	Discuss basic aspects of emotion
What Are Emotions?		
A Functionalist View of Emotion		
Regulation of Emotion		
Emotional Competence		
DEVELOPMENT OF EMOTION	**2**	Describe the development of emotion through the life span
Infancy		
Early Childhood		
Middle and Late Childhood		
Adolescence		
Adulthood		
TEMPERAMENT	**3**	Characterize variations in temperament and their significance
Describing and Classifying Temperament		
Biological Foundations and Experience		
Goodness of Fit		
Parenting and the Child's Temperament		
ATTACHMENT AND LOVE	**4**	Explain attachment and its development
Infancy and Childhood		
Adolescence		
Adulthood		

For many years, emotion was neglected in the study of life-span development. Today, emotion is increasingly important in conceptualizations of development. For example, even as infants, individuals show different emotional styles, display varying temperaments, and begin to form emotional bonds with their caregivers. In this chapter, we will study how temperament and attachment change across the human life span. But first, we will examine emotion itself, exploring the functions of emotions in people's lives and the development of emotion from infancy through late adulthood.

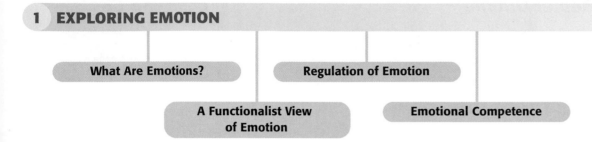

1 EXPLORING EMOTION

- What Are Emotions?
- A Functionalist View of Emotion
- Regulation of Emotion
- Emotional Competence

Imagine your life without emotion. Emotion is the color and music of life, as well as the tie that binds people together. How do psychologists define and classify emotions, and why are they important to development?

What Are Emotions?

We know emotion when we feel it, but defining emotion is difficult because it is a subjective experience. Is a child in an emotional state when her heart beats fast, her palms sweat, and her stomach churns? Is she in an emotional state when she smiles or grimaces? The body and face play important roles in emotion (Keltner & Ekman, 2000). However, psychologists debate how important each is in determining whether a person is in an emotional state. For our purposes, we will define **emotion** as a feeling that involves physiological arousal (a fast heartbeat, for example) and expressive behavior (a smile or grimace, for example).

When we think about emotions, a few dramatic feelings such as rage or glorious joy spring to mind. But emotions can be subtle as well, such as uneasiness in a new situation or the feeling a mother has when she holds her baby. Psychologists classify the broad range of emotions in many ways, but almost all classifications designate an emotion as either positive or negative. Positive emotions include enthusiasm, joy, and love. Negative emotions include anxiety, anger, guilt, and sadness.

Emotions are influenced by biological foundations and experience. In *The Expression of Emotions in Man and Animals,* Charles Darwin (1872/1965) stated that the facial expressions of humans are innate, not learned; are the same in all cultures around the world; and evolved from the emotions of animals. Darwin compared human snarls of anger with the growls of dogs and the hisses of cats. Today, psychologists still believe the emotions, especially facial expressions of emotions, have a strong biological foundation (Goldsmith, 2002). For example, children who are blind from birth and have never observed the smile or frown on another person's face smile and frown in the same way that children with normal vision do. Researchers also have found that facial expressions of basic emotions such as happiness, surprise, anger, and fear are the same across cultures.

However, *display rules*—when, where, and how emotions should be expressed—are not culturally universal (Shiraev & Levy, 2004; Triandis, 1994). For example, in cultures that are characterized by individuality—such as North America, Western Europe, and Australia—emotional displays tend to be long and intense. In contrast, Asians tend to conceal their emotions when in the presence of others. In Asian and other cultures that emphasize social connections, displays of emotions such as sympa-

emotion Feeling that involves a mixture of physical arousal and expressive behavior.

thy, respect, and shame are more common than in Western countries while negative emotions that might disrupt communication in a close-knit group are rarely displayed.

The biological foundations of emotion involve the development of the nervous system. Emotions are linked with early developing regions of the human nervous system, including structures of the limbic system and the brain stem (Thompson, 2003). The capacity of infants to show distress, excitement, and rage reflects the early emergence of these biologically rooted emotional brain systems. Significant advances in emotional responding occur during infancy and childhood as a result of changes in neurobiological systems (including the frontal regions of the cerebral cortex) that can exert control over the more primitive limbic system (Porges, Doussard-Roosevelt, & Maiti, 1994). As children develop, maturation of the cerebral cortex allows a decrease in unpredictable mood swings and an increase in the self-regulation of emotion.

Caregivers play a role in the infant's neurobiological regulation of emotions (Thompson, 2003). For example, by soothing the infant when the infant cries and shows distress, caregivers help infants to modulate their emotion and reduce the level of stress hormones (Gunnar, 2000; Gunnar & Davis, 2003).

In sum, biological evolution has endowed human beings to be *emotional,* but culture and relationships with others provide diversity in emotional experiences (Saarni, 1999, 2000). As we see next, this emphasis on the role of relationships in emotion is at the core of the functionalist view of emotion.

> *Blossoms are scattered by the wind
> And the wind cares nothing, but
> The blossoms of the heart
> No wind can touch.*
> —YOUSHIDA KENKO
> *Buddhist Monk, 14th Century*

A Functionalist View of Emotion

Developmentalists today tend to view emotions as the result of individuals' attempts to adapt to specific contextual demands (Campos, 1994, 2000). Thus, a person's emotional responses cannot be separated from the situations in which they are evoked. In many instances, emotions are elicited in interpersonal contexts. Thus, emotional expressions serve the important functions of signaling to others how one feels, regulating one's own behavior, and playing pivotal roles in social exchange.

One implication of the functionalist view is that emotions are *relational* rather than strictly internal, intrapsychic phenomena. Consider just some of the roles of emotion in parent-child relationships. The beginnings of an emotional bond between parents and an infant are based on affectively toned interchanges, as when an infant cries and the caregiver sensitively responds. By the end of the first year, a mother's facial expression—either smiling or fearful—influences whether an infant will explore an unfamiliar environment. And when children hear their parents quarreling, they often react with distressed facial expressions and inhibited play (Cummings, 1987). Well-functioning families often include humor in their interactions, sometimes making each other laugh and creating a light mood state to defuse conflict. When a positive mood has been induced in a child, the child is more likely to comply with a parent's directions.

A second implication of the functionalist view is that emotions are linked with an individual's goals in a variety of ways. Regardless of what the goal is, an individual who overcomes an obstacle to attain a goal experiences happiness. By contrast, a person who must relinquish a goal as unattainable experiences sadness. And a person who faces difficult obstacles in pursuing a goal often experiences anger.

The specific nature of the goal can affect the experience of a given emotion. For example, the avoidance of threat is linked with fear, the desire to atone is related to guilt, and the wish to avoid the scrutiny of others is associated with shame.

Regulation of Emotion

The ability to control one's emotions is a key dimension of development (Denham & others, 2003). *Emotional regulation* consists of effectively managing arousal to adapt and reach a goal. *Arousal* involves a state of alertness or activation, which can reach levels that are too high for effective functioning. Anger, for example, often requires regulation.

Here are some developmental trends in regulating emotion during childhood (Eisenberg, 1998, 2001):

- With increasing age in infancy and early childhood, regulation of emotion shifts gradually from external sources in the world (for example, parents) to self-initiated, internal resources. Caregivers soothe young children, manage young children's emotion by choosing the contexts in which they behave, and provide children with information (facial cues, narratives, and so on) to help them interpret events. With age and advances in cognitive development, children are better equipped to manage emotion themselves. For example, older children might minimize the escalation of negative emotion in an interpersonal conflict by monitoring their facial expressions (for example, avoiding sneering or looks of contempt).
- Cognitive strategies for regulating emotions, such as thinking about situations in a positive light, cognitive avoidance, and the ability to shift the focus of one's attention, increase with age.
- With greater maturity, children develop greater capacity to modulate their emotional arousal (such as controlling angry outbursts).
- With age, individuals become more adept at selecting and managing situations and relationships in ways that minimize negative emotion.
- With age, children become more capable of selecting effective ways to cope with stress.

Of course, there are wide variations in children's ability to modulate their emotions. Indeed, a prominent feature of adolescents with problems is that they often have difficulty managing their emotions.

Parents can help children learn to regulate their emotions. Depending on how they talk with their children about emotion, parents can be described as taking an *emotion-coaching* or an *emotion-dismissing* approach (Gottman, 2002). *Emotion-coaching parents* monitor their children's emotions, view their children's negative emotions as opportunities for teaching, assist them in labeling emotions, and coach them in how to deal effectively with emotions. In contrast, *emotion-dismissing parents* view their role as to deny, ignore, or change negative emotions. Researchers have found that when interacting with their children, emotion-coaching parents were less rejecting, used more scaffolding and praise, and were more nurturant than emotion-dismissing parents (Gottman & DeClaire, 1997). The children of emotion-coaching parents were better at physiologically soothing themselves when they got upset, were better at regulating their negative affect, could focus their attention better, and had fewer behavior problems than the children of emotion-dismissing parents.

**International Society for Research on Emotions
Emotion-Coaching Parents**

Emotional Competence

In chapter 8, we briefly described the concept of emotional intelligence ◀◀◀ P. 278. Here we will examine a closely related concept, emotional competence, that focuses on the adaptive nature of emotional experience. Carolyn Saarni (1999) believes that becoming emotionally competent involves developing a number of skills in social contexts that include:

SKILL	*EXAMPLE*
• *Awareness of one's emotional states*	Being able to differentiate whether one feels sad or anxious
• *Discerning others' emotions*	Understanding when another person is sad rather than afraid

• *Using the vocabulary of emotion terms in socially and culturally appropriate ways*	Appropriately describing a social situation in one's culture when a person is feeling distress
• *Empathic and sympathetic sensitivity to others' emotional experiences*	Being sensitive to other people when they are feeling distressed
• *Understanding that inner emotional states do not have to correspond to outer expressions; with maturity, understanding how one's emotionally expressive behavior may impact others and take this into account in the way one presents oneself*	Recognizing that one can feel very angry yet manage one's emotional expression so that it appears more neutral
• *Adaptively coping with negative emotions by using self-regulatory strategies that reduce the intensity or duration of such emotional states*	Reducing anger by walking away from an aversive situation and engaging in an activity that takes one's mind off of the aversive situation
• *Awareness that the expression of emotions plays a major role in the nature of relationships*	Knowing that expressing anger toward a friend on a regular basis is likely to harm the friendship
• *Viewing oneself overall as feeling the way one wants to feel*	Wanting to feel that one can cope effectively with stress and that one is successfully doing this

As children acquire these emotional competence skills in a variety of contexts, they are more likely to effectively manage their emotions, become resilient in the face of stressful circumstances, and develop more positive relationships (Denham & others, 2003; Saarni, 2000).

Review and Reflect: Learning Goal 1

1 Discuss basic aspects of emotion

REVIEW

- How is emotion defined?
- What characterizes functionalism in emotion?
- What are some developmental changes in the regulation of emotion?
- What constitutes emotional competence, according to Saarni?

REFLECT

- Think back to your childhood and adolescent years. How effective were you in regulating your emotion? Give some examples. Has your ability to regulate your emotions changed as you have grown older? Explain.

2 DEVELOPMENT OF EMOTION

Infancy	Middle and Late Childhood	Adulthood
Early Childhood	Adolescence	

Does an adult's emotional life differ from an adolescent's? Does the young child's emotional life differ from an infant's? Does an infant even have an emotional life? In this section, we will sketch an overview of the changes in emotion over the life span, looking not only at changes in emotional experience but also at the development of emotional competence.

First appearance	Emotion
Primary Emotions	
3 months	Joy Sadness Disgust
2 to 6 months	Anger
First 6 months	Surprise
6 to 8 months	Fear (peaks at 18 months)
Self-Conscious Emotions	
1½ to 2 years	Empathy Jealousy Embarrassment
2½ years	Pride Shame Guilt

FIGURE 10.1 The First Appearance of Different Emotions

Beginnings: Behaviors of a Newborn

primary emotions Emotions that are present in humans and animals, including surprise, joy, anger, sadness, fear, and disgust, that appear in the first six months of life.

self-conscious emotions Emotions that require cognition, especially consciousness; they include empathy, jealousy, and embarrassment, which first appear at about 1½ to 2 years and pride, shame, and guilt, which first appear at about 2½ years of age.

basic cry A rhythmic pattern usually consisting of a cry, a briefer silence, a shorter inspiratory whistle that is higher pitched than the main cry, and then a brief rest before the next cry.

anger cry A cry similar to the basic cry but with more excess air forced through the vocal cords (associated with exasperation or rage).

pain cry A sudden appearance of loud crying without preliminary moaning and a long initial cry followed by an extended period of breath holding.

Infancy

What are some early developmental changes in emotions? What functions do infants' cries serve? When do infants begin to smile?

Early Developmental Change in Emotion   In research on emotional development, two broad types of emotions are studied (Lewis, 2002) (see figure 10.1):

- **Primary emotions,** those that are present in humans and other animals. The primary emotions include surprise, joy, anger, sadness, fear, and disgust. They appear in the first six months of life.
- **Self-conscious emotions,** those which require cognition, especially consciousness. The self-conscious emotions include empathy, jealousy, and embarrassment, which first appear at about 1½ to 2 years (following the emergence of consciousness) and pride, shame, and guilt, which first appear at about 2½ years of age. In developing this second set of self-conscious emotions (referred to as *self-conscious evaluative emotions*), children acquire and are able to use societal standards and rules to evaluate their behavior.

Figure 10.2 shows infants expressing a number of the emotions we have described.

The ability of infants to communicate emotions permits coordinated interactions with their caregivers and the beginning of an emotional bond between them. Even when infants are only 3 months old, their face-to-face interactions with caregivers are mutually regulated. That is, not only do parents change their emotional expressions in response to infants' emotional expressions, but infants also modify their emotional expressions in response to their parents' emotional expressions. Because of this coordination, these interactions are described as *reciprocal* or *synchronous* when all is going well. Cries and smiles are two emotional expressions that infants display when interacting with parents, and they are babies' first forms of emotional communication.

Crying   Crying is the most important mechanism newborns have for communicating with their world. The first cry verifies that the baby's lungs have filled with air. Cries also may tell physicians and researchers something about the central nervous system.

Babies have at least three types of cries:

- **Basic cry:** a rhythmic pattern that usually consists of a cry, followed by a briefer silence, then a shorter inspiratory whistle that is somewhat higher in pitch than the main cry, then another brief rest before the next cry. Some infancy experts believe that hunger is one of the conditions that incite the basic cry.
- **Anger cry:** A variation of the basic cry associated with exasperation or rage, in which more excess air is forced through the vocal cords.
- **Pain cry:** A sudden long, initial loud cry followed by breath holding; no preliminary moaning is present. The pain cry is stimulated by a high-intensity stimulus.

Most adults can determine whether an infant's cries signify anger or pain (Zeskind, Klein, & Marshall, 1992). Parents can distinguish the cries of their own baby better than those of another baby.

To soothe or not to soothe—should a crying baby be given attention and soothed, or does this spoil the infant? Many years ago, the behaviorist John Watson (1928) argued that parents spend too much time responding to infant crying. As a consequence, he said, parents reward crying and increase its incidence. More recently, behaviorist Jacob Gewirtz (1977) found that a caregiver's quick, soothing response to crying increased crying. In contrast, infancy experts Mary Ainsworth (1979) and John Bowlby (1989) stress that you can't respond too much to infant crying in the first year of life. They believe that a quick, comforting response to the infant's cries is an important ingredient in the development of a strong bond between the infant and caregiver. In one of Ainsworth's studies, infants whose

Joy	**Sadness**	**Anger**
Fear	**Surprise**	**Pride**

FIGURE 10.2 Expression of Different Emotions in Infants

mothers responded quickly when they cried at 3 months of age cried less later in the first year of life (Bell & Ainsworth, 1972).

Controversy still characterizes the question of whether or how parents should respond to an infant's cries (Lewis & Ramsay, 1999). However, developmentalists increasingly argue that an infant cannot be spoiled in the first year of life, which suggests that parents should soothe a crying infant rather than be unresponsive. This reaction should help infants develop a sense of trust and secure attachment to the caregiver.

Smiling   Smiling is another important communicative behavior of the infant. Two types of smiling can be distinguished in infants:

- **Reflexive smile:** A smile that does not occur in response to external stimuli and appears during the first month after birth, usually during sleep.
- **Social smile:** A smile that occurs in response to an external stimulus, typically a face in the case of the young infant.

Social smiling does not occur until 2 to 3 months of age (Emde, Gaensbauer, & Harmon, 1976), although some researchers believe that infants grin in response to voices as early as 3 weeks of age (Sroufe & Waters, 1976). The power of the infant's smiles was captured by British theorist John Bowlby (1969): "Can we doubt that the more and better an infant smiles the better he is loved and cared for? It is fortunate for their survival that babies are so designed by nature that they beguile and enslave mothers."

www.mhhe.com/santrockldt2

Exploring Infant Crying

reflexive smile A smile that does not occur in response to external stimuli. It happens during the month after birth, usually during sleep.

social smile A smile in response to an external stimulus, which, early in development, typically is a face.

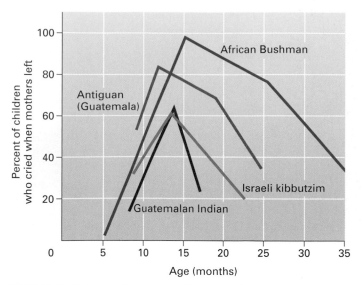

FIGURE 10.3 Separation Protest in Four Cultures

Note that separation protest peaked at about the same time in all four cultures in this study (13 to 15 months of age). However, a higher percentage (100 percent) of infants in an African Bushman culture engaged in separation protest compared with only about 60 percent of infants in Guatemalan Indian and Israeli kibbutzim cultures.

stranger anxiety An infant's fear of and wariness toward strangers; it tends to appear in the second half of the first year of life.

separation protest Occurs when infants experience a fear of being separated from a caregiver, which results in crying when the caregiver leaves.

social referencing "Reading" emotional cues in others to help determine how to act in a particular situation.

Fear As indicated in figure 10.1, fear typically first appears at about 6 months of age and peaks at about 18 months. The most frequent expression of an infant's fear involves **stranger anxiety,** in which an infant shows a fear and wariness of strangers. Stranger anxiety usually emerges gradually. It first appears at about 6 months of age in the form of wary reactions. By age 9 months, the fear of strangers is often more intense, and it continues to escalate through the infant's first birthday (Emde, Gaensbauer, & Harmon, 1976).

Not all infants show distress when they encounter a stranger. Besides individual variations, whether an infant shows stranger anxiety also depends on the social context and the characteristics of the stranger. Infants show less stranger anxiety when they are in familiar settings. For example, in one study, 10-month-olds showed little stranger anxiety when they met a stranger in their own home but much greater fear when they encountered a stranger in a research laboratory (Sroufe, Waters, & Matas, 1974). Also, infants show less stranger anxiety when they are sitting on their mothers' laps than when placed in an infant seat several feet away from their mothers (Bohlin & Hagekull, 1993). Thus, it appears that, when infants have a sense of security, they are less likely to show stranger anxiety.

Who the stranger is and how the stranger behaves also influence stranger anxiety in infants. Infants are less fearful of child strangers than adult strangers. They also are less fearful of friendly, outgoing, smiling strangers than of passive, unsmiling strangers (Bretherton, Stolberg, & Kreye, 1981).

In addition to stranger anxiety, infants experience fear of being separated from their caregivers. The result is **separation protest**—crying when the caregiver leaves. Separation protest tends to peak at about 15 months among U.S. infants. In fact, in one study, separation protest peaked at about 13 to 15 months in four different cultures (Kagan, Kearsley, & Zelazo, 1978). As indicated in figure 10.3, the percentage of infants who engaged in separation protest varied across cultures, but the infants reached a peak of protest at about the same age—just before the middle of the second year of life.

Social Referencing **Social referencing** involves "reading" emotional cues in others to help determine how to act in a particular situation. The development of social referencing helps infants to interpret ambiguous situations more accurately, as when they encounter a stranger and need to know whether to fear the person (Mumme, Fernald, & Herrera, 1996).

Infants become better at social referencing in the second year of life. At this age, they tend to "check" with their mother before they act; they look at her to see if she is happy, angry, or fearful. For example, in one study, 14- to 22-month-old infants were more likely to look at their mother's face as a source of information for how to act in a situation than were 6- to 9-month-old infants (Walden, 1991).

Emotional Regulation and Coping During the first year of life, the infant gradually develops an ability to inhibit, or minimize, the intensity and duration of emotional reactions (Eisenberg, 2001). From early in infancy, babies put their thumbs in their mouths as a self-soothing strategy. At first, infants mainly depend on caregivers to help them soothe their emotions, as when a caregiver rocks an infant to sleep, sings lullabyes to the infant, gently strokes the infant, and so on. Many developmentalists believe it is a good strategy for a caregiver to soothe an infant before the infant gets into an intense, agitated, uncontrolled state (Thompson, 1994).

Later in infancy, when they become aroused, infants sometimes redirect their attention or distract themselves in order to reduce their arousal (Grolnick, Bridges,

& Connell, 1996). By two years of age, toddlers can use language to define their feeling states and the context that is upsetting them (Kopp & Neufeld, 2002). A toddler might say, "Feel bad. Dog scare." This type of communication may help caregivers to help the child in regulating emotion.

Contexts can influence emotional regulation (Kopp & Neufeld, 2002; Saarni, 1999). Infants are often affected by fatigue, hunger, time of day, which people are around them, and where they are. Infants must learn to adapt to different contexts that require emotional regulation. Further, new demands appear as the infant becomes older and parents modify their expectations. For example, a parent may take it in stride if a 6-month-old infant screams in a restaurant but may react very differently if a 1½-year-old starts screaming.

Early Childhood

Young children, like adults, experience many emotions during the course of a day. At times, children also try to make sense of other people's emotional reactions and feelings.

Self-Conscious Emotions Recall our earlier description of *self-conscious emotions,* which require that children be able to refer to themselves and be aware of themselves as distinct from others (Lewis, 2002). We indicated that self-conscious evaluative emotions—pride, shame, and guilt—first appear at about 2½ years of age. Expression of these emotions indicates that children are beginning to acquire and are able to use societal standards and rules to evaluate their behavior.

Pride is expressed when children feel joy as a result of the successful outcome of a particular action (Lewis, 2002). Pride is often associated with achieving a particular goal.

Shame results when children judge their actions as failures in regard to their standards, rules, and goals (Lewis, 2002). Shame typically involves an evaluation of the entire self and can produce confusion and an inability to speak. Shame is not produced by any specific situation but by an individual's interpretation of an event.

Whereas shame arises from a global attribution of failure, *guilt* stems from a specific attribution (Lewis, 2002). In guilt, the attributional process focuses on an action rather than the total self (as in shame). The feeling produced in guilt is often not as intensely negative as the feeling generated by shame and does not lead to confusion and immobility. When they feel guilty, children often can take corrective action (although they don't always do so) to reduce the negative feeling and prevent it from occurring again.

Guilt and shame have different physical characteristics. When children experience shame, they often hunch over in an effort to hide or disappear; their bodies seem to shrink as if to disappear from the view of others (see figure 10.4). When they experience guilt, children usually move in space as if they are trying to repair the action.

In one study, girls showed more shame and pride than boys (Stipek, Recchia, & McClintic, 1992). This gender difference is interesting because girls are more at risk for internalizing disorders, such as anxiety and depression, in which feelings of shame and self-criticism are often evident (Cummings, Braungart-Rieker, & Du Rocher-Schudlich, 2003).

The development of evaluative, self-conscious emotions is especially influenced by parents' responses to children's behavior. For example, a young child may experience a twinge of guilt when a parent says, "You should feel bad about biting your sister."

Young Children's Emotion Language and Understanding of Emotion

Among the most important changes in emotional development in early childhood are an increased ability to talk about their own and others' emotions and to understand emotion (Kuebli, 1994). Between 2 and 4 years of age, children considerably

> *T*he experiences of the first three years of life are almost entirely lost to us, and when we attempt to enter into a small child's world, we come as foreigners who have forgotten the landscape and no longer speak the native tongue.
>
> —SELMA FRAIBERG
> *American Child Psychiatrist,*
> *20th Century*

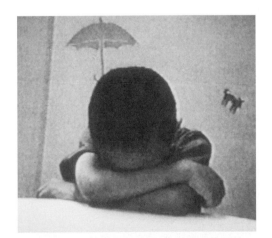

FIGURE 10.4 A Young Child Expressing the Emotion of Shame

FIGURE 10.5 Some Characteristics of Young Children's Emotion Language and Understanding

Approximate Age of Child	Description
2 to 3 years	Increase emotion vocabulary most rapidly
	Correctly label simple emotions in self and others and talk about past, present, and future emotions
	Talk about the causes and consequences of some emotions and identify emotions associated with certain situations
	Use emotion language in pretend play
4 to 5 years	Show increased capacity to reflect verbally on emotions and to consider more complex relations between emotions and situations
	Understand that the same event may call forth different feelings in different people and that feelings sometimes persist long after the events that caused them
	Demonstrate growing awareness about controlling and managing emotions in accord with social standards

increase the number of terms they use to describe emotions (Ridgeway, Waters, & Kuzaj, 1985). They also are learning about the causes and consequences of feelings (Denham, 1998; Denham & others, 2003).

When they are 4 to 5 years of age, children show an increased ability to reflect on emotions. During this time, they also begin to understand that the same event can elicit different feelings in different people. Moreover, they show a growing awareness that they need to manage their emotions to meet social standards (Bruce, Olen, & Jensen, 1999). Figure 10.5 summarizes the characteristics of young children's talk about emotion and their understanding of it.

Parents, teachers, and other adults can help children understand and control their emotions. They can talk with children to help them cope with distress, sadness, anger, or guilt. Learning to express some feelings and mask others is a common, everyday lesson in children's lives. Children who get angry because they have to wait their turn or who laugh at a crying child who has fallen and skinned a knee can be encouraged to consider other children's feelings. Children who boast about winning something can be reminded how sad it feels to lose.

Emotions play a strong role in whether a child's peer relationships are successful or not (Hubbard, 2001). Moody and emotionally negative children experience greater rejection by their peers, whereas emotionally positive children are more popular (Stocker & Dunn, 1990).

Emotional regulation is an important aspect of getting along with peers. In one study conducted in the natural context of young children's everyday peer interactions, self-regulation of emotion enhanced children's social competence (Fabes & others, 1999). Children who made an effort to control their emotional responses were more likely to respond in socially competent ways in an emotionally provocative peer situation (as when a peer made a hostile comment or took something away from the child). In sum, the ability to modulate one's emotions is an important skill that benefits children in their relationships with peers.

Middle and Late Childhood

These are some important developmental changes in emotions during the middle and late childhood years (Kuebli, 1994; Wintre & Vallance, 1994):

- An increased ability to understand such complex emotions as pride and shame (Kuebli, 1994). These emotions become more internalized (self-generated) and integrated with a sense of personal responsibility
- Increased understanding that more than one emotion can be experienced in a particular situation

- An increased tendency to take into fuller account the events leading to emotional reactions
- Marked improvements in the ability to suppress or conceal negative emotional reactions
- The use of self-initiated strategies for redirecting feelings

Adolescence

Adolescence has long been described as a time of emotional turmoil (Hall, 1904). Adolescents are not constantly in a state of "storm and stress," but emotional highs and lows do increase during early adolescence (Rosenblum & Lewis, 2003). Young adolescents can be on top of the world one moment and down in the dumps the next. In many instances, the intensity of their emotions seems out of proportion to the events that elicit them (Steinberg & Levine, 1997). Young adolescents might sulk a lot, not knowing how to adequately express their feelings. With little or no provocation, they might blow up at their parents or siblings, a response that might reflect the defense mechanism of displacing their feelings onto another person. For some adolescents, such emotional swings can reflect serious problems. Girls are especially vulnerable to depression in adolescence (Nolen-Hoeksema, 2004). But it is important for adults to recognize that moodiness is a *normal* aspect of early adolescence, and most adolescents make it through these moody times to become competent adults.

Reed Larson and Maryse Richards (1994) found that adolescents reported more extreme emotions and more fleeting emotions than their parents did. For example, adolescents were five times more likely to report being "very happy" and three times more likely to report being "very sad" than their parents (see figure 10.6). These findings lend support to the perception of adolescents as moody and changeable (Rosenblum & Lewis, 2003).

Researchers have also found that from the fifth through the ninth grades, both boys and girls experience a 50 percent decrease in being "very happy" (Larson & Lampman-Petraitis, 1989). In this same study, adolescents were more likely than preadolescents to report mildly negative mood states.

Emotional fluctuations in early adolescence may be related to the variability of hormones during this period. (Chapter 3 discussed the significant hormonal changes that characterize puberty.) Moods become less extreme as adolescents move into adulthood, and this decrease in emotional fluctuation may reflect adaptation to hormone levels (Rosenbaum & Lewis, 2003).

Researchers have discovered that pubertal change is associated with an increase in negative emotions (Archibald, Graber, & Brooks-Gunn, 2003; Dorn, Williamson, & Ryan, 2002; Brooks-Gunn, Graber, & Paikoff, 1994). However, most researchers conclude that hormonal influences are small and that when they occur they usually are associated with other factors, such as stress, eating patterns, sexual activity, and social relationships (Rosenbaum & Lewis, 2003; Susman, Dorn, & Schiefelbein, 2003; Susman & Rogol, 2004).

Indeed, environmental experiences may contribute more to the emotions of adolescence than hormonal changes. Recall from chapter 3 that in one study, social factors accounted for two to four times as much variance as hormonal factors in young adolescent girls' depression and anger (Brooks-Gunn & Warren, 1989) ◀|||| **P. 98.** In sum, both hormonal changes and environmental experiences are involved in the changing emotional landscape of adolescence.

Adulthood

Like children, adults adapt more effectively when they are emotionally intelligent—when they are skilled at perceiving and expressing emotion, understanding emotion, using feelings to facilitate thought, and managing emotions effectively. (In

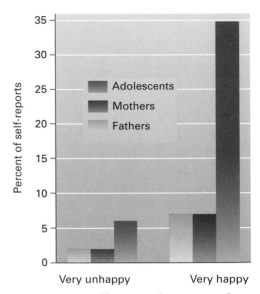

FIGURE 10.6 Self-Reported Extremes of Emotion by Adolescents, Mothers, and Fathers Using the Experience Sampling Method

In the study by Reed Larson and Maryse Richards (1994), adolescents and their mothers and fathers were beeped at random times by researchers using the experience sampling method. The researchers found that adolescents were more likely to report more emotional extremes than their parents.

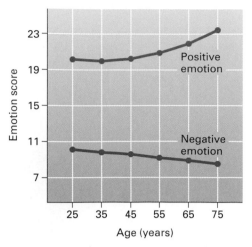

FIGURE 10.7 Changes in Positive and Negative Emotion Across the Adult Years

Positive and negative scores had a possible range of 6 to 30 with higher scores reflecting positive emotion and lower scores negative emotion. Positive emotion increased in the middle adulthood and late adulthood years while negative emotion declined.

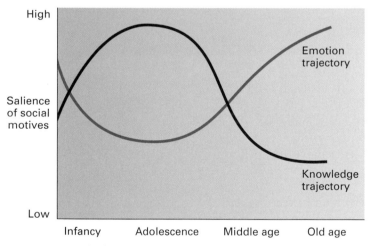

FIGURE 10.8 Idealized Model of Socioemotional Selectivity Through the Life Span

In Carstensen's theory of socioemotional selectivity, the motivation to reach knowledge-related and emotion-related goals changes across the life span.

socioemotional selectivity theory The theory that older adults become more selective about their social networks. Because they place high value on emotional satisfaction, older adults often spend more time with familiar individuals with whom they have had rewarding relationships.

chapter 14, "Families, Lifestyles, and Parenting," we will examine a number of aspects of relationships that involve emotions.) Researchers have found that across diverse samples—Norwegians, Catholic nuns, African Americans, Chinese Americans, and European Americans—older adults report better control of their emotions and fewer negative emotions than younger adults (Carstensen, Gottman, & Levensen, 1995; Carstensen & others, 2003; Charles, Mather, & Carstensen, 2003; Lawton & others, 1992; Mroczek, 2001).

Stereotypes would lead us to expect that the emotional landscape for older adults is bleak, that most live sad, lonely lives. Researchers have found a different picture (Charles, Mather, & Carstensen, 2003). One study of a very large U.S. sample examined emotions at different ages (Mroczek & Kolarz, 1998). Older adults reported experiencing more positive emotion and less negative emotion than younger adults, and positive emotion increased with age in adults at an accelerating rate (see figure 10.7). In another study, positive events (a child's birthday party, for example) and negative scenes (a burn victim, for example) were shown to adults of different ages while they were undergoing an MRI brain scan (Mather & others, in press). More activity in response to negative scenes occurred in the brains of the young adult, but greater activity in response to positive scenes occurred in the brains of the older adults. The activity differences were clearest in the amygdala, which is especially important in processing emotions.

Overall, compared with younger adults, the feelings of older adults mellow. Emotional life is on a more even keel, with fewer highs and lows. It may be that although older adults have less extreme joy, they have more contentment, especially when they are connected in positive ways with friends and family. In sum, researchers have found that the emotional life of older adults is more positive than stereotypes suggest (Carstensen, 1998; Carstenson & Charles, 2003; Carstensen & others, 2003; Mroczek, 2001; Pasupathi & Carstensen, in press).

One theory developed by Laura Carstensen (1991, 1993, 1995, 1998; Carstensen & others, 2003) stands out as important in thinking about developmental changes in adulthood, especially in older adults. **Socioemotional selectivity theory** states that older adults become more selective about their social networks. Because they place a high value on emotional satisfaction, older adults often spend more time with familiar individuals with whom they have had rewarding relationships. This theory argues that older adults deliberately withdraw from social contact with individuals peripheral to their lives while they maintain or increase contact with close friends and family members with whom they have had enjoyable relationships. This selective narrowing of social interaction maximizes positive emotional experiences and minimizes emotional risks as individuals become older. According to this theory, older adults systematically hone their social networks so that available social partners satisfy their emotional needs.

Is there research to support life-span differences in the composition of social networks? Longitudinal studies reveal far smaller social networks for older than for younger adults (Lee & Markides, 1990; Palmore, 1981). In one study of individuals 69 to 104 years of age, the oldest participants had fewer peripheral social contacts than the relatively younger participants but about the same number of close emotional relationships (Lang & Carstensen, 1994).

Socioemotional selectivity theory also focuses on the types of goals that individuals are motivated to achieve (Carstensen, Isaacowitz, & Charles, 1999; Carstensen & others, 2003; Löckenoff & Carstensen, 2003). According to the theory, motivation for knowledge-related goals starts relatively high in the early years of life, peaks in adolescence and early adulthood, then declines in middle and late adulthood (see figure 10.8).

The trajectory for emotion-related goals is high during infancy and early childhood, declines from middle childhood through early adulthood, and increases in middle and late adulthood.

One of the main reasons given for these changing trajectories in knowledge-related and emotion-related goals involves the perception of time (Carstensen & Charles, 2003; Carstensen, Isaacowitz, & Charles, 1999). Striving for knowledge is so important from late adolescence to middle age, it is pursued relentlessly, even at the cost of emotional satisfaction. But as older adults perceive that they have less time left in their lives, they are motivated to spend more time seeking emotion-related than knowledge-related goals.

> *Recent research paints a distinctly positive picture of aging in the emotion domain.*
>
> —**Laura Carstensen**
> *Contemporary Psychologist,*
> *Stanford University*

www.mhhe.com/santrockldt2

Laura Carstensen's Research

Review and Reflect: Learning Goal 2

2 Describe the development of emotion through the life span

REVIEW

- How does emotion develop in infancy?
- What characterizes emotional development in early childhood?
- What changes take place in emotion during middle and late childhood?
- How does emotion change in adolescence?
- What are some key aspects of emotional development in adulthood?

REFLECT

- A mother and father of an 8-month-old baby are having difficulty getting any sleep because the baby wakes up in the middle of the night crying. How would you recommend that they deal with this situation?

---

3 TEMPERAMENT

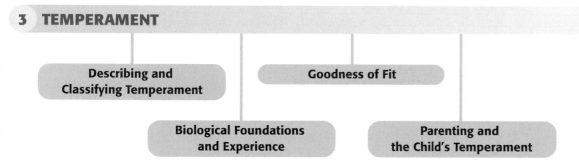

Do you get upset a lot? Does it take much to get you angry, or to make you laugh? Even at birth, babies seem to have different emotional styles. One infant is cheerful and happy much of the time; another baby seems to cry constantly. These tendencies reflect **temperament,** which is an individual's behavioral style and characteristic way of responding.

Temperament is closely linked with *personality,* the enduring personal characteristics of an individual. In fact, the lines between temperament and personality (which we will discuss in chapter 11) are often blurred. Temperament can be thought of as the biological and emotional foundations of personality. A baby's temperament inclines the baby toward a particular style of feeling and reacting, which makes it more likely that the baby's personality will take one shape or another.

Does temperament change over the life span? Does an infant's temperament predict how that infant will behave as a child or as an adult? Before these questions can be addressed, we need to examine how researchers describe or classify the temperaments of individuals.

temperament An individual's behavioral style and characteristic emotional response.

"Oh, he's cute, all right, but he's got the temperament of a car alarm."

Infancy and Toddlerhood:
Kagan Studies of Infant Temperament

easy child A temperament style in which the child is generally in a positive mood, quickly establishes regular routines, and adapts easily to new experiences.

difficult child A temperament style in which the child tends to react negatively and cry frequently, engages in irregular daily routines, and is slow to accept new experiences.

slow-to-warm-up child A temperament style in which the child has low activity level, is somewhat negative, shows low adaptability, and displays a low intensity of mood.

Describing and Classifying Temperament

How would you describe your temperament or the temperament of a friend? Researchers have described and classified the temperament of individuals in different ways. Here we will examine three ways of describing and classifying temperament.

Chess and Thomas' Classification   Psychiatrists Alexander Chess and Stella Thomas (Chess & Thomas, 1977; Thomas & Chess, 1991) identified three basic types, or clusters, of temperament:

- **Easy child.** This child is generally in a positive mood, quickly establishes regular routines in infancy, and adapts easily to new experiences.
- **Difficult child.** This child reacts negatively and cries frequently, engages in irregular daily routines, and is slow to accept change.
- **Slow-to-warm-up child.** This child has a low activity level, is somewhat negative, shows low adaptability, and displays a low intensity of mood.

In their longitudinal investigation, Chess and Thomas found that 40 percent of the children they studied could be classified as easy, 10 percent as difficult, and 15 percent as slow to warm up. Notice that 35 percent did not fit any of the three patterns. Researchers have found that these three basic clusters of temperament are moderately stable across the childhood years.

Kagan's Behavioral Inhibition   Another way of classifying temperament focuses on the differences between a shy, subdued, timid child and a sociable, extraverted, bold child. Jerome Kagan (1997, 2000, 2002, 2003; Kagan & Snidman, 1991) regards shyness with strangers (peers or adults) as one feature of a broad temperament category called *inhibition to the unfamiliar*. Inhibited children react to many aspects of unfamiliarity with initial avoidance, distress, or subdued affect, especially beginning about 7 to 9 months of age.

Kagan has found that inhibition shows considerable stability from infancy through early childhood. One recent study classified toddlers into extremely inhibited, extremely uninhibited, and intermediate groups (Pfeifer & others, 2002). Follow-up assessments occurred at 4 and 7 years of age. Continuity was demonstrated for both inhibition and lack of inhibition, although a substantial number of the inhibited children moved into the intermediate groups at 7 years of age.

Rothbart and Bates' Classification   New classifications of temperament continue to be forged (Rothbart & Putnam, 2002; Wachs & Kohnstamm, 2001). Mary Rothbart and John Bates (1998) have proposed this framework for classifying temperament:

- *Positive affect and approach.* Kagan's uninhibited children fit into this category.
- *Negative affectivity.* Children with this temperament are easily distressed; they may fret and cry often. Kagan's inhibited children fit this category.
- *Effortful control (self-regulation).* Infants who are high on effortful control show an ability to keep their arousal from getting too high and have strategies for soothing themselves. By contrast, children low on effortful control are often unable to control their arousal; they become easily agitated and intensely emotional (Eisenberg & others, 2002).

Biological Foundations and Experience

Physiological characteristics are associated with different temperaments (Rothbart & Bates, 1998). For example, inhibition is associated with a unique physiological pattern that includes high and stable heart rate, high cortisol levels, and high activity in the right frontal lobe of the brain (Kagan, 2002; Schmidt, Shahinfar, & Fox, 1996). Low levels of the neurotransmitter serotonin may increase an individual's vulnerability to fear and frustration, which can contribute to negative affectivity, such as depression (Hariri & others, 2002).

What is heredity's role in the biological foundations of temperament? Twin and adoption studies have found a heritability index for temperament in the range of .50 to .60, suggesting a moderate influence of heredity on temperament (Plomin & others, 1994). However, the strength of the association usually declines as infants become older (Goldsmith & Gottesman, 1981). This finding supports the belief that temperament becomes more malleable with experience. Alternatively, it may be that as a child becomes older, behavioral indicators of temperament are more difficult to spot.

Kagan (1997, 2002) argues that children inherit a physiology that biases them to have a particular type of temperament but that through experience they may learn to modify their temperament to some degree. For example, children may inherit a physiology that biases them to be fearful and inhibited, but they may learn to reduce their fear and inhibition.

What are some ways that developmentalists have classified infants' temperaments? Which classification makes the most sense to you, based on your observations of infants?

Developmental Connections   Do young adults show the same behavioral style and characteristic emotional responses as when they were infants or young children? Activity level is an important dimension of temperament. Are children's activity levels linked to their personality in early adulthood? In one longitudinal study, children who were highly active at age 4 were likely to be very outgoing at age 23, which reflects continuity (Franz, 1996). From adolescence into early adulthood, most individuals show fewer emotional mood swings, become more responsible, and engage in less risk-taking behavior, which reflects discontinuity (Caspi, 1998).

Is temperament in childhood linked with adjustment in adulthood? Here is what we know based on the few longitudinal studies that have been conducted on this topic (Caspi, 1998). In one longitudinal study, children who had an easy temperament at 3 to 5 years of age were likely to be well adjusted as young adults (Chess & Thomas, 1977). In contrast, many children who had a difficult temperament at 3 to 5 years of age were not well adjusted as young adults. Also, other researchers have found that boys with a difficult temperament in childhood are less likely as adults to continue their formal education, whereas girls with a difficult temperament in childhood are more likely to experience marital conflict as adults (Wachs, 2000).

Inhibition is another temperament characteristic that has been studied extensively (Kagan, 2000). Researchers have found that individuals with an inhibited temperament in childhood are less likely as adults to be assertive or to experience social support, and more likely to delay entering a stable job track (Wachs, 2000).

Yet another aspect of temperament involves emotionality and the ability to control one's emotions. In one longitudinal study, when 3-year-old children showed good control of their emotions and were resilient in the face of stress, they were likely to continue to handle emotions effectively as adults (Block, 1993). By contrast, when 3-year-olds had low emotional control and were not very resilient, they were likely to show problems in these areas as young adults.

In sum, these studies reveal some continuity between certain aspects of temperament in childhood and adjustment in early adulthood. However, keep in mind that these connections between childhood temperament and adult adjustment are based on only a small number of studies; more research is needed to verify these linkages.

Infant Temperament

Initial Temperament Trait: Inhibition

	Child A	Child B
Intervening Context		
Caregivers	Caregivers (parents) who are sensitive and accepting, and let the child set his or her own pace.	Caregivers who use inappropriate "low level control" and attempt to force the child into new situations.
Physical Environment	Presence of "stimulus shelters" or "defensible spaces" that the children can retreat to when there is too much stimulation.	The child continually encounters noisy, chaotic environments that allow no escape from stimulation.
Peers	Peer groups with other inhibited children with common interests, so the child feels accepted.	Peer groups consist of athletic extroverts, so the child feels rejected.
Schools	School is "undermanned" so inhibited children are more likely to be tolerated and feel they can make a contribution.	School is "overmanned" so inhibited children are less likely to be tolerated and more likely to feel undervalued.
Personality Outcomes		
	As an adult, individual is closer to extroversion (outgoing, sociable) and is emotionally stable.	As an adult, individual is closer to introversion and has more emotional problems.

FIGURE 10.9 Temperament in Childhood, Personality in Adulthood, and Intervening Contexts

Varying experiences with caregivers, the physical environment, peers, and schools may modify links between temperament in childhood and personality in adulthood. The example given here is for inhibition.

Developmental Contexts What accounts for the continuities and discontinuities between a child's temperament and an adult's personality? Physiological and heredity factors likely are involved in continuity. Theodore Wachs (1994, 2000) proposed ways that linkages between temperament in childhood and personality in adulthood might vary depending on the contexts in individuals' experience. Figure 10.9 summarizes how one characteristic might develop in different ways depending on the context.

Gender can be an important factor shaping the context that influences the fate of temperament. Parents might react differently to a child's temperament depending on whether the child is a boy or a girl and on the culture in which they live (Kerr, 2001). For example, in one study, mothers were more responsive to the crying of irritable girls than to the crying of irritable boys (Crockenberg, 1986).

Similarly, the reaction to an infant's temperament may depend, in part, on culture. For example, an active temperament might be valued in some cultures (such as the United States) but not in other cultures (such as China). Indeed, children's temperament can vary across cultures (Putnam, Sanson, & Rothbart, 2002). Behavioral inhibition is more highly valued in China than in North America, and researchers have found that Chinese children are more inhibited than Canadian infants (Chen & others, 1998). The cultural differences in temperament were linked to parent attitudes and behaviors. Canadian mothers of inhibited 2-year-olds were less accepting of their infants' inhibited temperament while Chinese mothers were more accepting.

In short, many aspects of a child's environment can encourage or discourage the persistence of temperament characteristics. One useful way of thinking about these relationships applies the concept of goodness of fit, which we examine next.

Goodness of Fit

goodness of fit The match between a child's temperament and the environmental demands the child must cope with.

Goodness of fit refers to the match between a child's temperament and the environmental demands the child must cope with (Matheny & Phillips, 2001). Consider an active child who is made to sit still for long periods of time or a slow-to-warm-up child who is abruptly pushed into new situations on a regular basis. Both children face a lack of fit between their temperament and environmental demands. Lack of fit can produce adjustment problems for the child.

Some temperament characteristics pose more parenting challenges than others, at least in modern Western societies. Children's proneness to distress, as exhibited by frequent crying and irritability, can contribute to the emergence of avoidant or coercive parental responses. In one research study, though, extra support and training for mothers of distress-prone infants improved the quality of mother-infant interaction (van den Boom, 1989).

What are some good strategies for parents to adopt when responding to their infant's temperament?

Parenting and the Child's Temperament

Many parents don't become believers in temperament's importance until the birth of their second child. Many parents view the first child's behavior as being solely a result of how they socialized the child. However, management strategies that worked with the first child might not be as effective with the second child. Problems experienced with the first child (such as those involved in feeding, sleeping, and coping with strangers) might not exist with the second child, but new problems might arise. Such experiences strongly suggest that children differ from each other very early in life, and that these differences have important implications for parent-child interaction (Kwak & others, 1999; Rothbart & Putnam, 2002).

What are the implications of temperamental variations for parenting? Although answers to this question necessarily are speculative because of the incompleteness of research, the conclusions described in the Applications in Life-Span Development interlude can be helpful.

Applications in Life-Span Development

Temperament and Adaptive Parenting

These conclusions regarding the best parenting strategies to use in relation to children's temperament were reached by temperament experts Ann Sanson and Mary Rothbart (1995):

- *Attention to and respect for individuality.* Parents need to be sensitive and flexible to the infant's signals and needs. One implication is that it is difficult to generate general prescriptions for "good parenting." A goal might be accomplished in one way with one child and in another way with another child, depending on the child's temperament.
- *Structuring the child's environment.* Crowded, noisy environments can pose greater problems for some children (such as a "difficult child") than others (such as an "easygoing" child). We might also expect that a fearful, withdrawing child would benefit from slower entry into new contexts.
- *The "difficult child" and packaged parenting programs.* Programs for parents often focus on dealing with children who have "difficult" temperaments. Acknowledgment that some children are harder to parent is often helpful, and advice on how to handle particular difficult characteristics can also be useful. However, whether a particular characteristic is difficult depends on its fit with the environment. To label a child "difficult" has the danger of becoming a self-fulfilling

prophecy. If a child is identified as "difficult," the labeling may maintain that categorization. Some critics argue that too often we are prone to pigeon-hole children into categories without examining the context in which temperament occurs (Rothbart & Bates, 1998; Saarni, 2000; Wachs, 2000). Nonetheless, children's temperament needs to be taken into account when considering caregiving behavior. Research does not yet allow for many highly specific recommendations, but, in general, caregivers should (1) be sensitive to the individual characteristics of the child, (2) be flexible in responding to these characteristics, and (3) avoid negative labeling of the child.

Review and Reflect: Learning Goal 3

3 Characterize variations in temperament and their significance

REVIEW

- How can temperament be described and classified?
- How is temperament influenced by biological foundations and experience?
- What is goodness of fit?
- What are some positive parenting strategies for dealing with a child's temperament?

REFLECT

- Consider your own temperament. We described a number of temperament categories. Which one best describes your temperament? Has your temperament changed as you have gotten older? If your temperament has changed, what factors contributed to the changes?

---

4 ATTACHMENT AND LOVE

Infancy and Childhood	Adolescence	Adulthood

So far, we have discussed how emotions and emotional competence change over the life span. We have also examined the role of emotional style; in effect, we have seen how emotions set the tone of our experiences in life. But emotions also write the lyrics because they are at the core of our relationships with others. Foremost among these relationships is attachment.

Attachment is a close emotional bond between two people. In this section, we will focus on two types of attachments: the attachment between children and their parents and romantic attachments.

Infancy and Childhood

A small curly-haired girl named Danielle, age 11 months, begins to whimper. After a few seconds, she begins to wail. Soon her mother comes into the room, and Danielle's crying ceases. Quickly, Danielle crawls over to where her mother is seated and reaches out to be held. Danielle has just demonstrated attachment to her mother.

Theories of Attachment   There is no shortage of theories about infant attachment. Two theorists discussed in chapter 1—Freud and Erikson—proposed influential views, as did John Bowlby.

Freud believed that infants become attached to the person or object that provides oral satisfaction. For most infants, this is the mother, since she is most likely

attachment A close emotional bond between two people.

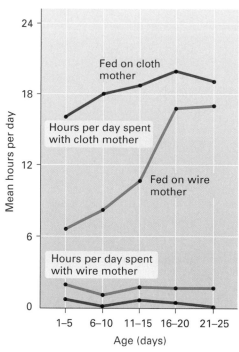

FIGURE 10.10 Contact Time with Wire and Cloth Surrogate Mothers
Regardless of whether the infant monkeys were fed by a wire or a cloth mother, they overwhelmingly preferred to spend contact time with the cloth mother.

**Infancy and Toddlerhood:
Harlow Studies of Infant Monkeys
Raised with Surrogate Mothers**

**Harry Harlow
Forming a Secure Attachment
Attachment Research**

to feed the infant. Is feeding as important as Freud thought? A classic study by Harry Harlow (1958) reveals that the answer is no (see figure 10.10). Harlow removed infant monkeys from their mothers at birth; for 6 months they were reared by surrogate (substitute) "mothers." One surrogate mother was made of wire, the other of cloth. Half of the infant monkeys were fed by the wire mother, half by the cloth mother. Periodically, the amount of time the infant monkeys spent with either the wire or the cloth mother was computed. Regardless of which mother fed them, the infant monkeys spent far more time with the cloth mother. This study clearly demonstrated that feeding is not the crucial element in the attachment process and that contact comfort is important.

Erik Erikson (1968) believed that the first year of life is the key time for the development of attachment. Recall his proposal (discussed in chapter 1) that the first year of life represents the stage of trust versus mistrust ◀▥ **P. 20.** A sense of trust requires a feeling of physical comfort and minimal fear or apprehension about the future. Trust in infancy sets the stage for a lifelong expectation that the world will be a good and pleasant place to be. Erikson also believed that responsive, sensitive parenting contributes to an infant's sense of trust.

The ethological perspective of British psychiatrist John Bowlby (1969, 1989) also stresses the importance of attachment in the first year of life and the responsiveness of the caregiver ◀▥ **P. 25.** Bowlby believes that an infant and its primary caregiver form an attachment. He argues that the newborn is biologically equipped to elicit attachment behavior (Weizmann, 2000). The baby cries, clings, coos, and smiles. Later, the infant crawls, walks, and follows the mother. The immediate result is to keep the primary caregiver nearby; the long-term effect is to increase the infant's chances of survival.

Attachment does not emerge suddenly but rather develops in a series of phases, moving from a baby's general preference for human beings to a partnership with primary caregivers. Here are four such phases based on Bowlby's conceptualization of attachment (Schaffer, 1996):

- *Phase 1: From birth to 2 months.* Infants instinctively direct their attachment to human figures. Strangers, siblings, and parents are equally likely to elicit smiling or crying from the infant.

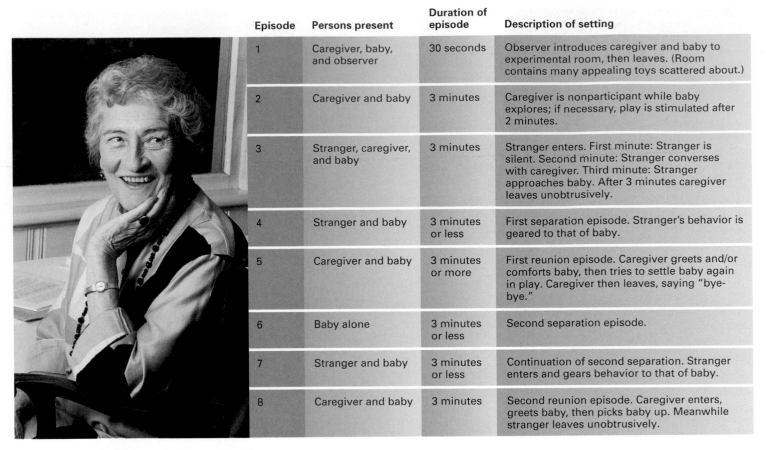

Episode	Persons present	Duration of episode	Description of setting
1	Caregiver, baby, and observer	30 seconds	Observer introduces caregiver and baby to experimental room, then leaves. (Room contains many appealing toys scattered about.)
2	Caregiver and baby	3 minutes	Caregiver is nonparticipant while baby explores; if necessary, play is stimulated after 2 minutes.
3	Stranger, caregiver, and baby	3 minutes	Stranger enters. First minute: Stranger is silent. Second minute: Stranger converses with caregiver. Third minute: Stranger approaches baby. After 3 minutes caregiver leaves unobtrusively.
4	Stranger and baby	3 minutes or less	First separation episode. Stranger's behavior is geared to that of baby.
5	Caregiver and baby	3 minutes or more	First reunion episode. Caregiver greets and/or comforts baby, then tries to settle baby again in play. Caregiver then leaves, saying "bye-bye."
6	Baby alone	3 minutes or less	Second separation episode.
7	Stranger and baby	3 minutes or less	Continuation of second separation. Stranger enters and gears behavior to that of baby.
8	Caregiver and baby	3 minutes	Second reunion episode. Caregiver enters, greets baby, then picks baby up. Meanwhile stranger leaves unobtrusively.

FIGURE 10.11 The Ainsworth Strange Situation

Mary Ainsworth *(left)* developed the Strange Situation to assess whether infants are securely or insecurely attached to their caregiver. The episodes involved in the Ainsworth Strange Situation are described here.

- *Phase 2: From 2 to 7 months.* Attachment becomes focused on one figure, usually the primary caregiver, as the baby gradually learns to distinguish familiar from unfamiliar people.
- *Phase 3: From 7 to 24 months.* Specific attachments develop. With increased locomotor skills, babies actively seek contact with regular caregivers, such as the mother or father.
- *Phase 4: From 24 months on.* Children become aware of others' feelings, goals, and plans and begin to take these into account in forming their own actions.

Individual Differences and the Strange Situation Although attachment to a caregiver intensifies midway through the first year, isn't it likely that some babies have a more positive attachment experience than others? Mary Ainsworth (1979) thinks so. Ainsworth created the **Strange Situation,** an observational measure of infant attachment in which the infant experiences a series of introductions, separations, and reunions with the caregiver and an adult stranger in a prescribed order (see figure 10.11). In using the Strange Situation, researchers hope that their observations will provide information about the infant's motivation to be near the caregiver and the degree to which the caregiver's presence provides the infant with security and confidence.

Based on how babies respond in the Strange Situation, they are described as being securely or insecurely attached to the caregiver:

- **Securely attached babies** use the caregiver as a secure base from which to explore the environment. When in the presence of their caregiver, securely

Strange Situation Ainsworth's observational measure of infant attachment to a caregiver that requires the infant to move through a series of introductions, separations, and reunions with the caregiver and an adult stranger in a prescribed order.

securely attached babies Babies who use the caregiver as a secure base from which to explore the environment.

attached infants explore the room and examine toys that have been placed in it. When the caregiver departs, securely attached infants might mildly protest, and when the caregiver returns these infants reestablish positive interaction with her, perhaps by smiling or climbing on her lap. Subsequently, they often resume playing with the toys in the room.

- **Insecure avoidant babies** show insecurity by avoiding the mother. In the Strange Situation, these babies engage in little interaction with the caregiver, display little distress when she leaves the room, usually do not reestablish contact with her on her return, and may even turn their back on her at this point. If contact is established, the infant usually leans away or looks away.

- **Insecure resistant babies** often cling to the caregiver and then resist her by fighting against the closeness, perhaps by kicking or pushing away. In the Strange Situation, these babies often cling anxiously to the caregiver and don't explore the playroom. When the caregiver leaves, they often cry loudly and push away if she tries to comfort them on her return.

- **Insecure disorganized babies** are disorganized and disoriented. In the Strange Situation, these babies might appear dazed, confused, and fearful. To be classified as disorganized, strong patterns of avoidance and resistance must be shown or certain select behaviors, such as extreme fearfulness around the caregiver, must be present.

Some critics believe that behavior in the Strange Situation—like other laboratory assessments—might not indicate what infants would do in a natural environment. Furthermore, as a measure of attachment it may be culturally biased. For example, German and Japanese babies often show different patterns of attachment than American infants. As shown in figure 10.12, German infants are more likely to show an avoidant attachment pattern and Japanese infants are less likely to show this pattern than U.S. infants (van IJzendoorn & Kroonenberg, 1988). The avoidant pattern in German babies likely occurs because their caregivers encourage them to be more independent (Grossmann & others, 1985). Also as shown in figure 10.12, Japanese babies are more likely than American babies to be categorized as resistant. This may have more to do with the Strange Situation as a measure of attachment than with attachment insecurity itself. Japanese mothers rarely let anyone unfamiliar with their babies care for them. Thus, the Strange Situation might create considerably more stress for Japanese infants than for American infants, who are more accustomed to separation from their mothers (Takahashi, 1990).

Even though there are cultural variations in attachment classification, the most frequent classification in every culture studied so far is secure attachment (van IJzendoorn & Kroonenberg, 1988). Further, researchers have found that infants' behaviors in the Strange Situation are closely related to how they behave at home in response to separation and reunion with their mothers (Pederson & Moran, 1996). Thus, many infant researchers believe the Strange Situation shows merit as a measure of infant attachment.

The Significance of Attachment
Do individual differences in attachment matter? Ainsworth believes that secure attachment in the first year of life provides an important foundation for psychological development later in life. The securely attached infant moves freely away from the mother but keeps track of where she is through periodic glances. The securely attached infant responds positively to being picked up by others and, when put back down, freely moves away to play.

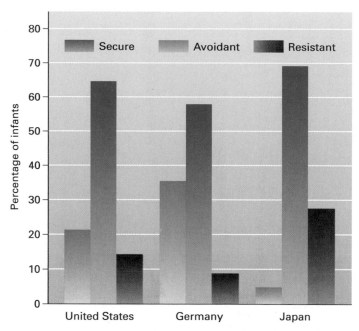

FIGURE 10.12 Cross-Cultural Comparison of Attachment

In one study, infant attachment in three countries—the United States, Germany, and Japan—was measured in the Ainsworth Strange Situation (van IJzendoorn & Kroonenberg, 1988). The dominant attachment pattern in all three countries was secure attachment. However, German infants were more avoidant and Japanese infants were less avoidant and more resistant than U.S. infants.

Infancy and Toddlerhood: Ainsworth Strange Situation

insecure avoidant babies Babies who show insecurity by avoiding the mother.

insecure resistant babies Babies who might cling to the caregiver, then resist her by fighting against the closeness, perhaps by kicking or pushing away.

insecure disorganized babies Babies who show insecurity by being disorganized and disoriented.

An insecurely attached infant, by contrast, avoids the mother or is ambivalent toward her, fears strangers, and is upset by minor, everyday separations.

If early attachment to a caregiver is important, it should relate to a child's social behavior later in development. For some children, early attachments seem to foreshadow later functioning (Egeland & Carlson, 2004; Sroufe, 2002). For other children, there is little continuity (Thompson, Easterbrooks, & Walker, 2003). For example, in one longitudinal study, attachment classification in infancy did not predict attachment classification at 18 years of age (Lewis, 1997). In this study, the best predictor of an insecure attachment classification at 18 was the occurrence of divorce in the intervening years. Consistency in caregiving over a number of years is likely an important factor in connecting early attachment and the child's functioning later in development.

Not all developmentalists believe that attachment in infancy is the only path to competence in life. Indeed, some developmentalists believe that too much emphasis has been placed on the attachment bond in infancy. Jerome Kagan (1987, 2000), for example, believes that infants are highly resilient and adaptive; he argues that they are evolutionarily equipped to stay on a positive developmental course, even in the face of wide variations in parenting. Kagan and others stress that genetic and temperament characteristics play more important roles in a child's social competence than the attachment theorists, such as Bowlby and Ainsworth, are willing to acknowledge (Chaudhuri & Williams, 1999; Young & Shahinfar, 1995). For example, infants may have inherited a low tolerance for stress. This, rather than an insecure attachment bond, may be responsible for their inability to get along with peers.

Another criticism of attachment theory is that it ignores the diversity of socializing agents and contexts that exists in an infant's world. In some cultures, infants show attachments to many people. Among the Hausa (who live in Nigeria), both grandmothers and siblings provide a significant amount of care for infants (Harkness & Super, 1995). Infants in agricultural societies tend to form attachments to older siblings, who are assigned a major responsibility for younger siblings' care.

Researchers recognize the importance of competent, nurturant caregivers in an infant's development (Maccoby, 1999; McHale & others, 2001; Parke, 2001). At issue, though, is whether or not secure attachment, especially to a single caregiver, is critical.

Despite such criticisms, there is ample evidence that security of attachment is important to development (Atkinson & Goldberg, 2004; Thompson, Easterbrooks, & Walker, 2003). Secure attachment in infancy is important because it reflects a positive parent-infant relationship and provides the foundation that supports healthy socioemotional development in the years that follow.

Caregiving Styles and Attachment Classification Is the style of caregiving linked with the quality of the infant's attachment? Securely attached babies have caregivers who are sensitive to their signals and are consistently available to respond to their infants' needs (Gao, Elliot, & Waters, 1999; Main, 2000). These caregivers often let their babies have an active part in determining the onset and pacing of interaction in the first year of life. One recent study found that maternal sensitivity in parenting was linked with secure attachment in infants in two different cultures: the United States and Colombia (Carbonell & others, 2002).

How do the caregivers of insecurely attached babies interact with them? Caregivers of avoidant babies tend to be unavailable or rejecting (Berlin & Cassidy, 2000). They often don't respond to their babies' signals and have little physical contact with them. When they do interact with their babies, they may behave in an angry and irritable way. Caregivers of resistant babies tend to be inconsistent; sometimes they respond to their babies' needs, and sometimes they don't. In general, they tend not to be very affectionate with their babies and show little synchrony when interact-

In the Hausa culture, siblings and grandmothers provide a significant amount of care for infants. *How might this practice affect attachment?*

ing with them. Caregivers of disorganized babies often neglect or physically abuse them (Barnett, Ganiban, & Cicchetti, 1999). In some cases, these caregivers are depressed.

Mothers and Fathers as Caregivers   Can fathers take care of infants as competently as mothers can? Observations of fathers and their infants suggest that fathers have the ability to act as sensitively and responsively as mothers with their infants (Parke, 1995, 2000, 2002). Perhaps the caregiving behavior of male humans resembles that of other male primates, who show notoriously low interest in their offspring. However, when forced to live with infants whose female caregivers are absent, the males can competently rear the infants. Remember, however, that although fathers can be active, nurturant, involved caregivers with their infants, many do not choose to follow this pattern (Silverstein, 2001).

Do fathers behave differently toward infants than mothers do? Maternal interactions usually center on child-care activities—feeding, changing diapers, bathing. Paternal interactions are more likely to include play (Parke, 2002). Fathers engage in more rough-and-tumble play. They bounce infants, throw them up in the air, tickle them, and so on (Lamb, 1986, 2000). Mothers do play with infants, but their play is less physical and arousing than that of fathers.

In one study, fathers were interviewed about their caregiving responsibilities when their children were 6, 15, 24, and 36 months of age (NICHD Early Child Care Research Network, 2000). Some of the fathers were videotaped while playing with their children at 6 and 36 months. Fathers were more involved in caregiving—bathing, feeding, dressing the child, taking the child to child care, and so on—when they worked fewer hours and mothers worked more hours, when mothers and fathers were younger, when mothers reported greater marital intimacy, and when the children were boys.

Child Care   Many parents worry whether care of their child by other people will adversely affect their children. They fear that child care by others will reduce their infants' emotional attachment to them, retard infants' cognitive development, fail to teach them how to control anger, and allow them to be unduly influenced by their peers. How extensive is child care by people other than parents? Are the worries of these parents justified?

Today in the United States, far more young children are in child care than at any other time in history; about 2 million children currently receive formal, licensed child care, and more than 5 million children attend kindergarten. Also, uncounted millions of children are cared for by unlicensed baby-sitters. Because the United States does not have a policy of paid leave for child care, child care in the United States has become a major national concern. In contrast, many European countries have well-developed child-care policies. For example, in Sweden, mothers or fathers are given paid maternity or paternity leave for up to nine months. For this reason, child care for Swedish infants under 1 year of age is usually not a major concern.

The types of child care that young children in the United States receive vary extensively (Scarr, 2000). Many child-care centers house large groups of children and have elaborate facilities. Some are commercial operations; others are nonprofit centers run by churches, civic groups, and employers. Child care is frequently provided in private homes, at times by child-care professionals, at others by mothers who want to earn extra money.

A special interest of researchers is the role of poverty in the quality of child care (Chase-Lansdale, Coley, & Grining, 2001). In one study, child-care centers that served high-income children delivered better-quality care than did centers that served middle- and low-income children (Phillips & others, 1994). Teacher-child ratios in subsidized centers for the poor were fairly good, but the quality of observed teacher-child interaction was lower than in high-income centers. Children who come from families with few resources (psychological, social, and economic) are more likely to experience low-quality child care than are children from more advantaged backgrounds (Lamb, 1994).

What constitutes a high-quality child-care program for infants? In a demonstration program at Harvard University, the child-care center included a pediatrician, a nonteaching director, and an infant-teacher ratio of 3 to 1 (Kagan, Kearsley, & Zelazo, 1978). Teachers' aides assisted at the center. The teachers and aides were trained to smile frequently, to talk with the infants, and to provide them with a safe environment, which included many stimulating toys. No adverse effects of child care were observed in this project. In the Research in Life-Span Development interlude, you can read about an ongoing national study of child care and its effects.

Research in Life-Span Development
A National Longitudinal Study of Child Care

Aware of the growing use of child care, the National Institute of Child Health and Human Development (NICHD) developed a comprehensive, longitudinal study of child-care experiences. The study began in 1991, and data were collected on a diverse sample of almost 1,400 children and their families at 10 locations across the United States over a period of seven years. Researchers are using multiple methods (trained observers, interviews, questionnaires, and testing) and measuring many facets of children's development, including physical health, cognitive development, and socioemotional development. Here are some of the results of this extensive study to date (NICHD Early Child Care Research Network, 2001, 2002, 2003):

- *Patterns of use.* There was high reliance on infant care, rapid entry into care after birth, and considerable instability in care. By 4 months of age, nearly three-fourths of the infants had entered some form of nonmaternal child care. Almost half of the infants were cared for by a relative when they first entered care and only 12 percent were enrolled in child-care centers. Socioeconomic factors were linked to the amount and type of care. For example, mothers with higher incomes and families that were more dependent on the mother's income placed their infants in child care at an earlier age. Mothers who believed that maternal employment has positive effects on children were more likely to place their infant in nonmaternal care for more hours. Low-income families were more likely than more affluent families to use child care, but infants from low-income families who were in child care averaged as many hours as infants from other income groups. In the preschool years, mothers who were single, those with more education, and families with higher incomes used more hours of center care than other families. Minority families and mothers with less education used more hours of care by relatives.
- *Quality of care.* Quality of care was judged by such characteristics as group size, child–adult ratio, physical environment, caregiver characteristics (such as formal education, specialized training, and child-care experience), and caregiver behavior (such as sensitivity to children). Infants from low-income families experienced lower quality of child care than infants from higher-income families. When quality of caregivers' care was high, children performed better on cognitive and language tasks, were more cooperative with their mothers during play, showed more positive and skilled interaction with peers, and had fewer behavior problems. Support was found for policies that improve state regulations for caregiver training and child-staff ratios, which were linked with higher cognitive and social competence at 54 months of age.

Higher-quality child care was related to higher-quality mother-child inter-action among the families that used nonmaternal care. Further, poor-quality care was related to an increase in insecure attachment to the mother at 15 months of age, but only when the mother was low in sensitivity and respon-siveness. However, child-care quality was not linked to attachment security at 36 months of age.

- *Amount of child care.* The quantity of child care predicted some outcomes. When children spent more hours in child care in their first three years, interactions with the mother (at 6, 15, 24, and 36 months) were less positive. Rates of ill-ness were higher when more hours of child care were experienced.
- *Family and parenting influences.* The results of this large national study indicated that the influence of families and parenting is not weakened by extensive child care. Parents played a significant role in helping children to regulate their emotions.

In sum, there continues to be concern about some aspects of child care in the United States. Experts increasingly recognize that child care may harm some chil-dren more than others (Langlois & Liben, 2003). Difficult children and those with poor self-control may be especially at risk in child care (Maccoby & Lewis, 2003). Thus, one intervention may involve teaching child-care providers how to foster self-regulatory skills in children (Fabes, Hanish, & Martin, 2003). Another intervention might involve more effort being invested in building attachment to the child-care center or school. For example, one study revealed that when children experienced their group, class, or school as a caring community, they showed increased concern for others, better conflict resolution skills, and decreased problem behaviors (Solomon & others, 2000).

Adolescence

Relationships between parents and children continue to be important into the ado-lescent years. But the adolescent's emotions may become more involved with peo-ple outside the family, especially with romantic partners. What do psychologists know about these relationships?

Attachment to Parents   The initial interest in attachment focused on infants and their caregivers. In the last decade, developmentalists have begun to explore the role of secure attachment and related concepts, such as connectedness to parents, dur-ing adolescence (Allen, Hauser, & Borman-Spurrell, 1996; Allen & others, 2003; Kenney & Barton, 2003; Kobak & others, 1993). Secure attachment to parents in adolescence may facilitate the adolescent's social competence and well-being, as reflected in such characteristics as self-esteem, emotional adjustment, and physical health (Cooper, Shaver, & Collins, 1998). In the research of Joseph Allen and his colleagues (Allen & others, 2002, 2003; Allen & Kuperminc, 1995), securely attached adolescents are somewhat less likely to engage in problem behaviors. In one study, secure attachment to both the mother and the father was related positively to ado-lescents' peer and friendship relations (Lieberman, Doyle, & Markiewicz, 1999).

Many studies that assess secure and insecure attachment in adolescence and adulthood use the Adult Attachment Interview (AAI) (George, Main, & Kaplan, 1984). This measure examines an individual's memories of significant attachment relationships. Based on the responses to questions on the AAI, individuals are clas-sified as *secure-autonomous* (which corresponds to secure attachment in infancy) or one of three insecure categories:

Dismissing/avoidant attachment is an insecure category in which individuals deemphasize the importance of attachment. This category is associated with

dismissing/avoidant attachment An inse-cure attachment style in which adolescents deemphasize the importance of attachment; is associated with consistent experiences of rejec-tion of attachment needs by caregivers.

consistent rejection of attachment needs by caregivers. One possible outcome of dismissing/avoidant attachment is that parents and adolescents may mutually distance themselves from each other, which lessens parents' influence. Dismissing/avoidant attachment is linked with violent and aggressive behavior in some adolescents.

- **Preoccupied/ambivalent attachment** is an insecure category in which adolescents are hypertuned to attachment experiences. This is thought to occur mainly because parents are inconsistently available to the adolescent, which may lead to considerable attachment-seeking behavior, mixed with anger. Conflict with parents may be too high for healthy development.
- **Unresolved/disorganized attachment** is an insecure category in which the adolescent has an unusually high level of fear and is often disoriented. This may result from such traumatic experiences as a parent's death or abuse by parents.

Dating and Romantic Relationships   Adolescents not only have attachments to their parents. Dating and romantic relationships also can lead to attachment. Adolescents spend considerable time either dating or thinking about dating, which has gone far beyond its original courtship function to become a form of recreation, a source of status and achievement, and a setting for learning about close relationships. One function of dating, though, continues to be mate selection.

Types of Dating and Developmental Changes   A number of developmental changes characterize dating (Furman, 2002). In one recent study, by the sixth grade, 40 percent of the individuals sampled had announced that "I like someone" (Buhrmester, 2001) (see figure 10.13). However, it was not until the tenth grade that 50 percent of the adolescents had a sustained romantic relationship that lasted two months or longer. By their senior year, 25 percent still had not engaged in this type of sustained romantic relationship. But a rather large portion of adolescents in dating relationships say that their relationships have per-

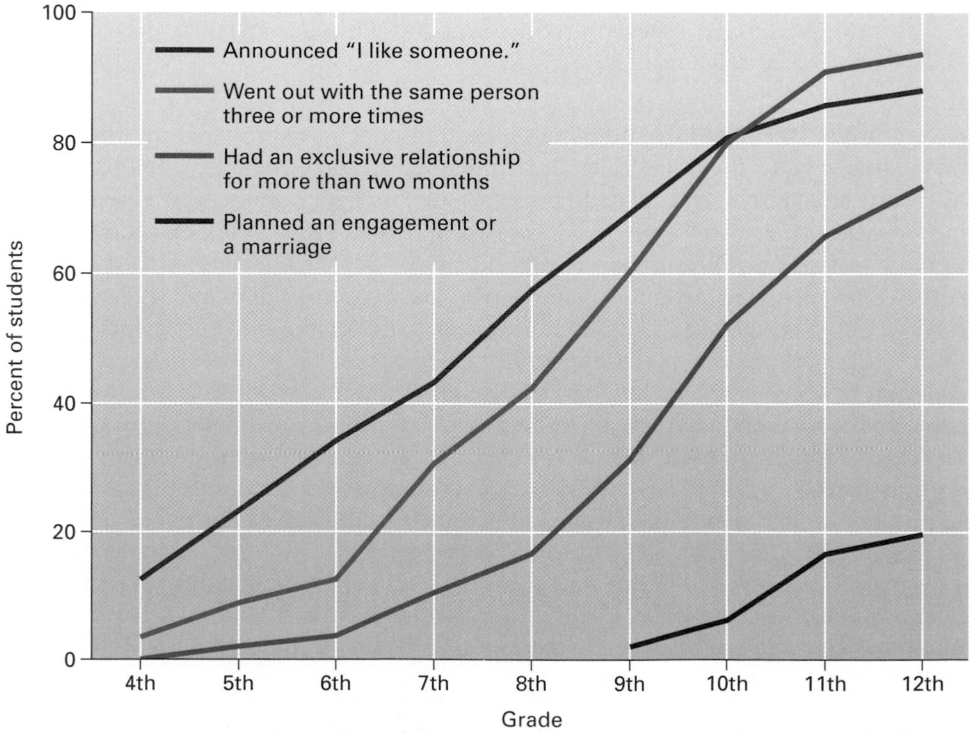

preoccupied/ambivalent attachment An insecure attachment style in which adolescents are hypertuned to attachment experiences. This is thought to occur mainly because parents are inconsistently available to the adolescent.

unresolved/disorganized attachment An insecure attachment style in which the adolescent has an unusually high level of fear and is disoriented. This may result from such traumatic experiences as a parent's death or abuse by parents.

FIGURE 10.13 Age Onset of Romantic Activity

sisted 11 months or longer: 20 percent of adolescents 14 or younger, 35 percent of 15- to 16-year-olds, and almost 60 percent of 17- and 18-year-olds (Carver, Joyner, & Udry, 2003).

In their early exploration of romantic relationships, today's adolescents often find comfort in numbers and hang out together in heterosexual groups. Sometimes they just hang out at someone's house or get organized enough to go to a mall or a movie (Peterson, 1997). Many adolescents are not motivated to fulfill attachment or even sexual needs in their early romantic relationships. Rather, these relationships serve as a context for adolescents to explore how attractive they are, how they should romantically interact with someone, and how all of this looks to the peer group (Brown, 1999). Only after adolescents acquire some basic competencies in interacting with romantic partners does the fulfillment of attachment and sexual needs become central to these relationships (Bouchey & Furman, 2003; Furman & Wehner, 1999).

A special concern is early dating and "going with" someone, which is associated with adolescent pregnancy and problems at home and school (Downey & Bonica, 1997; Metts, 2004). Among girls, early romantic involvement has been linked with lower grades, less active participation in class discussion, and school-related problems (Buhrmester, 2001).

Dating Scripts   For any social situation, people are likely to have a mental representation or *script* that describes the expected sequence of events. **Dating scripts** are the cognitive models that guide individuals' dating interactions. In one study, first dates were highly scripted along gender lines (Rose & Frieze, 1993). The boys followed a "proactive" dating script, asking for and planning the date, driving and opening doors, and initiating sexual interaction (making physical contact, making out, and kissing). The girls' script was "reactive," focused on concern about appearance, enjoying the date, being picked up, having doors opened, and responding to sexual overtures. These gender differences give males more power in the initial stage of a dating relationship.

Male and female adolescents also bring different motivations to the dating experience. In one study, 15-year-old girls were likely to describe romance in terms of interpersonal qualities, the boys in terms of physical attraction (Feiring, 1996). Also, the young adolescents were more likely to describe physical attraction in terms of appearance (being cute, pretty, or handsome) rather than in sexual terms (such as being a good kisser). But the failure to discuss sexual interests might reflect adolescents' discomfort in talking about such personal feelings with an unfamiliar adult.

Emotion and Romantic Relationships   The strong emotions of romantic relationships can thrust adolescents into a world in which ordinary reality recedes from view (Bouchey & Furman, 2003; Larson, Clore, & Wood, 1999). One 14-year-old reports that he is so in love he can't think about anything else. A 15-year-old girl is enraged by the betrayal of her boyfriend. She is obsessed with ways to get back at him. The daily fluctuations in the emotions of romantic relationships can make the world seem almost surreal. Although the strong emotions of romance can have disruptive effects on adolescents, they also provide a source for possible mastery and growth. Learning to manage these strong emotions can give adolescents a sense of competence.

Romantic relationships often are involved in an adolescent's emotional experiences (Collins, 2002). In one study of ninth- to twelfth-graders, girls gave real and fantasized heterosexual relationships as the explanation for more than one-third of their strong emotions and boys gave this reason for 25 percent of their strong emotions (Wilson-Shockley, 1995). Strong emotions were attached far less to school (13%), family (9%), and same-sex peer relations (8%). The majority of the emotions were reported as positive, but a substantial minority (42%) were reported as

Teen Chat

dating scripts Cognitive models that guide individuals' dating interactions.

negative, including feelings of anxiety, anger, jealousy, and depression. The most common trigger of the first episode of major depression in adolescence is a romantic breakup.

Sociocultural Contexts and Dating The sociocultural context exerts a powerful influence on adolescents' dating patterns. Values and religious beliefs of various cultures often dictate the age at which dating begins, how much freedom in dating is allowed, whether dates must be chaperoned by adults or parents, and the roles of males and females in dating. For example, Latino and Asian American cultures have more conservative standards regarding adolescent dating than does the Anglo-American culture.

Dating may be a source of cultural conflict for many adolescents whose families have come from cultures in which dating begins at a late age with little freedom, especially for adolescent girls. One recent study found that Asian American adolescents were less likely to be involved in a romantic relationship in the past 18 months than African American or Latino adolescents (Carver, Joyner, & Udry, 2003). In another recent study, Latina young adults in the midwestern United States reflected on their dating experiences during adolescence (Raffaelli & Ontai, 2001). They said that their parents placed strict boundaries on their romantic involvement. As a result, the young women recalled that their adolescent dating experiences were filled with tension and conflict. Over half of the Latinas engaged in "sneak dating" without their parents' knowledge.

Adulthood

Attachment and romantic relationships continue to be very important aspects of close relationships in adulthood. Let's explore attachment first, then different types of love.

Attachment What is the nature of attachment in adulthood? Although relationships with romantic partners differ from those with parents, romantic partners fulfill some of the same needs for adults as parents do for their children. Adults count on their romantic partners to be a secure base to which they can return and obtain comfort and security in stressful times.

In a number of studies, Cindy Hazan and Phillip Shaver (1987; Shaver & Hazan, 1993) have examined the continuity between childhood attachment relationships and romantic relationships. They interview adults about their relationship with their parents as they were growing up and about their current romantic relationship. They find that the quality of attachment is linked with the quality of adult romantic relationships. For example, adults who report that they were securely attached to their parents when they were growing up are more likely to say that they have a secure attachment to their romantic partner than their adult counterparts who report having had an insecure attachment to their parents. In one longitudinal study, individuals who were securely attached to caregivers at 1 year of age also were likely to have secure attachments to parents and romantic partners 20 years later (Waters & others, 2000).

In sum, there appear to be some important continuities between attachment to parents as a child and attachment to parents and romantic partners as a young adult. Nonetheless, not all individuals fit this pattern, and attachment styles are not cast in stone (Lewis, Feiring, & Rosenthal, 2000). For example, in the longitudinal study just described and in other studies, links between earlier and later attachments are lessened by stressful and disruptive life experiences (such as the death of a parent and instability of caregiving) (Collins & Laursen, 2000; Waters & others, 2000). Also, some individuals revise their attachment styles as they experience relationships in their adult years (Baldwin & Fehr, 1995). For example, in one study, approximately

30 percent of young adults changed their attachment style over a four-year period (Kirkpatrick & Hazan, 1994).

Romantic Love   Think for a moment about songs and books that hit the top of the charts. Chances are, they're about love. Poets, playwrights, and musicians through the ages have lauded the fiery passion of romantic love—and lamented the searing pain when it fails. **Romantic love** is also called *passionate love* or *eros*; it has strong components of sexuality and infatuation, and it often predominates in the early part of a love relationship.

Well-known love researcher Ellen Berscheid (1998) says that it is romantic love we mean when we say that we are "in love" with someone. It is romantic love, she believes, that we need to understand if we are to learn what love is all about. According to Berscheid, sexual desire is the most important ingredient of romantic love. We will discuss sexuality in more detail in chapter 12.

Romantic love includes a complex intermingling of emotions— fear, anger, sexual desire, joy, and jealousy, for example (Furman, 2002; Harris, 2002; Hendrick & Hendrick, 2004). Obviously, some of these emotions are a source of anguish. One study found that romantic lovers were more likely than friends to be the cause of depression (Berscheid & Fei, 1977).

Affectionate Love   Love is more than just passion. **Affectionate love,** also called companionate love, is the type of love that occurs when individuals desire to have the other person near and have a deep, caring affection for the person.

There is a growing belief that as love matures, passion tends to give way to affection (Berscheid, 2000; Berscheid & Reis, 1998). Phillip Shaver (1986) describes the initial phase of romantic love as a time that is fueled by a mixture of sexual attraction and gratification, a reduced sense of loneliness, uncertainty about the security of developing another attachment, and excitement about exploring the novelty of another human being. With time, he says, sexual attraction wanes, attachment anxieties either lessen or produce conflict and withdrawal, novelty is replaced with familiarity, and lovers either find themselves securely attached in a deeply caring relationship or distressed—feeling bored, disappointed, lonely, or hostile, for example. In the latter case, one or both partners may eventually seek another close relationship.

One investigation interviewed 102 happily married couples in early (average age 28), middle (average age 45), and late (average age 65) adulthood to explore the nature of age and sex differences in satisfying love relationships (Reedy, Birren, & Schaie, 1981). As indicated in figure 10.14, passion and sexual intimacy were more important in early adulthood, and feelings of affection and loyalty were more important in later-life love relationships. Young adult lovers also rated communication as more characteristic of their love than their older counterparts. Aside from the age differences, however, there were some striking similarities in the nature of satisfying love relationships. At all ages, emotional security was ranked as the most important factor in love, followed by respect, communication, help and play behaviors, sexual intimacy, and loyalty. The findings in this research also suggested that women believe emotional security is more important in love than men do.

Sternberg's Triarchic Theory of Love   Clearly, there is more to satisfying love relationships than sex. One theory of love that captures this idea was proposed by Robert J. Sternberg (1988). His **triangular theory of love** states that love has three

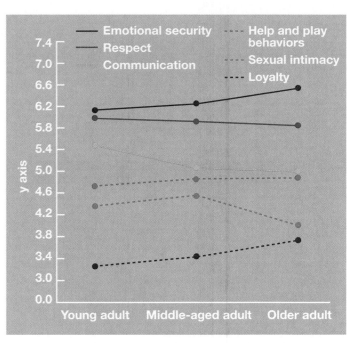

FIGURE 10.14 Changes in Satisfying Love Relationships Across the Adult Years

In the investigation by Reedy, Birren, and Schaie (1981), emotional security was the most important factor in love at all ages. Sexual intimacy was more important in early adulthood, while affection and loyalty were more important in the love relationships of older adults. Young adult lovers also rated communication as more important in love than their older counterparts.

Adult Attachment

Romance and Attraction

Intimacy

romantic love Also called passionate love or eros, this type of love has strong components of sexuality and infatuation, and it often predominates in the early part of a love relationship.

affectionate love Also called companionate love, this type of love occurs when individuals desire to have another person near and have a deep, caring affection for the person.

triangular theory of love Sternberg's theory that love includes three types—passion, intimacy, and commitment.

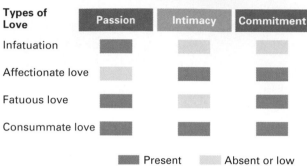

Types of Love	Passion	Intimacy	Commitment
Infatuation			
Affectionate love			
Fatuous love			
Consummate love			

Present   Absent or low

FIGURE 10.15 Sternberg's Triangle of Love

Sternberg identified three dimensions that shape the experience we call love: passion, intimacy, and commitment. Various combinations of the three dimensions produce particular types of love.

Early Adulthood: Sternberg's Triangular Theory of Love

main components or dimensions—passion, intimacy, and commitment (see figure 10.15):

- Passion, as described earlier, is physical and sexual attraction to another.
- Intimacy is the emotional feelings of warmth, closeness, and sharing in a relationship.
- Commitment is our cognitive appraisal of the relationship and our intent to maintain the relationship even in the face of problems.

According to Sternberg, if passion is the only ingredient (with intimacy and commitment low or absent), we are merely *infatuated*. This might happen in an affair or a "one-night stand." But varying combinations of the dimensions of love create three qualitatively different types of love:

- A relationship marked by intimacy and commitment but low or lacking in passion is called *affectionate love,* a pattern often found among couples who have been married for many years.
- If passion and commitment are present but intimacy is not, Sternberg calls the relationship *fatuous love,* as when one person worships another from a distance.
- If passion, intimacy, and commitment are all strong, the result is *consummate love,* the fullest type of love.

Our description of love has focused primarily on the concept of love in the United States. The Contexts of Life-Span Development interlude explores how love is viewed differently in Japan than in the United States.

Contexts of Life-Span Development

Love and Marriage in the United States and Japan

In U.S. culture, romantic love is the main reason people get married. Based on a review of many cross-cultural studies, the following conclusions were reached about contrasts between love and marriage in the United States and Japan (Rothbaum & others, 2000).

Traditionally, the Japanese family has had considerable influence on mate selection, and that influence continues to some degree today. Initial contacts leading to one-third to one-half of all marriages in Japan are still arranged by go-betweens (Hendry, 1995). It also is common practice for parents to investigate the background of potential spouses for children. In the United States, personal attraction dictates mate selection more than in Japan. Americans perceive that they have more choice and independence in selecting a mate than do Japanese (Markus & Kitayama, 1994).

In the United States romantic or passionate love is a strong factor in many marriages, especially early in the marital relationship; in Japan, loyalty and commitment are more important (Dion & Dion, 1993; Yamagishi & Yamagishi, 1994). Divorce statistics bear out the emphasis on loyalty and commitment in Japan. The divorce rate in the United States is more than three times that of Japan (Kumagai, 1995). Conflict is not readily accepted in marital relations in Japan; cohesion and cherishing the relationship are desired (Rothbaum & others, 2000). We will have much more to say about love and marriage in chapter 14, "Families, Lifestyles, and Parenting."

Review and Reflect: Learning Goal 4

4 Explain attachment and its development

REVIEW

- What is attachment? How does attachment develop in infancy and childhood? How are caregiving styles related to attachment? How is child care related to children's development?
- How does attachment develop in adolescence? What is the nature of dating and romantic relationships in adolescence?
- What are attachment and love like across the adulthood years?

REFLECT

- How would you describe your attachment style? Why do think you developed this attachment style?

Reach Your Learning Goals

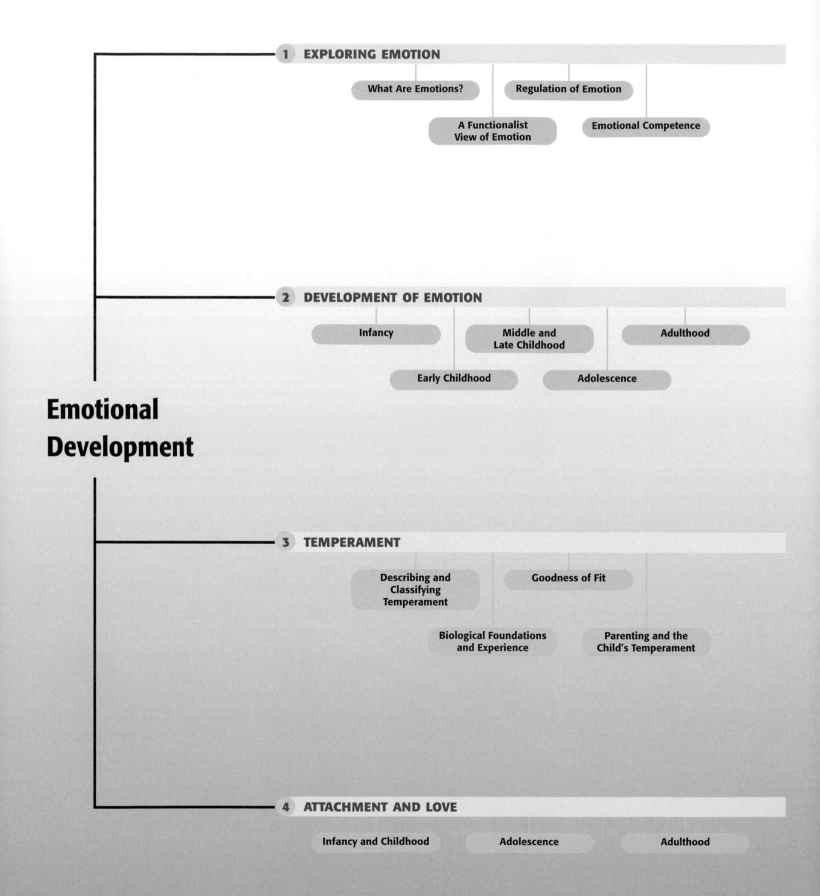

Emotional Development

1 EXPLORING EMOTION

What Are Emotions?

Regulation of Emotion

A Functionalist View of Emotion

Emotional Competence

2 DEVELOPMENT OF EMOTION

Infancy

Middle and Late Childhood

Adulthood

Early Childhood

Adolescence

3 TEMPERAMENT

Describing and Classifying Temperament

Goodness of Fit

Biological Foundations and Experience

Parenting and the Child's Temperament

4 ATTACHMENT AND LOVE

Infancy and Childhood

Adolescence

Adulthood

Summary

1 Discuss basic aspects of emotion

- Emotion is feeling, or affect, that involves a mixture of physiological arousal and expressive behavior. Emotions can be classified as positive or negative. Darwin described the evolutionary basis of emotions and today psychologists believe that emotions, especially facial expressions of emotions, have a biological foundation. Facial expressions of emotion are the same across cultures, but display rules are not culturally universal. Biological evolution endowed humans to be emotional but embeddedness in culture and relationships provides diversity in emotional experiences.

- The functionalist view of emotion emphasizes the importance of contexts and relationships in emotion. In this view, goals are involved in emotions in a variety of ways.

- The ability to control one's emotions is a key dimension of development. Emotional regulation consists of effectively managing arousal to adapt and reach a goal. In infancy and early childhood, regulation of emotion gradually shifts from external sources to self-initiated, internal sources. Also with increasing age, children are more likely to increase their use of cognitive strategies for regulating emotion, modulate their emotional arousal, become more adept at managing situations to minimize negative emotion, and choose effective ways to cope with stress. Parents can help children learn to regulate their emotion through emotion-coaching.

- Saarni believes that becoming emotionally competent involves developing a number of skills such as being aware of one's emotional states, discerning others' emotions, adaptively coping with negative emotions, and understanding the role of emotions in relationships.

2 Describe the development of emotion through the life span

- Two broad types of emotions are primary emotions (surprise, joy, anger, sadness, fear, and disgust, which appear in the first six months of life) and self-conscious emotions (empathy, jealousy, and embarrassment, which appear at 1½ to 2 years, and pride, shame, and guilt, which appear at 2½ years). Crying is the most important mechanism newborns have for communicating with their world. Babies have at least three types of cries—basic, anger, and pain cries. Controversy swirls about whether babies should be soothed when they cry, although increasingly experts recommend immediately responding in a caring way in the first year. Two types of smiling are reflexive and social. Two fears that infants develop are stranger anxiety and separation from a caregiver (which is reflected in separation protest). Social referencing increases in the second year of life. As infants develop it is important for them to engage in emotional regulation.

- Preschoolers become more adept at talking about their own and others' emotions. Two- and 3-year-olds substantially increase the number of terms they use to describe emotion and learn more about the causes and consequences of feelings. At 4 to 5 years of age, children increasingly reflect on emotions and understand that a single event can elicit different emotions in different people.

- In middle and late childhood, children show a growing awareness about controlling and managing emotions to meet social standards. Also in this age period, children increasingly understand complex emotions such as pride and shame and realize that more than one emotion can be expressed in a particular situation. They also increasingly take into account the events that led up to an emotional reaction, suppress and conceal their emotions, and initiate strategies to redirect their emotions.

- As individuals go through early adolescence they are less likely to report being very happy. Moodiness is a normal aspect of early adolescence. Although pubertal change is associated with an increase in negative emotions, hormonal influences are often small, and environmental experiences may contribute more to the emotions of adolescence than hormonal changes.

- Older adults are better at controlling their emotions than younger adults are, and older adults experience more positive and less negative emotions than younger adults do. An important theory regarding developmental changes in emotion during adulthood, especially late adulthood, is Carstensen's socioemotional selectivity theory. Knowledge-related and emotion-related goals change across the life span; emotion-related goals become more important when individuals get older.

3 Characterize variations in temperament and their significance

- Temperament is an individual's behavioral style and characteristic way of emotional responding. Developmentalists are especially interested in the temperament of infants. Chess and Thomas classified infants as (1) easy, (2) difficult, or (3) slow to warm up. Kagan believes that inhibition to the unfamiliar is an important temperament category. Rothbart and Bates' view of temperament emphasizes this classification: (1) positive affect and approach, (2) negative affectivity, and (3) effortful control (self-regulation).

- Physiological characteristics are associated with different temperaments, and a moderate influence of heredity has been found in studies of the heritability of temperament. Children inherit a physiology that biases them to have a particular type of temperament, but through experience they learn to modify their temperament style to some degree. Very active young children are likely to become outgoing adults. In some cases, a difficult temperament is linked with adjustment problems in early adulthood. The link between childhood temperament and adult personality depends in part on context, which helps shape the reaction to a child and thus the child's experiences. For example, the reaction to a child's temperament depends in part on the child's gender and on the culture.

- Goodness of fit refers to the match between a child's temperament and the environmental demands the child must cope with. Goodness of fit can be an important aspect of a child's adjustment.
- Although research evidence is sketchy at this point in time, some general recommendations are that caregivers should (1) be sensitive to the individual characteristics of the child, (2) be flexible in responding to these characteristics, and (3) avoid negative labeling of the child.

4 Explain attachment and its development

- Attachment is a close emotional bond between two people. In infancy, feeding is not an important aspect of attachment to a caregiver, although contact comfort and trust are. Bowlby's ethological theory stresses that the caregiver and the infant instinctively trigger attachment. Attachment develops in four phases. Securely attached babies use the caregiver, usually the mother, as a secure base from which to explore the environment. Three types of insecure attachment are avoidant, resistant, and disorganized. Ainsworth argued that secure attachment in the first year of life is optimal for development. She created the Strange Situation, an observational measure of attachment. Some critics argue that attachment theorists have not given adequate attention to genetics and temperament. Other critics stress that they have not adequately taken into account the diversity of social agents and contexts. Cultural variations in attachment have been found, but in all cultures studied to date secure attachment is the most common classification. Caregivers of secure babies are sensitive to the babies' signals and are consistently available to meet their needs. Caregivers of avoidant babies tend to be unavailable or rejecting. Caregivers of ambivalent-rejecting babies tend to be inconsistently available to their babies and usually are not very affectionate. Caregivers of disorganized babies often neglect or physically abuse their babies. The mother's role in the infant's development is often caregiving, the father's playful interaction. Child care has become a basic need of the American family. More children are now in child care in the United States than at any earlier point in history. The quality of child care is uneven, and day care remains a controversial topic. Quality child care can be achieved and seems to have few adverse effects on children. In the NICHD child-care study, infants from low-income families were found to receive the lowest quality of care. Also, higher quality of child care was linked with better performance on cognitive tasks and fewer child problems.
- Securely attached adolescents are referred to as secure-autonomous, while insecurely attached adolescents are referred to as dismissing-avoidant, preoccupied-ambivalent, or unresolved-disorganized. Dating, or thinking about dating, becomes an important aspect of many adolescents' lives. Early dating is associated with developmental problems. Culture can exert a powerful influence on dating.
- There appear to be some important continuities between attachment as a child and attachment to parents and romantic partners as a young adult, but attachment styles can change. Romantic love and affectionate love are two important types of love. Romantic love tends to be more important in early adulthood; affectionate love is more likely to be important in later-life love relationships.

Key Terms

emotion 332
primary emotions 336
self-conscious emotions 336
basic cry 336
anger cry 336
pain cry 336
reflexive smile 337
social smile 337
stranger anxiety 338

separation protest 338
social referencing 338
socioemotional selectivity
 theory 342
temperament 343
easy child 344
difficult child 344
slow-to-warm-up child 344
goodness of fit 346

attachment 348
Strange Situation 350
securely attached babies 350
insecure avoidant babies 351
insecure resistant babies 351
insecure disorganized
 babies 351
dismissing/avoidant
 attachment 355

preoccupied/ambivalent
 attachment 356
unresolved/disorganized
 attachment 356
dating scripts 357
romantic love 359
affectionate love 359
triangular theory of love 359

Key People

Carolyn Saarni 334
John Watson 336
Jacob Gewirtz 336
Mary Ainsworth 336
John Bowlby 336

Laura Carstensen 342
Alexander Chess and Stella
 Thomas 344
Jerome Kagan 344
Mary Rothbart 344

Theodore Wachs 346
Harry Harlow 349
Erik Erikson 349
Cindy Hazan and Phillip
 Shaver 358

Ellen Berscheid 359
Robert J. Sternberg 359

E-Learning Tools

Connect to **www.mhhe.com/santrockldt2** to research the answers and complete these exercises. In addition, you'll find a number of other resources and valuable study tools for chapter 10, "Emotional Development," on the Student CD-ROM that came with this book.

Taking It to the Net

1. Rebecca, a 20-year-old single mother, has had her 6-week-old daughter, who was born prematurely, home for a week. She tells her mother that the infant is the fussiest child she had ever seen. "I can see she is going to be a difficult child," Rebecca says. Is there some connection between premature birth and a fussy temperament?

2. For the past couple of months, 10-year-old Molly has exhibited some disturbing behavioral changes. She appears to be angry. She does not play with her friends in the neighborhood as much as she used to, and she often complains of headaches and stomach aches and begs her mother to let her stay home from school. She has been talking about wanting to die so that she can be with the family dog that died last year. Might Molly be suffering from depression?

3. Six months ago, 70-year-old Raymond lost his wife of 50 years to cancer. Raymond lives alone, has lost interest in spending time with his only child and three grandchildren, and has given up playing golf. He told his golfing buddies that life just did not seem worth living since his wife died. Raymond has an extensive gun collection. Is Raymond a suicide risk?

Self-Assessment

To explore attachment and romantic relationships in your life, complete these self-assessments:

- *My Attachment Style*
- *Am I Ready for a Committed Relationship?*
- *Am I a Giver or a Taker in a Romantic Relationship?*
- *What Is My Love Like?*
- *The Characteristics I Desire in a Potential Mate*

Health and Well-Being, Parenting, and Education

Build your decision-making skills by trying your hand at the health and well-being, parenting, and education "Scenarios."

The Self, Identity, and Personality

Learning Goals

1 Discuss the main ways the self is conceptualized

2 Explain the key facets of identity development

3 Describe personality and its development in adulthood

Think about yourself for a few moments. Who are you? What are you like as a person? This chapter seeks to answer such questions by exploring the self, identity, and personality. We will examine these dimensions of people at different points in the human life span, from infancy through late adulthood.

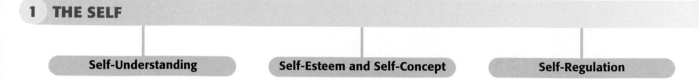

1 THE SELF

| Self-Understanding | Self-Esteem and Self-Concept | Self-Regulation |

What do we mean by the concepts of self, identity, and personality? Here are the definitions, and as you will see, there is considerable overlap in them:

- The **self** is all of the characteristics of a person.
- **Identity** is who a person is, representing a synthesis and integration of self-understanding.
- **Personality** refers to the enduring personal characteristics of individuals.

Theorists and researchers who focus on the self usually argue that the self is the central aspect of the individual's personality and that the self lends an integrative dimension to our understanding of different personality characteristics (Moore & Lemmon, 2001; Nurmi, 2004; Wilson & Dunn, 2004). Several aspects of the self have been studied more than others. These include self-understanding, self-esteem, and self-concept. Let's now turn our attention to how these aspects of the self develop across the human life span.

Self-Understanding

What is self-understanding? **Self-understanding** is the cognitive representation of the self, the substance of self-conceptions. For example, an 11-year-old boy understands that he is a student, a boy, a football player, a family member, a video game lover, and a rock music fan. A 13-year-old girl understands that she is a middle school student, in the midst of puberty, a girl, a cheerleader, a student council member, and a movie fan. Self-understanding is based, in part, on roles and membership categories (Harter, 1990, 1999). It provides the underpinnings for the development of identity (Damon & Hart, 1988). How does self-understanding develop across the life span?

Infancy Infants cannot verbally express their views and cannot understand complex instructions. Given these restrictions, how can researchers study infants' self-understanding? They test infants' *visual self-recognition* by presenting them with images of themselves.

For example, let's examine how the mirror technique works. An infant's mother puts a dot of rouge on the infant's nose. An observer watches to see how often the infant touches its nose. Next, the infant is placed in front of a mirror, and observers detect whether nose touching increases. The idea is that if the infant looks in the mirror and then tries to touch or rub off the rouge, the infant realizes that it is the self in the mirror but that something is not right because of the dot of rouge. In two investigations, infants recognized their own images in the mirror in the second half of the second year of life (Amsterdam, 1968; Lewis & Brooks-Gunn, 1979) (see figure 11.1). In sum, human infants develop a sense of rudimentary self-understanding called *self-recognition* at approximately 18 months of age (Hart & Karmel, 1996; Lewis & others, 1989).

Childhood Because children can verbally communicate, research on self-understanding in childhood is not limited to visual self-recognition, as it is during infancy. Mainly through interviews, researchers have probed many aspects of children's self-understanding.

self All of the characteristics of a person.

identity Who a person is, representing a synthesis of self-understanding.

personality The enduring personal characteristics of individuals.

self-understanding The individual's cognitive representation of the self, the substance of self-conceptions.

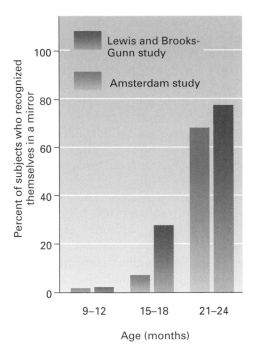

FIGURE 11.1 The Development of Self-Recognition in Infancy
The graph shows the findings of two studies in which infants less than 1 year of age did not recognize themselves in the mirror. A slight increase in the percentage of infant self-recognition occurred around 15 to 18 months of age. By 2 years of age, a majority of children recognized themselves.

How do preschool children understand the self? Young children generally confuse self, mind, and body (Broughton, 1978). Most young children conceive of the self as part of the body, which usually means the head. For them, the self can be described along many material dimensions, such as size, shape, and color.

Preschool children think of themselves and define themselves in physical terms. "Physical" in this case includes physical actions as well as body image and material possessions. Young children distinguish themselves from others through many physical and material attributes. Says 4-year-old Sandra, "I'm different from Jennifer because I have brown hair and she has blond hair." Says 4-year-old Ralph, "I am different from Hank because I am taller, and I am different from my sister because I have a bicycle." The *active dimension* is a central component of the self in early childhood (Keller, Ford, & Meacham, 1978). For example, preschool children often describe themselves in terms of activities such as play. In sum, in early childhood, children often describe themselves in terms of a physical self or an active self.

Preschool children also develop an awareness of how their present selves are causally bound to previous states of the self (Povinelli & Simon, 1998). For example in one study, 2-, 3-, and 4-year-old children briefly saw video images of themselves (Povinelli, Perilloux, & Landau, 1996). The images showed the children playing an unusual game and revealed that one experimenter had covertly placed a large sticker on each child's head. Few 2- and 3-year-olds reached up to their heads to remove the sticker while a majority of the 4- and 5-year-olds did so immediately after the delayed tape revealed that the experimenter had placed it there.

Middle and Late Childhood In middle and late childhood, self-understanding increasingly shifts away from defining the self in terms of external characteristics. Children develop a more complex self-understanding with three key characteristics.

First, in middle and late childhood, children shift toward defining themselves in terms of internal characteristics. They now recognize the difference between inner and outer states, and they are also more likely than young children to include subjective inner states in their definition of self. For example, in one investigation, second-grade children were much more likely than younger children to name psychological characteristics (such as preferences or personality traits) in their self-definition and less likely to name physical characteristics (such as eye color or possessions) (Aboud & Skerry, 1983). Eight-year-old Todd says, "I am smart and I am popular." Ten-year-old Tina

*K*now thyself, for once we know ourselves, we may learn how to care for ourselves, but otherwise we never shall.
—SOCRATES
Greek Philosopher, 5th Century B.C.

Concepts of Person and Self
Self-Development in Infancy

says about herself, "I am pretty good about not worrying most of the time. I used to lose my temper, but I'm better about that now. I also feel proud when I do well in school."

Second, in middle and late childhood, children begin to include *social aspects* such as references to social groups in their self-descriptions (Livesly & Bromley, 1973). For example, children might describe themselves as Girl Scouts, as Catholics, or as someone who has two close friends.

Third, children's self-understanding in middle and late childhood includes increasing reference to *social comparison*—how they compare with others. At this point in development, children are more likely to distinguish themselves from others in comparative rather than in absolute terms. That is, elementary-school-age children are likely to think about what they can do *in comparison with others*. For example, Diane Ruble (1983) gave children a difficult task and then offered feedback on their performance, as well as information about the performances of other children their age. The children were then asked for self-evaluations. Children younger than 7 made virtually no reference to the information about other children's performances. However, many children older than 7 included socially comparative information in their self-descriptions.

In short, during middle and late childhood, children tend to define themselves in terms of internal and social characteristics in comparison with others. The shift toward comparing themselves with others indicates an increased tendency to establish their differences as individuals apart from others.

The Role of Perspective Taking According to Piaget's theory, which we discussed in chapter 6, "Cognitive Developmental Approaches," young children are egocentric ◄‖‖ P. 208. As they develop, they move away from this self-centeredness. **Perspective taking** is the ability to assume another person's perspective and understand his or her thoughts and feelings.

Robert Selman (1980) has proposed a developmental theory of perspective taking that involves five stages, ranging from 3 years of age through adolescence (see figure 11.2). These stages begin with the egocentric viewpoint in early childhood and end with in-depth perspective taking in adolescence.

perspective taking The ability to assume another person's perspective and understand his or her thoughts and feelings.

Stage	Perspective-taking stage	Ages	Description
0	Egocentric viewpoint	3 to 5	Child has a sense of differentiation of self and other but fails to distinguish between the social perspective (thoughts, feelings) of other and self. Child can label other's overt feelings but does not see the cause-and-effect relation of reasons to social actions.
1	Social-informational perspective taking	6 to 8	Child is aware that other has a social perspective based on other's own reasoning, which may or may not be similar to child's. However, child tends to focus on one perspective rather than coordinating viewpoints.
2	Self-reflective perspective taking	8 to 10	Child is conscious that each individual is aware of the other's perspective and that this awareness influences self's and other's view of each other. Putting self in other's place is a way of judging other's intentions, purposes, and actions. Child can form a coordinated chain of perspectives but cannot yet abstract from this process to the level of simultaneous mutuality.
3	Mutual perspective taking	10 to 12	Adolescent realizes that both self and other can view each other mutually and simultaneously as subjects. Adolescent can step outside the two-person dyad and view the interaction from a third-person perspective.
4	Social and conventional system perspective taking	12 to 15	Adolescent realizes mutual perspective taking does not always lead to complete understanding. Social conventions are seen as necessary because they are understood by all members of the group (the generalized other), regardless of their position, role, or experience.

FIGURE 11.2 Selman's Stages of Perspective Taking

To study children's perspective taking, Selman interviews individual children, asking them to comment on such dilemmas as these:

> Holly is an 8-year-old girl who likes to climb trees. She is the best tree climber in the neighborhood. One day while climbing down from a tall tree, she falls . . . but does not hurt herself. Her father sees her fall. He is upset and asks her to promise not to climb trees anymore. Holly promises.
>
> Later that day, Holly and her friends meet Shawn. Shawn's kitten is caught in a tree and can't get down. Something has to be done right away or the kitten may fall. Holly is the only one who climbs trees well enough to reach the kitten and get it down but she remembers her promise to her father. (Selman, 1976, p. 302)

Subsequently, Selman asks each child a series of questions about the dilemma, such as these:

- Does Holly know how Shawn feels about the kitten?
- How will Holly's father feel if he finds out she climbed the tree?
- What does Holly think her father will do if he finds out she climbed the tree?
- What would you do in this situation?

By analyzing children's responses to these dilemmas, Selman (1980) concluded that children's perspective taking follows the developmental sequence described in figure 11.2.

Children's perspective taking can improve their peer group status and the quality of their friendships. For example, one investigation found that the most popular children in the third and eighth grades had competent perspective-taking skills (Kurdek & Krile, 1982). Children who are competent at perspective taking are better at understanding the needs of their companions, so they likely can communicate more effectively with them (Hudson, Forman, & Brion-Meisels, 1982).

Adolescence   The development of self-understanding in adolescence is complex and involves a number of aspects of the self (Harter, 1998, 1999; Nurmi, 2004). The tendency to compare themselves with others continues to increase in the adolescent years. However, when asked whether they engage in social comparison, most adolescents deny it because they are aware that it is somewhat socially undesirable to do so. Let's examine other ways in which the adolescent's self-understanding differs from the child's:

- ***Abstract and Idealistic*** Remember from our discussion of Piaget's theory of cognitive development in chapter 6 that many adolescents begin to think in more *abstract* and *idealistic* ways. When asked to describe themselves, adolescents are more likely than children to use abstract and idealistic labels. Consider 14-year-old Laurie's abstract description of herself: "I am a human being. I am indecisive. I don't know who I am." Also consider her idealistic description of herself: "I am a naturally sensitive person who really cares about people's feelings. I think I'm pretty good looking." Not all adolescents describe themselves in idealistic ways, but most adolescents distinguish between the real self and the ideal self.
- ***Self-Consciousness*** Adolescents are more likely than children to be *self-conscious* about and *preoccupied* with their self-understanding. This self-consciousness and self-preoccupation reflect adolescent egocentrism, which we discussed in chapter 6.
- ***The Fluctuating Self*** The adolescent's self-understanding fluctuates across situations and across time (Harter, 1990). The adolescent's self continues to be characterized by instability until the adolescent constructs a more unified theory of self, usually not until late adolescence or even early adulthood.
- ***Real and Ideal Selves*** The adolescent's emerging ability to construct ideal selves in addition to actual ones can be perplexing and agonizing to the adolescent. In one view, an important aspect of the ideal or imagined self is the **possible self**—what individuals might become, what they would like to become, and what they are afraid of (Markus

possible selves What individuals might become, what they would like to become, and what they are afraid of becoming.

Hazel Markus Talks About Selfways

& Nurius, 1986). Thus, adolescents' possible selves include both what adolescents hope to be as well as what they dread they will become (Bybee & Wells, 2003). The attributes of future positive selves (getting into a good college, being admired, having a successful career) can direct future positive states. The attributes of future negative selves (being unemployed, being lonely, not getting into a good college) can identify what is to be avoided. To read further about the important concept of multiple selves and culture in adolescence, see the Contexts of Life-Span Development interlude.

Contexts of Life-Span Development
Multiple Selves and Sociocultural Contexts

Differentiation of the self increases across the childhood, adolescent, and adult periods of development. Adolescents' portraits of themselves can change depending on whether they describe themselves when they are with their mother, father, close friend, romantic partner, or peer. They also can change depending on whether they describe themselves in the role of student, athlete, or employee. And adolescents might create different selves depending on their ethnic and cultural background and experiences.

The multiple selves of ethnically diverse youth reflect their experiences in navigating their multiple worlds of family, peers, school, and community (Cooper & others, 1995). Research with American youth of African, Chinese, Filipino, Latino, European, Japanese, and Vietnamese descent, as well as Japanese youth, shows that as youth move across cultural worlds, they can encounter barriers related to language, racism, gender, immigration, and poverty. In each of their different worlds they might also find resources in other people, in institutions, and in themselves. Youth who find it too difficult to move between worlds can become alienated from their school, family, and peers. However, youth who effectively navigate their various worlds can develop bicultural or multicultural selves and become "culture brokers" for others.

Hazel Markus and her colleagues (Markus, Mullaly, & Kitayama, 1999) believe that it is important to understand how multiple selves emerge through participation in cultural practices. They argue that all selves are culture-specific selves that emerge as individuals adapt to their cultural environments. Markus and her colleagues recognize that cultural groups are characterized by diversity, but nonetheless they conclude that it is helpful to understand the dominant aspects of multiple selves within a culture. Mainstream North American culture promotes and maintains individuality. North Americans, when given the opportunity to describe themselves, often provide not only portraits of their current selves but also notions of their future selves. They also frequently show a need to have multiple selves that are stable and consistent. In Japan, multiple selves are often described in terms of relatedness to others. Self-improvement also is an important aspect of the multiple selves of many Japanese.

- *Self-Integration* In late adolescence, self-understanding becomes more *integrative,* with the disparate parts of the self more systematically pieced together. Older adolescents are more likely to detect inconsistencies in their earlier self-descriptions as they attempt to construct a general theory of self, an integrated sense of identity.

Adulthood   Little has been written about developmental changes in self-understanding in young adults. However, many experts believe that as individuals move into the traditional college-age years and make the transition from adolescence to adulthood, they begin to engage in more self-reflection about what they want to do with their lives. The extended schooling that takes place in industrialized countries

like the United States and Japan provides time for further self-reflection and understanding of one's self.

Self-Awareness   An aspect of self-understanding that becomes especially important in
early adulthood is *self-awareness*. That is, how much is a young adult aware of his or
her psychological makeup, including strengths and weaknesses? (Notice that self-
awareness meshes with ideas about emotional intelligence and Howard Gardner's
(1983) category of intelligence referred to as insights about self in chapter 8, "Intelligence.")   ◀▥▥ PP. 274, 278. Many individuals do not have very good awareness of their
psychological makeup and skills. For example, how aware is the person that she or he
is a good or bad listener, uses the best strategies to solve personal problems, and is
assertive rather than aggressive or passive in resolving conflicts? Awareness of strengths
and weaknesses in these and many other aspects of life is an important dimension of
self-understanding throughout the adult years, and early adulthood is a time when
individuals can benefit considerably from improving some of their weaknesses.

   In one study, middle-aged adults were more likely to accept their good and bad
characteristics than younger adults were (Ryff, 1991). Although they acknowledged
both their good and bad qualities, middle-aged adults still had a generally positive
view of themselves. The middle-aged adults also were less concerned about the opinions of others and, more than the younger adults, perceived that they chose their
own standards.

Possible Selves   Another aspect of self-understanding that is important in the adult
years involves possible selves. Recall that we described *possible selves* as what individuals might become, what they would like to become, and what they are afraid
of becoming (Bybee & Wells, 2003; Cota-Robles, Neiss, & Hunt, 2000; Hooker, 1999;
Markus & Nurius, 1986). Adults in their twenties mention many possible selves that
they would like to become and might become. Some of these are unrealistic, such
as being happy all of the time and being very rich. As individuals get older, they
often describe fewer possible selves and portray them in more concrete and realistic ways. By middle age, individuals frequently describe their possible selves in terms
of areas of their life in which they already have performed, such as "being good at
my work" or "having a good marriage" (Cross & Markus, 1991). Health-related
selves achieve greater importance in late adulthood than earlier in adulthood
(Hooker, 1999).

   Many individuals continue to revise their possible selves as they go through the
adult years (Lalonde & Chandler, 2004). This ability to revise possible selves and
adapt them to find a better match between desired and achieved goals may be an
important aspect of maintaining positive self-esteem and psychological well-being as
individuals get older (Bengtson, Reedy, & Gordon, 1985).

Life Review   Another important aspect of self-understanding in adulthood is the
life review. Engaging in a life review involves looking back on one's experiences, evaluating them, interpreting them, and in some cases reinterpreting them.

   Life reviews can include just about any aspect of a person's life, such as work,
love, and play. Life reviews can include one's evaluation of success or failure in
work. They can include interpersonal dimensions, such as sharing and intimacy with
family members and friends. Life reviews also can include personal and value
dimensions, such as whether one has been a "giving" or "taking" individual,
whether one has had good moral values, and so on. In addition, life reviews can
include sociocultural dimensions, such as culture, ethnicity, and gender aspects of
one's life. These dimensions of the life review might unfold in a way that the pieces
do or do not make sense to the adult (Kenyon, Ruth, & Mader, 1999). In the final
analysis, the person's life review is to some degree unique.

   Middle-aged adults are more likely to engage in a life review than younger
adults are, but the greatest increase in life review likely occurs in older adults (Cully,

LaVoie, & Gfeller, 2001). As the past marches in review, the older adult surveys it, observes it, and reflects on it (Butler, 1996). Reconsideration of previous experiences and their meaning occurs, often with revision or expanded understanding taking place. This reorganization of the past may provide a more valid picture for the individual, providing new and significant meaning to one's life. It may also help prepare the individual for death, in the process reducing fear.

As the life review proceeds, the older adult may reveal to a spouse, children, or other close associates unknown characteristics and experiences that previously had been undisclosed. In return, they may reveal previously unknown or undisclosed truths. Hidden themes of great meaning to the individual may emerge, changing the nature of the older adult's sense of self.

Successful aging, though, doesn't mean thinking about the past all of the time. In one study, older adults who were obsessed about the past were less well adjusted than older adults who integrated their past and present (Wong & Watt, 1991).

Self-Esteem and Self-Concept

High self-esteem and a positive self-concept are important characteristics of children's and adults' well-being (Harter, 1999). **Self-esteem** refers to global evaluations of the self. Self-esteem is also referred to as *self-worth* or *image*. For example, a person may perceive that she or he is not merely a person but a *good* person. Of course, not all people have an overall positive image of themselves. **Self-concept** refers to domain-specific evaluations of the self. Individuals can make self-evaluations in many domains of their lives—academic, athletic, appearance, and so on. In sum, *self-esteem* refers to global self-evaluations, *self-concept* to domain-specific evaluations.

Investigators sometimes use the terms *self-esteem* and *self-concept* interchangeably and don't always precisely define them (Dusek & McIntyre, 2003). However, the distinction between self-esteem as global self-evaluation and self-concept as domain-specific self-evaluation should help you keep the terms straight.

Issues in Self-Esteem Does self-esteem fluctuate from day to day or remain stable? Most research studies have found it to be stable at least across a month or so (Baumeister, 1993; Tesser, 2000). But self-esteem can change, especially in response to transitions in life. For example, when children go from elementary school to middle school, their self-esteem usually drops (Hawkins & Berndt, 1985). Indeed, during and just after such life transitions, individuals' self-esteem often decreases. This decrease in self-esteem may occur during the transition from middle or junior high school to high school, and from high school to college.

Is self-esteem related to school and adult job performance? There are only modest correlations between school performance and self-esteem and these correlations do not indicate that high self-esteem causes good performance (Baumeister & others, 2003). Adult job performance is sometimes related to self-esteem, although the correlations vary considerably and the direction of the causation has not been documented (Judge & Bono, 2001). Occupational success may increase self-esteem, not necessarily the reverse. Nonetheless, self-esteem may be beneficial in some job contexts.

Is self-esteem linked to initiative? Individuals with high self-esteem have greater initiative and this can produce positive or negative outcomes (Baumeister & others, 2003). High-self-esteem individuals are prone to both prosocial and antisocial actions (for example, both defending victims against bullies and being a bully) compared with individuals with low self-esteems (Trzesniewsi & others, 2002). They initiate interactions and relationships (and sometimes exit them) more than their low-self-esteem counterparts (Glendinning & Inglis, 1999). High-self-esteem individuals are more likely to speak up in groups and experiment with sex (and perhaps drugs) (Gerrard & others, 2000; LePine & Van Dyne, 1998). They try harder in response to initial failure but they are willing to switch to something else if the present endeavor appears to be unpromising (Di Paula & Campbell, 2002).

self-esteem The global evaluative dimension of the self. Self-esteem is also referred to as self-worth or self-image.

self-concept Domain-specific evaluations of the self.

Is self-esteem related to happiness? Self-esteem is strongly related to happiness and it seems likely that high self-esteem increases happiness while depression lowers it (Baumeister & others, 2003). A large-scale international study of 13,000 college students from 49 different universities in 31 countries found that high self-esteem was strongly related to happiness (Diener & Diener, 1995). The correlation was stronger in individualist countries rather than collectivist countries. Other researchers have also found links between high self-esteem and happiness (Lyubomirksy & Lepper, 2002).

A large number of studies have found that individuals with low self-esteem report that they feel more depressed than individuals with high self-esteem (Arndt & Goldenberg, 2002; Baumeister & others, 2003; Harter, 1998). Low self-esteem has also been implicated in suicide attempts and anorexia nervosa (Fenzel, 1994).

Can a person have too much self-esteem? High self-esteem is a category that encompasses people who deserve their high self-esteem and are well adjusted as well as individuals who are narcissistic and conceited (Baumeister & others, 2003). *Narcissism,* refers to a self-centered and self-concerned approach in dealing with others. Typically, narcissistic individuals are unaware of their actual self and how others perceive them. This lack of awareness contributes to their adjustment problems. Narcissists are excessively self-centered and self-congratulatory, viewing their own needs and desires as paramount. As a result, narcissistic individuals rarely show any empathy toward others. In fact, narcissistic individuals often devalue people around them to protect their own precarious self-esteem, yet they often respond with rage and shame when others do not admire them and treat them in accordance with their grandiose fantasies about themselves. Narcissistic persons are at their most grandiose when their self-esteem is threatened. Narcissists may fly into a frenzy if they have given an unsatisfactory performance.

An important point needs to be made about much of the research on self-esteem: It is correlational rather than experimental. Remember from chapter 1 that correlation does not equal causation ◀◁▥ **P. 35**. Thus, if a correlational study finds an association between self-esteem and depression, it could be equally likely that depression causes low self-esteem or low self-esteem causes depression.

Developmental Changes   One recent cross-sectional study assessed the self-esteem of a very large, diverse sample of 326,641 individuals from 9 to 90 (Robins & others, 2002). About two-thirds of the participants were from the United States. The individuals were asked to respond to the item "I have high self-esteem" on a scale from 1 to 5 with 1 meaning "strongly agree" and 5 meaning "strongly disagree."

Self-esteem decreased in adolescence, increased in the twenties, leveled off in the thirties, rose in the fifties and sixties, and then dropped in the seventies and eighties (see figure 11.3). In most age periods, the self-esteem of males was higher than the self-esteem of females. Let's now explore developmental changes in self-esteem in more detail.

Childhood and Adolescence   Researchers have found that the accuracy of self-evaluations increases across the elementary school years (Harter, 1999). Young children tend to provide inflated views of themselves, but by about 8 years of age most children give more realistic appraisals of their skills (Harter, 1999). For example, older elementary school children who report a positive self-image of themselves in sports indeed are the ones who are reported by peers to be good at athletics.

Adolescents in general have long been described as having low self-esteem (Robins & others, 2002). However, the majority of adolescents actually have a positive self-image. In an extensive cross-cultural study, Daniel Offer and his colleagues (1988) sampled the self-images of adolescents around the world—in the United States, Australia, Bangladesh, Hungary, Israel, Italy, Japan, Taiwan, Turkey, and West Germany. Almost three-fourths of the adolescents had a healthy self-image.

Exploring Self-Esteem Research

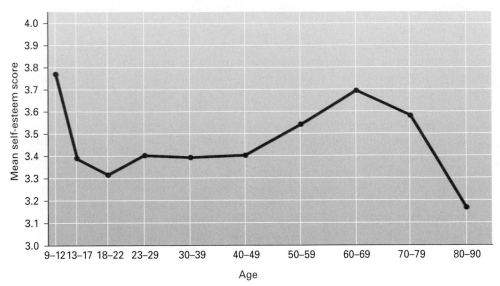

FIGURE 11.3 Self-Esteem Across the Life Span

One cross-sectional study found that self-esteem was high in childhood, dropped in adolescence, increased through early and middle adulthood, then dropped in the seventies and eighties (Robins & others, 2002). More than 300,000 individuals were asked the extent to which they have high self-esteem on a 5-point scale with 5 being "Strongly Agree" and 1 being "Strongly Disagree."

Some researchers believe that gender differences in self-esteem emerge by early adolescence, and this was found in the study just described (Robins & others, 2002). Girls and boys enter first grade with roughly equivalent levels of self-esteem. Yet some research studies have shown that by the middle school years girls' self-esteem is significantly lower than boys' (American Association of University Women, 1992; Gilligan, 1996). However, other researchers caution that the self-esteem of girls is only slightly lower than boys' and still in the positive range (Kling & others, 1999). We will discuss such gender differences in chapter 12, "Gender and Sexuality."

Adulthood Are there differences in the self-esteem of young, middle-aged, and older adults? In the self-esteem study described earlier, self-esteem dropped in late adulthood (Robbins & others, 2002). However, some researchers have not found any differences in self-esteem across the age periods of adulthood (McGue, Hirsch, & Lykken, 1993).

Given that older adults have more physical problems, why wouldn't they have lower self-esteem than young or middle-aged adults? One possible reason is that many older adults don't interpret their "losses" as negatively, and don't become as emotionally upset, as younger adults (Carstensen & Freund, 1994). For example, being asked to retire at age 63 may not be nearly as devastating as being fired from a job at 40. Furthermore, as we saw in chapter 10, "Emotional Development," Laura Carstensen (1998) argues that knowledge-related goals decrease in older adults while emotion-related goals increase ◀▥ **P. 342**. And many older adults have the ability to reach their emotion-related goals of honing their social network to spend most of their time with the people with whom they have enjoyed satisfying close relationships in the past. Finally, many older adults choose to compare themselves with other older adults rather than younger adults, which can help them maintain their positive self-image (Brandstädter, 1999; Brandstädter & Greve, 1994).

Increasing Self-Esteem Five ways self-esteem can be improved are through (1) identification of the causes of low self-esteem and the domains of competence important to the self, (2) emotional support and social approval, (3) taking responsibility for self-esteem, (4) achievement, and (5) coping.

Identifying sources of self-esteem—that is, competence in domains important to the self—is critical to improving self-esteem. Susan Harter (1990) points out that the self-esteem enhancement programs of the 1970s and 1980s, in which self-esteem itself was the target and individuals were encouraged to simply feel good about themselves, were ineffective. Rather, Harter believes that intervention must occur at the level of the *causes* of self-esteem if the individual's self-esteem is to improve significantly. Individuals have the highest self-esteem when they perform competently in domains that are important to them. Therefore, people should be encouraged to identify and value areas of competence.

Emotional support and social approval also powerfully influence self-esteem. Some children with low self-esteem come from conflicted families or conditions in which they experienced abuse or neglect—situations in which support was unavailable. In some cases, alternative sources of support can be implemented either informally through the encouragement of a teacher, a coach, or another significant adult or, more formally, through programs such as Big Brothers and Big Sisters. As peer approval becomes increasingly important during adolescence, peer support is an important influence on the adolescent's self-esteem.

Developing self-confidence and believing that one has the ability to do what it takes to improve self-esteem is another good strategy. Although it is helpful to have the social support and emotional approval of others, it is also very important for you to take the initiative to increase your self-esteem. In one recent study of more than 600 college students, there were costs when individuals sought high self-esteem for external reasons (Crocker, 2002). Seeking high self-esteem because of a motivation to look physically more attractive than others was linked with stress, drug and alcohol use, and disordered eating.

Achievement can also improve an individual's self-esteem (Baumeister & others, 2003). For example, self-esteem can be enhanced by the straightforward teaching of skills to individuals. People develop higher self-esteem because they know the important tasks to accomplish goals and by carrying out these tasks they are more likely to reach their goals.

Self-esteem often increases when individuals face a problem and try to cope with it rather than avoid it (Bednar, Wells, & Peterson, 1995). When coping prevails, the individual often faces problems realistically, honestly, and nondefensively, leading to favorable self-evaluative thoughts, which lead to the self-generated approval and higher self-esteem. The converse is true of low self-esteem. Unfavorable self-evaluations trigger denial, deception, and avoidance in an attempt to disavow that which has already been glimpsed as true. This process leads to self-generated disapproval as a form of feedback to the self about personal adequacy.

Self-Regulation

Self-regulation involves the ability to control one's behavior without having to rely on others' help. Self-regulation includes the self-generation and cognitive monitoring of thoughts, feelings, and behaviors in order to reach a goal. An individual might develop better self-control in the physical, cognitive, or socioemotional domain than in other domains.

Throughout most of the life span, individuals who engage in self-regulation are better achievers and more satisfied with their lives than their counterparts who let external factors dominate their lives (Carpara & Cervone, 2003; Pintrich, 2000, 2003; Schunk). For example, researchers have found that, compared with low-achieving students, high-achieving students engage in greater self-regulation. They do this by setting more specific learning goals, using more strategies to learn and adapt, self-monitoring more, and more systematically evaluating their progress toward a goal (Schunk & Zimmerman, 2003; Zimmerman, 2000). The Applications in Life-Span Development interlude describes a model for improving self-regulation.

self-regulation The ability to control one's behavior without having to rely on others for help.

Applications in Life-Span Development

Engaging in Self-Regulation

Teachers, tutors, mentors, counselors, and parents can help students become self-regulatory learners. Barry Zimmerman, Sebastian Bonner, and Robert Kovach (1996) developed a model for turning low-self-regulatory students into students who engage in these multistep strategies: (1) self-evaluation and monitoring, (2) goal setting and strategic planning, (3) putting a plan into action and monitoring it, and (4) monitoring outcomes and refining strategies (see figure 11.4).

Zimmerman and colleagues describe a seventh-grade student who is doing poorly in history and apply their self-regulatory model to her situation. In step 1, she self-evaluates her studying and test preparation by keeping a detailed record of them. The teacher gives her some guidelines for keeping these records. After several weeks, the student turns the records in and traces her poor test performance to low comprehension of difficult reading material.

In step 2, the student sets a goal—in this case improving reading comprehension—and plans how to achieve the goal. The teacher assists her in breaking the goal into components, such as locating main ideas and setting specific goals for understanding a series of paragraphs in her textbook. The teacher also provides the student with strategies, such as focusing initially on the first sentence of each paragraph and then scanning the others as a means of identifying main ideas. The teacher might offer the student tutoring in reading comprehension by an adult or a peer if it is available.

In step 3, the student puts the plan into action and begins to monitor her progress. Initially, she may need help from the teacher or tutor in identifying main ideas in the reading. This feedback can help her monitor her reading comprehension more effectively on her own.

In step 4, the student monitors her improvement in reading comprehension by evaluating whether it has had any impact on her learning outcomes. Most importantly: Has her improvement in reading comprehension led to better performance on history tests?

Self-evaluations reveal that the strategy of finding main ideas has only partly improved her comprehension, and only when the first sentence contained the paragraph's main idea. So the teacher recommends further strategies. As this continued refinement of self-evaluation and self-regulation takes place, the student's grades improve.

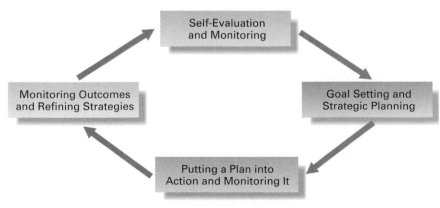

FIGURE 11.4 A Model of Self-Regulatory Learning

Infancy and Early Childhood In chapter 10, "Emotional Development," we discussed the importance of children learning to regulate their emotions as they develop ◀▦ **P. 338.** Emotional regulation is an important aspect of the overall development of self-regulation (Mischel & Mendoza-Denton, 2003). How do other aspects of self-regulation develop? Claire Kopp (1982, 1987) described a sequence for its development early in life. Initially, beginning at about 12 to 18 months of age, infants depend completely on caregivers for reminder signals about acceptable behaviors. At this age, infants begin to show compliance to caregivers' demands (Kaler & Kopp, 1990). For example, a parent might say, "No. Don't touch!" And the infant doesn't touch.

The next phase of developing self-regulation takes place at approximately 2 to 3 years of age. At this point, children begin to comply with the caregiver's expectations in the absence of external monitoring by the caregiver. Thus, most 2- to 3-year-old children are aware of where they may and may not play and which objects they may and may not touch if they are at home, on a playground, or in the homes of friends and relatives.

Nonetheless, at these young ages, there are clear limitations on self-regulation. Given a strong stimulus, such as a ball rolling down the street or the motivation to explore an interesting place, toddlers often ignore safety or exhortations. Also, only rudimentary aspects of delaying gratification are present at these early ages. For example, when 2-year-olds arc confronted with an unexpected delay (such as not being able go outside and play), they often whine and beg to engage in the activity. But there are clear signs of advances in self-initiated regulation, as when young children announce a toy cleanup without prompting from caregivers.

Preschoolers become better at self-control, learning how to resist temptation and giving themselves instructions that keep them focused (Kuczynski & Kochanska, 1990; Mischel & Patterson, 1978). Thus, toward the end of the preschool years, children might say to themselves, "No. I can't do that. I'm working," in response to a temptation to stop working and do something else, like play with an attractive toy (Mischel, Shode, & Peake, 1988).

Middle/Late Childhood and Adolescence Children increase their ability to regulate their behavior in the elementary school years, especially from about 5 or 6 ycars of agc to 7 or 8 years of age (Skinner & Connell, 1986). The increase coincides with the first several years of formal schooling and is likely due at least somewhat to the efforts of teachers to help children control their behavior.

Across the elementary school years, children increase their belief that their behavior is a result of their own effort and not due to luck (Skinner, Chapman, & Baltes, 1982). Also, from 8 to 14 years of age, perceived self-responsibility for failure (such as not doing well on a test) increases (Skinner & Connell, 1986).

Few studies of self-regulation have focused on adolescents (Clark-Plaskie & Lochman, 1999). On the one hand, advances in cognitive skills (logical thinking, for example), increased introspection, and the greater independence of adolescence might lead to increased self-control. Also, advances in cognitive abilities provide adolescents with a better understanding of the importance of delaying gratification for something desirable (such as a good grade in a class) rather than seeking immediate gratification (listening to rock music rather than studying). On the other hand, an increased sense of invincibility (which can lead to risk taking) and social comparison might produce less self-control.

Adulthood Self-control increases in early adulthood and on into the middle adult years (Gatz & Karel, 1993; Ryckman & Malikosi, 1975). However, it is important to consider not just general self-control but how people self-regulate their behavior in specific areas of their lives. One study examined individuals from 13 to 90 years of age. For the oldest group (60 to 90 years of age), self-control was lowest in the physical domain; for the youngest group (13 to 18 years of age), it was lowest in the social domain (Bradley & Webb, 1976). Other researchers have found a decline in perceived self-control in cognitive functioning in older adults (Bertrand & Lachman, 2003; Lachman, 1991; Lachman & others, 1982).

Although older adults are aware of age-related losses, most still effectively maintain a sense of self-control. The negative effects of age-typical problems, such as a decline in physical and cognitive skills and an increase in illness, may be buffered by a flexible, accommodating control style. Researchers have found that *accommodating control strategies* (changing one's goals to fit a given circumstance) increase in importance and *assimilative control strategies* (changing a situation to meet one's goals) decrease in importance beginning in middle adulthood (Brandstädter & Renner, 1990).

Late Adulthood: Paul Baltes' SOC Theory

Selective Optimization with Compensation   The need to accommodate to losses is an important aspect of self-regulation in aging adults. One theory that addresses this issue was proposed by Paul Baltes and his colleagues (Baltes & Baltes, 1990; Baltes, 2000, 2002, 2003; Krampe & Baltes, 2004). According to **selective optimization with compensation theory,** successful self-regulation in aging is linked with three main factors—selection, optimization, and compensation:

- Selection is based on the concept that older adults have a reduced capacity and loss of functioning, which require a reduction in performance in most life domains.
- Optimization suggests that it is possible to maintain performance in some areas through continued practice and the use of new technologies.
- Compensation becomes relevant when life tasks require a level of capacity beyond the older adult's performance potential. Older adults especially need to compensate in circumstances with high mental or physical demands, such as when thinking about and memorizing new material very fast, reacting quickly when driving a car, or running fast. When older adults develop an illness, the need for compensation is obvious.

When the late Arthur Rubinstein was interviewed at 80 years of age, he said that three factors were responsible for his ability to maintain his status as an admired concert pianist into old age. First, he mastered the weakness of old age by reducing the scope of his performances and playing fewer pieces (which reflects *selection*). Second, he spent more time at practice than earlier in his life (which reflects *optimization*). Third, he used special strategies such as slowing down before fast segments, thus creating the image of faster playing (which reflects *compensation*).

Selection of Priorities   In Baltes' view (2000, 2002, 2003; Baltes, Lindenberger, & Staudinger, 1998), the selection of domains and life priorities is an important aspect of development. Life goals and priorities likely vary across the life course for most people (Cantor & Blanton, 1996). In one study, younger adults were more likely to assess their well-being in terms of accomplishments and careers, whereas older adults were more likely to link well-being with good health and the ability to accept change. And as you read in chapter 10, emotion-related goals become increasingly important for older adults (Carstensen, 1998).

One cross-sectional study assessed the life investments of 25- to 103-year-olds (Staudinger, 1996; Staudinger & Fleeson, 1996) (see figure 11.5). From 25 to 34 years of age, participants said that they personally invest more time in work, friends, family, and independence, in that order. From 35 to 54 and 55 to 65 years of age, family became more important to them than friends in terms of their personal investment. Little changed in the rank ordering for those 70 to 84 years old, but for those 85 to 105 years old, health became the most important personal investment. Thinking about life showed up for the first time on the most important list for 85- to 105-year-olds. Other researchers have found similar ratings of domains across the life span (Heckhausen, 2002).

selective optimization with compensation theory The theory that successful self-regulation in aging is related to three main factors: selection, optimization, and compensation

25 to 34 Years	35 to 54 Years	55 to 65 Years	70 to 84 Years	85 to 100 Years
Work	**Family**	**Family**	**Family**	**Health**
Friends	Work	Health	Health	Family
Family	Friends	Friends	Cognitive fitness	Thinking about life
Independence	Cognitive fitness	Cognitive fitness	Friends	Cognitive fitness

FIGURE 11.5 Degree of Personal Life Investment at Different Points in Life

Shown here are the top four domains of personal life investment at different points in life. The highest degree of investment is listed at the top (for example, work was the highest personal investment from 25 to 34 years of age, family from 35 to 84, and health from 85 to 105).

Personal Control   Jutta Heckhausen and her colleagues (Heckhausen, 1997, 2001, 2002; Heckhausen & Schultz, 1995; Heckhausen, Wrosch, & Fleeson, 2001) believe it is important to examine control-related strategies and the ability of people to control important outcomes in their lives. They distinguish between primary control striving and secondary control striving:

- *Primary control striving* refers to individuals' efforts to change the external world so that it meets their needs and desires. Primary control strategies are directed at attaining personal goals and overcoming obstacles. Persistence in striving for a goal ("When things don't go according to my plans, my motto is: 'Where there is a will, there's a way'") is an example of a primary control strategy.
- *Secondary control striving* targets individuals' inner worlds and their own motivation, emotion, and mental representation. Examples of secondary control striving are positive reappraisal ("I find I usually learn something from a difficult situation") and lowering aspirations ("When my expectations are not being met, I lower them"). In most instances, primary control is more adaptive than secondary control because in primary control individuals change their environment to meet their own needs and seek gains in their life. In secondary control, they often are trying to minimize losses or maintain their standing.

Primary and secondary control are believed to change through the life span. The ability to control outcomes is expected to increase substantially during the child, adolescent, and early adult years, level off in middle adulthood, and then decline in late adulthood (see figure 11.6). Secondary control increases in a similar manner through the early adult years, but unlike primary control, continues to increase through adulthood (see figure 11.6). Increasing physical and social challenges to primary control lead older adults to increase the use of secondary control strategies (Grob, Little, & Wanner, 1999; Heckhausen & Schultz, 1995).

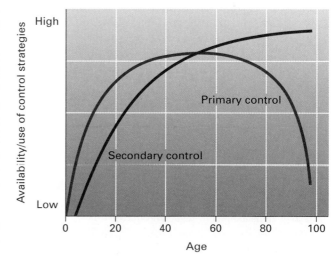

FIGURE 11.6 Theorized Changes in Primary and Secondary Control Strategies Across the Human Life Span

According to Heckhausen, primary control strategies increase in the child, adolescent, and early adult years, then level off in middle age, and finally decline in order adults. However, secondary control strategies continue to increase throughout the adult years.

One study focused on control strategies related to health or financial stress (Wrosch, Heckhausen, & Lachman, 2000). Primary control in the form of persistence in attaining a goal was positively related to perceived well-being in young adults. However, in middle and late adulthood, the secondary control strategy of positive reappraisal had a stronger link with perceived well-being than persistence. The secondary control strategy of lowering aspirations was negatively related to perceived well-being at all points in adulthood.

Review and Reflect: Learning Goal 1

1 Discuss the main ways the self is conceptualized

REVIEW

- How can the terms self, identity, and personality be defined? What is self-understanding, and how does it develop?
- What are self-esteem and self-concept, and how do they develop? How is self-esteem related to performance, initiative, and happiness? Is there a dark side to high self-esteem? What are some ways to increase self-esteem?
- What is self-regulation, and how does it develop?

REFLECT

- If a psychologist would have interviewed you when you were 8 years old, 14 years old, and again today, would your self-understanding and self-esteem be different? If so, how and why?

---

2 IDENTITY

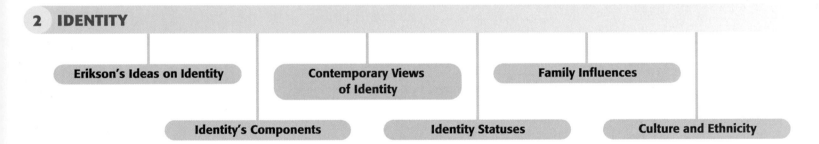

Erikson's Ideas on Identity · Identity's Components · Contemporary Views of Identity · Identity Statuses · Family Influences · Culture and Ethnicity

Who am I? What am I all about? What am I going to do with my life? What is different about me? How can I make it on my own? Not usually considered during childhood, these questions surface as common, virtually universal concerns during adolescence. Adolescents clamor for solutions to these questions that revolve around the concept of identity, and it was Erik Erikson (1950, 1968) who first understood how central such questions are to adolescent development. That today identity is believed to be a key concept in adolescent development is a result of Erikson's masterful thinking and analysis.

Erikson's Ideas on Identity

Recall from chapter 1 that Erik Erikson proposed that individuals go through eight stages during the life span ◀▥ P. 20. Erikson wrote extensively about the fifth of these eight stages: **Identity versus identity confusion,** which individuals experience during the adolescent years. At this time, adolescents examine who they are, what they are all about, and where they are going in life.

Adolescents are confronted with many new roles, such as vocational and romantic roles. **Psychosocial moratorium** is Erikson's term for the gap between childhood security and adult autonomy that adolescents experience as part of their identity exploration. As adolescents explore and search their culture's "identity files," they often experiment with different roles. Adolescents may emerge from this period

identity versus identity confusion Erikson's fifth stage of development, which occurs during the adolescent years; adolescents are faced with finding out who they are, what they are all about, and where they are going in life.

psychosocial moratorium Erikson's term for the gap between childhood security and adult autonomy that adolescents experience as part of their identity exploration.

either with a new sense of self or with identity confusion. Confusion either leads them to withdraw, isolating themselves from peers and family, or to immerse themselves in the world of peers and lose their identity in the crowd.

Erikson's ideas about adolescent identity development reveal rich insights into adolescents' thoughts and feelings. Reading one or more of his original writings is worthwhile. A good starting point is *Identity: Youth and Crisis* (1968). Other works that portray identity development are *Young Man Luther* (1962) and *Gandhi's Truth* (1969).

Identity's Components

Identity is a self-portrait composed of many pieces, including these:

- The career and work path the person wants to follow (vocational/career identity)
- Whether the person is conservative, liberal, or a middle-of-the-roader (political identity)
- The person's spiritual beliefs (religious identity)
- Whether the person is single, married, divorced, and so on (relationship identity)
- The extent to which the person is motivated to achieve and is intellectual (achievement, intellectual identity)
- Whether the person is heterosexual, homosexual, or bisexual (sexual identity)
- Which part of the world or country the person is from and how intensely the person identifies with his or her cultural heritage (cultural/ethnic identity)
- The kind of things the person likes to do, which can include sports, music, hobbies, and so on (interest)
- The individual's personality characteristics (such as being introverted or extraverted, anxious or calm, friendly or hostile, and so on) (personality)
- The individual's body image (physical identity)

At a bare minimum, identity formation involves commitment to a vocational direction, an ideological stance, and a sexual orientation.

Contemporary Views of Identity

Contemporary views of identity development see it as a gradual, lengthy process, not a cataclysmic transition (Baumeister, 1991; Kroger, 2003; Marcia, 1989; Marcia & Carpendale, 2004; Stewart, 2003; Stewart & McDermott, 2004). Identity formation neither begins nor ends with adolescence. It begins with the appearance of attachment, the development of a sense of self, and the emergence of independence in infancy, and reaches its final phase with a life review and integration in old age. What is important about identity development in adolescence, especially late adolescence, is that, for the first time, physical development, cognitive development, and socioemotional development advance to the point at which the individual can sort through and synthesize current and past identities. Questions such as "Who am I?" and "What aspects of my identities come out in different contexts?" are asked more frequently in adolescence than during childhood. Furthermore, adolescents are more likely to try to balance their needs for autonomy and for connectedness.

Identity formation does not happen neatly, and it usually does not happen cataclysmically. Synthesizing the identity components can be a long, drawn-out process, with many negations and affirmations of various roles and faces. Identity development gets done in bits and pieces. Decisions are not made once and for all, but have to be made again and again. And the decisions might seem trivial at the time: whom to date, whether or not to break up, whether or not to have intercourse, whether or not to take drugs, whether or not to go to college or finish high school and get a job, which major to choose, whether to study or to play, whether or not to be politically active, and so on. Over the years of adolescence and emerging adulthood, the decisions begin to form a core of what the individual is all about as a human being—what is called her or his identity.

"*W*ho are you?" said the caterpillar. Alice replied rather shyly, "I—I hardly know, sir, just at present—at least I know who I was when I got up this morning, but I must have changed several times since then."

—LEWIS CARROLL
English Writer, 19th Century

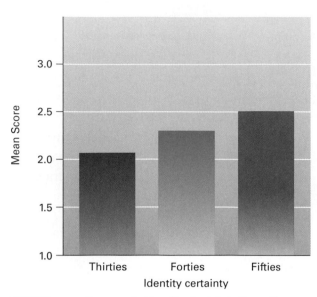

FIGURE 11.7 Changes in Identity Certainty from the Thirties Through the Fifties

Identity certainty increased in Smith College women as they aged from their thirties through their fifties (Stewart, Ostrove, & Helson, 2001). The women rated themselves on a 3-point scale indicating the extent to which they thought the statements about identity certainty were descriptive of their lives. Higher scores reflect greater identity certainty.

Resolution of the identity issue at adolescence does not mean that identity will be stable through the remainder of life. An individual who develops a healthy identity is flexible and adaptive, open to changes in society, in relationships, and in careers (Adams, Gulotta, & Montemayor, 1992). This openness means that numerous reorganizations of identity will occur throughout the individual's life.

Some of this identity reorganization may result from experiencing the changes theorized by Erikson. In one modification of Erikson's theory, it was proposed that Erikson's three adult stages—intimacy versus isolation (early adulthood), generativity versus stagnation (middle adulthood), and integrity versus despair (late adulthood)—are best viewed as developmental phases within identity. In this view, identity remains the central core of the self's development across all of the adult years but its main focus varies at different points in adult development (Whitbourne & Connolly, 1999).

However, as individuals move from early to middle adulthood they become more certain about their identity. For example, a longitudinal study of Smith College women found that identity certainty increased from the thirties through the fifties (Cole & Stewart, 1996; Roberts & Helson, 1997; Stewart, Ostrove, & Helson, 2001; Zucker, Ostrove, & Stewart, 2002) (see figure 11.7). Figure 11.8 describes the items that were used to assess identity certainty in the Smith College Study.

Identity Statuses

How does this process of forming an identity unfold? Eriksonian researcher James Marcia (1980, 1994; Marcia & Carpendale, 2004) developed an analysis of this question that some theorists and researchers consider a valuable contribution to understanding identity (Archer, 1989; Waterman, 1992).

According to Marcia, in forming an identity individuals go through periods of crisis and commitment. **Crisis** is a period of identity development during which the individual is exploring alternatives. (Most researchers use the term *exploration* rather than *crisis,* although, in the spirit of Marcia's formulation, the term *crisis* is used here.) **Commitment** is a part of identity development in which individuals show personal investment in what they are going to do.

Four Statuses The extent of an individual's crisis and commitment is used to classify the individual's position in the process of developing an identity—in other words, the person's *identity status.* The four statuses of identity are identity diffusion, identity foreclosure, identity moratorium, and identity achievement (see figure 11.9):

- **Identity diffusion** is the state adolescents are in when they have not yet experienced a crisis (that is, they have not explored meaningful alternatives) or made any commitments. Not only are they undecided about occupational and ideological choices, they are also likely to show little interest in such matters.
- **Identity foreclosure** is the state adolescents are in when they have made a commitment but not experienced a crisis. This occurs most often when parents hand down commitments to their adolescents, usually in an authoritarian way. In these circumstances, adolescents have not had adequate opportunities to explore different approaches, ideologies, and vocations on their own.
- **Identity moratorium** is the state adolescents are in when they are in the midst of a crisis but their commitments are either absent or only vaguely defined.
- **Identity achievement** is the state adolescents are in when they have undergone a crisis and made a commitment.

Let's explore some examples of Marcia's identity statuses. A 13-year-old adolescent has neither begun to explore her identity in any meaningful way nor made an identity commitment, so she is *identity diffused.* An 18-year-old boy's parents want him to be a medical doctor so he is planning to major in premedicine and has not explored

crisis A period of identity development during which the adolescent is choosing among meaningful alternatives.

commitment The part of identity development in which adolescents show a personal investment in what they are going to do.

identity diffusion Marcia's term for adolescents who have not yet experienced a crisis (explored meaningful alternatives) or made any commitments.

identity foreclosure Marcia's term for adolescents who have made a commitment but have not experienced a crisis.

identity moratorium Marcia's term for adolescents who are in the midst of a crisis, but their commitments are either absent or vaguely defined.

identity achievement Marcia's term for adolescents who have undergone a crisis and have made a commitment.

any other options; he is *identity foreclosed*. Nineteen-year-old Sasha is not quite sure what life paths she wants to follow, but she recently went to a counseling center to find out about different careers, so she is in *identity moratorium* status. Twenty-one-year-old Marcelo extensively explored different career options in college, eventually getting his degree in science education, and is looking forward to his first year of teaching high school students, so he is *identity achieved*. These examples focus on the career dimension, but remember that identity includes a number of dimensions.

The identity status approach has been sharply criticized by some researchers and theoreticians (Blasi, 1988; Cote & Levine, 1988; Lapsley & Power, 1988). They believe that the identity status approach distorts and trivializes Erikson's notions of crisis and commitment. For example, Erikson's idea of commitment loses the meaning of investing oneself in certain lifelong projects and is interpreted simply as having made a firm decision or not. Regarding commitment, Marcia (1996) believes that the first identity is just that—it is not and should not be expected to be the final product.

Developmental Changes in Identity Status   In Marcia's terms, young adolescents are primarily in the identity statuses of diffusion, foreclosure, or moratorium. What factors influence whether adolescents develop a positive identity? According to Marcia (1987, 1996), at least three aspects of the young adolescent's development are important in identity formation: Young adolescents must be confident that they have parental support, must have an established sense of industry, and must be able to adopt a self-reflective stance toward the future.

Some researchers believe the most important identity changes take place in emerging adulthood—from about 18 through 25 years of age—rather than in adolescence. Alan Waterman (1985, 1989, 1992) found that from the years preceding high school through the last years of college, the number of individuals who are identity achieved increases and the number of those who are identity diffused decreases. However, fewer college students have reached the identity-achieved status for religious beliefs and political ideology than for vocational choices. Thus, the timing of identity may vary with the particular life area involved; many college students are still wrestling with ideological commitments (Arehart & Smith, 1990).

Many researchers believe that a common pattern among individuals who develop positive identities is the "MAMA" cycle of *moratorium–achievement–moratorium–achievement* (Archer, 1989). These cycles may be repeated throughout life (Francis, Fraser, & Marcia, 1989). Personal, family, and societal changes are inevitable. As they occur, the flexibility and skill required to explore new alternatives and develop new commitments are likely to enhance an individual's coping skills.

The contexts of the individual's life influence identity development. Next, we will explore two such contexts: family and ethnicity.

Family Influences

Parents are important figures in the adolescent's development of identity. One approach to studying their influence examines parenting styles. *Democratic parents,* who encourage adolescents to participate in family decision making, foster identity achievement. *Autocratic parents,* who control the adolescent's behavior without giving the adolescent an opportunity to express opinions, encourage identity foreclosure. *Permissive parents,* who provide little guidance to adolescents and allow them to make their own decisions, promote identity diffusion (Enright & others, 1980).

Family atmosphere also influences the development of identity. According to Catherine Cooper and her colleagues (Carlson, Cooper & Hsu, 1990; Cooper & Grotevant, 1989; Grotevant & Cooper, 1985, 1998), a family atmosphere that promotes both individuality and connectedness fosters an adolescent's identity development:

Identity certainty
A sense of being my own person
Excitement, turmoil, confusion about my impulses and potential (reversed)
Coming near the end of one road and not yet finding another (reversed)
Feeling my life is moving well
Searching for a sense of who I am (reversed)
Wishing I had a wider scope to my life (reversed)
Anxiety that I won't live up to opportunities (reversed)
Feeling secure and committed

FIGURE 11.8 Items Used to Assess Identity Certainty

These items were used to assess identity certainty in the longitudinal study of Smith College women (Stewart, Ostrove, & Helson, 2001). In the assessment of identity certainty, five of the items involved reversed scoring (for example, if an individual scored high on the item "Searching for a sense of who I am," it was an indication of identity uncertainty rather identity certainty).

Erikson's Theory

Exploring Identity

The Society for Research on Identity Development

Identity Status Research

FIGURE 11.9 Marcia's Four Statuses of Identity

*O*nce formed, an identity furnishes individuals with a historical sense of who they have been, a meaningful sense of who they are now, and a sense of who they might become in the future.

—JAMES MARCIA
*Contemporary Psychologist,
Simon Fraser University*

- **Individuality** consists of two dimensions: self-assertion—the ability to have and communicate a point of view—and separateness—the use of communication patterns to express how one is different from others.
- **Connectedness** also consists of two dimensions: mutuality—which involves sensitivity to and respect for others' views—and permeability—which involves openness to others' views.

In general, Cooper's research reveals that identity formation is enhanced by family relationships that are both individuated, which encourages adolescents to develop their own point of view, and connected, which provides a secure base from which to explore the widening social worlds of adolescence. When connectedness is strong and individuation weak, adolescents often have an identity-foreclosure status. When connectedness is weak, adolescents often have an identity-confusion status (Archer & Waterman, 1994).

Culture and Ethnicity

Erikson was especially sensitive to the role of culture in identity development. Throughout the world, ethnic minority groups have struggled to maintain their cultural identities while blending into the dominant culture (Erikson, 1968). This struggle for an inclusive identity, or an identity within the larger culture, has been the driving force in the founding of churches, empires, and revolutions throughout history.

Questions about cultural identity make adolescence a special juncture for many ethnic minority individuals (Phinney, 2000, 2003; Spencer, 1999; Spencer & Dornbusch, 1990). They may have been aware of some ethnic and cultural differences as children, but they consciously confront their ethnicity for the first time in adolescence. In contrast to children, adolescents have the ability to interpret ethnic and cultural information, to reflect on the past, and to speculate about the future. They become acutely aware of the evaluations of their ethnic group made by the majority White culture (Comer, 1988). As one researcher commented, the young African American child may learn that Black is beautiful but conclude as an adolescent that White is powerful (Semaj, 1985). Ethnic minority youth's awareness of negative appraisals, restricted opportunities, and conflicting values can influence life choices and plans for the future (Spencer & others, 2001).

The contexts in which ethnic minority youth live influence their identity development. In the United States, many live in low-income urban areas, where support for developing a positive identity may be absent. Many of these youth live in pockets of poverty; they are exposed to drugs, gangs, and criminal activities; and they interact with other youths and adults who have dropped out of school and are unemployed. They lack successful ethnic minority role models with whom to identify. As one ethnic minority youth stated, "Why set goals? At least if you don't set any goals, you don't fail." In such settings, effective organizations and programs for youth can make important contributions to developing a positive identity (Ferrer-Wreder & others, 2002; Phinney, 2000).

Many ethnic minority adolescents must negotiate two value systems—that of their own ethnic group and that of the White society. Some adolescents reject the mainstream, foregoing the rewards controlled by White Americans. Others adopt the values and standards of the majority White culture; yet others take the difficult path of *biculturalism*, identifying in some ways with their ethnic culture, in other ways with the dominant culture.

Research reveals other differences in how adolescents deal with their ethnic identity. In one study, exploration of ethnic identity was higher among ethnic minority than among White American college students (Phinney & Alipura, 1990). These ethnic minority college students who had thought about and resolved issues involving their ethnicity had higher self-esteem than their ethnic minority counterparts who had not.

www.mhhe.com/santrockldt2

Exploring Ethnic Identities
Ethnic Identity Research

individuality It consists of two dimensions: self-assertion, the ability to have and communicate a point of view; and separateness, the use of communication patterns to express how one is different from others.

connectedness It consists of two dimensions: mutuality, sensitivity to and respect for others' views; and permeability, openness to others' views.

Another investigation studied the ethnic identity development of Asian American, African American, Latino, and White American tenth-grade students in Los Angeles (Phinney, 1989). In some instances, adolescents from different groups perceived different issues to be important in their resolution of ethnic identity. For the Asian American adolescents, pressures to achieve academically and concerns about quotas that make it difficult to get into good colleges were salient issues. Many of the African American girls discussed their realization that White American standards of beauty (especially hair and skin color) did not apply to them; the African American boys were concerned with possible job discrimination and the need to distinguish themselves from a negative stereotype. For the Latino adolescents, prejudice was a recurring theme, as was the conflict of values between their Latino cultural heritage and the majority culture.

Among immigrants to the United States, the problems and solutions connected to ethnic identity change with each succeeding generation (Phinney, 2003). The identity of the first generation of immigrants is likely to be secure and unlikely to change considerably. They may or may not develop an "American" identity. The degree to which they begin to feel American appears to be related to learning English, developing social networks beyond their ethnic group, and becoming culturally competent in the new context. For the second generation of immigrants, an "American" identity is more secure possibly because citizenship is granted with birth. Their ethnic identity is likely to be linked to retention of their ethnic language and social networks. For the third and later generations, the issues become more complex. Various historical, contextual, and political factors unrelated to acculturation may affect the extent to which their ethnic identity is retained. For non-European ethnic groups, racism and discrimination influence whether ethnic identity is retained.

Michelle Chin, age 16: "Parents do not understand that teenagers need to find out who they are, which means a lot of experimenting, a lot of mood swings, a lot of emotions and awkwardness. Like any teenager, I am facing an identity crisis. I am still trying to figure out whether I am a Chinese American or an American with Asian eyes."

Review and Reflect: Learning Goal 2

2 Explain the key facets of identity development

REVIEW

- What are Erikson's views of identity?
- What are the components of identity?
- What are some contemporary thoughts on identity?
- What are the four identity statuses and how are they formed? When do the key developmental changes in identity take place?
- How does the family influence identity?
- What roles do culture and ethnicity play in identity?

REFLECT

- Do you think your parents influenced your identity development? If so, how?

3 PERSONALITY

Trait Theories and the Big Five Factors of Personality

Generativity

Views on Adult Development

Stability and Change

Earlier we defined *personality* as the enduring personal characteristics of individuals ◀‖‖ **P. 368.** Personality psychologists use many strategies in trying to understand the enduring characteristics of individuals. Some of them study the entire personality of

Openness	**C**onscientiousness	**E**xtraversion	**A**greeableness	**N**euroticism (emotional stability)
• Imaginative or practical	• Organized or disorganized	• Sociable or retiring	• Softhearted or ruthless	• Calm or anxious
• Interested in variety or routine	• Careful or careless	• Fun-loving or somber	• Trusting or suspicious	• Secure or insecure
• Independent or conforming	• Disciplined or impulsive	• Affectionate or reserved	• Helpful or uncooperative	• Self-satisfied or self-pitying

FIGURE 11.10 The Big Five Factors of Personality

Each of the broad supertraits that encompasses more narrow traits and characteristics. Use the acronym OCEAN to remember the big five personality factors (*o*penness, *c*onscientiousness, and so on).

individuals; some come up with a list of traits that best describe individuals; others zero in on specific traits or characteristics, such as being introverted or extraverted.

In chapter 1, we described several major personality theories—psychoanalytic theories and the social cognitive theory of Bandura and Walter Mischel. You might wish to review those theories at this time ◀▥ **PP. 19, 24.** Here our exploration of personality will focus on trait theory, several views of personality development in adulthood, and studies of stability and change in personality during adulthood.

Trait Theories and the Big Five Factors of Personality

Trait theories state that personality consists of broad dispositions, called traits, that tend to produce characteristic responses. In other words, people can be described in terms of the basic ways they behave, such as whether they are outgoing or friendly or whether they are dominant and assertive. Although trait theorists disagree about which traits make up personality, they agree that traits are the fundamental units and building blocks of personality.

One trait theory that has received considerable attention is the **big five factors of personality,** the view that personality is made up of openness to experience, conscientiousness, extraversion, agreeableness, and neuroticism (emotional stability) (see figure 11.10). (Notice that if you create an acronym from these trait names, you will get the word OCEAN.) A number of research studies point toward these five factors as important dimensions of personality (Costa & McCrae, 1995, 1998; McCrae, 2001; McCrae & Costa, 2003). However, some personality researchers believe that they won't end up being the final list of major traits. For example, some support has been generated for two additional factors: excellent/ordinary and evil/decent. So the big five someday might become the "big seven" or some other number (Benet-Martinez & Waller, 1997).

The trait theories have identified a number of characteristics that are important to consider when attempting to understand an individual's personality. The trait approach also has led to advances in the assessment of personality through the development of numerous personality tests. However, some psychologists believe the trait approach gives too little attention to environmental factors and puts too much emphasis on stability. These criticisms initially were leveled by social cognitive theorist Walter Mischel (1968). Mischel argued that personality often changes according to the situation. Thus, an individual may behave very differently at a party or in the library.

Today, most personality psychologists believe that personality is a product of *trait-situation interaction*. In other words, both traits and situational (context) factors must be considered to understand personality (Ackerman, Kyllonen, & Roberts, 1999; Cervone & Mischel, 2002; Mischel, 2004). Also, some people are more consistent on some traits and other people are consistent on other traits.

Journal of Personality and Social Psychology

Personality Traits

Paul Costa's Research

trait theories Personality consists of broad dispositions, called traits, that tend to produce characteristic responses.

big five factors of personality The view that personality is made up of openness to experience, conscientiousness, extraversion, agreeableness, and neuroticism (emotional stability).

Views on Adult Development

Two important views on adult development are the stage-crisis view and the life-events approach.

The Stage-Crisis View   Erikson's theory, which we discussed earlier, is a stage-crisis view. Here we will describe the view of Daniel Levinson and examine the concept of a midlife crisis.

Levinson's Seasons of a Man's Life   In *The Seasons of a Man's Life,* clinical psychologist Daniel Levinson (1978) reported the results of extensive interviews with 40 middle-aged men. The interviews were conducted with hourly workers, business executives, academic biologists, and novelists. Levinson bolstered his conclusions with information from the biographies of famous men and the development of memorable characters in literature. Although Levinson's major interest focused on midlife change, he described a number of stages and transitions in the life span, ranging from 17 to 65 years of age, which are shown in figure 11.11.

Levinson emphasizes that developmental tasks must be mastered at each of these stages. In early adulthood, the two major tasks to be mastered are exploring the possibilities for adult living and developing a stable life structure. Levinson sees the twenties as a *novice phase* of adult development. At the end of one's teens, a transition from dependence to independence should occur. This transition is marked by the formation of a dream—an image of the kind of life the youth wants to have, especially in terms of a career and marriage. The novice phase is a time of reasonably free experimentation and of testing the dream in the real world.

From about the ages of 28 to 33, the man goes through a transition period in which he must face the more serious question of determining his goals. During the thirties, he usually focuses on family and career development. In the later years of this period, he enters a phase of Becoming One's Own Man (or BOOM, as Levinson calls it). By age 40, he has reached a stable location in his career, has outgrown his earlier, more tenuous attempts at learning to become an adult, and now must look forward to the kind of life he will lead as a middle-aged adult.

According to Levinson, the change to middle adulthood lasts about five years (ages 40 to 45) and requires the adult male to come to grips with four major conflicts that have existed in his life since adolescence: (1) being young versus being old, (2) being destructive versus being constructive, (3) being masculine versus being feminine, and (4) being attached to others versus being separated from them. Seventy to 80 percent of the men Levinson interviewed found the midlife transition tumultuous and psychologically painful, as many aspects of their lives came into question. According to Levinson, the success of the midlife transition rests on how effectively the individual reduces the polarities and accepts each of them as an integral part of his being.

The quality and quantity of the Levinson biographies are outstanding examples in the clinical tradition. However, the sample size of 40 in his study was small, not including enough men to generalize to all men. Further, because Levinson interviewed only middle-aged males, we can consider the data about middle adulthood more valid than the data about early adulthood. When individuals are asked to remember information about earlier parts of their lives, they may distort and forget things. The original Levinson data included no females, although Levinson (1987, 1996) reported that his stages, transitions, and the crisis of middle age hold for females as well as males.

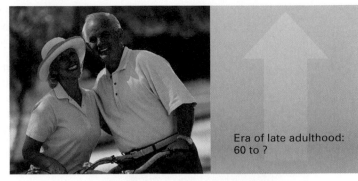

Late adult transition: Age 60 to 65

Era of late adulthood:
60 to ?

Middle adult transition: Age 40 to 45

Culminating life
structure for middle
adulthood: 55 to 60

Age 50 transition:
50 to 55

Entry life structure
for middle adulthood:
45 to 50

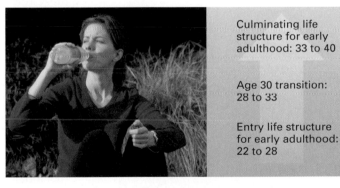

Early adult transition: Age 17 to 22

Culminating life
structure for early
adulthood: 33 to 40

Age 30 transition:
28 to 33

Entry life structure
for early adulthood:
22 to 28

FIGURE 11.11 Levinson's Periods of Adult Development

www.mhhe.com/santrockld2

Midlife Crisis
The MacArthur Foundation
Study of Midlife Development

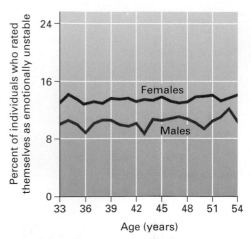

FIGURE 11.12 Emotional Instability and Age

In one longitudinal study, the emotional instability of individuals was assessed from age 33 to age 54 (McCrae & Costa, 1990). No significant increase in emotional instability occurred during the middle-aged years.

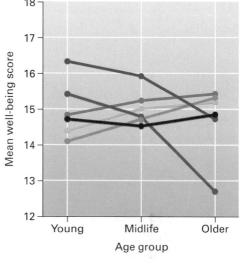

FIGURE 11.13 Age and Well-Being

In one study, six dimensions of well-being (self-acceptance, positive relations, personal growth, purpose in life, environmental mastery, and autonomy) were assessed in three different age groups of individuals (young adults, middle-aged adults, and older adults) (Keyes & Ryff, 1998). An increase or little change in most of the dimensions of well-being occurred during middle adulthood.

Levinson's work included no statistical analysis. However, the quality and quantity of the Levinson biographies are outstanding in the clinical tradition.

Midlife Crises Levinson (1978) views midlife as a crisis, believing that the middle-aged adult is suspended between the past and the future, trying to cope with this gap that threatens life's continuity. George Vaillant (1977) concludes that just as adolescence is a time for detecting parental flaws and discovering the truth about childhood, the forties are a decade of reassessing and recording the truth about the adolescent and adulthood years. However, whereas Levinson sees midlife as a crisis, Vaillant believes that only a minority of adults experience a midlife crisis:

> Just as pop psychologists have reveled in the not-so-common high drama of adolescent turmoil, also the popular press, sensing good copy, had made all too much of the mid-life crisis. The term mid-life crisis brings to mind some variation of the renegade minister who leaves behind four children and the congregation that loved him in order to drive off in a magenta Porsche with a 25-year-old striptease artiste. As with adolescent turmoil, mid-life crises are much rarer in community samples. (pp. 222–223)

Vaillant's study—called the *Grant Study*—involved a follow-up of Harvard University men in their early thirties and in their late forties who initially had been interviewed as undergraduates. Other research has also found that midlife is not characterized by pervasive crises. For example, a longitudinal study of 2,247 individuals found few midlife crises (McCrae & Costa, 1990). The emotional instability of these individuals did not significantly increase during their middle-aged years (see figure 11.12). In fact, these studies all documented psychological gains among middle-aged adults:

- One study assessed 3,032 American from 25 to 72 years of age (Brim, 1999). The individuals from 40 to 60 years of age were less nervous and worried than those under 40. The middle-aged adults reported a growing sense of control in their work as well as more financial security, greater environmental mastery (the ability to handle daily responsibilities), and more autonomy than their younger counterparts.
- A study found that adults experienced a peak of personal control and power in middle age (Clark-Plaskie & Lachman, 1999).
- A study of individuals described as young (average age 19), middle-aged (average age 46), and older (average age 73) adults found that their ability to manage their environmental surroundings (environmental mastery) and self-determination (autonomy) increased in middle age (Keyes & Ryff, 1998) (see figure 11.13). Their investment in living (purpose in life) and desire for continued self-realization (personal growth) dropped slightly from early to middle adulthood but still remained high before declining in late adulthood.

Adult development experts are virtually unanimous in their belief that midlife crises have been exaggerated (Bertrand & Lachman, 2003; Etaugh & Bridges, 2002; Reid & Willis, 1999; Lachman, 2004).

Conclusions About the Adult Stage Theories The perspectives of Erikson and Levinson emphasize the importance of developmental stages. Although this approach can help to identify themes that characterize many individuals at a particular point in development, there are several important issues to keep in mind when considering these perspectives:

- Little research has been conducted on the stage theories.
- The stage theories place too much emphasis on crises in development, especially midlife crises (Antonucci, Vandewater, & Lansford, 2000).
- There often is considerable individual variation in the way people experience the stages.

Next, we will explore an alternative to the stage approach as a way to examine adult personality development.

The Life-Events Approach An alternative to the stage approach to adult development is the life-events approach (Schwarzer & Schultz, 2003). In the early version of the life-events approach, life events were viewed as taxing circumstances for individuals, forcing them to change their personality (Holmes & Rahe, 1967). Such events as the death of a spouse, divorce, marriage, and so on were believed to involve varying degrees of stress, and therefore likely to influence the individual's development.

Today's life-events approach is more sophisticated (Cui & Vaillant, 1996; Hultsch & Plemons, 1979; McLeod, 1996). The **contemporary life-events approach** emphasizes that how life events influence the individual's development depends not only on the event but also on mediating factors (physical health, family supports, for example), the individual's adaptation to the life event (appraisal of the threat, coping strategies, for example), the life-stage context, and the sociohistorical context (see figure 11.14).

Consider how the life event of divorce might affect personality. A divorce is likely to be more stressful for individuals who are in poor health and have little family support. One individual may perceive it as highly stressful (less adaptive) rather than a challenge but develop coping strategies to effectively deal with it (more adaptive). And a divorce may be more stressful after many years of marriage when adults are in their fifties than when they have only been married several years and are in their twenties (an example of life-stage context) (Chiriboga, 1982). Finally, adults may be able to cope more effectively with divorce today than in the 1950s because divorce has become more commonplace and accepted in today's society (an example of sociohistorical context).

Though the life-events approach is a valuable addition to understanding adult development, it has its drawbacks (Dohrenwend & Dohrenwend, 1978). One of the most significant drawbacks is that the life-events approach places too much emphasis on change. It does not adequately recognize the stability that, at least to some degree, characterizes adult development. Another drawback is that it may not be life's major events that are the primary sources of stress, but our daily experiences (Pillow, Zautra, & Sandler, 1996). Enduring a boring but tense job or living in poverty does not show up on scales of major life events. Yet the everyday pounding from these conditions can add up to a highly stressful life and eventually illness. Greater insight into the source of life's stresses might come from focusing more on

> *M*id-life crises are greatly exaggerated in America.
> —GEORGE VAILLANT
> *Contemporary Psychologist, Harvard University*

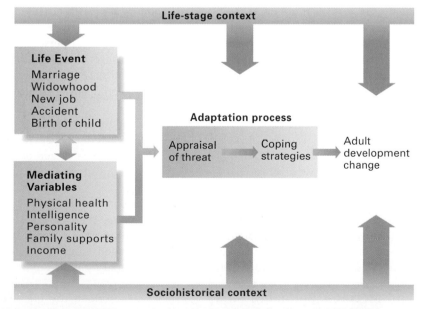

FIGURE 11.14 A Contemporary Life-Events Framework for Interpreting Adult Developmental Change

contemporary life-events approach
Emphasizes that how a life event influences the individual's development depends not only on the event but also on mediating factors, the individual's adaptation to the life event, the life-stage context, and the sociohistorical context.

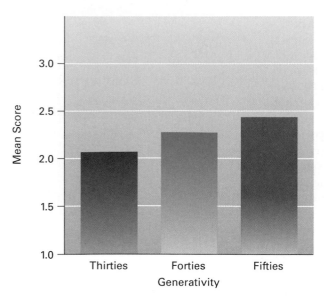

FIGURE 11.15 Changes in Generativity from the Thirties Through the Fifties

Generativity increased in Smith College women as they aged from their thirties through their fifties (Stewart, Ostrove, & Helson, 2001). The women rated themselves on a 3-point scale indicating the extent to which they thought the statements about generativity were descriptive of their lives. Higher scores reflect greater generativity.

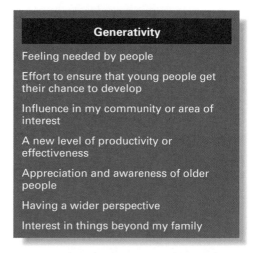

FIGURE 11.16 Items Used to Assess Generativity in the Smith College Study

generativity versus stagnation The seventh stage in Erikson's life-span theory that encompasses adults' desire to leave a legacy of themselves to the next generation.

daily hassles and daily uplifts (Lazarus & Folkman, 1984). Researchers have found that young and middle-aged adults experience a greater daily frequency of stressors than older individuals (Almeida & Horn, in press).

Generativity

Erikson (1968) believes that middle-aged adults face the issue of **generativity versus stagnation,** which is the name Erikson gave to the seventh stage in his life-span theory. Generativity encompasses adults' desire to leave a legacy of themselves to the next generation. By contrast, stagnation (sometimes called "self-absorption") develops when individuals sense that they have done nothing for the next generation.

In a longitudinal study of Smith College women, generativity increased from the thirties through the fifties (Cole & Stewart, 1996; Stewart, Ostrove, & Helson, 2001; Zucker, Ostrove, & Stewart, 2002) (see figure 11.15). Figure 11.16 describes the items that were used to assess generativity in the Smith College Study. In George Vaillant's (2002) longitudinal studies of aging, in middle age, generativity (defined in this study as "taking care of the next generation") was more strongly related than intimacy to whether individuals would have an enduring and happy marriage at 75 to 80 years of age. One participant in Vaillant's studies said, "From twenty to thirty I learned how to get along with my wife. From thirty to forty I learned how to be a success at my job, and at forty to fifty I worried less about myself and more about the children" (p.114).

Middle-aged adults can develop generativity in a number of ways (Kotre, 1984). Through biological generativity, adults conceive and give birth to an infant. Through parental generativity, adults provide nurturance and guidance to children. Through work generativity, adults develop skills that are passed down to others. And through cultural generativity, adults create, renovate, or conserve some aspect of culture that ultimately survives.

Stability and Change

Recall from chapter 1 that an important issue in life-span development is the extent to which individuals show stability in their development versus the extent to which they change ◀▥ **P. 16.** A number of longitudinal studies have assessed stability and change in the personality of individuals at different points in their lives. A common finding is that, in most cases, the less time between measurements of personality characteristics, the more stability they show. Thus, if we measure a person's introversion/extraversion at the age of 20 and then again at age 30, we are likely to find more stability than if we assess the person at the age of 20 and then again at the age of 40.

Neugarten's Kansas City Study One of the earliest longitudinal studies of adult personality development was conducted by Bernice Neugarten (1964). Known as the "Kansas City Study," it investigated individuals 40 to 80 years of age over a 10-year period. The adults were given personality tests and questionnaires, and they were interviewed.

Neugarten concluded that both stability and change characterized the adults as they aged. The characteristics that showed the most stability were styles of coping (such as avoiding problems or tackling them head on), being satisfied with life, and being goal-directed. In terms of change, as individuals aged from 40 to 60 they became more passive and were more likely to feel threatened by their environment.

Costa and McCrae's Baltimore Study Earlier we described the big five factors in personality as an important trait theory ◀▥ **P. 388.** Paul Costa and Robert McCrae (1995, 1998; McCrae & Costa, 2003) have studied the big five factors in approximately a thousand college-educated women and men from 20 to 96 years of age. Longitudinal data collection initially began in the 1950s to the mid-1960s on people of varying ages and is ongoing. Costa and McCrae found a great deal of stability across the adult years in the big five personality factors. However, their recent research highlights some differences in personality across the adult years (Costa & others, 2000). In the following Research in Life-Span Development interlude, you can read about age differences in the big five factors in personality in different cultures.

Research in Life-Span Development
Age Differences in Adult Personality Across Cultures

In one study, Robert McCrae and his colleagues (1999) found that there are some consistent age trends in personality in a number of cultures. In Germany, Croatia, Italy, Portugal, and Korea, older adults scored lower on extraversion and openness to experience than younger adults (see figure 11.17). In these countries, the older adults scored higher in agreeableness and conscientiousness than younger adults. Similar patterns of age changes also were found in another study of Chinese and American adults (Yang, McRae, & Costa, 1998). Few cultural variations were found in these studies.

In another recent study, 285 adults from the United States (the Midwest) and 450 adults from China (Bejing) who were 20 to 87 years of age were given the California Psychological Inventory (CPI) (Labouvie-Vief & others, 2000). The CPI is a standardized personality test in which individuals respond to a large number of items that reflect a number of personality traits by saying whether the items are like them or not like them. Analysis of the results indicated that older adults were less extraverted and less flexible than their younger adult counterparts. The older adults were more likely to show self-control and engage in normative behavior than younger adults were. The age differences were more pronounced for the Chinese than the American adults.

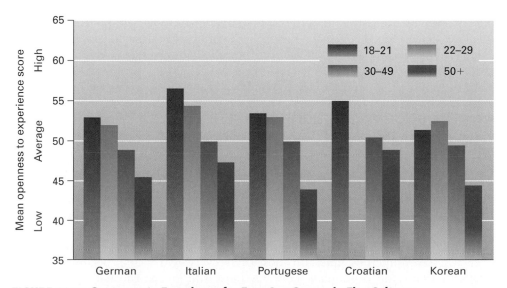

FIGURE 11.17 Openness to Experience for Four Age Groups in Five Cultures

Higher scores represent greater openness to experience. None of the Croatian respondents was aged 22 to 29.

Berkeley Longitudinal Studies Most longitudinal studies indicate that neither extreme stability nor extreme change characterizes most people's personality as they go through the adult years. One of the longest-running inquiries is the series of analyses called the Berkeley Longitudinal Studies. Initially, more than 500 children and their parents were studied in the late 1920s and early 1930s. The book *Present and Past in Middle Life* (Eichorn & others, 1981) profiles these individuals as they became middle-aged.

The results from early adolescence through a portion of midlife did not support either extreme in the debate over whether personality is characterized by stability or change. Some characteristics were more stable than others, however. The most stable characteristics were the degree to which individuals were intellectually oriented, self-confident, or open to new experiences. The characteristics that changed the most included the extent the individuals were nurturant or hostile and whether they had good self-control or not.

John Clausen (1993), one of the researchers in the Berkeley Longitudinal Studies, believes that too much attention has been given to discontinuities for all members of the human species, as exemplified in the adult stage theories. Rather, he believes that some people experience recurrent crises and change a great deal over the life course, while others have more stable, continuous lives and change far less.

Helson's Mills College Studies Another longitudinal investigation of adult personality development was conducted by Ravenna Helson and her colleagues (Helson, 1997; Helson, Mitchell, & Moane, 1984; Helson & Wink, 1992; Roberts, Helson, & Klohnen, 2002). They initially studied 132 women who were seniors at Mills College in California in the late 1950s. In 1981, when the women were 42 to 45 years old, they were studied again.

Helson and her colleagues distinguished three main groups among the Mills women: family-oriented, career-oriented (whether or not they also wanted families), and those who followed neither path (women without children who pursued only low-level work). Despite their different college profiles and their diverging life paths, the women in all three groups experienced some similar psychological changes over their adult years. However, the women in the third group changed less than those committed to career or family.

During their early forties, many of the women shared the concerns that stage theorists such as Levinson found in men: concern for young and old, introspectiveness, interest in roots, and awareness of limitations and death. However, the researchers in the Mills College Study concluded that rather than being in a midlife crisis, what was being experienced was *midlife consciousness*. They also indicated that commitment to the tasks of early adulthood—whether to a career or family (or both)—helped women learn to control their impulses, develop interpersonal skills, become independent, and work hard to achieve goals. Women who did not commit themselves to one of these lifestyle patterns faced fewer challenges and did not develop as fully as the other women (Rosenfeld & Stark, 1987). In the Mills study, some women moved toward becoming "pillars of society" in their early forties to early fifties (Helson & Wink, 1992).

George Vaillant's Studies George Vaillant (2002) has conducted three longitudinal studies of adult development and aging: (1) a sample of 268 socially advantaged Harvard graduates born about 1920 (called the "Grant Study"); (2) a sample of 456 socially disadvantaged inner-city men born about 1930; and (3) a sample of 90 middle-SES, intellectually gifted women born about 1910. These individuals have been assessed numerous times (in most cases every two years), beginning in the 1920s to 1940s and continuing today for those still living. The main assessments involve extensive interviews with the participants, their parents, and teachers.

Vaillant categorized 75- to 80-year-olds as "happy-well," "sad-sick," and "dead." He used data collected from these individuals when they were 50 years of age to predict which categories they were likely to end up in at 75 to 80 years of age. Alcohol abuse and smoking at age 50 were the best predictors of which individuals would be dead at 75 to 80 years of age. Other factors at age 50 were linked with being in the "happy-well" category at 75 to 80 years of age:

- Getting regular exercise
- Avoiding being overweight
- Being well educated
- Having a stable marriage
- Being future-oriented
- Being thankful and forgiving
- Empathizing with others
- Being active with other people
- Having good coping skills

Wealth and income at age 50 were not linked with being in the "happy-well" category at 75 to 80 years of age. The results for one of Vaillant's studies, the Grant Study of Harvard men, are shown in figure 11.18.

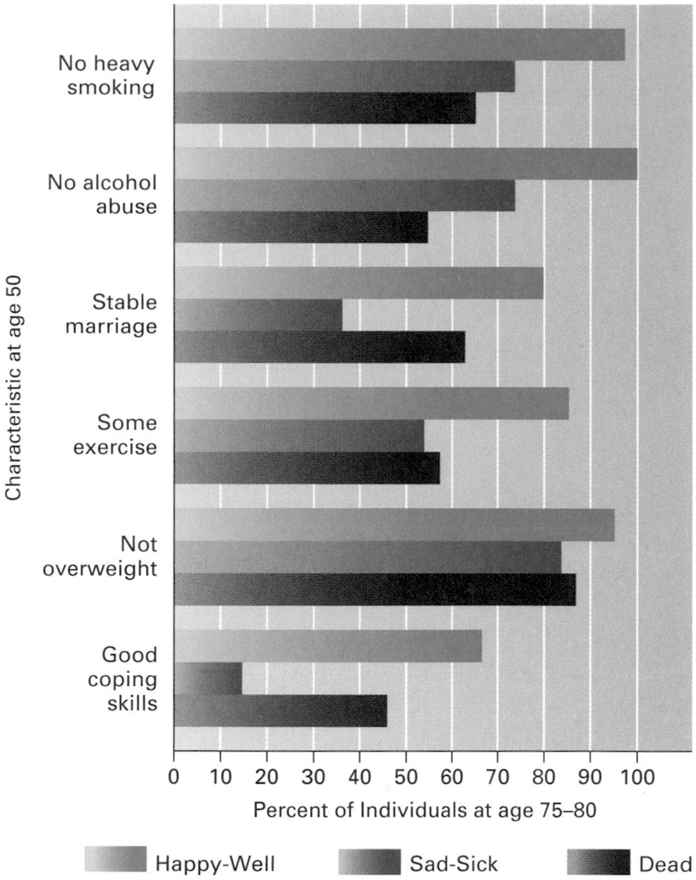

Conclusions   What can be concluded about stability and change in personality during the adult years? Avshalom Caspi and Brent Roberts (2001) recently concluded that the evidence does not support the conclusion that personality traits become completely fixed at a certain age in adulthood (Caspi & Roberts, 2001). However, they argue that change is typically limited, and in some cases the changes in personality are small. They also conclude that age is positively related to stability and that this link peaks in the fifties and sixties. That is, people show greater stability in their personality when they reach midlife than when they were younger adults. These findings support what is called a *cumulative personality model* of personality development, which states that with time and age people become more adept at interacting with their environment in ways that promote the stability of personality.

This does not mean that change is absent throughout midlife (Lachman, 2004). Ample evidence shows that social contexts, new experiences, and sociohistorical changes can affect personality development. However, Caspi and Roberts (2001) concluded, as people get older, stability increasingly outweighs change.

Other researchers argue that stability in personality begins to set in at about 30 years of age (Costa & McCrae, 2000; McCrae, 2001). However, some researchers conclude that personality change can be extensive in the adult years (Lewis, 2001). And some people likely change more than others. In sum, there still is disagreement on how much stability and change characterize personality development in adulthood (Bertrand & Lachman, 2003; Lachman, 2004).

FIGURE 11.18 Links Between Characteristics at Age 50 and Health and Happiness at Age 75 to 80

In a longitudinal study, the characteristics shown above at age 50 were related to whether individuals were happy-well, sad-sick, or dead at age 75 to 80 (Vaillant, 2002).

Review and Reflect: Learning Goal 3

3 Describe personality and its development in adulthood

REVIEW

- What are trait theories? What are the big five factors of personality?
- What are some views of adult development of personality?
- What is Erikson's view of middle-aged adults?
- What are some major longitudinal studies of adult personality development, and what implications do they have for the stability/change issue?

REFLECT

- Why is it important to examine longitudinal studies when investigating stability and change in development?

Reach Your Learning Goals

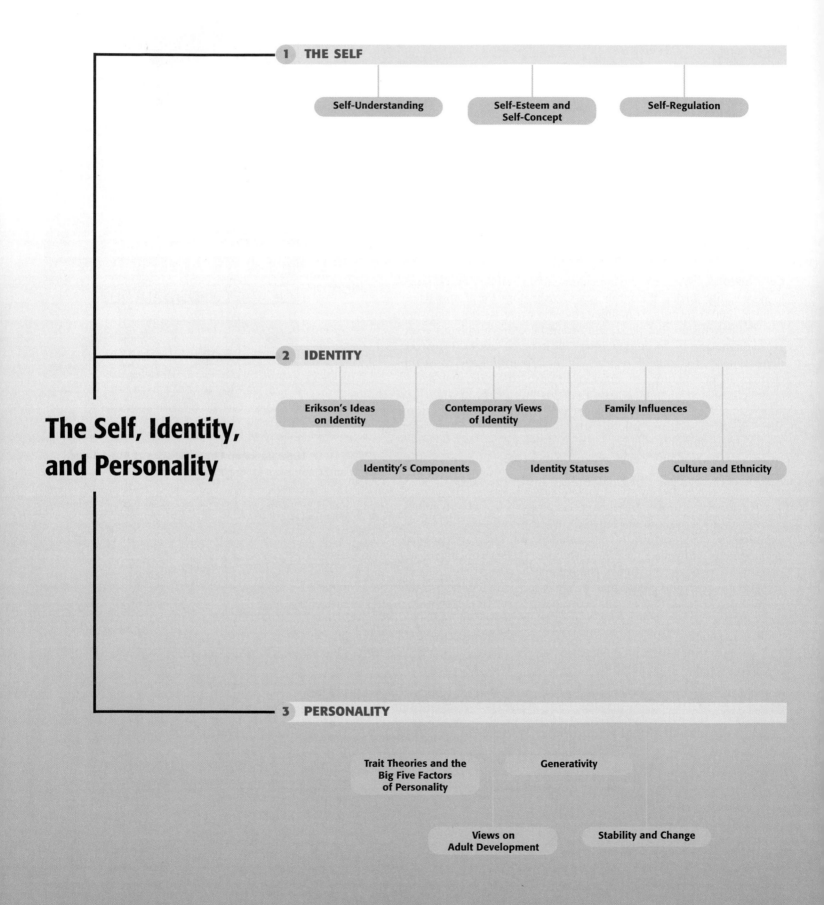

The Self, Identity, and Personality

1 THE SELF

Self-Understanding

Self-Esteem and Self-Concept

Self-Regulation

2 IDENTITY

Erikson's Ideas on Identity

Contemporary Views of Identity

Family Influences

Identity's Components

Identity Statuses

Culture and Ethnicity

3 PERSONALITY

Trait Theories and the Big Five Factors of Personality

Generativity

Views on Adult Development

Stability and Change

Summary

1 Discuss the main ways the self is conceptualized

- There is considerable overlap in the concepts of self, identity, and personality. *Self* is all characteristics of a person, *identity* is who a person is, and *personality* consists of the enduring personal characteristics of individuals. Self-understanding is the cognitive representation of the self, the substance of self-conceptions. Developmental changes in self-understanding include the construction of the self in infancy in terms of self-recognition and transformations in self-understanding in childhood (including perspective taking). Self-definition in adolescence is more abstract and idealistic, fluctuating, includes concern about the real self versus the ideal self, self-consciousness, and is more integrative. Developments in adulthood include expanded self-awareness and multiple selves and the life reviews of older adults.

- Self-esteem refers to global evaluations of the self; it is also called self-worth and self-image. Self-concept consists of domain-specific evaluations of the self. Self-esteem can change over time, and low self-esteem is linked with depression. The accuracy of self-evaluations increases across the elementary school years. Some studies have found that self-esteem decreases in adolescence, but overall, most adolescents still have positive self-esteem. Some important aspects of self-esteem include the degree to which it is linked to performance (this varies—only moderate correlations with school performance and varying correlations with job performance; individuals with high self-esteem have greater initiative and this can produce positive or negative outcomes; self-esteem is strongly correlated with happiness; there is a dark side to high self-esteem in that some individuals who have high self-esteem are conceited and narcissistic). Five ways to increase self-esteem are through (1) identification of the causes of low self-esteem and the domains of competence important to the self, (2) emotional support and social approval, (3) taking responsibility for self-esteem, (4) achievement, and (5) coping.

- Self-regulation involves the ability to control one's behavior without having to rely on others' help. Two-year-olds may show rudimentary forms of self-regulation, but many preschoolers show increased self-regulation. Elementary-school-aged children increase their self-regulation. In adolescence, some changes may increase self-regulation, others decrease it. Self-control increases in early and middle adulthood. Self-regulation may vary by domain. For example, older adults often show less self-regulation in the physical domain than younger adults. Baltes proposed the selective optimization with compensation theory of self-regulation. Many older adults show a remarkable ability to engage in self-regulation despite encountering losses. Heckhausen distinguishes between primary and secondary control strategies and has found that secondary control strategies increase through the adult years.

2 Explain the key facets of identity development

- Identity versus identity confusion is Erikson's fifth developmental stage, which individuals experience in the adolescent years. At this time, adolescents examine who they are, what they are all about, and where they are going in life. Erikson describes the psychological moratorium between childhood dependence and adult dependence that adolescents experience, which promotes identity exploration.

- Identity is a self-portrait with many pieces, including vocational/career identity, political identity, religious identity, relationship identity, sexual identity, and cultural/ethnic identity. At a minimum, identity involves commitment to a vocational direction, ideological stance, and sexual orientation.

- Contemporary views of identity argue that it is a gradual, lengthy process, not a cataclysmic transition. Identity development neither begins nor ends with adolescence, but adolescence is a key juncture in identity. At this point, the individual is able to sort through and synthesize past and current identities. The synthesis of identity components gets done in bits and pieces.

- According to Marcia, various combinations of crisis and commitment produce four identity statuses: identity diffused, identity foreclosed, identity moratorium, and identity achieved. A number of experts believe the key developmental changes in identity occur in the late teens and early twenties. "MAMA" cycles may continue throughout adulthood.

- Adolescents' identity development advances when their relationship with their parents includes both individuality and connectedness.

- Ethnic identity may present special issues for members of ethnic minority groups, and they may confront these issues for the first time in adolescence.

3 Describe personality and its development in adulthood

- Trait theories state that personality consists of broad dispositions, called traits, that tend to produce characteristic responses. One trait theory that has received considerable attention is the big five factors of personality, which consist of openness to experience, conscientiousness, extraversion, agreeableness, and neuroticism (emotional stability). Today most psychologists believe that personality is a product of trait-situation interaction.

- Two of the important adult developmental views are the stage-crisis view and the life-events approach. Levinson's and Erikson's theories are stage-crisis views. Midlife crises do not occur nearly as much as the stereotype suggests. What does arise is a midlife consciousness that focuses on such matters as how to adapt to aging. The life-events approach argues that life events and how people adapt to them are important in understanding adult development.

There is considerable variation in how people go through the adult stages of development and in how they experience and adapt to life events.

- Erikson believes that middle-aged adults face a significant issue in life—generativity versus stagnation, which is the name he gave to the seventh stage in his life-span theory. Generativity encompasses adults' desire to leave a legacy of themselves to the next generation.

- Five longitudinal studies that have addressed stability and change in adult development are Neugarten's "Kansas City Study," Costa and McCrae's Baltimore Study, the Berkeley Longitudinal Studies, Helson's Mills College Study, and Vaillant's studies. The longitudinal studies have shown that there is both stability and change in adult personality development.

Key Terms

self 368
identity 368
personality 368
self-understanding 368
perspective taking 370
possible selves 371
self-esteem 374
self-concept 374
self-regulation 377

selective optimization with
    compensation theory 380
identity versus identity
    confusion 382
psychosocial moratorium 382
crisis 384
commitment 384
identity diffusion 384

identity foreclosure 384
identity moratorium 384
identity achievement 384
individuality 386
connectedness 388
trait theories 388
big five factors of
    personality 388

contemporary life-events
    approach 391
generativity versus
    stagnation 392

Key People

Diane Ruble 370
Robert Selman 370
Hazel Markus 372
Susan Harter 377
Barry Zimmerman 378
Claire Kopp 379

Paul Baltes 380
Jutta Heckhausen 381
Erik Erikson 382
James Marcia 384
Alan Waterman 385
Catherine Cooper 385

Walter Mischel 388
George Vaillant 390
Bernice Neugarten 392
Paul Costa and Robert
    McCrae 392
John Clausen 394

Ravenna Helson 394
Avshalom Caspi and Brent
    Roberts 395

E-Learning Tools

Connect to **www.mhhe.com/santrockldt2** to research the answers and complete these exercises. In addition, you'll find a number of other resources and valuable study tools for chapter 11, "The Self, Identity, and Personality," on the Student CD-ROM that came with this book.

Taking It to the Net

1. Ted is the activities director at an adult retirement community. A friend who is a social worker suggested that Ted might want to develop a program in which the residents engage in the process of reminiscence and life review. What benefits might the residents gain from such an activity?

2. Janice, who has recently been appointed principal of a high school that has a large population of Middle Eastern, Asian, and Hispanic students, wants to conduct in-service training for the school's teachers to help them understand the challenges the ethnic students face as they strive to achieve their self-identity and ethnic identity. What challenges do the ethnic students face in resolving their identity crises, and how can the school assist them?

3. Eduardo is vice president for human resources at a 200-employee manufacturing plant. He wants to use a personality assessment for job selection and to help him plan interventions for employees who have job-related problems, such as poor motivation, personality problems with co-workers, and conflicts with supervisors. Would an assessment based on the five-factor model of personality be a good choice?

Self Assessment

To evaluate your self-esteem, identity, and personality, complete these self-assessments:

- *My Self-Esteem*
- *Exploring My Identity*
- *How Generative Am I?*
- *Am I Introverted or Extraverted?*

Health and Well-Being, Parenting, and Education

Build your decision-making skills by trying your hand at the health and well-being, parenting, and education "Scenarios."

Gender and Sexuality

Chapter Outline		*Learning Goals*

BIOLOGICAL, SOCIAL, AND COGNITIVE INFLUENCES ON GENDER   **1**

Biological Influences

Social Influences

Cognitive Influences

1 Explain biological, social, and cognitive influences on gender

---

GENDER COMPARISONS AND CLASSIFICATIONS   **2**

Gender Stereotyping

Gender Similarities and Differences

Masculinity, Femininity, and Androgyny

2 Discuss gender comparisons and classifications

GENDER DEVELOPMENT THROUGH THE LIFE SPAN   **3**

Childhood

Adolescence

Adulthood and Aging

3 Describe the development of gender through the life span

EXPLORING SEXUALITY   **4**

Biological and Cultural Factors

Sexual Orientation

Sexually Transmitted Infections

Forcible Sexual Behavior and Sexual Harassment

4 Characterize influences on sexuality, the nature of sexual orientation, and some sexual problems

---

SEXUALITY THROUGH THE LIFE SPAN   **5**

Child Sexuality

Adolescent Sexuality

Sexuality and Aging

5 Summarize how sexuality develops through the life span

As females and males, human beings are involved in the existence and continuation of life. Gender and sexuality—our lives as females and males—are important aspects of human development and are the topics of this chapter.

1 BIOLOGICAL, SOCIAL, AND COGNITIVE INFLUENCES ON GENDER

Biological Influences	Social Influences	Cognitive Influences

What exactly do we mean by gender? **Gender** refers to the social and psychological dimensions of being female or male. In contrast, **sex** designates the biological aspects of being female or male. A **gender role** is a set of expectations that prescribe how females and males should act, think, and feel. **Gender typing** is the process by which children acquire the thoughts, feelings, and behaviors that are considered appropriate for their gender in a particular culture. To understand how gender develops in our lives, we need to learn about biological, social, and cognitive influences on gender.

Biological Influences

It was not until the 1920s that researchers confirmed the existence of human sex chromosomes, the genetic material that determines our sex. Humans normally have 46 chromosomes, arranged in pairs. A 23rd pair with two X-shaped chromosomes produces a female. A 23rd pair with an X chromosome and a Y chromosome produces a male.

Hormones   In chapter 3 we discussed the two classes of hormones that have the most influence on gender, estrogens and androgens ◀▥ **P. 97.** Both estrogens and androgens occur in both females and males, but in very different concentrations.

Estrogens primarily influence the development of female physical sex characteristics and help regulate the menstrual cycle. Estrogens are a general class of hormones. An example of an important estrogen is estradiol. Estrogens are produced mainly by the ovaries.

Androgens primarily promote the development of male genitals and secondary sex characteristics. One important androgen is testosterone. Androgens are produced by the adrenal glands in males and females, and by the testes in males.

In the first few weeks of gestation, female and male embryos look alike. Male sex organs start to differ from female sex organs when a gene on the Y chromosome directs a small piece of tissue in the embryo to turn into testes. In females, there is no Y chromosome so the tissue turns into ovaries. Once the tissue has turned into testes, they begin to secrete testosterone.

To explore biological influences on gender, researchers have studied individuals who are exposed to unusual levels of sex hormones early in development. Here are four examples of the problems that may occur as a result (Lippa, 2002):

- *Congenital adrenal hyperplasia (CAH)*. Some girls have this condition, which is caused by a genetic defect. Their adrenal glands enlarge and produce abnormally high levels of androgens. CAH girls, although they are XX females, vary in how much their genitals look like male or female genitals. Their genitals may be surgically altered to look more like those of a typical female. Although CAH girls usually grow up to think of themselves as girls and women, they are less content with being a female and show a stronger interest in being a male than non-CAH girls (Berenbaum & Bailey, 2003; Ehrhardt & Baker, 1974; Slijper, 1984). They typically enjoy participating in rough-and-tumble play, sports, and dressing in masculine clothing, while disliking typical girl activities such as playing with dolls and wearing makeup and frilly clothes.

gender The social and psychological dimension of being female or male.

sex Designates the biological aspects of being female or male.

gender role A set of expectations that prescribe how females or males should think, act, or feel.

gender typing The process by which children acquire the thoughts, feelings, and behaviors that are considered appropriate for their gender in their culture.

estrogens A main class of sex hormones, an important one of which is estradiol, that influence the development of female sexual characteristics and help regulate the menstrual cycle.

androgens A main class of sex hormones, an important one of which is testosterone, that promote the development of male genitals and secondary sex characteristics.

- *Androgen-insensitive males.* Because of a genetic error, a small number of XY males do not have androgen receptors in their cells. They are called androgen-insensitive males. In the absence of androgen receptors, testosterone cannot affect cells. If androgen insensitivity is total, XY males develop as females in the sense that their bodies look completely female and they develop a female gender identity. They typically are romantically and sexually attracted to males (Wisniewski & others, 2000).

- *Pelvic field defect.* A small number of newborns have a disorder called pelvic field defect, which in boys involves a missing penis. For many years, doctors usually recommended that these genetic boys be raised as girls and undergo castration, which was required because they were born with testicles but not a penis. Thus, they were exposed to normal male amounts of testosterone prenatally but were castrated soon after birth. According to one study, despite efforts by parents to rear them as girls, most of the XY children insisted that they were boys (Reiner, 2001). Apparently, normal exposure to androgens prenatally had a stronger influence on their gender identity than being castrated and raised as girls.

- In another intriguing case, one of two identical twin boys lost his penis due to an errant circumcision (Lippa, 2002). The twin who lost his penis was surgically reassigned to be a girl and to be reared as a girl. Bruce—the real name of the boy—became Brenda. Early reports indicated that the sex assignment had been successful, but as Brenda grew up she reported that she never felt comfortable as a girl (Diamond & Sigmundson, 1997). As a young adult, Brenda became Bruce once again and now lives with a wife and adopted children (Colapinto, 2000). In sum, research suggests that biological factors, especially early hormonal production, play important roles in gender development (Lippa, 2002).

Although sex hormones alone, of course, do not determine behavior, researchers have found links between sex hormones levels and certain behaviors. The most established effects of testosterone on humans involve aggressive behavior and sexual behavior (Hyde, 2003). Levels of testosterone are correlated with sexual behavior in boys during puberty (Udry & others, 1985). Violent male criminals have above-average levels of testosterone (Dabbs & others, 1987), and professional football players have higher levels of testosterone than ministers do (Dabbs & Morris, 1990).

The Evolutionary Psychology View   In chapter 2 we described the approach of evolutionary psychology, which emphasizes that adaptation during the evolution of humans produced psychological differences between males and females (Buss, 1995, 2000, 2001, 2004) ◀||||| **P. 51.** Evolutionary psychologists argue that primarily because of their differing roles in reproduction, males and females faced different pressures in primeval environments when the human species was evolving. In particular, because having multiple sexual liaisons improves the likelihood that males will pass on their genes, natural selection favored males who adopted short-term mating strategies. These males competed with other males to acquire more resources in order to access females. Therefore, say evolutionary psychologists, males evolved dispositions that favor violence, competition, and risk taking.

In contrast, according to evolutionary psychologists, females' contributions to the gene pool was improved by securing resources for their offspring, which was promoted by obtaining long-term mates who could support a family. As a consequence, natural selection favored females who devoted effort to parenting and chose mates who could provide their offspring with resources and protection. Females developed preferences for successful, ambitious men who could provide these resources.

This evolutionary unfolding, according to some evolutionary psychologists, explains key gender differences in sexual attitudes and sexual behavior. For example, in one study, men said that ideally they would like to have more than 18 sexual partners in their lifetime, whereas women stated that ideally they would like to

"How is it gendered?"

© The New Yorker Collection 1999 Edward Koren from Cartoonbank.com. All rights reserved. Reprinted with permission.

*S*ex differences are adaptations to the differing restrictions and opportunities that a society provides for its men and women.

—ALICE EAGLY
Contemporary Psychologist,
Northwestern University

have only 4 or 5 (Buss & Schmidt, 1993). In another study, 75 percent of the men but none of the women approached by an attractive stranger of the opposite sex consented to a request for sex (Clark & Hatfield, 1989).

Such gender differences, says David Buss (1995, 2001, 2003, 2004), are exactly the type predicted by evolutionary psychology. Buss argues that men and women differ psychologically in those domains in which they have faced different adaptive problems during evolutionary history. In all other domains, predicts Buss, the sexes will be psychologically similar.

Critics of evolutionary psychology argue that its hypotheses are backed by speculations about prehistory, not evidence, and that in any event people are not locked into behavior that was adaptive in the evolutionary past. Critics also claim that the evolutionary view pays little attention to cultural and individual variations in gender differences.

Social Influences

Many social scientists do not locate the cause of psychological gender differences in biological dispositions. Rather, they argue that these differences are due to social experiences. Three theories that reflect this view have been influential.

Alice Eagly (2000, 2001) proposed **social role theory,** which states that gender differences result from the contrasting roles of women and men. In most cultures around the world, women have less power and status than men have and they control fewer resources (Wood, 2001). Compared with men, women perform more domestic work, spend fewer hours in paid employment, receive lower pay, and are more thinly represented in the highest levels of organizations. In Eagly's view, as women adapted to roles with less power and less status in society, they showed more cooperative, less dominant profiles than men. Thus, the social hierarchy and division of labor are important causes of gender differences in power, assertiveness, and nurture (Eagly & Diekman, 2003).

The **psychoanalytic theory of gender** stems from Freud's view that the preschool child develops a sexual attraction to the opposite-sex parent. At 5 or 6 years of age, the child renounces this attraction because of anxious feelings. Subsequently, the child identifies with the same-sex parent, unconsciously adopting the same-sex parent's characteristics. However, developmentalists do not believe gender development proceeds as Freud proposed (Callan, 2001). Children become gender-typed much earlier than 5 or 6 years of age, and they become masculine or feminine even when the same-sex parent is not present in the family.

The social cognitive approach discussed in chapter 1 provides an alternative explanation of how children develop gender-typed behavior (see figure 12.1) ◀▥ **P. 24.**

social role theory Eagly's theory that psychological gender differences are caused by the contrasting social roles of women and men.

psychoanalytic theory of gender Stems from Freud's view that preschool children develop a sexual attraction to the opposite-sex parent, then, at 5 to 6 years of age, renounce the attraction because of anxious feelings, subsequently identifying with the same-sex parent and unconsciously adopting the same-sex parent's characteristics.

Theory	Processes	Outcome
Psychoanalytic theory	Sexual attraction to opposite-sex parent at 3 to 5 years of age; anxiety about sexual attraction and subsequent identification with same-sex parent at 5 to 6 years of age	Gender behavior similar to that of same-sex parent
Social cognitive theory	Rewards and punishments of gender-appropriate and -inappropriate behavior by adults and peers; observation and initiation of models' masculine and feminine behavior	Gender behavior

FIGURE 12.1 A Comparison of the Psychoanalytic and Social Cognitive Views of Gender Development

Parents influence their children's development by action and example.

According to the **social cognitive theory of gender,** children's gender development occurs through observation and imitation, and through the rewards and punishments children experience for gender-appropriate and gender-inappropriate behavior (Bussey & Bandura, 1999). Parents often use rewards and punishments to teach their daughters to be feminine ("Karen, you are being a good girl when you play gently with your doll") and their sons to be masculine ("Keith, a boy as big as you is not supposed to cry"). Children also learn about gender from observing other adults in the neighborhood and on television (Fagot, Rodgers, & Leinbach, 2000). As children get older, peers become increasingly important. Peers extensively reward and punish gender behavior (Lott & Maluso, 2001). For example, when children play in ways that the culture says are sex-appropriate, they tend to be rewarded by their peers. Those who engage in activities that are considered inappropriate tend to be criticized or abandoned by their peers.

From 4 to about 12 years of age, children spend a large majority of their free play time exclusively with others of their own sex (Maccoby, 2002). What kind of socialization takes place in these same-sex play groups? In one study, researchers observed preschoolers over six months (Martin & Fabes, 2001). The more time boys spent interacting with other boys, the more their activity level, rough-and-tumble play, and sex-typed choice of toys and games increased, and the less time boys spent near adults. By contrast, the more time the preschool girls spent interacting with other girls, the more their activity level and aggression decreased, and the more their girl-type play activities and time spent near adults increased. After watching elementary school children repeatedly play in same-sex groups, two researchers characterized the playground as "gender school" (Luria & Herzog, 1985).

Cognitive Influences

Observation, imitation, rewards and punishment—these are the mechanisms by which gender develops according to social cognitive theory. Interactions between the child and the social environment are the main keys to gender development in this view. Some critics argue that this explanation pays too little attention to the child's own mind and understanding, and portrays the child as passively acquiring gender roles (Martin, Ruble, & Szkrybalo, 2002). Two cognitive theories—cognitive developmental theory and gender schema theory—stress that individuals actively construct their gender world:

- The **cognitive developmental theory of gender** states that children's gender typing occurs *after* children think of themselves as boys and girls. Once they consistently conceive of themselves as male or female, children prefer activities, objects, and attitudes consistent with this label.
- **Gender schema theory** states that gender typing emerges as children gradually develop gender schemas of what is gender-appropriate and gender-inappropriate in their culture. A *schema* is a cognitive structure, a network of associations that guide an individual's perceptions. A *gender schema* organizes the world in terms of female and male. Children are internally motivated to perceive the world and to act in accordance with their developing schemas.

Initially proposed by Lawrence Kohlberg (1966), the cognitive developmental theory of gender holds that gender development depends on cognition, and it applies the ideas of Piaget that we discussed in chapter 6 ◀▥▥ P. 209. As young children develop the conservation and categorization skills described by Piaget, said Kohlberg, they develop a concept of gender. What's more, they come to see that they will always be male or female. As a result, they begin to select models of their own sex to imitate. The little girl acts as if she is thinking, "I'm a girl, so I want to do girl things. Therefore, the opportunity to do girl things is rewarding."

Gender Resources
Alice Eagly's Research

*I*n childhood, boys and girls tend to gravitate toward others of their own sex. Boys' and girls' groups develop distinct cultures with different agendas.

—ELEANOR MACCOBY
Contemporary Psychologist,
Stanford University

social cognitive theory of gender The idea that children's gender development occurs through observation and imitation of gender behavior, as well as through the rewards and punishment children experience for behaviors believed to be appropriate or inappropriate for their gender.

cognitive developmental theory of gender The theory that children's gender typing occurs after they think of themselves as boys and girls. Once they consistently conceive of themselves as male or female, children prefer activities, objects, and attitudes that are consistent with this label.

gender schema theory The theory that gender typing emerges as children gradually develop gender schemas of what is gender-appropriate and gender-inappropriate in their culture.

FIGURE 12.2 The Development of Gender-Typed Behavior According to the Cognitive Developmental and Gender Schema Theories of Gender Development

Theory	Processes	Emphasis
Cognitive developmental theory	Development of gender constancy, especially around 6 to 7 years of age, when conservation skills develop; after children develop ability to consistently conceive of themselves as male or female, children often organize their world on the basis of gender, such as selecting same-sex models to imitate	Cognitive readiness facilitates gender identity
Gender schema theory	Sociocultural emphasis on gender-based standards and stereotypes; children's attention and behavior are guided by an internal motivation to conform to these gender-based standards and stereotypes, allowing children to interpret the world through a network of gender-organized thoughts	Gender schemas reinforce gender behavior

Notice that in this view gender-typed behavior occurs only after children develop *gender constancy,* which is the understanding that sex remains the same, even though activities, clothing, and hair style might change (Ruble, 2000). However, researchers have found that children do not develop gender constancy until they are about 6 or 7 years old. Even before this time, however, most little girls prefer girlish toys and clothes and games, and most little boys prefer boyish toys and games. Thus, contrary to Kohlberg's description of cognitive developmental theory, gender typing does not appear to depend on gender constancy.

Unlike cognitive developmental theory, gender schema theory does not require children to perceive gender constancy before they begin gender typing (see figure 12.2). Instead, gender schema theory states that gender typing occurs when children are ready to encode and organize information along the lines of what is considered appropriate for females and males in their society (Martin & Dinella, 2001; Martin & Halverson, 1981). Bit by bit, children pick up what is gender-appropriate and gender-inappropriate in their culture, and develop gender schemas that shape how they perceive the world and what they remember. Children are motivated to act in ways that conform with these gender schemas. Thus, gender schemas fuel gender typing.

In sum, cognitive factors contribute to the way children think and act as males and females. Through biological, social, and cognitive processes, children develop their gender attitudes and behaviors.

Review and Reflect: Learning Goal 1

1 Explain biological, social, and cognitive influences on gender

REVIEW

- What is gender? How does biology influence gender?
- What are three social theories of gender?
- What are two cognitive views of gender?

REFLECT

- Does any theory of gender development explain everything you know about differences between men and women? What might an eclectic view of gender development be like? (You might want to review the discussion of an eclectic theoretical orientation in chapter 1.)

2   GENDER COMPARISONS AND CLASSIFICATIONS

| Gender Stereotyping | Gender Similarities and Differences | Masculinity, Femininity, and Androgyny |

To what extent are there real behavioral differences between males and females? Are many of the reported differences just stereotypes? What are some ways that gender can be classified?

Gender Stereotyping

Gender stereotypes are general impressions and beliefs about females and males. For example, men are powerful; women are weak. Men make good mechanics; women make good nurses. Men are good with numbers; women are good with words. Women are emotional; men are not. All of these are stereotypes. They are generalizations about a group that reflect widely held beliefs (Diekman & Eagly, 2000).

Traditional Masculinity and Femininity   A classic study in the early 1970s assessed which traits and behaviors college students believed were characteristic of females and which they believed were characteristic of males (Broverman & others, 1972). The traits associated with males were labeled *instrumental:* They included characteristics such as being independent, aggressive, and power-oriented. The traits associated with females were labeled *expressive:* They included characteristics such as being warm and sensitive.

Thus, the instrumental traits associated with males suited them for the traditional masculine role of going out into the world as the breadwinner. The expressive traits associated with females paralleled the traditional feminine role of being the sensitive, nurturing caregiver in the home. These roles and traits, however, are not just different; they also are unequal in terms of social status and power. The traditional feminine characteristics are childlike, suitable for someone who is dependent and subordinate to others. The traditional masculine characteristics suit one to deal competently with the wider world and to wield authority.

Stereotyping and Culture   How widespread is gender stereotyping? In a far-ranging study of college students in 30 countries, stereotyping of females and males was pervasive (Williams & Best, 1982). Males were widely believed to be dominant, independent, aggressive, achievement-oriented, and enduring. Females were widely believed to be nurturant, affiliative, less esteemed, and more helpful in times of distress.

Of course, in the decades since this study was conducted, traditional gender stereotypes and gender roles have been challenged in many societies, and social inequalities between men and women have diminished. Do gender stereotypes change when the relationship between men and women changes? In a subsequent study, women and men who lived in relatively wealthy, industrialized countries perceived themselves as more similar than did women and men who lived in less developed countries (Williams & Best, 1989). In the more developed countries, the women were more likely to attend college and be gainfully employed. Thus, as sexual equality increases, gender stereotypes may diminish. However, recent research continues to find that gender stereotyping is pervasive (Best, 2001; Kite, 2001).

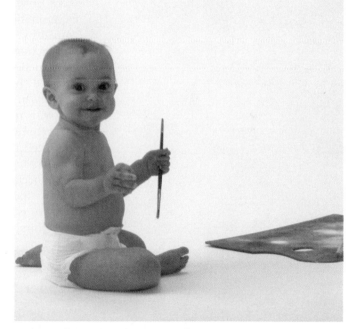

First imagine that this is a photograph of a baby girl. *What expectations would you have for her?* Then imagine that this is a photograph of a baby boy. *What expectations would you have for him?*

gender stereotypes Broad categories that reflect our impressions and beliefs about females and males.

Stereotyping of Occupations One area of gender stereotyping involves occupations. Even young children associate different occupations with men and women and aspire to occupations that are consistent with the cultural stereotypes for their own sex (Liben, Bigler, & Krogh, 2001). The Research in Life-Span Development interlude examines a study that attempted to reduce children's gender stereotyping.

Research in Life-Span Development
Reducing Children's Gender Stereotyping

One study focused on reducing children's gender stereotyping (Bigler & Liben, 1990). The researchers' goal was to decrease children's stereotyping of ten occupations commonly viewed as either feminine (beautician, fashion model, flight attendant, laundromat worker, and librarian) or masculine (construction worker, dentist, farmer, firefighter, and janitor). The participants in the study were 76 children from 6 through 11 years of age. During the first week of school, they were given a pretest to measure stereotyping and then randomly assigned to the experimental or the control group, each of which received a week of daily 20-minute lessons in occupations. The following week, the children were given a posttest measure of stereotyping.

The children in the experimental group were told that gender is irrelevant and that what's important is liking the job and having the skills needed for the job. For example, construction workers must learn to drive big machines. The children then were given practice problems. When the children gave gendered responses, the experimenter gave them corrective feedback. For example, in one practice problem Ann drove a bulldozer. Children were told "Ann loves to build things" and "Ann knows how to drive a bulldozer." The children then were asked, "Could Ann be a construction worker?" "How do you know?" If children said, "No, she couldn't because she is a girl," they were corrected for appealing to gender in their justifications. In the control group, children were given lessons on the same occupations but with no reference to or feedback about gender.

What were the results of this experiment? In the posttest, which was given after the week of gender instruction, the experimental group gave more nonstereotyped answers not only on the ten occupations they had been studying but also on many other occupations. For example, when children in the experimental group were asked which sex could do best at occupations like firefighting and being a librarian, they were more likely to say "both men and women" than the children in the control group, who were most likely to say "girls can't be firefighters."

Gender Similarities and Differences

What is the reality behind gender stereotypes? Let's examine some of the differences between the sexes, keeping in mind that

- the differences are averages and do apply to all females or all males;
- even when gender differences occur, there often is considerable overlap between males and females; and
- the differences may be due primarily to biological factors, sociocultural factors, or both.

First, we will examine physical differences, and then we will turn to cognitive and socioemotional differences.

Physical Similarities and Differences We could devote pages to describing physical differences between the average man and woman. For example, women have about twice the body fat of men, most concentrated around breasts and hips. In males, fat is more likely to go to the abdomen. On the average, males grow to be 10 percent taller than females. Androgens (the "male" hormones) promote the growth of long bones; estrogens (the "female" hormones) stop such growth at puberty.

Many physical differences between men and women are tied to health. From conception on, females have a longer life expectancy than males, and females are less likely than males to develop physical or mental disorders. Females are more resistant to infection, and their blood vessels are more elastic than males'. Males have higher levels of stress hormones, which cause faster clotting and higher blood pressure.

Does gender matter when it comes to brain structure and activity? Human brains are much alike, whether the brain belongs to a male or a female (Halpern, 2001). However, researchers have found some differences (Goldstein & others, 2001; Kimura, 2000); among the differences are:

"So according to the stereotype, you can put two and two together, but I can read the handwriting on the wall."

- One part of the hypothalamus involved in sexual behavior tends to be larger in men than women (Swaab & others, 2001).
- Portions of the corpus callosum—the band of tissues through which the brain's two hemispheres communicate—tend to be larger in females than males (Le Vay, 1994).
- An area of the parietal lobe that functions in visuospatial skills tends to be larger in males than females (Frederikse & others, 2000).
- The areas of the brain involved in emotional expression tend to show more metabolic activity in females than males (Gur & others, 1995).

Similarities and differences in the brains of males and females could be due to evolution and heredity, as well as social experiences.

Cognitive Similarities and Differences Many years ago, Eleanor Maccoby and Carol Jacklin (1974) concluded that males have better math and visuospatial skills (the kinds of skills an architect needs to design a building's angles and dimensions) than females, whereas females have better verbal abilities than males. Subsequently, Maccoby (1987) concluded that the verbal differences between females and males had virtually disappeared but that the math and visuospatial differences persisted. Today, some experts in gender, such as Janet Shibley Hyde (2004; Hyde & Mezulis, 2001), believe that the cognitive differences between females and males have been exaggerated. For example, Hyde points out that there is considerable overlap in the distributions of female and male scores on visuospatial tasks (see figure 12.3).

When researchers examine how children perform in school or on standardized tests, some differences between U.S. boys and girls persist. In a national study by the U.S. Department of Education (2000), boys did slightly better than girls at math and science. Overall, though, girls were far superior students, and they were significantly better than boys in reading. In another recent national study, females had higher reading achievement and better writing skills than males in grades 4, 8, and 12 with the gap widening as students progressed through school (Coley, 2001).

Keep in mind, though, that measures of achievement in school or scores on standardized tests may reflect many factors besides cognitive ability. For example, some test scores may reflect stereotype threat (as discussed in chapter 8). Performance in school may in part reflect attempts to conform to gender roles or differences in motivation, self-regulation, or other socioemotional characteristics.

Socioemotional Similarities and Differences Are "men from Mars" and "women from Venus"? Perhaps the gender differences that most fascinate people are those in how males and females relate to each other as

Adolescence: Adolescent Gender Differences in Science and Math

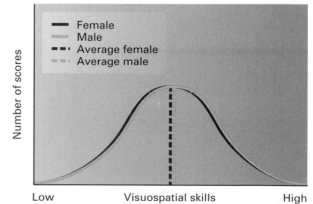

FIGURE 12.3 Visuospatial Skills of Males and Females

Notice that, although an average male's visuospatial skills are higher than an average female's, scores for the two sexes almost entirely overlap. Not all males have better visuospatial skills than all females—the overlap indicates that, although the average male score is higher, many females outperform most males on such tasks.

people. For just about every imaginable socioemotional characteristic, researchers have examined whether there are differences between males and females. Here we will examine just two that have been very closely studied: aggression and self-regulation.

One of the most consistent gender differences is that boys are more physically aggressive than girls. The difference occurs in all cultures and appears very early in children's development (White, 2001). The difference in physical aggression is especially pronounced when children are provoked.

Although boys are consistently more physically aggressive than girls, might girls be just as aggressive or even more aggressive than boys in other ways? The answer appears to be yes when two other types of aggression are considered. First, when researchers examine verbal aggression, such as yelling, females are often as aggressive or even more aggressive than males (Eagly & Steffen, 1986). Second, girls are more likely than boys to engage in *relational aggression,* which involves such behaviors as spreading malicious rumors in order to get others to dislike a child or ignoring someone when angry at him or her (Crick & others, 2001; Underwood, 2002).

Males usually show less self-regulation of emotions and behavior than females, and this low self-control can translate into behavioral problems (Eisenberg, Martin, & Fabes, 1996; Eisenberg & others, 2002; Eisenberg & Wang, 2003). In one study, children's low self-regulation was linked with greater aggression, teasing, overreaction to frustration, low cooperation, and inability to delay gratification (Block & Block, 1980).

Are psychological differences between males and females large or small? Alice Eagly (1996, 2001) argues that a belief that the differences are small arose from a feminist commitment to similarity between the sexes as a route to political equality, and from piecemeal and inadequate interpretations of research. Many feminists fear that differences between females and males will be interpreted as deficiencies in females and as biologically based, which could promote the old stereotypes that women are inferior to men (Unger & Crawford, 2000). According to Eagly, contemporary psychology has produced a large body of research that reveals behavior varies with gender and differences are socially induced. Recall, however, that evolutionary psychologist David Buss (2000) argues that there are substantial gender differences but, unlike Eagly, he emphasizes that they are evolutionary based. In sum, controversy continues over whether sex differences are rare and small or common and large, in part because gender is a political issue.

Gender in Context In thinking about gender, it is important to consider the context of behavior (Etaugh & Bridges, 2004; Fischer, 1999; Galliano, 2003). Gender behavior often varies across contexts. Consider helping behavior. Males are more likely to help in contexts in which a perceived danger is present and they feel competent to help (Eagly & Crowley, 1986). For example, males are more likely than females to help a person who is stranded by the roadside with a flat tire; automobile problems are an area about which many males feel competent. In contrast, when the context involves volunteering time to help a child with a personal problem, females are more likely to help than males are, because there is little danger present and females feel more competent at nurturing. In many cultures, girls show more caregiving behavior than boys do. However, in the few cultures where they both care for younger siblings on a regular basis, girls and boys are similar in their tendencies to nurture (Whiting, 1989).

Context is also relevant to gender differences in the display of emotions (Shields, 1991, 1998). Consider anger. Males are more likely to show anger toward strangers, especially other males, when they think they have been challenged. Males also are more likely than females to turn their anger into aggressive action, especially when the culture endorses such action (Tavris & Wade, 1984).

We find contextual variations regarding gender in specific situations, not only within a particular culture, but also across cultures (Nadien & Denmark, 1999).

In China, females and males are usually socialized to behave, feel, and think differently. The old patriarchal traditions of male supremacy have not been completely uprooted. Chinese women still make considerably less money than Chinese men do, and, in rural China (such as here in the Lixian Village of Sichuan) male supremacy still governs many women's lives.

Sociocultural contexts determine what is considered to be gender-appropriate and gender-inappropriate socioemotional behavior. Not too long ago it was accepted that boys are made of "snips and snails and puppy dogs' tails" and that girls are made of "sugar and spice and all that's nice. " The well-adjusted female was expected to display expressive traits, such as being dependent, nurturant, and uninterested in power. The well-adjusted male was expected to show instrumental traits, such as being independent, aggressive, and power-oriented.

In many cultures around the world, traditional gender roles continue to guide the behavior of males and females. In China and Iran, for instance, it is still widely accepted for males to engage in dominant behavior and females to behave in subordinate ways. Many Western cultures, such as the United States, have become more flexible about gender behavior and allow for more diversity. For example, although a girl's father might promote traditional femininity, her friends might engage in many traditionally masculine activities, and her teachers might encourage her to be assertive. One recent study found that societal changes are leading females to have more instrumental traits (Spence & Buckner, 2000).

Androgyny

Masculinity, Femininity, and Androgyny

In the 1970s, as both males and females became dissatisfied with the burdens imposed by their stereotyped roles, alternatives to "masculinity" and "femininity" were explored. Instead of thinking of masculinity and femininity as a continuum, with more of one meaning less of the other, it was proposed that individuals could show both expressive and instrumental traits. This thinking led to the development of the concept of **androgyny,** the presence of a high degree of masculine and feminine characteristics in the same individual (Bem, 1977; Spence & Helmreich, 1978). The androgynous individual might be a male who is assertive (masculine) and sensitive to others' feelings (feminine), or a female who is dominant (masculine) and caring (feminine).

Measures have been developed to assess androgyny. One of the most widely used gender measures, the *Bem Sex-Role Inventory,* was constructed by a leading early proponent of androgyny, Sandra Bem (1977). Based on their responses to the items in the Bem Sex-Role Inventory, individuals are classified as having one of four gender-role orientations: masculine, feminine, androgynous, or undifferentiated (see figure 12.4):

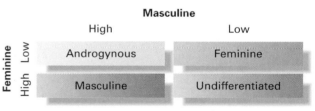

FIGURE 12.4 Gender-Role Classification

- The androgynous individual is simply a female or a male who has a high degree of both feminine (expressive) and masculine (instrumental) traits.
- A feminine individual is high on feminine (expressive) traits and low on masculine (instrumental) traits.
- A masculine individual is high on instrumental traits and low on expressive traits.
- An undifferentiated person is low on both feminine and masculine traits.

Androgynous women and men, according to Bem, are more flexible and more mentally healthy than either masculine or feminine individuals; undifferentiated individuals are the least competent. To some degree, though, *context* influences which gender role is most adaptive. In close relationships, a feminine or androgynous gender role may be more desirable because of the expressive nature of close relationships. However, a masculine or androgynous gender role may be more desirable in academic and work settings because of their demands for action and assertiveness. And the culture in which individuals live also plays an important role in determining what is adaptive. On the one hand, increasing numbers of children in the United States and other modernized countries such as Sweden are being raised to behave in androgynous ways. But traditional gender roles continue to dominate the cultures of many countries around the world.

androgyny The presence of a high degree of feminine and masculine characteristics in the same individual.

Some critics of androgyny say enough is enough and that there is too much talk about gender. An alternative to androgyny is **gender-role transcendence,** the view that when an individual's competence is at issue, it should be conceptualized on a person basis rather than on the basis of masculinity, femininity, or androgyny (Pleck, 1983). That is, we should think about ourselves as people, not as masculine, feminine, or androgynous. Parents should rear their children to be competent individuals, not masculine, feminine, or androgynous, say the gender-role critics. They believe such gender-role classification leads to too much stereotyping.

Review and Reflect: Learning Goal 2

2 Discuss gender comparisons and classifications

REVIEW

- What is gender stereotyping and how extensive is it?
- What are some physical, cognitive, and socioemotional differences between men and women?
- What are some ways that gender roles can be classified?

REFLECT

- Several decades ago, the word *dependency* was used to describe the relational orientation of femininity. Dependency took on a negative connotation for females—for instance, that females can't take care of themselves while males can. Today, the term *dependency* is being replaced by the term *relational abilities,* which has more positive connotations (Caplan & Caplan, 1999). Rather than being thought of as dependent, women are now more often described as skilled in forming and maintaining relationships. Make up a list of words that you associate with masculinity and femininity. Do these words have any negative connotations for males and females? For the words that do have negative connotations, are there words that could replace them?

---

3 GENDER DEVELOPMENT THROUGH THE LIFE SPAN

Childhood	Adolescence	Adulthood and Aging

Here we will focus further on gender-related developmental changes in the childhood years and discuss some changes that take place in adolescence and adulthood as well.

Childhood

Do gender lessons have to be hammered into children's heads year after year? Apparently not, according to gender expert Carole Beal (1994). Instead, what girls and boys learn about gender seems to be learned quickly at certain points in development, especially when new abilities first emerge. For example, toddlers learn a lot about gender when they make their first bids for autonomy and begin to talk. Children form many ideas about what the sexes are like from about 1½ to 3 years of age. Many parents don't really start to think about gender issues involving their child until preschool or kindergarten, but at that point children have already altered their behavior and learned to think of themselves as a girl or a boy. Few parents have to tell their little boys not to wear pink pants to the first grade! Children show a clear preference for same-sex peers (Vaughn & others, 2001).

gender-role transcendence The view that people should be evaluated as persons, not in terms of femininity, masculinity, or androgyny.

The amount, timing, and intensity of gender socialization is different for girls and boys (Beal, 1994). Boys receive earlier and more intense gender socialization than girls do. The social cost of deviating from the expected male role is higher for boys than is the cost for girls of deviating from the expected female role, in terms of peer rejection and parental disapproval. Imagine a girl who is wearing a toy holster, bandanna, and cowboy hat, running around in the backyard pretending to herd cattle. Now imagine a boy who is wearing a flowered hat, ropes of pearls, and lipstick, pretending to cook dinner on a toy stove. Which of these do you have a stronger reaction to—the girl's behavior or the boy's? Probably the boy's. Researchers have found that "effeminate" behavior in boys elicits much more negative reaction than does "masculine" behavior in girls (Martin, 1990).

Boys might have a more difficult time learning the masculine gender role because male models are less accessible to young children and messages from adults about the male role are not always consistent. For example, most mothers and teachers would like for boys to behave in masculine ways, but also to be neat, well-mannered, and considerate. However, fathers and peers usually want boys to behave in another way—independent and engaging in rough-and-tumble play. The mixed messages make it difficult for boys to figure out how to act.

Although gender roles have become more flexible in recent years, the flexibility applies more for girls than for boys (Beal, 1994). Girls can now safely be ambitious, competitive, and interested in sports, but relatively few adults are equally supportive of boys' being gentle, interested in fashion, and motivated to sign up for ballet classes. Instrumental traits and masculine gender roles may be evolving into a new norm for everyone.

Concern about the ways boys are being brought up has been called a "national crisis of boyhood" by William Pollack (1999) in his book *Real Boys.* Pollack says that little has been done to change what he calls the "boy code." Boy code tells boys they should not show their feelings and should act tough, says Pollack. Boys learn the boy code in many contexts—sandboxes, playgrounds, schoolrooms, camps, hangouts—and are taught the code by parents, peers, coaches, teachers, and other adults. Pollack, as well as many others, believes that boys would benefit from being socialized to express their anxieties and concerns and to better regulate their aggression.

Adolescence

Early adolescence is another transitional point that seems to be especially important in gender development. Young adolescents have to cope with the enormous changes of puberty. These changes are intensified by their expanding cognitive abilities, which make them acutely aware of how they appear to others. Relations with others change extensively as dating relationships begin and sexuality is experienced.

As females and males experience the physical and social changes of early adolescence, they must to come to terms with new definitions of their gender roles (Belansky & Clements, 1992). During early adolescence, individuals develop the adult, physical aspects of their sex ◀ ‖‖ **P. 99.** Some theorists and researchers have proposed that, with the onset of puberty, girls and boys experience an intensification of gender-related expectations. Puberty might signal to socializing others—parents, peers, and teachers, for example—that the adolescent is beginning to approach adulthood and, therefore, should begin to act more in ways that resemble the stereotypical female or male adult. The **gender-intensification hypothesis** states that psychological and behavioral differences between boys and girls become greater during early adolescence because of increased pressures to conform to traditional masculine and feminine gender roles (Hill & Lynch, 1983).

Some researchers have reported evidence of gender intensification in early adolescence (Hill & Lynch, 1983). For example, in one study, sex differences in

Early Childhood: Gender Role Behavior in Preschool

Middle and Later Childhood: Gender Differences in Middle and Later Childhood

gender-intensification hypothesis The view that psychological and behavioral differences between boys and girls become greater during early adolescence because of increased socialization pressures to conform to traditional gender roles.

gender-role attitudes increased across the early adolescent years. Gender-role attitudes were measured by the Attitudes Toward Women Scale (Galambos & others, 1985), which assesses the extent to which adolescents approve of gender-based division of roles. For example, the adolescent is asked such questions as whether girls should have the same freedom as boys. However, not every female and male shows gender intensification during puberty, and the family context influences how strongly gender intensification occurs (Crouter, Manke, & McHale, 1995). The jury is still out on the validity of the gender-intensification hypothesis (Galambos, 2004).

Gender intensification may create special problems for boys. Adopting a strong masculine role in adolescence is increasingly being found to be associated with problem behaviors. Joseph Pleck (1995) believes that what has defined traditional masculinity includes behaviors that do not have social approval but nonetheless validate the adolescent boy's masculinity. That is, in the male adolescent culture, male adolescents perceive that they will be thought of as more masculine if they engage in premarital sex, drink alcohol, take drugs, and participate in delinquent activities.

Male adolescent culture as well as the "mixed messages" that boys receive during gender socialization may also play a part in creating gender differences in school achievement (Koch, 2003). For example, recent evidence suggests that boys dominate in the academic bottom half of high school classes (DeZolt & Hull, 2001). That is, although many boys perform at the average or advanced level, the bottom 50 percent academically is made up mainly of boys. Males are more likely than females to be assigned to special/remedial education classes. Females are more likely to be engaged with academic material, be attentive in class, put forth more academic effort, and participate more in class than boys are (DeZolt & Hull, 2001).

Adulthood and Aging

How might women's and men's development vary as they go through their adult years? How might gender be linked with aging?

Women's Development Jean Baker Miller (1986) concluded that when researchers examine what women have been doing in their lives, a large part of it is active participation in the development of other people. In Miller's view, women often try to interact with others in ways that will foster the other person's development along many dimensions—emotionally, intellectually, and socially. Most experts believe it is important for women not only to maintain their competency in relationships but also to be self-motivated (Donelson, 1998). Miller believes that through increased self-determination, coupled with already developed relationship skills, many women will gain greater power in American culture. And as Harriet Lerner (1989) concluded in her book *The Dance of Intimacy*, it is important for women to bring to their relationships nothing less than a strong, assertive, independent, and authentic self. She believes competent relationships are those in which the separate "I-ness" of both persons can be appreciated and enhanced while still staying emotionally connected to each other.

Communication Between Men and Women Deborah Tannen (1990) analyzed the talk of women and men. She reported that a common complaint that wives have about their husbands is "He doesn't listen to me anymore." Another is "He doesn't talk to me anymore." Lack of communication, though high on women's lists of reasons for divorce, is mentioned much less often by men.

Tannen distinguishes rapport talk from report talk. **Rapport talk** is the language of conversation. It is a way of establishing connections and negotiating relationships. Women enjoy rapport talk more, and men's lack of interest in rapport talk bothers many women. In contrast, **report talk** is talk that is designed to give infor-

rapport talk The language of conversation; a way to establish connections and negotiate relationships; preferred by women.

report talk Language designed to give information, including public speaking; preferred by men.

mation, which includes public speaking. Men prefer to engage in report talk. Men hold center stage through such verbal performances as telling stories and jokes. They learn to use talk as a way of getting and keeping attention.

Recent studies continue to reveal gender differences in communication. One study of a sampling of students' e-mails found that people could guess the writer's gender two-thirds of the time (Thomson & Murachver, 2001). Another study revealed that women make 63 percent of phone calls and when talking to another woman stay on the phone longer (7.2 minutes) than men do when talking with other men (4.6 minutes) (Smoreda & Licoppe, 2000).

Women's dissatisfaction with men's silence at home is captured in a typical cartoon setting: a husband and wife sitting at the breakfast table. He's reading the newspaper; she's glaring at the back of the newspaper. Or he's opening a newspaper and asking his wife, "Is there anything you want to say to me before I begin reading the newspaper?" The reader knows there isn't, but that as soon as he starts reading the paper, she will think of something. To him, talk is for information. So when his wife interrupts his reading, it must be to inform him of something he needs to know—so she might as well tell him what she thinks he needs to know before he starts reading. But for her, talk is for interaction. She believes that saying things is a way to show involvement; listening is a way to show caring and interest.

The problem, then, might not be an individual man, or even men's styles alone, but the difference between women's and men's styles. If so, both men and women can make adjustments. A woman can push herself to speak up without being invited, or begin to speak even at the slightest pause in talk. The adjustment should not be one-sided. Rather than hogging public talk, men can warmly encourage women to speak in a group.

Men's Development   The male of the species—what is he really like? What are his concerns? According to Joseph Pleck's (1981, 1995) *role-strain view*, male roles are contradictory and inconsistent. Men not only experience stress when they violate men's roles, they also are harmed when they do act in accord with men's roles (Levant, 1996). Here are some of the areas where men's roles can cause considerable strain (Levant & Brooks, 1997):

- *Health.* Men's life expectancy is 8 to 10 years less than women's. Men have higher rates of stress-related disorders, alcoholism, car accidents, and suicide. Men are more likely than women to be the victims of homicide. In sum, the male role is hazardous to men's health.
- *Male-female relationships.* Too often, the male's role involves images that men should be dominant, powerful, and aggressive and should control women. Also, the male role has involved looking at women in terms of their bodies rather than their minds and feelings. Earlier, we described Deborah Tannen's (1990) concept that men show too little interest in rapport talk and relationships. And the male role has included the view that women should not be considered equal to men in work, earnings, and many other aspects of life. Too often these dimensions of the male role have produced men who have disparaged women, been violent toward women, and been unwilling to have equal relationships with women.
- *Male-male relationships.* Too many men have had too little interaction with their fathers, especially fathers who are positive role models (Day & Acock, 2004). Nurturing and being sensitive to others have been considered aspects of the female role, and not the male role. And the male role emphasizes competition rather than cooperation. All of these aspects of the male role have left men with inadequate positive emotional connections with other males.

To reconstruct masculinity in more positive ways, Ron Levant (1996) believes, every man should (1) reexamine his beliefs about manhood, (2) separate out the

**Gender and Communication
Women's Issues**

**Psychological Study of
Men and Masculinity**

Men's Issues

Tom Cruise (*left*) played Jerry Maguire in the movie *Jerry Maguire* with 6-year-old Ray, son of Jerry's love interest. The image of nurturing and nurtured males was woven throughout the movie. Jerry's relationship with Ray was a significant theme in the movie. It is through the caring relationship with Ray that Jerry makes his first genuine movement toward emotional maturity. The boy is guide to the man (Shields, 1998). Many experts on gender believe that men and boys would benefit from engaging in more nurturant behaviors.

valuable aspects of the male role, and (3) get rid of those parts of the masculine role that are destructive. All of this involves becoming more "emotionally intelligent"— that is, becoming more emotionally self-aware, managing emotions more effectively, reading emotions better (one's own emotions and others'), and being motivated to improve close relationships.

Gender and Aging   One view of changing gender roles during the adult years was created by David Gutmann (1975, 1997). He proposed the **parental imperative,** which states that mothers and fathers adopt different gender roles so they can raise children more effectively. In his research, Gutmann has found that in many cultures young and middle-aged men must engage in masculine behaviors to feed and protect their families, and in many cultures young and middle-aged women must engage in feminine behaviors to nurture and care for their children and provide for their families' emotional needs.

Gutmann believes that at some point in middle adulthood, though, men and women become freed from the parental imperative. At this point, he says, men become less active and more sensitive in relationships. At about the same time, middle-aged women become more active and assertive. Thus, he argues that as aging sets in, men become more "feminine" by engaging in traditionally feminine traits while women become more "masculine" by displaying an increase in traditionally masculine traits.

Some researchers have found that older men do become more feminine (nurturant, sensitive) but that many older women do not necessarily become more masculine (assertive, dominant) (Turner, 1982). Keep in mind that cohort effects are especially important to consider in areas like gender roles. As sociohistorical changes take place and are assessed more frequently in life-span investigations, what were

parental imperative Gutmann's view that mothers and fathers adopt different gender roles so they can raise children more effectively.

once perceived to be age effects may turn out to be cohort effects (Jacobs, 1994). This may be especially true if increasing numbers of adults adopt androgynous gender roles.

One study found that time spent in committed activities by older adults had shifted in opposite ways for women and men (Verbrugge, Gruber-Baldini, & Fozard, 1996). Between 1958 and 1992, older men decreased their time in paid work and spent more time doing housework, home repairs, yard work, shopping, and child care. In contrast, older women engaged in more paid work and decreased their time in housework.

A possible double jeopardy also faces many women—the burden of both ageism and sexism (Lopata, 1994). The poverty rate for elderly females is almost double that of elderly males. According to Congresswoman Mary Rose Oakar, the number one priority for midlife and older women should be economic security. She predicts that 25 percent of all women working today can expect to be poor in old age. Yet only recently has scientific and political interest in the aging woman developed. For many years, the aging woman was virtually invisible in aging research and in protests involving rights for the elderly (Markson, 1995). An important research and political agenda for the twenty-first century is increased interest in the aging and the rights of older women.

Not only is it important to be concerned about older women's double jeopardy of ageism and sexism, but special attention also needs to be devoted to older females from ethnic minority groups. They face triple jeopardy—ageism, sexism, and racism (Burton, 1996; Markides, 1995). The Contexts of Life-Span Development interlude explores further aspects of gender and ethnicity in aging women.

Contexts of Life-Span Development
Being Female, Ethnic, and Old

Part of the unfortunate history of ethnic minority groups in the United States has been the negative stereotypes against members of their groups. Many with immigrant origins may also have faced special difficulties because they are not fluent or literate in English, may not be aware of the values and norms involved in American social interaction, and may have lifestyles that differ from those of mainstream America (Organista, 1994). Often included in these cultural differences is the role of women. Many, but not all, immigrant ethnic groups traditionally have relegated the woman's role to family maintenance. Many important decisions might be made by a woman's husband or parents, and she is often not expected to seek an independent career or enter the workforce except in the case of dire financial need.

Some ethnic minority groups may define an older woman's role as unimportant, but in some ethnic groups, a woman's social status improves as she gets older. For example, older African American women can express their own needs and be given status and power in the community.

Despite their positive status in the African American family and the African American culture, African American women over the age of 70 are the poorest population group in the United States. Three of five older African American women live alone; most of them are widowed. The low incomes of older African American women translate into less than adequate access to health care.

A portrayal of older African American women in cities reveals some of their survival strategies. They highly value the family as a system of mutual support and aid, adhere to the American work ethic, and view religion as a source of strength (Perry & Johnson, 1994). The use of religion as a way to cope with stress has a long

A special concern is the stress faced by African American elderly women. *What are some ways they cope with stress?*

history in the African American culture, with roots in the slave experience. The African American church came to fulfill needs and functions once met by religion-based tribal and community organizations that African Americans brought from Africa. In one study, older African American women valued church organizations more than their male counterparts did, especially valuing the church's group activities and organizations (Taylor, 1982).

In sum, older African American women have faced considerable stress in their lives (Edmonds, 1993). In the face of this stress, they have shown remarkable adaptiveness, resilience, responsibility, and coping skills.

Review and Reflect: Learning Goal 3

3 Describe the development of gender through the life span

REVIEW

- What are some developmental changes in gender in childhood?
- How does gender change during adolescence?
- How does gender change during adulthood?

REFLECT

- How have your gender attitudes and behavior changed since childhood? Are the changes mainly age changes or do they reflect cohort effects?

---

4 EXPLORING SEXUALITY

Biological and Cultural Factors	Sexually Transmitted Infections

Sexual Orientation	Forcible Sexual Behavior and Sexual Harassment

Now that we have studied the gender aspects of being female and male, let's turn our attention to the sexual aspects. To explore sexuality, we will examine biological and cultural factors, sexual orientation, sexually transmitted infections, forcible sexual behavior, and sexual harassment.

Biological and Cultural Factors

We don't need sex for everyday survival, the way we need food and water, but we do need it for the survival of the species. With this important role of sex in mind, let's examine some biological and cultural factors involved in sexuality.

Biological Factors In our discussion of gender, we described the two main classes of sex hormones: estrogens (which primarily promote the development of female physical sex characteristics) and androgens (which mainly promote the development of male physical sex characteristics). As we discussed in chapter 3, the pituitary gland monitors hormone levels, but it itself is regulated by the hypothalamus ◀||||| **P. 97.** The pituitary gland sends out a signal to the testes or ovaries to manufacture a hormone, then the pituitary gland, through interaction with the hypothalamus, detects when the optimal level of the hormone is reached and maintains this level.

As we move from the lower to the higher animals, the role of hormones becomes less clear, especially in females. For human males, higher androgen levels are associated with sexual motivation and orgasm frequency (Knussman, Christiansen, & Couwenbergs, 1986). Nonetheless, sexual behavior is so individualized in humans that it is difficult to specify the effects of hormones.

Cultural Factors   Sexual motivation also is influenced by cultural factors (Caron, 1998; Tolman & Diamond, 2001). The range of sexual values across cultures is substantial. Some cultures consider sexual pleasures "weird" or "abnormal." Consider the people who live on the small island of Ines Beag off the coast of Ireland. They are some of the most sexually repressed people in the world. They know nothing about tongue kissing or hand stimulation of the penis, and they detest nudity. For both females and males, premarital sex is out of the question. Men avoid most sexual experiences because they believe that sexual intercourse reduces their energy level and is bad for their health. Under these repressive conditions, sexual intercourse occurs only at night and takes place as quickly as possible as the husband opens his nightclothes under the covers and the wife raises her nightgown. As you might suspect, female orgasm is rare in this culture (Messinger, 1971).

In contrast, consider the Mangaian culture in the South Pacific. In Mangaia, young boys are taught about masturbation and are encouraged to engage in it as much as they like. At age 13, the boys undergo a ritual that initiates them into sexual manhood. First, their elders instruct them about sexual strategies, including how to help their female partner have orgasms. Then, two weeks later, the boy has intercourse with an experienced woman who helps him hold back ejaculation until she can achieve orgasm with him. By the end of adolescence, Mangaians have sex virtually every day. Mangaian women report a high frequency of orgasms.

As reflected in the behavior of the people in these two different cultures, our sexual motivation is influenced by **sexual scripts** (Krahe, 2000). These are stereotyped patterns of expectancies for how people should behave sexually. Two well-known sexual scripts are the traditional religious script and the romantic script. In the **traditional religious script,** sex is accepted only within marriage. Extramarital sex is taboo, especially for women. Sex means reproduction and sometimes affection. In the **romantic script,** sex is synonymous with love. If we develop a relationship with someone and fall in love, it is acceptable to have sex with the person whether we are married or not.

You probably are familiar with some sex differences in sexual scripts. Females tend to link sexual intercourse with love more than males do, and males are more likely to emphasize sexual conquest. Some sexual scripts involve a double standard, such that it is okay for male adolescents to have sex but not females, and that if the female gets pregnant it's her fault for not using contraception.

Sexual Orientation

Our exploration of sexual orientation focuses on heterosexual and homosexual attitudes and behaviors.

Heterosexual Attitudes and Behavior   In a well-designed study, Robert Michael and his colleagues (1994) interviewed nearly 3,500 people from 18 to 50 years of age who were randomly selected (a sharp contrast from earlier samples such as the famous study by Alfred Kinsey and his colleagues in the 1940s). Among the key findings from the 1994 survey:

---

*W*e are born twice over; the first time for existence, the second time for life; once as human beings and later as men or as women.

—JEAN-JACQUES ROUSSEAU
*French-Born Swiss Philosopher,
18th Century*

sexual scripts Stereotyped patterns of expectancies for how people should behave sexually.

traditional religious script Sex is accepted only within marriage; extramarital sex is taboo, especially for women, and sex means reproduction and sometimes affection.

romantic script Sex is synonomous with love: If we develop a relationship with someone and fall in love, it is acceptable to have sex with the person whether we are married or not.

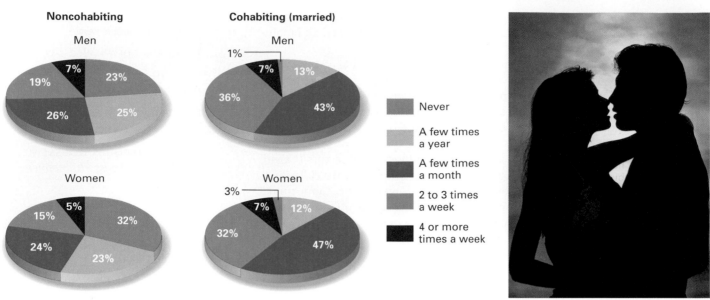

Noncohabiting

Men

7% | 23% | 19% | 26% | 25%

Women

5% | 32% | 15% | 24% | 23%

Cohabiting (married)

Men

1% | 7% | 13% | 36% | 43%

Women

3% | 7% | 12% | 32% | 47%

Never

A few times a year

A few times a month

2 to 3 times a week

4 or more times a week

FIGURE 12.5 The 1994 Sex in America Survey

Percentages show noncohabiting and cohabiting (married) males' and females' responses to the question "How often have you had sex in the past year?"

The Kinsey Institute

- Americans tend to fall into three categories: One-third have sex twice a week or more, one-third a few times a month, and one-third a few times a year or not at all.

- Married couples have sex the most often and also are the most likely to have orgasms when they do. Figure 12.5 portrays the frequency of sex for married and noncohabiting individuals in the past year.

- Most Americans do not engage in kinky sexual acts. When asked what their favorite sexual acts were, the vast majority (96 percent) said that vaginal sex was "very" or "somewhat" appealing. Oral sex was in third place, after an activity that many have not labeled a sexual act—watching a partner undress.

- Adultery is clearly the exception rather than the rule. Nearly 75 percent of the married men and 85 percent of the married women indicated that they have never been unfaithful.

- Men think about sex far more than women do—54 percent of the men said they think about it every day or several times a day, whereas 67 percent of the women said they think about it only a few times a week or a few times a month.

In sum, one of the most powerful messages in the 1994 survey was that Americans' sexual lives are more conservative than previously believed. Although 17 percent of the men and 3 percent of the women said they have had sex with at least 21 partners, the overall impression from the survey was that sexual behavior is ruled by marriage and monogamy for most Americans.

So far, we have mentioned several gender differences in sexuality, such as men thinking about sex more often than women do and women linking sexual intercourse with love more than men do. A recent review of research also concluded that (Baumeister, Catanese, & Vohs, 2001) men report more frequent feelings of sexual arousal, have more frequent sexual fantasies, and rate the strength of their own sex drive higher than women. Men also are more likely to masturbate, have more permissive attitudes about casual premarital sex, and have a more difficult time adhering to their vows of celibacy when they become married (Oliver & Hyde, 1993; Peplau, 2002).

Homosexual Attitudes and Behavior   Until the end of the nineteenth century, it was generally believed that people were either heterosexual or homosexual.

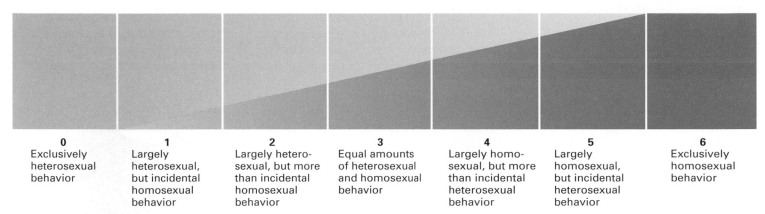

0	1	2	3	4	5	6
Exclusively heterosexual behavior	Largely heterosexual, but incidental homosexual behavior	Largely heterosexual, but more than incidental homosexual behavior	Equal amounts of heterosexual and homosexual behavior	Largely homosexual, but more than incidental heterosexual behavior	Largely homosexual, but incidental heterosexual behavior	Exclusively homosexual behavior

FIGURE 12.6 Continuum of Sexual Orientation

The continuum ranges from exclusive heterosexuality, which Kinsey and associates (1948) labeled 0, to exclusive homosexuality, labeled 6. People who are about equally attracted to both sexes, 2 to 4, are bisexual.

Today, it is more accepted to view sexual orientation along a continuum from exclusive heterosexuality to exclusive homosexuality rather than as an either/or proposition (see figure 12.6). Some individuals are also **bisexual,** being sexually attracted to people of both sexes. In the Sex in America survey, 2.7 percent of the men and 1.3 percent of the women indicated that they had had homosexual sex in the past year (Michael & others, 1994).

Why are some individuals homosexual and others heterosexual? Speculation about this question has been extensive, but no firm answers are available. Homosexuals and heterosexuals have similar physiological responses during sexual arousal and seem to be aroused by the same types of tactile stimulation. Investigators find no differences between homosexuals and heterosexuals in a wide range of attitudes, behaviors, and adjustments (Bell, Weinberg, & Hammersmith, 1981). Homosexuality once was classified as a mental disorder, but both the American Psychiatric Association and the American Psychological Association discontinued this classification in the 1970s.

Recently, researchers have explored the possible biological basis of homosexuality (Gladue, 1994). The results of hormone studies have been inconsistent. If male homosexuals are given male sexual hormones (androgens), their sexual orientation does not change. Their sexual desire merely increases. A very early prenatal critical period might influence sexual orientation. In the second to fifth months after conception, exposure of the fetus to hormone levels characteristic of females might cause the individual (male or female) to become attracted to males (Ellis & Ames, 1987). If this critical-period hypothesis turns out to be correct, it would explain why clinicians have found that sexual orientation is difficult, if not impossible, to modify.

With regard to anatomical structures, neuroscientist Simon LeVay (1991) found that an area of the hypothalamus that governs sexual behavior is twice as large (about the size of a grain of sand) in heterosexual males as in homosexual males. Homosexual males and heterosexual females had about equal-sized areas in this part of the hypothalamus. Critics of this research point out that many of the homosexuals in the study had AIDS and their brains could have been altered by the disease.

An individual's sexual orientation—heterosexual, homosexual, or bisexual—most likely is determined by a combination of genetic, hormonal, cognitive, and environmental factors (Baldwin & Baldwin, 1998). Most experts on homosexuality believe that no one factor alone causes homosexuality and that the relative weight of each factor can vary from one individual to the next. No one knows exactly why some individuals are homosexual (Herek, 2000).

www.mhhe.com/santrockldt2

The International Lesbian and Gay Association

bisexual Being sexually attracted to people of both sexes.

Scientists have a clearer picture of what does not cause homosexuality. For example, children raised by gay or lesbian parents or couples are no more likely to be homosexual than children raised by heterosexual parents (Patterson, 2000). There also is no evidence that male homosexuality is caused by a dominant mother or a weak father, or that female homosexuality is caused by girls choosing male role models.

Many gender differences that appear in heterosexual relationships also occur in homosexual relationships. Like heterosexual women (Peplau, 2002):

- lesbians' sexual fantasies are more likely than gay men's to be personal and romantic,
- lesbians have fewer sex partners than gay men, and
- lesbians have less permissive attitudes about casual sex and sex outside a primary relationship than gay men.

Thus, whether they have a heterosexual or homosexual orientation, for many women, sexuality is strongly linked to a close relationship with the best context for enjoyable sex being a committed relationship. This is less so for men (Peplau, 2002; Peplau, Fingerhut, & Beals, 2004).

How can gays and lesbians adapt to a world in which they are a minority? According to psychologist Laura Brown (1989), gays and lesbians experience life as a minority in a dominant majority culture. Brown believes that gays and lesbians adapt best when they don't define themselves in polarities, such as trying to live in an separate gay or lesbian world or completely accepting the majority culture. Instead, developing a bicultural identity and balancing the demands of the two cultures can often lead to more effective coping for homosexuals, says Brown.

Sexually Transmitted Infections

Sexually transmitted infections (STIs) are diseases that are contracted primarily through sexual contact. This contact includes oral-genital and anal-genital contact as well as vaginal intercourse. STIs are an increasing health problem. The main STIs are three caused by bacterial infections—gonorrhea, syphilis, and chlamydia—and three STIs caused by viruses—genital herpes, HPV (human papillomavirus), and AIDS (acquired immune deficiency syndrome).

Gonorrhea *Gonorrhea* is a sexually transmitted infection that is commonly called the "drip" or the "clap." It is one of the most common STIs in the United States and is caused by the bacterium *Neisseria gonorrhoeae,* which thrives in the mucous membranes lining the mouth, throat, vagina, cervix, urethra, and anal tract. The bacterium is spread by contact between the infected moist membranes of one individual and the membranes of another.

Gonorrhea can be successfully treated in its early stages with penicillin or other antibiotics. Untreated, gonorrhea can lead to infections that can move to various organs and can cause infertility. More than 650,000 cases are reported in the United States annually (Centers for Disease Control and Prevention, 2002a).

Syphilis *Syphilis* is a sexually transmitted infection caused by the bacterium *Treponema pallidum,* a spirochete. The spirochete needs a warm, moist environment to survive, and it is transmitted by penile-vaginal, oral-genital, or anal contact. It can also be transmitted from a pregnant woman to her fetus after the fourth month of pregnancy. If the mother is treated before this time with penicillin, syphilis will not be transmitted to the fetus.

In its early stages, syphilis can be effectively treated with penicillin. In its advanced stages, syphilis can cause paralysis or even death. Approximately 40,000 cases of syphilis are reported in the United States each year.

Chlamydia *Chlamydia,* the most common of all sexually transmitted infections in the United States, is named for *Chlamydia trachomatis,* a bacterium that spreads by sexual contact and infects the genital organs of both sexes. Although fewer individuals have heard of chlamydia than have heard of gonorrhea and syphilis, its incidence is much higher (Centers for Disease Control and Prevention, 2002a). About 4 million Americans are infected with chlamydia each year. About 10 percent of all college students have chlamydia. This STI is highly infectious, and women run a 70 percent risk of contracting it in a single sexual encounter. The male risk is estimated at between 25 and 50 percent.

Males with chlamydia often get treatment because of noticeable symptoms in the genital region; however, most females are asymptomatic. Therefore, many females go untreated and chlamydia spreads to the upper reproductive tract, where it can cause pelvic inflammatory disease (PID). PID, in turn, can result in ectopic pregnancies (a pregnancy in which the fertilized egg is implanted outside the uterus) or infertility. One-quarter of females who have PID become infertile; multiple cases of PID increase the rate of infertility to half. Some researchers suggest that chlamydia is the number one preventable cause of female infertility.

Genital Herpes *Genital herpes* is a sexually transmitted infection caused by a large family of viruses with many different strains. These strains produce other, nonsexually transmitted infections such as chicken pox and mononucleosis. Three to five days after contact, itching and tingling can occur, followed by an eruption of sores and blisters. The attacks can last up to three weeks and may recur in a few weeks or a few years.

Although drugs such as acyclovir alleviate symptoms, there is no known cure for herpes. The virus can be transmitted through nonlatex condoms and foams, making infected individuals reluctant to have sex, angry about the unpredictability of their lives, and fearful that they won't be able to cope with the pain and stress of the next attack. For these reasons, support groups for individuals with herpes have been established.

HPV *HPV* is a virus (human papillomavirus) that causes genital warts on people. The warts can be as large as nickels or so small that they cannot be seen. There are more than a million new cases of HPV each year in the United States. The most common way to contract HPV is by having sex with, or touching the genitals of, someone who already has the virus.

Women with HPV face an increased risk for cervical cancer. Genital warts can be removed by physicians. Sometimes the warts are frozen off; at other times a laser is used to remove them. Although the warts can be removed, it generally is believed that once the virus is acquired, HPV does not go away.

AIDS No single STI has had a greater impact on sexual behavior, or created more public fear, in the last several decades than AIDS. **AIDS** is a sexually transmitted infection that is caused by the *human immunodeficiency virus (HIV),* which destroys the body's immune system. A person who has contracted HIV is vulnerable to infections that a normal immune system could destroy (Carey & Vanable, 2003).

Of the AIDS cases reported through June 2001, in the United States, 82 percent were men, 18 percent were women. Overall, 47 percent of the AIDS cases were gay men, 25 percent were injection drug users, 10 percent were persons infected heterosexually, and 2 percent were individuals infected through blood or blood products (Centers for Disease Control and Prevention, 2002b).

Because of education and the development of more effective drug treatments, deaths due to AIDS have begun to decline in the United States (Centers for Disease Control and Prevention, 2002b). Multidrug combinations can suppress the HIV virus to low levels for an extended time (Carey & Vanable, 2003). However, in

AIDS A sexually transmitted infection caused by the human immunodeficiency virus (HIV), which destroys the body's immune system.

many locations around the world AIDS is increasing. For example, in Africa more than 4 million people had AIDS in 2000. To put this in perspective, a total of 774,467 cases of AIDS had been reported to the Centers for Disease Control and Prevention (2002b) through the end of 2000, in the United States.

Experts say that AIDS can be transmitted only by (Kalichman, 1996)

- sexual contact,
- sharing hypodermic needles,
- blood transfusion (which in the last few years has been tightly monitored),
- other direct contact of cuts or mucous membranes with blood and sexual fluids, or
- mother-baby transmission.

Remember that it is not who you are, but what you do, that puts you at risk for getting HIV. Anyone who is sexually active or uses intravenous drugs is at risk. *No one* is immune. Once an individual is infected, the prognosis is likely illness and possibly death. The only safe behavior is abstinence from sex, which most individuals do not perceive as an option. Beyond abstinence, there is only "safer" behavior, such as sexual behavior without exchange of semen, vaginal fluids, or blood, and sexual intercourse with a condom (Strong & others, 2005).

Just asking a date about his or her sexual behavior does not guarantee protection from AIDS and other sexually transmitted infections (Noam, Zimmerman, & Atwood, 2004). For example, in one investigation, 655 college students were asked to answer questions about lying and sexual behavior (Cochran & Mays, 1990). Of the 422 respondents who said they were sexually active, 34 percent of the men and 10 percent of the women said they had lied so that their partner would be more inclined to have sex with them. Much higher percentages—47 percent of the men and 60 percent of the women—said they had been lied to by a potential sexual partner. When asked what aspects of their past they would be most likely to lie about, more than 40 percent of the men and women said they would understate the number of their sexual partners. Twenty percent of the men, but only 4 percent of the women, said they would lie about results from an HIV blood test.

Protecting Against STIs   What are some good strategies for protecting against AIDS and other sexually transmitted infections? They include these:

- *Know your and your partner's risk status.* Anyone who has had previous sexual activity with another person might have contracted an STI without being aware of it. Get to know a prospective partner before you have sex. Use this time to inform the other person of your STI status and inquire about your partner's. Remember that many people lie about their STI status.
- *Obtain medical examinations.* Many experts recommend that couples who want to begin a sexual relationship should have a medical checkup to rule out STIs before they engage in sex. If cost is an issue, contact your campus health service or a public health clinic.
- *Have protected, not unprotected, sex.* When correctly used, latex condoms help to prevent many STIs from being transmitted. Condoms are more effective in preventing gonorrhea, syphilis, chlamydia, and HIV than herpes.
- *Don't have sex with multiple partners.* One of the best predictors of getting an STI is having sex with multiple partners. Having more than one sex partner elevates the likelihood that you will encounter an infected partner.

CDC National Prevention Network
American Social Health Association
Sexually Transmitted Infections Resources
Center for AIDS Prevention Studies

Forcible Sexual Behavior and Sexual Harassment

Too often, sex involves the exercise of power. Here we will briefly look at two of the problems that may result: rape and sexual harassment.

Rape   *Rape* is forcible sexual intercourse with a person who does not give consent. Legal definitions of rape differ from state to state. For example, in some states, husbands are not prohibited from forcing their wives to have intercourse, although this has been challenged in several states. Because victims may be reluctant to suffer the consequences of reporting rape, the actual incidence is not easily determined. It appears that rape occurs most often in large cities, where it has been reported that 8 of every 10,000 women 12 years and older are raped each year. Nearly 200,000 rapes are reported each year in the United States.

An increasing concern is *date or acquaintance rape,* which is coercive sexual activity directed at someone with whom the victim is at least casually acquainted. By some estimates, two-thirds of college freshman women report having been date-raped or having experienced an attempted date rape at least once (Watts & Zimmerman, 2002). About two-thirds of college men admit that they fondle women against their will, and one-half admit to forcing sexual activity.

A major study that focused on campus sexual assault involved a phone survey of 4,446 women attending two- or four-year colleges (Fisher, Cullen, & Turner, 2000). In this study, slightly less than 3 percent said that they either had experienced a rape or an attempted rape during the academic year. About 1 of 10 college women said that they had experienced rape in their lifetime. Unwanted or uninvited sexual contacts were widespread, with more than one-third of the college women reporting these incidents. As shown in figure 12.7, in this study, most women (about 9 of 10) knew the person who sexually victimized them. Most of the women attempted to take protective actions against their assailants but were then reluctant to report the victimization to the police. Several factors were associated with sexual victimization: living on campus, being unmarried, getting drunk frequently, and experiencing prior sexual victimization.

Although most victims of rape are women, male rape does occur (Ellis, 2002). Men in prisons are especially vulnerable to rape, usually by heterosexual males who use rape as a means of establishing their dominance and power. Though it might seem impossible for a man to be raped by a woman, a man's erection is not

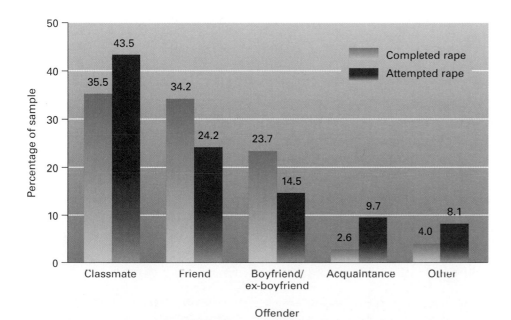

FIGURE 12.7 Completed Rape and Attempted Rape of College Women According to Victim-Offender Relationship

completely under his voluntary control, and some cases of male rape by women have been reported (Sarrel & Masters, 1982). Male victims account for fewer than 5 percent of all rapes.

Why does rape occur so often in the United States? Among the causes given are that males are socialized to be sexually aggressive, to regard women as inferior beings, and to view their own pleasure as the most important objective. Researchers have found that male rapists share the following characteristics: Aggression enhances their sense of power or masculinity; they are angry at women in general; and they want to hurt and humiliate the victim (Browne & Williams, 1993).

Rape is a traumatic experience for the victims and those close to them (Christopher & Sprecher, 2000; Koss & Boeschen, 1998). Victims initially feel shock and numbness and are often acutely disorganized. Some show their distress through words and tears; others internalize their suffering. As victims strive to get their lives back to normal, they may experience depression, fear, and anxiety for months or years (Thompson & others, 2003). Sexual dysfunctions, such as reduced sexual desire and an inability to reach orgasm, occur in 50 percent of female rape victims (Sprei & Courtois, 1988). Many victims make changes in their lives—such as moving to a new apartment or refusing to go out at night. Recovery depends on coping abilities, psychological adjustments prior to the assault, and social support. Parents, boyfriend or husband, and others close to the victim are important factors in recovery, as is the availability of professional counseling (Kelly, 2004; Mein & others, 2003).

Sexual Harassment Sexual harassment takes many forms—from sexist remarks and physical contact (patting, brushing against their bodies) to blatant propositions and sexual assaults (Ogashi, 2001; Paludi, 2002). Millions of women experience sexual harassment each year in work and educational settings. Sexual harassment of men by women also occurs but to a far lesser extent than sexual harassment of women by men.

Sexual harassment can result in serious psychological consequences for the victim. Sexual harassment is a manifestation of power of one person over another. The elimination of such exploitation requires the development of work and academic environments that provide equal opportunities to develop a career and obtain education in a climate free of sexual harassment (Koch, 2003; Marks & Nelson, 1993).

www.mhhe.com/santrockldt2

Sexual Assault
Sexual Harassment

Review and Reflect: Learning Goal 4

4 Characterize influences on sexuality, the nature of sexual orientation, and some sexual problems

REVIEW

- How do biology and culture influence sexuality?
- What is the nature of heterosexual and homosexual attitudes and behavior?
- What are some common sexually transmitted infections? What are some good strategies for protecting against STIs?
- What is the nature of forcible sexual behavior and sexual harassment?

REFLECT

- Do you think sex is a matter of doing what comes naturally—that is, sexual behavior is essentially determined by a person's biological drive? Explain your answer.

5 SEXUALITY THROUGH THE LIFE SPAN

Child Sexuality	Adolescent Sexuality	Sexuality and Aging

So far we have discussed a number of aspects of human sexuality. Now, let's explore sexuality at different points in development, beginning with childhood.

Child Sexuality

Most psychologists doubt Freud's claim that preschool children have a strong sexual attraction to the parent of the other sex. But what are some aspects of child sexuality?

A majority of children engage in some sex play, usually with friends or siblings (Crooks & Bauer, 2002; DeLamater & Friedrich, 2002). Child sex play includes exhibiting or inspecting the genitals. Much of this child sex play is likely motivated by curiosity. There does not appear to be any link between such sexual play and sexual adjustment in adolescence or adulthood.

As the elementary school years progress, sex play with others usually declines, although romantic interest in peers may be present. Curiosity about sex remains high in the elementary school years, and children may ask many questions about reproduction and sexuality (Gordon & Gordon, 1989). However, the main surge in sexual interest takes place not in childhood but in early adolescence.

Adolescent Sexuality

Adolescence is a bridge between the asexual child and the sexual adult (Feldman, 1999). It is a time of sexual exploration and experimentation with sexual fantasies and realities, of incorporating sexuality into one's identity (Christopher, 2001). Most adolescents have an almost insatiable curiosity about sexuality's mysteries. They think about whether they are sexually attractive, how to do sex, and what the future holds for their sexual lives. The majority of adolescents eventually manage to develop a mature sexual identity, but for most there are times of vulnerability and confusion.

Every society pays some attention to adolescent sexuality. In some societies, adults clamp down and protect adolescent females from males by chaperoning them. Other societies promote very early marriage. Yet other societies, such as the United States, allow some sexual experimentation, although there is controversy about just how far sexual experimentation should be allowed to go. Most adolescents have healthy sexual attitudes and engage only in sexual practices that will not compromise their development (Feldman, 1999).

How do adolescents develop a sexual identity and how does sexual behavior change during adolescence? Those questions are the focus of our discussion of adolescent sexuality, but we also will consider how adolescents deal with the prospect of pregnancy and sexually transmitted infections.

Developing a Sexual Identity Mastering emerging sexual feelings and forming a sexual identity are multifaceted (Archibald, Graber, & Brooks-Gunn, 2003; Brooks-Gunn & Graber, 1999). Adolescents face the challenge of learning to manage sexual feelings such as sexual arousal and attraction, developing new forms of intimacy, and learning to regulate sexual behavior to avoid undesirable consequences. They must synthesize their developing sexual identity with other facets of their identity.

Sexual arousal emerges as a new phenomenon in adolescence, and it is important to view sexuality as a normal aspect of adolescent development.

—SHIRLEY FELDMAN
Contemporary Psychologist, Stanford University

An adolescent's sexual identity involves sexual orientation, activities, interests, and styles of behavior (Buzwell & Rosenthal, 1996). For example, some adolescents have considerable anxiety about sex, while others show little anxiety about it. Some adolescents are strongly aroused sexually, others less so. Some adolescents are very active sexually, others are virgins. Some adolescents are sexually inactive because of a strong religious upbringing; other religious adolescents are sexually active (Thorton & Canburn, 1989).

The development of gay or lesbian identity is often referred to as *coming-out*. In one comprehensive survey of almost 35,000 junior and senior high school students in Minnesota, 4.5 percent reported predominantly homosexual attractions (Remafedi & others, 1992). Homosexual identities, attractions, and behaviors increased with age. More than 6 percent of the 18-year-olds said they had predominantly homosexual attractions. How many of these youths later become gay is not known. Many adolescents who engage in homosexual behavior in adolescence do not continue the practice into adulthood.

It is commonly believed that most gay and lesbian individuals quietly struggle with same-sex attractions in childhood, do not engage in heterosexual dating, and gradually recognize that they are gay or lesbian in mid to late adolescence (Diamond, 2003). Many youths do follow this developmental pathway but others do not. For example, many youths have no recollection of same-sex attractions and experience a more abrupt sense of their same-sex attraction in late adolescence (Savin-Williams, 2001; Savin-Williams & Diamond, 2004). Researchers also have found that the majority of adolescents with same-sex attractions also experience some degree of other-sex attractions (Garofalo & others, 1999).

It is also commonly believed that adolescents who are attracted to same-sex individuals always fall in love with these individuals. However, some youth claim that their same-sex attractions are purely physical, others assert that they have more to do with emotional attachment (Savin-Williams, 2001; Savin-Williams & Diamond, 2004). In sum, these adolescents have diverse patterns of initial attraction, often have bisexual attractions, and may have physical or emotional attraction to same-sex individuals, but do not always fall in love with them (Diamond, 2003).

Adolescent Sexual Behaviors Adolescents engage in a rather consistent progression of sexual behaviors (DeLamater & MacCorquodale, 1979). Kissing usually comes first, followed by petting. Next comes intercourse, or, in some cases, oral sex,

What are some developmental pathways involved in homosexuality?

Adolescence: Gay and Lesbian Teenagers

which has increased substantially among adolescents in recent years. In a study of 452 individuals 18 to 25 years of age who were asked about their sexual experiences (Feldman, Turner, & Araujo, 1999), males reported engaging in these sexual behaviors approximately 1 year earlier than females.

A national survey of U.S. adolescents revealed the following information about the timing of sexual activities (Alan Guttmacher Institute, 1998):

- Most young adolescents have not had sexual intercourse: 8 in 10 girls and 7 in 10 boys are virgins at age 15.
- The probability that adolescents will have sexual intercourse increases steadily with age.
- Initial sexual intercourse occurs in the mid to late adolescent years for a majority of teenagers, about 8 years before they marry. More than one-half of 17-year-olds have had sexual intercourse; 1 in 5 individuals have not yet had sexual intercourse by age 19.
- Of adolescent females' first voluntary sexual partners, the majority are younger, the same age, or no more than two years older; 27 percent are three to four years older; and 12 percent are five or more years older.

In sum, by the end of adolescence, the majority of individuals have had sexual intercourse. One study found that African American adolescents have a less restrictive timetable than other ethnic groups, while Asian American adolescents have a more restrictive one (Feldman, Turner, & Araujo, 1999) (see figure 12.8). Male, African American, and inner-city adolescents report being the most sexually active (Feldman, Turner, & Araujo, 1999).

The timing of sexual initiation varies widely by country and gender. In one recent study, the proportion of girls who had intercourse by age 17 ranged from 72 percent in Mali to 47 percent in the United States and 45 percent in Tanzania (Singh & others, 2000). The proportion of boys who had intercourse by age 17 ranged from 76 percent in Jamaica to 64 percent in the United States and 63 percent in Brazil. But in almost every region of the world, sexual activity by 15- to 19-year-olds follows different patterns for males and females (Singh & others, 2000). The vast majority of sexually experienced males in this age group are unmarried, while two-thirds or more of the sexually experienced females at these ages are married.

Many adolescents are not emotionally prepared to handle sexual experiences, especially in early adolescence. In one study, the earlier in adolescence U.S. boys and girls engaged in sexual intercourse, the more likely they were to show adjustment problems (Bingham & Crockett, 1996). Sexual activity before the age of 16 is linked with excessive drinking, drug use, delinquency, and school-related problems (Dryfoos, 1990). In one recent longitudinal study, sexual involvement by girls at an early age was linked with lower self-esteem, greater depression, greater sexual activity, and lower grades in high school (Buhrmester, 2001). Early sexual involvement by boys was related to greater substance abuse and sexual activity. Furthermore,

Sexual timetable (years)	White	African American	Latino	Asian American
Kiss	14.3	13.9	14.5	15.7
French kiss	15.0	14.0	15.3	16.2
Touch breast	15.6	14.5	15.5	16.9
Touch penis	16.1	15.0	16.2	17.8
Touch vagina	16.1	14.6	15.9	17.1
Sexual intercourse	16.9	15.5	16.5	18.0
Oral sex	17.1	16.9	17.1	18.3

FIGURE 12.8 Sexual Timetables of White, African American, Latino, and Asian American Adolescents

What evidence is there that early sexual intercourse in adolescence is a risk factor for developmental problems?

adolescents who engage in sex before age 16 and experience a number of partners are the least effective users of contraception and are at risk for unintended pregnancy and for sexually transmitted infections.

Contraceptive Use The risks of unwanted pregnancy and sexually transmitted infections can be reduced significantly by using contraception and barriers (such as condoms). A sexually active adolescent who does not use contraception has a 90 percent chance of pregnancy within one year (Alan Guttmacher Institute, 1998). Gay and lesbian youth who do not experiment with heterosexual intercourse are spared the risk of pregnancy but they still face the risk of sexually transmitted infections.

The good news is that adolescents are increasing their use of contraceptives (Child Trends, 2000). By 1995, adolescent girls' contraceptive use at first intercourse reached 78 percent, with two-thirds of that figure involving condom use. The method adolescent girls use most frequently is the pill (44 percent), followed by the condom (38 percent) (Alan Guttmacher Institute, 1998). Of course, the pill provides no protection against sexually transmitted infections.

Although adolescent contraceptive use is increasing, many sexually active adolescents still do not use contraceptives, or they use them inconsistently (Ford, Sohn, & Lepkowski, 2001; Niccolai & others, 2003; Paukku & others, 2003). Sexually active younger adolescents are less likely than older adolescents to take contraceptive precautions. Younger adolescents are more likely to use a condom or withdrawal, whereas older adolescents are more likely to use the pill or a diaphragm. In one study, adolescent females reported changing their behavior in the direction of safer sex practices more than did adolescent males (Rimberg & Lewis, 1994).

Sexually Transmitted Infections Earlier, we described sexually transmitted infections. Here we will focus on their appearance in adolescents. Every year more than 3 million American adolescents (about one in four who are sexually experienced) acquire an STI (Alan Guttmacher Institute, 1999). In a single act of unprotected sex with an infected partner, a teenage girl has a 1 percent risk of getting HIV, a 30 percent risk of acquiring genital herpes, and a 50 percent chance of contracting gonorrhea. In some areas, as many as 25 percent of sexually active adolescents have contracted chlamydia. Adolescents have a higher incidence of gonorrhea and of chlamydia than young adults.

A special concern is the high incidence of AIDS in sub-Saharan Africa (World Health Organization, 2000). Adolescent girls in many African countries are vulnerable to being infected with the HIV virus by adult men. Approximately six times as many adolescent girls as boys have AIDS in these countries, while in the United States adolescent males are more likely to have AIDS than their female counterparts (Centers for Disease Control and Prevention, 2001a). In Kenya, 25 percent of 15- to 19-year-old girls are HIV positive compared with 4 percent of the boys.

Adolescence: Teen Pregnancy and Childbearing

Adolescent Pregnancy Adolescents have an increased risk of unintended pregnancy if they have sex before the age of 16, as we noted earlier, and if they have multiple partners. In addition, a recent research review found that living in a dangerous or low-income neighborhood is a risk factor for adolescent pregnancy (Miller, Benson, & Galbraith, 2001). A close relationship with a parent, parental regulation of activities, and parental values against intercourse or unprotected intercourse in adolescence were linked with reduced risk of adolescent pregnancy.

The United States continues to have one of the highest rates of adolescent pregnancy and childbearing in the developed world, despite a considerable decline in the 1990s (Alan Guttmacher Institute, 2002; Centers for Disease Control and

Prevention, 2001b). U.S. adolescent pregnancy rates are nearly twice those of Canada and Great Britain, and at least four times the rates in France and Sweden (see figure 12.9).

U.S. adolescents are no more sexually active than their counterparts in countries such as France and Sweden. Why, then, are U.S. adolescent pregnancy rates so high? Four reasons based on cross-cultural studies are (Alan Guttmacher Institute, 2002):

- *Childbearing regarded as adult activity.* European countries, as well as Canada, have a strong consensus that childbearing belongs in adulthood when young people have completed their education, have become employed, are independent from their parents, and are living in stable relationships. In the United States, this belief is not as strong and varies across groups and areas of the country.
- *Clear messages about sexual behavior.* Although adults in other countries strongly encourage adolescents to wait until they have established themselves before having children, they are usually more accepting of adolescents having sex than are American adults. In France and Sweden, adolescent sexual expression is viewed as normal and positive, but there are widespread expectations that the sex will take place within a committed relationship. Indeed, U.S. adolescent sexual relationships tend to be more sporadic and short-lived than such relationships in European countries. Equally strong is the expectation that adolescents who are having sex will take precautions to protect themselves and their partners from pregnancy and sexually transmitted infections. In keeping with this view, schools in Great Britain, France, Sweden, and most of Canada have sex education programs that provide more comprehensive information about prevention than U.S. schools. In addition, the media are used more often in government-sponsored campaigns for promoting responsible sexual behavior in these countries than in the United States. Also, the United States is the only country with formal policies directing state and federal funds toward educational programs that have as their sole purpose the promotion of abstinence. More than one-third (35 percent) of all local U.S. school districts that have policies on sex education require that abstinence be taught as the only appropriate option for unmarried individuals and that contraception either be presented as ineffective in preventing pregnancy or not be covered at all. Among school districts in the South—where birth rates to adolescent mothers are substantially higher than the national average—that figure rises to 55 percent.
- *Access to family planning services.* In countries with a more accepting attitude toward adolescent sexual relationships, adolescents have easier access to reproductive health services than they do in the United States. For example, in Canada, France, Great Britain, and Sweden, contraceptive services are integrated into other types of primary health care and are available free or at a low cost for adolescents. Generally, adolescents in these countries know where to obtain such services and know that they will receive competent, confidential, nonjudgmental care. In the United States, where attitudes about adolescent sexual relationships are more conflicted, adolescents have a more difficult time obtaining contraceptive services. Many do not have health insurance and cannot get birth control as part of their basic health care.
- *Youth development.* France, Sweden, and to some extent Canada and Great Britain, help adolescents with vocational training and education. They also help adolescents find work and unemployment benefits, if needed. By contrast, the U.S. approach emphasizes individual responsibility for one's welfare. Education, training, and employment are for the most part up to adolescents themselves, with the help of their families.

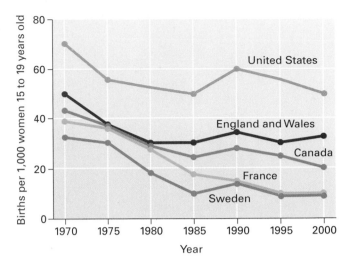

FIGURE 12.9 Cross-Cultural Comparisons of Adolescent Pregnancy Rates

The Alan Guttmacher Institute

Adolescent Pregnancy

Decreasing U.S. Adolescent Pregnancy Rates   Despite the negative comparisons of the United States with many other developed countries, there are encouraging trends in U.S. adolescent pregnancy rates (Ventura & others, 2001). In 2000, births to adolescent girls fell to the lowest rate in the six decades this statistic has been kept (Centers for Disease Control and Prevention, 2001a). The rate of births to adolescent girls has dropped 22 percent since 1991. Reasons for the decline include increased contraceptive use, fear of sexually transmitted infections such as AIDS, health classes, and the economic prosperity of the 1990s, which may have caused many adolescents to delay starting a family so that they could take jobs.

The greatest drop in the U.S. adolescent pregnancy rate in the 1990s was for 15- to 17-year-old African American girls. Latino adolescents are more likely than African American and non-Latino White adolescents to become pregnant (Child Trends, 2001). Births to Latino and African American adolescents are more likely to be repeat births than births to non-Latino White adolescents.

Consequences of Adolescent Pregnancy   The consequences of adolescent pregnancies are cause for concern. Adolescent pregnancy creates health risks for both the offspring and the mother. Infants born to adolescent mothers are more likely to have low birth weights—a prominent factor in infant mortality—as well as neurological problems and childhood illness (Dryfoos, 1990). Adolescent mothers often drop out of school. However, often it is not pregnancy alone that leads to negative consequences for an adolescent mother and her offspring (Leadbetter & Way, 2000). Adolescent mothers are more likely to come from low-income backgrounds (Hoffman, Foster, & Furstenberg, 1993). Many adolescent mothers also were not good students before they became pregnant. One recent study found that adolescent childbearers were more likely to have a history of conduct problems, less educational attainment, and low socioeconomic status than later childbearers (Jaffee, 2002). However, early childbearing increased the difficulties associated with these risks.

Keep in mind that not every adolescent female who bears a child lives a life of poverty and low achievement. Some adolescent mothers do well in school and have positive outcomes (Ahn, 1994; Whitman, Barkowski, & Keogh, 2001). But most adolescent mothers need help in obtaining competent child care and in planning for

These are not adolescent mothers, but rather adolescents who are participating in the Teen Outreach Program (TOP) which engages adolescents in volunteer community service. These adolescents are serving as volunteers in a child-care center for crack babies. Researchers have found that such volunteer experiences can reduce the rate of adolescent pregnancy.

the future. Serious, extensive efforts are also needed to help pregnant adolescents and young mothers enhance their educational and occupational opportunities. In the Applications in Life-Span Development interlude, you can read about social policy and adolescent sexuality.

Applications in Life-Span Development
Adolescent Sexuality and Education

Adolescents should learn about human sexuality and reproduction early, *before* they become sexually active. Programs that promote sexual health should not begin any later than early adolescence. Information about preventing transmission of the AIDS virus should be included in education about sexuality. For example, many young adolescents do not know that the incubation period for AIDS can be 10 or more years and that a pregnant female can transmit HIV to her fetus. Programs should teach adolescents how to avoid or to manage sexually oriented encounters. Schools, families, and the media can contribute to this effort.

Adolescent pregnancy is also an important target of social policy initiatives (Dannhausen-Brun, Shalowitz, & Berry, 1997; Larson, Brown, & Mortimer, 2003). Most adolescent pregnancies are unintended. Any sound educational approach needs to make it very clear that becoming a parent at the right time—after adolescence—is critical to optimal development, for both the parent and the offspring.

The Carnegie Foundation's report *Starting Points: Meeting the Needs of Our Youngest Children* (1994) emphasized the importance of preparing adolescents for responsible parenthood. When individuals make an informed, thoughtful commitment to having children, they are more likely to become good parents. Individuals who are unprepared for the opportunities and responsibilities of parenthood create great risks for their children.

Our nation needs a substantial expansion of efforts to educate adolescents about parenthood. Families are an important source of such information, but so are schools, places of worship, and community organizations. Adolescents should be encouraged to do community service in child-care centers, because this experience will help them understand what is required to raise young children.

Sexuality and Aging

Earlier in our coverage of sexual orientation, we covered a number of basic ideas about heterosexual and homosexual attitudes and behavior. Much of what we said there applies to young adults. Here we will focus on changes in middle adulthood and late adulthood.

Middle Adulthood What kind of changes characterize the sexuality of women and men as they go through middle age? As we discussed in chapter 3, **climacteric** is a term that is used to describe the midlife transition in which fertility declines. Recall that **menopause** is the time in middle age, usually in the late forties or early fifties, when a woman's menstrual periods cease. The average age at which U.S. women have their last period is 52. There is a dramatic decline in the production of estrogen by the ovaries, which in some women produces "hot flashes," nausea, fatigue, rapid heartbeat, or other symptoms (Sommer, 2001). In a large-scale study of Americans in midlife, almost two-thirds of postmenopausal women said they felt relief that their periods had stopped (Brim, 1999). Just over 50 percent of middle-aged women said they did not have hot flashes.

climacteric The midlife transition in which fertility declines.

menopause The complete cessation of a woman's menstruation, which usually occurs in the late forties or early fifties.

Frequency of Sex

Age groups	Not at all	A few times a year	A few times a month	2 to 3 times a week	4 or more times a week
Men					
18 to 24	15	21	24	28	12
25 to 29	7	15	31	36	11
30 to 39	8	15	37	23	6
40 to 49	9	18	40	27	6
50 to 59	11	22	43	20	3
Women					
18 to 24	11	16	32	29	12
25 to 29	5	10	38	37	10
30 to 39	9	16	36	33	6
40 to 49	15	16	44	20	5
50v59	30	22	35	12	2

FIGURE 12.10 The Sex in America Survey: Frequency of Sex at Different Points in Adult Development

www.mhhe.com/santrockldt2

Menopause

Medline: Menopause

Menopause Guide

Medline: Middle-Age Sexuality

Midlife Male Hormone Changes

Although testosterone production begins to decline about 1 percent a year during middle adulthood, and sperm count usually shows a slow decline, men do not lose their fertility in middle age. The drop in testosterone levels, however, can reduce men's sexual drive. Their erections are less full and less frequent, and require more stimulation to achieve them. As much as 75 percent of the erectile dysfunctions in middle-aged men stem from physiological problems. Smoking, diabetes, hypertension, and elevated cholesterol levels are at fault in many erectile problems in middle-aged men (Crooks & Bauer, 2002).

Recently, Viagra became a popular drug used to conquer impotence. Its success rate is in the range of 60 to 80 percent for men. Viagra is not an aphrodisiac; it won't work in the absence of desire. The possible downside of Viagra involves headaches in 1 of 10 men, seeing blue (about 3 percent of users develop temporary vision problems ranging from blurred vision to a blue or green halo effect), and blackouts (Viagra can trigger a sudden drop in blood pressure). Also, scientists do not know the long-term effects of taking the drug, although in short-term trials it appears to be a relatively safe drug.

Although the ability of men and women to function sexually shows little biological decline in middle adulthood, sexual activity usually occurs less frequently than in early adulthood. Career interests, family matters, energy level, and routine may contribute to this decline. In the recent Sex in America survey, frequency of having sex was greatest for individuals aged 25 to 29 years old (47 percent had sex twice a week or more) and dropped off for individuals in their fifties (23 percent of 50- to 59-year-old males said they had sex twice a week or more, while only 14 percent of the females in this age group reported this frequency) (Michael & others, 1994). Figure 12.10 shows the age trends in frequency of sex from the Sex in America survey.

A spouse or live-in partner makes all the difference in whether sexual activity occurs, especially for women over 40 years of age. In one study, 95 percent of women in their forties with partners said that they have been sexually active in the last six months, compared with only 53 percent of those without partners (Brim, 1999). By their fifties, 88 percent of women living with a partner have been sexually active in the last six months, but only 37 percent of those who are neither married nor living with someone say they have had sex in the last six months.

Late Adulthood Aging does induce some changes in human sexual performance, more so in men than in women (Atchley & Barusch, 2004; Carbone & Seftel, 2002). Orgasm becomes less frequent in males, occurring in every second to third act of intercourse rather than every time. More direct stimulation usually is needed to produce an erection. From 65 to 80 years of age, approximately one out of four men have serious problems getting or keeping erections; for those over 80 years of age, the percentage rises to one out of two men (Butler & Lewis, 2002). Even when intercourse is impaired by infirmity, other relationship needs persist, among them closeness, sensuality, and being valued as a man or a woman (Johnson, 1996).

In the absence of two circumstances—actual disease and the belief that old people are or should be asexual—sexuality can be lifelong. This view is contrary to folklore and to the beliefs of many. Fortunately, many older adults have gone on having sex, unabashed by the destructive social images of the dirty old man and the asexual, undesirable old woman (Burgess, 2004).

In one study of adults in their sixties, many were still having sex (Wiley & Bortz, 1996). The women rated kissing as one of the most satisfying sexual activities, while the men rated oral sex as the most satisfying. In another study of more than 1,200 older adults (mean age = 77), almost 30 percent had participated in sexual activity in the past month (Matthias & others, 1997). Two-thirds of the older adults were satisfied with their current level of sexual activity.

At this point, we have discussed many aspects of sexuality, but we have not examined three influential factors: an individual's morality, values, and religion. In chapter 13, we will explore these topics.

Review and Reflect: Learning Goal 5

5 Summarize how sexuality develops through the life span

REVIEW

- What is the nature of child sexuality?
- How do adolescents develop a sexual identity? How does sexual behavior develop? What are some risk factors for sexual problems during adolescence?
- How does sexuality change in middle adulthood? How does sexuality change in late adulthood?

REFLECT

- How would you describe your sexual identity? What contributed to this identity?

Reach Your Learning Goals

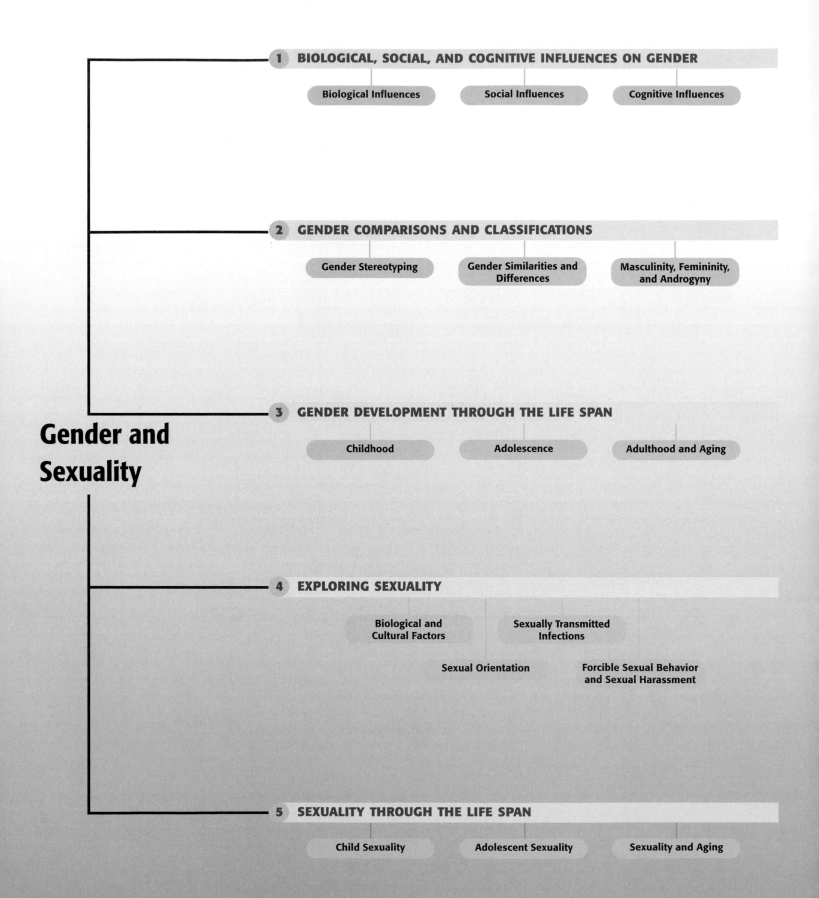

Gender and Sexuality

1 BIOLOGICAL, SOCIAL, AND COGNITIVE INFLUENCES ON GENDER

- Biological Influences
- Social Influences
- Cognitive Influences

2 GENDER COMPARISONS AND CLASSIFICATIONS

- Gender Stereotyping
- Gender Similarities and Differences
- Masculinity, Femininity, and Androgyny

3 GENDER DEVELOPMENT THROUGH THE LIFE SPAN

- Childhood
- Adolescence
- Adulthood and Aging

4 EXPLORING SEXUALITY

- Biological and Cultural Factors
- Sexually Transmitted Infections
- Sexual Orientation
- Forcible Sexual Behavior and Sexual Harassment

5 SEXUALITY THROUGH THE LIFE SPAN

- Child Sexuality
- Adolescent Sexuality
- Sexuality and Aging

Summary

1 Explain biological, social, and cognitive influences on gender

- *Gender* refers to the social and psychological aspects of being female or male; sex designates the biological aspects of being female or male. Key aspects of gender include gender roles and gender typing (the process by which children acquire the thoughts, feelings, and behaviors that are considered appropriate for their gender). Biological influences on gender include heredity, hormones, and evolution. The 23rd pair of chromosomes with two X-shaped chromosomes produces a female; a 23rd pair with an X and a Y chromosome produces a male. Estrogens primarily influence the development of female physical sex characteristics and help regulate the menstrual cycle. Androgens primarily promote the development of male genitals and secondary sex characteristics. To explore biological influences on gender, researchers have studied individuals who are exposed to unusual levels of sex hormones early in development. Evolutionary psychology argues that adaptation during the evolution of humans produced psychological differences between males and females.

- Three theories have been influential in arguing that psychological differences between the genders are due to social factors. Social role theory states that gender differences result from the contrasting roles of women and men. The psychoanalytic theory of gender stems from Freud's view that the preschool child develops a sexual attraction to the opposite-sex parent. The social cognitive theory of gender states that children learn about gender through observation, imitation, reward, and punishment.

- Two cognitive theories stress that individuals cognitively construct their gender world. The cognitive developmental theory of gender states that children's gender typing occurs *after* they think of themselves as boys and girls. Gender schema theory states that gender typing emerges as children gradually develop gender schemas of what is gender-appropriate and gender-inappropriate in their culture.

2 Discuss gender comparisons and classifications

- Gender stereotypes are general impressions and beliefs about males and females. Gender stereotypes are widespread.

- There are a number of physical differences in males and females, small or nonexistent cognitive differences, and some socioemotional differences (males are more physically aggressive and active, but engage in less self-regulation; females show a stronger interest in relationships). Gender in context is an important concept.

- Gender roles can be classified as androgynous, masculine, feminine, or undifferentiated. Androgyny is the presence of a high degree of masculine and feminine characteristics in the same individual. Gender-role transcendence is an alternative.

3 Describe the development of gender through the life span

- Children form many ideas about what the sexes are like from about 1½ to 3 years of age. The amount, timing, and intensity of gender socialization is different for girls and boys. Boys receive earlier and more intense gender socialization than girls do.

- There is continued controversy about whether young adolescents experience gender intensification.

- Many experts argue that it is important for women to retain their relationship strengths but also put more energy into self-development. Tannen stresses that many women prefer rapport talk and many men prefer report talk. Men have been successful at achieving, but the male role involves considerable strain. There is diversity in men's experiences, just as there is in women's. Gutmann proposed the parental imperative. Men seem to become more nurturant and sensitive when they get older, but the evidence about whether women tend to become more assertive and dominant when they are older is mixed.

4 Characterize influences on sexuality, the nature of sexual orientation, and some sexual problems

- The role of hormones in human sexual behavior is difficult to specify. Sexual motivation is also influenced by cultural factors. Sexual scripts in cultures influence sexual behavior. In the 1994 Sex in America survey, Americans' sexual lives were reported to be more conservative than in earlier surveys. It is generally accepted to view sexual orientation along a continuum.

- An individual's sexual preference likely is the result of a combination of genetic, hormonal, cognitive, and environmental factors.

- Sexually transmitted infections (STIs) are contracted primarily through sexual contact. The STI that has received the most attention in recent years is AIDS. Gonorrhea, syphilis, chlamydia, genital herpes, and HPV are among the most common STIs. Some good strategies for protecting against STIs include knowing your and your partner's risk status; obtaining medical exams; having protected, not unprotected, sex; and not having sex with multiple partners.

- Rape is forcible sexual intercourse with a person who does not give consent. Rape usually produces traumatic reactions in its victims. Sexual harassment occurs when one person uses his or her power over another individual in a sexual manner.

5 Summarize how sexuality develops through the life span

- A majority of children engage in sexual play, but their motivation is probably mainly curiosity.

- Mastering sexual feelings and forming a sense of identity involve a number of factors. The progression of sexual behaviors usually is kissing, petting, and sexual intercourse or oral sex. By age 19, four of five U.S. individuals have had sexual intercourse. Early sexual activity, not using contraception, and poverty are risk factors for sexual problems. Adolescents are increasingly using contraceptives, but many still do not use them. More than one in four sexually active adolescents has an STI. The United States has one of the highest adolescent pregnancy rates in the Western world. Adolescent pregnancy can have negative consequences for the mother and the offspring.

- Menopause usually occurs in the late forties or early fifties. Men do not experience an inability to father children in middle age, although their testosterone level drops. In late adulthood, sexual changes do occur, more so for men than women.

Key Terms

gender 402
sex 402
gender role 402
gender typing 402
estrogens 402
androgens 402
social role theory 404
psychoanalytic theory of gender 404

social cognitive theory of gender 405
cognitive developmental theory of gender 405
gender schema theory 405
gender stereotypes 407
androgyny 411
gender-role transcendence 412

gender-intensification hypothesis 413
rapport talk 414
report talk 414
parental imperative 416
sexual scripts 419
traditional religious script 419
romantic script 419

bisexual 421
AIDS 423
climacteric 433
menopause 433

Key People

Alice Eagly 404
Sigmund Freud 404
Lawrence Kohlberg 405
Eleanor Maccoby and Carol Jacklin 409

Janet Shibley Hyde 409
Sandra Bem 411
Joseph Pleck 414
Jean Baker Miller 414

Harriet Lerner 414
Deborah Tannen 414
Ron Levant 415
David Gutmann 416

Robert Michael 419
Alfred Kinsey 419
Laura Brown 422

E-Learning Tools

Connect to **www.mhhe.com/santrockldt2** to research the answers and complete these exercises. In addition, you'll find a number of other resources and valuable study tools for chapter 12, "Gender and Sexuality," on the Student CD-ROM that came with this book.

Taking It to the Net

1. Travis is gay. One of his classmates, who admits that he thinks that homosexuality is a sin, asked, "Why don't you go to therapy and get over your problem?" Travis says he doesn't have a problem. Does Travis need therapy to "get over" being gay?

2. Denise, the only female employee in the parts department of a large automobile dealer, tells her mother that she is disgusted by the pornographic calendars hanging on the office wall and tired of the men addressing her as "honey" and "baby doll." Her mother tells her that she might have a sexual harassment claim against her employer. Does she? And if so, what can Denise do about it?

3. Maureen is 48 years old and approaching menopause. Her gynecologist recommends hormone replacement therapy. Maureen wants to find out more about it before she makes her decision. What drugs are used in HRT? What are the medical risks of HRT?

Self-Assessment

To evaluate yourself on various aspects of gender and sexuality, complete these self-assessments:

- *Am I Androgynous?*
- *My Attitudes Toward Women*
- *How Much Do I Know about STIs?*
- *My Romantic and Sexual Involvement in Adolescence*
- *My Knowledge of Sexual Myths and Realities*

Health and Well-Being, Parenting, and Education

Build your decision-making skills by trying your hand at the health and well-being, parenting, and education "Scenarios."

Moral Development, Values, and Religion

Chapter Outline

Learning Goals

1 Discuss theory and research on moral thought, behavior, and feeling

2 Explain how parents and schools influence moral development

3 Describe the development of prosocial and antisocial behavior

4 Characterize the development of values, religion spirituality, and meaning in life

Just as a person's emotional life and sexual life change with age, a person's moral life and spiritual life also develop through the life span. This chapter examines how moral development proceeds. We will also explore how people go beyond questions of right and wrong to search for values, religion, spirituality, and meaning at different points in their lives.

1 DOMAINS OF MORAL DEVELOPMENT

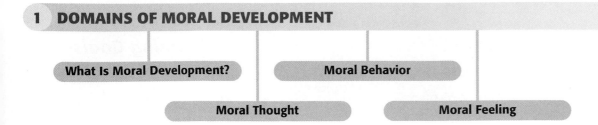

What Is Moral Development?

Moral Behavior

Moral Thought

Moral Feeling

Moral development has been a topic of greatest concern to societies, communities, and families. It is also one of the oldest topics of interest to those who are curious about human nature. Philosophers and theologians have talked about and written about it for many centuries. In the twentieth century, psychologists began theorizing and studying moral development.

What Is Moral Development?

Moral development involves changes in thoughts, feelings, and behaviors regarding standards of right and wrong. Moral development has an *intrapersonal* dimension, which regulates a person's activities when she or he is not engaged in social interaction, and an *interpersonal* dimension, which regulates social interactions and arbitrates conflict (Gibbs, 2003; Walker, 1996; Walker & Pitts, 1998). To understand moral development, we need to consider three basic questions:

First, how do individuals *reason* or *think* about moral decisions?
Second, how do individuals actually *behave* in moral circumstances?
Third, how do individuals *feel* about moral matters?

The next three sections focus on these three domains of moral development—thought, behavior, and feelings. Keep in mind that thoughts, behaviors, and feelings often are interrelated. For example, if the focus is on an individual's behavior, it is still important to evaluate the person's reasoning. Also, emotions can distort moral reasoning.

> "*M*orality involves voluntary actions that, at least potentially, have social or interpersonal implications and are governed by internal cognitive and emotional processes.
>
> —LAWRENCE WALKER
> *Contemporary Psychologist,
> University of British Columbia*

Moral Thought

How do individuals think about what is right and wrong? Are children able to evaluate moral questions in the same way that adults can? Piaget had some thoughts about these questions. So did Lawrence Kohlberg.

moral development Changes in thoughts, feelings, and behaviors regarding standards of right and wrong.

heteronomous morality (Piaget) The first stage of moral development in Piaget's theory, occurring at 4 to 7 years of age. Justice and rules are conceived of as unchangeable properties of the world, removed from the control of people.

Piaget's Theory Interest in how children think about moral issues was stimulated by Piaget (1932), who extensively observed and interviewed children from the ages of 4 through 12. Piaget watched children play marbles to learn how they used and thought about the game's rules. He also asked children about ethical issues—theft, lies, punishment, and justice, for example. Piaget concluded that children go through two distinct stages in how they think about morality.

- From 4 to 7 years of age, children display **heteronomous morality,** the first stage of moral development in Piaget's theory. Children think of justice and rules as unchangeable properties of the world, removed from the control of people.

- From 7 to 10 years of age, children are in a transition, showing some features of the first stage of moral reasoning and some stages of the second stage, autonomous morality.
- From about 10 years age and older, children show **autonomous morality,** the second stage of moral development. They become aware that rules and laws are created by people, and in judging an action, they consider the actor's intentions as well as the consequences.

A heteronomous thinker judges the rightness or goodness of behavior by considering the consequences of the behavior, not the intentions of the actor. For example, the heteronomous thinker says that breaking twelve cups accidentally is worse than breaking one cup intentionally. For the moral autonomist, the actor's intentions assume paramount importance. The heteronomous thinker also believes that rules are unchangeable and are handed down by all-powerful authorities. When Piaget suggested to young children that they use new rules in a game of marbles, they resisted. By contrast, older children—moral autonomists—accept change and recognize that rules are merely convenient conventions, subject to change.

The heteronomous thinker also believes in **immanent justice,** *Piaget's concept that if a rule is broken, punishment will be meted out immediately.* The young child believes that a violation is connected automatically to its punishment. Thus, young children often look around worriedly after committing a transgression, expecting inevitable punishment. Immanent justice also implies that if something unfortunate happens to someone, the person must have transgressed earlier. Older children, who are moral autonomists, recognize that punishment occurs only if someone witnesses the wrongdoing and that, even then, punishment is not inevitable.

Piaget argued that, as children develop, they become more sophisticated in thinking about social matters, especially about the possibilities and conditions of cooperation. Piaget believed that this social understanding comes about through the mutual give-and-take of peer relations. In the peer group, where others have power and status similar to the child's, plans are negotiated and coordinated, and disagreements are reasoned about and eventually settled. Parent-child relations, in which parents have the power and children do not, are less likely to advance moral reasoning, because rules are often handed down in an authoritarian way.

Kohlberg's Theory

Like Piaget, Lawrence Kohlberg (1958, 1976, 1986) stressed that moral reasoning unfolds in stages. The stages, Kohlberg believed, are universal. Children, adolescents, and adults construct their moral thoughts as they pass from one stage to the next.

Kohlberg arrived at his view after 20 years of using a unique interview with children. In the interview, children are presented with a series of stories in which characters face moral dilemmas. Here is the most popular Kohlberg dilemma:

> In Europe a woman was near death from a special kind of cancer. There was one drug that the doctors thought might save her. It was a form of radium that a druggist in the same town had recently discovered. The drug was expensive to make, but the druggist was charging ten times what the drug cost him to make. He paid $200 for the radium and charged $2,000 for a small dose of the drug. The sick woman's husband, Heinz, went to everyone he knew to borrow the money, but he could only get together $1,000, which is half of what it cost. He told the druggist that his wife was dying and asked him to sell it cheaper or let him pay later. But the druggist said, "No, I discovered the drug, and I am going to make money from it." So Heinz got desperate and broke into the man's store to steal the drug for his wife. (Kohlberg, 1969, p. 379)

This story is one of 11 that Kohlberg devised to investigate the nature of moral thought. After reading the story, the interviewee answers a series of questions about the moral dilemma. Should Heinz have stolen the drug? Was stealing it right or wrong? Why? Is it a husband's duty to steal the drug for his wife if he can get

Exploring Moral Development

Lawrence Kohlberg, who created a provocative theory of moral development. In his view, "Moral development consists of a sequence of qualitative changes in the way an individual thinks."

autonomous morality The second stage of moral development in Piaget's theory, displayed by older children (about 10 years of age and older). The child becomes aware that rules and laws are created by people and that, in judging an action, one should consider the actor's intentions as well as the consequences.

immanent justice Piaget's concept that if a rule is broken, punishment will be meted out immediately.

LEVEL 1 Preconventional Level No Internalization	LEVEL 2 Conventional Level Intermediate Internalization	LEVEL 3 Postconventional Level Full Internalization
Stage 1 Heteronomous Morality *Children obey because adults tell them to obey. People base their moral decisions on fear of punishment.*	**Stage 3** Mutual Interpersonal Expectations, Relationships, and Interpersonal Conformity *Individuals value trust, caring, and loyalty to others as a basis for moral judgments.*	**Stage 5** Social Contract or Utility and Individual Rights *Individuals reason that values, rights, and principles undergird or transcend the law.*
Stage 2 Individualism, Purpose, and Exchange *Individuals pursue their own interests but let others do the same. What is right involves equal exchange.*	**Stage 4** Social Systems Morality *Moral judgments are based on understanding of the social order, law, justice, and duty.*	**Stage 6** Universal Ethical Principles *The person has developed moral judgments that are based on universal human rights. When faced with a dilemma between law and conscience, a personal, individualized conscience is followed.*

FIGURE 13.1 Kohlberg's Three Levels and Six Stages of Moral Development

preconventional reasoning The lowest level in Kohlberg's theory of moral development. The individual's moral reasoning is controlled primarily by external rewards and punishment.

heteronomous morality (Kohlberg) Kohlberg's first stage of preconventional reasoning, in which moral thinking is tied to punishment.

individualism, instrumental purpose, and exchange The second Kohlberg stage of moral development. At this stage, individuals pursue their own interests but also let others do the same.

conventional reasoning The second, or intermediate, level in Kohlberg's theory of moral development. At this level, individuals abide by certain standards but they are the standards of others such as parents or the laws of society.

mutual interpersonal expectations, relationships, and interpersonal conformity Kohlberg's third stage of moral development. At this stage, individuals value trust, caring, and loyalty to others as a basis of moral judgments.

social systems morality The fourth stage in Kohlberg's theory of moral development. Moral judgments are based on understanding the social order, law, justice, and duty.

it no other way? Would a good husband steal? Did the druggist have the right to charge that much when there was no law setting a limit on the price? Why or why not?

The Kohlberg Stages From the answers interviewees gave for this and other moral dilemmas, Kohlberg hypothesized three levels of moral thinking, each of which is characterized by two stages (see figure 13.1).

Preconventional reasoning is the lowest level of moral reasoning, said Kohlberg. At this level, good and bad are interpreted in terms of external rewards and punishments.

- *Stage 1.* **Heteronomous morality** is the first stage in preconventional reasoning. At this stage, moral thinking is tied to punishment. For example, children think that they must obey because they fear punishment for disobedience.
- *Stage 2.* **Individualism, instrumental purpose, and exchange** is the second stage of preconventional reasoning. At this stage, individuals reason that it is okay to pursue one's own interests but let others do the same. Thus, they think that what is right involves an equal exchange. People reason that if they are nice to others, others will be nice to them in return.

Conventional reasoning is the second, or intermediate, level in Kohlberg's theory of moral development. At this level, individuals abide by certain standards (internal), but they are the standards of others (external), such as parents or the laws of society.

- *Stage 3.* **Mutual interpersonal expectations, relationships, and interpersonal conformity** is Kohlberg's third stage of moral development. At this stage, individuals value trust, caring, and loyalty to others as a basis of moral judgments. Children and adolescents often adopt their parents' moral standards at this stage, seeking to be thought of by their parents as a "good girl" or a "good boy."
- *Stage 4.* **Social systems morality** is the fourth stage in Kohlberg's theory of moral development. At this stage, moral judgments are based on understanding the social order, law, justice, and duty. For example, adolescents may reason that in order for a community to work effectively, it needs to be protected by laws that are adhered to by its members.

Postconventional reasoning is the highest level in Kohlberg's theory of moral development. At this level, the individual recognizes alternative moral courses, explores the options, and then decides on a personal moral code.

- *Stage 5.* **Social contract or utility and individual rights** is the fifth Kohlberg stage. At this stage, individuals reason that values, rights, and principles undergird or transcend the law. A person evaluates the validity of actual laws, and social systems can be examined in terms of the degree to which they preserve and protect fundamental human rights and values.
- *Stage 6.* **Universal ethical principles** is the sixth and highest stage in Kohlberg's theory of moral development. At this stage, the person has developed a moral standard based on universal human rights. When faced with a conflict between law and conscience, the person will follow conscience, even though the decision might involve personal risk.

To further help you understand the Kohlberg stages, figure 13.2 provides examples of responses to the "Heinz and the druggist" dilemma for each stage.

Kohlberg believed that these levels and stages occur in a sequence and are age related: Before age 9, most children use level 1, preconventional reasoning, when they consider moral choices. By early adolescence, they reason in more conventional ways. Most adolescents reason at stage 3, with some signs of stages 2 and 4.

Kohlberg's Moral Dilemmas

Adolescence: Adolescent Moral Development

Stage	Pro	Con
1	He should steal the drug. It is not really bad to take it. It is not like he did not ask to pay for it first. The drug he would take is only worth $200; he is not really taking a $2,000 drug.	He should not steal the drug; it is a big crime. He did not get permission; he used force and broke and entered. He did a lot of damage stealing a very expensive drug and breaking up the store, too.
2	It is alright to steal the drug, because she needs it and he wants her to live. It is not that he wants to steal, but it is the way he has to use to get the drug to save her.	He should not steal it. The druggist is not wrong or bad; he just wants to make a profit. That is what you are in business for, to make money.
3	He should steal the drug. He is only doing something that is natural for a good husband to do. You cannot blame him for doing something out of love for his wife; you would blame him if he did not love his wife enough to save her.	He should not steal it. If his wife dies, he cannot be blamed. It is not because he is heartless or that he does not love her enough to do everything that he legally can. The druggist is the selfish or heartless one.
4	You should steal it. If you did nothing, you would be letting your wife die. It is your responsibility if she dies. You have to take it with the idea of paying the druggist.	It is a natural thing for Heinz to want to save his wife, but it is also wrong to steal. He still knows he is stealing and taking a valuable drug from the man who made it.
5	The law was not set up for these circumstances. Taking the drug in this situation is not really right, but it is justified to do it.	You cannot completely blame someone for stealing, but extreme circumstances do not really justify taking the law into your own hands. You cannot have everyone stealing whenever they get desperate. The end may be good, but the ends do not justify the means.
6	This is a situation that forces him to choose between stealing and letting his wife die. In a situation where the choice must be made, it is morally right to steal. He has to act in terms of the principle of preserving and respecting life.	Heinz is faced with a decision of whether to consider the other people who need the drug just as badly as his wife. Heinz ought to act not according to his particular feelings toward his wife, but considering the value of all the lives involved.

FIGURE 13.2 Examples of Responses at Each Stage to the "Heinz and the Druggist" Dilemma

postconventional reasoning The highest level in Kohlberg's theory of moral development. At this level, the individual recognizes alternative moral courses, explores the options, and then decides on a personal moral code.

social contract or utility and individual rights The fifth Kohlberg stage. At this stage, individuals reason that values, rights, and principles undergird or transcend the law.

universal ethical principles The sixth and highest stage in Kohlberg's theory of moral development. Individuals develop a moral standard based on universal human rights.

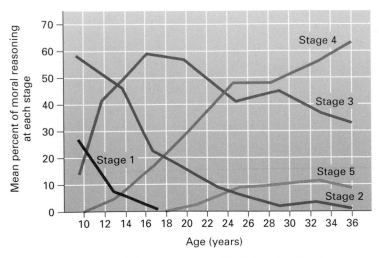

FIGURE 13.3 Age and the Percentage of Individuals at Each Kohlberg Stage

In one longitudinal study of males from 10 to 36 years of age, at age 10 most moral reasoning was at stage 2 (Colby & others, 1983). At 16 to 18 years of age, stage 3 became the most frequent type of moral reasoning, and it was not until the mid-twenties that stage 4 became the most frequent. Stage 5 did not appear until 20 to 22 years of age and it never characterized more than 10 percent of the individuals. In this study, the moral stages appeared somewhat later than Kohlberg envisioned and stage 6 was absent.

By early adulthood, a small number of individuals reason in postconventional ways.

What evidence supports this developmental description? In a 20-year longitudinal investigation, the use of stage 1 and 2 reasoning decreased with age (Colby & others, 1983) (see figure 13.3). Stage 4, which did not appear at all in the moral reasoning of 10-year-olds, was reflected in the moral thinking of 62 percent of the 36-year-olds. Stage 5 did not appear until age 20 to 22 and never characterized more than 10 percent of the individuals.

Thus, the moral stages appeared somewhat later than Kohlberg initially envisioned, and reasoning at the higher stages, especially stage 6, was rare. Recently, stage 6 was removed from the Kohlberg moral judgment scoring manual, but it still is considered to be theoretically important in the Kohlberg scheme of moral development.

Shortly before his death, Kohlberg was contemplating the addition of a seventh stage to his theory, the *cosmic perspective*. He believed that at this level individuals move beyond considerations of justice and see themselves not just as part of humanity but as part of the universe (Kohlberg & Ryncarz, 1990). In this stage, individuals reflect on such questions as: Why be moral? Why be a just person in a world that appears to be unjust? Stage 7 has much in common with the emphasis on self-transcendence in Eastern philosophy and religion. Stage 7 thinkers recognize that in experiencing oneness with the universe everything is connected, which means that one person's actions affect everyone else and the consequences revert back to the doer.

Influences on the Kohlberg Stages What factors influence movement through Kohlberg's stages? Several investigators have attempted to advance individuals' levels of moral development by having a model present arguments that reflect moral thinking one stage above the individuals' established levels. These studies are based on the cognitive developmental concepts of equilibrium and conflict. By presenting moral information slightly beyond the children's cognitive level, a disequilibrium is created that motivates them to restructure their moral thought. The upshot of these studies is that virtually any plus-stage discussion format, for any length of time, seems to promote more advanced moral reasoning (Walker, 1982).

Kohlberg believed that peer interaction is a critical part of the social stimulation that challenges children to change their moral orientation. Whereas adults characteristically impose rules and regulations on children, the give-and-take among peers gives children an opportunity to take the perspective of another person and to generate rules democratically. Kohlberg stressed that perspective-taking opportunities can, in principle, be engendered by encounters with any peers.

Kohlberg's Critics Kohlberg's theory provoked debate, research, and criticism (Carr, 2002; Gibbs, 2003; Lapsley, 1996; Lapsley & Narvaez, 2004; Rest, 1999; Smetana & Turiel, 2003). Key criticisms involve the link between moral thought and moral behavior, assessment of moral reasoning, the role of culture and the family in moral development, and the significance of concern for others.

Moral Thought and Moral Behavior Kohlberg's theory has been criticized for placing too much emphasis on moral thought and not enough emphasis on moral behavior. Moral reasons can sometimes be a shelter for immoral behavior. Bank embezzlers and presidents endorse the loftiest of moral virtues when commenting about moral dilemmas, but their own behavior may be immoral. We don't have to look further than the recent scandals involving Enron and WorldCom executives to find evidence for the presence of lofty moral thoughts and immoral behaviors. No one wants a nation of cheaters and thieves who can reason at the postconventional level. The cheaters and thieves may know what is right yet still do what is wrong. Heinous actions can be cloaked in a mantle of moral virtue.

The mantle of virtue is not necessarily a ruse; it is often taken on sincerely. Social cognitive theorist Albert Bandura (1999, 2002) argues that people usually do not engage in harmful conduct until they have justified the morality of their actions to themselves. Immoral conduct is made personally and socially acceptable by portraying it as serving socially worthy or moral purposes or even as doing God's will. Bandura provides the example of Islamic extremists who mount jihad (holy war) as self-defense against tyrannical, decadent people who they see as seeking to enslave the Islamic world.

Assessment of Moral Reasoning Some developmentalists fault the quality of Kohlberg's research and believe that more attention should be paid to the way moral development is assessed (King & Mayhew, 2002; Thoma, 2002). For example, James Rest (1986, 1999) argued that alternative methods should be used to collect information about moral thinking instead of relying on a single method that requires individuals to reason about hypothetical moral dilemmas. Rest also said that Kohlberg's stories are extremely difficult to score. To help remedy this problem, Rest developed his own measure of moral development, called the Defining Issues Test (DIT).

Unlike Kohlberg's procedure, the DIT attempts to determine which moral issues individuals feel are crucial in a given situation by presenting a series of dilemmas and a list of definitions of the major issues involved. In the dilemma of Heinz and the druggist, individuals might be asked whether a community's laws should be upheld or whether Heinz should be willing to risk being injured or caught as a burglar. They might also be asked to list the most important values that govern human interaction. They are given six stories and asked to rate the importance of each issue involved in deciding what ought to be done. Then they are asked to list what they believe are the four most important issues. Rest argued that this method provides a more valid and reliable way to assess moral thinking than Kohlberg's method (Rest & others, 1999).

Researchers also have found that the hypothetical moral dilemmas posed in Kohlberg's stories do not match the moral dilemmas many children and adults face in their everyday lives (Walker, de Vries, & Trevethan, 1987). Most of Kohlberg's stories focus on the family and authority. However, when one researcher invited adolescents to write stories about their own moral dilemmas, the adolescents generated dilemmas that were broader in scope, focusing on friends, acquaintances, and other issues, as well as family and authority (Yussen, 1977). The adolescents' moral dilemmas also were analyzed in terms of their content. As shown in figure 13.4, the moral issues that concerned adolescents more than any others involved interpersonal relationships.

Some moral development researchers believe that it is valuable to have research participants recall and discuss dilemmas from their own experience (Walker, deVries, & Trevethan, 1987). This strategy may provide information not only about their moral stage but also about how they interpret moral situations. Using Kohlberg's scoring system, one study found no significant differences between the moral reasoning about real-life conflicts displayed by 16- to 19-year-olds and that of 18- to 25-year-olds, but 35- to 48- and 65- to 84-year-olds reasoned at higher levels than the two younger age groups (Walker, deVries, & Trevethan, 1987, 1995).

Culture and Moral Reasoning Yet another criticism of Kohlberg's view is that it is culturally biased (Banks, 1993; Miller, 1995). One review of 45 studies in 27 diverse world cultures provided support for the universality of Kohlberg's first four stages, but there was more cultural diversity at stages 5 and 6 (Snarey, 1987). This review

Story Subject	Grade		
	7	9	12
	Percentage		
Alcohol	2	0	5
Civil rights	0	6	7
Drugs	7	10	5
Interpersonal relations	38	24	35
Physical safety	22	8	3
Sexual relations	2	20	10
Smoking	7	2	0
Stealing	9	2	0
Working	2	2	15
Other	11	26	20

FIGURE 13.4 Actual Moral Dilemmas Generated by Adolescents

concluded that moral reasoning is more culture-specific than Kohlberg envisioned and that Kohlberg's scoring system does not recognize the higher-level moral reasoning of certain cultural groups (Snarey, 1987). Examples of higher-level moral reasoning that would not be scored as such by Kohlberg's system are values related to communal equity and collective happiness in Israel, the unity and sacredness of all life forms in India, and the relation of the individual to the community in New Guinea. These examples of moral reasoning would not be scored at the highest level in Kohlberg's system because they do not emphasize the individual's rights and abstract principles of justice. One study assessed the moral development of 20 adolescent male Buddhist monks in Nepal (Huebner & Garrod, 1993). The issue of justice, a basic theme in Kohlberg's theory, was not of paramount importance in the monk's moral views, and their concerns about the prevention of suffering and the role of compassion are not captured by Kohlberg's theory.

In sum, although Kohlberg's approach does capture much of the moral reasoning voiced in various cultures around the world, his approach misses or misconstrues some important moral concepts in particular cultures (Fang & others, 2002; Walker, 1996). In the Contexts of Life-Span Development interlude, you can read more about cultural variations in moral reasoning.

Contexts of Life-Span Development
Moral Reasoning in the United States and India

Cultural meaning systems vary around the world, and these systems shape children's morality. Consider a comparison of American and Indian Hindu Brahman children (Schweder, Mahapatra, & Miller, 1987). Like people in many other non-Western societies, Indians view moral rules as part of the natural world order. This means that Indians do not distinguish between physical, moral, and social regulation, as Americans do. For example, in India, violations of food taboos and marital restrictions can be just as serious as acts intended to cause harm to others. In India, social rules are seen as inevitable, much like the law of gravity.

According to William Damon (1988), where culturally specific practices take on profound moral and religious significance, as in India, the moral development of children focuses extensively on their adherence to custom and convention. In contrast, Western moral doctrine tends to elevate abstract principles, such as justice and welfare, to a higher moral status than customs or conventions. As in India, socialization practices in many Third World countries actively instill in children a great respect for their culture's traditional codes and practices.

How might Asian Indian children and American children reason differently about moral issues?

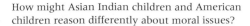

Families and Moral Development Kohlberg believed that family processes are essentially unimportant in children's moral development. As noted earlier, he argued that parent-child relationships usually provide children with little opportunity for give-and-take or perspective taking. Rather, Kohlberg said that such opportunities are more likely to be provided by children's peer relations (Brabeck, 2000).

Did Kohlberg underestimate the contribution of family relationships to moral development? A number of developmentalists emphasize that *inductive discipline*, which uses reasoning and focuses children's attention on the consequences of their actions for others, positively influences moral development (Hoffman, 1970). They also stress that parents' moral values influence children's developing moral thoughts (Gibbs, 1993). Nonetheless, most developmentalists agree with Kohlberg (and Piaget) that peers play an important role in the development of moral reasoning.

Gender and the Care Perspective Carol Gilligan (1982, 1992, 1996; Gilligan & others, 2003) argues that Kohlberg's theory is based on a male norm that puts abstract principles above relationships and concern for others. Kohlberg's theory takes a **justice perspective,** which is a moral perspective that focuses on the rights of the individual; individuals stand alone and independently make moral decisions. In contrast, Gilligan argues for a **care perspective,** which is a moral perspective that views people in terms of their connectedness with others and emphasizes interpersonal communication, relationships with others, and concern for others. According to Gilligan, Kohlberg greatly underplayed the care perspective—perhaps because he was a male, because most of his research was with males rather than females, and because he used male responses as a model for his theory.

In extensive interviews with girls from 6 to 18 years of age, Gilligan and her colleagues found that girls consistently interpret moral dilemmas in terms of human relationships and base these interpretations on listening and watching other people (Gilligan, 1992, 1996). According to Gilligan, girls have the ability to sensitively pick up different rhythms in relationships and often are able to follow the pathways of feelings.

Gilligan believes that girls reach a critical juncture in their development when they reach adolescence. Usually around 11 to 12 years of age, girls become aware that their intense interest in intimacy is not prized by the male-dominated culture, even though society values women as caring and altruistic. Girls are presented with a choice that makes them look either selfish or selfless. Gilligan believes that, as adolescent girls experience this dilemma, they increasingly silence their "distinctive voice."

A recent meta-analysis (a statistical analysis that combines the results of many studies) casts doubt on Gilligan's claim of substantial gender differences in moral judgment (Jaffee & Hyde, 2000). In this study, no substantial overall differences in moral orientation were found between males and females. When differences occurred, they were better explained by the nature of the dilemma than by gender. For example, both males and females tended to use care reasoning when dealing with interpersonal dilemmas; both males and females tended to use justice reasoning to handle societal dilemmas.

Social Conventional Reasoning

Some theorists and researchers argue that it is important to distinguish between moral reasoning and social conventional reasoning, something they believe Kohlberg did not adequately do (Lapsley, 1996; Smetana & Turiel, 2003; Turiel, 1998, 2003). **Social conventional reasoning** focuses on thoughts about social consensus and convention. In contrast, moral reasoning emphasizes ethical issues. Conventional rules are created to control behavioral irregularities and maintain the social system. Conventional rules are arbitrary and subject to individual judgment. For example, using a fork and spoon at meals is a social conventional rule, as is raising one's hand in class before speaking.

In contrast, moral rules are not arbitrary and determined by whim. They also are not created by social consensus. Rather, moral rules are obligatory, widely

Carol Gilligan, who argues that Kohlberg's view does not give adequate attention to relationships.

"**M**any girls seem to fear, most of all, being alone—without friends, family, or relationships.
—CAROL GILLIGAN
Contemporary Psychologist, Harvard University

www.mhhe.com/santrockldt2

Gilligan's Care Perspective
Exploring Girls' Voices

justice perspective A moral perspective that focuses on the rights of the individual; individuals independently make moral decisions.

care perspective The moral perspective of Carol Gilligan; views people in terms of their connectedness with others and emphasizes interpersonal communication, relationships with others, and concern for others.

social conventional reasoning Thoughts about social consensus and convention, as opposed to moral reasoning that stresses ethical issues.

accepted, and somewhat impersonal (Turiel, 1998). Thus, rules pertaining to lying, cheating, stealing, and physically harming another person are moral rules because violation of these rules affronts ethical standards that exist apart from social consensus and convention. In sum, moral judgments involve concepts of justice, whereas social conventional judgments are concepts of social organization.

Moral Behavior

What are the basic processes responsible for moral behavior? What is the nature of self-control and resistance to temptation? How do social cognitive theorists view moral development?

Basic Processes The processes of reinforcement, punishment, and imitation have been invoked to explain how individuals learn certain responses and why their responses differ from one another. When individuals are reinforced for behavior that is consistent with laws and social conventions, they are likely to repeat that behavior. When provided with models who behave morally, individuals are likely to adopt their actions. Finally, when individuals are punished for immoral behaviors, those behaviors can be eliminated, but at the expense of sanctioning punishment by its very use and of causing emotional side effects for the individual.

These general conclusions come with some important qualifiers. The effectiveness of reward and punishment depends on the consistency and timing with which they are administered. The effectiveness of modeling depends on the characteristics of the model and the cognitive skills of the observer.

Behavior is situationally dependent. Thus, individuals do not consistently display moral behavior in different situations. How consistent is moral behavior? In a classic investigation of moral behavior, one of the most extensive ever conducted, Hugh Hartshorne and Mark May (1928–1930) observed the moral responses of 11,000 children who were given the opportunity to lie, cheat, and steal in a variety of circumstances—at home, at school, at social events, and in athletics. A completely honest or a completely dishonest child was difficult to find. Situation-specific behavior was the rule. Children were more likely to cheat when their friends put pressure on them to do so and when the chance of being caught was slim. However, other analyses suggest that although moral behavior is influenced by situational determinants, some children are more likely than others to cheat, lie, and steal (Burton, 1984).

Resistance to Temptation and Self-Control When pressures mount for individuals to cheat, lie, or steal, it is important to ask whether they have developed the ability to resist temptation and to exercise self-control (Bandura, 1991; Mischel, 1987). Walter Mischel (1974) argues that self-control is strongly influenced by cognitive factors. Researchers have shown that children can instruct themselves to be more patient and, in the process, show more self-control. In one investigation, preschool children were asked to perform a very dull task (Mischel & Patterson, 1976). Close by was a very enticing talking mechanical clown that tried to persuade the children to play with it. The children who had been trained to say to themselves, "I'm not going to look at Mr. Clown when Mr. Clown says to look at him" were more likely to control their behavior and continue working on the dull task than were children who were not given the self-instructional strategy.

There has been considerable interest in the effects of punishment on children's ability to resist temptation (Parke, 1972, 1977). For the most part, offering children cognitive rationales (such as reasons why a child should not play with a forbidden toy) enhances most forms of punishment. Cognitive rationales are more effective in getting children to resist temptation over a period of time than punishments that do not use reasoning, such as placing children in their rooms without explaining the consequences for others of the children's deviant behavior.

Social Cognitive Theory The role of cognitive factors in resistance to temptation and self-control illustrates ways in which cognitions mediate the link between environmental experiences and moral behavior ◀▥ **P. 24**. The relationships between these three elements—environment, cognition, and behavior—are highlighted by social cognitive theorists. The **social cognitive theory of morality** emphasizes a distinction between an individual's moral competence (the ability to perform moral behaviors) and moral performance (performing those behaviors in specific situations) (Mischel & Mischel, 1975). *Moral competencies* include what individuals are capable of doing, what they know, their skills, their awareness of moral rules and regulations, and their cognitive ability to construct behaviors. Moral competence is the outgrowth of cognitive-sensory processes. *Moral performance*, or behavior, however, is determined by motivation and the rewards and incentives to act in a specific moral way.

Albert Bandura (1991, 1999, 2002) also believes that moral development is best understood by considering a combination of social and cognitive factors, especially those involving self-control. Bandura (2002) argues that in developing a moral self, individuals adopt standards of right and wrong that serve as guides and deterrents for conduct. In this self-regulatory process, people monitor their conduct and the conditions under which it occurs, judge it in relation to moral standards, and regulate their actions by the consequences they apply to themselves. They do things that provide them satisfaction and a sense of self-worth. They often refrain from violating their moral standards in order to avoid self-condemnation. Thus, self-sanctions keep conduct in line with internal standards. In Bandura's view, morality is rooted in self-regulation rather than abstract reasoning.

Moral Feeling

Think about when you do something you sense is wrong. Does it affect you emotionally? Maybe you get a twinge of guilt. And when you give someone a gift, you might feel joy. What role do emotions play in moral development, and how do these emotions develop?

Psychoanalytic Theory According to Sigmund Freud, guilt and the desire to avoid feeling guilty are the foundation of moral behavior. In Freud's theory, as we discussed in chapter 1, the *superego* is the moral branch of personality ◀▥ **P. 19**. The superego consists of two main components, the ego ideal and conscience. The **ego ideal** rewards the child by conveying a sense of pride and personal value when the child acts according to ideal standards approved by the parents. The **conscience** punishes the child for behaviors disapproved by the parents by making the child feel guilty and worthless.

How do the superego and hence guilt develop? According to Freud, children fear losing their parents' love and being punished for their unacceptable sexual wishes toward the opposite-sex parent. To reduce anxiety, avoid punishment, and maintain parental affection, children identify with the same-sex parent. Through this identification, children *internalize* the parent's standards of right and wrong, which reflect societal prohibitions, and hence develop the superego. Also, the child turns inward the hostility that was previously aimed externally at the same-sex parent. This inwardly directed hostility is then experienced self-punitively (and unconsciously) as guilt. In the psychoanalytic account of moral development, children conform to societal standards to avoid guilt. In this way, self-control replaces parental control.

Freud's claims regarding the formation of the ego ideal and conscience cannot be verified. However, researchers can examine the extent to which children feel guilty when they misbehave. In one recent study, 106 preschool children were observed in laboratory situations in which they were led to believe that they had damaged valuable objects (Kochanska & others, 2002). In these mishaps, the behavioral indicators

social cognitive theory of morality The theory that distinguishes between moral competence—the ability to produce moral behaviors—and moral performance—those behaviors in specific situations.

ego ideal The component of the superego rewards the child by conveying a sense of pride and personal value when the child acts according to ideal standards approved by the parents.

conscience The component of the superego that punishes the child for behaviors disapproved of by parents by making the child feel guilty and worthless.

of guilt that were coded by observers included avoiding gaze (looking away or down), body tension (squirming, backing away, hanging head down, covering face with hands), and distress (looking uncomfortable, crying). Girls expressed more guilt than boys did. Children with a more fearful temperament expressed more guilt. Children of mothers who used power-oriented discipline (such as spanking, slapping, and yelling) displayed less guilt.

As children develop socially and cognitively, the triggers for guilt change as well. In one study of fifth-, eighth-, and eleventh-graders, parents were the individuals most likely to evoke guilt (Williams & Bybee, 1994). With development, guilt evoked by family members was less prevalent, but guilt engendered by girlfriends or boyfriends was more frequent. At the higher grade levels, the percentage of students reporting guilt about aggressive, externalizing behaviors declined, whereas those mentioning guilt over internal thoughts and inconsiderateness increased. Males were more likely to report guilt over externalizing behaviors, while females reported more guilt over violating norms of compassion and trust.

Empathy Positive feelings, such as empathy, contribute to the child's moral development. Feeling **empathy** means reacting to another's feelings with an emotional response that is similar to the other's feelings (Damon, 1988). To empathize is not just to sympathize; it is to put oneself in another's place emotionally.

Although empathy is an emotional state, it has a cognitive component—the ability to discern another's inner psychological states, or what we have previously called *perspective taking* (Eisenberg & others, 1991). Infants have the capacity for some purely empathic responses, but for effective moral action, children must learn to identify a wide range of emotional states in others and to anticipate what kinds of action will improve another person's emotional state.

What are the milestones in children's development of empathy? According to an analysis by child developmentalist William Damon (1988), changes in empathy take place in early infancy, at 1 to 2 years of age, in early childhood, and at 10 to 12 years of age.

Global empathy is the young infant's empathic response in which clear boundaries between the feelings and needs of the self and those of another have not yet been established. For example, one 11-month-old infant fought off her own tears, sucked her thumb, and buried her head in her mother's lap after she had seen another child fall and hurt himself. Not all infants cry every time someone else is hurt, though. Many times, an infant will stare at another's pain with curiosity. Although global empathy is observed in some infants, it does not consistently characterize all infants' behavior.

When they are 1 to 2 years of age, infants may feel genuine concern for the distress of other people, but only when they reach early childhood can they respond appropriately to another person's distress. This ability depends on children's new awareness that people have different reactions to situations. By late childhood, they may begin to feel empathy for the unfortunate. To read further about Damon's description of the developmental changes in empathy from infancy through adolescence, see figure 13.5.

The Contemporary Perspective on the Role of Emotion in Moral Development

We have seen that classical psychoanalytic theory emphasizes the power of unconscious guilt in moral development but that other theorists, such as Damon, emphasize the role of empathy. Today, many child developmentalists believe that both positive feelings—such as empathy, sympathy, admiration, and self-esteem—and negative feelings—such as anger, outrage, shame, and guilt—contribute to children's moral development (Damon, 1988; Eisenberg & Fabes, 1998; Roberts & Strayer, 1996). When strongly experienced, these emotions influence children to act in accord with standards of right and wrong.

empathy Reacting to another's feelings with an emotional response that is similar to the other's feelings.

Age Period	Nature of Empathy
Early infancy	Characterized by global empathy, the young infant's empathic response does not distinguish between feelings and needs of self and others.
1 to 2 years of age	Undifferentiated feelings of discomfort at another's distress grow into more genuine feelings of concern, but infants cannot translate realization of other's unhappy feelings into effective action.
Early childhood	Children become aware that every person's perspective is unique and that someone else may have a different reaction to a situation. This awareness allows the child to respond more appropriately to another person's distress.
10 to 12 years of age	Children develop an emergent orientation of empathy for people who live in unfortunate circumstances—the poor, the handicapped, and the socially outcast. In adolescence, this newfound sensitivity may give a humanitarian flavor to the individual's ideological and political views.

FIGURE 13.5 Damon's Description of Developmental Changes in Empathy

Such emotions as empathy, shame, guilt, and anxiety over other people's violations of standards are present early in development and undergo developmental change throughout childhood and beyond (Damon, 1988). These emotions provide a natural base for children's acquisition of moral values, motivating them to pay close attention to moral events. However, moral emotions do not operate in a vacuum to build a child's moral awareness, and they are not sufficient in themselves to generate moral responses. They do not give the "substance" of moral regulation—the rules, values, and standards of behavior that children need to understand and act on. Moral emotions are inextricably interwoven with the cognitive and social aspects of children's development.

www.mhhe.com/santrockldt2

Developing Empathy in Children and Youth

Review and Reflect: Learning Goal 1

1 **Discuss theory and research on moral thought, behavior, and feeling**

REVIEW

- What is moral development?
- What are Piaget's and Kohlberg's theories of moral development? What are some criticisms of Kohlberg's theory? What is social conventional reasoning?
- What processes are involved in moral behavior? What is the social cognitive theory of moral development?
- How are moral feelings related to moral development?

REFLECT

- What do you think about these circumstances?

  A man who had been sentenced to serve 10 years for selling a small amount of marijuana walked away from a prison camp after serving only six months of his sentence. Twenty-five years later he was caught. He is now in his fifties and is a model citizen. Should he be sent back to prison? Why or why not? At which Kohlberg stage should your response be placed?

  A young woman who had been in a tragic accident is "brain dead" and has been kept on life support systems for four years without ever regaining consciousness. Should the life support systems be removed? Explain your response. At which Kohlberg stage should your response be placed?

2 CONTEXTS OF MORAL DEVELOPMENT

Parenting

Schools

So far, we have examined the three main domains of moral development—thoughts, behaviors, and feelings. We noted that both Piaget and Kohlberg believed that peer relations exert an important influence on moral development. What other contexts play a role in moral development? In particular, what are the roles of parents and schools?

Parenting

Both Piaget and Kohlberg held that parents do not provide unique or essential inputs to children's moral development. Parents, in their view, are responsible for providing role-taking opportunities and cognitive conflict, but peers play the primary role in moral development. Research reveals that both parents and peers contribute to children's moral maturity (Walker, Hennig, & Krettenauer, 2000). A general Socratic style of eliciting the other's opinion and checking for understanding is effective in advancing moral maturity in both parent and peer contexts. Here we will focus more on the role of parental discipline in moral development and then draw some conclusions about parenting and moral development.

Parental Discipline Discipline techniques used by parents can be classified as love withdrawal, power assertion, and induction (Hoffman, 1970, 1988):

- **Love withdrawal** is a discipline technique in which a parent withholds attention or love from the child, as when the parent refuses to talk to the child or states a dislike for the child. For example, the parent might say, "I'm going to leave you if you do that again" or "I don't like you when you do that."
- **Power assertion** is a discipline technique in which a parent attempts to gain control over the child or the child's resources. Examples include spanking, threatening, or removing privileges.
- **Induction** is the discipline technique in which a parent uses reasoning and explains the consequences for others of the child's actions. Examples of induction include, "Don't hit him. He was only trying to help" and "Why are you yelling at her? She didn't mean to trip you."

How are these techniques likely to affect moral development? Moral development theorist and researcher Martin Hoffman (1970) believes that any discipline produces arousal on the child's part. Love withdrawal and power assertion are likely to evoke a very high level of arousal, with love withdrawal generating considerable anxiety and power assertion considerable hostility.

When a parent uses power assertion or love withdrawal, the child may be so aroused that even if the parent explains the consequences of the child's actions for others, the child might not pay attention. Also, power assertion presents parents as weak models of self-control—as individuals who cannot control their feelings. Accordingly, children may imitate this model of poor self-control when they face stressful circumstances.

In contrast to love withdrawal and power assertion, induction is more likely to produce a moderate level of arousal in children, a level that permits them to attend to the cognitive rationale parents offer. Furthermore, induction focuses the child's attention on the action's consequences for others, not on the child's own shortcomings. For these reasons, Hoffman (1988) believes that parents should use induction to encourage children's moral development.

love withdrawal A discipline technique in which a parent withholds attention or love from the child.

power assertion A discipline technique in which a parent attempts to gain control over the child or the child's resources.

induction A discipline technique in which a parent uses reasoning and explains the consequences for others of the child's actions.

In research contrasting parenting techniques, findings vary according to children's developmental level and socioeconomic status, but generally induction is more positively related to moral development than is love withdrawal or power assertion. Induction works better with elementary-school-age children than with preschool children (Brody & Shaffer, 1982), and it works better with middle-socioeconomic-status (middle-SES) than with lower-SES children (Hoffman, 1970). Older children are probably better able to understand the reasons given to them and are better at perspective taking. Some theorists believe that the internalization of society's moral standards is more likely among middle-SES than among lower-SES individuals, because internalization is more rewarding to those in the middle-SES culture (Kohn, 1977).

Parenting Recommendations   Parental discipline does contribute to children's moral development, but other aspects of parenting also play an important role, such as providing opportunities for perspective taking and modeling moral behavior and thinking. Nancy Eisenberg and her colleagues (Eisenberg & Murphy, 1995; Eisenberg & Valiente, 2002) summarized the findings from the research literature on ways in which parenting can influence children's moral development. They concluded that, in general, moral children tend to have parents who

- are warm and supportive rather than punitive—one recent study found that maternal warmth was linked with children's empathy through the mother's positive expression of emotions (Zhou & others, 2002);
- use inductive discipline;
- provide opportunities for the children to learn about others' perspectives and feelings;
- involve children in family decision making and in the process of thinking about moral decisions; and
- model moral behaviors and thinking themselves and provide opportunities for their children to model moral behaviors and thinking.

Parents who show this configuration of behaviors likely foster concern and caring about others in their children, and create a positive parent-child relationship. These parents also provide information about what behaviors are expected of the child and why, and they promote an internal rather than an external sense of morality.

Schools

However parents treat their children at home, they may feel that they have little control over a great deal of their children's moral education. Children spend extensive time away from their parents at school. How do schools influence children's moral development?

The Hidden Curriculum   More than 60 years ago, educator John Dewey (1933) recognized that even when schools do not have specific programs in moral education, they provide moral education through a "hidden curriculum." The **hidden curriculum** is conveyed by the moral atmosphere that is a part of every school. The moral atmosphere is created by school and classroom rules, the moral orientation of teachers and school administrators, and text materials. Teachers serve as models of ethical or unethical behavior. Classroom rules and peer relations at school transmit attitudes about cheating, lying, stealing, and consideration of others. And through its rules and regulations, the school administration infuses the school with a value system.

Character Education   In the 1980s and 1990s, critics of U.S. public schools claimed that the "hidden curriculum" was teaching moral relativism. Through books such as

> *$\mathcal{B}$oth theory and empirical data support the conclusion that parents play an important role in children's moral development.*
>
> —**NANCY EISENBERG**
> *Contemporary Psychologist, Arizona State University*

hidden curriculum The pervasive moral atmosphere that characterizes schools.

Exploring Character Education

The Center for the Fourth and Fifth Rs

Exploring Values Education

Give Five

Volunteer Matching Online

William Bennet's *Book of Virtues* (1993) and William Damon's *Greater Expectations* (1995), these critics promoted **character education,** which teaches students "moral literacy" to prevent them from engaging in immoral behavior. Proponents of character education argue that certain behaviors are wrong and that students should be taught that they are wrong throughout their education. Every school should have an explicit moral code that is clearly communicated to students. Any violations of the code should be met with sanctions (Bennett, 1993). Instruction in moral concepts can take the form of example and definition, class discussions and role-playing, or rewarding students for proper behavior.

Values Clarification

A second approach to providing moral education is **values clarification,** which means helping people to clarify what their lives are for and what is worth working for. Unlike character education, which tells students what their values should be, values clarification encourages students to define their own values and understand the values of others (Williams & others, 2003).

In the following values clarification example, students are asked to select from among ten people the six who will be admitted to a safe shelter because a third world war has broken out (Johnson, 1990):

> You work for a government agency in Washington and your group has to decide which six of the following ten people will be admitted to a small fallout shelter. Your group has only 20 minutes to make the decision. These are your choices:
> * A 30-year-old male bookkeeper
> * The bookkeeper's wife, who is six months pregnant
> * A second-year African American male medical student who is a political activist
> * A 42-year-old male who is a famous historian-author
> * A Hollywood actress who is a singer and dancer
> * A female biochemist
> * A 54-year-old male rabbi
> * A male Olympic athlete who is good in all sports
> * A female college student
> * A policeman with a gun

In this exercise, there are no right or wrong answers. The clarification of values is left to the individual student.

Advocates of values clarification say it is value-free. However, critics argue that its content offends community standards and that the exercises undermine accepted values and fail to stress right behavior.

Cognitive Moral Education

A third approach to moral education, **cognitive moral education,** is based on the belief that students should learn to value such things as democracy and justice as their moral reasoning develops. Kohlberg's theory has served as the foundation for a number of cognitive moral education programs. In a typical program, high school students meet in a semester-long course to discuss a number of moral issues. The instructor acts as a facilitator rather than as a director of the class. The hope is that students will develop more advanced notions of such concepts as cooperation, trust, responsibility, and community.

Toward the end of his career, Kohlberg (1986) recognized that the moral atmosphere of the school is more important than he initially envisioned. For example, in one study, a semester-long moral education class based on Kohlberg's theory was successful in advancing moral thinking in three democratic schools but not in three authoritarian schools (Higgins, Power, & Kohlberg, 1983).

Service Learning

Another approach to moral education—service learning—takes education out into the community (Flanagan, 2002; Levesque & Prosser, 1996; Youniss & others, 2002, 2003). **Service learning** is a form of education that promotes social

---

character education A direct moral education approach that involves teaching students a basic moral literacy to prevent them from engaging in immoral behavior or doing harm to themselves or others.

values clarification Helping people clarify what their lives are for and what is worth working for. Students are encouraged to define their own values and understand others' values.

cognitive moral education Education based on the belief that students should learn to value things like democracy and justice as their moral reasoning develops; Kohlberg's theory has been the basis for many of the cognitive moral education approaches.

service learning A form of education that promotes social responsibility and service to the community.

responsibility and service to the community. In service learning, adolescents might tutor, help the elderly, work in a hospital or a child-care center, or clean up a vacant lot to make a play area.

An important goal of service learning is to help adolescents become less self-centered and more strongly motivated to help others (Pritchard & Whitehead, 2004; Waterman, 1997). One eleventh-grade student worked as a reading tutor for students from low-income backgrounds with poor reading skills. She commented that until she did the tutoring she did not realize how many students had not experienced the same opportunities that she had when she was growing up. Thus, service learning can benefit adolescents as well as the recipients of their service.

Researchers have found that service learning benefits adolescents in a number of ways:

• Their grades improve, they become more motivated, and set more goals (Johnson & others, 1998; Search Institute, 1995; Serow, Ciechalski, & Daye, 1990).
• Their self-esteem improves (Hamburg, 1997; Johnson & others, 1998).
• They have an improved sense of being able to make a difference for others (Search Institute, 1995).
• They become less alienated (Calabrase & Schumer, 1986).
• They increasingly reflect on society's political organization and moral order (Yates, 1995).

Adolescent volunteers tend to share certain characteristics, such as extraversion, a commitment to others, and a high degree of self-understanding (Eisenberg & Morris, 2004). Also, adolescent girls are more likely to volunteer to engage in service learning than adolescent boys (Eisenberg & Morris, 2004).

More than just about anything else, 12-year-old Katie Bell (*at bottom*) wanted a playground in her New Jersey town. She knew that other kids also wanted one, so she put together a group, which generated fundraising ideas for the playground. They presented their ideas to the town council. Her group got more youth involved. They helped raise money by selling candy and sandwiches door-to-door. Katie says, "We learned to work as a community. This will be an important place for people to go and have picnics and make new friends." Katie's advice, "You won't get anywhere if you don't try." *What are some possible effects of volunteering on adolescent development?*

Review and Reflect: Learning Goal 2

2 Explain how parents and schools influence moral development

REVIEW

• How does parental discipline affect moral development? What are some effective parenting strategies for advancing children's moral development?
• What is the hidden curriculum? What are some contemporary approaches to moral education?

REFLECT

• What type of discipline did your parents use with you? What effect do you think this has had on your moral development?

3 PROSOCIAL AND ANTISOCIAL BEHAVIOR

Prosocial Behavior   **Antisocial Behavior**

Service learning encourages positive moral behavior. This behavior is not just moral behavior but behavior that is intended to benefit other people, and psychologists call it *prosocial behavior* (Eisenberg & Morris, 2004). Of course, people have always engaged in antisocial behavior as well. In this section, we will take a closer look at prosocial and antisocial behavior, focusing on how they develop.

Prosocial Behavior

Caring about the welfare and rights of others, feeling concern and empathy for them, and acting in a way that benefits others are all components of prosocial behavior. What motivates this behavior and how does it develop in children?

Altruism and Reciprocity   The purist forms of prosocial behavior are motivated by **altruism,** an unselfish interest in helping another person (Eisenberg & Wang, 2003). Human acts of altruism are plentiful. Think of the hardworking laborer who places $5 in a Salvation Army kettle, the volunteers at homeless shelters, the person who donates a kidney so someone else can live. Altruism is found throughout the human world. It is also taught by every widely practiced religion in the world—Christianity, Judaism, Islam, Hinduism, Buddhism. The circumstances most likely to evoke altruism are empathy for an individual in need or a close relationship between the benefactor and the recipient (Batson, 1989).

One recent study of 423 older adult couples who were followed for five years revealed the benefits of altruism (Brown, in press). At the beginning of the study, the couples were asked about the extent to which they had given or received emotional or practical help in the past year. Five years later, those who said they had helped others were half as likely to have died. One possible reason for this finding is that helping others may reduce the output of stress hormones, which improves cardiovascular health and strengthens the immune system (Kenrick, Neuberg, & Cialdini, 2002).

Some people, though, argue that true altruism does not exist because behind any action one can propose some benefit to the person performing the action so that it is not truly unselfish. Whether this is the case or not, many prosocial behaviors that appear altruistic are in fact motivated by the norm of *reciprocity*, which is the obligation to return a favor with a favor.

The notion of reciprocity pervades human interactions all over the world. Fundraisers try to exploit the norm of reciprocity when they send free calendars or other knickknacks in the mail, hoping that you'll feel obligated to reciprocate with a donation to their cause. People feel guilty when they do not reciprocate, and they may feel angry if someone else does not reciprocate. Reciprocity or altruism may motivate many important prosocial behaviors, including sharing (Piliavin, 2003).

Sharing and Fairness   William Damon (1988) has described a developmental sequence by which sharing develops in children. Most sharing during the first three years of life is done for nonempathic reasons, such as for the fun of the social play ritual or out of imitation. Then, at about 4 years of age, a combination of empathic awareness and adult encouragement produces a sense of obligation on the part of the child to share with others. Most 4-year-olds are not selfless saints, however. Children believe they have an obligation to share but do not necessarily think they should be as generous to others as they are to themselves. Neither do their actions always support their beliefs, especially when they covet an object. What is important developmentally is that the child has developed a belief that sharing is an obligatory part of a social relationship and involves a question of right and wrong. These early ideas about sharing set the stage for giant strides that children make in the years that follow.

By the start of the elementary school years, children begin to express more complicated notions of what is fair. Throughout history varied definitions of fairness have been used as the basis for distributing goods and resolving conflicts. These definitions involve the principles of equality, merit, and benevolence:

- *Equality* means that everyone is treated the same.
- *Merit* means giving extra rewards for hard work, a talented performance, or other laudatory behavior.
- *Benevolence* means giving special consideration to individuals in a disadvantaged condition.

altruism An unselfish interest in helping another person.

Equality is the first of these principles used regularly by elementary school children. It is common to hear 6-year-old children use the word *fair* as synonymous with *equal* or *same*. By the mid to late elementary school years, children also believe that equity means special treatment for those who deserve it—a belief that applies the principles of merit and benevolence.

Missing from the factors that guide children's sharing is one that many adults might expect to be the most influential: the motivation to obey adult authority figures. Surprisingly, a number of studies have shown that adult authority has only a small influence on children's sharing. For example, when Nancy Eisenberg (1982) asked children to explain their own spontaneous acts of sharing, they mainly gave empathic and pragmatic reasons. Not one of the children referred to the demands of adult authority.

Parental advice and prodding certainly foster standards of sharing, but the give-and-take of peer requests and arguments provide the most immediate stimulation of sharing. Parents can set examples that children carry into their interactions and communication with peers, but parents are not present during all of their children's peer exchanges. The day-to-day construction of fairness standards is done by children in collaboration and negotiation with each other. Over the course of many years and thousands of encounters, children's understanding of such notions as equality, merit, benevolence, and compromise deepens. With this understanding comes a greater consistency and generosity in children's sharing (Damon, 1988).

Prosocial behavior occurs more often in adolescence than in childhood, although examples of caring for others and comforting someone in distress occur even during the preschool years (Eisenberg & Fabes, 1998; Eisenberg & Morris, 2004). The Research in Life-Span Development interlude focuses on a research study that examines the consistency and development of prosocial behavior.

Research in Life-Span Development

The Consistency and Development of Prosocial Behavior

Nancy Eisenberg and her colleagues (1999) studied 32 individuals from the time they were 4 to 5 years of age to when they were in their early twenties. They were assessed on eleven occasions through a variety of procedures, including observations, interviews, parents' reports, and friends' reports. Observations of prosocial behavior in preschool focused on behaviors of sharing, helping, and offering comfort. In elementary school, the children were given an opportunity to anonymously donate to a charity for needy children (the experimenter had given them 8 nickels). They were also given an opportunity to help the experimenter pick up dropped paper clips. In the later elementary school years, adolescence, and in their early twenties, the individuals filled out a self-report scale of items that focused on altruism.

The results indicated that the observed prosocial behaviors in preschool (sharing, helping, and offering comfort) were related to the children's prosocial behavior in the elementary school years and in the early twenties. These findings support the view that prosocial behavior is rather stable from the early childhood years into at least the first part of early adulthood.

Gender and Prosocial Behavior   Are there gender differences in prosocial behavior during adolescence? Adolescent females view themselves as more prosocial and empathic and also engage in more prosocial behavior than males (Eisenberg & Morris, 2004). For example, a review of research found that across childhood and adolescence, females engaged in more prosocial behavior (Eisenberg & Fabes, 1998).

The biggest gender difference occurred for kind and considerate behavior with a smaller difference in sharing.

Antisocial Behavior

Most children and adolescents at one time or another act out or do things that are destructive or troublesome for themselves or others. If these behaviors occur often, psychiatrists diagnose them as conduct disorders. If these behaviors result in illegal acts by juveniles, society labels them *delinquents.* Both problems are much more common in males than females.

Conduct Disorder **Conduct disorder** refers to age-inappropriate actions and attitudes that violate family expectations, society's norms, and the personal or property rights of others. Children with conduct problems show a wide range of rule-violating behaviors, from swearing and temper tantrums to severe vandalism, theft, and assault (Cimbora & McIntosh, 2003; Harada & others, 2002). Conduct disorder is much more common among boys than girls.

Consider 4-year-old Andy, who threw his booster seat in his mother's face and thought it was funny. He was acting up even though he had already received one time-out for yelling and screaming at the table. Then he picked up a fork and threw it at his sister, barely missing her eye. Consider also 10-year-old Nick who, when he was only 2 years old, put two unopened cans of cat food on the stove and lit the burner. One of the cans exploded. Over the next 10 years, Nick killed several family pets, set fires, beat up classmates, stole money, and regularly terrorized his younger sister. Both of these children's behaviors suggest that they have a conduct disorder (Mash & Wolfe, 1999).

As part of growing up, most children and youth break the rules from time to time—they fight, skip school, break curfew, steal, and so on. As many as 50 percent of the parents of 4- to 6-year-old children report that their children steal, lie, disobey, or destroy property at least some of the time (Achenbach, 1997). Most of these children show a decrease in antisocial behavior from 4 to 18 years of age, but adolescents who are referred to psychological clinics for therapy still show high rates of antisocial behavior (Achenbach, 1997).

It has been estimated that about 5 percent of children show serious conduct problems, like those of Nick. These children are often described as showing an *externalizing* or *undercontrolled* pattern of behavior. Children who show this pattern often are impulsive, overactive, and aggressive and engage in delinquent actions.

Conduct problems in children are best explained by a confluence of causes, or risk factors, operating over time (Dodge & Pettit, 2003). These include possible genetic inheritance of a difficult temperament, ineffective parenting, and living in a neighborhood where violence is the norm.

Despite considerable efforts to help children with conduct problems, there is a lack of consensus on what works (Mash & Wolfe, 1999). A multisystem treatment is sometimes recommended, which is carried out with all family members, school personnel, juvenile justice staff, and other individuals in the child's life (Farmer & others, 2002; Frick, 2001).

Juvenile Delinquency Closely linked with conduct disorder is **juvenile delinquency,** which refers to a broad range of behaviors, ranging from socially unacceptable behavior such as acting out in school to criminal acts such as burglary. For legal purposes, a distinction is made between index offenses and status offenses:

- *Index offenses* are criminal acts, whether they are committed by juveniles or adults. They include such acts as robbery, aggravated assault, rape, and homicide.
- *Status offenses,* such as running away, truancy, underage drinking, sexual promiscuity, and uncontrollability, are less serious acts. They are illegal only when they are performed by youth under a specified age.

conduct disorder Age-inappropriate actions and attitudes that violate family expectations, society's norms, and the personal or property rights of others.

juvenile delinquency Refers to a great variety of behaviors, ranging from unacceptable behavior to status offenses to criminal acts.

States differ in the age used to classify individuals as juveniles or adults. Approximately three-fourths of the states have established age 18 as a maximum for defining juveniles. Two states use age 19 as the cutoff, seven states use age 17, and four states use age 16. Thus, running away from home at age 17 may be a status offense in some states but not others.

U.S. government statistics reveal that 8 of 10 cases of juvenile delinquency involve males (Snyder & Sickmund, 1999). In the last two decades, however, there has been a greater increase in female delinquency than male delinquency (Snyder & Sickmund, 1999). For both male and female delinquents, rates for property offenses are higher than for other types of offenses (such as toward persons, drug offenses, and public order offenses).

Delinquency rates among African Americans, other minority groups, and low-SES youths are especially high in proportion to the overall population of these groups. However, these groups have less influence and may be judged delinquent more readily than adolescents who are White or have middle socioeconomic status.

Should adolescents who commit a crime be tried as adults (Steinberg & Cauffman, 2001)? In one study, trying adolescent offenders as adults increased rather than reduced their crime rate (Myers, 1999). The study evaluated more than 500 violent youths in Pennsylvania, which has adopted a "get tough" policy. Although these 500 offenders had been given harsher punishment than a comparison group retained in juvenile court, they were *more* likely to be rearrested—and rearrested more quickly—for new offenses once they were returned to the community. This suggests that the short-term gain in safety attained by prosecuting juveniles as adults might increase the number of criminal offenses over the long run.

Antecedents of Delinquency How do children grow up to be delinquents? One portrait of the paths they take comes from the Pittsburgh Youth Study, a longitudinal study of more than 1,500 inner-city boys. Three pathways to delinquency were identified (Loeber & Farrington, 2001; Loeber & others, 1998, 2002; Stouthamer-Loeber & others, 2002):

- *Authority conflict.* Youth on this pathway showed stubbornness prior to age 12, and then moved on to defiance and avoidance of authority.
- *Covert.* Minor covert acts such as lying were followed by property damage and moderately serious delinquency, then serious delinquency.
- *Overt.* Minor aggression was followed by fighting and violence.

The study found that by the eighth grade, many boys had been exhibiting problem behaviors for about six years before they appeared in court (Loeber & others, 2002).

Another recent study examined the developmental trajectories of childhood disruptive behaviors and adolescent delinquency (Broidy & others, 2003). For boys, early problem behavior involving aggression was linked with delinquency in adolescence. However, no connection between early aggression problems and later delinquency was found for girls.

Let's look at several other factors that are related to delinquency. Erik Erikson (1968) believes that adolescents whose development has restricted their access to acceptable social roles or made them feel that they cannot measure up to the demands placed on them may choose a *negative identity*. Adolescents with a negative identity may find support for their delinquent image among peers, reinforcing the negative identity. For Erikson, delinquency is an attempt to establish an identity, although it is a negative identity.

Although delinquency is less exclusively a lower-SES phenomenon than it was in the past, some characteristics of lower-SES culture can promote delinquency. The norms of many low-SES peer groups and gangs are antisocial, or counterproductive, to the goals and norms of society at large. Getting into and staying out of

Juvenile Delinquency
Oregon Social Learning Center
Center for the Prevention of School Violence

A current special concern in low-income areas is escalating gang violence. *What are some of the possible causes of juvenile delinquency?*

trouble are prominent features of life for some adolescents in low-income neighborhoods. Adolescents from low-income backgrounds may sense that they can gain attention and status by performing antisocial actions. Being "tough" and "masculine" are high-status traits for low-SES boys, and these traits are often measured by the adolescent's success in performing and getting away with delinquent acts. Adolescents in a community with a high crime rate observe many models who engage in criminal activities. These communities may be characterized by poverty, unemployment, and feelings of alienation toward higher-SES individuals. Quality schooling, educational funding, and organized neighborhood activities may be lacking in these communities (Flannery & others, 2003; Tolan, Gorman-Smith, & Henry, 2003).

Inadequate family support systems are also associated with delinquency (Feldman & Weinberger, 1994). Parents of delinquents are less skilled in discouraging antisocial behavior and in encouraging skilled behavior than are parents of nondelinquents. Parental monitoring of adolescents is especially important in determining whether an adolescent becomes a delinquent (Patterson, DeBaryshe, & Ramsey, 1989). One recent longitudinal study found that when parents knew less about their adolescents' whereabouts, activities, and peers, the adolescents were more likely to engage in delinquent behavior (Laird & others, 2003). Family discord and inconsistent and inappropriate discipline are also associated with delinquency. An increasing number of studies have found that siblings can have a strong influence on delinquency (Conger & Reuter, 1996). In one recent study, high levels of hostile sibling relationships and older sibling delinquency were linked with younger sibling delinquency in both brother and sister pairs (Slomkowski & others, 2001).

Preventing Delinquency   One program that seeks to prevent juvenile delinquency is called *Fast Track* (Dodge, 2001; The Conduct Problems Prevention Research Group, 2002). Children who showed conduct problems at home and at kindergarten were identified. Then, during the elementary school years, the at-risk children and their families are given support and training in parenting, problem-solving and coping skills, peer relations, classroom atmosphere and curriculum, academic achievement, and home-school relations. Ten project interventionists work with the children, their families, and schools to increase the protective factors and decrease the risk factors in these areas. Thus far, comparisons with high-risk children who did not experience the intervention show that the intervention improved parenting practices and children's problem-solving and coping skills, peer relations, reading achievement, and behavior at home and school during the elementary school years.

Violence and Youth Youth violence is a special concern in the United States today (U.S. Department of Health and Human Services, 2001). In one study, 17 percent of U.S. high school students reported carrying a gun or other weapon the past 30 days (National Center for Health Statistics, 2000). In this same study, a smaller percentage (7 percent) reported bringing a gun or other weapon onto school property.

These factors often are present in at-risk youths and seem to propel them toward violent acts (Walker, 1998):

- Early involvement with drugs and alcohol
- Easy access to weapons, especially handguns
- Association with antisocial, deviant peer groups
- Pervasive exposure to violence in the media

Many at-risk youths also are easily provoked to rage: They react aggressively to real or imagined slights and act upon them, sometimes with tragic consequences. They might misjudge the motives and intentions of others because of hostility and agitation (Coie & Dodge, 1998). Consequently, they frequently engage in hostile confrontations with peers and teachers. It is not unusual to find anger-prone youth threatening bodily harm to others.

A few years ago a rash of murders was committed by adolescents, with the targets of their violence being classmates or school personnel. In April 1999, two students at Columbine High School (in Littleton, Colorado), Eric Harris (age 18) and Dylan Klebold (age 17), shot and killed 12 students and a teacher, and wounded 23 others. In 2001, 15-year-old Charles "Andy" Williams fired shots at Santana High School in Southern California that killed two classmates and injured 13 others. According to students at the school, Andy was a victim of bullying and had joked the previous weekend of his violent plans, but no one took him seriously after he said he was just kidding.

Is there any way to predict whether a youth will turn violent? It's a complex task, but psychologists have pieced together some clues (Cowley, 1998; Harter & Whitesell, 2001). Violent youth are overwhelmingly male, and many are driven by feelings of powerlessness. Violence seems to infuse these youth with a sense of power.

Small-town shooting sprees attract attention, but youth violence is far greater in poverty-infested areas of inner cities. Urban poverty fosters powerlessness and hence rage. Living in poverty is frustrating, and many inner-city neighborhoods provide almost daily opportunities to observe violence. Many urban youth who live in poverty also lack adequate parental involvement and supervision. Many youth give clear indications of their future violence but aren't taken seriously. Boston College psychologist James Garbarino (1999, 2001) says there is a lot of ignoring that goes on in these situations. Parents often don't want to acknowledge what might be a very upsetting reality. Harris and Klebold, for example, were members of the Trenchcoat Mafia clique of Columbine outcasts. The two had even made a video for a class that depicted them walking down the halls and shooting other students.

The Applications in Life-Span Development interlude offers some recommendations for reducing youth violence.

> Youth who kill often have a distorted perspective on what is right and wrong. This distorted perspective can become a self-justifying rationale for violence.
>
> —James Garbarino
> *Contemporary Developmental Psychologist, Cornell University*

Andy Williams, escorted by police after being arrested for killing two classmates and injuring 13 others at Santana High School in 2001. *What factors might contribute to youth murders?*

Applications in Life-Span Development

Reducing Youth Violence

These are some of the Oregon Social Learning Center's recommendations for reducing youth violence (Walker, 1998):

- *Recommit to raising children safely and effectively.* This includes engag- ing in parenting practices that have been shown to produce healthy, well-adjusted children. Such practices include consistent, fair discipline that is not harsh or severely punitive, careful monitoring and supervision, positive family management techniques, involvement in the child's daily life, daily debriefings about the child's experiences, and teaching problem-solving strategies.
- *Make prevention a reality.* Too often lip service is given to prevention strategies without investing in them at the necessary levels to make them effective.
- *Give more support to schools, which are struggling to educate a population that includes many at-risk children.*
- *Forge effective partnerships among families, schools, social service systems, churches, and other agencies to create the socializing experiences that will provide all youth with the opportunity to develop in positive ways.*

Review and Reflect: Learning Goal 3

3 **Describe the development of prosocial and antisocial behavior**

REVIEW

- How is altruism defined? How does prosocial behavior develop?
- What is conduct disorder? What are key factors in the development of juvenile delinquency and youth violence? What are some recommendations for reducing youth violence?

REFLECT

- As the head of a major government agency responsible for reducing delinquency in the United States, what programs would you try to implement?

---

4 VALUES, RELIGION, SPIRITUALITY, AND MEANING IN LIFE

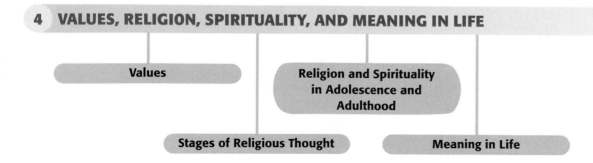

Values

Religion and Spirituality in Adolescence and Adulthood

Stages of Religious Thought

Meaning in Life

---

spirituality Involves a sense of connectedness to a sacred other (God, nature, a higher power).

James Garbarino (1999) has interviewed a number of young killers. He concludes that nobody really knows precisely why a tiny minority of youth kill, but that the cause might be a lack of a spiritual center. In many of the youth killers he interviewed, Garbarino found a spiritual or emotional emptiness in which the youth sought meaning in the dark side of life. In contrast, **spirituality** involves a sense

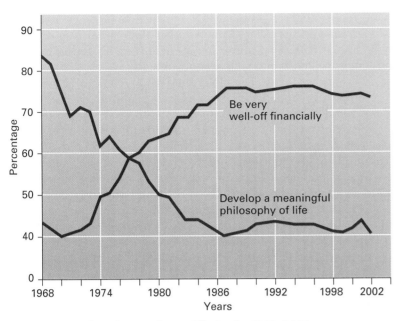

FIGURE 13.6 Changing Freshmen Life Goals, 1968–2002

In the last three decades, a significant change has occurred in freshmen students' life goals. A far greater percentage of today's college freshmen state that a "very important" life goal is to be well-off financially, and far fewer state that developing a meaningful philosophy of life is a "very important" life goal.

of connectedness to a sacred other (God, nature, a higher power). Are spirituality and religion important in your life? How much time have you spent thinking about the meaning of life? What are your values?

Values

Values are beliefs and attitudes about the way things should be. They involve what is important to us. We attach value to all sorts of things: politics, religion, money, sex, education, helping others, family, friends, career, cheating, self-respect, and so on. We carry with us values that influence our thoughts, feelings, and actions.

One way of measuring what people value is to ask them what their goals are. Over the past two decades, traditional-aged college students have shown an increased concern for personal well-being and a decreased concern for the well-being of others, especially for the disadvantaged (Sax & others, 2002). As shown in figure 13.6, today's college freshmen are more strongly motivated to be well-off financially and less motivated to develop a meaningful philosophy of life than were their counterparts of 20 or even 10 years ago. The percentage of students who viewed becoming very well-off financially as a "very important" reason for attending college reached a record high in the 1996 survey—73 percent compared with 50 percent in 1971.

Two aspects of values that increased during the 1960s continue to characterize many of today's youth: self-fulfillment and self-expression (Conger, 1981, 1988). But today, many people seek "self-fulfillment" by paying attention to their physical health and well-being. If self-fulfillment and self-expression are one's only goals, self-destruction, loneliness, or alienation can result. For successful adjustment in life, it is important to seek self-fulfillment *and* have a strong commitment to others. There are some signs that U.S. college students are shifting toward a stronger interest in the welfare of society. For example, the percentage of college freshman who said they would very likely participate in volunteer or community service work in the coming year increased from 17 percent in 1990 to 25 percent in 2002 (Sax & others, 2002).

Research on adolescents in seven countries revealed that family values of compassion and social responsibility were the values that were most consistently linked with adolescent participation in community service, commitment to serving their country, and empathy for disenfranchised groups (Bowes & Flanagan, 2000; Flanagan

values Beliefs and attitudes about the way things should be.

Values of American College Freshmen

& others, 1998). One recent analysis revealed that middle school civics textbooks are far more likely to discuss an individual's rights rather than social responsibility (Simmons & Avery, in press). Thus, adolescents may benefit from a stronger emphasis on social responsibility in both family and school contexts.

Other research on values has found that adolescents who are involved in groups that connect them to others in school, their communities, or faith-based institutions report higher levels of social trust, altruism, commitments to the common good of people, and endorsements of the rights of immigrants for full inclusion in society (Flanagan & Faison, 2001). In this research, adolescents who were uninvolved in such groups were more likely to endorse self-interest and materialistic values.

In one recent study, 459 students from 20 high school classrooms participated in focus group discussions about the most important values they perceived that youth could possess (Steen, Kachorek, & Peterson, 2003). The students especially endorsed leadership, practical intelligence, wisdom, love of learning, spirituality, and the capacity to love and be loved. The students believed that these traits are mainly learned rather than innate and that these strengths develop through real-world experiences rather than through formal instruction.

Stages of Religious Thought

Can children understand religious ideas? How does thinking about religion develop from childhood through adulthood?

Applying Piaget's Stages to Religious Thought   The cognitive developmental theory of Jean Piaget (1952) provides a theoretical backdrop for understanding religious development in children and adolescents ◀‖‖ P. 202. For example, in one study children were asked about their understanding of certain religious pictures and Bible stories (Goldman, 1964). The children's responses fell into three stages closely related to Piaget's theory.

In the first stage (up to 7 or 8 years of age)—*preoperational intuitive religious thought*—children's religious thoughts were unsystematic and fragmented. The children often either did not fully understand the stories or did not consider all of the evidence. For example, asked "Why was Moses afraid to look at God?" (Exodus 3:6) one child answered, "Because God had a funny face!"

In the second stage (from 7 or 8 to 13 or 14 years of age)—*concrete operational religious thought*—children focused on particular details of pictures and stories. For example, in response to the question about why Moses was afraid to look at God, one child said, "Because it was a ball of fire. He thought he might burn him." Another child replied, "It was a bright light and to look at it might blind him."

In the third stage (age 14 through the remainder of adolescence)—*formal operational religious thought*—adolescents revealed a more abstract religious understanding. For example, one adolescent said that Moses was afraid to look at God because "God is holy and the world is sinful." Another youth responded, "The awesomeness and almightiness of God would make Moses feel like a worm in comparison."

Other researchers have found similar developmental changes in children and adolescents. For example, in one study, at about 17 or 18 years of age adolescents increasingly commented about freedom, meaning, and hope—abstract concepts—when making religious judgments (Oser & Gmnder, 1991).

Fowler's Developmental Theory   Piaget's stages are part of the basis for a more comprehensive theory of religious development proposed by James Fowler (1981, 1996). Fowler focused on the motivation to discover meaning in life, either within or outside of organized religion, and drew on the theories of Erikson, Piaget, and Kohlberg (Torney-Purta, 1993) (see figure 13.7):

Stage 1. Intuitive-projective faith (early childhood). After infants learn to trust their caregiver (Erikson's formulation), they invent their own intuitive images of good

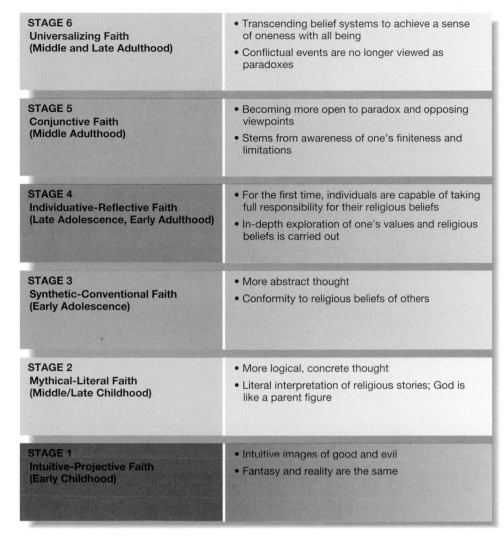

STAGE 6 **Universalizing Faith** **(Middle and Late Adulthood)**	• Transcending belief systems to achieve a sense of oneness with all being • Conflictual events are no longer viewed as paradoxes
STAGE 5 **Conjunctive Faith** **(Middle Adulthood)**	• Becoming more open to paradox and opposing viewpoints • Stems from awareness of one's finiteness and limitations
STAGE 4 **Individuative-Reflective Faith** **(Late Adolescence, Early Adulthood)**	• For the first time, individuals are capable of taking full responsibility for their religious beliefs • In-depth exploration of one's values and religious beliefs is carried out
STAGE 3 **Synthetic-Conventional Faith** **(Early Adolescence)**	• More abstract thought • Conformity to religious beliefs of others
STAGE 2 **Mythical-Literal Faith** **(Middle/Late Childhood)**	• More logical, concrete thought • Literal interpretation of religious stories; God is like a parent figure
STAGE 1 **Intuitive-Projective Faith** **(Early Childhood)**	• Intuitive images of good and evil • Fantasy and reality are the same

FIGURE 13.7 Fowler's Stage Theory of Religious Development

and evil. As children move into Piaget's preoperational stage, their cognitive worlds open up a variety of new possibilities. Fantasy and reality are taken as the same thing. Right and wrong are seen in terms of consequences to the self. Children readily believe in angels and spirits.

Stage 2. Mythical-literal faith (middle and late childhood). As children move into Piaget's concrete operational stage, they begin to reason in a more logical but not abstract way. They see the world as orderly. Grade-school children interpret religious stories literally, and they perceive God as being much like a parent figure who rewards the good and punishes the bad. What is right is often perceived as fair exchange.

Stage 3. Synthetic-conventional faith (transition between childhood and adolescence, early adolescence). As adolescents develop formal operational thought, they begin to integrate what they have learned about religion into a coherent belief system. According to Fowler, although the synthetic-conventional faith stage is more abstract than the previous stages, young adolescents still mainly conform to the religious beliefs of others and have not yet analyzed alternative religious ideologies. Questions of right and wrong are evaluated in terms of the effect on relationships or in terms of what others might say. The faith of adolescents often involves a personal relationship with God. God is thought of as "always there for me." Fowler believes that most adults never move on to higher stages of religious development.

Stage 4. Individuative-reflective faith (transition between adolescence and adulthood, early adulthood). At this stage, individuals for the first time take full responsibility for their religious beliefs. Young adults start to realize that they can choose the course of their lives and that they must expend effort to follow a particular life course. Individuals come face-to-face with such decisions as these: "Should I consider myself first, or should I consider the welfare of others first?" "Are the religious doctrines that were taught to me when I was growing up absolute, or are they relative?" Fowler believes that both formal operational thought and the intellectual challenges to an individual's values and religious ideologies that often develop in college are essential to developing individuative-reflective faith.

Stage 5. Conjunctive faith (middle adulthood). This stage involves being open to paradox and opposing viewpoints. This openness stems from people's awareness of their finiteness and limitations. One woman Fowler placed at this stage said: "Whether you call it God or Jesus or Cosmic Flow or Reality or Love, it doesn't matter what you call it, it is there" (Fowler, 1981, p. 192). Fowler believes that only a small number of adults reach this stage of conjunctive faith.

Stage 6. Universalizing faith (middle adulthood or late adulthood). Fowler's highest stage of religious development involves transcending specific belief systems to achieve a sense of oneness with all being and a commitment to breaking down the barriers that divide people. Conflictual events are no longer seen as paradoxes. Fowler says that very, very few people achieve this elusive, highest stage of religious development.

Although Fowler's theory has received considerable attention, little research has tested the theory (Day & Youngman, 2003). There is increasing research, however, regarding the role that religion plays in the lives of adolescents and adults, and we will examine that research in the next section.

Religion and Spirituality in Adolescence and Adulthood

How important are religious issues to adolescents? What role does religion play in the lives of adults?

Adolescence Religious issues are important to adolescents (Paloutzian & Santrock, 2000). In one survey, 95 percent of 13- to 18-year-olds said that they believe in God or a universal spirit (Gallup & Bezilla, 1992). Almost three-fourths of adolescents said that they pray, and about one-half indicated that they had attended religious services within the past week. Almost half of the youth said that it is very important for a young person to learn religious faith.

The Positive Role of Religion in Adolescents' Lives Researchers have found that various aspects of religion are linked with positive outcomes for adolescents. In one recent study, adolescents who viewed religion as a meaningful part of their life and a way to cope with problems were half as likely to use drugs than adolescents who did not view religion as important (Wills & Sandy, 2003). In another recent study of 9,700 adolescents, going to church was linked with better grades for students from low-income backgrounds (Regnerus, 2001). Churchgoing may benefit students because religious communities encourage socially acceptable behavior, which includes doing well in school. Churchgoing also may benefit students because churches often offer positive role models for students.

Many religious adolescents also internalize their religion's message about caring and concern for people (Ream & Savin-Williams, 2003). For example, in one survey, religious youth were almost three times as likely to engage in community service as nonreligious youth (Youniss, McLellan, & Yates, 1999).

Religion is often an asset to the communities in which adolescents live (Ream & Savin-Williams, 2003). In some instances, religious institutions are the only organization that initiates efforts to work with adolescents in inner cities. For inner-city

Many children and adolescents show an interest in religion, and many religious institutions created by adults (such as this Muslim school in Malaysia) are designed to introduce them to religious beliefs and ensure that they will carry on a religious tradition.

youth, as well as other youth, religion offers possible answers to questions about meaning, purpose, and direction in life (Trulear, 2000).

Parenting and Religion Societies use many methods—such as Sunday schools, parochial education, and parental teaching—to ensure that people will carry on a religious tradition. Does this religious socialization work? In many cases it does (Paloutzian, 2000).

In general, adults tend to adopt the religious teachings of their upbringing. For instance, individuals who are Catholics by the time they are 25 years of age, and who were raised as Catholics, likely will continue to be Catholics throughout their adult years. If a religious change or reawakening occurs, it is most likely to take place during adolescence. However, it is important to consider the quality of the parent-adolescent relationship (Ream & Savin-Williams, 2003). Adolescents who have a positive relationship with their parents or are securely attached to them are likely to adopt the religious orientation of their parents (Dudley, 1999). Adolescents who have a negative relationship with their parents or are insecurely attached to them may disaffiliate from religion or seek religion-based attachments that are missing in their family system (Streib, 1999).

Religiousness and Sexuality in Adolescence One area of religion's influence on adolescent development involves sexual activity. Although variability and change in church teachings make it difficult to characterize religious doctrines simply, most churches discourage premarital sex. Thus, the degree of adolescent participation in religious organizations may be more important than religious affiliation as a determinant of premarital sexual attitudes and behavior. Adolescents who attend religious services frequently might hear messages about abstaining from sex. Involvement of adolescents in religious organizations also enhances the probability that they will become friends with adolescents who have restrictive attitudes toward premarital sex.

One recent national study of 3,356 adolescents (mean age = 16 years) focused on four aspects of religiousness (Miller & Gur, 2002):

1. *Attendance at religious events* ("In the past 12 months, how often did you attend religious services?" and "Many churches, synagogues, and other places of worship

*R*eligion enlightens, terrifies, subdues; it gives faith, inflicts remorse, inspires resolutions, and inflames devotion.

—HENRY NEWMAN
English Churchman and Writer, 19th Century

have special activities for teenagers, such as youth groups, Bible classes, or choir. In the past 12 months, how often did you attend such youth activities?")

2. *Personal conservatism* ("Do you agree or disagree that the sacred scriptures of your religion are the word of God and are completely without any mistakes?" and "Do you think of yourself as a born-again Christian?")

3. *Personal devotion* ("How often do you pray?" and "How important is religion to you?")

4. *Religious denomination*

The results indicated that personal devotion was linked with fewer sexual partners outside a romantic relationship. Frequent attendance at religious events was related to a greater perception of risk of contracting HIV or pregnancy from unprotected intercourse and a responsible and planned use of birth control. Personal conservativism was linked with unprotected sex. In another study, links between religion and sexuality also occurred (Fehring & others, 1998). In college students, guilt, prayer, organized religious activity, and religious well-being were associated with fewer sexual encounters.

Adulthood and Aging What role do religion and spirituality play in the lives of adults? Is there a point in adult development at which understanding of the meaning of life increases? What is religion like in the lives of older adults?

Religion and Spirituality in Adulthood Religion is an important aspect of people's lives around the world—98 percent of respondents in India, 88 percent in Italy, 72 percent in France, and 63 percent in Scandanavia say that they believe in God (Gallup, 1987). In the MacArthur Study of Midlife Development, more than 70 percent of U.S. individuals surveyed said they are religious and consider spirituality a major part of their lives (Brim, 1999). However, about half said they attend religious services less than once a month or never. In another study, about three-fourths of Americans said that they pray (*Religion in America,* 1993).

Females have consistently shown a stronger interest in religion than males have (Bijur & others, 1993). Compared with men, they participate more in both organized and personal forms of religion, are more likely to believe in a higher power or presence, and are more likely to feel that religion is an important dimension of their lives.

A series of recent studies have found that Americans are becoming less committed to particular religious denominations (such as Baptist or Catholic). They are more tolerant of other faiths and more focused on their own spiritual journeys (Paloutzian, 2000). This change may be partly generational, a consequence of baby boomers' emphasis on experimentation and independent thinking. Americans also report declining faith in mainstream religious institutions, in religious leaders, and in the spiritual and moral stature of the nation (*Religion in America,* 1993; Sollod, 2000).

In thinking about religion and adult development, it is important to consider individual differences. Religion is a powerful influence in some adults' lives, whereas it plays little or no role in others' lives (Myers, 2000). Further, the influence of religion in people's lives may change as they develop. In John Clausen's (1993) longitudinal investigation, some individuals who had been strongly religious in their early adult years became less so in middle age; others became more religious in middle age.

Are people who have a meaningful faith happier than those who do not? Reviews of the happiness literature suggest that happy people do tend to have a meaningful religious faith (Diener, Lucas, & Oishi, 2002). Remember, though, that knowing that two factors correlate does not mean that one causes the other. A number of researchers have found that religiously active individuals report greater happiness than do those who are religiously inactive (Diener, Lucas, & Oishi, 2002). However, we don't know whether this connection means that faith enhances happiness or that happiness induces faith.

Religion in Older Adults In a recent study of individuals from their early thirties through their late sixties/early seventies, a significant increase in spirituality occurred between late middle adulthood (mid-fifties/early sixties) and late adulthood (late sixties/mid-seventies) (Wink & Dillon, 2002) (see figure 13.8). The spirituality of women increased more than that of men. In this study, spirituality in late adulthood was linked with religiosity in early adulthood (thirties). This supports the idea that early religious involvement predisposes individuals to further spiritual development.

Individuals over 65 years of age are more likely than younger people to say that religious faith is the most significant influence in their lives, that they try to put religious faith into practice, and that they attend religious services (Gallup & Bezilla, 1992). In one analysis, most older African Americans and older Whites attended religious services several times a month, said religion was important in their lives, read religious materials, listened to religious programming, and prayed frequently (Levin, Taylor, & Chatters, 1994). Also, in this analysis, older women had a stronger interest in religion than did older men.

Is religion related to a sense of well-being and life satisfaction in old age? In one study of 836 older persons, it was. Religious practices—such as prayer and scripture reading—and religious feelings were associated with a sense of well-being, especially for women and individuals over 75 years of age (Koenig, Smiley, & Gonzales, 1988). In one study, older adults' self-esteem was highest when they had a strong religious commitment and lowest when they had little religious commitment (Krause, 1995). In another study, a commitment to religion was linked with health and well-being in young, middle-aged, and older African American adults (Levin, Chatters, & Taylor, 1995). In another study, older adults who derived a sense of meaning in life from religion had higher levels of life-satisfaction, self-esteem, and optimism (Krause, 2003). African American older adults were more likely to find meaning in religion than non-Latino White older adults.

Religion can meet some important psychological needs in older adults, helping them to face impending death, to find and maintain a sense of meaningfulness in life, and to accept the inevitable losses of old age (Fry, 1999 Koenig & Larson, 1998). In one recent study, although church attendance decreased among older adults during their last year of life, their feelings of religiousness and the strength or comfort they received from religion were either stable or increased (Idler, Kasl, & Hays, 2001). Socially, the religious community can serve many functions for older adults, such as social activities, social support, and the opportunity to assume teaching and leadership roles. Older adults can become deacons, elders, or religion teachers, assuming leadership roles they might have been unable to take on before they retired (Cox & Hammonds, 1988). In many societies around the world, older adults are the spiritual leaders in their churches and communities.

Might praying or meditating actually be associated with longevity? In one recent study, they were (McCullough & others, 2000). Nearly 4,000 women and men 65 years and older, mostly Christians, were asked about their health and whether they prayed or meditated. Those who said they rarely or never prayed had about a 50 percent greater risk of dying during the six-year study compared with those who prayed or meditated at least once a month. In this study, the researchers controlled for many factors known to place people at risk for dying, such as smoking, drinking, and social isolation. It is possible that prayer and meditation lower the incidence of death in older adults because they reduce stress and dampen the body's production of stress hormones such as adrenaline. A decrease in stress hormones is linked with a number of health benefits, including a stronger immune system (McCullough & others, 2000).

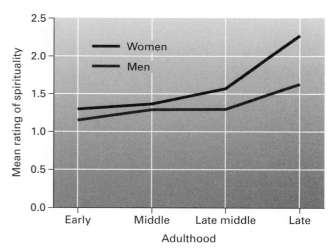

FIGURE 13.8 Level of Spirituality in Four Adult Age Periods

In one recent study, spirituality increased between late middle adulthood (mid-fifties/early sixties) and late adulthood (late sixties/mid-seventies)(Wink & Dillon, 2002). Spirituality, defined as the importance of a personal quest for a sense of connectedness with a sacred other (God, nature, a higher power), was assessed through interviews with the adults and rated on a 5-point scale with

5 = central role in daily life

4 = have personal spiritual experiences and consistently incorporate spiritual practices in their daily lives

3 = have personal spiritual experiences and occasionally engage in spiritual practices

2 = some interest in spiritual matters or some spiritual experiences but do not engage in spiritual practices

1 = denial of any interest in spiritual matters

Exploring the Psychology of Religion

Psychology of Religion Journals

During late adulthood, many individuals increasingly engage in prayer. *What are some other aspects of religion in the lives of older adults?*

Meaning in Life

Austrian psychiatrist Victor Frankl's mother, father, brother, and wife died in the concentration camps and gas chambers in Auschwitz, Poland. Frankl survived the concentration camp and went on to write about meaning in life. In his book *Man's Search for Meaning,* Frankl (1984) emphasized each person's uniqueness and the finiteness of life. He believes that examining the finiteness of our existence and the certainty of death adds meaning to life. If life were not finite, says Frankl, we could spend our life doing just about whatever we please because time would continue forever.

Frankl said that the three most distinct human qualities are spirituality, freedom, and responsibility. Spirituality, in his view, does not have a religious underpinning. Rather, it refers to a human being's uniqueness—to spirit, philosophy, and mind. Frankl proposed that people need to ask themselves such questions as why they exist, what they want from life, and what the meaning of their life is.

It is in middle adulthood that individuals begin to be faced with death more often, especially the deaths of parents and other older relatives. Also, faced with less time in their own lives, many individuals in middle age begin to ask the questions that Frankl proposed.

Roy Baumeister (1991; Baumeister & Vohs, 2002) argues that the quest for a meaningful life can be understood in terms of four main needs for meaning:

- *Need for purpose.* Present events draw meaning from their connection with future events. Purposes can be divided into (1) goals and (2) fulfillments. Life can be oriented toward a future anticipated state, such as living happily ever after or being in love.
- *Need for values.* Frankl (1984) emphasized value as the main form of meaning that people need. Values can lend a sense of goodness to life and justify certain courses of action.
- *Need for a sense of efficacy.* This involves the belief that one can make a difference. In a life with purposes and values but no efficacy, a person knows what is desirable but cannot do anything with that knowledge. With a sense of efficacy, people believe that they can control their environment, which has physical and mental health benefits (Bandura, 2001).

• *Need for self-worth.* Most individuals want to be good, worthy persons. Self-worth can be pursued individually, such as finding out that one is very good at doing something, or collectively, as when people find self-esteem from belonging to a group or category of people.

Review and Reflect: Learning Goal 4

4 Characterize the development of values, religion, spirituality, and meaning in life

REVIEW

• What are values? How are the values of U.S. college students changing?
• What are two stage theories of religious development?
• What are some developmental changes in religion and spirituality?
• How do people seek meaning in life?

REFLECT

• What are the most important aspects of meaning in life? Might the components of meaning in life vary depending on how old someone is? Explain.

Reach Your Learning Goals

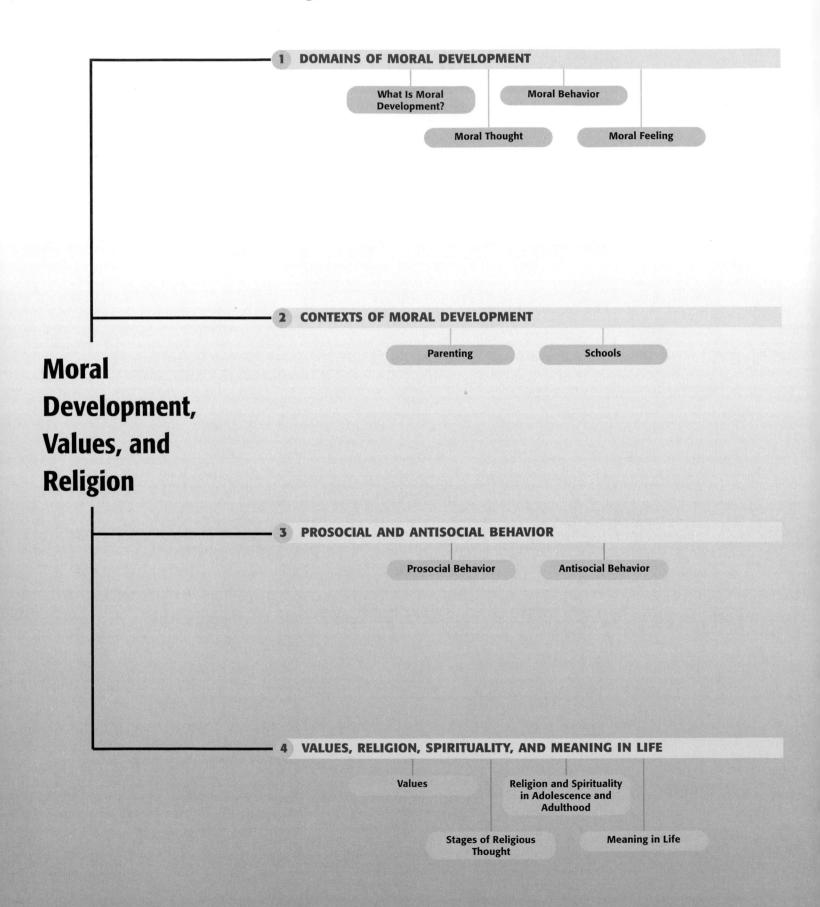

Moral Development, Values, and Religion

1 DOMAINS OF MORAL DEVELOPMENT

What Is Moral Development?

Moral Behavior

Moral Thought

Moral Feeling

2 CONTEXTS OF MORAL DEVELOPMENT

Parenting

Schools

3 PROSOCIAL AND ANTISOCIAL BEHAVIOR

Prosocial Behavior

Antisocial Behavior

4 VALUES, RELIGION, SPIRITUALITY, AND MEANING IN LIFE

Values

Religion and Spirituality in Adolescence and Adulthood

Stages of Religious Thought

Meaning in Life

Summary

1 Discuss theory and research on moral thought, behavior, and feeling

- Moral development involves changes in thoughts, feelings, and behaviors regarding right and wrong. Moral development consists of intrapersonal and interpersonal dimensions.

- Piaget distinguished between the heteronomous morality of younger children and the autonomous morality of older children. Kohlberg developed a provocative theory of moral reasoning. He argued that development of moral reasoning consists of three levels—preconventional, conventional, and postconventional—and six stages (two at each level). Kohlberg believed that these stages were age-related. Influences on the Kohlberg stages include cognitive development, imitation and cognitive conflict, peer relations, and perspective taking. Criticisms of Kohlberg's theory have been made, especially by Gilligan, who advocates a stronger care perspective. Other criticisms focus on the inadequacy of moral reasoning to predict moral behavior, the assessment of moral reasoning, and culture and family influences. A distinction can be made between moral reasoning and social conventional reasoning, which concerns social consensus and conventions.

- The processes of reinforcement, punishment, and imitation have been used to explain the acquisition of moral behavior, but they provide only a partial explanation. Situational variability is stressed by behaviorists. Cognitions can play a role in resistance to temptation and self-control. Social cognitive theory emphasizes a distinction between moral competence and moral performance.

- In Freud's theory, the superego is the moral branch of personality. The superego consists of the ego ideal and the conscience. According to Freud, guilt is the foundation of children's moral behavior. Empathy is an important aspect of moral feelings and it changes developmentally. In the contemporary perspective, both positive and negative feelings contribute to moral development.

2 Explain how parents and schools influence moral development

- Love withdrawal, power assertion, and induction are discipline techniques. Induction is most likely to be linked with positive moral development, at least in middle-SES children. Moral development can be advanced by these parenting strategies: being warm and supportive rather than punitive; using inductive discipline; providing opportunities to learn about others' perspectives and feelings; involving children in family decision making; and modeling moral behaviors.

- The hidden curriculum, initially described by Dewey, is the moral atmosphere of a school. Contemporary approaches to moral education include character education, values education, and cognitive moral education. Service learning is increasing.

3 Describe the development of prosocial and antisocial behavior

- Altruism, which is an unselfish interest in helping another person, and reciprocity often motivate prosocial behaviors such as sharing. Damon described a sequence by which children develop their understanding of fairness and come to share more consistently. Peers play a key role in this development.

- Conduct disorder involves age-inappropriate actions and attitudes that violate family expectations, society's norms, and the personal or property rights of others. The disorder is more common in boys than in girls. Juvenile delinquency involves a broad range of behaviors, from socially unacceptable behavior to status offenses to criminal behavior. In the Pittsburgh Youth Study, pathways to delinquency included conflict with authority, minor covert acts followed by property damage and more serious acts, minor aggression followed by fighting and violence. Heavy peer influence, low parental monitoring, ineffective discipline, having an older sibling who is a delinquent, and living in an urban, high-crime area are also linked with delinquency. Early involvement with drugs and violence, easy access to weapons, associations with antisocial peer groups, and pervasive exposure to violent content in the media are associated with violent youth. Recommendations for reducing youth violence include effective parenting, prevention, support for schools, and forging effective partnerships among families, schools, and communities.

4 Characterize the development of values, religion, spirituality, and meaning in life

- Values are beliefs and attitudes about the way people think things should be. Over the last two decades traditional-age college students have shown an increased interest in personal well-being and a decreased interest in the welfare of others.

- Piaget's theory provides a foundation for understanding developmental changes in children's and adolescents' conceptions of religion. Fowler proposed a life-span theory of spiritual and religious development with six stages.

- Many children and adolescents show an interest in religion. Adolescence may be a special juncture in religious development for many individuals. Various aspects of religion are linked with positive outcomes in adolescent development. When adolescents have a positive relationship with parents or are securely attached to them, they often adopt their parents' religious beliefs. Links have been found between adolescent sexuality and religiousness. Religion is an important dimension of many American adults' lives as well as the lives of people around the world. Females have a stronger interest in religion than males do. Religious interest often increases in late adulthood.

- Frankl argued that people need to face the finiteness of their life before they understand life's meaning. Faced with the death of older relatives and less time to live themselves, middle-aged adults increasingly examine life's meaning. Baumeister described four main needs that guide how people try to make sense of their lives: (1) need for purpose, (2) need for values, (3) need for a sense of efficacy, and (4) need for self-worth.

Key Terms

Key People

E-Learning Tools

Connect to **www.mhhe.com/santrockldt2** to research the answers and complete these exercises. In addition, you'll find a number of other resources and valuable study tools for chapter 13, "Moral Development, Values, and Religion," on the Student CD-ROM that came with this book.

Taking It to the Net

1. Isabelle is working in an after-school program in an inner-city community center that has a high level of violence and gang activity. Isabelle wants to start a program that will educate parents about what they can do at home to raise caring and kind children. What can parents do?

2. Howard, chairperson of his Methodist church's outreach committee, struggled with problem drinking when he was a young man and credits involvement in the church with his ability to give up alcohol. He wants the church to organize a support group for substance abusers and drug addicts, thinking that if his faith helped him, it can help others. What is the relationship between religious faith and spirituality and recovery from substance abuse?

3. Liz is worried about her 8-year-old son. Ever since he got a Nintendo for Christmas and a game called Mortal Kombat, she can't keep him away from it. He sneaks into the downstairs rec room and plays it when she thinks he is outside. He seems to have become more aggressive, but she wonders if that is just her imagination. Can playing violent video games make children more aggressive?

Self-Assessment

Complete these self-assessments to explore your values, spiritual well-being, and meaning in life:

- *Comparing My Attitudes and Values with Those of Other College Students*
- *My Spiritual Well-Being*
- *What Is My Purpose in Life?*

Health and Well-Being, Parenting, and Education

Build your decision-making skills by trying your hand at the health and well-being, parenting, and education "Scenarios."

Social Contexts of Development

Generations will depend on the ability of every procreating individual to face his children.

—ERIK ERIKSON
American Psychotherapist, 20th Century

As children develop, their small world widens as they discover new contexts and people. As they grow through childhood, their parents still cradle their lives, but their lives also are shaped by successive choirs of peers and friends. Parents can give adolescents both roots and wings. When some adults become parents, they recognize for the first time how much effort their parents put in to rearing them. Increasing numbers of adults choose to get married later or not at all. As people age, they come to sense that the generations of living things pass in a short while, and like runners, they pass on the torch of life.

Section 5 contains three chapters: "Families, Lifestyles, and Parenting" (chapter 14), "Peers and the Sociocultural World" (chapter 15), and "Schools, Achievement, and Work" (chapter 16).

Families, Lifestyles, and Parenting

Love and attachment are two aspects of family life that we discussed in chapter 10. Beyond these emotional ties, what else goes on in families that influences development? And how do the choices that adults make about family life affect their development and the development of their children? These are some of the questions that we will consider in this chapter.

1 ANALYZING FAMILY LIFE

The Family Life Cycle	Family Processes

No two families are the same; they vary as much as their individual members. Nevertheless, families do share some common features. In particular, they all change over time, and certain processes operate in all of them. As a basis for examining how families influence development, let's first consider some of these changes and processes.

The Family Life Cycle

As we go through life, our families go through a life cycle. The stages of the family life cycle are (Carter & McGoldrick, 1989) (see figure 14.1):

Leaving home and becoming a single adult is the first stage in the family life cycle, and it involves **launching,** the process in which youth move into adulthood and exit their family of origin. In a successful launching, the young adult separates from the family of origin without cutting off ties completely or fleeing to some substitute emotional refuge. Complete cutoffs from parents rarely solve emotional problems. Launching is a time to formulate life goals, to develop an identity, and to become more independent before joining with another person to form a new family. This is a time for young people to sort out emotionally what they will take along from the family of origin, what they will leave behind, and what they will create themselves into.

Young adults no longer feel compelled to comply with parental expectations and wishes. They shift to dealing with their parents adult-to-adult, which requires a mutually respectful form of relating, in which young adults can appreciate and accept their parents as they are.

The **new couple** is the second stage in the family life cycle. Marriage is usually described as the union of two individuals from separate families, but in reality it is the union of two entire family systems and the development of a new, third system. This stage involves not only the development of a new marital system, but also a realignment as the families of origin and friends

leaving home and becoming a single adult The first stage in the family life cycle that involves launching.

launching The process in which youth move into adulthood and exit their family of origin.

new couple The second stage in the family life cycle that involves marriage, which is not just the union of two individuals but the union of two families.

Doonesbury

BY GARRY TRUDEAU

include the spouse. Changes in gender roles, marriage of partners from divergent cultural backgrounds, and physical distances between family members increase the burden on couples to define their relationships for themselves. Some experts on marriage and the family believe that marriage represents such a different phenomenon for women and men that we need to speak of "her" marriage and "his" marriage. In American society, women have anticipated marriage with greater enthusiasm and more positive expectations than men have.

Becoming parents and a family with children is the third stage in the family life cycle. When they enter this stage, adults move up a generation and become caregivers to the younger generation. Moving through this lengthy stage successfully requires a commitment of time as a parent, an understanding of the parenting role, and a willingness to adapt to developmental changes in children. Couples in this stage may face struggles with each other about their responsibilities, as well as a refusal or inability to function as competent parents.

The **family with adolescents** represents the fourth stage of the family life cycle. Adolescence is a period in which individuals push for autonomy and seek to develop their own identity. This is a lengthy process, transpiring over at least 10 to 15 years. Compliant children may become noncompliant adolescents. In response, parents may either clamp down, pressuring the adolescent to conform to parental values, or become more permissive, giving the adolescent extensive freedom. Neither is a wise strategy. A flexible, adaptive approach is best.

The **family at midlife** is the fifth stage in the family life cycle. It is a time of launching children, linking generations, and adapting to midlife changes. Until about a generation ago, most families were involved in raising their children for much of their adult lives until old age. Because of the lower birth rate and longer life of most adults, parents now launch their children about 20 years before retirement, which frees many midlife parents to pursue other activities.

The **family in later life** is the sixth and final stage in the family life cycle. Retirement alters a couple's lifestyle, requiring adaptation. Grandparenting also characterizes many families in this stage.

Some critics argue that talking about stages of the family life cycle is misleading. They argue that clearly defined stages often do not develop and that the stages do not always occur in a sequential fashion (Azar, 2003; Elder, 1998). Further, they state that it is the variability associated with the stages that should be emphasized. For example, some people have children early during adolescence or their forties; some have children outside of marriage. Entry into these stages is increasingly independent from age. Further, many individuals have multiple families (such as children from a first marriage and children from a remarriage), and these families may develop at different points in the person's life course.

Family Processes

As we examine the family and other social contexts of development, keep Urie Bronfenbrenner's (1986, 2000) ecological theory, which we discussed in chapter 1, in mind. Recall that Bronfenbrenner analyzes the social contexts of development in terms of five environmental systems:

- The microsystem or the setting in which the individual lives, such as a family, the world of peers, schools, work, and so on
- The mesosystem, which consists of links between microsystems, such as the connection between family processes and peer relations
- The exosystem, which consists of influences from another setting (such as parents' work) that the individual does not experience directly
- The macrosystem or the culture in which the individual lives, such as a nation or an ethnic group

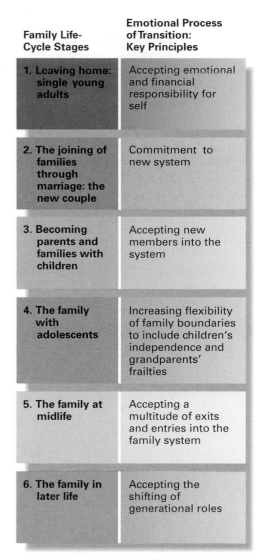

Family Life-Cycle Stages	Emotional Process of Transition: Key Principles
1. Leaving home: single young adults	Accepting emotional and financial responsibility for self
2. The joining of families through marriage: the new couple	Commitment to new system
3. Becoming parents and families with children	Accepting new members into the system
4. The family with adolescents	Increasing flexibility of family boundaries to include children's independence and grandparents' frailties
5. The family at midlife	Accepting a multitude of exits and entries into the family system
6. The family in later life	Accepting the shifting of generational roles

FIGURE 14.1 The Family Life Cycle

becoming parents and a family with children The third stage in the family life cycle in which adults move up a generation and become caregivers for the younger generation.

family with adolescents The fourth stage in the family life cycle in which adolescents push for autonomy and an identity.

family at midlife The fifth stage in the family life cycle, a time for launching children, linking generations, and adapting to midlife changes.

family in later life The sixth and final stage in the family life cycle, involving adaptation to retirement and grantparenting.

Journal of Family Psychology

Family Relations

Marriage and Family Therapy

*W*e never know the love of our parents until we have become parents.

—HENRY WARD BEECHER
American Clergyman, 19th Century

• The chronosystem or sociohistorical circumstances, such as the increase in the numbers of working mothers, divorced parents, and stepparent families in the United States in the last 30 to 40 years.

Let's begin our examination of family processes with the process of reciprocal socialization, which occurs at the level of the microsystem.

Reciprocal Socialization   Socialization between parents and children is not a one-way process. Parents do socialize children, but socialization in families is reciprocal. **Reciprocal socialization** is socialization that is bidirectional; children socialize parents just as parents socialize children (Crouter & Booth, 2003; Patterson & Fisher, 2002).

For example, the interaction of mothers and their infants is sometimes symbolized as a dance in which successive actions of the partners are closely coordinated. This coordinated dance can assume the form of *mutual synchrony,* which means that each person's behavior depends on the partner's previous behavior. Or the interaction can be *reciprocal* in a precise sense, which means that the actions of the partners can be matched, as when one partner imitates the other or when there is mutual smiling (Cohn & Tronick, 1988).

One important example of early synchronized interaction is mutual gaze or eye contact (Fogel, Toda, & Kawai, 1988). In one investigation, the mother and infant engaged in a variety of behaviors while they looked at each other; by contrast, when they looked away from each other, the rate of such behaviors dropped considerably (Stern & others, 1977). And in one investigation, synchrony in parent-child relationships was positively related to children's social competence (Harrist, 1993).

In short, the behaviors of infants and parents involve substantial synchronization. Another example occurs in **scaffolding,** which means adjusting the level of guidance to fit the child's performance, as we discussed in chapter 6. The parent responds to the child's behavior with scaffolding, which in turn affects the child's behavior. For example, in the game peek-a-boo, parents initially cover their babies, then remove the covering, and finally register "surprise" at the babies' reappearance. As infants become more skilled at peek-a-boo, infants gradually do some of the covering and uncovering. Parents try to time their actions in such a way that the infant takes turns with the parent. In addition to peek-a-boo, pat-a-cake and "so-big" are other caregiver games that exemplify scaffolding and turn-taking sequences. In one investigation, infants who had more extensive scaffolding experiences with their parents, especially in the form of turn-taking, were more likely to engage in turn-taking as they interacted with their peers (Vandell & Wilson, 1988). Scaffolding, as our discussions in earlier chapters indicated, can be used to support children's efforts at any age.

Family As a System   As a social system, the family can be thought of as a constellation of subsystems defined in terms of generation, gender, and role (Davis, 1996; Rothbaum & others, 2002). Divisions of labor among family members define particular subunits, and attachments define others. Each family member is a participant in several subsystems—some *dyadic* (involving two people), some *polyadic* (involving more than two people). The father and child represent one dyadic subsystem, the mother and father another; the mother-father-child represent one polyadic subsystem, the mother and two siblings another (Piotrowski, 1997).

These subsystems interact and influence each other. Thus, as figure 14.2 illustrates, marital relations, parenting, and infant/child behavior can have both direct and indirect effects on each other (Belsky, 1981). The link between marital relationships and parenting has recently received increased attention. The most consistent findings are that compared with unhappily married parents, happily married

reciprocal socialization   Socialization is bidirectional in that children socialize parents just as parents socialize children.

scaffolding   Adjusting the level of guidance to fit the child's performance.

parents are more sensitive, responsive, warm, and affectionate toward their children (Grych, 2002).

Researchers have found that promoting marital satisfaction often leads to good parenting. The marital relationship is an important support for parenting (Belsky & Hsieh, 1998; Cummings & others, 2002). When parents report more intimacy and better communication in their marriage, they are more affectionate to their children (Grych, 2002). One recent study found parents were more likely to frequently and intensely physically punish their children when they had a high level of marital conflict (Kanoy & others, 2003). Thus, marriage-enhancement programs may end up improving parenting and helping children. Programs that focus on parenting skills might also benefit from including attention to the participants' marriages.

Sociocultural and Historical Changes   Family development does not occur in a social vacuum. Important sociocultural and historical influences affect family processes, which reflect Bronfenbrenner's concepts of the macrosystem and chronosystem (Conger, Lorenz, & Wickrama, 2004; Elder & Conger, 2000; Parke, 2004; Parke & Buriel, 1998). Both great upheavals such as war, famine, or mass immigration and subtle transitions in ways of life may stimulate changes in families. One example is the effect on U.S. families of the Great Depression of the 1930s. During its height, the Depression produced economic deprivation, adult discontent, and depression about living conditions. It also increased marital conflict, inconsistent child rearing, and unhealthy lifestyles—heavy drinking, demoralized attitudes, and health disabilities—especially in fathers (Elder, 1980).

Subtle changes in a culture that have significant influences on the family were described by anthropologist Margaret Mead (1978). Such changes include the longevity of older adults, movement to urban and suburban areas, television, and a general dissatisfaction and restlessness.

Fifty years ago, the older people who survived were usually hearty and still closely linked to the family, often helping to maintain the family's existence. Today, older people live longer, which means that their middle-aged children are often pressed into a caretaking role for their parents or the elderly parents may be placed in a nursing home. Older parents may have lost some of their socializing role in the family during the twentieth century as many of their children moved great distances away.

Many of these family moves were away from farms and small towns to urban and suburban settings. In the small towns and farms, individuals were surrounded by lifelong neighbors, relatives, and friends. Today, neighborhood and extended-family support systems are not nearly as prevalent. Families now move all over the country, often uprooting the child from a school and peer group he or she has known for a considerable length of time. And for many families, this type of move occurs every year or two, as one or both parents are transferred from job to job.

The media and technology also play a major role in the changing family. Many children who watch television find that parents are too busy working to share this experience with them. Children increasingly experience a world that their parents are not a part of. Instead of participating in neighborhood peer groups, children come home after school and plop down in front of the television set or a computer screen. And television allows children and their families to see new ways of life. Lower-SES families can look into the family lives of middle-SES families by simply pushing a button.

Another change in families has been an increase in general dissatisfaction and restlessness. The result of such restlessness and the tendency to divorce and remarry has been a hodgepodge of family structures, with far greater numbers of single-parent and stepparent families than ever before in history. Later in the chapter, we discuss such aspects of the changing social world of the child and the family in greater detail.

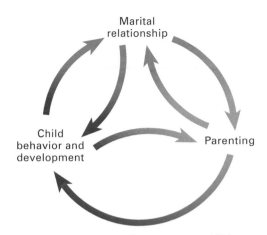

FIGURE 14.2 Interaction Between Children and Their Parents: Direct and Indirect Effects

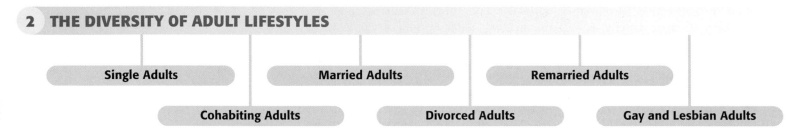

Review and Reflect: Learning Goal 1

1 Describe the family life cycle and family processes

REVIEW

*   What are the six stages of the family life cycle?
*   What are some important family processes?

REFLECT

*   What do you predict will be some major changes in families in the twenty-first century?

2 THE DIVERSITY OF ADULT LIFESTYLES

| Single Adults | Married Adults | Remarried Adults |
| Cohabiting Adults | Divorced Adults | Gay and Lesbian Adults |

One of the most striking social changes in recent decades is the decreased stigma attached to people who do not maintain what were long considered conventional families. Adults today choose many lifestyles and form many types of families. They live alone, cohabit, marry, divorce, remarry, or live with someone of the same sex. Let's explore each of these lifestyles and how they affect adults.

Single Adults

There is no rehearsal. One day you don't live alone, the next day you do. College ends. Your wife walks out. Your husband dies. Suddenly, you live in this increasingly modern condition, living alone. Maybe you like it, maybe you don't. Maybe you thrive on the solitude, maybe you ache as if in exile. Either way, chances are you are only half prepared, if at all, to be sole proprietor of your bed, your toaster, and your time. Most of us were raised in the din and clutter of family life, jockeying for a place in the bathroom in the morning, fighting over the last piece of cake, and obliged to compromise on the simplest of choices—the volume of the stereo, the channel on the TV, for example. Few of us grew up thinking that home would be a way station in our life course.

There has been a dramatic rise in the percentage of single adults. In 2000, 25 percent of American adults lived alone (U.S. Bureau of the Census, 2002). This is more than three times the percentage in 1970 (8 percent). As illustrated in figure 14.3, the percentage of those in their early thirties who were single showed a similar increase.

Myths and stereotypes are associated with being single, ranging from the "swinging single" to the "desperately lonely, suicidal" single. Of course, most single adults are somewhere between these extremes. Common problems of single adults include forming intimate relationships with other adults, confronting loneliness, and finding a niche in a society that is marriage-oriented.

Advantages of being single include time to make decisions about one's life course, time to develop personal resources to meet goals, freedom to

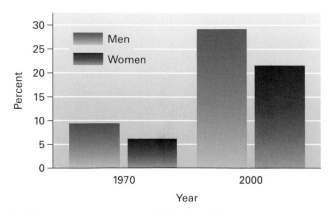

FIGURE 14.3 Percentage of Single Adults 30 to 34 Years of Age in 1970 and 2000

In three decades, the percentage of single adults 30 to 34 years of age in the United States more than tripled.

make autonomous decisions and pursue one's own schedule and interests, opportunities to explore new places and try out new things, and privacy.

One woman who never married commented, "I enjoy knowing that I can satisfy my own whims without someone else's interferences. If I want to wash my hair at two o'clock in the morning, no one complains. I can eat when I'm hungry and watch my favorite television shows without contradictions from anyone. I enjoy these freedoms."

Once adults reach the age of 30, there can be increasing pressure to settle down and get married. This is when many single adults make a conscious decision to marry or to remain single. As one 30-year-old male recently commented, "It's real. You are supposed to get married by 30—that is a standard. It is part of getting on with your life that you are supposed to do. You have career and who-am-I concerns in your twenties. In your thirties, you have to get on with it, keep on track, make headway, financially and family-wise." But, to another 30-year-old, getting married is less important than buying a house and some property. A training manager for a computer company, Jane says, "I'm competent in making relationships and being committed, so I don't feel a big rush to get married. When it happens, it happens."

The older aging adults become, the greater are their odds of living alone. The majority of older adults living alone are widowed. As with younger adults, older adults living alone are not necessarily lonely; they may have regular exchanges with relatives, neighbors, and friends.

Cohabiting Adults

Cohabitation refers to living together in a sexual relationship without being married. Cohabitation has undergone considerable changes in recent years (Jamieson & others, 2003; Means & others, 2003; Oppenheimer, 2003; U.S. Bureau of the Census, 2003) (see figure 14.4). The percentage of U.S. couples who cohabit before marriage has increased from approximately 11 percent in 1970 to almost 60 percent at the beginning of the twenty-first century (Bumpass & Lu, 2000). Cohabiting rates are even higher in some countries—in Sweden, cohabitation before marriage is virtually universal (Hoem, 1995). In the United States, cohabiting arrangements tend to be short-lived, with one-third lasting less than a year (Hyde & DeLamater, 2003). Less than 1 out of 10 lasts 5 years. Of course, it is easier to dissolve a cohabitation relationship than to divorce. A number of couples view their cohabitation not as a precursor to marriage but as an ongoing lifestyle. These couples do not want the official aspects of marriage.

Do cohabiting relationships differ from marriage in other ways? Relationships between cohabiting men and women tend to be more equal than those between husbands and wives (Wineberg, 1994).

Although cohabitation offers some advantages, it also can produce some problems (Cohan & Kleinbaum, 2002; Solot & Miller, 2002). Disapproval by parents and other family members can place emotional strain on the cohabiting couple. Some cohabiting couples have difficulty owing property jointly. Legal rights on the dissolution of the relationship are less certain than in a divorce.

Does cohabiting help or harm the chances that a couple will have a stable and happy marriage? Some researchers have found no differences in marital quality between individuals who earlier cohabited and those who did not (Newcomb & Bentler, 1980; Watson & DeMeo, 1987). Other researchers have found lower rates of marital satisfaction in couples who lived together before getting married (Booth & Johnson, 1988). For example, in one study of 13,000 individuals, married couples

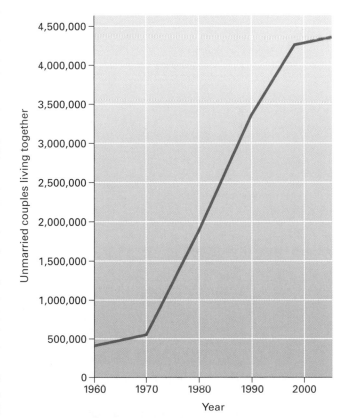

FIGURE 14.4 The Increase in Cohabitation in the United States

Since 1970, there has been a dramatic increase in the number of unmarried adults living together in the United States.

who cohabited prior to their marriage reported lower levels of happiness with and commitment to their marital relationship than their counterparts who had not previously cohabited (Nock, 1995). In another study, couples who had cohabited before marriage were more likely to divorce than couples who had not cohabited (DeMaris & Rao, 1992). And in one recent study, after 10 years of marriage, 40 percent of couples who lived together before marriage had divorced, whereas 31 percent of those who had not cohabited first had divorced (Centers for Disease Control and Prevention, 2002).

In sum, researchers have found either that cohabitation leads to no differences or that cohabitation is not good for a marriage. What might explain the finding that cohabiting is linked with divorce more than not cohabiting? The most frequently given explanation is that the more nontraditional lifestyle of cohabitation may attract less conventional individuals who are not great believers in marriage in the first place (Manning & Smock, 2002; Whitehead & Popenoe, 2003). An alternative explanation is that the experience of cohabiting changes people's attitudes and habits in ways that increase their likelihood of divorce (Solot & Miller, 2002).

Cohabitation is also increasing among older adults (Allen, Blieszner, & Roberto, 2000). By the 1990s, approximately 2.4 percent of older adults were cohabiting, compared with almost 0 percent in 1960 (Chevan, 1996). Older men are more likely to cohabit than older women. In some cases, older adults cohabit because of poverty.

Married Adults

The second stage in the family life cycle is becoming a couple. In chapter 10, we discussed attachment and love in adults. You might want to review that material because it describes important aspects of marital relationships. Let's now explore marriage in greater detail, focusing on some marital trends, what makes marriages work, the benefits of a good marriage, and developmental changes in marriage in middle and late adulthood.

Marital Trends   Until about 1930, stable marriage was widely accepted as the endpoint of adult development. In the last 60 years, however, personal fulfillment both inside and outside marriage has emerged as a goal that competes with marital stability. The changing norm of male-female equality in marriage has produced marital relationships that are more fragile and intense than they were earlier in the twentieth century (Bradbury, Fincham, & Beach, 2000). More adults are remaining single longer today, and the average duration of a marriage in the United States is currently just over nine years. In 2002, the U.S. average age for a first marriage climbed to just over 27 years for men and just over 25 years for women, higher than at any point in history (U.S. Bureau of the Census, 2003) (see figure 14.5).

However, the United States is still a marrying society. In 1998, 118 million individuals in the United States were married, about 60 percent of the total population, which is a drop of only about 5 percent since 1980. The divorce rate has begun to slow down, although it remains high. And the proportion of women who never marry remained at about 7 percent throughout the twentieth century.

The sociocultural context is a powerful influence on marriage. The age at which individuals marry, expectations about what the marriage will be like, and the developmental course of the marriage vary not only across historical time within a given culture, but also across cultures. For example, as part of China's efforts to control population growth, a 1981 law sets the minimum age for marriage at 22 years for males, 20 for females. More information about marriage in different cultures appears in the Contexts of Life-Span Development interlude.

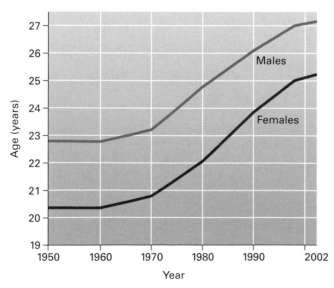

FIGURE 14.5 Increase in Age at First Marriage in the United States

Shown here are average ages at first marriage in the United States. Notice that since the 1960s, the age at which this important life event occurs has steadily increased.

Contexts of Life-Span Development

Marriage Around the World

The traits that people look for in a marriage partner vary around the world (Hamon & Ingoldsby, 2003). In one large-scale study of 9,474 adults from 37 cultures on six continents and five islands, people varied most regarding how much they valued chastity—desiring a marital partner with no previous experience in sexual intercourse (Buss & others, 1990). Chastity was the most important characteristic in selecting a marital partner in China, India, Indonesia, Iran, Taiwan, and the Palestinian Arab culture. Adults from Ireland and Japan placed moderate importance on chastity. In contrast, adults in Sweden, Finland, Norway, the Netherlands, and Germany generally said that chastity was not important in selecting a marital partner.

Domesticity is also valued in some cultures and not in others. In this study, adults from the Zulu culture in South Africa, Estonia, and Colombia placed a high value on housekeeping skills in their marital preference. By contrast, adults in the United States, Canada, and all Western European countries except Spain said that housekeeping skill was not an important trait in their partner.

Religion plays an important role in marital preferences in many cultures. For example, Islam stresses the honor of the male and the purity of the female. It also emphasizes the woman's role in childbearing, child rearing, educating children, and instilling the Islamic faith in their children.

International comparisons of marriage also reveal that individuals in Scandinavian countries marry later than Americans, whereas their counterparts in Eastern Europe marry earlier (Bianchi & Spani, 1986). In Denmark, for example, almost 80 percent of the women and 90 percent of the men aged 20 to 24 have never been married. In Hungary, less than 40 percent of the women and 70 percent of the men the same age have never been married. In Scandinavian countries, cohabitation is popular among young adults; however, most Scandinavians eventually marry. Only 5 percent of the women and 11 percent of the men in their early forties have never been married. Some countries, such as Hungary, encourage early marriage and childbearing to offset declines in the population. Like Scandinavian countries, Japan has a high proportion of unmarried young people. However, rather than cohabiting as the Scandinavians do, unmarried Japanese young adults live at home longer with their parents before marrying.

(a)

(b)

(a) In Scandinavian countries, cohabitation has been popular; only a small percentage of 20- to 24-year-olds are married. *(b)* Islam has stressed male honor and female purity.

What Makes Marriages Work   John Gottman (1994; Gottman & Notarius, 2000; Gottman & Silver, 1999; Gottman & others, 1998) has been studying married couples' lives since the early 1970s. He uses many methods to analyze what makes marriages work. Gottman interviews couples about the history of their marriage, their philosophy about marriage, and how they view their parents' marriages. He videotapes them talking to each other about how their day went and evaluates what they say about the good and bad times of their marriages. Gottman also uses physiological measures to measure their heart rate, blood flow, blood pressure, and immune functioning moment by moment. He also checks back in with the couples every year to see how their marriage is faring. Gottman's research represents the most extensive assessment of marital relationships available. Currently he and his colleagues are following 700 couples in seven studies.

In his research, Gottman has found that seven main principles determine whether a marriage will work or not:

- *Establishing love maps.* Individuals in successful marriages have personal insights and detailed maps of each other's life and world. They aren't psychological

*W*hen two people are under the influence of the most violent, most insane, most delusive, and most transient of passions, they are required to swear that they will remain in that excited, abnormal, and exhausting condition continuously until death do them part.

—GEORGE BERNARD SHAW
Irish Playwright, 20th Century

strangers. In good marriages, partners are willing to share their feelings with each other. They use these "love maps" to express not only their understanding of each other but also their fondness and admiration.

- *Nurturing fondness and admiration.* In successful marriages, partners sing each other's praises. More than 90 percent of the time, when couples put a positive spin on their marriage's history, the marriage is likely to have a positive future.

- *Turning toward each other instead of away.* In good marriages, spouses are adept at turning toward each other regularly. They see each other as friends. This friendship doesn't keep arguments from occurring, but it can prevent differences from overwhelming the relationship. In these good marriages, spouses respect each other and appreciate each other's point of view despite disagreements.

- *Letting your partner influence you.* Bad marriages often involve one spouse who is unwilling to share power with the other. Although power-mongering is more common in husbands, some wives also show this trait. A willingness to share power and to respect the other person's view is a prerequisite to compromising.

- *Solving solvable conflicts.* Two types of problems occur in marriage: (1) perpetual and (2) solvable. Perpetual problems include differences about whether to have children and how often to have sex. Solvable problems include not helping each other reduce daily stresses and not being verbally affectionate. Unfortunately, more than two-thirds of marital problems fall into the perpetual category—those that won't go away. Fortunately, marital therapists have found that couples often don't have to solve their perpetual problems for the marriage to work. In his research, Gottman has found that resolving conflicts works best when couples start out solving the problem with a soft rather than a harsh approach, try to make and receive repair attempts, regulate their emotions, compromise, and are tolerant of each other's faults. Conflict resolution is not about one person making changes, it is about negotiating and accommodating each other (Driver & others, 2003).

    Work, stress, in-laws, money, sex, housework, a new baby: these are among the typical areas of marital conflict, even in happy marriages. When there is conflict in these areas, it usually means that a husband and wife have different ideas about the tasks involved, their importance, or how they should be accomplished. If the conflict is perpetual, no amount of problem-solving expertise will fix it. The tension will decrease only when both partners feel comfortable living with the ongoing difference. However, when the issue is solvable, the challenge is to find the right strategy for dealing with it. Strategies include:
Scheduling formal griping sessions about stressful issues
Learning to talk about sex in a way that both partners feel comfortable with
Creating lists of who does what to see how household labor is divided

- *Overcoming gridlock.* One partner wants the other to attend church, the other is an atheist. One partner is a homebody, the other wants to go out and socialize a lot. Such problems often produce gridlock. Gottman believes the key to ending gridlock is not to solve the problem, but to move from gridlock to dialogue and be patient.

- *Creating shared meaning.* The more partners can speak candidly and respectfully with each other, the more likely it is that they will create shared meaning in their marriage. This also includes sharing goals with one's spouse and working together to achieve each other's goals.

The Benefits of a Good Marriage   Are there any benefits to having a good marriage? There are. An unhappy marriage increases an individual's risk of getting sick by approximately one-third and can even shorten a person's life by an average of four years (Gove, Style, & Hughes, 1990). Individuals who are happily married live

What makes marriages work? What are the benefits of having a good marriage?

longer, healthier lives than either divorced individuals or those who are unhappily married (Cotten, 1999; Gallo & others, 2003).

What are the reasons for these benefits of a happy marriage? People in happy marriages likely feel less physically and emotionally stressed, which puts less wear and tear on a person's body. Such wear and tear can lead to numerous physical ailments, such as high blood pressure and heart disease, as well as psychological problems such as anxiety, depression, and substance abuse.

Marriage in Middle and Late Adulthood What is marriage like for middle-aged adults? How does marriage change in late adulthood?

Middle Adulthood Even some marriages that were difficult and rocky during early adulthood turn out to be better adjusted during middle adulthood (Wickrama & others, 2004). Although the partners may have lived through a great deal of turmoil, they eventually discover a deep and solid foundation on which to anchor their relationship. In middle adulthood, the partners may have fewer financial worries, less housework and chores, and more time with each other. Partners who engage in mutual activities usually view their marriage as more positive at this time.

Most individuals in midlife who are married voice considerable satisfaction with being married. In one recent large-scale study of individuals in middle adulthood, 72 percent of those who were married said their marriage was either "excellent" or "very good" (Brim, 1999). Possibly by middle age, many of the worst marriages already have dissolved.

Late Adulthood The time from retirement until death is sometimes referred to as the "final stage in the marriage process." Retirement alters a couple's lifestyle, requiring adaptation. The greatest changes occur in the traditional family, in which the husband works and the wife is a homemaker. The husband may not know what to do with his time, and the wife may feel uneasy having him around the house all of the time. In traditional families, both partners may need to move toward more expressive roles. The husband must adjust from being the good provider to being a helper around the house; the wife must change to being even more loving and understanding. Marital happiness as an older adult is also affected by each partner's ability to deal with personal conflicts, including aging, illness, and eventual death (Field, 1996).

www.mhhe.com/santrockld2

John Gottman's Ideas

G row old with me!
The best is yet to be,
The last of life,
For which the first was made.
—ROBERT BROWNING
English Poet, 19th Century

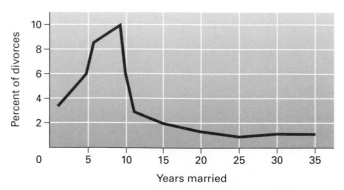

FIGURE 14.6 The Divorce Rate in Relation to Number of Years Married

Shown here is the percentage of divorces as a function of how long couples have been married. Notice that most divorces occur in the early years of marriage, peaking in the fifth to tenth years of marriage.

Divorced Adults

The divorce rate in the United States reached 10 percent of the population at the beginning of the twenty-first century, but it has been declining since the 1980s. Disadvantaged groups have a higher incidence of divorce. Youthful marriage, premarital pregnancy, low educational level, and low income are associated with increases in divorce.

Even those adults who initiated their divorce experience challenges after a marriage dissolves (Amato, 2000; Hetherington, 2000). Both divorced women and divorced men complain of loneliness, diminished self-esteem, anxiety about the unknowns in their lives, and difficulty in forming satisfactory new intimate relationships.

Timing of Divorce and Age of Divorced Adults If a divorce is going to occur, it usually takes place early in a marriage; most occur in the fifth to tenth year of marriage (National Center for Health Statistics, 2000) (see figure 14.6). It may be that although a marriage is troubled, some partners stay in it and try to work things out. If after several years these efforts don't improve the relationship, they may seek a divorce.

Are there any differences in the factors that predict whether couples will divorce in midlife compared with when they were younger adults? In a 14-year longitudinal study, John Gottman and Robert Levenson (2000) recently found that couples who divorce in midlife tend to have a profile like the couple played by Annette Bening and Kevin Spacey in the movie *American Beauty:* cool, distant, and with suppressed emotions. The midlife divorcing couples were alienated and avoidant. They were the kind of people you see in a restaurant who aren't talking with each other. It is a distant relationship with little or no laughter, love, or interest in each other. One of the divorcing midlife parents often feels like his or her life is "empty." In contrast, the researchers found that when divorce occurs among younger adults (often in the first seven years of a marriage), it is characterized by heated emotions that tend to burn out the marriage early. The young divorcing couples frequently were volatile and expressive, full of disappointment that they let each other know about.

Very few older adults divorce: only about 1 percent of all who divorce in any given year in the United States. However, divorce recently has started to rise slightly among older adults (National Center for Health Statistics, 2000).

Mental and Physical Health The stress of separation and divorce places both men and women at risk for psychological and physical difficulties (Hetherington & Stanley-Hagan, 2002). Separated and divorced women and men have higher rates of psychiatric disorders, admission to psychiatric hospitals, clinical depression, alcoholism, and psychosomatic problems, such as sleep disorders, than do married adults. There is increasing evidence that stressful events of many types—including marital separation—reduce the immune system's capabilities, rendering separated and divorced individuals vulnerable to disease and infection. In one study, the most recently separated women (one year or less) were more likely to show impaired immunological functioning than women whose separations had occurred one to six years earlier (Kiecolt-Glaser & Glaser, 1988). Also in this study, unhappily married individuals had immune systems that were not functioning as effectively as those of happily married individuals.

Concerns of Custodial and Noncustodial Parents Custodial parents have concerns about child rearing and overload in their lives. Noncustodial parents register complaints about alienation from or lack of time with their children. (We will discuss the effects of divorce on children later in this chapter.) Men show only modest declines in income following a divorce, but women face a significant decline, with estimates of the decline ranging from 20 to 35 percent. For divorced women, the financial decline means living in a less desirable neighborhood with fewer resources, less effective schools, and more deviant peer groups for their children. However, the economic decline for women following a divorce has diminished as fewer women follow the conventional role of stay-at-home homemaker and more have experience in the workforce before divorce.

Diversity of Pathways Out of Divorce Psychologically, one of the most common characteristics of divorced adults is difficulty in trusting someone else in a romantic relationship. Following a divorce, though, people's lives can take diverse turns. In E. Mavis Hetherington's research, men and women took six common pathways in exiting divorce (Hetherington & Kelly, 2002):

- *The enhancers.* Accounting for 20 percent of the divorced group, these females grew more competent, well-adjusted, and self-fufilled following their divorce. They were competent in multiple areas of life, showed a remarkable ability to bounce back from stressful circumstances, and create something meaningful out of the problems they encountered.
- *The good-enoughs.* Consistently the largest group of divorced individuals, they were described as the average man and woman coping with divorce. They showed some strengths and some vulnerabilities, some success and some problems. When they encountered a problem, they tried to solve it. Many of them attended night classes, made new friends, created active social lives, and sought higher-paying jobs. However, they were less proactive and less persistent than the enhancers. Good-enough women usually married men who educationally and economically looked like their first husbands, often moving into marriages that were not a great improvement over the first one.
- *The seekers.* This group was eager to find a new mate as soon as possible. At one year postdivorce, 40 percent of the men and 38 percent of women were classified as seekers. As individuals found new partners over time or became more secure or satisfied in their single life, the seeker category shrank and came to be predominated by men.
- *The libertines.* They often spent more time in single bars and had more casual sex than their counterparts in the other divorce categories. However, by the end of the first year postdivorce, they often grew disillusioned with their sensation-seeking lifestyle and longed for a stable relationship.
- *The competent loners.* These individuals, which made up only about 10 percent of the divorced group, were well-adjusted, self-sufficient, and socially skilled. They had a successful career, an active social life, and a wide range of interests. However, unlike enhancers, competent loners had little interest in sharing their life with anyone else.
- *The defeated.* Some of these individuals had problems before their divorce, which worsened after the breakup when they found that the added stress of a failed marriage was more than they could handle. Others had problems because they had a spouse who had supported them, or in the case of a drinking problem, restricted them.

Strategies for Divorced Adults Hetherington recommends these strategies for divorced adults (Hetherington & Kelly, 2002):

- Look at divorce as an opportunity for personal growth and for building more fulfilling relationships.
- Think carefully about your decisions. The consequences of choices about work, lovers, and children may last a lifetime.
- Focus more on the future than the past. Set priorities and goals, and then work toward them.

www.mhhe.com/santrockldt2

Divorced Adults

- Capitalize on your strengths and the resources available to you.
- Don't expect to be successful and happy in everything you do. The road to a more satisfying life is likely to be bumpy and have many detours.
- Be aware that you are never trapped by one pathway. Most of the divorced adults who were categorized as defeated immediately after divorce in Hetherington's research gradually moved on to a better life, but moving forward usually requires a great deal of effort.

Remarried Adults

On average, divorced adults remarry within four years after their divorce, with men doing this sooner than women. Stepfamilies come in many sizes and forms. The custodial and noncustodial parents and stepparent all might have been married and divorced, in some cases more than once. These parents might have residential children from prior marriages and a large network of grandparents and other relatives. Regardless of their form and size, the newly reconstituted families face some unique tasks. The couple must define and strengthen their marriage and at the same time renegotiate the biological parent-child relationships and establish stepparent-stepchild and stepsibling relationships (Coleman, Ganong, & Fine, 2000; Hetherington & Stanley-Hagan, 2002).

The complex histories and multiple relationships make adjustment difficult in a stepfamily (Coleman, Ganong, & Weaver, 2001; Rice, 2002; Thomson & others, 2001). Only one-third of stepfamily couples stay remarried (Gerlach, 1998).

Why do remarried adults find it so difficult to stay remarried? For one thing, many remarry not for love but for financial reasons, for help in rearing children, and to reduce loneliness. They also might carry into the stepfamily negative patterns that produced failure in an earlier marriage. Remarried couples also experience more stress in rearing children than parents in never-divorced families (Ganong & Coleman, 1994).

Among the strategies that help remarried couples cope with the stress of living in a stepfamily are these (Visher & Visher, 1989):

- *Have realistic expectations.* Allow time for loving relationships to develop, and look at the complexity of the stepfamily as a challenge to overcome.
- *Develop new positive relationships within the family.* Create new traditions and ways of dealing with difficult circumstances. Allocation of time is especially important because so many people are involved. The remarried couple needs to allot time alone for each other.

What are the research findings regarding the development and psychological well-being of children raised by gay and lesbian couples?

www.mhhe.com/santrockldt2

Gay and Lesbian Relationships

Gay and Lesbian Adults

The legal and social context of marriage creates barriers to breaking up that do not usually exist for same-sex partners. But in other ways researchers have found that gay and lesbian relationships are similar—in their satisfactions, loves, joys, and conflicts—to heterosexual relationships (Hyde & DeLamater, 2003; Julien & others, 2003; Peplau & Beals, 2002). For example, like heterosexual couples, gay and lesbian couples need to find the balance of romantic love, affection, autonomy, and equality that is acceptable to both partners (Kurdek, 2003). Lesbian couples especially place a high priority on equality in their relationships (Kurdek, 1995). Indeed, some researchers have found that gay and lesbian couples are more flexible in their gender roles than heterosexual individuals are (Marecek, Finn, & Cardell, 1988). In one study, gay and lesbian couples listed the areas of conflict in order of frequency: finances, driving style, affection and sex, being overly critical, and household tasks (Kurdek, 1995). The components of this list are likely to be familiar to heterosexual couples.

There are a number of misconceptions about homosexual couples. Contrary to stereotypes, one partner is masculine and the other feminine in only a small percentage of homosexual couples. Only a small segment of the gay male population have a large number of sexual partners and this is uncommon among lesbians. Furthermore, researchers have found that homosexuals prefer long-term, committed relationships (Peplau & Beals, 2002). About half of committed gay male couples do have an open relationship that allows the possibility of sex (but not affectionate love) outside of the relationship. Lesbian couples usually do not have this open relationship.

Increasingly, gay and lesbian couples are creating families that include children (see figure 14.7). Researchers have found that children growing up in gay or lesbian families are just as popular with their peers, and there are no differences in the adjustment and mental health of children living in these families when they are compared with children in heterosexual families (Anderssen, Amlie, & Ytteroy, 2002; Hyde & DeLamater, 2003). Also, the overwhelming majority of children growing up in a gay or lesbian family have a heterosexual orientation (Patterson, 1995, 2000, 2002).

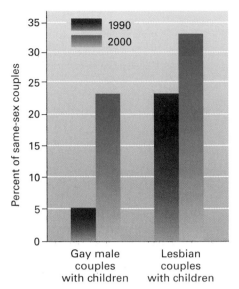

FIGURE 14.7 Amount of Same Sex Couples with Children

Review and Reflect: Learning Goal 2

2 Discuss the diversity of adult lifestyles and how they influence people's lives

REVIEW

- What characterizes single adults?
- What are the lives of cohabiting adults like?
- What are some key aspects of the lives of married adults?
- How does divorce affect adults?
- What are the lives of remarried parents like?
- What characterizes the lifestyles of gay and lesbian adults?

REFLECT

- Which type of lifestyle are you living today? What do you think are its advantages and disadvantages for you? If you could have a different lifestyle, which one would it be? Why?

3 PARENTING

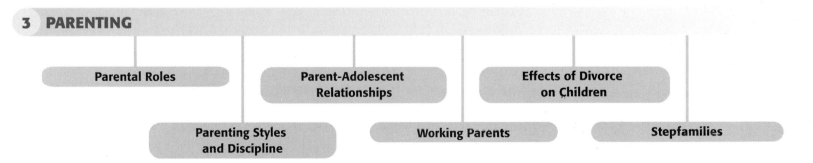

How does a parent's choice of lifestyle affect a child? The answers change as the child passes through the stages of the family life cycle. Before examining these changes, let's consider parenting itself.

Parental Roles

Many adults plan when to be parents and consider how parenting will fit with their economic situation. For others, the discovery that they are about to become parents is a startling surprise. In either event, the prospective parents may have mixed

I looked on child rearing not only as a work of love and duty but as a profession that was fully as interesting and challenging as any honorable profession in the world and one that demanded the best that I could bring to it.

—ROSE KENNEDY
U.S. Public Figure, Philanthropist, 20th Century

Parenting

emotions and romantic illusions about having a child. The needs and expectations of parents have stimulated many myths about parenting:

- The birth of a child will save a failing marriage.
- As a possession or extension of the parent, the child will think, feel, and behave like the parents did in their childhood.
- Children will take care of parents in old age.
- Parents can expect respect and get obedience from their children.
- Having a child means that the parents will always have someone who loves them and is their best friend.
- Having a child gives the parents a "second chance" to achieve what they should have achieved.
- If parents learn the right techniques, they can mold their children into what they want.
- It's the parents' fault when children fail.
- Mothers are naturally better parents than fathers.
- Parenting is an instinct and requires no training.

Currently, there is a tendency to have fewer children. The number of one-child families is increasing. Is there a best time to have children? Is there a best way to raise them? These are some of the questions we will now consider.

Timing of Parenthood As birth control has become common practice, many individuals choose when they will have children and how many children they will raise. They are not only marrying later, but also having children later (Azar, 2003; Grolnick & Gurland, 2001). What are some of the advantages of having children early or late?

Some of the advantages of having children early (in the twenties) are these: The parents are likely to have more physical energy; for example, they can cope better with such matters as getting up in the middle of the night with infants and waiting up until adolescents come home at night. The mother is likely to have fewer medical problems with pregnancy and childbirth. And the parents may be less likely to build up expectations for their children, as do many couples who have waited many years to have children.

There are also advantages to having children later (in the thirties): The parents will have had more time to consider their goals in life, such as what they want from their family and career roles. The parents will be more mature and will be able to benefit from their experiences to engage in more competent parenting. And the parents will be better established in their careers and have more income for child-rearing expenses.

Are U.S. women who have focused on their careers anxious about being childless? A recent book, *Creating a Life: Professional Women and the Quest for Children* (Hewlett, 2002), described the results of interviews with 1,186 high-achieving career women (income in the top 10 percent of their age group) from 28 to 55 years of age. Among the findings were:

- Thirty-three percent were childless at age 40.
- Forty-two percent who worked in corporations were childless.
- Forty-nine percent of "ultra-achievers" (earning more than $100,000 a year) were childless.
- Twenty-five percent of childless high achievers who were from 41 to 55 years of age would still like to have a child and 31 percent of "ultra-achievers" would still like to have one.
- No high achiever from 41 to 55 years of age had a first child after age 39 and no "ultra-achiever" had a child after age 36.

Many of the study's childless women in their forties and fifties recommended that younger women spend more time envisioning what their life will be like when they become middle-aged and whether they want their life to include a child. They argue that many high-achieving women will ultimately be happier if they have a child in their twenties or thirties. Critics respond that the optimal age for mother-hood depends on the individual and that many women become mothers after they are 35 years of age.

The Transition to Parenting   Whether people become parents through pregnancy, adoption, or stepparenting, they face disequilibrium and must adapt (Cox & others, 2004; Heincke, 2002). Parents want to develop a strong attachment with their infant, but they still want to maintain strong attachments to their spouse and friends, and possibly continue their careers. Parents ask themselves how this new being will change their lives. A baby places new restrictions on partners; no longer will they be able to rush out to a movie on a moment's notice, and money may not be readily available for vacations and other luxuries. Dual-career parents ask, "Will it harm the baby to place her in child care? Will we be able to find responsible baby-sitters?"

In a longitudinal investigation of couples from late pregnancy until 3½ years after the baby was born, couples enjoyed more positive marital relations before the baby was born than after (Cowan & others, 1995; Cowan & Cowan, 2000). Still, almost one-third showed an increase in marital satisfaction. Some couples said that the baby had both brought them closer together *and* moved them farther apart; being parents enhanced their sense of themselves and gave them a new, more stable identity as a couple. Babies opened men up to a concern with intimate relationships, and the demands of juggling work and family roles stimulated women to manage family tasks more efficiently and pay attention to their own personal growth.

At some point during the early years of the child's life, parents face the difficult task of juggling their roles as parents and as self-actualizing adults. Until recently, nurturing children and having a career were thought to be incompatible and the nurturing was supposed to be the mother's job. Fortunately, we have come to recognize that a balance between caring and achieving, nurturing and working—although difficult—can be accomplished (Hoffman & Youngblood, 1999).

Parenting Styles and Discipline

Parenting requires interpersonal skills and makes emotional demands, yet there is little in the way of formal education for this task. Most parents learn parenting practices from their own parents—some they accept, some they discard. Husbands and wives may bring different views of parenting to the marriage. Unfortunately, when parenting methods are passed on from one generation to the next, both desirable and undesirable practices are perpetuated.

Parents want their children to grow into socially mature individuals, and they may feel frustrated in trying to discover the best way to accomplish this. Developmentalists have long searched for the ingredients of parenting that promote competent socioemotional development (Brooks, 1999; Parke, 2004). The work of Diana Baumrind (1971) has been especially influential.

Baumrind's Classification of Parenting Styles   Baumrind believes that parents should be neither punitive nor aloof. Rather, they should develop rules for their children and be affectionate with them. She identified four types of parenting styles:

- **Authoritarian parenting** is a restrictive, punitive style in which parents exhort the child to follow their directions and to respect their work and effort. The authoritarian parent places firm limits and controls on the child and allows little verbal exchange. For example, an authoritarian parent might say, "You do it my way or else." Authoritarian parents also might spank the child frequently,

authoritarian parenting A restrictive, punitive style in which parents exhort the child to follow their directions and to respect their work and effort. Firm limits are placed on the child and little verbal exchange is allowed.

	Accepting, responsive	Rejecting, unresponsive
Demanding, controlling	Authoritative	Authoritarian
Undemanding, uncontrolling	Indulgent	Neglectful

FIGURE 14.8 Classification of Parenting Styles

The four types of parenting styles (authoritative, authoritarian, indulgent, and neglectful) involve the dimensions of acceptance and responsiveness, on the one hand, and demand and control on the other. For example, authoritative parenting involves being both accepting/responsive and demanding/controlling.

authoritative parenting A style that encourages children to be independent but still places limits and controls on children's actions; extensive verbal give-and-take is allowed and parents are warm and nurturant toward the child.

neglectful parenting A style in which the parent is very uninvolved in the child's life.

indulgent parenting A style in which parents are very involved with their children but place few demands or controls on them.

enforce rules rigidly but not explain them, and show rage toward the child. Children of authoritarian parents are often unhappy, fearful, and anxious about comparing themselves with others; they tend to fail to initiate activity and have weak communication skills.

- **Authoritative parenting** encourages children to be independent but still places limits and controls on their actions. Extensive verbal give-and-take is allowed, and parents are warm and nurturant toward the child. An authoritative parent might put his arm around the child in a comforting way and say, "You know you should not have done that. Let's talk about how you can handle the situation better next time." Authoritative parents support children's constructive behavior. They also expect mature, independent, and age-appropriate behavior of children. Children whose parents are authoritative are often cheerful, self-controlled, self-reliant, and achievement-oriented; they maintain friendly relations with peers, cooperate with adults, and cope well with stress.

- **Neglectful parenting** is a style in which the parent is very uninvolved in the child's life. Children whose parents are neglectful develop the sense that other aspects of the parents' lives are more important than they are. These children tend to be socially incompetent. Many have poor self-control and don't handle independence well. They frequently have low self-esteem, are immature, and may be alienated from the family. In adolescence, they may show patterns of truancy and delinquency.

- **Indulgent parenting** is a style of parenting in which parents are very involved with their children but place few demands or controls on them. These parents let their children do what they want. Children never learn to control their own behavior and always expect to get their way. Some parents deliberately rear their children in this way because they believe that the combination of warm involvement and few restraints will produce a creative, confident child. However, children whose parents are indulgent rarely learn respect for others and have difficulty controlling their behavior. They might be domineering, egocentric, noncompliant, and have difficulties in peer relations.

These four styles of parenting involve combinations of acceptance and responsiveness on the one hand and demand and control on the other. How these dimensions combine to produce authoritarian, authoritative, neglectful, and indulgent parenting is shown in figure 14.8. Research studies continue to document more positive links between authoritative parenting and the well-being of children and adolescents than for the other three types (Slicker & Thornberry, 2003).

Why is authoritative parenting likely to be the most effective style? These reasons have been given (Steinberg & Silk, 2002):

1. Authoritative parents establish an appropriate balance between control and autonomy, giving children opportunities for self-initiative while providing the standards, limits, and guidance that children need (Rueter & Conger, 1995).
2. Authoritative parents are more likely to engage children in verbal give-and-take and allow children to express their views (Kuczynski & Lollis, 2002). This type of family discussion is likely to help children to understand social relationships and what is required for being a socially competent person.
3. The warmth and parental involvement provided by authoritative parents make children more receptive to parental influence (Sim, 2000).

Do the benefits of authoritative parenting transcend the boundaries of ethnicity, socioeconomic status, and household composition? Although occasional exceptions to patterns have been found, the evidence linking authoritative parenting with

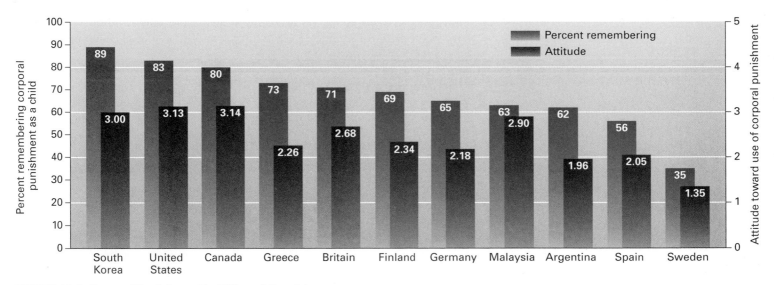

FIGURE 14.9 Corporal Punishment in Different Countries

A 5-point scale was used to assess attitudes toward corporal punishment with scores closer to 1 indicating an attitude against its use and scores closer to 5 suggesting an attitude for its use.

competence on the part of the adolescent has been found in research across a wide range of ethnic groups, social strata, cultures, and family structures (Steinberg & Silk, 2002).

Punishment and Discipline For centuries, corporal (physical) punishment, such as spanking, has been considered a necessary and even desirable method of disciplining children (Greven, 1991). Use of corporal punishment is legal in every state in America, and it is estimated that 70 to 90 percent of American parents have spanked their children (Straus, 1991). A recent cross-cultural comparison found that individuals in the United States and Canada were among the most favorable toward corporal punishment and remembered it being used by their parents (Curran & others, 2001) (see figure 14.9).

Despite the widespread use of corporal punishment, there have been surprisingly few research studies on physical punishment, and those that have been conducted are correlational (Baumrind, Larzelere, & Cowan, 2002). Clearly, it would be highly unethical to randomly assign parents to either spank or not spank their children in an experimental study. Recall that cause and effect cannot be determined in a correlational study. In one correlational study, spanking by parents was linked with children's antisocial behavior, including cheating, telling lies, being mean to others, bullying, getting into fights, and being disobedient (Strauss, Sugarman, & Giles-Sims, 1997). In a recent study of White, African American, and Latino families, spanking by parents predicted an increase in children's problems over time in all three groups (McLoyd & Smith, 2002). However, when parents showed strong emotional support of the child, the link between spanking and child problems was reduced.

A recent research review concluded that corporal punishment by parents is associated with higher levels of immediate compliance and aggression among children, and lower levels of moral internalization and mental health (Gershoff, 2002). Some critics, though, argue that the research evidence is not yet sound enough to warrant a blanket injunction against corporal punishment (Baumrind, Larzelere, & Cowan, 2002).

What are some reasons for avoiding spanking or similar punishments? The reasons include:

- Punishment where adults yell, scream, or spank presents children with out-of-control models for handling stressful situations. Children may imitate this aggressive, out-of-control behavior.
- Punishment can instill fear, rage, or avoidance. For example, spanking the child may cause the child to avoid being around the parent and fear the parent.
- Punishment tells children what not to do rather what to do. Children should be given feedback, such as "Why don't you try this?"
- Punishment can be abusive. When parents discipline their children, they might not intend to be abusive but become so aroused when they are punishing the child that they become abusive (Baumrind, Larzelere, & Cowan, 2002).

Because of reasons such as these, Sweden passed in a law in 1979 forbidding parents to physically punish (spank or slap, for example) children. Since the law was enacted, youth rates of delinquency, alcohol abuse, rape, and suicide have dropped in Sweden (Durrant, 2002). These improvements may have occurred for other reasons, such as changing attitudes and opportunities for youth. Nonetheless, the Swedish experience suggests that physical punishment of children may be unnecessary. Other countries that have passed antispanking laws include Finland (1984), Denmark (1986), Norway (1987), Austria (1989), Cyprus (1994), Latvia (1998), Croatia (1999), Germany (2000), and Israel (2000).

Most child psychologists recommend reasoning with the child, especially explaining the consequences of the child's actions for others, as the best way to handle children's misbehaviors. Time-out, in which the child is removed from a setting where the child experiences positive reinforcement, can also be effective. For example, when the child has misbehaved, a parent might take away TV viewing for a specified period of time.

Child Abuse Unfortunately, punishment sometimes leads to the abuse of infants and children. In 2001, an estimated 903,000 U.S. children were victims of child abuse (U.S. Department of Health and Human Services, 2003). Eighty-four percent of these children were abused by a parent or parents. Laws in many states now require doctors and teachers to report suspected cases of child abuse, yet many cases go unreported, especially those of battered infants.

Many people have difficulty understanding parents who abuse or neglect their children. Our response is often outrage and anger at the parent. This outrage focuses attention on parents as bad, sick, monstrous, sadistic individuals who cause their children to suffer. Experts on child abuse believe that this view is too simple and deflects attention away from the social context of the abuse and the parents' coping skills. It is important to recognize that child abuse is a diverse condition, that it is usually mild to moderate in severity, and that it is only partially caused by personality characteristics of the parent (Azar, 2002; Field, 2000). Most often, the abuser is not a raging, uncontrolled physical abuser but an overwhelmed single mother in poverty who neglects the child.

Whereas the public and many professionals use the term *child abuse* to refer to both abuse and neglect, developmentalists increasingly use the term *child maltreatment* (Cicchetti, 2001; Kotch, 2003). This term does not have quite the emotional impact of the term *abuse* and acknowledges that maltreatment includes diverse conditions.

Types of Maltreatment The four main types of child maltreatment are physical abuse, child neglect, sexual abuse, and emotional abuse (National Clearinghouse on Child Abuse and Neglect Information, 2002):

- *Physical abuse* is characterized by the infliction of physical injury as result of punching, beating, kicking, biting, burning, shaking, or otherwise harming a child. The parent or other person may not have intended to hurt the child; the injury may have resulted from excessive physical punishment.

- *Child neglect* is characterized by failure to provide for the child's basic needs (Golden, Samuels, & Southall, 2003). Neglect can be physical, educational, or emotional:

  Physical neglect includes refusal of, or delay in, seeking health care; abandonment; expulsion from the home or refusal to allow a runaway to return home; and inadequate supervision.

  Educational neglect involves the allowance of chronic truancy, failure to enroll a child of mandatory school age in school, and failure to attend to a special education need.

  Emotional neglect includes such actions as marked inattention to the child's needs for affection; refusal of or failure to provide necessary psychological care; spouse abuse in the child's presence; and permitting drug or alcohol use by the child.

- *Sexual abuse* includes fondling a child's genitals, intercourse, incest, rape, sodomy, exhibitionism, and commercial exploitation through prostitution or the production of pornographic materials. Many experts believe that sexual abuse is the most underreported type of child maltreatment because of the secrecy or "conspiracy of silence" that so often characterizes sexual abuse cases (Bouvier, 2003).

- *Emotional abuse (psychological/verbal abuse/mental injury)* includes acts or omissions by parents or other caregivers that have caused, or could cause, serious behavioral, cognitive, or emotional problems. Some cases of emotional abuse may not reveal any harm in the child's behavior or condition but are serious enough to warrant intervention by child protective services. For example, parents or others may use unusual types of punishment, such as confining a child in a dark closet. Less severe acts, such as frequent belittling and rejection of the child, are often difficult to prove and make it difficult for child protective services to intervene.

Although any of these forms of child maltreatment may be found separately, they often occur in combination. Emotional abuse is almost always present when other forms are identified.

The Cultural Context of Abuse

The extensive violence that takes place in American culture is reflected in the occurrence of violence in the family (Azar, 2002). A regular diet of violence appears on television screens, and parents often resort to power assertion as a disciplinary technique. In China, where physical punishment is rarely used to discipline children, the incidence of child abuse is reported to be very low. In the United States, many abusing parents report that they do not have sufficient resources or help from others. This may be a realistic evaluation of the situation of many low-income families.

Family Influences

To understand abuse in the family, the interactions of all family members need to be considered, regardless of who performs the violent acts against the child (Margolin, 1994). For example, even though the father may be the one who physically abuses the child, contributions by the mother, the child, and siblings also should be evaluated. Many parents who abuse their children come from families in which physical punishment was used. These parents view physical punishment as a legitimate way of controlling the child's behavior.

Were parents who abuse children abused by their own parents? About one-third of parents who were abused themselves when they were young abuse their own children (Cicchetti & Toth, 1998). Thus, some, but not a majority, of parents are locked into an intergenerational transmission of abuse. Mothers who break out of the intergenerational transmission of abuse often have at least one warm, caring

National Clearinghouse on Child Abuse and Neglect

Child Abuse Prevention Network

International Aspects of Child Abuse

*C*hild maltreatment involves grossly inadequate and destructive aspects of parenting.

—DANTE CICCHETTI
Contemporary Developmental Psychologist, University of Rochester

Early Childhood: Child Maltreatment

adult in their background; have a close, positive marital relationship; and have received therapy (Egeland, Jacobvitz, & Sroufe, 1988).

Developmental Consequences of Abuse Among the developmental consequences of child maltreatment are poor emotion regulation, attachment problems, problems in peer relations, difficulty in adapting to school, and other psychological problems (Azar, 2002; Maughan & Cicchetti, 2002; Shonk & Cicchetti, 2001). Maltreated infants may show excessive negative affect or blunted positive affect. Maltreated children appear to be poorly equipped to develop successful peer relations, due to their aggressiveness, avoidance, and aberrant responses to both distress and positive approaches from peers (Bolger & Patterson, 2001; Mueller & Silverman, 1989).

Being physically abused has been linked with children's anxiety, personality problems, depression, conduct disorder, and delinquency (Shonk & Cicchetti, 2001; Zielinski & others, 2003). Later, during the adult years, maltreated children show increased violence toward other adults, dating partners, and marital partners, as well as increased substance abuse, anxiety, and depression (Malinosky-Rummell & Hansen, 1993). In sum, maltreated children are at risk for developing a wide range of problems and disorders (Bissada & Briere, 2002).

Coparenting A dramatic increase in research on *coparenting* has occurred in the last two decades. The theme of this research is that poor coordination between parents, undermining of the other parent, lack of cooperation and warmth, and disconnection by one parent are conditions that place children at risk for problems (McHale & others, 2002). By contrast, parental cooperation and warmth are linked with children's prosocial behavior and competence in peer relations. For example, in one study, 4-year-old children from families characterized by low levels of mutuality and support in coparenting were more likely than their classmates to show difficulties in social adjustment on the playground (McHale, Johnson, & Sinclair, 1999).

Good Parenting Takes Time and Effort In U.S. society today, there is an unfortunate theme suggesting that parenting can be done quickly, with little or no inconvenience (Sroufe, 2000). One example is the practice of playing Mozart CDs in the hope that they will enrich infants' and young children's brains. One-minute bedtime stories are being marketed successfully for parents to read to their children (Walsh, 2000). Most of these are brief summaries of longer stories. There are one-minute bedtime bear books, puppy books, and so on. These parents know it is good to read to their children, but they don't want to spend a lot of time doing it.

Judith Harris' (1998) book *The Nurture Assumption* (which states that heredity and peer relations are the key factors in children's development) fits into this theme that parents don't need to spend much time with their children. Why did it become so popular? Perhaps in part because it made people who don't spend much time with their children feel less guilty.

What is wrong with these quick-fix approaches to parenting? Good parenting takes a lot of time and a lot of effort (Hoghugi & Long, 2004). You can't do it in a minute here and a minute there. You can't do it with CDs.

Parent-Adolescent Relationships

Even the best parents may find their relationship with their child strained during adolescence. Important aspects of parent-adolescent relationships include autonomy/attachment and conflict.

Autonomy and Attachment The adolescent's push for autonomy and responsibility puzzles and angers many parents. Parents see their teenager slipping from their

*P*arenting is a very important profession, but no test of fitness for it is ever imposed in the interest of children.

—GEORGE BERNARD SHAW
Irish Playwright, 20th Century

grasp. They may have an urge to take stronger control as the adolescent seeks autonomy and responsibility. Heated emotional exchanges may ensue, with either side calling names, making threats, and doing whatever seems necessary to gain control. Most parents anticipate that their teenager will have some difficulty adjusting to the changes that adolescence brings, but few parents can imagine and predict just how strong an adolescent's desires will be to spend time with peers or how much adolescents will want to show that it is they—not their parents—who are responsible for their successes and failures.

The ability to attain autonomy and gain control over one's behavior in adolescence is acquired through appropriate adult reactions to the adolescent's desire for control. At the onset of adolescence, the average individual does not have the knowledge to make mature decisions in all areas of life. As the adolescent pushes for autonomy, the wise adult relinquishes control in those areas in which the adolescent can make reasonable decisions but continues to guide the adolescent to make reasonable decisions in areas in which the adolescent's knowledge is more limited. Gradually, adolescents acquire the ability to make mature decisions on their own (Zimmer-Gembeck & Collins, 2003).

Gender differences characterize autonomy-granting in adolescence, with boys being given more independence than girls. In one recent study, this was especially true in those U.S. families that had a traditional gender-role orientation (Bumpus, Crouter, & McHale, 2001).

Cultural differences also characterize adolescent autonomy. In one study, U.S. adolescents sought autonomy earlier than Japanese adolescents (Rothbaum & others, 2000). In the transition to adulthood, Japanese youth are less likely to live outside the home than Americans (Hendry, 1999).

Even while adolescents seek autonomy, parent-child attachment remains important. Recall from chapter 10 that researchers have linked adolescents' secure attachment to their parents with the adolescents' well-being. For example, Joseph Allen and his colleagues (Allen & Hauser, 1994; Allen & Kuperminc, 1995; Allen & others, 2003) found that securely attached adolescents were less likely than those who were insecurely attached to engage in problem behaviors, such as juvenile delinquency and drug abuse. In other research, securely attached adolescents had better peer relations than their insecurely attached counterparts (Cassidy & Shavor, 1999; Kobak, 1999; Laible, Carlo, & Raffaeli, 2000).

Parent-Adolescent Conflict Although attachment to parents may remain strong during adolescence, the connectedness is not always smooth. Early adolescence is a time when conflict with parents escalates (Adams & Laursen, 2001; Holmbeck, 1996; Steinberg & Silk, 2002). Much of the conflict involves the everyday events of family life, such as keeping a bedroom clean, dressing neatly, getting home by a certain time, and not talking forever on the phone. The conflicts rarely involve major dilemmas, such as drugs and delinquency.

The increased conflict in early adolescence may be due to a number of factors: the biological changes of puberty, cognitive changes involving increased idealism and logical reasoning, social changes focused on independence and identity, maturational changes in parents, and expectations that are violated by parents and adolescents (Collins & Laursen, 2004). Adolescents compare their parents to an ideal standard and then criticize their flaws. Many parents see their adolescent changing from a compliant child to someone who is noncompliant, oppositional, and resistant to parental standards.

It is not unusual to hear parents of young adolescents ask, "Is it ever going to get better?" Things usually do get better as adolescents move from early to late adolescence. Conflict with parents often escalates during early adolescence, remains somewhat stable during the high school years, and then lessens as the adolescent reaches 17 to 20 years of age. Parent-adolescent relationships become more positive

Old Model	New Model
Autonomy, detachment from parents; parent and peer worlds are isolated	Attachment and autonomy; parents are important support systems and attachment figures; adolescent-parent and adolescent-peer worlds have some important connections
Intense, stressful conflict throughout adolescence; parent-adolescent relationships are filled with storm and stress on virtually a daily basis	Moderate parent-adolescent conflict common and can serve a positive developmental function; conflict greater in early adolescence, especially during the apex of puberty

FIGURE 14.10 Old and New Models of Parent-Adolescent Relationships

> When I was a boy of 14, my father was so ignorant I could hardly stand to have the man around. But when I got to be 21, I was astonished at how much he had learnt in 7 years.
>
> —MARK TWAIN
> *American Writer and Humorist,*
> *20th Century*

if adolescents go away to college than if they stay at home and go to college (Sullivan & Sullivan, 1980).

The everyday conflicts that characterize parent-adolescent relationships may serve a positive function. These minor disputes and negotiations facilitate the adolescent's transition from being dependent on parents to becoming an autonomous individual. For example, in one study, adolescents who expressed disagreement with their parents explored identity development more actively than did adolescents who did not express disagreement with their parents (Cooper & others, 1982). One way for parents to cope with the adolescent's push for independence and identity is to recognize that adolescence is a 10- to 15-year transitional period in the journey to adulthood, rather than an overnight accomplishment. Recognizing that conflict and negotiation can serve a positive developmental function can tone down parental hostility too. Understanding parent-adolescent conflict, though, is not simple (Conger & Ge, 1999; Riesch & others, 2003).

In sum, the old model of parent-adolescent relationships suggested that parent-adolescent conflict is intense and stressful throughout adolescence. The new model emphasizes that most parent-adolescent conflict is moderate rather than intense and that the moderate conflict can serve a positive function. Figure 14.10 summarizes the old and new models of parent-adolescent relationships, which include changes in thinking about attachment and autonomy.

Still, a high degree of conflict characterizes some parent-adolescent relationships. According to one estimate, parents and adolescents engage in prolonged, intense, repeated, unhealthy conflict in about one in five families (Montemayor, 1982). In other words, 4 to 5 million American families encounter serious, highly stressful parent-adolescent conflict. And this prolonged, intense conflict is associated with a number of adolescent problems—movement out of the home, juvenile delinquency, school dropout, pregnancy and early marriage, membership in religious cults, and drug abuse (Brook & others, 1990).

Some cultures are marked by less parent-adolescent conflict than others. American psychologist Reed Larson (1999) studied middle-socioeconomic-status adolescents and their families in India. He observed that in India there seems to be little parent-adolescent conflict and that many families likely would be described as "authoritarian" in Baumrind's categorization. Larson also observed that in India adolescents do not go through a process of breaking away from their parents and that parents choose their youths' marital partners. Researchers have also found considerably less conflict between parents and adolescents in Japan than in the United States (Rothbaum & others, 2000).

Conclusions   We have seen that parents play very important roles in adolescent development. Although adolescents are moving toward independence, they still need to stay connected with families (Collins & Laursen, 2004; Roth & Brooks-Gunn, 2000). In the National Longitudinal Study on Adolescent Health (Council of Economic Advisors, 2000) of more than 12,000 adolescents, those who did not eat dinner with a parent five or more days a week had dramatically higher rates of smoking, drinking, marijuana use, getting into fights, and initiation of sexual activity. In another recent study, parents who played an active role in monitoring and guiding their adolescents' development were more likely to have adolescents with positive peer relations and lower drug use than parents who had a less active role (Mounts, 2002).

Competent adolescent development is most likely when adolescents have parents who (Small, 1990):

- Show them warmth and mutual respect
- Demonstrate sustained interest in their lives
- Recognize and adapt to their cognitive and socioemotional development
- Communicate expectations for high standards of conduct and achievement
- Display constructive ways of dealing with problems and conflict

These ideas coincide with Diana Baumrind's (1971, 1991) authoritative parenting style.

Working Parents

More children and adolescents are growing up in diverse family structures than ever before. The increased number of mothers in the labor force represents one source of change in U.S. families and U.S. society. Many mothers spend the greatest part of their day away from their children, even their infants. More than one of every two mothers with a child under the age of 5 is in the labor force; more than two of every three with a child from 6 to 17 years of age is. What are the implications?

Recall that in Bronfenbrenner's ecological theory, the exosystem is an environmental system in which experiences in another social context—in which the individual does not have an active role—influence what the individual experiences in an immediate social context. The link between the social context of parents' work and the social context of the family illustrates the concept of exosystem.

Because household operations have become more efficient and family size has decreased in America, it is not certain that when both parents work outside the home, children receive less attention than children in the past whose mothers were not employed. Parents might spend less time than in the past keeping the house clean or pursuing hobbies. Time once split among children might now be focused on one or two. It also cannot be assumed that if the mother did not go to work, the child would benefit from the extra time and attention. Parenting does not always have a positive effect on the child. Parents may overinvest in their children, worrying excessively and discouraging the child's independence. The needs of the growing child require the mother to give increasing independence to the child, which may be easier for women whose job provides an additional source of identity and self-esteem.

As Lois Hoffman (1989) commented, maternal employment is a part of modern life. It is not an aberrant aspect of it but a response to other social changes. A number of researchers have found no detrimental effects of maternal employment on children's development (Gottfried, Gottfried, & Bathurst, 2002; Hoffman & Youngblade, 1999). Work can produce positive and negative effects on parenting. Work-related stress can spill over and harm parenting, but a sense of well-being produced by work can lead to more positive parenting.

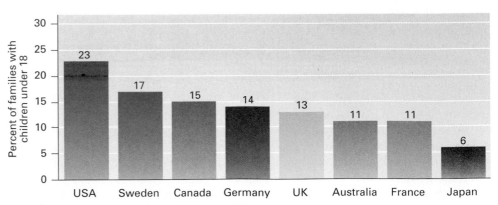

FIGURE 14.11 Single-Parent Families in Different Countries

Family and the Workplace

However, when a child's mother works in the first year of life it can have a negative effect on the child's later development (Belsky & Eggebeen, 1991; Hill & others, 2001). For example, a recent major longitudinal study found that the 3-year-old children of mothers who went to work before the children were 9 months old had poorer cognitive outcomes than 3-year-old children whose mothers had stayed at home with them in the first nine months of the child's life (Brooks-Gunn, Han, & Waldfogel, 2002). The negative effects of going to work during the child's first nine months were less pronounced when the mothers worked less than 30 hours a week, the mothers were more sensitive (responsive and comforting) in their caregiving, and the child care the children received outside the home was higher in quality.

Effects of Divorce on Children

The increasing number of children growing up in single-parent families is staggering. As shown in figure 14.11, the United States has the highest percentage of single-parent families, compared with virtually all other countries. Many of these families are the result of divorce. Let's examine some important questions about the effects of divorce on children.

Are children better adjusted in intact, never divorced families than in divorced families? Most researchers agree that children from divorced families show poorer adjustment than their counterparts in nondivorced families (Amato & Keith, 1991; Harvey & Fine, 2004; Hetherington & Stanley-Hagan, 2002) (see figure 14.12). Those that have experienced multiple divorces are at greater risk. Children in divorced families are more likely than children in nondivorced families to have academic problems, to show externalized problems (such as acting out and delinquency) and internalized problems (such as anxiety and depression), to be less socially responsible, to have less competent intimate relationships, to drop out of school, to become sexually active at an early age, to take drugs, to associate with antisocial peers, and to have low self-esteem (Conger & Chao, 1996). Keep in mind that a majority of children in divorced families do not have significant adjustment problems.

Should parents stay together for the sake of the children? Whether parents should stay in an unhappy or conflicted marriage for the sake of their children is one of the most commonly asked questions about divorce (Hetherington, 1999, 2000). If the stresses and disruptions associated with an unhappy marriage that erode the well-being of children are reduced by the move to a divorced, single-parent family, divorce can be advantageous. However, if the diminished resources and increased risks associated with divorce also are accompanied by inept parenting and sustained or increased conflict (not only between the divorced couple but also among parents, children, and siblings), the best choice for the children would be for

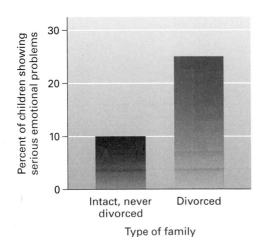

FIGURE 14.12 Divorce and Children's Emotional Problems

In Hetherington's research, 25 percent of children from divorced families showed serious emotional problems compared with only 10 percent of children from intact, never-divorced families. However, keep in mind that a substantial majority (75 percent) of the children from divorced families did not show serious emotional problems.

an unhappy marriage to be retained (Hetherington & Stanley-Hagan, 2002). These are "ifs," and it is difficult to determine how these will play out. Note that marital conflict may have negative consequences for children in the context of marriage or divorce (Cummings, Braungart-Rieker, & Du Rocher-Schudlich, 2003; Cummings & Davies, 2002; Hetherington & Kelly, 2002).

How much do family processes matter in divorced families? Family processes matter a lot (Emery & others, 2001; Hetherington & Stanley-Hagan, 2002; Kelly, 2001; Weinraub, Horvath, & Gringlas, 2002). When divorced parents' relationships with each other is harmonious and when they use authoritative parenting, the adjustment of children improves (Hetherington, Bridges, & Insabella, 1998). A number of researchers have shown that a disequilibrium, which includes diminished parenting skills, occurs in the year following the divorce but that, by two years after the divorce, restablization has occurred and parenting skills have improved (Hetherington, 1989).

What factors are involved in the child's individual risk and vulnerability in a divorced family? Among the factors involved in the child's risk and vulnerability are the child's adjustment prior to the divorce, as well as the child's personality and temperament, gender, and custody situation (Hetherington & Stanley-Hagan, 2002). Children whose parents later divorce show poorer adjustment before the breakup (Amato & Booth, 1996). Children who are socially mature and responsible, who show few behavioral problems, and who have an easy temperament are better able to cope with their parents' divorce. Children with a difficult temperament often have problems in coping with their parents' divorce (Hetherington, 1999).

Earlier studies reported gender differences in response to divorce, with divorce being more negative for girls than boys in mother-custody families. However, more recent studies have shown that gender differences are less pronounced and consistent than was previously believed. Some of the inconsistency may be due to the increase in father custody, joint custody, and increased involvement of noncustodial fathers, especially in their sons' lives. There appear to be few advantages of joint custody over custody by one parent (Hetherington, Bridges, & Insabella. 1998). Some studies have shown that boys adjust better in father-custody families, girls in mother-custody families, while other studies have not (Santrock & Warshak, 1979; Maccoby & Mnookin, 1992).

What role does socioeconomic status play in the lives of children in divorced families? Custodial mothers experience the loss of about one-fourth to one-half of their predivorce income, in comparison with a loss of only one-tenth by custodial fathers (Emery, 1999). This income loss for divorced mothers is accompanied by increased workloads, high rates of job instability, and residential moves to less desirable neighborhoods with inferior schools.

In the Applications in Life-Span Development interlude, you can read about some good strategies for communicating with children about divorce.

Children and Divorce

Divorce Resources

Father Custody

Middle and Later Childhood: Divorce and Child Development

Applications in Life-Span Development

Communicating with Children About Divorce

Ellen Galinsky and Judy David (1988) developed a number of guidelines for communicating with children about divorce.

Explaining the Separation

As soon as the daily activities in the home make it obvious that one parent is leaving, tell the children. If possible, both parents should be present when the children are made aware of the separation to come. The reasons for the separation are very difficult for young children to understand. No matter what parents tell children, children can find reasons to argue against the separation. A child may say something like "If you don't love each other anymore, you need to start trying harder." One set of parents told their 4-year-old, "We both love you. We will both always love you and take care of you, but we aren't going to live in the same house anymore. Daddy is moving to an apartment near the stores where we shop." It is extremely important for parents to tell the children who will take care of them and to describe the specific arrangements for seeing the other parent.

Explaining That the Separation Is Not the Child's Fault

Young children often believe their parents' separation or divorce is their own fault. Therefore, it is important to tell children that they are not the cause of the separation. Parents need to repeat this a number of times.

Explaining That It May Take Time to Feel Better

It is helpful to tell young children that it's normal to not feel good about what is happening and that lots of other children feel this way when their parents become separated. It is also okay for divorced parents to share some of their emotions with children, by saying something like "I'm having a hard time since the separation just like you, but I know it's going to get better after a while." Such statements are best kept brief and should not criticize the other parent.

Keeping the Door Open for Further Discussion

Tell your children that anytime they want to talk about the separation to come to you. It is healthy for children to express their pent-up emotions in discussions with their parents and to learn that the parents are willing to listen to their feelings and fears.

Providing as Much Continuity as Possible

The less children's worlds are disrupted by the separation, the easier their transition to a single-parent family will be. This means maintaining the rules already in place as much as possible. Children need parents who care enough to not only give them warmth and nurturance but also to set reasonable limits. If the custodial parent has to move to a new home, it is important to preserve as much of what is familiar to the child as possible. In one family, the child helped arrange her new room exactly as it had been prior to the divorce. If children must leave friends behind, it is important for parents to help the children stay in touch by phone or by letter. Keeping the children busy and involved in the new setting can also keep their minds off stressful thoughts about the separation.

Providing Support for Your Children and Yourself

After a divorce or separation, parents are as important to children as before the divorce or separation. Divorced parents need to provide children with as much support as possible. Parents function best when other people are available to give them support as adults and as parents. Divorced parents can find people who provide practical help and with whom they can talk about their problems. One divorced parent commented, "I've made a mess of my life. I don't deserve anybody's help." Seeking out others for support and feedback about problems can make the transition to a single-parent family more bearable.

Stepfamilies

Not only are parents divorcing more, they are also getting remarried more (Dunn & others, 2001). The number of remarriages involving children has grown steadily in recent years. About half of all children whose parents divorce will have a stepparent within four years of parental separation. However, divorces occur at a 10 percent higher rate in remarriages than in first marriages (Cherlin & Furstenberg, 1994).

In some cases, the stepfamily may have been preceded by the death of the spouse. However, by far the largest number of stepfamilies are preceded by divorce rather than death.

Three common types of stepfamily structure are (1) stepfather, (2) stepmother, and (3) blended or complex. In stepfather families, the mother typically had custody of the children and remarried, introducing a stepfather into her children's lives. In stepmother families, the father usually had custody and remarried, introducing a stepmother into his children's lives. In a blended or complex stepfamily, both parents bring children from previous marriages to live in the newly formed stepfamily.

Children's relationships with custodial parents (mothers in stepfather families, fathers in stepmother families) are often better than with stepparents (Santrock, Sitterle, & Warshak, 1988). Also, children in simple families (stepmother, stepfather) often show better adjustment than their counterparts in complex (blended) families (Anderson & others, 1999; Hetherington & Kelly, 2002).

Children in stepfamilies show more adjustment problems than children in nondivorced families (Hetherington, Bridges, & Isabella, 1998). The adjustment problems are similar to those in divorced children—academic problems and lower self-esteem, for example (Anderson & others, 1999). However, like divorced children, a majority of children in stepfamilies do not have problems. In one recent analysis, 20 percent of children from stepfamilies showed adjustment problems compared with 10 percent in intact, never-divorced families (Hetherington & Kelly, 2002; Hetherington & Stanley-Hagan, 2002). In another recent study, children's depressive symptoms increased in the first few years after a stepfamily was formed but the longer they were in the stepfamily the fewer depressive symptoms they had (Sweeney, 2003).

Early adolescence is an especially difficult time for the formation of a stepfamily (Anderson & others, 1999). It may be that becoming part of a stepfamily exacerbates normal adolescent concerns about identity, sexuality, and autonomy. To read further about stepfamilies, see the Research in Life-Span Development interlude.

Stepfamily Support

Research in Life-Span Development
Family Functioning and Adolescent Adjustment in Stepfamilies

In a longitudinal study, E. Mavis Heth-erington and her colleagues (1999) examined family relationships and the adjustment of two adolescent siblings (who varied in degree of biological relatedness) in non-stepfamilies and in simple and complex stepfamilies. *Simple stepfamilies* were those in which all of the children were fully biologically related siblings from the mother's previous marriage. *Complex stepfamilies* were those in which both residential siblings had different relationships to the biological parents. All couples in stepfamilies had been remarried for a minimum of five years and an average of nine years. The families were seen twice, three years apart. Family relationships and adolescent adjustment were assessed using interviews and questionnaires with the mothers, fathers/stepfathers, and the two siblings. Observations of family interaction also were conducted in the home.

There were few differences between non-stepfamily and simple stepfamily members. However, being in a complex stepfamily was linked with more family relationship problems, such as parent-adolescent conflict and the adolescent being less well adjusted—with lower social responsibility and more externalized problems.

Review and Reflect: Learning Goal 3

3 **Characterize parenting and how it affects children's development**

REVIEW

- What are parental roles?
- What are four main parenting styles and how are they linked with children's development? Is physical punishment a wise choice by parents? What is the nature of child abuse? Does coparenting have positive effects on children? Can parenting be done quickly?
- How can parent-adolescent relationships be described?
- What is the link between working mothers and children's development?
- How does divorce affect children's development?
- What influence does growing up in a stepfamily have on children's development?

REFLECT

- What stereotypes exist about children from these types of families: working mother; divorced; and stepfamily?

---

4 OTHER FAMILY RELATIONSHIPS

Sibling Relationships and Birth Order	Grandparenting	Intergenerational Relationships

Important as child-parent relationships are to children's development, other family relationships are also significant. Here we briefly examine sibling relationships, grandparenting, and intergenerational relationships.

Sibling Relationships and Birth Order

More than 80 percent of American children have one or more siblings. Any of you who have grown up with siblings probably have a rich memory of aggressive, hostile interchanges. But sibling relationships also have many pleasant, caring moments (Zukow-Goldring, 2002). Children's sibling relationships include helping, sharing, teaching, fighting, and playing. Siblings can act as emotional supports, rivals, and communication partners (Zukow-Goldring, 2002). One recent study found that adolescent siblings spent an average of 10 hours a week together with an average of 12 percent of that time spent in constructive time (creative activities such as art, music, and hobbies; sports; religious activities; and games)

*B*ig sisters are the crabgrass in the lawn of life.
—CHARLES SCHULZ
American Cartoonist, 20th Century

and 25 percent in nonconstructive time (watching TV and hanging out) (Tucker, McHale, & Crouter, 2003). Also, in one study, positive sibling relationships in adolescence contributed to a sense of emotional and school-related support (Seginer, 1998).

Because there are so many possible sibling combinations, it is difficult to generalize about sibling influences. Among the factors to consider are the number of siblings, the ages of siblings, birth order, age spacing, the sex of siblings, and whether sibling relationships are different from parent-child relationships (Teti, 2001).

Sibling relationships persist over the entire life span for most adults (Teti, 2001; White, 2001). Eighty-five percent of today's adults have at least one living sibling. Sibling relationships in adulthood may be extremely close, apathetic, or highly rivalrous. The majority of sibling relationships in adulthood have been found to be close (Cicirelli, 1991). Those siblings who are psychologically close to each other in adulthood tended to be that way in childhood. It is rare for closeness between siblings to develop for the first time in adulthood (Dunn, 1984).

Does it matter whether a child is a firstborn in a family or a later-born or only child? Researchers have found links between certain characteristics and birth order within the family. They usually explain these differences by pointing to variations in how parents and siblings interact with a child, depending on the child's position in the family. This is especially true in the case of the firstborn child (Teti, 2001).

Parents have higher expectations for firstborn children than for later-born children. They put more pressure on them for achievement and responsibility. They also interfere more with their activities (Rothbart, 1971). Given these differences, it is not surprising that firstborns and later-borns have different characteristics (Rodgers, 2000; Zajonc, 2001). Firstborn children are more adult-oriented, helpful, conforming, anxious, and self-controlled than their siblings. They excel in academic and professional endeavors. Firstborns are overrepresented in *Who's Who* and Rhodes scholars, for example. However, firstborns also have more guilt, anxiety, and difficulty in coping with stressful situations, as well as higher admission to child guidance clinics. Parents give more attention to firstborns, and this is related to firstborns' nurturant behavior (Stanhope & Corter, 1993).

What is the only child like? The popular conception is that the only child is a self-centered "spoiled brat," with such undesirable characteristics as dependency and lack of self-control. But researchers present a more positive portrayal of the only child, who often is achievement-oriented and displays a desirable personality, especially in comparison with later-borns and children from large families (Falbo & Poston, 1993; Jiao, Ji, & Jing, 1996).

Keep in mind, though, that birth order by itself often is not a good predictor of behavior. Factors such as age spacing, the sex of siblings, heredity, temperament, parenting styles, peer influences, school influences, sociocultural factors, and so forth are often more important in determining a child's behavior than birth order.

The one-child family is becoming much more common in China because of the strong motivation to limit the population growth in the People's Republic of China. The effects of this policy have not been fully examined. *In general, what have researchers found the only child to be like?*

Early Childhood: Motor Skills and Birth Order

Grandparenting

As more individuals live to an old age, and as more families live in varied family structures, we can expect the nature of the grandparent's role and social interaction with grandchildren to change (Reitzes & Mutran, 2004; Smith & Drew, 2002). How satisfying is it to be a grandparent? What roles do grandparents assume, and what styles do they use with their grandchildren?

Satisfaction with Grandparenting   A majority of grandparents say that grandparenting is easier than parenting. In one study, frequent contact with grandchildren predicted high levels of satisfaction with grandparenting for both grandmothers and

Foundation of Grandparenting

Grandparent Visitation Rights

grandfathers (Peterson, 1999). Opportunities to observe their grandchildren's development and share in their activities were described as the best features of being a grandparent; lack of frequent contact with grandchildren was pointed to as the worst feature. Only a small minority (8 percent) of Australian grandparents said that they were more dissatisfied than satisfied with their grandparenting role (Peterson, 1999).

Grandparent Roles and Styles   What is the meaning of the grandparent role? Three prominent meanings are attached to being a grandparent (Neugarten & Weinstein, 1964). For some older adults, being a grandparent is a source of biological reward and continuity. For others, being a grandparent is a source of emotional self-fulfillment, generating feelings of companionship and satisfaction that may have been missing in earlier adult-child relationships (Sanders & Trygstad, 1993). And for yet others, being a grandparent is a remote role.

The grandparent role may have different functions in different families, in different ethnic groups and cultures, and in different situations (Kivnick & Sinclair, 1996). For example, in one study of White, African American, and Mexican American grandparents and grandchildren, the Mexican American grandparents saw their grandchildren more frequently, provided more support for the grandchildren and their parents, and had more satisfying relationships with their grandchildren (Bengtson, 1985). And in a study of three generations of families in Chicago, grandmothers had closer relationships with their children and grandchildren and gave more personal advice than grandfathers did (Hagestad, 1985).

The diversity of grandparenting was also apparent in an early investigation of how grandparents interacted with their grandchildren (Neugarten & Weinstein, 1964). Three styles were dominant—formal, fun-seeking, and distant. In the formal style, the grandparent performed what was considered to be a proper and prescribed role. These grandparents showed a strong interest in their grandchildren, but were careful not to give child-rearing advice. In the fun-seeking style, the grandparent was informal and playful. Grandchildren were a source of leisure activity; mutual satisfaction was emphasized. A substantial portion of grandparents were distant figures. In the distant-figure style, the grandparent was benevolent but interaction was infrequent. Grandparents who were over the age of 65 were more likely to display a formal style of interaction; those under 65 were more likely to display a fun-seeking style.

The Changing Profile of Grandparents   In 1997, the U.S. Bureau of the Census issued its first detailed portrait of living arrangements involving grandparents. Especially noticeable was the increasing number of grandchildren living with their grandparents (Fuller-Thompson & Minkler, 2001). In 1980, 2.3 million grandchildren lived with their grandparents, but in 2000 that figure had reached 5.6 million (U.S. Bureau of the Census, 2001). Forty-two percent of those grandparents are responsible for their grandchildren. Divorce, adolescent pregnancies, and drug use by parents are the main reasons that grandparents are thrust back into the "parenting" role they thought they had shed.

Almost half of the grandchildren who move in with grandparents are raised by a single grandmother. These families are mainly African American (53 percent). When both grandparents are raising grandchildren, the families are overwhelmingly White.

Grandparents who take in grandchildren are in better health, are better educated, are more likely to be working outside the home, and are younger than grandparents who move in with their children. Less than 20 percent of grandparents whose grandchildren move in with them are 65 years old or older. In one recent study of grandparents raising their grandchildren, younger grandparents, grandchildren with physical and psychological problems, and low family cohesion were associated with stress (Sands & Goldberg-Glen, 2000).

According to the 2000 U.S. Census report, a majority of the grandparents living with their children contributed to the family income and provided child care while parents worked. Only about 10 percent of the grandparents who move in with their children and grandchildren are in poverty. Almost half of the grandparents who move in with their children are immigrants. Partly because women live longer than men, there are more grandmothers than grandfathers (2.9 million versus 1.7 million) who live with their children. About 70 percent of the grandparents who move in with their children are grandmothers.

As divorce and remarriage have become more common, a special concern of grandparents is visitation privileges with their grandchildren. In the last 10 to 15 years, more states have passed laws giving grandparents the right to petition a court for visitation privileges with their grandchildren, even if a parent objects. Whether such forced visitation rights for grandparents are in the child's best interest is still being debated.

Intergenerational Relationships

With each new generation, personality characteristics, attitudes, and values are replicated or changed. As older family members die, their biological, intellectual, emotional, and personal legacies are carried on in the next generation. Their children become the oldest generation and their grandchildren the second generation. As adult children become middle-aged they often develop more positive perceptions of their parents (Field, 1999). In one study, conflicts between mothers and daughters decreased across the life course in both the United States and Japan (Akiyama & Antonucci, 1999).

For the most part, family members maintain considerable contact across generations (Allen, Blieszener, & Roberto, 2000; Bengtson, 2001; Miller-Day, 2004). As we continue to stay connected with our parents and our children as we age, both similarity and dissimilarity across generations are found (Palkovitz & others, 2003). For example, similarity between parents and an adult child is most noticeable in religion and politics, least in gender roles, lifestyle, and work orientation.

What are the most common conflicts that arise in relationships between parents and adult children? In one study, they included communication and interaction style (such as "He is always yelling" and "She is too critical"), habits and lifestyle choices (such as sexual activity, living arrangements), child-rearing practices and values (such as decisions about having children, being permissive or controlling), politics, religion, and ideology (such as lack of religious involvement) (Clarke & others, 1999). In this study, there were generational differences in the perception of the main conflicts. Parents most often listed habits and lifestyle choices; adult children cited communication and interaction style.

A consistent finding in intergenerational research is that parents and their young adult children differ in the way they describe their relationship. For example, in one study, middle-aged parents were especially likely to report that the relationship was closer (Acquilino, 1999). A longitudinal study found that parents continued to give more favorable evaluations of their relationships with adult children across 17 years (Giarrusso & Du Feng, 1999).

The relationship between parents and their adult children is related to the nature of their earlier relationship as these studies indicate:

- In a New Zealand study, supportive family environments and parenting when the children were 3 to 15 years of age were linked with more positive relationships (in terms of contact, closeness, conflict, and reciprocal assistance) between the children and their middle-aged parents when the children were 26 years old (Belsky & others, 2001).

What is the nature of intergenerational relationships?

The Sandwich Generation

*I*n case you're worried about what's going to become of the younger generation, it's going to grow up and start worrying about the younger generation.

—ROGER ALLEN
American Writer, 20th Century

- In another study, individuals who felt trusted by their parents in adolescence reported greater closeness to their parents in early adulthood (Jacobs & Tanner, 1999). Also in this study, daughters who had experienced long-term lack of trust during adolescence were more alienated from their parents as young adults than sons who had similar experiences.

- In yet another study, the motivation of adult children to provide social support to their older parents was linked with earlier family experiences (Silverstein & others, 2002). Children who spent more time in shared activities with their parents and were given more financial support by them earlier in their lives provided more support to their parents when they became older.

Converging findings across a broad range of research populations in various countries suggest that problematic parenting develops in part through learning the behavior modeled by one's parents (Capaldi & others, 2003; Conger & others, 2003; Serbin & Karp, 2003). Also, problematic parenting seems to be an extension of an individual's early style of aggressive and problematic social behavior (Serbin & Karp, 2004; Thornberry & others, 2003). For example, parents with a history of childhood aggression tend to have continuing social, behavioral, and health difficulties, as do their offspring (Fagot & others, 1998; Serbin & others, 1998). Conversely, parental involvement, cognitive stimulation, and warmth appear to have important protective effects for offspring (Serbin & Stack, 1998). And educational achievement appears to be a powerful buffer against problematic parenting, protecting families from the transfer of risk across generations (Serbin & Karp, 2003).

Gender differences also characterize intergenerational relationships (Bengtson, 2001; Brown & Roodin, 2003; Etaugh & Bridges, 2001; Krishnakumar & Black, 2003; Norris, Pratt, & Kulack, 2003). In one study, mothers and their daughters had much closer relationships during their adult years than mothers and sons, fathers and daughters, and fathers and sons (Rossi, 1989). Also in this study, married men were more involved with their wives' kin than with their own. And maternal grandmothers and maternal aunts were cited twice as often as their counterparts on the paternal side of the family as the most important or loved relative.

Middle-aged adults play an important role in intergenerational relationships (Fingerman & Lang, 2004; Williams & Nussbaum, 2001). They have been described as the "sandwich," "squeeze," or "overload" generation because of the responsibilities they have for their adolescent and young adult children on the one hand and their aging parents on the other (Etaugh & Bridges, 2001). Daughters are almost three times more likely than are sons to give their parents assistance in daily living activities (Dwyer & Coward, 1991). These simultaneous pressures from adolescents or young adult children and aging parents may contribute to stress in middle adulthood.

Fewer middle-aged adults act as caregivers to both a parent and to their own children than reports in the media might suggest (Hoyer & Roodin, 2003). In one large-scale study, a large majority of middle-aged children did not provide direct care for their parents (Rosenthal, Martin-Matthews, & Matthews, 1996). When this responsibility was required, it most often was assumed by daughters in their mid to late fifties who did not simultaneously have direct child-care or child-rearing responsibilities. In another study, the point at which adult children took responsibility for caring for their parents usually coincided with the launching of their adult children (Soldo, 1996).

Many middle-aged adults experience considerable stress when their parents become very ill and die (Lachman, 2004). One survey found that when adults enter midlife, 41 percent have both parents alive but that 77 percent leave midlife with no parents alive (Bumpass & Acquilino, 1994).

Review and Reflect: Learning Goal 4

4 **Explain other aspects of family relationships**

REVIEW

- How do siblings interact with each other? How is birth order linked with developmental outcomes?
- What is the nature of grandparenting?
- How do intergenerational relationships influence development?

REFLECT

- Do you have a sibling(s)? If so, what is your relationship like? Has it changed over the years? If you don't have a sibling, how do you think your life would have been different with one or more siblings?

Reach Your Learning Goals

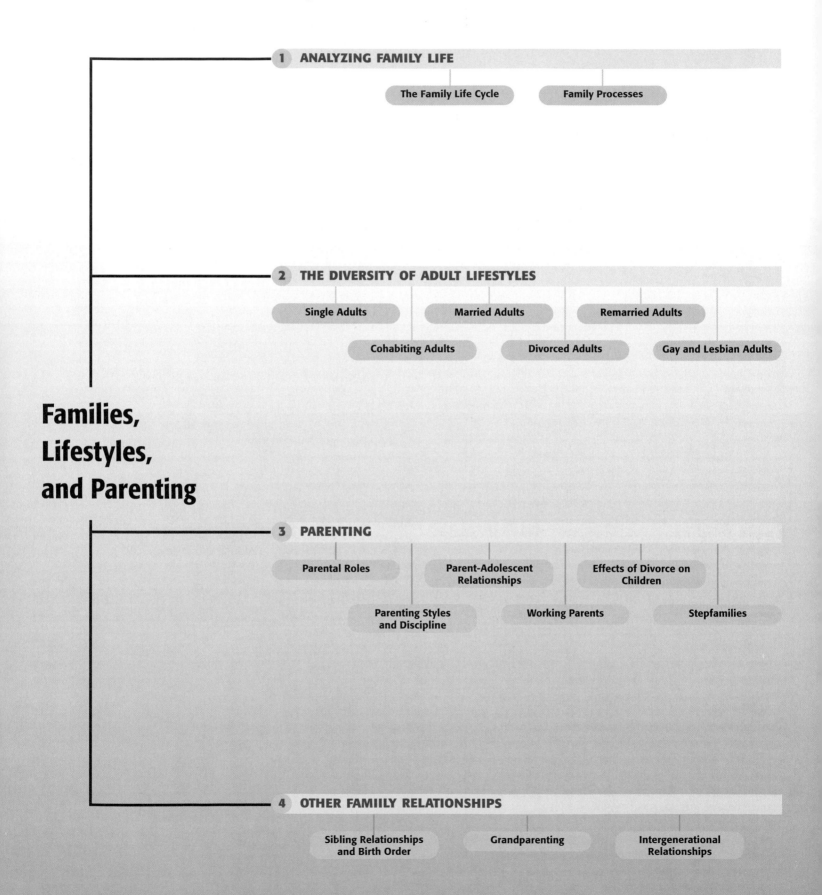

Families, Lifestyles, and Parenting

1 ANALYZING FAMILY LIFE

The Family Life Cycle

Family Processes

2 THE DIVERSITY OF ADULT LIFESTYLES

Single Adults

Married Adults

Remarried Adults

Cohabiting Adults

Divorced Adults

Gay and Lesbian Adults

3 PARENTING

Parental Roles

Parent-Adolescent Relationships

Effects of Divorce on Children

Parenting Styles and Discipline

Working Parents

Stepfamilies

4 OTHER FAMIILY RELATIONSHIPS

Sibling Relationships and Birth Order

Grandparenting

Intergenerational Relationships

Summary

1   Describe the family life cycle and family processes

- The family life cycle consists of six stages: (1) leaving home and becoming a single adult, (2) the new couple, (3) becoming parents and a family with children, (4) becoming a family with adolescents, (5) the family at midlife, and (6) the family in later life.
- Among the most important aspects of family processes are reciprocal socialization, the family as a system, and sociocultural and historical changes.

2   Discuss the diversity of adult lifestyles and how they influence people's lives

- Being single has become an increasingly prominent lifestyle. Myths and stereotypes about singles abound, ranging from "swinging single" to "desperately lonely, suicidal single." There are advantages and disadvantages to being single, autonomy being one of the advantages. Intimacy, loneliness, and finding a positive identity in a marriage-oriented society are concerns of single adults.
- Cohabitation is an increasing lifestyle for many adults. Cohabitation offers some advantages as well as problems. Cohabitation does not lead to greater marital happiness but rather to no differences or differences suggesting that cohabitation is not good for a marriage.
- Even though adults are remaining single longer and the divorce rate is high, Americans still show a strong predilection for marriage. The age at which individuals marry, expectations about what the marriage will be like, and the developmental course of marriage vary not only over time within a culture, but also across cultures. Gottman has conducted the most extensive research on what makes marriages work. In his research these principles characterize good marriages: establishing love maps, nurturing fondness and admiration, turning toward each other instead of away, letting your partner influence you, solving solvable conflicts, overcoming gridlock, and creating shared meaning. The benefits of marriage include better physical and mental health and a longer life. A majority of middle-aged adults who are married say their marriage is good or excellent. The time from retirement until death is sometimes called the final stage in the marital process.
- The U.S. divorce rate increased dramatically in the twentieth century but began to decline in the 1980s. Divorce is complex and emotional. In the first year following divorce, a disequilibrium in the divorced adult's behavior occurs, but by several years after the divorce, more stability has been achieved. The divorced displaced homemaker may encounter excessive stress. Men do not go through a divorce unscathed either.
- Stepfamilies are complex and adjustment is difficult. Only about one-third of remarried adults with children stay remarried.
- One of the most striking findings about gay and lesbian couples is how similar they are to heterosexual couples. Researchers have found that the children of gay and lesbian parents are as well adjusted as those of heterosexual couples. The overwhelming number of children in gay and lesbian families grow up to be heterosexual.

3   Characterize parenting and how it affects children's development

- There are many myths about the parenting role. Currently, there is a trend toward having fewer children and choosing when to have children. The transition to parenting involves a great deal of adaptation for many people.
- Authoritarian, authoritative, neglectful, and indulgent are four main parenting styles. Authoritative parenting is the style most often associated with children's social competence. Physical punishment is widely used by U.S. parents, but there are a number of reasons why it is not a good choice. The four main types of child abuse are physical abuse, child neglect, sexual abuse, and emotional abuse. An understanding of child abuse requires information about cultural, familial, and community influences. Child maltreatment places the child at risk for a number of developmental problems. Coparenting has positive effects on children's development. In today's society, an unfortunate theme is that parenting can be done quickly. However, good parenting takes extensive time and effort.
- Adolescents seek to be independent but secure attachment to parents is positive for development. Conflict with parents often increases in adolescence but it usually is moderate rather than severe.
- For many children, when both parents work full-time outside the home there are no negative long-term effects on children. However, in specific circumstances, as when both parents work in the first year of the infant's life, negative effects have recently been found.
- Overall, divorce is linked with adjustment problems in children, but not for all children. Whether parents should stay together for the sake of the children is a difficult question to answer. Family processes, such as harmony between parents, quality of parenting, and support systems, matter in divorced children's development. So does socioeconomic status.
- Children in stepparent families have more problems than their counterparts in nondivorced families. Adolescence is an especially difficult time for remarriage of parents to occur. Restabilization takes longer in stepfamilies than divorced families.

4   Explain other aspects of family relationships

- Siblings interact with each other in positive and negative ways. Birth order is related in certain ways to child characteristics, but some critics argue that birth order is not a good predictor of behavior.

- A large majority of grandparents are satisfied with their grandparenting role. The grandparent role can have different meanings. The grandparent role may have different functions in different families, ethnic groups, cultures, and situations. The changing profile of grandparents involves an increasing number of grandchildren living with their grandparents.

- Continuing contact across generations in families usually occurs. Mothers and daughters have the closest relationship. The middle-age generation has been called the"sandwich" generation. The middle-age generation plays an important role in linking generations.

Key Terms

leaving home and becoming a
  single adult 482
launching 482
new couple 482

becoming parents and a family
  with children 483
family with adolescents 483
family at midlife 483

family in later life 483
reciprocal socialization 484
scaffolding 484
authoritarian parenting 497

authoritative parenting 498
neglectful parenting 498
indulgent parenting 498

Key People

John Gottman 489

E. Mavis Hetherington 493

Diana Baumrind 497

Lois Hoffman 505

E-Learning Tools

Connect to **www.mhhe.com/santrockldt2** to research the answers and complete these exercises. In addition, you'll find a number of other resources and valuable study tools for chapter 14, "Families, Lifestyles, and Parenting," on the Student CD-ROM that came with this book.

Taking It to the Net

1. Chad is a paralegal in his mother's law firm. His mother just took the case of a woman who announced that she is lesbian, left her husband of 10 years, and is fighting for custody of her two girls, ages 5 and 7. Chad's mother has asked him to find out what the research says about the gender identity and sexual orientation of girls raised by lesbian mothers. What will Chad find?

2. Jocelyn, who feels that she was not a very good mother to her son, Jack, now 30 and with two children of his own, has tried to make up for it by being a devoted grandmother. Jocelyn is devastated to hear that Jack and his wife are divorcing and Jack has agreed to give custody of the children to his wife. Jack told Jocelyn not to count on seeing the children much, because his wife and Jocelyn never got along. What legal rights does Jocelyn have to continue having a relationship with her grandchildren?

3. Ellen, expecting her first child in a month, told her mother of her plans to return to work when the baby is 6 months old. "I wish you would reconsider," her mother said. "I was just reading last week about how bad it is for the kids to be in child care, especially so early." "Oh, mother," Ellen said. "That is old news. The latest research is that child care is good for kids." Who is right?

Self-Assessment

To evaluate your ideas about the best ways to parent children and the extent to which your parents monitored your behavior in adolescence, complete this self-assessment:

- *My Beliefs About Parenting*
- *How Much Did My Parents Monitor My Behavior in Adolescence?*

Health and Well-Being, Parenting, and Education

Build your decision-making skills by trying your hand at the health and well-being, parenting, and education "Scenarios."

Peers and the Sociocultural World

Chapter Outline

Learning Goals

PEER RELATIONS IN CHILDHOOD AND ADOLESCENCE

1   Discuss peer relations in childhood and adolescence

Functions of Peer Groups

Adult-Child and Peer Relations

Developmental Changes

Social Cognition

Peer Statuses

Bullying

Gender and Peer Relations

Adolescent Peer Relations

FRIENDSHIP

2   Explain the role of friendship through the life span

Functions of Friendship

Friendship During Childhood

Friendship During Adolescence

Adult Friendship

PLAY AND LEISURE

3   Describe the developmental aspects of play and leisure

Childhood

Adolescence

Adulthood

AGING AND THE SOCIAL WORLD

4   Summarize the social aspects of aging

Social Theories of Aging

Stereotyping of Older Adults

Social Support and Social Integration

Successful Aging

SOCIOCULTURAL INFLUENCES

5   Evaluate sociocultural influences on development

Culture

Socioeconomic Status and Poverty

Ethnicity

The social worlds outside of the family play important roles in life-span development. As we go through life, we interact with a convoy of people through peer relations, friendships, cliques, and support systems in many different cultural worlds.

1 PEER RELATIONS IN CHILDHOOD AND ADOLESCENCE

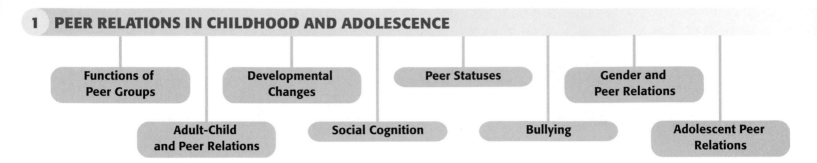

As children grow older, peer relations consume increasing amounts of their time. What is the function of a child's peer group?

Functions of Peer Groups

Peers are individuals of about the same age or maturity level. Same-age peer interaction fills a unique role in our culture (Hartup, 1983). Even if schools were not graded by age and children were left alone to determine the composition of their own societies, they would form peer groups. Peer groups provide a source of information and comparison about the world outside the family. Children receive feedback about their abilities from their peer group. They evaluate what they do in terms of whether it is better than, as good as, or worse than what other children do. It is hard to do this at home because siblings are usually older or younger.

Are peers necessary for development? When peer monkeys who have been reared together are separated, they become depressed and regress socially (Suomi, Harlow, & Domek, 1970). The human development literature contains a classic example of the importance of peers in social development. Anna Freud (Freud & Dann, 1951) studied six children from different families who banded together after their parents were killed in World War II. Intensive peer attachment was observed; the children formed a tightly knit group, dependent on one another and aloof with outsiders. Even though deprived of parental care, they became neither delinquent nor psychotic.

Both Jean Piaget (1932) and Harry Stack Sullivan (1953) stressed that children learn reciprocity through interaction with their peers. Children explore the meanings of fairness and justice by working through disagreements with peers. They also learn to be keen observers of peers' interests and perspectives in order to smoothly integrate themselves into ongoing peer activities.

Of course, peer influences can be negative as well as positive (McHale & others, 2003). Being rejected or overlooked by peers leads some children to feel lonely or hostile. Further, rejection and neglect by peers are related to an individual's subsequent mental health and criminal problems. Withdrawn children who are rejected by peers or victimized and lonely are at risk for depression. Children who are aggressive with their peers are at risk for developing a number of problems, including delinquency and dropping out of school. Peers can also undermine parental values and control.

Keep in mind that the influences of peer experiences vary according to the way peer experience is measured, the outcomes specified, and the developmental trajectories traversed (Hartup, 1999). For example, "peer group" might refer to

peers Individuals of about the same age or maturity level.

acquaintances, clique, neighborhood associates, a friendship network, or an activity group (Brown, 1999).

Adult-Child and Peer Relations

What are some of the differences between peer relations and adult-child relationships? Rough-and-tumble play occurs mainly with other children, not with adults, and children often turn to their parents rather than their peers in times of stress. Peer relations also are likely to be much more equal than are parent-child relations. Because parents have greater knowledge and authority, children must often learn how to conform to rules laid down by parents. With peers, children learn to form and assert their own opinions, appreciate the perspective of peers, cooperatively resolve disagreements, and evolve mutually acceptable standards of conduct.

Parents influence peer relations in numerous ways (Kerr & others, 2003). Their choices of neighborhoods, churches, schools, and their own friends influence the pool from which their children might select possible friends (Cooper & Ayers-Lopez, 1985). In addition, parents may recommend strategies to their children, such as how to handle disputes or how to become less shy. They may encourage their children to be tolerant or to resist peer pressure. And parent-child relationships can provide the emotional basis for exploring and enjoying peer relations (Ladd & Pettit, 2002; Schneider, Atkinson, & Tardif, 2001).

Carollee Howes and her colleagues have conducted a number of research studies to demonstrate that relationships with teachers, as well as parents, can benefit children's socioemotional development and peer relations. In one study, children in child-care settings who had secure attachment relationships with their teachers were more gregarious and less hostile toward their peers than were their counterparts with insecure attachments with their teachers (Howes, Matheson, & Hamilton, 1994). In another study, young children who were more sociable with parents *and* teachers also were more sociable with peers than were children who were less sociable with these adults (Howes & Clements, 1994). In yet another study, children's secure attachments with teachers compensated for insecure attachments with parents in terms of the children's social competence (Howes & others, 1988). In sum, parent-child and peer worlds are coordinated and connected, but they also are distinct.

Developmental Changes

Some researchers believe that peer interaction in infancy provides valuable information about social development (Vandell, 1985). For example, in one investigation, positive affect in infant peer relations was related to easy access to peer play groups and to peer popularity in early childhood (Howes, 1985).

The frequency of peer interaction picks up considerably during early childhood (Hartup, 1983). Although aggressive interaction and rough-and-tumble play increase, the *proportion* of aggressive exchanges, compared with friendly exchanges, decreases.

Children spend an increasing amount of time in peer interaction during middle and late childhood. In one investigation, children interacted with peers 10 percent of their day at age 2, 20 percent at age 4, and more than 40 percent between the ages of 7 and 11. In a typical school day, episodes with peers totaled 299 per day (Barker & Wright, 1951).

Social Cognition

With age, children tend to acquire more mature ways of relating to peers. This maturing in part reflects their changing social cognitions. *Social cognitions* involve thoughts about social matters (Lewis & Carpendale, 2002). Children who are unable

www.mhhe.com/santrockldt2

Peer Relations

Child Development CD

Early Childhood: Peer Relations and Exploration in Early Childhood

to interact effectively with each other may lack necessary cognitive skills (Rabiner & others, 1991). What skills are important to their peer relations? Three possibilities are perspective-taking ability, social knowledge, and social information-processing skills.

Perspective Taking As we discussed in chapter 13, "Moral Development, Values, and Religion" *perspective taking* involves taking another's point of view ◀◀▥ **P. 446.** As children enter the elementary school years, both their peer interaction and their perspective-taking ability increase. Reciprocity is especially important in peer interchanges at this point in development as children play games, function in groups, and cultivate friendships.

Researchers have documented the link between perspective-taking skills and the quality of peer relations, especially in the elementary school years (LeMare & Rubin, 1987). Perspective-taking skills probably help peer relations in part because they improve communication effectiveness. One investigation evaluated the communication exchanges among peers at kindergarten, first-, third-, and fifth-grade levels (Krauss & Glucksberg, 1969). Children were asked to instruct a peer in how to stack a set of blocks. The peer sat behind a screen with blocks similar to those the other child was stacking (see figure 15.1). The kindergarten children made numerous errors in telling the peer how to duplicate the novel block stack. The older children, especially the fifth-graders, were much more efficient in communicating to a peer how to stack the blocks. They were sensitive to the communication demands of the task and were far superior at perspective taking and figuring out how they had to talk for the peer to understand them. In elementary school, children also become more efficient at understanding complex messages, so the listening skills of the peer in this experiment probably helped the communicating peer as well.

Social Knowledge Social knowledge also is involved in children's ability to get along with peers. In particular, they need to know which goals to pursue in ambiguous situations and which *scripts* to follow to get children to be their friends. For example, it helps to know that saying nice things, regardless of what the peer does or says, will make the peer like the child more.

Social Information-Processing Skills How do children process information about peer relations? For example, a boy accidentally trips and knocks another boy's

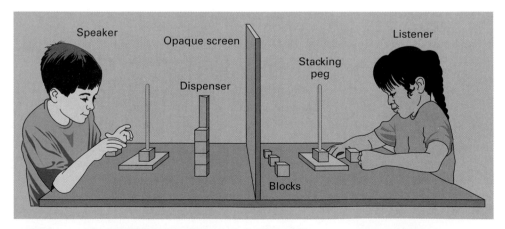

FIGURE 15.1 The Development of Communication Skills

This is an experimental arrangement of speaker and listener in the investigation of the development of communication skills.

soft drink out of his hand. How does the other boy interpret his action? Suppose he misinterprets the encounter as hostile, which leads him to retaliate aggressively against the boy who tripped him. If he has repeated encounters of this kind, other peers come to perceive the aggressor as habitually acting inappropriately.

Peer relations researcher Kenneth Dodge (1993) has found that aggressive boys are more likely to perceive another child's actions as hostile when the child's intention is ambiguous. And when aggressive boys search for clues to determine a peer's intention, they respond more rapidly, less efficiently, and less reflectively than nonaggressive children. Children who respond in these ways are often rejected by their peers, and as we will see shortly, they can be helped through social skills training.

Peer Statuses

The term *sociometric status* is used to describe the extent to which children are liked or disliked by their peer group. Sociometric status is typically assessed by asking children to rate how much they like or dislike each of their classmates. Or it may be assessed by asking children to nominate the children they like the most and those they like the least.

Developmentalists have distinguished five types of peer statuses (Wentzel & Asher, 1995):

- **Popular children** are frequently nominated as a best friend and are rarely disliked by their peers.
- **Average children** receive an average number of both positive and negative nominations from their peers.
- **Neglected children** are infrequently nominated as a best friend but are not disliked by their peers.
- **Rejected children** are infrequently nominated as someone's best friend and are actively disliked by their peers.
- **Controversial children** are frequently nominated both as someone's best friend and as being disliked.

Popular children have a number of social skills that contribute to their being well liked. Researchers have found that popular children give out reinforcements, listen carefully, maintain open lines of communication with peers, are happy, control their negative emotions, act like themselves, show enthusiasm and concern for others, and are self-confident without being conceited (Hartup, 1983; Rubin, Bukowski, & Parker, 1998).

Neglected children engage in low rates of interaction with their peers and are often described as shy by peers. Rejected children often have more serious adjustment problems than those who are neglected (Parker & Asher, 1987). For example, one recent study found that in kindergarten, rejected children were less likely to engage in classroom participation, express a desire to avoid school, and more likely to report being lonely (Buhs & Ladd, 2002).

Rejection and aggressiveness are an especially problematic mix. In one study, 112 fifth-grade boys were evaluated over a period of seven years until the end of high school (Kupersmidt & Coie, 1990). The best predictor of whether rejected children would engage in delinquent behavior or drop out of school later during adolescence was aggression toward peers in elementary school. Another recent study found that when third-grade boys were highly aggressive and rejected by their peers, they showed markedly higher levels of delinquency as adolescents and young adults (Miller-Johnson, Coie, & Malone, 2003).

Not all rejected children are aggressive (Haselager & others, 2002; Hymel, McDougall, & Renshaw, 2002). Aggression and its related characteristics of impulsiveness and disruptiveness underlie rejection about half the time, but approximately 10 to 20 percent of rejected children are shy.

*P*eer rejection contributes to subsequent problems of adaptation, including antisocial behavior.

—JOHN COIE
Contemporary Psychologist, Duke University

popular children Children who are frequently nominated as a best friend and are rarely disliked by their peers.

average children Children who receive an average number of both positive and negative nominations from their peers.

neglected children Children who are infrequently nominated as a best friend but are not disliked by their peers.

rejected children Children who are infrequently nominated as a best friend and are actively disliked by their peers.

controversial children Children who are frequently nominated both as someone's best friend and as being disliked.

How can neglected children and rejected children be trained to interact more effectively with their peers? Many training programs for neglected children aim to help them attract attention from their peers in positive ways and to hold their attention by asking questions, by listening in a warm and friendly way, and by saying things about themselves that relate to the peers' interests. They also are taught to enter groups more effectively. Rejected children may be taught to more accurately assess whether the intentions of their peers are negative. Rejected children also may be asked to engage in role playing or to discuss hypothetical situations involving negative encounters with peers, such as when a peer cuts into a line ahead of them. In some programs, children are shown videotapes of appropriate peer interaction; then they are asked to comment on them and to draw lessons from what they have seen (Ladd, Buhs, & Troop, 2002).

Bullying

Significant numbers of students are victimized by bullies (Bukowski & Sippola, 2001; Espelage & Swearer, 2004; Pellegrini, 2002; Rigby, 2002; Swearer & others, 2004). In one recent national survey of more than 15,000 sixth- through tenth-grade students, nearly one of every three students said that they had experienced occasional or frequent involvement as a victim or perpetrator in bullying (Nansel & others, 2001). In this study, *bullying* was defined as verbal or physical behavior intended to disturb someone less powerful. Boys and younger middle school students were most likely to be affected. As shown in figure 15.2, being belittled about looks or speech was the most frequent type of bullying. Children who said they were bullied reported more loneliness and difficulty in making friends, while those who did the bullying were more likely to have low grades and to smoke and drink alcohol.

Victims of bullying have certain characteristics (Card, Isaacs & Hodges, 2000; Coleman & Byrd, 2003; Ladd & Kochenderfer-Ladd, 2002; Nansel & Overpeck, 2002; Pellegrini, 2002). In one recent study, victims had parents who were intrusive, demanding, and unresponsive with their children (Ladd & Kochenderfer-Ladd, 1998). Also, parent-child relationships characterized by intense closeness were linked with higher levels of peer victimization in boys. Overly close and emotionally intense relationships between parents and sons might promote self-doubts and worries that male peer groups perceive as weaknesses. Another study (Olweus, 1980) found that bullies' parents were more likely to be rejecting, authoritarian, or permissive about their sons' aggression, whereas victims' parents were more likely to be anxious and overprotective.

Victims of bullies can suffer both short-term and long-term effects (Limber, 1997). Short-term, they can become depressed, lose interest in schoolwork, or even avoid going to school. The effects of bullying can persist into adulthood. One longitudinal study of male victims who were bullied during childhood found that in their twenties they were more depressed and had lower self-esteem than their counterparts who had not been bullied in childhood (Olweus, 1993). Bullies may also display long-lasting problems. In the study just mentioned, about 60 percent of the boys who were identified as bullies in middle school had at least one criminal conviction (and about one-third had three or more convictions) in their twenties, rates that are far higher than the rates for nonbullies.

Some strategies that teachers can use to reduce bullying are (Limber, 1997, 2004; Olweus, 1993):

- getting older peers to serve as monitors for bullying and intervening when they see it taking place,
- developing school-wide rules and sanctions against bullying and posting them throughout the school,
- forming friendship groups for adolescents who are regularly bullied by peers, and

Peer Conflicts

Reducing Bullying

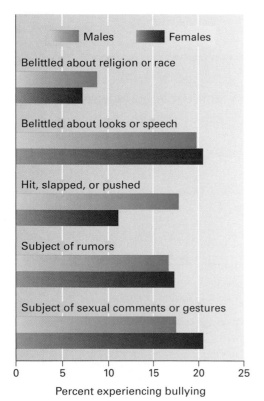

FIGURE 15.2 Bullying Behaviors Among U.S. Youth

This graph shows the type of bullying most often experienced by U.S. youth (Nansel & others, 2001). The percentages reflect the extent to which bullied students said that they had experienced a particular type of bullying. In terms of gender, note that when they were bullied, boys were more likely to be hit, slapped, or pushed than girls were.

- incorporating the message of the antibullying program into church, school, and other community activities.

Gender and Peer Relations

We noted that boys are far more likely to be involved in bullying than girls are. Indeed, there is increasing evidence that gender plays an important role in peer relations (Espelage, Mebane, & Swearer, 2004; McHale & others, 2003; Sebanc & others, 2003). Gender influences the composition of children's groups, their size, and the interaction within groups (Maccoby, 1998, 2002):

- *Gender composition.* Around the age of 3, children already prefer to spend time with same-sex playmates. From 4 to 12 years of age, this preference for playing in same-sex groups increases (see figure 15.3).
- *Group size.* From about 5 years of age onward, boys tend to associate in larger clusters than girls do. Girls are more likely than boys to play in groups of two or three.
- *Interaction in same-sex groups.* Boys are more likely to participate in organized group games than girls are. They also are more likely to engage in rough-and-tumble play, competition, conflict, ego displays, risk taking, and dominance seeking. And more than girls' groups, boys' groups seek to attain a group goal (Benenson, Apostolaris, & Parnass, 1997). By contrast, girls are more likely to engage in "collaborative discourse."

Participation in same-sex groups is linked with gender-typed behavior. One study found that over the course of six months, the more time boys spent playing with other boys, the more their activity level, rough-and-tumble play, and sex-typed choices of toys and games increased, and the less time they spent near adults (Martin & Fabes, 2001). By contrast, the more time girls spent playing with girls, the lower was their aggression and activity level, the higher their choices of girl-type play and activities, and the more time they spent near adults.

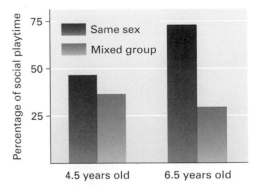

FIGURE 15.3 Developmental Changes in Percentage of Time Spent in Same-Sex and Mixed-Group Settings

Observations of children show that they are more likely to play in same-sex than mixed-sex groups. This tendency increases between 4 and 6 years of age.

Adolescent Peer Relationships

Adolescent Peer Relations

Peer relations play powerful roles in the lives of adolescents. When you think back to your adolescent years, many of your most enjoyable moments probably were spent with peers—on the telephone, in school activities, in the neighborhood, at dances, or just hanging out. Peer relations undergo important changes in adolescence. In childhood, the focus of peer relations is on being liked by classmates and being included in games or lunchroom conversations. Beginning in early adolescence, teenagers typically prefer to have a smaller number of friendships that are more intense and intimate than those of young children. Cliques are formed and shape the social lives of adolescents as they begin to "hang out" together (Brown, 2004).

Peer Pressure and Conformity Adolescents conform more to peer standards than children do. Consider this statement made by an adolescent girl:

> Peer pressure is extremely influential in my life. I have never had very many friends, and I spend quite a bit of time alone. The friends I have are older. . . . The closest friend I have had is a lot like me in that we are both sad and depressed a lot. I began to act even more depressed than before when I was with her. I would call her up and try to act even more depressed than I was because that is what I thought she liked. In that relationship, I felt pressure to be like her.

Around the ninth grade, conformity to peers—especially to their antisocial standards—peaks (Berndt, 1979; Leventhal, 1994) (see figure 15.4).

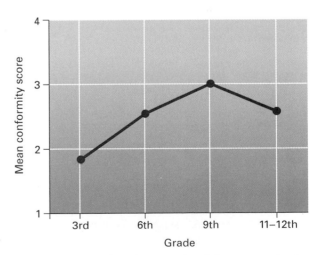

FIGURE 15.4 Conformity to Antisocial Peer Standards from the Third Through the Twelfth Grades

Higher scores indicate greater conformity to antisocial peer standards. Notice that conformity to antisocial peer standards increased through the child and early adolescent years, peaking in the ninth grade, and then dropping in the twelfth grade.

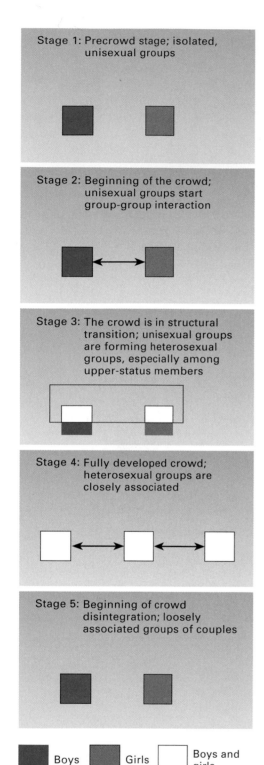

Stage 1: Precrowd stage; isolated, unisexual groups

Stage 2: Beginning of the crowd; unisexual groups start group-group interaction

Stage 3: The crowd is in structural transition; unisexual groups are forming heterosexual groups, especially among upper-status members

Stage 4: Fully developed crowd; heterosexual groups are closely associated

Stage 5: Beginning of crowd disintegration; loosely associated groups of couples

Boys   Girls   Boys and girls

FIGURE 15.5 Dunphy's Progression of Peer Group Relations in Adolescence

cliques Small groups that range from 2 to 12 individuals and average about 5 to 6 individuals.

crowds Peer groups that are larger and less personal than cliques.

At this point in development, an adolescent is most likely to go along with a peer to steal hubcaps, draw graffiti on a wall, or steal cosmetics from a store counter. But conformity to peer pressure in adolescence can be positive as well as negative. A great deal of peer conformity, such as dressing like one's friends and wanting to spend huge chunks of time with members of a clique, is not negative and reflects the desire to be involved in the peer world.

Cliques and Crowds Cliques and crowds assume more important roles in the lives of adolescents than children (Brown, 2003, 2004). **Cliques** are small groups that range from 2 to about 12 individuals and average about 5 to 6 individuals. The clique members are usually of the same sex and about the same age. Cliques can form because adolescents engage in similar activities, such as being in a club or on a sports team. Some cliques also form because of friendship. Several adolescents may form a clique because they have spent time with each other and enjoy each other's company. Not necessarily friends, they often develop a friendship if they stay in the clique. What do adolescents do in cliques? They share ideas, hang out together, and often develop an in-group identity, believing that their clique is better than other cliques.

Crowds are larger and less personal than cliques. Adolescents are usually members of a crowd based on reputation; members of a crowd may or may not spend much time together. Many crowds are defined by the activities adolescents engage in (such as "jocks" who are good at sports or "druggies" who take drugs).

Membership in a crowd is also linked with self-esteem. In one study, the crowds included jocks (athletically oriented), populars (well-known students who led social activities), normals (middle-of-the-road students who made up the masses), druggies or toughs (known for illicit drug use or other delinquent activities), and nobodies (low in social skills or intellectual abilities) (Brown & Lohr, 1987). The self-esteem of the jocks and the populars was highest, whereas that of the nobodies was lowest. One group of adolescents not in a crowd had self-esteem equivalent to that of the jocks and the populars; this group was the independents, who indicated that crowd membership was not important to them. Keep in mind that these data are correlational; self-esteem could increase an adolescent's probability of becoming a crowd member, just as crowd membership could increase the adolescent's self-esteem.

Adolescent Groups Versus Child Groups Adolescent groups differ from child groups in several important ways. Cross-sex peer relations increase. During the adolescent years, groups tend to include a broader array of members, beyond the friends or neighborhood acquaintances that often make up the members of child groups. Also, in adolescent peer groups, rules are usually more defined than in children's peer groups. For example, captains or leaders are usually formally elected or appointed in adolescent peer groups.

A well-known observational study by Dexter Dunphy (1963) supports the notion that participation in mixed-sex groups increases during adolescence. In late childhood, boys and girls participate in small, same-sex cliques. As they move into the early adolescent years, the same-sex cliques begin to interact with each other. Gradually, the leaders and high-status members form further cliques based on mixed-sex relationships. Eventually, the newly created mixed-sex cliques replace the same-sex cliques. The mixed-sex cliques interact with each other in large crowd activities, too—at dances and athletic events, for example. In late adolescence, the crowd begins to dissolve as couples develop more-serious relationships (see figure 15.5).

Peers play an important role in the development of individuals in all cultures. However, as indicated in the Contexts of Life-Span Development interlude, cultures vary in how strong the socializing role of peers is.

Contexts of Life-Span Development

Cross-Cultural Comparisons of Peer Relations

Adolescence : Peer Relations in Early Adolescence

In some countries, adults restrict adolescents' access to peers. For example, in many areas of rural India and in Arab countries, opportunities for peer relations are severely restricted, especially for girls (Brown & Larson, 2002). If girls attend school in these regions of the world, it is usually in sex-segregated schools. In these countries, interaction with the other sex or opportunities for romantic relationships are restricted (Booth, 2002).

In chapter 14, we indicated that Japanese adolescents seek autonomy later from their parents and have less conflict with them than American adolescents do. In a recent cross-cultural analysis, the peer group was more important to U.S. adolescents than to Japanese adolescents (Rothbaum & others, 2000). Japanese adolescents spend less time outside the home, have less recreational leisure time, and engage in fewer extracurricular activities with peers than U.S. adolescents (White, 1993). Also, U.S. adolescents are more likely to put pressure on their peers to resist parental influence than Japanese adolescents are (Rothbaum & others, 2000).

A trend, though, is that in societies in which adolescents' access to peers has been restricted, adolescents are engaging in more peer interaction during school and in shared leisure activities, especially in middle-socioeconomic-status contexts (Brown & Larson, 2002). For example, in Southeast Asia and some Arab regions, adolescents are starting to rely more on peers for advice and share interests with them (Booth, 2002; Santa Maria, 2002).

In many countries and regions, though, peers play more prominent roles in adolescents' lives (Brown & Larson, 2002). For example, in sub-Saharan Africa, the peer group is a pervasive aspect of children's and adolescents' lives (Nsamenang, 2002). Throughout Europe and North America, the peer group also is a ubiquitous part of adolescent life (Arnett, 2002).

Review and Reflect: Learning Goal 1

1 Discuss peer relations in childhood and adolescence

REVIEW

- What are the functions of peer groups? What are Piaget's and Sullivan's views on peers?
- How are the worlds of parents and peers distinct but coordinated?
- What is the developmental course of peer relations in childhood?
- How is social cognition involved in peer relations?
- Describe five types of peer statuses.
- What is the nature of bullying?
- How is gender involved in children's peer relations?
- What is peer pressure and conformity like in adolescence? How are cliques and crowds involved in adolescent development? How do adolescent groups differ from child groups?

REFLECT

- Think back to your childhood and adolescent years. Which peer status would you use to describe yourself? How important do you think your peer status was in your development?

2 FRIENDSHIP

```
Functions of Friendship        Friendship During Adolescence

        Friendship During Childhood        Adult Friendship
```

The world of peers is one of varying acquaintances; we interact with some people we barely know, and with others we know well, every day. It is to the latter type—friends—that we now turn.

Functions of Friendship

Friendships serve six functions (Gottman & Parker, 1987):

1. *Companionship.* Friendship provides a familiar partner, someone who is willing to engage in collaborative activities.
2. *Stimulation.* Friends provide interesting information, excitement, and amusement.
3. *Physical support.* Friends provide resources and assistance.
4. *Ego support.* Friendship provides the expectation of support, encouragement, and feedback that helps individuals maintain an impression of themselves as competent, attractive, and worthwhile.
5. *Social comparison.* Friends provide information about where individuals stand.
6. *Intimacy/affection.* Friendship provides a warm, close, trusting relationship with another individual, a relationship that involves self-disclosure. In most research, **intimacy in friendship** is defined narrowly as self-disclosure or sharing of private thoughts. Private or personal knowledge about a friend has been used as an index of intimacy (Selman, 1980; Sullivan, 1953).

Harry Stack Sullivan (1953) was the most influential theorist to discuss the importance of friendships. In contrast to other psychoanalytic theorists' narrow emphasis on parent-child relationships, Sullivan contended that friends also play important roles in well-being and development. In terms of well-being, he argued that all people have a number of basic social needs, including the need for tenderness (secure attachment), playful companionship, social acceptance, intimacy, and sexual relations. Whether or not these needs are fulfilled largely determines our emotional well-being. For example, if the need for playful companionship goes unmet, then we become bored and depressed; if the need for social acceptance is not met, we suffer a lowered sense of self-worth.

What are the main functions of friendship?

Middle and Later Childhood: Friends in Middle and Later Childhood

Friendship During Childhood

Willard Hartup (1996, 2000), who has studied peer relations across four decades, has concluded that many children use friends as cognitive and social resources on a regular basis. Hartup also commented that transitions, such as moving from elementary to middle school, are negotiated more competently by children who have friends than by those who don't.

Not all friendships and not all friends are equal. The quality of friendship is important to consider. Supportive friendships between socially skilled individuals are developmentally advantageous, whereas coercive and conflict-ridden friendships are not (Berndt, 2002; Hartup & Abecassis, 2000). Friendship and its developmental significance can vary from one child to another. Children's characteristics, such as temperament ("easy" versus "difficult" for example), likely influence the nature of their friendships.

Throughout the childhood years, friends are generally similar—in terms of age, sex, ethnicity, and many other factors (Luo, Fang, & Aro, 1995). Friends often have similar attitudes toward school, similar educational aspirations, and closely aligned

intimacy in friendship Self-disclosure and the sharing of private thoughts.

achievement orientations. Friends like the same music, wear the same kind of clothes, and prefer the same leisure activities (Berndt, 1982, 1999). If friends have different attitudes about school, one of them may want to play basketball or go shopping rather than do homework. If the other friend insists on completing homework, the conflict may weaken the friendship, and the two may drift apart.

Friendship During Adolescence

Sullivan argued that there is a dramatic increase in the psychological importance and intimacy of close friends during early adolescence. Thus the ups and downs of experiences with friends increasingly shape adolescents' well-being. In particular, Sullivan believed that the need for intimacy intensifies during early adolescence, motivating teenagers to seek out close friends. He felt that if adolescents failed to forge such close friendships, they would experience painful feelings of loneliness coupled with a reduced sense of self-worth.

Research findings support many of Sullivan's ideas. For example, adolescents report disclosing intimate and personal information to their friends more often than do younger children (Buhrmester, 1998; Buhrmester & Furman, 1987) (see figure 15.6). When young children talk about their friendships, they rarely comment about intimate self-disclosure or mutual understanding. In one investigation, friendship intimacy was more prominent in 13- to 16-year-olds than in 10- to 13-year-olds (Buhrmester, 1990). Adolescents also say they depend more on friends than on parents to satisfy their needs for companionship, reassurance of worth, and intimacy (Furman & Buhrmester, 1992). In one study, daily interviews with 13- to 16-year-old adolescents over a five-day period were conducted to find out how much time they spent engaged in meaningful interactions with friends and parents (Buhrmester & Carbery, 1992). Adolescents spent an average of 103 minutes per day in meaningful interactions with friends, compared with just 28 minutes per day with parents.

In addition, the quality of friendship is more strongly linked to feelings of well-being during adolescence than during childhood. Teenagers with superficial friendships, or no close friendships at all, report feeling lonelier and more depressed and have a lower sense of self-esteem than do teenagers with intimate friendships (Yin, Buhrmester, & Hibbard, 1996). In another study, friendship in early adolescence was a significant predictor of self-worth in early adulthood (Bagwell, Newcomb, & Bukowski, 1994).

Friendships are often important sources of support (Berndt, 1999). Sullivan described how adolescent friends support one another's sense of personal worth. When close friends disclose their mutual insecurities and fears about themselves, they discover that they are not "abnormal" and that they have nothing to be ashamed of. Friends also act as important confidants, providing both emotional support and advice, during times of trouble (such as difficulties with parents or the breakup of romance). Friends can also protect "at risk" adolescents from victimization by peers (Bukowski, Sippola, & Boivin, 1995). In addition, friends can become active partners in building a sense of identity. During countless hours of conversation, friends act as sounding boards as teenagers explore issues ranging from future plans to stances on religious and moral issues.

Intimacy The most consistent finding in the last two decades of research on adolescent friendships is that intimacy is an important feature of these friendships (Berndt & Perry, 1990; Bukowski, Newcomb, & Hoza, 1987). When young adolescents are asked what they want from a friend or how they can tell someone is their best friend, they frequently say that a best friend will share problems with them, understand them, and listen when they talk about their own thoughts or feelings.

Are the friendships of adolescent girls more intimate than the friendships of adolescent boys? When asked to describe their best friends, girls refer to intimate conversations and faithfulness more than boys do. For example, girls are more likely to describe their best friend as "sensitive just like me" or "trustworthy just like me"

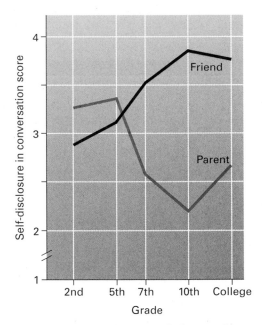

FIGURE 15.6 Developmental Changes in Self-Disclosing Conversations

Self-disclosing conversations with friends increased dramatically in adolescence while declining in an equally dramatic fashion with parents. However, self-disclosing conversations with parents began to pick up somewhat during the college years. The measure of self-disclosure involved a 5-point rating scale completed by the children and youth with a higher score representing greater self-disclosure. The data shown represent the means for each age group.

(Duck, 1975). Boys may discourage one another from openly disclosing their problems (Maccoby, 1998). Boys make themselves vulnerable to being called "wimps" if they can't handle their own problems and insecurities.

Mixed-Age Friendships Like children, adolescents tend to form friendships with individuals who are similar to themselves. Most adolescents develop friendships with individuals who are close to their own age. However, some adolescents become best friends with younger or older individuals. Parents often fear that adolescents who have older friends will be encouraged to engage in delinquent behavior or early sexual behavior. Researchers have found that adolescents who interact with older youths do engage in these behaviors more frequently, but it is not known whether the older youths guide younger adolescents toward deviant behavior or whether the younger adolescents were already prone to deviant behavior before they developed the friendship with the older youths (Billy, Rogers, & Udry, 1984).

In a longitudinal study of eighth-grade girls, early-maturing girls developed friendships with girls who were chronologically older but biologically similar to them (Magnusson, 1988). The early-maturing girls were more likely than their peers to engage in a number of deviant behaviors, such as being truant from school, getting drunk, and stealing. Also, as adults (26 years of age), the early-maturing girls were more likely to have had a child and were less likely to be vocationally and educationally oriented than their later-maturing counterparts. Thus, parents do seem to have reason to be concerned when their adolescents become close friends with individuals who are considerably older than they are.

Adult Friendship

What are friendships like in adulthood? As in childhood, adult friends tend to be similar in a number of ways—occupational status, ethnicity, age, marital status, income, education, gender, and religion (Pruchno & Rosenbaum, 2003; Rawlins, 2004). Although both family and friends are important to an individual's psychological well-being, some developmentalists argue that friends are often more important than family members. Explanations for this difference include (Pruchno & Rosenbaum, 2003):

- *Family relationships are obligatory, friendships optional.* Family members should be available for support, so if they are absent, it is felt as a deficit. Since friends do not have to be available, their presence is perceived more strongly as a benefit.
- *Family relationships are ascribed, friendships chosen.* Individuals cannot choose to replace their parents and siblings, even when relationships are highly stressful, but they can replace their friends. Relationships with family members are more difficult to sever, and throughout the life span people report that family members get on their nerves more than friends (Antonucci & Akiyama, 1995). Further, the sense of being desirable that is elicited by friendships may enhance self-esteem and well-being. Researchers have found that friendships are more often a source of enjoyment and socializing, which can contribute to psychological well-being.
- *Friends are often similar in age, family members from different generations.* Because friends are typically members of the same age group, they often share personal characteristics, cohort experiences, and lifestyles. These similarities may promote better communication and understanding with friends than with family members.

Gender Differences As in the childhood years, there are gender differences in adult friendships (Clark & Grote, 2003; Winstead & Griffin, 2001). Women have more close friends than men do, and their friendships are more intimate. When adult female friends get together, they often talk, whereas adult male friends are more likely to engage in activities, especially outdoors. Thus, the adult male pattern of friendship often involves keeping one's distance while sharing useful information. When women talk with their friends, they expect to be able to express their feelings, reveal their weaknesses, and discuss their problems. They anticipate that their friends will listen at length and be sympathetic. In contrast, men are less likely to talk about their weaknesses with their friends, and they want practical solutions to their problems rather than sympathy (Tannen, 1990). Also, adult male friendships are more competitive than those of women (Sharkey, 1993). For example, male friends disagree with each other more. Keep in mind, however, that these differences in same-sex adult friendship tend to be small (Sabini, 1995).

What about female-male friendship? Cross-gender friendships are more common among adults than among elementary school children, but not as common as same-gender friendships (Fehr, 1996). Cross-gender friendships can provide both opportunities and problems. The opportunities involve learning more about common feelings and interests and shared characteristics, as well as acquiring knowledge and understanding of beliefs and activities that historically have been typical of one gender.

Problems can arise in cross-gender friendships because of different expectations. For example, a woman might expect sympathy from a male friend but might receive a directive solution rather than a shoulder to cry on (Tannen, 1990). Another problem that can plague adult cross-gender friendship is unclear sexual boundaries, which can produce tension and confusion (Swain, 1992).

Friendship in Late Adulthood   How does friendship change during late adulthood? Friends play an important role in the support systems of older adults (Troll, 1999). Friendships with unrelated adults may help to replace the warmth, companionship, and nurturance no longer supplied by distant families. As discussed in chapter 10, older adults tend to narrow their social networks. Aging expert Laura Carstensen (1998) concluded that people choose close friends over new friends as they grow older.

Gender differences in friendship continue among older adults. In one recent study of 128 married older adults, women were more depressed than men if they did not have a best friend, but women who did have a friend reported lower levels of depression (Antonucci, Lansford, & Akiyama, 2001). Women who did not have a best friend were less satisfied with life than women who did. One study of friendships among young-old and old-old adult friendships found more changes among older adult males than females (Field, 1999). Among older men, the number of new friends, desire for close friendships, and involvement beyond the family declined, whereas older women did not change in these areas.

What happens when older adults' friends die? Some older adults deal with this loss by loosening their requirements for whom they consider a friend (Troll, 1999). "Friends" come to include the woman passed in the hall or the deliverer of meals-on-wheels.

> *A man's growth is seen in the successive choirs of his friends.*
>
> —RALPH WALDO EMERSON,
> *American Poet and Essayist,*
> *19th Century*

Review and Reflect: Learning Goal 2

2 Explain the role of friendship through the life span

REVIEW

- What are six functions of friendship?
- What is the developmental significance of friendship in childhood?
- How can adolescents' friendships be characterized? What is Sullivan's view on friendship?
- How do friendships vary in adulthood based on gender and age?

REFLECT

- Rank the six functions of friendship from most (1) to least (6) important as you were growing up.

3 PLAY AND LEISURE

| Childhood | Adolescence | Adulthood |

Peers and friends often engage in play and enjoy leisure activities together. Let's explore the developmental aspects of play and leisure.

Childhood

An extensive amount of peer interaction during childhood involves play; however, social play is but one type of play. **Play** is a pleasurable activity that is engaged in for its own sake.

www.mhhe.com/santrockldt2

Play

Functions of Play Play is essential to a young child's health. Play increases affiliation with peers, releases tension, advances cognitive development, and increases exploration. Play increases the probability that children will converse and interact with each other. During this interaction, children practice the roles they will assume later in life.

Many theorists have emphasized various functions of play. According to Freud and Erikson, play helps children master anxieties and conflicts. In play, children work off excess physical energy and release pent-up tensions. They may feel less threatened and be more likely to express their feelings during play. Thus, therapists use **play therapy** as a means of letting children work off frustrations while analyzing their conflicts and coping methods (Drewes, Carey, & Schaefer, 2003).

According to Piaget (1962), play reflects children's cognitive development but also advances that development. During play, children practice their competencies and skills in a relaxed, pleasurable way. For example, children who have just learned to add or multiply begin to play with numbers in different ways as they perfect these operations, laughing as they do so.

Vygotsky (1962) also believed that play is an excellent setting for cognitive development. He was especially interested in the symbolic and make-believe aspects of play, as when a child rides a stick as if it were a horse. For young children, the imaginary situation is real. Parents should encourage such imaginary play, which advances the child's cognitive development, especially creative thought.

Daniel Berlyne (1960) described play as exciting and pleasurable because it satisfies the exploratory drive. This drive involves curiosity and a desire for information about something new or unusual. Through play, children can safely explore and seek out new information. Play encourages exploratory behavior by offering the possibilities of novelty, complexity, uncertainty, surprise, and incongruity.

Parten's Classic Study of Play Many years ago, Mildred Parten (1932) developed an elaborate classification of children's play. Based on observations of children in free play at nursery school, Parten arrived at these play categories:

- **Unoccupied play** is not play as it is commonly understood. The child may stand in one spot or perform random movements that do not seem to have a goal. In most nursery schools, unoccupied play is less frequent than other forms of play.
- **Solitary play** happens when the child plays alone, independently of others. The child seems engrossed in the activity. Two- and 3-year-olds engage more frequently in solitary play than older preschoolers do.
- **Onlooker play** takes place when the child watches other children play. The child may talk with other children and ask questions but does not play with them. The child's active interest in other children's play distinguishes onlooker play from unoccupied play.

play A pleasurable activity that is engaged in for its own sake.

play therapy Therapy that lets children work off frustrations while therapists analyze their conflicts and coping methods.

unoccupied play Play in which the child is not engaging in play as it is commonly understood and might stand in one spot or perform random movements that do not seem to have a goal.

solitary play Play in which the child plays alone, independently of others.

onlooker play Play in which the child watches other children play.

Mildred Parten classified play into six categories. *In this photograph, which of her categories are reflected in the behavior of the children?*

- **Parallel play** occurs when the child plays separately from others but with toys like those the others are using or in a manner that mimics their play. The older children are, the less frequently they engage in parallel play. However, even older preschool children engage in parallel play quite often.
- **Associative play** involves social interaction with little or no organization. During associative play, children seem more interested in each other than in what they are doing.
- **Cooperative play** consists of social interaction in a group with a sense of group identity and organized activity. Formal games, competitions, and groups formed by the teacher for doing things together are examples of cooperative play. Cooperative play is the prototype for the games of middle childhood. Little cooperative play is seen during the preschool years.

Types of Play   Parten's categories represent one way of thinking about the types of play. Her categories emphasize the role of play in the child's social world. The contemporary perspective on play emphasizes the cognitive as well as the social aspects of play. Among the most widely studied types of children's play today are sensorimotor and practice play, pretense/symbolic play, social play, constructive play, and games (Bergen, 1988). These types are not mutually exclusive. Children's play can combine the categories.

Sensorimotor and Practice Play   **Sensorimotor play** is behavior by infants to derive pleasure from exercising their sensorimotor schemes. It develops along with sensorimotor thought, which we discussed in chapter 6. Infants initially engage in sensorimotor play in the second quarter of the first year of life. At 9 months of age, infants begin to select novel objects for exploration and play, especially those that respond, such as toys that make noise or bounce. At 12 months of age, infants enjoy making things work and exploring cause and effect.

parallel play Play in which the child plays separately from others, but with toys like those the others are using or in a manner that mimics their play.

associative play Play that involves social interaction with little or no organization.

cooperative play Play that involves social interaction in a group with a sense of group identity and organized activity.

sensorimotor play Behavior by infants to derive pleasure from exercising their sensorimotor schemes.

Activity	Nonindustrial, unschooled populations	Postindustrial, schooled populations		
		United States	Europe	East Asia
TV viewing	Insufficient data	1.5 to 2.5 hours	1.5 to 2.5 hours	1.5 to 2.5 hours
Talking	Insufficient data	2 to 3 hours	Insufficient data	45 to 60 minutes
Sports	Insufficient data	30 to 60 minutes	20 to 80 minutes	0 to 20 minutes
Structured voluntary activities	Insufficient data	10 to 20 minutes	10 to 20 minutes	0 to 10 minutes
Total free time	4 to 7 hours	6.5 to 8.0 hours	5.5 to 7.5 hours	4.0 to 5.5 hours

Note: The estimates in the table are averaged across a 7-day week, including weekdays and weekends. The data for nonindustrial, unschooled populations comes primarily from rural peasant populations in developing countries.

FIGURE 15.7 Average Daily Leisure Time of Adolescents in Different Regions of the World

Practice play involves the repetition of behavior when new skills are being learned or when mastery and coordination of skills are required for games or sports. Sensorimotor play, which often involves practice play, is primarily confined to infancy, whereas practice play occurs throughout life. During the preschool years, children often engage in play that involves practicing various skills. Although practice play declines in the elementary school years, practice play activities such as running, jumping, sliding, twirling, and throwing balls or other objects are still frequent.

Pretense/Symbolic Play **Pretense/symbolic play** occurs when the child transforms the physical environment into a symbol. Between 9 and 30 months of age, children increase their use of objects in symbolic play. They transform objects—substituting them for other objects and acting toward them as if they were these other objects. For example, a preschool child treats a table as if it were a car and says, "I'm fixing the car," as he grabs a leg of the table.

Many experts on play consider the preschool years the "golden age" of symbolic/pretense play that is dramatic or sociodramatic (Fein, 1986). This type of make-believe play often appears at about 18 months of age and reaches a peak at 4 to 5 years of age, then gradually declines.

Social Play **Social play** is play that involves interaction with peers. Parten's categories, described earlier, are oriented toward social play. Social play increases dramatically during the preschool years.

Games **Games** are activities that are engaged in for pleasure and include rules. They often involve competition. During the preschool years, children may begin to participate in social game play that involves simple rules of reciprocity and turn taking. However, games take on a much stronger role in the lives of elementary school children. In one study, the highest incidence of game playing occurred between 10 and 12 years of age (Eiferman, 1971). After age 12, games decline in popularity (Bergin, 1988).

Adolescence

Leisure refers to the pleasant times when individuals are free to pursue activities and interests of their own choosing—hobbies, sports, or reading, for example. How much leisure time do U.S. adolescents have compared with adolescents in other countries? How do U.S. adolescents use their leisure time?

Figure 15.7 indicates that U.S. adolescents spend more time in leisure activities than adolescents in other industrialized countries (Larson & Varma, 1999). About 40 to 50 percent of U.S. adolescents' waking hours (not counting summer vaca-

practice play Play that involves repetition of behavior when new skills are being learned or when mastery and coordination of skills are required for games or sports. Sensorimotor play, which often involves practice play, is primarily confined to infancy, whereas practice play occurs throughout life.

pretense/symbolic play Play that occurs when a child transforms the physical environment into a symbol.

social play Play that involves social interactions with peers.

games Activities that are engaged in for pleasure and include rules.

leisure The pleasant times when individuals are free to pursue activities and interests of their own choosing.

tions) is spent in leisure activities compared with 25 to 35 percent in East Asia and 35 to 45 percent in Europe. Whether this additional leisure time is a liability or an asset for U.S. adolescents, of course, depends on how they use it.

The largest amounts of U.S. adolescents' free time are spent using the media and playing, hanging out, and unstructured leisure activities, often with friends. U.S. adolescents spend more time in voluntary structured activities—such as sports, hobbies, and organizations—than East Asian adolescents.

According to Reed Larson (2001), for optimal development, U.S. adolescents may have too much unstructured time because when adolescents are allowed to choose what they do with their time, they typically engage in unchallenging leisure activities such as hanging out and watching TV. Although relaxation and social interaction are important aspects of adolescence, it seems unlikely that spending large numbers of hours per week in unchallenging activities fosters development. Structured voluntary activities may provide more promise for adolescent development than unstructured time, especially if adults give responsibility to adolescents, challenge them, and provide competent guidance in these activities (Larson, 2001; Mahoney, Larson, & Eccles, 2004; Mahoney & others, 2004).

Adulthood

As adults, not only must we learn how to work well, but we also need to learn how to relax and enjoy leisure (Iwasaki, 2003; Strain & others, 2002). In view of the work ethic on which America was based, it is not surprising to find that many adults view leisure as boring and unnecessary. But even Aristotle recognized leisure's importance in life, stressing that we should not only work well but use leisure well. He described leisure as better because it was the end of work.

Some workers today have more control over their work schedule than their counterparts in the early twentieth century. Flex time options—such as working 12-hour shifts over three consecutive days followed by four days off, working at home via computer, completing projects by working on weekends, and banking extra hours to use for free time and vacations—allow some of today's workers to control when they have time for leisure (Hoyer & Roodin, 2003). However, dual obligations to career and family may leave some workers with less time to pursue leisure pursuits than workers had 20 years ago (Brett & Stroh, 2003).

What is leisure in middle adulthood like? When Mark became 40 years old, he decided that he needed to develop some leisure activities and interests. He bought a personal computer and joined a computer club. Now Mark looks forward to coming home from work and "playing with his toy." At the age of 43, Barbara sent her last child off to college and told her husband that she was going to spend the next several years reading the many books she had bought but had never found time to read. Mark and Barbara chose different leisure activities, but their actions suggest that middle adulthood is a time when leisure activities assume added importance. For example, some developmentalists believe that middle adulthood is a time of questioning how time should be spent and of reassessing priorities (Gould, 1978).

Leisure can be an especially important aspect of middle adulthood because of the changes many individuals experience at this point in the life span (Mannell, 2000). The changes include physical changes, changes in relationship with spouse and children, and career changes. By middle adulthood, more money is available to many individuals, and there may be more free time and paid vacations. These midlife changes may produce expanded opportunities for leisure. For many individuals, middle adulthood is the first time in their lives when they have the opportunity to diversify their interests.

In one study, 12,338 men 35 to 57 years of age were assessed each year for five years regarding whether they took vacations (Gump & Matthews, 2000). Then the researchers examined the medical and death records over nine years for men who lived for at least a year after the last vacation survey. Compared with those who never took vacations, men who went on annual vacations were 21 percent less likely to die over the nine years and 32 percent less likely to die of coronary heart disease. The qualities that lead men to pass on a vacation tend to promote heart disease, such as not trusting anyone to fill in while you are gone or fearing that you will get behind in your work and someone will replace you. (These behaviors sometimes have been described as part of the Type A behavioral pattern.)

Adults at midlife need to begin preparing psychologically for retirement (Bernard & Phillipson, 2004). Constructive and fulfilling leisure activities in middle adulthood are an important part of this preparation (Kelly, 1996). If an adult develops leisure activities that can be continued into retirement, the transition from work to retirement can be less stressful.

Review and Reflect: Learning Goal 3

3 Describe the developmental aspects of play and leisure

REVIEW

- What are the functions of play? How would you describe Parten's classic study of play? What are the different types of play?
- What is leisure? How do adolescents use their discretionary time?
- What are some key aspects of leisure in adulthood?

REFLECT

- Do you think most young children's and adults' lives today are too structured? Do children and adults have too little time to play? Do U.S. adolescents have too much? Explain.

---

4 AGING AND THE SOCIAL WORLD

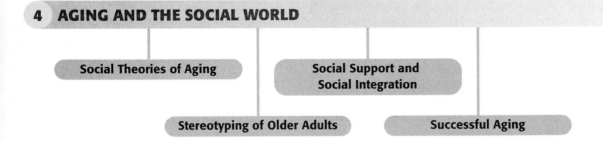

Social Theories of Aging

Social Support and Social Integration

Stereotyping of Older Adults

Successful Aging

The death of peers as well as family members is an expected part of old age. Does it follow that our social world must shrink as we get older? How do social experiences influence the aging process? Let's explore some theories of aging that give social experiences an important role.

Social Theories of Aging

In chapter 10, "Emotional Development," we discussed *socioemotional selectivity theory,* which states that older adults become more selective about their social networks and may seek greater emotional quality in relationships with friends and family ◀‖‖ P. 342. Let's consider three other social theories of aging.

Disengagement theory states that to cope effectively, older adults should gradually withdraw from society. This theory was proposed almost half a century ago (Cumming & Henry, 1961). In this view, older adults develop increasing self-preoccupation, lessen emotional ties with others, and show decreasing interest in

disengagement theory The theory that, to cope effectively, older adults should gradually withdraw from society.

society's affairs. By following these strategies of disengagement, it was believed that older adults would enjoy enhanced life satisfaction.

This theory generated a storm of protest and met with a quick death. We present it because of its historical relevance. Although not formally proposed until 1961, it summarized the prevailing beliefs about older adults in the first half of the twentieth century.

Activity theory states that the more active and involved older adults are, the more likely they will be satisfied with their lives. Thus, activity theory is the exact opposite of disengagement theory. Researchers have found strong support for activity theory, beginning in the 1960s and continuing into the twenty-first century (Neugarten, Havighurst, & Tobin, 1968). One longitudinal study found that a greater overall activity level (which included social activities such as visiting relatives or friends, solitary activities such as hobbies, and productive activities such as volunteer work and gardening) at the beginning of the study was related to greater happiness, better physical and cognitive functioning, and reduced mortality six years later (Menec, 2003). In sum, when older adults are active, energetic, and productive, they age more successfully and are happier than if they disengage from society (Antonucci, Vandewater, & Lansford, 2000).

Activity theory suggests that many individuals will achieve greater life satisfaction if they continue their middle adulthood roles into late adulthood. If these roles are stripped from them (as in early retirement), it is important for them to find substitute roles that keep them active and involved.

A third social theory of aging is **social breakdown–reconstruction theory** (Kuypers & Bengtson, 1973). This theory argues that aging is promoted through negative psychological functioning brought about by negative views of older adults and inadequate services for them. Social breakdown begins with negative social views and ends with identifying and labeling oneself as incompetent. Social reconstruction can be brought about by viewing older adults as competent, by applying positive labels (such as helpers, self-controlled, wise, and competent) to them, and by providing them with adequate support systems.

Thus, both activity theory and social breakdown–reconstruction theory argue that older adults' capabilities and competence are far greater than society has acknowledged in the past. Older adults' active participation in society can increase their life satisfaction and positive feelings about themselves.

Stereotyping of Older Adults

Social participation by older adults is often discouraged by **ageism,** which is prejudice against others because of their age, especially prejudice against older adults (Hepworth, 2004; Hummert & others, 2004). They are often perceived as incapable of thinking clearly, learning new things, enjoying sex, contributing to the community, or holding responsible jobs. Many older adults face painful discrimination and might be too polite and timid to attack it (Glover & Branine, 2003; McMullin & Marshall, 2001; Perdue, 2000). Because of their age, older adults might not be hired for new jobs or might be eased out of old ones; they might be shunned socially; and they might be edged out of their family life.

The personal consequences of negative stereotyping about aging can be serious. A physician (60 years old himself) recently told an 80-year-old: "Well, of course, you are tired. You just need to slow down. Don't try to do so much. After all you are very old." Many older adults accept this type of advice even though it is rooted in age stereotyping rather than medical records.

Ageism is widespread; the most frequent form is disrespect for older adults, followed by assumptions about ailments or frailty caused by age (Palmore, 2001). However, the increased number of adults living to an older age has led to active efforts to improve society's image of the elderly, obtain better living conditions for older adults, and gain political clout.

**Social Psychology of Aging
Ageism Resources**

activity theory The theory that the more active and involved older adults are, the more likely they are to be satisfied with their lives.

social breakdown–reconstruction theory The theory that aging is promoted through negative psychological functioning brought about by negative views of older adults and inadequate services for them; social reconstruction can be brought about by viewing older adults as competent.

ageism Prejudice against other people because of their age, especially prejudice against older adults.

Social Support and Social Integration

In the *social convoy* model of social relations, individuals go through life embedded in a personal network of individuals from whom they give and receive social support (Antonucci & Akiyama, 2002; Antonnuci, Akiyama, & Lansford, 1998; Antonucci, Lansford, & Akiyama, 2001; Kahn & Antonucci, 1990). Social support can help individuals of all ages cope more effectively. More specifically, social support can improve the physical and mental health of older adults (Oxman & Hall, 2001; Pruchno & Rosenbaum, 2003; Reinhardt, 2001). Social support is linked with a reduction in symptoms of disease and with the ability to meet one's own health-care needs (Cohen, Teresi, & Holmes, 1985). Social support also decreases the probability that an older adult will be institutionalized (Antonucci, 1990). And social support is associated with a lower incidence of depression in older adults (Joiner, 2000).

Social integration plays an important role in the lives of many older adults (Antonucci, Vandewater, & Lansford, 2000; Muszcz & Giles, 2002). Remember from our earlier discussion of socioemotional selectivity theory that many older adults choose to have fewer peripheral social contacts and more emotionally positive contacts with friends and family. Thus, a decrease in the overall social activity of many older adults may reflect their greater interest in spending more time in the small circle of friends and families where they are less likely to have negative emotional experiences. However, being lonely and socially isolated is a significant health risk factor in older adults (Rowe & Kahn, 1997). In one study, being part of a social network was related to longevity, especially for men (House, Landis, & Umberson, 1988). A longitudinal study found that poor social connections, infrequent participation in social activities, and social disengagement predicted cognitive decline in older adults (Zunzunegui & others, 2003). And in another longitudinal study, both women and men with more organizational memberships lived longer than their counterparts with low participation in organizations (Tucker & others, 1999).

Social support has very positive effects on older adults, but giving that support can be stressful if those adults need a great deal of care. We explore this topic in the Research in Life-Span Development interlude.

Research in Life-Span Development
The Stress of Caring for Older Adults

A special concern that has emerged in recent years is the stress on caregivers who care for an older person (Anderson, Kiecolt-Glaser, & Glaser, 1994; Caswell & others, 2003; Clark & Standard, 1996; Kiecolt-Glaser & others, 2003; Martire & Schultz, 2001). Janice Kiecolt-Glaser and her colleagues (1991) have found that individuals with long-term caregiving responsibilities, such as caring for an ailing spouse, are at risk for becoming clinically depressed and also have immune systems that do not respond well to standard challenges. In their research, caregivers did not mount as good an immune response after getting a flu vaccination as did individuals not involved in long-term caregiving responsibilities. Further, the persons with high levels of caregiving responsibilities did not show significant psychological or immunological improvement up to three years after their spouse's death. These findings suggest a special concern for the aging population. For people 75 years of age and older, influenza and pneumonia are among the leading causes of death. With immune response suppression lingering after years of caregiving, the risk for these caregiving individuals is likely increased.

Successful Aging

For too long, the positive dimensions of late adulthood were ignored (Aspinwall & Staudinger, 2003; Carstensen & Charles, 2003; Nussbaum & Coupland, 2004; Rowe & Kahn, 1997; Ryff & Singer, 2003). Throughout this book, we have called attention to the positive aspects of aging. There are many robust, healthy older adults. With a proper diet, an active lifestyle, mental stimulation and flexibility, positive coping skills, good social relationships and support, and the absence of disease, many abilities can be maintained or in some cases even improved as we get older. Even when individuals develop a disease, improvements in medicine mean that increasing numbers of older adults can still lead active, constructive lives.

Being active is especially important to successful aging (Varo & others, 2003). Older adults who get out and go to meetings, participate in church activities, go on trips, and exercise regularly are more satisfied with their lives than their counterparts who disengage from society (Menec, 2003). Older adults who are emotionally selective, optimize their choices, and compensate effectively for losses increase their chances of aging successfully (Baltes, 2000; Baltes & Freund, 2003).

Successful aging also involves perceived control over the environment. In chapter 4, "Health," we described how perceived control over the environment had a positive effect on nursing home residents' health and longevity ◀Ⅲ **P. 141**. In recent years, the term *self-efficacy* has often been used to describe perceived control over the environment and the ability to produce positive outcomes (Bandura, 2000; DeVellis & DeVellis, 2001). Researchers have found that many older adults are quite effective in maintaining a sense of control and have a positive view of themselves (Brandstädter, Wentura, & Greve, 1993). Examining the positive aspects of aging is an important trend in life-span development and is likely to benefit future generations of older adults.

Review and Reflect: Learning Goal 4

4 Summarize the social aspects of aging

REVIEW

- What are three social theories of aging?
- How extensively are older adults stereotyped?
- What roles do social support and social integration play in the development of older adults?
- What are some important aspects of successful aging?

REFLECT

- How might aging successfully in late adulthood be related to what people have done earlier in their lives?

5 SOCIOCULTURAL INFLUENCES

Culture   **Socioeconomic Status and Poverty**   **Ethnicity**

Personal relations with friends and other peers form only part of the social world outside the family that influences development. As we have seen throughout this book, development is also influenced by the sociocultural context. Here we will take a closer

Individualistic	Collectivistic
Focuses on individual	Focuses on groups
Self is determined by personal traits independent of groups; self is stable across contexts	Self is defined by in-group terms; self can change with context
Private self is more important	Public self is most important
Personal achievement, competition, power are important	Achievement is for the benefit of the in-group; cooperation is stressed
Cognitive dissonance is frequent	Cognitive dissonance is infrequent
Emotions (such as anger) are self-focused	Emotions (such as anger) are often relationship based
People who are the most liked are self-assured	People who are the most liked are modest, self-effacing
Values: pleasure, achievement, competition, freedom	Values: security, obedience, in-group harmony, personalized relationships
Many casual relationships	Few, close relationships
Save own face	Save own and other's face
Independent behaviors: swimming, sleeping alone in room, privacy	Interdependent behaviors: co-bathing, co-sleeping
Relatively rare mother-child physical contact	Frequent mother-child physical contact (such as hugging, holding)

FIGURE 15.8 Characteristics of Individualistic and Collectivistic Cultures

look at three aspects of that context: culture, socioeconomic status, and ethnicity.

Culture

Culture refers to the behavior, patterns, beliefs, and all other products of a group of people that are passed on from generation to generation. It results from the interaction between people and their environment over many years.

The concept of culture is broad; it includes many components and can be analyzed in many ways (Berry, 2000). Cross-cultural expert Richard Brislin (1993) described a number of characteristics of culture:

- Culture is made up of ideals, values, and assumptions about life that guide people's behavior.
- Culture consists of those aspects of the environment that people make.
- Culture is transmitted from generation to generation, with responsibility for the transmission resting on the shoulders of parents, teachers, and community leaders.
- When their cultural values are violated or their cultural expectations are ignored, people react emotionally.
- It is not unusual for people to accept a cultural value at one point in their lives and reject it at another point. For example, rebellious adolescents and young adults might accept a culture's values and expectations after having children of their own.

Research by American psychologist Donald Campbell and his colleagues (Brewer & Campbell, 1976; Campbell & LeVine, 1968) revealed that people in all cultures tend to:

- believe that what happens in their culture is "natural" and "correct" and that what happens in other cultures is "unnatural" and "incorrect"
- perceive their cultural customs as universally valid—that is, believe that "what is good for us is good for everyone"
- behave in ways that favor their cultural group
- feel hostile toward other cultural groups

In other words, people in all cultures tend to display **ethnocentrism,** the tendency to consider one's own group superior to others.

The Relevance of Culture for the Study of Life-Span Development For the most part, the study of children has been ethnocentric, emphasizing American values, especially those of middle-socioeconomic-status White males (Matsumoto, 2000, 2004). Students of life-span development in the twenty-first century will need to give increased attention to the study of culture and move beyond ethnocentrism (Greenfield, 2000; Padilla & Perez, 2003; Shriaev & Levy, 2004). The future is likely to bring increased contact between people from varied cultural backgrounds in schools and neighborhoods. Immigrants, refugees, and ethnic minority individuals increasingly refuse to become part of a homogeneous melting pot, instead requesting that schools, employers, and governments honor many of their cultural customs.

Global interdependence is an inescapable reality. Children, adolescents, and adults are not just citizens of one country; they are citizens of the world—a world that, through advances in transportation and technology, has become increasingly connected. By better understanding cultures around the world, we may be able to interact more effectively with each other and make this planet a more hospitable, peaceful place (Matsumoto, 2000, 2004).

culture The behavior patterns, beliefs, and all other products of a group of people that are passed on from generation to generation.

ethnocentrism The tendency to favor one's own group over other groups.

Individualism and Collectivism   What cultural differences are significant in life-span development? One finding in cross-cultural research is that cultures around the world tend to take two very different orientations to life and social relations (Gilovitch & others, 2003). That is, cultures tend to emphasize either individualism or collectivism:

- **Individualism** involves giving priority to personal goals rather than to group goals; it emphasizes values that serve the self, such as feeling good, personal distinction and achievement, and independence.
- **Collectivism** emphasizes values that serve the group by subordinating personal goals to preserve group integrity, interdependence of the members, and harmonious relationships.

Figure 15.8 on page 542 summarizes some of the main characteristics of individualistic and collectivistic cultures. Many Western cultures, such as those of the United States, Canada, Great Britain, and the Netherlands, are described as individualistic; many Eastern cultures, such as those of China, Japan, India, and Thailand, are described as collectivistic.

Many of the assumptions about contemporary ideas in fields like life-span development were developed in individualistic cultures (Triandis, 1994, 2001). Consider the flurry of *self-* terms in psychology that have an individualistic focus: *self-actualization, self-awareness, self-efficacy, self-reinforcement, self-criticism, self-serving, selfishness,* and *self-doubt* (Lonner, 1988).

Self-conceptions are related to culture. In one study, American and Chinese college students completed 20 sentences beginning with "I am _____ (Trafimow, Triandis, & Goto, 1991). As indicated in figure 15.9, the American college students were much more likely to describe themselves with personal traits ("I am assertive," for example), while the Chinese students were more likely to identify themselves by their group affiliations ("I am a member of the math club," for example).

Critics of the individualism of psychology point out that human beings have always lived in groups and have always needed one another for survival. They argue that the Western emphasis on individualism may undermine our basic need for relatedness (Kagitcibasi, 1988, 1995). Some social scientists believe that many problems in Western cultures are intensified by the Western cultural emphasis on individualism. Individualistic cultures have higher rates than collectivistic cultures of suicide, drug abuse, crime, teenage pregnancy, divorce, child abuse, and mental disorders. Regardless of their cultural background, people need a positive sense of both self *and* connectedness to others.

Rites of Passage   As a concrete example of significant cultural differences, consider **rites of passage,** which are ceremonies or rituals that mark an individual's transition from one status to another, especially into adulthood. Some societies have elaborate rites of passage that signal the adolescent's transition to adulthood; others do not. In many premodern cultures, rites of passage are the avenue through which adolescents gain access to sacred adult practices, knowledge, and sexuality (Sommer, 1978). The transformation usually is characterized by some form of ritual death and rebirth, or by means of contact with the spiritual world.

This kind of ritual provides a forceful, abrupt entry into the adult world. It facilitates the adolescent's separation from the immediate family, especially the mother. At the same time, bonds are forged between the adolescent and the adult instructors through shared rituals, hazards, and secrets to allow the adolescent to enter the adult world.

Americans do not have formal rites of passage that mark the transition from adolescence to adulthood. Some religious and social groups do have initiation ceremonies that serve a similar function—the Jewish bar mitzvah, the Catholic confirmation, and social debuts, for example. School graduation ceremonies come the closest to being culture-wide rites of passage in the United States. Nonetheless, high school graduation does not result in universal change. Many high school graduates

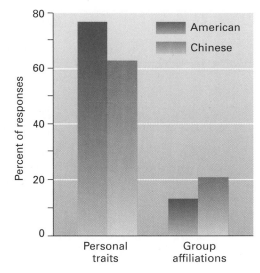

FIGURE 15.9 American and Chinese Self-Conceptions

College students from the United States and China completed 20 "I am _____" sentences. Both groups filled in personal traits more than group affiliations. However, the U.S. college students more often filled in the blank with personal traits, the Chinese with group affiliations.

individualism Giving priority to personal goals rather than to group goals; emphasizing values that serve the self, such as feeling good, personal distinction and achievement, and independence.

collectivism Emphasizing values that serve the group by subordinating personal goals to preserve group integrity, interdependence of members, and harmonious relationships.

rites of passage Ceremonies or rituals that mark an individual's transition from one status to another, especially into adulthood.

The Apache Indians of the American Southwest celebrate a girl's entrance into puberty with a four-day ritual that includes special dress, day-long activities, and solemn spiritual ceremonies.

Cultures differ in the amount of prestige they give to older adults. In Navajo culture, older adults are especially treated with respect because of their wisdom and extensive life experiences. *What are some other factors that are linked with respect for older adults in a culture?*

www.mhhe.com/santrockldt2

The Web of Culture

Global Internet Communication

Cross-Cultural Comparisons

Old Age Across Time and Culture

continue to live with their parents, to be economically dependent on them, and to be undecided about career and lifestyle matters.

The absence in the United States of clear-cut rites of passage to adulthood makes the attainment of adult status ambiguous. Many individuals are unsure whether they have reached adult status. For example, in Texas, the age for beginning employment is 15, but many younger adolescents and even children are employed. The age for driving is 16, but when emergency need is demonstrated, a driver's license can be obtained at age 15. Even at age 16, some parents might not allow their son or daughter to obtain a driver's license. The age for voting is 18, and the age for drinking has been raised to 21. Exactly when adolescents become adults is not clearly delineated in the United States.

Aging and Culture What factors are associated with whether older adults are accorded a position of high status in a culture? Seven factors are most likely to predict high status for the elderly in a culture (Sangree, 1989):

- Older persons have valuable knowledge.
- Older persons control key family or community resources.
- Older persons are permitted to engage in useful and valued functions as long as possible.
- There is role continuity throughout the life span.
- Age-related role changes involve greater responsibility, authority, and advisory capacity.
- The extended family is a common family arrangement, and the older person is integrated into the extended family.
- The culture is more collectivistic than individualistic.

Socioeconomic Status and Poverty

Analyzing cultures represents just one way to understand the social context of life-span development. Another approach focuses on inequalities present in every society. That is, how do people in a particular society differ in their access to economic, social, and psychological resources, and how do these differences affect their development through life?

What Is Socioeconomic Status?   Generally, members of a society have (1) occupations that vary in prestige, and some individuals have more access than others to higher-status occupations; (2) different levels of educational attainment, and some individuals have more access than others to better education; (3) different economic resources; and (4) different degrees of power to influence a community. These differences go together. That is, people with prestigious occupations tend also to have higher levels of educational attainment, more economic resources, and more power. Together these differences in the ability to control resources and to participate in society's rewards produce **socioeconomic status (SES),** which refers to a grouping of people with similar occupational, educational, and economic characteristics.

The number of different socioeconomic statuses depends on the community's size and complexity. In most investigators' descriptions of socioeconomic status, two broad categories, low SES and middle SES, are used, although as many as five categories are delineated. Sometimes low SES is described as low-income, working class, or blue collar; sometimes middle SES is described as middle-income, managerial, or white collar. Examples of low-SES occupations are factory worker and maintenance worker. Examples of middle-SES occupations include manager and professional (doctor, lawyer, teacher, accountant, and so on).

Socioeconomic Variations in Neighborhoods, Schools, and Families   A parent's SES is likely linked to the neighborhoods in which children live and the schools they attend. Children whose parents have high SES are likely to live in attractive houses and neighborhoods, and attend schools where the mix of students is primarily from middle- and upper-SES backgrounds. Children whose parents have low SES do not live in very attractive houses and neighborhoods, and they attend schools where the mix of students is mainly from lower-SES backgrounds.

Such variations in neighborhood settings can influence children's adjustment (Leffert & Blyth, 1996; Leventhal & Brooks-Gunn, 2003). For example, neighborhood crime and isolation have been linked with low self-esteem and psychological distress in children (Roberts, Jacobson, & Taylor, 1996). Furthermore, schools in low-income neighborhoods have fewer resources than schools in higher-income neighborhoods, and they are more likely to have more students with lower achievement test scores and low rates of graduation with small percentages of students going to college (Garbarino & Asp, 1981).

In the United States and most Western cultures, differences have been found in child rearing among different socioeconomic (SES) groups (Hoff, Laursen, & Tardif, 2002). Compared with higher-SES parents, lower-SES parents are more concerned that their children conform to society's expectations, create a home atmosphere in which it is clear that parents have authority over children, use physical punishment more in disciplining their children, and are more directive and less conversational with their children.

Compared with lower-SES parents, higher-SES parents are more concerned with developing children's initiative and delay of gratification; they create a home atmosphere in which children are more nearly equal participants and in which rules are discussed rather than being laid out in an authoritarian manner; they are less likely to use physical punishment; and they are less directive and more conversational with their children.

There also are socioeconomic differences in the way that parents think about education (Hoff, Laursen, & Tardiff, 2002; Magnuson & Duncan, 2002). Middle- and upper-income parents more often think of education as something that should be mutually encouraged by parents and teachers. By contrast, low-income parents are more likely to view education as the teacher's job. Increased school-family linkages can especially benefit children from low-income families.

Keep in mind that a sizeable portion of children from low-SES backgrounds perform well in school; some perform better than many middle-SES students. When children from low-SES backgrounds achieve well in school, it is not unusual to find

socioeconomic status (SES) A grouping of people with similar occupational, educational, and economic characteristics.

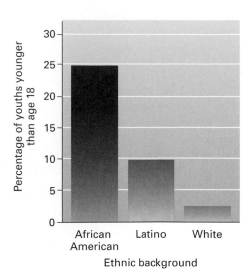

Note: A distressed neighborhood is defined by high levels (at least one standard deviation above the mean) of (1) poverty; (2) female-headed families; (3) high school dropouts; (4) unemployment; and

FIGURE 15.10 Percentages of Youth Under 18 Who Are Living in Distressed Neighborhoods

*W*hat happens to a dream deferred? Does it dry up like a raisin in the sun?

—LANGSTON HUGHES
*American Poet and Author,
20th Century*

feminization of poverty The fact that far more women than men live in poverty. Women's low income, divorce, and the resolution of divorce cases by the judicial system, which usually leaves women with less money than they and their children need to adequately function, are the likely causes.

a parent or parents making special sacrifices to provide the conditions that contribute to academic success.

Poverty   When sixth-graders in a poverty-stricken area of St. Louis were asked to describe a perfect day, one boy said he would erase the world, then he would sit and think. Asked if he wouldn't rather go outside and play, the boy responded, "Are you kidding, out there?" (Children's Defense Fund, 1992). The world is a dangerous and unwelcoming place for too many of America's children, especially those who live in poverty (Edelman, 1997). Some children are resilient and cope with the challenges of poverty without any major setbacks, but too many struggle unsuccessfully (Books, 2004; Magnuson & Duncan, 2002). Each child of poverty who reaches adulthood unhealthy, unskilled, or alienated keeps our nation from being as competent and productive as it can be (Children's Defense Fund, 1992).

Poverty Rates   In 2000, 16.2 percent of U.S. children were living in families below the poverty line (Children's Defense Fund, 2001). This was the lowest rate of poverty for children in two decades. However, it is much higher than the poverty rate for children in other industrialized nations. For example, Canada has a child poverty rate of 9 percent and Sweden has a rate of 2 percent.

Poverty in the United States tends to follow ethnic lines. Almost 50 percent of African American and 40 percent of Latino children live in poverty. Compared with White children, ethnic minority children are more likely to experience persistent poverty over many years and live in isolated poor neighborhoods where social supports are minimal and threats to positive development abundant (Jarrett, 1995) (see figure 15.10).

Why is poverty among American children so high? Three reasons are apparent (Huston, McLoyd, & Coll, 1994): Economic changes have eliminated many blue-collar jobs that paid reasonably well so that many workers do not earn enough to support a family. The percentage of children living in single-parent families headed by mothers has increased. Government benefits were reduced during the 1970s and 1980s.

Psychological Ramifications of Poverty   Poor children are often exposed to poor health conditions, inadequate housing and homelessness, environmental toxins, and violence. What are the psychological ramifications of living in poverty? First, the poor are often powerless. At work, they rarely are the decision makers; rules are handed down to them. Second, the poor are often vulnerable to disaster. They are not likely to be given notice before they are laid off from work, and they usually do not have financial resources to fall back on when problems arise. Third, their alternatives are restricted. Only a limited number of jobs are open to them. Even when alternatives are available, the poor might not know about them or be prepared to make a wise decision, because of inadequate education and inability to read well. Fourth, being poor means having less prestige.

Persistent and long-standing poverty can have especially damaging effects on children. In one study, the longer children lived in families with income below the poverty line, the lower was the quality of their home environments (Garrett, Ng'andu, & Ferron, 1994). Also in this study, improvements in family income had their strongest effects on the home environments of chronically poor children. In another study, children in families experiencing both persistent and occasional poverty had lower IQs and more internalized behavior problems than never-poor children, but persistent poverty had a much stronger negative effect on IQ and behavioral problems than occasional poverty did (Duncan, Brooks-Gunn, & Klebanov, 1994). Further, one recent study of more than 30,000 individuals from birth into the adult years found that the greater risk for developmental outcomes took place with persistent and accumulating socioeconomic disadvantage throughout childhood and adolescence (Schoon & others, 2002).

Feminization of Poverty   The term **feminization of poverty** refers to the fact that far more women than men live in poverty. More than one-third of single mothers live in poverty, compared with 10 percent of single fathers. Among the reasons for the high poverty rate of single mothers are women's low pay, infrequent alimony, and poorly enforced child support from fathers. Divorce usually leaves women with less money than they and their children need. Vonnie McLoyd (1990, 1998) concludes that because poor, single mothers are more distressed than their middle-SES counterparts are, they often show low support, nurturance, and involvement with their children.

Families and Poverty   One recent study documented the important links among economic well-being, parenting behavior, and social adjustment (Mistry & others 2002). Lower levels of economic well-being and elevated perceptions of economic pressure were linked with parenting behavior. Distressed parents reported feeling less effective and capable in disciplining their children and were observed to be less affectionate in parent-child interactions. In turn, less optimal parenting predicted lower teacher ratings of children's social behavior and higher ratings of behavior problems.

Benefits provided to parents may have important effects on children. In one study, work-based antipoverty programs for parents were linked to enhanced school performance and social behavior of children (Huston & others, 2001). In this study, wage supplements sufficient to raise family income above the poverty threshold and subsidies for child care and health insurance were given to adults who worked full-time. Positive effects were found for boys' academic achievement, classroom behavior skills, problem behaviors, and educational and occupational aspirations. Possibly the effects were more positive for boys than girls because boys have more behavioral and school-related problems to begin with.

In another recent study, an experimental welfare program in Minnesota resulted in positive outcomes for children (Gennetian & Miller, 2002). This program includes financial incentives to encourage work and mandatory participation in employment-focused activities. The program was linked with increased employment rates, decreased poverty, decreased problem behaviors among children, and improved school performance by children.

Poverty and Aging   Older adults who live in poverty are a special concern. Although the overall number of older people living in poverty has declined since the 1960s, the percentage of older persons living in poverty has remained in the 10 to 12 percent range since the early 1980s (U.S. Bureau of the Census, 2000). Furthermore, poverty rates soar among some groups of older Americans. More than 25 percent of older women who live alone live in poverty. Poverty rates among ethnic minorities are two to three times higher than the rate for Whites. Combining sex and ethnicity, 60 percent of older African American women and 50 percent of older Latino women who live alone live in poverty.

The majority of older adults face a life of reduced income. The average income of retired Americans is only about half of what they earned when they were fully employed. Middle-aged Americans who will retire in 20 to 25 years will need an income equal to 75 percent of their current annual expenditures (adjusted for inflation) to maintain their current middle-aged lifestyle.

Ethnicity

As our discussion of poverty and aging indicated, differences in SES often overlap with ethnic differences. The United States is a showcase for these differences because it has been a great magnet for people from many ethnic groups. Cultural heritages from every continent have collided and mixed here. Native Americans, European Americans, African Americans, Latinos, Chinese Americans, and other groups have retained parts of their culture of origin, lost other parts, and seen some elements transformed as they became part of the mainstream culture.

No one is quite sure whether the results of all these ethnic groups coming together is more like a mosaic or a tapestry, a melting pot or a quilt. What is certain is that the United States is more ethnically diverse than ever before. Ninety-three

Jason Leonard, age 15: "I want America to know that most of us Black teens are not troubled people from broken homes and headed to jail. . . . In my relationships with my parents, we show respect for each other and we have values in our house. We have traditions we celebrate together, including Christmas and Kwanzaa."

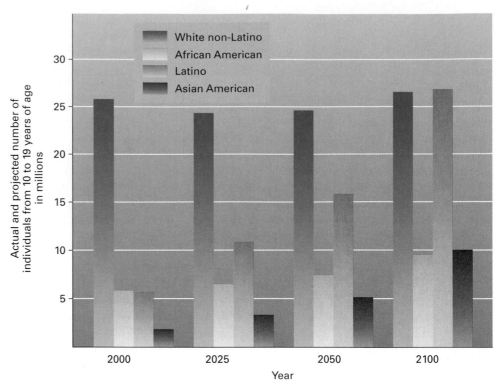

FIGURE 15.11 Actual and Projected Number of U.S. Adolescents Aged 10 to 19, 2000–2100

In 2000, there were more than 25 million White non-Latino adolescents aged 10 to 19 years of age in the United States, while the numbers for ethnic minority groups were substantially lower. However, projections for 2025 through 2100 reveal dramatic increases in the number of Latino and Asian American adolescents to the point at which in 2100 it is projected that there will be more Latino than non-Latino Whites in the United States and more Asian American than African American adolescents.

languages are spoken in Los Angeles alone. Does it matter which ethnic group a person belongs to? The Contexts of Life-Span Development interludes throughout this book have given some examples of how ethnicity can influence development. In chapter 1 we noted that *ethnicity* is based on cultural heritage and includes characteristics such as nationality, race, religion, and language. Here we will explore some additional examples of the role ethnicity plays in development.

Immigration   Relatively high rates of minority immigration have contributed to the growth in the proportion of ethnic minorities in the U.S. population (Cushner, McClelland, & Safford, 2003; McLoyd, 2000). And this growth of ethnic minorities is expected to continue throughout the twenty-first century. Asian Americans are expected to be the fastest-growing ethnic group of adolescents, with a growth rate of almost 600 percent growth by 2100. Latino adolescents are projected to increase almost 400 percent by 2100. Figure 15.11 shows the actual numbers of adolescents in different ethnic groups in the year 2000, as well as the numbers projected through 2100. Notice that by 2100, Latino adolescents are expected to outnumber non-Latino White adolescents.

Immigrants often experience special stressors. These include language barriers, separations from support networks, changes in SES, and the struggle both to preserve ethnic identity and to adapt to the majority culture (Barrera & others, 2004; Cushner, 2003; Fulgini & Yoshikawa, 2003; Romero & Roberts, 2003).

Parents and children may be at different stages of *acculturation,* the process of adapting to the majority culture. The result may be conflict over cultural values (Buki & others, 2003; Chun & Akutsu, 2003; Kwak, 2003; Roosa & others, 2002;

Samaniego & Gonzales, 1999; Santiseban & Mitrani, 2003). One study examined values in immigrant (Vietnamese, Armenian, and Mexican) and nonimmigrant families (African American and European American) (Phinney, 1996). In all groups, parents endorsed family obligations more than adolescents did, and the differences between generations generally increased with time in the United States.

Research increasingly shows links between acculturation and adolescent problems (Cuellar, Siles, & Bracamontes, 2004; Gonzales & others, in press). For example, more-acculturated Latino youths in the United States experience higher rates of conduct problems, substance abuse, and risky sexual behavior than their less-acculturated counterparts (Brook & others, 1998).

Ethnicity and Socioeconomic Status   Research has often failed to tease apart the influences of ethnicity and socioeconomic status (SES). Ethnicity and SES can interact in ways that exaggerate the negative influence of ethnicity because ethnic minority individuals are overrepresented in the lower socioeconomic levels of American society (Barbarin, McCandies, & Coleman, 2003; Borrayo & Jenkins, 2003; Bradley & Corwyn, 2003; Coll & Pachter, 2002; Spencer & Dornbusch, 1990). Consequently, too often researchers have given ethnic explanations for differences that were largely based on socioeconomic status, not ethnicity. For example, decades of research on group differences in self-esteem failed to consider the socioeconomic status of African American and White American children (Hare & Castenell, 1985). When the self-esteem of African American children from low-SES backgrounds is compared with that of White American children from middle-SES backgrounds, the differences are often large but not informative because of the confounding of ethnicity and SES (Scott-Jones, 1995).

Ethnicity and Families   Families within different ethnic groups in the United States differ in their size, structure, composition, reliance on kinships networks, and levels of income and education (Coll & Pachter, 2002; Parke & Buriel, 1998). Large and extended families are more common among minority groups than among the White majority. For example, 19 percent of Latino families have three or more children, compared with 14 percent of African American and 10 percent of White families. African American and Latino children interact more with grandparents, aunts, uncles, cousins, and more-distant relatives than do White children.

Single-parent families are more common among African Americans and Latinos than among White Americans (Weinraub, Houruath, & Gringlas, 2002). In comparison with two-parent households, single parents often have more limited resources of time, money, and energy. Ethnic minority parents also are less educated and more likely to live in low-income circumstances than their White counterparts. Still, many impoverished ethnic minority families manage to find ways to raise competent children (Coll & Pachter, 2002).

One recent research study examined the home environments of four ethnic groups: European American, African American, Latino, and Asian American (Bradley & others, 2001). In this study, both similarities and differences characterized the home environments of children from different ethnic groups in terms of the percentage of children who were exposed to various events and conditions. For example, about 90 percent of all mothers (regardless of ethnic group) spoke to their infants during the home visit. About 85 percent of the play environments of infants (regardless of ethnic group) appeared to be safe. Further, relatively few mothers (5 to 11 percent) restricted their preschool children during the home visit. Also, about 75 percent of the elementary school children (regardless of ethnic group) were encouraged to talk during the home visit.

There were some ethnic differences in the observations of home environments. For example, in this study, African American mothers were less likely than

Exploring Diversity
Migration and Ethnic Relations
Immigration and Ethnicity: Research Centers

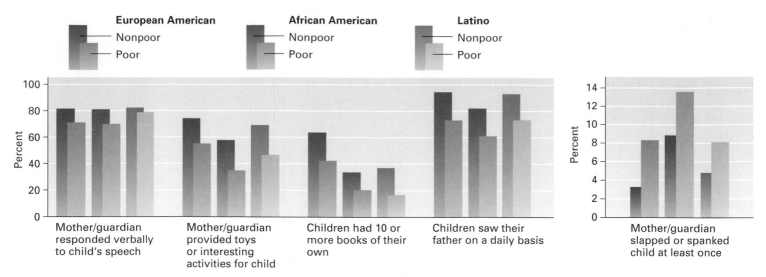

FIGURE 15.12 Home Environments of Infants by Ethnicity and Poverty Status

These data are based on home observations and maternal interviews obtained in the first three years of children's lives. Although there are some differences across ethnic groups, the most consistent differences were found between families classified as poor and nonpoor. For example, regardless of their ethnic group, children growing up in nonpoor home environments were more likely to have their speech responded to, be provided with toys or interesting activities, have ten or more books of their own, see their father on a daily basis, and be less likely to be slapped or spanked. Similar findings occurred when children were older.

mothers in the other ethnic groups to display physical affection to their children, and they reported using physical punishment more. The fathers were also less likely to be present in the African American homes than the other three groups. In addition, compared with African American and Latino homes, European American and Asian American homes were more likely to contain materials for learning and recreation, and the European American and Asian American mothers were also more likely to read to their children than the other two groups. The most consistent results, however, involved poverty, which was a more powerful indicator of the type of home environment children experienced than ethnicity was (see figure 15.12).

Poverty contributes to the stressful life experiences of many ethnic minority children (Coll & Pachter, 2002). But even when they are not poor, economic advantage does not enable ethnic minority children to escape entirely the prejudice and discrimination directed at them (Harwood & others, 2002; McAdoo, 2002). Although middle-SES ethnic minority children have more resources available to counter the destructive influences of prejudice and discrimination, they still cannot completely avoid the pervasive influence of negative stereotypes about ethnic minority groups.

Vonnie McLoyd (1990) concluded that ethnic minority children experience a disproportionate share of the adverse effects of poverty and unemployment in America today. Thus, many ethnic minority children experience a double disadvantage: (1) prejudice and discrimination because of their ethnic minority status, and (2) the stressful effects of poverty.

Some aspects of home life can help protect ethnic minority children from injustice. The community and the family can filter out destructive racist messages, and parents can present alternative frames of reference to those presented by the majority. The extended family also can serve as an important buffer to stress (McAdoo, 2002). In the Applications in Life-Span Development interlude, you can read about how the cultural context can influence ethnic minority parenting.

Applications in Life-Span Development

Acculturation and Ethnic Minority Parenting

Cynthia Garcia Coll and Lee Pachter (2002) recently described how the cultural context can influence ethnic minority parenting. A summary of their view follows.

Ethnic minority children and their parents are expected to transcend their own cultural background and incorporate aspects of the dominant culture into their development. Young children's expectations and opportunities for acculturation are mainly influenced by their parents and the extended family system. The level of family acculturation can affect parenting style by influencing expectations for children's development, parent-child interactions, and the role of the extended family. Conflict about caregiving practices may arise between less acculturated and more acculturated family members. For example, in one study, the level of acculturation and maternal education were the strongest predictors of maternal-infant interaction patterns in Latino families (Perez-Febles, 1992).

In early childhood, ethnic minority children learn about the dominant culture's values and may be expected to adapt to unfamiliar cultural norms (such as focusing on winning, expressing emotions, and being responsible for one's self). For example, an African American mother may prefer to leave her children with extended family members while she is at work because historically this had been seen as the best way to cope with an absent mother. However, this well-intentioned, culturally appropriate decision might place the child at an educational and social disadvantage relative to other children of the same age who benefit from preschool experiences that support the transition to the elementary school.

In middle and late childhood and adolescence, disparity between the acculturation of children, their parents, and the extended family can be magnified. In adolescence, individuals often make decisions about their acculturation more independently from their family. When immigrant adolescents choose to adopt the values of the dominant U.S. culture (such as unchaperoned dating), they often clash with parents and extended family members who have more traditional values.

It is important to recognize the complexity and individual variation in the acculturative aspects of ethnic minority parenting. This complexity and variation involve the generation of the family members, the recency of their immigration, their socioeconomic status, national origin, and many aspects of the dominant culture in which they now live (such as racial attitudes, quality of schooling, and community support groups).

Differences and Diversity   Historical, economic, and social experiences produce differences between various ethnic minority groups, and between ethnic minority groups and the majority White group (Halonen & Santrock, 1999). Individuals living in a particular ethnic group adapt to the values, attitudes, and stresses of that culture. Recognizing and respecting differences is an important aspect of getting along with others in a diverse, multicultural world (Velásquez, Arellano, & McNeill, 2004). Children, like all of us, need to take the perspective of individuals from ethnic groups that are different than their own and think, "If I were in their shoes, what kind of experiences might I have had?" "How would I feel if I were a member of their ethnic group?" "How would I think and behave if I had grown up in their world?" Such perspective taking often increases empathy and understanding of individuals from ethnic and cultural groups different from one's own.

Unfortunately, the emphasis often placed by our society and science on the differences between ethnic minority groups and the White majority in the United

*C*onsider the flowers of a garden: Though differing in kind, color, form, and shape, yet, inasmuch as they are refreshed by the waters of one spring, revived by the breath of one wind, invigorated by the rays of one sun, this diversity increases their charm and adds to their beauty. . . . How unpleasing to the eye if all the flowers and plants, the leaves and blossoms, the fruits, the branches, and the trees of that garden were all of the same shape and color! Diversity of hues, form, and shape enriches and adorns the garden and heightens its effect.

—'ABDU'L BAHA
Persian Baha'i Religious Leader, 19th/20th Century

States has been damaging to ethnic minority individuals. Ethnicity has defined who will enjoy the privileges of citizenship and to what degree and in what ways (Jones, 1997). An individual's ethnic background has determined whether the individual will be alienated, oppressed, or disadvantaged.

For too long, differences between any ethnic minority group and Whites were conceptualized as *deficits* or inferior characteristics on the part of the ethnic minority group. Indeed, research on ethnic minority groups often focused only on a group's negative, stressful aspects. For example, research on African American adolescent females invariably examined such topics as poverty, unwed mothers, and dropping out of school. The current emphasis underscores the strengths of various ethnic groups and is long overdue. For example, the extended-family support system that characterizes many ethnic groups is now recognized as an important factor in coping.

As we noted in chapter 1, there also is considerable diversity within each ethnic group (Banks, 2002, 2003; Cushner, 2003). Ethnic minority groups are not homogeneous; they have different social, historical, and economic backgrounds. For example, Mexican, Cuban, and Puerto Rican immigrants are often lumped together as Latinos, but the typical member of each of these groups had different reasons for migrating, came from varying socioeconomic backgrounds in their native countries, and experience different rates and types of employment in the United States (Coll & others, 1995). The U.S. federal government now recognizes 511 *different* Native American tribes, each having a unique background. The category "Asian Americans" includes people with Chinese, Japanese, Filipino, Korean, and Southeast Asian ancestry. The diversity of Asian Americans is reflected in their educational attainment: For example, 90 percent of Korean American males graduate from high school, but only 71 percent of Vietnamese American males do.

Sometimes, well-meaning individuals fail to recognize the diversity within an ethnic group (Sue, 1990). For example, a sixth-grade teacher went to a human relations workshop and was exposed to the necessity of incorporating more ethnicity into her instructional planning. Since she had two Mexican American adolescents in her class, she asked them to be prepared to demonstrate to the class on the following Monday how they danced at home. The teacher expected both of them to perform Mexican folk dances, reflecting their ethnic heritage. The first boy got up in front of the class and began dancing in a typical American fashion. The teacher said, "No, I want you to dance like you and your family do at home, like you do when you have Mexican American celebrations." The boy informed the teacher that his family did not dance that way. The second boy demonstrated a Mexican folk dance to the class. The first boy was highly assimilated into the American culture and did not know how to dance Mexican folk dances. The second boy was less assimilated and came from a Mexican American family that had retained more of its Mexican heritage.

This example illustrates the diversity and individual differences that exist within any ethnic minority group. Failure to recognize diversity and individual variations results in the stereotyping of an ethnic minority group.

Ethnicity and Aging As we saw in our discussion of poverty, ethnic minority groups are overrepresented in the poverty category of older adults (Hayward, Friedman, & Chen, 1996). Ethnic minority adults face possible double jeopardy. They confront problems related to *both* ageism and racism (Jackson, Chatters, & Taylor, 1993). Both the wealth and the health of ethnic minority older adults decrease more rapidly than for non-Latino White older adults (Edmonds, 1993). Ethnic minority older adults are more likely to become ill but less likely to receive treatment. They are also more likely to have a history of less education, unemployment, worse housing conditions, and shorter life expectancies than their non-Latino White older adult counterparts (Himes, Hogan, & Eggebeen, 1996). And many ethnic minority workers never enjoy the Social Security and Medicare benefits to which their earnings contribute, because they die before reaching the age of eligibility for benefits.

Despite the stress and discrimination faced by older adult ethnic minority individuals, many of these older adults have developed successful coping mechanisms that allow them to survive in the dominant non-Latino White world (Markides & Rudkin, 1996). Extensions of family networks, ethnic neighborhoods, and churches provide avenues for meaningful social participation, feelings of power, satisfaction, and a sense of belonging and being loved. Thus, it always is important to consider individual variations in the lives of aging minorities.

Review and Reflect: Learning Goal 5

5 Evaluate sociocultural influences on development

REVIEW

- How can culture, cross-cultural comparisons, and individualism/collectivism be defined? How is culture related to development?
- What is socioeconomic status? How are socioeconomic status and poverty linked to development?
- What is ethnicity? How is ethnicity involved in development? What are some important aspects of ethnicity to recognize?

REFLECT

- No matter how well intentioned people are, their life circumstances likely have given them some prejudices. If they don't have prejudices toward people with different cultural and ethnic backgrounds, other kinds of people may bring out prejudices in them. For example, prejudices can be developed about people who have certain religious or political conventions, people who are unattractive or too attractive, people with a disability, and people in a nearby town. As a parent or teacher, how would you attempt to reduce children's prejudices?

Reach Your Learning Goals

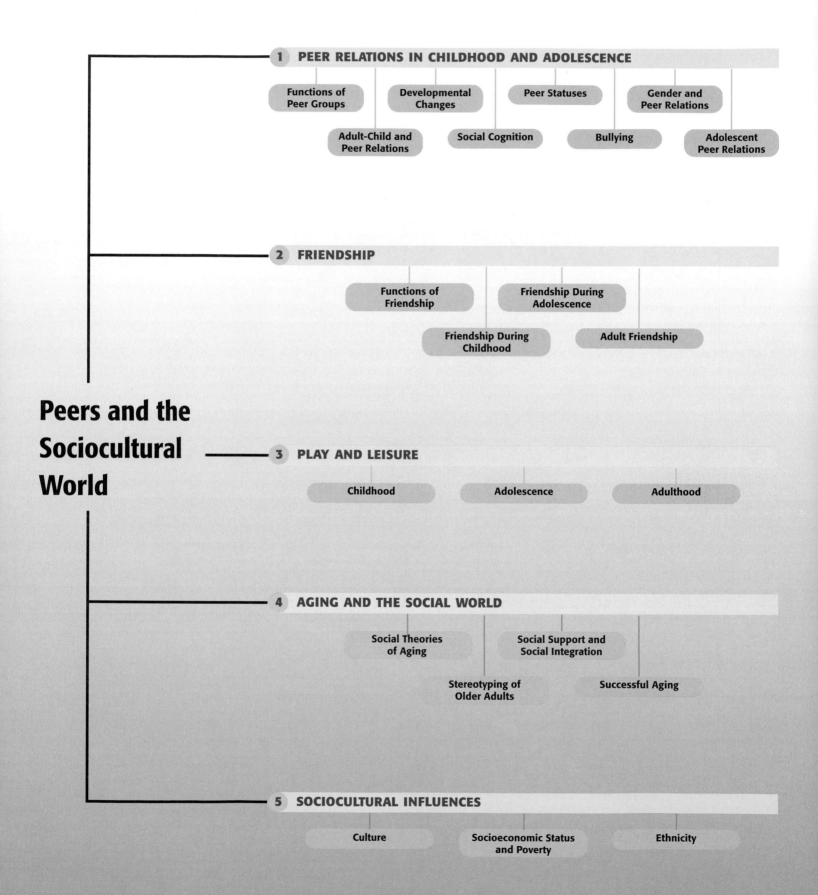

Peers and the Sociocultural World

1 PEER RELATIONS IN CHILDHOOD AND ADOLESCENCE

- Functions of Peer Groups
- Developmental Changes
- Peer Statuses
- Gender and Peer Relations
- Adult-Child and Peer Relations
- Social Cognition
- Bullying
- Adolescent Peer Relations

2 FRIENDSHIP

- Functions of Friendship
- Friendship During Adolescence
- Friendship During Childhood
- Adult Friendship

3 PLAY AND LEISURE

- Childhood
- Adolescence
- Adulthood

4 AGING AND THE SOCIAL WORLD

- Social Theories of Aging
- Social Support and Social Integration
- Stereotyping of Older Adults
- Successful Aging

5 SOCIOCULTURAL INFLUENCES

- Culture
- Socioeconomic Status and Poverty
- Ethnicity

Summary

1 Discuss peer relations in childhood and adolescence

- Peers are individuals who are at about the same age or maturity level. Peers provide a means of social comparison and a source of information about the world outside the family. Good peer relations may be necessary for normal social development. The inability to "plug in" to a social network is associated with a number of problems. Peer relations can be both positive and negative. Piaget and Sullivan stressed that peer relations provide the context for learning the reciprocal aspects of relationships.

- Healthy family relations usually promote healthy peer relations. Parents can model or coach their children in ways of relating to peers. Parents' choices of neighborhoods, churches, schools, and their own friends influence the pool from which their children might select possible friends. Rough-and-tumble play occurs mainly in peer relations rather than in parent-child relations. In times of stress, children usually turn to parents rather than peers. Peer relations have a more equal basis than parent-child relations.

- Some researchers believe that the quality of social interaction with peers in infancy provides valuable information about social development. As increasing numbers of infants have attended child care, infant peer relations have increased. The frequency of peer interaction, both positive and negative, increases in the preschool years. Children spend even more time with peers in the elementary and secondary school years.

- Perspective taking, social information-processing skills, and social knowledge are important dimensions of social cognition in peer relations.

- Popular children are frequently nominated as a best friend and are rarely disliked by their peers. Average children receive an average number of both positive and negative nominations from their peers. Neglected children are infrequently nominated as a best friend but are not disliked by their peers. Rejected children are rarely nominated as a best friend and are disliked by their peers. Controversial children are frequently nominated both as one's best friend and as being disliked by peers.

- Significant numbers of students are bullied, and this can result in short-term and long-term negative effects for the victim.

- Gender is linked to peer relations in several ways. From 4 to 12 years of age, preference for playing same-sex groups increases. Boys' groups are larger and they participate in more organized games than girls. Boys are more likely to engage in rough-and-tumble play, competition, ego displays, risk taking, and dominance, while girls are more likely to engage in collaborative discourse. The more time boys spend playing with boys, the higher their levels of aggression and activity, while the more time girls spend playing with girls, the lower their levels of aggression and activity.

- The pressure to conform to peers is strong during adolescence, especially around the ninth grade. Cliques and crowds assume more importance in the lives of adolescents than children. Membership in certain crowds—especially jocks and populars—is associated with increased self-esteem. Independents also show high self-esteem. Child groups are less formal and less heterogeneous than adolescent groups; child groups are also more likely to have same-sex participants.

2 Explain the role of friendship through the life span

- The functions of friendship include companionship, stimulation, physical support, ego support, social comparison, and intimacy/affection. Sullivan contended that friendships play important roles in well-being and development, especially fulfilling social needs.

- The developmental significance of friendship may vary from child to child, but many children use friends as a cognitive and social resource on a regular basis. Throughout childhood and adolescence, friends are generally similar—in terms of age, sex, ethnicity, and many other factors.

- Sullivan argued that there is a dramatic increase in the psychological importance of intimacy of close friends in adolescence. Friendships are important sources of support for adolescents. Research findings generally support his view. Adolescents who become friends with older individuals engage in more deviant behaviors than their counterparts with same-age friends.

- Friendships play an important role in adult development, especially in providing emotional support. Female, male, and female-male friendships often have different characteristics. Regardless of age, friendship is an important aspect of relationships. In old age, there often is more change in male than in female friendships.

3 Describe the developmental aspects of play and leisure

- The functions of play include affiliation with peers, tension release, advances in cognitive development, and exploration. Parten examined these categories of social play: unoccupied, onlooker, parallel, associative, and cooperative. Three-year-olds engaged in more solitary and parallel play, 5-year-olds in more cooperative and associative play. The contemporary perspective emphasizes both social and cognitive aspects of play. The most widely studied types of play include sensorimotor and practice play, pretend/symbolic play, social play, and games.

- Leisure refers to the pleasant times when individuals are free to pursue activities and interests of their own choosing—hobbies, sports, or reading, for example. U.S. adolescents have more discretionary time than adolescents in other industrialized countries and they often fill this time with unchallenging activities such as hanging out and watching television. U.S. adolescents spend more time in voluntary unstructured activities—such as hobbies, sports, and organizations—than East Asian adolescents. Some scholars argue that U.S. adolescents have too much unstructured discretionary time that should be replaced with more challenging activities.

- As adults, we not only need to learn to work well, but we also need to learn to enjoy leisure. Midlife may be an especially important time for leisure because of the physical changes that occur and because of preparation for an active retirement.

4 Summarize the social aspects of aging

- Disengagement theory has not held up but activity theory and social breakdown–reconstruction theory are viable theories of aging.
- There is extensive stereotyping of older adults, and ageism is a common occurrence.
- Social support is an important aspect of helping people cope with stress. Older adults usually have less integrated social networks and engage in less social activity than their younger counterparts, although these findings may be influenced by cohort effects.
- Increasingly, the positive aspects of aging are being studied. Factors that are linked with successful aging include an active lifestyle, positive coping skills, good social relationships and support, and self-efficacy.

5 Evaluate sociocultural influences on development

- Culture refers to the behavior patterns, beliefs, and all other products of a group of people that are passed on from generation to generation. Cross-cultural comparisons involve the comparison of one culture with one or more cultures, which provides information about the degree to which information is universal or culture-specific. One way that the influence of culture has been studied is to characterize cultures as individualistic (giving priority to personal rather than group goals) or collectivistic (emphasizing values that serve the group). Rites of passage are ceremonies that mark an individual's transition from one status to another, especially into

adulthood. In premodern cultures, rites of passage are well defined, but in contemporary America they are not. Respect for the aged may vary across cultures. Factors that predict high status for the older adults across cultures range from the perception that they have valuable knowledge to the belief that they serve useful functions.

- Socioeconomic status (SES) is the grouping of people with similar occupational, educational, and economic characteristics. The neighborhoods, schools, and families of children have SES characteristics that are related to the child's development. Parents from low-SES families are more concerned that their children conform to society's expectations, have an authoritarian parenting style, use physical punishment more in disciplining their children, and are more directive and less conversational with their children than higher-SES parents. Poverty is defined by economic hardship. The subculture of the poor is often characterized not only by economic hardship but also by social and psychological difficulties. When poverty is persistent and long-lasting, it especially has adverse effects on children's development. Older adults who live in poverty are a special concern. The majority of older adults face a life of reduced income.
- Ethnicity is based on cultural heritage, nationality characteristics, race, religion, and language. Immigration brings a number of challenges as children adapt to their new culture. Too often researchers have not teased apart ethnic and socioeconomic status effects. Although not all ethnic minority families are poor, poverty contributes to the stress of many ethnic minority families and between ethnic minority groups and the White majority. African American and Latino children are more likely than White American children to live in single-parent families and larger families and to have extended family connections. Recognizing differences in ethnicity is an important aspect of getting along with others in a diverse, multicultural world. Too often differences have been described as deficits on the part of ethnic minority individuals. Ethnic groups are not homogeneous. Failure to recognize this diversity results in stereotyping. A special concern involves ethnicity and aging.

Key Terms

Key People

E-Learning Tools

Connect to **www.mhhe.com/santrockldt2** to research the answers and complete these exercises. In addition, you'll find a number of other resources and valuable study tools for chapter 15, "Peers and the Sociocultural World," on the Student CD-ROM that came with this book.

Taking It to the Net

1. Charise is completing her course work for a Ph.D. in developmental psychology. She does not want to teach and she is not interested in working in a research lab. But she is very creative and loves young children. Her dissertation advisor suggested that she look into working for a toy company. What role do developmental psychologists play in developing the toys that young children play with?

2. Jeff is the director of the local YMCA's family programs. He has an idea for conducting a seminar for parents on how to help their children cope with peer pressure. What things can parents do to help their children resist negative peer pressure?

3. Patricia, public affairs director for a national advocacy organization for older adults, is planning a public education campaign focusing on poverty among the nation's over-65 population. How many of the country's over-65 population live in poverty, and how does the picture change with advanced age? What age, race, gender, and marital factors create the greatest risk for poverty after the age of 85?

Self-Assessment

To examine your ideas about stereotyping related to race and aging, complete these self-assessments:

- *Do I Engage in Racial and Aging Stereotyping?*
- *My Beliefs About Aging*

Health and Well-Being, Parenting, and Education

Build your decision-making skills by trying your hand at the health and well-being, parenting, and education "Scenarios."

Schools, Achievement, and Work

This chapter is about becoming educated, achieving, and working. We will explore such topics as contemporary approaches to student learning, becoming motivated to reach goals, careers, developmental changes in work, and retirement.

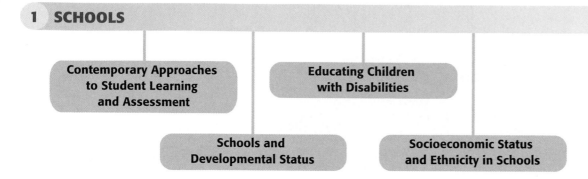

We have discussed many aspects of schools throughout this book but especially in Section 3, "Cognitive Processes and Development." Recall our coverage of applications of Piaget's and Vygotsky's theories to education in chapter 6, strategies for encouraging children's critical thinking in schools in chapter 7, applications of Gardner's and Sternberg's theories of intelligence to education in chapter 8, and bilingual education in chapter 9. Among the topics related to schools that we will explore here are contemporary approaches to student learning, education for individuals at different developmental levels, educating children with disabilities, and socioeconomic status and ethnicity in schools.

Contemporary Approaches to Student Learning and Assessment

Controversy swirls about the best way for children to learn in school and about how to assess their learning.

Direct Instruction and Constructivist Approaches   The back-to-basics movement has many advocates who believe that schools should use a **direct instruction approach,** a teacher-centered approach that is characterized by teacher direction and control, mastery of academic skills, high expectations for students, and maximum time spent on learning tasks.

In the 1990s, interest in school reform focused on constructivist approaches (Santrock, 2004). **Cognitive constructivist approaches** emphasize the child's active, cognitive construction of knowledge and understanding. The teacher's role is to provide support for students to explore their world and develop understanding. Piaget's theory, which we discussed in chapter 6, is the main developmental theory that is linked with cognitive constructivist approaches ◀∥∥∥ P. 202. **Social constructivist approaches** focus on the importance of collaboration with others to produce knowledge and understanding (John-Steiner & Mahn, 2003). The implication is that teachers should create many opportunities for students to learn with the teacher and with peers in co-constructing understanding. Vygotsky's theory, which we also discussed in chapter 6, is the main developmental theory that has served as the foundation for social constructivist approaches ◀∥∥∥ P. 218.

In short, constructivist approaches place the learner, not the teacher, at the center of the education process; they apply *learner-centered principles* (Duffy & Kirkley, 2004; McCombs, 2003). Figure 16.1 summarizes 14 learner-centered principles. These principles were constructed by a prestigious group of scientists and educators from a wide range of disciplines and published by the American Psychological Association in *Learner-Centered Principles: A Framework for School Reform and Redesign* (Learner-Centered Principles Work Group, 1997).

direct instruction approach A teacher-centered approach characterized by teacher direction and control, mastery of academic material, high expectations for students' progress, and maximum time spent on learning tasks.

cognitive constructivist approach An approach that emphasizes the child's active, cognitive construction of knowledge and understanding; Piaget's theory is an example of this approach.

social constructivist approach An approach that focuses on collaboration with others to produce knowledge and understanding; Vygotsky's theory is an example of this approach.

FIGURE 16.1 Learner-Centered Psychological Principles

Cognitive and Metacognitive Factors

1. Nature of the Learning Process
   The learning of complex subject matter is most effective when it is an intentional process of constructing meaning from information and experience.

2. Goals of the Learning Process
   The successful learner, over time and with support and instructional guidance, can create meaningful, coherent representations of knowledge.

3. Construction of Knowledge
   The successful learner, can link new information with existing knowledge in meaningful ways.

4. Strategic Thinking
   The successful learner, can create a repertoire of thinking and reasoning strategies to achieve complex goals.

5. Thinking about Thinking
   Higher-order strategies for selecting and monitoring mental operations facilitate creative and critical thinking.

6. Context of Learning
   Learning is influenced by environmental factors, including culture, technology, and instructional practices.

Motivational and Instructional Factors

7. Motivational and Emotional Influences on Learning
   What and how much is learned is influenced by the learner's motivation. Motivation to learn, in turn, is influenced by the learner's emotional states, beliefs, interests, goals, and habits of thinking.

8. Intrinsic Motivation to Learn
   The learner's creativity, higher-order thinking, and natural curiosity all contribute to motivation to learn. Intrinsic motivation is stimulated by tasks of optimal novelty and difficulty, relevant to personal interests, and providing for personal choice and control.

9. Effects of Motivation on Effort
   Acquisition of complex knowledge and skills requires extended learner effort and guided practice. Without learners' motivation to learn, the willingness to exert this effort is unlikely without coercion.

Developmental and Social Factors

10. Developmental Influences on Learning
    As individuals develop, there are different opportunities and constraints for learning. Learning is most effective when development within and across physical, cognitive, and socioemotional domains is taken into account.

11. Social Influences on Learning
    Learning is influenced by social interactions, interpersonal relations, and communication with others.

Individual Difference Factors

12. Individual Differences in Learning
    Learners have different strategies, approaches, and capabilities for learning that are a function of prior experience and heredity.

13. Learning and Diversity
    Learning is most effective when differences in learners' linguistic, cultural, and social backgrounds are taken into account.

14. Standards and Assessment
    Setting appropriately high and challenging standards and assessing the learner as well as learning progress—including diagnostic, process, and outcome assessment—are integral parts of the learning process.

Advocates of the cognitive and social constructivist and learner-centered approaches argue that the direct instruction approach turns children into passive learners and does not adequately challenge them to think in critical and creative ways. The direct instruction enthusiasts say that the constructivist approaches do not give enough attention to the content of a discipline, such as history or

Ask ERIC

Pathways to School Improvement

I touch the future. I teach.

—CHRISTA MCAULIFFE
*American Educator and Astronaut,
20th Century*

science. They also believe that the constructivist approaches are too relativistic and vague.

Accountability   Whether the direct instruction or a constructivist approach is used in a school, how do parents or taxpayers know if that school is educating children effectively? As the public and government have demanded increased accountability from schools, state-mandated tests have taken on a powerful role (Hambleton, 2002; McMillan, 2004). Most states have or are in the process of identifying objectives that every student in the state is expected to achieve. Teachers are strongly encouraged to incorporate these objectives into their planning and instruction.

Proponents argue that state-mandated testing will have a number of positive effects. These include improved student performance; more time teaching the subjects of tests; high expectations for all students; identification of poorly performing schools, teachers, and administrators; and improved confidence in schools as test scores increase.

Critics of state-mandated tests argue that they lead to these negative consequences (McMillan, 2002):

- *Dumbing down the curriculum.* State-mandated tests place more emphasis on rote memorization than on problem solving and critical thinking. One recent analysis found that state tests focus on less-demanding knowledge and skills (Quality Counts, 2001).
- *Teaching to the test.* Teachers increasingly teach knowledge and skills that are to be covered on state tests (Firestone, Monfils, & Schorr, 2004; Hicks & others, 2004). They spend inordinate amounts of time on testlike activities and practice tests and less time on actual teaching of important content and skills. One recent survey found that six of ten U.S. teachers said that state tests have led to teaching that focuses too heavily on state tests (Quality Counts, 2001).
- *Discrimination against low-socioeconomic-status (SES) and ethnic minority children.* This results when disproportionate percentages of these children do not meet the state standards (Camilli & Monfils, 2004).

For reasons such as these, the American Psychological Association, the American Educational Research Association, and the National Council on Measurement in Education have issued standards for the use of tests. They note that test scores are too limited and unstable to be used as the sole source of information for many major decisions about student placement or promotion. Test scores should always be used in combination with other sources of information about student achievement when making important decisions about students (National Research Council, 2001).

Schools and Developmental Status

Let's now explore how schools work at different developmental levels of students, beginning with early childhood education.

Early Childhood Education   There are many variations in the way young children are educated (Brewer, 2004; Vecchiotti, 2003). First, we will explore child-centered kindergarten, then turn our attention to developmentally appropriate and inappropriate education, and finally discuss a current controversy in early childhood education.

The Child-Centered Kindergarten   In the 1840s, Friedrich Froebel's concern for quality education for young children led to the founding of the kindergarten—literally, "a garden for children." The founder of the kindergarten understood that, like growing plants, children require careful nurturing. Unfortunately, too many of today's kindergartens have forgotten the importance of careful nurturing (Krogh & Slentz, 2001).

The **child-centered kindergarten** emphasizes the education of the whole child and concern for his or her physical, cognitive, and socioemotional development. Instruction is organized around the child's needs, interests, and learning styles. Emphasis is on the process of learning, rather than what is learned (White & Coleman, 2000). The child-centered kindergarten recognizes that each child follows a unique developmental pattern, that young children learn best through firsthand experiences with people and materials, and that play is extremely important in the child's total development. *Experimenting, exploring, discovering, trying out, restructuring, speaking,* and *listening* are all themes that describe excellent kindergarten programs. Such programs are closely attuned to the developmental status of 4- and 5-year-old children (Goelman & others, 2003).

Reggio Emilia
NAEYC
Head Start Resources

Developmentally Appropriate and Inappropriate Education   It is time for number games in a kindergarten class at the Greenbrook School in South Brunswick, New Jersey. With little prodding from the teacher, 23 5- and 6-year-old children fetch geometric puzzles, playing cards, and counting equipment from the shelves lining the room. At one round table, some young children fit together brightly colored shapes. One girl forms a hexagon out of triangles. Other children gather around her to count up how many parts were needed to make the whole. After about half an hour, the children prepare for story time. They put away their counting equipment and sit in a circle around one young girl. She holds up a giant book about a character named Mrs. Wishywashy, who insists on giving the farm animals a bath. The children recite the whimsical lines, clearly enjoying one of their favorite stories. The hallway outside the kindergarten is lined with drawings depicting the children's own interpretations of the book. After the first reading, volunteers act out various parts of the book. Not one face in the room looks bored.

This is not reading, writing, and arithmetic the way most individuals remember it. A growing number of educators and psychologists believe that preschool and young elementary school children learn best through active, hands-on teaching methods such as games and dramatic play. They know that children develop at varying rates and that schools need to allow for these individual differences (Golbeck, 2001; Henninger, 1999; Jalongo & Isenberg, 2000). They also believe that schools should focus on improving children's social development, as well as their cognitive development. Educators refer to this type of schooling as **developmentally appropriate practice;** it is based on knowledge of the typical development of children within an age span (age appropriateness) as well as the uniqueness of the child (individual appropriateness). In contrast, developmentally inappropriate practice for young children relies on abstract paper-and-pencil activities presented to large groups.

A comprehensive document regarding developmentally appropriate practice in early childhood programs is the position statement by the National Association for the Education of Young Children (NAEYC) (Bredekamp, 1987, 1997; NAEYC, 1986). Figure 16.2 presents some of the NAEYC's descriptions of developmentally appropriate practice.

One recent study compared 182 children from five developmentally appropriate and five developmentally inappropriate kindergarten classrooms in a Louisiana school system (Hart & others, 2003). Developmentally appropriate classrooms had hands-on activities and integrated curriculum tailored to meet age group, cultural, and individual learning styles; developmentally inappropriate classrooms featured an academic, direct instruction emphasis with extensive use of workbooks/worksheets, seatwork, and rote drill/practice activities. Children from the two types of classrooms did not differ in prekindergarten readiness, and the classrooms were balanced in terms of sex and socioeconomic status. Teacher ratings of child behavior and scores on the California Achievement Test were obtained through the third grade. Children who were in developmentally inappropriate classrooms had slower growth in

child-centered kindergarten Education that involves the whole child by considering both the child's physical, cognitive, and social development and the child's needs, interests, and learning styles.

developmentally appropriate practice Education that focuses on the typical developmental patterns of children (age appropriateness) and the uniqueness of each child (individual appropriateness). Such practice contrasts with developmentally inappropriate practice, which ignores the concrete, hands-on approach to learning. Direct teaching largely through abstract paper-and-pencil activities presented to large groups of young children is believed to be developmentally inappropriate.

Component	Appropriate practice	Inappropriate practice
Language development, literacy, and cognitive development	Children are provided many opportunities to see how reading and writing are useful before they are instructed in letter names, sounds, and word identification. Basic skills develop when they are meaningful to children. An abundance of these activities is provided to develop language and literacy: listening to and reading stories and poems; taking field trips; dictating stories; participating in dramatic play; talking informally with other children and adults; and experimenting with writing.	Reading and writing instruction stresses isolated skill development, such as recognizing single letters, reading the alphabet, singing the alphabet song, coloring within predefined lines, and being instructed in correct formation of letters on a printed line.
	Children develop an understanding of concepts about themselves, others, and the world around them through observation, interaction with people and real objects, and the seeking of solutions to concrete problems. Learning about math, science, social studies, health, and other content areas is integrated through meaningful activities.	Instruction stresses isolated skill development through memorization. Children's cognitive development is seen as fragmented in content areas, such as math or science, and times are set aside for each of these.
Physical development	Children have daily opportunities to use large muscles, including running, jumping, and balancing. Outdoor activity is planned daily so children can freely express themselves.	Opportunity for large muscle activity is limited. Outdoor time is limited because it is viewed as interfering with instructional time, rather than as an integral part of the children's learning environment.
	Children have daily opportunities to develop small muscle skills through play activities, such as puzzles, painting, and cutting.	Small motor activity is limited to writing with pencils, coloring predrawn forms, and engaging in similar structured lessons.
Aesthetic development and motivation	Children have daily opportunities for aesthetic expression and appreciation through art and music. A variety of art media are available.	Art and music are given limited attention. Art consists of coloring predrawn forms or following adult-prescribed directions.
	Children's natural curiosity and desire to make sense of their world are used to motivate them to become involved in learning.	Children are required to participate in all activities to obtain the teacher's approval; to obtain extrinsic rewards, such as stickers or privileges; or to avoid punishment.

FIGURE 16.2 NAEYC Recommendations for Developmentally Appropriate and Inappropriate Education

vocabulary, math application, and math computation. In another recent study, the academic achievement of mostly African American and Latino children who were attending Head Start was assessed in terms of whether they were in schools emphasizing developmentally appropriate or inappropriate practices (Huffman & Speer, 2000). The young children in the developmentally appropriate classrooms were more advanced in letter/word identification and showed better performance in applying problems over time. In the Applications in Life-Span Development interlude, you can read about a developmentally appropriate education program for young children.

Applications in Life-Span Development

Reggio Emilia's Children

The Reggio Emilia approach is an educational program for young children that was developed in the northern Italian city of Reggio Emilia (Gandini & Edwards, 2000). Children of single parents and children with disabilities have priority in admission; other children are admitted according to a scale of needs. Parents pay on a sliding scale based on income.

The children are encouraged to learn by investigating and exploring topics that interest them. A wide range of stimulating media and materials is available for children to use as they learn—music, movement, drawing, painting, sculpting, collages, puppets and disguises, and photography, for example.

In this program, children often explore topics in a group, which fosters a sense of community, respect for diversity, and a collaborative approach to problem solving. Two co-teachers are present to serve as guides for children. The Reggio Emilia teachers consider a project as an adventure, which can start from an adult's suggestion, from a child's idea, or from an event, such as a snowfall or something else unexpected. Every project is based on what the children say and do. The teachers allow children enough time to think and craft a project.

At the core of the Reggio Emilia approach is the image of children who are competent and have rights, especially the right to outstanding care and education (Bredekamp, 1993). Parent participation is considered essential, and cooperation is a major theme in the schools (Gandini, 1993). Many early childhood education experts believe the Reggio Emilia approach provides a supportive, stimulating context in which children are motivated to explore their world in a competent and confident manner (Cadwell, 1997, 2002; Firlik, 1996).

A Reggio Emilia classroom in which young children explore topics that interest them.

Middle and Later Childhood: Starting First Grade Around the World

As children make the transition to elementary school, they interact and develop relationships with new and significant others. School provides them with a rich source of new ideas to shape their sense of self.

ERIC Clearinghouse on Teachers Elementary Education

Controversy in Early Childhood Education Currently there is controversy about what the curriculum of U.S. early childhood education should be (Goelman & others, 2003). On one side are those who advocate a child-centered, constructivist approach much like that emphasized by the NAEYC description of developmentally appropriate practice. On the other side are those who advocate an academic, direct instruction approach.

In reality, many high-quality early childhood education programs include both academic and constructivist approaches. Many education experts like Lilian Katz (1999), though, worry about academic approaches that place too much pressure on young children to achieve and don't provide any opportunities to actively construct knowledge. Early childhood programs should focus on cognitive development *and* socioemotional development, not exclusively on cognitive development (Anderson & others, 2003; NAEYC, 2002).

Elementary School For many children, entering the first grade signals a change from being a "home-child" to being a "school-child"—a situation in which new roles and obligations are experienced. Children take up the new role of being a student, interact, develop new relationships, adopt new reference groups, and develop new standards by which to judge themselves. School provides children with a rich source of new ideas to shape their sense of self.

Evidence is mounting that early schooling proceeds mainly on the basis of negative feedback. For example, children's self-esteem in the latter part of elementary school is lower than it is in the earlier part, and older children rate themselves as less smart, less good, and less hardworking than do younger ones (Blumenfeld & others, 1981; Eccles, 2003; Eccles, Wigfield, & Byrnes, 2003).

Elementary teachers often feel pressured to "cover the curriculum." Frequently, teachers do so by tightly scheduling discrete time segments for each subject. This approach ignores the fact that children often do not need to distinguish learning by subject area. For example, they advance their knowledge of reading and writing when they work on social studies projects; they learn mathematical concepts through music and physical education (Katz & Chard, 1989). Thus, to facilitate learning, the classroom might include a publishing center, complete with materials for writing, illustrating, typing, and binding student-made books; a science area, with animals and plants for observation and books to study; and other similar areas. Classrooms should also provide opportunities for spontaneous play, recognizing that elementary school children continue to learn in all areas through unstructured play.

Many contemporary education experts believe children should be active, constructivist learners and taught through concrete, hands-on experience (Bonk & Cunningham, 1999). Let's examine an elementary school classroom based on these principles (Katz & Chard, 1989). In this example, the children were investigating a school bus. They wrote to the district's school superintendent and asked if they could have a bus parked at their school for a few days. They studied the bus, discovered the functions of its parts, and discussed traffic rules. Then, in the classroom, they built their own bus out of cardboard. The children had fun, but they also practiced writing, problem solving, and even some arithmetic. When the class had their parents' night, the teacher was ready with reports on how each child was doing. However, all that the parents wanted to see was the bus because their children had been talking about it at home for weeks.

Educating Adolescents Let's explore what the transition to middle/junior high school is like and the nature of effective schools for young adolescents.

The Transition to Middle or Junior High School The emergence of junior high schools in the 1920s and 1930s was justified on the basis of the physical, cognitive, and social changes that characterize early adolescence, as well as the need for more schools for the growing student population. Old high schools became junior high schools, and new regional high schools were built. In most systems, the ninth grade remained a part of the high school in content, although physically separated from it in a 6-3-3 system. Gradually, the ninth grade was restored to the high school, as many school systems developed middle schools that include the seventh and eighth grades, or sixth, seventh, and eighth grades. The creation of middle schools was influenced by the earlier onset of puberty in recent decades.

The transition to middle school has several benefits for students. They are more likely to feel grown up, have more subjects from which to select, and have more opportunities to spend time with peers and to locate compatible friends. They enjoy increased independence from direct parental monitoring, and they may be more challenged intellectually by academic work.

Despite these potential benefits, the first year of middle or junior high school is difficult for many students (Hawkins & Berndt, 1985). For example, in one study of the transition from sixth grade in an elementary school to the seventh grade in a junior high school, adolescents' perceptions of the quality of their school life plunged in the seventh grade (Hirsch & Rapkin, 1987). In the seventh grade, the students were less satisfied with school, were less committed to school, and liked their teachers less. The drop in school satisfaction occurred regardless of how academically successful the students were.

In short, the transition to middle school or junior high school can be stressful (Eccles, 2003, 2004; Seidman, 2000). Why? The transition takes place at a time when many changes—in the individual, in the family, and in school—are occurring simultaneously. These changes include puberty and related concerns about body image; the emergence of at least some aspects of formal operational thought, including accompanying changes in social cognition; increased responsibility; and decreased dependency on parents. Changes in the school include a switch to a larger, more impersonal classroom; to having many teachers; to having a larger, more heterogeneous set of peers; and to an increased focus on achievement and performance. Also, when students make the transition to middle or junior high school, they experience the **top-dog phenomenon,** the circumstance of moving from the top position (being the oldest, biggest, and most powerful students in elementary school) to the lowest position (being the youngest, smallest, and least powerful in middle or junior high school).

Effective Schools for Young Adolescents   Some critics of today's junior high and middle schools argue that they have become watered-down versions of high schools. Instead of offering curricular and extracurricular activities geared to the biological and psychological development of young adolescents, say the critics, middle and junior high schools mimic the curricular and extracurricular schedules of high schools.

What makes a successful middle school? Joan Lipsitz (1984) and her colleagues searched the nation for the best middle schools. Based on the recommendations of education experts and observations in schools in different parts of the United States, four middle schools were chosen for their outstanding ability to educate young adolescents. What were these middle schools like?

The most striking feature was their willingness and ability to adapt all school practices to their students' individual differences in physical, cognitive, and social development. The schools took seriously the knowledge we have developed about young adolescents. For example, one middle school fought to keep its schedule of mini-courses on Friday, so that every student could be with friends and pursue personal interests. Two other middle schools expended considerable energy on a complex school organization, so that small groups of students worked with small groups of teachers who could vary the tone and pace of the school day, depending on the students' needs. Another middle school developed an advisory scheme, so that each student had daily contact with an adult who was willing to listen, explain, comfort, and prod the adolescent. Such school policies reflect thoughtfulness and personal concern about individual students.

Middle Schools
Schools for Adolescents

top-dog phenomenon The circumstance of moving from the top position in elementary school to the lowest position in middle or junior high school.

The transition from elementary to middle or junior high school occurs at the same time as a number of other developmental changes. *What are some of these other developmental changes?*

Another characteristic of the effective middle schools was that early in their existence—the first year in three of the schools and the second year in the fourth school—they emphasized the importance of creating an environment that was positive for adolescents' social and emotional development. This goal was established not only because such environments contribute to academic excellence but also because the schools considered the socioeomotional development of their students as intrinsically important.

The vast majority of U.S. middle schools do not approach the excellent schools described by Lipsitz. In a 1989 report, "Turning Points: Preparing American Youth for the 21st Century," the Carnegie Foundation concluded that most young adolescents in the United States attend massive, impersonal schools; learn from seemingly irrelevant curricula; trust few adults in school; and lack access to health care and counseling. Here are some recommendations of the Carnegie Foundation (1989) report:

- Develop smaller "communities" or "houses" to lessen the impersonal nature of large middle schools.
- Lower student-to-counselor ratios from several hundred-to-1 to 10-to-1.
- Involve parents and community leaders in schools.
- Develop curricula that produce students who are literate, understand the sciences, and have a sense of health, ethics, and citizenship.
- Have teachers team teach in more flexibly designed curriculum blocks that integrate several disciplines, instead of presenting students with disconnected, rigidly separated 50-minute segments.
- Boost students' health and fitness with more in-school programs, and help students who need public health care to get it.

In *Turning Points 2000,* there was continued emphasis on the earlier Turning Points recommendations (Jackson & Davis, 2002). Some of the new emphases in the 2000 recommendations focused on teaching a curriculum grounded in rigorous academic standards, using instructional methods designed to prepare all students to achieve higher standards, providing a safe and healthy school environment, and involving parents and communities in supporting student learning and healthy

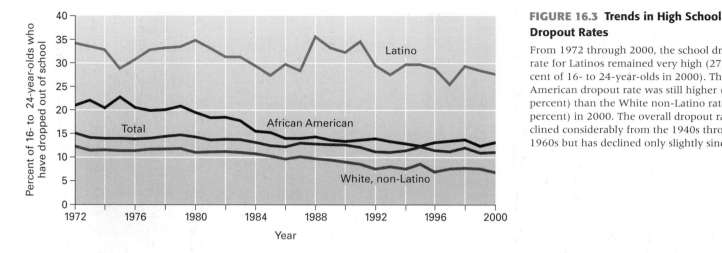

FIGURE 16.3 **Trends in High School Dropout Rates**

From 1972 through 2000, the school dropout rate for Latinos remained very high (27.8 percent of 16- to 24-year-olds in 2000). The African American dropout rate was still higher (13.1 percent) than the White non-Latino rate (6.9 percent) in 2000. The overall dropout rate declined considerably from the 1940s through the 1960s but has declined only slightly since 1972.

development. In sum, middle schools throughout the nation need a major redesign if they are to be effective in educating adolescents for becoming competent adults in the twenty-first century.

High School Just as there are concerns about U.S. middle school education, so are there concerns about U.S. high school education (Dornbusch & Kaufman, 2001; Hemmings, 2004; Kaufman, 2001). Many students graduate from high school with inadequate reading, writing, and mathematical skills, including many who go on to college and must enroll in remediation classes there. Other students drop out of high school and do not have skills that will allow them to advance in the work world.

In the last half of the twentieth century, high school dropout rates declined overall (National Center for Education Statistics, 2001). For example, in the 1940s, more than half of U.S. 15- to 24-year-olds had dropped out of school; in 2000, this figure had decreased to only 10.9 percent. Figure 16.3 shows the trends in high school dropout rates from 1972 through 2000. Notice that the dropout rate of Latino adolescents remains high (27.8 percent of 16- to 24-year-old Latino adolescents had dropped out of school in 2000). The highest dropout rate in the United States, though, occurs for Native American youth—only about 10 percent finish their high school education.

Students drop out of schools for many reasons. In one study, almost 50 percent of the dropouts cited school-related reasons for leaving school, such as not liking school or being expelled or suspended (Rumberger, 1995). Twenty percent of the dropouts (but 40 percent of the Latino students) cited economic reasons for leaving school. One-third of the female students dropped out for personal reasons, such as pregnancy or marriage.

An increasing number of educators believe that the nation's high schools need a new mission for the twenty-first century that addresses these problems (National Commission on the High School Senior Year, 2001):

1. More support is needed to enable all students to graduate from high school with the knowledge and skills needed to succeed in postsecondary education and careers. Many parents and students, especially those in low-income and minority communities, are unaware of the knowledge and level of skills required to succeed in postsecondary education.
2. High schools need to have higher expectations for student achievement. A special concern is the senior year of high school, which has become too much of a party time.

In the Contexts of Life-Span Development interlude, you can read about similarities and differences between U.S. secondary schools and secondary schools in a number of other countries.

Contexts of Life-Span Development
Cross-Cultural Comparisons of Secondary Schools

Secondary schools in different countries share a number of features, but differ on others (Cameron & others, 1983). Let's explore the similarities and differences in secondary schools in five countries: Australia, Brazil, Germany, Japan, and the United States.

Most countries mandate that children begin school at 6 to 7 years of age and stay in school until they are 14 to 16 years of age. Brazil requires students to go to school only until they are 14 years of age; Germany, Japan, Australia, and the United States require school attendance until 15 to 16 years of age.

Most secondary schools around the world are divided into two or more levels, such as middle school (or junior high school) and high school. However, Germany's schools are divided according to three educational ability tracks. By age 11 or 12, top students are headed for high school, or Gymnasium, where they eventually take the high school exit exam that enables them to go to a university. Others enter a less challenging track that trains them for white collar jobs. And less intellectually gifted students are routed to a track where they learn trade skills.

Japanese secondary schools have an entrance exam, but secondary schools in the other four countries do not. Only Australia and Germany have comprehensive exit exams.

The United States is the only country in the world in which sports are an integral part of the public school system. Only a few private schools in other countries have their own sports teams, sports facilities, and highly organized sports events.

In Brazil, students are required to take Portuguese (the native language) and four foreign languages (Latin, French, English, and Spanish). Brazil requires these languages because of the country's international character and emphasis on trade and commerce. Seventh-grade students in Australia take courses in sheep husbandry and weaving, two areas of economic and cultural interest in the country. In Japan, students take Western literature and languages (in addition to Japanese literature and language), Western physical education (in addition to Japanese martial arts classes), and Western sculpture and handicrafts (in addition to Japanese calligraphy). The Japanese school year is also much longer than that of other countries (225 days, versus 180 days in the United States, for example).

The juku, or "cramming school," is available to Japanese adolescents in the summertime and after school. It provides coaching to help them improve their grades and their entrance exam scores for high schools and universities. The Japanese practice of requiring an entrance exam for high school is a rarity among the nations of the world. *What are some differences between secondary schools in Japan and the United States?*

College and Adult Education Going to college offers many practical benefits, even beyond an education. The more education individuals have, the more income they will earn (*Occupational Outlook Handbook,* 2002–2003). Also, individuals with a college education live two years on the average longer than their counterparts who only graduate from high school. What is the transition to college like? Are adults seeking more education than in the past?

Transition to College Like the transition to middle or junior high school, the transition from high school to college involves change and possible stress. In many instances, there are parallel changes in the two transitions. Going from being a senior in high school to being a freshman in college replays the top-dog phenomenon (moving from being the oldest, most powerful group of students to the youngest, least powerful group of students), which occurred as adolescence began. The transition from high school to college also usually involves movement to a larger, more impersonal school structure; interaction with peers from more diverse backgrounds; and increased focus on achievement and its assessment.

But like the transition to middle or junior high school, the transition to college can involve positive features. Students are more likely to feel grown up and have more subjects from which to select, more time to spend with peers, and more opportunities to explore different lifestyles and values; they are likely to enjoy greater independence from parental monitoring and to be challenged intellectually by academic work (Santrock & Halonen, 2004).

However, today's college students experience more stress and are more depressed than in the past, according to a national study of more than 300,000 freshmen at more than 500 colleges and universities (Sax & others, 2002). In 2002, 27 percent (up from 16 percent in 1985) said they frequently "felt overwhelmed with what I have to do." The pressure to succeed in college, get a great job, and make lots of money were pervasive concerns of these students.

The United States is becoming a more educated country. In 1998, 24 percent of the population over 25 years old had completed 4 years or more years of college, compared with only 17 percent in 1980 (U.S. Department of Education, 1999). Total college enrollment is expected to increase during this decade.

What is college attendance like around the world? Canada has the largest percentage of 18- to 21-year-olds enrolled in college (41 percent), followed by Belgium (40 percent), France (36 percent), the United States (35 percent), Ireland (31 percent), and New Zealand (25 percent) (U.S. Department of Education, 1999). The greatest percentage increase in college attendance is taking place in Africa—128 percent from 1980 through 1996.

Adult Education   An increasing number of adults older than the traditional college age go to school. *Adult education* refers to all forms of schooling and learning in which adults participate. Adult education includes literacy training, community development,

Many immigrants to the United States take adult education classes, such as this Spanish-speaking man and woman enrolled in an English class. *What are some trends in adult education?*

The American College Freshman

American Association for Adult and Continuing Education

university credit programs, on-the-job training, and continuing professional education (Corley, 2000). Institutions that offer education to adults include colleges, libraries, museums, government agencies, businesses, and churches.

In 1985, individuals over the age of 25 represented 45 percent of the enrollment in credit courses in the United States. At the beginning of the twenty-first century, that figure is now slightly over 50 percent. The increase in adult education is a result of increased leisure time for some individuals and the need to update information and skills for others. Some older adults simply take educational courses because they enjoy learning and want to keep their minds active.

Women represent the majority of adult learners—almost 60 percent. In the 35 and over age group, women constitute an even greater percentage of the enrollment in adult education—almost 70 percent. Some of these women devoted their early adult lives to homemaking and parenting and decided to go back to school to enter a new career.

Going back to a classroom after being away from school for a long time can be stressful. However, returning students should realize that they bring a wealth of experience to college and should feel good about the contributions they can make.

Educating Children with Disabilities

So far we have discussed schools as they are experienced by the majority of U.S. students. But approximately 10 percent of children in the United States receive special education or related services. Figure 16.4 shows the approximate percentages of children with various disabilities who receive special education services (U.S. Department of Education, 2000). Within this group, a little more than half have a learning disability. Substantial percentages of children also have speech or language impairments (19 percent of those with disabilities), mental retardation (11 percent), and serious emotional disturbance (8 percent).

Learning Disabilities Bobby's second-grade teacher complains that his spelling is awful. Eight-year-old Tim says reading is really hard for him, and a lot of times

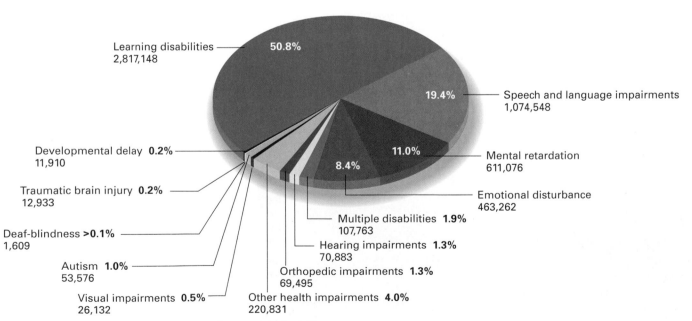

FIGURE 16.4 The Diversity of Children Who Have a Disability

Note: The figures represent children with a disability who received special education services in the 1998–1999 school year. Children with multiple disabilities also have been counted under various single disabilities.

the words don't make much sense. Alisha has good oral language skills but has considerable difficulty in computing correct answers to arithmetic problems. Each of these students has a learning disability.

Characteristics Three criteria have mainly been used to define learning disabilities (Siegel, 2003):

- *Exclusionary criteria.* Learning disabilities are not a result of some other condition. Learning disabilities are not the result of inadequate education; the child does not have sensory deficits, such as hearing or visual impairment; the child does not have serious neurological disorders that might restrict learning; and the child does not have major socioemotional problems that might interfere with learning.
- *IQ-achievement discrepancy.* A learning disability exists only if there is a discrepancy between potential (as measured by an IQ test) and achievement, with achievement being significantly lower than would be predicted by IQ. IQ-achievement discrepancy is a highly controversial aspect of the definition of learning disabilities (Lyons, 1996). Critics argue, for example, that IQ scores are an inadequate assessment of children's specific cognitive skills and that a gap between IQ and achievement may not predict whether a child will have a reading disability (Siegel & Himel, 1998; Toth & Siegel, 1994).
- *Specificity.* The learning problem is specific, usually confined to one or two cognitive areas. Some experts argue that the concept of a general, homogeneous group of learning-disabled (LD) children should be abandoned and that a child with a learning disability should be considered as part of a more specifically defined subtype (Stanovich, 1986). The two subtypes of learning disabilities that have most often been described are (1) reading disability and (2) arithmetic disability.

After examining the research on learning disabilities, leading expert Linda Siegel (2003) recently concluded that a definition of **learning disabilities** should include these components: (1) a minimum IQ level; (2) a significant difficulty in a school-related area (especially reading or mathematics); and (3) exclusion of only severe emotional disorders, second-language background, sensory disabilities, and specific neurological deficits.

About three times as many boys as girls are classified as having a learning disability (U.S. Department of Education, 1996). Among the explanations for this gender difference are a greater biological vulnerability among boys and *referral bias* (that is, boys are more likely to be referred by teachers for treatment because of their behavior) (Bender, 2004).

About 5 percent of all school-age children in the United States receive special education or related services because of a learning disability. (In the federal classification of children receiving special education and related services, attention deficit hyperactivity disorder [ADHD] is included in the learning disabilities category. Because of the significant interest in ADHD today, we will discuss it in a separate subsection.) In the past two decades, the percentage of children classified as having a learning disability has increased substantially—from less than 30 percent of all children receiving special education and related services in 1977 to a little more than 50 percent today. Some experts say that the dramatic increase reflects poor diagnostic practices and overidentification. They believe that teachers sometimes are too quick to label children with the slightest learning problem as having a learning disability, instead of recognizing that the problem may rest in their ineffective teaching. Other experts say the increase in children being labeled with a "learning disability" is justified (Hallahan & Kaufmann, 2003).

Dyslexia The most common problem that characterizes children with a learning disability involves reading (Grigorenko, 2001; Ho & others, 2004; Rittey, 2003; Thompson, 2003). Such children especially show problems in phonological skills (recall from chapter

learning disability Includes three components: (1) a minimum IQ level; (2) a significant difficulty in a school-related area (especially reading or mathematics); and (3) exclusion of only severe emotional disorders, second-language background, sensory disabilities, and specific neurological deficits.

Exploring Disabilities
Learning Disabilities
ADHD

**Middle and Later Childhood:
Attention Deficit Disorder**

9, "Language Development," that these involve being able to understand how sounds and letters match up to make words). **Dyslexia** is a category that is reserved for individuals who have a severe impairment in their ability to read and spell.

Children with a learning disability often have difficulties in handwriting, spelling, or composition (Raymond, 2004). Their writing may be extremely slow, their writing products may be virtually illegible, and they may make numerous spelling errors because of their inability to match up sounds and letters.

Linda Siegel (2003) recently provided these recommendations for helping children with learning disabilities:

- To improve word recognition skills, use a word family approach to draw attention to common word patterns (such as cat, bat, sat, fat, rat, and mat).
- Use talking books and/or textbooks on tape.
- Use high-interest, low-vocabulary books.
- Use a language experience approach, which involves dictating stories then using the words from these stories as a basis for reading vocabulary.
- Encourage children to use a word processor on a computer to help them improve their written work.
- Consider alternatives such as class handouts or tape recording oral lessons because copying from the blackboard is difficult for children.
- Have children with a math computation disability use a calculator to help them with arithmetic facts and multiplication tables.

Attention Deficit Hyperactivity Disorder   Matthew has attention deficit hyperactivity disorder, and the outward signs are fairly typical. He has trouble attending to the teacher's instructions and is easily distracted. He can't sit still for more than a few minutes at a time, and his handwriting is messy. His mother describes him as very fidgety.

Characteristics   Attention deficit hyperactivity disorder **(ADHD)** is a disability in which children consistently show one or more of these characteristics over a period of time: (1) inattention, (2) hyperactivity, and (3) impulsivity. Children who are inattentive have difficulty focusing on any one thing and may get bored with a task after only a few minutes. Children who are hyperactive show high levels of physical activity, almost always seeming to be in motion. Children who are impulsive have difficulty curbing their reactions and don't do a good job of thinking before they act. Depending on the characteristics they display, children with ADHD can be diagnosed as (1) ADHD with predominantly inattention, (2) ADHD with predominantly hyperactivity/impulsivity, or (3) ADHD with both inattention and hyperactivity/impulsivity.

Diagnosis and Developmental Characteristics   The number of children diagnosed and treated for ADHD has increased substantially, by some estimates doubling in the 1990s. The disorder occurs as much as four to nine times more in boys than in girls. There is controversy about the increased diagnosis of ADHD (Terman & others, 1996), however. Some experts attribute the increase mainly to heightened awareness of the disorder. Others are concerned that many children are being diagnosed without undergoing extensive professional evaluation with input from multiple sources.

Signs of ADHD may be present in the preschool years. Parents and preschool or kindergarten teachers may notice that the child has an extremely high activity level and a limited attention span. They may say the child is "always on the go," "can't sit still even for a second," or "never seems to listen." Many children with ADHD are difficult to discipline, have a low frustration tolerance, and have problems in peer relations. Other common characteristics of children with ADHD include general immaturity and clumsiness.

Although signs of ADHD are often present in the preschool years, their classification often doesn't take place until the elementary school years (Stein & Perrin, 2003). The increased academic and social demands of formal schooling, as well as

dyslexia A category of learning disabilities involving a severe impairment in the ability to read and spell.

attention deficit hyperactivity disorder (ADHD) A disability in which children consistently show one or more of the following characteristics: (1) inattention, (2) hyperactivity, and (3) impulsivity.

stricter standards for behavioral control, often illuminate the problems of the child with ADHD. Elementary school teachers typically report that this type of child has difficulty in working independently, completing seat work, and organizing work. Restlessness and distractibility are often noted. These problems are more likely to be observed in repetitive or taxing tasks or tasks that the child perceives to be boring (such as completing worksheets or doing homework).

It used to be thought that ADHD decreased in adolescence, but current estimates suggest that ADHD decreases in only about one-third of adolescents. Increasingly, it is thought that these problems may continue into adulthood.

Causes and Treatment Definitive causes of ADHD have not been found. However, a number of causes have been proposed, such as low levels of certain neurotransmitters (chemical messengers in the brain), prenatal and postnatal abnormalities, and environmental toxins, such as lead (Biderman & Faraone, 2003). Thirty to 50 percent of children with ADHD have a sibling or parent who has the disorder (Faraone & Doyle, 2001; Whalen, 2001; Woodrich, 1994).

Many experts recommend a combination of academic, behavioral, and medical interventions to help students with ADHD learn and adapt more effectively (Medd, 2003; Rapport & others, 2001). This intervention requires cooperation and effort on the part of parents, teachers, administrators, special educators, school psychologists, and health-care professionals (Whalen, 2001).

About 85 to 90 percent of children with ADHD are taking medication such as Ritalin or Adderall (which has fewer side effects than Ritalin) to control their behavior (Denney, 2001). Ritalin and Adderall are stimulants, and for most individuals, they speed up the nervous system and behavior (Fararone & others, 2004). However, in many children with ADHD they have the opposite effect, slowing down their nervous system and behavior. Scientists are still not sure why these drugs work in such opposite ways for children with ADHD and those who do not have the disorder (Johnson & Leung, 2001). Researchers have found that a combination of medication (such as Ritalin) and behavior management improves the behavior of children with ADHD better than medication alone or behavior management alone (Swanson & others, 2001). Critics argue that many physicians are too quick in prescribing stimulants for children with mild forms of ADHD (Timimi & Taylor, 2004).

Educational Issues The legal requirement that U.S. schools serve all children with a disability is fairly recent. Until laws were passed in the 1970s that mandated services for children with disabilities, most public schools either refused enrollment to children with a disability or inadequately served them. In 1975, *Public Law 94-142*, the Education for All Handicapped Children Act, required that all students with disabilities be given a free, appropriate public education.

In 1990, Public Law 94-142 was renamed the *Individuals with Disabilities Education Act (IDEA)*. IDEA spells out broad mandates for services to all children with disabilities. These include the requirements that students with disabilities be given an individualized education plan (IEP) and be educated in the least restrictive environment (LRE) (Smith, 2004; Smith & others, 2004).

An **individualized education plan (IEP)** is a written statement that spells out a program that is specifically tailored for the student with a disability. In general, the IEP should be (1) related to the child's learning capacity, (2) specifically constructed to meet the child's individual needs and not merely a copy of what is offered to other children, and (3) designed to provide educational benefits.

The **least restrictive environment (LRE)** is a setting that is as similar as possible to the one in which children who do not have a disability are educated. This provision of the IDEA has given a legal basis to efforts to educate children with a disability in the regular classroom (Dettmer, Dyck, & Thurston, 2002). The term **inclusion** describes educating a child with special education needs full-time in the regular classroom (Chaote, 2004; Friend & Busuck, 2002; Wardle, 2003).

Public Law 94-142 mandates free, appropriate education for all children. *What are the aspects of this education?*

Education of Children Who Are Exceptional

individualized education plan (IEP) A written statement that spells out a program tailored to a child with a disability. The plan should be (1) related to the child's learning capacity, (2) specially constructed to meet the child's individual needs and not merely a copy of what is offered to other children, and (3) designed to provide educational benefits.

least restrictive environment (LRE) The concept that a child with a disability must be educated in a setting that is as similar as possible to the one in which children who do not have a disability are educated.

inclusion Educating a child with special education needs full-time in the regular classroom.

Socioeconomic Status and Ethnicity in Schools

Children from low-income, ethnic minority backgrounds have more difficulties in school than do their middle-socioeconomic-status, White counterparts. Why? Critics argue that schools have not done a good job of educating low-income, ethnic minority students (Scott-Jones, 1995). Let's further explore the roles of socioeconomic status and ethnicity in schools.

The Education of Students from Low Socioeconomic Backgrounds

Many children in poverty face problems at home that present barriers to their learning (Books, 2004; Bradley & Corwyn, 2002; Cooter, 2004). They might have parents who don't set high educational standards for them, who are incapable of reading to them, and who don't have enough money to pay for educational materials and experiences, such as books and trips to zoos and museums. They might be malnourished and live in areas where crime and violence are a way of life.

As a result, children from low-SES families are likely to begin school several steps behind other children. In an attempt to give these children a better chance to succeed, the federal government began **Project Head Start** in the summer of 1965, funded by the Economic Opportunity Act, and it continues to serve disadvantaged children today. Project Head Start is a compensatory education program designed to provide preschool children from low-income families the opportunity to acquire the skills and experiences important for success in school.

Evaluations support the positive influence of compensatory education on both the cognitive and social worlds of disadvantaged young children (Reynolds, 1999; Schweinhart, 1999). Model preschool programs have been linked with long-term effects such as lower rates of placement in special education, dropping out of school, grade retention, delinquency, and use of welfare programs. However, one estimate is that 40 percent of the 1,400 Head Start programs are of questionable quality (Zigler & Styfco, 1994). More attention needs to be given to developing consistently high-quality Head Start programs (Bronfenbrenner, 1995; Maxwell, 2000).

Children from a low SES-background face another obstacle: their schools (Bradley & Corwyn, 2002). Compared with schools in higher-income areas, schools in low-income areas are more likely to have more students with low achievement test scores, low graduation rates, and small percentages of students going to college; they are more likely to have young teachers with less experience; and they are more likely to encourage rote learning (Spring, 2001). Too few schools in low-income neighborhoods provide students with environments that are conducive to learning. Many of the schools' buildings and classrooms are old and crumbling.

Jonathan Kozol (1991) vividly described some of the problems that children of poverty face in their neighborhood and at school in *Savage Inequalities.* Following are some of his observations in one inner-city area. East St. Louis, Illinois, has no obstetric services, no regular trash collection, and few jobs. Nearly one-third of the families live on less than $7,500 a year, and 75 percent of its population lives on welfare of some form. Blocks upon blocks of housing consist of dilapidated, skeletal buildings. Residents breathe the chemical pollution of nearby Monsanto Chemical Company. Raw sewage repeatedly backs up into homes. Lead from nearby smelters poisons the soil. Child malnutrition and fear of violence are common. The problems of the streets spill over into the schools, where sewage also backs up from time to time. Classrooms and hallways are old and unattractive, athletic facilities inadequate. Teachers run out of chalk and paper, the science labs are 30 to 50 years out of date, and the school's heating system has never worked correctly. A history teacher has 110 students but only 26 books. Anyone who visits places like East St. Louis, says Kozol, comes away profoundly shaken.

Ethnicity in Schools

East St. Louis is 98 percent African American. Kozol's interest was in describing what life is like in the nation's inner-city neighborhoods and schools, which are predominantly African American and Latino. More than one-third

Diversity and Education

Project Head Start Compensatory education designed to provide children from low-income families the opportunity to acquire the skills and experiences important for school success.

of all African American and almost one-third of all Latino students attend schools in the 47 largest city school districts in the United States, compared with only 5 percent of all White and 22 percent of all Asian American students. Many of these inner-city schools are still segregated, are grossly underfunded, and do not provide adequate opportunities for children to learn effectively. Thus, as discussed in chapter 15, the effects of SES and the effects of ethnicity are often intertwined **P. 549.**

School segregation is still a factor in U.S. education. Almost one-third of all African American and Latino students attend schools in which 90 percent or more of the students are from minority groups (Banks, 2002, 2003).

The school experiences of students from different ethnic groups vary considerably (Bennett, 2003; Taylor & Whittaker, 2003). African American and Latino students are much less likely than non-Latino White or Asian American students to be enrolled in academic, college preparatory programs and are much more likely to be enrolled in remedial and special education programs. Asian American students are far more likely than other ethnic minority groups to take advanced math and science courses in high school. African American students are twice as likely as Latinos, Native Americans, or Whites to be suspended from school.

Some experts say that a form of institutional racism permeates many American schools by which teachers accept a low level of performance from children of color (Ogbu & Stern, 2001; Spencer, 1990). American anthropologist John Ogbu (1989) proposed that ethnic minority students are placed in a position of subordination and exploitation in the American educational system. He believes that students of color, especially African Americans and Latinos, have inferior educational opportunities, are exposed to teachers and school administrators who have low academic expectations for them, and encounter negative stereotypes (Ogbu & Stern, 2001). In one study of middle schools in predominantly Latino areas of Miami, Latino and White teachers rated African American students as having more behavioral problems than African American teachers rated the same students as having (Zimmerman & others, 1995).

Here are some strategies for improving relationships among ethnically diverse students (Santrock, 2004):

- *Turn the class into a jigsaw classroom.* When Eliot Aronson was a professor at the University of Texas at Austin, the school system contacted him for ideas on how to reduce the increasing racial tension in classrooms. Aronson (1986) developed the concept of the "jigsaw classroom," in which students from different cultural backgrounds are placed in a cooperative group in which they have to construct different parts of a project to reach a common goal. Aronson used the term *jigsaw* because he saw the technique as much like a group cooperating to put pieces together to complete a jigsaw puzzle. How might this work? Team sports, drama productions, and music performances are examples of contexts in which students cooperate to reach a common goal.
- *Use technology to foster cooperation with students from around the world.*
- *Encourage students to have positive personal contact with diverse other students.* Contact alone does not do the job of improving relationships with diverse others. For example, busing ethnic minority students to predominantly White schools, or vice versa, has not reduced prejudice or improved interethnic relations (Minuchin & Shapiro, 1983). What matters is what happens after children get to school. Especially beneficial in improving interethnic relations is sharing one's worries, successes, failures, coping strategies, interests, and other personal information with people of other ethnicities. When this happens, people are seen more as individuals than as a heterogeneous cultural group.
- *Encourage students to engage in perspective taking.* Exercises and activities that help students see others' perspectives can improve interethnic relations. This helps students "step into the shoes" of peers who are culturally different and feel what it is like to be treated in fair or unfair ways.

James Comer (left) is shown with some of the inner-city African American children who attend a school that became a better learning environment because of Comer's intervention. Comer is convinced that a strong, familylike atmosphere is a key to improving the quality of inner-city schools.

- *Help students think critically and be emotionally intelligent when cultural issues are involved.* Students who learn to think critically and deeply about interethnic relations are likely to decrease their prejudice. Becoming more emotionally intelligent includes understanding the causes of one's feelings, managing anger, listening to what others are saying, and being motivated to share and cooperate.
- *Reduce bias.* Teachers can reduce bias by displaying images of children from diverse ethnic and cultural groups, selecting play materials and classroom activities that encourage cultural understanding, helping students resist stereotyping, and working with parents.
- *View the school and community as a team to help support teaching efforts.* James Comer (1988; Comer & others, 1996) believes that a community, team approach is the best way to educate children. Three important aspects of the Comer Project for Change are (1) a governance and management team that develops a comprehensive school plan, assessment strategy, and staff development plan; (2) a mental health or school support team; and (3) a parent's program. Comer believes that the entire school community should have a cooperative rather than an adversarial attitude. The Comer program is currently operating in more than 600 schools in 26 states.
- *Be a competent cultural mediator.* Teachers can play a powerful role as a cultural mediator by being sensitive to racist content in materials and classroom interactions, learning more about different ethnic groups, being sensitive to children's ethnic attitudes, viewing students of color positively, and thinking of positive ways to get parents of color more involved as partners with teachers in educating children (Jones & Fuller, 2003).

Review and Reflect: Learning Goal 1

1 **Describe the role of schools in development**

REVIEW

- What are some contemporary approaches to student learning?
- How do schools change as children develop?
- What is involved in educating children with disabilities?
- What roles do socioeconomic status and ethnicity play in schools?

REFLECT

- What was your middle or junior high school like? How did it measure up to Lipsitz' criteria for effective schools for young adolescents and the Carnegie Foundation's recommendations?

---

2 ACHIEVEMENT

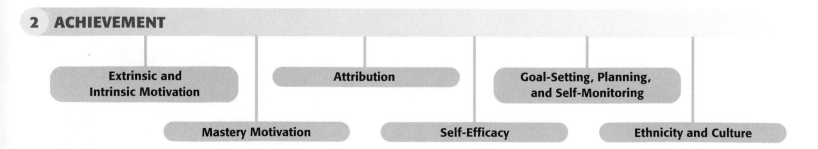

| Extrinsic and Intrinsic Motivation | Attribution | Goal-Setting, Planning, and Self-Monitoring |
| Mastery Motivation | Self-Efficacy | Ethnicity and Culture |

In any classroom, whoever the teacher is and whatever approach is used, some children achieve more than others. Why? Among the reasons for variations in achievement are characteristics of the child and sociocultural contexts related to motivation.

Calvin and Hobbes   by Bill Watterson

Extrinsic and Intrinsic Motivation

The behavioral perspective emphasizes the importance of extrinsic motivation. **Extrinsic motivation** involves doing something to obtain something else (the activity is a means to an end). Extrinsic motivation is often influenced by external incentives such as rewards and punishments. For example, a student may study for a test in order to obtain a good grade.

While the behavioral perspective emphasizes extrinsic motivation in achievement, the cognitive perspective stresses the importance of intrinsic motivation. **Intrinsic motivation** involves the internal motivation to do something for its own sake (the activity is an end in itself). For example, a student may study hard for a test because he or she enjoys the content of the course.

Current evidence strongly favors establishing a classroom climate in which students are intrinsically motivated to learn (Brophy, 2004; Eccles, 2004; Hennesey & Amabile, 1998; Wigfield & Eccles, 2002). Students are more motivated to learn when they are given choices, become absorbed in challenges that match their skills, and receive rewards that have informational value but are not used for control. Praise also can enhance students' intrinsic motivation. To see why these things are so, let's first consider the intrinsic motivation of self-determination and personal choice. Then, we will examine how external rewards can either enhance or undermine intrinsic motivation. Finally, we will identify some developmental changes in intrinsic and extrinsic motivation as students move up the educational ladder.

Self-Determination and Choice   One view of intrinsic motivation emphasizes that students want to believe that they are doing something because of their own will, not because of external success or rewards (Deci, Koestner, & Ryan, 2001; Deci & Ryan, 1994). Students' internal motivation and intrinsic interest in school tasks increase when they have opportunities to make choices and take responsibility for their learning (Stipek, 1996, 2002). For example, in one study, high school science students who were encouraged to organize their own experiments demonstrated more care and interest in the laboratory than did their counterparts who had to follow detailed instructions and directions (Rainey, 1965). In another study, those students who were given some choice of activities and when to do them, and were encouraged to take personal responsibility for their behavior, had higher achievement gains and were more likely to graduate from high school than a control group (deCharms, 1984).

Extrinsic Rewards and Internal Motivation   In some situations, rewards can actually undermine learning. For example, in one study, students who had a strong

extrinsic motivation Response to external incentives such as rewards and punishments.

intrinsic motivation Internal motivational factors such as self-determination, curiosity, challenge, and effort.

interest in art spent more time drawing when they did not expect a reward than did their counterparts who also had a strong interest in art but knew they would be rewarded (Lepper, Greene, & Nisbett, 1973). Other researchers have found similar effects (Morgan, 1984).

However, classroom rewards can be useful (Cameron, 2001). Rewards can serve (1) as an incentive to engage in tasks, in which case the goal is to control the student's behavior; and (2) to convey information about mastery (Bandura, 1982; Deci, 1975). Rewards used as incentives lead to perceptions that the student's behavior was caused by the external reward and not by the student's own motivation. In contrast, when rewards convey information about mastery, students' feelings of competence are likely to be enhanced. It is not the reward itself that causes the effect but rather the offer or the expectation of the reward (Schunk, 2001).

To better understand the difference between using rewards to control students' behavior and using them to provide information about mastery, consider this example (Schunk, 2000, 2004). A teacher puts a reward system in place in which the more work students accomplish, the more points they will earn. Students will be motivated to work to earn points because the points can be exchanged for privileges, but the points also provide information about their capabilities. That is, the more points students earn, the more work they have accomplished. As they accumulate points, students are more likely to feel competent. In contrast, if points are provided simply for spending time on a task, the task might become a means to an end. Because the points don't convey anything about capabilities, students are likely to perceive that the rewards control their behavior.

Thus, rewards that convey information about students' mastery can increase intrinsic motivation by increasing their sense of competence. However, negative feedback, such as criticism, that carries information that students are incompetent can undermine intrinsic motivation, especially if students doubt their ability to become competent (Stipek, 2002).

Developmental Shifts in Intrinsic and Extrinsic Motivation Many psychologists and educators believe that it is important for children to develop intrinsic motivation as they grow older. However, as students move from the early elementary school years to the high school years, intrinsic motivation tends to drop (Harter, 1996). In one study, the biggest drop in intrinsic motivation and largest increase in extrinsic motivation occurred between the sixth and seventh grade (Harter, 1981). In another study, as students moved from the sixth to the eighth grade, they increasingly said that school is boring and irrelevant (Harter, 1996). In this study, students who were intrinsically motivated were doing much better academically than those who were extrinsically motivated.

Why the shift toward extrinsic motivation as children move to higher grades? One explanation is that grading practices reinforce external motivation. That is, as students get older, they lock into the increasing emphasis on grades and their internal motivation drops.

Jacquelynne Eccles and her colleagues (Eccles, 2003, 2004; Eccles & Midgley, 1989; Eccles & Wigfield, 2002; Wigfield, Eccles, & Pintrich, 1996) identified some specific changes in the school context that help to explain the decline in intrinsic motivation. Middle and junior high schools are more impersonal, more formal, more evaluative, and more competitive than elementary schools. Students compare themselves more with other students because they are increasingly graded in terms of their relative performance on assignments and standardized tests.

Mastery Motivation

The increasingly competitive, impersonal atmosphere of middle schools obviously does not discourage all students. To some, these characteristics represent a challenge.

Researchers have found that how students typically respond to challenges has a lot to do with how much they achieve.

Carol Dweck and her colleagues (Dweck & Elliott, 1983; Dweck & Leggett, 1988) have found that children show two distinct responses to difficult or challenging circumstances: a mastery orientation or a helpless orientation. Children with a **mastery orientation** focus on the task rather than on their ability, have positive affect (suggesting they enjoy the challenge), and generate solution-oriented strategies that improve their performance. Mastery-oriented students often instruct themselves to pay attention, to think carefully, and to remember strategies that worked for them in the past (Anderman, Maehr, & Midgley, 1996).

In contrast, children with a **helpless orientation** focus on their inadequacies, often attribute their difficulty to a lack of ability, and display negative affect (including boredom and anxiety). This orientation undermines their performance. Figure 16.5 describes some behaviors that might reflect a helpless orientation.

A mastery orientation can also be contrasted with a **performance orientation,** which involves being concerned with the outcome rather than the process. For performance-oriented students, winning is what matters. For mastery-oriented students, what matters is the sense that they are effectively interacting with their environment. Mastery-oriented students do like to win, but winning isn't as important as it is for performance-oriented students. Developing their skills is more important.

The student:

- Says "I can't"
- Doesn't pay attention to teacher's instructions
- Doesn't ask for help, even when it is needed
- Does nothing (e.g., stares out the window)
- Guesses or answers randomly without really trying
- Doesn't show pride in successes
- Appears bored, uninterested
- Is unresponsive to teacher's exhortations to try
- Is easily discouraged
- Doesn't volunteer answers to teacher's questions
- Maneuvers to get out of or to avoid work (e.g., has to go to the nurse's office)

FIGURE 16.5 Behaviors That Suggest a Helpless Orientation

Intrinsic Motivation

Attribution

Attribution

Attribution theory states that individuals are motivated to discover the underlying causes of behavior as part of the effort to make sense out of the behavior. In a way, attribution theorists say, people are like intuitive scientists, seeking the cause behind what happens.

The reasons individuals behave the way they do can be classified in a number of ways, but one basic distinction stands out above all others—the distinction between internal causes, such as the actor's personality traits or motives, and external causes, which are environmental, situational factors such as rewards or task difficulty (Heider, 1958). If college students do not do well on a test, do they attribute it to the teacher making the test too difficult (external cause) or to their not studying hard enough (internal cause)? The answer to such a question influences how people feel about themselves. If students believe that their poor performance is the teacher's fault, they will not feel as badly as when they do poorly because they do not spend enough time studying.

An extremely important aspect of internal causes for achievement is *effort* (Alderman, 2004). Unlike many causes of success, effort is under a person's control and amenable to change. The importance of effort in achievement is recognized even by children. In one study, third- to sixth-grade students felt that effort was the most effective strategy for good school performance (Skinner, Wellborn, & Connell, 1990).

Self-Efficacy

Albert Bandura (1997, 2001), whose social cognitive theory we described in chapter 1, believes that a critical factor in whether or not students achieve is **self-efficacy,** the belief that one can master a situation and produce favorable outcomes ◀ ▥ **P. 24.** Self-efficacy is the belief that "I can"; helplessness is the belief that

mastery orientation An orientation in which one is task-oriented and, instead of focusing on one's ability, is concerned with learning strategies.

helpless orientation An orientation in which one seems trapped by the experience of difficulty and attributes one's difficulty to a lack of ability.

performance orientation An orientation in which one focuses on achievement outcomes; winning is what matters most, and happiness is thought to result from winning.

attribution theory The theory that, in their effort to make sense out of their own behavior or performance, individuals are motivated to discover its underlying causes. Attributions are perceived causes of outcomes.

self-efficacy The belief that one can master a situation and produce favorable outcomes.

"I cannot" (Bandura & Locke, 2003; Maddux, 2002; Stipek, 2002). Students with high self-efficacy endorse such statements as "I know that I will be able to learn the material in this class" and "I expect to be able to do well at this activity."

Dale Schunk (1991, 2001) has applied the concept of self-efficacy to many aspects of students' achievement. In his view, self-efficacy influences a student's choice of activities. Students with low self-efficacy for learning may avoid many learning tasks, especially those that are challenging. By contrast, high-self-efficacy counterparts eagerly work at learning tasks (Schunk & Zimmerman, 2003). High-self-efficacy students are more likely to expend effort and persist longer at a learning task than low-self-efficacy students.

Goal-Setting, Planning, and Self-Monitoring

Self-efficacy and achievement improve when individuals set goals that are specific, proximal, and challenging (Bandura, 2001; Schunk, 2001). A nonspecific, fuzzy goal is "I want to be successful." A more concrete, specific goal is "I want to make the honor roll by the end of the semester."

Students can set both long-term (distal) and short-term (proximal) goals. It is okay for individuals to set some long-term goals, such as "I want to graduate from high school" or "I want to go to college," but they also need to create short-term goals, which are steps along the way. "Getting an A on the next math test" is an example of a short-term, proximal goal. So is "Doing all of my homework by 4 P.M. Sunday." David McNally (1990), author of *Even Eagles Need a Push*, advises that when individuals set goals and plan, they should be reminded to live their lives one day at a time. They should make their commitments in bite-size chunks. A house is built one brick at a time, a cathedral one stone at a time. The artist paints one stroke at a time. The student should also work in small increments.

Another good strategy is to set challenging goals. A challenging goal is a commitment to self-improvement. Strong interest and involvement in activities are sparked by challenges. Goals that are easy to reach generate little interest or effort. However, goals should be optimally matched to the individual's skill level. If goals are unrealistically high, the result will be repeated failures that lower the individual's self-efficacy.

Carol Dweck (1996; Dweck & Leggett, 1988) and John Nicholls (1979) define goals in terms of immediate achievement-related focus and definition of success. For example, Nicholls distinguishes between ego-involved goals, task-involved goals, and work-avoidant goals. Individuals who have ego-involved goals strive to maximize favorable evaluations and minimize unfavorable ones. For example, ego-involved individuals focus on how smart they will look and how effectively they can outperform others. In contrast, individuals who have task-involved goals focus on mastering tasks. They concentrate on how they can do the task and what they will learn. Individuals with work-avoidant goals try to exert as little effort as possible when faced with a task.

It is not enough just to set goals. In order to achieve, it also is important to plan how to reach those goals. Being a good planner means managing time effectively, setting priorities, and being organized.

Individuals should not only plan their next week's activities but also monitor how well they are sticking to their plan. Once engaged in a task, they need to monitor their progress, judge how well they are doing on the task, and evaluate the outcomes to regulate what they do in the future (Eccles, Wigfield, & Schiefele, 1998). High-achieving children are often self-regulatory learners (Schunk, 2004; Schunk & Zimmerman, 2001, 2003; Zimmerman, 2001; Zimmerman & Schunk, 2004). For example, high-achieving children monitor their learning and systematically evaluate their progress toward a goal more than low-achieving students do. Encouraging children to monitor their learning conveys the message that they are responsible for their own behavior and that learning requires their active, dedicated participation.

In sum, we have seen that a number of internal factors influence children's achievement. Especially important are intrinsic motivation, a mastery orientation, and goal-setting, planning, and self-regulation (Pintrich, 2003; Pintrich & Schunk, 2002; Schunk & Zimmerman, 2003; Zimmerman & Schunk, 2004).

Ethnicity and Culture

How do ethnicity and culture influence children's achievement? Of course, diversity exists within every group in terms of achievement. But Americans have been especially concerned about two questions related to ethnicity and culture. First, does their ethnicity deter ethnic minority children from high achievement in school? And second, is there something about American culture that accounts for the poor performance of U.S. children in math and science?

Ethnicity   As we discussed in chapter 15, analyzing the effects of ethnicity in the United States is complicated by the fact that a disproportionate number of ethnic minorities have low socioeconomic status P. 549. Disentangling the effects of SES and ethnicity can be difficult, and many investigations overlook the socioeconomic status of ethnic minority students. In many instances, when ethnicity *and* socioeconomic status are investigated, socioeconomic status predicts achievement better than ethnicity does. Students from middle- and upper-income families fare better than their counterparts from low-income backgrounds in a host of achievement situations—for example, expectations for success, achievement aspirations, and recognition of the importance of effort (Gibbs, 1989).

Sandra Graham (1986, 1990) has conducted a number of studies that reveal stronger socioeconomic-status than ethnic differences in achievement. She is struck by how consistently middle-income African American students, like their White middle-income counterparts, have high achievement expectations and understand that failure is usually due to a lack of effort.

A special challenge for many ethnic minority students is dealing with negative stereotypes and discrimination. Many ethnic minority students living in poverty must also deal with conflict between the values of their neighborhood and those of the majority culture, a lack of high-achieving role models, and as we discussed earlier, poor schools (McLoyd, 2000). Even students who are motivated to learn and achieve may find it difficult to perform effectively in such contexts.

Cross-Cultural Comparisons   In the past decade, the poor performance of American children in math and science has become well publicized. For example, in one cross-national comparison of the math and science achievement of 9- to 13-year-old students, the United States finished 13th (out of 15) in science and 15th (out of 16) in math achievement (Educational Testing Service, 1992). In this study, Korean and Taiwanese students placed first and second, respectively. Critics of cross-national comparisons argue that, in many comparisons, virtually all U.S. children are being compared with a "select" group of children from other countries; therefore, they conclude, it is no wonder that American students don't fare so well. That criticism holds for some international comparisons. However, when the top 25 percent of students in different countries were compared, U.S. students moved up some, but not a lot (Mullis & others, 1998). In the Research in Life-Span Development interlude, you can read about Harold Stevenson's efforts to find out why American students fare so poorly in mathematics.

Research in Life-Span Development

Cross-Cultural Comparisons in Learning Math and Math Instruction

The University of Michigan's Harold Stevenson has been conducting research on children's learning for five decades. His current research explores reasons for the poor performance of American students. Stevenson and his colleagues (Stevenson, 1995, 2000; Stevenson, Hofer, & Randel, 1999; Stevenson & others, 1990) have completed five cross-cultural comparisons of students in the United States, China, Taiwan, and Japan. In these studies, Asian students consistently outperform American students. And, the longer the students are in school, the wider the gap becomes between Asian and American students—the lowest difference is in the first grade, the highest in the eleventh grade (the highest grade studied).

To learn more about the reasons for these large cross-cultural differences, Stevenson and his colleagues spent thousands of hours observing in classrooms, as well as interviewing and surveying teachers, students, and parents. They found that the Asian teachers spent more of their time teaching math than did the American teachers. For example, more than one-fourth of total classroom time in the first grade was spent on math instruction in Japan, compared with only one-tenth of the time in the U.S. first-grade classrooms. Also, the Asian students were in school an average of 240 days a year, compared with 178 days in the United States.

In addition, differences were found between the Asian and American parents. The American parents had much lower expectations for their children's education and achievement than did the Asian parents. Also, the American parents were more likely to believe that their children's math achievement was due to innate ability; the Asian parents were more likely to say that their children's math achievement was the consequence of effort and training (see figure 16.6). The Asian students were more likely to do math homework than were the American students, and the Asian parents were far more likely to help their children with their math homework than were the American parents (Chen & Stevenson, 1989).

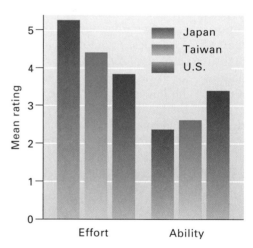

FIGURE 16.6 Mothers' Beliefs About the Factors Responsible for Children's Math Achievement in Three Countries

In one study, mothers in Japan and Taiwan were more likely to believe that their children's math achievement was due to effort rather than innate ability, while U.S. mothers were more likely to believe their children's math achievement was due to innate ability (Stevenson, Lee, & Stigler, 1986). If parents believe that their children's math achievement is due to innate ability and their children are not doing well in math, the implication is that they are less likely to think their children will benefit from putting forth more effort.

Review and Reflect: Learning Goal 2

2 Explain the key aspects of achievement

REVIEW

- What are intrinsic and extrinsic motivation? How are they related to achievement?

- How are mastery, helpless, and performance orientations linked with achievement?
- What is attribution and how is it linked with achievement?
- What is self-efficacy and how is it related to achievement?
- Why are goal-setting, planning, and self-monitoring important in achievement?
- How do cultural, ethnic, and socioeconomic variations influence achievement?

REFLECT

- Think about several of your own past schoolmates who showed low motivation in school. Why do you think they behaved that way? What teaching strategies may have helped them?

3 CAREERS, WORK, AND RETIREMENT

| Career Development | Work | Retirement |

The quality of schooling children experience and the achievement orientation they develop provide the foundation for career success and work when they become adults. Choosing a career, developing in a career, working, and coping with retirement—these are important themes in adulthood.

Career Development

When you were a child, what were your thoughts about a career? How did your thinking about careers change as you became an adolescent? What are they now?

Developmental Changes Many children have idealistic fantasies about what they want to be when they grow up. For example, young children may want to be a superhero, a sports star, or a movie star. In the high school years, they often have begun to think about careers on a somewhat less idealistic basis. In their late teens and early twenties, their career decision making has usually turned more serious as they explore different career possibilities and zero in on the career they want to enter. In college, this often means choosing a major or specialization that is designed to lead to work in a particular field. By their early and mid-twenties, many individuals have completed their education or training and started to enter a full-time occupation. Through the remainder of early adulthood, individuals often seek to establish their emerging career, move up the career ladder, and improve their financial standing.

FIGURE 16.7 Holland's Model of Personality Types and Career Choices

Personality Types **Personality type theory** is John Holland's (1987) view that it is important for individuals to select a career that matches up well with their personality type. Holland believes that when individuals find careers that fit their personality, they are more likely to enjoy the work and stay in the job longer than their counterparts who work at jobs not suited to their personality. Holland proposed six basic career-related personality types: realistic, investigative, artistic, social, enterprising, and conventional (see figure 16.7):

personality type theory John Holland's view that it is important to match an individual's personality with a particular career.

- *Realistic.* They like the outdoors and manual activities. They often are less social, have difficulty in demanding situations, and prefer to work alone. This personality type matches up best with jobs in labor, farming, truck driving, construction, engineering, and piloting.
- *Investigative.* They are interested in ideas more than people, are rather indifferent to social relationships, are troubled by emotional situations, and are often aloof and intelligent. This personality type matches up well with scientific, intellectually oriented professions.
- *Artistic.* They are creative and enjoy working with ideas and materials that allow them to express themselves in innovative ways. They value nonconformity, freedom, and ambiguity. Sometimes they have difficulties in social relationships. Not many jobs match up with the artistic personality type. Consequently, some artistic individuals work in jobs that are their second or third choices and express their artistic interests through hobbies and leisure.
- *Social.* They like to work with people and tend to have a helping orientation. They like doing social things considerably more than intellectual tasks. This personality type matches up with jobs in teaching, social work, and counseling.
- *Enterprising.* They also are more oriented toward people than things or ideas. They may try to dominate others to reach their goals. They are often good at persuading others to do things. The enterprising type matches up with careers in sales, management, and politics.
- *Conventional.* They function best in well-structured situations and are skilled at working with details. They often like to work with numbers and perform clerical tasks rather than working with ideas or people. The conventional type matches up with such jobs as accountant, bank teller, secretary, or file clerk.

If all individuals (and careers) fell conveniently into Holland's personality types, career counselors would have an easy job. However, individuals are typically complex. Holland (1987) states that individuals rarely are pure types, and most persons are a combination of two or three types. Still, the basic idea of matching the abilities and attitudes of individuals to particular careers is an important contribution to the career development field. Holland's personality types are incorporated into the Strong-Campbell Interest Inventory, a widely used measure in career guidance.

Values and Careers   An important aspect of choosing a career is that it also match up with your values. When people know what they value most—what is important to them in life—they can refine their career choice more effectively. Some values are reflected in Holland's personality types, such as whether a person values working in a career that involves helping others or in a career in which creativity is valued. Among the values that some individuals consider important in a career are working with people they like, working in a career with prestige, making a lot of money, being happy, not having to work long hours, being mentally challenged, having plenty of time for leisure pursuits, working in the right geographical location, and working where physical and mental health are important.

Monitoring the Occupational Outlook   It is a good idea for individuals to keep up with the occupational outlook for various fields. An excellent source is *The Occupational Outlook Handbook* (2004–2005), which is revised every two years.

Service-producing industries will account for most new jobs: business, health, and professional services are projected to account for nearly 75 percent of job growth from 2000 to 2010. Employment in computer and data-processing services is projected to grow 86 percent in this time, ranking it as the fastest-growing industry. Indeed, the seven occupations with the fastest projected growth are all in the computer area. No matter what their career aspirations, individuals will need computer skills to perform their job competently.

Jobs that require college degrees will be the fastest-growing and highest-paying. Jobs that require an associate degree from a community college are projected to increase more than 30 percent from 1998 to 2008, those that require a bachelor's degree or doctoral degree more than 25 percent, and those that require a master's degree more than 20 percent. All but a few of the highest-paying occupations require a college degree.

The labor force participation rates of women in nearly all age groups are projected to increase while that of men is anticipated to remain unchanged. The Asian American and Latino American labor forces are expected to increase faster than other ethnic groups, by 40 and 37 percent, respectively. It has been projected that by 2008, the Latino American labor force will be larger than the African American labor force.

Occupational Outlook
Career and Job-Hunting Resources
What Color Is Your Parachute?
Job Interviewing

Work

Work defines individuals in fundamental ways (Osipow, 2000; Vondracek & Porfeli, 2003). Individuals identify with their work, and work shapes their lives in many ways. It is an important influence on their financial standing, housing, the way they spend their time, where they live, friendships, and health.

Work in Adolescence   One of the greatest changes in adolescents' lives in recent years has been the increased number of adolescents who work part-time and still attend school on a regular basis. Our discussion of adolescents and work focuses on the sociohistorical context of adolescent work and the advantages and disadvantages of part-time work.

Sociohistorical Context of Adolescent Work   Over the past century, the percentage of youth who work full-time as opposed to those who are in school has decreased dramatically. In the late 1800s, fewer than one of every twenty high school age adolescents in the United States was in school. Many adolescents learned a trade from their father or some other adult member of the community. Today, more than nine of every ten U.S. adolescents receive high school diplomas.

Even though education keeps many of today's youth from holding full-time jobs, it has not prevented them from working part-time while going to school. In 1940, only 1 of 25 tenth-grade males attended school and simultaneously worked part-time. In the 1970s, the number had increased to 1 in 4. Today, 3 of 4 combine school and part-time work.

What kinds of jobs are U.S. adolescents working at today? The typical part-time job for high school seniors involves 16 to 20 hours of work per week, although 10 percent work 30 hours or more. About 17 percent of adolescents who work do so in restaurants, such as McDonald's and Burger King, waiting on customers and cleaning up. Other adolescents work in retail stores as cashiers or salespeople (about 20 percent), in offices as clerical assistants (about 10 percent), or as unskilled laborers (about 10 percent).

Work Profiles of Adolescents Around the World   How does work in adolescence vary in countries around the world? In many developing countries, where it is common for adolescents to not attend school on a regular basis, boys often spend more time in income-generating labor than girls do (Larson & Verma, 1999). In these developing countries, adolescent girls often engage in unpaid household labor. For adolescents in the lowest socioeconomic status, the figure was 5.9 hours per day for boys and 3.5 hours for girls.

Income-generating labor outside the home is less prevalent in developed countries, and enforcement of child labor laws restricts it to the mid- to late-adolescent years. In the high school years, employment is more common for U.S. adolescents than in many other developed countries. For example, in one study, 80 percent of Minneapolis eleventh-graders had part-time jobs compared to only 27 percent of Japanese eleventh-graders and 26 percent of Taiwanese eleventh-graders (Crystal & others, 1994).

Advantages and Disadvantages of Part-Time Work in Adolescence

Do part-time jobs bring benefits for U.S. adolescents? In one study, adolescents reported that their jobs encouraged good work habits and that they were using their earnings for high school or college costs (Marsh, 1991). Work may especially benefit adolescents in low-income, urban contexts by providing them with economic benefits and adult monitoring. This may increase school engagement and decrease delinquency. In one recent study, low-income, urban adolescents who never worked had more school-related difficulties than those who did work (Leventhal, Graber, & Brooks-Gunn, 2001). Stable work increased the likelihood of going to college more for adolescent males in low-income, urban contexts than for females.

Other evidence of the effects of work on adolescents comes from research conducted by Ellen Greenberger and Laurence Steinberg (1981, 1986), who examined the work experiences of students in four California high schools. The work experiences of the adolescents helped them to understand how the business world works, how to get and how to keep a job, and how to manage money. Working also helped adolescents to learn to budget their time, to take pride in their accomplishments, and to evaluate their goals.

The findings of Greenberger and Steinberg also disproved some common myths. For example, generally it is assumed that adolescents receive extensive on-the-job training when they are hired for work. The reality is that they got little training at all. Also, it is assumed that youths—through work experiences—learn to get along better with adults. However, adolescents reported that they rarely felt close to the adults with whom they worked.

Furthermore, working adolescents often have to give up sports, social affairs with peers, and sometimes sleep. And they have to balance the demands of work, school, family, and peers. Greenberger and Steinberg asked students about their grade point averages, school attendance, satisfaction from school, and the number of hours spent studying and participating in extracurricular activities since they began working. They found that the working adolescents had lower grade point averages than nonworking adolescents. More than one of four students reported that their grades dropped when they began working; only one of nine said that their grades improved.

It was not just working that affected adolescents' grades—more important was how long they worked. Tenth-graders who worked more than 14 hours a week suffered a drop in grades. Eleventh-graders worked up to 20 hours a week before their grades dropped. When adolescents spend more than 20 hours per week working, there is little time to study for tests and to complete homework assignments.

In addition, working adolescents felt less involved in school, were absent more, and said that they did not enjoy school as much as their nonworking counterparts did. Adolescents who worked also spent less time with their families—but just as much time with their peers—as their nonworking counterparts. Adolescents who worked long hours also were more frequent users of alcohol and marijuana. Other researchers have also found detrimental effects of work on adolescent development (Bachman & Schulenberg, 1993).

How does the quality of the job shape the costs and benefits of working in adolescence? In one longitudinal study, adolescents in jobs with opportunities for advancement showed increases in mastery motivation, heightened work values, and reduced depression (Mortimer & others, 1996). Jobs that youth described as extrinsically rather than intrinsically rewarding appear to detract from schoolwork (Mortimer, Harley, & Johnson, 1998).

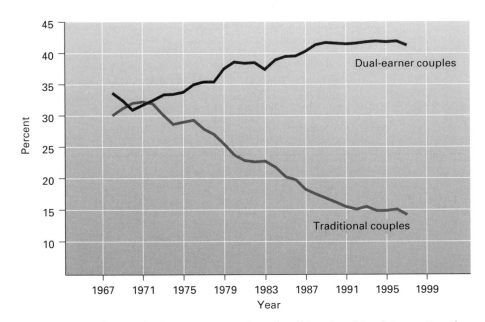

FIGURE 16.8 Changes in the Percentage of U.S. Traditional and Dual-Career Couples
Notice the dramatic increase in dual-earner couples in the last three decades. Traditional couples are those in which the husband is the sole breadwinner.

Overall, the weight of the evidence suggests that spending large amounts of time in paid labor has limited developmental benefits for youth, and for some it is associated with risky behavior and costs to physical health (Larson & Verma, 1999; Larson & Wilson, 2004). Some youth, though, are engaged in challenging work activities, are provided constructive supervision by adults, and experience favorable work conditions, However, in general, given the repetitive nature of most labor carried out by adolescents around the world, it is difficult to argue that there are developmental gains provided by working 15 to 25 hours per week in such labor (Larson & Verma, 1999).

Work in Adulthood Both Sigmund Freud and the Russian Count Leo Tolstoy described love and work as the two most important things that adults need to do well. We discussed love in chapter 10. Let's now explore work in the adult years.

Most individuals spend about one-third of their adult lives at work. In one recent survey, 35 percent of Americans worked 40 hours a week (Center for Survey Research at the University of Connecticut, 2000). Almost half of the individuals worked more than 40 hours a week. Only 10 percent worked less than 30 hours a week.

Work creates a structure and rhythm to life that individuals often miss when they do not work for an extended time. When unable to work, many individuals experience emotional distress and low self-esteem.

However, some aspects of work also create stress. Four main aspects of work settings are linked with employee stress and health problems (Moos, 1986): high job demands such as having a heavy workload and time pressure; inadequate opportunities to participate in decision making; high level of supervisor control; and lack of clarity about what it takes for competent performance.

Changing Gender Roles Although single-earner married families still make up a sizeable minority of U.S. families, this is the era of the two-earner couple (Barnett, 2001) (see figure 16.8). The increase in dual-earner couples has led to increased attention to how couples divide household and family responsibilities (Barnett, 2001; Hyde &

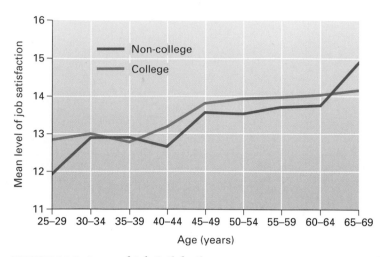

FIGURE 16.9 Age and Job Satisfaction

Job satisfaction increases with age, for both college- and non-college-educated adults. Among the reasons for increased satisfaction are more income, higher-status jobs, greater job security, and stronger job commitment.

Barnett, 2001). Recent research suggests that (Barnett, 2001; Barnett & others, 2001):

- *Men are increasing their responsibility for maintaining the home.* Men in dual-career families do about 45 percent of the housework. The decreasing gap between the time women and men spend in household and child-care tasks is likely due to both increases in time spent by men and decreases in time spent by women.
- *Women are increasing their responsibility for breadwinning.* In terms of hourly earnings, a growing percentage of wives earn as much as or more than their husbands. This role reversal is present in about one-third of two-earner couples.
- *Men are showing greater interest in family and parenting.* The twenty-first century is the first time that young men are reporting that family is at least as important to them as work (Barnett & others, 2001). Among men with more egalitarian attitudes, fatherhood is linked with a decrease of 9 hours per week at work, while among men with more traditional views, fatherhood is associated with an increase of almost 11 hours per week.

Job Satisfaction Work satisfaction increases steadily throughout the work life—from age 20 to at least age 60, for both college-educated and non-college-educated adults (Rhodes, 1983) (see figure 16.9). This pattern has been found for both women and men. Satisfaction probably increases because as we get older we get paid more, we are in higher positions, and we have more job security.

There is also a greater commitment to the job as we get older. We take our jobs more seriously, have lower rates of avoidable absenteeism, and are more involved with our work in middle adulthood than in early adulthood. Younger adults are still experimenting with their work and still searching for the right occupation. They may be inclined to seek out what is wrong with their current job rather than focusing on what is right about it. For the most part, researchers have found the highest levels of physical and psychological well-being among those people who are doing as much paid work as they would like to do (House, 1998; House & others, 1992).

Careers and Work in Middle Adulthood In the United States, approximately 80 percent of individuals 40 to 59 years of age are employed. In the 51 to 59 age group, slightly less than 25 percent do not work. More than half of the 51 to 59 age group say that a health condition or an impairment limits the type of paid work that they do (Sterns & Huyck, 2001). However, one recent study found that women who are 50 and older who work are healthier and have a more positive attitude than those who do not work (National Center for Women & Aging, 2002). For those 55 and older, U.S. labor force participation is projected to grow substantially (Schwerha & McMullin, 2002). Most of the increase is expected to come from jobs in the service industry.

Mental and physical capabilities will not be a major impediment for many middle-aged adults if they want to continue working. Nevertheless, the current middle-aged worker faces challenges in the twenty-first century (Avolio & Sosik, 1999). Many jobs traditionally held by males have been moved overseas in the search for cheaper labor. The proliferation of computer technology compels middle-aged adults to become increasingly computer literate (Csaja, 2001). And when companies decide to reduce their workforce, they may offer incentives to middle-aged employees to retire early—in their fifties, or in some cases even forties, rather than their sixties.

Some midlife career changes are the consequence of losing one's job; others are self-motivated (Moen, 1998; Moen & Wethington, 1999). For many people, midlife is a time of evaluation, assessment, and reflection in terms of the work they do and want to do in the future. Among the work issues that some people face in midlife are recognizing limitations in career progress, deciding whether to change jobs or careers, whether to rebalance family and work, and planning for retirement (Sterns & Huyck, 2001).

Some individuals in middle age decide that they don't want to do the same work they have been doing (Hoyer & Roodin, 2003). Middle adulthood involves adjusting idealistic hopes to realistic possibilities in light of how much time individuals have before they retire and how fast they are reaching their occupational goals (Levinson, 1978, 1996). If individuals perceive that they are behind schedule, if their goals are unrealistic, they don't like the work they are doing, or their job has become too stressful, they could become motivated to change jobs.

Work in Late Adulthood Aging and work expert James House (1998) believes that many middle-aged workers would like to do less paid work while many older adults would like to do more. What percentage of older adults continue to work? How productive are they?

The percentage of U.S. men over the age of 65 who continue to work full-time today is as much as 70 percent less than at the beginning of the twentieth century. However, the percentage of older adults who work part-time has steadily increased since the 1960s (Elder & Pavalko, 1993).

In the National Longitudinal Survey of Older Men, good health, a strong psychological commitment to work, and a distaste for retirement were the most important characteristics related to continued employment into their seventies and eighties (Parnes & Sommers, 1994). The probability of employment also was positively correlated with educational attainment and being married to a working wife.

With the aging of baby boomers—78 million people who will begin to reach traditional retirement age in 2010—we are likely to see increasing numbers of older adults continue to work (Cowell & others, 2003; Yeats, Folts, & Knapp, 1999). Also, an increasing number of middle-aged and older adults are embarking on a second or a third career (Moen & Wethington, 1999). In some cases, this is an entirely different type of work or a continuation of previous work but at a reduced level.

Cognitive ability is one of the best predictors of job performance in older adults (Park, 1994). Some individuals maintain their productivity throughout their lives. Some of these older workers work as many or more hours than younger workers. And older workers have lower rates of absenteeism, fewer accidents, and increased job satisfaction, compared with their younger counterparts (Warr, 1994). Recall that substantively complex work is linked with a higher level of intellectual functioning (Schooler, 2001). This likely is a reciprocal relation—that is, individuals with higher cognitive ability likely continue to work as older adults, and when they work in substantively complex jobs, this likely enhances their intellectual functioning (Schooler, 2001).

Many older adults participate in unpaid work—as a volunteer or as an active participant in a voluntary association. These options afford older adults opportunities for productive activity, social interaction, and a positive identity.

Efforts to end age discrimination have increased the ability of older workers to continue working if they choose. In 1967, the Age Discrimination Act made it federal policy to prohibit the firing of employees because of their age before they reach the mandatory retirement age. In 1986, Congress voted to ban mandatory retirement for all but a few occupations, such as police officer, firefighter, and airline pilot, where safety is an issue. Federal law now prohibits employers from firing older

Ninety-two-year-old Russell "Bob" Harrell *(right)* puts in 12-hour days at Sieco Consulting Engineers in Columbus, Indiana. A highway and bridge engineer, he designs and plans roads. James Rice (age 48), a vice-president of client services at Sieco, says that "Bob" wants to learn something new every day and that he has learned many life lessons from being around him. Harrell says he is not planning on retiring. *What are some variations in work and retirement in older adults?*

workers, who have seniority and higher salaries, just to save money. As mandatory retirement continues to lessen, more older workers will face the decision of when to retire rather than being forced into retirement.

Retirement

AARP

At what age do most people retire in the United States? Do many people continue to work part-time even though they are retired? What is retirement like in other countries? How do people adjust to retirement?

The option to retire is a late-twentieth-century phenomenon in the United States (Atchley, 1996). It exists largely thanks to the implementation in 1935 of the Social Security system, which gives benefits to older workers when they retire. On the average, today's workers will spend 10 to 15 percent of their lives in retirement.

Significant numbers of retirees only partially retire, moving to part-time employment by either reducing the number of hours they work on their career jobs or by taking on new (and frequently lower-paying) jobs (Han & Moen, 1998). Self-employed men are especially likely to continue paid employment, either on the same job or on a new job. Nearly one-third of the men who take on a part-time job do not do so until two years after their retirement (Burkhauser & Quinn, 1989).

In a recent survey, 80 percent of baby boomers said that they expect to work during the retirement years (Roper Starch Worldwide, 2000). The main reason they plan to continue working is to engage in part-time work for interest or enjoyment (35 percent), followed by income (23 percent), desire to start a business (17 percent), and the desire to try a different field of work (5 percent). In another recent survey, nearly 70 percent of current employees said that they expect to work for pay once they retire, mainly because they enjoy working and want to stay active and involved (Anthony Greenwald & Associates, 2000).

In many European countries, officials have experimented with financial inducements designed to reduce unemployment by encouraging the retirement of older workers. Germany, Sweden, Great Britain, Italy, France, Czechoslovakia, Hungary, and Russia are among the nations that are moving toward earlier retirement. In the Netherlands, however, there is currently an effort to recruit retired persons to reenter the workforce because of low unemployment.

Retirement is a process, not an event (Kim & Moen, 2001). Much of the research on retirement has been cross-sectional rather than longitudinal and has focused on men rather than women. One recent study found that men had higher morale when they had retired within the last two years compared with men who had been retired for longer periods of time (Kim & Moen, 2002).

Older adults who adjust best to retirement are healthy, have adequate income, are active, are better educated, have an extended social network including both friends and family, and usually were satisfied with their lives before they retired (Bernard & Phillipson, 2004; Elovainio & others, 2003; Gall, Evans, & Howard, 1997; Lee, 2003; Moen & Quick, 1998; Palmore & others, 1985). Older adults with inadequate income and poor health, and who must adjust to other stress that occurs at the same time as retirement, such as the death of a spouse, have the most difficult time adjusting to retirement (Nusbaum, 2003; Stull & Hatch, 1984).

Flexibility is also a key factor in whether individuals adjust well to retirement. When people retire, they no longer have the structured environment they had when they were working, so they need to be flexible and discover and pursue their own interests (Eisdorfer, 1996). Cultivating interests and friends unrelated to work improves adaptation to retirement (Zarit & Knight, 1996).

Individuals who view retirement planning only in terms of finances don't adapt as well to retirement as those who have a more balanced retirement plan (Birren, 1996). It is important not only to plan financially for retirement, but to consider

*S*ignificant numbers of retirees undergo "partial" rather than full retirement.

—PHYLLIS MOEN
Contemporary Psychologist,
Cornell University

other areas of your life as well (Choi, 2001; Cole, 2003). What are you going to do with your leisure time? What are you going to do to stay active? What are you going to do socially? What are you going to do to keep your mind active?

Review and Reflect: Learning Goal 3

3 Discuss career development, work, and retirement

REVIEW

- What is involved in the development of a career?
- What are some key aspects of work?
- What characterizes retirement?

REFLECT

- At what age would you like to retire? Or would you prefer to continue working as long as you are healthy? At what age did your father and/or mother retire? How well did they adjust to retirement?

Reach Your Learning Goals

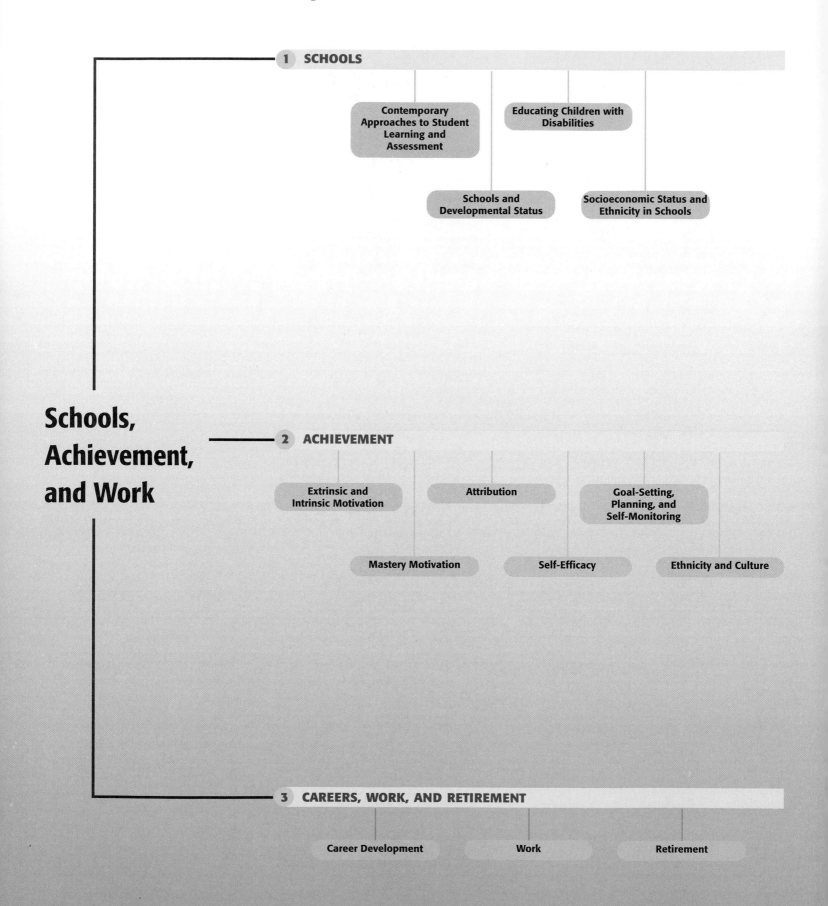

Schools, Achievement, and Work

1 SCHOOLS

- Contemporary Approaches to Student Learning and Assessment
- Educating Children with Disabilities
- Schools and Developmental Status
- Socioeconomic Status and Ethnicity in Schools

2 ACHIEVEMENT

- Extrinsic and Intrinsic Motivation
- Attribution
- Goal-Setting, Planning, and Self-Monitoring
- Mastery Motivation
- Self-Efficacy
- Ethnicity and Culture

3 CAREERS, WORK, AND RETIREMENT

- Career Development
- Work
- Retirement

Summary

1 Describe the role of schools in development

- Contemporary approaches to student learning include direct instruction, cognitive constructivist, and social constructivist. A number of learner-centered principles with a constructivist theme have been advocated by a team of experts convened by the American Psychological Association. Increased concern about the effectiveness of schools in the United States has produced extensive state-mandated testing, which has both strengths and weaknesses, and is controversial.

- Early childhood education has many variations but developmentally appropriate education is an important theme. A special concern is that early elementary school education proceeds too much on the basis of negative feedback to children. The transition from elementary school to middle or junior high school can be stressful. Successful schools for young adolescents focus on individual differences, show a deep concern for what is known about early adolescence, and emphasize social as well as cognitive development. There are concerns about dropping out of school and improving the high school experience. The transition to college can involve a number of positive and negative experiences.

- An estimated 10 percent of U.S. children with a disability receive education services. Slightly more than 50 percent of these children are classified as having a learning disability. A learning disability includes three components: (1) a minimum IQ level; (2) a significant difficulty in a school-related area; and (3) exclusion of only severe emotional disorders, second-language background, sensory disabilities, and specific neurological deficits. Dyslexia is a category of learning disabilities that involves a severe impairment in the ability to read and spell. Attention deficit hyperactivity disorder (ADHD) is a disability in which individuals consistently show problems in one or more of these areas: (1) inattention, (2) hyperactivity, and (3) impulsivity. ADHD has been increasingly diagnosed. A number of laws have been passed in the United States to ensure that children with a disability receive a free, appropriate education and are provided adequate services.

- Children in poverty face problems at home and at school that present barriers to learning. The school experiences of children from different ethnic groups vary considerably. A number of strategies can be adopted to improve relationships with diverse others.

2 Explain the key aspects of achievement

- Extrinsic motivation involves doing something to obtain something else (a means to an end). Intrinsic motivation involves the internal motivation to do something for its own sake (an end in itself). Overall, most experts recommend that teachers create a classroom climate in which students are intrinsically motivated to learn. One view of intrinsic motivation emphasizes its self-determining characteristics.

Giving students some choice and providing opportunities for personal responsibility increase intrinsic motivation. When rewards are used, they should convey information about task mastery rather than external control. Researchers have found that as students move from the early elementary school years to high school, their intrinsic motivation declines, especially during the middle school years.

- A mastery orientation focuses on the task rather than ability, involves positive affect, and includes solution-oriented strategies. A helpless orientation focuses on personal inadequacies, attributing difficulty to lack of ability. Negative affect (boredom, anxiety, for example) also is present. A performance orientation involves being concerned with achievement outcome rather than achievement process. Mastery orientation is the preferred achievement orientation.

- The main classification of attributions distinguishes attributions to internal causes, especially effort, and attributions to external causes. It is especially important to emphasize the internal factor of effort in making attributions about achievement.

- Self-efficacy is the belief that one can master a situation and produce positive outcomes. Bandura believes that self-efficacy is a critical factor in whether students will achieve. Schunk argues that self-efficacy influences a student's choice of tasks, with low-efficacy students avoiding many learning tasks.

- Setting specific, proximal (short-term), and challenging goals benefits students' self-efficacy and achievement. Dweck and Nicholls define goals in terms of immediate achievement-related focus and definition of success. Being a good planner means managing time effectively, setting priorities, and being organized. Self-monitoring is a key aspect of self-regulation and benefits student learning.

- In most investigations, socioeconomic status predicts achievement better than ethnicity. U.S. children do more poorly on math and science achievement tests than children in Asian countries such as China, Taiwan, and Japan.

3 Discuss career development, work, and retirement

- Many young children have idealistic fantasies about a career. In the late teens and early twenties, their career thinking has usually become more serious. By their early to mid-twenties, many individuals have started in a career. In the remainder of early adulthood, they seek to establish their career and start moving up the career ladder. John Holland proposed that it is important for individuals to choose a career that is compatible with their personality type. It is also important to match up a career to your values. Service-producing industries will account for the most jobs in America in the next decade. Jobs that require a college education will be the fastest growing and highest paying. Labor force participation of women will increase and so will that of Latinos and African Americans.

- Work defines people in fundamental ways and is a key aspect of their identity. Today, the majority of U.S. adolescents work part-time while attending school. There are both advantages and disadvantages to part-time work in adolescence. U.S. adolescents engage in more work than their counterparts in many developed countries. Most individuals spend about one-third of their adult life at work. People often become stressed if they are unable to work but work also can produce stress. The increasing number of women who work in careers outside the home has led to new work-related issues. For many people midlife is a time of reflection, assessment, and evaluation of their current work and what they plan to do in the future. Work satisfaction increases steadily throughout life—from age 20 to at least age 60. Midlife job or career changes can be self-motivated or forced on individuals. Today, the percentage of men over 65 who continue to work full-time is less than at the beginning of the twentieth century. An important change in older adults' work patterns is the increase in part-time work.

- A retirement option for older workers is a very recent phenomenon in the United States. While the United States has moved toward increasing the age for retirement, many European countries have lowered it. A number of characteristics of individuals before retirement are linked to how well adjusted they are after retirement.

Key Terms

direct instruction approach 560
cognitive constructivist approach 560
social constructivist approach 560
child-centered kindergarten 563

developmentally appropriate practice 563
top-dog phenomenon 567
learning disability 573
dyslexia 574
attention deficit hyperactivity disorder (ADHD) 574

individualized education plan (IEP) 575
least restrictive environment (LRE) 575
inclusion 575
Project Head Start 576
extrinsic motivation 579

intrinsic motivation 579
mastery orientation 581
helpless orientation 581
performance orientation 581
attribution theory 581
self-efficacy 581
personality type theory 585

Key People

Friedrich Froebel 562
Joan Lipsitz 567
Linda Siegel 573

Jonathan Kozol 576
John Ogbu 577
Carol Dweck 581

Albert Bandura 581
Dale Schunk 582
Harold Stevenson 584

John Holland 585
Ellen Greenberger and Laurence Steinberg 588

E-Learning Tools

Connect to **www.mhhe.com/santrockldt2** to research the answers and complete these exercises. In addition, you'll find a number of other resources and valuable study tools for chapter 16, "Schools, Achievement, and Work," on the Student CD-ROM that came with this book.

Taking It to the Net

1. A State's representative to the U.S. Congress wants to decrease funding to Head Start. In a debate on the House floor, he maintains that the program is no more than expensive child care. What should the representative know about the latest research on how Head Start benefits low-income children and their parents?

2. Charles and Joanne are preparing for their first IEP meeting concerning the education of their 7-year-old daughter, Kara, who has autism. What should they do to prepare for the IEP meeting? What are some things they need to do at the meeting?

3. Juan and Carmen have been married—and employed—for 30 years. They have enough savings that they don't need to work, and they plan to retire at the end of this year. What should they know about the effect of retirement on their marriage and their individual social and emotional well-being?

Self-Assessment

To evaluate your career interests, assertiveness in job hunting, and perceptions of older workers, complete these self-assessments:

- *Evaluating My Career Interests*
- *How Assertive Will I Be in Searching for a Job?*
- *My Perception of Older Workers*

Health and Well-Being, Parenting, and Education

Build your decision-making skills by trying your hand at the health and well-being, parenting, and education "Scenarios."

Endings

SECTION

6

Years following years steal something every day: At last they steal us from ourselves away.

—ALEXANDER POPE
English Poet, 18th Century

Our life ultimately ends—when we approach life's grave sustained and soothed with unfaltering trust or rave at the close of day; when at last years steal us from ourselves; and when we are linked to our children's children's children by an invisible cable that runs from age to age. This final section contains one chapter: "Death and Grieving" (chapter 17).

Death and Grieving

Learning Goals

1 Evaluate issues in determining death and decisions regarding death

2 Describe the roles of sociohistorical and cultural contexts in understanding death

3 Discuss death and attitudes about it at different points in development

4 Explain the psychological aspects involved in facing one's own death and the contexts in which people die

5 Identify ways to cope with the death of another person

In this final chapter of the book, we will explore many aspects of death and dying. Among the questions that we will ask are: How can death be defined? How is death viewed in other cultures? What are some links between development and death? How do people face their own death? How do people cope with the death of someone they love?

1 DEFINING DEATH AND LIFE/DEATH ISSUES

Issues in Determining Death

Decisions Regarding Life, Death, and Health Care

Is there one point in the process of dying that is *the* point at which death takes place, or is death a more gradual process? What are some decisions individuals can make about life, death, and health care?

Issues in Determining Death

Twenty-five years ago, determining if someone was dead was simpler than it is today. The end of certain biological functions, such as breathing and blood pressure, and the rigidity of the body (rigor mortis) were considered to be clear signs of death. In the past several decades, defining death has become more complex (Corr, Nabe, & Corr, 2003; Kyba, 2002; Rodabough, 2003). Consider the circumstance of Philadelphia Flyers hockey star Pelle Lindbergh, who slammed his Porsche into a cement wall on November 10, 1985. The newspaper headline the next day read, "Flyers' Goalie is Declared Brain Dead." In spite of the claim that he was "brain dead," the story reported that Lindbergh was listed in "critical condition" in the intensive care unit of a hospital.

Brain death is a neurological definition of death, which states that a person is brain dead when all electrical activity of the brain has ceased for a specified period of time. A flat EEG (electroencephalogram) recording for a specified period of time is one criterion of brain death. The higher portions of the brain often die sooner than the lower portions. Because the brain's lower portions monitor heartbeat and respiration, individuals whose higher brain areas have died may continue breathing and have a heartbeat. The definition of brain death currently followed by most physicians includes the death of both the higher cortical functions and the lower brain stem functions.

Some medical experts argue that the criteria for death should include only higher cortical functioning. If the cortical death definition were adopted, then physicians could claim a person is dead who has no cortical functioning even though the lower brain stem is functioning. Supporters of the cortical death policy argue that the functions we associate with being human, such as intelligence and personality, are located in the higher cortical part of the brain. They believe that when these functions are lost, the "human being" is no longer alive.

Decisions Regarding Life, Death, and Health Care

In cases of catastrophic illness or accidents, patients might not be able to respond adequately to participate in decisions about their medical care. To prepare for this situation, some individuals make choices earlier.

Natural Death Act and Advanced Directive For many patients in a coma, it has not been clear what their wishes regarding termination of treatment might be

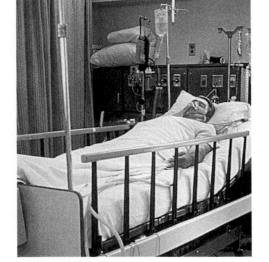

Advances in medical technology have complicated the definition of death. *What is the nature of the controversy about the criteria that should be used for determining when death occurs?*

brain death A neurological definition of death. A person is brain dead when all electrical activity of the brain has ceased for a specified period of time. A flat EEG recording is one criterion of brain death.

if they still were conscious (Aiken, 2000). Recognizing that terminally ill patients might prefer to die rather than linger in a painful or vegetative state, the organization "Choice in Dying" created the living will. This document is designed to be filled in while the individual can still think clearly; it expresses the person's desires regarding extraordinary medical procedures that might be used to sustain life when the medical situation becomes hopeless.

Physicians' concerns over malpractice suits and the efforts of people who support the Living Will concept have produced natural death legislation in many states. For example, California's Natural Death Act permits individuals who have been diagnosed by two physicians as terminally ill to sign an *advanced directive,* which states that life-sustaining procedures shall not be used to prolong their lives when death is imminent. An advanced directive must be signed while the individual still is able to think clearly. Laws in all fifty states now accept advanced directives as reflecting an individual's wishes.

Euthanasia Euthanasia ("easy death") is the act of painlessly ending the lives of individuals who are suffering from an incurable disease or severe disability. Sometimes euthansia is called "mercy killing." Distinctions are made between two types of euthanasia: passive and active.

- **Passive euthanasia** occurs when a person is allowed to die by withholding available treatment, such as withdrawing a life-sustaining device. For example, this might involve turning off a respirator or a heart-lung machine.
- **Active euthanasia** occurs when death is deliberately induced, as when a lethal dose of a drug is injected.

Technological advances in life-support devices raise the issue of quality of life (Asch & Christakis, 1996; Jecker, 1996). Should individuals be kept alive in undignified and hopeless states? The trend is toward acceptance of passive euthanasia in the case of terminally ill patients. The inflammatory argument that once equated this practice with suicide rarely is heard today. However, experts do not yet entirely agree on the precise boundaries or the exact mechanisms by which treatment decisions should be implemented (Jennekens & Kater, 2002; Leeman, 2002; Walker, 2003). Can a comatose patient's life-support systems be disconnected when the patient has left no written instructions to that effect? Does the family of a comatose patient have the right to overrule the attending physician's decision to continue life-support systems? These questions have no simple or universally agreed-upon answers (Kelly & McLoughlin, 2002). In one study of Canadian health-care workers, there was considerable variability in their decisions about whether to withdraw life support from critically ill patients (Cook & others, 1995).

The most widely publicized cases of active euthanasia involve "assisted suicide" (Ardelt, 2003; Bosshard & others, 2003; Hendin, 2002; Paterson, 2003; Paterson & Forbes, 2003). Jack Kevorkian, a Michigan physician, has assisted a number of terminally ill patients to end their lives (Roscoe & others, 2002). After a series of trials, Kevorkian was convicted of second-degree murder and given a long prison sentence.

Active euthanasia is a crime in most countries and in all states in the United States except one—Oregon (Hedberg, Hopkins, & Kohn, 2003). In 1994, the state of Oregon passed the Death with Dignity Act, which allows active euthanasia. Through 2001, ninety-one individuals were known to have died by active euthanasia in Oregon. Active euthanasia is legal in the Netherlands and Uruguay (Sheldon, 2002).

A survey of more than 900 physicians assessed their attitudes about active euthanasia (Walker, Gruman, & Blank, 1999). Most opposed active euthanasia, said that adequate pain control often eliminates the need for it, and commented that the primary role of the physician is to preserve life. They also reported that the

Late Adulthood: Advanced Directives

Choice in Dying
Assisted Suicide
Exploring Euthanasia

Dr. Jack Kevorkian assisted a number of people in Michigan to end their lives through active euthanasia. *Where do you stand on the use of active euthanasia?*

euthanasia The act of painlessly ending the lives of persons who are suffering from incurable diseases or severe disabilities; sometimes called "mercy killing."

passive euthanasia The withholding of available treatments, such as life-sustaining devices, allowing the person to die.

active euthanasia Death induced deliberately, as by injecting a lethal dose of a drug.

potential for abuse in active euthanasia is substantial, and many believe that it is morally wrong.

Needed: Better Care for Dying Individuals   Death in America is often lonely, prolonged, and painful (Institute of Medicine, 1997). Dying individuals often get too little or too much care. Scientific advances sometimes have made dying harder by delaying the inevitable (Muth, 2000). Also, even though painkillers are available, too many people experience severe pain during the last days and months of life (Fine & Peterson, 2002). Many health-care professionals have not been trained to provide adequate end-of-life care or to understand its importance. In 1997, a panel of experts recommended that regulations be changed to make it easier for physicians to prescribe painkillers for dying patients who need them (Institute of Medicine, 1997).

End-of-life care should include respect for the goals, preferences, and choices of the patient and his or her family (Kirchhoff, 2002; Wilson & Truman, 2002). Many patients who are nearing death want companionship.

There are few fail-safe measures for avoiding pain at the end of life. Still, you can follow these suggestions (Cowley & Hager, 1995):

- Make a living will, and be sure there is someone who will draw your doctor's attention to it.
- Give someone the power of attorney and make sure this person knows your wishes regarding medical care.
- Give your doctors specific instructions—from "Do not resuscitate" to "Do everything possible"—for specific circumstances.
- If you want to die at home, talk it over with your family and doctor.
- Check to see whether your insurance plan covers home care and hospice care.

Hospice is a program committed to making the end of life as free from pain, anxiety, and depression as possible. Whereas a hospital's goals are to cure illness and prolong life, hospice care emphasizes **palliative care,** which involves reducing pain and suffering and helping individuals die with dignity (Goodwin & others, 2003; Kaasa & Loge, 2003). Health-care professionals work together to treat the dying person's symptoms, make the individual as comfortable as possible, show interest in the person and the person's family, and help them cope with death (Chochinov, 2002; Ersek & Wilson, 2003; Simpson, 2003; Williams & Wheeler, 2001).

The hospice movement began toward the end of the 1960s in London, when a new kind of medical institution, St. Christopher's Hospice, opened. Little effort is made to prolong life at St. Christopher's—there are no heart-lung machines and there is no intensive care unit, for example. A primary goal is to bring pain under control and to help dying patients face death in a psychologically healthy way. The hospice also makes every effort to include the dying individual's family; it is believed that this strategy benefits not only the dying individual but family members as well, probably diminishing their guilt after the death (Mulholland, 2002; Reb, 2003).

The hospice movement has grown rapidly in the United States (Leming, 2003). More than 1,500 community groups are involved nationally in establishing hospice programs. Hospices are more likely to serve people with terminal cancer than those with other life-threatening conditions (Kastenbaum, 2000). Hospice adovates underscore that it is possible to control pain for almost any dying individual and that it is possible to create an environment for the patient that is superior to that found in most hospitals (Hayslip, 1996).

Today more hospice programs are home-based, a blend of institutional and home care designed to humanize the end-of-life experience for the dying person. Whether the hospice program is carried out in the dying person's home, through a blend of home and institutional care, or in an institution often depends on medical needs and the availability of caregivers, including family and friends.

www.mhhe.com/santrockldt2

Hospice Net

Hospice Foundation of America

Better Care for the Dying

hospice A program committed to making the end of life as free from pain, anxiety, and depression as possible. The goals of hospice contrast with those of a hospital, which are to cure disease and prolong life.

palliative care Emphasized in hospice care, involves reducing pain and suffering and helping individuals die with dignity.

2 DEATH AND CULTURAL CONTEXTS

Changing Historical Circumstances

Death in Different Cultures

When, where, and how people die have changed historically in the United States. Also, attitudes toward death vary across cultures.

Changing Historical Circumstances

We have already described one of the historical changes involving death—the increasing complexity of determining when someone is truly dead. Another historical change involves the age group in which death most often strikes. Two hundred years ago, almost one of every two children died before the age of 10, and one parent died before children grew up. Today, death occurs most often among older adults (Lamb, 2004). Life expectancy has increased from 47 years for a person born in 1900 to 77 years for someone born today (U.S. Bureau of the Census, 2000). In 1900, most people died at home, cared for by their family. As our population has aged and become more mobile, more older adults die apart from their families. In the United States today, more than 80 percent of all deaths occur in institutions or hospitals. The care of a dying older person has shifted away from the family and minimized our exposure to death and its painful surroundings.

Death in Different Cultures

Cultural variations characterize the experience of death and attitudes about death (Gire, 2002; Morgan & Laungani, 2003). To live a full life and die with glory was the prevailing goal of the ancient Greeks. Individuals are more conscious of death in times of war, famine, and plague. Whereas Americans are conditioned from early in life to live as though they were immortal, in much of the world this fiction cannot be maintained. Death crowds the streets of Calcutta in daily overdisplay, as it does the scrubby villages of Africa's Sahel. Children live with the ultimate toll of malnutrition and disease, mothers lose as many babies as survive into adulthood, and it is rare that a family remains intact for many years. Even in peasant areas where life is better, and health and maturity may be reasonable expectations, the presence of dying people in the house, the large attendance at funerals, and the daily contact with aging adults prepare the young for death and provide them with guidelines on how to die. By contrast, in the United States it is not uncommon to reach adulthood without having seen someone die.

FIGURE 17.1 A Ritual Associated with Death
Family memorial day at the national cemetery in Seoul, Korea.

www.mhhe.com/santrockld2

Dying and Medicine in America

Culture and Death

Most societies throughout history have had philosophical or religious beliefs about death, and most societies have a ritual that deals with death (see figure 17.1). Death may be seen as a punishment for one's sins, an act of atonement, or a judgment of a just God. For some, death means loneliness; for others, death is a quest for happiness. For still others, death represents redemption, a relief from the trials and tribulations of the earthly world. Some embrace death and welcome it; others abhor and fear it. For those who welcome it, death may be seen as the fitting end to a fulfilled life. From this perspective, how we depart from earth is influenced by how we have lived.

In most societies, death is not viewed as the end of existence—though the biological body has died, the spiritual body is believed to live on (Emmons, 2003; Morgan, 2003). This religious perspective is favored by most Americans as well (Gowan, 2003). Cultural variations in attitudes toward death include belief in reincarnation, which is an important aspect of the Hindu and Buddhist religions (Dillon, 2004; Truitner & Truitner, 1993). In the Gond culture of India, death is believed to be caused by magic and demons. The members of the Gond culture react angrily to death. In the Tanala culture of Madagascar, death is believed to be caused by natural forces. The members of the Tanala culture show a much more peaceful reaction to death than their counterparts in the Gond culture.

In many ways, we in the United States are death avoiders and death deniers (Taylor, 2003). This denial can take many forms:

- The tendency of the funeral industry to gloss over death and fashion lifelike qualities in the dead
- The adoption of euphemistic language for death—for example, *exiting, passing on, never say die,* and *good for life,* which implies forever
- The persistent search for a fountain of youth
- The rejection and isolation of the aged, who may remind us of death
- The adoption of the concept of a pleasant and rewarding afterlife, suggesting that we are immortal
- The medical community's emphasis on prolonging biological life rather than on diminishing human suffering

---

Review and Reflect: Learning Goal 2

2 **Describe the roles of sociohistorical and cultural contexts in understanding death**

REVIEW
- What are some changing sociohistorical circumstances regarding death?
- What are some variations in death across cultures?

REFLECT
- Why is the United States such a death-denying culture? How could this be changed?

---

3   A DEVELOPMENTAL PERSPECTIVE ON DEATH

| Causes of Death | Attitudes Toward Death at Different Points in the Life Span | Suicide |

Do the causes of death vary across the human life span? Do we have different expectations about death as we develop through the life span? What are our attitudes toward death at different points in our development? What causes people to commit suicide?

Causes of Death

Death can occur at any point in the human life span. Death can occur during prenatal development through miscarriages or stillborn births. Death can also occur during the birth process or in the first few days after birth, which usually happens because of a birth defect or because infants have not developed adequately to sustain life outside the uterus. In chapter 3, "Physical Development and Biological Aging," we described *sudden infant death syndrome (SIDS)*, in which infants stop breathing, usually during the night, and die without apparent cause (Corr & Corr, 2003) ◀▥ **P. 116.** SIDS currently is the leading cause of infant death in the United States, with the risk highest at 4 to 6 weeks of age (American Academy of Pediatrics Task Force on Infant Sleep Position and SIDS, 2000).

In childhood, death occurs most often because of accidents or illness. Accidental death in childhood can be the consequence of such things as an automobile accident, drowning, poisoning, fire, or a fall from a high place. Major illnesses that cause death in children are heart disease, cancer, and birth defects.

Compared with childhood, death in adolescence is more likely to occur because of motor vehicle accidents, suicide, and homicide. Many motor vehicle accidents that cause death in adolescence are alcohol-related. We will examine suicide in greater depth shortly.

Older adults are more likely to die from chronic diseases, such as heart disease and cancer, whereas younger adults are more likely to die from accidents. Older adults' diseases often incapacitate before they kill, which produces a course of dying that slowly leads to death. Of course, many young and middle-aged adults die of diseases, such as heart disease and cancer.

Attitudes Toward Death at Different Points in the Life Span

The ages of children and adults influence the way they experience and think about death. A mature, adultlike conception of death includes an understanding that death

www.mhhe.com/santrockldt2

Discussing Death with Young Children

Grieving Children

Association for Death Education and Counseling

is final and irreversible, that death represents the end of life, and that all living things die. Most researchers have found that as children grow, they develop a more mature approach to death (Hayslip & Hansson, 2003).

Childhood Most researchers believe that infants do not have even a rudimentary concept of death. However, as infants develop an attachment to a caregiver, they can experience loss or separation and an accompanying anxiety. But young children do not perceive time the way adults do. Even brief separations may be experienced as total losses. For most infants, the reappearance of the caregiver provides a continuity of existence and a reduction of anxiety. We know very little about the infant's actual experiences with bereavement, although the loss of a parent, especially if the caregiver is not replaced, can negatively affect the infant's health.

Even children 3 to 5 years of age have little or no idea of what death means. They may confuse death with sleep or ask in a puzzled way, "Why doesn't it move?" Preschool-aged children rarely get upset by the sight of a dead animal or by being told that a person has died. They believe that the dead can be brought back to life spontaneously by magic or by giving them food or medical treatment. Young children often believe that only people who want to die, or who are bad or careless, actually die. They also may blame themselves for the death of someone they know well, illogically reasoning that the event may have happened because they disobeyed the person who died.

Sometime in the middle and late childhood years more realistic perceptions of death develop. In one early investigation of children's perception of death, children 3 to 5 years of age denied that death exists, children 6 to 9 years of age believed that death exists but only happens to some people, and children 9 years of age and older recognized death's finality and universality (Nagy, 1948). In a review of research on children's conception of death, it was concluded that children probably do not view death as universal and irreversible until about 9 years of age (Cuddy-Casey & Orvaschel, 1997). Most children under 7 do not see death as likely. Those who do, perceive it as reversible.

An expert on death and dying, Robert Kastenbaum (1997) takes a different view of developmental dimensions of death and dying. He believes that even very young children are acutely aware of and concerned about *separation* and *loss,* just as attachment theorist John Bowlby (1980) does. Kastenbaum also says that many children work hard at trying to understand death. Thus, instead of viewing young children as having illogical perceptions of death, Kastenbaum thinks a more accurate stance is to view them as having concerns about death and striving to understand it.

Most psychologists believe that honesty is the best strategy in discussing death with children. Treating the concept as unmentionable is thought to be an inappropriate strategy, yet most of us have grown up in a society in which death is rarely discussed. In one study, the attitudes of 30,000 young adults toward death were evaluated (Shneidman, 1973). More than 30 percent said they could not recall any discussion of death during their childhood. An equal number said that, although death was discussed, the discussion took place in an uncomfortable atmosphere. Almost one of every two respondents said that the death of a grandparent was their first personal encounter with death.

In addition to honesty, what other strategies can be adopted in discussing death with children? The best response to the child's query about death might depend on the child's maturity level (Aiken, 2000). For example, the preschool child requires a less elaborate explanation than an older child. Death can be explained to preschool children in simple physical and biological terms. Actually, what young children need more than elaborate explanations of death is reassurance that they are loved and will not be abandoned. Regardless of children's age, adults should be sensitive and sympathetic, encouraging them to express their own feelings and ideas.

It is not unusual for terminally ill children to distance themselves from their parents as they approach the final phase of their illness. The distancing may be due to the depression that many dying patients experience, or it may be a child's way of protecting parents from the overwhelming grief they will experience at the death. Most dying children know they have a terminal illness. Their developmental level, social support, and coping skills influence how well they cope with knowing they will die.

Adolescence   In adolescence, the prospect of death, like the prospect of aging, is regarded as a notion so remote that it does not have much relevance. The subject of death may be avoided, glossed over, kidded about, neutralized, and controlled by a cool, spectator-like orientation. This perspective is typical of the adolescent's self-conscious thought; however, some adolescents do show a concern for death, both in trying to fathom its meaning and in confronting the prospect of their own demise (Baxter, Stuart, & Stewart, 1998).

Adolescents develop more abstract conceptions of death than children do. For example, adolescents describe death in terms of darkness, light, transition, or nothingness (Wenestam & Wass, 1987). They also develop religious and philosophical views about the nature of death and whether there is life after death.

You will also recall (from chapter 6, "Cognitive Developmental Approaches") the concepts of adolescent egocentrism and personal fable—adolescents' preoccupation with themselves and their belief that they are invincible and unique P. 214. Thus, it is not unusual for adolescents to think that they are somehow immune to death and that death is something that happens to other people but not to them.

Adulthood   There is no evidence that a special orientation toward death develops in early adulthood. An increase in consciousness about death accompanies individuals' awareness that they are aging, which usually intensifies in middle adulthood. In our discussion of middle adulthood, we indicated that midlife is a time when adults begin to think more about how much time is left in their lives. Researchers have found that middle-aged adults actually fear death more than do young adults or older adults (Kalish & Reynolds, 1976). Older adults, though, think about death more and talk about it more in conversation with others than do middle-aged and young adults. They also have more direct experience with death as their friends and relatives become ill and die (Hayslip & Hansson, 2003). Older adults are forced to examine the meanings of life and death more frequently than are younger adults.

Younger adults who are dying often feel cheated more than do older adults who are dying (Kalish, 1987). Younger adults are more likely to feel they have not had the opportunity to do what they want to with their lives. Younger adults perceive they are losing what they might achieve; older adults perceive they are losing what they have.

In old age, one's own death may take on an appropriateness it lacked in earlier years. Some of the increased thinking and conversing about death, and an increased sense of integrity developed through a positive life review, may help older adults accept death. Older adults are less likely to have unfinished business than are younger adults. They usually do not have children who need to be guided to maturity, their spouses are more likely to be dead, and they are less likely to have work-related projects that require completion. Lacking such anticipations, death may be less emotionally painful to them. Even among older adults, however, attitudes toward death vary. One 82-year-old woman declared that she had lived her life and was ready to see it come to an end. Another 82-year-old woman declared that death would be a regrettable interruption of her participation in activities and relationships.

> We keep on thinking and rethinking death after we have passed through childhood's hour.
>
> —ROBERT KASTENBAUM
> *Contemporary Gerontologist, Arizona State University*

Suicide

What are some of the factors that place people at risk for suicide? They include serious physical illnesses, feelings of hopelessness, social isolation, failure in school and work, loss of loved ones, serious financial difficulties, and depression (Davison & Neale, 2004).

Adolescence Suicide is rare in childhood but escalates in adolescence (Peck, 2003). Suicide is the third leading cause of death in 10- to 19-year-olds today in the United States (National Center for Health Statistics, 2002). Although the incidence of suicide in adolescence has increased in recent years, it is still a relatively rare event. In 2000, 1,921 individuals from 10 to 19 years of age committed suicide in the United States (National Center for Health Statistics, 2002).

Far more adolescents contemplate or attempt suicide unsuccessfully (Borowsky, Ireland, & Resnick, 2001; Seroczynski, Jacquez, & Cole, 2003). In a national study, 19 percent of U.S. high school students said that they had seriously considered or attempted suicide in the last 12 months (National Center for Health Statistics, 2002). Less than 3 percent reported a suicide attempt that resulted in an injury, poisoning, or drug overdose that had been treated by a doctor. Females were more likely to attempt suicide than males, but males were more likely to commit suicide. Males use more lethal means, such as a gun, in their suicide attempts than females; adolescent females are more likely to cut their wrists or take an overdose of sleeping pills.

There is controversy about whether homosexual adolescents are more likely to attempt or commit suicide than heterosexual adolescents (Harrison, 2003). In one study of 12,000 adolescents, approximately 15 percent of gay and lesbian youth said that they had attempted suicide compared with 7 percent of heterosexual youth (Russell & Joyner, 2001). However, in another study, gay and lesbian adolescents were only slightly more likely than heterosexual adolescents to attempt suicide (Savin-Williams, 2001). According to a leading researcher on gay youth, Richard Savin-Williams (2001), the earlier studies likely exaggerated the suicide rates for gay adolescents because they only surveyed the most disturbed youth who were attending support groups or hanging out at shelters for gay youth.

Both early and later experiences may be involved in suicide attempts. The adolescent might have a long-standing history of family instability and unhappiness. Lack of affection and emotional support, high control, and pressure for achievement by parents during childhood are likely to show up as factors in suicide attempts. The adolescent might also lack supportive friendships. Recent and current stressful circumstances, such as getting poor grades in school and experiencing the breakup of a romantic relationship, may trigger suicide attempts (Antai-Oton, 2003; Rudd, 2003).

Genetic factors are also associated with suicide. The closer a person's genetic relationship to someone who has committed suicide, the more likely that person is to also commit suicide.

What is the psychological profile of the suicidal adolescent? Suicidal adolescents often have depressive symptoms (American Academy of Pediatrics, 2000; Rudd, 2003). Although not all depressed adolescents are suicidal, depression is the most frequently cited factor associated with adolescent suicide (Pelkonen & Marttunen, 2003). A sense of hopelessness, low self-esteem, and high self-blame are also associated with adolescent suicide (Guillon, Crocq, & Bailey, 2003; Harter & Marold, 1992; Harter & Whitesell, 2001; Seroczynski, Jacquez, & Cole, 2003).

Adulthood and Aging U.S. suicide rates increase in adulthood, reaching their highest level in the 85 and over age group (see figure 17.2) (U.S. Bureau of the Census, 2002). Older White men are more likely to commit suicide than any other group. For all adult age groups (as for adolescents) males are more likely to commit suicide than females.

Older adults are less likely to communicate their suicide intentions than are younger adults and adolescents, and they make fewer attempts. However, when older adults attempt suicide, they use more lethal methods and more often succeed (McIntosh, 1995). A surviving spouse is especially at risk for depression or suicide (De Leo, 2002; McIntosh, 2003; Turvey & others, 1999).

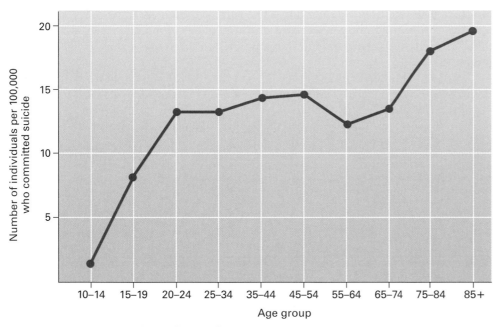

FIGURE 17.2 **U.S. Rate of Suicide in Different Age Groups**

Review and Reflect: Learning Goal 3

3 **Discuss death and attitudes about it at different points in development**

REVIEW

- What are some developmental changes in the cause of death?
- What are some attitudes about death at different points in development?
- Why do people commit suicide? What are some links of suicide to development?

REFLECT

- What is your current attitude about death? Has it changed since you were an adolescent? If so, how?

4   FACING ONE'S OWN DEATH

| Kübler-Ross' Stages of Dying | Perceived Control and Denial | The Contexts in Which People Die |

Knowledge of death's inevitability permits us to establish priorities and structure our time accordingly. As we age, these priorities and structurings change in recognition of diminishing future time. Values concerning the most important uses of time also change. For example, when asked how they would spend six remaining

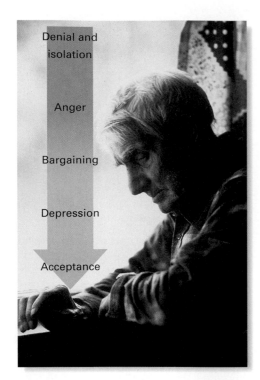

FIGURE 17.3 Kübler-Ross' Stages of Dying

According to Elisabeth Kübler-Ross, we go through five stages of dying: denial and isolation, anger, bargaining, depression, and acceptance. *Does everyone go through these stages, or go through them in the same order? Explain.*

denial and isolation Kübler-Ross' first stage of dying, in which the dying person denies that she or he is really going to die.

anger Kübler-Ross' second stage of dying, in which the dying person's denial gives way to anger, resentment, rage, and envy.

bargaining Kübler-Ross' third stage of dying, in which the dying person develops the hope that death can somehow be postponed.

depression Kübler-Ross' fourth stage of dying, in which the dying person comes to accept the certainty of her or his death. A period of depression or preparatory grief may appear.

acceptance Kübler-Ross' fifth stage of dying, in which the dying person develops a sense of peace, an acceptance of her or his fate, and, in many cases, a desire to be left alone.

months of life, younger adults described such activities as traveling and accomplishing things they previously had not done; older adults described more inner-focused activities—contemplation and meditation, for example (Kalish & Reynolds, 1976).

Most dying individuals want an opportunity to make some decisions regarding their own life and death (Kastenbaum, 2000). Some individuals want to complete unfinished business; they want time to resolve problems and conflicts and to put their affairs in order. Might there be a sequence of stages we go through as we face death?

Kübler-Ross' Stages of Dying

Elisabeth Kübler-Ross (1969) divided the behavior and thinking of dying persons into five stages: denial and isolation, anger, bargaining, depression, and acceptance.

Denial and isolation is Kübler-Ross' first stage of dying, in which the person denies that death is really going to take place. The person may say, "No, it can't be me. It's not possible." This is a common reaction to terminal illness. However, denial is usually only a temporary defense. It is eventually replaced with increased awareness when the person is confronted with such matters as financial considerations, unfinished business, and worry about surviving family members.

Anger is Kübler-Ross' second stage of dying, in which the dying person recognizes that denial can no longer be maintained. Denial often gives way to anger, resentment, rage, and envy. The dying person's question is, "Why me?" At this point, the person becomes increasingly difficult to care for as anger may become displaced and projected onto physicians, nurses, family members, and even God. The realization of loss is great, and those who symbolize life, energy, and competent functioning are especially salient targets of the dying person's resentment and jealousy.

Bargaining is Kübler-Ross' third stage of dying, in which the person develops the hope that death can somehow be postponed or delayed. Some persons enter into a bargaining or negotiation—often with God—as they try to delay their death. Psychologically, the person is saying, "Yes, me, but . . ." In exchange for a few more days, weeks, or months of life, the person promises to lead a reformed life dedicated to God or to the service of others.

Depression is Kübler-Ross' fourth stage of dying, in which the dying person comes to accept the certainty of death. At this point, a period of depression or preparatory grief may appear. The dying person may become silent, refuse visitors, and spend much of the time crying or grieving. This behavior is normal and is an effort to disconnect the self from love objects. Attempts to cheer up the dying person at this stage should be discouraged, says Kübler-Ross, because the dying person has a need to contemplate impending death.

Acceptance is Kübler-Ross' fifth stage of dying, in which the person develops a sense of peace, an acceptance of one's fate, and in many cases, a desire to be left alone. In this stage, feelings and physical pain may be virtually absent. Kübler-Ross describes this fifth stage as the end of the dying struggle, the final resting stage before death. A summary of Kübler-Ross' dying stages is presented in figure 17.3.

What is the current evaluation of Kübler-Ross' approach? According to Robert Kastenbaum (1998, 2000), there are some problems with Kübler-Ross' approach:

- The existence of the five-stage sequence has not been demonstrated by either Kübler-Ross or independent research.
- The stage interpretation neglected the patients' situations, including relationship support, specific effects of illness, family obligations, and institutional climate in which they were interviewed.

However, Kübler-Ross' pioneering efforts were important in calling attention to those who are attempting to cope with life-threatening illnesses. She did much to encourage attention to the quality of life for dying persons and their families.

Because of the criticisms of Kübler-Ross' stages, some psychologists prefer to describe them not as stages but as potential reactions to dying. At any one moment, a number of emotions may wax and wane. Hope, disbelief, bewilderment, anger, and acceptance may come and go as individuals try to make sense of what is happening to them.

In facing their own death, some individuals struggle until the end, desperately trying to hang on to their lives. Acceptance of death never comes for them. Some psychologists believe that the harder individuals fight to avoid the inevitable death they face and the more they deny it, the more difficulty they will have in dying peacefully and in a dignified way; other psychologists argue that not confronting death until the end may be adaptive for some individuals (Lifton, 1977).

The extent to which people have found meaning and purpose in their lives is linked with how they approach death. A recent study of 160 individuals with less than three months to live revealed that those who had found purpose and meaning in their lives felt the least despair in the final weeks, while dying individuals who saw no reason for living were the most distressed and wanted to hasten death (McClain, Rosenfeld, & Breitbart, 2003). In this and other studies, spirituality helped to buffer dying individuals from severe depression (Smith, McCullough, & Poll, in press).

Perceived Control and Denial

Perceived control may work as an adaptive strategy for some older adults who face death. When individuals are led to believe they can influence and control events—such as prolonging their lives—they may become more alert and cheerful. Remember from chapter 4 that giving nursing home residents options for control improved their attitudes and increased their longevity (Rodin & Langer, 1977).

Denial also may be a fruitful way for some individuals to approach death. It can be adaptive or maladaptive. Denial can be used to avoid the destructive impact of shock by delaying the necessity of dealing with one's death. Denial can insulate the individual from having to cope with intense feelings of anger and hurt; however, if denial keeps us from having a life-saving operation, it clearly is maladaptive. Denial is neither good nor bad; its adaptive qualities need to be evaluated on an individual basis.

The Contexts in Which People Die

For dying individuals, the context in which they die is important. More than 50 percent of Americans die in hospitals, and nearly 20 percent die in nursing homes. Some people spend their final days in isolation and fear (Clay, 1997). An increasing number of people choose to die in the humane atmosphere of a hospice.

Hospitals offer several important advantages to the dying individual; for example, professional staff members are readily available, and the medical technology present may prolong life. But a hospital may not be the best place for many people to die. Most individuals say they would rather die at home (Kalish & Reynolds, 1976). Many feel, however, that they will be a burden at home, that there is limited space there, and that dying at home may alter relationships. Individuals who are facing death also worry about the competency and availability of emergency medical treatment if they remain at home.

Kübler-Ross on Dying

'Man is the only animal that finds his own existence a problem he has to solve and from which he cannot escape. In the same sense man is the only animal who knows he must die.

—ERICH FROMM
American Psychotherapist,
20th Century

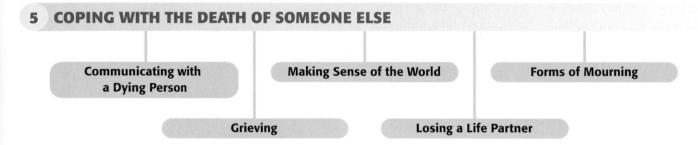

Review and Reflect: Learning Goal 4

4 **Explain the psychological aspects involved in facing one's own death and the contexts in which people die**

REVIEW

• What are Kübler-Ross' five stages of dying? What conclusions can be reached about them?
• What roles do perceived control and denial play in facing one's own death?
• What are the contexts in which people die?

REFLECT

• How do you think you will psychologically handle facing facing your own death?

5 COPING WITH THE DEATH OF SOMEONE ELSE

Communicating with a Dying Person

Grieving

Making Sense of the World

Losing a Life Partner

Forms of Mourning

Loss can come in many forms in our lives—divorce, a pet's death, loss of a job—but no loss is greater than that which comes through the death of someone we love and care for—a parent, sibling, spouse, relative, or friend. In the ratings of life's stresses that require the most adjustment, death of a spouse is given the highest number. How should we communicate with a dying individual? How do we cope with the death of someone we love?

Communicating with a Dying Person

Most psychologists believe that it is best for dying individuals to know that they are dying and that significant others know they are dying so they can interact and communicate with each other on the basis of this mutual knowledge. What are some of the advantages of this open awareness for the dying individual? First, dying individuals can close their lives in accord with their own ideas about proper dying. Second, they may be able to complete some plans and projects, can make arrangements for survivors, and can participate in decisions about a funeral and burial. Third, dying individuals have the opportunity to reminisce, to converse with others who have been important in their life, and to end life conscious of what life has been like. And fourth, dying individuals have more understanding of what is happening within their bodies and what the medical staff is doing to them (Kalish, 1981).

In addition to keeping communication open, what are some suggestions for conversing with a dying individual? Some experts believe that conversation should not focus on mental pathology or preparation for death but should focus on strengths of the individual and preparation for the remainder of life. Since external accomplishments are not possible, communication should be directed more at internal growth. Keep in mind also that important support for a dying individual may come not only from mental health professionals, but also from nurses, physicians, a spouse, or intimate friends (De-Spelder & Strickland, 2004). In the Applications in Life-Span Development interlude, you can read further about effective communication strategies with a dying person.

www.mhhe.com/santrockldt2

Exploring Death and Dying

Death and Dying Resources

Applications in Life-Span Development

Communicating with a Dying Person

Effective strategies for communicating with a dying person include these:

1. Establish your presence, be at the same eye level; don't be afraid to touch the dying person—dying individuals are often starved for human touch.
2. Eliminate distraction—for example, ask if it is okay to turn off the TV. Realize that excessive small talk can be a distraction.
3. Dying individuals who are very frail often have little energy. If the dying person you are visiting is very frail, you may not want to visit for very long.
4. Don't insist that the dying person feel acceptance about death if the dying person wants to deny the reality of the situation; on the other hand, don't insist on denial if the dying individual indicates acceptance.
5. Allow the dying person to express guilt or anger; encourage the expression of feelings.
6. Don't be afraid to ask the person what the expected outcome for the illness is. Discuss alternatives, unfinished business.
7. Sometimes dying individuals don't have access to other people. Ask the dying person if there is anyone he or she would like to see that you can contact.
8. Encourage the dying individual to reminisce, especially if you have memories in common.
9. Talk with the individual when she or he wishes to talk. If this is impossible, make an appointment and keep it.
10. Express your regard for the dying individual. Don't be afraid to express love, and don't be afraid to say good-bye.

Grieving

Our exploration of grief focuses on dimensions of grieving, as well as cultural diversity in healthy grieving.

Dimensions of Grieving   **Grief** is the emotional numbness, disbelief, separation anxiety, despair, sadness, and loneliness that accompany the loss of someone we love. Grief is not a simple emotional state but rather a complex, evolving process with multiple dimensions (Adams, 2003; Jacobs & others, 1987). In this view, pining for the lost person is one important dimension. Pining or yearning reflects an intermittent, recurrent wish or need to recover the lost person. Another important dimension of grief is separation anxiety, which not only includes pining and pre-occupation with thoughts of the deceased person but also focuses on places and things associated with the deceased, as well as crying or sighing. Grief may also involve despair and sadness, which include a sense of hopelessness and defeat, depressive symptoms, apathy, loss of meaning for activities that used to involve the person who is gone, and growing desolation (Giddens & Giddens, 2000; Ringdal & others, 2001).

These feelings occur repeatedly shortly after a loss. As time passes, pining and protest over the loss tend to diminish, although episodes of depression and apathy may remain or increase. The sense of separation anxiety and loss may continue to the end of one's life, but most of us emerge from grief's tears, turning our attention once again to productive tasks and regaining a more positive view of life (Powers & Wampold, 1994).

grief The emotional numbness, disbelief, separation anxiety, despair, sadness, and loneliness that accompany the loss of someone we love.

The grieving process is more like a roller-coaster ride than an orderly progression of stages with clear-cut time frames (Lund, 1996). The ups and downs of grief often involve rapidly changing emotions, meeting the challenges of learning new skills, detecting personal weaknesses and limitations, creating new patterns of behavior, and forming new friendships and relationships (Bruce, 2002; Mitchell & Catron, 2002). For most individuals, grief becomes more manageable over time, with fewer abrupt highs and lows. But many grieving spouses report that even though time has brought some healing, they have never gotten over their loss. They have just learned to live with it.

Long-term grief is sometimes masked and can predispose individuals to become depressed and even suicidal (Davis, 2001; Kastenbaum, 1998, 2000). Good family communication can help reduce the incidence of depression and suicidal thoughts. For example, in one study, family members who communicated poorly with each other had more negative grief reactions six months later than those who communicated effectively with each other just after the loss of a family member (Schoka & Hayslip, 1999).

Cultural Diversity in Healthy Grieving Some approaches to grieving emphasize the importance of breaking bonds with the deceased and returning to autonomous lifestyles. People who persist in holding on to the deceased are believed to be in need of therapy. Recent analyses, however, have cast doubt on whether this recommendation is always the best therapeutic advice (Reisman, 2001; Stroebe & others, 1992).

Analyses of non-Western cultures suggest that beliefs about continuing bonds with the deceased vary extensively. Maintenance of ties with the deceased is accepted and sustained in the religious rituals of Japan. In the Hopi of Arizona, the deceased are forgotten as quickly as possible and life is carried on as usual. Their funeral ritual concludes with a break-off between mortals and spirits. The diversity of grieving is nowhere more clear than in two Muslim societies—one in Egypt, the other in Bali. In Egypt, the bereaved are encouraged to dwell at length on their grief, surrounded by others who relate similarly tragic accounts and express their own sorrow. By contrast, in Bali, the bereaved are encouraged to laugh and be joyful.

In a longitudinal study of bereavement in the Netherlands, many people tended to maintain contact with the deceased, despite the contemporary emphasis on breaking such bonds (Stroebe & Stroebe, 1991). Many of the widowed persons were not planning a major break with their pasts, but rather were integrating the loss

> *E*veryone can master grief but he who has it.
>
> —WILLIAM SHAKESPEARE
> *English Playwright, 17th Century*

How might grieving vary across individuals and cultures?

experience into their lifestyles and trying to carry on much as before the death of a loved one. Well over half "consulted" the deceased when having to make a decision. One widow said that she gained considerable comfort from knowing that her decision was exactly what her deceased husband would have wanted her to do.

Similar findings have been reported among American widows and among the parents of sons who died in two Israeli wars, 13 and 4 years earlier (Rubin & Malkinson, 2001; Schuchter & Zook, 1993). Even many years after the death of their son, the Israeli parents showed a strong involvement with him. They idealized the lost son in ways that were not present in the descriptions by a control group of parents of sons who had recently left home.

In summary, people grieve in a variety of ways (Matzo & others, 2003). The diverse grieving patterns are culturally embedded practices (Haas, 2003). Thus, there is no one right, ideal way to grieve. There are many different ways to feel about a deceased person and no set series of stages that the bereaved must pass through to become well adjusted. The stoic widower may need to cry out over his loss at times. The weeping widow may need to put her husband's wishes aside as she becomes the financial manager of her estate. What is needed is an understanding that healthy coping with the death of a loved one involves growth, flexibility, and appropriateness within a cultural context.

Making Sense of the World

One beneficial aspect of grieving is that it stimulates many individuals to try to make sense of their world (Kalish, 1981, 1987). A common occurrence is to go over again and again all of the events that led up to the death. In the days and weeks after the death, the closest family members share experiences with each other, sometimes reminiscing over family experiences. In one recent study, women who became widowed in midlife were challenged by the crisis of their husband's death to examine meaningful directions for their lives (Danfroth & Glass, 2001).

Each individual may offer a piece of death's puzzle. "When I saw him last Saturday, he looked as though he were rallying," says one family member. "Do you think it might have had something to do with his sister's illness?" remarks another. "I doubt it, but I heard from an aide that he fell going to the bathroom that morning," comments yet another. "That explains the bruise on his elbow," says the first individual. "No wonder he told me that he was angry because he could not seem to do anything right," chimes in a fourth family member. So it goes in the attempt to understand why someone who was rallying on Saturday was dead on Wednesday.

When a death is caused by an accident or a disaster, the effort to make sense of it is pursued more vigorously. As added pieces of news come trickling in, they are integrated into the puzzle. The bereaved want to put the death into a perspective that they can understand—divine intervention, a curse from a neighboring tribe, a logical sequence of cause and effect, or whatever it may be.

Meaning-making is increasingly believed to be an important aspect of coping (Folkman & Moskowitz, 2004). Bert Hayslip and Robert Hansson (2003) described three types of meaning-making coping involving death: (1) personal, (2) family, and (3) community:

- *Personal meaning-making coping.* Finding a meaningful, satisfactory explanation for the loss of a loved one—cognitive acceptance—may be an important aspect of coping and recovery (Neimeyer, 2001; Weiss, 1988). Meaning-making can serve two important coping functions (Davis & Nolen-Hoeksema, 2001). First, an unexpected, untimely, or traumatic death can threaten one's assumptions about the world and what life is all about. Thus, an important coping strategy is to construct a personal meaning for the death that helps to reestablish one's sense of security. A second function of meaning-making coping is to help the bereaved individual to understand that successfully coping with the death can produce personal growth, a broadening of personal and philosophical perspectives, and increased appreciation of one's other close relationships.

Mary Assanful (front right with other former restaurant workers) worked at Windows on the World restaurant located in the World Trade Center and lost her job when terrorist attacks came. She says that she still is not herself and regularly has nightmares. A Ghana native, Mary is still unemployed. She has joined several other workers who are now planning to return by opening a restaurant near Ground Zero. They hope the new restaurant will honor their coworkers who died and provide a focus and meaning for their still-unsettled lives. Mary says that since they have been working on this new project, her mind has calmed somewhat.

- *Family meaning-making coping.* Many family members support each other as they try to understand a death (Nadeau, 2001). Family members may have different thoughts regarding the cause and implications of the death. As they share their beliefs about the death, they may search for common factors, encourage shy members to participate, help each other to rethink the troubling aspects of the death, and suggest coping strategies. Younger family members who lack the life experiences, maturity, or resources necessary to effectively cope with the death may especially benefit from family discussion of the event.

- *Community-meaning coping.* The meaning and implications of death present not only at the level of the individual and the family, but also at the broader level of the community and even the nation. Some deaths, such as those of John F. Kennedy, Princess Diana, and the victims of the terrorist attacks on the World Trade Center in New York and the Pentagon in Washington, D.C., September 11, 2001, can startle a community and nation and lead to a collective search for meaning. This collective search for meaning often involves a focus on healing the community, reaffirming purpose and the future, and memoralizing the dead.

Losing a Life Partner

Those left behind after the death of an intimate partner suffer profound grief and often endure financial loss, loneliness, increased physical illness, and psychological disorders, including depression (Hungerford, 2001; Stroebe & others, 1998). How they cope with the crisis varies considerably. Widows outnumber widowers by the ratio of 5 to 1, because women live longer than men, because women tend to marry men older than themselves, and because a widowed man is more likely to remarry. Widowed women are probably the poorest group in America. One study found that most widows in the United States and Germany experienced a decline in living standards in the year following their husband's death, and many fell into poverty when they became widows (Hungerford, 2001). Also, a recent study of Mexican Americans revealed that widows were more likely than widowers to report financial strain, welfare dependency, and use of Medicaid than widowers (Angel, Douglas, & Angel, 2003). In this study, widows received more emotional support than widowers.

Many widows are lonely. The poorer and less educated they are, the lonelier they tend to be. The bereaved are also at increased risk for many health problems, including death (Corr, Nable, & Corr, 2000; Manor & Eisenbach, 2003; Valdimarsdottir & others, 2003).

The following Research in Life-Span Development interlude examines the relation of widowhood to health.

Research in Life-Span Development

The Women's Health Initiative Study of Widowhood and Health

One recent three-year longitudinal study of more than 130,000 women aged 50 to 79 years of age in the United States as part of the Women's Health Initiative examined the relation of widowhood to physical and mental health, health behaviors, and health outcomes (Wilcox & others, 2003). Women were categorized as 1) remaining married, 2) transitioning from married to widowed, 3) remaining widowed, and 4) transitioning from widowed to married. Widows were further subdivided into the recently widowed (widowed for less than one year) and longer-term widowed (widowed for more than one year).

The measures used to assess the older women's health were:

- *Physical health.* Blood pressure was assessed after five minutes of quiet rest using the average of two readings with 30 seconds between the readings. Hypertension was defined as more than 140/90. Body mass index (BMI) was calculated and used to determine whether a woman was obese. A health survey assessed physical function and health status.
- *Mental health.* Depressive symptoms were assessed by a six-item depression scale with participants rating the frequency of their depressed thoughts during the past week. The participant's self-report of antidepressant medicine use was also obtained. Information about social functioning and mental health was based on participants' responses on the Social Functioning Scale (Ware & others, 2000).
- *Health Behaviors.* Dietary behaviors were assessed with a modified version of the National Cancer Institute-Health Habits and History Questionnaire (Patterson & others, 1999). Participants also were asked if they smoked tobacco, and if so, how much. To assess physical activity, participants were asked how often they walked outside the home each week and the extent to which they engaged in strenuous or moderate exercise. To assess health care use, they were asked whether they had visited their doctor in the past year.
- *Health Outcomes.* Cardiovascular disease and cancer occurrences were assessed annually and any overnight hospitalizations were noted.

At the beginning of the three-year study, married women reported better physical and mental health than, and better health in general, than widowed women. Women who remained married over the the 3-year-period of the study showed stability in mental health, recent widows experienced marked impairments in mental health, and longer-term widows showed stability or slight improvements in mental health. Both groups of widows (recent and longer-term) reported more unintentional weight loss across the three years. The findings underscore the resilience of older women and their capacity to reestablish connections but point to the need for services that strengthen social support for those who have difficulty during the transition from married to widowhood.

Optimal adjustment after a death depends on several factors (Leming & Dickinson, 2002). Women do better than men largely because, in our society, women are responsible for the emotional life of a couple, whereas men usually manage the finances and material goods (Fry, 2001). Thus, women have better networks of friends, closer relationships with relatives, and experience in taking care of themselves psychologically (Antonucci & others, 2001). Older widows do better than younger widows, perhaps because the death of a partner is more expected for older women. For their part, widowers usually have more money than widows do, and they are much more likely to remarry.

For either widows or widowers, social support helps them adjust to the death of a spouse (Boerner & Wortman, 1998; Kastenbaum, 1998). The Widow-to-Widow program, begun in the 1960s, provides support for newly widowed women. Volunteer widows reach out to other widows, introducing them to others who may have similar problems, leading group discussions, and organizing social activities. The program has been adopted by the American Association of Retired Persons and disseminated throughout the United States as the Widowed Person's Service. The model has since been adopted by numerous community organizations to provide support for those going through a difficult transition.

One recent study found that psychological and religious factors—such as personal meaning, optimism, the importance of religion, and access to religious support—were related to the psychological well-being of older adults following the loss of a spouse (Fry, 2001). Other studies have indicated that religiosity and coping skills are related to well-being following the loss of a spouse in late adulthood (Fry, 1999).

Grief and Bereavement
WidowNet

Princess Diana's sons, William and Harry, placed white flowers and a letter to their mother on her coffin. *What are some ways that people mourn a death and grieve?*

www.mhhe.com/santrockldt2

Buddhist Funeral Rites

Forms of Mourning

One decision facing the bereaved is what to do with the body. Approximately 80 percent of corpses are disposed of by burial, the remaining 20 percent by cremation (Aiken, 2000; Cremation Association of America, 2000). Cremation is more popular in the Pacific region of the United States, less popular in the South. Cremation also is more popular in Canada than in the United States and most popular of all in Japan and many other Asian countries.

The funeral is an important aspect of mourning in many cultures. In one recent study, bereaved individuals who were personally religious derived more psychological benefits from a funeral, participated more actively in the rituals, and adjusted more positively to the loss (Hayslip, Edmondson, & Guarnaccia, 1999).

The funeral industry has been the source of controversy in recent years. Funeral directors and their supporters argue that the funeral provides a form of closure to the relationship with the deceased, especially when there is an open casket. Their critics claim that funeral directors are just trying to make money and that embalming is grotesque. One way to avoid being exploited during bereavement is to purchase funeral arrangements in advance. However, in one survey, only 24 percent of individuals 60 and over had made any funeral arrangements (Kalish & Reynolds, 1976).

In some cultures, a ceremonial meal is held after death; in others, a black armband is worn for one year following a death. Cultures vary in how they practice mourning (Adamolekun, 2001; Shepard, 2002). To learn about two cultures with extensive mourning systems, see the Contexts of Life-Span Development interlude.

Contexts of Life-Span Development
The Amish, Traditional Judaism, and Mourning

The family and the community have important roles in mourning in some cultures. Two of those cultures are the Amish and traditional Judaism (Worthington, 1989).

The Amish are a conservative group with approximately 80,000 members in the United States, Ontario, and several small settlements in South and Central America. The Amish live in a family-oriented society in which family and community support are essential for survival. Today, they live at the same unhurried pace as that of their ancestors, using horses instead of cars and facing death with the same steadfast faith as their forebears. At the time of death, close neighbors assume the responsibility of notifying others of the death. The Amish community handles virtually all aspects of the funeral.

The funeral service is held in a barn in warmer months and in a house during colder months. Calm acceptance of death, influenced by a deep religious faith, is an integral part of the Amish culture. Following the funeral, a high level of support is given to the bereaved family for at least a year. Visits to the family, special scrapbooks and handmade items for the family, new work projects started for the widow, and quilting days that combine fellowship and productivity are among the supports given to the bereaved family.

The family and community also have specific and important roles in mourning in traditional Judaism. The program of mourning is divided into graduated time periods, each with its appropriate practices. The observance of these practices is required of the spouse and the immediate blood relatives of the deceased. The first period is *aninut,* the period between death and burial. The next two periods make up *avelut,* or mourning proper. The first of these is *shivah,* a period of seven days, which commences with the burial. It is followed by *sheloshim,* the 30-day period following the burial, including shivah. At the end of sheloshim, the mourning process is considered over for all but one's parents. For parents, mourning continues for 11 months, although observances are minimal.

The seven-day period of the shivah is especially important in traditional Judaism. The mourners, sitting together as a group through an extended period, have an opportunity to project their feelings to the group as a whole. Visits from others during shivah may help the mourner deal with feelings of guilt. After shivah, the mourner is encouraged to resume normal social interaction. In fact, it is customary for the mourners to walk together a short distance as a symbol of their return to society. In its entirety, the elaborate mourning system of traditional Judaism is designed to promote personal growth and to reintegrate the individual into the community.

An Amish funeral procession in Pennsylvania. *How does the way the Amish engage in mourning differ from that of other cultural groups?*

Review and Reflect: Learning Goal 5

5 **Identify ways to cope with the death of another person**

REVIEW

- What are some strategies for communicating with a dying person?
- What is the nature of grieving?
- How is making sense of the world a beneficial outcome of grieving?
- What are some characteristics and outcomes of losing a life partner?
- What are some forms of mourning? What is the nature of the funeral?

REFLECT

- Is there a best or worst way to grieve? Explain.

We have arrived at the end of this book. I hope this book and course have been a window to the life span of the human species and a window to your own personal journey in life.

Our study of the human life span has been long and complex. You have read about many physical, cognitive, and socioemotional changes that take place from conception through death. This is a good time to reflect on what you have learned. Which theories, studies, and ideas were especially interesting to you? What did you learn about your own development?

Following this chapter is an appendix titled "Careers in Life-Span Development." There you will find descriptions of many exciting careers and Web connections in this field.

I wish you all the best in the remaining years of your journey though the human life span.

John W. Santrock

Reach Your Learning Goals

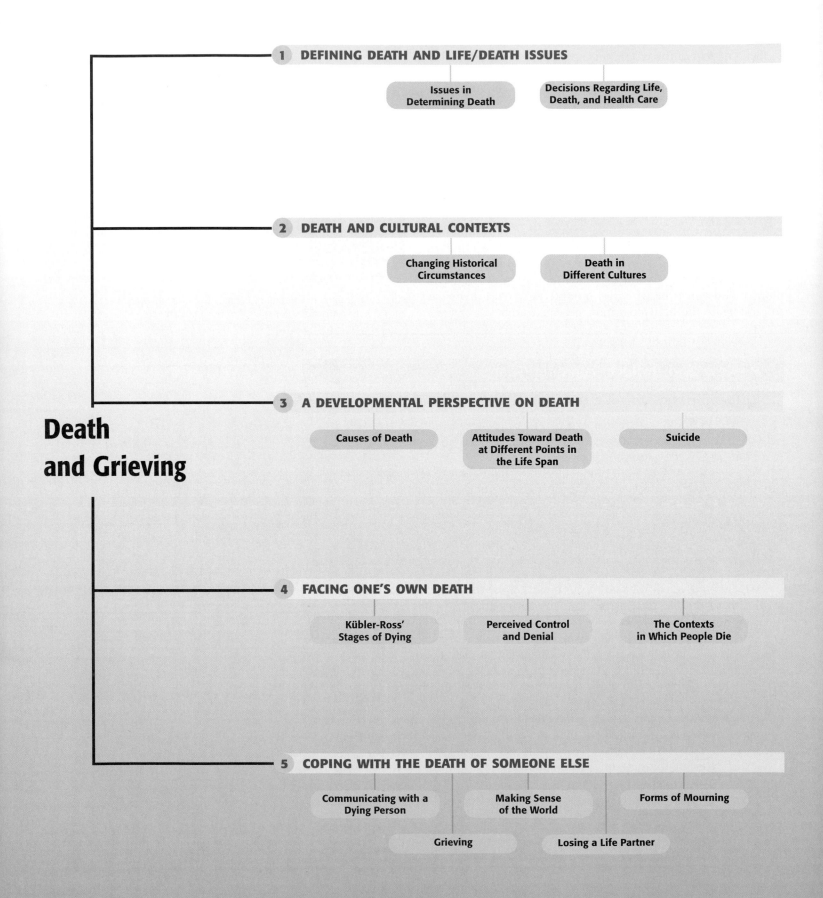

Death and Grieving

1 DEFINING DEATH AND LIFE/DEATH ISSUES

- Issues in Determining Death
- Decisions Regarding Life, Death, and Health Care

2 DEATH AND CULTURAL CONTEXTS

- Changing Historical Circumstances
- Death in Different Cultures

3 A DEVELOPMENTAL PERSPECTIVE ON DEATH

- Causes of Death
- Attitudes Toward Death at Different Points in the Life Span
- Suicide

4 FACING ONE'S OWN DEATH

- Kübler-Ross' Stages of Dying
- Perceived Control and Denial
- The Contexts in Which People Die

5 COPING WITH THE DEATH OF SOMEONE ELSE

- Communicating with a Dying Person
- Making Sense of the World
- Forms of Mourning
- Grieving
- Losing a Life Partner

Summary

1 Evaluate issues in determining death and decisions regarding death

- Twenty-five years ago, determining if someone was dead was simpler than it is today. Brain death is a neurological definition of death, which states that a person is brain dead when all electrical activity of the brain has ceased for a specified period of time. Medical experts debate whether this should mean the higher and lower brain functions or just the higher cortical functions. Currently, most states have a statute endorsing the cessation of brain function (both higher and lower) as a standard for determining death.

- Decisions regarding life, death, and health care can involve whether to have a living will, euthanasia, and hospice care. Living wills and advanced directives are increasingly used. Euthanasia is the act of painlessly ending the life of a person who is suffering from an incurable disease or disability. Distinctions are made between active and passive euthanasia. Hospice care emphasizes reducing pain and suffering rather than prolonging life.

2 Describe the roles of sociohistorical and cultural contexts in understanding death

- When, where, and why people die have changed historically. Today, death occurs most often among older adults. More than 80 percent of all deaths in the United States now occur in a hospital or other institution; our exposure to death in the family has been minimized. Most societies throughout history have had philosophical or religious beliefs about death, and most societies have rituals that deal with death.

- Most cultures do not view death as the end of existence—spiritual life is thought to continue. The United States has been described as a death-denying and death-avoiding culture.

3 Discuss death and attitudes about it at different points in development

- Although death is more likely to occur in late adulthood, death can come at any point in development. In children and younger adults, death is more likely to occur because of accidents; in older adults, death is more likely to occur because of chronic diseases.

- Infants do not have a concept of death. Preschool children also have little concept of death. Preschool children sometimes blame themselves for a person's death. In the elementary school years, children develop a more realistic orientation toward death. Most psychologists believe honesty is the best strategy for helping children cope with death. Death may be glossed over in adolescence. Adolescents have more abstract, philosophical views of death than children do. There is no evidence that a special orientation toward death emerges in early adulthood. Middle adulthood is a time when adults show a heightened consciousness about death and death anxiety. The deaths of some persons, especially children and younger adults, are often perceived to be more tragic than those of others, such as very old adults, who have had an opportunity to live a long life. Older adults often show less death anxiety than middle-aged adults, but older adults experience and converse about death more. Attitudes about death may vary considerably among adults of any age.

- Among the factors that place people at risk for suicide are serious physical illnesses, feelings of hopelessness, social isolation, failure in school and work, loss of loved ones, serious financial difficulties, and depression. Suicide behavior is rare in childhood but escalates in adolescence. Both early and later experiences can be involved in suicide. The suicide rate increases in a linear fashion from adolescence through late adulthood.

4 Explain the psychological aspects involved in facing one's own death and the contexts in which people die

- Kübler-Ross proposed five stages: denial and isolation, anger, bargaining, depression, and acceptance. Not all individuals go through the same sequence.

- Perceived control and denial may work together as an adaptive orientation for the dying individual. Denial can be adaptive or maladaptive, depending on the circumstance.

- Most deaths in the United States occur in hospitals; this has advantages and disadvantages. Most individuals say they would rather die at home, but they worry that they will be a burden and they worry about the lack of medical care.

5 Identify ways to cope with the death of another person

- Most psychologists recommend an open communication system with the dying. Communication should not dwell on pathology or preparation for death but should emphasize the dying person's strengths.

- Grief is the emotional numbness, disbelief, separation, anxiety, despair, sadness, and loneliness that accompany the loss of someone we love. Grief is multidimensional and in some cases may last for years. There are cultural variations in grieving.

- The grieving process may stimulate individuals to strive to make sense out of their world; each individual may contribute a piece to death's puzzle.

- Usually the most difficult loss is the death of a spouse. The bereaved are at risk for many health problems. Social support benefits widows and widowers.

- Forms of mourning vary across cultures. Approximately 80 percent of corpses are disposed of by burial, 20 percent by cremation. An important aspect of mourning in many cultures is the funeral. In recent years, the funeral industry has been the focus of controversy. In some cultures, a ceremonial meal is held after death.

Key Terms

brain death 602
euthanasia 603
passive euthanasia 603

active euthanasia 603
hospice 604
palliative care 604

denial and isolation 612
anger 612
bargaining 612

depression 612
acceptance 612
grief 615

Key People

Richard Savin-Williams 610

Robert Kastenbaum 608

Elisabeth Kübler-Ross 612

E-Learning Tools

Connect to **www.mhhe.com/santrockldt2** to research the answers and complete these exercises. In addition, you'll find a number of other resources and valuable study tools for chapter 17, "Death and Grieving," on the Student CD-ROM that came with this book.

Taking It to the Net

1. Herman's mother has Parkinson's disease. He wants her to make some difficult end-of-life decisions while she still can. He and his mother discuss the options of a health-care power of attorney, a living will, and/or a DNR. What are the different purposes of these documents and what is the family's involvement in these decisions?

2. Letitia, a recent widow, is interested in starting a program for widowed women in her community. In order to start the process to request funding, she is exploring her options in foundation grants. As part of this process, she will need to investigate the available data on the nature and extent of widowhood in the United States today, including the age, sex, and socioeconomic status of widowed people. What type of information is available to her and her group?

3. Ellen has taken care of her mother throughout her long, lingering illness that has just been diagnosed as terminal. Ellen does not think she alone can provide the type of care necessary to take care of her mother in her final weeks. Her neighbor suggested she contact the local hospice. What does a hospice offer to families in this situation and how is it different from a nursing home?

Self-Assessment

To evaluate your anxiety about death and to complete a living will, complete these self-assessments:

- *How Much Death Anxiety Do I Have?*
- *The Living Will*

Health and Well-Being, Parenting, and Education

Build your decision-making skills by trying your hand at the health and well-being, parenting, and education "Scenarios."

Appendix *Careers in Life-Span Development*

Some of you may be quite sure about what you plan to make your life's work. Others of you might not have decided on a major yet and might be uncertain about which career path you want to follow. Each of us wants to find a rewarding career and enjoy the work we do. The field of life-span development offers an amazing breadth of career options that can provide extremely satisfying work.

If you decide to pursue a career in life-span development, what career options are available to you? Many. College and university professors teach courses in many different areas of life-span development, education, family development, nursing, and medicine. Teachers impart knowledge, understanding, and skills to children and adolescents. Counselors, clinical psychologists, nurses, and physicians help people of different ages to cope more effectively with their lives and improve their well-being. Various professionals work with families to improve the quality of family functioning.

Although an advanced degree is not absolutely necessary in some areas of life-span development, you usually can considerably expand your opportunities (and income) by obtaining a graduate degree. Many careers in life-span development pay reasonably well. For example, psychologists earn well above the median salary in the United States. Also, by working in the field of life-span development, you can guide people in improving their lives, understand yourself and others better, possibly advance the state of knowledge in the field, and have an enjoyable time while you are doing these things.

If you are considering a career in life-span development, would you prefer to work with infants? children? adolescents? older adults? As you go through this term, try to spend some time with people of different ages. Observe their behavior. Talk with them about their lives. Think about whether you would like to work with people of this age in your life's work.

Another important aspect of exploring careers is to talk with people who work in various jobs. For example, if you have some interest in becoming a school counselor, call a school, ask to speak with a counselor, and set up an appointment to discuss the counselor's career and work. If you have an interest in becoming a nurse, think about whether you would rather work with babies, children, adolescents, or older adults. Call the nursing department at a hospital, ask to speak with the nursing department, and set up an appointment to speak with the nursing coordinator about a nursing career.

Something else that should benefit you is to work in one or more jobs related to your career interests while you are in college. Many colleges and universities have internships or work experiences for students who major in such fields as life-span development. Some of these opportunities are for course credit or pay; others are strictly on a volunteer basis. Take advantage of these opportunities. They can provide you with valuable experiences to help you decide if this is the right career area for you, and they can help you get into graduate school, if you decide you want to go.

In the upcoming sections, we will profile a number of careers in four areas: education/research; clinical/counseling; medical/nursing/physical; and families/relationships. These are not the only career options in life-span development, but they should provide you with an idea of the range of opportunities available and information about some of the main career avenues you might pursue. In profiling these careers, we will address the amount of education required, the nature of the training, and a description of the work.

By going to the website for this book **(www.mhhe.com/santrockldt2),** you can obtain more detailed career information about the various careers in life-span development described in this appendix.

EDUCATION/RESEARCH

There are numerous career opportunities in life-span development that involve education and/or research. These range from being a college professor to child-care director to school psychologist.

College/University Professor

Courses in life-span development are taught in many different programs and schools in college and universities, including psychology, education, nursing, child and family studies, social work, and medicine. A Ph.D. or master's degree almost always is required to teach in some area of life-span development in a college or university. Obtaining a doctoral degree usually takes four to six years of graduate work. A master's degree requires approximately two years of graduate work. The professional job might be at a research university with one or more master's or Ph.D. programs in life-span development, at a four-year college with no graduate programs, or at a community college.

The training involves taking graduate courses, learning to conduct research, and attending and presenting papers at professional meetings. Many graduate students work as teaching or research assistants for professors in an apprenticeship relationship that helps them to become competent teachers and researchers. The work that college professors do includes teaching courses either at the undergraduate or graduate level (or both), conducting research in a specific area, advising students and/or directing their research, and serving on college or university committees. Some college instructors do not conduct research as part of their job but instead focus mainly on teaching. However, research is part of the job description at most universities with master's and Ph.D. programs.

If you are interested in becoming a college or university professor, you might want to make an appointment with your instructor in this class on life-span development to learn more about their profession and what their work is like.

Researcher

Some individuals in the field of life-span development work in research positions. Most have either a master's or a Ph.D. in some area of life-span development. They might work at a university, in some cases in a university professor's research program, in government at such agencies as the National Institute of Mental Health, or in private industry. Individuals who have full-time research positions in life-span development generate innovative research ideas, plan studies, and carry out the research by collecting data, analyzing the data, and then interpreting it. Then, they will usually attempt to publish the research in a scientific journal. A researcher often works in a collaborative manner with other researchers on a project and may present the research at scientific meetings, where she or he also learns about other research. One researcher might spend much of his or her time in a laboratory; another researcher might work out in the field, such as in schools, hospitals, and so on.

Elementary or Secondary School Teacher

Becoming an elementary or secondary school teacher requires a minimum of an undergraduate degree. The training involves taking a wide range of courses with a major or concentration in education as well as completing a supervised practice teaching internship. The work of an elementary or secondary school teacher involves teaching in one more subject areas, preparing the curriculum, giving tests, assigning grades, monitoring students' progress, conducting parent-teacher conferences, and attending in-service workshops.

Exceptional Children (Special Education) Teacher

Becoming a teacher of exceptional children requires a minimum of an undergraduate degree. The training consists of taking a wide range of courses in education and a concentration of courses in educating children with disabilities or children who are gifted. The work of a teacher of exceptional children involves spending concentrated time with individual children who have a disability or are gifted. Among the children a teacher of exceptional children might work with include children with learning disabilities, ADHD, mental retardation, or a physical disability such as cerebral palsy. Some of this work will usually be done outside of the student's regular classroom; some of it will be carried out when the student is in the regular classroom. The exceptional children teacher works closely with the student's regular classroom teacher and parents to create the best educational program for the student. Teachers of exceptional children often continue their education after obtaining their undergraduate degree and attain a master's degree.

Early Childhood Educator

Early childhood educators work on college faculties and have a minimum of a master's degree in their field. In graduate school, they take courses in early childhood education and receive supervisory training in day care or early childhood programs. Early childhood educators usually teach in community colleges that award an associate degree in early childhood education.

Preschool/Kindergarten Teacher

Preschool teachers teach mainly 4-year-old children, and kindergarten teachers primarily teach 5-year-old children. They usually have an undergraduate degree in education, specializing in early childhood education. State certification to become a preschool or kindergarten teacher usually is required. These teachers direct the educational activities of young children.

Family and Consumer Science Educator

Family and consumer science educators may specialize in early childhood education or instruct middle and high school students about such matters as nutrition, interpersonal relationships, human sexuality, parenting, and human development. Hundreds of colleges and universities throughout the United States offer two- and four-year degree programs in family and consumer science. These programs usually include an internship requirement. Additional education courses may be needed to obtain a teaching certificate. Some family and consumer educators go on to graduate school for further training, which provides a background for possible jobs in college teaching or research.

Educational Psychologist

An educational psychologist most often teaches in a college or university and conducts research in such areas of educational psychology as learning, motivation, classroom management, and assessment. Most educational psychologists have a doctorate in education, which takes four to six years of graduate work. They help train students who will take various positions in education, including educational psychology, school psychology, and teaching.

School Psychologist

School psychologists focus on improving the psychological and intellectual well-being of elementary, middle/junior, and high school students. They usually have a master's or doctoral degree in school psychology. In graduate school, they take courses in counseling, assessment, learning, and other areas of education and psychology. School psychologists may work in a centralized office in a school district or in one or more schools. They give psychological tests, interview students and their parents, consult with teachers, and may provide counseling to students and their families.

Gerontologist

Gerontologists usually work in research in some branch of the federal or state government. They specialize in the study of aging with a particular focus on government programs for older adults, social policy, and delivery of services to older adults. In their research, gerontologists define problems to be studied, collect data, interpret the results, and make recommendations for social policy. Most gerontologists have a master's or doctoral degree and have taken a concentration of coursework in adult development and aging.

CLINICAL/COUNSELING

There are a wide variety of clinical and counseling jobs that are linked with life-span development. These range from child clinical psychologist to adolescent drug counselor to geriatric psychiatrist.

Clinical Psychologist

Clinical psychologists seek to help people with psychological problems. They work in a variety of settings, including colleges and universities, clinics, medical schools, and private practice. Clinical psychologists have either a Ph.D. (which involves clinical and research training) or a Psy.D. degree (which only involves clinical training). This graduate training usually takes five to seven years and includes courses in clinical psychology and a one-year supervised internship in an accredited setting toward the end of the training. In most cases, they must pass a test to become licensed in a state and to call themselves a clinical psychologist. Some clinical psychologists only conduct psychotherapy, others do psychological assessment and psychotherapy, and some also do research.

In regard to life-span development, clinical psychologists might specialize in a particular age group, such as children (child clinical psychologist) or older adults (often referred to as a geropsychologist). Many geropsychologists pursue a year or two of postdoctoral training.

Psychiatrist

Psychiatrists obtain a medical degree and then do a residency in psychiatry. Medical school takes approximately four years, and the psychiatry residency another three to four years. Unlike psychologists (who do not go to medical school), psychiatrists can administer drugs to clients.

Like clinical psychologists, psychiatrists might specialize in working with children (child psychiatry) or with older adults (geriatric psychiatry). Psychiatrists might work in medical schools in teaching and research roles, in a medical clinic, or in private practice. In addition to administering drugs to help improve the lives of people with psychological problems, psychiatrists also may conduct psychotherapy.

Counseling Psychologist

Counseling psychologists go through much of the same training as clinical psychologists, although in a graduate program in counseling rather than clinical psychology. Counseling psychologists have either a master's degree or a doctoral degree. They also must go through a licensing procedure. One type of master's degree in counseling leads to the designation of licensed professional counselor. They work in the same settings as clinical psychologists, and may do psychotherapy, teach, or conduct research. Many counseling psychologists do not do therapy with individuals who have more severe mental disorders, such as schizophrenia.

School Counselor

School counselors help identify students' abilities and interests, guide students in developing academic plans, and explore career options with students. They may help students cope with adjustment problems. They may work with students individually, in small groups, or even in a classroom. They often consult with parents, teachers, and school administrators when trying to help students with their problems. School counselors usually have a master's degree in counseling.

High school counselors advise students on choosing a major, admissions requirements for college, taking entrance exams, applying for financial aid, and appropriate vocational and technical training. Elementary school counselors are mainly involved in counseling students about social and personal problems. They may observe children in the classroom and at play as part of their work.

Career Counselor

Career counselors help individuals to identify what the best career options are for them and guide them in applying for jobs. They may work in private industry or at a college or university. They usually interview individuals and give them vocational and/or psychological tests to help provide students with information about appropriate careers that fit their interests and abilities. Sometimes they help individuals to create professional resumes or conduct mock interviews to help them feel comfortable in a job interview. They might create and promote job fairs or other recruiting events to help individuals obtain jobs.

Social Worker

Many social workers are involved in helping people with social or economic problems. They may investigate, evaluate, and attempt to rectify reported cases of abuse, neglect, endangerment, or domestic disputes. They can intervene in families if necessary and provide counseling and referral services to individuals and families. They have a minimum of an undergraduate degree from a school of social work that includes course work in various areas of sociology and psychology. Some social workers also have a master's or doctoral degree. They often work for publicly funded agencies at the city, state, or national level, although increasingly they work in the private sector in areas such as drug rehabilitation and family counseling.

In some cases, social workers specialize in a certain area, as is true of a medical social worker, who has a master's degree in social work (M.S.W.). This involves graduate coursework and supervised clinical experiences in medical settings. A medical social worker might coordinate a variety of support services to people with a severe or long-term disability. Family-care social workers often work with families with children or an older adult who needs support services.

Drug Counselor

Drug counselors provide counseling to individuals with drug-abuse problems. They may work on an individual basis with a substance abuser or conduct group therapy sessions. At a minimum, drug counselors go through an associate's or certificate program. Many have an undergraduate degree in substance-abuse counseling, and some have master's and doctoral degrees. They may work in private practice, with a state or federal government agency, with a company, or in a hospital setting. Some drug counselors specialize in working with adolescents or older adults. Most states provide a certification procedure for obtaining a license to practice drug counseling.

Rehabilitation Counselor

Rehabilitation counselors work directly with individuals who have a physical disability that may have developed because of a disease or an injury. They try to help them function as competently as possible. In their efforts, they consult with other professionals and coordinate services.

Becoming a rehabilitation counselor requires a master's or Ph.D. degree in rehabilitation counseling. This includes graduate coursework, clinical training, training in physical therapy, and possibly research training.

MEDICAL/NURSING/PHYSICAL

This third main area of careers in life-span development includes a wide range of careers in the medical and nursing areas, as well as jobs pertaining to improving some aspect of the person's physical development.

Obstetrician/Gynecologist

An obstetrician/gynecologist prescribes prenatal and postnatal care and performs deliveries in maternity cases. The individual also treats diseases and injuries of the female reproductive system. Becoming an obstetrician/gynecologist requires a medical degree plus three to five years of residency in obstetrics/gynecology. Obstetricians may work in private practice, in a medical clinic, a hospital, or in a medical school.

Pediatrician

A pediatrician monitors infants' and children's health, works to prevent disease or injury, helps children attain optimal health, and treats children with health problems. Pediatricians have attained a medical degree and then do a three- to five-year residency in pediatrics.

Pediatricians may work in private practice, in a medical clinic, in a hospital, or in a medical school. As a medical doctor, they can administer drugs to children and may counsel parents and children on ways to improve the children's health. Many pediatricians on the faculty of medical schools also teach and conduct research on children's health and diseases.

Geriatric Physician

A geriatric physician has a medical degree and has specialized in geriatric medicine by doing a three- to five-year residency. Geriatric physicians diagnose medical problems of older adults, evaluate treatment options, and make recommendations for nursing care or other arrangements. As with other doctors, they may work in private practice, in a medical clinic, in a hospital, or in a medical school. They also may primarily treat the diseases and health problems of older adults, but geriatric physicians in medical school settings also may teach future physicians and conduct research.

Neonatal Nurse

A neonatal nurse is involved in the delivery of care to the newborn infant. The neonatal nurse may work to improve the health and well-being of infants born under normal circumstances or be involved in the delivery of care to premature and critically ill neonates. A minimum of an undergraduate degree in nursing with a specialization in the newborn is required. This training involves coursework in nursing and the biological sciences, as well as supervisory clinical experiences.

Nurse-Midwife

A nurse-midwife formulates and provides comprehensive care to selected maternity patients, cares for the expectant mother as she prepares to give birth and guides her through the birth process, and cares for the postpartum patient. The nurse-midwife also may provide care to the newborn, counsel parents on the infant's development and parenting, and provide guidance about health practices. Becoming a nurse-midwife generally requires an undergraduate degree from a school of nursing. A nurse-midwife most often works in a hospital setting.

Pediatric Nurse

Pediatric nurses have a degree in nursing that takes two to five years to complete. Some also may go on to obtain a master's or doctoral degree in pediatric nursing. Pediatric nurses take courses in biological sciences, nursing care, and pediatrics, usually in a school of nursing. They also undergo supervised clinical experiences in medical settings. They monitor infants' and children's health, work to prevent disease or injury, and help children attain optimal health. They may work in hospitals, schools of nursing, or with pediatricians in private practice or at a medical clinic.

Geriatric Nurse

Geriatric nurses seek to prevent or intervene in the chronic or acute health problems of older adults. They take courses in a school of nursing and obtain a degree in nursing. This takes anywhere from two to five years. As in the case of a pediatric nurse, a geriatric nurse also may obtain a master's or doctoral degree in his or her speciality. Geriatric nurses take courses in biological sciences, nursing care, and mental health. They also experience supervised clinical training in geriatric settings. They may work in hospitals, nursing homes, schools of nursing, or with geriatric medical specialists or psychiatrists in a medical clinic or in private practice.

Physical Therapist

Physical therapists usually have an undergraduate degree in physical therapy and are licensed by a state. They take courses and experience supervised training in physical therapy. Many physical therapists work with people of all ages, although some specialize in working with a specific age group, such as children or older adults. They work directly with these individuals who have a physical problem either due to disease or injury to help them function as competently as possible. They may consult with other professionals and coordinate services for the individual.

Occupational Therapist

Occupational therapists may have an associate, bachelor's, master's, and/or doctoral degree with education ranging from two to six years. Training includes occupational therapy courses in a specialized program. National certification is required and licensing/registration is required in some states. Occupational therapy is a health and rehabilitation profession that helps people regain, develop, and build skills that are important for independent functioning, health, well-being, security and happiness. The occupational therapist initiates the evaluation of clients and manages the treatment process for clients with various impairments.

Therapeutic/Recreation Therapist

Therapeutic/recreation therapists maintain or improve the quality of life for people with special needs through intervention, leisure education, and recreation participation. They work in hospitals, rehabilitation centers, local government agencies, at-risk youth programs, as well as other settings. Becoming a therapeutic/recreation therapist requires an undergraduate degree with coursework in leisure studies and a concentration in therapeutic recreation. National certification is usually required. Coursework in anatomy, special education, and psychology are beneficial.

Audiologist

An audiologist has a minimum of an undergraduate degree in hearing science. This includes courses and supervisory training. Audiologists assess and identify the presence and severity of hearing loss, as well as problems in balance. Some audiologists also go on to obtain a master's or doctoral degree. They may work in a medical clinic, with a physician in private practice, in a hospital, or in a medical school.

Speech Therapist

Speech therapists are health-care professionals who are trained to identify, assess, and treat speech and language problems. They may work with physicians, psychologists, social workers, and other health-care professionals in a team approach to help individuals with physical or psychological problems in which speech and language are involved in the problem. Speech pathologists have a minimum of an undergraduate degree in speech and hearing science or communications disorders area. They may work in private practice, in hospitals and medical schools, and in government agencies with individuals of any age. Some may specialize in working with children, others with the elderly, or in a particular type of speech disorder.

Genetic Counselor

Genetic counselors are health professionals with specialized graduate degrees and experience in the areas of medical genetics and counseling. Most enter the field after majoring in undergraduate school in such disciplines as biology, genetics, psychology, nursing, public health, and social work.

Genetic counselors work as members of a health-care team, providing information and support to families who have members with birth defects or genetic disorders and to families who may be at risk for a variety of inherited conditions. They identify families at risk and provide supportive counseling. They serve as educators and resource people for other health-care professionals and the public. Almost half work in university medical centers, and another one-fourth work in private hospital settings.

FAMILIES/RELATIONSHIPS

A number of careers and jobs are available for working with families and relationship problems across the life span. These range from being a home health aide to working as a marriage and family therapist.

Home Health Aide

No education is required for this position. There is brief training by an agency. A home health aide provides direct services to older adults in the older adults' homes, providing assistance in basic self-care tasks.

Child Welfare Worker

A child welfare worker is employed by the Child Protective Services unit of each state. The child welfare worker protects the child's rights, evaluates any maltreatment of the child, and may have the child removed from the home if necessary. A child social worker has a minimum of an undergraduate degree in social work.

Child Life Specialist

Child life specialists work with children and their families when the child needs to be hospitalized. They monitor the child's activities, seek to reduce the child's stress, help the child cope effectively, and assist the child in enjoying the hospital experience as much as possible. Child life specialists may provide parent education and develop individualized treatment plans based on an assessment of the child's development, temperament, medical plan, and available social supports. Child life specialists have an undergraduate degree, and they take courses in child development and education, as well as usually taking additional courses in a child life program.

Marriage and Family Therapist

Marriage and family therapists work on the principle that many individuals who have psychological problems benefit when psychotherapy is provided in the context of a marital or family relationship. Marriage and family therapists may provide marital therapy, couple therapy to individuals in a relationship who are not married, and family therapy to two or more members of a family.

Marriage and family therapists have a master's or doctoral degree. They go through a training program in graduate school similar to a clinical psychologist but with the focus on marital and family relationships. In most states, it is necessary to go through a licensing procedure to practice marital and family therapy.

WEBSITE CONNECTIONS FOR CAREERS IN LIFE-SPAN DEVELOPMENT

By going to the website for this book (**www.mhhe.com/santrockldt2**), you can obtain more detailed career information about the various careers in life-span development described in this appendix. Go to the Web connections in the Careers Appendix section, where you will read about a description of the websites. Then click on the title and you will be able to go directly to the website described. Here are the website labels:

Education/Research

Careers in Psychology
Elementary and Secondary School Teaching
Exceptional Children Teachers
Early Childhood Education
Family and Consumer Science Education
Educational Psychology
School Psychology

Clinical Counseling

Clinical Psychology
Psychiatry
Counseling Psychology
School Counseling
Social Work
Drug Counseling
Gerontology

Medical/Nursing/Physical Development

Obstetrics and Gynecology
Pediatrics
Nurse-Midwife
Neonatal Nursing
Pediatric Nursing
Gerontological Nursing
Physical Therapy
Occupational Therapy
Therapeutic/Recreation Therapy
Audiology and Speech Pathology
Genetic Counseling

Families/Relationships

Child Welfare Worker
Child Life Specialist
Marriage and Family Therapist

Glossary

A

AB̄error The Piagetian object-permanence concept in which an infant progressing into substage 4 makes frequent mistakes, selecting the familiar hiding place (A) rather than the new hiding place (B̄).   207

acceptance Kübler-Ross' fifth stage of dying, in which the dying person develops a sense of peace, an acceptance of her or his fate, and, in many cases, a desire to be left alone.   612

accommodation Piagetian concept of adjusting schemes to fit new information and experiences.   200

accommodation of the eye The eye's ability to focus and maintain an image on the retina.   185

active euthanasia Death induced deliberately, as by injecting a lethal dose of a drug.   603

active (niche-picking) genotype-environment correlations Correlations that exist when children seek out environments they find compatible and stimulating.   63

activity theory The theory that the more active and involved older adults are, the more likely they are to be satisfied with their lives.   539

addiction A pattern of behavior characterized by an overwhelming involvement with using a drug and securing its supply.   155

adolescent egocentrism The heightened self-consciousness of adolescents, which is reflected in adolescents' beliefs that others are as interested in them as they are in themselves, and in adolescents' sense of personal uniqueness and invincibility.   214

adoption study A study in which investigators seek to discover whether, in behavior and psychological characteristics, adopted children are more like their adoptive parents, who provided a home environment, or more like their biological parents, who contributed their heredity. Another form of the adoption study is to compare adoptive and biological siblings.   62

aerobic exercise Sustained activity that stimulates heart and lung functioning.   152

affectionate love Also called companionate love, this type of love occurs when individuals desire to have another person near and have a deep, caring affection for the person.   359

affordances Opportunities for interaction offered by objects that are necessary to perform activities.   178

ageism Prejudice against other people because of their age, especially prejudice against older adults.   539

AIDS A sexually transmitted infection caused by the human immunodeficiency virus (HIV), which destroys the body's immune system.   423

altruism An unselfish interest in helping another person.   458

Alzheimer's disease A progressive, irreversible brain disorder characterized by a gradual deterioration of memory, reasoning, language, and, eventually, physical function.   139

androgens A main class of sex hormones, an important one of which is testosterone, that promote the development of male genitals and secondary sex characteristics.   97

androgens The main class of male sex hormones.   402

androgyny The presence of a high degree of feminine and masculine characteristics in the same individual.   411

anger Kübler-Ross' second stage of dying, in which the dying person's denial gives way to anger, resentment, rage, and envy.   612

anger cry A cry similar to the basic cry but with more excess air forced through the vocal cords (associated with exasperation or rage).   336

animism A facet of preoperational thought—the belief that inanimate objects have "lifelike" qualities and are capable of action.   208

anorexia nervosa An eating disorder that involves the relentless pursuit of thinness through starvation.   147

Apgar Scale A widely used method to assess the health of newborns at 1 and 5 minutes after birth. The Apgar Scale evaluates infants' heart rate, respiratory effort, muscle tone, body color, and reflex irritability.   86

aphasia A language disorder resulting from brain damage that involves a loss of the ability to use words.   319

assimilation Piagetian concept of the incorporation of new information into existing schemes.   200

associative play Play that involves social interaction with little or no organization.   535

attachment A close emotional bond between two people.   348

attention Concentrating and focusing mental resources.   237

attention deficit hyperactivity disorder (ADHD) A disability in which children consistently show one or more of the following characteristics: (1) inattention, (2) hyperactivity, and (3) impulsivity.   574

attribution theory The theory that, in their effort to make sense out of their own behavior or performance, individuals are motivated to discover its underlying causes. Attributions are perceived causes of outcomes.   581

authoritarian parenting A restrictive, punitive style in which parents exhort the child to follow their directions and to respect their work and effort. Firm limits are placed on the child and little verbal exchange is allowed.   498

authoritative parenting A style that encourages children to be independent but still places limits and controls on children's actions; extensive verbal give-and-take is allowed and parents are warm and nurturant toward the child.   498

automaticity The ability to process information with little or no effort.   234

autonomous morality The second stage of moral development in Piaget's theory, displayed by older children (about 10 years of age and older). The child becomes aware that rules and laws are created by people and that, in judging an action, one should consider the actor's intentions as well as the consequences.   443

average children Children who receive an average number of both positive and negative nominations from their peers.   525

B

bargaining Kübler-Ross' third stage of dying, in which the dying person develops the hope that death can somehow be postponed.   612

basal metabolism rate (BMR) The minimal amount of energy a person uses in a resting state.   145

basic cry A rhythmic pattern usually consisting of a cry, a briefer silence, a shorter inspiratory whistle that is higher pitched than the main cry, and then a brief rest before the next cry.   336

basic-skills-and-phonetics approach An approach that emphasizes that reading instruction should teach phonetics and its basic rules for translating written symbols into sounds.   315

Bayley Scales of Infant Development Developed by Nancy Bayley, these scales are widely used in assessing infant development. The current version has three parts: a Mental Scale, a Motor Scale, and the Infant Behavior Profile.   287

becoming parents and a family with children The third stage in the family life cycle in which adults move up a generation and become caregivers for the younger generation.   483

behavior genetics The field that seeks to discover the influence of heredity and environment on individual differences in human traits and development.   62

behavioral and social cognitive theories Theories that hold that development can be best described in terms of the behaviors learned through interactions with the environment.   24

big five factors of personality The view that personality is made up of openness to experience, conscientiousness, extraversion, agreeableness, and neuroticism (emotional stability).   388

biological age A person's age in terms of biological health.   15

bio-psycho-social health model The approach in which health is viewed in terms of a combination of biological, psychological, and social factors.   132

bisexual Being sexually attracted to people of both sexes.   421

bonding The formation of a connection, especially a physical bond, between parents and the newborn in the period shortly after birth.   87

brain death A neurological definition of death. A person is brain dead when all electrical activity of the brain has ceased for a specified period of time. A flat EEG recording is one criterion of brain death.   602

Brazelton Neonatal Behavioral Assessment Scale A test given shortly after birth to assess newborns' neurological development, reflexes, and reactions to people.   86

Broca's area An area of the brain's left frontal lobe that directs the muscle movements involved in speech production.   319

bulimia nervosa An eating disorder in which the individual consistently follows a binge-purge eating pattern.   148

C

canalization The process by which characteristics are restricted to a narrow developmental course, apparently protecting a person from environmental extremes.   58

care perspective The moral perspective of Carol Gilligan; views people in terms of their connectedness with others and emphasizes interpersonal communication, relationships with others, and concern for others.   449

case study An in-depth examination of an individual.   34

cataracts A thickening of the lens of the eye that causes vision to become cloudy, opaque, and distorted.   186

cellular clock theory Leonard Hayflick's theory that the maximum number of times that human cells can divide is about 75 to 80. As we age, our cells have less capability to divide.   124

centration The focusing of attention on one characteristic to the exclusion of all others.   209

cephalocaudal pattern The sequence in which the fastest growth occurs at the top—the head—with physical growth in size, weight, and feature differentiation gradually working from top to bottom.   94

character education A direct moral education approach that involves teaching students a basic moral literacy to prevent them from engaging in immoral behavior or doing harm to themselves or others.   456

child-centered kindergarten Education that involves the whole child by considering both the child's physical, cognitive, and social development and the child's needs, interests, and learning styles.   563

child-directed speech Language spoken in a higher pitch than normal with simple words and sentences.   321

chromosomes Threadlike structures that contain the genetic substance DNA.   53

chronic disorders Disorders characterized by slow onset and long duration.   138

chronological age The number of years that have elapsed since a person's birth; what is usually meant by "age."   15

climacteric The midlife transition in which fertility declines.   103, 433

cliques Small groups that range from 2 to 12 individuals and average about 5 to 6 individuals.   528

cognitive constructivist approach An approach that emphasizes the child's active, cognitive construction of knowledge and understanding; Piaget's theory is an example of this approach.   560

cognitive developmental theory of gender The theory that children's gender typing occurs *after* they think of themselves as boys and girls. Once they consistently conceive of themselves as male or female, children prefer activities, objects, and attitudes that are consistent with this label.   405

cognitive moral education Education based on the belief that students should learn to value things like democracy and justice as their moral reasoning develops; Kohlberg's theory has been the basis for many of the cognitive moral education approaches.   456

cohort effects Effects that are due to a subject's time of birth or generation but not age.   38

collectivism Emphasizing values that serve the group by subordinating personal goals to preserve group integrity, interdependence of members, and harmonious relationships.   543

commitment The part of identity development in which adolescents show a personal investment in what they are going to do.   384

concrete operational stage Piaget's third stage, which lasts from approximately 7 to 11 years of age; children can perform concrete operations, and logical reasoning replaces intuitive reasoning as long as the reasoning can be applied to specific, concrete examples.   211

conduct disorder Age-inappropriate actions and attitudes that violate family expectations, society's norms, and the personal or property rights of others.   460

connectedness It consists of two dimensions: mutuality, sensitivity to and respect for others' views; and permeability, openness to others' views.   386

conscience The component of the superego that punishes the child for behaviors disapproved of by parents by making the child feel guilty and worthless.   451

conservation The idea that an amount stays the same regardless of how its container changes.   209

contemporary life-events approach Emphasizes that how a life event influences the individual's development depends not only on the event but also on mediating factors, the individual's adaptation to the life event, the life-stage context, and the sociohistorical context.   391

continuity-discontinuity issue The debate about the extent to which development involves gradual, cumulative change (continuity) or distinct stages (discontinuity).   17

controversial children Children who are frequently nominated both as someone's best friend and as being disliked.   525

conventional reasoning The second, or intermediate, level in Kohlberg's theory of moral development. At this level, individuals abide by certain standards but they are the standards of others such as parents or the laws of society.   444

convergent thinking Thinking that produces one correct answer; characteristic of the kind of thinking required on conventional intelligence tests.   294

cooperative play Play that involves social interaction in a group with a sense of group identity and organized activity.   535

correlation coefficient A number based on statistical analysis that is used to describe the degree of association between two variables.   36

correlational research The goal is to describe the strength of the relation between two or more events or characteristics.   35

creativity The ability to think in novel and unusual ways and come up with unique solutions to problems.   293

crisis A period of identity development during which the adolescent is choosing among meaningful alternatives.   384

critical thinking Thinking reflectively and productively, and evaluating the evidence.   252

cross-cultural studies Comparisons of one culture with one or more other cultures. These provide information about the degree to which children's development is similar, or universal, across cultures, and the degree to which it is culture-specific.   28

cross-sectional approach A research strategy in which individuals of different ages are compared at one time.   37

crowds Peer groups that are larger and less personal than cliques.   528

crystallized intelligence Accumulated information and verbal skills, which increase with age, according to Horn.   289

culture The behavior patterns, beliefs, and all other products of a group of people that are passed on from generation to generation.   542

culture-fair tests Intelligence tests that are intended to not be culturally biased.   285

dating scripts Cognitive models that guide individuals' dating interactions.   357

dementia A global term for any neurological disorder in which the primary symptoms involve a deterioration of mental functioning.   138

denial and isolation Kübler-Ross' first stage of dying, in which the dying person denies that she or he is really going to die.   612

depression Kübler-Ross' fourth stage of dying, in which the dying person comes to accept the certainty of her or his death. A period of depression or preparatory grief may appear.   612

descriptive research This type of research aims to observe and record behavior.   35

development The pattern of change that begins at conception and continues through the life span.   6

developmental quotient (DQ) An overall developmental score that combines subscores on motor, language, adaptive, and personal-social domains in the Gesell assessment of infants.   287

developmentally appropriate practice Education that focuses on the typical developmental patterns of children (age appropriateness) and the uniqueness of each child (individual appropriateness). Such practice contrasts with developmentally inappropriate practice, which ignores the concrete, hands-on approach to learning. Direct teaching largely through abstract paper-and-pencil activities presented to large groups of young children is believed to be developmentally inappropriate.   563

dialect A variety of language that is distinguished by its vocabulary, grammar, or pronunciation.   317

difficult child A temperament style in which the child tends to react negatively and cry frequently, engages in irregular daily routines, and is slow to accept new experiences.   344

direct instruction approach A teacher-centered approach characterized by teacher direction and control, mastery of academic material, high expectations for students' progress, and maximum time spent on learning tasks.   560

disease model of addiction The view that addictions are biologically based, lifelong diseases that involve a loss of control over behavior and require medical and/or spiritual treatment for recovery.   155

disengagement theory The theory that, to cope effectively, older adults should gradually withdraw from society.   538

dishabituation The recovery of a habituated response after a change in stimulation.   180

dismissing/avoidant attachment An insecure attachment style in which adolescents deemphasize the importance of attachment; is associated with consistent experiences of rejection of attachment needs by caregivers.   355

divergent thinking Thinking that produces many answers to the same question; characteristic of creativity.   294

divided attention Concentrating on more than one activity at a time.   237

DNA A complex molecule that contains genetic information.   53

Down syndrome A chromosomally transmitted form of mental retardation, caused by the presence of an extra (47th) chromosome.   58

dynamic systems theory A theory, proposed by Esther Thelen, that seeks to explain how motor behaviors are assembled for perceiving and acting.   166

dyslexia A category of learning disabilities involving a severe impairment in the ability to read and spell.   574

easy child A temperament style in which the child is generally in a positive mood, quickly establishes regular routines, and adapts easily to new experiences.   344

eclectic orientation An approach that selects and uses whatever is considered the best in many theories.   31

ecological theory Bronfenbrenner's view that development is influenced by five environmental systems—microsystem, mesosystem, exosystem, macrosystem, and chronosystem. These emphasize the role of social contexts in human development.   27

ecological view The view, proposed by the Gibsons, that people directly perceive information in the world around them. Perception brings people in contact with the environment in order to interact with it and adapt to it.   178

ego ideal The component of the superego rewards the child by conveying a sense of pride and personal value when the child acts according to ideal standards approved by the parents.   451

egocentrism An important feature of preoperational thought—the inability to distinguish between one's own and someone else's perspective.   208

elaboration Engaging in more extensive processing of information, which benefits memory.   245

embryonic period The period of prenatal development that occurs two to eight weeks after conception. During the embryonic period, the rate of cell differentiation intensifies, support systems for the cells form, and organs appear.   66

emotion Feeling that involves a mixture of physical arousal and expressive behavior.   332

emotional intelligence The ability to perceive and express emotions accurately and adaptively, to understand emotion and emotional knowledge, to use feelings to facilitate thought, and to manage emotions in oneself and others.   278

empathy Reacting to another's feelings with an emotional response that is similar to the other's feelings.   452

encoding The mechanism by which information gets into memory.   234

epigenetic view Emphasizes that development is the result of an ongoing, bi-directional interchange between heredity and environment.   64

episodic memory Retention of information about the where and when of life's happenings.   246

equilibration A mechanism that Piaget proposed to explain how children shift from one stage of thought to the next. The shift occurs as children experience cognitive conflict, or disequilibrium, in trying to understand the world. Eventually, they resolve the conflict and reach a balance, or equilibrium, of thought.   201

Erikson's theory A psychoanalytic theory in which eight stages of psychosocial development unfold throughout the human life span. Each stage consists of a unique developmental task that confronts individuals with a crisis that must be faced.   20

estrogens A main class of sex hormones, an important one of which is estradiol, that influence the development of female sexual characteristics and help regulate the menstrual cycle.   97

estrogens The main class of female sex hormones.   402

ethnicity A range of characteristics rooted in cultural heritage, including nationality, race, religion, and language.   28

ethnocentrism The tendency to favor one's own group over other groups.   542

ethological theory of development An approach that stresses that behavior is strongly influenced by biology, tied to evolution, and characterized by critical or sensitive periods.   25

euthanasia The act of painlessly ending the lives of persons who are suffering from incurable diseases or severe disabilities; sometimes called "mercy killing."   603

evocative genotype-environment correlations Correlations that exist when the child's genotype elicits certain types of physical and social environments.   63

evolutionary psychology Emphasizes the importance of adaptation, reproduction, and "survival of the fittest" in shaping behavior.   51

expanding Restating, in a linguistically sophisticated form, what a child has said.   321

experiment A carefully regulated procedure in which one or more of the factors believed to influence the behavior being studied is manipulated and all other factors are held constant. Experimental research permits the determination of cause.   36

expertise Having extensive, highly organized knowledge and understanding of a particular domain.   259

explicit memory Conscious memory of facts and experiences.   242

extrinsic motivation Response to external incentives such as rewards and punishments.   579

factor analysis A statistical procedure that correlates test scores to identify underlying clusters, or factors.   274

family at midlife The fifth stage in the family life cycle, a time for launching children, linking generations, and adapting to midlife changes.   483

family in later life The sixth and final stage in the family life cycle, involving adaptation to retirement and grantparenting.   483

family with adolescents The fourth stage in the family life cycle in which adolescents push for autonomy and an identity.   483

feminization of poverty The fact that far more women than men live in poverty. Women's low income, divorce, and the resolution of divorce cases by the judicial system, which usually leaves women with less money than they and their children need to adequately function, are the likely causes.   546

fetal alcohol syndrome (FAS) A cluster of abnormalities that appears in the offspring of mothers who drink alcohol heavily during pregnancy.   72

fetal period The prenatal period of development that begins two months after conception and lasts for seven months, on the average.   67

fine motor skills Motor skills that involve finely tuned movements, such as any activity that requires finger dexterity.   174

fluid intelligence The ability to reason abstractly, which steadily declines from middle adulthood on, according to Horn.   289

formal operational stage Piaget's fourth and final stage, which occurs between the ages of 11 and 15; individuals move beyond concrete experiences and think in more abstract and logical ways.   213

fragile X syndrome A genetic disorder involving an abnormality in the X chromosome, which becomes constricted and often breaks.   59

free-radical theory A microbiological theory of aging that states that people age when their cells metabolize energy, they generate waste that includes unstable oxygen molecules known as free radicals that damage DNA and other cellular structures.   124

games Activities that are engaged in for pleasure and include rules.   536

gender The psychological and sociocultural dimensions of being female or male.   29, 402

gender-intensification hypothesis The view that psychological and behavioral differences between boys and girls become greater during early adolescence because of increased socialization pressures to conform to traditional gender roles.   413

gender role A set of expectations that prescribe how females or males should think, act, or feel.   402

gender–role transcendence The view that people should be evaluated as persons, not in terms of femininity, masculinity, or androgyny.   412

gender schema theory The theory that gender typing emerges as children gradually develop gender schemas of what is gender-appropriate and gender-inappropriate in their culture.   405

gender stereotypes Broad categories that reflect our impressions and beliefs about females and males.   407

gender typing The process by which children acquire the thoughts, feelings, and behaviors that are considered appropriate for their gender in their culture.   402

generativity versus stagnation The seventh stage in Erikson's life-span theory that encompasses adults' desire to leave a legacy of themselves to the next generation.   392

genes Units of hereditary information composed of DNA. Genes direct cells to reproduce themselves and manufacture the proteins that maintain life.   53

genotype A person's genetic heritage; the actual genetic material.   55

germinal period The period of prenatal development that takes place in the first two weeks after conception. It includes the creation of the zygote, continued cell division, and the attachment of the zygote to the uterine wall.   66

gifted Having high intelligence (an IQ of 130 or higher) or superior talent for something.   292

glaucoma Damage to the optic nerve because of the pressure created by a buildup of fluid in the eye.   186

goodness of fit The match between a child's temperament and the environmental demands the child must cope with.   346

grasping reflex A neonatal reflex that occurs when something touches the infant's palms. The infant responds by grasping tightly.   168

grief The emotional numbness, disbelief, separation anxiety, despair, sadness, and loneliness that accompany the loss of someone we love.   615

gross motor skills Motor skills that involve large-muscle activities, such as walking.   169

habituation Decreased responsiveness to a stimulus after repeated presentations of the stimulus.   180

helpless orientation An orientation in which one seems trapped by the experience of difficulty and attributes one's difficulty to a lack of ability.   581

heritability The fraction of the variance in a population that is attributed to genetics.   280

heteronomous morality (Kohlberg)
Kohlberg's first stage of preconventional reasoning, in which moral thinking is tied to punishment.   444

heteronomous morality (Piaget) The first stage of moral development in Piaget's theory, occurring at 4 to 7 years of age. Justice and rules are conceived of as unchangeable properties of the world, removed from the control of people.   442

hidden curriculum The pervasive moral atmosphere that characterizes schools.   455

horizontal décalage Piaget's concept that similar abilities do not appear at the same time within a stage of development.   211

hormonal stress theory The theory that aging in the body's hormonal system can lower resistance to stress and increase the likelihood of disease.   125

hormones Powerful chemical substances secreted by the endocrine glands and carried through the body by the bloodstream.   96

hospice A program committed to making the end of life as free from pain, anxiety, and depression as possible. The goals of hospice contrast with those of a hospital, which are to cure disease and prolong life.   604

hypotheses Assertions or predictions, often derived from theories, that can be tested.   18

hypothetical-deductive reasoning Piaget's formal operational concept that adolescents have the cognitive ability to develop hypotheses about ways to solve problems and can systematically deduce which is the best path to follow in solving the problem.   214

I

identity Who a person is, representing a synthesis of self-understanding.   368

identity achievement Marcia's term for adolescents who have undergone a crisis and have made a commitment.   384

identity diffusion Marcia's term for adolescents who have not yet experienced a crisis (explored meaningful alternatives) or made any commitments.   384

identity foreclosure Marcia's term for adolescents who have made a commitment but have not experienced a crisis.   384

identity moratorium Marcia's term for adolescents who are in the midst of a crisis, but their commitments are either absent or vaguely defined.   384

identity versus identity confusion Erikson's fifth stage of development, which occurs during the adolescent years; adolescents are faced with finding out who they are, what they are all about, and where they are going in life.   382

imaginary audience The aspect of adolescent egocentrism that involves attention-getting behavior motivated by a desire to be noticed, visible, and "on stage."   214

immanent justice Piaget's concept that if a rule is broken, punishment will be meted out immediately.   443

implicit memory Memory without conscious recollection: memory of skills and routine procedures that are performed automatically.   242

inclusion Educating a child with special education needs full-time in the regular classroom.   575

individualism Giving priority to personal goals rather than to group goals; emphasizing values that serve the self, such as feeling good, personal distinction and achievement, and independence.   543

individualism, instrumental purpose, and exchange The second Kohlberg stage of moral development. At this stage, individuals pursue their own interests but also let others do the same.   444

individuality It consists of two dimensions: self-assertion, the ability to have and communicate a point of view; and separateness, the use of communication patterns to express how one is different from others.   386

individualized education plan (IEP) A written statement that spells out a program tailored to a child with a disability. The plan should be (1) related to the child's learning capacity, (2) specially constructed to meet the child's individual needs and not merely a copy of what is offered to other children, and (3) designed to provide educational benefits.   575

induction A discipline technique in which a parent uses reasoning and explains the consequences for others of the child's actions.   454

indulgent parenting A style in which parents are very involved with their children but place few demands or controls on them.   498

infinite generativity The ability to produce an endless number of meaningful sentences using a finite set of words and rules.   304

information-processing approach An approach that focuses on the ways children process information about their world—how they manipulate information, monitor it, and create strategies to deal with it.   23, 232

innate goodness Rousseau's view that children are born inherently good.   7

insecure avoidant babies Babies who show insecurity by avoiding the mother.   351

insecure disorganized babies Babies who show insecurity by being disorganized and disoriented.   351

insecure resistant babies Babies who might cling to the caregiver, then resist her by fighting against the closeness, perhaps by kicking or pushing away.   351

intelligence Thinking skills and the ability to adapt to and learn from life's everyday experiences.   270

intelligence quotient (IQ) An individual's mental age divided by chronological age multiplied by 100; devised in 1912 by William Stern.   271

intermodal perception The ability to integrate information about two or more sensory modalities, such as vision and hearing.   190

intimacy in friendship Self-disclosure and the sharing of private thoughts.   530

intrinsic motivation Internal motivational factors such as self-determination, curiosity, challenge, and effort.   579

intuitive thought substage The second substage of preoperational thought, occurring between approximately 4 and 7 years of age. Children begin to use primitive reasoning and want to know the answers to all sorts of questions.   209

J

justice perspective A moral perspective that focuses on the rights of the individual; individuals independently make moral decisions.   449

juvenile delinquency Refers to a great variety of behaviors, ranging from unacceptable behavior to status offenses to criminal acts.   460

K

Klinefelter syndrome A chromosomal disorder in which males have an extra X chromosome, making them XXY instead of XY.   59

kwashiorkor A condition caused by a deficiency in protein in which the child's face, legs, and abdomen swell with water.   144

L

labeling Identifying the names of objects.   321

laboratory A controlled setting.   32

language A form of communication, whether spoken, written, or signed, that is based on a system of symbols.   304

language acquisition device (LAD) Chomsky's term that describes a biological endowment that enables the child to detect the features and rules of language, including phonology, syntax, and semantics.   319

lateralization Specialization of function in one hemisphere of the cerebral cortex.   106

launching The process in which youth move into adulthood and exit their family of origin.   482

learning disability Includes three components: (1) a minimum IQ level; (2) a significant difficulty in a school-related area (especially reading or mathematics); and (3) exclusion of only severe emotional disorders, second-language background, sensory disabilities, and specific neurological deficits.   573

least restrictive environment (LRE) The concept that a child with a disability must be educated in a setting that is as similar as possible to the one in which children who do not have a disability are educated.   575

leaving home and becoming a single adult The first stage in the family life cycle that involves launching.   482

leisure The pleasant times after work when individuals are free to pursue activities and interests of their own choosing.   536

life expectancy The number of years that a person is expected to live on average when born in a particular year.   8

life-history records Information about events and activities over a lifetime.   35

life-process model of addiction The view that addiction is not a disease but a habitual response and a source of gratification and security that can be understood only in the context of social relationships and experiences.   155

life span The upper boundary of life, the maximum number of years an individual can live. The maximum life span of human beings is about 120 years of age.   119

longitudinal approach A research strategy in which the same individuals are studied over a period of time, usually several years or more.   38

long-term memory A relatively permanent and unlimited type of memory.   243

love withdrawal A discipline technique in which a parent withholds attention or love from the child.   454

low birth weight infant An infant who weighs less than 5½ pounds at birth.   82

macular degeneration A vision problem in the elderly that involves deterioration of the retina.   186

marasmus A wasting away of body tissues in the infant's first year, caused by insufficient caloric intake.   144

mastery orientation An orientation in which one is task-oriented and, instead of focusing on one's ability, is concerned with learning strategies.   581

meiosis A specialized form of cell division that occurs to form eggs and sperm (or gametes).   55

memory Retention of information over time.   239

menarche A girl's first menstrual period.   98

menopause The time in middle age, usually in the late forties or early fifties, when a woman's menstrual periods cease.   103, 433

mental age (MA) An individual's level of mental development relative to others.   271

mental retardation A condition of limited mental ability in which the individual (1) has a low IQ, usually below 70 on a traditional intelligence test, (2) has difficulty adapting to everyday life, and (3) has an onset of these characteristics by age 18.   291

metacognition Cognition about cognition, or "knowing about knowing."   234

metamemory Knowledge about memory.   261

metaphor An implied comparison between two unlike things.   317

mitochondrial theory The theory that aging is caused by the decay of mitochondria, tiny cellular bodies that supply energy for function, growth, and repair.   124

mitosis Cellular reproduction in which the cell's nucleus duplicates itself with two new cells being formed, each containing the same DNA as the parent cell, arranged in the same 23 pairs of chromosomes.   54

moral development Changes in thoughts, feelings, and behaviors regarding standards of right and wrong.   442

Moro reflex A neonatal startle response that occurs in reaction to a sudden, intense noise or movement. When startled, the newborn arches its back, throws its head back, and flings out its arms and legs. Then the newborn rapidly closes its arms and legs to the center of the body.   167

morphology Units of meaning involved in word formation.   305

multiple-factor theory L. L. Thurstone's theory that intelligence consists of seven primary mental abilities: verbal comprehension, number ability, word fluency, spatial visualization, associative memory, reasoning, and perceptual speed.   274

mutual interpersonal expectations, relationships, and interpersonal conformity Kohlberg's third stage of moral development. At this stage, individuals value trust, caring, and loyalty to others as a basis of moral judgments.   444

natural childbirth Developed in 1914 by Dick-Read, this method attempts to reduce the mother's pain by decreasing her fear through education about childbirth and relaxation techniques during delivery.   82

naturalistic observation Observation that occurs in a real-world setting without an attempt to manipulate the situation.   33

nature-nurture issue The debate about the extent to which development is influenced by nature and by nurture. Nature refers to an organism's biological inheritance, nurture to its environmental experiences.   16

neglected children Children who are infrequently nominated as a best friend but are not disliked by their peers.   525

neglectful parenting A style in which the parent is very uninvolved in the child's life.   498

neo-Piagetians Developmentalists who have elaborated on Piaget's theory, emphasizing the importance of information processing.   218

neuron Nerve cell that handles information processing.   105

new couple The second stage in the family life cycle that involves marriage, which is not just the union of two individuals but the union of two families.   482

nonnormative life events Unusual occurrences that have a major impact on a person's life. The occurrence, pattern, and sequence of these events are not applicable to many individuals.   11

nonshared environmental experiences The child's own experiences, both within the family and outside the family, that are not shared by another sibling. Thus, experiences occurring within the family can be part of the "nonshared environment."   63

normal distribution A symmetrical distribution with a majority of the cases falling in the middle of the possible range of scores and few scores appearing toward the extremes of the range.   272

normative age-graded influences Biological and environmental influences that are similar for individuals in a particular age group.   11

normative history-graded influences Biological and environmental influences that are associated with history. These influences are common to people of a particular generation.   11

object permanence The Piagetian term for one of an infant's most important accomplishments: understanding that objects and events continue to exist even when they cannot directly be seen, heard, or touched.   204

onlooker play Play in which the child watches other children play.   534

operations Internalized sets of actions that allow children to do mentally what before they had done physically. Operations also are reversible mental actions.   207

organization Piaget's concept of grouping isolated behaviors into a higher-order, more smoothly functioning cognitive system; the grouping or arranging of items into categories. 201

original sin Based on Christian doctrine, the view that children are born into the world corrupted with an inclination toward evil. 7

osteoporosis A disorder of aging that involves an extensive loss of bone tissue and is the main reason many older adults walk with a marked stoop. Women are especially vulnerable to osteoporosis. 138

P

pain cry A sudden appearance of loud crying without preliminary moaning and a long initial cry followed by an extended period of breath holding. 336

palliative care Emphasized in hospice care, involves reducing pain and suffering and helping individuals die with dignity. 604

parallel play Play in which the child plays separately from others, but with toys like those the others are using or in a manner that mimics their play. 535

parental imperative Gutmann's view that mothers and fathers adopt different gender roles so they can raise children more effectively. 416

passive euthanasia The withholding of available treatments, such as life-sustaining devices, allowing the person to die. 603

passive genotype-environment correlations Correlations that occur because the biological parents, who are genetically related to the child, provide a rearing environment for the child. 62

peers Individuals of about the same age or maturity level. 522

perception The interpretation of sensation. 178

performance orientation An orientation in which one focuses on achievement outcomes; winning is what matters most, and happiness is thought to result from winning. 581

personal fable The part of adolescent egocentrism that involves an adolescent's sense of uniqueness and invincibility. 215

personality The enduring personal characteristics of individuals. 368

personality type theory John Holland's view that it is important to match an individual's personality with a particular career. 585

perspective taking The ability to assume another person's perspective and understand his or her thoughts and feelings. 370

phenotype The way an individual's genotype is expressed in observed and measurable characteristics. 55

phenylketonuria (PKU) A genetic disorder in which an individual cannot properly metabolize an amino acid. PKU is now easily detected but, if left untreated, results in mental retardation and hyperactivity. 59

phonology Rules regarding how sounds are perceived as different and which sound sequences may occur in the language. 304

Piaget's theory The theory that children construct their understanding of the world and go through four stages of cognitive development. 22

play A pleasurable activity that is engaged in for its own sake. 534

play therapy Therapy that lets children work off frustrations while therapists analyze their conflicts and coping methods. 534

popular children Children who are frequently nominated as a best friend and are rarely disliked by their peers. 525

possible selves What individuals might become, what they would like to become, and what they are afraid of becoming. 371

postconventional reasoning The highest level in Kohlberg's theory of moral development. At this level, the individual recognizes alternative moral courses, explores the options, and then decides on a personal moral code. 445

postformal thought Thinking that is reflective, relative, and contextual; provisional; realistic; and open to emotions and subjective. 225

power assertion A discipline technique in which a parent attempts to gain control over the child or the child's resources. 454

practice play Play that involves repetition of behavior when new skills are being learned or when mastery and coordination of skills are required for games or sports. Sensorimotor play, which often involves practice play, is primarily confined to infancy, whereas practice play occurs throughout life. 536

pragmatics The appropriate use of language in context. 306

preconventional reasoning The lowest level in Kohlberg's theory of moral development. The individual's moral reasoning is controlled primarily by external rewards and punishment. 444

preoccupied/ambivalent attachment An insecure attachment style in which adolescents are hypertuned to attachment experiences. This is thought to occur mainly because parents are inconsistently available to the adolescent. 356

preoperational stage The second Piagetian developmental stage, which lasts from about 2 to 7 years of age; children begin to represent the world with words, images, and drawings. 207

prepared childbirth Developed by French obstetrician Ferdinand Lamaze, this childbirth strategy is similar to natural childbirth but includes a special breathing technique to control pushing in the final stages of labor and a more detailed anatomy and physiology course. 82

pretense/symbolic play Play that occurs when a child transforms the physical environment into a symbol. 536

preterm infant An infant born three weeks or more before the pregnancy has reached its full term. 82

primary emotions Emotions that are present in humans and animals, including surprise, joy, anger, sadness, fear, and disgust, that appear in the first six months of life. 336

Project Head Start Compensatory education designed to provide children from low-income families the opportunity to acquire the skills and experiences important for school success. 576

prospective memory Involves remembering to do something in the future. 249

proximodistal pattern The sequence in which growth starts at the center of the body and moves toward the extremities. 94

psychoanalytic theories Theories that hold that development depends primarily on the unconscious mind and is heavily couched in emotion, that behavior is merely a surface characteristic, that it is important to analyze the symbolic meanings of behavior, and that early experiences are important in development. 19

psychoanalytic theory of gender Stems from Freud's view that preschool children develop a sexual attraction to the opposite-sex parent, then, at 5 to 6 years of age, renounce the attraction because of anxious feelings, subsequently identifying with the same-sex parent and unconsciously adopting the same-sex parent's characteristics. 404

psychological age An individual's adaptive capacities compared with those of other individuals of the same chronological age. 15

psychosocial moratorium Erikson's term for the gap between childhood security and adult autonomy that adolescents experience as part of their identity exploration. 382

puberty A period of rapid physical maturation involving hormonal and bodily changes during early adolescence. 96

R

rapport talk The language of conversation; a way to establish connections and negotiate relationships; preferred by women. 414

reaction range The range of possible phenotypes for each genotype, suggesting the importance of an environment's restrictiveness or richness. 57

recasting Rephrasing a statement that a child has said, perhaps turning it into a question. 321

reciprocal socialization Socialization is bidirectional in that children socialize parents just as parents socialize children. 484

reciprocal teaching Individuals take turns leading small-group discussions. 253

reflexive smile A smile that does not occur in response to external stimuli. It happens during the month after birth, usually during sleep. 337

rejected children Children who are infrequently nominated as a best friend and are actively disliked by their peers. 525

report talk Language designed to give information, including public speaking; preferred by men. 414

reproduction The process that, in humans, begins when a female gamete (ovum) is fertilized by a male gamete (sperm). 55

restrained eaters Individuals who chronically restrict their food intake to control their weight. Restrained eaters are often on diets, are very conscious of what they eat, and tend to feel guilty after splurging on sweets. 149

rites of passage Ceremonies or rituals that mark an individual's transition from one status to another, especially into adulthood. 543

romantic love Also called passionate love or eros, this type of love has strong components of sexuality and infatuation, and it often predominates in the early part of a love relationship. 359

romantic script Sex is synonomous with love: If we develop a relationship with someone and fall in love, it is acceptable to have sex with the person whether we are married or not. 419

rooting reflex A newborn's built-in reaction that occurs when the infant's cheek is stroked or the side of the mouth is touched. In response, the infant turns its head toward the side that was touched, in an apparent effort to find something to suck. 167

S

satire The use of irony, derision, or wit to expose folly or wickedness. 317

scaffolding In cognitive development, Vygotsky used this term to describe the changing support over the course of a teaching session, with the more-skilled person adjusting guidance to fit the child's current performance level. 219, 484

schemas Mental frameworks that organize concepts and information. 240

schema theory States that people mold memories to fit information that already exists in their minds. 240

schemes In Piaget's theory, actions or mental representations that organize knowledge. 200

securely attached babies Babies who use the caregiver as a secure base from which to explore the environment. 350

selective attention Focusing on a specific aspect of experience that is relevant while ignoring others that are irrelevant. 237

selective optimization with compensation theory The theory that successful self-regulation in aging is related to three main factors: selection, optimization, and compensation. 380

self All of the characteristics of a person. 368

self-concept Domain-specific evaluations of the self. 374

self-conscious emotions Emotions that require cognition, especially consciousness; they include empathy, jealousy, and embarrassment, which first appear at about 1½ to 2 years and pride, shame, and guilt, which first appear at about 2½ years of age. 336

self-efficacy The belief that one can master a situation and produce favorable outcomes. 581

self-esteem The global evaluative dimension of the self. Self-esteem is also referred to as self-worth or self-image. 374

self-regulation The ability to control one's behavior without having to rely on others for help. 377

self-understanding The individual's cognitive representation of the self, the substance of self-conceptions. 368

semantic memory A person's knowledge about the world, including fields of expertise, general academic knowledge, and "everyday knowledge" about meaning of words, famous individuals, important places, and common things. 246

semantics The meanings of words and sentences. 306

sensation Reaction that occurs when information contacts sensory receptors—the eyes, ears, tongue, nostrils, and skin. 178

sensorimotor play Behavior by infants to derive pleasure from exercising their sensorimotor schemes. 536

sensorimotor stage The first of Piaget's stages, which lasts from birth to about 2 years of age; infants construct an understanding of the world by coordinating sensory experiences (such as seeing and hearing) with motoric actions. 202, 535

separation protest Occurs when infants experience a fear of being separated from a caregiver, which results in crying when the caregiver leaves. 338

sequential approach A combined cross-sectional, longitudinal design. 38

seriation The concrete operation that involves ordering stimuli along a quantitative dimension (such as length). 213

service learning A form of education that promotes social responsibility and service to the community. 456

sex Designates the biological aspects of being female or male. 402

sexual scripts Stereotyped patterns of expectancies for how people should behave sexually. 419

shape constancy Recognition that an object remains the same even though its orientation to us changes. 183

shared environmental experiences Siblings' common experiences, such as their parents' personalities and intellectual orientation, the family's socioeconomic status, and the neighborhood in which they live. 63

short-term memory Retention of information for up to 15 to 30 seconds, without rehearsal of the information. Using rehearsal, individuals can keep the information in short-term memory longer. 243

sickle-cell anemia A genetic disorder that affects the red blood cells and occurs most often in people of African descent. 59

size constancy Recognition that an object remains the same even though the retinal image of the object changes. 182

slow-to-warm-up child A temperament style in which the child has low activity level, is somewhat negative, shows low adaptability, and displays a low intensity of mood. 344

small for date infant Also called small for gestational age infant, this infant's birth weight is below normal when the length of pregnancy is considered. A small for date infant may be preterm or full term. 83

social age Social roles and expectations related to a person's age. 15

social breakdown–reconstruction theory The theory that aging is promoted through negative psychological functioning brought about by negative views of older adults and inadequate services for them; social reconstruction can be brought about by viewing older adults as competent. 539

social cognitive theory The theory that behavior, environment, and person/cognitive factors are important in understanding development. 24

social cognitive theory of gender The idea that children's gender development occurs through observation and imitation of gender behavior, as well as through the rewards and punishment children experience for behaviors believed to be appropriate or inappropriate for their gender. 405

social cognitive theory of morality The theory that distinguishes between moral competence—the ability to produce moral behaviors—and moral performance—those behaviors in specific situations. 405, 451

social constructivist approach An emphasis on the social contexts of learning and the construction of knowledge through social interaction. Vygotsky's theory reflects this approach.   222, 560

social contract or utility and individual rights The fifth Kohlberg stage. At this stage, individuals reason that values, rights, and principles undergird or transcend the law.   445

social conventional reasoning Thoughts about social consensus and convention, as opposed to moral reasoning that stresses ethical issues.   449

social play Play that involves social interactions with peers.   536

social referencing "Reading" emotional cues in others to help determine how to act in a particular situation.   338

social role theory Eagly's theory that psychological gender differences are caused by the contrasting social roles of women and men.   404

social smile A smile in response to an external stimulus, which, early in development, typically is a face.   337

social systems morality The fourth stage in Kohlberg's theory of moral development. Moral judgments are based on understanding the social order, law, justice, and duty.   444

socioeconomic status (SES) A grouping of people with similar occupational, educational, and economic characteristics.   544

socioemotional selectivity theory The theory that older adults become more selective about their social networks. Because they place high value on emotional satisfaction, older adults often spend more time with familiar individuals with whom they have had rewarding relationships.   342

solitary play Play in which the child plays alone, independently of others.   534

source memory The ability to remember where something is learned.   249

spermarche A boy's first ejaculation of semen.   98

spirituality Involves a sense of connectedness to a sacred other (God, nature, a higher power).   464

stability-change issue The debate about the degree to which early traits and characteristics persist through life or change.   16

standardized test A test that is given with uniform procedures for administration and scoring.   34

stereotype threat The anxiety that one's behavior might confirm a negative stereotype about one's group.   286

Strange Situation Ainsworth's observational measure of infant attachment to a caregiver that requires the infant to move through a series of introductions, separations, and reunions with the caregiver and an adult stranger in a prescribed order.   350

stranger anxiety An infant's fear of and wariness toward strangers; it tends to

appear in the second half of the first year of life.   338

strategy construction Discovering a new procedure for processing information.   234

sucking reflex A newborn's built-in reaction of automatically sucking an object placed in its mouth. The sucking reflex enables the infant to get nourishment before it has associated a nipple with food.   167

sudden infant death syndrome (SIDS) A condition that occurs when an infant stops breathing, usually during the night, and suddenly dies without an apparent cause.   116

sustained attention The state of readiness to detect and respond to small changes occurring at random times in the environment; also called vigilance.   237

symbolic function substage The first substage of preoperational thought, occurring roughly between the ages of 2 and 4. In this substage, the young child gains the ability to represent mentally an object that is not present.   208

syntax The ways words are combined to form acceptable phrases and sentences.   305

tabula rasa Locke's view that children are born as "blank slates" and acquire their characteristics through experience.   7

telegraphic speech The use of short and precise words without grammatical markers such as articles, auxiliary verbs, and other connectives.   309

temperament An individual's behavioral style and characteristic emotional response.   343

teratogen Any agent that causes a birth defect. The field of study that investigates the causes of birth defects is called teratology.   70

theory A coherent set of ideas that helps to explain data and to make predictions.   18

theory of mind Thoughts about how mental processes work, such as a child's becoming aware that the mind exists and understanding cognitive connections to the physical world.   261

thinking Manipulating and transforming information in memory, usually to form concepts, reason, think critically, and solve problems.   252

top-dog phenomenon The circumstance of moving from the top position in elementary school to the lowest position in middle or junior high school.   567

traditional religious script Sex is accepted only within marriage; extramarital sex is taboo, especially for women, and sex means reproduction and sometimes affection.   419

trait theories Personality consists of broad dispositions, called traits, that tend to produce characteristic responses.   388

transitivity If a relation holds between a first object and a second object, and holds between the second object and a third object, then it holds between the first object and the third object. Piaget believed that an understanding of transitivity is characteristic of concrete operational thought.   213

triangular theory of love Sternberg's theory that love includes three types—passion, intimacy, and commitment.   359

triarchic theory of intelligence Sternberg's theory that intelligence consists of compotential intelligence, experiential intelligence, and contextual intelligence.   276

Turner syndrome A chromosomal disorder in females in which either an X chromosome is missing, making the person XO instead of XX, or the second X chromosome is partially deleted.   59

twin study A study in which the behavioral similarity of identical twins is compared with the behavioral similarity of fraternal twins.   62

two-factor theory Spearman's theory that individuals have both general intelligence, which he called *g*, and a number of specific intelligences, referred to as *s*.   274

universal ethical principles The sixth and highest stage in Kohlberg's theory of moral development. Individuals develop a moral standard based on universal human rights.   445

unoccupied play Play in which the child is not engaging in play as it is commonly understood and might stand in one spot or perform random movements that do not seem to have a goal.   534

unresolved/disorganized attachment An insecure attachment style in which the adolescent has an unusually high level of fear and is disoriented. This may result from such traumatic experiences as a parent's death or abuse by parents.   356

values Beliefs and attitudes about the way things should be.   465

values clarification Helping people clarify what their lives are for and what is worth working for. Students are encouraged to define their own values and understand others' values.   456

visual preference method A method developed by Fantz to determine whether infants can distinguish one stimulus from another by measuring the length of time they attend to different stimuli. 180

Vygotsky's theory A sociocultural cognitive theory that emphasizes how culture and social interaction guide cognitive development. 22

Wernicke's area An area of the brain's left hemisphere that is involved in language comprehension. 319

whole-language approach An approach that stresses that reading instruction should parallel children's natural language learning. Reading materials should be whole and meaningful. 314

wisdom Expert knowledge about the practical aspects of life that permits excellent judgment about important matters. 290

working memory A mental "workbench" where individuals manipulate and assemble information when making decisions, solving problems, and comprehending written and spoken language. 243

XYY syndrome A chromosomal disorder in which males have an extra Y chromosome. 59

zone of proximal development (ZPD) Vygotsky's term for tasks too difficult for children to master alone but that can be mastered with assistance. 218

zygote A single cell formed through fertilization. 55

References

AAP (American Academy of Pediatricians). (2001). *Recommended childhood immunization schedule.* Washington, DC: American Academy of Pediatrics.

Aartson, M. J., Martin, M., & Zimprich, D. (2003). Gender differences in level and change in cognitive functioning: Results from the longitudinal aging study in Amsterdam. *Gerontology, 50,* 35–38.

Abbott, A. (2003). Restless nights, listless days. *Nature, 4235,* 896–898.

Abel, E. L., Kruger, M., & Burd, L. (2002). Effects of maternal and paternal age on Caucasian and Native American preterm births and birth weights. *American Journal of Perinatology, 19,* 49–54.

Aboud, F., & Skerry, S. (1983). Self and ethnic concepts in relation to ethnic constancy. *Canadian Journal of Behavioral Science, 15,* 3–34.

Achenbach, T. M. (1997). What is normal? What is abnormal? Developmental perspectives on behavioral and emotional problems. In S. S. Luthar, J. A. Burack, D. Cicchetti, & J. R. Weisz (Eds.), *Developmental psychopathology: Perspectives on adjustment, risk, and disorder.* New York: Cambridge University Press.

Ackerman, P. L., Kyllonen, P. C., & Roberts, R. D. (Eds.) (1999). *Learning and individual differences: Process, trait, and content determinants.* Washington, DC: American Psychological Association.

Acquilino, W. (1999). Two views of one relationship: Comparing parents' and young adult children's reports of the quality of intergenerational relations. *Journal of Marriage and the Family, 61,* 858–870.

Acredolo, L. P., & Hake, J. L. (1982). Infant perception. In B. B. Wolman (Ed.), *Handbook of developmental psychology.* Englewood Cliffs, NJ: Prentice Hall.

Adamolekun, K. (2001). Survivors' motives for extravagant funerals among the Yorubas of western Nigeria. *Death Studies, 25,* 609–619.

Adams, C. A. (2003). *ABCs of grief: A handbook for survivors.* Amityville, NY: Baywood.

Adams, G. R., Gulotta, T. P., & Montemayor, R. (Eds.). (1992). *Adolescent identity formation.* Newbury Park, CA: Sage.

Adams, R. J. (1989). Newborns' discrimination among mid- and long-wavelength stimuli. *Journal of Experimental Child Psychology, 47,* 130–141.

Adams, R., & Laursen, B. (2001). The organization and dynamics of adolescent conflict with parents and friends. *Journal of Marriage and the Family, 63,* 97–110.

Adler, S. A., & Haith, M. M. (2003). The nature of infants' visual expectations for event content. *Infancy, 4,* 389–411.

Adolph, K. E. (1997). Learning in the development of infant locomotion. *Monographs of the Society for Research in Child Development, 62* (3, Serial No. 251).

Adolph, K. E. (2002). Learning to keep balance. In R. Kail (Ed.), *Advances in child development and behavior.* San Diego: Academic Press.

Adolph, K. E., & Avolio, A. M. (2000). Walking infants adapt locomotion to changing body dimensions. *Journal of Experimental Psychology: Human Perception and Performance, 26,* 1148–1166.

Adolph, K. E., & Eppler, M. A. (2002). Flexibility and specificity in infant motor skill acquisition. In J. Fagan & M. Hayne (Eds.), *Progress in infancy research* (Vol. 2). Mahwah, NJ: Erlbaum.

Adolph, K. E., Vereijken, B., & Shrout, P. E. (2003). What changes in infant walking and why. *Child Development, 74,* 475–497.

Adolph, K. E., Weise, I., & Marin, L. (2003). Motor development. *Encyclopedia of Cognitive Science.* London: Macmillan Reference Ltd.

Aertgeerts, B., & Buntinx, F. (2002). The relation between alcohol abuse or dependence and academic performance in first-year college students. *Journal of Adolescent Health, 31,* 223–225.

Aguiar, A., & Baillargeon, R. (2002). Developments in young infants' reasoning about occluded objects. *Cognitive Psychology, 45,* 263–336.

Ahluwalia, I. B., Tessaro, I., Grumer-Strawn, L. M., MacGowan, C., & Benton-Davis, S. (2000). Georgia's breastfeeding promotion program for low-income women. *Pediatrics, 105,* E-85–E-87.

Ahmad, M., & Lachs, M. S. (2002). Elder abuse and neglect: What physicians can and should do. *Cleveland Clinic Journal of Medicine, 69,* 801–808.

Ahn, N. (1994). Teenage childbearing and high school completion: Accounting for individual heterogeneity. *Family Planning Perspectives, 26,* 17–21.

Aiken, L. R. (2003). *Psychological testing and assessment* (11th ed.). Boston: Allyn & Bacon.

Ainsworth, M. D. S. (1979). Infant-mother attachment. *American Psychologist, 34,* 932–937.

Akiyama, H., & Antonucci, T. C. (1999, November). *Mother-daughter dynamics over the life course.* Paper presented at the meeting of the Gerontological Association of America, San Francisco.

Alan Guttmacher Institute. (1998). *Teen sex and pregnancy.* New York: Author.

Alan Guttmacher Institute. (1999). *Facts in brief: Teen sex and pregnancy.* New York: Author.

Alan Guttmacher Institute. (2002). Teen pregnancy: Trends and lessons learned. In *Policy analysis: Issues in brief.* New York: Author.

Alderman, M. K. (2004). *Motivation and achievement.* Mahwah, NJ: Erlbaum.

Alexander, J. M., McIntire, D. D., & Leveno, K. J. (2001). Prolonged pregnancy: Induction of labor and cesarean births. *Obstetrics and Gynecology, 97,* 911–915.

Alexopoulos, G., Buckwalter, K., Olin, J., Martinez, R., Wainscott, C., & Krishnan, K. (2002). Comorbidity of late life depression: An opportunity for research on mechanisms and treatment. *Biological Psychiatry, 52,* 543.

Allen, J. P., & Hauser, S. T. (1994, February). *Adolescent-family interactions as predictors of qualities of parental, peer, and romantic relationships at age 25.* Paper presented at the meeting of the Society for Research on Adolescence, San Diego.

Allen, J. P., Hauser, S. T., & Borman-Spurrell, E. (1996). Attachment security and related sequelae of severe adolescent psychopathology: An eleven-year follow-up study. *Journal of Consulting and Clinical Psychology, 64,* 254–263.

Allen, J. P., & Kuperminc, G. P. (1995, March). *Adolescent attachment, social competence, and problematic behavior.* Paper presented at the meeting of the Society for Research in Child Development, Indianapolis.

Allen, J. P., March, P., McFarland, C., McElhaney, K. B., Land, D. J., Jodl, K., & Peck, S. (2002). Attachment and autonomy as predictors of the development of social skills and delinquency during midadolescence. *Journal of Consulting and Clinical Psychology, 70,* 56–66.

Allen, J. P., McElhaney, K. B., Land, D. J., Kuperminc, G. P., Moore, C. W., O'Beirne-Kelly, H., & Kilmer, S. L. (2003). A secure base in adolescence: Markers of attachment security in the mother-adolescent relationship. *Child Development, 74,* 292–307.

Allen, K. R., Blieszener, R., & Roberto, K. A. (2000). Families in middle and later years: A review and critique of research in the 1990s. *Journal of Marriage and the Family, 62,* 911–926.

Allen, M., Brown, P., & Finlay, B. (1992). *Helping children by strengthening families.* Washington, DC: Children's Defense Fund.

Almeida, D. M., & Horn, M. C. (in press). Is daily life more stressful during middle adulthood? In C. D. Ryff & R. C. Kessler (Eds.), *A portrait of midlife in the United States.* Chicago: University of Chicago Press.

Amato, P. R. (2000). The consequences of divorce for adults and children. *Journal of Marriage and the Family, 62,* 1269–1287.

Amato, P. R., & Booth, A. (1996). A prospective study of divorce and parent-child relationships. *Journal of Marriage and the Family, 58,* 356–365.

Amato, P. R., & Keith, B. (1991). Parental divorce and the well-being of children: A meta-analysis. *Psychological Bulletin, 110,* 26–46.

American Academy of Pediatrics (AAP) Committee on Drugs. (1994). The transfer of drugs and other chemicals into human milk. *Pediatrics, 93,* 137–150.

American Academy of Pediatrics (AAP) Work Group of Breastfeeding. (1997). Breastfeeding and the use of human milk. *Pediatrics, 100,* 1035–1039.

American Academy of Pediatrics (AAP). (2000). Suicide and suicide attempts in adolescence. *Pediatrics, 105,* 871–874.

American Academy of Pediatrics (AAP). (2001). Children adolescents, and television. *Pediatrics, 107,* 423–426.

American Academy of Pediatrics Task Force on Infant Sleep Position and SIDS. (2000). Changing concepts of sudden infant death syndrome. *Pediatrics, 105,* 650–656.

American Association of University Women. (1992). *How schools shortchange girls: A study of major findings on girls and education.* Washington, DC: Author.

American Association on Mental Retardation, Ad Hoc Committee on Terminology and Classification. (1992). *Mental retardation* (9th ed.). Washington, DC: Author.

Amisola, R. V., & Jacobson, M. S. (2003). Physical activity, exercise, and sendentary activity: Relationship to the causes and treatment of obesity. *Adolescent Medicine, 14,* 23–35.

Amsterdam, B. K. (1968). *Mirror behavior in children under two years of age.* Unpublished doctoral dissertation, University of North Carolina, Chapel Hill.

Anantharaju, A., Feller, A., & Chedid, A. (2002). Aging liver: A review. *Gerontology, 48,* 343–348.

Anastasi, A., & Urbina, S. (1996). *Psychological testing* (7th ed.). Upper Saddle River, NJ: Prentice Hall.

Anderman, E. M., Maehr, M. L., & Midgley, C. (1996). Declining motivation after the transition to middle school: Schools can make a difference. Unpublished manuscript, University of Kentucky, Lexington.

Anderson, B. L., Kiecolt-Glaser, J. K., & Glaser, R. (1994). A biobehavioral model of cancer stress and disease course. *American Psychologist, 49,* 389–404.

Anderson, D. R., Lorch, E. P., Field, D. E., Collins, P. A., & Nathan, J. G. (1986, April). *Television viewing at home: Age trends in visual attention and time with TV. Child Development, 57,* 1024–1033.

Anderson, E., Greene, S. M., Hetherington, E. M., & Clingempeel, W. G. (1999). The dynamics of parental remarriage. In E. M. Hetherington (Ed.), *Coping with divorce, single parenting, and remarriage.* Mahwah, NJ: Erlbaum.

Anderson, L. M., Shinn, C., Fullilove, M. T., Serimshaw, S. C., Fielding, J. E., Normand, J., & Carande-Kulis, V. G. (2003). The effectiveness of early childhood development programs: A systematic review. *American Journal of Preventive Medicine, 24* (Suppl. 3), 32–46.

Andersen, R. E., Franckowiak, S. C., Bartlett, S. J., & Fontaine, K. R. (2002). Physiologic changes after diet combined with structured aerobic exercise or lifestyle activity. *Metabolism, 51,* 1528–1533.

Anderson, S. E., Dallal, G. E., & Must, A. (2003). Relative weight and race influence average age at menarche: Results from two nationally representative surveys of U.S. girls studied 25 years apart. *Pediatrics, 111,* 844–850.

Anderssen, N., Amlie, C., & Ytteroy, E. A. (2002). Outcomes for children with lesbian or gay parents. A review of studies from 1978 to 2000. *Scandanavian Journal of Psychology, 43,* 335–351.

Andersson, J. (2001). Net effect of memory collaboration: How is collaboration affected by factors such as friendship, gender, and age? *Scandinavian Journal of Psychology, 42,* 367–375.

Andrist, L. C. (2003). Media images, body dissatisfaction, and disordered eating in adolescent women. *MCN American Journal of Maternal and Child Nursing, 28,* 119–123.

Angel, J. L., Douglas, N., & Angel, R. J. (2003). Gender, widowhood, and long-term care in the older Mexican population. *Journal of Women and Aging, 15,* 89–105.

Angold, A., Costello, E. J., & Worthman, C. M. (1998). Puberty and depression: The roles of age, pubertal status and pubertal timing. *Psychological Medicine, 28,* 51–61.

Antai-Otong, D. (2003). Suicide: Life span considerations. *Nursing Clinics of North America, 38,* 137–150.

Anthony Greenwald & Associates. (2000). *Current views toward retirement; A poll.* New York: Author.

Antonucci, T. C. (1990). Social supports and social relationships. In R. H. Binstock & L. K. George (Eds.), *Handbook of aging and the social sciences* (3rd. ed.). San Diego: Academic Press.

Antonucci, T. C., & Akiyama, H. (1995). Convoys of social relations: Family and friendships within a lifespan context. In R. Blieszner & V. H. Bedford (Eds.), *Handbook of aging and the family* (pp. 355–371). Westport, CT: Greenwood Press.

Antonucci, T. C., Akiyama, H., & Lansford, J. E. (1998). Negative effects of close social relations. *Family Relations, 47,* 379–384.

Antonucci, T. C. & Akiyama, H. (2002). Aging and close relationships over the life span. *International Society for the Study of Behavioural Development Newsletter* (1, Serial No. 41), 2–5.

Antonucci, T. C., Lansford, J. E., & Akiyama, H. (2001). The impact of positive and negative aspects of marital relationships and friendships on the well-being of older adults. In J. P. Reinhardt (Ed.), *Negative and positive support.* Mahwah, NJ: Erlbaum.

Antonucci, T. C., Lansford, J. E., & Schaabeg, L., Smith, J., Baltes, M., Akiyama, H., Takahashi, K., & Fuhrer, R. (2001). Widowhood and illness: A comparison of social network characteristics in France, Germany, Japan, and the United States. *Psychology and Aging, 16,* 655–665.

Antonucci, T. C., Vandewater, E. A., & Lanford, J. E. (2000). Adulthood and aging: Social processes and development. In A. Kazdin (Ed.), *Encyclopedia of psychology.* Washington, DC, & New York: American Psychological Association and Oxford University Press.

Arbuckle, T. Y., Maag, U., Pushkar, D., & Chalkelsen, J. S. (1998). Individual differences in trajectory of intellectual development over 45 years of adulthood. *Psychology and Aging, 13,* 663–675.

Archer, S. L. (1989). The status of identity: Reflections on the need for intervention. *Journal of Adolescence, 12,* 345–359.

Archer, S. L., & Waterman, A. S. (1994). Adolescent identity development: Contextual perspectives. In C. B. Fisher & R. M. Lerner (Eds.), *Applied developmental psychology.* New York: McGraw-Hill.

Archibald, A. B., Graber, J. A., & Brooks-Gunn, J. (2003). Pubertal processes and physical growth in adolescence. In

G. Adams & M. Berzonsky (Eds.), *Blackwell handbook of adolescence*. Malden, MA: Blackwell.

Archibald, A. B., Graber, J. A., & Brooks-Gunn, J. (1999). Associations among parent-adolescent relationships, pubertal growth, dieting, and body image in young adolescent girls: A short-term longitudinal study. *Journal of Research on Adolescence, 9*, 395–415.

Archibald, A. B., Graber, J. A., & Brooks-Gunn, J. (2003). Pubertal processes and physical growth in adolescence. In G. R. Adams & M. Berzonsky (Eds.), *Handbook on adolescence*. Malden, MA: Blackwell.

Archibald, S. L., Fennema-Notetine, C., Gamst, A., Riley, E. P., Mattson, S. N., & Jernigan, T. L. (2001). Brain dysmorphology in individuals with severe prenatal alcohol exposure. *Developmental Medicine and Child Neurology, 43*, 148–154.

Ardelt, M. (2004). Physician-assisted suicide. In C. D. Bryant (Ed.), *Handbook of death and dying*. Thousand Oaks, CA: Sage.

Arehart, D. M., & Smith, P. H. (1990). Identity in adolescence: Influences on dysfunction and psychosocial task issues. *Journal of Youth and Adolescence, 19*, 63–72.

Arendt, R., Angelopouos, J., Salvator, A., & Singer, L. (1999). Motor development of cocaine-exposed children at age two years. *Pediatrics, 103*, 86–92.

Ariès, P. (1962). *Centuries of childhood* (R. Baldrick, Trans.). New York: Knopf.

Arndt, J., & Goldenberg, J. L. (2002). From threat to sweat: The role of physiological arousal in the motivation to maintain self-esteem. In A. Tesser, D. A. Stapel, & J. V. Wood (Eds.), *Self and motivation: Emerging psychological perspectives* (pp. 43–69). Washington, DC: American Psychological Association.

Arnett, J. (1990). Contraceptive use, sensation seeking, and adolescent egocentrism. *Journal of Youth and Adolescence, 19*, 171–180.

Arnett, J. J. (2002). Adolescents in Western countries in the 21st century: Vast opportunities—for all? In B. B. Brown, R. W. Larson, & T. S. Saraswathi (Eds.), *The world's youth*. New York: Cambridge University Press.

Aronson, E. (1986, August). *Teaching students things they think they already know about: The case of prejudice and desegregation.* Paper presented at the meeting of the American Psychological Association, Washington, DC.

Aronson, J. M. (2002). Stereotype threat: Contending and coping with unnerving expectations. *Improving academic achievement.* San Diego: Academic Press.

Aronson, J. M., Fried, C. B., & Good, C. (2002). Reducing the effects of stereotype threat on African American college students by shaping theories of intelligence. *Journal of Experimental Social Psychology, 38*, 113–125.

Aronson, J. M., Lustina, M. J., Good, C., Keough, K., Steele, C. M., & Brown, J. (1999). When white men can't do math: Necessary and sufficient factors in stereotype threat. *Journal of Experimental Social Psychology, 35*, 29–46.

Arshad, S. H. (2001). Food allergen avoidance in primary prevention of food allergy. *Allergy, 56*, 113–116.

Asch, D. A., & Christakis, N. A. (1996). Why do physicians prefer to withdraw some forms of life support over others? Intrinsic attributes of life-sustaining treatments are associated with physicians' preferences. *Medical Care, 34*, 103–111.

Asher, J., & Garcia, R. (1969). The optimal age to learn a foreign language. *Modern Language Journal, 53*, 334–341.

Aslin, R. N. (1987). Visual and auditory development in infancy. In J. Osofsky (Ed.), *Handbook of infant development* (2nd ed.). New York: Wiley.

Aslin, R. N., Jusczyk, P. W., & Pisoni, D. B. (1998). Speech and auditory processing during infancy: Constraints on and precursors to language. In W. Damon (Ed.), *Handbook of child psychology* (5th ed., Vol. 2). New York: Wiley.

Aspinwall, L. G., & Staudinger, U. M. (2003). A psychology of human strengths: Some central issues in an emerging field. In L. G. Aspinwall & U. M. Staudinger (Eds.), *A psychology of human strengths*. New York: Oxford University Press.

Astin, A. W. (1993). *What matters in college.* San Francisco: Jossey-Bass.

Atchley, R. C. (1976). *The sociology of retirement.* Cambridge, MA: Schenkman.

Atchley, R. C., & Barusch, A. (2004). *Social forces of aging (10th Ed.).* Belmont, CA: Wadsworth.

Atkinson, L., & Goldberg, S. (Eds.) (2004). *Attachment issues in psychopathology and intervention.* Mahwah, NJ: Erlbaum.

Atkinson, R. M., Ryan, S. C., & Turner, J. A. (2001). Variation among aging alcoholic patients in treatment. *American Journal of Geriatric Psychiatry, 9*, 275–282.

Attie, I., & Brooks-Gunn, J. (1989). Development of eating problems in adolescent girls: A longitudinal study. *Developmental Psychology, 25*, 70–79.

Avidan, A. Y. (2002). Sleep changes and disorders in the elderly patient. *Current Neurology and Neuroscience Reports, 2*, 178–185.

Avolio, B. J., & Sosik, J. J. (1999). A life-span framework for assessing the impact of work on white-collar workers. In S. L. Willis & J. D. Reid (Eds.), *Life in the middle: Psychological and social development in middle age.* San Diego: Academic Press.

Azar, S. T. (2002). Parenting and child maltreatment. In M. H. Bornstein (Ed.), *Handbook of parenting* (Vol. 4, 2nd ed.). Mahwah, NJ: Erlbaum.

Azar, S. T. (2003). Adult development and parenting. In J. Demick & C. Andreoletti (Eds.), *Handbook of adult development.* New York: Kluwer.

Babalola, O. E., Murdoch, I. E., Cousens, S., Abiose, A., & Jones, B. (2003). Blindness: How to assess numbers and causes. *British Journal of Ophthalmology, 87*, 282–284.

Bachman, D. L. (1992). Sleep disorders with aging: Evaluation and treatment. *Geriatrics, 47*, 53–61.

Bachman, J. G., & Schulenberg, J. (1993). How part-time work intensity relates to drug use, problem behavior, time use, and satisfaction among high school seniors: Are these consequences or just correlates? *Developmental Psychology, 29*, 220–235.

Bachman, J. G., O'Malley, P. M., Schulenberg, J., Johnston, L. D., Bryant, A. L., & Merline, A. C. (2002). *The decline of substance abuse in young adulthood.* Mahwah, NJ: Erlbaum.

Baddeley, A. (1990). *Human memory: Theory and practice.* Boston: Allyn & Bacon.

Baddeley, A. (1998). *Human memory* (rev. ed.). Boston: Allyn & Bacon.

Baddeley, A. (2001). *Is working memory still working?* Paper presented at the meeting of the American Psychological Association, San Francisco.

Bagwell, C. L., Newcomb, A. F., & Bukowski, W. M. (1994, February). *Early adolescent friendship as a predictor of adult adjustment: A twelve year follow-up investigation.* Paper presented at the biennial meeting of the Society for Research on Adolescence, San Diego.

Bahado-Singh, R. O., Choic, S. J., Oz, U., Mendilciolglu, I., Rowther, M., & Persutte, W. (2003). Early second-trimester individualized estimation of trisomy 18 risk by ultrasound. *Obstetrics and Gynecology, 101*, 463–468.

Bahrick, H. P. (1984). Semantic memory content in permastore: Fifty years of memory for Spanish learned in school. *Journal of Experimental Psychology: General, 113*, 1–35.

Bahrick, H. P., Bahrick, P. O., & Wittlinger, R. P. (1975). Fifty years of memory for names and faces: A cross-sectional approach. *Journal of Experimental Psychology: General, 104*, 54–75.

Baillargeon, R. (1995). The object concept revisited: New directions in the investigation of infants' physical knowledge, In C. E. Granrud (Ed.), *Visual perception and cognition in infancy.* Hillsdale, NJ: Erlbaum.

Baillargeon, R. (2002). The acquisition of physical knowledge in infancy: A summary in eight lessons. In U. Goswami (Ed.), *Handbook of childhood cognitive development.* Malden, MA: Blackwell.

Baillargeon, R., & Devos, J. (1991). Object Permanence in Young Children: Further Evidence, *Child Development, 62*, 1227–1246.

Baird, A. A., Gruber, S. A., Cohen, B. M., Renshaw, R. J., & Yureglun-Todd, D. A. (1999). MRI of the amygdala in children and adolescents. *American Academy of Child and Adolescent Psychiatry, 38,* 195–199.

Bakeman, R., & Brown, J. V. (1980). Early interaction: Consequences for social and mental development at three years. *Child Development, 51,* 437–447.

Baldwin, J. D., & Baldwin, J. I. (1998). Sexual behavior. In H. S. Friedman (Ed.), *Encyclopedia of mental health* (Vol. 3). San Diego: Academic Press.

Baldwin, M., & Fehr, B. (1995). On the instability of attachment ratings. *Personal Relationships, 2,* 247–261.

Balota, D. A., Dolan, P. O., & Ducheck, J. M. (2000). Memory changes in healthy older adults. In E. Tulving & F. I. M. Craik (Eds.), *The Oxford handbook of memory.* New York: Oxford University Press.

Baltes, P. B. (1987). Theoretical propositions of life-span developmental psychology: On the dynamics between growth and decline. *Developmental Psychology, 23,* 611–626.

Baltes, P. B. (1993). The aging mind: Potentials and limits. *Gerontologist, 33,* 580–594.

Baltes, P. B. (1995, September). Unpublished review of J. W. Santrock's *Life-span development,* 6th ed. New York: McGraw-Hill.

Baltes, P. B. (2000). Life-span developmental theory. In A. Kazdin (Ed.), *Encyclopedia of psychology.* Washington, DC, & New York: American Psychological Association and Oxford University Press.

Baltes, P. B. (2002). On the incomplete architecture of human ontogeny. *Psychology: Journal of the Hellenic (Greek) Psychological Society, 9,* 252–279.

Baltes, P. B. (2003). On the incomplete architecture of human ontogeny: Selection, optimization, and compensation as foundation of developmental theory. In U. M. Staudinger & U. Lindenberger (Eds.), *Understanding human development.* Boston: Kluwer.

Baltes, P. B., & Baltes, M. M. (1990). Psychological perspectives on successful aging: The model of selective optimization with compensation. In P. B. Baltes & M. M. Baltes (Eds.), *Successful aging: Perspectives from the behavioral sciences.* New York: Cambridge University Press.

Baltes, P. B., Glück, J., & Kunzmann, U. (2002). Wisdom: Its structure and function in regulating successful life span development. In C. R. Synder & S. J. Lopez (Eds.), *Handbook of positive psychology.* New York: Oxford University Press.

Baltes, P. B., & Kunzmann, U. (2003). Wisdom. *The Psychologist, 16,* 131–133.

Baltes, P. B., & Lindenberger, U. (1997). Emergence of a powerful connection between sensory and cognitive functions across the adult life span: A new window to the study of cognitive aging? *Psychology and Aging, 12,* 12–21.

Baltes, P. B., Lindenberger, U., & Staudinger, U. M. (1998). Life-span theory in developmental psychology. In W. Damon (Ed.), *Handbook of child psychology* (5th ed., Vol. 1). New York: Wiley.

Baltes, P. B., & Smith, J. (1990). Toward a psychology of wisdom and its ontogenesis. In R. J. Sternberg (Ed.), *Wisdom: Its nature, origin, and development.* New York: Cambridge University Press.

Baltes, P. B., & Smith, J. (2003). New frontiers in the future of aging: From successful aging of the young old to the dilemmas of the fourth age. *Gerontology, 49,* 123–135.

Baltes, P. B., Staudinger, U. M., & Lindenberger, U. (1999). Life-span psychology: Theory and application to intellectual functioning. *Annual Review of Psychology, 50,* 471–507.

Bandstra, E. S., Morrow, C. E., Anthony, J. C., Haynes, V. L., Johnson, A. L., Xue, L., & Audrey, Y. (2000, May). *Effects of prenatal cocaine exposure on attentional processing in children through five years of age.* Paper presented at the joint meetings of the Pediatric Academic Societies and the American Academy of Pediatrics, Boston.

Bandura, A. (1982). Self-efficacy mechanism in human agency. *American Psychologist, 37,* 122–147.

Bandura, A. (1986). *Social foundations of thought and action: A social cognitive theory.* Englewood Cliffs, NJ: Prentice Hall.

Bandura, A. (1991). Social cognitive theory of moral thought and action. In W. M. Kurtines & J. L. Gewirtz (Eds.), *Handbook of moral behavior and development* (Vol. 1). Hillsdale, NJ: Erlbaum.

Bandura, A. (1997). *Self-efficacy.* New York: W. H. Freeman.

Bandura, A. (1998, August). *Swimming against the mainstream: Accentuating the positive aspects of humanity.* Paper presented at the meeting of the American Psychological Association, San Francisco.

Bandura, A. (1999). Moral disengagement in the perpetuation of inhumanities. *Personality and Social Psychology Review, 3,* 193–209.

Bandura, A. (2000). Social cognitive theory. In A. Kazdin (Ed.), *Encyclopedia of psychology.* Washington, DC, & New York: American Psychological Association and Oxford University Press.

Bandura, A. (2001). Social cognitive theory. *Annual Review of Psychology* (Vol. 52). Palo Alto, CA: Annual Reviews.

Bandura, A. (2002). Selective moral disengagement in the exercise of moral agency. *Journal of Moral Education, 31,* 101–119.

Bandura, A., & Locke, E. A. (2003). Negative self-efficacy and goals revisited. *Journal of Applied Psychology, 88,* 87–99.

Banks, E. C. (1993, March). *Moral education curriculum in a multicultural context: The Malaysian primary curriculum.* Paper presented at the biennial meeting of the Society for Research in Child Development, New Orleans.

Banks, J. A. (2002). *Introduction to multicultural education* (3rd ed.). Boston: Allyn & Bacon.

Banks, J. A. (2003). *Teaching strategies for ethnic studies* (7th ed.). Boston: Allyn & Bacon.

Banks, M. S., & Salapatek, P. (1983). Infant visual perception. In P. H. Mussen (Ed.), *Handbook of child psychology* (4th ed., Vol. 2). New York: Wiley.

Baraket, L. P., Kunin-Batson, A., & Kazak, A. E. (2003). Child health psychology. In I. B. Weiner (Ed.), *Handbook of psychology* (Vol. IX). New York: Wiley.

Barbarin, O., McCandies, T., & Coleman, C. (2003, April). *Socio-cultural niches: Implications of SES and ethnic variations in home environments for child development.* Paper presented at the meeting of the Society for Research in Child Development, Tampa.

Barker, R., & Wright, H. F. (1951). *One boy's day.* New York: Harper & Row.

Barnett, D., Ganiban, J., & Cicchetti, D. (1999). Maltreatment, negative expressivity, and the development of type D attachments from 12 to 24 months of age. In J. I. Vondra & D. Barnett (Eds.), *Monograph of the Society for Research in Child Development, 64* (3, Serial No. 258), 97–118.

Barnett, R. C. (2001). Work-family balance. In J. Worell (Ed.), *Encyclopedia of women and gender.* San Diego: Academic Press.

Barnett, R. C., Gareis, K. C., James, J. B., & Steele, J. (2001, August). *Planning ahead: College seniors' concerns about work-family conflict.* Paper presented at the meeting of the American Psychological Association, San Francisco.

Barnett, S. B., & Maulik, D. (2001). Guidelines and recommendations for safe use of Doppler ultrasound in perinatal applications. *Journal of Maternal and Fetal Medicine, 10,* 75–84.

Baron, N. S. (1992). *Growing up with language.* Reading, MA: Addison-Wesley.

Barr, H. M., & Streissguth, A. P. (2001). Identifying maternal self-reported alcohol use associated with fetal alcohol disorders. *Alcoholism: Clinical and Experimental Research, 25,* 283–287.

Barrera, M., Gonzales, N. A., Lopez, V., & Fernandez, A. C. (2004). Problem behaviors of Chicana/o and Latina/o adolescents. In M. Schaller & L. S. Crandall (Eds.), *The psychological foundations of culture.* Mahwah, NJ: Erlbaum.

Barrett, D. E., Radke-Yarrow, M., & Klein, R. E. (1982). Chronic malnutrition and child behavior. Effects of calorie supplementation on social and emotional functioning at school age. *Developmental Psychology, 18,* 541–556.

Bartlett, F. C. (1932). *Remembering.* Cambridge: Cambridge University Press.

Bates, A. S., Fitzgerald, J. F., Dittus, R. S., & Wollinsky, F. D. (1994). Risk factors for underimmunization in poor urban infants. *Journal of the American Medical Association, 272,* 1105–1109.

Bates, E., Harris, C., Marchman, V., Wulfeck, B., & Kritchevsky, M. (1995). Production of complex syntax in normal aging and Alzheimer's disease. *Language and Cognitive Processes, 10,* 487–539.

Batson, C. D. (1989). Personal values, moral principles, and the three path model of prosocial motivation. In N. Eisenberg & J. Reykowski (Eds.), *Social and moral values.* Hillsdale, NJ: Erlbaum.

Bauer, P. J. (2002). Long-term recall memory: Behavioral and neuro-developmental changes in the first 2 years of life. *Current Directions in Psychological Science, 11,* 137–141.

Bauer, P. J., Wenner, J. A., Dropik, P. L., & Wewerka, S. S. (2000). Parameters of remembering and forgetting in the transition from infancy to early childhood. *Monographs of the Society for Research in Child Development, 65* (4, Serial No. 263).

Bauer, P. J., Wiebe, S. A., Carver, L. J., Waters, J. M., & Nelson, C. A. (2003). Developments in long-term explicit memory late in the first year of life: Behavioral and electrophysiological indices. *Psychological Science, 14,* 629–635.

Baum, A. S. (2000). Genetic disorders. In A. Kazdin (Ed.), *Encyclopedia of psychology.* Washington, DC, & New York: American Psychological Association and Oxford University Press.

Baum, A., Revenson, T. A., & Singer, J. E. (Eds.), (2001). *Handbook of health psychology.* Mahwah, NJ: Erlbaum.

Baumeister, R. F. (1991). Identity crisis. In R. M. Lerner, A. C. Petersen, & J. Brooks-Gunn (Eds.), *Encyclopedia of adolescence* (Vol. 1). New York: Garland.

Baumeister, R. F. (1991). *Meaning of life.* New York: Guilford.

Baumeister, R. F. (1993). *Self-esteem: The puzzle of low self-regard.* New York: Plenum Press.

Baumeister, R. F., Campbell, J. D., Krueger, J. I., & Vohs, K. D. (2003). Does high self-esteem cause better performance, interpersonal success, happiness, or healthier lifestyles? *Psychological Science in the Public Interest, 4,* (No. 1). 1–44.

Baumeister, R. F., Catanese, K. R., & Vohs, K. D. (2001). Is there a gender difference in strength of sex drive? *Personality and Social Psychology Review, 5,* 242–273.

Baumeister, R. F., & Vohs, K. D. (2002). The pursuit of meaningfulness in life. In C. R. Snyder & S. J. Lopez (Eds.), *Handbook of positive psychology.* New York: Oxford University Press.

Baumrind, D. (1971). Current patterns of parental authority. *Developmental Psychology Monographs, 4* (1, Pt. 2).

Baumrind, D. (1991). Effective parenting during the early adolescent transition. In P. A. Cowan & E. M. Hetherington (Eds.), *Advances in family research* (Vol. 2). Hillsdale, NJ: Erlbaum.

Baumrind, D. (1999, November). Unpublished review of J. W. Santrock's *Child development,* 9th ed. (New York: McGraw-Hill).

Baumrind, D., Larzelere, R. E., & Cowan, P. A. (2002). Ordinary physical punishment: Is it harmful? Comment on Gershoff. *Psychological Bulletin, 128,* 590–595.

Baxter, G. W., Stuart, W. J., & Stewart, W. J. (1998). *Death and the adolescent.* Toronto: University of Toronto Press.

Baxter, M. G. (2003). Age-related memory impairment: Is the cure worse than the disease? *Neuron, 40,* 669–670.

Bayley, N. (1943). Mental growth during the first three years. In R. G. Barker, J. S. Kounin, & H. F. Wright (Eds.), *Child behavior and development.* New York: McGraw-Hill.

Bayley, N. (1969). *Manual for the Bayley Scales of Infant Development.* New York: Psychological Corporation.

Beal, C. R. (1994). *Boys and girls: The development of gender roles.* New York: McGraw-Hill.

Bean, C. J., Schaner, C. E., & Kelly, W. G. (2004). Meiotic pairing and imprinted X Chromatin assembly in Caenorhabditis elegans. *Nature Genetics, 36,* 100–105.

Bearison, D. J., & Dorval, B. (2002). *Collaborative cognition.* Westport, CT: Ablex.

Bearman, P., & Bruckner, H. (1999). *Peer effects on adolescent sexual debut and pregnancy.* Paper prepared for the National Campaign to Prevent Teen Pregnancy, Washington, DC.

Bechtold, A. G., Busnell, E. W., & Salapatek, P. (1979, April). *Infants' visual localization of visual and auditory targets.* Paper presented at the meeting of the Society for Research in Child Development, San Francisco.

Bednar, R. L., Wells, M. G., & Peterson, S. R. (1995). *Self-esteem* (2nd ed.). Washington, DC: American Psychological Association.

Begley, S. (1997). How to build a baby's brain. *Newsweek Special Issue.* Spring/Summer, 28–32.

Beins, B. (2004). *Research methods.* Boston: Allyn & Bacon.

Belansky, E. S., & Clements, P. (1992, March). *Adolescence: A crossroads for gender-role transcendence or gender-role intensification.* Paper presented at the meeting of the Society for Research on Adolescence, Washington, DC.

Bell, A. P., Weinberg, M. S., & Hammersmith, S. K. (1981). *Sexual preference.* New York: Simon & Schuster.

Bell, S. M., & Ainsworth, M. D. S. (1972). Infant crying and maternal responsiveness. *Child Development, 43,* 1171–1190.

Bellinger, D., Leviton, A., Waternaux, C., Needleman, H., & Rabinowitz, M. (1987). Longitudinal analysis of prenatal and postnatal lead exposure and early cognitive development. *New England Journal of Medicine, 316,* 1037–1043.

Belloc, N. B., & Breslow, L. (1972). Relationships of physical health status and health practices. *Preventive Medicine, 1,* 409–421.

Belsky, J. (1981). Early human experience: A family perspective. *Developmental Psychology, 17,* 3–23.

Belsky, J., & Eggebeen, D. (1991). Early and extensive maternal employment/child care and 4–6-year-olds socioemotional development: Children of the National Longitudinal Survey of Youth. *Journal of Marriage and the Family, 53,* 1083–1099.

Belsky, J., & Hsieh, K. (1998). Patterns of marital change during the early childhood years: Parent personality, coparenting, and division-of-labor correlates. *Developmental Psychology, 12,* 511–528.

Belsky, J., Jaffe, S., Hsieh, K., & Silva, P. (2001). Child-rearing antecedents of intergenerational relations in young adulthood: A prospective study. *Developmental Psychology, 37,* 801–813.

Bem, S. L. (1977). On the utility of alternative procedures for assessing psychological androgyny. *Journal of Consulting and Clinical Psychology, 45,* 196–205.

Bendelius, J. (2003). The nutritional challenge of genetic enzyme-deficiency syndromes. *School Nurse News, 20,* 16–17.

Bender, W. N. (2004). *Learning disabilities (5th Ed.).* Boston: Allyn & Bacon.

Bendersky, M., & Sullivan, M. W. (2002). Basic methods in infant research. In A. Slater & M. Lewis (Eds.), *Introduction to infant development.* New York: Oxford University Press.

Benenson, J. F., Apostolaris, N. H., & Parnass, J. (1997). Age and sex differences in dyadic and group interaction. *Developmental Psychology, 33,* 538–543.

Benet-Martinez, V. & Waller, N. G. (1997). Further evidence for the cross-cultural generality of the 'Big Seven' model: Imported and indigenous Spanish personality constructs. *Journal of Personality, 65,* 567–598.

Bengtson, V. L. (1985). Diversity and symbolism in grandparental roles. In V. L. Bengtson & J. Robertson (Eds.), *Grandparenthood.* Newbury Park, CA: Sage.

Bengtson, V. L. (2001). Beyond the nuclear family: The increasing importance of multi-generational bonds. *Journal of Marriage and the Family, 63,* 1–16.

Bengtson, V. L., Reedy, M. N., & Gordon, C. (1985). Aging and self-conceptions: Personality processes and social contexts. In J. E. Birren & K. W. Schaie (Eds.), *Handbook of the psychology of aging.* New York: Van Nostrand Reinhold.

Bennett, C. I. (2003). *Comprehensive multicultural education* (5th ed.). Boston: Allyn & Bacon.

Bennett, W. (1993). *The book of virtues.* New York: Simon & Schuster.

Bennett, W. I., & Gurin, J. (1982). *The dieter's dilemma: Eating less and weighing more.* New York: Basic Books.

Benson, E. (2003, February). Intelligence across cultures. *Monitor on Psychology, 34* (No. 2). 56–58.

Berado, F. M. (2004). Widowhood and its social implications. In C.D. Bryant (Ed.), *Handbook of death and dying.* Thousand Oaks, CA: Sage.

Berardi, A., Parasuraman, R., & Haxby, J. V. (2001). Overall vigilance and sustained attention decrements in healthy aging. *Experimental Aging Research, 27,* 19–39.

Berenbaum, S. A., & Bailey, J. M. (2003). Effects on gender identity of prenatal androgens and genital appearance: Evidence from girls with congenital adrenal hyperplasia. *Journal of Clinical Endocrinology and Metabolism, 88,* 1102–1106.

Bergen, D. (1988). Stages of play development. In D. Bergen (Ed.), *Play as a medium for learning and development.* Portsmouth, NH: Heinemann.

Berger, S. E. & Adolph, K. E. (2003). Infants use handrails as tools in a locomotor task. *Developmental Psychology, 39,* 594–605.

Bergmann, K. E., Bergmann, R. L., Von Kries, R., Bohm, R., Richter, R., Dudenhausen, J. W., & Wahn, U. (2003). Early determinants of childhood overweight and adiposity in a birth cohort study: Role of breastfeeding. *International Journal of Obesity and Related Metabolic Disorders, 27,* 162–172.

Berk, L. E. (1994). Why children talk to themselves. *Scientific American, 271*(5), 78–83.

Berk, L. E., & Spuhl, S. T. (1995). Maternal interaction, private speech, and task performance in preschool children. *Early Childhood Research Quarterly, 10,* 145–169.

Berko Gleason, J. (2000). Language: An overview. In A. Kazdin (Ed.), *Encyclopedia of psychology.* Washington, DC, & New York: American Psychological Association and Oxford University Press.

Berko Gleason, J. (2002). Review of J. W. Santrock's *Life-span development,* 9th ed. New York: McGraw-Hill.

Berko, J. (1958). The child's learning of English morphology. *World, 14,* 150–177.

Berlin, L., & Cassidy, J. (2000). Understanding parenting: Contributions of attachment theory and research: in J. D. Osofsky & H. E. Fitzgerald (Eds.), *WAIMH handbook of infant mental health* (Vol. 3). New York: Wiley.

Berlyne, D. E. (1960). *Conflict, arousal, and curiosity.* New York: McGraw-Hill.

Bernard, M., & Phillipson, C. (2004). Retirement and leisure. In J. F. Nussbaum & J. Coupland (Eds.), *Handbook of communication and aging.* Mahwah, NJ: Erlbaum.

Berndt, T. J. (1979). Developmental changes in conformity to peers and parents. *Developmental Psychology, 15,* 608–616.

Berndt, T. J. (1982). The features and effects of friendships in early adolescence. *Child Development, 53,* 1447–1460.

Berndt, T. J. (1999). Friends' influence on children's adjustment. In W. A. Collins & B. Laursen (Eds.), *Relationships as developmental contexts.* Mahwah, NJ: Erlbaum.

Berndt, T. J. (2002). Friendship quality and social development. *Current Directions in Psychological Science, 11,* 7–10.

Berndt, T. J., & Perry, T. B. (1990). Distinctive features and effects of early adolescent friendships. In R. Montemayor (Ed.), *Advances in adolescent research.* Greenwich, CT: JAI Press.

Bernier, M. O., Plu-Bureau, G., Bossard, N., Ayzac, L., Thalabard, J. C. (2000). Breastfeeding and risk of breast cancer: A meta-analysis of published studies. *Human Reproduction Update, 6*(4), 374–386.

Berr, C. (2002). Oxidative stress and cognitive impairment in the elderly. *Journal of Nutrition, Health, and Aging, 6,* 261–266.

Berry, J. (2000). Cultural foundations of human behavior. In A. Kazdin (Ed.), *Encyclopedia of psychology.* Washington, DC, and New York: American Psychological Association and Oxford University Press.

Berscheid, E. (1988). Some comments on love's anatomy: Or, whatever happened to old-fashioned lust? In R. J. Sternberg (Ed.), *Anatomy of love.* New Haven, CT: Yale University Press.

Berscheid, E. (2000). Attraction. In A. Kazdin (Ed.), *Encyclopedia of psychology.* Washington, DC, & New York: American Psychological Association and Oxford University Press.

Berscheid, E., & Fei, J. (1977). Sexual jealousy and romantic love. In G. Clinton & G. Smith (Eds.), *Sexual jealousy.* Englewood Cliffs, NJ: Prentice Hall.

Berscheid, E., & Reis, H. T. (1998). Attraction and close relationships. In D. T. Gilbert, S. T. Fiske, & G. Lindzey (Eds.), *Handbook of social psychology* (4th ed., Vol. 2). New York: McGraw-Hill.

Bertenthal, B. I., & Clifton, R. K. (1998). Perception and action. In W. Damon (Ed.), *Handbook of child psychology* (5th ed. Vol. 2). New York: Wiley.

Bertrand, R. M., & Lachman, M. E. (2003). Personality development in adulthood and old age. In I. B. Weiner (Ed.), *Handbook of psychology* (Vol. VI). New York: Wiley.

Best, D. (2001). Cross-cultural gender roles. In J. Worrell (Ed.), *Encyclopedia of women and gender.* San Diego: Academic Press.

Best, J. W., & Kahn, J. V. (2003). *Research in education* (9th ed.). Boston: Allyn & Bacon.

Beyene, Y. (1986). Cultural significance and physiological manifestations of menopause: A biocultural analysis. *Culture, Medicine, and Psychiatry, 10,* 47–71.

Bialystok, E. (1997). Effects of bilingualism and biliteracy on children's emerging concepts of print. *Developmental Psychology, 33,* 429–440.

Bialystok, E. (1999). Cognitive complexity and attentional control in the bilingual mind. *Child Development, 70,* 537–804.

Bialystok, E. (2001). Metalinguistic aspects of bilingual processing. *Annual Review of Applied Linguistics, 21,* 169–181.

Bianchi, S. M., & Spani, D. (1986). *American women in transition.* New York: Russell Sage Foundation.

Biderman, J., & Faraone, S. V. (2003). Current concepts on the neurobiology of attention-deficit/hyperactivity disorder. *Journal of Attention Disorders, 6* (Suppl. 1), S7–S16.

Bigler, R. S., & Liben, L. S. (1990). The role of attitudes and interventions in gender-schematic processing. *Child Development, 61,* 1440–1452.

Bijur, P. E., Wallston, K. A., Smith, C. A., Lifrak, S., & Friedman, S. B. (1993, August). *Gender differences in turning to religion for coping.* Paper presented at meeting of the American Psychological Association, Toronto.

Billman, J. (2003). *Observation and participation in early childhood settings: A practicum guide* (2nd ed.). Boston: Allyn & Bacon.

Billy, J. O. G., Rodgers, J. L., & Udry, J. R. (1984). Adolescent sexual behavior and friendship choice. *Social Forces, 62,* 653–678.

Bingham, C. R., & Crockett, L. J. (1996). Longitudinal adjustment patterns of boys and girls experiencing early, middle, and late sexual intercourse. *Developmental Psychology, 32,* 647–658.

Birren, J. E. (Ed.), (1996). *Encyclopedia of gerontology.* San Diego: Academic Press.

Birren, J. E. (2002). Unpublished review of J. W. Santrock's *Topical life-span development,* 2nd ed. (New York: McGraw-Hill.)

Birren, J. E., & Schaie, K. W. (Eds.) (2001). *Handbook of the psychology of aging* (5th ed.). San Diego: Academic Press.

Birren, J. E., Woods, A. M., & Williams, M. V. (1980). Behavioral slowing with age: Causes, organization, & consequences. In L. W. Poon (Ed.), *Aging in the 1980s: Psychological issues.* Washington, DC: American Psychological Association.

Bissada, A., & Briere, J. (2002). Child abuse: Physical and sexual. In J. Worell (Ed.), *Encyclopedia of women and gender.* San Diego: Academic Press.

Bjorklund, D. F. (2000). *Children's thinking: Developmental function and individual differences* (3rd ed.). Belmont, CA: Wadsworth.

Bjorklund, D. F., & Pellegrini, A. D. (2002). *The origins of human nature.* New York: Oxford University Press.

Bjorklund, D. F., & Rosenbaum, K. (2000). Middle childhood: Cognitive development. In A. Kazdin (Ed.), *Encyclopedia of psychology.* Washington, DC, & New York:

American Psychological Association and Oxford University Press.

Black, J. E. (2001, April). *Complex and interactive effects of enriched experiences on brain development.* Paper presented at the meeting of the Society for Research in Child Development, Minneapolis.

Black, M., & Matula, K. (1999). *Essentials of Bayley Scales of Infant Development II: Assessment.* New York: John Wiley.

Black, M. M., Baqui, A. H., Zaman, K., Persson, L. A., El Arifeen, S., Le, K., McNary, S. W., Parveen, M., & Black, R. E. (2003, April). *Iron and zinc supplementation promote motor development and exploratory behavior in Bangladesh infants.* Paper presented at the meeting of the Society for Research in Child Development, Tampa.

Blair, C., & Ramey, C. (1996). Early intervention with low birth weight infants: The path to second generation research. In M. J. Guralnick (Ed.). *The effectiveness of early intervention.* Baltimore: Paul H. Brookes.

Blair, S. N. (1990, January). Personal communication. Aerobics Institute, Dallas.

Blair, S. N., Kohl, H. W., Paffenbarger, R. S., Clark, D. G., Cooper, K. H., & Gibbons, L. W. (1989). Physical fitness and all-cause mortality: A prospective study of healthy men and women. *Journal of the American Medical Association, 262,* 2395–2401.

Blasi, A. (1988). Identity and the development of the self. In D. Lapsley & F. C. Power (Eds.), *Self, ego, and identity.* New York: Springer-Verlag.

Blickstein, I. (2003). Motherhood at or beyond the edge of reproductive age. *International Journal of Fertility and Women's Medicine, 48,* 17–24.

Block, J. (1993). Studying personality the long way. In D. Funder, R. D. Parke, C. Tomlinson-Keasey, & K. Widaman (Ed.), *Studying lives through time.* Washington, DC: American Psychological Association.

Block, J. H., & Block, J. (1980). The role of ego-control and ego-resiliency in the organization of behavior. In W. A. Collins (Ed.), *Minnesota symposium on child psychology* (Vol. 13). Minneapolis: University of Minnesota Press.

Bloom, B. (1985). *Developing talent in young people.* New York: Ballentine.

Bloom, L. (1998). Language acquisition in its developmental context. In W. Damon (Ed.), *Handbook of child psychology* (5th ed., Vol. 2). New York: Wiley.

Bloom, L., Lifter, K., & Broughton, J. (1985). The convergence of early cognition and language in the second year of life: Problems in conceptualization and measurement. In M. Barrett (Ed.), *Single word speech.* London: Wiley.

Bloom, P. (2002). *How children learn the meaning of words.* Cambridge, MA: MIT Press.

Bloor, C., & White, F. (1983). Unpublished manuscript. University of California at San Diego, La Jolla, CA.

Blumenfeld, P. C., Pintrich, P. R., Wessles, K., & Meece, J. (1981, April). *Age and sex differences in the impact of classroom experiences on self-perceptions.* Paper presented at the biennial meeting of the Society of Research in Child Development, Boston.

Blundell, J. E. (1984). Systems and interactions: An approach to the pharmacology of feeding. In A. J. Stunkard & E. Stellar (Eds.), *Eating and its disorders.* New York: Raven Press.

Bodrova, E., & Leong, D. J. (2003). Learning and development of preschool children from the Vygotskian perspective. In A. Kozulin, B. Gindis, Ageyev, V. S. & Miller, S. M. (Eds.), *Vygotsky's educational theory in cultural context.* New York: Cambridge University Press.

Boerner, K., & Wortman, C. B. (1998). Grief and loss. In H. S. Freeman (Ed.), *Encyclopedia of mental health* (Vol. 2). San Diego: Academic Press.

Bogenschneide, K. (Ed.). (2002). *Family policy matters.* Mahwah. NJ: Erlbaum.

Bohlin, G., & Hagekull, B. (1993). Stranger wariness and sociability in the early years. *Infant Behavior and Development, 16,* 53–67.

Bolen, J. C., Bland, S. D., & Sacks, J. J. (1999, April). *Injury prevention behaviors: Children's use of occupant restraints and bicycle helmets.* Paper presented at the meeting of the Society for Research in Child Development, Albuquerque.

Bolger, K. E., & Patterson, C. J. (2001). Developmental pathways from child maltreatment to peer rejection. *Child Development, 72,* 339–351.

Bonk, C. J., & Cunningham, D. J. (1999). Searching for learner-centered, constructivist, and sociocultural components of collaborative educational learning tools. In C. J. Bonk & K. S. King (Eds.), *Electronic collaborators.* Mahwah, NJ: Erlbaum.

Bonnel, S., Mohand-Said, S., & Sahel, J. A. (2003). The aging of the retina. *Experimental Gerontology, 38,* 825–831.

Books, S. (2004). *Poverty and schooling in the U.S.* Mahwah, NJ: Erlbaum.

Books, S. (2004). *Poverty and schooling.* Mahwah, NJ: Erlbaum.

Bookstein, F. L., Streissguth, A. P., Sampson, P. D., Connor, P. D., & Barr, H. M. (2002). Corpus callosum shape and neuropsychological deficits in adult males with heavy fetal alcohol exposure. *Neuroimage, 15,* 233–251.

Booth, A., & Johnson, D. (1988). Premarital cohabitation and marital success. *Journal of Family Issues, 9,* 255–272.

Booth, A., Johnson, D. R., Granger, D. A., Crouter, A. C., & McHale, S. (2003). Testosterone and child and adolescent adjustment: The moderating role of parent-child relationships. *Developmental Psychology, 39,* 85–98.

Booth, M. (2002). Arab adolescents facing the future: Enduring ideals and pressures to change. In B. B. Brown, R. W. Larson, & T. S. Saraswathi (Eds.), *The world's youth.* New York: Cambridge University Press.

Bornstein, M. H., & Arterberry, M. E. (1999). Perceptual development. In M. H. Bornstein & M. E. Lamb (Eds.), *Developmental psychology: An advanced textbook* (4th ed.). Mahwah, NJ: Erlbaum.

Bornstein, M. H., & Sigman, M. D. (1986). Continuity in mental development from infancy. *Child Development, 57,* 251–274.

Borowsky, I. W., Ireland, M., & Resnick, M. D. (2001). Adolescent suicide attempts: Risks and protectors. *Pediatrics, 107,* 485–493.

Borrayo, E. A., & Jenkins, S. R. (2003). Feeling frugal: Socioeconomic status, acculturation, and cultural health beliefs among women of Mexican descent. *Cultural Diversity and Ethnic Minority Psychology, 9* 197–206.

Bosshard, G., Germini, D., Eisenhart, D., & Bar, W. (2003). Assisted suicide bordering on active euthanasia. *International Journal of Legal Medicine, 117,* 106–108.

Bossy-Wetzel, E., Barsoum, M. J., Godzik, A., Schwarzenbacher, R., & Lipton, S. A. (2003). Mitochondrial fission in apoptosis, neurogenesis, and aging. *Current Opinions in Cell Biology, 15,* 706–716.

Bourchey, H. A., & Furman, W. (2003). Dating and romantic relationships in adolescence. In G. Adams & M. Berzonsky (Eds.), *Blackwell handbook of adolescence.* Malden, MA: Blackwell.

Bouvier, P. (2003). Child sexual abuse: vicious circles of fate or paths to resilience? *Lancet, 361,* 446–447.

Bower, B. (1985). The left hand of math and verbal talent. *Science News, 127,* 263.

Bower, T. G. R. (1966). Slant perception and shape constancy in infants. *Science, 151,* 832–834.

Bower, T. G. R. (2002). Space and objects. In A. Slater & M. Lewis (Eds.), *Introduction to infant development.* New York: Oxford University Press.

Bowes. J., & Flanagan, C. A. (2000, July). The relationship of empathy, sympathy, and altruism in adolescence: International comparisons. In L. Sherrod (Chair), *Youth civic engagement.* Symposium at the meeting of the International Society for the Study of Behavioral Development, Beijing, China.

Bowlby, J. (1969). *Attachment and loss* (Vol. 1). London: Hogarth Press.

Bowlby, J. (1980). *Attachment and loss:* Vol. 3. *Loss, sadness, and depression.* New York: Basic Books.

Bowlby, J. (1989). *Secure and insecure attachment.* New York: Basic Books.

Boyer, K., & Diamond, A. (1992). Development of memory for temporal order in infants and young children. In A. Diamond (Ed.), *Development and neural bases of higher cognitive function.* New York: New York Academy of Sciences.

Brabeck, M. M. (2000). Kohlberg, Lawrence. In A. Kazdin (Ed.), *Encyclopedia of psychology*. Washington, DC, and New York: American Psychological Association and Oxford University Press.

Brabeck, M. M., & Shore, E. L. (2003). Gender differences in intellectual and moral development. In J. Demick & C. Andreoletti: (Eds.), *Handbook of adult development*. New York: Kluwer.

Brabyn, J. A., Schneck, M. E., Haegerstrom-Portnoy, G., & Lott, L. (2001). The Smith-Kettlewell Institute (SKI) Longitudinal Study of Vision Function and Its Impact Among the Elderly: An overview. *Ophthamology and Vision Science, 78*, 2464–2469.

Bradbury, F. D., Fincham, F. D., & Beach, S. R. H. (2000). Research on the nature and determinants of marital satisfaction: A decade in review. *Journal of Marriage and the Family, 62*, 964–980.

Bradley, R. E., & Webb, R. (1976). Age-related differences in locus of control orientation in three behavior domains. *Human Development, 19*, 49–55.

Bradley, R. H., & Corwyn, R. F. (2002). Socioeconomic status and child development. *Annual Review of Psychology* (Vol. 53). Palo Alto, CA: Annual Reviews.

Bradley, R. M., & Corwyn, R. F. (2003). Age and ethnic variations in family process mediators of SES. In M. H. Bornstein & R. H. Bradley (Eds.) *Socioeconomic status, parenting, and child development* Mahwah, NJ: Erlbaum.

Bradley, R. H., Corwyn, R. F., McAdoo, H. P., & Coll, C. G. (2001). The home environments of children in the United States. Part I: Variations by age, ethnicity, and poverty status. *Child Development, 72*, 1844–1867.

Brandstadter, J. (1999). Sources of resilience in the aging self: Toward integrated perspectives. In T. M. Hess & F. Blanchard-Fields (Eds.), *Social cognition and aging*. San Diego: Academic Press.

Brandstadter, J., & Greve, W. (1994). The aging self: Stabilizing and protective processes. *Development Review, 14*, 52–80.

Brandstadter, J., & Renner, G. (1990). Tenacious goal pursuit and flexible goal adjustment: Explication and age-related analysis of assimilative and accommodative strategies of coping. *Psychology and Aging, 5*, 58–67.

Brandstadter, J., Wentura, D., & Greve, W. (1993). Adaptive resources of the aging self: Outlines of an emergent perspective. *Journal of Behavioral Development, 16*, 323–349.

Brazelton, T. B. (1956). Sucking in infancy. *Pediatrics, 17*, 400–404.

Brazelton, T. B., Nugent, J. K., & Lester, B. M., (1987). Neonatal behavioral assessment scale. In J. D. Osofsky (Ed.), *Handbook of infant development* (2nd ed.). New York: Wiley.

Bredekamp, S. (1987). *Developmentally appropriate practice in early childhood programs serving children from birth through age 8.* Washington, DC: National Association for the Education of Young Children.

Bredekamp, S. (1993). Reflections on Reggio Emilia. *Young Children, 49*, 13–16.

Bredekamp, S. (1997). NAEYC issues revised position statement on developmentally appropriate practice in early childhood programs. *Young Children, 52*, 34–40.

Brent, R. L., & Fawcett, L. B. (2000, May). *Environmental causes of human birth defects: What have we learned about the mechanism, nature, and etiology of congenital malformations in the past 50 years?* Paper presented at the joint meetings of the Pediatric Academic Societies and the American Academy of Pediatrics, Boston.

Bretherton, I., Stolberg, U., & Kreye, M. (1981). Engaging strangers in proximal interaction: Infants' social initiative. *Developmental Psychology, 17*, 746–755.

Brett, J. M., & Stroh, L. K. (2003). Working 61 plus hours a week: Why do managers do it? *Journal of Applied Psychology, 88*, 67–78.

Brewer, J. A. (2004). *Introduction to early childhood education.* Boston: Allyn & Bacon.

Brewer, M. B., & Campbell, D. T. (1976). *Ethnocentrism and intergroup attitudes.* New York: Wiley.

Brim, O. (1999). *The MacArthur Foundation study of midlife development.* Vero Beach, FL: MacArthur Foundation.

Brislin, R. (1993). *Understanding culture's influence on behavior.* Fort Worth, TX: Harcourt Brace.

Brodaty, H., Draper, B. M., Millar, J., Low, L. F., Lie, D., Sharah, S., & Paton, H. (2003). Randomized controlled trial of different models of care for nursing home residents with dementia complicated by depression or psychosis. *Journal of Clinical Psychiatry, 64*, 63–72.

Brody, G. H., & Ge, X. (2001). Linking parenting processes and self-regulation to psychological functioning and alcohol use during early adolescence. *Journal of Family Psychology, 15*, 82–94.

Brody, G. H., & Shaffer, D. R. (1982). Contributions of parents and peers to children's moral socialization. *Developmental Review, 2*, 31–75.

Brody, J. E. (1994, April 6). The value of breast milk. *New York Times*, p. C11.

Brody, N. (2000). Intelligence. In A. Kazdin (Ed.), *Encyclopedia of psychology*. Washington, DC, & New York: American Psychological Association and Oxford University Press.

Broidy, L. M., Nagin, D. S., Tremblay, R. E., Bates, J. E., Dodge, K. A., Fegusson, D., Horwood, J. L., Loeber, R., Laird, R., Lynam, D. R., Moffitt, T. E., Pettit, G. S., & Vitaro, F. (2003). Developmental trajectories of childhood disruptive behaviors and adolescent delinquency: A six-site, cross-national study. *Developmental Psychology, 39*, 222–245.

Bronfenbrenner, U. (1986). Ecology of the family as a context for human development: Research perspectives. *Developmental Psychology, 22*, 723–742.

Bronfenbrenner, U. (1995). Developmental ecology through space and time: A future perspective. In P. Moen, G. H. Elder, & K. Lüscher (Eds.), *Examining lives in context*. Washington, DC: American Psychological Association.

Bronfenbrenner, U. (1995, March). *The role research has played in Head Start.* Paper presented at the meeting of the Society for Research in Child Development, Indianapolis.

Bronfenbrenner, U. (2000). Ecological theory. In A. Kazdin (Ed.), *Encyclopedia of psychology*. Washington, DC, & New York: American Psychological Association and Oxford University Press.

Bronfenbrenner, U., & Morris, P. (1998). The ecology of developmental processes. In W. Damon (Ed.), *Handbook of child psychology* (5th ed., Vol. 1). New York: Wiley.

Brook, J. S., Brook, D. W., Gordon, A.S., Whiteman, M., & Cohen, P. (1990). The psychological etiology of adolescent drug use: A family interactional approach. *Genetic, Social, and General Psychology Monographs, 116*, 110–267.

Brook, J. S., Whiteman, M., Balka, E. B., Win, P. T., & Gursen, M. D. (1998). Drug use among Puerto Ricans: Ethnic identity as a protective factor. *Hispanic Journal of Behavioral Sciences, 20*, 241–254.

Brooks, J. B. (1999). *The process of parenting* (5th ed.). Mountain View, CA: Mayfield.

Brooks, J. G., & Brooks, M. G. (1993). *The case for constructivist classrooms.* Alexandria, VA: Association for Supervision and Curriculum.

Brooks, J. G., & Brooks, M. G. (2001). *The case for constructivist classrooms* (2nd ed.). Upper Saddle River, NJ: Erlbaum.

Brooks-Gunn, J. (1988). Antecedents and consequences of variations in girls' maturational timing. In M. D. Levine & E. R. McAnarney (Eds.), *Early adolescent transitions.* Lexington, MA: Lexington Books.

Brooks-Gunn, J. (2003). Do you believe in magic?: What we can expect from early childhood programs. *Social Policy Report, Society for Research in Child Development, XVII* (No. 1), 1–13.

Brooks-Gunn, J., & Graber, J. (1999). *What's sex got to do with it? The development of health and sexual identities during adolescence.* Unpublished manuscript, Columbia University, New York City.

Brooks-Gunn, J., Graber, J. A., & Paikoff, R. L. (1994). Studying links between hormones and negative affect: Models and measures. *Journal of Research on Adolescence, 4*, 469–486.

Brooks-Gunn, J., Han, W. J., & Waldfogel, J. (2002). Maternal employment and child cognitive outcomes in the first three years of life: The NICHD Study of Early Child Care. *Child Development, 73*, 1052–1072.

Brooks-Gunn, J., & Paikoff, R. (1993). "Sex is a gamble, kissing is a game": Adolescent sexuality, contraception, and sexuality. In S. P. Millstein, A. C. Petersen, & E. O. Nightingale (Eds.), *Promoting the health behavior of adolescents.* New York: Oxford University Press.

Brooks-Gunn, J., & Warren, M. P. (1989). The psychological significance of secondary sexual characteristics in 9- to 11-year-old girls. *Child Development, 59,* 161–169.

Brophy, J. (2004). *Motivating students to learn (2nd Ed.).* Mahwah, NJ: Erlbaum.

Broughton, J. M. (1978). Development of concepts of self, mind, reality and knowledge. In W. Damon (Ed.), *Social cognition.* San Francisco: Jossey-Bass.

Broverman, I., Vogel. S., Broverman, D., Clarkson, F., & Rosenkranz, P. (1972). Sex-role stereotypes: A current appraisal. *Journal of Social Issues, 28,* 59–78.

Brown, A. L. (1990). Domain-specific principles affect learning and transfer in children. *Cognitive Science, 14,* 107–133.

Brown, A. L. (1997). Transforming schools into communities of learners. *American Psychologist, 52,* 399–409.

Brown, A. L. (1998, April). *Reciprocal teaching.* Paper presented at the meeting of the American Educational Research Association, San Diego.

Brown, A. L., & Campione, J. C. (1996). Psychological learning theory and the design of innovative environments. In L. Schauble & R. Glaser (Eds.), *Contributions of instructional innovation to understanding learning.* Mahwah, NJ: Erlbaum.

Brown, A. L., & Day, J. D. (1983). Macrorules for summarizing texts: The development of expertise. *Journal of Verbal Learning and Verbal Behavior, 22,* 1–14.

Brown, A. L., Kane, M. J., & Echols, K. (1986). Young children's mental models determine analogical transfer across problems with a common goal structure. *Cognitive Development, 1,* 103–122.

Brown, B. B. (1999). "You're going with whom?!": Peer group influences on adolescent romantic relationships. In W. Furman, B. B. Brown, & C. Feiring (Eds.), *The development of romantic relationships in adolescence.* Cambridge: Cambridge University Press.

Brown, B. B. (1999). Measuring the peer environment of American adolescents. In S. L. Friedman & T. D. Wachs (Eds.), *Measuring environment across the life span.* Washington, DC: American Psychological Association.

Brown, B. B. (2003). Crowds, cliques, & friendships. In G. Adams & M. Berzonsky (Eds.), *Blackwell handbook of adolescence.* Malden, MA: Blackwell.

Brown, B. B. (2004). Adolescents' relationships with peers. In R. Lerner & L. Steinberg (Eds.), *Handbook of adolescent Psychology.* New York: Wiley.

Brown, B. B., & Larson, R. W. (2002). The kaleidoscope of adolescence: Experiences of the world's youth at the beginning of the 21st century. In B. B. Brown, R. W. Larson, & T. S. Saraswathi (Eds.), *The world's youth.* New York: Cambridge University Press.

Brown, B. B., & Lohr, M. J. (1987). Peer-group affiliation and adolescent self-esteem: An integration of ego-identity and symbolic-interaction theories. *Journal of Personality and Social Psychology, 52,* 47–55.

Brown, E. (2003). When breast just isn't best. *Practicing Midwife, 6,* 42.

Brown, J. D., & Siegel, J. D. (1988). Exercise as a buffer of life stress: A prospective study of adolescent health. *Health Psychology, 7,* 341–353.

Brown, L. H., & Roodin, P. A. (2003). Grandparent-grandchild relationships and the life course perspective. In J. Dement & C. Andreoletti (Eds.). *Handbook of adult development.* New York: Kluwer.

Brown, L. S. (1989). New voices, new visions: Toward a lesbian/gay paradigm for psychology. *Psychology of Women Quarterly, 13,* 445–458.

Brown, R. (1973). *A first language: The early stages.* Cambridge, MA: Harvard University Press.

Brown, S. (in press). Spirituality and longevity. *Psychological Science.*

Browne, A., & Williams, R. R. (1993). Gender, intimacy, and lethal violence. Trends from 1976 through 1987. *Gender and Society, 7,* 78–98.

Brownell, K. (2000). Dieting. In A. Kazdin (Ed.), *Encyclopedia of psychology.* Washington, DC, & New York: American Psychological Association and Oxford University Press.

Brownell, K. D., & Cohen, L. R. (1995). Adherence to dietary regimens. *Behavioral Medicine, 20,* 226–242.

Brownell, K. D., & Rodin, J. (1994). The dieting maelstrom: Is it possible to lose weight? *American Psychologist, 9,* 781–791.

Brownlee, S. (1998, June 15). Baby talk. *U.S. News & World Report,* 48–54.

Bruce, C. A. (2002). The grief process for patient, family, and physician. *Journal of the American Osteopathic Association, 102, (9, Supplement 3),* S28–S32.

Bruce, J. M., Olen, K., & Jensen S. J. (1999, April). *The role of emotion and regulation in social competence.* Paper presented at the meeting of the Society for Research in Child Development, Albuquerque.

Bruck, M., & Ceci, S. J. (1997). The suggestibility of young children. *Current Directions in Psychological Science, 6,* 75–79.

Bruck, M., & Ceci, S. J. (1999). The suggestibility of children's memory. *Annual Review of Psychology, 50,* 419–439.

Bruck, M., Ceci, S. J., & Hembrooke, H. (1998). Reliability and credibility of young children's reports: From research to policy and practice, *American Psychologist, 53(2),* 136–151.

Bruner, J. S. (1983). *Child talk.* New York: W. W. Norton.

Bruner, J. S. (1996). *The culture of education.* Cambridge, MA: Harvard University Press.

Budwig, N. (1993). *A developmental functionalist approach to child language.* Hillsdale, NJ: Erlbaum.

Buhrmester, D. (1990). Friendship, interpersonal competence, and adjustment in preadolescence and adolescence. *Child Development, 61,* 1101–1111.

Buhrmester, D. (1998). Need fulfillment, interpersonal competence, and the developmental contexts of early adolescent friendship. In W. M. Bukowski & A. F. Newcomb (Eds.), *The company they keep: Friendship in childhood and adolescence.* New York: Cambridge University Press.

Buhrmester, D. (2001, April). *Does age at which romantic involvement start matter?* Paper presented at the meeting of the Society for Research in Child Development, Minneapolis.

Buhrmester, D., & Carbery, J. (1992, March). *Daily patterns of self-disclosure and adolescent adjustment.* Paper presented at the biennial meeting of the Society for Research on Adolescence, Washington, DC.

Buhrmester, D., & Furman, W. (1987). The development of companionship and intimacy. *Child Development, 58,* 1101–1113.

Buhs, E. S., & Ladd, G. W. (2002). Peer rejection as an antecedent of young children's school adjustment: An examination of mediating processes. *Developmental Psychology, 37,* 550–560.

Buki, L. P., MA, T., Strom, R. D., & Strom, S. K. (2003). Chinese immigrant mothers of adolescents: Self-perceptions of acculturation effects on parenting. *Cultural Diversity and Ethnic Minority Parenting, 9* 127–140.

Bukowski, W. M., Newcomb, A. F., & Hoza, B. (1987). Friendship conceptions among early adolescents: A longitudinal study of stability and change. *Journal of Early Adolescence, 7,* 143–152.

Bukowski, W. M., & Sippola, L. K. (2001). Groups, individuals, and victimization: A view of the peer system. In J. Juvonen and S. Graham (Eds.), *Peer harassment in school: The plight of the vulnerable and victimized.* New York: Guilford.

Bukowski, W. M., Sippola, L. K., & Boivin, M. (1995, March). *Friendship protects "at risk" children from victimization by peers.* Paper presented at the meeting of the Society for Research in Child Development, Indianapolis.

Bulterys, M. (2001). Preventing vertical HIV transmissions in the year 2000. *Placenta, 22,* 5–12.

Bumpass, L. L., & Aquilino, W. (1994). *A social map of midlife: Family and work over the middle life course.* Center for Demography and Ecology, University of Wisconsin, Madison.

Bumpass, L. L., & Lu, H. H. (2000). Trends in cohabitation and implications for children's family contexts in the United States. *Population Studies, 54,* 29–41.

Bumpus, M. F., Crouter, A. C., & McHale, S. M. (2001). Parental autonomy granting during adolescence: Exploring gender differences in context. *Developmental Psychology, 37,* 161–173.

Burgess, E. O. (2004). Sexuality in midlife and later life couples. In J. H. Harvey & A. Wetzel (Eds.), *The handbook of sexuality in close relationships.* Mahwah, NJ: Erlbaum.

Burke, H. M., Zautra, A. J., Davis, M. C., Schultz, A. S., & Reich, J. W. (2003). Arthritis and musculoskeletal conditions. In I. B. Weiner (Ed.), *Handbook of psychology* (Vol. IX). New York: Wiley.

Burkhauser, R. V., & Quinn, J. F. (1989). American patterns of work and retirement. In W. Schmall (Ed.), *Redefining the process of retirement.* Berlin: Springer.

Burton, L. M. (1996). The timing of childbearing, family structure, and the role of responsibilities of aging Black women. In E. M. Hetherington & E. A. Blechman (Eds.), *Stress, coping, and resilience in children and families.* Hillsdale, NJ: Erlbaum.

Burton, R. V. (1984). A paradox in theories and research in moral development. In W. M. Kurtines & J. L. Gewirtz (Eds.), *Morality, moral behavior, and moral development.* New York: Wiley.

Bus, A. G., van IJzendoorn, M. H., & Pellegrini, A. D. (1995). Joint book reading makes for success in learning to read: A meta-analysis on intergenerational transmission of literacy. *Review of Educational Research, 65,* 1–21.

Bush, P. G., Mayhew, T. M., Abramovich, D. R., Aggett, P. J., Burke, M. D., & Page, K. R. (2001). Maternal cigarette smoking and oxygen diffusion across the placenta. *Placenta, 21,* 824–833.

Buss, D. M. (1995). Evolutionary psychology: A new paradigm for psychological science. *Psychological Inquiry, 6,* 1–30.

Buss, D. M. (2000). Evolutionary psychology. In A. Kazdin (Ed.), *Encyclopedia of psychology.* Washington, DC, & New York: American Psychological Association and Oxford University Press.

Buss, D. M. (2001). Human nature and culture: An evolutionary psychology perspective. *Journal of Personality, 69,* 955–978.

Buss, D. M. (2003). *The evolution of desire: Strategies of human mating (rev. ed.).* New York: Basic Books.

Buss, D. M. (2004). *Evolutionary psychology* (2nd ed.). Boston: Allyn & Bacon.

Buss, D. M., & others. (1990). International preferences in selecting mates: A study of 37 cultures. *Journal of Cross-Cultural Psychology, 21,* 5–47.

Buss, D. M., & Schmitt, D. P. (1993). Sexual strategies theory: An evolutionary perspective on human mating. *Psychological Review, 100,* 204–232.

Bussey, K., & Bandura, A. (1999). Social cognitive theory of gender development and differentiation. *Psychological Review, 106,* 676–713.

Butler, R. N. (1996). Life review. In J. E. Birren (Ed.), *Encyclopedia of gerontology* (Vol. 2). San Diego: Academic Press.

Butler, R. N., & Lewis, M. (2002). *The new love and sex after 60.* New York: Ballentine.

Buzwell, S., & Rosenthal, D. (1996). Constructing a sexual self: Adolescents' sexual self-perceptions and sexual risk-taking. *Journal of Research on Adolescence, 6,* 489–513.

Bybee, J. A., & Wells. Y. V. (2003). The development of possible selves during adulthood. In J. Demick & C. Andreoletti (Eds.), *Handbook of adult development.* New York: Kluwer.

Byrnes, J. P. (1997). *The nature and development of decision making.* Mahwah, NJ: Erlbaum.

Byrnes, J. P. (2001). *Minds, brains, and learning.* New York: Guilford.

Byrnes, J. P. (2003). Cognitive development during adolescence. In G. Adams & M. Berzonsky (Eds.), *Blackwell handbook of adolescence.* Malden, MA: Blackwell.

Cabeza, R. (2002). Hemispheric asymmetry reduction in older adults: The HAROLD model. *Psychology and Aging, 17,* 85–100.

Cadwell, L. B. (1997). *Bringing Reggio Emilia home.* New York: Teachers College Press.

Cadwell, L. B. (2002). *Bringing learning to life.* New York: Teachers College Press.

Cahill, L., Haier, R. J., White, N. S., Fallon, J., Kilparaick, L., Lawrence, C., Potkin, S. G., & Alkire, M. T. (2001). Sex-related differences in amygdala activity during emotionally influenced memory storage. *Neurobiology of Learning and Memory, 75,* 1–9.

Calabrese, R. L., & Schumer, H. (1986). The effects of service activities on adolescent alienation. *Adolescence, 21,* 675–687.

Callan, J. E. (2001). Gender development: Psychoanalytic perspectives. In J. Worrell (Ed.), *Encyclopedia of women and gender.* San Diego: Academic Press.

Callender, E. S., Rickard, L., Rinksy-Eng, J. (2001). Knowledge and use of folic acid supplementation: A study of Colorado women whose pregnancies were affected by a fetal neural tube defect. *Clinical Investigations in Medicine, 24,* 124–128.

Cameron, J. (2001). Negative effects of reward on intrinsic motivation—a limited phenomenon. *Review of Educational Research, 71,* 29–42.

Cameron, J., Cowan, L., Holmes, B., Hurst, P., & McLean, M. (Eds.), (1983). *International handbook of educational systems.* New York: Wiley.

Camilli, G., & Monfils, L. (2004). Test scores and equity. In W. A. Firestone, L. F. Monfils, & R. Y. Schoor (Eds.), *The ambiguity of teaching to the test.* Mahwah, NJ: Erlbaum.

Campbell, D. T., & LeVine, K. A. (1968). Ethnocentrism and intergroup relations. In R. Abelson & others (Eds.), *Theories and cognitive consistency: A sourcebook.* Chicago: Rand-McNally.

Campbell, F. A., Pungello, E. P., Miller-Johnson, S., Burchinal, M., & Ramey, C. T. (2001). The development of cognitive and academic abilities: Growth curves from an early childhood educational experiment. *Development Psychology, 37,* 231–243.

Campbell, K., Waters, E., O'Meara, S., & Summerbell, C. (2001). Interventions for preventing obesity in childhood: A systematic review. *Obesity Review, 2,* 49–57.

Campbell, L., Campbell, B., & Dickinson, D. (2004). *Teaching and learning through multiple intelligences* (3rd ed.). Boston: Allyn & Bacon.

Campos, J. J., (1994, spring). The new functionalism in emotions. *SRCD Newsletter,* pp. 1, 7, 9–11, 14.

Campos, J. J., (2001, April). *Emotion in emotional development: Problems and prospects.* Paper presented at the meeting of the Society for Research in Child Development. Minneapolis.

Campos, J. J., Anderson, D. I., Barbu-Roth, M. A., Hubbard, E. M., Hertenstein, J. J., & Witherington, D. (2000). Travel broadens the mind. *Infancy, 1,* 149–219.

Campos, J. J., Langer, A., & Krowitz, A. (1970). Cardiac responses on the visual cliff in prelocomotor human infants. *Science, 170,* 196–197.

Campos, J. J., Kermoian, R., & Zumbahlen, M. R. (1992). Socio-emotional transformation in the family system following infant crawling onset. In N. Eisenberg & R. A. Fabes (Eds.), *New directions for child development.* San Francisco: Jossey-Bass.

Camps, P., & Munoz-Torrero, D. (2002). Cholinergic drugs in pharmacotherapy of Alzheimer's disease. *Mini-Review of Medicinal Chemistry, 2,* 11–25.

Canfield, R. L., & Haith, M. M. (1991). Young infants' visual expectations for symmetric and asymmetric stimulus sequences. *Developmental Psychology, 27,* 198–208.

Cantor, N., & Blanton, H. (1996). Effortful pursuit of personal goals in daily life. In P. M. Gollwitzer & J. A. Bargh (Eds.), *The psychology of the action: Linking cognition and motivation to behavior.* New York: Guilford Press.

Capaldi, D. M., Pears, K. C., Patterson, G. R., & Owen, L. D. (2003). Continuity of parenting practices across generations in an at-risk sample: A prospective comparison of direct and mediated associations. *Journal of Abnormal Child Psychology, 31,* 127–142.

Caplan, P. J., & Caplan, J. B. (1999). *Thinking critically about research on sex and gender.* (2nd ed.). New York: HarperCollins.

Caporael, L. R. (2001). Evolutionary psychology *Annual Review of Psychology* (Vol. 52). Palo Alto, CA: Annual Reviews.

Capparelli, E. V., Mirocnick, M., Danker, W. M., Blanchard, S., Mofenson, L., McSherry, G. D., Gay, H., Ciupak, G., Smith, B., & Connor, J. D. (2003). Pharmacokinetics and tolerance of zidovudine in preterm infants. *Journal of Pediatrics, 142,* 47–52.

Caprara, G. V., & Cervone, D. (2003). A conception of personality as an agenetic, self-regulating system. In L. G. Aspinwall & U. M. Staudinger (Eds.), *A psychology of human strengths.* Washington, DC: American Psychological Association.

Carbone, D. J., & Seftel, A. D. (2002). Erectile dysfunctions: Diagnosis and treatment in older men. *Geriatrics, 57(9),* 18–24.

Carbonell, O. A., Alzte, G., Bustamante, M. R., & Quiceno, J. (2002). Maternal caregiving and infant security in two cultures. *Developmental Psychology, 38,* 67–78.

Carbonne, B., Tsatsaris, V., & Goffinet, F. (2001). The new tocolytics. *Gynecology, Obstetrics, and Fertility, 29,* 316–319.

Card, N. A., Isaacs, J., & Hodges, E. V. E. (2000, April). *Dynamics of interpersonal aggression in the school context: Who aggresses against whom?* Paper presented at the meeting of the Society for Research on Adolescence, Chicago.

Cardelle-Elawar, M. (1992). Effects of teaching metacognitive skills to students with low mathematics ability. *Teaching and Teacher Education* (Vol. 8, No. 2), 109–121.

Carey, M. P., & Vanable, P. A. (2003). AIDS/HIV. In I. B. Weiner (Ed.), *Handbook of psychology* (Vol. 9). New York: Wiley.

Carey, S. (1977). The child as word learner. In M. Halle, J. Bresman, & G. Miller (Eds.), *Linguistic theory and psychological reality* Cambridge, MA: MIT Press.

Carey, S. (2000). Science education as conceptual change. *Journal of Applied Developmental Psychology, 21,* 13–20.

Carlson, C., Cooper, C., & Hsu, J. (1990, March). *Predicting school achievement in early adolescence: The role of family process.* Paper presented at the meeting of the Society for Research in Adolescence, Atlanta.

Carnegie Foundation. (1989). *Turning points: Preparing youth for the 21st century.* New York: Author.

Carnegie Foundation. (1994). *Starting points: Meeting the needs of our youngest children.* New York: Author.

Caron, S. L. (1998). *Cross-cultural perspectives on sexuality.* Boston: Allyn & Bacon.

Carr, D. (2002). Moral education and the perils of developmentalism. *Journal of Moral Education, 31,* 5–19.

Carr, D., House, J. S., Kessler, R. C., Nesse, R. M., Sonnege, J., & Wortman, C. (2000). Marital quality and psychological adjustment to widowhood among older adults: A longitudinal analysis. *Journal of Gerontology: Social Sciences, 55B,* No. 4., S197–S207.

Carroll, J. (1993). *Human cognitive abilities.* Cambridge: Cambridge University Press.

Carskadon, M. A., Acebo, C., & Seifer, R. (2001). Extended nights, sleep loss, and recovery sleep in adolescents. *Archives of Italian Biology, 139,* 301–312.

Carskadon, M. A., Labyak, S. E., Acebo, C., & Seifer, R. (1999). Intrinsic circadian period of adolescent humans measured in conditions of forced desynchrony. *Neuroscience Letters, 260,* 129–132.

Carskadon, M. A., Wolfson, A. R., Acebo, C., Tzischinsky, O., & Seifer, R. (1998). Adolescent sleep patterns, circadian timing, and sleepiness at a transition to early school days. *Sleep, 21,* 873–884.

Carstensen, L. L. (1991). Selectivity theory: Social activity in life-span context. *Annual Review of Gerontology and Geriatrics, 11,* 195–217.

Carstensen, L. L. (1993). Motivation for social contact across the life span: A theory of socioemotional selectivity. In J. E. Jacobs (Ed.), *Nebraska symposium on motivation.* Lincoln: University of Nebraska Press.

Carstensen, L. L. (1995). Evidence for life-span theory of socioemotional selectivity. *Current Direction in Psychological Science, 4,* 151–156.

Carstensen, L. L. (1998). A life-span approach to social motivation. In J. Heckhausen & C. Dweck (Eds.), *Motivation and self-regulation across the life span.* New York: Cambridge University Press.

Carstensen, L. L., & Charles, S. T. (2003). Human aging: Why is even good news taken badly? In L. G. Aspinwall & U. M. Staudinger (Eds.), *A psychology of human strengths.* New York: Oxford University Press.

Carstensen, L. L., Charles, S. T., Isaacowitz, D., & Kennedy, Q. (2003). Life-span development and emotion. In R. J. Davidson, K. Scherer, & H. H. Goldsmith (Eds.), *Handbook of affective sciences.* New York: Oxford University Press.

Carstensen, L. L., & Freund, A. M. (1994). Commentary: The resilience of the aging self. *Developmental Review, 14,* 81–92.

Carstensen, L. L., Gottman, J. M., & Levenson, R. W. (1995). Emotional behavior in long-term marriage. *Psychology and Aging, 10,* 140–149.

Carstensen, L. L., Isaacowitz, D. M., & Charles, S. T. (1999). Taking time seriously: A theory of socioemotional selectivity. *American Psychologist, 54,* 165–181.

Carter, B., & McGoldrick, M. (1989). Overview: The changing family life cycle—A framework for family therapy. In B. Carter & M. McGoldrick (Eds.), *The changing family life cycle* (2nd ed.). Boston: Allyn & Bacon.

Carter-Saltzman, L. (1980). Biological and sociocultural effects on handedness: Comparison between biological and adoptive families. *Science, 209,* 1263–1265.

Carver, K., Joyner, K., Udry, J. R. (2003). National estimates of adolescent romantic relationships. In P. Florsheim (Ed.), *Adolescent romantic relationships and sexual behavior.* Mahwah, NJ: Erlbaum.

Carver, L. J, & Bauer, P. J. (2001). The dawning of a past: The emergence of long-term explicit memory in infancy. *Journal of Experimental Psychology: General, 130(4),* 726–745.

Case, R. (1987). Neo-Piagetian theory: Retrospect and prospect. *International Journal of Psychology, 22,* 773–791.

Case, R. (1992). The role of the frontal lobes in the regulation of cognitive development. *Brain and Cognition, 20,* 51–73.

Case, R. (1999). Conceptual development in the child and the field: A personal view of the Piagetian legacy. In E. K. Skolnick, K. Nelson, S. A. Gelman, & P. H. Miller (Eds.), *Conceptual development.* Mahwah, NJ: Erlbaum.

Case, R., Kurland, D. M., Goldberg, J. (1982). Operational efficiency and the growth of short-term memory span. *Journal of Experimental Child Psychology, 33,* 386–404.

Case, R., & Mueller, M. P. (2001). Differentiation, integration, and covariance mapping as fundamental processes in cognitive and neurological growth. In J. L. McClelland & R. S. Siegler (Eds.), *Mechanisms of cognitive development.* Mahwah, NJ: Erlbaum.

Casey, B., Giedd, J., & Thomas, K. (2000). Structural and functional brain development and its relation to cognitive development. *Biological Psychology, 54,* 241–257.

Casey, B. J., Durston, S., & Fossella, J. A. (2001). Evidence for a mechanistic model of cognitive control. *Clinical Neuroscience Research, 1,* 267–282.

Casey, B. M., McIntire, D. D., & Leveno, K. J. (2001). The continuing value of the Apgar score for the assessment of newborn infants. *New England Journal of Medicine, 344,* 467–471.

Caspi, A. (1998). Personality development across the life course. In W. Damon (Ed.), *Handbook of child psychology* (Vol. 3). New York: Wiley.

Caspi, A., & Roberts, B. W. (2001). Personality development across the life course: The argument for change and continuity. *Psychological Inquiry, 12,* 49–66.

Cassidy, J., & Shaver, P. R. (Eds.) (1999). *Handbook of attachment: Theory, research, and clinical applications.* New York: Guilford.

Castle, N. G. (2001). Innovation in nursing homes. *The Gerontologist, 41,* No. 2, 161–172.

Castoldi, A. F., Coccini, T., & Manzo, L. (2003). Neurotoxic and molecular effects of methylmercury in humans. *Review of Environmental Health, 18,* 19–31.

Castro, L. C., & Avina, R. L. (2002). Maternal obesity: Pregnancy outcomes. *Current Opinions in Obstetrics and Gynecology, 14,* 601–616.

Caswell, L. W., Vitaliano, P. P., Croyle, K. L., Scanlan, J. M., Zhang, J., & Daruwala, A. (2003). Negative associations of chronic stress and cognitive performance in older adult caregivers. *Experimental Aging Research, 29,* 303–318.

Cauffman, B. E. (1994, February). *The effects of puberty, dating, and sexual involvement on dieting and disordered eating in young adolescent girls.* Paper presented at the meeting of the Society for Research on Adolescence, San Diego.

Caulfield, R. A. (2001). *Infants and toddlers.* Upper Saddle River, NJ: Prentice Hall.

Cavanaugh, J. C. (2000, January). Commentary. *American Psychologist, 31,* p. 25.

Cavanaugh, J. C., & Whitbourne, S. K. (2003). Research methods in adult development. In J. Demick & C. Andreoletti (Eds.), *Handbook of adult development.* New York: Kluwer.

Cave, R. K. (2002, August). *Early adolescent language: A content analysis of child development and educational psychology textbooks.* Unpublished doctoral dissertation, University of Nevada–Reno, Reno.

Cavill, S., & Bryden, P. (2003). Development of handedness: comparison of questionnaire and performance-based measure of preference. *Brain and Cognition, 53,* 149–151.

Ceci, S. J. (1996). Unpublished review of *Child Development* (8th ed.) by J. W. Santrock. New York: McGraw-Hill.

Ceci, S. J. (2000). Bronfenbrenner, Urie. In A. Kazdin (Ed.), *Encyclopedia of psychology.* Washington, DC, & New York: American Psychological Association and Oxford University Press.

Ceci, S. J., & Bruck, M. (1993). The suggestibility of the child witness: A historical review and synthesis. *Psychological Bulletin, 113,* 403–439.

Ceci, S. J., & Gilstrap, L. L. (2000), Determinants of intelligence: Schooling and intelligence. In A. Kazdin (Ed.), *Encyclopedia of Psychology.* Washington, DC, & New York: American Psychological Association and Oxford University Press.

Center for Survey Research at the University of Connecticut. (2000). *Hours on the job.* Storrs: University of Connecticut, Center for Survey Research.

Centers for Disease Control and Prevention. (2000). *HIV/AIDS surveillance report.* Atlanta: Author.

Centers for Disease Control and Prevention. (2001a). *Sexually transmitted disease.* Atlanta: Author.

Centers for Disease Control and Prevention. (2001b). *Data and statistics: Adolescent pregnancy.* Atlanta: Author.

Centers for Disease Control and Prevention. (2002). *Cohabitation.* Atlanta: Author.

Centers for Disease Control and Prevention. (2002a). *Sexually transmitted diseases.* Atlanta: Author.

Centers for Disease Control and Prevention. (2002b). *AIDS.* Atlanta: Author.

Cervone, D., & Mischel, W. (2002). Personality Science. In D. Cervone & W. Mischel (Eds.), *Personality Science.* New York: Guilford.

Chall, J. S. (1979). The great debate: Ten years later with a modest proposal for reading stages. In L. B. Resnick & P. A. Weaver (Eds.), *Theory and practice of early reading.* Hillsdale, NJ: Erlbaum.

Chan, A., Keane, R. J., & Robinson, J. S. (2001). The contribution of maternal smoking to preterm birth, small for gestational age, and low birth weight among Aboriginal and non-Aboriginal births in South Australia. *Medical Journal of Australia, 174,* 389–393.

Chan-Yeung, M., & Dimich-Ward, H. (2003). Respiratory health effects of exposure to environmental tobacco smoke. *Respirology, 8,* 131–139.

Charles, S. T., Mather, M., & Carstensen, L. L. (in press). Aging and emotional memory: The forgettable nature of negative images for older adults. *Journal of Experimental Psychology: General.*

Charness, N., & Bosman, E. A. (1992). Human factors and aging. In F. I. M. Craik & T. A. Salthouse (Eds.), *The handbook of aging and cognition.* Hillsdale, NJ: Erlbaum.

Charness, N., Krampe, R. T., & Mayr, U. (1996). The role of practice and coaching in entrepreneurial skill domains: An international comparison of life-span chess skill acquisition. In K. A. Ericsson (Ed.), *The road to excellence: The acquisition of expert performance in the arts, sciences, sports, and games.* Mahwah, NJ: Erlbaum.

Chase-Lansdale, P. L., Coley, R. L., & Grining, C. P. L. (2001, April). *Low-income families and child care.* Paper presented at the meeting of the Society for Research in Child Development, Minneapolis.

Chaudhry, V., Cornblath, D. R., Corse, A., Freimer, M., Simmons-O'Brien, E., & Vogelsang, G. (2002). Thalidomide-induced neuropathy. *Neurology, 59,* 1872–1875.

Chauhuri, J. H., & Williams, P. H. (1999, April). *The contribution of infant temperament and parent emotional availability to toddler attachment.* Paper presented at the meeting of the Society for Research in Child Development, Albuquerque.

Chavkin, W. (2001). Cocaine and pregnancy—time to look at the evidence. *Journal of the American Medical Association, 285,* 1626–1628.

Chen, C., & Stevenson, H. W. (1989). Homework: A cross-cultural examination. *Child Development, 60,* 551–561.

Chen, X., Hastings, P. D., Rubin, K. H., Chen, H., Cen, G., & Stewart, S. L. (1998). Childrearing attitudes and behavioral inhibition in Chinese and Canadian toddlers: A cross-cultural study. *Developmental Psychology, 34,* 677–686.

Cherif, H., Tarry, J. L., Ozanne, S. E., & Hales, C. N. (2003). Aging and telomeres: A study into organ- and gender-specific telomere shortening. *Nucleic Acids Research, 31,* 1576–1583.

Cherlin, A. J., & Furstenberg, F. F. (1994). Stepfamilies in the United States: A reconsideration, In J. Blake & J. Hagen (Eds.) *Annual review of sociology.* Palo Alto, CA: Annual Reviews.

Cherry, K. E., & LeCompte, D. L. (1999). Age and individual differences influence prospective memory. *Psychology and Aging, 14,* 60–76.

Chess, S., & Thomas, A. (1977). Temperamental individuality from childhood to adolescence. *Journal of Child Psychiatry, 16,* 218–226.

Chevan, A. (1996). As cheaply as one: Cohabitation in the older population. *Journal of Marriage and the Family, 58,* 656–667.

Chi, M. T. (1978). Knowledge structures and memory development. In R. S. Siegler (Ed.), *Children's thinking: What develops?* Hillsdale, NJ: Erlbaum.

Chi, M. T. (1981). Knowledge development and memory performance. In J. P. Das & N. O'Conner (Eds.), *Intelligence and learning.* New York: Plenum Press.

Child Trends. (2000). Trends in sexual activity and contraceptive use among teens. *Child trends research brief.* Washington, DC: Author.

Child Trends. (2001). *Trends among Hispanic children, youth, and families.* Washington, DC: Author.

Children's Defense Fund. (1992). *The state of America's children, 1992.* Washington, DC: Author.

Children's Defense Fund. (2001). *A fair start.* Washington, DC: Author.

Chiriboga, D. A. (1982). Adaptation to marital separation in later and earlier life. *Journal of Gerontology, 37,* 109–114.

Choate, J. S. (2004). *Successful inclusive teaching (4th Ed.).* Boston: Allyn & Bacon.

Chochinov, H. M. (2002). Dignity-conserving care—a new model for palliative care: Helping the patient feel valued. *Journal of the American Medical Association, 287,* 2253–2260.

Choi, N. G. (2001). Relationship between life satisfaction and postretirement employment among older women. *International Journal of Aging and Human Development, 52,* 45–70.

Chomsky, N. (1957). *Syntactic structures*. The Hague: Mouton.

Chopdar, A., Chakravarthy, U., & Verma, D. (2003). Age related macular degeneration. *British Journal of Medicine, 326*, 485–488.

Chopra, M. (2003). Risk factors for undernutrition of young children in a rural area of South Africa. *Public Health Nursing, 6*, 645–652.

Christensen, L. (1996). *Diet-behavior relationships*. Washington, DC: American Psychological Association.

Christian, K., Bachnan, H. J., & Morrison, F. J. (2001). Schooling and cognitive development. In R. J. Sternberg & E. L. Grigorenko (Eds.), *Environmental effects on cognitive development*. Mahwah, NJ: Erlbaum.

Christiansen, L. B. (2004). *Experimental methodology* (9th Ed.). Boston: Allyn & Bacon.

Christopher, F. S. (2001). *To dance the dance*. Mahwah, NJ: Erlbaum.

Christopher, F. S., & Sprecher, S. (2000). Sexuality in marriage, dating, and other relationships: Decade review. *Journal of Marriage and Family, 62*, 999–1017.

Chun, K. M., & Akutsu, P. D. (2003). Acculturation among ethnic minority families. In K. M. Chun, P. B. Organista, & G. Marin (Eds.), *Acculturation*. Washington, DC: American Psychological Association.

Churchill, J. D., Galvez, R., Colcombe, S., Swain, R. A., Kramer, A. F., & Greenough, W. T. (2002). Exercise, experience, and the aging brain. *Neurobiology of Aging, 23*, 941–955.

Cicagles, M., Field, T., Hossain, Z., Pelaez-Nogueras, M., & Gewirtz, J. (1996). Touch among children at nursery school. *Early Child Development and Care, 126*, 101–110.

Cicchetti, D. (2001). How a child builds a brain. In W. W. Hartup & R. A. Weinberg (Eds.), *Child psychology in retrospect and prospect*. Mahwah, NJ: Erlbaum.

Cicchetti, D., & Toth, S. L. (1998). Perspectives on research and practice in developmental psychology. In W. Damon (Ed.), *Handbook of child psychology* (Vol. 4). New York: Wiley.

Cicirelli, V. G. (1991). Sibling relationships in adulthood. *Marriage and Family Review, 16*, 291–310.

Cimbora, D. M., & McIntosh, D. N. Emotional responses to antisocial acts in adolescent males with conduct disorder: A link to affective morality. *Journal of Child and Adolescent Psychology, 32*, 296–301.

Clampet-Lundquist, S., Edin, K., London, A., Scott, E., & Hunter, V. (2004). "Making a way out of no way": How mother meet the basic family needs while moving from welfare to work. In A. C. Crouter & A. Booth (Eds.), *Work-family challenges for low-income families and their children*. Mahwah, NJ: Erlbaum.

Clancy, S. M., & Hoyer, W. J. (1994). Age and skill in visual search. *Developmental Psychology, 30*, 545–552.

Clark, E. (2000). Language acquisition. In A. Kazdin (Ed.), *Encyclopedia of psychology*. Washington, DC, & New York: American Psychological Association and Oxford University Press.

Clark, M. S., & Grote, N. K. (2003). Close relationships. In I. B. Weiner (Ed.), *Handbook of psychology* (Vol. 5). New York: Wiley.

Clark, M. S., & Standard, P. L. (1996). Caregiver burden and the structural family model. *Family and Community Health, 18*, 58–66.

Clark, R. D., & Hatfield, E. (1989). Gender differences in receptivity to sexual offers. *Journal of Psychology and Human Sexuality, 2*, 39–55.

Clarke, E. J., Preston, M., Raksin, J., & Bengtson, V. L. (1999). Types of conflicts and tensions between older adults and adult children. *Gerontologist, 39*, 261–270.

Clark-Plaskie, M., & Lachman, M. E. (1999). The sense of control in midlife. In S. L. Willis & J. D. Reid (Eds.), *Life in the middle*. San Diego: Academic Press.

Clausen, J. A. (1993). *American lives*. New York: Free Press.

Clay, R. A. (1997, April). Helping dying patients let go of life in peace. *APA Monitor*, p. 42.

Clifton, R. K., Morrongiello, B. A., Kulig, J. W., & Dowd, J. M. (1981). Developmental changes in auditory localization in infancy. In R. N. Aslin, J. R. Alberts, & M. R. Petersen (Eds.), *Development of perception* (Vol. 1). Orlando, FL: Academic Press.

Clifton, R. K., Muir, D. W., Ashmead, D. H., & Clarkson, M. G. (1993). Is visually guided reaching in early infancy a myth? *Child Development, 64*, 1099–1110.

Clinchy, B. M., Mansfield, A. F., & Schott, J. L. (1995, March). *Development of narrative and scientific modes of thought in middle childhood*. Paper presented at the meeting of the Society for Research in Child Development, Indianapolis.

Cnattinugius, S., Bergstrom, R., Lipworth, L., & Kramer, M. S. (1998). Prepregnancy weight and the risk of adverse pregnancy outcomes. *New England Journal of Medicine, 338*, 147–152.

Cochran, S. D., & Mays, V. M. (1990). Sex, lies, and HIV. *New England Journal of Medicine, 332*, 774–775.

Cocking, R. R., Mestre, J. P., & Brown, A. L. (2001). New developments in the science of learning: Using research to help students learn science and mathematics. *Journal of Applied Developmental Psychology, 21*, 1–11.

Cohan, C. L., & Kleinbaum, S. (2002). Toward a greater understanding of the cohabitation effect: Premarital cohabitation and marital communication. *Journal of Marriage and Family, 64*, 180–192.

Cohen, C. I., Teresi, J., & Holmes, D. (1985). Social networks, stress, adaptation, and health. *Research on Aging, 7*, 409–431.

Cohen, G. J. (2000). *American Academy of Pediatrics guide to your child's sleep: Birth through adolescence*. New York: Villard Books.

Cohen, R. J., & Swerdlik, M. E. (2002). *Psychological testing and assessment* (5th ed.). New York: McGraw-Hill.

Cohn, J. F., & Tronick, E. Z. (1988). Mother-infant face-to-face interaction. Influence is bidirectional and unrelated to periodic cycles in either partner's behavior. *Developmental Psychology, 24*, 396–397.

Coie, J. D., & Dodge, K. A. (1998). Aggression and antisocial behavior. In W. Damon (Ed.), *Handbook of child psychology* (5th ed., Vol. 3). New York: Wiley.

Colapinto, J. (2000). *As nature made him*. New York: Simon & Schuster.

Colby, A., Kohlberg, L., Gibbs, J., & Lieberman, M. (1983). A longitudinal study of moral judgment. *Monographs of the Society for Research in Child Development, 48*, (21, Serial No. 201).

Colcombe, S. J., Erickson, K. I., Raz, N., Webb, A. G., Cohen, N. J., McAuley, E., & Kramer, A. F. (2003). Aerobic fitness reduces brain tissue loss in aging humans. *Journal of Gerontology: Biological Sciences and Medical Sciences, 58A*, M176–M180.

Colcombe, S. J., & Kramer, A. F. (in press). Fitness effects on the cognitive function of older adults: A meta-analytic study. *Psychological Science*.

Cole, A. (2003). Retirement: Into extra time. *Health Services Journal, 113*, 26–28.

Cole, E. R., & Stewart, A. J. (1996). Black and White women's political activism: Personality development, political identity and social responsibility. *Journal of Personality and Social Psychology, 71*, 130–140.

Cole, M., & Cole, S. (2001). *The development of children* (4th ed.). New York: Worth.

Coleman, M., Ganong, L., & Fine, M. (2000). Reinvestigating remarriage: Another decade of progress. *Journal of Marriage and the Family, 62*, 1288–1307.

Coleman, M., Ganong, L., & Weaver, S. E. (2001). Relationship maintenance and enhancement in remarried families. In J. H. Harvey & A. Wenzel (Eds.), *Close romantic relationships*. Mahwah, NJ: Erlbaum.

Coleman, P. D. (1986, August). *Regulation of dendritic extent: Human aging brain and Alzheimer's disease*. Paper presented at the meeting of the American Psychological Association, Washington, DC.

Coleman, P. K., & Byrd, C. P. (2003). Interpersonal correlates of peer victimization among young adolescents. *Journal of Youth and Adolescence, 32*, 301–314.

Coley, R. (2001). *Differences in the gender gap: Comparisons across/racial/ethnic groups in the United States*. Princeton, NJ: Educational Testing Service.

Coll, C. T. G., Erkut, S., Alarcon, O., Garcia, H. A. V., & Tropp, L. (1995, March). *Puerto Rican adolescents and families: Lessons in construct and instrument development.* Paper presented at the meeting of the Society for Research in Child Development, Indianapolis.

Coll, C. T. G., & Pachter, L. M. (2002). Ethnic and minority parenting. In M. H. Bornstein (Ed.), *Handbook of parenting* (2nd ed., Vol. 4). Mahwah, NJ: Erlbaum.

Collins, W. A. (2002, April). *More than a myth: The developmental significance of romantic relationships during adolescence.* Presidential address delivered at the Meeting of the Society for Research on Adolescence, New Orleans.

Collins, W. A., & Laursen, B. (2000). Adolescent relationships: The art of fugue. In C. Hendrick & S. S. Hendrick (Eds.), *Close relationships: A sourcebook.* Thousand Oaks, CA: Sage.

Collins, W. A., & Laursen, B. (2004). Parent-adolescent relationships and influences. In R. Lerner & L. Steinberg (Eds.), *Handbook of adolescence.* New York: Wiley.

Collins, W. A., Maccoby, E. E., Steinberg, L., Hetherington, E. M., & Bornstein, M. H. (2000). Contemporary research on parenting: The case for nature and nurture. *American Psychologist, 55,* 218–232.

Collins, W. A., Maccoby, E. E., Steinberg, L., Hetherington, E. M., & Bornstein, M. H. (2001). Toward nature WITH nurture. *American Psychologist, 56,* 171–173.

Comer, J. P. (1988). Educating poor minority children. *Scientific American, 259,* 42–46.

Comer, J. P., Haynes, N. M., Joyner, E. T., & Ben-Avie, M. (1996). *Rallying the whole village: The Comer process for reforming urban education.* New York: Teachers College Press.

Committee on Drugs. (2000). Use of psychoactive medication during pregnancy and possible effects on the fetus and newborn. *Pediatrics, 105,* 880–887.

Committee on Fetus and Newborn. (2000). Prevention and management of pain and stress in the newborn. *Pediatrics, 105,* 454–461.

Committee on Substance Abuse. (2000). Fetal alcohol syndrome an alcohol-related neurodevelopmental disorders. *Pediatrics, 106,* 258–261.

Commoner, B. (2002). Unraveling the DNA myth: The spurious foundation of genetic engineering. *Harper's Magazine, 304,* 39–47.

Commons, M. L., & Richards, F. A. (2003). Four postformal stages. In J. Demick & C. Andreoletti (Eds.), *Handbook of Adult Development.* New York: Kluwer.

Commons, M. L., Sinnott, J. D., Richards, F. A., & Armon, C. (1989). *Adult development. Vol. 1: Comparisons and applications of developmental models.* New York: Praeger.

Condry, K. F., Smith, W. C., & Spelke, E. S. (2001). Development of perceptual organization. In F. Lacerda, C. von Hofsten, & M. Heimann (Eds.), *Emerging cognitive abilities in infancy.* Mahwah, NJ: Erlbaum.

Conger, F. O., Lorenz, F. O., & Wickrama, K. A. S. (2004). Changing families in changing times. In R. D. Conger, F. O. Lorenz, & K. A. S. Wickrama (Eds.), *Continuity and change in family relations.* Mahwah, NJ: Erlbaum.

Conger, J. J. (1981). Freedom and commitment: Families, youth, and social change. *American Psychologist, 36,* 1475–1484.

Conger, J. J. (1988). Hostages to the future: Youth, values, and the public interest. *American Psychologist, 43,* 291–300.

Conger, R. D., & Chao, W. (1996). Adolescent depressed mood. In R. L. Simons (Ed.), *Understanding differences between divorced and intact families: Stress, interaction, and child outcome.* Thousand Oaks, CA: Sage.

Conger, R. D., & Ge, X. (1999). Conflict and cohesion in parent-adolescent relations: Changes in emotional expression. In M. J. Cox & J. Brooks-Gunn (Eds.), *Conflict and cohesion in families.* Mahwah, NJ: Erlbaum.

Conger, R. D., Neppl, T., Kim, K. J., & Scaramella, I. (2003). Angry and aggressive behavior across three generations: A prospective, longitudinal study of parents and children. *Journal of Abnormal Child Psychology, 31,* 143–160.

Conger, R. D., & Reuter, M. (1996). Siblings, parents, and peers: A longitudinal study of social influences in adolescent risk for alcohol use and abuse. In G. H. Brody (Ed.), *Sibling relationships: Their causes and consequences.* Norwood, NJ: Ablex.

Connell, C. M., & Janevic, M. R. (2003). Health and human development. In I. B. Weiner (Ed.), *Handbook of psychology* (Vol. VI). New York: Wiley.

Cook, D. J., Guyatt, G. H., Jaeschke, R., Reeve, J., Spanier, A., King, D., Molloy, D., Willan, A., & Streiner, D. (1995). Determinants in Canadian health care workers of the decision to withdraw life support from the critically ill. *Journal of the American Medical Association, 273,* 703–708.

Cook, M., & Birch, R. (1984). Infant perception of the shapes of tilted plane forms. *Infant Behavior and Development, 7,* 389–402.

Cooper, C. R., & Ayers-Lopez, S. (1985). Family and peer systems in early adolescence: New models of the role of relationships in development. *Journal of Early Adolescence, 5,* 9–22.

Cooper, C. R., & Grotevant, H. D. (1989, April). *Individual and connectedness in the family and adolescent's self and relational competence.* Paper presented at the meeting of the Society for Research in Child Development, Kansas City.

Cooper, C. R., Grotevant, H. D., Moore, M. S., & Condon, S. M. (1982, August). *Family support and conflict: Both foster adolescent identity and role taking.* Paper presented at the meeting of American Psychological Association, Washington, DC.

Cooper, C. R., Jackson, J. F., Azmitia, M., Lopez, E., & Dunbar, N. (1995). Bridging students' multiple worlds: African American and Latino youth in academic outreach programs. In R. F. Macias & R. G. Garcia-Ramos (Eds.), *Changing schools for changing students.* Santa Barbara: University of California Linguistic Minority Research Institute.

Cooter, R. B. (Ed.) (2004). *Perspectives on rescuing urban literacy education.* Mahwah, NJ: Erlbaum.

Copper, M. L., Shaver, P. R., & Collins, N. L. (1998). Attachment styles, emotional regulation, and adjustment in adolescence. *Journal of Personality and Social Psychology, 74,* 1380–1397.

Corley, E. (2000). Adult education. Retrieved from the World Wide Web at *http://encarta.msn.com.*

Corr, C. A., & Corr, D. M. (2004). Sudden infant death syndrome. In C. D. Bryant (Ed.), *Handbook of death and dying.* Thousand Oaks, CA: Sage.

Corr, C. A., Nabe, C. M., & Corr, D. M. (2003). *Death and dying, life and living* (4th ed.). Belmont, CA: Wadsworth.

Corrigan, R. (1981). The effects of task and practice on search for invisibly displaced objects. *Developmental Review, 1,* 1–17.

Corsica, J. A., & Perri, M. G. (2003). Obesity. In I. B. Weiner (Ed.), *Handbook of psychology* (Vol. IX). New York: Wiley.

Corso, J. F. (1977). Auditory perception and communication. In J. E. Birren & K. W. Schaie (Eds.), *Handbook of the psychology of aging* (2nd ed.). New York: Van Nostrand Reinhold.

Cosey, E. J., & Bechtel, G. A. (2001). Family support and prenatal care among unmarried African American teenage primiparas. *Journal of Community Health and Nursing, 18,* 107–114.

Cosmides, L., Tooby, J., Cronin, H., & Curry, O. (Eds.). (2003). *What is evolutionary psychology? Explaining the new science of the mind.* New Haven, CT: Yale University Press.

Costa P. T., Herbst J. H., McCrae R. R., & Siegler, I. C. (2000). Personality at midlife: Stability, intrinsic maturation, and response to life events. *Assessment, 7,* 367–380.

Costa, P. T., & McCrae, R. R. (1995). Solid ground on the wetlands of personality: A reply to Black. *Psychological Bulletin, 117,* 216–220.

Costa, P. T., & McCrae, R. R. (1998). Personality assessment. In H. S. Friedman (Ed.), *Encyclopedia of mental health* (Vol. 3). San Diego: Academic Press.

Costa, P. T., & McCrae, R. R. (2000). Contemporary personality psychology. In C. E. Coffey and J. L. Cummings (Eds.), *Textbook of geriatric neuropsychology.* Washington, DC: American Psychiatric Press.

Cota-Robles, S., Neiss, M., & Hunt, C. (2000, April). *Future parent, future scholars: A longitudinal study of adolescent "possible selves" and adult outcomes.* Paper presented at the meeting of the Society for Research on Adolescence, Chicago.

Cote, J. E., & Levine, C. (1988). On critiquing the identity crisis paradigm: A rejoinder to Waterman, *Development Review, 8,* 209–218.

Cotton, S. R. (1999). Marital status and mental health revisited: Examining the importance of risk factors and resources. *Family Relations, 48,* 225–233.

Council of Economic Advisors. (2000). *Teens and their parents in the 21st century: An examination of trends in teen behavior and the role of parent involvement.* Washington, DC: Author.

Courtenay, W. H., McCreary, D. R., & Merighi, J. R. (2002). Gender and ethnic differences in health beliefs and behaviors. *Journal of Health Psychology, 7,* 219–231.

Cowan, C.P., & Cowan, P. A. (2000). *When partners become parents.* Mahwah, NJ: Erlbaum.

Cowan, C.P., Cowan, P. A., Heming, G., & Boxer, C. (1995). *Preventive interventions with parents of preschoolers on the children's adaptation to kindergarten.* Paper presented at the meeting of the Society for Research in Child Development New Orleans.

Cowell, R., Weeks, S., Humm, C., & John, M. (2003). Work until you drop. *Nursing Standards, 17,* 23.

Cowley, G. (1998, April 6). Why children turn violent. *Newsweek,* 24–25.

Cowley, G., & Hager, M. (1995, December 4). Terminal care: Too painful, too prolonged. *Newsweek,* pp. 74–75.

Cox, H., & Hammonds, A. (1998). Religiosity, aging, and life satisfaction. *Journal of Religion and Aging, 5,* 1–21.

Cox, M. J., Burchinal, M., Taylor, L. C., Frosch, B., Goldman, B., & Kanoy, K. (2004). The transition to parenting: Continuity and change in early parenting behavior and attitudes. In R. D. Conger, F. O. Lorenz, & K. A. S. Wickrama (Eds.), *Continuity and change in family relations.* Mahwah, NJ: Erlbaum.

Crano, W., & Brewer, M. (2002). *Principles and Methods of social research* (2nd ed.). Mahwah, NJ: Erlbaum.

Cremation Association of America. (2000). *Fact sheet.* Milwaukee, WI: Author.

Crick, N. R., Nelson, D. A., Morales, J. R., Cullerton-Sen, C., Casas, J. F., Hickman, S. (2001). Relational victimization in childhood and adolescence: I hurt you through the grapevine. In J. Juvonen & S. Graham (Eds.), *Peer harassment in school: The plight of the vulnerable and victimized.* New York: Guilford Press.

Crockenberg, S. B. (1986). Are temperamental differences in babies associated with predictable differences in caregiving? In J. V. Lerner & R. M. Lerner (Eds.), *Temperament and social interaction during infancy and childhood.* San Francisco: Jossey-Bass.

Crocker, J. (2002). The costs of seeking self-esteem. *Journal of Social Issues, 58,* 597–615.

Cronin, C. (2003). First-time mothers—identifying their needs, perceptions, and experiences. *Journal of Clinical Nursing, 12,* 260–267.

Crooks, R., & Bauer, K. (2002). *Our sexuality* (8th ed.). Belmont, CA: Wadsworth.

Cross, S., & Markus, H. (1991). Possible selves across the lifespan. *Human Development, 34,* 230–255.

Crouter, A. C., & Booth, A. (Eds.). (2003). *Children's influence on family dynamics.* Mahwah, NJ: Erlbaum.

Crouter, A. C., & Booth, A. (Eds.) (2004). *Work-family challenges for low-income families and their children.* Mahwah, NJ: Erlbaum.

Crouter, A. C., Manke, B. A., & McHale, S. M. (1995). The family context of gender intensification in early adolescence. *Child Development, 66,* 317–329.

Crowley, K., Callahan, M. A., Tenenbaum, H. R., & Allen, E. (2001). Parents explain more to boys than to girls during shared scientific thinking. *Psychological Science, 12,* 258–261.

Croyle, R. T. (2000). Genetic counseling. In A. Kazdin (Ed.), *Encyclopedia of psychology.* Washington, DC, & New York: American Psychological Association and Oxford University Press.

Cruz, O. L., Kasse, C. A., & Leonhart, F. D. (2003). Efficacy of surgical treatment of chronic otitis media. *Otolaryngology, Head, and Neck Surgery, 128,* 263–266.

Crystal, D. S., Chen, C., Fuligni, A., Stevenson, H. W., Hsu, C., Ko, H., Kitamura, S., & Kimura, S. (1994). Psychological maladjustment and academic achievement: A cross-cultural study of Japanese, Chinese, and American high school students. *Child Development, 65*(4), 738–753.

Csaja, S. J. (2001). Technological change and the older worker. In J. E. Birren & K. W. Schaie (Eds.), *Handbook of the psychology of aging* (5th ed.). San Diego: Academic Press.

Csikszentmihalyi, M. (1996). *Creativity.* New York: HarperCollins.

Csikszentmihalyi, M. (1997). *Finding flow: The psychology of engagement with everyday life.* New York: Basic Books.

Csikszentmihalyi, M., & Rathunde, K. (1998). The development of the person: An experiential perspective on the ontogenesis of psychological complexity. In W. Damon (Ed.), *Handbook of child psychology* (5th ed., Vol. 1). New York: Wiley.

Cuddy-Casey, M., & Orvaschel, H. (1997). Children's understanding of death in relation to child suicidality and homicidality. *Death Studies, 17.* 33–45.

Cuellar, I., Siles, E., & Bracamontes, E. (2004). Acculturation. In M. Schaller & C. S. Crandall (Eds.), *The psychological foundations of culture.* Mahwah, NJ: Erlbaum.

Cui, X., & Vaillant, G. E. (1996). Antecedents and consequents of negative life events in adulthood: A longitudinal study. *American Journal of Psychiatry, 153,* 123–126.

Cullen, K. (2001). *Context and eating behavior in children.* Unpublished research, Children's Nutrition Research Center, Baylor School of Medicine, Houston.

Cully, J. A., LaVoie, D., & Gfeller, J. D. (2001). Reminiscence, personality, and psychological functioning in older adults. *The Gerontologist, 41,* No. 1, 89–95.

Cumming, E., & Henry, W. (1961). *Growing old.* New York: Basic Books.

Cummings, E. M. (1987). Coping with background anger in early childhood. *Child Development, 58,* 976–984.

Cumming, E. M., Braungart-Rieker, J. M., & Du Rocher-Schudlich, T. (2003). Emotion and personality development. In I. B. Weiner (Ed.), *Handbook of psychology* (Vol. 6). New York: Wiley.

Cummings, E. M., & Davies, P. T. (2002). Effects of marital conflict on children: Recent advances and emerging themes in process-oriented research. *Journal of Child Psychology and Psychiatry, 43,* 31–63.

Cummings, E. M., Goeke-Morey, M. C., Papp, L. M., & Dukewich, T. L. (2002). Children's responses to mothers' and fathers' emotionality and tactics in marital conflict in the home. *Journal of Family Psychology, 16,* 478–492.

Curran, K., DuCette, J., Eisenstein, J., & Hyman, I. A. (2001, August). *Statistical analysis of the cross-cultural data: The third year.* Paper presented at the meeting of the American Psychological Association, San Francisco.

Curtiss, S. (1977). *Genie.* New York: Academic Press.

Cushner, K. H. (2003). *Human diversity in action* (2nd ed.). New York: McGraw-Hill.

Cushner, K. H., McClelland, A., & Safford, P. (2003). *Human diversity in action: An integrative approach* (4th ed.). New York: McGraw-Hill.

Dabbs, J. M., Jr., Frady, R. I., Carr, T. S., & Besch, M. F. (1987). Saliva, testosterone, and criminal violence in young adult prison inmates. *Psychosomatic Medicine, 49,* 174–182.

Dabbs, J. M., Jr., & Morris, R. (1990). Testosterone, social class, and antisocial behavior in a sample of 4,462 men. *Psychological Science, 1,* 209–211.

Dahl, R. E., & Lewin, D. S. (2002). Pathways to adolescent health sleep regulation and behavior. *Journal of Adolescent Health, 31* (Suppl.), 175–184.

Damon, W. (1988). *The moral child.* New York: Free Press.

Damon, W. (1995). *Greater expectations.* New York: Free Press.

Damon, W., & Hart, D. (1998). *Self-understanding in childhood and adolescence.* New York: Cambridge University Press.

Danforth, M. M., & Glass, J. C. (2001). Listen to my words, give meaning to my sorrow: A study in cognitive constructs in middle-aged bereaved widows. *Death Studies, 25,* 513–548.

Daniels, S. (2001). Cardiovascular disease risk factors and atherosclerosis in children and adolescents. *Current Atherosclerosis Reports, 3,* 479–485.

Danner, D., Snowdon, D., & Friesen, W. (2001). Positive emotions in early life and longevity: Findings from the Nun Study. *Journal of Personality and Social Psychology, 80(5),* 804–813.

Dannhausen-Brun, C. A., Shalowitz, M. U., & Berry, C. A. (1997, April). *Challenging the assumptions: Teen moms and public policy.* Paper presented at the meeting of the Society for Research in Child Development, Washington, DC.

Darwin, C. (1859). *On the origin of species.* London: John Murray.

Darwin, C. (1965). *The expression of the emotions in man and animals.* Chicago: University of Chicago Press. (Original work published 1872).

Dasen, P. R. (1977). Are cognitive processes universal? A contribution to cross-cultural Piagetian psychology. In N. Warran (Ed.), *Studies in cross-cultural psychology* (Vol. 1). London: Academic Press.

Dasen, P. R., Ngini, L., & Lavalée, M. (1979). Cross-cultural training studies of concrete operations. In L. H. Eckenberger, W. J. Lonner, & Y. H. Poortinga (Eds.), *Cross-cultural contributions to psychology.* Boston: Allyn & Bacon.

Dattilio, F. M. (Ed.). (2001). *Case studies in couple and family therapy.* New York: Guilford.

Davidson, D. (1996). The effects of decision characteristics on children's selective search of predecisional information. *Acta Psychologica, 92,* 263–281.

Davies, K. (2001). *Cracking the genome.* New York: Free Press.

Davis, C. G., & Nolen-Hoeksema, S. (2001). Loss and meaning: How do people make sense of loss? *American Behavioral Scientist, 44,* 726–741.

Davis, G. F. (2001). Loss and duration of grief. *Journal of the American Medical Association, 285,* 1152–1153.

Davis, K. (1996). *Families.* Pacific Grove, CA: Brooks/Cole.

Davison, G. C., & Neale, J. M. (2001). *Abnormal psychology* (8th ed.). New York: Wiley.

Davison, G. C., & Neale, J. M. (2004). *Abnormal psychology* (9th ed.). New York: Wiley.

Davisson, M. T., Gardiner, K., & Costa, A. C. (2001). Report of the ninth international workshop on the molecular biology of human chromosome 21 and Down syndrome. *Cytogenetic Cell Genetics, 92,* 1–22.

Daws, D. (2000). *Through the night.* San Francisco: Free Association Books.

Day, J. M., & Youngman, D. J. (2003). Discursive practices and their interpretation in the psychology of religious development. In J. Demick & C. Andreoletti (Eds.), *Handbook of adult development.* New York: Kluwer.

Day, N. L., Leech, S. L., Richardson, G. A., Cornelius, M. D., Robles, N., & Larkby, C. (2002). Prenatal alcohol exposure predicts continued deficits in offspring size at 14 years of age. *Alcohol: Clinical and Experimental Research, 26,* 1584–1591.

Day, R. D., & Acock, A. (2004). Youth ratings of family processes and father role performance of resident and nonresident fathers. In R. D. Day & M. E. Lamb (Eds.), *Conceptualizing and measuring father involvement.* Mahwah, NJ: Erlbuam.

Day, R. H., & McKenzie, B. E. (1973). Perceptual shape constancy in early infancy. *Perception, 2,* 315–320.

de la Rocheborchard, E., & Thonneau, P. (2002). Paternal age and maternal age are risk factors for miscarriage: Results of a multicentre European study. *Human Reproduction, 17,* 1649–1656.

De Leo, D. (2002). Struggling against suicide: The need for an integrative approach. *Crisis, 23,* 23–31.

De Villers, M. J. (2003). Documentation of preventive education and screening for osteoporosis. *Outcomes Management, 7,* 28–32.

DeCasper, A. J., & Spence, M. J. (1986). Prenatal maternal speech influences newborn's perception of speech sounds. *Infant Behavior and Development, 9,* 133–150.

deCharms, R. (1984). Motivation enhancement in educational settings. In R. Ames & C. Ames (Eds.). *Research on motivation in education* (Vol. 1). Orlando: Academic Press.

Deci, E. L. (1975). *Intrinsic motivation.* New York: Plenum Press.

Deci, E. L., Koestner, R., & Ryan, R. M. (2001). Extrinsic rewards and intrinsic motivation in education: Reconsidered once again. *Review of Educational Research, 71,* 1–28.

Deci, E. L., & Ryan, R. (1994). Promoting self-determined education. *Scandinavian Journal of Educational Research, 38,* 3–14.

DeLamater, J., & Friedrich, W. (2002). Human sexual development. *Journal of Sex Research, 39,* 10–14.

DeLoache, J. S. (1989). The development of representation in young children. In H. W. Reese (Ed.), *Advances in child development and behavior.* New York: Academic Press.

DeLoache, J. S. (2001). The symbol-mindedness of young children. In W. W. Hartup & R. A. Weinberg (Eds.), *Child psychology in retrospect and prospect.* Mahwah, NJ: Erlbaum.

DeLoache. J. S., Miller, K. F., & Pierroutsakos, S. L. (1998). Reasoning and problem solving. In D. Kuhn & R. S. Siegler (Eds.), *Handbook of child psychology* (5th ed., Vol. 2). New York: Wiley.

DeMaris, A., & Rao, K. (1992). Premarital cohabitation and subsequent marital stability in the United States: A reassessment. *Journal of Marriage and the Family, 54,* 178–190.

Dement, W. C., & Vaughn, C. (2000). *The promise of sleep.* New York: Dell.

Demetriou, A. (2001, April). *Towards a comprehensive theory of intellectual development: Integrating psychometric and post–Piagetian theories.* Paper presented at the meeting of the Society for Research in Child Development, Minneapolis.

Demetriou, A., Christou, C., Spanoudis, G., & Platsidou, M. (2002). The development of mental processing: Efficiency, working memory, and thinking. *Monographs of the Society for Research in Child Development, 67* (1, Serial No. 268).

Demorest, R. A., & Landry, A. G. (2003). Prevention of pediatric sports injuries. *Current Sports Medicine Reports, 2,* 337–343.

Dempster, F. N. (1981). Memory span: Sources of individual and developmental differences. *Psychological Bulletin, 80,* 63–100.

Denham, S. A. (1998). *Emotional development in young children.* New York: Guilford.

Denham, S. A., Blair, K. A., DeMulder, E., Levitas, J., Sawyer, K., Auerbach-Major, S., & Queenan, P. (2003). Preschool emotional competence: Pathway to social competence? *Child Development, 74,* 238–256.

Denney, N. W. (1986, August). *Practical problem solving.* Paper presented at the meeting of the American Psychological Association, Washington, DC.

Denney, N. W. (1990). Adult age differences in traditional and practical problem solving. *Advances in Psychology, 72,* 329–349.

Denny, C. B. (2001). Stimulant effects in attention deficit hyperactivity disorder. *Journal of Clinical Child Psychology, 30,* 98–109.

DeSpelder, L. A., & Strickland, A. L. (2000). *The last dance: Encountering death and dying* (6th ed.). Mountain View, CA: Mayfield.

Dettmer, P., Dyck, N., & Thurston, L. (2002). *Consultation, collaboration, and teamwork for students with special needs* (4th ed.). Boston: Allyn & Bacon.

DeVellis, B. M., & DeVellis, R. F. (2001). Self-efficacy and health. In A. Baum, T. A. Revenson, & J. E. Singer (Eds.), *Handbook of health psychology.* Mahwah, NJ: Erlbaum.

Dewey, J. (1933). *How we think.* Lexington, MA: D. C. Heath.

Dezolt, D. M., & Hull, S. H. (2001). Classroom and school climate. In J. Worell (Ed.), *Encyclopedia of women and gender.* San Diego: Academic Press.

Di Paula, A., & Campbell, J. D. (2002). Self-esteem and persistence in the face of failure. *Journal of Personality and Social Psychology, 83,* 711–724.

Diamond, A. D. (1985). Development of the ability to use recall to guide action, as indicated by infants' performance on AB. *Child Development, 56,* 868–883.

Diamond, A. D. (2001). A model system for studying the role of dopamine in the prefrontal cortex during early development in humans: Early and continuously treated phenylketonuria. In C. Nelson & M. Luciana (Eds.), *Handbook of developmental cognitive neuroscience.* Cambridge, MA: MIT Press.

Diamond, L. M. (2003). Love matters: Romantic relationships among sexual-minority adolescents. In P. Florsheim (Ed.), *Adolescent romantic relations and sexual behavior.* Mahwah, NJ: Erlbaum.

Diamond, M., & Sigmundson, H. K. (1997). Sex reassignment at birth: Long-term review and clinical implications. *Archives of Pediatric and Adolescent Medicine, 151,* 298–304.

Dickman, A. B., & Eagly, A. H. (2000). Stereotypes as dynamic constructs: Women and men of the past, present, and future. *Personality and Social Psychology Bulletin, 26,* 1171–1188.

Diener, E. (2004). *Frequently Asked questions (FAQs) about Subjective well-being* (happiness and life-satisfaction). Champaign, IL: University of Illinois, Department of Psychology.

Diener, E., & Diener, M. (1995). Cross-cultural correlates of life satisfaction and self-esteem. *Journal of Personality and Social Psychology, 68,* 653–663.

Diener, E., Lucas, R. E., & Oishi, S. (2002). Subjective well-being: the science of happiness and life-satisfaction. In C. R. Synder & S. J. Lopez (Eds.), *Handbook of positive psychology.* New York: Oxford University Press.

DiLalla, L. F. (2000). Development of intelligence: Current research and theories. *Journal of School Psychology, 38,* 3–8.

Dillin, A., Hsu, A. L., Arantes-Oliveira, N., Lehrer-Graiwere, J., Hsin, H., Fraser, A. G., Kamath, R. S., Ahringer, J., & Kenyon, C. (2002). Rates of behavior and aging specified by mitochondrial function during development. *Science, 298,* 2398–2401.

Dillon, J. (2004). Reincarnation: The technology of death. In C. D. Bryant (Ed.), *Handbook of death and dying.* Thousand Oaks, CA: Sage.

DiMauro, S., Tanji, K., Bonilla, E., Palloti, F., & Schon, E. A. (2002). Mitochondrial abnormalities in muscle and other aging cells: Classification, causes, and effects. *Muscle and Nerve, 26,* 597–607.

Dion, K. K., & Dion, K. L. (1993). Individualistic and collectivistic perspectives on gender and the cultural context of love and intimacy. *Journal of Social Issues, 49,* 53–69.

Dishion, T. (2001, April). *Understanding and preventing adolescent drug use.* Paper presented

at the meeting of the Society for Research in Child Development, Minneapolis.

Dixit, N. K., Gerton, B. K., Dohn, P., Meyer-Lindenberg, A., & Berman, K. F. (2000, June). *Age-related changes in rCBF activation during an N-Back working memory paradigm occur prior to age 50.* Paper presented at the Human Brain Mapping meeting, San Antonio, TX.

Dixon, R. A., & Cohen, A. (2003). Cognitive development in adulthood. In I. B. Weiner (Ed.), *Handbook of psychology* (Vol. 6). New York: Wiley.

Dixon, R. A., Kurzman, D., & Friesen, I. C. (1993). Handwriting performance in younger and older adults: Age, familiarity, and practice effects. *Psychology and Aging, 8(3),* 360–370.

Dodge, K. A. (1993). Social cognitive mechanisms in the development of conduct disorder and depression. *Annual Review of Psychology, 44,* 559–584.

Dodge, K. A. (2001). The science of youth violence prevention: Progressing from developmental psychopathology to efficacy to effectiveness in public policy. *American Journal of Preventive Medicine, 20,* 63–70.

Dodge, K. A., & Pettit, G. S. (2003). A biopsychosocial model of the development of chronic conduct problems in adolescence. *Developmental Psychology, 39,* 349–371.

Dohrenwend, B. S., & Dohrenwend, B. P. (1978). Some issues in research on stressful life events. *Journal of Nervous and Mental Disease, 166,* 7–15.

Dolcini, M. M., Coh, L. D., Adler, N. E., Millstein, S. G., Irwin, C. E., Kegeles, S. M., & Stone, G. C. (1989). Adolescent egocentrism and feelings of invulnerability: Are they related? *Journal of Early Adolescence, 9,* 409–418.

Donelson, F. E. (1998), *Women's experiences.* Mountain View, CA: Mayfield.

Donovan, C. A., & Smolkin, L. B. (2002). Children's genre knowledge: An examination of K–5 students' performance on multiple tasks providing different levels of scaffolding. *Reading Research Quarterly, 37,* 428–465.

Dorn, L. D., Williamson, D. E., & Ryan, N. D. (2002, April). *Maturational hormone differences in adolescents with depression and risk for depression.* Paper presented at the meeting of the Society for Research on Adolescence, New Orleans.

Dornbusch, S., & Kaufman, J. (2001). The social structure of the U.S. high school. In T. Urdan & F. Pajares (Eds.), *Adolescence and education.* Greenwich, CT: IAP.

Downey, G., & Bonica, C. A. (1997, April). *Characteristics of early adolescent dating relationships.* Paper presented at the meeting of the Society for Research in Child Development, Washington, DC.

Drewes, A. A., Carey, L. J., & Schaefer, C. E. (Eds.), (2003). *School-based play therapy.* New York: Wiley.

Driver, J., Tabares, A., Shapiro, A., Nahm, E. Y., & Gottman, J. M. (2003). Interactional patterns in marital success and failure: Gottman laboratory studies. In F. Walsh (Ed.), *Normal family processes* (3rd ed.). New York: Guilford.

Drum, B. A. (2003). Aberration analyses needed for FDA evaluation of safety and effectiveness of wavefront-guided refractive surgical devices. *Journal of Refractive Surgery, 19,* S588–S591.

Dryfoos, J. G. (1990). *Adolescents at risk: Prevalence and prevention.* New York: Oxford University Press.

Duck, S. W. (1975). Personality similarity and friendship choices by adolescents. *European Journal of Social Psychology, 5,* 351–365.

Dudley, R. L. (1999). Youth religious commitment over time: Longitudinal study of retention. *Review of Religious Research, 41,* 110–121.

Duffy, T. M., & Kirkley, J. R. (Eds.), (2004) *Learner-centered theory and practice in distance education.* Mahwah, NJ: Erlbaum.

Dunbar, K. (2001). What scientific thinking reveals about the nature of cognition. In K. Crowley, C. D. Schunn, & T. Okada (Eds.), *Designing for science.* Mahwah, NJ: Erlbaum.

Duncan, G. J., Brooks-Gunn, J., & Klebanov, P. K. (1994). Economic deprivation and early childhood development. *Child Development, 65,* 296–318.

Dunkel-Schetter, C. (1998). Maternal stress and preterm delivery. *Prenatal and Neonatal Medicine, 3,* 39–42.

Dunkel-Schetter, C., Gurung, R. A. R., Lobel, M., & Wadhwa, P. D. (2001). Stress processes in pregnancy and birth. In A. Baum, T. A. Revenson, & J. E. Singer (Eds.), *Handbook of health psychology.* Mahwah, NJ: Erlbaum.

Dunn, A. L., & Blair, S. N. (2002). Translating evidence-based physical activity interventions into practice., *American Journal of Preventive Medicine; 22,* (No. 4, Suppl.), 8–9.

Dunn, J. (1984). Sibling studies and the developmental impact of critical incidents. In P. B. Baltes & O. G. Brim (Eds.), *Life-span development and behavior* (Vol. 6). Orlando, FL: Academic Press.

Dunn, J., Davies, L. C., O'Connor, T. G., & Sturgess, W. (2001). Family lives and friendships: The perspectives of children in step-, single-parent, and nonstop families. *Journal of Family Psychology, 15,* 272–287.

Dunphy, D. C. (1963). The social structure of urban adolescent peer groups. *Society, 26,* 230–246.

Durkin, D. (2004). *Teaching them to read (6th Ed.).* Boston: Allyn & Bacon.

Durrant, J. E. (2002). Trends in youth crime and well-being since the abolition of corporal punishment in Sweden. *Youth and Society, 3,* 437–455.

Durrant, R., & Ellis, B. (2003). Evolutionary psychology. In I. B. Weiner (Ed.), *Handbook of psychology* (Vol. III). New York: Wiley.

Dusek, J. B., & McIntyre, J. G. (2003). Self-concept and self-esteem development. In G. Adams & M. Berzonsky (Eds.), *Blackwell handbook of adolescence.* Malden, MA: Blackwell.

Dweck, C. (1996). Social motivation: Goals and social-cognitive processes. In J. Juvonen & K. R. Wentzel (Eds.), *Social motivation.* New York: Cambridge University Press.

Dweck, C., & Elliott, E. (1983). Achievement Motivation. In P. Mussen (Ed.), *Handbook of child psychology* (4th ed., Vol. 4). New York: Wiley.

Dweck, C., & Leggett, E. (1988). A social cognitive approach to motivation and personality: *Psychological Review, 95.* 256–273.

Dwyer, J. W., & Coward, R. T. (1991). A multivariate comparison of the involvement of adult sons versus daughters in the care of impaired parents. *Journal of Gerontology: Social Sciences, 46,* S259–S269.

Eacott, M. J., & Crawley, R. A. (1998). The offset of childhood amnesia: Memory for events that occurred before age 3. *Journal of Experimental Psychology: General, 127,* 22–33.

Eagly, A. H. (1996). Differences between women and men. *American Psychologist, 51,* 158–159.

Eagly, A. H. (2000). Gender roles. In A. Kazdin (Ed.), *Encyclopedia of psychology.* Washington, DC, & New York: American Psychological Association and Oxford University Press.

Eagly, A. H. (2001). Social role theory of sex differences and similarities. In J. Worrell (Ed.), *Encyclopedia of women and gender.* San Diego: Academic Press.

Eagly, A. H., & Crowley, M. (1986). Gender and helping behavior: A meta-analytic review of the social psychological literature. *Psychological Bulletin, 100,* 283–308.

Eagly, A. H., & Diekman, A. B. (2003). The malleability of sex differences in response to social roles. In L. G. Aspinwall & V. M. Staudinger (Eds.). *A psychology of human strengths.* Washington, DC: American Psychological Association.

Eagly, A. H., & Steffen, V. J. (1986). Gender and aggressive behavior: A meta-analytic review of the social psychological literature. *Psychological Bulletin, 100,* 309–330.

Eaves, L. J., & Silberg, J. L. (2003). Modulation of gene expression by genetic and environmental heterogeneity in timing of developmental milestones. *Behavior Genetics, 33,* 1–6.

Eccles, J. S. (2003). Education: Junior and high school. In G. Adams & M. Berzonsky (Eds.), *Blackwell handbook of adolescence.* Malden, MA: Blackwell.

Eccles, J. S. (2004). Schools, academic motivation, and stage-environment fit. In R. Lerner & L. Steinberg (Eds.), *Handbook of adolescent psychology.* New York: Wiley.

Eccles, J. S., & Midgley, C. (1989). Stage-environment fit: Developmentally appropriate classrooms for young adolescents. In C. Ames & R. Ames (Eds.), *Research on motivation in education* (Vol. 3). Oriando: Academic Press.

Eccles, J. S., Wigfield, A., & Byrnes, J. (2003). Cognitive development in adolescence. In 1. B. Weiner (Ed.), *Handbook of psychology* (Vol. VI). New York: Wiley.

Eccles, J. S., Wigfield, A., & Schiefele, U. (1998). Motivation to succeed. In W. Damon (Ed.), *Handbook of child psychology* (5th ed., Vol. 3), New York: Wiley.

Echevarria, J., Vogt, M., & Short, D. J. (2004). *Making content comprehensible for English language learners.* Boston: Allyn & Bacon.

Edelman, M. W. (1996). *The state of America's children.* Washington, DC: Children's Defense Fund.

Edelman, M. W. (1997, April). *Children, families and social policy.* Paper presented at the meeting of the Society for Research in Child Development, Washington, DC.

Edmonds, M. M. (1993). Physical health. In J. S. Jackson, L. M. Chatters, & R. J. Taylor (Eds.), *Aging in Black America.* Newbury Park, CA: Sage.

Educational Testing Service. (1992, February). *Cross-national comparison of 9–13 year olds' science and math achievement.* Princeton, NJ: Educational Testing Service,.

Egeland, B., & Carlson, B. (2004). Attachment and psychopathology. In L. Atkinson & S. Goldberg (Eds.), *Attachment issues in psychopathology and intervention.* Mahwah, NJ: Erlbaum.

Egeland, B., Jacobvitz., D., & Sroufe, L. A. (1988). Breaking the cycle of abuse. *New Directions for Child Development, 11,* 77–92.

Eichorn, D. H., Clausen, J. A., Haan, N., Honzik, M. P., & Mussen, P. H. (Eds.). (1981). *Present and past in middle life.* New York: Academic Press.

Eiferman, R. R. (1971). Social play in childhood. In R. Herron & B. Sutton-Smith (Eds.), *Child's play.* New York: Wiley.

Eiger, M. S., & Olds, S. W. (1999). *The complete book of breastfeeding* (3rd ed.). New York: Bantam.

Einstein, G. O., McDaniel, M. A., Manzi, M., Cochran, B., & Baker, M. (2000). Prospective memory and aging: Forgetting intentions over short delays. *Psychology and Aging, 15,* 671–683.

Eisdorfer, C. (1996, December). Interview. *APA Monitor,* p. 35.

Eisenberg, N. (1998). Introduction. In N. Eisenberg (Ed.), *Handbook of child psychology* (5th ed., Vol. 3). New York: Wiley.

Eisenberg, N. (2001). Emotion-regulated regulation and its relation to quality of social functioning. In W. W. Hartup & R. A. Weinberg (Eds.), *Child psychology in retrospect and prospect.* Mahwah, NJ: Erlbaum.

Eisenberg, N. (Ed.). (1982). *The development of prosocial behavior.* New York: Wiley.

Eisenberg, N., & Fabes, R. A. (1998). Prosocial development. In W. Damon (Ed.), *Handbook of child psychology* (5th ed., Vol. 3). New York: Wiley.

Eisenberg, N., Fabes, R. A., Guthrie, I. K., & Reiser, M. (2002). The role of emotionality and regulation in children's social competence and adjustment. In L. Pulkkinen & A. Caspi (Eds.), *Paths to successful development.* New York: Cambridge University Press.

Eisenberg, N., Gutherie, I. K., Murphy, B. C., Shepard, S. A., Cumberland, A., & Carlo, G. (1999). Consistency and development of prosocial dispositions: A longitudinal study. *Child Development, 70,* 1360–1372.

Eisenberg, N., Martin, C. L., & Fabes, R. A. (1996). Gender development and gender effects. In D. C. Berliner & R. C. Calfee (Eds.), *Handbook of educational psychology.* New York: Macmillan.

Eisenberg, N., & Morris, A. S. (2004). Moral cognitions and prosocial responding in adolescence. In R. Lerner & L. Steinberg (Eds.), *Handbook of adolescence.* New York: Wiley.

Eisenberg, N., & Murphy, B. (1995). Parenting and children's moral development. In M. H. Bornstein (Ed.), *Children and parenting* (Vol. 4). Hillsdale, NJ: Erlbaum.

Eisenberg, N., Shea, C. I., Carolo, G., & Knight, G. P. (1991). Empathy-related responding and cognition: A chicken and egg dilemma. In W. M. Kurtines & J. Gewirtz (Eds.), *Moral behavior and development* (Vol. 2). Hillsdale, NJ: Erlbaum.

Eisenberg, N., & Valiente, C. (2002). Parenting and children's prosocial and moral development. In M. H. Bornstein (Ed.), *Handbook of parenting* (2nd ed., Vol. 5). Mahwah, NJ: Erlbaum.

Eisenberg, N., & Wang, V. O. (2003). Toward a positive psychology: Social developmental and cultural contributions. In L. G. Aspinwall & U. Staudinger (Eds.), *A psychology of human strengths.* Washington, DC: American Psychological Association.

Eisinger, F., & Burke, W. (2003). Breast cancer and breastfeeding. *Lancet, 361,* 176–177. Dewey, K. G. (2003). Is breastfeeding protective against childhood obesity? *Journal of Human Lactation, 19,* 9–18.

Ekwo, E. E., & Moawad, A. (2002). Maternal age and preterm births in a black population. *Pediatric Perinatal Epidemiology, 2,* 145–151.

Elder, G. H. (1980). Adolescence in historical perspective. In J. Adelson (Ed.), *Handbook of adolescent psychology.* New York: Wiley.

Elder, G. H. (1998). The life course and human development. In W. Damon (Ed.), *Handbook of child development* (5th Ed.). New York: Wiley.

Elder, G. H., & Conger, R. D. (2000). *Children of the land.* Chicago: University of Chicago Press.

Elder, G. H., & Pavalko, E. K. (1993). Work careers in men's later years: Transitions, trajectories, and historical change. *Journal of Gerontology, 48,* S180–S191.

Elkind, D. (1976). *Child development and education: A Piagetian perspective.* New York: Oxford University Press.

Elkind, D. (1978). Understanding the young adolescent. *Adolescence, 13,* 127–134.

Ellis, C. D. (2002). Male rape. *Collegian, 9,* 34–39.

Ellis, L., & Ames, M. A. (1987). Neurohormonal functioning and sexual orientation. *Psychological Bulletin, 101,* 233–258.

Elmes, D. G., Kantowitz, B. H., & Roedinger, H. L. (2003). *Research methods in psychology* (7th ed.). Belmont, CA: Wadsworth.

Elovainio, M., Kivimaki, M., Vahtera, J., Ojanlatva, A., Korkeila, K., Suominen, S., Helenius, H., & Koskenvuo, M. (2003). Social support, early retirement, and a retirement preference: A study of 10,489 Finnish adults. *Journal of Occupational and Environmental Medicine, 45,* 433–439.

Emde, R. N., Gaensbauer, T. G., & Harmon, R. J. (1976). Emotional expression in infancy: A biobehavioral study. *Psychological Issues: Monograph Series, 10* (37).

Emery, C. A. (2003). Risk factors for injury in child and adolescent sport: a systematic review of the literature. *Clinical Journal of Sport Medicine, 13,* 256–268.

Emery, R. E. (1999). *Renegotiating family relationships* (2nd ed.). New York: Guilford Press.

Emery, R. E., Laumann-Billings, L., Waldron, M. C., Sbarra, D. A., & Dillon, P. (2001). Child custody mediation and litigation: Custody, contract, and coparenting 12 years after initial dispute resolution. *Journal of Consulting and Clinical Psychology, 69,* 323–332.

Emmons, C. F. (2004). The spiritualist movement. In C. D. Bryant (Ed.), *Handbook of death and dying.* Thousand Oaks, CA: Sage.

Enck, G. E. (2004). The dying process. In C. D. Bryant (Ed.)., *Handbook of death and dying.* Thousand Oaks, CA: Sage.

Engelhart, M. J., Geerlings, M. I., Ruitenberg, A., van Swieten, J. C., Hofman, A., Witteman, J. C. M., & Breteler, M. B. (2002). Dietary intake of antioxidants and risk of Alzheimer's disease. *Journal of the American Medical Association, 287,* 3223–3229.

England, L. J., Kendrick, J. S., Gargiullo, P. M., Zhniscr, S. C., & Hannon, W. H. (2001). Measures of maternal tobacco exposure and infant birth weight at term. *American Journal of Epidemiology, 153,* 954–960.

Enoch, M. A., & Goldman, D. (2002). Problem drinking and alcoholism: Diagnosis and treatment. *American Family Physician, 65,* 441–448.

Enright, R. D., Lapsley, D. K., Dricas, A. S., & Fehr, L. A. (1980). Parental influence on the development of adolescent autonomy and identity. *Journal of Youth and Adolescence, 9,* 529–546.

Enstrom, J. E. (1999). Smoking cessation and mortality trends among two United States populations. *Journal of Clinical Epidemiology, 52,* 813–825.

Erdem, A., Erdem, M., Arslan, M., Yazici, G., Eskandari, R., & Himmetogulu, O. (2002). The effects of maternal anemia and iron deficiency on fetal erythropoiesis: Comparison between serum erythropoietin, hemoglobin and ferritin levels in mothers and newborns. *Journal of Maternal, Fetal, and Neonatal Medicine, 11,* 329–332.

Ericsson, K. A., Krampe, R., & Tesch-Romer, C. (1993). The role of deliberate practice in the acquisition of expert performance. *Psychological Review, 100,* 363–406.

Erikson, E. H. (1950). *Childhood and society.* New York: W. W. Norton.

Erikson, E. H. (1962). *Young man Luther.* New York: W. W. Norton.

Erikson, E. H. (1968). *Identity: Youth and crisis.* New York: W. W. Norton.

Erikson, E. H. (1969). *Gandhi's truth.* New York: Norton.

Ersek, M., & Wilson, S. A. (2003). The challenges and opportunities of providing end-of-life care in nursing homes. *Journal of Palliative Medicine, 6,* 45–57.

Eskenazi, B., Stapleton, A. L., Kharrazi, M., & Chee, W. Y. (1999). Associations between maternal decaffeinated and caffeinated coffee consumption and fetal growth and gestational duration. *Epidemiology, 10,* 242–249.

Espelage, D. L., & Swearer, S. M. (Eds.). (2003). *Bullying in American schools.* Mahwah, NJ: Erlbaum.

Espelage, D. L., Mebane, S. M., & Swearer, S. M. (2004). Gender differences in bullying: Moving beyond the mean. In D. L. Espelage & S. M. Swearer (Eds.), *Bullying in American schools.* Mahwah, NJ: Erlbaum.

Etaugh, C. A., & Bridges, J. S. (2001). Midlife transitions. In J. Worell (ed.), *Encyclopedia of women and gender.* San Diego: Academic Press.

Etaugh, C., & Bridges, J. S. (2004). The *Psychology of Women (2ⁿᵈEd.).* Boston: Allyn & Bacon.

Etelson, D., Brand, D. A., Patrick, P. A., & Shirali, A. (2003). Childhood obesity: Do Parents recognize the risk? *Obesity Research, 11,* 1362–1368.

Etzel, R. (1988, October). *Children of smokers.* Paper presented at the American Academy of Pediatrics meeting, New Orleans.

Evert, J., Lawler, E., Bogan, H., & Perls, T. (2003). Morbidity profiles of centenarians: Survivors, delayers, and escapers. *Journal of Gerontology: Biological Sciences and Medical Sciences, 58,* M232–M237.

Fabel, K., Fabel, K., Tam, B., Kaufer, D., Aiker, A., Simmons, N., Kuo, C. J., & Palmer, T. D. (2003). VEGF is necessary for exercise-induced adult hippocampal neurogenesis. *European Journal of Neuroscience, 18,* 2803–2812.

Fabes, R. A., Eisenberg, N., Jones, S., Smith, M., Gutherie, I., Poulin, R., Shepard, S., & Friedman, J. (1999). Regulation, emotionality, and preschoolers' socially competent peer interactions. *Child Development, 70,* 432–442.

Fabes, R. A., Hanish, L. D., & Martin, C. L. (2003). Children at play: The role of peers in understanding the effects of child care. *Child Development, 74,* 1039–1043.

Fagan, J. F. (1992). Intelligence: A theoretical viewpoint. *Current Directions in Psychological Science, 1,* 82–86.

Fagot, B. J., Pears, K. C., Capaldi, D. M., Crosby, L., & Leve, C. S. (1998). Becoming an adolescent father: Precursors and parenting. *Developmental Psychology, 34,* 1209–1219.

Fagot, B. J., Rodgers, C. S., & Leinbach, M. D. (2000). Theories of gender socialization. In T. Eckes & H. M. Trautner (Eds.), *The developmental social psychology of gender.* Mahwah, NJ: Erlbaum.

Fairfield, K. M., & Fletcher, R. H. (2002). Vitamins for chronic disease prevention in adults. *Journal of the American Medical Association, 287,* 3116–3126.

Falbo, T., & Poston, D. L. (1993). The academic, personality, and physical outcomes of only children in China. *Child Development, 64,* 18–35.

Famy, C., Streissguth, A. P., & Unis, A. S. (1998). Mental illness in adults with fetal alcohol syndrome or fetal alcohol effects. *American Journal of Psychiatry, 155,* 552–554.

Fang, G., Fang, F. X., Keller, M., Edelstein, W., Kehle, T. J., & Bray, M. A. (2002). Social moral reasoning in Chinese children: A developmental study. *Psychology in the Schools, 40,* 125–138.

Fang, J., Madhaven, S., & Alderman, M. H. (1999). Low birth weight: Race and maternal nativity—Impact of community income. *Pediatrics, 103,* e5.

Fantz, R. L. (1963). Pattern vision in newborn infants. *Science, 140,* 296–297.

Faraone, S. V., & Doyle, A. E. (2001). The nature and heritability of attention deficit hyperactivity disorder. *Child and Adolescent Psychiatric Clinics of North America, 10,* 299–316.

Faraone, S. V., Spencer, T., Aleardi, M., Pagano, C., & Biederman, J. (2004). Meta-analysis of the efficacy of methylpendiate for treating adult attention deficit hyperactivity disorder. *Journal of Clinical Psychopharmacology, 24,* 24–29.

Farmer, E. M., Compton, S. N., Bums, B. J., & Robertson, E. (2002). Reviews of the evidence for treatment of childhood psychopathology: Externalizing disorders. *Journal of Consulting and Clinical Psychology, 70,* 1267–1302.

Federal Interagency Forum on Child and Family Statistics. (2002). *Key national indicators of well-being.* Washington, DC: U.S. Government Printing Office.

Fehr, B. (1996). *Friendship processes.* Thousand Oaks, CA: Sage.

Fehring, R. J., Cheever, K. H., German, K., & Philpot, C. (1998). Religiosity and sexual activity among older adolescents. *Journal of Religion and Health, 37,* 229–239.

Fein, G. G. (1986). Pretend play. In D. Görlitz & J. F. Wohlwill (Eds.), *Curiosity, imagination, and play.* Hillsdale, NJ: Erlbaum.

Feinberg, M., & Hetherington, E. M. (2001). Differential parenting as a within-family variable. *Journal of Family Psychology, 15,* 22–37.

Feiring, C. (1996). Concepts of romance in 15-year-old adolescents. *Journal of Research on Adolescence, 6,* 181–200.

Feldhusen, J. (1999). Giftedness and creativity. In M. A. Runco & S. Pritzker (Eds.), *Encyclopedia of creativity.* San Diego: Academic Press.

Feldman, D. H. (1997, August). *Hitting middle C: Toward a more comprehensive domain for creativity research.* Paper presented at the meeting of the American Psychological Association, Chicago.

Feldman, S. S. (1999). Unpublished review of J. W. Santrock's *Adolescence,* 8th ed. New York: McGraw-Hill.

Feldman, S. S., Turner, R., & Araujo, K. (1999). Interpersonal context as an influence on sexual timetables of youths: Gender and ethnic effects. *Journal of Research on Adolescence, 9,* 25–52.

Feldman, S. S., & Weinberger, D. A. (1994). Self-restraint as a mediator of family influences on boy's delinquent behavior: A longitudinal study. *Child Development, 65,* 195–211.

Fenzel, L. M. (1994, February). *A prospective study of the effects of chronic strains on early adolescent self-worth and school adjustment.* Paper presented at the meeting of the Society for Research on Adolescence, San Diego.

Ferguson, D. M., Harwood, L. J., & Shannon, F. T. (1987). Breastfeeding and subsequent social adjustment in 6- to 8-year-old children. *Journal of Child Psychology and Psychiatry, 28,* 378–386.

Fernandes, O., Sabharwal, M., Smiley, T., Pastuszak, A., Koren, G., & Einarson, T. (1998). Moderate to heavy caffeine consumption during pregnancy and relationship to spontaneous abortion and abnormal fetal growth: A meta-analysis. *Reproductive Toxicology; 12,* 435–444.

Ferrer-Wreder, L., Lorene, C. C., Kurtines, W., Briones, E., Bussell, J., Berman, S., & Arrufat, O. (2002). Promoting identity development in marginalized youth. *Journal of Adolescent Research, 17,* 168–187.

Fiatarone, M. A., Marks, E. C., Meredith, C. N., Lipsitz, L. A., & Evans, W. J. (1990). High intensity strength training in nonagenarians: Effects on skeletal muscle. *Journal of the American Medical Association, 263,* 3029–3034.

Field, A. E., Cambargo, C. A., Taylor, C. B., Berkey, C. S., Roberts, S. B., & Colditz, G. A. (2001). Peer, parent, and media influences on the development of weight concerns and frequent dieting among preadolescent and adolescent girls and boys. *Pediatrics, 107,* 54–60.

Field, D. (1996). Review of relationships in old age by Hansson & Carpenter. *Contemporary Psychology, 41,* 44–45.

Field, D. (1999). A cross-cultural perspective on continuity and change in social relations in old age: Introduction to a special issue. *International Journal of Aging and Human Development, 48,* 257–262.

Field, T. M. (1992, September). Stroking babies helps growth, reduces stress. *Brown University Child and Adolescent Behavior Letter,* pp. 1, 6.

Field, T. M. (1998). Massage therapy effects. *American Psychologist, 53,* 1270–1281.

Field, T. M. (2000). Child abuse. In A. Kazdin (Ed.), *Encyclopedia of psychology.* Washington, DC, & New York: American Psychological Association and Oxford University Press.

Field, T. M. (2001). Massage therapy facilitates weight gain in preterm infants. *Current Directions in Psychological Science, 10,* 51–54.

Field, T. M. (2002). *Touch.* Cambridge, MA: MIT Press.

Field, T. M. (2003). Stimulation of preterm infants. *Pediatric Review, 24,* 4–11.

Field, T. M., Grizzle, N., Scafidi, F., & Schanberg, S. (1996). Massage and relaxation therapies' effects on depressed adolescent mothers. *Adolescence, 31,* 903–911.

Field, T. M., Henteleff, T., Hernandez-Reif, M., & others. (1998). Children with asthma have improved pulmonary functions after massage therapy. *Journal of Pediatrics, 132,* 854–858.

Field, T. M., Hernandez-Reif, M., Seligman, S., Krasnegor, J., & Sunshine, W. (1997). Juvenile rheumatoid arthritis: Benefits from massage therapy. *Journal of Pediatric Psychology, 22,* 607–617.

Field, T. M., Hernandez-Reif, M., Taylor, S., Quintino, O., & Burman, I. (1997). Labor pain is reduced by massage therapy. *Journal of Psychosomatic Obstetrics and Gynecology, 18,* 286–291.

Field, T. M., Lasko, D., Mundy, P., Henteleff, T., Kabat, S., Talpins, S., & Dowling, M. (1997). Brief report: Autistic children's attentiveness and responsivity improve after touch therapy. *Journal of Autism and Developmental Disorders, 27,* 333–338.

Field, T. M., Quintino, O., Hernandez-Reif, M., & Koslosky, G. (1998). Adolescents with attention deficit hyperactivity disorder benefit from massage therapy. *Adolescence, 33,* 103–108.

Field, T. M., Schanberg, S. M., Scafidi, F., Bauer, C. R., Vega-Lahr, N., Garcia, R., Nystrom, J., & Kuhn, C. M. (1986). Tactile/kinesthetic stimulation effects on preterm neonates. *Pediatrics, 77,* 654–658.

Fields, R. (2004). *Drugs in perspective (5th Ed.).* New York: McGraw-Hill.

Finch, C. E., & Seeman, T. E. (1999). Stress theories of aging. In V. L. Bengtson, & K. W. Schaie (Eds.), *Handbook of theories of aging.* New York: Springer.

Fine, P. G., & Peterson, D. (2002). Caring what dying patients care about caring. *Journal of Pain Symptom Management, 23,* 267–268.

Fingerman, K. L., & Lang, F. R. (2004). Coming together: A perspective on relationships across the life span. In F. R. Lang & K. L. Fingerman (Eds.), *Growing together.* New York: Cambridge University Press.

Firestone, W. A., Monfils, L. F., & Schorr, R. Y. (Eds.) (2004). *The Ambiguity of teaching to the test.* Mahwah, NJ: Erlbaum.

Firlik, R. (1996). Can we adapt the philosophies and practices of Reggio Emilia, Italy, for use in American schools? *Young Children, 51,* 217–220.

Fischer, A. H. (Ed.). (1999). *Gender and emotion.* New York: Cambridge University Press.

Fischer, K. W., & Bidell, T. R. (1998). Dynamic development of psychological structures in action and thought. In W. Damon (Ed.), *Handbook of child psychology* (Vol. 1). New York: Wiley.

Fischer, K. W., & Lazerson, A. (1984). *Human development.* San Francisco: W. H. Freeman.

Fischer, K. W., & Pruyne, E. (2003). Reflective thinking in adulthood. In J. Demick & C. Andreoletti (Eds.), *Handbook of adult development.* New York: Kluwer.

Fisher, B. S., Cullen, F. T., & Turner, M. G. (2000). *The sexual victimization of college women.* Washington, DC: National Institute of Justice.

Fitzpatrick, L. A. (2003). Osteoporosis: Alternatives to estrogen treatment. *Minnesota Medicine, 86,* 36–41.

Fivush, R. (1993). Developmental perspectives on autobiographical recall. In G. S. Goodman & B. Bottoms (Eds.), *Child victims and child witnesses: Understanding and improving testimony.* New York: Guilford.

Fixler, J., & Styles, L. (2002). Sickle-cell disease. *Pediatric Clinics of North America, 49,* 1193–1210.

Flanagan, C. (2002, April). *Inclusion and reciprocity: Development sources of social trust and civic hope.* Paper presented at the meeting of the Society for Research on Adolescence, New Orleans.

Flanagan, C., Bowes, J., Jonsson, B., Caspo, B., & Sheblanova, E. (1998). Ties that bind: Correlates of male and female adolescents' civic commitments in seven countries. *Journal of Social Issues, 54,* 457–476.

Flanagan, C., & Faison, N. (2001). Youth civic development: Implications for social policy and programs. *SRCD Social Policy Report, XV* (No. 1), 1–14.

Flannery, D. J., Hussey, D., Biebelhausen, L., & Wester, K. (2003). Crime, delinquency, and youth gangs. In G. Adams & M. Berzonsky (Eds.), *Blackwell handbook of adolescence.* Malden, MA: Blackwell.

Flavell, J. H. (1999). Cognitive development. *Annual Review of Psychology* (Vol. 50). Palo Alto. CA: Annual Reviews.

Flavell, J. H., Friedrichs, A., & Hoyt, J. (1970). Developmental changes in memorization processes. *Cognitive Psychology, 1,* 324–340.

Flavell, J. H., Miller, P. H., & Miller, S. A. (2002). *Cognitive development* (4th ed.). Upper Saddle River, NJ: Prentice Hall.

Flick, L., White, D. K., Vemulapalli, C., Stulac, B. B., & Kemp, J. S. (2001). Sleep position and the use of soft bedding during bed sharing among African American infants at increased risk for sudden infant death syndrome. *Journal of Pediatrics, 138,* 338–343.

Flohr, J. W., Atkins, D. H., Bower, T. G. R., & Aldridge, M. A. (2001, April). *Infant music preferences.* Paper presented at the meeting of the Society for Research in Child Development, Minneapolis.

Floyd, J. A. (2002). Sleep and aging. *Nursing Clinics of North America, 37,* 719–731.

Floyd, R. A., & Hensley, K. (2002). Oxidative stress in brain aging. Implications for therapeutics of neurogenerative diseases. *Neurobiology of Aging, 23,* 795–807.

Flynn, J. R. (1999). Searching for justice: The discovery of IQ gains over time. *American Psychologist. 54,* 5–20.

Fogel, A. (2001). *Infancy* (4th ed.). Belmont, CA: Wadsworth.

Fogel, A., Toda, S., & Kawai, M. (1988). Mother-infant face-to-face interaction in Japan and the United States: A laboratory comparison using 3-month-old infants. *Developmental Psychology, 24,* 398–406.

Fogoros, R. N. (2001). *Does stress really cause heart disease?* Retrieved October 10, 2001, from http://www.about.com

Folkman, S., & Moskowitz, J. T. (2004). Coping: Pitfalls and promises. *Annual Review of Psychology* (Vol. 55). Palo Alto, CA: Annual Reviews.

Ford, K., Sohn, W., & Lepkowski, J. (2001). Characteristics of adolescents' sexual partners and their association with use of condoms and other contraceptive methods. *Family Planning Perspectives, 33,* 100–105, 132.

Foss, C., & Sundby, J. (2003). The construction of the gendered patient: Hospital staff's attitudes to female and male patients. *Patient Education and Counseling, 49,* 45–52.

Fowler, J. W. (1981). *Stages of faith: The psychology of human development and the quest for faith.* New York: HarperCollins.

Fowler, J. W. (1996). *Faithful change.* Nashville, TN: Abingdon Press.

Fox, B., & Hull, M. (2002). *Phonics for the teacher of reading* (8th ed.). Upper Saddle River, NJ: Merrill.

Fozard, J. L. (2000). Sensory and cognitive changes with age. In K. W. Schaie & M. Pietrucha (Eds.), *Mobility and transportation in the elderly.* New York: Springer.

Fozard, J. L., & Gordon-Salant, S. (2001). Changes in vision and hearing with aging. In J. E. Birren & K. W. Schaie (Eds.), *Handbook of the psychology of aging* (5th ed.). San Diego: Academic Press.

Francis, J., Fraser, G., & Marcia, J. E. (1989). *Cognitive and experimental factors in moratorium-achievement (MAMA) cycles.* Unpublished manuscript, Department of Psychology, Simon Fraser University, Burnaby, British Columbia.

Frank, D. A., Augustyn, M., Knight, W. G., Pell, T., & Zuckerman, B. (2001). Growth, development, and behavior in early childhood following prenatal cocaine exposure: a systematic review. *Journal of the American Medical Association, 285,* 1613–1625.

Frankl, V. (1984). *Man's search for meaning.* New York: Basic Books.

Franz, C. E. (1996). The implications of preschool tempo and motoric activity level for personality decades later. Reported in Caspi, A. (1998). Personality development across the life course. In W. Damon (Ed.), *Handbook of child psychology* (Vol. 3). New York: Wiley, p. 337.

Fraser, S. (Ed.). (1995). *The bell curve wars: Race, intelligence, and the future of America.* New York: Basic Books.

Frede, E. C. (1995). The role of program quality in producing early childhood program benefits. *The Future of Children.* (Vol. 5, No. 3), 115–132.

Frederikse, M., Lu, A., Aylward, E., Barta, P., Sharma, T., & Pearlson, G. (2000). Sex differences in inferior lobule volume in schizophrenia. *American Journal of Psychiatry, 157,* 422–427.

Fredrickson, D. D. (1993). Breastfeeding research priorities, opportunities, and study criteria: What we learned from the smoking trail. *Journal of Human Lactation, 3,* 147–150.

Freeman, K. E., & Gehl, K. S. (1995, March). *Beginnings, middles, and ends: 24-month-olds' understanding of analogy.* Paper presented at the meeting of the Society for Research in Child Development, Indianapolis.

Freeman-Fobbs, P. (2003). Feeding our children to death. *Journal of the National Medical Association, 95,* 119.

Frenn, M., Malin, S., Bansal, N., Delgado, M., Greer, Y., Havice, M., Ho, M., & Schweizer, H. (2003). Addressing health disparities in middle school students' nutrition and exercise. *Journal of Community Health Nursing, 20,* 1–14.

Freud, A., & Dann, S. (1951). Instinctual anxiety during puberty. In A. Freud (Ed.), *The ego and its mechanisms of defense.* New York: International Universities Press.

Freud, S. (1917). *A general introduction to psychoanalysis.* New York: Washington Square Press.

Freund, A. M., & Riediger, M. (2003). Successful aging. In I. B. Weiner (Ed.), *Handbook of psychology* (Vol. VI). New York: Wiley.

Frias, J. L., & Davenport, M. L. (2003). Health supervision for children with Turner syndrome. *Pediatrics, 111,* 692–702.

Frick, P. J. (2001). Effective interventions for children and adolescents with conduct disorder. *Canadian Journal of Psychiatry, 46,* 597–608.

Fried, P. A., & Smith, A. M. (2001). A literature review of the consequences of prenatal marijuana exposure. An emerging theme of a deficiency in executive function. *Neurotoxicology and Teratology, 23,* 1–11.

Fried, P. A., & Watkinson, B. (1990). 36- and 48-month neurobehavioral follow-up of children prenatally exposed to marijuana, cigarettes, and alcohol. *Developmental and Behavioral Pediatrics, 11,* 49–58.

Friend, M., & Bursuck, W. D. (2002). *Including students with special needs* (3rd ed.). Boston: Allyn & Bacon.

Friesch, R. E. (1984). Body fat, puberty and fertility. *Biological Review, 59,* 161–188.

Frieske, D. A., & Park D. C. (1999). Memory for news in young and old adults. *Psychology and Aging, 14,* 90–98.

Fry, P. S. (1999, November). *Significance of religiosity and spirituality to psychological well being of older adults.* Paper presented at the meeting of the Gerontological Society of America, San Francisco.

Fry, P. S. (1999, November). *Widows' regrets of action and inaction in coping with spousal loss: A follow-up.* Paper presented at the meeting of the Gerontological Society of America, San Francisco.

Fry, P. S. (2001). The unique contribution of key existential factors to the prediction of psychological well-being of older adults following spousal loss. *The Gerontologist, 41,* 69–81.

Frye, D., Zelazo, P. D., Brooks, P. J., & Samuels, M. C. (1996). Inference and action in early causal reasoning. *Developmental Psychology, 32,* 120–131.

Fujii, K., & Demura, S. (2003). Relationship between change in BMI with age and delayed menarche in female athletes. *Journal of Physiological Anthropology and Applied Human Science, 22,* 97–104.

Fulgini, A. J., & Yoshikawa, H. (2003). Socioeconomic resources, parenting and child development among immigrant families. In M. H. Bornstein & R. H. Bradley (Eds.), *Socioeconomic status, parenting, and child development.* Mahwah, NJ: Erlbaum.

Fuller-Thomson, E., & Minkler, M. (2001). American grandparents providing extensive care to their grandchildren: Prevalence and profile. *The Gerontologist, 41* (No. 2), 201–209.

Furman, W. (2002). The emerging field of adolescent romantic relationships. *Current Directions in Psychological Science, 11,* 177–180.

Furman, W., & Buhrmester, D. (1992). Age and sex differences in perceptions of networks of personal realtionships. *Child Development, 63,* 103–115.

Furman, W., & Wehner, E. A. (1999). Adolescent romantic relationships: A developmental perspective. In S. Shulman & W. A. Collins (Eds.), *New directions for child development: Adolescent romantic relationships.* San Francisco: Jossey-Bass.

Furth, H. G., & Wachs, H. (1975). *Thinking goes to school.* New York: Oxford University Press.

Gabbard, C. P. (2000). *Lifelong motor development* (3rd ed.). Boston: Allyn & Bacon.

Gaillard, W. D., Balsamo, L. M., Ibrahim, Z., Sachs, B. C., & Xu, B. (2003). MRI identifies regional specialization of neural networks for reading in young children. *Neurology, 60,* 94–100.

Galambos, N. L. (2004). Gender and gender role development in adolescence. In R. Lerner & L. Steinberg (Eds.), *Handbook of adolescence.* New York: Wiley.

Galambos, N. L., Petersen, A. C., Richards, M., & Gitleson, I. B. (1985). The Attitudes toward Women Scale for Adolescents (AWSA): A study of reliability and validity. *Sex Roles, 13,* 343–356.

Galinsky, E., & David, J. (1988). *The preschool years: Family strategies that work—from experts and parents.* New York: Times Books.

Gall, M. D., Borg, W. R., & Gall, J. P. (2003). *Educational research* (7th ed.). Boston: Allyn & Bacon.

Gall, T. L., Evans, D. R., & Howard, J. (1997). The retirement adjustment process: Changes in well-being of male retirees across time. *Journal of Gerontology, 52B,* P110–P117.

Galliano, G. (2003). *Gender.* Belmont, CA: Wadsworth.

Gallo, L. C., Troxel. W. M., Matthews, K. A., & Kuller, L. W. (2003). Marital status and quality in middle-aged women: associations

with levels and trajectories of cardiovascular risk factors. *Health Psychology, 22,* 453–462.

Gallup, G. W. (1987). *The Gallup poll: Public opinion 1986.* Wilmington, DE: Scholarly Resources.

Gallup., G. W., & Bezilla, R. (1992). *The religious life of young Americans.* Princeton, NJ: Gallup Institute.

Galotti, K. M., & Kozberg, S. F. (1996). Adolescents' experience of a life-framing decision. *Journal of Youth and Adolescence, 25,* 3–16.

Galvin, M., David, J. P., Delacourte, A., Luna, J., & Mena, R. (2002). Sequence of neurofibrillary changes in aging and Alzheimer's disease: A confocal study with phospho-tau antibody AD2. *Journal of Alzheimer's Disease, 4,* 417–425.

Gandini, L. (1993). Fundamentals of the Reggio Emilia approach to early childhood education. *Young Children, 49,* 4–8.

Gandini, L., & Edwards, C. P. (2000). *Bambini: The Italian approach to infant/toddler care.* New York: Teachers College Press.

Ganong, L. H., & Coleman, M. (1994). *Remarried family relationships.* Thousand Oaks, CA: Sage.

Gao, Y., Elliott, M. E., & Waters, E. (1999, April). *Maternal attachment representations and support for three-year-olds' secure base behavior.* Paper presented at the meeting of the Society for Research in Child Development, Albuquerque.

Garbarino, J. (1999). *Lost boys: Why our sons turn violent and how we can save them.* New York: Free Press.

Garbarino, J. (2001). Violent children. *Archives of Pediatrics & Adolescent Medicine, 155,* 1–2.

Garbarino, J., & Asp, C. E. (1981). *Successful schools and competent students.* Lexington, MA: Lexington Books.

Garcia, E., & Willis, A. I. (2001). Framework for understanding multicultural literacies. In P. R. Schmidt & P. B. Mosenthal (Eds.), *Reconceptualizing literacy in the new age of multiculturalism and pluralism.* Greenwich, CT: IAP.

Garcia-Bournissen, F., Feig, D. S., & Koren, G. (2003). Maternal-fetal transport of hypoglycaemic drugs. *Clinical Pharmacokinetics, 42,* 303–313.

Gard, J. W., Alexander, J. M., Bawdon, R. E., & Albrecht, J. T. (2002). Oxytocin preparation stability in several common intravenous solutions. *American Journal of Obstetrics and Gynecology, 186,* 496–498.

Gardner, H. (1983). *Frames of mind.* New York: Basic Books.

Gardner, H. (1985). *The mind's new science.* New York: Basic Books.

Gardner, H. (1993). *Multiple intelligences.* New York: Basic Books.

Gardner, H. (1999). *The disciplined mind.* New York: Simon & Schuster.

Gardner, H. (2001, March 13). *An education for the future.* Paper presented to the Royal Symposium, Amsterdam.

Gardner, H. (2002). The pursuit of excellence through education. In M. Ferrari (Ed.), *Learning from extraordinary minds.* Mahwah, NJ: Erlbaum.

Garofalo, R., Wolf, R. C., Wissow, L. S., Woods, E. R., & Goodman, E. (1999). Sexual orientation and risk of suicide attempts among a representative sample of youth. *Archives of Pediatrics and Adolescent Medicine, 153,* 487–493.

Garrett, P., Ng'andu, N., & Ferron, J. (1994). Poverty experiences of young children and the quality of their home environments. *Child Development, 65,* 331–345.

Gatz, M., & Karel, M. J. (1993). Individual change in perceived control over 20 years. Special Issue: Planning and control processes across the life span, *International Journal of Behavioral Development, 16*(2), 305–322.

Gavrilov, L. A, & Gavrilova, N. S. (2002). Evolutionary theories of aging and longevity. *The Scientific World Journal, 2,* 339–356.

Gaylor, E. E., Anders, T. F., & Goodlin-Jones, B. L. (1999, April). *Sleep problems in early childhood: Continuity from 12 months.* Paper presented at the meeting of the Society for Research in Child Development, Albuquerque.

Gazzaniga, M. S. (1986). *The social brain.* New York: Plenum.

Gazzaniga, M. S., Ivry, R. B., & Mangum, G. R. (2002). *Cognitive neuroscience* (2nd ed.). New York: W. W. Norton.

Geary, D. C., & Huffman, K. J. (2002). Brain and cognitive evolution: Forms of modularity and functions of mind. *Psychological Bulletin, 128,* 667–698.

Geller, P. A., Graf, M. C., & Dyson-Washington, F. (2003). Women's health psychology. In I. B. Weiner (Ed.),. *Handbook of psychology,* (Vol. IX). New York: Wiley.

Gelman, R. (1969). Conservation acquisition: A problem of learning to attend to relevant attributes. *Journal of Experimental Child Psychology, 7,* 67–87.

Gelman, R., & Williams, E. M. (1998). Enabling constraints for cognitive development and learning. In W. Damon (Ed.), *Handbook of child psychology* (5th ed., Vol. 4). New York: Wiley.

Gelman, S. A., & Opfer, J. E. (2002). Development of the animate-inanimate distinction. In U. Goswami (Ed.), *Blackwell handbook of childhood cognitive development.* Malden, MA: Blackwell.

Gennetian, L. A., & Miller, C. (2002). Children and welfare reform: A view from an experimental welfare program in Minnesota. *Child Development, 73,* 601–620.

George, C., Main, M., & Kaplan, N. (1984). *Attachment interview with adults.*

Unpublished manuscript, University of California, Berkeley.

Gerlach, P. (1998). *Stepfamily in formation.* Chicago: Stepfamily Association of Illinois.

Gerrard, J. A., & Chudasama, G. (2003). Screening to reduce HIV transmission from mother to baby. *Nursing Times, 99,* 44–45.

Gerrard, M., Gibbons, F. X., Reis-Bergan, M., & Russell, D. W. (2000). Self-esteem, self-serving cognitions, and health risk behavior. *Journal of Personality, 68,* 1177–1201.

Gerrotsen, M., Berg, I., Deelman, B., Visser-Keizer, A., & Jong, B. (2003). Speed of information processing after unilateral stroke. *Journal of Clinical and Experimental Neuropsychology, 25,* 1–13.

Gershoff, E. T. (2002). Corporal punishment by parents and associated child behaviors and experiences: A meta-analysis and theoretical review. *Psychological Bulletin, 128,* 539–579.

Gescheider, G. A. (1997). *Psychophysics: The fundamentals.* Mahwah, NJ: Erlbaum.

Geschwind, N., & Behan, P. O. (1984). Laterality, hormones, and immunity. In N. Geschwind & A. M. Galaburda (Eds.), *Cerebral dominance: The biological foundations.* Cambridge, MA: Harvard University Press.

Gesell, A. L. (1934). *Infancy and human growth.* New York: Macmillan.

Gewirtz, J. (1977). Maternal responding and the conditioning of infant crying: Directions of influence within the attachment-acquisition process. In B. C. Etzel, J. M. LeBlanc, & D. M. Baer (Eds.), *New developments in behavioral research.* Hillsdale, NJ: Erlbaum.

Giarrusso, R., & Feng, D. (1999, November). *The influence of life transitions on the intergenerational stake phenomenon.* Paper presented at the meeting of the Gerontological Association of America, San Francisco.

Giavecchio, L. (2001, April). *Sustained attention and receptive language in preschool Head Start story time.* Paper presented at the meeting of the Society for Research in Child Development, Minneapolis.

Gibbs, J. C. (1993, March). *Inductive discipline's contribution to moral motivation.* Paper presented at the biennial meeting of the Society for Research in Child Development, New Orleans.

Gibbs, J. C. (2003). *Moral development and reality.* Thousand Oaks, CA: Sage.

Gibbs, J. T. (1989). Black American adolescents. In J. T. Gibbs & L. N. Huang (Eds.), *Children of color.* San Francisco: Jossey-Bass.

Gibbs, J. T., & Huang, L. N. (1989). A conceptual framework for assessing and treating minority youth. In J. T. Gibbs & L. N. Huang (Eds.), *Children of color.* San Francisco: Jossey-Bass.

Gibson, E, J., Riccio, G., Schmuckler, M. A., Stoffregen, T. A., Rosenberg, D., & Taormina, J. (1987). Detection of the traversability of surfaces by crawling and walking infants. *Journal of Experimental Psychology: Human Perception and Performance, 13,* 533–544.

Gibson, E. J. (1969). *Principles of perceptual learning and development.* New York: Appleton-Century-Crofts.

Gibson, E. J. (1989). Exploratory behavior in the development of perceiving, acting, and the acquiring of knowledge. *Annual Review of Psychology, 39.* Palo Alto, CA: Annual Reviews.

Gibson, E. J. (2001). *Perceiving the affordances.* Mahwah, NJ: Erlbaum.

Gibson, E. J., & Walk, R. D. (1960). The "visual cliff." *Scientific American, 202,* 64–71.

Gibson, J. H., Harries, M., Mitchell, A., Godfrey, R., Lunt, M., & Reeve, J. (2000). Derminants of bone density and prevalence of osteopenia among female runners in their second to seventh decades of age *Bone, 26,* 591–598.

Gibson, J. J. (1966). *The senses considered as perceptual systems.* Boston: Houghton Mifflin.

Gibson, J. J. (1979). *The ecological approach to visual perception.* Boston: Houghton Mifflin.

Giddens, S., & Giddens, O. (2000). *Coping with grieving and loss.* New York: Rosen.

Giedd, J., Jeffries, N., Blumenthal, J., Castellanos, F., Vaituzis, A., Fernandez, T., Hamburger, S., Liu, H., Nelson, J., Bedwell, J., Tran, L., Lenane, M., Nicolson, R., & Rapoport, J. (1999). Childhood-onset schizophrenia: Progressive brain changes during adolescence. *Biological Psychiatry, 46,* 892–898.

Gilligan, C. (1982). *In a different voice.* Cambridge, MA: Harvard University Press.

Gilligan, C. (1992, May). *Joining the resistance: Girls' development in adolescence.* Paper presented at the symposium on development and vulnerability in close relationships, Montreal, Quebec.

Gilligan, C. (1996). *Minding women: Reshaping the education realm.* Cambridge, MA: Harvard University Press.

Gilligan, C. (1996). The centrality of relationships in psychological development: A puzzle, some evidence, and a theory. In G. G. Noam & K. W. Fischer (Eds.), *Development and vulnerability in close relationships.* Hillsdale, NJ: Erlbaum.

Gilligan, C., Spencer, R., Weinberg, M. K., & Bertsch, T. (2003). On the listening guide: A voice-centered relational model. In P. M. Carnic, & J. E. Rhodes (Eds.), *Qualitative research in psychology.* Washington, DC: American Psychological Association.

Gilliland, A. L. (2002). Beyond holding hands: The modern role of the professional doula. *Journal of Obstetrics, Gynecologic, and Neonatal Nursing, 31,* 762–769.

Gilovitch, T., Wang, R. F., Regan, D., & Sadafumi, N. (2003). Regrets of action and inaction across cultures. *Journal of Cross-Cultural Psychology, 34,* 61–71.

Gire, J. T. (2002). How death imitates life: Cultural influences on conceptions of death and dying. In W. J. Lonner, D. L. Dinnel, S. A. Hayes, & D. N. Sattler (Eds.), *Online Readings in Psychology and Culture* (Unit 14, Chapter 2), (http://www.wwu.edu/~culture), Center for Cross-Cultural Research, Western Washington University, Bellingham, Washington.

Gladue, B. A. (1994). The biopsychology of sexual orientation. *Current Directions in Psychological Science, 3,* 150–154.

Glendinning, A., & Inglis, D. (1999). Smoking behavior in youth: The problem of low self-esteem? *Journal of Adolescence, 22,* 673–682.

Glover, I., & Branine, M. (2003). Ageism in work and employment. *Personnel Psychology, 56,* 265–268.

Goelman, H., Anderson, C. J., Anderson, J., Gouzaousasis, P., Kendrick, M., Kindel, A. M., Porath, M., & Koh, J. (2003). Early childhood education. In I. B. Weiner (Ed.), *Handbook of psychology* (Vol. 7). New York: Wiley.

Golbeck, S. L. (Ed.). (2001). *Psychological perspectives on early childhood education.* Mahwah, NJ: Erlbaum.

Golden, M. H., Samuels, M. P., & Southall, D. P. (2003). How to distinguish between neglect and deprivational abuse. *Archives of Diseases in Childhood, 88,* 105–107.

Goldman, R. (1964). *Religious thinking from childhood to adolescence.* London: Routledge & Kegan Paul.

Goldsmith, H. H. (2002). Genetics of emotional development. In R. J. Davidson, K. R. Scherer, & H. H. Goldsmith (Eds.), *Handbook of affective sciences.* New York: Oxford University Press.

Goldsmith, H. H., & Gottesman, I. I. (1981). Origins of variation in behavioral style: A longitudinal study of temperament in young twins. *Child Development, 52,* 91–103.

Goldstein, J. M., Seidman, L. J., Horton, N. J., Makris, N., Kennedy, D. N., Caviness, V. S., Faraone, S. V., & Tsuang, M. T. (2001). Normal sexual dimorphism of the adult human brain assessed by in vivo magnetic resonance imaging. *Cerebral Cortex, 11,* 490–497.

Goldwater, P. N. (2001). SIDS: More facts and controversies. *Medical Journal of Australia, 174,* 302–304.

Goleman, D. (1995). *Emotional intelligence.* New York: Basic Books.

Goleman, D., Kaufman, P., & Ray, M. (1993). *The creative mind.* New York: Plume.

Gonzales, N. A., Knight, G. P., Morgan Lopez, A., Saenz, D., & Sirolli, A. (in press). Acculturation and the mental health of Latino youths: An integration and critique of the literature. In J. M. Contreras, K. A. Kerns, & A. M. Neal-Barnett (Eds.), *Latino children and families in the United States.* Westport, CT: Greenwood.

Gonzalez-del Angel, A. A., Vidal, S., Saldan, Y, del Castillo, V., Angel, M., Macias, M., Luna, P., & Orozco, L. (2000). Molecular diagnosis of the fragile X and FRAXE syndromes in patients with mental retardation of unknown cause in Mexico. *Annals of Genetics, 43,* 29–34.

Goodman, G. S. (2000). *101 things parents should know before volunteering to coach their kids' sport teams.* New York: Contemporary Books.

Goodman, G. S., Batterman-Faunce, J. M., & Kenney, R. (1992). Optimizing children's testimony: Research and social policy issues concerning allegations of child sexual abuse. In D. Cicchetti & S. Toth (Eds.), *Child abuse, child development, and social policy.* Norwood, NJ: Ablex.

Goodman, R. A., Mercy, J. A., Loya, F., Rosenberg, M. L., Smith, J. C., Allen, N. H., Vargas, L., & Kolts, R. (1986). Alcohol use and interpersonal violence: Alcohol detected in homicide victims. *American Journal of Public Health, 76,* 144–149.

Goodstadt, L., & Ponting, C. P. (2001). Sequence variation and disease in the wake of the draft human genome. *Human Molecular Genetics, 20,* 2209–2214.

Goodwin, D. M., Higginson, I. J., Myers, K., Douglas, H. R., & Normand, C. E. (2003). Effectiveness of palliative care in improving pain, symptom control, and quality of life. *Journal of Pain and Symptom Management, 25,* 202–212.

Gordon, S., & Gordon, J. (1989). *Raising a child conservatively in a sexually permissive world.* New York: Simon & Schuster.

Gotesdam, K. G., & Agras, W. S. (1995). General population-based epidemiological survey of eating disorders in Norway. *International Journal of Eating Disorders, 18,* 119–126.

Goto, S., Takashasi, R., Araki, S., & Nakamoto, H. (2002). Dietary restriction initiated in late adulthood can reverse age-related alterations of protein and protein metabolism. *Annals of the New York Academy of Science, 959,* 50–60.

Gottfried, A. E., Gottfried, A. W., & Bathurst, K. (2002). Maternal and dual-earner employment status and parenting. In M. H. Bornstein (Ed.), *Handbook of parenting* (2nd ed., Vol. 2). Mahwah: NJ: Erlbaum.

Gottlieb, G. (1998). Normally occurring environmental and behavioral influences on gene activity: From central dogma to probabilistic epigenesis. *Psychological Review, 105,* 792–802.

Gottlieb, G. (2000). Nature and nurture theories. In A. Kazdin (Ed.), *Encyclopedia of psychology.* Washington, DC, & New York: American Psychological Association and Oxford University Press.

Gottlieb, G. (2002). Origin of the species: The potential significance of early experience for evolution. In W. W. Hartup & R. A. Weinberg (Eds.), *Child psychology in retrospect and prospect.* Mahwah, NJ: Erlbaum.

Gottlieb, G. (2003). *Developmental behavior genetics and the statistical concept of Interaction.* Unpublished manuscript, Department of Psychology, University of North Carolina, Chapel Hill.

Gottlieb, G. (2004). Normally occuring environmental and behavioral influences on gene activity. In C. G. Coll, E. L. Bearer, & R. M. Lerner (Eds.), *Nature and nurture,* Mahwah, NJ: Erlbaum.

Gottlieb, G., Wahlsten, D., & Lickliter, R. (1998). The significance of biology for human development: A developmental psychobiological systems view. In W. Damon (Ed.), *Handbook of child psychology* (5th ed., Vol. 1). New York: Wiley.

Gottman, J. M. (1994). *Why marriages succeed or fail.* New York: Simon & Schuster.

Gottman, J. M. (2002). *Four parenting styles: The Emotion-coaching parent.* Seattle, WA: Talaris Research Institute.

Gottman, J. M., Coan, J., Carrere, S., & Swanson, C. (1998). Predicting marital happiness and stability from newlywed interaction. *Journal of Marriage and the Family, 60,* 5–22.

Gottman, J. M., & DeClaire, J. (1997). *The heart of parenting: Raising an emotionally intelligent child.* New York: Simon & Schuster.

Gottman, J. M., & Levenson, R. W. (2000). The timing of divorce: Predicting when a couple will divorce over a 14-year period. *Journal of Marriage and the Family, 62,* 737–745.

Gottman, J. M., & Notarius, C. I. (2000). Decade review: Observing marital interaction. *Journal of Marriage and the Family, 62,* 927–947.

Gottman, J. M., & Parker, J. G. (Eds.). (1987). *Conversations of friends.* New York: Cambridge University Press.

Gottman, J. M., Ryan, K. D., Carrere, S., & Erley, A. M. (2002). Toward a scientifically based marital therapy. In H. A. Liddle & D. A. Santisteban (Eds.), *Family psychology.* Washington, DC: American Psychological Association.

Gottman, J. M., & Silver, N. (1999). *The seven principles for making marriages work.* New York: Crown.

Gould, E., Reeves, A. J., Graziano, M. S., & Gross, C. G. (1999). Neurogenesis in the neocortex of adult primates. *Science, 286,* 548–552.

Gould, R. L. (1978). *Transformations: Growth and change in adult life.* New York: Simon & Schuster.

Gould, S. J. (1981). *The mismeasure of man.* New York: W. W. Norton.

Gove, W. R., Style, C. B., & Hughes, M. (1990). The effect of marriage on the well-being of adults: A theoretical analysis. *Journal of Health and Social Behavior, 24,* 122–131.

Gowan, D. E. (2004). Christian beliefs concerning death and life after death. In C. D. Bryant (Ed.), *Handbook of death and dying.* Thousand Oaks, CA: Sage.

Graber, J. A., & Brooks-Gunn, J. (2001). *Co-occurring eating and depressive problems: An 8-year study of adolescent girls.* Unpublished manuscript, Center for Children and Families, Columbia University.

Graber, J. A., & Brooks-Gunn, J. (2002). Adolescent girls' sexual development. In G. M. Wingood & R. J. DiClemente (Eds.), *Handbook of sexual and reproductive health.* New York: Plenum.

Graham, K. M. (2001, April). *Child survival: A right, not a need.* Paper presented at the meeting of the Society for Research in Child Development, Minneapolis.

Graham, S. (1986, August). *Can attribution theory tell us something about motivation in blacks?* Paper presented at the meeting of the American Psychological Association, Washington, DC.

Graham, S. (1990). Motivation in Afro-Americans. In G. L. Berry & J. K. Asamen (Eds.), *Black students: Psychosocial issues and academic achievement.* Newbury Park, CA: Sage.

Graham, S. (1997). Executive control in the revising of students with learning and writing difficulties. *Journal of Educational Psychology, 89,* 223–234.

Grandjean, P., White, R. F., Weihe, P., & Jorgensen, P. J. (2003). Neurotoxic risk caused by stable and variable exposure to methylmercury from seafood. *Ambulatory Pediatrics, 1,* 18–23.

Grant, J. (1997). *State of the world's children.* New York: UNICEF and Oxford University Press.

Gratton, M. A., & Vasquez, A. E. (2003). Age-related hearing loss: current research. *Current Opinions in Otolaryngology, Head, and Neck Surgery, 11,* 367–371.

Graves, M. F., Juel, C., & Graves, B. B. (2004). *Teaching reading in the 21st century.* Boston: Allyn & Bacon.

Greenberger, E., & Steinberg, L. (1981). *Project for the study of adolescent work: Final report.* Report prepared for the National Institute of Education, U.S. Department of Education, Washington, DC.

Greenberger, E., & Steinberg, L. (1986). *When teenagers work: The psychological social costs of adolescent employment.* New York: Basic Books.

Greene, V. L., Lovely, M. E., Miller, M. D., & Ondrich, J. I. (1995). Reducing nursing home use through community long-term care: An optimization analysis. *Journal of Gerontology: Social Sciences, 50B,* S259–S268.

Greenfield, P. M. (1966). On culture and conservation. In J. S. Bruner, R. P. Oliver, & P. M. Greenfield (Eds.), *Studies in cognitive growth.* New York: Wiley.

Greenfield, P. M. (2000). Culture and development. In A. Kazdin (Ed.), *Encyclopedia of psychology.* Washington, DC, & New York: American Psychological Association and Oxford University Press.

Greenfield, P. M. (2003, February). Commentary. *Monitor on Psychology, 34* (No. 2), p. 58.

Greenfield, P. M., Keller, H., Fulgini, A., & Maynard, A. (2003). Cultural pathways through universal development. *Annual Review of Psychology, 54*, 461–490.

Greenfield, P. M., & Suzuki, L. K. (1998). Culture and human development. In I. E. Siegel & K. A. Renninger (Eds.), *Handbook of child psychology* (5th ed., Vol. 4). New York: Wiley.

Greenough, W. T. (1997, April 21). Commentary in article, "Politics of biology." *U.S. News & World Report.* p. 79.

Greenough, W. T. (1999, April). *Experience, brain development, and links to mental retardation.* Paper presented at the meeting of the Society for Research in Child Development, Albuquerque.

Greenough, W. T. (2000). Brain development. In A. Kazdin (Ed.), *Encyclopedia of psychology.* Washington, DC, & New York: American Psychological Association and Oxford University Press.

Greenough, W. T. (2001, April). *Nature and nurture in the brain development process.* Paper presented at the meeting of the Society for Research in Child Development, Minneapolis.

Greenough, W. T., Klintsova, A. Y., Irvan, S. A., Galvez, R., Bates, K. E., & Weiler, I. J. (2001). Synaptic regulation of protein synthesis and the fragile X protein. *Proceedings of the National Academy of Science USA, 98,* 7101–7106.

Gregory, R. L. (2004). *Psychological testing (4th Ed.).* Boston: Allyn & Bacon.

Greven, P. (1991). *Spare the child: The religious roots of punishment and the psychological impact of physical abuse.* New York: Knopf.

Grigorenko, E. (2000). Heritability and intelligence. In R. J. Sternberg (Ed.), *Handbook of intelligence.* New York: Cambridge University Press.

Grigorenko, E. L. (2001). Developmental dyslexia: An update on genes, brains, and environments. *Journal of Child Psychology and Psychiatry, 42,* 91–125.

Grigorenko, E. L., (2001). The invisible danger: The impact of ionizing radiation on cognitive development and functioning. In R. J. Sternberg & E. L. Grigorenko (Eds.), *Environmental effects on cognitive abilities.* Mahwah, NJ: Erlbaum.

Grigorenko, E. L., Geissler, P., Prince, R., Okatcha, F., Nokes, C., Kenney, D. A., Bundy, D. A., & Sternberg, R. J. (2001). The organization of Luo conceptions of intelligence: A study of implicit theories in a Kenyan village. International *Journal of Behavioral Development, 25,* 367–378.

Grimes, B., & Mattimore, K. (1989, April). *The effects of stress and exercise on identity formation in adolescence.* Paper presented at the biennial meeting of the Society for Research in Child Development, Kansas City.

Grob. A., Little, T. D., & Wanner, B. (1999). Control judgements across the lifespan. *International Journal of Behavioral Decisions, 23,* 833–854.

Grodzinsky, Y. (2001). The neurology of syntax: Language use without Broca's area. *Behavior and Brain Sciences, 23,* 1–21.

Grolnick, W. S., Bridges, L. J., & Connell, J. P. (1996). Emotion regulation in two-year-olds: Strategies and emotional expression in four contexts. *Child Development, 67,* 928–941.

Grolnick, W. S., & Gurland, S. T. (2001). Mothering: Retrospect and prospect. In J. P. McHale & W. S. Grolnick (Eds.), *Retrospect and prospect in the psychological study of families.* Mahwah, NJ: Erlbaum.

Gross, R. T. (1984). Patterns of maturation: Their effects on behavior and development. In M. D. Levine & P. Satz (Eds.), *Middle childhood: Development and dysfunction.* Baltimore: University Park Press.

Grossmann, K., Grossmann, K. E., Spangler, G., Suess, G., & Unzner, L. (1985). Maternal sensitivity and newborns' orientation responses as related to quality of attachment in northern Germany. In I. Bretherton & E. Waters (Eds.), Growing points of attachment theory and research. *Monographs of the Society for Research in Child Development, 50* (Serial No. 209), 1–2.

Grotevant, H. D., & Cooper, C. R. (1985). Patterns of interaction in family relationships and the development of identity exploration in adolescence. *Child Development, 56,* 415–428.

Grotevant, H. D., & Cooper, C. R. (1998). Individuality and connectedness in adolescent development: Review and prospects for research on identity, relationships, and context. In E. Skoe & A. von der Lippe (Eds.), *Personality development in adolescence: A cross-national and life-span perspective,* London: Routledge.

Groth, K. E., Gilmore, G. C., & Thomas, C. W. (2003). Impact of stimulus integrity on age differences in letter matching. *Experimental Aging Research, 29,* 155–172.

Grumbach, M. M., & Styne, D. M. (1992). Puberty: Ontogeny, neuroendocrinology, physiology, and disorders. In J. D. Wilson & P. W. Foster (Eds.), *Williams textbook of endocrinology* (pp. 1139–1231). Philadelphia: W. B. Saunders.

Grych, J. H. (2002). Marital relationships and parenting. In M. H. Bornstein (Ed.), *Handbook of Parenting* (2nd ed.). Mahwah, NJ: Erlbaum.

Guercio, G., Rivarola, M. A., Chaler, E., Maceiras, M., & Belgorosky, A. (2003). Relationship between the growth hormone/insulin-like growth factor-I axis, insulin sensitivity, and adrenal androgens in normal prepubertal and pubertal girls. *Journal of Clinical Endocrinology and Metabolism, 88,* 1389–1393.

Guilford, J. P. (1967). *The structure of intellect.* New York: McGraw-Hill.

Guillon, M. S., Crocq, M. A., & Bailey, P. E. (2003). The relationship between self-esteem and psychiatric disorders in adolescents. *European Psychiatry, 18,* 59–62.

Gump, B., & Matthews, K. (20__). *Annual vacations, health, and death.* __ presented at the meeting of America__ Psychosomatic Society, Savannah, GA__

Gunnar, M. R. (2000). Early adversity__ the development of stress reactivity and __ regulation. In C. A. Nelson (Ed.), *The effec__ early adversity on neurobehavioral development. The Minnesota Symposia on Child Psychology* (Vol. 31) (pp. 163–200). Mahwah, NJ: Erlbaum.

Gunnar, M. R., & Davis, E. P. (2003). Stress and emotion in early childhood. In I. B. Weiner (Ed.), *Handbook of psychology* (Vol. 6). New York: Wiley.

Gunnar, M. R., Malone, S., & Fisch, R. O. (1987). The psychobiology of stress and coping in the human neonate: Studies of the adrenocortical activity in response to stress in the first week of life. In T. Field, P. McCabe, & N. Scheiderman (Eds.). *Stress and coping.* Hillsdale, NJ: Erlbaum.

Guo, S. S., Wu, W., Chumlea, W. C., & Roche, A. F. (2002). Predicting overweight and obesity in adulthood from body mass index values in childhood and adolescence. *American Journal of Clinical Nutrition, 76,* 653–658.

Gur, R. C., Mozley, L. H., Mozley, P. D., Resnick, S. M., Karp, J. S., Alavi, A., Arnold, S. E., & Gur, R. E. (1995). Sex differences in regional cerebral glucose metabolism during a resting state. *Science, 267,* 528–531.

Gutmann, D. L. (1975). Parenthood: A key to the comparative study of the life cycle. In N. Datan & L. Ginsberg (Eds.), *Life-span developmental psychology: Normative life crises.* New York: Academic Press.

Gutmann, D. L. (1997). *The human elder in nature, culture, and society.* Boulder, CO: Westview Press.

Haas, F. (2003). Bereavement care: Seeing the body. *Nursing Standards, 17,* 33–37.

Hadley, E. C., Dutta, C., Finkelstein, J., Harris, T., Lane, M., Roth, G., Sherman, S., & Starke-Reed, P. (2001). Human implications of caloric restriction's effects on aging in laboratory animals. *Journal of Gerontology, 56A* (Suppl.), 5–7.

Hagestad, G. O. (1985). Continuity and connectedness. In V. L. Bengtson (Ed.), *Grandparenthood.* Beverly Hills, CA: Sage.

Hahn, W. K. (1987). Cerebral lateralization of function: From infancy through childhood. *Psychological Bulletin, 101,* 376–392.

Haig, D. (2003). Behavioral genetics: Family matters. *Nature, 421,* 491–492.

Haith, M. M., & Benson, J. B. (1998). Infant cognition. In W. Damon (Ed.). *Handbook of child psychology* (5th ed., Vol. 2). New York: Wiley.

Haith, M. M., Hazen, C., & Goodman, G. S. (1988). Expectation and anticipation of dynamic visual events by 3.5 month old babies. *Child Development, 59,* 467–479.

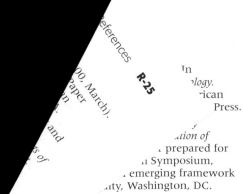

...logy.
...rican
Press.

...tion of
... prepared for
... Symposium,
... emerging framework
...ity, Washington, DC.

...alystok, E., & Wiley, E.
...cal evidence: A test of the
...period hypothesis for second-language
...isition. *Psychological Science. 14,* 31–38.

Hakuta, K., Butler, Y. G., & Witt, D.
(2000). *How long does it take English learners to attain proficiency?* Berkeley, CA: The University of California Linguistic Minority Research Institute Policy Report 2000–1.

Hale, S. (1990). A global developmental trend in cognitive processing speed. *Child Development, 61,* 653–663.

Hall, G. S. (1904). *Adolescence* (Vols. 1 & 2). Englewood Cliffs, NJ: Prentice Hall.

Hallahan, D. P., & Kaufman, J. M. (2003). *Exceptional learners* (9th ed.). Boston: Allyn & Bacon.

Halonen, J., & Santrock, J. W. (1999). *Psychology: The contexts of behavior* (3rd ed.). New York: McGraw-Hill.

Halpern, D. (2001). Sex difference research: Cognitive abilities. In J. Worell (Ed.), *Encyclopedia of women.* San Diego: Academic Press.

Hambleton, R. K. (2002). How can we make NAEP and state test score reporting scales and reports more understandable? In R. W. Lissitz & W. D. Schafer (Eds.), *Assessment in educational reform: Both means and ends.* Boston: Allyn & Bacon.

Hamburg, D. A. (1997). Meeting the essential requirements for healthy adolescent development in a transforming world. In R. Takanishi & D. Hamburg (Eds.), *Preparing adolescents for the 21st century.* New York: Cambridge University Press.

Hamon, R. R., & Ingoldsby, B. B. (Eds.) (2003). *Mate selection across cultures.* Newbury Park, CA: Sage.

Han, S. K., & Moen, P. (1998). *Clocking out: Multiplex time use in retirement.* Bronfenbrenner Life Course Center Working Paper Series #98-03m. Ithaca, NY: Cornell University.

Hanson, L. A., & Korotkova, A. (2002). The role of breastfeeding in prevention of neonatal infection. *Seminars in Neonatology, 7,* 257–281.

Hanson, L. A., Korotkova, M., Haversen, L., Mattsby-Baltzer, I., Hah-Zoric, M., Silferdal, S. A., Strandvick, B., & Telemo, E. (2002). Breastfeeding, a complex support system for the offspring. *Pediatrics International, 44,* 347–352.

Hanson, L. A., Korotkova, M., Lundin, S., Haversen, L., Silfverdal, S. A., Masttsbuy-

Baltzer, I., Strandvik, B., & Telemo, E. (2003). The transfer of immunity from mother to child. *Annals of the New York Academy of Science, 987,* 199–206.

Harada, Y., Satho, Y., Sakuma, A., Imai, J., Tamura, T., Takashai, T., & Amano, N. (2002). Behavioral and developmental disorders among conduct disorder. *Psychiatry and Clinical Neurosciences, 56,* 621–625.

Hardin, L. E. (2003). Problem-solving concepts and theories. *Journal of Veterinary Medicine and Education, 30,* 226–229.

Hare, B. R., & Castenell, L. A. (1985). No place to run, no place to hide: Comparative status and future prospects of black boys. In M. B. Spencer, G. K. Brookins, & W. R. Allen (Eds.), *Beginnings: The social and affective development of black children.* Hillsdale, NJ: Erlbaum.

Hariri, A. R., Mattay, V. S., Tessitore, A., Kolachana, B., Fera, F., Goldman, D., Egan, M. F., & Weinberger, D. R. (2002). Seratonin transporter genetic variation and the response of the human amygdala. *Science, 297,* 400–403.

Harkins, S. W., Price, D. D., & Martinelli, M. (1986). Effects of age on pain perception. *Journal of Gerontology, 41,* 58–63.

Harkness, S., & Super, E. M. (1995). Culture and parenting. In M. H. Bornstein (Ed.), *Handbook of parenting* (Vol. 3). Hillsdale, NJ: Erlbaum.

Harlow, H. F. (1958). The nature of love. *American Psychologist, 13,* 673–685.

Harris, C. R. (2002). Sexual and romantic jealousy in heterosexual and homosexual adults. *Psychological Science, 13,* 7–12.

Harris, G., Thomas, A., & Booth, D. A. (1990). Development of salt taste in infancy. *Developmental Psychology, 26,* 534–538.

Harris, J. R. (1998). *The nurture assumption: Why children turn out the way they do: Parents matter less than you think and peers matter more.* New York: Free Press.

Harris, K. R., & Graham, S. (1996). *Making the writing process work: Strategies for composition and self-regulation.* Cambridge, MA: Brookline Books.

Harris, L. (1975). *The myth and reality of aging in America.* Washington, DC: National Council on Aging.

Harris, L. (1997). *A national poll of children and exercise.* Washington, DC: Lou Harris & Associates.

Harris, R. J., Schoen, L. M., & Hensley, D. L., (1992). A cross-cultural study of story memory. *Journal of Cross-Cultural Psychology, 23,* 133–147.

Harrison, T. W. (2003). Adolescent homosexuality and concerns regarding disclosure. *Journal of School Health, 73,* 107–112.

Harrist, A. W. (1993, March). *Family interaction styles as predictors of children's competence: The role of synchrony and nonsynchrony.* Paper presented at the biennial

meeting of the Society for Research in Child Development, New Orleans.

Hart, B., & Risley, T. R. (1995). *Meaningful differences.* Baltimore, MD: Paul Brookes.

Hart, C., Yang, C., Charlesworth, R., & Burts, D. C. (2003). *Kindergarten teaching practices: Associations with later child academic and social/emotional adjustment to school.* Paper presented at the meeting of the Society for Research in Child Development, Tampa.

Hart, D., & Karmel, M. P. (1996). Self-awareness and self-knowledge in humans, great apes, and monkeys. In A. Russon, K. Bard, & S. Parker (Eds.), *Reaching into thought.* New York: Cambridge University Press.

Harter, S. (1981). A new self-report scale of intrinsic versus extrinsic orientation in the classroom: Motivational and informational components. *Developmental Psychology, 17,* 300–312.

Harter, S. (1990). Self and identity development. In S. S. Feldman & G. R. Elliott (Eds.), *At the threshold: The developing adolescent.* Cambridge, MA: Harvard University Press.

Harter, S. (1996). Teacher and classmate influences on scholastic motivation, self-esteem, and level of voice in adolescents. In J. Juvonen & K. R. Wentzel (Eds.), *Social motivation.* New York: Cambridge University Press.

Harter, S. (1998). The development of self-representations. In W. Damon (Ed.), *Handbook of child psychology* (5th ed., Vol. 3). New York: Wiley.

Harter, S. (1999). *The construction of the self.* New York: Guilford.

Harter, S., & Marold, D. B. (1992). Psychological risk factors contributing to adolescent suicide ideation. In G. Noam & S. Borst (Eds.), *Child and adolescent suicide.* San Francisco: Jossey Bass.

Harter, S., & Whitesell, N. (2001, April). *What we have learned from Columbine: The impact of self-esteem on suicidal and violent ideation among adolescents.* Paper presented at the meeting of the Society for Research in Child Development, Minneapolis.

Hartshorne, H., & May, M. S. (1928–1930). *Moral studies in the nature of character: Studies in deceit* (Vol. 1); *Studies in self-control* (Vol. 2). *Studies in the organization of character* (Vol. 3). New York: Macmillan.

Hartup, W. W. (1983). The peer system. In P. H. Mussen (Ed.), *Handbook of child psychology* (4th ed., Vol. 4). New York: Wiley.

Hartup, W. W. (1996). The company they keep: Friendships and their development significance. *Child Development, 67,* 1–13.

Hartup, W. W. (1999, April). *Peer relations and the growth of the individual child.* Paper presented at the meeting of the Society for Research in Child Development, Albuquerque.

Hartup, W. W. (2000). Middle childhood: Socialization and social context. In A. Kazdin (Ed.), *Encyclopedia of psychology.* Washington,

DC, & New York: American Psychological Association and Oxford University Press.

Hartup, W. W., & Abecassis, M. (2002). Friends and enemies. In P. K. Smith & C. H. Hart (Eds.), *Blackwell handbook of chilhood social development.* Malden, MA: Blackwell.

Hartwell, L., Hood, M. L., Siler, L. M., Veres, R. C., & Reynolds, A. (2004). *Genetics* (2nd Ed.). New York: McGraw-Hill.

Harvey, J. H., & Fine, M. A. (2004). *Children of divorce.* Mahwah, NJ: Erlbaum.

Harwood, R., Leyendecker, B., Carlson, V., Asencio, M., & Miller, A. (2002). Parenting among Latino families in the U.S. In M. H. Bornstein (Ed.), *Handbook of parenting* (2nd ed., Vol. 4). Mahwah, NJ: Erlbaum.

Haselager, G. J. T., Cilessen, A. H. N., Van Lieshout, C. F. M., Riksen-Walraen, J. M. A., & Hartup, W. W. (2002). Heterogeneity among peer-rejected boys across middle childhood: Developmental pathways of social behavior. *Developmental Psychology, 38,* 446–456.

Hasher, L. (2003, February 28). Commentary in "The wisdom of the wizened." *Science, 299,* 1300–1302.

Hasher, L., Chung, C., May, C. P., & Foong, N. (2002). Age, time of testing, and proactive interference. *Canadian Journal of Experimental Psychology, 56,* 200–207.

Hasnis, E., & Reznick, A. Z. (2003). Antioxidants and healthy aging. *Israel Medical Association, 5,* 368–370.

Hauck, F. R., Moore, C. M., Herman, S. M., Donovan, M., Kalekar, M., Christoffel, K. K., Hoffman, H. J., & Rowley, D. (2002). The contribution of prone sleeping position to the racial disparity in sudden infant death syndrome: The Chicago Infant Mortality Study. *Pediatrics, 110,* 772–780.

Hauck, S. J., & Bartke, A. (2001). Free radical defenses in the liver and kidney of human growth hormone transgenic mice. *Journal of Gerontology, 56A, No. 4,* B153–B162.

Hauselmann, H. J., & Rizzoli, R. (2003). A comprehensive review of treatments for postmenopausal osteoporosis. *Osteoporosis International, 14,* 2–12.

Havighurst, R. J. (1973). History of developmental psychology: Socialization and personality development through the life span. In P. B. Baltes & K. W. Schaie (Eds.), *Life-span developmental psychology.* New York Academic Press.

Hawkins, D. N., & Whitman, S. D. (2004). Balancing work and family: Problems and solutions with low-income families. In A. C. Crouter & A. Booth (Eds.), *Work-family challenges for low-income families and their children.* Mahwah, NJ: Erlbaum.

Hawkins, J. A., & Berndt, T. J. (1985, April). *Adjustment following the transition to junior high school.* Paper presented at the Society for Research in Child Development meeting, Toronto.

Hay, P., & Bacaltchuk, J. (2003). Bulimia nervosa. *Clinical Evidence, 8,* 914–926.

Hayflick, L. (1997). The cellular basis for biological aging. In C. E. Finch & L. Hayflick (Eds.), *Handbook of the biology of aging.* New York: Van Nostrand.

Hayslip, B. (1996). Hospice. In J. E. Birren (ed.), *Encyclopedia of gerontology* (Vol. 1). San Diego: Academic Press.

Hayslip, B., Edmondson, R., & Guarnaccia, C. (1999, November). *Religiousness, perceptions of funerals, and bereavement adjustment in adulthood.* Paper presented at the meeting of the Gerontological Society of America, San Francisco.

Hayslip, B., & Hansson, R. (2004). Death awareness and adjustment across the life span. In C. D. Bryant (Ed.), *Handbook of death and dying.* Thousand Oaks, CA: Sage.

Hayward, M. D., Friedman, S., & Chen, H. (1996) Race inequities in men's retirement. *Journal of Gerontology, 51A,* S1–S10.

Hazan, C., & Shaver, P. R. (1987). Romantic love conceptualized as an attachment process. *Journal of Personality and Social Psychology, 52,* 522–524.

Health Management Resources. (2001). *Child health and fitness.* Boston: Author.

Heckhausen, J. (1997). Developmental regulation across adulthood: Primary and secondary control of age-related challenges. *Developmental Psychology, 33,* 176–187.

Heckhausen, J. (2001). Adaptation and resilience in midlife. In M. E. Lachman (Ed.), *Handbook of midlife development.* New York: John Wiley.

Heckhausen, J. (2002). Developmental regulation of life-course transitions: A control theory approach. In L. Pulkkinen & A. Caspi (Eds.), *Paths to successful development: Personality in the life course.* New York: Cambridge University Press.

Heckhausen, J., & Schultz, R. (1995). A life-span theory of control. *Psychological Review, 102,* 284–304.

Heckhausen, J., Wrosch, C., & Fleeson, W. (2001). Developmental regulation before and after a developmental decline: The sample case of "biological clock" for childbearing. *Psychology and Aging, 16,* 400–413.

Hedberg, K., Hopkins, D., & Kohn, M. (2003). Five years of legal physician-assisted suicide in Oregon. *New England Journal of Medicine, 348,* 961–964.

Hedden, T., & Park, D. C. (2003). Contributions of source and inhibitory mechanisms to age-related retroactive interference in verbal working memory. *Journal of Experimental Psychology: General, 132,* 93–112.

Heider, F. (1958). *The psychology of interpersonal relations.* New York: Wiley.

Heilman, A. W., Blair, T. R., & Rupley, W. H. (2002). *Principles and practices of teaching reading* (10th ed.). Upper Saddle River, NJ: Merrill.

Heinicke, C. M. (2000). The transition to parenting. In M. H. Bornstein (Ed.), *Handbook of parenting* (2nd ed.). Mahwah, NJ: Erlbaum.

Helmuth, L. (2003, February 28). The wisdom of the wizened. *Science, 299,* 1300–1302.

Helson, R. (1997, August). *Personality change: When is it adult development?* Paper presented at the meeting of the American Psychological Association, Chicago.

Helson, R., Mitchell, V., & Moane, G. (1984). Personality change in women from college to midlife. *Journal of Personality and Social Psychology, 53,* 176–186.

Helson, R., & Wink, P. (1992). Personality change in women from the early 40s to early 50s. *Psychology and Aging, 7,* 46–55.

Hemmings, A. (2004). *Coming of age in U. S. high schools.* Mahwah, NJ: Erlbaum.

Hendin, H. (2002). Assisted suicide, euthanasia, and the right to end-of-life care. *Crisis, 23,* 40–41.

Hendrick, C., & Hendrick, S. S. (2004). Sex and romantic love. In J. H Harvey, A. Wenzel, & S. Sprecher (Eds.), *The handbook of sexuality in close relationships.* Mahwah, NJ: Erlbaum.

Hendry, J. (1995) *Understanding Japanese society.* London: Routledge.

Hendry, J. (1999). *Social anthropology.* New York: Macmillan.

Hennessey, B. A., & Amabile, T. M. (1998). Reward, intrinsic motivation, and creativity. *American Psychologist, 53,* 674–675.

Henninger, M. L. (1999). *Teaching young children.* Columbus, OH: Merrill.

Hepper, P. G., Shahidullah, S., & White, R. (1990). Origins of fetal handedness. *Nature, 347,* 431.

Hepworth, M. (2004). Images of aging. In J. F. Nussbaum & J. Coupland (Eds.), *Handbook of communication and aging.* Mahwah, NJ: Erlbaum.

Herbst, M. A., Mercer, B. M., Beasley, D., Meyer, N., & Carr, T. (2003). Relationship of prenatal care and perinatal morbidity in low-birth-weight infants. *American Journal of Obstetrics and Gynecology, 189,* 930–933.

Herek, G. (2000). Homosexuality. In A. Kazdin (Ed.), *Encyclopedia of psychology.* Washington, DC, & New York: American Psychological Association and Oxford University Press.

Herman-Giddens, M. E., Slora, E. J., Wasserman, R. C., Bourdony, C. J., Bhapkar, M. V., Koch, G. G., & Hasemeier, C. (1997). Secondary sexual characteristics and menses in young girls seen in office practice: A study from the Pediatric Research in Office Settings Network. *Pediatrics, 99,* 505–512.

Herrnstein, R. J., & Murray, C. (1994). *The bell curve: Intelligence and class structure in American life.* New York: Macmillan.

Hess, T. M., Auman, C., Colcombe, S. J., & Rahhal, T. A. (2003). The impact of stereotype threat on age differences in memory performance. *Journals of Gerontology: Psychological Sciences and Social Sciences, 58B*, P3–P11.

Hetherington, E. M. (1989). Coping with family transitions: Winners, losers, and survivors. *Child Developments, 60*, 1–14.

Hetherington, E. M. (1993). An overview of the Virginia Longitudinal Study of Divorce and Remarriage with a focus on early adolescence. *Journal of Family Psychology, 7*, 39–56.

Hetherington, E. M. (1999). Social capital and the development of youth from non-divorced, divorced, and remarried families. In W. A. Collins & B. Laursen (Eds.), *Relationships as developmental contexts.* Mahwah, NJ: Erlbaum.

Hetherington, E. M. (2000). Divorce. In A. Kazdin (Ed.), *Encyclopedia of psychology.* Washington, DC, & New York: American Psychological Association and Oxford University Press.

Hetherington, E. M., Bridges, M., & Insabella, G. M. (1998). What matters? What does not? Five perspectives on the association between marital transitions and children's adjustment. *American Psychologist, 53*, 167–184.

Hetherington, E. M., & Kelly, J. (2002). *For better or for worse: Divorce reconsidered.* New York: W. W. Norton.

Hetherington, E. M., & Stanley-Hagan, M. (2002). Parenting in divorced and remarried families. In M. Bornstein (Ed.), *Handbook of parenting* (2nd ed.). Mahwah, NJ: Erlbaum.

Hetherington, E. M., Henderson, S. H., Reiss, D., & others. (1995). Adolescent siblings in stepfamilies: Family functioning and adolescent adjustment, *Monographs of the Society for Research in Child Development, 64* (No. 4).

Hetherington, E. M., Reiss, D., & Plomin, R. (Eds.). (1994). *Separate social worlds of siblings: The impact of nonshared environment on development.* Hillsdale, NJ: Erlbaum.

Heuwinkel, M. K. (1996). New ways of learning: 5 new ways of teaching. *Childhood Education, 72*, 27–31.

Hewlett, S. A. (2002). *Creating a life: Professional women and the quest for children.* New York: Talk Miramax Books.

Hicks, J., Martinez, M. C., Schoor, R. Y., & Camilli, G. (2004). Teaching to the test. In W. A. Firestone, L. F. Monfils, & R. Y. Schoor (Eds.), *The ambiguity of teaching to the test.* Mahwah, NJ: Erlbaum.

Hiebert, E. H., & Raphael, T. E. (1996). Psychological perspectives on literacy and extensions to educational practice. In D. C. Berliner & R. C. Calfee (Eds.), *Handbook of educational psychology:* New York: Macmillan.

Higgins, A., Power, C., & Kohlberg, L. (1983, April). *Moral atmosphere and moral judgment.* Paper presented at the biennial meeting of the Society for Research in Child Development, Detroit.

Hill, J. O., & Trowbridge, F. L. (1998). Childhood obesity: Future directions and research priorities. *Pediatrics, 101*, 570–574.

Hill, J. P., & Lynch, M. E. (1983). The intensification of gender-related role expectations during early adolescence. In J. Brooks-Gunn & A. C. Petersen (Eds.), *Girls at puberty: Biological and psychosocial perspectives.* New York: Plenum Press.

Hill, J., Waldfogel, J., Brooks-Gunn, J., & Han, W. (2001, November). *Towards a better estimate of causal links in child policy: The case of maternal employment and child outcomes.* Paper presented at the Association for Public Policy Analysis and Management Fall Research Conference, Washington, DC.

Himes, C. L., Hogan, D. P., & Eggebeen, D. J. (1996). Living arrangements of minority elders. *Journal of Gerontology. 51A*, S42–S48.

Hinde, R. A. (1992). Developmental psychology in the context of other behavioral sciences. *Developmental Psychology, 28*, 1018–1029.

Hiort, O. (2002). Androgens and puberty. *Best Practice and Research: Clinical Endocrinology and Metabolism, 16*, 31–41.

Hirsch, B. J., & Rapkin, B. D. (1987). The transition to junior high school: A longitudinal study of self-esteem, psychological symptomatology, school life, and social support. *Child Development, 58*, 1235–1243.

Ho, C. S., Chan, D. W., Lee, S. H., Tsang, S. M., & Luan, V. H. (2004). Cognitive profiling and preliminary subtyping in Chinese developmental dyslexia. *Cognition, 91*, 43–75.

Hobel, C. J., Dunkel-Schetter, C., Roesch, S. C., Castro, L. C., & Arora, C. P. (1999). Maternal plasma corticotrophin-releasing hormone associated with stress at 20 weeks' gestation in pregnancies ending in preterm delivery. *American Journal of Obstetrics and Gynecology, 180*, S257–S263.

Hobson, A. (2000). Dreams. In A. Kazdin (Ed.), *Encyclopedia of psychology.* Washington, DC, New York: American Psychological Association and Oxford University Press.

Hodges, E. A. (2003). A primer on early childhood obesity and parental influence. *Pediatric Nursing, 29*, 13–16.

Hodges, J. R. (2000). Memory in the dementias. In E. Tulving & F. I. M. Craik (Eds.), *The Oxford handbook of memory.* New York: Oxford University Press.

Hoem, B. (1995). Sweden. In H.-P. Blossfeld (Ed.), *The new role of women: Family formation in modern societies.* Boulder, CO: Westview Press.

Hoff, E., Laursen, B., & Tardiff, T. (2002). Socioeconomic status and parenting. In M. H. Bornstein (Ed.), *Handbook of Parenting* (2nd ed., Vol. 2) Mahwah, NJ: Erlbaum.

Hoffman, L. W. (1989). Effects of maternal employment in two-parent families. *American Psychologist, 44*, 283–293.

Hoffman, L. W., & Youngblade, L. M. (1999). *Mothers at work: Effects on children's well-being.* New York: Cambridge.

Hoffman, M. L. (1970). Moral development. In P. H. Mussen (Ed.), *Manual of child psychology* (3rd ed., Vol. 2). New York: Wiley.

Hoffman, M. L. (1988). Moral development. In M. H. Bornstein & E. Lamb (Eds.), *Developmental psychology: An advanced textbook* (2nd ed.). Hillsdale, NJ: Erlbaum.

Hoffman, S. (2003). Sleep in the older adult: implications for nurses. *Geriatric Nursing, 24*, 210–214.

Hoffman, S., Foster, E., & Furstenberg, F. (1993). Reevaluating the costs of teenage childbearing. *Demography, 30*, 1–13.

Hogan, D. M., & Tudge, J. (1999). Implications of Vygotsky's theory for peer learning. In A. M. O'Donnell & A. King (Eds.), *Cognitive perspectives on peer learning.* Mahwah, NJ: Erlbaum.

Hogan, M. J. (2003). Divided attention in older but not younger adults is impaired by anxiety. *Experimental Aging Research, 29*, 111–136.

Hoghughi, M. S., & Long, N. (Eds.). (2004). *Handbook of parenting.* Newbury Park, CA: Sage.

Holding, S. (2002). Current state of screening for Down syndrome. *Annals of Clinical Biochemistry, 39*, 1–11.

Holland, J. L. (1987). Current status of Holland's theory of careers: Another perspective. *Career Development Quarterly, 36*, 24–30.

Holmbeck, G. N. (1996.) A model of family relational transformations during the transition to adolescence: Parent-adolescent conflict and adaptation, In J. A. Graber, J. Brooks-Gunn, & A. C. Petersen (Eds.), *Transitions through adolescence.* Hillsdale, NJ: Erlbaum.

Holmes, T. H., & Rahe, R. H. (1967). The social readjustment rating scale. *Journal of Psychosomatic Research, 11*, 213–218.

Holtzen, D. W. (2000). Handedness and professional tennis. *International Journal of Neuroscience, 105*, 101–119.

Honein, M. A., Paulozzi, L. J., Mathews, T. J., Erickson, J. D., & Wong, L. Y. (2001). Impact of folic acid fortification of the U.S. food supply on the occurrence of tube defects. *Journal of the American Medical Association, 285*, 2981–2986.

Honzik, M. P., MacFarlane, I. W., & Allen, L. (1948). The stability of mental test performance between two and eighteen years. *Journal of Experimental Education, 17*, 309–324.

Hood, B. (1995). Gravity rules for 2–4 year olds? *Cognitive Development, 10*, 577–598.

Hooker, K. (1999). Possible selves in adulthood. In T. M. Hess & F.

Blanchard-Fields (Eds.), *Social cognition and aging*. San Diego: Academic Press.

Hopkins, B. (1991). Facilitating early motor development: An intracultural study of West Indian mothers and their infants living in Britain. In J. K. Nugent, B. M. Lester, & T. B. Brazelton (Eds.), *The cultural context of infancy: Vol. 2. Multicultural and interdisciplinary approaches to parent-infant relations*. Norwood, NJ: Ablex.

Hopkins, B., & Westra, T. (1988). Maternal handling and motor development: An intracultural study. *Genetic Psychology Monographs, 14*, 377–420.

Hopkins, B., & Westra, T. (1990). Motor development, maternal expectations, and the role of handling. *Infant Behavior and Development, 13*, 117–122.

Hopkins, J. R. (2000). Erikson, E. H. (2000). In A. Kazdin (Ed.), *Encyclopedia of psychology*. Washington, DC, & New York: American Psychological Association and Oxford University Press.

Hoppu, U., Kalliomaki, M., Laiho, K., & Isolauri, E. (2001). Breast milk—immunomodulatory signals against allergenic diseases, *Allergy, 56*, 23–26.

Horn, J. L., & Donaldson, G. (1980). Cognitive development II: Adulthood development of human abilities. In O. G. Brim & J. Kagan (Eds.), *Constancy and change in human development*. Cambridge, MA: Harvard University Press.

Horne, R. S., Franco, P., Adamson, T. M., Groswasser, U., & Kahn, A. (2002). Effects of body position on sleep and arousal characteristics in infants. *Early Human Development, 69*, 25–33.

Horton, D. M. (2001). The disappearing bell curve. *Journal of Secondary Gifted Education, 12*, 185–188.

Hotchner, T. (1997). *Pregnancy and childbirth*. New York: Avon.

House, J. S. (1998). Commentary: Age, work, and well-being, In K. W. Schaie & C. Schooler (Eds.). *The impact of work on older adults*. New York: Springer.

House, J. S., Kessler, R. C., Herzog, R. C., Mero, R. P., Kinney, A. M., & Breslow, M. J. (1992). Social stratification, age, and health. In K. W. Schaie, D. Blazer, & J. S. House (Eds.), *Aging, health behaviors, and health outcomes*. Mahwah, NJ: Erlbaum.

House, J. S., Landis, K. R., & Umberson, D. (1988). Social relationships and health. *Science, 241*, 540–545.

Howard, R. W. (2001). Searching the real world for signs of rising population intelligence. *Personality & Individual Differences, 30*, 1039–1058.

Howe, L. J. (2003). Management of age related macular degeneration: Still room for improvement. *British Journal of Ophthalmology, 87*, 375.

Howe, M. J. A., Davidson, J. W., Moore, D. G., & Sloboda, J. A. (1995). Are there early childhood signs of musical ability? *Psychology of Music, 23*, 162–176.

Howell, E. M. (2001). The impact of Medicaid expansions for pregnant women: A synthesis of the evidence. *Medical Care Research Review, 58*, 3–30.

Howes, C. (1985, April). *Predicting preschool sociometric status from toddler peer interaction*. Paper presented at the meeting of the Society for Research in Child Development, Toronto.

Howes, C., & Clements, D. (1994). Adult socialization of children's play in child care. In H. Goelman (Ed.), *Play and child care*. Albany: State University of New York Press.

Howes, C., Matheson, C. C., & Hamilton, C. E. (1994). Maternal, teacher, and child care history. Correlates of children's relationships with peers. *Child Development, 65*, 264–272.

Howes, C., Rodning, C., Galluzzo, D. C., & Myers, L. (1988). Attachment and child care: Relationships with mother and caregiver. *Early Childhood Research Quarterly 3*(4), 403–416.

Hoyer, W. J. & Roodin, P. A. (2003). *Adult development and aging* (5th ed.). New York: McGraw-Hill.

Hoyer, W. J., & Touron, D. R. (2003). Learning in adulthood. In J. Demick & C. Andreoletti (Eds.), *Handbook of adult development*. New York: Kluwer.

Hoyle, R. H., & Judd, C. M. (2002). *Research methods in social psychology* (7th ed.). Belmont, CA: Wadsworth.

Hu, P., Seeman, T. E., Harris, T. B., & Reuben, D. B. (2003). Docs inflammation or undernutrition explain the low cholesterol-mortality association in high-functioning older persons? MacArthur Studies of Successful Aging, *51*, 80–84.

Huang, H., Appel, L. J., Croft, K. D., Miller, E. R., Mori, T. A., & Puddey, I. B. (2002). Effects of vitamin C and vitamin E on in vivo lipid peroxidation: Results of a randomized clinical trial. *The American Journal of Clinical Nutrition, 76*, 549–555.

Huang, Y. L., Liu, R. Y., Wang, Q. S., Van Someren, E. J., Xu, H., & Zhou, J. N. (2002). Age-associated difference in circadian sleep-wake and rest-activity rhythms. *Physiology and Behavior, 76*, 597–603.

Hubbard, J. A. (2001). Emotion expression processes in children's peer interaction: The role of peer rejection, aggression, and gender. *Child Development, 72*, 1426–1438.

Hudson, L. M., Forman, E. R., & Brion-Meisels, S. (1982). Role-taking as a predictor of prosocial behavior in cross-age tutors. *Child Development, 53*, 1320–1329.

Huebner, A. M., & Garrod, A. C. (1993). Moral reasoning among Tibetan monks: A study of Buddhist adolescents and young adults in Nepal. *Journal of Cross-Cultural Psychology, 24*, 167–185.

Huffman, L. R., & Speer, P. W. (2000). Academic performance among at-risk children: The role of developmentally appropriate practices. *Early Childhood Research Quarterly, 15*, 167–184.

Hughes, P. C. Reported in Fozard, J. L., & Popkin, S. J. (1978). Optimizing adult development. *American Psychologist, 33*, 975–989.

Hulse, G. K., O'Neill, G., Pereira, C., & Brewer, C. (2001). Obstetric and neonatal outcomes associated with maternal naltrexone exposure. *Australian and New Zealand Journal of Obstetrics and Gynecology, 41*, 424–428.

Hultdin, M., Rosenquist, R., Thunberg, U., Tobin, G., Norrback, K. E., Johnson, A., Sundstrom, C., & Roos, G. (2003). Association between telomere length and V(II) gene mutation status in chronic lymphocyctic leukemia: Clinical and biological implications. *British Journal of Cancer, 88*, 593–598.

Hultsch, D. F., Hertzog, C., Small, B. J., & Dixon, R. A. (1999). Use it or lose it: Engaged lifestyle as a buffer of cognitive decline in aging? *Psychology and Aging, 14*, 245–263.

Hultsch, D. F., & Plemons, J. K. (1979). Life events and life-span development. In P. B. Baltes & O. G. Brim (Eds.), *Life-span development and behavior*. New York: Academic Press.

Humm, C. (2001). Sleep patterns in older people. *Nursing Times, 97*, 40–41.

Hummert, T. A., Garstka, E. B., Ryan, J. L., & Bonnesen, J. L. (2004). The role of age stereotypes in interpersonal communication. In J. F. Nussbaum & J. Coupland (Eds.), *Handbook of communication and aging*. Mahwah, NJ: Erlbaum.

Humphcys, K. (2000). Alcoholics Anonymous. In A. Kazdin (Ed.), *Encyclopedia of psychology*. Washington, DC, & New York: American Psychological Association and Oxford University: Press.

Humphrey, D. G., & Kramer, A. F. (1997). Age differences in visual search for feature, conjunction, and triple-conjunction targets. *Psychology and Aging, 12*, 704–717.

Huncharek, M., Kupelnick, B., & Klassen, H. (2002). Paternal smoking during pregnancy and the risk of childhood brain tumors: Results of a meta-analysis. *In Vivo,15*, 535–541.

Hungerford, T. L. (2001). The economic consequences of widowhood on elderly women in the United States and Germany. *The Gerontologist, 41*, 103–110.

Hunt, C. E., Lesko, S. M., Vezina, R. M., McCoy, R., Corwin, J. J., Mandell, F., Willinger, M., Hoffman, H. J., & Mitchell, A. A. (2003). Infant sleep position and associated health outcomes. *Archives of Pediatric and Adolescent Medicine, 157*, 469–474.

Hunt, E. (1995). *Will we be smart enough? A cognitive analysis of the coming work force*. New York: Russell Sage.

Huston, A. C., Duncan, G. J., Grander, R., Bos, J., McLoyd, V., Mistry, R., Crosby, D.,

Gibson, C., Magnuson, K., Romich, J., & Ventura, A. (2001). Work-based antipoverty programs for parents can enhance the school performance and social behavior of children. *Child Development, 72,* 318–336.

Huston, A. C., McLoyd, V. C., & McColl, C. G. (1994). Children and poverty: Issues in contemporary research. *Child Development, 65,* 275–282.

Huttenlocher. J., & Cymerman, E. (1999). Unpublished data on speech syntax. Chicago: University of Chicago.

Huttenlocher, J., Haight, W., Bruk, A., Seltzer, M., & Lyons, T. (1991). Early vocabulary growth: Relation to language input and gender. *Developmental Psychology, 27,* 236–248.

Huttenlocher, J., Levine, S., & Vevea, J. (1998). Environmental input and cognitive growth: A study using time-period comparisons. *Child Development, 69,* 1012–1029.

Huttenlocher, P. R., & Dabholkar, A. S. (1997). Regional differences in synaptogenesis in human cerebral cortex. *Journal of Comparative Neurology, 37(2),* 167–178.

Huyck, M. H., & Hoyer, W. J. (1982). *Adult development and aging.* Belmont, CA: Wadsworth.

Hyde, J. S. (2003). Unpublished review of Santrock, J. W., *Topical life-span development* (2nd ed.). New York: McGraw-Hill.

Hyde, J. S. (2004). *Half the human experience* (5th ed.). Boston: Houghton Mifflin.

Hyde, J. S., & Barnett, R. C. (2001). Women, men, work and family: A new theoretical view. *The American Psychologist, 56(10),* 781–796.

Hyde, J. S., & DeLamater, J. D. (2003). *Human Sexuality* (8th ed.). New York: McGraw-Hill.

Hyde, J. S., & Mezulis, A. H. (2001). Gender difference research: Issues and critique. In J. Worrell (Ed.), *Encyclopedia of women and gender.* San Diego: Academic Press.

Hyde, J. S., & Mezulis, A. H. (2001). Gender difference research: Issues and critique. In J. Worrell (Ed.), *Encyclopedia of women and gender.* San Diego: Academic Press.

Hylton, C., Congdon, N., Friedman, D., Kempen, J., Quigley, H., Bass, E., & Jampel, H. (2003). Cataract after glaucoma filtration surgery. *American Journal of Ophthalmology, 135,* 231–232.

Hyman, E. E., & Loftus, E. F. (2001). In M. L. Eisen, J. A. Quas, & G. S. Goodman (Eds.), *Memory and suggestibility in the forensic interview.* Mahwah, NJ: Erlbaum.

Hymel, S., McDougall, P., & Renshaw, P. (2002). Peer acceptance/rejection. In P. K. Smith & C. H. Hart (Eds.), *Blackwell handbook of childhood social development.* Malden, MA: Blackwell.

Iannucci, L. (2000). *Birth defects.* New York: Enslow.

Iannuzi, A., Celentano, P., Galasso, R., Covetti, G., Sacchetti, L., Zarrilli, F., De Michele, M., & Rubba, P. (2002). Dietary and circulating antioxidant vitamins in relation to carotid plaques in middle-aged women. *The American Journal of Clinical Nutrition, 76,* 582–587.

Idler, E. L., Stanislav, V. K., & Hays, J. C. (2001). Patterns of religious practice and belief in the last year of life. *Journal of Gerontology: Psychological Sciences and Social Sciences, 56B,* S326–S334.

Ikonomovic, M. D., Mufson, E. J., Wuu, J., Cochran, E. J. Bennett, D. A., & DeKosky, S. T. (2003). Cholinergic plasticity in the hippocampus of individuals with mild cognitive impairment: Correlation with Alzheimer's neuropathy. *Journal of Alzheimer's Disease, 5,* 39–48.

Ingelhart, R., & Rabier, J. (1986). Aspirations adapt to situations—but why are the Belgians so much happier than the French? A cross-cultural analysis of the subjective quality of life. In F. M. Andrews (Ed.), *Research on the quality of life.* Ann Arbor: University of Michigan, Institution of Social Research.

Ingersoll, E. W., & Thoman, E. B. (1999). Sleep/wake states of preterm infants: Stability, developmental change, diurnal variation, and relation with caregiving activity. *Child Development, 170,* 1–10.

Insel, P. M., & Roth, W. T. (2004). *Core concepts in health (9th Ed. Updated).* New York: McGraw-Hill.

Institute of Medicine. (1997, June). *Approaching death: Improving care at the end of life.* Washington, DC: National Academy of Sciences.

Irshad, M., & Chaudhuri, P. S. (2003). Oxidant-antioxidant system: role of significance in the human body. *Indian Journal of Experimental Biology, 40,* 1233–1239.

Irwin, C. E. (1993). The adolescent, health, and society: From the perspective of the physician. In S. G. Millstein, A. C. Petersen, & E. O. Nightingale (Eds.), *Promoting the health of adolescents.* New York: Oxford University Press.

Ito, S., & Lee, A. (2003). Drug excretion into breast milk: Overview. *Advances in Drug Delivery: Review, 29,* 617–627.

Iverson, P. & Kuhl, P. K. (1996). Influences of phonetic identification and category goodness on American listeners' perception of /r/ and /l/. *Journal of the Acoustical Society of America, 99,* 1130–1140.

Iverson, P., Kuhl, P. K., Akahane-Yamada, R., Diesch, E., Tohkura, Y., Ketterm, P., & Siebert, C. (2003). A perceptual interference account of acquisition difficulties in non-native phonemes. *Cognition 87,* B47–B57.

Iwaski, Y. (2003). Roles of leisure in coping with stress among university students: A repeated-assessment field study. *Anxiety, Stress, and Coping, 16,* 31–57.

Jackson, A. W., & Davis, G. A. (2002). *Turning Points 2000.* New York: Teachers College Press.

Jackson, J. S., Chatters, L. M., & Taylor, R. J. (Eds.) (1993). *Aging in Black America.* Newbury Park, CA: Sage.

Jacob, N., Van Gestel, S. Derom, C., Theiry, E., Vernon, P., Derom, R., & Vlietinck, R. (2001). Heritability estimates of intelligence in twins: Effect of chorion type. *Behavior Genetics, 31,* 209–217.

Jacobs, J. E., & Klaczynski, P. A. (2002). The development of judgment and decision making during childhood and adolescence. *Current Directions in Psychological Science, 11,* 145–149.

Jacobs, J. E., & Potenza, M. (1990, March). *The use of decision-making strategies in late adolescence.* Paper presented at the meeting of the Society for Research in Adolescence, Atlanta.

Jacobs, J. E., & Tanner, J. L. (1999, August). *Stability and change in perceptions of parent-child relationships.* Paper presented at the meeting of the Gerontological Association of America, San Francisco.

Jacobs, R. H. (1994). His and her aging: Differences, difficulties, dilemmas, delights. *Journal of Geriatric Psychiatry, 27,* 113–128.

Jacobs, S. C., Dosten, T. R., Kasl, S. V., Ostfield, A. M., Berkman, L., & Charpentier, M. P. H. (1987). Attachment theory and multiple dimensions of grief. *Omega, 18,* 41–52.

Jacobson, J. L., & Jacobson, S. W. (2002). Association of prenatal exposure to an environmental contaminant with intellectual function in childhood. *Journal of Toxicology—Clinical Toxocology, 40,* 467–475.

Jacobson, J. L., Jacobson, S. W., Fein, G. G., Schwartz. P. M., & Dowler, J. (1984). Prenatal exposure to an environmental toxin: A test of the multiple-effects model. *Developmental Psychology, 20,* 523–532.

Jadelis, K., Miller, M., Ettinger, W., & Messier, S. (2001). Strength, balance, and the modifying effects of obesity and knee pain: results from the Observational Arthritis Study in Seniors (OASIS). *Journal of the American Geriatric Society, 49,* 884–891.

Jaffe, S. R. (2002). Pathways to adversity in young adulthood among early childbearers. *Journal of Family Psychology, 16,* 38–49.

Jaffee, S., & Hyde, J. S. (2000). Gender differences in moral orientation: A meta-analysis. *Psychological Bulletin, 126,* 703–726.

Jakicic, J. M., & Gallagher, K. I. (2003). Exercise considerations for the sedentary, overweight adult. *Exercise and Sport Science Review, 31,* 91–95.

Jakicic, J. M., Marcus, B. H., Gallagher, K. I., Napolitano, M., & Lang, W. (2003). Effect of exercise duration and intensity on weight loss in overweight, sedentary women: A randomized trial. *Journal of the American Medical Association, 290,* 1323–1330.

Jalongo, M. R., & Isenberg, J. P. (2000). *Exploring your role: A practitioner introduction to early childhood education.* Columbus, OH: Merrill.

James, W. (1890/1950). *The principles of psychology.* New York: Dover.

Jamieson, L., Anderson, M., McCrone, D., Bechhofer, F., Stewart, R., & Li, Y. (2003). Cohabitation and commitment: Partnership plans of young men and young women. *Sociological Review, 50,* 356–377.

Jarrett, R. L. (1995). Growing up poor: The family experiences of socially mobile youth in low-income African-American neighborhoods. *Journal of Adolescent Research, 10,* 111–135.

Jecker, N. S. (1996). Ethics and euthanasia. In J. E. Birren (Ed.), *Encyclopedia of gerontology* (Vol. 1). San Diego: Academic Press.

Jencks, C. (1979). *Who gets ahead? The determinants of economic success in America.* New York: Basic Books.

Jencks, C. (1979). *Who gets ahead? The determinants of economic success in America.* New York: Basic Books.

Jenkins, J. M., & Astington, J. W. (1996). Cognitive factors and family structure associated with theory of mind development in young children. *Developmental Psychology, 32,* 70–78.

Jennekens, F. G., & Kater, L. (2002). Physician-assisted death. *New England Journal of Medicine, 347,* 1043.

Jensen, A. R. (1969). How much can we boost IQ and scholastic achievement? *Harvard Educational Review, 39,* 1–123.

Jessor, R., Turbin, M. S., & Costa, F. (1998). Protective factors in adolescent health behavior. *Journal of Personality and Social Psychology, 75,* 788–800.

Ji, B. T., Shu, X. O., Linet, M. S., Zheng, W., Wacholde, S., Gao, Y. T., Ying, D. M., & Jin, F. (1997). Paternal cigarette smoking and the risk of childhood cancer among offspring of nonsmoking mothers. *Journal of the National Cancer Institute, 89,* 238–244.

Jiao, S., Ji, G., & Jing, Q. (1996). Cognitive development of Chinese urban only children and children with siblings. *Child Development, 67,* 387–395.

Jin, S. H., Kim, T. I., Han, D. S., Shin, S. K., & Kim, W. H. (2002). Thalidomide suppresses the interleukin 1 beta-induced NFκB signaling pathway in colon cancer cells. *Annals of the New York Academy of Science, 973,* 414–418.

Jirtle, R. L., Sander, M., & Barrett, J. C. (2000). Genomic imprinting and environmental disease susceptibility. *Environmental Health Perspectives, 108,* 271 278.

Johannes, L. (2002, June 3). The surprising rise of a radical diet: "Calorie restriction." *The Wall Street Journal,* pp. A1, A10.

Johnson, B. K. (1996). Older adults and sexuality. A multidimensional perspective. *Journal of Gerontological Nursing, 22,* 6–15.

Johnson, D. W. (1990). *Teaching out: Interpersonal effectiveness and self-actualization.* Upper Saddle River, NJ: Prentice Hall.

Johnson, J. S., & Newport, E. L. (1991). Critical period effects on universal properties of language: The status of subjacency in the acquisition of a second language. *Congnition, 39,* 215–258.

Johnson, M. H. (2000). Infancy: Biological processes. In A. Kazdin (Ed.), *Encyclopedia of psychology.* Washington, DC, & New York: American Psychological Association and Oxford University Press.

Johnson, M. H. (2001). Functional brain development during infancy. In A. Fogel & G. Bremner (Eds.), *Blackwell handbook of infant development.* London: Blackwell.

Johnson, M. K., Beebe, T., Mortimer, J. T., & Snyder, M. (1998). Volunteerism in adolescence: A process perspective. *Journal of Research on Adolescence, 8,* 309–332.

John-Steiner, V., & Mahn, H. (2003). Sociocultural contexts for teaching and learning. In I. B. Weiner (Ed.), *Handbook of psychology* (Vol. VII). New York: Wiley.

Johnston, C., & Leung, D. W. (2001). Effects of medication, behavioral, and combined treatments on parents' and children's attributions for the behavior of children with attention-deficit hyperactivity disorder, *Journal of Consulting and Clinical Psychology, 69,* 67–76.

Johnston, L. D., O'Malley, P. M., & Bachman, J. G. (1996). *National survey results on drug use from the monitoring the Future Study. Vol. 2: College students.* Ann Arbor: University of Michigan, Institute of Social Research.

Johnston, L. D., O'Malley, P. M., & Bachman, J. G. (2001, December). *Monitoring the future, 2001.* Ann Arbor, MI: Institute for Social Research, University of Michigan.

Johnston, L. D., O'Malley, P. M., & Bachman, J. G. (2003). *Monitoring the future national results on adolescent drug use: Overview of key findings, 2002.* Bethesda, MD: National Institute of Drug Abuse.

Joiner, T. E. (2000). Depression: Current developments and controversies. In S. H. Qualls & N. Abeles (Eds.), *Psychology and the aging revolution.* Washington, DC: American Psychological Association.

Jones, G., Riley, M., & Dwyer, T. (2000). Breastfeeding early in life and bone mass in prepubertal children: A longitudinal study. *Osteoporosis International, 11,* 146–152.

Jones, J. H. (1997). *Prejudice and racism* (2nd ed.). New York: McGraw-Hill.

Jones, M. C. (1965). Psychological correlates of somatic development. *Child Development, 36,* 899–911.

Jones, T. G., & Fuller, M. L. (2003). *Teaching Hispanic children.* Boston: Allyn & Bacon.

Joseph, C. L. M. (1989). Identification of factors associated with delayed antenatal care. *Journal of the American Medical Association, 81,* 57–63.

Judge, T. A., & Bono, J. E. (2001). Relationship of core self-evaluations traits—self-esteem, generalized self-efficacy, locus of control, and emotional stability—with job satisfaction and job performance: A meta-analysis. *Journal of Applied Psychology, 86,* 80–92.

Julien, D., Chartranol, E., Bouthillier, D., & Begin, J. (2003). Conflict, social support, and relationship quality: An observational study of heterosexual, gay male, and lesbian couples. *Journal of Family Psychology, 20,* 411–436.

Jusczyk, P. W. (2000). *The discovery of spoken language.* Cambridge, MA: MIT Press.

Jusczyk, P. W. (2002). Language development: From speech perception to words. In A. Slater & M. Lewis (Eds.), *Introduction to infant development.* New York: Oxford University Press.

Jusczyk, P. W., & Hohne, E. A. (1997). Infants' memory for spoken words. *Science, 277,* 1984–1986.

Kaasa, S., & Loge, J. II. (2003). Quality of life in palliative care: Principles and practice. *Palliative Medicine, 17,* 7–8.

Kaasinen, V., & Rinne, J. O. (2002). Functional imaging studies of the dopamine system and cognition in normal aging and Parkinson's disease. *Neuroscience and Biobehavioral Review, 26,* 785–793.

Kagan, J. (1984). *The nature of the child.* New York: Basic Books.

Kagan, J. (1987). Perspectives on infancy. In J. D. Osofsky (Ed.), *Handbook on infant development* (2nd ed.). New York: Wiley.

Kagan, J. (1997). Temperament and the reactions to unfamiliarity. *Child Development, 68,* 139–143.

Kagan, J. (1998). The biology of the child. In W. Damon (Ed.), *Handbook of child psychology* (5th ed., Vol. 3). New York: Wiley.

Kagan, J. (2000). Temperament. In A. Kazdin (Ed.), *Encyclopedia of psychology.* Washington, DC, & New York: American Psychological Association and Oxford University Press.

Kagan, J. (2002). Behavioral inhibition as a temperamental category. In R. J. Davidson, K. R. Scherer, & H. H. Goldsmith (Eds.), *Handbook of affective sciences.* New York: Oxford University Press.

Kagan, J. (2003). Biology, context, and development. *Annual Review of Psychology, 54.* Palo Alto, CA: Annual Reviews.

Kagan, J. J., Kearsley, R. B., & Zelazo, P. R. (1978). *Infancy: Its place in human development.* Cambridge, MA: Harvard University Press.

Kagan, J., & Snidman, N. (1991). Infant predictors of inhibited and uninhibited behavioral profiles. *Psychological Science, 2,* 40–44.

Kagitcibasi, C. (1988). Diversity of socialization and social change. In P. R. Dasen,

J. W. Berry, & N. Sartorious (Eds.), *Health and cross-cultural psychology: Toward applications.* Newbury Park, CA: Sage.

Kagitcibasi, C. (1995). Is psychology relevant to global human development issues? Experience from Turkey. *American Psychologist, 50,* 293–300.

Kahn, A., Swaguchi, T., Swaaguchi, A., Groswasser, J., Franco, P., Scaillet, S., Kelmanson, I., & Dan, B. (2002). Sudden infant deaths: From epidemiology to physiology. *Forensic Science International, 130* (Suppl.), 8.

Kahn, R., & Antonucci, T. C. (1990). Convoys over the life course: Attachment, roles, and social support. In P. B. Baltes & O. Brim (Eds.), *Life-span development and behavior.* San Diego: Academic Press.

Kail, R. (1988). Reply to Stigler, Nusbaum, and Chalip. *Child Development, 59,* 1154–1157.

Kail, R. (2000). Speed of information processing: Developmental change and links to intelligence. *Journal of School Psychology, 38,* 51–62.

Kaler, S. R., & Kopp, C. B. (1990). Compliance and comprehension in very young toddlers. *Child Development, 61,* 1997–2003.

Kalichman, S. (1996). *Answering your questions about AIDS.* Washington, DC: American Psychological Association.

Kalil, A., & DeLeire, T. (Eds.) (2004). *Family investments in children's potential.* Mahwah, NJ: Erlbaum.

Kalish, R. A. (1981). *Death, grief, and caring relationships.* Monterey, CA: Brooks/Cole.

Kalish, R. A. (1987). Death. In G. L. Maddox (Ed.), *Encyclopedia of aging.* New York: Springer.

Kalish, R. A., & Reynolds, D. K. (1976). *An overview of death and ethnicity.* Farmingdale, NY: Baywood.

Kamii, C. (1985). *Young children reinvent arithmetic: Implications of Piaget's theory.* New York: Teachers College Press.

Kamii, C. (1989). *Young children continue to reinvent arithmetic.* New York: Teachers College Press.

Kang, D., & Hamasaki, N. (2003). Mitochondrial oxidative stress and mitochondrial DNA. *Clinical Chemistry and Laboratory Medicine, 41,* 1281–1288.

Kanoy, K., Ulku-Steiner, B., Cox, M., & Burchinal, M. (2003). Marital relationship and individual psychological characteristics that predict physical punishment of children. *Journal of Family Psychology, 17,* 20–28.

Kaplow, J. B., Curran, P. J., & Dodge, K. A. (2002). Child, parent, and peer predictors of early-onset substance use: A multisite longitudinal study. *Journal of Abnormal Child Psychology, 30,* 199–216.

Karns, J. T. (2001). Health, nutrition, and safety. In A. Fogel & G. Bremmer (Eds.), *Blackwell handbook of infant development.* London: Blackwell.

Kastenbaum, R. J. (1997). Unpublished review of J. W. Santrock's *Life-span development,* 7th ed. New York: McGraw-Hill.

Kastenbaum, R. J. (1998). *Death, society, and human experience* (6th ed.). Upper Saddle River, NJ: Prentice Hall.

Kastenbaum, R. J. (2000). *The psychology of death* (3rd ed.). New York: Springer.

Katchadourian, H. (1987). *Fifty: Midlife in perspective.* New York: W. H. Freeman.

Katz, L. (1999). Curriculum disputes in early childhood education. *ERIC Clearinghouse on Elementary and Early Childhood Education,* Document EDO-PS-99-13.

Katz, L., & Chard, S. (1989). *Engaging the minds of young children: The project approach.* Norwood, NJ: Ablex.

Kaufman, P. (2001). Dropping out of school: Detours in the life course. In T. Urdan & F. Pajares (Eds.), *Adolescence and education.* Greenwich, CT: IAP.

Kaugers, A. S., Russ, S. W., & Singer, L. T. (2000, May). *Self-regulation among cocaine-exposed four-year-old children.* Paper presented at the joint meetings of the Pediatric Academic Societies and the American Academy of Pediatrics, Boston.

Kausler, D. H. (1994). *Learning and memory in normal aging.* San Diego: Academic Press.

Keating, D. P. (1990). Adolescent thinking. In S. S. Feldman & G. R. Elliott (Eds.), *At the threshold: The developing adolescent.* Cambridge, MA: Harvard University Press.

Keating, D. P. (2003, April). *Cognitive integration in adolescence: The next sensitive period.* Paper presented at the meeting of the Society for Research in Child Development, Tampa.

Keating, D. P. (2004). Cognitive and brain development. In R. Lerner & L. Steinberg (Ed.), *Handbook of adolescent psychology.* New York: Wiley.

Keller, A., Ford, L., & Meacham, J. (1978). Dimensions of self-concept in preschool children. *Developmental Psychology, 14,* 483–489.

Kellman, P. J., & Banks, M. S. (1998). Infant visual perception. In W. Damon (Ed.), *Handbook of child psychology* (5th ed., Vol. 2). New York: Wiley.

Kelly, B. D., & McLoughlin, D. M. (2002). Euthanasia, assisted suicide, and psychiatry: A Pandora's box. *British Journal of Psychiatry, 181,* 278–279.

Kelly, G. F. (2004). *Sexuality today (7th ed. updated).* New York: McGraw-Hill.

Kelly, J. B. (2001). Legal and educational interventions for families in residence and contact disputes. *Australian Journal of Family Law, 15,* 92–113.

Kelly, J. R. (1996). Leisure. In J. E. Birren (Ed.), *Encyclopedia of gerontology* (Vol. 2). San Diego: Academic Press.

Keltner, D., & Ekman, P. (2000). Emotion: An overview. In A. Kazdin (Ed.), *Encyclopedia*

of psychology. Washington, DC, & New York: American Psychological Association and Oxford University Press.

Kemper, S., Greiner, L. H., Marquis, J. G., Prenovost, K., Mitzner, T. L. (2001). Language decline across the life span: Findings from the Nun Study *Psychology and Aging, 16*(2), 227–239.

Kempermann, G, van Pragg, H., & Gage, F. H. (2000). Activity-dependent regulation of neuronal plasticity and self repair. *Progress in Brain Research, 127,* 35–48.

Kennell, J. H., & McGrath, S. K. (1999). Commentary: Practical and humanistic lessons from the third world for perinatal caregivers everywhere. *Birth, 26,* 9–10.

Kenney, M. E., & Barton, C. E. (2003). Attachment theory and research. In J. Demick & C. Andreoletti (Eds.), *Handbook of adult development.* New York: Kluwer.

Kenrick, D. T., Li, N. P., Butner, J. (2003). Dynamical evolutionary psychology: Individual decision rules and emergent social norms. *Psychological Review, 110,* 3–28.

Kenrick, D. T., Neuberg, S. L., & Cialdini, R. B. (2002). *Social Psychology: Unraveling the Mystery* (2nd ed.). Boston: Allyn & Bacon.

Kenyon, G. M., Ruth, J.-R., & Mader, W. (1999). Elements of a narrative gerontology. In V. L. Bengtson & K. W. Schaie (Eds.), *Handbook of theories of aging.* New York: Springer.

Kerr, M. (2001). Culture as a context for temperament. In T. D. Wachs & G. A. Kohnstamm (Eds.), *Temperament in context.* Mahwah, NJ: Erlbaum.

Kerr, M., Stattin, H., Biesecker, G., & Ferrer-Wreder, L. (2003). Relationships with parents and peers in adolescence. In I. B. Weiner (Ed.), *Handbook of psychology* (Vol. 6). New York: Wiley.

Kessen, W., Haith, M. M., & Salapatek, P. (1970). Human infancy. In P. H. Mussen (Ed.), *Manual of child psychology* (3rd ed., Vol. 1). New York: Wiley.

Ketcham, C. J., & Stelmack, G. E. (2001). Age-related declines in motor control. In J. E. Birren & K. W. Schaie (Eds.), *Handbook of the psychology of aging.* (5th ed.). San Diego: Academic Press.

Keyes, C. L. M., & Ryff, C. D. (1998). Generativity in adult lives: Social structure contours and quality of life consequences. In D. P. McAdams & E. de St. Aubin (Eds.), *Generativity and adult development: How and why we care for the next generation.* Washington, DC: American Psychological Association.

Khedr, E. M., Hamed, E., Said, A., & Basahi, J. (2002). Handedness and language cerebral lateralization. *European Journal of Applied Physiology, 87,* 469–473.

Khodr, B., Howard, J., Watson, K., & Khalil, Z. (2003). Effect of short-term and long-term antioxidant therapy on primary and secondary aging neurovascular processes. *Journals of Gerontology A: Biological Science and Medical Science, 58,* 698–708.

Kiecolt-Glaser, J. K., Dura, J. R., Specher, C. E., Trask, O. J., & Glaser, R. (1991). Spousal caregivers of dementia victims. *Psychosomatic Medicine, 53,* 345–362.

Kiecolt-Glaser, J. K., & Glaser, R. (1988). Behavioral influences on immune function. In T. Field, P. McCabe, & N. Schneiderman (Eds.), *Stress and coping across development.* Hillsdale, NJ: Erlbaum.

Kiecolt-Glaser, J. K., Preacher, K. J., MacCallum, R. C., Atkinson, C., Malarkey, W. B., & Glaser, R. (2003). Chronic stress and age-related increases in the Proinflammatory cytokine IL-6. *Proceedings of the National Academy of Science, USA, 100,* 9090–9095.

Kiess, W., Galler, A., Reich, A., Muller, G., Kapellen, T., Deutscher, J., Raile, K., & Kratzch, J. (2001). Clinical aspects of obesity in childhood and adolescence. *Obesity Reviews, 2,* 29–36.

Kilbride, H. W., Thorstad, K. K., & Daily, D. K. (2000, May). *Preschool outcome for extremely low birth weight infants compared to their full term siblings.* Paper presented at the joint meeting of the Pediatric Academic Societies and American Academy of Pediatrics, Boston.

Kim, J. E., & Moen, P. (2001). Is retirement good or bad for subjective well-being? *Current Directions in Psychological Science, 3,* 83–87.

Kim, J. E., & Moen, P. (2002). Retirement transitions, gender, and psychological well-being: A life-course, ecological model. *Journal of Gerontology: Psychological Sciences, 57b,* P212–P222.

Kimm, S. Y., Glynn, N. W., Kriska, A. M., Barton, B. A., Kronsberg, S. S., Daniels, S. R., Crawford, P. B., Sabry, Z. I., & Liu, K. (2002). Decline in physical activity in black girls and white girls during adolescence. *New England Journal of Medicine, 347,* 709–715.

Kimm, S. Y., & Obarzanek, E. (2002). Childhood obesity: A new pandemic of the new millenium. *Pediatrics, 110,* 1003–1007.

Kimura, D. (2000). *Sex and cognition.* Cambridge, MA: MIT Press.

King, P. M., & Mayhew, M. J. (2002). Moral judgment in higher education: Insights from the Defining Issues Test. *Journal of Moral Education, 31,* 247–269.

Kinginger, C. (2002). Defining the zone of proximal development in U.S. foreign language education. *Applied Linguistics, 23,* 240–261.

Kinsey, A. C., Pomeroy, W. B., & Martin, E. E. (1948). *Sexual behavior in the human male.* Philadelphia: W. B. Saunders.

Kirchhoff, K. T. (2002). Promoting a peaceful death in the ICU. *Critical Care Nursing Clinics of North America, 14,* 201–206.

Kirk, K. L. (2001). Dietary restriction and aging. *Journal of Gerontology, 56A* (No. 2), B123–B129.

Kirkpatrick, L. A., & Hazan, C. (1994). Attachment styles and close relationships: A four-year prospective study. *Personal Relationships, 1,* 123–142

Kisilevsky, B. S. (1995). The influence stimulus and subject variables on human fetal responses to sound and vibration. In J-P. Lecaunet, W. P. Fifer, M. A. Krasnegor, & W. P. Smotherman (Eds.), *Fetal development.* Hillsdale, NJ: Erlbaum.

Kitchener, K. S., & King, P. M. (1981). Reflective judgment: Concepts of justification and their relationship to age and education. *Journal of Applied Developmental Psychology, 2,* 89–111.

Kite, M. (2001). Gender stereotypes. In J. Worrell (Ed.), *Encyclopedia and women and gender.* San Diego: Academic Press.

Kivnick. H. Q., & Sinclair, H. M. (1996). Grandparenthood. In J. E. Birren (Ed.), *Encyclopedia of gerontology* (Vol. 1). San Diego: Academic Press.

Klaczynski, P. A., & Narasimham, G. (1998). Development of scientific reasoning biases: Cognitive versus ego-protective explanations. *Developmental Psychology, 34,* 175–187.

Klaus, M. H., & Kennell, H. H. (1976). *Maternal-infant bonding.* St. Louis: Mosby.

Klaus, M. H., Kennell, J. H., & Klaus, P. H. (1993). *Mothering the mother.* Reading, MA: Addison-Wesley.

Klenka, J. C., & Manning, D. (2003). Sudden infant death syndrome: Bed sharing with mothers who smoke. *Archives of Diseases in Childhood, 88,* 112–113.

Klesges, L. M., Johnson, K. C., Ward, K. D., & Barnard, M. (2001). Smoking cessation in pregnant women. *Obstetrics and Gynecological Clinics of North America, 28,* 269–282.

Kliegel, M., McDaniel, M. A., & Einstein, G. O. (2000). Plan formation, retention, and execution in prospective memory: A new approach and age-related effects. *Memory and Cognition, 28,* 1041–1049.

Kliegl, R., & Baltes, P. B. (1987). Theory-guided analysis of mechanisms of development and aging through testing-the-limits and research on expertise. In C. Schooler & K. W. Schaie (Eds.), *Cognitive functioning and social structure over the life course.* Norwood, NJ: Ablex.

Kliegl, R., Smith, J., & Baltes, P. B. (1990). On the locus and process of magnification of age differences during mnemonic training. *Developmental Psychology, 26,* 894–904.

Kling, K. C., Hyde, J. S., Showers, C. J., & Buswell, B. N. (1999). Gender differences in self-esteem: A meta-analysis. *Psychological Bulletin, 125,* 470–500.

Knecht, S., Drager, B., Deppe, M., Bobe, L., Lohmann, H., Floel, A., Ringelstein, E. B., & Henningsen, H. (2000). Handedness and hemispheric language dominance in healthy humans. *Brain, 135,* 2512–2518.

Knect, S., Jansen, A., Frank, A., van Randenborgh, J., Sommer, J., Kanowksi, M., & Heinze, H. J. (2003). How atypical is atypical language dominance? *Neuroimage, 18,* 917–927.

Knussmann, R., Christiansen, K., & Couwenbergs, C. (1986). Relations between sex hormone levels and sexual behavior in men. *Archives of Sexual Behavior, 15,* 429–445.

Kobak, R. (1999). The emotional dynamics of disruptions in attachment relationships: Implications for theory, research, and clinical intervention. In J. Cassidy & P. Shaver (Eds.), *Handbook of attachment.* New York: Guilford.

Kobark, R., Cole, C., Fleming, W., Ferenz-Gilles, R., & Bamble, W. (1993). Attachment and emotional regulation during mother-teen problem-solving: A control theory analysis. *Child Development, 64,* 231–245.

Koch, J. (2003). Gender issues in the classroom. In I. B. Weiner (Ed.), *Handbook of psychology* (Vol. 7). New York: Wiley.

Kochanska, G., Gross, J. N., Lin, M., & Nichols, K. E. (2002). Guilt in young children: Development, determinants, and relations with a broader set of standards. *Child Development, 73,* 461–482.

Koenig, H. G. (2001). Religion and medicine II: Religion, mental health, and related behaviors. *International Journal of Psychiatry, 31,* 97–109.

Koenig, H. G., & Larson, D. B. (1998). Religion and mental health. In H. S. Friedman (Ed.), *Encyclopedia of mental health* (Vol. 3). San Diego: Academic Press.

Koenig, H. G., Smiley, M., & Gonzales, J. A. T. (1988). *Religion, health, and aging.* New York: Greenwood Press.

Kohlberg, L. (1958). *The development of modes of moral thinking and choice in the years 10 to 16.* Unpublished doctoral dissertation, University of Chicago.

Kohlberg, L. (1966). A cognitive-developmental analysis of children's sex-role concepts and attitudes. In E. E. Maccoby (Ed.), *The development of sex differences.* Palo Alto, CA: Stanford University Press.

Kohlberg, L. (1969). Stage and sequence: The cognitive-developmental approach to socialization. In D. A. Goslin (Ed.), *Handbook of socialization theory and research.* Chicago: Rand McNally.

Kohlberg, L. (1976). Moral stages and moralization: The cognitive-developmental approach. In T. Lickona (Ed.), *Moral development and behavior.* New York: Holt, Rinehart & Winston.

Kohlberg, L. (1986). A current statement on some theoretical issues. In S. Modgil & C. Modgil (Eds.), *Lawrence Kohlberg.* Philadelphia: Falmer.

Kohlberg, L., & Ryncarz, R. A. (1990). Beyond justice reasoning: Moral development and consideration of a seventh stage. In C. N. Alexander & E. J. Langer (Eds.), *Higher stages of human development.* New York: Oxford University Press.

Kohn, M., & Golden, N. H. (2001). Eating disorders in children and adolescents. *Pediatric Drugs, 3,* 91–99.

Kohn. M. L. (1977). *Class and conformity: A study in values* (2nd ed.). Chicago: University of Chicago Press.

Kopp, C. B. (1982). The antecedents of self-regulation. *Developmental Psychology, 18,* 199–214.

Kopp, C. B. (1987). The growth of self-regulation: Caregivers and children. In N. Eisenberg (Ed.), *Contemporary topics in developmental psychology.* New York: Wiley.

Kopp, C. B., & Neufeld, S. J. (2002). Emotional development in infancy. In R. Davidson & K. Scherer (Eds.), *Handbook of affective sciences.* New York: Oxford University Press.

Kornhaber, M., Fierros, E., & Veenema, S. (2004). *Multiple intelligences: Best ideas from research and practice.* Boston: Allyn & Bacon.

Kosnik, W., Winslow, L., Kline, D., Rasinski, K., & Sekuler, R. (1989). Visual changes in daily life through adulthood. *Journal of Gerontology: Psychological Sciences, 43,* P63–P70.

Koss, M., & Boeschen, L. (1998). Rape. In H. S. Friedman (Ed.), *Encyclopedia of mental health* (Vol. 3). San Diego: Academic Press.

Kotch, J. B. (2003). Psychological maltreatment. *Pediatrics, 111,* 444–445.

Kotovsky, L., & Baillargeon, R. (1994). Calibration-based reasoning about collision events in 11-month-old infants. *Cognition, 51,* 107–129.

Kotre, J. (1984). *Outliving the self: Generativity and the interpretation of lives.* Baltimore: The Johns Hopkins University Press.

Kozol, J. (1991). *Savage inequalities.* New York: Crown.

Kozulin, A. (2000). Vygotsky. In A. Kazdin (Ed.), *Encyclopedia of psychology.* Washington, DC, & New York: American Psychological Association and Oxford University Press.

Kozulin, A., Gindis, B., Ageyev, V. S., & Miller, S. M. (Eds.) (2003). *Vygotsky's educational theory in cultural context.* New York: Cambridge University Press.

Krahe, B. (2000). Sexual scripts and heterosexual aggression. In T. Eckes & H. M. Trautner (Eds.), *The developmental social psychology of gender.* Mahwah, NJ: Erlbaum.

Kramer, A. F., Hahn, S., Cohen, N. J., Banich, M. T., McAuley, E., Harrison, C. R., Chason, J., Vakil, E., Bardell, L., Boileau, R. A., & Colocombe, A. (1999). Aging, fitness, and neurocognitive function. *Nature, 400,* 418–419.

Kramer, A. F., & Willis, S. L. (2002). Enhancing the cognitive vitality of older adults. *Current Directions in Psychological Research, 11,* 173–177.

Kramer, D. A. (2003). The ontogeny of wisdom in its variations. In J. Demick & C. Andreoletti (Eds.), *Handbook of adult development.* New York: Kluwer.

Kramer, D., Kahlbaugh, P. E., & Goldston, R. B. (1992). A measure of paradigm beliefs about the social world. *Journal of Gerontology: Psychological Sciences, 47,* P180–P189.

Kramer, M. (2003). Commentary: Breastfeeding and child health, growth, and survival. *International Journal of Epidemiology, 32,* 96–98.

Kramer, M. S., & others (2001). Promotion of breastfeeding intervention trial. *Journal of the American Medical Association, 285* (No. 4), 413–420.

Krampe, R. T., & Baltes, P. B. (2004). Intelligence as adaptive resource development and resource allocation: A new look through the lenses of SOC and expertise. In R. J. Sternberg & E. L. Grigorenko (Eds.), *Perspectives on the psychology of abilities, competencies, and expertise.* New York: Cambridge University Press.

Krause, N. (1995). Religiosity and self-esteem among older adults. *Journal of Gerontology: Psychological Sciences, 50B,* P236–P246.

Krause, N. (2003). Religious meaning and subjective well-being in late life. *Journal of Gerontology: Psychological Sciences and Social Sciences, 58B,* S160–S170.

Krauss, R. A., & Glucksberg, S. (1969). The development of communication: Competence as a function of age. *Child Development, 40,* 255–266.

Kreutzer, M., Leonard, C., & Flavell, J. H. (1975). An interview study of children's knowledge about memory. *Monographs of the Society for Research in Child Development, 40* (1, Serial No. 159).

Krimel, L. S., & Goldman-Rakic, P. S. (2001). Prefrontal microcircuits. *Journal of Neuroscience, 21,* 3788–3796.

Krishnakumar, A., & Black, M. M. (2003). Family processes within three-generation Households and adolescent mothers' satisfaction with father involvement. *Journal of Family Psychology, 17,* 488–498.

Kroger, J. (2003). Identity development during adolescence. In G. Adams & M. Berzonsky (Eds.), *Blackwell handbook of adolescence.* Malden, MA: Blackwell.

Krogh, K. L., & Slentz, S. L. (2001). *Teaching young children.* Mahwah, NJ: Erlbaum.

Kübler-Ross, E. (1969). *On death and dying.* New York: Macmillan.

Kuchenbecker, S. (2000). *Raising winners.* New York: Times Books/Random House.

Kuczynski, L., & Kochanska, G. (1990). Development of children's noncompliance strategies from toddlerhood to age 5. *Developmental Psychology, 26,* 398–408.

Kuczynski, L., & Lollis, S. (2002). Four foundations for a dynamic model of parenting. In J. R. M. Gerris (Ed.), *Dynamics of parenting.* Hillsdale, NJ: Erlbaum.

Kuebli, J. (1994, March). Young children's understanding of everyday emotions. *Young Children,* pp. 36–48.

Kuhl, P. K. (1993). Infant speech perception: A window on psycholinguistic development. *International Journal of Psycholinguistics, 9,* 33–56.

Kuhl, P. K. (2000). A new view of language acquisition. *Proceedings of the National Academy of Science, 97*(22), 11850–11857.

Kuhn, D. (1998). Afterward to Volume 2: Cognition, perception, and language. In W. Damon (Ed.), *Handbook of child psychology* (5th ed., Vol. 2). New York: Wiley.

Kuhn, D. (2000). Adolescence: Adolescent thought processes. In A. Kazdin (Ed.), *Encyclopedia of psychology.* Washington, DC, & New York: American Psychological Association and Oxford University Press.

Kuhn, D., Amsel, E., & O'Laughlin, M. (1988). *The development of scientific thinking skills.* Orlando, FL: Academic Press.

Kuhn, D., Schauble, L., & Garcia-Mila, M. (1992). Cross-domain development of scientific reasoning. *Cognition and Instruction, 9,* 285–327.

Kumagai, F. (1995). Families in Japan: Beliefs and realities. *Journal of Comparative and Family Studies, 18,* 135–163.

Kumari, A. S. (2002). Pregnancy outcome in women with morbid obesity. *International Journal of Gynecology and Obstetrics, 73,* 101–107.

Kunzmann, U., & Baltes, P. B. (2003). Beyond the traditional scope of intelligence: Wisdom in action. In R. J. Sternberg, J. Lautrey, & T. I. Lubert (Eds.), *Models of intelligence: International perspectives.* Washington, DC: American Psychological Association.

Kupersmidt, J. B., & Coie, J. D. (1990). Preadolescent peer status, aggression, and school adjustment as predictors of externalizing problems in adolescence. *Child Development, 61,* 1350–1363.

Kurdek, L. A. (1995). Developmental changes in relationship quality in gay and lesbian cohabiting couples. *Developmental Psychology, 31,* 86–94.

Kurdek, L. A. (2003). Differences between gay and lesbian cohabiting couples. *Journal of Social and Personal Relationships, 20,* 411–436.

Kurdek, L. A., & Krile, D. (1982). A developmental analysis of the relation between peer acceptance and both interpersonal understanding and perceived social self-competence. *Child Development, 53,* 1485–1491.

Kurtz, D. A., Cantu, C. L., & Phinney, J. S. (1996, March). *Group identities as predictors of self-esteem among African American, Latino, and White adolescents.* Paper presented at the meeting of the Society for Research on Adolescence, Boston.

Kuypers, J. A., & Bengtson, V. L. (1973). Social breakdown and competence. A model of normal aging. *Human Development, 16,* 181–201.

Kwak, H. K., Kim, M., Cho, B. H., & Ham, Y. M. (1999, April). *The relationship between children's temperament, maternal control strategies, and children's compliance.* Paper presented at the meeting of the Society for Research in Child Development, Albuquerque.

Kwak, K. (2003). Adolescents and their parents: A review of intergenerational family relations for immigrant and non-immigrant families. *Human Development, 46,* 115–136.

Kwon, S. (1999, November). *Control beliefs and cognitive intervention gains: Early-dementia identification by non-intellective factors.* Paper presented at the meeting of the Gerontological Society of America, San Francisco.

Kyba, F. C. (2002). Legal and ethical issues in end-of-life care. *Critical Care and Nursing Clinics of North America, 14,* 141–155.

Labouvie-Vief, G. (1986, August). *Modes of knowing and life-span cognition.* Paper presented at the meeting of the American Psychological Association, Washington, DC.

Labouvie-Vief, G. (1996). Knowledge and the construction of women's development. In P. B. Baltes & U. Staudinger (Eds.), *Interactive minds: Life-span perspectives on the social foundations of cognition.* New York: Cambridge University Press.

Labouvie-Vief, G., Diehl, M., Tarnowksi, A., & Shen, J. (2000). Age differences in personality: Findings from the United States and China. *Journal of Gerontology: Psychological Sciences, 55B,* P4–P17.

Lachman, M. E. (1991). Perceived control over memory aging: Developmental and intervention perspective. *Journal of Social Issues, 47*(4), 159–175.

Lachman, M. E. (2004). Development in midlife. *Annual Review of Psychology,* Vol. 55. Palo Atto, CA: Annual Reviews.

Lachman, M. E., Baltes, P. B., Nesselroade, J. R., & Willis, S. L. (1982). Examination of personality-ability relationships in the elderly: The role of the contextual (interface) assessment mode. *Journal of Research in Personality, 16,* 485–501.

Ladd, G. W., Buhs, E., & Troop, W. (2002). School adjustment and social skills training. In P. K. Smith & C. H. Hart (Eds.), *Blackwell handbook of childhood social development.* Malden, MA: Blackwell.

Ladd, G. W., & Kochenderfer-Ladd, B. (1998). Parenting behaviors and parent-child relationships: Correlates of peer victimization in kindergarten. *Developmental Psychology, 34,* 1450–1458.

Ladd, G. W., & Kochenderfer-Ladd, B. (2002). Identifying victims of peer aggression from early to middle childhood: Analysis of cross-informant data for concordance, incidence of victimization, characteristics of identified victims, and estimation of relational adjustment. *Psychological Assessment, 14,* 74–96.

Ladd, G. W., & Pettit, G. S. (2002). Parenting and the development of children's peer relationships. In M. H. Bornstein (Ed.), *Handbook of parenting* (2nd ed., Vol. 5). Mahwah, NJ: Erlbaum.

Laible, D. J., Carlo, G., & Raffaeli, M. (2000). The differential relations of parent and peer attachment to adolescent adjustment. *Journal of Youth and Adolescence, 29,* 45–53.

Laird, R. D., Pettit, G. S., Bates, J. E., & Dodge, K. A. (2003). Parents' monitoring-relevant knowledge and adolescents' delinquent behavior: Evidence of correlated developmental changes and reciprocal influences. *Child Development, 74,* 752–768.

Lakatta, E. S. (1992, December 6). Commentary in "We can age successfully." *Parade Magazine,* p. 15.

Lalonde, C., & Chandler, M. (2004). Culture, selves, and time. In C. Lightfoot, C. Lalonde, & M. Chandler (Eds.), *Changing conceptions of psychological life.* Mahwah, NJ: Erlbaum.

Lamb, M. E. (1986). *The father's role: Applied perspectives.* New York: Wiley.

Lamb, M. E. (1994). Infant care practices and the application of knowledge. In C. B. Fisher & R. M. Lerner (Eds.), *Applied developmental psychology.* New York: McGraw-Hill.

Lamb, M. E. (2000). The history of research on father involvement: An overview. *Marriage and Family Review, 29,* 23–42.

Lamb, V. L. (2004). Historical and epidemiological trends in mortality in the United States. In C. D. Bryant (Ed.), *Handbook of death and dying.* Thousand Oaks, CA: Sage.

Lane, H. (1976). *The wild boy of Aveyron.* Cambridge, MA: Harvard University Press.

Lane, H. B., & Pullen, P. C. (2004). *Phonological awareness assessment and instruction.* Boston: Allyn & Bacon.

Lang, F. R., & Carstensen, L. L. (1994). Close emotional relationships in late life: Further support for proactive aging in the social domain. *Psychology and Aging, 9,* 315–324.

Langley-Evans, S. C., & Langley-Evans, A. J. (2002). Use of folic acid supplements in the first trimester of pregnancy. *Journal of the Royal Society of Health, 122,* 181–186.

Langlois, J. H., & Liben, L. S. (2003). Child care research: An editorial perspective. *Child Development, 74,* 969–1226.

Langston, W. (2002). *Research methods manual for psychology.* Belmont, CA: Wadsworth.

Lapsley, D. K. (1996). *Moral psychology.* Boulder, CO: Westview Press.

Lapsley, D. K., & Narvacz, D. (Eds.) (2004). *Moral development, self, and identity.* Mahwah, NJ: Erlbaum.

Lapsley, D. K., & Power, F. C. (Eds.). (1988). *Self, ego, and identity.* New York: Springer-Verlag.

Larsen, R. J., & Buss, D. M. (2002). *Personality psychology: Domains of knowledge about human nature.* New York: McGraw-Hill.

Larson, R. W. (1999, September). Unpublished review of J. W. Santrock's *Adolescence,* 8th ed. (New York: McGraw-Hill).

Larson, R. W. (2001). How U.S. children spend time: What it does (and doesn't) tell us about their development. *Current Directions in Psychological Science, 10,* 160–164.

Larson, R. W., Brown, B., & Mortimer, J. (2003). *Adolescents' preparation for the future: Perils and promises.* Malden, MA: Blackwell.

Larson, R. W., Clore, G. L., & Wood, G. A. (1999). The emotions of romantic relationships. In W. Furman, B. B. Brown, & C. Feiring (Eds.), *Contemporary perspectives on romantic relationships.* New York: Cambridge University Press.

Larson, R. W., & Lampman-Petraitis, C. (1989). Daily emotional states as reported by children and adolescents. *Child Development, 60,* 1250–1260.

Larson, R. W. & Richards, M. H. (1994). *Divergent realities* New York: Basic Books.

Larson, R. W., & Verma, S. (1999). How children and adolescents spend their time around the world: Work, play, and developmental opportunities. *Psychological Bulletin, 125,* 701–736.

Larson, R. W. & Wilson, S. (2004). Adolescence across place and time: Globalization and the changing pathways to adulthood. In R. Lerner & L. Steinberg (Eds.), *Handbook of Adolescent Psychology.* New York: Wiley.

Lawton, M. P., Kleban, M. H., Rajagopal, D., & Dean, J. (1992). The dimensions of affective experience in three age groups. *Psychology and Aging, 7,* 171–184.

Lazarus, R. S., & Folkman, S. (1984). *Stress, appraisal, and coping.* New York: Springer.

Leach, P. (1990). *Your baby and child: From birth to age five.* New York: Knopf.

Leadbeater, B. J., & Way, N. (2000). *Growing up fast.* Mahwah, NJ: Erlbaum.

Learner-Centered Principles Work Group (1997). *Learner-centered psychological principles: A framework for school redesign and reform.* Washington, DC: American Psychological Association.

Leary, M. R. (2004). *Introduction to behavioral research* (4th Ed.). Boston: Allyn & Bacon.

LeDoux, J. E. (2000). Emotion circuits in the brain. *Annual Review of Neuroscience, 23,* 155–184.

LeDoux, J. E. (2002). *The synaptic self.* New York: Viking.

Lee, D. J., & Markides, K. S. (1990). Activity and mortality among aged persons over an eight-year period. *Journals of Gerontology: Social Sciences, 45,* S39–S42.

Lee, I. M., Hsieh, C., & Paffenbarger, O. (1995). Exercise intensity and longevity in men. *Journal of the American Medical Association, 273,* 1179–1184.

Lee, I. M., Manson, J. E., Hennekens, C. H., & Paffenbarger, R. S. (1993). Bodyweight and mortality: A 27-year-follow-up. *Journal of the American Medical Association, 270,* 2823–2828.

Lee, I. M., & Skerrett, P. J. (2001). Physical activity and all-cause mortality: What is the dose-response relation? *Medical Science and Sports Exercise, 33* (6 Suppl.), S459–S471.

Lee, M. M. (2003). Is treatment with luteinizing hormone-releasing hormone agonist justified in short adolescents? *New England Journal of Medicine, 348,* 942–945.

Lee, S. Y., Kim, M. T., Kim, S. W., Song, M. S., & Yoon, S. J. (2003). Effect of lifetime lactation on breast cancer risk: A Korean women's cohort study. *International Journal of Cancer, 105,* 390–393.

Lee, W. K. (2003). Women and retirement planning: Towards the "feminization of poverty" in an aging Hong Kong. *Journal of Women and Aging, 15,* 31–53.

Leeman, C. P. (2002). Physician-assisted death. *New England Journal of Medicine, 347,* 1041–1042.

Leffert, N., & Blyth, D. A. (1996, March). *The effects of community contexts on early adolescents.* Paper presented at the meeting of the Society for Research on Adolescence, Boston.

Lehman, H. C. (1960). The age decrement in outstanding scientific creativity. *American Psychologist, 15,* 128–134.

Lehrer, R., Schauble, L., & Petrosino, A. (2001). Reconsidering the role of the experiment in science. In K. Crowley, C. Schunn, & T. Okada (Eds.), *Designing for science.* Mahwah, NJ: Erlbaum.

Leith, L. M. (1998). Exercise and mental health. In H. S. Friedman (Ed.), *Encyclopedia of mental health* (Vol. 2). San Diego: Academic Press.

LeMare, L. J., & Rubin, K. H. (1987). Perspective taking and peer interaction: Structural and developmental analyses. *Child Development, 58,* 306–315.

Leming, M. R. (2004). The history of the hospice approach. In C. D. Bryant (Ed.), *Handbook of death and dying.* Thousand Oaks, CA: Sage.

Leming, M. R., & Dickinson, G. E. (2002). *Understanding death, dying, and bereavement* (5th ed.). Belmont. CA: Wadsworth.

Lenders, C. M., McElrath, T. F., & Scholl, T. O. (2000). Nutrition in pregnancy. *Current Opinions in Pediatrics, 12,* 291–296.

Lenneberg, E. (1967). *The biological foundations of language.* New York: Wiley.

Lenoir, C. P., Mallet, E., & Calenda, E. (2000). Siblings of sudden infant death syndrome and near miss in about 30 families: Is there a genetic link? *Medical Hypotheses, 54,* 408–411.

Leonards, U., Ibanez, V., & Giannakopoulos, P. (2002). The role of stimulus type in age-related changes of visual working memory. *Experimental Brain Research, 146,* 172–183.

LePine. J. A., & Van Dyne, L. (1998). Predicting voice behavior in work groups. *Journal of Applied Psychology, 83,* 853–868.

Lepper, M., Greene, D., & Nisbett, R. (1973). Undermining children's intrinsic interest with intrinsic rewards: A test of the overjustification hypothesis. *Journal of Personality and Social Psychology, 28,* 129–137.

Lerner, H. G. (1989). *The role of intimacy.* New York: Harper & Row.

Lerner, R. (2002). *Concepts and theories of human development* (3rd ed.). Mahwah, NJ: Erlbaum.

Lerner, R., & Steinberg, L. (Eds.), (2004). *Handbook of adolescent psychology.* New York: Wiley.

Lesaux, N. K., & Siegel, L. S. (2003). The development of reading in children who speak English as a second language. *Developmental Psychology, 39,* 1005–1019.

Lester, B. M., Tronick, E. Z., LaGasse, L., Seifer, R., Bauer, C. R., Shankaran, S., Bada, H. S., Wright L. L., Smeriglio, V. L., Lu, J., Finnegan, L. P., & Maza, P. L. (2002). The maternal lifestyle study: Effects of substance exposure during pregnancy on neurodevelopmental outcome in 1-month-old infants. *Pediatrics, 110,* 1182–1192.

Levant, R. F. (1996). The male code and parenting: A psychoeducational approach. In M. P. Andronico (Ed.), *Men in groups.* Washington, DC: American Psychological Association.

Levant, R. F., & Brooks, G. R. (1997). *Men and sex: New psychological perspectives.* New York: Wiley.

LeVay, S. (1991). A difference in the hypothalamic structure between heterosexual and homosexual men. *Science, 253,* 1034–1037.

Levelt, W. J. M. (1989). *Speaking: From intention to articulation.* Cambridge, MA: MIT Press.

Leventhal, A. (1994, February). *Peer conformity during adolescence: An integration of developmental, situational, and individual characteristics.* Paper presented at the meeting of the Society for Research on Adolescence, San Diego.

Leventhal, A. G., Wang, Y., Pu, M., Zhou, Y., & Ma, Y. (2003). GABA and its agonists improved visual cortical function in senescent monkeys. *Science, 300,* 812–815.

Leventhal, T., & Brooks-Gunn, J. (2003). Children and youth in neighborhood contexts. *Current Directions in Psychological Science, 12,* 27–31.

Leventhal, T., Graber, J.A., & Brooks-Gunn, J. (2001). Adolescent transition into young adulthood: Antecedents, correlates and consequences of adolescent employment. *Journal of Research on Adolescence, 11(3),* 297–323.

Levesque, J., & Prosser, T. (1996). Service learning connections. *Journal of Teacher Education, 47,* 325–334.

Levin, J. S., Chatters, L.M., & Taylor, R. J. (1995). Religious effects on health status and life satisfaction among Black Americans. *Journal of Gerontology: Social Sciences, 50B,* S154–S163.

Levin, J. S., Taylor, R. J., & Chatters, L. M. (1994). Race and gender differences in religiosity among older adults: Findings from four national surveys. *Journal of Gerontology, 49,* S137–S145.

Levinson, D. J. (1978). *The seasons of a man's life.* New York: Knopf.

Levinson, D. J. (1987, August). *The seasons of a woman's life.* Paper presented at the meeting of the American Psychological Association, New York.

Levinson, D. J. (1996). *Seasons of a woman's life.* New York: Alfred Knopf.

Levy, B. R., Jennings, P., & Langer, E. J. (2001). Improving attention in old age. *Journal of Adult Development, 8,* 189–192.

Lewis, C., & Carpendale, J. (2002). Social cognition. In P. K. Smith & C. H. Hart (Eds.), *Blackwell handbook of childhood social development.* Malden, MA: Blackwell.

Lewis, M. (1997). *Altering fate: Why the past does not predict the future.* New York: Guilford Press.

Lewis, M. (2001). Issues in the study of personality development. *Psychological Inquiry, 12,* 67–83.

Lewis, M. (2002). Early emotional development. In A. Slater & M. Lewis (Eds.), *Infant development.* New York: Oxford University Press.

Lewis, M., & Brooks-Gunn, J. (1979). *Social cognition and the acquisition of the self.* New York: Plenum.

Lewis, M., Feiring, C., & Rosenthal, S. (2000). Attachment over time. *Child Development, 71,* 707–720.

Lewis, M., & Ramsay, D. S. (1999). Effect of maternal soothing and infant stress response. *Child Development, 70,* 11–20.

Lewis, M., Sullivan, M. W., Sanger, C., & Weiss, M. (1989). Self-development and self-conscious emotions. *Child Development, 60,* 146–156.

Lewis, R. (2003). *Human genetics* (5th ed.). New York: McGraw-Hill.

Lewis, R., Gaffin, D., Hoefnagels, M., & Parker, B. (2004). *Life (5th Ed.).* New York: McGraw-Hill.

Lewis, V. G., Money, J., & Bobrow, N. A. (1977). Idiopathic pubertal delay beyond the age of 15: Psychological study of 12 boys. *Adolescence, 12,* 1–11.

Li, A. M., Chan, D., Wong, E., Yin J., Nelson, E. A., & Fok, T. F. (2003). The effects of obesity on pulmonary function. *Archives of Diseases in Childhood, 88,* 361–363.

Li, D. K., Petitti, D. B., Willinger, M., McMahon, R., Odouli, R., Vu, H., & Hoffman, H. J. (2003). Infant sleeping position and the risk of sudden infant death syndrome in California, 1997–2000. *American Journal of Epidemiology, 157,* 446–455.

Li, S. J., Li, Z., Wu, G., Zhang, M. J., Franczak, M., & Antuono, P. G. (2002). Alzheimer disease: Evaluation of functional

MR imaging index as a marker. *Radiology, 225*, 253–259.

Liben, L. S., Bigler, R. S., & Krogh, H. R. (2001). Pink and blue collar jobs: Children's judgements of job status and job aspirations in relation to sex of worker. *Journal of Experimental Child Psychology, 79(4)*, 346–363.

Lickliter, R., & Bahrick, L. E. (2000). The development of infant intersensory perception: Advantages of a comparative convergent-operations approach. *Psychological Bulletin, 126*, 260–280.

Lie, E., & Newcombe, N. (1999). Elementary school children's explicit and implicit memory for faces of preschool classmates. *Developmental Psychology, 35*, 102–112.

Lieberman, M., Doyle, A., & Markiewicz, D. (1999). Developmental patterns in security of attachment to mother and father in late childhood and early adolescence: Associations with peer relations. *Child Development, 70*, 202–213

Lifton, R. J. (1977). The sense of immortality: On death and the continuity of life. In H. Feifel (Ed.), *New meanings of death.* New York: McGraw-Hill.

Light, L. L. (2000). Memory changes in adulthood. In S. H. Qualls & N. Abeles (Eds.), *Psychology and the aging revolution.* Washington, DC: American Psychological Association.

Lightwood, J. M., Phibbs, C. S., & Glantz, S. A. (1999). Short-term health and economic benefits of smoking cessation. *Pediatrics, 104*, 1312–1320.

Limbar, S. P. (2004). Implementation of the Olweus bullying prevention program in American schools: Lessons learned from the field. In D. L. Espelage & S. M. Swearer (Eds.), *Bullying in American schools.* Mahwah, NJ: Erlbaum.

Limber, S. P. (1997). Preventing violence among school children. *Family Futures, 1*, 27–28.

Lindbohm, M. (1991). Effects of paternal occupational exposure in spontaneous abortions. *American Journal of Public Health, 121*, 1029–1033.

Lippa, R. A. (2002). *Gender, nature, and nurture.* Mahwah, NJ: Erlbaum.

Lipsitz, J. (1984). *Successful schools for young adolescents.* New Brunswick, NJ: Transaction.

Litovsky, R. Y., & Ashmead, D. II. (1997). Development of binaural and spatial hearing in infants and children. In R. H. Gilkey & T. R. Anderson (Eds.), *Binaural and spatial hearing in real and virtual environments,* Mahwah, NJ: Erlbaum.

Lively, W., & Bromley, D. (1973). *Person perception in childhood and adolescence.* New York: Wiley.

Lobel, M., Yali, A. M., Zhu, W., DeVincent, C. J., & Meyer, B. A. (2002). Beneficial associations between optimistic disposition and emotional distress in high-risk pregnancy. *Psychology and Health, 17*, 77–95.

Lock, A. (2002). Preverbal communication. In U. Goswami (Ed.), *Blackwell handbook of childhood cognitive development.* Malden, MA: Blackwell.

Löckenhoff, C. E., & Carstensen, L. L. (2003). Is the life-span theory of control a theory of development or a theory of coping? In S. Zarit, L. Pearlin, & K. W. Schaie, (Eds.), *Personal Control in Social and Life Span Contexts.* New York: Springer.

Lockman, J. J. (2000). A perception-action perspective on tool use development. *Child Development, 71*, 137–144.

Loeber, R., DeLamatre, M., Keenan, K., & Zhang, Q. (1998). A prospective replication of developmental pathways in disruptive and delinquent behavior. In R. Cairns, L. Bergman, & J. Kagan (Eds.), *Methods and models for studying the individual.* Thousand Oaks, CA: Sage.

Loeber, R., & Farrington, D. P. (Eds.). (2001). *Child delinquents: Development, intervention and service needs.* Thousand Oaks, CA: Sage.

Loeber, R., Farrington, D. P., Stouthamer-Loeber, M., Moffitt, T. E., Caspi, A., & Lynam, D. (2002). Male mental health problems, psychopathy, and personality traits: Key findings from the first 14 years of the Pittsburgh Youth Study. *Clinical Child and Family Psychology Review, 4(4)*, 273–297.

Loftus, E. F. (2002) Memory faults and fixes. *Issues in Science and Technology,* XVIII (No. 4) 41–50.

London, M. L., Ladewig, P. W., Olds, S. B., & Ladewig, P. W. (2000). *Maternal newborn nursing care* (4th ed.). Boston: Addison-Wesley.

Lonner, W. J. (1988, October). *The introductory psychology text and cross-cultural psychology: A survey of cross-cultural psychologists.* Bellingham: Western Washington University, Center for Cross-cultural Research.

Lopata, H. Z. (1994). *Circles and settings: Role changes of American women.* Albany State University of New York Press.

Lorenz, K. Z. (1965). *Evolution and the modification of behavior.* Chicago: University of Chicago Press.

Lott, B., & Maluso, D. (2001). Gender development: Social learning. In J. Worrell (Ed.), *Encyclopedia of women and gender.* San Diego: Academic Press.

Louv, R. (1990). *Childhood's future.* Boston: Houghton Mifflin.

Lowe, X., Eskenazi, B., Nelson, D. O., Kidd, S., Alme, A., & Wyrobek, A. J. (2001). Frequency of XY sperm increases with age in fathers of boys with Klinefelter syndrome. *American Journal of Human Genetics, 69*, 1046–1054.

Lubart, T. I. (2003). In search of creative intelligence. In R. J. Sternberg, J. Lautrey, & T. I. Lubert (Eds.), *Models of intelligence: International perspectives.* Washington, DC: American Psychological Association.

Lubinski, D. (2000). Measures of intelligence: Intelligence tests. In A. Kazdin (Ed.), *Encyclopedia of Psychology.* Washington, DC, & New York: American Psychological Association and Oxford University Press.

Luciana, M., Sullivan, J., & Nelson, C. A. (2001). Associations between phenylalanine-to-tyrosine ratios and performance on tests of neuropsychological function in adolescents treated early and continuously for phenylketonuria. *Child Development, 72*, 1637.

Lucurto, C. (1990). The malleability of IQ as judged from adoption studies. *Intelligence, 14*, 275–292.

Luffy, R., & Grove, S. K. (2003). Examining the validity, reliability, and preference of three pediatric pain measurement tools in African-American children. *Pediatric Nursing, 29*, 54–59.

Lumeng, J. C., Gannon, K., Cabral, H. J., Frank, D. A., & Zuckerman, B. (2003). Association between clinically meaningful behavior problems and overweight in children. *Pediatrics, 112*, 1138–1145,

Lund, D. A. (1996). Bereavement and loss. In J. E. Birren (Ed.), *Encyclopedia of gerontology* (Vol. 1). San Diego: Academic Press.

Luo, Q., Fang, X., & Aro, P. (1995, March). *Selection of best friends by Chinese adolescents.* Paper presented at the meeting of the Society for Research in Child Development, Indianapolis.

Luria, A., & Herzog, E. (1985, April). *Gender segregation across and within settings.* Paper presented at the biennial meeting of the Society for Research in Child Development, Toronto.

Lynn, R. (1996). Racial and ethnic differences in intelligence in the U.S. on the Differential Ability Scale. *Personality and Individual Differences, 26*, 271–273.

Lyon, G. R. (1996). Learning disabilities. *Future of Children, 6(1)* 54–76.

Lyon, T. D., & Flavell, J. H. (1993). Young children's understanding of forgetting over time. *Child Development, 64*, 789–800.

Lyubomirsky, S., & Lepper, H. S. (2002). *What are the differences between happiness and self-esteem?* Unpublished manuscript, U. of California, Riverside.

Maas, J. B. (1998). *Power sleep.* New York: Villard Books.

Maccoby, E. E. (1987, November). Interview with Elizabeth Hall: All in the family. *Psychology Today,* pp. 54–60.

Maccoby, E. E. (1998). *The two sexes: Growing up apart, coming together.* Cambridge, MA: Harvard University Press.

Maccoby, E. E. (1999). The uniqueness of the parent-child relationship. In W. A. Collins & B. Laursen (Eds.), *Relationships as developmental contexts.* Mahwah, NJ: Erlbaum.

Maccoby, E. E. (2002). Gender and group process: A developmental perspective. *Current Directions in Psychological Science, 11*, 54–57.

Maccoby, E. E. (2002). Parenting effects. In J. G. Borkowski, S. L. Ramey, & M. Bristol-Power (Eds.), *Parenting and the child's world.* Mahwah, NJ: Erlbaum.

Maccoby, E. E., & Jacklin, C. N. (1974). *The psychology of sex differences.* Palo Alto, CA: Stanford University Press.

Maccoby, E. E., & Lewis, C. C. (2003). Less daycare or better daycare? *Child Development, 74,* 1069–1075.

Maccoby, E. E., & Mnookin, R. H. (1992). *Dividing the child: Social and legal dilemmas of custody.* Cambridge, MA: Harvard University Press.

MacDorman, M. F., Minino, A. M., Strobino, D. M., & Guyer, B. (2002). Annual summary of vital statistics—2001. *Pediatrics, 110,* 1037–1052.

MacDorman, M. F., & Singh, G. K. (1998). Midwifery care, social and medical factors, and birth outcomes in the USA. *Journal of Epidemiology and Community Health, 52,* 310–317.

MacFarlane, J. A. (1975). Olfaction in the development of social preferences in the human neonate. In *Parent-infant interaction.* Ciba Foundation Symposium No. 33. Amsterdam: Elsevier.

Maciokas, J. B., & Crognale, M. A. (2003). Cognitive and attentional changes with age: Evidence from attentional blink deficits. *Experimental Aging Research, 29,* 137–153.

MacKay, D. G., & Abrams L. (1996). Language, memory, and aging: Distributed deficits and the structure of new-versus-old connections. In J. E. Birren & K. W. Schaie (Eds.), *Handbook of the psychology of aging.* San Diego: Academic Press.

MacLean, W. E. (2000). Down syndrome. In A. Kazdin (Ed.), *Encyclopedia of psychology.* Washington, DC, & New York: American Psychological Association and Oxford University Press.

Madden, D. J. (2001). Speed and timing of behavioral processes. In J. E. Birren & K. W. Schaie (Eds.), *Handbook of the psychology of aging* (5th ed.). San Diego: Academic Press.

Madden, D. J. (2001). Speed and timing of behavioral processes. In J. E. Birren & K. W. Schaie (Eds.), *Handbook of the psychology of aging* (5th ed.). San Diego: Academic Press.

Madden, D. J., Gottlob, L. R., Denny, L. L., Turkington, T. G., Provenzale, J. M., Hawk. T. C., et al. (1999). Aging and recognition memory: Changes in regional cerebral blood flow associated with components of reaction time distributions. *Journal of Cognitive Neuroscience, 11,* 511–520.

Maddux, J. (2002). The power of believing you can. In C. R. Snyder & S. J. Lopez (Eds.), *Handbook of positive psychology.* New York: Oxford University Press.

Magnuson, K. A., & Duncan, G. J. (2002). Parents in poverty. In M. H. Bornstein (Ed.), *Handbook of parenting* (2nd ed. Vol. 4). Mahwah, NJ: Erlbaum.

Magnusson, D. (1988). *Individual development from an interactional perspective: A longitudinal study.* Hillsdale, NJ: Erlbaum.

Mahakunakorn, P., Tohda, M., Murakami, 'Y., Matsumot, K., & Watanabe, H. (2004). Antioxidant and free-radical-scavenging activity of Choto-san and its related Constituents. *Biological & Pharmaceutical Bulletin, 27,* 38–46

Mahoney, J. L., Larson, R. W., & Eccles, J. S. (Eds.) (2004). *Organized activities as contexts of development.* Mahwah, NJ: Erlbaum.

Mahoney, J. L., Larson, R. W., Eccles, J. S., & Lord, H. (2004). Organized activites as contexts for child and adolescent development. In J. L. Mahoney, R. W. Larson, & J. S. Eccles (Eds.), *Organized activities as contexts of development.* Mahwah, NJ: Erlbaum.

Main, M. (2000). Attachment theory. In A. Kazdin (Ed.), *Encyclopedia of psychology.* Washington, DC, & New York: American Psychological Association and Oxford University Press.

Makrides, M., Neumann, M., Simmer, K., Pater, J., & Gibson, R. (1995). Are long-chain polyunsaturated fatty acids essential nutrients in infancy? *Lancet, 345,* 1463–1468.

Malinosky-Rummell, R., & Hansen, D. J. (1993). Long-term consequences of childhood physical abuse. *Psychological Bulletin, 114,* 68–79.

Mandler, J. (2000). Unpublished review of J. W. Santrock's *Life-span development,* 8th ed. New York: McGraw-Hill.

Mandler, J. M. (2003). Conceptual categorization. In D. Rakison & L. M. Oakes (Eds.), *Early category and concept development.* New York: Oxford University Press.

Mandler, J. M., & McDonough, L. (1995). Long-term recall in infancy. *Journal of Experimental Child Psychology, 59,* 457–474.

Manis, F. R., Keating, D. P., & Morrison, F. J. (1980). Developmental differences in the allocation of processing capacity. *Journal of Experimental Child Psychology, 29,* 156–169.

Manne, S. (2003). Coping and social support. In I. B. Weiner (Ed.), *Handbook of psychology* (Vol. IX). New York: Wiley.

Mannell, R. C. (2000). Older adults, leisure, and wellness. *Journal of Leisurability, 26,* 3–10.

Manning, W. D., & Smock, P. J. 2002. First comes cohabitation and then comes marriage. *Journal of Family Issues, 23,* 1065–1087.

Manor, O., & Eisenbach, Z. (2003). Mortality after spousal loss: Are there sociodemographic differences? *Social Science and Medicine, 56,* 405–413.

Mantzoros, C. S. (2000). Role of leptin in reproduction. *Annals of the New York Academy of Sciences, 900,* 174–183.

Many, J. E. (2002). An exhibition and analysis of verbal tapestries: Understanding how scaffolding is woven into the fabric of instructional conversations. *Reading Research Quarterly, 37,* 376–407.

Maratsos, M. (1998). The acquisition of grammar. In D. Kuhn & R. S. Siegler (Eds.), *Handbook of child psychology* (5th ed., Vol. 2). New York: Wiley.

Marchman, V. (2003). Review of Santrock, J. W. *Child Development,* 10th Ed. New York: McGraw-Hill.

Marcia, J., & Carpendale, J. (2004). Identity: Does thinking make it so? In C. Lightfoot, C. Lalonde, & M. Chandler (Eds.), *Changing conceptions of psychological life.* Mahwah, NJ: Erlbaum.

Marcia, J. E. (1980). Ego identity development. In J. Adelson (Ed.), *Handbook of adolescent psychology.* New York: Wiley.

Marcia, J. E. (1987). The identity status approach to the study of ego identity development. In T. Honess & K. Yardley (Eds.), *Self and identity: Perspectives across the lifespan.* London: Routledge & Kegan Paul.

Marcia, J. E. (1989). Identity in adolescence. *Journal of Adolescence, 12,* 401–410.

Marcia, J. E. (1996). Unpublished review of J. W. Santrock's *Adolescence,* 7th ed. Dubuque, IA: Brown & Benchmark.

Marcus, D. L., Mulrine, A., & Wong, K. (1999, September 13). How kids learn. *U.S. News & World Report,* pp. 44–50.

Marecek, J., Finn, S. E., & Cardell, M. (1988). Gender roles in the relationships of lesbians and gay man. In J. P. De Cecco (Ed.), *Gay relationships.* New York: Harrington Park Press.

Margolin, L. (1994). Child sexual abuse by uncles. *Child Abuse and Neglect, 18,* 215–224.

Markides, K. S. (1995). Aging and ethnicity. *Gerontologist, 35,* 276–277.

Markides, K. S., & Rudkin, L. (1996). Race and ethnic diversity. In J. E. Birren (Ed.), *Encyclopedia of gerontology* (Vol. 2). San Diego: Academic Press.

Markowitz, M. (2000). Lead poisoning. *Pediatrics in Review, 21,* 327–335.

Marks, D. F., Sykes, C. M., & Mckinley, J. M. (2003). Health psychology: Overview and professional issues. In I. B. Weiner (Ed.), *Handbook of psychology* (Vol. IX). New York: Wiley.

Marks, M. A., & Nelson, E. S. (1993). Sexual harassment on campus: Effects of professor gender on perception of sexually harassing behaviors. *Sex Roles, 28,* 207–218.

Markson, E. W. (1995). Older women: The silent majority? *Gerontologist, 35,* 278–281.

Markus, H. R., & Kitayama, S. (1994). The cultural construction of self and emotion: Implications for social behavior. In S. Kitayama & H. R. Markus (Eds.), *Emotion and culture.* Washington, DC: American Psychological Association.

Markus, H. R., & Nurius, P. (1986). Possible selves. *American Psychologist, 41,* 954–969.

Markus, H. R., Mullally, P. R., & Kitayama, S. (1999). *Selfways: Diversity in modes of cultural participation.* Unpublished manuscript, Department of Psychology, University of Michigan.

Marsh, H. W. (1991). Employment during high school: Character building or a subversion of academic goals? *Sociology of Education, 64,* 172–189.

Marsiske, M., Klumb, P. L., & Baltes, M. M. (1997). Everyday activity patterns and sensory functioning in old age. *Psychology and Aging, 12,* 444–457.

Marsiske, M., Lang, F. R., Baltes, R. B., & Baltes, M. M. (1995). Selective optimization with compensation. In R. A. Dixon & L. Backman (Eds.), *Compensating for psychological deficits and declines.* Hillsdale, NJ: Erlbaum.

Martin, C. L. (1990). Attitudes and expectations about children with nontraditional traditional gender roles. *Sex Roles, 22,* 151–165.

Martin, C. L., & Dinella, L. (2001). Gender development: Gender schema theory. In J. Worell (Ed.), *Encyclopedia of women and gender.* San Diego: Academic Press.

Martin, C. L., & Fabes, R. A (2001). The stability and consequences of young children's segregated social play. *Developmental Psychology, 37,* 431–446.

Martin, C. L., & Halverson, C. F. (1981). A schmetic processing model of sex typing and stereotyping in children. *Child Development, 52,* 1119–1134.

Martin, C. L., Ruble, D. N., & Szkrybalo, J. (2002). Cognitive theories of early gender development. *Psychological Bulletin, 128,* 903–933.

Martin, J. A., & Buckwalter, J. A. (2001). Biomarkers of aging. *Journal of Gerontology, 56A, No. 4,* B172-B179.

Martire, L. M., & Schultz, R. (2001). Informal caregiving to older adults. In A. Baum, T. A. Revenson, & J. E. Singer (Eds.), *Handbook of health psychology.* Mahwah, NJ: Erlbaum.

Mash, E. J., & Wolfe, D. A. (1999). *Abnormal child psychology.* Belmont, CA: Wadsworth.

Mason, J. A., & Hermann, K. R. (1998). Universal infant hearing screening by automated auditory brainstem response measurement. *Pediatrics, 101,* 221–228.

Masten, A. S. (1999). Resilience comes of age: Reflections on the past and outlook for the next generation of research. In M. D. Glantz, J. Johnson, & L. Huffman (Eds.), *Resilience and development. New York:* Plenum Press.

Masten, A. S. (2001). Ordinary magic: Resilience processes in development. *American Psychologist, 56,* 227–238.

Matheny, A. P., & Phillips, K. (2001). Temperament and context: Correlates of home environment with temperament continuity and change. In T. D. Wachs & G. A. Kohnstamm (Eds.), *Temperament in context.* Mahwah, NJ: Erlbaum.

Mather, M., Canli, T., English, T., Whitfield, S., Wais, P., Ochsner, K., Gabrieli, J. D. E., Carstensen, L. L. (in press). Amygdala responses to emotionally valenced stimuli in older and younger adults. *Psychological Science.*

Matlin, M. W. (2004). The *Psychology of women* (5th Ed.). Belmont, CA: Wadsworth.

Matsumoto, D. (2000). *Culture and psychology: People around the world* (2nd ed.). Belmont, CA: Wadsworth.

Matsumoto, D. (2004). *Culture and psychology* (3rd Ed.). Belmont, CA: Wadsworth.

Matthias, R. F., Lubben, J. E., Atchison, K. A., & Schweitzer, S. O. (1997). Sexual activity and satisfaction among very old adults: Results from a community-dwelling Medicare population survey. *Gerontologist, 37,* 6–14.

Mattson, M. P., & Liu, D. (2002). Energetics and oxidative stress in synaptic plasticity and neurogenerative disorders. *Neuromuscular Medicine, 2,* 215–231.

Mattson, M. P., Duan, W., Chan, S. L., Cheng, A., Haughey, N., Gary, D. S., Guo, Z., Lee, J., & Furukawa, K. (2002). Neuroprotective and neurorestorative signal transduction mechanisms in brain aging: Modification by genes, diet, and behavior. *Neurobiology of Aging, 23,* 707.

Matzo, M. L., Sherman, D. W., Lo, K., Egan, K. A., Grant, M., & Rhome, A. (2003). Strategies for teaching loss, grief, and bereavement. *Nursing Education, 28,* 71–76.

Maughan, A., & Cicchetti, D. (2002). Impact of child maltreatment and interadult violence on children's emotion regulation difficulties and socioemotional adjustment. *Child Development, 73,* 1525–1542.

Maulik, D. (2003). New directions in prenatal care. *Journal of Maternal, Fetal, and Neonatal Medicine, 13,* 361.

Mauro, V. P., Wood, I. C., Krushel, L., Crossin, K. L., & Edelman, G. M. (1994). Cell adhesion alters gene transcription in chicken embryo brain cells and mouse embryonal carcinoma cells. *Proceedings of the National Academy of Sciences USA, 91,* 2868–2872.

Maxon, S. (2003). Behavioral genetics. In I. B. Weiner (Ed.), *Encyclopedia of psychology* (Vol. III). New York: Wiley.

Maxwell, C. B. (2000). Head Start. In A. Kazdin (Ed.), *Encyclopedia of psychology.* Washington, DC, & New York: American Psychological Association and Oxford University Press.

Mayer, J. D., Salovey, P., & Caruso, D. R. (2002). *Mayer-Salovey-Caruso Emotional Intelligence Test (MSCEIT): User's Manual.* Toronto, Ontario, Canada: Multi-Health Systems.

Mayer, R. E. (2003). *Learning and instruction.* Boston: Allyn & Bacon.

Mayer, R. E. (2003). Memory and information processes. In I. B. Weiner (Ed.), *Handbook of psychology* (Vol. VII). New York: Wiley.

Mayes, L. (2003). Unpublished review of J. W. Santrock's *Topical life-span development,* 2nd ed. New York: McGraw-Hill.

Maynard, L. M., Galuska, D. A., Blanck, H. M., & Serdula, M. K. (2003). Maternal perceptions of weight status of children. *Pediatrics, 111,* 1226–1231.

McAdoo, H. P. (2002). African-American parenting. In M. H. Bornstein (Ed.), *Handbook of parenting* (2nd ed., Vol. 4.) Mahwah, NJ: Erlbaum.

McAuliff, B., Kovera, M., & Viswesvaran, C. (1998). *Methodological issues in child suggestibility research: A meta-analysis.* Paper presented at the meeting of the American Psychology and Law Society, Redondo Beach, CA.

McCabe, M. P., & Ricciardelli, L. A. (2003). Sociocultural influences on body image and body changes among adolescent boys and girls. *Journal of Social Psychology, 143,* 5–26.

McCall, R. B., Applebaum, M. I., & Hogarty, P. S. (1973). Developmental changes in mental performance. *Monographs of the Society for Research in Child Development, 38* (Serial No. 150).

McCarty, M. E., & Ashmead, D. H. (1999). Visual control of reaching and grasping in infants. *Developmental Psychology, 35,* 620–631.

McClain, C. S., Rosenfeld, B., & Breitbart, W. S. (2003, March). *The influence of spirituality on end-of-life despair in cancer patients close to death.* Paper presented at the meeting of American Psychosomatic Society, Phoenix.

McCombs, B. L. (2003). Research to policy for guiding educational reform. In I. B. Weiner (Ed.), *Handbook of psychology* (Vol. VII). New York: Wiley.

McCormick, C. B. (2003). Metacognition and learning. In I. B. Weiner (Ed.), *Handbook of psychology* (Vol. VII). New York: Wiley.

McCormick, C. B., & Pressley, M. (1997). *Educational psychology.* New York: Longman.

McCormick, M. C. (2001). Prenatal care—necessary, but not sufficient. *Health Services Research, 36,* 399–403.

McCrae, R. R. (2001). Traits through time. *Psychological Inquiry, 12,* 85–87.

McCrae, R. R., & Costa, P. T. (1990). *Personality in adulthood.* New York: Guilford.

McCrae, R. R., & Costa, P. T. (2003). *Personality in adulthood* (2nd ed.). New York: Guilford.

McCrae, R. R., Costa, P. T., Lima, M. P., Simoes, A., Ostendorf, F., et al. (1999). Age differences in personality across the adult lifespan: Parallels in five cultures. *Developmental Psychology, 35,* 466–477.

McCullough, M. E., Hoyt, W. T., Larson, D. B., Koenig, H. G., & Thoresen, C. (2000). Religious involvement and mortality: A meta-analytic review. *Health psychology, 19,* 211–222.

McDougall, G. J., Strauss, M. E., Holston, E. C., & Martin, M. (1999, November). *Memory self-efficacy and memory-anxiety as predictors of memory performance in at-risk elderly.* Paper presented at the meeting of the Gerontological Society of America, San Francisco.

McDowd, J. M., Filion, D. L., Pohl, P. S., Richards, L. G., & Stiers, W. (2003). Attentional abilities and functional outcomes following a stroke. *Journals of Gerontology: Psychological Sciences and Social Sciences, 58B,* P45–P53.

McFarlane, T., Polivy, J., & Herman, C. P. (1998). Dieting. In H. S. Friedman (Ed.), *Encyclopedia of mental health* (Vol. 1). San Diego: Academic Press.

McGee, L. M., & Richgels, D. J. (2004). *Literacy's beginnings (4th Ed.).* Boston: Allyn & Bacon.

McGue, M., Bouchard, T. J., Iacono, W. G., & Lykken, D. T. (1993). Behavioral genetics of cognitive ability: A life-span perspective. In R. Plomin & G. E. McClearn (Eds.), *Nature, nurture, and psychology.* Washington, DC: American Psychological Association.

McGue, M., Hirsch, B., & Lykken, D. T. (1993). Age and the self-perception of ability: A twin analysis. *Psychology and Aging, 8,* 72–80.

McGuire, F. (2000). What do we know? Not much. The state of leisure and aging research. *Journal of Leisurability, 26,* 97–100.

McHale, J. P., Luretti, A., Talbot, J., & Pouquette, C. (2001). Retrospect and prospect in the psychological study of marital and couple relationships. In J. P. McHale & W. S. Grolnick (Eds.), *Retrospect and prospect in the psychological study of families.* Mahwah, NJ: Erlbaum.

McHale, J., Johnson, D., & Sinclair, R. (1999). Family dynamics, preschoolers' family representations, and preschool peer relationships. *Early Education and Development, 10,* 373–401.

McHale, J., Khazan, I., Erera, P., Rotman, T., DeCourcey, W., & McConnell, M. (2002). Coparenting in diverse family systems. In M. H. Bornstein (Ed.), *Handbook of parenting* (2nd ed., Vol. 3). Mahwah, NJ: Erlbaum.

McHale, S., Dariotis, J. K., & Kauh, T. J. (2003). Social development and social relationships in middle childhood. In I. B. Weiner (Ed.), *Handbook of psychology* (Vol. 6). New York: Wiley.

McIntosh, J. L. (1995). Suicide prevention in the elderly (65–99). In M. M. Silverman & R. W. Maris (Eds.), *Suicide prevention toward the year 2000* (pp. 180–192). New York: Guilford Press.

McIntosh, J. L. (2003). Suicide survivors. In C. D. Bryant (Ed.), *Handbook of death and dying.* Thousand Oaks, CA: Sage.

McKenna, J. J., Mosko, S. S., & Richard, C. A. (1997). Bedsharing promotes breastfeeding. *Pediatrics, 100,* 214–219.

McKnight, A. J., & McKnight A. S. (1993). The effect of cellular phone use upon driver attention. *Accident Analysis and Prevention, 25,* 259–265.

McLeod, J. D. (1996). Life events. In J. E. Birren (Ed.), *Encylcopedia of gerontology* (Vol. 1). San Diego: Academic Press.

McLoyd, V. C. (1990). The impact of economic hardship on Black families and children: Psychological distress, parenting, and socioemotional development. *Child Development, 61,* 311–346.

McLoyd, V. C. (1998). Children in poverty: Development, public policy, and practice. In W. Damon (Ed.), *Handbook of child psychology* (5th ed., Vol. 4). New York: Wiley.

McLoyd, V. C. (2000). Poverty. In A. Kazdin (Ed.), *Encyclopedia of psychology.* Washington, DC, & New York: American Psychological Association and Oxford University Press.

McLoyd, V. C., & Smith, J. (2002). Physical discipline and behavior problems in African American, European American, and Hispanic children: Emotional support as a moderator. *Journal of Marriage and Family, 64,* 40–53.

McMillan, J. H. (2002). *Policy issues.* Richmond, VA: Virginia Commonwealth University.

McMillan, J. H. (2004). *Classroom assessment (3rd Ed.).* Boston: Allyn & Bacon.

McMullin, J. A., & Marshall, V. W. (2001). Ageism, age relations, and garment industry work in Montreal. *The Gerontologist, 41, No. 1,* 111–119.

McNally, D. (1990). *Even eagles need a push.* New York: Dell.

McNamara, F., & Sullivan, C. E. (2000). Obstructive sleep apnea in infants. *Journal of Pediatrics, 136,* 318–323.

McVey, G. L., Pepler, D., Davis, D., Flett, G. L., & Abdolell, M. (2002). Risk and protective factors associated with disordered eating during early adolescence. *Journal of Early Adolescence, 22,* 75–95.

Mead, M. (1978, Dec. 30–Jan. 5). The American family: An endangered species. *TV Guide,* pp, 21–24.

Means, C., Adrienne, J., Snyder, D. K., & Negy, C. (2003). Assessing nontraditional couples. *Journal of Marital and Family Therapy, 29,* 69–83.

Medd, S. E. (2003). Children with ADHD need our advocacy. *Journal of Pediatric Health Care, 17,* 102–104.

Meeker, A. K., & De Marzo, A. M. (2004). Recent advances in telomere biology: Implications for human cancer. *Current Opinions in Oncology, 16,* 32–38.

Mehler, J., Jusczyk, P. W., Lambertz, G., Halsted, N., Bertoncini, J., & Amiel-Tison, C. (1998). A precursor of language acquisition in young infants. *Cognition, 29.* 132–178.

Meijer, J., & Elshout, J. J. (2001). The predictive and discriminant validity of the zone of proximal development. *British Journal of Educational Psychology, 71,* 93–113.

Mein, J. K., Palmer, C. M., Shand, M. C., Templeton, D. J., Parekh, V., Mobbs, M., Haig, K., Huffam, S. E., & Young, L. (2003). Management of acute sexual assault. *Medical Journal of Australia, 178,* 226–230.

Meis, P. J. (2003, February 6). *Effects of progesterone on preterm births.* Paper presented at the meeting of the Society for Maternal-Fetal Medicine, San Francisco.

Melamed, B. G., Roth, B., & Fogel, J. (2001). Childhood health issues across the life span. In A. Baum, T. A. Revenson, & J. E. Singer (Eds.), *Handbook of health psychology.* Mahwah, NJ: Erlbaum.

Melinder, K. A., & Andersson, R. (2001). The impact of structural factors on the injury rate in different European countries. *European Journal of Public Health, 11,* 301–308.

Meltzoff, A. N. (2000). Learning and cognitive development. In A. Kazdin (Ed.), *Encyclopedia of psychology.* Washington, DC, & New York: American Psychological Association and Oxford University Press.

Meltzoff, A. N., & Gopnik, A. (1997). *Words, thoughts, and theories.* Cambridge, MA: MIT Press.

Memmler, R. L., Cohen, B. J., Wood, D. L., & Schwegler, J. (1995). *The human body in health and disease* (8th ed.). Philadelphia: Lippincott Williams & Wilkins.

Menec, V. H. (2003). The relation between everyday activities and successful aging: A 6-year longitudinal study. *Journals of Gerontology: Psychological Sciences and Social Sciences, 58B,* 574–582.

Menyuk, P., Liebergott, J., & Schultz, M. (1995). *Early language development in full-term and premature infants.* Hillsdale, NJ: Erlbaum.

Meredith, N. V. (1978). Research between 1960 and 1970 on the standing height of young children in different parts of the world. In H. W. Reece & L. P. Lipsitt (Eds.), *Advances in child development and behavior* (Vol. 12). New York: Academic Press.

Merrick, J., Aspler, S., & Schwartz, G. (2001). Should adults with phenylketonuria have diet treatment? *Mental Retardation, 39,* 215–217.

Merrill, S. S., & Verbrugge, L. M. (1999). Health and disease in midlife. In S. L. Willis & J. D. Reid (Eds.), *Life in the middle: Psychological and social development in middle age.* San Diego: Academic Press.

Messinger, J. C. (1971). Sex and repression in an Irish folk community. In D. S. Marshall & R. C. Suggs (Eds.), *Human Sexual behavior: Variations in the ethnic spectrum.* New York: Basic Books.

Metts, S. (2004). First sexual involvement in romantic relationships. In J. H. Harvey, A. Wenzel, & S. Sprecher (Eds.), *The handbook of sexuality in close relationships.* Mahwah, NJ: Erlbaum.

Mhatre, M. C., Fernandes, G., & Ticku, M. K. (1991). Aging reduces the mRNA of alpha 1 GABAA receptor subunit in rat cerebral cortex. *European Journal of Pharmacology, 208,* 171–174.

Michael, R. T., Gagnon, J. H., Laumann, E. O., & Kolata, G. (1994). *Sex in America.* Boston: Little, Brown.

Michel, G. L. (1981). Right-handedness: A consequence of infant supine head-orientation preference? *Science, 212,* 685–687.

Miller, B. C., Benson, B., & Galbraith, K. A. (2001). Family relationships and adolescent pregnancy risk: A research synthesis. *Developmental Review, 21,* 1–38.

Miller, G. A. (1981). *Language and speech.* New York: W. H. Freeman.

Miller, J. B. (1986). *Toward a new psychology of women* (2nd ed.). Boston: Beacon Press.

Miller, J. G. (1995, March). *Culture, context, and personal agency: The cultural grounding of self and morality.* Paper presented at the meeting of the Society for Research in Child Development, Indianapolis.

Miller, L., & Gur, M. (2002). Religiousness and sexual responsibility in adolescent girls. *Journal of Adolescent Health, 31,* 401–406.

Miller, M., Rejeski, W., Reboussin, B., Ten Have, T., & Ettinger, W. (2000). Physical activity, functional limitations, and disability in older adults. *Journal of the American Geriatric Society, 48,* 1264–1272.

Miller-Day, M. A. (2004). *Communication among grandmothers, mothers, and adult daughters.* Mahwah, NJ: Erlbaum.

Miller-Johnson, S., Coie, J. D., & Malone, P. (2003, April). *Do aggression and peer rejection predict early adult outcomes?* Paper presented at the meeting of the Society for Research in Child Development, Tampa.

Miller-Jones, D. (1989). Culture and testing. *American Psychologist, 44,* 360–366.

Millstein, S. G. (1993). A view of health from the adolescent's perspective. In S. G. Millstein, A. C. Petersen, & E. O. Nightingale (Eds.), *Promoting the health of adolescents.* New York: Oxford University Press.

Minuchin, P. O., & Shapiro, E. K. (1983). The school as a context for social development. In P. H. Mussen (Ed.), *Handbook of child psychology* (4th ed., Vol. 4). New York: Wiley.

Mischel, W. (1968). *Personality and assessment.* New York: Wiley.

Mischel, W. (1973). Toward a cognitive social learning reconceptualization of personality. *Psychological Review, 80,* 252–283.

Mischel, W. (1974). Process in delay of gratification. In L. Berkowitz (Ed.), *Advances in experimental social psychology* (Vol. 7). New York: Academic Press.

Mischel, W. (1987). *Personality* (4th ed.). New York: Holt, Rinehart & Winston.

Mischel, W. (1995, August). *Cognitive-affective theory of person-environment psychology.* Paper presented at the meeting of the American Psychological Association, New York City.

Mischel, W. (2004). Toward an integrative science of the person. *Annual Review of Psychology, 55.* Palo Alto, CA: Annual Reviews.

Mischel, W., & Mendoza-Denton, R. (2003). Harnessing willpower and socioemotional intelligence to enhance human agency potential. In L. G. Aspinwall & U. M. Staudinger (Eds.), *A psychology of human strengths.* Washington DC: American Psychological Association.

Mischel, W., & Mischel, H. (1975, April). *A cognitive social-learning analysis of moral development.* Paper presented at the meeting of the Society for Research in Child Development, Denver.

Mischel, W., & Patterson, C. J. (1976). Substantive and structural elements of effective plans for self-control. *Journal of Social and Personality Psychology, 34,* 942–950.

Mischel, W., & Patterson, C. J. (1978). Effective plans for self-control. In W. A. Collins (Ed.), *Minnesota symposia on child psychology* (Vol. 2). Hillsdale, NJ: Erlbaum.

Mischel, W., Shoda, Y., & Peake, P. K. (1988). The nature of adolescent competencies predicted by preschool delay of gratification. *Journal of Personality and Social Psychology, 54,* 687–696.

Mistry, J., & Rogoff, B. (1994). Remembering in cultural context. In W. J. Lonner & R. Malpass (Eds.), *Psychology and culture.* Boston: Allyn & Bacon.

Mistry, R. S., Vandewater, E. A., Huston, A. C., & McLoyd, V. C. (2002). Economic well-being and children's social adjustment: The role of family process in an ethnically diverse low-income sample. *Child Development, 3,* 935–951.

Mitchell, E. A., Stewart, A. W., Crampton, P., & Salmond, C. (2000). Deprivation and sudden infant death syndrome. *Social Science and Medicine, 51,* 147–150.

Mitchell, M., & Catron, G. (2002). Teaching grief and bereavement: Involving support groups in educating student midwives. *The Practicing Midwife, 5,* 26–27.

Miyake, Y., Yura, A., & Iki, M. (2003). Breastfeeding and the prevalence of symptoms of allergic disorders in Japanese adolescents. *Clinical and Experimental Allergy, 33,* 312–316.

Modell, J., & Elder, G. H. (2002). Child development in history: So what's new. In W. W. Hartup & R. A. Weinberg (Eds.), *Child psychology in retrospect and prospect.* Mahwah, NJ: Erlbaum.

Moen, P. (1998). Recasting careers: Changing reference groups, risks, and realities. *Generations, 22,* 40-45.

Moen, P., & Quick, H. E. (1998). Retirement. In H. S. Friedman (Ed.), *Encyclopedia of mental health* (Vol. 3). San Diego: Academic Press.

Moen, P., & Wethington, E. (1999). Midlife development in a life course context. In S. L. Willis & J. D. Reid (eds.), *Life in the middle: Psychological and social development in middle age.* San Diego: Academic Press.

Mohan, R. M., Golding, S., & Paterson, D. J. (2001). Intermittent hypoxia improves atrial tolerance to subsequent anoxia and reduces stress protein expression. *Acta Physiology Scandinavia, 172,* 89–95.

Monk, C., Fifer, W. P., Sloan, R. P., & Myers, M. M. (2000, May). *Individual differences in fetal cardiac reactivity are associated with maternal anxiety and infant birth weight.* Paper presented at the joint meetings of the Pediatric Academic Societies and the American Academy of Pediatrics, Boston.

Montemayor, R. (1982). The relationship between parent-adolescent conflict and the amount of time adolescents spend with parents, peers, and alone. *Child Development, 53,* 1512–1519.

Moore, C., & Lemmon, K. (2001). *The self in time.* Mahwah, NJ: Erlbaum.

Moore, C. L. (2004). Can behavioral evolution be measured on a staircase? A commentary. *Development Psychobiology, 44,* 16–20.

Moore, D. (2001). *The dependent gene.* New York: W. H. Freeman.

Moos, R. H. (1986). Work as a human context. In M. S. Pallack & R. Perloff (Eds.), *Psychology and work: Productivity, change, and employment.* Washington, DC: American Psychological Association.

More, J. (2003). New guidelines on infant feeding in the first 12 months of life. *Journal of Family Health Care, 13,* 89–90.

Morgan, J. D. (2004). Spirituality. In C. D. Bryant (Ed.), *Handbook of death and dying.* Thousand Oaks, CA: Sage.

Morgan, J. D., & Laungani, P. (Eds.). (2003). *Death and bereavement around the world. Vol. 4.: Death and bereavement in Asia, Australia, and New Zealand.* Amityville, NY: Baywood.

Morgan, M. (1984). Reward-induced decrements and increments in intrinsic motivation. *Review of Educational Research, 54,* 5–30.

Morris, J. C., Storandt, M., Miller, J. P., McKeel, D., Price, J., Rubin, E. H., & Berg, L. (2001). Mild cognitive impairment represents early-stage Alzheimer's disease. *Archives of Neurology, 58,* 397–405.

Morris, J. K., Wald, N. J., Mutton, D. E., & Alberman, E. (2003). Comparison of models of maternal age-specific risk for Down syndrome live births. *Prenatal Diagnostics, 23,* 252–258.

Morrison, J., & MacKenzie, I. Z. (2003). Cesarean section on demand. *Seminars in Perinatology, 27,* 20–33.

Morrongiello, B. A., Fenwick, K. D., & Chance, G. (1990). Sound localization acuity in very young infants: An observer-based testing procedure. *Developmental Psychology, 26,* 75–84.

Mortimer, J. A., Snowdon, D. A., & Markesbery, W. R. (2003). Head circumference, education, and risk of dementia: Findings from the Nun study. *Journal of Clinical and Experimental Neuropsychology, 25,* 671–679.

Mortimer, J. T., Harley, C., & Johnson, M. K. (1998, February). *Adolescent work quality and the transition to adulthood.* Paper presented at the meeting of the Society for Research on Adolescence, San Diego, CA.

Mortimer, J., Finch, M., Ryu, S., Shanahan, M., & Call, K. (1996). The effects of work intensity on adolescent mental health, achievement, and behavioral adjustment: New evidence from a prospective study. *Child Development, 67,* 1243–1261.

Moses, J., Steptoe, A., Mathews, A., & Edwards, S. (1989). The effects of exercise training on mental well-being in a normal population: A controlled trial. *Journal of Psychosomatic Research, 33,* 47–61.

Mounts, N. S. (2002). Parental management of adolescent peer relationships in context: The role of parenting style. *Journal of Family Psychology, 16,* 58–69.

Moyo, N. T. (2003). Midwives and women together for the family of the world: The place of research. *Midwifery, 19,* 10–16.

Mozingo, J. N., Davis, M. W., Droppleman, P. G., & Merideth, A. (2000). "It wasn't working." Women's experiences with short-term breast feeding. *American Maternal Journal of Nursing, 25,* 120–126.

Mroczek, D. K. (2001). Age and emotion in adulthood. *Current Directions in Psychological Science, 10,* 87–90.

Mroczek, D. K., & Kolarz, C. M. (1998). The effect of age on positive and negative affect: A developmental perspective on happiness. *Journal of Personality and Social Psychology, 75,* 1333–1349.

Mueller, N., & Silverman, N. (1989). Peer relations in maltreated children. In D. Cicchetti & V. Carlson (Eds.), *Child maltreatment.* New York: Cambridge University Press.

Mulholland, H. (2002). Hospice care: A few home truths. *Nursing Times, 98* (40), 11.

Muller, D., & Nikonenko, I. (2003). Dynamic presynaptic varicosities: A role in activity-dependent synaptogenesis. *Trends in Neuroscience, 26,* 573–575.

Mullis, I. V. S., Martin, M. O., Beaton, A. E., Gonzales, E. J., Kelly, D. L., & Smith, T. A. (1998). *Mathematics and science achievement in the final year of secondary school.* Chestnut Hill, MA: TIMSS International Study Center, Boston College.

Mumme, D. L., Fernald, A., & Herrera, C. (1996). Infant's responses to facial & emotional signals in a social referencing paradigm. *Child Development, 67,* 3219–3237.

Mungas, D., Reed, B. R., Jagust, W. J., DeCarli, C., Mack, W. J., Kramer, J. H., Weiner, M. W., Schuff, N., & Chui, H. C. (2002). Volumetric MRI predicts rate of cognitive decline related to AD and cerebrovascular disease. *Neurology, 59,* 867–873.

Mussen P. H., Honzik, M., & Eichorn, D. (1982). Early adult antecedents of life satisfaction at age 70. *Journal of Gerontology, 37,* 316–322.

Muszcz, M., & Giles, L. (2002). Benefits of close social relationships for health and longevity of older adults. *International Society for the Study of Behavioural Development Newsletter* (1, Serial No. 41) 15–16.

Muth, A. S. (Ed.). (2000). *Death and dying sourcebook: Basic consumer health information for the layperson about end-of-life care and related ethical issues.* Detroit: Omnigraphics.

Myers, A., & Hansen, C. (2002). *Experimental psychology* (5th ed.). Belmont, CA: Wadsworth.

Myers, D. G. (2000). *The American paradox.* New Haven, CT: Yale University Press.

Myers, D. L. (1999). *Excluding violent youths from juvenile court: The effectiveness of legislative waiver.* Doctoral dissertation, University of Maryland, College Park.

Myerson, J., Rank, M. R., Raines, F. Q., & Schnitzler, M. A. (1998). Race and general cognitive ability: The myth of diminishing returns in education. *Psychological Science, 9,* 139–142.

Nadeau, J. W. (2001). Meaning making in a family bereavement: A family systems approach. In M. S. Stroebe, R. O. Hansson, W. Stroebe, & H. Schut (Eds.), *Handbook of bereavement research: Consequences, coping, and care.* Washington, DC: American Psychological Press.

Nadelman, L. (Ed.) (2004). *Research manual in child development.* Mahwah, NJ: Erlbaum.

Nadien, M. B., & Denmark, F. L. (Eds.). (1999). *Females and autonomy: A life-span perspective.* Boston: Allyn & Bacon.

NAEYC. (2002). *Early learning standards: Creating the conditions for success.* Washington, DC: National Association for the Education of Young Children.

Nagy, M. (1948). The child's theories concerning death. *Journal of Genetic Psychology, 73,* 3–27.

Nansel, T. R., Overpeck, M., Pilla, R., Ruan, W., Simons-Morton, B., & Scheidt, P. (2001). Bullying behaviors among U.S. youth. *Journal of the American Medical Association, 285,* 2094–2100.

Nansel, T. R. & Overpeck, M. (2002, April). *The relationship of bullying and being bullied to aggression/violence in a nationally representative sample of U.S. youth.* Paper presented at the meeting of the Society for Research on Adolescence, New Orleans.

Narang, A., & Jain, N. (2001). Haemolytic disease of newborn. *Indian Journal of Pediatrics, 68,* 167–172.

Nash, J. M. (1997, February 3). Fertile minds. *Time,* pp. 50–54.

National Assessment of Educational Progress. (2000). *Reading achievement.* Washington, DC: National Center for Education Statistics.

National Association for the Education of Young Children. (1986). Position statement on developmentally appropriate practice in programs for 4- and 5- year-olds. *Young Children 41,* 20–29.

National Association for the Education of Young Children. (1998). *Learning to read and write.* Washington, DC: Author.

National Center for Addiction and Substance Abuse. (2001). *2000 teen survey.* New York: National Center for Addiction and Substance Abuse, Columbia University.

National Center for Education Statistics. (2000). *Children's reading and mathematics achievement in kindergarten and first grade.* Bethesda, MD: Author.

National Center for Education Statistics. (2001). *Dropout Rates in the United States: 2000.* Washington, DC: U.S. Department of Education.

National Center for Health Statistics. (2000). *Growth charts of children,* Washington, DC: Author.

National Center for Health Statistics. (2000). *Health United States, 1999.* Atlanta: Centers for Disease Control and Prevention.

National Center for Health Statistics. (2001). *Health statistics by sex and race/ethnicity.* Atlanta: Centers for Disease Control and Prevention.

National Center for Health Statistics. (2002). *Health United States, 2002.* Hyattsville, MD: U.S. Department of Health and Human Services.

National Center for Health Statistics. (2002). *National Vital Statistics Report: Death statistics.* Bethesda, MD: Author.

National Center for Health Statistics. (2003). *Health: United States.* Atlanta: Center for Disease Control and Prevention.

National Center for Women & Aging. (2002, November). *Majority of women over 50 say aging is better than they expected.* Press Release. Waltham, MA: Brandeis University.

National Clearinghouse on Child Abuse and Neglect. (2002). *What is child maltreatment?* Washington. DC: Administration for Children and Families.

National Commission on Sleep Disorders. (1993, January). *Report of the National Commission on Sleep Disorders Research.* Washington, DC: U.S. Department of Health and Human Services.

National Commission on the High School Year. (2001). *Youth at the crossroads: Facing high school and beyond.* Washington, DC: The Education Trust.

National Community Service Coalition. (1995). *Youth volunteerism.* Washington, DC: Author.

National Institute of Drug Abuse. (2001). *Marijuana.* Washington, DC: National Institutes of Health.

National Institute of Neurological Disorders and Stroke. (2003). *Understanding Sleep.* Bethesda, MD: Author.

National Institutes of Health. (2003). *Alzheimer's disease.* Bethesda, MD: Author.

National Reading Panel. (2000). *Teaching children to read.* Washington, DC: National Institute of Child Health and Human Development.

National Research Council. (1999). *How people learn.* Washington, DC: National Academy Press.

National Research Council. (1999). *Starting out right: A guide to promoting children's reading success.* Washington, DC: National Academy Press.

National Research Council. (2001). *Knowing what students know.* Washington, DC: National Academy Press.

Natsopoulos, D., Kiosseoglou, G., Xeroxmeritou, A., & Alevriadou, A. (1998). Do the hands talk on the mind's behalf? Differences in language between left- and right-handed children. *Brain and Language, 64,* 184 214.

Natsopoulos, D., Koutselini, M., Kiosseoglou, G., & Koundouris, F. (2002). Differences in language performance in variations of lateralization. *Brain and Language, 82,* 223–240.

Navarrete, C., Martinez, I., & Salamanca, F. (1994). Paternal line of transmission in chorea of Huntington with very early onset. *Genetic Counseling, 5,* 175–178.

Neimeyer, R. A. (Ed.). (2001). *Meaning reconstruction and the experience of loss.* Washington, DC: American Psychological Press.

Neisser, U., Boodoo, G., Bouchard, T. J., Boykin, A. W., Brody, N., Ceci, S. J., Halpern, D. F., Loehlin, J. C., Perloff, R. J., Sternberg, R., & Urbina, S. (1996). Intelligence: Knowns and unknowns. *American Psychologist, 51,* 77–101.

Nelson, C. A. (1999). Research description. *Institute of Child Development biennial report.* Minneapolis: Institute of Child Development.

Nelson, C. A. (2000). Neural plasticity and human development: The role of early experience in sculpting memory systems. *Developmental Science, 3,* 115–130.

Nelson, C. A. (2001). The development and neural bases of face recognition. *Infant and Child Development, 10,* 3–18.

Nelson, C. A. (2003). Neural development and lifelong plasticity. In R. M. Lerner, F. Jacobs, & D. Wertlieb (Eds.), *Handbook of applied developmental science* (Vol. 1). Thousand Oaks, CA: Sage.

Nelson, C. A. (2003, April). *Gray matters: A neuroconstructivist perspective on cognitive development.* Paper presented at the meeting of the Society for Research on Child Development, Tampa.

Nelson, H., Bernstein, P. S., Schmidt, M. C., Von Tress, M. S., & Askew, E. W. (2003). Dietary modification and moderate antioxidant supplementation differentially affect serum carotenoids, antioxidant levels, and markers of oxidative stress in humans. *Journal of Nutrition, 133,* 3117–3123.

Nelson, K. (1999). Levels and modes of representation: Issues for the theory of conceptual change and development. In E. K. Skolnick, K. Nelson, S. A. Gelman, & P. H. Miller (Eds.), *Conceptual Development.* Mahwah, NJ: Erlbaum.

Nelson, M. E., Fiatarone, M. A., Moranti, C. M., Trice, I., Greenberg, R. A., & Evans, W. J. (1994). Effects of high-intensity strength training on multiple risk factors for osteoporotic fractures: A randomized controlled trial. *Journal of the American Medical Association, 272,* 1909–1914.

Neugarten, B. L. (1964). *Personality in middle and late life.* New York: Atherton.

Neugarten, B. L. (1988, August). *Policy issues for an aging society.* Paper presented at the meeting of the American Psychological Association, Atlanta.

Neugarten, B. L., & Weinstein, K. K. (1964). The changing American grandparent. *Journal of Marriage and the Family, 26,* 199–204.

Neugarten, B. L., Havighurst, R. J., & Tobin, S. S. (1968). Personality and patterns of aging. In B. L. Neugarten (Ed.), *Middle age and aging.* Chicago: University of Chicago.

Newcomb, M. D., & Bentler, P. M. (1988). Substance use and abuse among children and teenagers. *American Psychologist, 44,* 242–248.

Newcomb, M., & Bentler, P. (1980). Assessment of personality and demographic aspects of cohabitation and marital success. *Journal of Personality Development, 4,* 11–24.

Newcombe, N. S., Drummey, A. B., Fox, N. A., Lile, E., & Ottinger-Alberts, W. (2000). Remembering early childhood: How much, how, and why (or why not). *Current Directions in Psychological Science, 9,* 55–58.

Newcombe, N., & Fox, N. (1994). Infantile amnesia: Through a glass darkly. *Child Development, 65,* 31–40.

Newell, K., Scully, D. M., McDonald, P. V., & Baillargeon, R. (1989). Task constraints and infant grip configurations. *Developmental Psychobiology, 22,* 817–832.

Ngo-Metzger, Q., Massgli, M. P., Clarridge, B. R., Manocchia, M., Davis, R. B., Iczzoni, L. I., & Phillips, R. S. (2003). Linguistic and cultural barriers to care. *Journal of General and Internal Medicine, 18,* 44–52.

Niccolai, L. M., Ethier, K. A., Kershaw, T. S., Lewis, J. B., & Ickovics, J. R. (2003). Pregnant adolescents at risk: Sexual behaviors and sexually transmitted disease presence. *American Journal of Obstetrics and Gynecology, 188,* 63–70.

NICHD Early Child Care Research Network. (2000). Factors associated with fathers' caregiving activities and sensitivity with young children. *Developmental Psychology, 14,* 200–219.

NICHD Early Child Care Research Network. (2001). Nonmaternal care and family factors in early development: An overview of the NICHD Study of Early Child Care. *Journal of Applied Developmental Psychology. 22,* 457–492.

NICHD Early Child Care Research Network. (2002). Structure→Process→ Outcome: Direct and indirect effects of child care quality on young children's development. *Psychological Science, 13,* 199–206.

NICHD Early Child Care Research Network. (2003). Does amount of time spent in child care predict socioemotional adjustment during the transition to kindergarten. *Child Development, 74,* 976–1005.

Nicholls, J. G. (1979). Development of perception of own attainment and causal attribution for success and failure in reading. *Journal of Educational Psychology, 71,* 94–99.

Nichols, F. H., & Humenick, S. S. (2000). *Childbirth education* (2nd ed.). London: Harcourt International.

Nicklas, B. J., Dennis, K. E., Berman, D. M., Sorkin, J., Ryan, A. S., & Goldberg, A. P. (2003). Lifestyle intervention of hypocaloric dieting and walking reduces abdominal obesity and improves coronary heart disease factors in obese, postmenopausal, African-American and caucasian women. *Journal of Gerontology: Biological Sciences and Medical Sciences, 58A,* M181–M189.

Nielsen, S. J., Siega-Riz, A. M., & Popkin, B. M. (2002). Trends in energy intake in U.S. between 1977 and 1996: Similar shifts seen across age groups. *Obesity Research, 10,* 370–378.

Nieman, Y. F. (2004). Stereotypes of Chicanas and Chicanos. In R. J. Velásquez, L. M. Arellano, & B. W. McNeil (Eds.), *The handbook of Chicana/Chicano psychology and mental health.* Mahwah. NJ: Erlbaum.

Nies, M. A., Reisenberg, C. E., Dhursical, H. L., & Artibee K. (2003). Southern women's response to walking intervention. *Public Health Nursing, 20,* 146–152.

Nisbett, R. (2003). The *geography of thought.* New York: Free Press.

Noar, S. M., Zimmerman, R. S., & Atwood, K. A. (2004). Safer sex and sexually transmitted infections from a relationship perspective. In J. H. Harvey & A. Wetzel (Eds.), *The handbook of sexuality in close relationships.* Mahwah, NJ: Erlbaum.

Nocenteni, U., Goulet, P., Roberts, P. M., & Joanette, Y. (2001). The effects of left- versus right-hemisphere lesions on the sensitivity to intra- and interconceptual semantic relationships. *Neuropsychologia, 39,* 443–451.

Nock, S. (1995). A comparison of marriages and cohabitating relationships. *Journal of Family Issues, 16,* 53–76.

Noguera-Obenza, M., Ochoa, T. J., Gomez, H. F., Guerrero, M. L., Herrera-Insua, I., Morrow, A. L., Ruiz-Palacios, G., Pickering, L. K., Guzman, C. A., & Cleary, T. G. (2003). Human milk secretory antibodies against attaching and effacing Escherichia coli antigens. *Emerging and Infectious Diseases, 9,* 545–551.

Nolan, K., Schell, L. M., Stark, A. D., & Gomez, M. I. (2002). Longitudinal study of energy and nutrient intakes for infants from low-income, urban families. *Public Health Nutrition, 5,* 405–412.

Nolen-Hoeksema, S. (2004). *Abnormal psychology* (3rd ed.). New York: McGraw-Hill.

Norris, J. E., Pratt, M. W., & Kuiak, S. L. (2003). Parent-child relations in adulthood: An intergenerational family systems perspective. In L. Kuczynski (Ed.), *Handbook of dynamics in parent-child relations.* Newbury Park, CA: Sage.

Nottebohm, F. (2002). Neuronal replacement in the adult brain. *Brain Research Bulletin, 57,* 737–750.

Nottelmann, E. D., Susman, E. J., Blue, J. H., Inoff-Germain, G., Dorn, L. D., Loriaux, D. L., Cutler, G. B., & Chrousos, G. P. (1987). Gonadal and adrenal hormone correlates of adjustment in early adolescence. In R. M. Lerner & T. T. Foch (Eds.), *Biological-psychological interactions in early adolescence.* Hillsdale, NJ: Erlbaum.

Nowak, C. A. (1977). Does youthfulness equal attractiveness? In L. E. Troll, J. Israel, & K. Israel (Eds.), *Looking ahead: A woman's guide to the problems and joys of growing older.* Englewood Cliffs, NJ: Prentice Hall.

Nsamenang, A. B. (2002). Adolescence in sub-Saharan Africa: An image constructed from Africa's triple heritage. In B. B. Brown, R. W. Larson, & T. S. Saraswathi (Eds.), *The world's youth.* New York: Cambridge University Press.

Nugent, K., & Brazelton, T. B. (2000). Preventive infant mental health: Uses of the Brazelton scale. In J. D. Osofsky & H. E. Fitzgerald (Eds.), *WAIMH Handbook of infant mental health* (Vol. 2). New York: Wiley.

Nurmi, J. (2004). Socialization and self-development: Channeling, selection, adjustment, and reflection. In R. Lerner & L. Steinberg (Eds.), *Handbook of adolescent psychology.* New York: Wiley.

Nusbaum, N. J. (2003). Preparation for healthy retirement. *Journal of the American Geriatric Association, 51,* 429.

Nussbaum, J. F., & Coupland, J. (Eds.) (2004) . *Handbook of communication and aging.* Mahwah, NJ: Erlbaum.

Nyberg, L., Sandblom, J., Jones, S., Neely, A. S., Peterson, K. M., Ingvar, M., & Backman, L. (2003). Neural correlates of training-related memory improvements in adulthood and aging. *Proceedings of the National Academy of Science, 100,* 13728–13733.

Nyiti, R. M. (1982). The validity of "cultural differences explanations" for cross-cultural variation in the rate of Piagetian cognitive development. In D. Wagner & H. Stevenson (Eds.), *Cultural perspectives on child development.* New York: W. H. Freeman.

O'Callahan, M., Andrews, A. M., & Krantz, D. S. (2003). Coronary heart disease and hypertension. In I. B. Weiner (Ed.), *Handbook of psychology* (Vol. IX). New York: Wiley.

O'Connor, M. G., & Kaplan, E. F. (2003). Age-related changes in memory. In J. Demick & C. Andreoletti (Eds.), *Handbook of adult development.* New York: Kluwer.

O'Donnell, M. P., & Wood, M. (2004). *Becoming a reader (3rd Ed.).* Boston: Allyn & Bacon.

O'Donnell, W. T., & Warren, S. T. (2003). A decade of molecular studies of fragile X syndrome. *Annual Review of Neuroscience, 25,* 315–338.

O'Leary, C. (2004). Fetal alcohol syndrome. *Journal of Pediatric Child Health, 40,* 2–7.

O'Neill, P. (2002). Acute otitis media. *Clinical Evidence, 8,* 251–261.

Obler, L. K. (1993). Language beyond childhood. In J. B. Gleason (Ed.), *The development of language* (3rd ed.). New York: Macmillan.

Oboro, V. O., & Tabowei, T. O. (2003). A randomized controlled trial of misoprostol versus oxytocin in the active management of the third stage of labor. *Journal of Obstetrics and Gynecology, 23,* 13–16.

Occupational Outlook Handbook. (2002–2003). Washington, DC: U.S. Department of Labor.

Oddy, W. H. (2002). The impact of breastmilk on infant and child health. *Breastfeeding Review, 10,* 5–18.

Offer, D., Ostrov, E., Howard, K. I., & Atkinson, R. (1988). *The teenage world: Adolescents' self-image in ten countries.* New York: Plenum Press.

Ogashi, K. (2001). Academic harassment. *Lancet, 357,* 396–397.

Ogbu, J. U. (1989, April). *Academic socialization of Black children: An innoculation against future failure?* Paper presented at the meeting of the Society for Research in Child Development, Kansas City.

Ogbu, J., & Stern, P. (2001). Caste status and intellectual ability. In R. J. Sternberg & E. L. Grigorenko (Eds.), *Environmental effects on cognitive abilities.* Mahwah, NJ: Erlbaum.

Ogden, C. L., Flegal, K. M., Carroll, M. D., & Johnson, C. L. (2002). Prevalence and trends in overweight among U.S. children and adolescents. *Journal of the American Medical Association, 288,* 1728–1732.

Ohgi, S., Arisawa, K., Takahashi, T., Kusumoto, T., Goto, Y., & Saito, A. T. (2003). Neonatal behavioral assessment scale as a predictor of later developmental disabilities of low birth-weight and/or premature infants. *Brain Development, 25,* 313–321.

Olivardia, R., Pope, H. G., Mangweth, B., & Hudson, J. I. (1995). Eating disorders in college men. *American Journal of Psychiatry, 152,* 1279–1284.

Oliver, M. B., & Hyde, J. S. (1993). Gender differences in sexuality: A meta-analysis. *Psychological Bulletin, 114,* 29–51.

Olsho, L. W., Harkins, S. W., & Lenhardt, M. L. (1985). Aging and the auditory system. In J. E. Birren & K. W. Schaie (Eds.), *Handbook of the psychology of aging* (2nd ed.). New York: Van Nostrand Reinhold.

Olson, H. C. (2000). Fetal alcohol syndrome. In A. Krazdin (Ed.), *Encyclopedia of psychology.* Washington, DC, & New York: American Psychological Association and Oxford University Press.

Olszewski-Kubilius, P. (2003). Gifted education programs and procedures. In I. B. Weiner (Ed.), *Handbook of psychology* (Vol VII). New York: Wiley.

Olweus, D. (1980). Bullying among schoolboys. In R. Barnen (Ed.), *Children and violence.* Stockholm: Academic Litteratur.

Olweus, D. (1993). *Bullying at school.* Cambridge, MA: Blackwell.

Onwuegbuzi, A. J., & Daley, C. E. (2001). Racial differences in IQ revisited: A synthesis of nearly a century of research. *Journal of Black Psychology, 27,* 209–220.

Oppenheimer, V. K. (2003). Cohabiting and marriage during young men's career-development process. *Demography, 40,* 127–149.

Orbanic, S. (2001). Understanding bulimia. *American Journal of Nursing, 101,* 35–41.

Organista, K. C. (1994). Overdue overview of elderly Latino mental health. *Contemporary Psychology, 39,* 61–62.

Ornstein, P. A., & Haden, C. A. (2001). False childhood memories and eyewitness suggestibility. In M. L. Eisen, J. A. Quas, & G. S. Goodman (Eds.), *Memory and suggestibility in the forensic interview.* Mahwah, NJ: Erlbaum.

Ornstein, P., Gordon, B. N., & Larus, D. (1992). Children's memory for a personally experienced event: Implications for testimony. *Applied Cognition and Psychology, 6,* 49–60.

Oser, F., & Gmünder, P. (1991). *Religious judgment: A developmental perspective.* Birmingham, AL: Religious Education Press.

Osipow, S. (2000). Work, In A. Kazdin (Ed.), *Encyclopedia of psychology.* Washington, DC, & New York: American Psychological Association and Oxford University Press.

Ouellette, M. M., & others. (2000). Subsenescent telomere lengths in fibroblasts immortalized by lasting amounts of telomerase. *Journal of Biological Chemistry, 275,* 10072–10076.

Overton, W. F. (2003). Development across the life span. In I. B. Weiner (Ed.), *Handbook of psychology* (Vol. VI). New York: Wiley.

Overton, W. F., & Byrnes, J. P. (1991). Cognitive development. In R. M. Lerner, A. C. Petersen, and J. Brooks-Gunn (Eds.), *Encyclopedia of adolescence* (Vol.1). New York: Garland.

Oxman, T. E., & Hall, J. G. (2001). Social support and treatment response in older depressed primary care patients. *Journal of Gerontology, 56B* (No. 1), P35–P45.

Padilla, A. M., & Perez, W. (2003). Acculturation, social identity, and social cognition: A new perspective. *Hispanic Journal of Behavioral Sciences, 25,* 35–55.

Paffenbarger, R. S., Hyde, R. T., Wing, A. L., Lee, I., Jung, D. L., & Kampter, J. B. (1993). The association of changes in physical-activity level and other life-style characteristics with mortality among men. *New England Journal of Medicine, 328,* 538–545.

Palkovitz, R., Marks, L. D., Appleby, D. W., & Holmes, E. K. (2003). Parenting and development: Contexts, processes, and products. In L. Kuczynski (Ed.), *Handbook of dynamics in parent-child relations.* Newbury Park, CA: Sage.

Palmore, E. B. (1981). *Social patterns in normal aging: Findings from the Duke Longitudinal Study.* Durham, NC: Duke University Press.

Palmore, E. B. (2001). The ageism survey: First findings. *The Gerontologist, 41,* 572–575.

Palmore, E. B., Burchett, B. M., Fillenbaum, C. G., George, L. K., & Wallman, L. M. (1985). *Retirement: Causes and consequences.* New York: Springer.

Paloutzian, R. F. (2000). *Invitation to the psychology of religion* (3rd ed.). Needham Heights, MA: Allyn & Bacon.

Paloutzian, R. F., & Santrock, J. W. (2000). The psychology of religion. In J. W. Santrock, *Psychology* (6th ed.). New York: McGraw-Hill.

Paludi, M. A. (2002). *Psychology of women* (2nd Ed.). Upper Saddle River, NJ: Prentice Hall.

Papp, C., & Papp, Z. (2003). Chorionic villus sampling and amniocentesis: What are the risks in current practice? *Current Opinions in Obstetrics and Gynecology, 15,* 159–165.

Parazzini, F., Chatenoud, L., Surace, M., Tozzi, L., Salerio, B., Bettoni, G., & Benzi, G. (2003). Moderate alcohol drinking and risk of preterm birth. *European Journal of Clinical Nutrition, 57,* 1345–1349.

Park, D. C. (1994). Aging, cognition, and work. *Human Performance, 7,* 181–205.

Park, D. C., & Gutchess, A. H. (2002). Aging, cognition, and culture: A neuroscientific perspective. *Neuroscience and Biobehavior Reviews, 26,* 859–867.

Park, D. C., Lautenschalger, G., Hedden, T., Davidson, N. S., Smith, A. D., & Smith, P. K. (2002). Models of visuospatial and verbal memory across the adult life span. *Psychology and Aging, 17,* 299–320.

Parke, R. D. (1972). Some effects of punishment on children's behavior. In W. W. Hartup (Ed.), *The young child* (Vol. 2). Washington, DC. National Association for the Education of Young Children.

Parke, R. D. (1977). Some effects of punishment on children's behavior—Revisited. In E. M. Hetherington & R. D. Parke (Eds.), *Readings in comtemporary child psychology.* New York: McGraw-Hill.

Parke, R. D. (1995). Fathers and families. In M. H. Bornstein (Ed.), *Children and parenting* (Vol. 3). Hillsdale, NJ: Erlbaum.

Parke, R. D. (2000). Father involvement: A developmental psychology perspective. *Marriage and Family Review, 29,* 43–58.

Parke, R. D. (2001). Parenting in the new millenium. In J. P. McHale & W. S. Grolnick (Eds.), *Retrospect and prospect in the psychological study of families.* Mahwah, NJ: Erlbaum.

Parke, R. D. (2002). Fathering. In M. H. Bornstein (Ed.), *Handbook of parenting* (2nd ed.). Mahwah, NJ: Erlbaum.

Parke, R. D. (2004). Development in the family. *Annual Review of Psychology, Vol. 55.* Palo Alto, CA: Annual Reviews.

Parke, R. D., & Buriel, R. (1998). Socialization in the family. Ethnic and ecological perspectives. In W. Damon (Ed.), *Handbook of child psychology* (5th ed., Vol. 3). New York: Wiley.

Parke, R. D., & Clarke-Stewart, K. A. (2003). Developmental psychology. In I. B. Weiner (Ed.), *Handbook of psychology* (Vol. 1). New York: Wiley.

Parker, J. G., & Asher, S. R. (1987). Peer relations and later personal adjustment: Are low accepted children at risk? *Psychological Bulletin, 102,* 357–389.

Parmar, R. C., Muranjan, M. N., & Swami, S. (2002). Trisomy 21 with XYY. *Indian Journal of Pediatrics, 11,* 979–981.

Parnes, H. S., & Sommers, D. G. (1994). Shunning retirement: Work experiences of men in their seventies and early eighties. *Journal of Gerontology, 49,* S117–S124.

Parsons, P. A. (2003). From the stress theory of aging to energetic and evolutionary expectations for longevity. *Biogerontology, 4,* 63–73.

Parten, M. (1932). Social play among preschool children. *Journal of Abnormal Social Psychology, 27,* 243–269.

Pasupathi, M., & Carstensen, L. L. (in press). Age and emotional experience during mutual reminiscing. *Psychology and Aging.*

Paterson, I. (2003). The ethics of assisted suicide. *Nursing Times, 99,* 30–31.

Paterson, I., & Forbes, S. (2003). Should assisted suicide be legalized? *Nursing Times, 99,* 18–19.

Patterson, C. J. (1995). Sexual orientation and human development: An overview. *Developmental Psychology, 31,* 3–11.

Patterson, C. J. (2000). Family relationships of lesbians and gay men. *Journal of Marriage and the Family, 62,* 1052–1069.

Patterson, C. J. (2002). Lesbian and gay parenthood. In M. H. Bornstein (Ed.), *Handbook of parenting* (2nd ed., Vol. 3). Mahwah, NJ: Erlbaum.

Patterson, G. R., & Fisher, P. A. (2002). Recent developments in our understanding of parenting. Bidirectional effects, causal models, and a search for parsimony. In M. H. Bornstein (Ed.), *Handbook of parenting* (2nd ed.). Mahwah, NJ: Erlbaum.

Patterson, G. R., DeBaryshe, B. D., & Ramsey, E. (1989). A developmental perspective on antisocial behavior. *American Psychologist, 44,* 329–355.

Paukku, M., Quan, J., Darvey, P., & Raine, T. (2003). Adolescents' contraceptive use and pregnancy history. *Obstetrics and Gynecology, 101,* 534–538.

Pavlov, I. P. (1927). In G. V. Anrep (Trans.), *Conditioned reflexes.* London: Oxford University Press.

Payer, L. (1991). The menopause in various cultures. In H. Burger & M. Boulet (Eds.), *A portrait of menopause.* Park Ridge, NJ: Parthenon.

Pearlin, L. I. (1994). The study of the oldest-old: Some promises and puzzles. *International Journal of Aging and Human Development, 38,* 91–98.

Peck, D. L. (2004). Suicide and suicide trends in the United States, 1900–1999. In C. D. Bryant (Ed.), *Handbook of death and dying.* Thousand Oaks, CA: Sage.

Pederson, D. R., & Moran, G. (1996). Expressions of the attachment relationship outside of the Strange Situation. *Child Development, 67,* 915–927.

Pelkonen, M., & Marttunen, M. (2003). Child and adolescent suicide: Epidemiology, risk factors, and approaches to prevention. *Pediatric Drugs, 5,* 243–265.

Pellegrini, A. (2002). Bullying, victimization, and sexual harassment during transition to middle school. *Educational Psychologist, 37,* 151–163.

Penninx, B. W., Rejeski, W. J., Pandya, J., Miller, M. E., Di Bari, M., Applegate, W. B., & Pahor, M. (2002). Exercise and depressive symptoms: A comparison of aerobic and resistance exercise effects on emotional and physical function in older persons with high and low depressive symptomatology. *Journal of Gerontology: Psychological and Social Sciences, 57,* P124–P132.

Peplau, L. A. (2002). *Current research on gender and sexuality.* Paper presented at the meeting of the American Psychological Association, Chicago.

Peplau, L. A. (2003). Human sexuality: How do men and women differ? *Current Directions in Psychological Science, 12,* 37–40.

Peplau, L. A., & Beals, K. P. (2002). Lesbians, gays, and bisexuals in relationships.

In J. Worell (Ed.), *Encyclopedia of women and gender*. San Diego: Academic Press.

Peplau, L. A., Fingerhut, A., & Beals, K. P. (2004). Sexuality in the relationships of lesbians and gay men. In J. H. Harvey & A. Wetzel (Eds.), *The handbook of sexuality in close relationships*. Mahwah, NJ: Erlbaum.

Perdue, C. W. (2000). Ageism. In A. Kazdin (Ed.), *Encyclopedia of psychology*. Washington, DC, & New York: American Psychological Association and Oxford University Press.

Peregoy, S., & Boyle, O. (2001). *Reading, writing, and learning in ESL* (3rd ed.). Boston: Allyn & Bacon.

Pérez, B. (2004). *Becoming literate*. Mahwah, NJ: Erlbaum.

Perez-Febles, A. M. (1992). *Acculturation and interactional styles of Latina mothers and their infants*. Unpublished honors thesis, Brown University, Providence, RI.

Perkins, D. (1994, September). Creativity by design. *Educational Leadership*, pp. 18–25.

Perkins, D., & Tishman, S. (1997, March). Commentary in "Teaching today's pupils to think more critically." *APA Monitor*, p. 51.

Perls, T. (1999, November). *An Internet-based life expectancy calculator*. Paper presented at the meeting of the Gerontological Association of America, San Francisco.

Perls, T., Lauerman, J. F., & Silver, M. H. (1999). *Living to 100*. New York: Basic Books.

Perry, C. L., Kelder, S. H., & Komro, K. A. (1993). The social world of adolescents. In S. G. Millstein, A. C. Petersen, & E. O. Nightingale (Eds.), *Promoting the health of adolescents*. New York: Oxford University Press.

Perry, C. M., & Johnson, C. L. (1994). Families and support networks among African American oldest-old. *International Journal of Aging of Human Development, 38*, 41–50.

Perry, W. G. (1970). *Forms of intellectual and ethical development in the college years*. New York: Holt, Rinehart & Winston.

Peskin, E. G., & Rein, G. M. (2002). A guest editorial: What is the correct cesarian rate and how do we get there? *Obstetrics and Gynecological Survey, 57*, 189–190

Peskin, H. (1967). Pubertal onset and ego functioning. *Journal of Abnormal Psychology, 72*, 1–15.

Petersen, A. C. (1979, January). Can puberty come any faster? *Psychology Today*, pp. 45–56.

Petersen, A. C. (1993). Creating adolescents: The role of context and process in developmental trajectories. *Journal of Research on Adolescence, 3*, 1–18.

Peterson, C. (1999). Grandfathers' and grandmothers' satisfaction with the grandparenting role: Seeking new answers to old questions. *International Journal of Aging and Human Development, 49*, 61–78.

Peterson, K. S. (1997, September 3). In high school, dating is a world into itself. *USA Today*, pp. 1–2D.

Petrill, S. A. (2003). The development of intelligence: Behavioral genetic approaches. In R. J. Sternberg, J. Lautrey, & T. I. Lubert (Eds.), *Models of intelligence: International perspectives*. Washington, DC: American Psychological Association.

Pettito, L. A., Kovelman I., & Harasymowycz, U. (2003, April). *Bilingual language development: Does learning the new damage the old*. Paper presented at the meeting of the Society for Research in Child Development, Tampa.

Pfeifer, M., Goldsmith, H. H., Davidson, R. J., & Rickman, M. (2002). Continuity and change in inhibited and uninhibited children. *Child Development, 73*, 1474–1485.

Phillips, D. A., Voran, K., Kisker, E., Howes, C., & Whitebook, M. (1994). Child care for children in poverty: Opportunity or inequity? *Child Development, 65*, 472–492.

Phillips, S. (2003). Adolescent health. In I. B. Weiner (Ed.), *Handbook of psychology* (Vol. IX). New York: Wiley.

Phillips, W. T., Kiernan, R. M., & King, A. C. (2001). The effects of physical activity on physical and psychological health. In A. Baum, T. A. Revenson, & J. E. Singer (Eds.), *Handbook of health psychology*. Mahwah, NJ: Erlbaum.

Phinney, J. S. (1989). Stages of ethnic identity development in minority group adolescents. *Journal of Early Adolescence, 9*, 34–49.

Phinney, J. S. (1996). When we talk about American ethnic groups, what do we mean? *American Psychologist, 51*, 918–927.

Phinney, J. S. (2000). Ethnic identity. In A. Kazdin (Ed.), *Encyclopedia of psychology*. Washington, DC, & New York: American Psychological Association and Oxford University Press.

Phinney, J. S. (2003). Ethnic identity and acculturation. In K. M. Chun, P. B. Organista, & G. Marin (Eds.), *Acculturation*. Washington, DC: American Psychological Association.

Phinney, J. S., & Alipuria, L. L. (1990). Ethnic identity in college students from four ethnic groups, *Journal of Adolescence, 13*, 171–183.

Piaget, J. (1932). *The moral judgment of the child*. New York: Harcourt Brace Jovanovich.

Piaget, J. (1952). *The origins of intelligence in children*. (M. Cook, Trans.). New York: International University Press.

Piaget, J. (1954). *The construction of reality in the child*. New York: Basic Books.

Piaget, J. (1962). *Play, dreams, and imitation in childhood*. New York: W. W. Norton.

Piaget, J., & Inhelder, B. (1969). *The child's conception of space* (F. J. Langdon & J. L. Lunger, Trans.). New York: W. W. Norton.

Pianta, R., Hamre, B., & Stuhlman, M. (2003). Relationships between teachers and children. In I. B. Weiner, *Handbook of Psychology* (Vol. 7). New York: Wiley.

Piccini, P., Pavese, N., & Brooks, D. J. (2003). Endogenous dopamine release after pharmacological challenges in Parkinson's disease. *Annals of Neurology, 53*, 647–653.

Pick, H. L. (1997). Review of J. W. Santrock's *Child development*, 8th ed. New York: McGraw-Hill.

Pickering, T. G. (2001). Mental stress as a causal factor in the development of hyper-tension and cardiovascular disease. *Current Hypertension Reports, 3*, 249–254.

Pickrell, J., & Loftus, E. F. (2001). *Creating false memories*. Paper presented at the meeting of the American Psychological Society, Toronto.

Pierson, R. N. (2003). Body composition in aging: A biological perspective. *Current Opinion in Clinical Nutrition and Metabolic Care, 6*, 15–20.

Piliavin, J. A., (2003). Doing well by doing good: Benefits for the benefactor. In C. L. M. Keys & J. Haidt (Eds.), *Flourishing: Positive psychology and the life well-lived*. Washington, DC: American Psychological Association.

Pillow, D. R., Zautra, A. J., & Sandler, I. (1996). Major life events and minor stressors: Identifying mediational links in the stress process. *Journal of Personality and Social Psychology, 70*, 381–394.

Pinette, M. G., Wax, J., Blackstone, J., Crtin, A., & McCrann, D. (2004). Timing of early amniocentesis as afunction of membrane fusion. *Journal of Clinical Utrasound, 32*, 8–11.

Pinker, S. (1994). *The language instinct*. New York: William Morrow.

Pinn, V. W. (2003). Sex and gender factors in medical studies: Implications for health and clinical practice. *Journal of the American Medical Association, 289*, 397–400.

Pintrich, P. R. (2000). The role of goal orientation in self-regulated learning. In M. Boekaerts, P. R. Pintrich, & M. Zeidner (Eds.), *Handbook of self-regulation*. San Diego: Academic Press.

Pintrich, P. R. (2003). Motivation and classroom learning. In I. B. Weiner (Ed.), *Handbook of psychology* (Vol. 7). New York: Wiley.

Pintrich, P. R., & Schunk, D. H. (2002). *Motivation in education* (2nd ed.). Upper Saddle River, NJ: Prentice Hall.

Piolino, P., Desgranges, B., Benali, K., & Eustache, F. (2002). Episodic and semantic remote autobiographical memory in aging. *Memory, 10*, 239–357.

Piotrowski, C. C. (1997, April). *Mother and sibling triads in conflict: Linking conflict style and the quality of sibling relationships*. Paper presented at the meeting of the Society for Research in Child Development, Washington DC.

Pittman, K., & Diversi, M. (2003). Social policy for the 21st century. In R. Larson, B. Brown, & J. Mortimer (Eds.), *Adolescents' preparation for the future: Perils and promise*. Malden, MA: Blackwell.

Pittman, K., Diversi, M., Irby, M., & Fabber, T. (2003). Social policy implications. In R. Larson, B. Brown, & J. Mortimer (Eds.), *Adolescents' preparation for the future: Perils and promise.* Malden, MA: Blackwell.

Pleck, J. (1995). The gender role strain paradigm: An update. In R. F. Levant & W. S. Pollack (Eds.), *A new psychology of men.* New York: Basic Books.

Pleck, J. H. (1981). *The myth of masculinity.* Beverly Hills, CA: Sage.

Pleck, J. H. (1983). The theory of male sex role identity: Its rise and fall, 1936–present. In M. Levin (Ed.), *In the shadow of the past: Psychology portrays the sexes.* New York: Columbia University Press.

Pleck, J. H. (1995). The gender-role strain paradigm. In R. F. Levant & W. S. Pollack (Eds.), *A new psychology of men.* New York: Basic Books.

Plomin, R. (1993, March). *Human behavioral genetics and development: An overview and update.* Paper presented at the biennial meeting of the Society for Research in Child Development, New Orleans.

Plomin, R. (1999). Genetics and general cognitive ability. *Nature. 402* (Suppl.), C25–C29.

Plomin, R. (2003). 50 years of DNA. *American Psychological Society, 16,* 7–8.

Plomin, R., & McGuffin, P. (2003). Psychopathology in the postgenomic era. *Annual Review of Psychology, 54,* 205–228.

Plomin, R., Asbury, K., & Dunn, J. (2001). Why are children in the same family so different? Nonshared environment a decade later. *Canadian Journal of Psychiatry, 46,* 225–233.

Plomin, R., DeFries, J. C., Craig, I. W., & McGuffin, P. (Eds). (2003). *Behavioral genetics in the postgenomic era.* APA Books: Washington, DC.

Plomin, R., DeFries, J. C., McClearn, G. E., & McGuffin, P. (2001). *Behavioral genetics* (4th ed.). New York: Worth.

Plomin, R., Fulker, D. W., Corley, R., & DeFries, J. C. (1997). Nature, nurture, and cognitive development from 1 to 16 years: A parent-offspring adoption study. *Psychological Science, 8,* 442–447.

Plomin, R., Reiss, D., Hetherington, E. M., & Howe, G. W. (1994). Nature and nurture: Contributions to measures of the family environment. *Developmental Psychology, 30,* 32–43.

Polivy, J., Herman, C. P., Mills, J., & Brock, H. (2003). Eating disorders in adolescence. In G. Adams & M. Berzonsky (Eds.), *Blackwell handbook of adolescence.* Malden, MA: Blackwell.

Pollack, H. A., & Frohna, J. G. (2001). A competing risk model of sudden death syndrome incidence in two U.S. birth cohorts. *Journal of Pediatrics, 138,* 661–667.

Pollack, W. (1999). *Real boys.* New York: Owl Books.

Pollak, C. P., & Bright, D. (2003). Caffeine consumption and weekly sleep patterns in U.S. seventh-, eighth-, and ninth-graders. *Pediatrics, 111,* 42–46.

Pollitt, E. P., Gorman, K. S., Engle, P. L., Martorell, R., & Rivera, J. (1993). Early supplementary feeding and cognition. *Monographs of the Society for Research in Child Development, 58* (7, Serial No. 235).

Polychronakos, C. (2003). Impact of the human genome project on pediatric endocrinology. *Hormone Research, 55–65.*

Pomerleau, O. (2000). Smoking. In A. Kazdin (Ed.), *Encyclopedia of psychology.* Washington, DC, & New York: American Psychological Association and Oxford University Press.

Poole, D. A., & Lindsey, D. S. (1996). *Effects of parents' suggestions, interviewing techniques, and age on young children's event reports.* Presented at the NATO Advanced Study Institute, Port de Bourgenay, France.

Porac, C., & Searleman, A. (2002). The effects of hand preference side and hand preference switch history on measures of psychological and physical well-being and cognitive performance in a sample of older adult right- and left-handers. *Neuropsychologia, 40,* 2074–2083.

Porges, S. W., Doussard-Roosevelt, J. A., & Maiti, A. K. (1994). Vagal tone and the physiological regulation of emotion. In N. A. Fox (Ed.), *Emotion regulation: Behavioral and biological considerations. Monographs of the Society for Research in Child Development, 59* (Serial No. 240), 167–196.

Potter, S. M., Zelazo, P. R., Stack, D. M., & Papageorgiou, A. N. (2000). Adverse effects of fetal cocaine exposure on neonatal auditory information processing. *Pediatrics, 105,* e40–e41.

Potvin, L., Champagne, F., & Laberge-Nadeau, C. (1988). Mandatory driver training and road safety: The Quebec experience. *American Journal of Public Health, 78,* 1206–1212.

Poulton, S., & Sexton, D. (1996). Feeding young children: Developmentally appropriate considerations for supplementing family care. *Childhood Education, 73,* 66–71.

Povinelli, D. J., & Simon, B. B. (1998). Young children's reactions to briefly versus extremely delayed images of the self: Emergence of the autobiographical stance. *Developmental Psychology, 34,* 188–194.

Povinelli, D. J., Perilloux, H. K., & Landau, K. R. (1996). Self-recognition in young children using delayed versus live feedback: Evidence of a developmental asynchrony. *Child Development, 67,* 1540–1554.

Powers, L. E., & Wampold, B. E. (1994). Cognitive-behavioral factors in adjustment to adult bereavement. *Death Studies, 18,* 1–24.

Powers, S. K., & Howley, E. T. (2004). *Exercise physiology (5th Ed.).* New York: McGraw-Hill.

Pratt, H. D., Patel, D. R., & Greydanus, D. E. (2003). Behavioral aspects of children's sports. *Pediatric Clinics of North America, 50,* 879–899.

Prescott, S. L. (2003). Early origins of allergic disease. *Current Opinions on Allergy and Clinical Immunology, 3,* 125–132.

Pressley, M. (1983). Making meaningful materials easier to learn. In M. Pressley & J. R. Levin (Eds.), *Cognitive strategy research: Educational applications* (pp. 239–266). New York: Springer-Verlag.

Pressley, M. (2003). Psychology of literacy and literacy instruction. In I. B. Weiner (Ed.), *Handbook of psychology* (Vol. VII). New York: Wiley.

Pressley, M., Cariligia-Bull, T., Deane, S., & Schneider, W. (1987). Short-term memory, verbal competence, and age as predictors of imagery instructional effectiveness. *Journal of Experimental Child Psychology, 43,* 194–211.

Prickaerts, J., Koopmans G., Blokland, A., & Scheepens, A. (2004). Learning and adult neurogenesis. *Neurobiology of learning and memory, 81,* 1–11.

Pritchard, F. F., & Whitehead, G. I. (2004). *Implementing and evaluating service learning in middle and high schools.* Mahwah, NJ: Erlbaum.

Provenzo, E. F. (2002). *Teaching, learning, and schooling in American culture: A critical perspective.* Boston: Allyn & Bacon.

Pruchno, R., & Rosenbaum, J. (2003). Social relationships in adulthood and old age. In I. B. Weiner (Ed.), *Handbook of psychology,* (Vol. 6). New York: Wiley.

Putnam, S. P., Sanson, A. V., & Rothbart, M. K. (2002). Child temperament and parenting. In M. H. Bornstein (Ed.), *Handbook of parenting* (2nd ed.). Mahwah, NJ: Erlbaum.

Quadflieg, N., & Fichter, M. M. (2003). The course and outcome of bulimia nervosa. *European Child and Adolescent Psychiatry, 12* (Suppl. 1), I199–I209.

Quality Counts. (2001). *A better balance: Standards, tests, and the tools to succeed.* Bethesda, MD: Education Week on the Web.

Qutub, M., Klapper, P., Vallely, P., & Cleator, G. (2001). Genital herpes in pregnancy: Is screening cost effective? *International Journal of STD and AIDS, 12,* 14–16.

Rabiner, D. L., Gordon, L., Klumb, D., & Thompson, L. B. (1991, April). *Social problem solving deficiencies in rejected children: Motivational factors and skill deficits.* Paper presented at the meeting of the Society for Research in Child Development, Seattle.

Rabinowitz, V. C., & Sechzur, J. (1994). Feminist methodologies. In F. L. Denmark & M. A. Paludi (Eds.), *Handbook on the psychology of women.* Westport, CT: Greenwood Press.

Raffaelli, M., & Ontai, L. (2001). "She's sixteen years old and there's boys calling over to the house": An exploratory study of sexual socialization in Latino families. *Culture, Health and Sexuality, 3,* 295–310.

Rahhal, T. A., May, C. P., & Hasher, L. (2002). Truth and character: Sources that older adults can remember. *Psychological Science, 13,* 101–105.

Rainey, R. (1965). The effects of directed vs. non-directed laboratory work on high school chemistry achievement. *Journal of Research in Science Teaching, 3,* 286–292.

Ramey, C. T, Ramey, S. L., & Lanzi, R. G. (2001). Intelligence and experience. In R. J. Sternberg & E. L. Grigorenko (Eds.), *Environment effects on cognitive development.* Mahwah, NJ: Erlbaum.

Ramey, C. T., & Campbell, F. A. (1984). Preventive education for high-risk children: Cognitive consequences of the Carolina Abecedarian Project. *American Journal of Mental Deficiency, 88,* 515–523.

Ramey, C. T., & Ramey, S. L. (1998). Early prevention and early experience. *American Psychologist, 53,* 109–120.

Ramphal, C. (1962). *A study of three current problems in education.* Unpublished doctoral dissertation, University of Natal, India.

Ransjo-Arvidson, A. B., Matthiesen, A. S., Nissen, L. G., Widstrom, A. M., & Uvnas-Moberg, K. (2001). Maternal analgesia during labor disturbs newborn behavior: Effects on breastfeeding, temperature, and crying. *Birth, 28,* 5–12.

Rapaport, S. (1994, November 28). Interview. *U.S. News & World Report,* p. 94.

Rapport, M. D., Chung, K. M., Shore, G., & Issacs, P. (2001). A conceptual model of child psychopathology: Implications for understanding a deficit hyperactivity disorder and treatment effectiveness. *Journal of Clinical Child Psychology, 30,* 48–58.

Raudenbush, S. (2001). Longitudinal data analysis. *Annual Review of Psychology* (Vol. 52). Palo Alto, CA: Annual Reviews.

Raven, P. H., & Johnson, G. B. (2002). *Biology* (6th ed.). New York: McGraw-Hill.

Rawlins, W. K. (2004). Friendship in later life. In J. F. Nussbaum & J. Coupland (Eds.), *Handbook of communication and aging.* Mahwah, NJ: Erlbaum.

Ray, O. S., & Ksir, C. J. (2004). *Drugs, society, and behavior (10th Ed.).* New York: McGraw-Hill.

Raymond, E. B. (2004). *Learners with mild disabilities (2nd Ed.).* Boston: Allyn & Bacon.

Ream, G. L., & Savin-Williams, R. (2003). Religious development in adolescence. In G. Adams & M. Berzonksy (Eds.), *Blackwell handbook of adolescence.* Malden, MA: Blackwell.

Reb, A. M. (2003). Palliative and end-of-life care: Policy analysis. *Oncology Nursing Forum, 30,* 35–50.

Redinbaugh, E. M., MacCallum, J., & Kiecolt-Glaser, J. K. (1995). Recurrent syndromal depression in caregivers. *Psychology and Aging, 10,* 358–368.

Reedy, M. N., Birren, J. E., & Schaie, K. W. (1981). Age and sex differences in satisfying relationships across the adult life span. *Human Development, 24,* 52–66.

Regan, J., & Alderson, A. (2003). Obesity: A growing and serious epidemic for children and adolescents. *Tennessee Medicine, 96,* 229–230.

Regenerus, M. D. (2001). *Making the grade: The influence of religion upon the academic performance of youth in disadvantaged communities.* Report 01-04, Center for Research on Religion and Urban Civil Council, University of Pennsylvania.

Reid, J. D., & Willis, S. L. (1999). Middle age: New thoughts, new directions. In S. L. Willis & J. D. Reid (Eds.), *Life in the middle.* San Diego: Academic Press.

Reifman, A. (2001). Models of parenting and adolescent drinking. *American Psychologist, 56,* 170–171.

Reiner, W. G. (2001). Gender identity and sex reassignment. In L. King, B. Belman, & S. Kramer (Eds.), *Clinical pediatric urology* (3rd ed.). London: ISIS Medical.

Reinhardt, J. P. (2001): Social support and well-being in later life. In J. P. Reinhardt (Ed.), *Negative and positive support.* Mahwah, NJ: Erlbaum.

Reis, D., Neiderhiser, J. M., Hetherington, E. M., & Plomin, R. (2000). *The relationship code.* Cambridge, MA: Harvard University Press.

Reisman, A. S. (2001). Death of a spouse: Basic assumptions and continuation of bonds. *Death Studies, 25,* 445–460.

Reitzes, D. C., & Mutran, E. J. (2004). Grandparenthood: Factors influencing frequency of grandparent-grandchildren contact and grandparent role satisfaction. *Journals of Gerontology B: Psychological and Social Sciences, 59,* S9–S16.

Relier, J. P. (2001). Influence of maternal stress on fetal behavior and brain development. *Biology of the Neonate, 79,* 168–171.

Religion in America. (1993). Princeton, NJ: Princeton Religious Research Center.

Remafedi, G., Resnick, M., Blum, R., & Harris, L. (1992). The demography of sexual orientation in adolescents. *Pediatrics, 89,* 714–721.

Rest, J. (1999). *Postconventional moral thinking.* Mahwah, NJ: Erlbaum.

Rest, J. R. (1986). *Moral development: Advances in theory and research.* New York: Praeger.

Rest, J., Narvaez, D., Bebeau, M. J., & Thomas, S. J. (1999). *Postconventional moral thinking.* Mahwah, NJ: Erlbaum.

Reuter-Lorenz, P. A., Jonides, J., Smith, E. S., Hartley, A., Miller, A., Marshuetz, C., et al. (2000). Age differences in the frontal lateralization of verbal and spatial working memory revealed by PET. *Journal of Cognitive Neuroscience, 12,* 174–187.

Reynolds, A. J. (1999, April). *Pathways to long-term effects in the Chicago Child-Parent Center Program.* Paper presented at the meeting of the Society for Research in Child Development, Albuquerque.

Rhodes, S. R. (1983). Age-related differences in work attitudes and behavior: A review and conceptual analysis. *Psychological Bulletin, 93,* 329–367.

Ribeiro, J., Guerra, S., Pinto, A., Oliveria, J., Duarte, J., & Mota, J. (2003). Overweight and obesity in children and adolescents: Relationship with blood pressure and physical activity. *Annals of Human Biology, 30,* 203–213.

Rice, J. (2002). Family roles and patterns: Contemporary trends. In J. Worrel (Ed.), *Encyclopedia of women and gender.* San Diego: Academic Press.

Richardson, B. A., & Hughes, J. P. (2003). Modeling breastmilk infectivity in HIV-1 infected mothers. *Biometrics, 59,* 179–185.

Richardson, G. A., Ryan, C., Willford, J., Day, N. L., & Goldschmidt, L. (2002). Prenatal alcohol and marijuana exposure: Effects on neuropsychological outcomes at 10 years. *Neurotoxicology and Teratology, 24,* 309–320.

Rickards, A. L., Kelly, E. A., Doyle, L. W., & Callahan, C. (2001). Cognition, academic progress, behavior, and self-concept at 14 years of very low birthweight children. *Journal of Developmental and Behavioral Pediatrics, 22,* 11–18.

Ridgeway, D., Waters, E., & Kuczaj, S. A. (1985). Acquisition of emotion-descriptive language: Receptive and productive vocabulary norms for ages 18 months to 6 years. *Developmental Psychology, 21,* 901–908.

Riesch, S. K., Gray, J., Hoefs, M., Keenan, T., Ertil, T., & Mathison, K. (2003). Conflict and conflict resolution: parent and young teen perceptions. *Journal of Pediatric Health Care, 17,* 22–31.

Rietveld, M. J., Dolan, C. V., van Baal, G. C., & Boomsma, D. I. (2003). A twin study of differentiation of cognitive abilities in childhood. *Behavior Genetics, 33,* 367–381

Rigby, K. (2002). Bullying in childhood. In P. K. Smith & C. H. Hart (Eds.), *Blackwell handbook of childhood social development.* Malden, MA: Blackwell.

Riley, E. P., Mattson, S. N., Li, T. K., Jacobsen, S. W., Coles, C. D., Kodituwakku, P. W., Adams, C. M., & Workman, M. I. (2003). Neurobehavioral consequence of Prenatal alcohol exposure: An international perspective. *Alcohol: Clinical and Experimental Research, 27,* 362–373.

Riley, K. P., Snowdon, D. A., & Markesbery, W. R. (2002). Alzheimer's neurofibrillary pathology and the spectrum of cognitive function: Findings from the nun study. *Annals of Neurology, 5,* 567–577.

Rimberg, H. M., & Lewis, R. J. (1994). Older adolescents and AIDS: Correlates of self-reported safer sex practices. *Journal of Research on Adolescence, 4,* 453–464.

Rinehart, S. D., Stahl, S. A., & Erickson, L. G. (1986). Some effects of summarization training on reading and studying. *Reading Research Quarterly, 21,* 422–438.

Ringdal, G. I., Jordhoy, M. S., Ringdal, K., & Kaasa, S. (2001). The first year of grief and bereavement in close family members to individuals who have died of cancer. *Palliative Medicine, 15,* 91–105.

Rittey, C. D. (2003). Learning difficulties: What the neurologist needs to know. *Journal of Neurology and Neurological Psychiatry, 74,* (Suppl. 1), 30–36.

Roberts, B. L., Dunkle, R., & Haug, M. (1994). Physical, psychological, and social resources as moderators of stress to mental health of the very old. *Journal of Gerontology, 49,* S35–S43.

Roberts, B. W., & Helson, R. (1997). Changes in culture, changes in personality: The influence of individualism in a longitudinal study of women. *Psychology and Aging, 17,* 423–434.

Roberts, B. W., Helson, R., & Klohnen, E. C. (2002). Personality development and growth in women across 30 years: Three perspectives. *Journal of Personality, 70,* 79–102.

Roberts, D., Jacobson, L., & Taylor, R. D. (1996, March). *Neighborhood characteristics, stressful life events, and African-American adolescents' adjustment.* Paper presented at the meeting of the Society for Research on Adolescence, Boston.

Roberts, W., & Strayer, J. (1996). Empathy, emotional expressiveness, and prosocial behavior. *Child Development, 67,* 471–489.

Robins, R. W., Trzesniewski, K. H., Tracy, J. L., Gosling, S. D., & Potter, J. (2002). Global self-esteem across the life span. *Psychology and Aging, 17,* 423–434.

Rodabough, T. (2003). The evolution of the legal definition of death. In C. D. Bryant (Ed.), *Handbook of death and dying.* Thousand Oaks, CA: Sage.

Rode, S. S., Chang, P., Fisch, R. O., & Sroufe, L. A. (1981). Attachment patterns of infants separated at birth. *Developmental Psychology, 17,* 188–191.

Rodgers, J. L. (2000). Birth orders. In A. Kazdin (Ed.), *Encyclopedia of psychology.* Washington, DC, & New York: American Psychological Association and Oxford University Press.

Rodin, J. (1983). Behavioral medicine: Beneficial effects of self-control training in aging. *International Review of Applied Psychology, 32,* 153–181.

Rodin, J., & Langer, E. J. (1977). Long-term effects of a control-relevant intervention with the institutionalized aged. *Journal of Personality and Social Psychology, 35,* 397–402.

Roemmich, J. N., Clark, P. A., Berr, S. S., Mai, V., Mantzoros, C. S., Flier, J. S., Weltman, A., & Rogol, A. D. (1998) Gender differences in leptin levels during puberty are related to the subcutaneous fat

depot and sex steroids. *American Journal of Physiology, 275,* E543–E551.

Roemmich, J. N., Wright, S. M. & Epstein, L. H. (2002). Dietary restraint and stress-induced snacking in youth. *Obesity Research, 10,* 1120–1126.

Rogers, W. A., & Fisk, A. D. (2001). Attention in cognitive aging research. In J. E. Birren & K. W. Schaie (Eds.), *Handbook of the psychology of aging* (5th ed.). San Diego: Academic Press.

Rogoff, B. (1990). *Apprenticeship in thinking.* New York: Oxford University Press.

Rogoff, B. (1998). Cognition as a collaborative process. In W. Damon (Ed.), *Handbook of child psychology* (5th ed., Vol. 2). New York: Wiley.

Rogoff, B. (2001, April). *Examining cultural processes in developmental research.* Paper presented at the meeting of the Society for Research in Child Development, Minneapolis.

Rogoff, B. (2003). *The cultural nature of human development.* New York: Oxford University Press.

Rogoff, B., & Morelli, G. (1989). Perspectives on children's development from cultural psychology. *American Psychologist, 44,* 343–348.

Rogoff, B., Turkanis, C. G., & Bartlett, L. (Eds.) (2001). *Learning together.* New York: Oxford University Press.

Rogol, A. D., Roemmich, J. N., & Clark, P. A. (1998, September). *Growth at puberty.* Paper presented at the workshop Physical Development, Health Futures of Youth II: Pathways to Adolescent Health, Maternal and Child Health Bureau, Annapolis, MD.

Rogol, A. D., Roemmich, J. N., & Clark, P. A. (2002). Growth at puberty. *Journal of Adolescent Health, 31* (Suppl.), 192–200.

Romero, A. J., & Roberts, R. E. (2003). Stress within a bicultural context for adolescents of Mexican descent. *Cultural Diversity and Ethnic Minority Psychology, 9,* 171–184.

Roosa, M. W., Dumka, L. E., Gonzales, N. A., & Knight, G. P. (2002). Cultural/ethnic issues and the prevention scientist in the 21st century. *Prevention & Treatment, 5,* 1–13.

Roper Starch Worldwide. (2000). *Attitudes toward retirement: A poll.* New York Author.

Roscoe, L. A., Malphurs, J. E., Dragovic, L. J., & Cohen, D. (2002). A comparison of characteristics of Kevorkian euthanasia cases and physician-assisted suicides in Oregon. *The Gerontologist, 41,* 439–446.

Rose, A. A., Feldman, J. F., McCarton, C. M., & Wolfson, J. (1988). Information processing in seven-month-old infants as a function of risk status. *Child Development, 59,* 489–603.

Rose, L. C., & Gallup, A. M. (2000). The 32nd annual Phi Delta Kappa/Gallup Poll of

the public's attitudes toward the public schools. *Phi Delta Kappan, 82* (No. 10), 41–58.

Rose, S. A., Feldman, J. F., & Wallace, I. F. (1992). Infant information processing in relation to six-year cognitive outcomes. *Child Development, 63,* 1126–1141.

Rose, S., & Frieze, I. R. (1993). Young singles' contemporary dating scripts. *Sex Roles, 28,* 499–509.

Rosenblith, J. F. (1992). *In the beginning* (2nd ed.). Newbury Park, CA: Sage.

Rosenblum, G. D., & Lewis, M. (2003). Emotional development in adolescence. In G. Adams & M. Berzonsky (Eds.), *Blackwell Handbook of Adolescence.* Malden, MA: Blackwell.

Rosenfield, R. L., Bachrach, L. K., Chernausek, S. D., & others. (2000). Current age of onset of puberty [Letters to the editor], *Pediatrics, 106,* 622.

Rosenstein, D., & Oster, H. (1988). Differential facial responses to four basic tastes in newborns. *Child Development, 59,* 1555–1568.

Rosenthal, C. J., Martin-Matthews, A., & Matthews, S. H. (1996). Caught in the middle? Occupancy in multiple roles and help to parents in a national probability sample of Canadian adults. *Journal of Gerontology: Social Sciences, 51b:* S274–S283.

Rosenthal, R., & Jacobsen, L. (1968). *Pygmalion in the classroom.* Ford Worth: Harcourt Brace.

Rosenzweig, M. R. (1969). Effects of heredity and environment on brain chemistry, brain anatomy, and learning ability in the rat. In M. Monosevitz, G. Lindzey, & D. D. Thiessen (Eds.), *Behavioral genetics.* New York: Appleton-Century-Crofts.

Rosenzweig, M. R. (2000). Ethology. In A. Kazdin (Ed.), *Encyclopedia of psychology.* Washington, DC, & New York: American Psychological Association and Oxford University Press.

Rosnow, R. L. (1995). Teaching research ethics through role-playing and discussion. In M. E. Ware & D. E. Johnson (Eds.), *Demonstrations and activities in teaching psychology* (Vol. 1). Mahwah, NJ: Erlbaum.

Rosnow, R. L., & Rosenthal, R. (1996). *Beginning behavioral research* (2nd ed.). Upper Saddle River, NJ: Prentice Hall.

Rossi, A. S. (1989). A life-course approach to gender, aging, and intergenerational relations. In K. W. Schaie & C. Schooler (Eds.), *Social structure and aging.* Hillsdale, NJ: Erlbaum.

Roth, G. S., Lane, M. A., Ingram, D. K., Mattison, J. A., Elahi, D., Tobin, J. D., Muller, D., & Metter, E. J. (2002). Biomarkers of caloric restriction may predict longevity in humans. *Science, 297,* 811.

Roth, J., & Brooks-Gunn, J. (2000). What do adolescents need for healthy development? Implications for youth policy. *Social Policy*

Report, Society for Research in Child Development, 13(1), 1–19.

Rothbart, M. K., & Bates, J. E. (1998). Temperament. In W. Damon (Ed.). *Handbook of child psychology* (5th ed., Vol. 3). New York: Wiley.

Rothbart, M. K., & Putnam, S. P. (2002). Temperament and socialization. In L. Pulkkinen & A. Caspi (Eds.), *Paths to successful development.* New York: Cambridge University Press.

Rothbart, M. L. K. (1971). Birth order and mother-child interaction, *Dissertation Abstracts, 27,* 45–57.

Rothbaum, F., Pott, M., Azuma, H., Miyake, K., & Weisz, J. (2000). The development of close relationships in Japan and the United States: Paths of symbiotic harmony and generative tension. *Child Development, 71,* 1121–1142.

Rothbaum, F., Rosen, K., Ujiie, T., & Uchida, N. (2002). Family systems theory, attachment theory, and culture. *Family Processes, 41,* 328–350.

Rothstein, R. (1998, May). Bilingual education: The controversy. *Phi Delta Kappan,* pp. 672–678.

Rovee-Collier, C. (1987). Learning and memory in children. In J. D. Osofsky (Ed.), *Handbook of infant development* (2nd ed.). New York: Wiley.

Rovee-Collier, C. (2001). Infant learning and memory. In A. Fogel & G. Bremner (Eds.), *Blackwell handbook of infant development.* London: Blackwell.

Rovee-Collier, C. (2002). Infant learning and memory. In U. Goswami (Ed.), *Blackwell handbook of childhood cognitive development.* Malden, MA: Blackwell.

Rowe, D. C. (2001). The nurture assumption persists *American Psychologist, 56,* 168–169.

Rowe, J. W., & Kahn, R. L. (1997). *Successful aging.* New York: Pantheon Books.

Rowe, J. W., & Kahn, R. L. (1998). *Successful aging.* New York: Pantheon.

Rowe, S. M., & Wertsch, J. V. (2002). Vygotsky's model of cognitive development. In U. Goswami (Ed.), *Blackwell handbook of child development.* Malden, MA: Blackwell.

Rubenstein, L. Z., Josephson, K. R., Trueblood, P. R., Loy, S., Harker, J. O., Pietruszka, F. M., & Robbins, A. S. (2000). Effects of group exercise program on strength, mobility, and falls among fall-prone elderly men. *Journal of Gerontology: Medical Sciences, 55A,* M317–M321.

Rubia, K., Overmeyer, S., Taylor, E., Brammer, M., Williams, S., Simmons, A., Andrew, C., & Bullmore, E. (2000). Functional frontalisation with age: Mapping neurodevelopmental trajectories with fMRI. *Neuroscience & Biobehavioral Reviews, 24,* 13–19.

Rubin, D. H., Krasilnikoff, P. A., Leventhal, J. M., Weile, B., & Berget, A. (1986, August 23). Effect of passive smoking on birthweight. *The Lancet,* 415–417.

Rubin, K. H., Bukowski, W., & Parker, J. G. (1998). Peer interactions, relationships, and groups. In N. Eisenberg (Ed.), *Handbook of child psychology* (5th ed., Vol. 3). New York: Wiley.

Rubin, S. & Malkinson, R. (2001) *Parental response to child loss across the life-cycle: Clinical and research perspectives.* In M. Stroebe, R. Hansson, W. Stroebe & H. Schut (Eds), *Handbook of bereavement research: consequences, coping and care.* Washington, DC: American Psychological Association.

Ruble, D. (1983). The development of social comparison processes and their role in achievement-related self-socialization. In E. Higgins, D. Ruble, & W. Hartup (Eds.), *Social cognitive development: A social-cultural perspective.* New York: Cambridge University Press.

Ruble, D. N. (2000). Gender constancy. In A. Kazdin (Ed.), *Encyclopedia of psychology.* Washington DC, and New York: American Psychological Association and Oxford University Press.

Rudd, M. D. (2003). Warning signs for suicide? *Suicide and Life-Threatening Behavior, 33,* 99–100.

Rudolph, K. L., Chang, S., Lee, H., Gottlieb, G. J., Greider, C., & DePinho, R. A. (1999). Longevity, stress response, and cancer in aging telomerase-deficient mice. *Cell, 96,* 701–712.

Rueter, M., & Conger, R. (1995). Antecedents of parent-adolescent disagreements. *Journal of Marriage and the Family, 57,* 435–448.

Ruff, H. A., & Capozzoli, M. C. (2003). Development of attention and distractibility in the first 4 years of life. *Developmental Psychology, 39,* 877–890.

Rumberger, R. W. (1995). Dropping out of middle school: A multilevel analysis of students and schools. *American Educational Research Journal, 3,* 583–625.

Runco, M. (1999). Critical thinking. In M. A. Runco & S. Pritzker (Eds.), *Encyclopedia of creativity.* San Diego: Academic Press.

Runco, M. (2004). Creativity. *Annual Review of Psychology* (Vol. 54). Palo Alto, CA: Annual Reviews.

Rusak, B., Robertson, H. A., Wisden, W., & Hunt, S. P. (1990). Light pulses that shift rhythms induce gene expression in the suprachiasmatic nucleus. *Science, 248,* 1237–1240.

Russell, S. T., & Joyner, K. (2001). Adolescent sexual orientation and suicide risk: Evidence from a national study. *American Journal of Public Health, 91,* 1276–1281.

Rutter, M. (2002). Nature, nurture, and development: From evangelism through science toward policy and practice. *Child Development, 73,* 1–21.

Ryan, A. S. (1997). The resurgence of breastfeeding in the United States. *Pediatrics, 99,* E-12.

Ryan, A. S., Wenjun, Z., & Acosta, A. (2002). Breastfeeding continues to increase into the new millenium. *Pediatrics, 110,* 1103–1109.

Ryckman, R. M., & Malikosi, M. (1975). Relationship between locus of control and chronological age. *Psychological Reports, 36,* 655–658.

Ryff, C. D. (1991). Possible selves in adulthood and old age: A tale of shifting horizons. *Psychology and Aging, 6,* 286–295.

Ryff, C. D., & Singer, B. (2003). Ironies of the human condition: Well-being and health on the way to mortality. In L. G. Aspinwall & U. M. Staudinger (Eds.), *A psychology of human strengths.* New York: Oxford University Press.

Rymer, R. (1992). *Genie.* New York: HarperCollins.

Saarni, C. (1999). The *development of emotional competence.* New York: Guilford.

Saarni, C. (2000). Emotional competence: A developmental perspective. In R. Bar-On & J. D. Parker (Eds.). *The handbook of emotional intelligence.* San Francisco: Jossey-Bass.

Sabini, J. (1995). *Social psychology* (2nd ed.). New York: Norton.

Sackett, P. (2003, February). Commentary on stereotype threat. *Monitor on Psychology, 34,* p. 52.

Saczynski, J., & Willis, S. L. (2001). *Cognitive training and maintenance of intervention effects in the elderly.* Unpublished manuscript. University Park, PA: Pennsylvania State University.

Sadeh, A., Raviv, A., & Gruber, R. (2000). Sleep patterns and sleep disruptions in school-age children. *Developmental Psychology, 36,* 291–301.

Sagan, C. (1977). *The dragons of Eden.* New York: Random House.

Saigal, S., den Ouden, L., Wolke, D., Hoult, L., Paneth, N., Streiner, D. L., Whitaker, A., & Pinto-Martin, J. (2003). School-age outcomes in children who were extremely low birth weight from four international population-based cohorts. *Pediatrics, 112,* 943–950.

Salat, D. H., Kaye, J. A., & Janowsky, J. S. (2002). Greater orbital prefrontal lobe selectively predicts worse working memory performance in older adults. *Cerebral Cortex, 12,* 494–505.

Salovey, P., & Mayer, J. D. (1990). Emotional intelligence. *Imagination, Cognition, and Personality, 9,* 185–211.

Salovey, P., & Pizarro, D. A. (2003). The value of emotional intelligence. In R. J. Sternberg, J. Lautrey, & T. I. Lubert (Eds.), *Models of intelligence: International perspectives.* Washington, DC: American Psychological Association.

Salthouse, T. A. (1988). Cognitive aspects of motor functioning. *Annals of the New York Academy of Science, 515,* 33–41.

Salthouse, T. A. (1991). *Theoretical perspectives on cognitive aging.* Hillsdale, NJ: Erlbaum.

Salthouse, T. A. (1994). The nature of the influence of speed on adult age differences in cognition. *Developmental Psychology, 30,* 240–259.

Salthouse, T. A. (1996). General and specific speed mediation of adult age differences in memory. *Journal of Gerontology, 51A,* P30–P42.

Salthouse, T. A. (2000). Adult development and aging: Cognitive processes and development. In A. Kazdin (Ed.), *Encyclopedia of psychology.* Washington, DC, & New York: American Psychological Association and Oxford University Press.

Salthouse, T. A., & Miles, J. D. (2002). Aging and time-sharing aspects of executive control. *Memory and Cognition, 30,* 572–582.

Samaniego, R. Y., & Gonzales, N. A. (1999). Multiple mediators of the effects of acculturation status on delinquency for Mexican American adolescents. *American Journal of Community Psychology, 27,* 189–210.

Samour, P. Q., Helm, K. K., & Lang, C. E. (Eds.). (2000). *Handbook of pediatric nutrition* (2nd ed.). Aspen, CO: Aspen.

Samuels, M., & Samuels, N. (1996). *New well pregnancy book.* New York: Fireside.

Sanders, G. F., & Trygstad, D. W. (1993). Strengths in the grandparent-grandchild relationship. *Activities, Adaptation, and Aging, 17,* 43–50.

Sandler, D. P., Comstock, G. W., Helsing, K. J., & Shore, D. L. (1989). Deaths from all causes in nonsmokers who lived with smokers. *American Journal of Public Health, 79,*163–167.

Sands, R. G., & Goldberg-Glen, R. S. (2000). Factors associated with stress among grandparents raising their grandchildren. *Family Relations, 49,* 97–105.

Sangree, W. H. (1989). Age and power: Life-course trajectories and age structuring of power relations in East and West Africa. In D. I. Kertzer & K. W. Schaie (Eds.), *Age structuring in comparative perspective.* Hillsdale, NJ: Erlbaum.

Sanson, A., & Rothbart, M. K. (1995). Child temperament and parenting. In M. H. Bornstein (Ed.), *Handbook of parenting* (Vol. 4). Hillsdale, NJ: Erlbaum.

Santa Maria, M. (2002).Youth in Southeast Asia: Living within the continuity of tradition and the turbulence of change. In B. B. Brown, R. W. Larson, & T. S. Saraswathi (Eds.), *The world's youth.* New York: Cambridge University Press.

Santiago-Delefosse, M. J., & Delefosse, J. M. O. (2002). Three positions on child thought and language. *Theory and Psychology, 12,* 723–747.

Santilli, N. R., Falbo, M. C., & Harris, J. T. (2002, April). *The role of volunteer services, self perceptions, and relationships with others on prosocial development.* Paper presented at the meeting of the Society for Research on Adolescence, New Orleans.

Santiseban, D. A., & Mitrani, V. B. (2003). The influence of acculturation processes on the family. In K. M. Chun, P. B. Organista, & G. Marin (Eds.), *Acculturation.* Washington, DC: American Psychological Association.

Santrock, J. W. (2004). *Educational psychology* (2nd ed.). New York: McGraw-Hill.

Santrock, J. W., & Halonen, J. A. (2004). *Your guide to college success* (3rd ed.). Belmont, CA: Wadsworth.

Santrock, J. W., Sitterle, K. A., & Warshak. R. A. (1988). Parent–child relationships in stepfather families. In P. Bronstein & C. P. Cowan (Eds.), *Fatherhood today: Men's changing roles in the family.* New York: Wiley.

Santrock, J. W., & Warshak, R. A. (1979). Father custody and social development in boys and girls. *Journal of Social Issues, 35,* 112–125.

Saraswathi, T. S., & Mistry, J. (2003). The cultural context of child development. In I. B. Weiner (Ed.), *The handbook of psychology* (Vol. VI). New York: Wiley.

Sarigiani, P. A., & Petersen, A. C. (2000). Adolescence: Puberty and biological maturation. In A. Kazdin (Ed.), *Encyclopedia of psychology.* Washington, DC, & New York: American Psychological Association and Oxford University Press.

Sarks, A. J. (2002). Age related macular degeneration. *Clinical Evidence, 8,* 614–628.

Sarrel, P., & Masters, W. (1982). Sexual molestation of men by women. *Archives of Human Sexuality, 11,* 117–131.

Savin-Williams, R. C. (2001). *Mom, dad, I'm gay.* Washington, DC: American Psychological Association.

Savin-Williams, R. C. (2001). Suicide attempts among sexual-minority youths: Population and measurement issues. *Journal of Consulting and Clinical Psychology, 69,* 983–991.

Savin-Williams, R., & Diamond, L. (2004). SEX. In R. Lerner & L. Steinberg. *Handbook of adolescent psychology.* New York: Wiley

Sax, L. J., Lindholm, J. A., Astin, A. W., Korn, W. S., & Mahoney, K. M. (2002). *The American freshman: National norms for fall 2002.* Los Angeles: Higher Education Research Institute, UCLA.

Scafidi, F., & Field, T. M. (1996). Massage therapy improves behavior in neonates born to HIV-positive mothers. *Journal of Pediatric Psychology, 21,* 889–897.

Scarr, S. (1984, May). Interview. *Psychology Today,* pp. 59–63.

Scarr, S. (1993). Biological and cultural diversity: The legacy of Darwin for development. *Child Development, 64,* 1333–1353.

Scarr, S. (2000). Day care. In A. Kazdin (Ed.), *Encyclopedia of Psychology.* Washington, DC, & New York: American Psychological Association and Oxford University Press.

Scarr, S., & Weinberg, R. A. (1983). The Minnesota adoption studies: Genetic differences and malleability. *Child Development, 54,* 182–259.

Schachter, S. C., & Ransil, B. J. (1996). Handedness distributions in nine professional groups. *Perceptual and Motor Skills, 82,* 51–63.

Schacter, D. L. (2001). *The seven sins of memory.* Boston: Houghton Mifflin.

Schaffer, H. R. (1996). *Social development.* Cambridge, MA: Blackwell.

Schaie, K. W. (1977). Toward a stage theory of adult cognitive development. *Aging and Human Development, 8,* 129–138.

Schaie, K. W. (1983). Consistency and changes in cognitive functioning of the young-old and old-old. In M. Bergner, U. Lehr, E. Lang, & R. Schmidt-Scherzer (Eds.), *Aging in the eighties and beyond.* New York: Springer.

Schaie, K. W. (1993). The Seattle longitudinal studies of adult intelligence. *Current Directions in Psychological Science, 2,* 171–175.

Schaie, K. W. (1994). The life course of adult intellectual abilities. *American Psychologist, 49,* 304–313.

Schaie, K. W. (1996). *Intellectual development in adulthood: The Seattle Longitudinal Study.* New York: Cambridge University Press.

Schaie, K. W. (1997). Unpublished review of J. W. Santrock's *Life-span development* (7th ed.). New York: McGraw-Hill.

Schaie, K. W. (2000). The impact of longitudinal studies on understanding development from young adulthood to old age. *International Journal of Behavioral Development, 24,* 257–266.

Schaie, K. W. (2000). Unpublished review of J. W. Santrock's *Life-span development,* 8th ed. New York: McGraw-Hill.

Schauble, L. (1996). The development of scientific reasoning in knowledge-rich contexts. *Developmental Psychology, 32,* 102–119.

Schiffman, S. S. (1996). Smell and taste. In J. E. Birren (Ed.), *Encyclopedia of gerontology.* San Diego: Academic Press.

Schmidt, L. A., Shahinfar, A., & Fox, N. A. (1996). Frontal EEG correlates of dysregulated social behavior in children. *Psychophysiology, 33,* S8.

Schmidt, U. (2003). Aetiology of eating disorders in the 21st century: New answers to old questions. *European Child and Adolescent Psychiatry, 12* (Suppl. 1), I130–I137.

Schneider, B. H., Atkinson, L., & Tardif, C. (2001). Child-parent attachment and children's peer relations: A quantitative review. *Developmental Psychology, 37,* 86–100.

Schneider, W., & Pressley, M. (1997). *Memory development between two and twenty.* Mahwah, NJ: Erlbaum.

Schnorr, T. M., & others. (1991). Video-display terminals and the risk of spontaneous abortion. *New England Journal of Medicine, 324,* 727–733.

Schoendorf, K. C., & Kiely, J. L. (1992). Relationship of sudden infant death syndrome to maternal smoking during and after pregnancy. *Pediatrics, 90,* 905–908.

Schoka, E., & Hayslip, B. (1999, November). *Grief and the family system: The roles of communication, affect, and cohesion.* Paper presented at the meeting of the Gerontological Society of America, San Francisco.

Schooler, C. (2001). The intellectual effects of the demands of the work environment. In R. J. Sternberg & E. L. Grigorenko (Eds.), *Environmental effects on cognitive abilities.* Mahwah, NJ: Erlbaum.

Schoon, I., Bynner, J., Joshi, H., Parsons, S., Wiggins, R. D., & Sacker, A. (2002). The influence of context, timing, and duration of risk experiences for the passage from childhood to midadulthood. *Child Development, 73,* 1486–1504.

Schrag, S. G., & Dixon, R. L. (1985). Occupational exposure associated with male reproductive dysfunction. *Annual Review of Pharmacology and Toxicology, 25,* 467–592.

Schugens, M. M., Daum, I., Spindler, M., & Birbaumer, N. (1997). Differential effects of aging on explicit and implicit memory. *Aging, Neuropsychology, and Cognition, 4,* 33–44.

Schulpis, K. H., Tsakiris, S., Karikas, G. A., Moukas, M., & Behrakis, P. (2003). Effect of diet on plasma total antioxidant status in phenylketonuric patients. *European Journal of Clinical Nutrition, 57,* 383–387.

Schultz, R., & Curnow, C. (1988). Peak performance and age among super athletes: Track and field, swimming, baseball, tennis, and golf. *Journal of Gerontology, 43,* P113–P120.

Schunk, D. H. (1991). Self-efficacy and academic motivation. *Educational Psychologist, 25,* 71–86.

Schunk, D. H. (2000). *Theories of learning* (3rd Ed.) Upper Saddle River, NJ: Prentice-Hall.

Schunk, D. H. (2001). Social cognitive theory and self-regulated learning. In B. J. Zimmerman & D. H. Schunk (Eds.), *Self-regulated learning and achievement* (2nd ed.). Mahwah, NJ: Erlbaum.

Schunk, D. H. (2004). *Learning theories* (4th Ed.) Upper Saddle River, NJ: Prentice Hall.

Schunk, D. H., & Zimmerman, B. J. (Eds.). (2001). *Self-regulated learning and academic achievement.* Mahwah, NJ: Erlbuam.

Schunk, D. N., & Zimmerman, B. J. (2003). Self-regulation and learning. In I. B. Weiner (Ed.), *Handbook of psychology,* (Vol. 7). New York: Wiley.

Schunn, C. D., & Anderson, J. (2001). Acquiring expertise in science. In K. Crowley, C. D. Schunn, & T. Okada (Eds.), *Designing for Science.* Mahwah, NJ: Erlbaum.

Schwartz, M. B., & Puhl, R. (2003). Childhood obesity: A societal problem to solve. *Obesity Review, 4,* 57–71.

Schwarzer, R., & Schultz, U. (2003). Stressful life events. In I. B. Weiner (Ed.), *Handbook of psychology* (Vol. IX). New York: Wiley.

Schweinhart, L. J. (1999, April). *Generalizing from High/Scope longitudinal studies.* Paper presented at the Meeting of the Society for Research in Child Development, Albuquerque.

Schwerha, D. J., & McMullin, D. L. (2002). Prioritizing ergonomic research in aging for the 21st century American workforce. *Experimental Aging Research, 28,* 99–110.

Schwimmer, J. B., Burwinkle, T. M., & Varni, J. W. (2003). Health-related quality of life of severely obese children and adolescents. *Journal of the American Medical Association, 289,* 1813–1819.

Scott, C. M., & Popovich, D. J. (2001). Undiagnosed alcoholism and prescription drug misuse among the elderly. *Caring, 20,* 20–23.

Scott-Jones, D. (1995, March). *Incorporating ethnicity and socioeconomic status in research with children.* Paper presented at the meeting of the Society for Research in Child Development, Indianapolis.

Search Institute. (1995). *Barriers to participation in youth programs.* Unpublished manuscript, the Search Institute, Minneapolis.

Search Institute. (1999). Does service learning make a difference? *Search Institute Source, 15* (1), pp. 1–2.

Sears, R. R., & Feldman, S. S. (Eds.). (1973). *The seven ages of man.* Los Altos, CA: Kaufmann.

Sebanc, A. M., Pierce, S. L., Cheatham, C. L., & Gunnar, M. R. (2003). Gendered social worlds in preschool: Dominance, peer acceptance, and assertiveness skills in boys' and girls' peer groups. *Social Development, 12,* 91–106.

Seeman, T. E., Berkman, L. F., Charpentier, P. A., Balzer, D. G., Albert, M. S., & Tinetti, M. E. (1995). Behavioral and psychological predictors of physical performance: MacArthur Studies of Successful Aging. *Journal of Gerontology: Medical Sciences, 50A,* M177–M183.

Segerberg, O. (1982). *Living to be 100: 1200 who did and how they did it.* New York: Scribner's.

Seginer, R. (1998). Adolescents' perception of relationships with older sibling in the context of other close relationships. *Journal of Research on Adolescence, 8,* 287–308.

Seidman, E. (2000). School transitions. In A. Kazdin (Ed.), *Encyclopedia of psychology.* Washington, DC, & New York: American Psychological Association and Oxford University Press.

Seifer, R. (2001). Socioeconomic status, multiple risks, and development of intelligence. In R. J. Sternberg &

E. L. Grigorenko (Eds.), *Environmental effects on cognitive abilities.* Mahwah, NJ: Erlbaum.

Selman, R. L. (1976). Social-cognitive understanding. In T. Lickona (Ed.), *Moral development and behavior.* New York: Holt, Rinehart & Winston.

Selman, R. L. (1980). *The growth of interpersonal understanding.* New York: Academic Press.

Semaj, L. T. (1985). Afrikanity, cognition, and extended self-identity. In M. B. Spencer, G. K. Brookins, & W. R. Allen (Eds.), *Beginnings: The social and affective development of Black children.* Hillsdale, NJ: Erlbaum.

Serbin, L. A., Cooperman, J. M., Peters, P. L., Lehoux, P. M., Stack, D. M. & Schwartzman, A. E. (1988). Intergenerational transfer of psychosocial risk in women with childhood histories of aggression, withdrawal, or aggression and withdrawal. *Developmental Psychology, 34,* 1246–1262.

Serbin, L. A., & Karp, J. (2003). Intergenerational studies of parenting and the transfer of risk from parent to child. *Current Directions in Psychological Science, 12,* 138–142.

Serbin, L. A., & Karp, J. (2004). The intergenerational transfer of psychosocial risk. *Annual Review of Psychology, Vol. 55.* Palo Alto, CA: Annual Reviews.

Serbin, L. A., & Stack, D. M. (Eds.). (1998). Longitudinal studies of inter-generational continuity and the transfer of psycho-social risk [Special section]. *Developmental Psychology. 34,* 1159–1273.

Seroczynski, A. D., Jacquez, F. M., & Cole, D. (2003). Depression and suicide during adolescence. In G. Adams & M. Berzonsky (Eds.), *Blackwell handbook of adolescence.* Malden, MA: Blackwell.

Serow, R. C., Ciechalski, J., & Daye, C. (1990). Students as volunteers. *Urban Education, 25,* 157–168.

Serpell, R. (1974). Aspects of intelligence in a developing country. *African Social Research, 17,* 576–596.

Serpell, R. (1982). Measures of perception, skills, and intelligence. In W. W. Hartup (Ed.), *Review of child development research* (Vol. 6, pp. 392–440). Chicago: University of Chicago Press.

Serpell, R. (2000). Culture and intelligence. In A. Kazdin (Ed.), *Encyclopedia of psychology.* Washington, DC, & New York: American Psychological Association and Oxford University Press.

Shapiro, K., & Caramazza, A. (2003). The representation of grammatical categories in the brain. *Trends in Cognitive Science, 7,* 201–206.

Sharkey, W. (1993). Who embarrasses whom? Relational and sex differences in the use of intentional embarrassment. In P. J. Kalbfleisch (Ed.), *Interpersonal communication.* Mahwah, NJ: Erlbaum.

Shatz, M., & Gelman, R. (1973). The development of communication skills: Modifications in the speech of young children as a function of the listener. *Monographs of the Society for Research in Child Development, 38* (Serial No. 152).

Shaver, P. R. (1986, August). *Being lonely, falling in love: Perspectives from attachment theory.* Paper presented at the meeting of the American Psychological Association, Washington, DC.

Shaver, P. R., & Hazan, C. (1993). Adult romantic attachment: Theory and evidence. In W. H. Jones & D. Perlman (Eds.), *Advances in personal relationships.* London: Jessica Kingsley.

Shaw, G. M. (2001). Adverse human reproductive outcomes and electromagnetic fields. *Bioelectromagnetics, 5* (Suppl.), S5–S18.

Shay, J. W., & Wright, W. E. (1999). Telomeres and telomerase in the regulation of cellular aging. In V. A. Bohr, B. F. Clark, & T. Stevenser (Eds.), *Molecular biology of aging.* Copenhagen, Denmark: Munksgaard.

Shay, J. W., & Wright, W. E. (2000). The use of telomerized cells for tissue engineering. *Nature Biotechnology, 18,* 22–23.

Shay, J. W., & Wright, W. E. (2002). Telomerase: A target for cancer therapeutics. *Cancer Cell, 2,* 257–265.

Shedlock, D. J., & Cornelius, S. W. (2003). Psychological approaches to wisdom and its development. In J. Demick & C. Andreoletti (Eds.), *Handbook of adult development.* New York: Kluwer.

Sheldon, T. (2002). World Medical Association isolates Netherlands on euthanasia. *British Medical Journal, 325,* 675.

Shepard, G. H. (2002). Three days for weeping: Dreams, emotions, and death in Peruvian Amazon. *Medical Anthropology Quarterly, 16,* 200–209.

Sherwood, A., Light, K. C., & Blumenthal, J. A. (1989). Effects of aerobic exercise training on hemodynamic responses during psychosocial stress in normotensive and borderline hypertensive Type A men: A preliminary report. *Psychosomatic Medicine, 51,* 123–136.

Shields, S. A. (1991). Gender in the psychology of emotion: A selective research review. In K. T. Strongman (Ed.), *International review of studies on emotion* (Vol. 1). New York: Wiley.

Shields, S. A. (1998, August). *What Jerry Maguire can tell us about gender and emotion.* Paper presented at the meeting of the International Society for Research on Emotions, Würzburg, Germany.

Shiono, P. H., & Behrman, R. E. (1995, spring). Low birth weight: Analysis and recommendations. *Future of Children, 5*(1), 4–18.

Shiraev, E., & Levy, D. (2004), *Cross-cultural psychology (2nd Ed.)* Boston. Allyn & Bacon.

Shneidman, E. S. (1973). *Deaths of man.* New York: Quadrangle/New York Times.

Shonk, S. M., & Cicchetti, D. (2001). Maltreatment, competency deficits, and risk for academic and behavioral maladjustment. *Developmental Psychology, 37,* 3–17.

Shuchter, S., & Zisook S. (1993). The course of normal grief. In M. Stroebe, W. Stroebe, & R. O. Hanson (Eds.), *Handbook of bereavement.* New York: Cambridge University Press.

Shweder, R., Mahapatra, M., & Miller, J. (1987). Culture and moral development. In J. Kagan & S. Lamb (Eds.), *The emergence of morality in young children.* Chicago: University of Chicago Press.

Siegel, L. S. (2003). Learning disabilities. In I. B. Weiner (Ed.), *Handbook psychology* (Vol. 7). New York: Wiley.

Siegel L. S., & Himel, N. (1998). Socioeconomic status, age and the classification of dyslexic and poor readers: Further evidence of the irrelevancy of IQ to reading disability. *Dyslexia, 4,* 90–104.

Siegfried, T. (2002, January 16). Explaining aging requires complicated brains. *Dallas Morning News,* p. 3F.

Siegler, I. C., Kaplan, B. H., Von Dras, D. D., & Mark, D. B. (1999). Cardiovascular health: A challenge for midlife. In S. L. Willis & J. D. Reid (Eds.), *Life in the middle: Psychological and social development in middle age.* San Diego: Academic Press.

Siegler, R. S. (1976). Three aspects of cognitive development. *Cognitive Psychology, 8,* 481–520.

Siegler, R. S. (1998). *Children's thinking* (3rd ed.). Upper Saddle River, NJ: Prentice Hall.

Siegler, R. S. (2001). Cognition, instruction, and the quest for meaning. In S. M. Carver & D. Klahr (Eds.), *Cognition and instruction.* Mahwah, NJ: Erlbaum.

Siegler, R. S. (2003). Relations between short-term and long-term cognitive development. *Psychological Science Agenda, 16,* 8–10.

Sigman, M., Cohen, S. E., & Beckwith, L. (2000). Why does infant attention predict adolescent intelligence? In D. Muir & A. Slater (Eds.), *Infant development: Essential readings.* Malden, MA: Blackwell.

Signore, C. (2001). Rubella. *Primary Care Update in Obstetrics and Gynecology, 8,* 133–137.

Silva, C., & Martins, M. (2003). Relations between children's invented spelling and children's phonological awareness. *Educational Psychology, 23,* 3–16.

Silverstein, L. B. (2001). Father and families. In J. P. McHale & W. S. Grolnick (Eds.), *Retrospect and prospect in the psychological study of families.* Mahwah, NJ: Erlbaum.

Silverstein, M., Conroy, S. J., Wang, H., Giarrusso, R., & Bengtson, V. L. (2002). Reciprocity in parent-child relations over the adult life course. *Journal of Gerontology: Psychological Sciences and Social Sciences, 57B,* S3–S13.

Sim, T. (2000). Adolescent psychosocial competence: The importance and role of regard for parents. *Journal of Research on Adolescence, 10,* 49–64.

Simmons, A. M., & Avery, P. G. (in press). Civic life as conveyed in U.S. civics and history textbooks. *Journal of Social Education.*

Simmons, R. G., & Blyth, D. A. (1987). *Moving into adolescence.* Hawthorne, NY: Aldine.

Simons-Morton, B., Haynie, D. L., Crump, A. D., Eitel, P., & Saylor, K. E. (2001). Peer and parent influences on smoking and drinking among early adolescents. *Health Education and Behavior, 28,* 95–107.

Simonton, D. K. (1996). Creativity. In J. E. Birren (Ed.), *Encyclopedia of aging.* San Diego: Academic Press.

Simpson, M. (2003). Developing education and support for community nurses: Principles and practice of palliative care. *Nursing Management, 9,* 9–12.

Singer, L. T., Arendt, R., Fagan, J., Minnes, S., Salvator, A., Bolek, T., & Becker, M. (1999). Neonatal visual information processing in cocaine-exposed and non-exposed infants. *Infant Behavior and Development, 22,* 1–15.

Singer, T., Lindenberger, U., & Baltes, P. B. (2003). Plasticity of memory for new learning in very old age: Six-year longitudinal findings in the Berlin Aging Study (BASE). *Psychology and Aging, 18,* 318–331.

Singh, M. A. F. (2002). Exercise comes of age: Rationale and recommendations for a geriatric exercise prescription. *Journal of Gerontology: Medical Sciences, 57A,* M262–M282.

Singh, N. A., Clements, K. M., & Fiatarone, M. A. (1997). A randomized controlled trial of progressive resistance training in depressed elders. *Journal of Gerontology, 52A,* M27–M35.

Singh, S., Wulf, D., Samara, R., & Cuca, Y. P. (2000). Gender differences in the timing of first intercourse: Data from 14 countries. *International Family Planning Perspectives, 26,* 21–28, 43.

Sinnott, J. D. (2003). Postformal thought and adult development: Living in balance. In J. Demick & C. Andreolett: (Eds.), *Handbook of adult development.* New York: Kluwer.

Skinner, B. F. (1938). *The behavior of organisms: An experimental analysis.* New York: Appelton-Century-Crofts.

Skinner, B. F. (1957). *Verbal behavior.* New York: Appleton-Century-Crofts.

Skinner, E. A., Chapman, M., & Baltes, P. B. (1982). *The causality, agency, and control interview.* Max Planck Institute for Human Development and Education, Berlin, West Germany.

Skinner, E. A., & Connell, J. P. (1986). Control understanding: Suggestions for a developmental framework. In M. M. Baltes &

P. B. Baltes (Eds.), *The psychology of control and aging* (pp. 35–69). Hillsdale, NJ: Erlbaum.

Skinner, E. A., Wellborn, J. G., & Connell, J. P. (1990). What it takes to do well in school and whether I've got it. *Journal of Educational Psychology, 82,* 22–32.

Slade J. M., Miszko, T. A., Laity, J. H., Agrawal, S. K., & Cress, M. E. (2002). Anaerobic power and physical function in strength-trained and non-strength-trained older adults. *Journal of Gerontology: Biological Sciences and Medical Sciences, 57A,* M168–M172.

Slater, A. (2002). Visual perception, In A. Fogel & G. Bremner (Eds.), *Blackwell handbook of infant development.* London: Blackwell.

Slater, A., Field, T., & Hernandez-Reif, M. (2002). The development of the senses. In A. Slater & M. Lewis (Eds.), *Introduction to infant development.* New York: Oxford University Press.

Slater, A., Morison, V., & Somers, M. (1988). Orientation discrimination and cortical function in the human newborn. *Perception, 17,* 597–602.

Slicker, E. K., & Thornberry, I. (2003). Older adolescent well-being and authoritative parenting. *Adolescent & Family Health, 3,* 9–19.

Slijper, F. M. E. (1984). Androgens and gender role behavior in girls with congenital adrenal hyperplasia (CAH). *Progress in Brain Research, 61,* 417–422.

Slobin, D. (1972, July). Children and language: They learn the same way around the world. *Psychology Today,* 71–76.

Slomkowski, C., Rende, R., Conger, K. J., Simons, R. L., & Conger, R. D. (2001). Sisters, brothers, and delinquency: Social influence during early and middle adolescence. *Child Development, 72,* 271–283.

Small, D. H., & Fodero, L. R. (2002). Cholinergic regulation of synaptic plasticity as a therapeutic target in Alzheimer's disease. *Journal of Alzheimer's disease, 4,* 349–355.

Small, S. A. (1990). *Preventive programs that support families with adolescents.* Washington, DC: Carnegie Council on Adolescent Development.

Smentana, J., & Turiel, E. (2003). Moral development during adolescence. In G. Adams & M. Berzonsky (Eds.), *The Blackwell handbook of adolescence.* Malden, MA: Blackwell.

Smith, D. (2004). *Introduction to special education* (5th ed.). Boston: Allyn & Bacon.

Smith, F. (2004). *Understanding reading (6th Ed.).* Mahwah, NJ: Erlbaum.

Smith, L. B., & Samuelson, L. K. (2003). Different is good: connectionism and dynamic systems theory are complementary emergentist approaches to development. *Developmental Science, 6,* 434–439.

Smith, L. M., Chang, L., Yonekura, M. L., Gilbride, K., Kuo, J., Poland, R. E.,

Walot, I., & Ernst, T. (2001). Brain proton magnetic resonance spectroscopy and imaging in children exposed to cocaine in utero. *Pediatrics, 107,* 227.

Smith, L., & Hattersley, J. (2000). *The smart guide to preventing SIDS.* New York: Smart.

Smith, L., Muir, D. W., & Kisilevsky, B. (2001, April). *Preterm infants' responses to auditory stimulation of varying intensity.* Paper presented at the meeting of the Society for Research in Child Development, Minneapolis.

Smith, P. K., & Drew, L. M. (2002). Grandparenthood. In M. H. Bornstein (Ed.), *Handbook of parenting* (2nd ed.). Mahwah, NJ: Erlbaum.

Smith, T. B., McCullough, M. E., & Poll, J. (in press). Religiousness and depression: Evidence for a main effect and the moderating influence of stressful life events. *Psychological Bulletin.*

Smith, T. E. C., Polloway, E. A., Patton, J. R., & Dowdy, C. A. (2004). *Teaching students with special needs in inclusive settings (4th Ed.).* Boston: Allyn & Bacon.

Smoreda, Z., & Licoppe, C. (2000). Gender-specific use of the domestic telephone. *Social Psychology Quarterly, 63,* 238–252.

Snarey, J. (1987, June). A question of morality. *Psychology Today,* pp. 6–8.

Snowdon, D. A. (1995). An epidemiological study of aging in a select population and its relationship to Alzheimer's disease. Unpublished manuscript, Sanders Brown Center on Aging, Lexington, KY.

Snowdon, D. A. (1997). Aging and Alzheimer's disease: Lessons from the nun study. *Gerontologist, 37,* 150–156.

Snowdon, D. A. (2002). *Aging with grace: What the nun study teaches us about leading longer, healthier, and more meaningful lives.* New York: Bantam.

Snowdon, D. A. (2003). Healthy aging and dementia: Findings from the Nun study. *Annals of Internal Medicine, 139,* 450–454.

Snowdon, D. A., Tully, C. L., Smith, C. D., Riley, K. P., & Markesbery, W. R. (2000). Serum folate and the severity of atrophy of the neocortex in Alzheimer's disease: Findings from the nun study. *American Journal of Clinical Nutrition, 71,* 993–998.

Snyder, H. N., & Sickmund, M. (1999, October). *Juvenile offenders and victims: 1999 national report.* Washington, DC: National Center for Juvenile Justice.

Soldo, B. J. (1996). Cross-pressures on middle-aged adults: A broader view. *Journal of Gerontology: Psychological Sciences and Social Sciences, 51B,* S271–S273.

Sollod, R. N. (2000). Religious and spiritual practices. In A. Kazdin (Ed.), *Encyclopedia of psychology.* Washington, DC, & New York: American Psychological Association and Oxford University Press.

Solomon, D., Battistich, V., Watson, M., Schaps, E., & Lewis C. (2000). A six-district study of educational change: Direct and mediated effects of the Child Development Project. *Social Psychology of Education, 4,* 3–51.

Solot, D., & Miller, M. (2002). *Unmarried to each other.* New York: Marlowe.

Soltero, S. W. (2004). *Dual language.* Boston: Allyn & Bacon.

Sommer, B. (2001). Menopause. In J. Worell (Ed.), *Encyclopedia of women and gender.* San Diego: Academic Press.

Sommer, B. B. (1978). *Puberty and adolescence.* New York: Oxford University Press.

Sophian, C. (1985). Perseveration and infants' search: A comparison of two- and three-location tasks. *Developmental Psychology, 21,* 187–194.

Sorof, J., & Daniels, S. (2002). Obesity hypertension in children: A problem of epidemic proportions. *Hypertension, 40,* 441–447.

Sowell, E., & Jernigan, T. (1998). Further MRI evidence of late brain maturation: Limbic volume increases and changing asymmetries during childhood and adolescence. *Developmental Neuropsychology, 14,* 599–617.

Sowter, B., Doyle, L. W., Morley, C. J., Altmann, A., & Halliday, J. (1999). Is sudden infant death syndrome still more common in very low birth weight infants in the 1990s? *Medical Journal of Australia, 171,* 411–413.

Spandel, V. (2004). *Creating young writers.* Boston: Allyn & Bacon.

Spear, H. J., & Kulbok, P. A. (2001). Adolescent health behaviors and related factors: A review. *Public Health Nursing, 18,* 82–93.

Spearman, C. E. (1927). *The abilities of man.* New York: Macmillan.

Spelke, E. S. (1979). Perceiving bimodally specified events in infancy. *Developmental Psychology, 5,* 626–636.

Spelke, E. S. (1991). Physical knowledge in infancy: Reflections on Piaget's theory. In S. Carey & R. Gelman (Eds.), *The epigenesis of mind: Essays on biology and cognition.* Hillsdale, NJ: Erlbaum.

Spelke, E. S. (2000). Core knowledge. *American Psychologist, 55,* 1233–1243.

Spelke, E. S., Breinlinger, K., Macomber, J., & Jacobson, K. (1992). Origins of knowledge. *Psychological Review, 99,* 605–632.

Spelke, E. S., & Hespos, S. J. (2001). Continuity, competence, and the object concept. In E. Dupoux (Ed.), *Language, brain, and behavior.* Cambridge, MA: Bradford/MIT Press.

Spelke, E. S., & Newport, E. L. (1998). Nativism, empiricism, and the development of knowledge. In W. Damon (Ed.), *Handbook of child psychology* (5th ed., Vol. 2). New York: Wiley.

Spelke, E. S., & Owsley, C. J. (1979). Intermodal exploration and knowledge in infancy. *Infant Behavior and Development, 2,* 13–28.

Spence, J. T., & Buckner, C. E. (2000). Instrumental and expressive traits, trait stereotypes, and sexist attitudes: What do they signify? *Psychology of Women Quarterly, 24,* 44–62.

Spence, J. T., & Helmreich, R. (1978). *Masculinity and feminity: Their psychological dimensions.* Austin: University of Texas Press.

Spence, M. J., & DeCasper, A. J. (1987). Prenatal experience with low-frequency maternal voice sounds influences neonatal perception of maternal voice samples. *Infant Behavior and Development, 10,* 133–142.

Spencer, J. P., Vereijken, B., Diedrich, F. J., & Thelen, E. (2000). Posture and the emergence of manual skills. *Developmental Science, 3,* 216–233.

Spencer, M. B. (1990). Commentary in Spencer, M. B., & Dornbusch, S. Challenges in studying ethnic minority youth. In S. S. Feldman & G. R. Elliott (Eds.), *At the threshold: The developing adolescent.* Cambridge, MA: Harvard University Press.

Spencer, M. B. (1999). Social and cultural influences on school adjustment: The application of an identity-focused cultural ecological perspective. *Educational Psychologist, 34,* 43–57.

Spencer, M. B., & Dornbusch, S. M. (1990). Challenges in studying minority youth. In S. S. Feldman & G. R. Elliott (Eds.), *At the threshold: The developing adolescent.* Cambridge, MA: Harvard University Press.

Spencer, M. B., Noll, E., Stoltzfuz, J., & Harpalani, V. (2001). Identity and school adjustment: Revisiting the "acting white" assumption. *Educational Psychologist, 36,* 21–30.

Sprei, J. E., & Courtois, C. A. (1988). The treatment of women's sexual dysfunctions arising from sexual assault. In R. A. Brown & J. R. Fields (Eds.), *Treatment of sexual problems in individual and couples therapy.* Great Neck, NY: PMA.

Spring, J. (2001). *The intersection of cultures* (2nd ed.). New York: McGraw-Hill.

Springer, S. P., & Deutsch, G. (1985). *Left brain, right brain.* San Francisco: Freeman.

Sroufe, L. A. (2000, Spring). The inside scoop on child development: Interview. *Cutting through the hype.* Minneapolis: College of Education and Human Development, University of Minnesota.

Sroufe, L. A. (2002). From infant attachment to promotion of adolescent autonomy. In J. G. Borkowski, S. L. Ramey, & M. Bristol-Power (Eds.), *Parenting and the child's world.* Mahwah, NJ: Erlbaum.

Sroufe, L. A., Dugal, S., Weinfield, N. S., & Carlson, E. (2001). Relationships, development, and pathology. In A. J. Sameroff, M. Lewis, & S. M. Miller (Eds.), *Handbook of developmental psychopathology* (2nd ed.). New York: Plenum.

Sroufe, L. A., & Waters, E. (1976). The ontogenesis of smiling and laughter: A perspective on the organization of development in infancy. *Psychological Review, 83,* 173–198.

Sroufe, L. A., Waters, E., & Matas, L. (1974). Contextual determinants of infant affectional response. In M. Lewis & L. Rosenblum (Eds.), *Origins of fear.* New York: Wiley.

St. Pierre, R., Layzer, J., & Barnes, H. (1996). *Regenerating two-generation programs.* Cambridge, MA: Abt Associates.

Stahl, S. (2002. January). *Effective reading instruction in the first grade.* Paper presented at the Michigan Reading Recovery conference, Dearborn, MI.

Stanhope, L., & Corter, C. (1993, March). *The mother's role in the transition to siblinghood.* Paper presented at the biennial meeting of the Society for Research in Child Development, New Orleans.

Stanovich, K. E. (1986). Cognitive processes and the reading problems of learning disabled children: Evaluating the assumption of specificity. In J. Torgesen & B. Wong (Eds.), *Psychological and educational perspectives on learning disabilities.* Orlando, FL: Academic Press.

Stattin, H., & Magnusson, D. (1990). *Pubertal maturation in female development: Paths through life* (Vol. 2). Hillsdale, NJ: Erlbaum.

Staudinger, U. M. (1996). Psychologische Produktivitat und Selbstenfaltung im Alter. In M. M. Baltes & L. Montada (Eds.), *Produktives Leben im Alter.* Frankfurt: Campus.

Staudinger, U. M., & Fleeson, W. (1996). *Life investment is a sample of 20 to 105 year olds.* Unpublished manuscript. Max Planck Institute for Human Development and Education, Berlin.

Stearns, S. C. (2002). A cross-cultural analysis of the behavior of women and men: Implications for the origins of sex differences. *Psychological Bulletin, 128,* 699–727.

Steele, C. M., & Aronson, J. (1995). Stereotype threat and the intellectual test performance of African-Americans. *Journal of Personality and Social Psychology, 69,* 797–811.

Steen, T. A., Kachorek, L. V., & Peterson, C. (2003). Character strengths among youth. *Journal of Youth and Adolescence, 32,* 5–16.

Steiger, H., Bruce, K. R., & Israel, M. (2003). Eating disorders. In I. B. Weiner (Ed.), *Handbook of psychology* (Vol. VIII). New York: Wiley.

Stein, M. T., & Perrin, J. M. (2003). Diagnosis and treatment of ADHD in school-age children in primary care settings: A synopsis of the AAP practice guidelines. *Pediatric Review, 24,* 92–98.

Steinberg, L. D., & Levine, A. (1997). *You and your adolescent* (2nd ed.). New York: Harper Perennial.

Steinberg, L. D., & Silk, J. S. (2002). Parenting adolescents. In M. H. Bornstein (Ed.), *Handbook of parenting.* Mahwah, NJ: Erlbaum.

Steinberg, L., & Caufmann, E. (2001). Adolescents as adults in court. *Social Policy Report,* XV (No. 4), 1–13.

Steiner, J. E. (1979). Human facial expressions in response to taste and smell stimulation. In H. Reese & L. Lipsitt (Eds.), *Advances in child development and behavior* (Vol. 13). New York: Academic Press.

Steiner, M., Dunn, E., & Born, L. (2003). Hormones and mood: From menarche to menopause and beyond. *Journal of Affective Disorders, 74,* 67–83.

Steinman, M. A., Landefeld, C. S., & Gonzales, R. (2003). Predictors of broad-spectrum antibiotic prescribing for acute respiratory infections in adult primary care. *Journal of the American Medical Association, 289,* 719–725.

Stepanuk, K. M., Tolosa, J. E., Lewis, D., Myers, V., Royds, C., Sabogal, J. C., & Librizzi, R. (2002). Folic acid supplementation use among women who contact a teratology information service. *American Journal of Obstetrics and Gynecology, 187,* 964–967.

Stern, D. N., Beebe, B., Jaffe, J., & Bennett, S. L. (1977). The infant's stimulus world during social interaction: A study of caregiver behaviors with particular reference to repetition and timing. In H. R. Schaffer (Ed.), *Studies in mother-infant interaction.* London: Academic Press.

Sternberg, R. J. (1986). *Intelligence applied.* Fort Worth: Harcourt Brace.

Sternberg, R. J. (1988). *The triangle of love.* New York: Basic Books.

Sternberg, R. J. (1993). *Sternberg Triarchic Abilities Test (STAT).* Unpublished test, Department of Psychology, Yale University, New Haven, CT.

Sternberg, R. J. (1997). Educating intelligence: Infusing the triarchic theory into instruction. In R. J. Sternberg & E. Grigorenko (Eds.), *Intelligence, heredity, and environment.* New York: Cambridge University Press.

Sternberg, R. J. (1999). Intelligence. In M. A. Runco & S. Pritzker (Eds.), *Encyclopedia of creativity.* San Diego: Academic Press.

Sternberg, R. J. (2001). Is there a heredity-environment paradox? In R. J. Sternberg & E. L. Grigorenko (Eds.), *Environmental effects on cognitive abilities.* Mahwah, NJ: Erlbaum.

Sternberg, R. J. (2002). Intelligence: The triarchic theory of intelligence. In J. W. Gutherie (Ed.), *Encyclopedia of education* (2nd ed.). New York: Macmillan.

Sternberg, R. J. (2003). Contemporary theories of intelligence. In I. B. Weiner (Ed.), *Handbook of psychology* (Vol. 7). New York: Wiley.

Sternberg, R. J., Castejøn, J. L., Prieto, M. D., Hautamäki, J., & Grigorenko, E. L. (2001a). Confirmatory factory analysis of the Sternberg triarchic abilities test in three international samples: An empirical test of the triarchic theory of intelligence. *European Journal of Psychological Assessment, 17*(1), 1–16.

Sternberg, R. J., & Grigorenko, E. L. (Eds.). (2001). *Environmental effects on cognitive abilities.* Mahwah. NJ: Erlbaum.

Sternberg, R. J., & Nigro, C. (1980). Developmental patterns in the solution of verbal analogies. *Child Development, 51,* 27–38.

Sternberg, R. J., Nokes, K., Geissler, P. W., Prince, R., Okatcha, F., Bundy, D. A., & Grigorenko, E. L. (2001b). The relationship between academic and practical intelligence: A case study in Kenya. *Intelligence, 29,* 401–418.

Sternberg, R. J., & O'Hara, L. A. (2000). Intelligence and creativity. In R. J. Sternberg (Ed.), *Handbook of intelligence.* New York: Cambridge University Press.

Sternberg, R. J., & Rifkin, B. (1979). The development of analogical reasoning processes. *Journal of Experimental Child Psychology, 27,* 195–232.

Sterns, H. L., Barrett, G. V., & Alexander, R. A. (1985). Accidents and the aging individual. In J. E. Birren & K. W. Schaie (Eds.), *Handbook of the psychology of aging.* New York: Van Nostrand Reinhold.

Sterns, H. L., & Huyck, H. (2001). The role of work in midlife. In M. E. Lachman (Ed.), *Handbook of midlife development.* New York: John Wiley.

Stevenson, H. G., Lee, S., & Stigler, J. W. (1986). Mathematics achievement of Chinese, Japanese, and American children. *Science, 231,* 693–699.

Stevenson, H. W. (1995). Mathematics achievement of American students: First in the world by the year 2000? In C. A. Nelson (Ed.), *Basic and applied perspectives on learning, cognition, and development.* Minneapolis: University of Minnesota Press.

Stevenson, H. W. (2000). Middle childhood: Education and schooling. In A. Kazdin (Ed.), *Encyclopedia of psychology.* Washington, DC, & New York: American Psychological Association and Oxford University Press.

Stevenson, H. W., Hofer, B. K., & Randel, B. (1999). *Middle childhood: Education and schooling.* Unpublished manuscript, Dept. of Psychology, University of Michigan, Ann Arbor.

Stevenson, H. W., Lee, S., Chen, C., Stigler, J. W., Hsu, C., & Kitamura, S. (1990). Contexts of achievement. *Monograph of the Society for Research in Child Development, 55* (Serial No. 221).

Stewart, A. J. (2003). Gender, race, and generation in a Midwest high school: Using ethnographically-informed methods in psychology. *Psychology of Women Quarterly, 27,* 1–11.

Stewart, A. J., & McDermott, C. (2004). Gender in psychology. *Annual Review of Psychology, 55.* Palo Alto, CA: Annual Reviews.

Stewart, A. J., Ostrove, J. M., & Helson, R. (2001). Middle aging in women: Patterns of personality change from the 30s to the 50s. *Journal of Adult Development, 8,* 23–37.

Stice, E., Presnell, K., & Spangler, D. (2002). Risk factors for binge eating onset in adolescent girls: A 2-year prospective investigation. *Health Psychology, 21,* 131–138.

Stigler, J. W., Nusbaum, H. C., & Chalip, L. (1988). Developmental changes in speed of processing: Central limiting mechanism or skill transfer. *Child Development, 59,* 1144–1153.

Stine, E. A. L., Soederberg, L. M., & Morrow, D. G. (1996). Language and discourse processing through adulthood. In F. Blanchard-Fields & T. M. Hess (Eds.), *Perspectives on cognitive change in adulthood and aging.* New York: McGraw-Hill.

Stine-Morrow, E. A. L., & Soederberg Miller, L. M. (1999). Basic cognitive processes. In J. C. Cavanaugh & S. K. Whitbourne (Eds.), *Gerontology: An interdisciplinary perspective.* New York: Oxford University Press.

Stipek, D. J. (1996). Motivation and instruction. In D. C. Berliner & R. C. Calfee (Eds.). *Handbook of educational psychology.* New York: Macmillan.

Stipek, D. J. (2002). *Motivation to learn* (4th ed.). Boston: Allyn & Bacon.

Stipek, D. J., Recchia, S., & McClintic, S. (1992). Self-evaluation in young children. *Monographs of the Society for Research in Child Development, 57,* (Serial No. 226), 2–3.

Stocker, C., & Dunn, J. (1990). Sibling relationships in childhood: Links with friendships and peer relationships. *British Journal of Developmental Psychology, 8,* 227–244.

Stouthamer-Loeber, M., Loeber, R., Wei, E., Farrington, D. P., & Wikstrom, P. H. (2002). Risk and promotive effects in the explanation of persistent serious delinquency in boys. *Journal of Consulting and Clinical Psychology, 70,* 111–123.

Stowell, J. R., McGuire, L., Glaser, R., & Kiecolt-Glaser, J. (2003). Psychoneuroimmunology. In I. B. Weiner (Ed.), *Handbook of psychology* (Vol. IX). New York: Wiley.

Strain, L. A., Grabusie, C. C., Searle, M. S., & Dunn, N. J. (2002). Continuing and ceasing leisure activities in later life: A longitudinal study. *The Gerontologist, 42,* 217–223.

Straus, M. A. (1991). Discipline and deviance: Physical punishment of children and violence and other crimes in adulthood. *Social Problems, 38,* 133–154.

Strauss, M. A., Sugarman, D. B., & Giles-Sims, J. (1997). Spanking by parents and subsequent anti-social behavior in children. *Archives of Pediatrics and Adolescent Medicine, 151,* 761–767.

Streib, H. (1999). Off-road religion? A narrative approach to fundamentalist and occult orientations of adolescents. *Journal of Adolescence, 22,* 255–267.

Streissguth, A. P., Martin, D. C., Sandman, B. M., Kirchner, G. L., &

Darby, B. L. (1984). Intrauterine alcohol and nicotine exposure: Attention and reaction time in four-year-old children. *Developmental Psychology, 20,* 533–543.

Strickland, B. (1988). Sex-related differences in health and illness. *Psychology of Women Quarterly, 12,* 381–399.

Striegel-Moore, R. H., Silberstein, L. R., & Rodin, J. (1993). The social self in bulimia nervosa: Public self-consciousness, social anxiety, and perceived fraudulence. *Journal of Abnormal Psychology, 102,* 297–303.

Stroebe, M., Gergen, M. H., Gergen, K. J., & Stroebe, W. (1992). Broken hearts or broken bonds: Love and death in historical perspective. *American Psychologist, 47,* 1205–1212.

Stroebe, M., & Stroebe, W. (1991). Does "grief work" work? *Journal of Consulting and Clinical Psychology, 59,* 57–65.

Stroebe, M., Stroebe, W., Schut, H., & van den Bout, J. (1998). Bereavement. In H. S. Friedman (Ed.), *Encyclopedia of mental health* (Vol. 1). San Diego: Academic Press.

Strong, B., Sayad, B. W., DeVault, C., & Yarber, W. (2005). *Human Sexuality* (5th Ed.). New York, McGraw-Hill

Stull, D. E., & Hatch, L. R. (1984). Unraveling the effects of multiple life changes. *Research on Aging 6,* 560–571.

Stunkard, A. (2000). Obesity. In A. Kazdin (Ed.), *Encyclopedia of psychology.* Washington, DC, & New York: American Psychological Association and Oxford University Press.

Substance Abuse and Mental Health Services Administration. (2002). *Aging and substance abuse.* Washington, DC: U.S. Department of Health and Human Services.

Sue, S. (1990, August). *Ethnicity and culture in psychological research and practice.* Paper presented at the meeting of the American Psychological Association, Boston.

Sullivan, H. S. (1953). *The interpersonal theory of psychiatry.* New York: W. W. Norton.

Sullivan, J. L. (2003). Prevention to mother-to-child transmission of HIV—what next? *Journal of Acquired Immune Deficiency Syndrome, 34,* Supplement 1: S67–S72.

Sullivan, K., & Sullivan, A, (1980). Adolescent-parent separation. *Developmental Psychology, 16,* 93–99.

Suomi, S. J., Harlow, H. F., & Domek, C. J. (1970). Effect of repetitive infant-infant separations of young monkeys. *Journal of Abnormal Psychology, 76,* 161–172.

Super, C., & Harkness, S. (1997). The cultural structuring of child development. In J. W. Berry, Y. H. Poortinga, & J. Pandey (Eds.), *Handbook of cross-cultural psychology: Vol. 2. Theory and method.* Boston: Allyn & Bacon.

Susman, E. J., Dorn, L. D., & Schiefelbein, V. L. (2003). Puberty, sexuality, and health. In I. B. Weiner (Ed.), *Handbook of psychology* (Vol. VI). New York: Wiley.

Susman, E. J., Dorn, L. D., & Schiefelbein, V. L. (2003). Puberty, sexuality, and health. In R. M. Lerner, M. A. Easterbrooks, & J. Mistry (Eds.), *Comprehensive handbook of psychology: Developmental psychology* (Vol. 6). New York: Wiley.

Susman, E. J., Finkelstein, J. W., Chinchilli, V. M., Schwab, J., Liben, L. S., & others. (1998). The effect of sex hormone replacement therapy on behavior problems and moods in adolescents with delayed puberty. *Journal of Pediatrics, 133* (4), 521–525.

Susman, E. J., & Rogol, A. (2004). Puberty and psychological development. In R. Lerner & L. Steinberg (Eds.), *Handbook of adolescent psychology.* New York: Wiley.

Suzman, R. M., Harris, T., Hadley, E. C., Kovar, M. G., & Weindruch, R. (1992). The robust oldest old: Optimistic perspectives for increasing healthy life expectancy. In R. M. Suzman, D. P. Willis, & K. G. Manton (Eds.), *The oldest old.* New York: Oxford University Press.

Swaab, D. F., Chung, W. C., Kruijver, F. P., Hofman, M. A., & Ishunina, T. A. (2001). Structural and functional sex differences in the human hypothalamus. *Hormones and Behavior, 40,* 93–98.

Swain, S. O. (1992). Men's friendships with women. In P. M. Nardi (Ed.), *Gender in intimate relationships.* Belmont, CA: Wadsworth.

Swanson, H. L. (1999). What develops in working memory? A life span perspective. *Developmental Psychology, 35,* 986–1000.

Swanson, J. M., & others. (2001). Clinical relevance of the primary findings of MTA: Success rates based on severity of ADHD and ODD symptoms at the end of treatment. *Journal of the American Academy of Child and Adolescent Psychiatry, 40,* 168–179.

Swearer, S. M., Grills, A. E., Haye, K. M., & Cary, P. T. (2004). Internalizing problems in students involved in bullying and victimization. In D. L. Espelage & S. M. Swearer (Eds.), *Bullying in American schools.* Mahwah, NJ: Erlbaum.

Sweeney, M. M. (2003, April). *Are stepfamilies associated with the physical and emotional well-being of adolescents?* Paper presented at the meeting of the Society for Research in Child Development, Tampa.

Sweet, M. P., Hodgman, J. E., Pena, I., Barton, L., Pavlova, Z., & Ramanathan, R. (2003). Two-year outcome of infants weighing 600 grams or less at birth and born 1994 through 1998. *Obstetrics and Gynecology, 101,* 18–23.

Szaflarksi, J. P., Binder, J. R., Possing, E. T., McKiernan, K. A., Ward, B. D., & Hammeke, T. A. (2002). Language lateralization in left-handed and ambidextrous people: fMRI data. *Neurology, 59,* 238–244.

Tahir, L., & Gruber, H. E. (2003). Developmental trajectories and creative work in late life. In J. Demick & C. Andreoletti (Eds.), *Handbook of adult development.* New York: Kluwer.

Takahashi, K. (1990). Are the key assumptions of the "Strange Situation" procedure universal? A view from Japanese research. *Human Development, 33,* 23–30.

Tanaka-Matsumi, J. (2001). Abnormal psychology and culture. In D. Matsumoto (Ed.), *The handbook of culture and psychology.* New York: Oxford University Press.

Tang, M. P., Chon, H. C, Tsao, P. n., Tson, K. I., & Hsich, W. S. (2004). Outcome of very low birth weight infants with sonographic enlarged occipital horn. *Pediatric Neurology, 30,* 42–45

Tannen, D. (1990). *You just don't understand: Women and men in conversation.* New York: Ballantine.

Tappan, M. B. (1998). Sociocultural psychology and caring psychology: Exploring Vygotsky's "hidden curriculum." *Educational Psychologist, 33,* 23–33.

Tavris, C., & Wade, C. (1984). *The longest war: Sex differences in perspective* (2nd ed.). San Diego: Harcourt Brace Jovanovich.

Taylor, H. G., Klein, N., & Hack, M. (1994). Academic functioning in < 750 gm birthweight children who have normal cognitive abilities: Evidence for specific learning disabilities. *Pediatric Research 35,* 289A.

Taylor, L. S., & Whittaker, C. R. (2003). *Bridging multiple worlds.* Boston: Allyn & Bacon.

Taylor, M. R. (2004). Dealing with death: Western philosophical strategies. In C. D. Bryant (Ed.), *Handbook of death and dying.* Thousand Oaks, **CA: Sage.**

Taylor, S. E. (2003). *Health psychology* (5th ed.). New York: McGraw-Hill.

Taylor, S. P. (1982). Mental health and successful coping among Black women. In R. C. Manuel (Ed.), *Minority aging.* Westport, CT: Greenwood Press.

Teasdale, T. W., & Owen, D. R. (2001). Cognitive abilities in left-handers: Writing posture revisited. *Neuropsychologia, 39,* 881–884.

Temple, C., Nathan, R., Temple, F., & Burris, N. A. (1993). *The beginnings of writing* (3rd ed.). Boston: Allyn & Bacon.

Tercyak, K. P., Johnson, S. B., Roberts, S. E., & Cruz, A. Z. (2001). Psychological response to prenatal genetic counseling and amniocentesis. *Patient Educational Counseling, 43,* 73–84.

Terman, D. L., Larner, M. B., Stevenson, C. S., & Behrman, R. E. (1996). Special education for students with disabilities: Analysis and recommendations. *The Future of Children, 6*(1) 4–24.

Terman, L. (1925). *Genetic studies of genius. Vol. 1: Mental and physical traits of a thousand gifted children.* Stanford, CA: Stanford University Press.

Terry, W. S. (2003). *Learning and memory* (2nd ed.). Boston: Allyn & Bacon.

Tershakovec, A. M., Kuppler, K. M., Zemel, B. S., Katz, L., Weinzimer, S., Harty, M. P., & Stallings, V. A. (2003). Body composition and metabolic factors in obese children and adolescents. *International Journal of Obesity and Related Metabolic Disorders, 27,* 19–24.

Tesser, A. (2000). Self-esteem. In A. Kazdin (Ed.), *Encyclopedia of psychology.* Washington, DC, & New York: American Psychological Association and Oxford University Press.

Teti, D. (2001). Retrospect and prospect in the psychological study of sibling relationships. In J. P. McHale & W. S. Grolnick (Eds.), *Retrospect and prospect in the psychological study of families.* Mahwah, NJ: Erlbaum.

Tharp, R. G. (1994). Intergroup differences among Native Americans in socialization and child cognition: An erthogenetic analysis. In P. M. Greenfield & R. Cocking (Eds.), *Cross-cultural roots of minority child development.* Mahwah, NJ: Erlbaum.

Tharp, R. G., & Gallimore, R. (1988). *Rousing minds to life: Teaching, learning, and schooling in social context.* New York: Cambridge University Press.

Thayer, J. F., Rossy, I., Sollers, J., Friedman, B. H., & Allen, M. T. (1996, March). *Relationships among heart period variability and cardiodynamic measures vary as a function of fitness.* Paper presented at the meeting of the American Psychosomatic Society, Williamsburg. VA.

The Conduct Problems Prevention Research Group. (2002). Evaluation of the first 3 years of the Fast Track prevention trial with children at high risk for adolescent conduct problems. *Journal of Abnormal Child Psychology, 30,* 19–35.

Thelen, E. (1995). Motor development: A new synthesis. *American Psychologist, 50,* 79–95.

Thelen, E. (2000). Perception and motor development. In A. Kazdin (Ed.), *Encyclopedia of psychology.* Washington, DC, & New York: American Psychological Association and Oxford University Press.

Thelen, E. (2001). Dynamic mechanisms of change in early perceptual-motor development. In J. L. McClelland & R. S. Siegler (Eds.), *Mechanisms of cognitive developmental.* Mahwah, NJ: Erlbaum.

Thelen, E., & Smith, L. B. (1998). Dynamic systems theory. In W. Damon (Ed.), *Handbook of child psychology* (5th ed., Vol. 1.). New York: Wiley.

Thoma, S. J. (2002). An overview of the Minnesota approach to moral development. *Journal of Moral Education, 31,* 225–245.

Thomas, A., & Chess, S. (1991). Temperament in adolescence and its functional significance. In R. M. Lerner, A. C. Petersen, & J. Brooks-Gunn (Eds.), *Encyclopedia of adolescence* (Vol. 2). New York: Garland.

Thompson, J. L., & Hansen, L. A. (2003). Thalidomide dosing in patients with relapsed or refractory multiple myeloma. *Annals of Pharmacotherapy, 37,* 571–576.

Thompson, J. W., Ryan, K. W., Pindiya, S. D., & Bost, J. E. (2003). Quality of care for children in commercial and Medicaid managed care. *Journal of the American Medical Asssociation, 290,* 1486–1493.

Thompson, K. M., Crosby, R. D., Wonderlich, S. A., Mitchell, J. E., Redline, J., Demuth, G., Smyth, J., & Haseltine, B. (2003). Psychopathology and sexual trauma in childhood and adulthood. *Journal of Traumatic Stress, 16,* 35–38.

Thompson, P. M., Giedd, J. N., Woods, R. P., MacDonald, D., Evans, A. C., & Toga, A. W. (2000). Growth patterns in the developing brain detected by using continuum mechanical tensor maps. *Nature, 404,* 190–193.

Thompson, R. A. (1994). Emotion regulation: A theme in search of a definition. *Monographs of the Society for Research in Child Development, 59* (Serial No. 240), 2–3.

Thompson, R. A., Easterbrooks, M. A., & Walker, L. (2003). Social and emotional development in infancy. In I. B. Weiner (Ed.), *Handbook of psychology* (Vol. 6). New York: Wiley.

Thompson, R. A., & Murachver, T. (2001). Predicting gender from electronic discourse. *British Journal of Social Psychology, 40,* 193–208.

Thompson, R. A., & Nelson, C. A. (2001). Developmental science and the media. *American Psychologist, 56,* 5–15.

Thomson, E., Mosley, J., Hanson, T. L., McLanahan S. S. (2001). Remarriage, cohabitation, and changes in mothering behavior. *Journal of Marriage and the Family, 63,* 370–380.

Thomson, M. (2003). Monitoring dyslexics' intelligence and attainments: A follow-up Study. *Dyslexia, 9,* 3–17.

Thornberry, T. P., Freeman-Gallant, A., Lizotto, A. J., Krohn, M. D., & Smith, C. A. (2003). Linked lives: The intergenerational transmission of antisocial behavior. *Journal of Abnormal Child Psychology, 31,* 171–184.

Thorton, A., & Camburn, D. (1989). Religious participation and sexual behavior and attitudes. *Journal of Marriage and the Family, 49,* 117–128.

Thurstone, L. L. (1938). *Primary mental abilities.* Chicago: University of Chicago Press.

Timimi, S., & Taylor, E. (2004). ADHD is best understood as a cultural construct. *British Journal of Psychiatry, 184,* 8–9.

Tolan, P. H., Gorman-Smith, D., & Hendry, D. B. (2003). The developmental ecology of urban male youth violence. *Developmental Psychology, 39,* 274–291.

Tolman, D. L., & Diamond, L. M. (2001). Desegregating sexuality research. Cultural and biological perspectives on gender and desire. *Annual Review of Sex Research, 12,* 33–74.

Torney-Purta, J. (1993, August). *Cross-cultural examination of stages of faith development.* Paper presented at the meeting of the American Psychological Association, Toronto.

Toseland, R. W., McCallion, P., Gerber, T., & Banks, S. (2002). Predictors of health and human services use by persons with dementia and their family caregivers. *Social Science and Medicine, 55,* 1255–1266.

Toth, G., & Siegel, L. S. (1994). A critical evaluation of the IQ-achievement discrepancy based definition of dyslexia. In K. P. van den Bos, L. S. Siegel, D. J. Bakker, & D. L. Share (Eds.), *Current directions in dyslexia research.,* Lisse, The Netherlands: Swets & Zeitlinger.

Tough, S. C., Newburn-Cook, C., Johnston, D. W., Svenson, L. W., Rose, S., & Belik, J. (2002). Delayed childbearing and its impact on population rate changes in lower birth weight, multiple birth, and preterm delivery. *Pediatrics, 109,* 399–403.

Trafimow, D., Triandis, H. C., & Goto, S. G. (1991). Some tests of the distinction between the private and collective self. *Journal of Personality and Social Psychology, 60,* 649–655.

Trappe, R., Laccone, F., Cobilanschi, J., Meins, M., Huppke, P., Hanefeld, F., & Engel, W. (2001). MECP2 mutations in sporadic cases of Rett syndrome are almost exclusively of paternal origin. *American Journal of Human Genetics, 68,* 1093–1101.

Trasler, J. (2000). Paternal exposures: Altered sex ratios. *Teratology, 62,* 6–7.

Treffers, P. E., Eskes, M., Kleiverda, G., & van Alten, D. (1990). Home births and minimal medical interventions. *Journal of the American Medical Association, 246,* 2207–2208.

Trehub, S. E., Schneider, B. A., Thorpe, L. A., & Judge, P. (1991). Observational measures of auditory sensitivity in early infancy. *Developmental Psychology, 27,* 40–49.

Treuth, M. S., Sunehag, A. L., Trautwein, L. M., Bier, D. M., Haywood, M. W., & Butte, N. F. (2003). Metabolic adaptation to high-fat and high-carbohydrate diets in children and adolescents. *American Journal of Clinical Nutrition, 77,* 479–489.

Triandis, H. C. (1994). *Culture and social behavior.* New York: McGraw-Hill.

Triandis, H. C. (2001). Individualism and collectivism. In D. Matsumoto (Ed.), *The handbook of culture and psychology.* New York: Oxford University Press.

Trinidad, D. R., & Johnson, C. A. (2002). The association between emotional intelligence and early adolescent tobacco and alcohol use. *Personality and Individual Differences, 32,* 95–105.

Trinklein, N. D., Aldred, S. F., Hartman, S. J., Schroeder, D. L., Otillar, R. P., & Myers, R. M. (2004). An abundance of bidirectional promoters in the human genome. *Genome Research, 14,* 62–66

Troen, B. R. (2003). The biology of aging. *Mount Sinai Journal of Medicine, 70,* 3–22.

Troiano, R. P., & Flegal, K. M. (1998). Overweight children and adolescents: Description, epidemiology, and demographics. *Pediatrics, 101,* 497–504.

Troll, L. E. (1999). Questions for future studies: Social relationships in old age. *International Journal of Aging and Human Development, 48,* 347–351.

Truitner, K., & Truitner, N. (1993). Death and dying in Buddhism. In D. P. Irish & K. F. Lundquist (Eds.), *Ethnic variations in dying, death, and grief: Diversity in universality.* Washington, DC: Taylor & Francis.

Trulear, H. D. (2000). *Faith-based institutions and high-risk youth: First report to the field.* Philadelphia: Public/Private Ventures.

Trzesniewski, K. H., Donnellan, M. B., Robins, R. W., Moffitt, T. E., & Caspi, A. (2002, February). *Do juvenile delinquents have high or low self-esteem?* Paper presented at the annual meeting of the Society for Personality and Social Psychology, Savannah, GA.

Tucker, C. J., McHale, S. M., & Crouter, A. C. (2003, April). *Adolescent sibling involvement and sibling personal qualities matter.* Paper presented at the meeting of the Society for Research in Child Development, Tampa.

Tucker, J. S., Schwartz, J. E., Clark, K. M., & Friedman, H. S. (1999). Age-related changes in the associations of social network ties with mortality risk. *Psychology and Aging, 14,* 564–571.

Tudge, J., & Scrimsher, S. (2003). Lev S. Vygotsky on education: A cultural-historical, interpersonal, and individual approach to development. In B. J. Zimmerman & D. H. Schunk (Eds.), *Educational psychology: A century of contributions.* Mahwah, NJ: Erlbaum.

Tulving, E. (2000). Concepts of memory. In E. Tulving & F. I. M. Craik (Eds.), *The Oxford handbook of memory.* New York: Oxford University Press.

Turiel, E. (1998). The development of morality. In N. Eisenberg (Ed.), *Handbook of child psychology* (5th ed., Vol. 3). New York: Wiley.

Turiel, E. (2003). *The culture of morality.* New York: Cambridge University Press.

Turk, D. C., Rudy, T. E., & Salovey, P. (1984). Health protection: Attitudes and behaviors of LPN's teachers, and college students. *Health Psychology, 3,* 189–210.

Turner, B. F. (1982). Sex-related differences in aging. In B. B. Wolman (Ed.), *Handbook of developmental psychology.* Englewood Cliffs, NJ: Prentice Hall.

Turvey, C. L., Carney, C., Arndt, S., & Wallace, R. B. (1999, November). *Conjugal loss and syndromal depression in a sample of elders ages 70 years and older.* Paper presented at the meeting of the Gerontological Society of America, San Francisco.

Tutka, P., Wielosz, M., & Zatonski, W. (2003). Exposure to environmental tobacco smoke and children's health. *International Journal of Occupational, Medical, and Environmenal Health, 15*, 325–335.

U.S. Bureau of the Census (2003). *People.* Washington, DC: Author.

U.S. Department of Education. (1999). *Digest of education statistics.* Washington, DC: Author.

U.S. Department of Education. (2000). *To assure a free and appropriate public education of all children with disabilities.* Washington, DC: U.S. Office of Education.

U.S. Department of Education. (2000). *Trends in educational equity for girls and women.* Washington, DC: Author.

U.S. Food and Drug Administration. (2001). *Mercury in fish.* Washington, DC: Author.

U.S. Bureau of the Census. (2000). *Statistical abstracts of the United States.* Washington, DC: U.S. Government Printing Office.

U.S. Bureau of the Census. (2002). *Death Statistics.* Washington, DC: Author.

U.S. Department of Education. (1996). *Number and disabilities of children and youth served under IDEA.* Washington, DC: Office of Special Education Programs, Data Analysis System.

U.S. Department of Energy. (2001). *The human genome project.* Washington, DC: Author.

U.S. Department of Health and Human Services (2003). *Child abuse and neglect statistics.* Washington. DC: Author.

U.S. Department of Health and Human Services. (2001). *Youth violence.* Rockville, MD: Author.

U.S. General Accounting Office. (1987, September). *Prenatal care: Medicaid recipients and uninsured women obtain insufficient care.* A report to the Congress of the United States, HRD-97-137. Washington, DC: GAO.

U.S. Bureau of the Census. (2002). *Census data: 2000.* Washington, DC: Author.

Udry, J. R. & others (1985). Serum androgenic hormones motivate sexual behavior in adolescent boys. *Fertility and Sterility, 43,* 90–94.

Underwood, M. (2002). Sticks and stones and social exclusion: Aggression among boys and girls. In P. K. Smith & C. H. Hart (Eds.), *Blackwell handbook of childhood social development.* Malden, MA: Blackwell.

Unger, B., Kemp, J. S., Wilins, D., Psara, R., Ledbetter, T., Graham, M., Case, M., & Thach, B. T. (2003). Racial disparity and modifiable risk factors among infants dying suddenly and unexpectedly. *Pediatrics, 111,* E127–E131.

Unger, R., & Crawford, M. (2000). *Women and gender* (4th ed.). New York: McGraw-Hill.

UNICEF. (2001). *UNICEF statistics: Low birthweight.* Geneva: Author.

UNICEF. (2003). *The State of the world's children: 2003.* Geneva: Author.

University of Louisville Birth Defects Center. (2001). FDA says some fish unsafe for pregnant women. *Birth Defects Center Research Newsletter, 9,* p. 3.

Vaillant, G. E. (1977). *Adaptation to life.* Boston: Little, Brown.

Vaillant, G. E. (2002). *Aging well.* Boston: Little Brown.

Valdimarsdottir, U., Helgason, A. R., Furst, C. J., Adolfsson, J., & Steineck, G. (2003) Long-term effects of widowhood after terminal cancer: A Swedish nationwide follow-up. *Scandinavian Journal of Public Health, 31,* 31–36.

Van Beveren, T. T. (2002). *Prenatal development and the newborn.* Unpublished manuscript, University of Texas at Dallas, Richardson.

van den Boom, D. C. (1989). Neonatal irritability and the development of attachment. In G. A. Kohnstamm, J. E. Bates, & M. K. Rothbart (Eds.), *Temperament in childhood.* New York: Wiley.

Van Goozen, S. H. M., Matthys, W., Cohen-Kettenis, P. T., Thisjssen, J. H. H., & van Engeland, H. (1998). Adrenal androgens and aggression in conduct disorder prepubertal boys and normal control. *Biological Psychiatry, 43,* 156–158.

van IJzendoorn, M. H., & Kroonenberg, P. M. (1988). Cross-cultural patterns of attachment: A meta-analysis of the Strange Situation. *Child Development, 59,* 147–156.

Vandell, D. L. (1985, April). *Relationship between infant-peer and infant-mother interactions: What have we learned?* Paper presented at the meeting of the Society for Research in Child Development, Toronto.

Vandell, D. L., & Wilson, K. S. (1988). Infants' interactions with mother, sibling, and peer: Contrasts and relations between interaction systems. *Child Development, 48,* 176–186.

Varo, J. J, Martinez-Gonzales, M. A., De Irala-Estevez, J., Kearney, J., Gibney, M., & Martinez, J. A. (2003). Distribution and determinants of sedentary life styles in the European union. *International Journal of Epidemiology, 32,* 138–146.

Vaughn, B. E., Colvin, T. N., Azria, M. R., Caya, L., & Krzysik, L. (2001). Dyadic analyses of friendship in a sample of preschool-aged children attending Headstart. *Child Development, 72,* 862–878.

Veach, J. E. (2003). Glaucoma case report: a nutritional response. *Optometry, 74,* 775–781.

Vecchiotti, S. (2003). Kindergarten: An overlooked educational policy priority. *SRCD Social Policy Report, XVII* (No. 11), 1–19.

Velasquez, R. J., Arellano, L. M., & McNeill, B. W. (Eds.) (2004). *The handbook of Chicano/a psychology and mental health.* Mahwah, NJ: Erlbaum.

Velez-Pardo, C., Lopera, F., Del Rio, J. M. (2002). DNA damage does not correlate with beta-plaques and neurofibrillary tangles in familial Alzheimer's disease Presenilin-1 mutation. *Journal of Alzheimer's Disease, 2.* 47–57.

Venter, J. C. (2003). A part of the human genome sequence. *Science, 299,* 1183–1184.

Ventura, S. J., Martin, J. A., Curtin, S. C., & Mathews, T. J. (1997, June 10). *Report of final natality statistics, 1995.* Washington, DC: National Center for Health Statistics.

Ventura, S. J., Mosher, W. D., Curtin, S. C., Abma, J. C., & Henshaw, S. (2001). Trends in pregnancy rates for the United States, 1976–1997: An update. *National Vital Statistics Reports, 49,* 1–9.

Verbrugge, L. M., Gruber-Baldini, A. L., & Fozard, J. L. (1996). Age differences and age changes in activities: Baltimore Longitudinal Study of Aging. *Journal of Gerontology: Social Sciences, 51B,* S30–S41.

Verklan, M. T. (2002). Physiological variability during transition to extrauterine life. *Critical Care Nursing Quarterly, 24,* 41–56.

Vidaeff, A. C., & Mastrobattista, J. M. (2003). In utero cocaine exposure: a thorny mix of science and mythology. *American Journal of Perinatology, 20,* 165–172.

Vidal, F. (2000). Piaget, Jean. In A. Kazdin (Ed.), *Encyclopedia of psychology.* Washington, DC, & New York: American Psychological Association and Oxford University Press.

Visher, E., & Visher, J. (1989). Parenting coalitions after remarriage: Dynamics and therapeutic guidelines. *Family Relations, 38,* 65–70.

Vogels, W. W., Dekker, M. R., Brouwer, W. H., & de Jong, R. (2002). Age-related changes in event-related prospective memory performance: A comparison of four prospective memory tasks. *Brain and Cognition, 49,* 341–362.

Vondracek, F. W., & Porfeli, E. J. (2003). The world of work and careers. In G. Adams & M. Berzonsky (Eds.), *Blackwell handbook of adolescence.* Malden, MA: Blackwell.

Vreugdenhil, H. J., Llijper, F. M., Mulder, P. G., & Weisglas-Kuperus, N. (2002). Effects of perinatal exposure to PCBs and dioxins on play behavior in Dutch children at school age. *Environmental Health Perspectives, 110,* A593–A591.

Vygotsky, L. S. (1962). *Thought and language.* Cambridge, MA: MIT Press.

Wachs, T. D. (1994). Fit, context and the transition between temperament and personality. In C. Halverson, G. Kohnstamm, & R. Martin (Eds.), *The developing structure of personality from infancy to adulthood.* Hillsdale, NJ: Erlbaum.

Wachs, T. D. (2000). *Necessary but not sufficient.* Washington, DC: American Psychological Association.

Wachs, T. D., & Kohnstamm, G. A. (Eds.). (2001). *Temperament in context.* Mahwah, NJ: Erlbaum.

Wadden, T. A., Foser, G. D., Stunkard, A. J., & Conill, A. M. (1996). Effects of weight cycling on the resting energy expenditure and body composition of obese women. *Eating Disorders, 19,* 5–12.

Waddington, C. H. (1957). *The strategy of the genes.* London: Allen & Son.

Wagner, R. K. (1997). Intelligence, training, and employment. *American Psychologist, 52,* 1059–1069.

Wagner, R. K., & Sternberg, R. J. (1986). Tacit knowledge and intelligent functioning in the everyday world. In R. J. Sternberg & R. K. Wagner (Eds.), *Practical intelligence.* New York: Cambridge University Press.

Wahlster, D. (2003). Genetics and the development of brain and behavior. In J. Valsiner & K. J. Connolly (Eds.). *Handbook of developmental psychology.* Thousand Oaks, CA: Sage.

Walden, T. (1991). Infant social referencing. In J. Garber & K. Dodge (Eds.), *The development of emotional regulation and dysregulation.* New York: Cambridge University Press.

Walker, C., Gruman, C., & Blank, K. (1999, November). *Physician-assisted suicide: Looking beyond the numbers.* Paper presented at the meeting of the Gerontological Society of America, San Francisco.

Walker, E. F. (2002). Adolescent neurodevelopment and psychopathology. *Current Directions in Psychological Science, 11,* 24–28.

Walker, G. C. (2004). Medical euthanasia. In C. D. Bryant (Ed.), *Handbook of death and dying.* Thousand Oaks, CA: Sage.

Walker, H. (1998, May 31). Youth violence: Society's problem. *Eugene Register Guard,* p. 1C.

Walker, L. J. (1982). The sequentiality of Kohlberg's stages of moral development. *Child Development, 53,* 1130–1136.

Walker, L. J. (1996). Unpublished review of J. W. Santrock's *Child development,* 8th ed. (New York: McGraw-Hill).

Walker, L. J., deVries, B., & Trevethan, S. D. (1987). Moral stages and moral orientation in real-life and hypothetical dilemmas. *Child Development, 58,* 842–858.

Walker, L. J., Henning, K. H., & Krettenauer, T. (2000). Parent and peer contexts for children's moral development. *Child Development, 71,* 1033–1048.

Walker, L. J., & Pitts, R. C. (1998). Naturalistic conceptions of moral maturity. *Developmental Psychology, 34,* 403–419.

Walker, L. J., Pitts, R. C., Hennig, K. H., & Matsuba M. K. (1995). Reasoning about morality and real-life moral problems. In M. Kilen & D. Hart (Eds.), *Morality of everyday life.* New York: Cambridge University Press.

Walker, N., Philbin, D. A., & Fisk, A. D. (1997). Age-related differences in movement control: adjusting submovement structure to optimize performance. *Journal of Gerontology, 52B(1),* P40–P52.

Wallace, M., Mills, B., & Browning, C. (1997). Effects of cross-training on markers of insulin resistance/hyperinsulinemia. *Medical Science and Sports Exercise, 29,* 1170–1175.

Walsh, L. A. (2000, Spring). The inside scoop on child development: Interview. *Cutting through the hype.* Minneapolis: College of Education & Human Development, University of Minnesota.

Walters, E., & Kendler, K. S. (1994). Anorexia nervosa and anorexia-like symptoms in a population based twin sample. *American Journal of Psychiatry, 152,* 62–71.

Wanagat, J., Lopez, M. E., & Aiken, J. M. (2001). Alterations in the mitochondrial genome. In E. J. Masoro & S. N. Austad (Eds.), *Handbook of the biology of aging.* (5th ed.). San Diego: Academic Press.

Wang, X., Zuckerman, B., Kautman, G., Pearson, C., Wang, G., Chen, C., Wise, P., Bauchner, H., & Xu, X. (2000, May). *Maternal cigarette smoking, genetic susceptibility, and birthweight.* Paper presented at the joint meeting of the Pediatric Academic Societies and the American Academy of Pediatrics, Boston.

Ward, B. M., Lambert, S. B., & Lester, R. A. (2001). Rubella vaccination in prenatal and postnatal women: Why not use MMR? *Medical Journal of Australia, 174,* 311–312.

Wardle, F. (2003). *Introduction to special education.* Boston: Allyn & Bacon.

Warner, H. (2002, September 16). Commentary. *The Dallas Morning News,* p. 6F.

Warner, H. R., & Hodes, R. J. (2000, Spring). Telomere length, telomerase, and aging: Hype, hope, and reality. *Generations, 24,* 48–53.

Warner, J., & Butler, R. (2002). Dementia. *Clinical Evidence, 7,* 846–866.

Warr, P. (1994). Age and employment. In M. Dunnette, L. Hough, & H. Triandis (Eds.), *Handbook of industrial and organizational psychology* (Vol. 4). Palo Alto, CA: Consulting Psychologists Press.

Wasik, B. H. (Ed.) (2004). *Handbook of family literacy.* Mahwah, NJ: Erlbaum.

Watenberg, N., Silver, S., Harel, S., & Lerman-Sagie, T. (2002). Significance of microencephaly among children with developmental disabilities. *Journal of Child Neurology, 17,* 117–122.

Waterman, A. S. (1985). Identity in the context of adolescent psychology. In A. S. Waterman (Ed.), *Identity in adolescence: Processes and contents.* San Francisco: Jossey-Bass.

Waterman, A. S. (1989). Curricula interventions for identity change: Substantive and ethical considerations. *Journal of Adolescence, 12,* 389–400.

Waterman, A. S. (1992). Identity as an aspect of optimal psychological functioning. In G. R. Adams, T. P. Gullotta, & R. Montemayor (Eds.), *Adolescent identity formation.* Newbury Park, CA: Sage.

Waterman, A. S. (1997). An overview of service-learning and the role of research and evaluation in service-learning programs. In A. S. Waterman (Ed.), *Service learning.* Mahwah, NJ: Erlbaum.

Waters, E., & Cummings, M. (2000). A secure base from which to explore relationships. *Child Development, 71,* 164–172.

Waters, E., Merrick, S., Albersheim, L., Treboux, D., & Crowell, J. (2000). Attachment theory from infancy to adulthood: A 20-year-longitudinal study of relations between infant Strange Situation classification and attachment representations in adulthood. *Child Development, 71,* 684–689.

Watras, J. (2002). *The foundations of educational curriculum and diversity: 1565 to the present.* Boston: McGraw-Hill.

Watson, J. B. (1928). *Psychological care of infant and child.* New York: W. W. Norton.

Watson, J. B., & Rayner, R. (1920). Conditioned emotional reactions. *Journal of Experimental Psychology, 3,* 1–14.

Watson, R., & DeMeo, P. (1987). Premarital cohabitation vs. traditional courtship and subsequent marital adjustment: A replication and follow-up. *Family Relations, 36,* 193–197.

Watts, C., & Zimmerman, C. (2002). Violence against women: Global scope and magnitude. *Lancet, 359,* 1232–1237.

Watts, D. H., Brown, Z. A., Money, D., Selke, S., Huang, M. L., Sacks, S. L., & Corey, L. (2003). A double-blind, randomized, placebo-controlled trial of acyclovir in late pregnancy for the reduction of herpes simplex virus shedding and cesarean delivery. *American Journal of Obstetrics and Gynecology, 188,* 836–843.

Weale, R. A. (1992). *The senescence of human vision.* New York: Oxford University Press.

Weatherford, W. (1999, October 31). Alzheimer's disease—What's new? *Dallas Morning News,* p. 4P.

Wechsler, D. (1939). *The measurement of adult intelligence.* Baltimore: Williams & Wilkins.

Wechsler, H., Davenport, A., Sowdall, G., Moetykens, B., & Castillo, S. (1994). Health and behavioral consequences of binge drinking in college. *Journal of the American Medical Association, 272,* 1672–1677.

Wechsler, H., Lee, J. E., Kuo, M., Seibring, M., Nelson, T. F., & Lee, H. (2002). Trends in college binge drinking during a period of increased prevention efforts: Findings from 4 Harvard School of Public Health College Alcohol Study surveys: 1993–2001. *Journal of American College Health, 50,* 203–217.

Weincke, J. K., Thurston, S. W., Kelsey, K. T., Varkonyi, A., Wain, J. C., Mark, E. J., & Christiani, D. C. (1999). Early age at smoking initiation and tobacco carcinogen DNA damage in the lung. *Journal of the National Cancer Institute, 91,* 614–619.

Weinraub, M., Horuath, D. L., & Gringlas, M. B. (2002). Single parenthood. In M. H. Bornstein (Ed.), *Handbook of parenting* (2nd ed., Vol. 3). Mahwah, NJ: Erlbaum.

Weinraub, M., Horvath, D. L., & Gringlas, M. B. (2002). Single parenthood. In M. H. Bornstein (Ed.), *Handbook of parenting* (2nd ed., Vol. 3). Mahwah, NJ: Erlbaum.

Weinstein, N. D. (1984). Reducing unrealistic optimism about illness susceptibility. *Health Psychology, 3,* 431–457.

Weiss, R. S. (1988). Loss and recovery. *Journal of Social Issues, 44* (3), 37–52.

Weissburg, R. P., & Greenberg, M. T. (1998). School and community competence-enhancement and prevention programs. In W. Damon (ed.), *Handbook of child psychology* (5th ed., Vol. 4). New York: Wiley.

Weizmann, F. (2000). In A. Kazdin (Ed.), *Encyclopedia of psychology.* Washington, DC, & New York: American Psychological Association and Oxford University Press.

Welch, R. A., Blessed, W. B., & Lacoste, H. (2003). Five-year experience with midsemester amniocentesis performed by a single group of obstetrician-gynecologists at a community hospital. *American Journal of Obstetrics and Gynecology, 188,* 600–601.

Welford, A. T. (1984). Between bodily changes and performance: some possible reasons for slowing with age. *Experimental Aging Research, 10(2),* 73–88.

Wellman, H. M. (1997, April). *Ten years of theory of mind: Telling the story backwards.* Paper presented at the meeting of the Society for Research in Child Development, Washington, DC.

Wellman, H. M. (2000). Early childhood. In A. Kazdin (Ed.), *Encyclopedia of psychology.* Washington, DC, & New York: American Psychological Association and Oxford University Press.

Wellman, H. M. (2002). Understanding the psychological world: Developing a theory of mind. In U. Goswami (Ed.), *Blackwell handbook of childhood cognitive development.* Malden, MA: Blackwell.

Wellman, H. M., Cross, D., & Watson, J. (2001). Meta-analysis of theory-of-mind development: The truth about false belief. *Child Development, 72,* 655–684.

Wenestam, C. G., & Wass, H. (1987). Swedish and U.S. Children's thinking about death: A qualitative study and cross-cultural comparison. *Death Studies, 11,* 99–121.

Wentzel, K. R., & Asher, S. R. (1995). The academic lives of neglected, rejected, popular, and controversial children. *Child Development, 66,* 754–763.

West, R., & Craik, F. I. M. (2001). Influences on the efficiency of prospective memory in younger and older adults. *Psychology and Aging, 16,* 682–696.

Whalen, C. K. (2001). ADHD treatment in the 21st century: Pushing the envelope. *Journal of Clinical Child Psychology, 30,* 136–140.

White, B., Castle, P., & Held, R. (1964). Observations on the development of visually directed reaching. *Child Development, 35,* 349–364.

White, C. W., & Coleman, M. (2000). *Early childhood education.* Columbus, OH: Merrill.

White, J. W. (2001). Aggression and gender. In J. Worrell (Ed.), *Encyclopedia of women and gender.* San Diego: Academic Press.

White, L. (2001). Sibling relationships over the life course. *Journal of Marriage and the Family, 63,* 555–568.

White, M. (1993). *The material child: Coming of age in Japan and America.* New York: Free Press.

Whitebourne, S. K., & Connolly, L. A. (1999). The developing self in midlife. In S. L. Willis & J. D. Reid (Eds.), *Life in the middle.* San Diego: Academic Press.

Whitehead, B. D., & Popenoe, D. (2003) *The state of our unions.* New Brunswick, NJ: Rutgers University

Whitfield, K. E., Weidner, G., Clark, R., & Anderson, N. B. (2003). Cultural aspects of health psychology. In I. B. Weiner (Ed.), *Handbook of psychology* (Vol. IX). New York: Wiley.

Whiting, B. B. (1989, April). *Culture and interpersonal behavior.* Paper presented at the biennial meeting of the Society for Research in Child Development, Kansas City.

Whitley, B. E. (2002). *Principles of research in behavioral science* (2nd ed.). New York: McGraw-Hill.

Whitman, T. L., Bortkowski, J. G., Keogh, D. A., & Weed, K. (2001). *Interwoven lives.* Mahwah, NJ: Erlbaum.

Wickelgren, I. (1999). Nurture helps to mold able minds. *Science, 283,* 1832–1834.

Wickrama, K. A. S., Brynt, C. M., Conger, R. D., & Meehan, J. M. (2004). Change and continuity in marital relationships during the middle years. In R. D. Conger, F. O. Lorenz, & K. A. S. Wickrama (Eds.), *Continuity and change in family relations.* Mahwah, NJ: Erlbaum.

Wigfield, A., & Eccles, J. S. (Eds.). (2002). *Development of achievement motivation.* San Diego: Academic Press.

Wigfield, A., Eccles, J. S., & Pintrich, P. R. (1996). Development between the ages of 11 and 25. In D.C. Berliner & R. C. Calfee (Eds.), *Handbook of educational Psychology.* New York: Macmillan.

Wilcox, S., Evenson, K. R., Aragaki, A., Wassertheil-Smoller, S., Mouton, C.P., & Loevinger, B. L. (2003). The effects of widowhood on physical and mental health, health behaviors, and health outcomes: the women's health initiative. *Health Psychology, 22,* 513–522.

Wiley, D., & Bortz, W. M. (1996). Sexuality and aging—usual and successful. *Journal of Gerontology, 51A,* M142–M146.

Willcox, B. J., Willcox, M. D., & Suzuki, M. (2002). *The Okinawa program.* New York: Crown.

Williams, A., & Nussbaum, J. F. (2001). *Intergenerational communication across the life span.* Mahwah, NJ: Erlbaum.

Williams, C., & Bybee, J. (1994). What do children feel guilty about? Developmental and gender differences. *Developmental Psychology, 30,* 617–623.

Williams, D. D., Yancher, S. C., Jensen, L. C., & Lewis, C. (2003). Character education in a public high school: A multi-year inquiry into unified studies. *Journal of Moral Education, 32,* 3–33.

Williams, J. E., & Best, D. L. (1982). *Measuring sex stereotypes: A thirty-nation study.* Newbury Park, CA: Sage.

Williams, J. E., & Best, D. L. (1989). *Sex and psyche: Self-concept viewed cross-culturally.* Newbury Park, CA: Sage.

Williams, M. A., & Wheeler, M. S. (2001). Palliative care: What is it? *Home Healthcare Nurse, 19,* 550–556.

Williams, M. E. (1995). *The American geriatric society's complete guide to aging and health.* New York: Harmony Books.

Williams, R. B. (2001). Hostility (and other psychosocial risk factors): Effects on health and the potential for successful behavioral approaches to prevention and treatment. In A. Baum, T. A. Revenson, & J. E. Singer (Eds.), *Handbook of health psychology.* Mahwah, NJ: Erlbaum.

Willis, S. L., & Nesselroade, C. S. (1990). Long-term effects of fluid ability training in old age. *Developmental Psychology, 26,* 905–910.

Willis, S. L., & Schaie, K. W. (1986). Training the elderly on the ability factors of spatial orientation and inductive reasoning. *Psychology and Aging, 1,* 239–247.

Willis, S. L., & Schaie, K. W. (1994). Assessing everyday competence in the elderly. In C. Fisher & R. Lerner (Eds.), *Applied developmental psychology.* Hillsdale, NJ: Erlbaum.

Willis, S. L., & Schaie, K. W. (1999). Intellectual functioning in midlife. In S. L. Willis & J. D. Reid (Eds.), *Life in the middle: Psychological and social development in middle age.* San Diego: Academic Press.

Wills, T. A., & Sandy, J. M. (2003). Buffering effect of religiosity for adolescent substance abuse. *Psychology of Addictive Behaviors, 17,* 24–31.

Wilson, D. M., & Truman, C. D. (2002). Addressing myths about end-of-life care: Research into the use of acute care hospitals over the last five years of life. *Journal of Palliative Care, 18,* 29–38.

Wilson, R. M., Hall, M. A., Leu, D. J., & Kinzer, C. K. (2001). *Phonics phonemic awareness, and word analysis for teachers* (7th ed.). Upper Saddle River, NJ: Merrill.

Wilson, R. S., Mendes de Leon, C. F., Barnes, L. L., Schneider, J. A., Bienias, J., Evans, D. A., & Bennett, D. A. (2002). Participation in cognitively stimulating activities and risk of incident Alzheimer disease. *Journal of the American Medical Association, 287,* 742–748.

Wilson, T. D., & Dunn, E. W. (2004). Self-knowledge: Its limits, value, and potential for improvement. *Annual Review of Psychology, Vol. 55.* Palo Alto, CA: Annual Reviews.

Wilson-Shockley, S. (1995). *Gender differences in adolescent depression: The contribution of negative affect.* M. S. thesis, University of Illinois at Urbana-Champaign.

Windle, M., & Windle, R. C. (2003). Alcohol and other substance use and abuse. In G. Adams & M. Berzonsky (Eds.), *Blackwell handbook of adolescence.* Malden, MA: Blackwell.

Windle, W. F. (1940). *Physiology of the human fetus.* Philadelphia: W. B. Saunders.

Wineberg, H. (1994). Marital reconciliation in the United States: Which couples are successful? *Journal of Marriage and the Family, 56,* 80–88.

Wing, R. R., & Polley, B. A. (2001). In A. Baum, T. A. Revenson, & J. E. Singer (Eds.), *Handbook of health psychology.* Mahwah, NJ: Erlbaum.

Wingfield, A., & Kahana, M. J. (2002). The dynamics of memory retrieval in older adulthood. *Canadian Journal of Experimental Psychology, 56*(3), 187–199.

Wink, P., & Dillon, M. (2002). Spiritual development across the adult life course: Findings from a longitudinal study. *Journal of Adult Development, 9,* 79–94.

Winner, E. (1986, August). Where pelicans kiss seals. *Psychology Today,* pp. 24–35.

Winner, E. (1996). *Gifted children: Myths and realities.* New York: Basic Books.

Winner, E. (2000). The origins and ends of giftedness. *American Psychologist, 55,* 159–169.

Winsler, A., Carlton, M. P., & Barry, M. J. (2000). Age-related changes in preschool children's systematic use of private speech in a natural setting. *Journal of Child Language, 27,* 665–687.

Winsler, A., Caverly, S. L, Willson-Quayle, A., Carlton, M. P., & Howell, C. (2002). The social and behavioral ecology of mixed-age and same-age preschool classrooms: A natural experiment. *Journal of Applied Developmental Psychology, 23,* 305–330.

Winsler, A., Diaz, R. M., & Montero, I. (1997). The role of private speech in the transition from collaborative to independent task performance in young children. *Early Childhood Research Quarterly, 12,* 59–79.

Winstead, B., & Griffin, J. L. (2001). Friendship styles. In J. Worell (Ed.), *Encyclopedia of women and gender.* San Diego: Academic Press.

Wintre, M. G., & Vallance, D. D. (1994). A developmental sequence in the comprehension of emotions: Intensity, multiple emotions, and valence. *Developmental Psychology, 30,* 509–514.

Wisniewski, A. B., Migeon, C. J., Meyer-Behlburg, H. F. L., Gearhart, J. P., Berkovitz, G. D., Brown, T. R., & Money, J. (2000). Complete androgen insensitivity syndrome: Long-term medical, surgical, and psychosexual outcome. *The Journal of Clinical Endocrinology and Metabolism, 85,* 2664–2669.

Wisotsky, W., & Swencionis, C. (2003). Cognitive-behavioral approaches to the management of obesity. *Adolescent Medicine, 14,* 37–48.

Witkin, H. A., Mednick, S. A., Schulsinger, R., Bakkestrom, E., Christiansen, K. O., Goodenbough, D. R., Hirchhorn, K., Lunsteen, C., Owen, D. R., Philip, J., Ruben, D. B., & Stocking, M. (1976). Criminality in XYY and XXY men. *Science, 193,* 547–555.

Women's Sports Foundation. (2001). *The 10 commandments for parents and coaches in youth spots.* Eisenhower Park, NY: Author.

Wong, D. L., Hockenberry, M. J., Wilson, D., Winkelstein, M. L., & Kline, N. E. (2003). *Whaley & Wong's nursing care of infants and children.* St. Louis: Mosby.

Wong, D. L., Perry, S. E., & Hockenberry, M. (2001), *Maternal child nursing care* (2nd ed.). St. Louis: Mosby.

Wong, P. T. P., & Watt, L. M. (1991). What types of reminiscence are associated with successful aging? *Psychology and Aging, 6,* 272–279.

Wood, J. M. (2002). Age and visual impairment decrease driving performance as measured on a closed-road circuit. *Human Factors, 44,* 482–494.

Wood, J. T. (2001). *Gendered lives.* Belmont, CA: Wadsworth.

Wood, M. D., Vinson, D. C., & Shr, K. J. (2001). Alcohol use and misuse. In A. Baum, T. A. Revenson, & J. E. Singer (Eds.), *Handbook of health psychology.* Mahwah, NJ: Erlbaum.

Woodrich, D. L. (1994). *Attention-deficit hyperactivity disorder: What every parent should know.* Baltimore: Paul H. Brookes.

Woodward, A. L., & Markman, E. M. (1998). Early word learning. In D. Kuhn & R. S. Siegler (Eds.), *Handbook of child psychology* (5th ed., Vol. 2). New York: Wiley.

Woodward, N. J., & Wallston, B. S. (1987). Age and health-care beliefs: Self-efficacy as a mediator of low desire for control. *Psychology and Aging, 2,* 3–8.

Wooley, S. C., & Garner, D. M. (1991). Obesity treatment: The high cost of false hope. *Journal of the American Dietetic Association, 91,* 1248–1251.

Worell, J. (Ed.). (2001). *Encyclopedia of women and gender.* New York: Oxford University Press.

World Health Organization. (2000). *The world health report.* Geneva: Author.

World Health Organization. (February 2, 2000). *Adolescent health behavior in 28 countries.* Geneva: Author.

Worobey, J., & Belsky, J. (1982). Employing the Brazelton scale to influence mothering: An experimental comparison of three strategies. *Developmental Psychology, 18,* 736–743.

Worthington, E. L. (1989). Religious faith across the life span: Implications for counseling and research. *Counseling Psychologist, 17,* 555–612.

Wozniak, R. (2004). An introduction to scientific research. In L. Nadelman (Ed.), *Research manual in child development* (2nd Ed.). Mahwah, NJ: Erlbaum.

Wright, M. R. (1989). Body image satisfaction in adolescent girls and boys. *Journal of Youth and Adolescence, 18,* 71–84.

Wrosch, C., Heckhausen, J., & Lachman, M. E. (2000). Primary and secondary control strategies for managing health and financial stress across adulthood. *Psychology and Aging, 15,* 387–399.

Yamagishi, T., & Yamagishi, M. (1994). Trust and commitment in the United States and Japan. *Motivation and Emotion, 18,* 129–166.

Yang, J., McCrae, R. R., & Costa, P. T. (1998). Adult age differences in personality traits in the United States and the People's Republic of China. *Journal of Gerontology: Psychological Sciences, 53B,* P375–P383.

Yang, S., & Sternberg, R. J. (1997). Taiwanese Chinese people's conceptions of intelligence. *Intelligence, 25,* 21–36.

Yanovski, J. A., Rose, S. R., Municchi, G., Pescovitz, O. H., Hill, S. C., Cassorla, F. G., & Cutler, G. B. (2003). Treatment with a luteinizing hormone-releasing hormone agonist in adolescents with short stature. *New England Journal of Medicine, 348,* 908–917.

Yates, M. (1995, March). *Community service and political-moral discussions among Black urban adolescents.* Paper presented at the meeting of the Society for Research in Child Development, Indianapolis.

Yeats, D. E., Folts, W. E., & Knapp, J. (1999). Older workers' adaptation to a changing workplace: Employment issues for the 21st century. *Educational Gerontology, 25,* 331–347.

Yekin, Y. (2002). Do environmental and hereditary factors affect the psychophysiology and left-right shift in left-handers? *International Journal of Neuroscience, 110,* 109–134.

Yin, Y., Buhrmester, D., & Hibbard, D. (1996, March). *Are there developmental changes in the influence of relationships with parents and friends on adjustment during early adolescence?* Paper presented at the meeting of the Society for Research on Adolescence, Boston.

Young, D. (2001). The nature and management of pain: What is the evidence? *Birth, 28,* 149–151.

Young, K. T. (1990). American conceptions of infant development from 1955 to 1984: What the experts are telling parents. *Child Development, 61,* 17–28.

Young, S. K., & Shahinfar, A. (1995, March). *The contributions of maternal sensitivity and child temperament to attachment status at 14 months.* Paper presented at the meeting of the Society for Research in Child Development, Indianapolis.

Youniss, J., McLellan, J. A., & Yates, M. (1999). Religion, community service, and identity in American youth. *Journal of Adolescence, 22,* 243–253.

Youniss, J., Silbereisen, R., Christmas-Best, V., Bales, S., Diversi, M., & McLaughlin, M. (2003). Civic and community engagement of adolescents in the 21st century. In R. Larson, B. Brown, & J. Mortimer (Eds.), *Adolescents' preparation for the future: Perils and promise.* Malden, MA: Blackwell.

Youniss, J., Silbereisen, R., Christmas-Best, V., Bales, S., Diversi, M., & McLaughlin, M. (2003). Civic and community engagement of adolescents in the 21st century. In R. Larson, B. Brown, & J. Mortimer (Eds.), *Adolescents' preparation for the future: Perils and promises.* Malden, MA: Blackwell.

Yu, B. P., Lim, B. O., & Sugano, M. (2002). Dietary restriction downregulates free radical and lipid peroxide production: Plausible mechanism for elongation of life span. *Journal of Nutritional Science, and Vitaminology, 48,* 257–284.

Yu, C. W., Sung, R. Y., So, R., Lam, K., Nelson, F. A., Li, A. M., Yuanb, Y., & Lam, P. K. (2002). Energy expenditure and physical activity of obese children: Cross-sectional study. *Hong Kong Medical Journal, 8,* 313–317.

Yu, V. Y. (2000). Developmental outcome of extremely preterm infants. *American Journal of Perinatology, 17,* 57–61.

Yussen, S. R. (1997). Characteristics of moral dilemmas written by adolescents. *Developmental Psychology, 13,* 162–163.

Zajonc, R. B. (2001). The family dynamics of intellectual development. *American Psychologist. 56,* 523–524.

Zarit, S. H., & Downs, M. G. (1999, Fall). State of the art for practice in dementia: Introduction. *Generations,* pp. 6–8.

Zarit, S. H., & Knight, B. G. (Eds.), (1996). *A guide to psychotherapy and aging.* Washington, DC: American Psychological Association.

Zarof, C. M., Knutelska, M., & Frumkes, T. E. (2003). Variation in stereoacuity: Normative description, fixation disparity, and the roles of aging and gender. *Investigative Ophthalmology and Vision Science, 44,* 891–900.

Zaslow, M. (2004). Childcare for low-income families: Problems and promises. In A. C. Crouter & A. Booth (Eds.), *Work-family challenges for low-income families and their children.* Mahwah, NJ: Erlbaum.

Zeskind, P. S., Klein, L., Marshall, T. R. (1992). Adults' perceptions of experimental modifications of durations and expiratory sounds in infant crying. *Developmental Psychology, 28,* 1153–1162.

Zhou, Q., Eisenberg, N., Losoya, S. H., Fabes, R. A., Reiser, M., Gutherie, I. K., Murphy, B. C., Cumberland, A. J., & Shepard, S. A. (2002). The relations of parental warmth and expressiveness to children's empathy-related responding and social functioning: A longitudinal study. *Child Development, 73,* 893–915.

Zielinksi, D. S., Campa, M. I., Eckenrode, J. J. (2003, April). *Child maltreatment and the early onset of problem behaviors: A follow-up at 19 years.* Paper presented at the meeting of the Society for Research in Child Development, Tampa.

Zigler, E., & Styfco, S. J. (1994). Head Start: Criticisms in a constructive context. *American Psychologist, 49,* 127–132.

Zimmer-Gembeck, M. J., & Collins, A. W. (2003). Autonomy development during adolescence. In G. Adams & M. Berzonsky (Eds.), *Blackwell handbook of adolescence.* Malden, MA: Blackwell.

Zimmerman, B. J. (2000). Attaining self-regulation: A social cognitive perspective. In M. Boekaerts, P. Pintrich, & M. Zeidner (Eds.), *Self-regulation: Theory, research, and application.* Orlando, FL: Academic Press.

Zimmerman, B. J. (2001). Developing self-fulfilling cycles of academic regulation: An analyis of exemplary instructional models. In D. H. Schunk & B. J. Zimmerman (Eds.), *Self-regulated learning and academic achievement.* Mahwah, NJ: Erlbaum.

Zimmerman, B. J., Bonner, S., & Kovach, R. (1996). *Developing self-regulated learners.* Washington, DC: American Psychological Association.

Zimmerman, B. J., & Schunk, D. H. (2004). Self-regulating intellectual processes and outcomes. In D. Y. Dai & R. J. Sternberg (Eds.), *Motivation, emotion, and cognition.* Mahwah, NJ: Erlbaum.

Zimmerman, R. S., Khoury, E., Vega, W. A., Gil, A. G., & Warheit, G. J. (1995). Teacher and student perceptions of behavior problems among a sample of African American, Hispanic, and non-Hispanic White students. *American Journal of Community Psychology, 23,* 181–197.

Zitnik, G., & Martin, G. M. (2002). Age-related decline in neurogenesis: Old cells or new environment? *Journal of Neuroscience Research, 70,* 258–263.

Zoppi, M. A., Ibba, R. M., Putzolu, M., Floris, M., & Monni, K. G. (2001). Nuchal translucency and the acceptance of invasive prenatal chromosomal diagnosis in women aged 35 and older. *Obstetrics and Gynecology, 97,* 916–920.

Zucker, A. N., Ostrove, J. M., & Stewart, A. J. (2002). College educated women's personality development in adulthood: Perceptions and age differences. *Psychology and Aging, 17,* 236–244.

Zukow-Goldring, P. (2002). Sibling caregiving, In M. H. Bornstein (Ed.), *Handbook of parenting* (2nd ed., Vol. 3). Mahwah, NJ: Erlbaum.

Zunzunequi, M., Alvarado, B. E., Del Ser, T., & Otero, A. (2003). Social networks, social integration, and social engagement determine cognitive decline in community-dwelling Spanish older adults. *Journal of Gerontology Series B: Psychological and Social Sciences, 58,* S93–S100.

Zvara, A., Hackler, L., Nagy, Z. B., Micsik, T., & Puskas, L. S. (2003). New molecular methods for classification, diagnosis, and therapy prediction of hematological malignancies. *Pathology and Oncology Research, 8,* 231–240.

Credits

Line Art and Text

Chapter 1

Figure 1.1 From John Santrock, *Psychology* 7th ed. Copyright © 2003 by The McGraw-Hill Companies. Reproduced with permission of The McGraw-Hill Companies. **Figure 1.2** Source: U.S. Census Data; Social Security Administration, *The Statistical History of the United States,* 1976. **Figure 1.3** From John Santrock, *Life-Span Development* 8th ed. Copyright © 2002 by The McGraw-Hill Companies. Reproduced with permission of The McGraw-Hill Companies. **Figure 1.4** From John Santrock, *Life-Span Development* 8th ed. Copyright © 2002 by The McGraw-Hill Companies. Reproduced with permission of The McGraw-Hill Companies. **Figure 1.5** From Robert Inglehart in *Cultures Shift in Advanced Industrial Society.* Copyright © 1990 by Princeton University Press. Reprinted by permission of Princeton University Press. **Figure 1.6** From John Santrock, *Life-Span Development* 8th ed. Copyright © 2002 by The McGraw-Hill Companies. Reproduced with permission of The McGraw-Hill Companies. **Figure 1.7** From John Santrock, *Life-Span Development* 8th ed. Copyright © 2002 by The McGraw-Hill Companies. Reproduced with permission of The McGraw-Hill Companies. **Figure 1.8** From John Santrock, *Child Development* 9th ed. Copyright © 2001 by The McGraw-Hill Companies. Reproduced with permission of The McGraw-Hill Companies. **Figure 1.9** From John Santrock, *Child Development* 9th ed. Copyright © 2001 by The McGraw-Hill Companies. Reproduced with permission of The McGraw-Hill Companies. **Figure 1.10** From John Santrock, *Children* 5th ed. Copyright © 1997 by The McGraw-Hill Companies. Reproduced with permission of The McGraw-Hill Companies. **Figure 1.11** From Kopp/Krakow, *The Child,* 1982, p. 648. Reprinted by permission of Pearson Education, Inc. **Figure 1.14** From Crowley, et al., 2001, "Parents Explain More to Boys Than Girls During Shared Scientific Thinking," *Psychological Science,* 12, 258-261. Reprinted by permission of Blackwell Publishing Ltd. **Figure 1.15** From John Santrock, *Children* 5th ed. Copyright © 1997 by The McGraw-Hill Companies. Reproduced with permission of The McGraw-Hill Companies. **Figure 1.16** From John Santrock, *Child Development* 9th ed. Copyright ©2001 by The McGraw-Hill Companies. Reproduced with permission of The McGraw-Hill Companies.

Chapter 2

Figure 2.1 After Bonner, J.T. (1988). *The Evolution of Culture in Animals.* Princeton, NJ: Princeton University Press. **Figure 2.2** With permission, from Baltes, P. B., Staudinger, U. M., & Lindenberger, U. (1999). Lifespan psychology, *Annual Review of Psychology,* Volume 50 ©1999 by Annual Reviews www.AnnualReviews.org. Also reprinted by permission of Dr. Paul B. Baltes. **Figure 2.3** From John Santrock, *Child Development* 9th ed. Copyright © 2001 by The McGraw-Hill Companies. Reproduced with permission of The McGraw-Hill Companies. **Figure 2.5** From John Santrock, *Psychology* 7th ed. Copyright © 2003 by The McGraw-Hill Companies. Reproduced with permission of The McGraw-Hill Companies. **Figure 2.6** From John Santrock, *Children* 5th ed. Copyright © 1997 by The McGraw-Hill Companies. Reproduced with permission of The McGraw-Hill Companies. **Figure 2.8** From John Santrock, *Life-Span Development* 8th ed. Copyright © 2002 by The McGraw-Hill Companies. Reproduced with permission of The McGraw-Hill Companies. **Figure 2.9** From John Santrock, *Life-Span Development* 8th ed. Copyright © 2002 by The McGraw-Hill Companies. Reproduced with permission of The McGraw-Hill Companies. **Figure 2.10** From NOVA, 2001 at www.pbs.org/wgbh/nova/genome/survey.html. Copyright ©2002 WGBH/Boston. Used with permission. **Figure 2.11** From John Santrock, *Children* 7th ed. Copyright © 2002 by The McGraw-Hill Companies. Reproduced with permission of The McGraw-Hill Companies. **Figure 2.13** From John Santrock, *Children* 5th ed. Copyright ©1997 by The McGraw-Hill Companies. Reproduced with permission of The McGraw-Hill Companies. **Figure 2.14** (text) From John Santrock, *Children* 5th ed. Copyright © 1997 by The McGraw-Hill Companies. Reproduced with permission of The McGraw-Hill Companies. **Figure 2.16** From John Santrock, *Life-Span Development* 9th ed. Copyright © 2003 by The McGraw-Hill Companies. Reproduced with permission of The McGraw-Hill Companies. **Figure 2.17** From T. Fields, S. M. Schanberg, F. Scafidi, C. R. Bauer, N. Vega-Lahr, R. Garcia, J. Nystrom, & C. M. Kuhn, "Tactile/Kinesthetic Stimulation Effects on Preterm Neonates," *Pediatrics,* 77, p. 657, Figure 1. Reproduced with permission from *Pediatrics.* Copyright © 1986 American Academy of Pediatrics.

Chapter 3

Figure 2.18 From Virginia A. Apgar, 1975, "A Proposal for a New Method of Evaluation of a Newborn Infant," in *Anesthesia and Analgesia,* Vol. 32, pp. 260–267. Reprinted by permission. **Figure 3.1** From John Santrock, *Children* 7th ed. Copyright © 2003 by The McGraw-Hill Companies. Reproduced with permission of The McGraw-Hill Companies. **Figure 3.2** From John Santrock, *Adolescence* 8th ed. Copyright © 2001 by The McGraw-Hill Companies. Reproduced with permission of The McGraw-Hill Companies. **Figure 3.3** From John Santrock, *Adolescence* 8th ed. Copyright © 2001 by The McGraw-Hill Companies. Reproduced with permission of The McGraw-Hill Companies. **Figure 3.4** From "Earlier Maturation in Man" by J. M. Tanner, *Scientific American,* January 1968. Copyright © 1968 by Scientific American, Inc. Used with permission. **Figure 3.5** Adapted from *Newsweek,* Health for Life, special section, Fall/Winter 2001. Copyright © 2001 Newsweek, Inc. All rights reserved. Reprinted by permission. **Figure 3.6** Adapted from *Newsweek,* Health for Life, special section, Fall/Winter 2001. Copyright © 2001 Newsweek, Inc. All rights reserved. Reprinted by permission. **Figure 3.8** From John Santrock, *Children* 7th ed. Copyright © 2003 by The McGraw-Hill Companies. Reproduced with permission of The McGraw-Hill Companies. **Figure 3.9** From John Santrock, *Child Development* 9th ed. Copyright © 2001 by The McGraw-Hill Companies. Reproduced with permission of The McGraw-Hill Companies. **Figure 3.10** From John Santrock, *Children* 7th ed. Copyright © 2003 by The McGraw-Hill Companies. Reproduced with permission of The McGraw-Hill Companies. **Figure 3.13** Reprinted by permission of the publisher from *The Postnatal Development of the Human Cerebral Cortex,* Vol. 1–VIII, by Jesse LeRoy Concl. Cambridge, MA: Harvard University Press, Copyright © 1939, 1975 by the President and Fellows of Harvard College. **Figure 3.14** From John Santrock, *Psychology* 7th ed. Copyright © 2003 by The McGraw-Hill Companies. Reproduced with permission of The McGraw-Hill Companies. **Figure 3.15** From *Human Biology and Ecology,* 2nd ed., by Albert Damon. Copyright © 1977 by W.W. Norton & Company, Inc. Used by permission of W.W. Norton & Company, Inc. **Figure 3.16** From John Santrock, *Life-Span Development* 9th ed. Copyright © 2003 by The McGraw-Hill Companies. Reproduced with permission of The McGraw-Hill Companies. **Figure 3.17** From John Santrock, *Life-Span Development* 9th ed. Copyright ©2003 by The McGraw-Hill Companies. Reproduced with permission of The McGraw-Hill Companies. **Figure 3.19** Reprinted with permission from H. P. Roffwarg, J. N. Muzio, and W. C. Dement, "Ontogenetic Development of Human Dream-Sleep-Cycle," *Science,* 152, 604–609. Copyright ©1966 American Association for the Advancement of Science. **Figure 3.20** From *The Psychology of Death, Dying and Bereavement* by Richard Schultz. Copyright © 1978 by The McGraw-Hill Companies.

Reproduced with the permission of The McGraw-Hill Companies. **Figure 3.21** From *The Okinawa Program* by Bradley J. Willcox, D. Craig Willcox and Makoto Suzuki. Copyright © 2001 by Bradley J. Willcox, D. Craig Willcox and Makoto Suzuki. Used by permission of Clarkson Potter Publishers, a division of Random House, Inc.

Chapter 4

Figure 4.4 Source: U.S. Dept. of Health and Human Services (1999). *Health United States: 1999* with Health and Aging Chartbook. Hyattsville, MD: National Center for Health Statistics (PHS No. 99–1232). **Figure 4.5** From John Santrock, *Life-Span Development* 9th ed. Copyright © 2003 by The McGraw-Hill Companies. Reproduced with permission of The McGraw-Hill Companies. **Figure 4.11** (bar graph) Reprinted from *Journal of Psychosomatic Research,* Vol. 29, S. C. Kobasa, S. R. Maddi, M. C. Pucette, and M. Zola, pp. 525–533. Copyright © 1986 Elsevier Science. With permission from Elsevier Science. **Figure 4.12** Source: Johnson, L. D., O'Malley, P. M., & Bachman, J. G., 2001, "The Monitoring of the Future: National Results on Adolescent Drug Use," Washington, DC: National Institute on Drug Abuse. **Figure 4.13** From John Santrock, *Psychology* 7th ed. Copyright © 2003 by The McGraw-Hill Companies. Reproduced with permission of The McGraw-Hill Companies. **Figure 4.15** Source: National Center for Health Statistics, *Health United States: 2002,* Table 67.

Chapter 5

Figure 5.1 From John Santrock, *Children* 5th ed. Copyright © 1997 by The McGraw-Hill Companies. Reproduced with permission of The McGraw-Hill Companies. **Figure 5.3** From Santrock, *Child Development* 9th ed. Copyright © 2001 by The McGraw-Hill Companies. Reproduced with permission of The McGraw-Hill Companies. **Figure 5.4** From John Santrock, *Life-Span Development* 9th ed. Copyright © 2003 by The McGraw-Hill Companies. Reproduced with permission of The McGraw-Hill Companies. **Figure 5.5** Adapted from Alexander Semenoick, in R. L. Frantz, "The Origin of Form Perception," *Scientific American,* 1961. **Figure 5.6** From A. Slater, V. Morison, and M. Somers, "Orientation Discrimination and Cortical Functions in the Human Newborn" in *Perception,* Vol. 17, 1988, pp. 597–602, Figure 1 and Table 1. Reprinted by permission of Pion, Ltd. **Figure 5.8** From John Santrock, *Child Development* 9th ed. Copyright © 2001 by The McGraw-Hill Companies. Reproduced with permission of The McGraw-Hill Companies. **Figure 5.11** After graph by Dr. John Brabyn, The Smith-Kettlewell Eye Research Institute. **Figure 5.13** Vision and hearing decline in old age and late old age. Credit: From John Santrock, *Life-Span Development* 8th ed. Copyright © 2002 by The McGraw-Hill Companies. Reproduced with permission of The McGraw-Hill Companies.

Chapter 6

Figure 6.2 From John Santrock, *Child Development* 9th ed. Copyright © 2001 by The McGraw-

Hill Companies. Reproduced with permission of The McGraw-Hill Companies. **Figure 6.4** From Baillargeon, R., and DeVoe, J., "Object permanence in young children: Further evidence" in *Child Development,* 62, 1227–1246. Copyright © 1991 Society for Research in Child Development. Reprinted with permission. **Figure 6.5** From John Santrock, *Life-Span Development* 8th ed. Copyright © 2002 by The McGraw-Hill Companies. Reproduced with permission of The McGraw-Hill Companies. **Figure 6.7** From John Santrock, *Life-Span Development* 8th ed. Copyright © 2002 by The McGraw-Hill Companies. Reproduced with permission of The McGraw-Hill Companies. **Figure 6.8** From John Santrock, *Life-Span Development* 8th ed. Copyright © 2002 by The McGraw-Hill Companies. Reproduced with permission of The McGraw-Hill Companies. **Figure 6.9** From John Santrock, *Life-Span Development* 8th ed. Copyright © 2002 by The McGraw-Hill Companies. Reproduced with permission of The McGraw-Hill Companies. **Figure 6.10** From John Santrock, *Life-Span Development* 8th ed. Copyright © 2002 by The McGraw-Hill Companies. Reproduced with permission of The McGraw-Hill Companies.

Chapter 7

Figure 7.1 Adapted from *Human Biology and Ecology,* 2nd ed., by Albert Damon. Copyright © 1977 by W.W. Norton & Company, Inc. Used by permission of W.W. Norton & Company, Inc. **Figure 7.3** From John Santrock, *Psychology* 7th ed. Copyright © 2003 by The McGraw-Hill Companies. Reproduced with permission of The McGraw-Hill Companies. **Figure 7.4** From John Santrock, *Psychology* 7th ed. Copyright © 2003 by The McGraw-Hill Companies. Reproduced with permission of The McGraw-Hill Companies. **Figure 7.5** From J. C. Bartlett, *Remembering,* 1932. Reprinted with permission of Cambridge University Press. **Figure 7.8** From John Santrock, *Psychology* 7th ed. Copyright © 2003 by The McGraw-Hill Companies. Reproduced with permission of The McGraw-Hill Companies. **Figure 7.9** From John Santrock, *Child Development* 10th ed. Copyright © 2003 by The McGraw-Hill Companies. Reproduced with permission of The McGraw-Hill Companies. **Figure 7.10** From M. T. H. Chi, "Knowledge Structures and Memory Development" in *Children's Thinking: What Develops?,* R. S. Siegler (ed.). Copyright © 1978 Lawrence Erlbaum Associates. Reprinted by permission. **Figure 7.12** From John Santrock, *Psychology* 7th ed. Copyright © 2003 by The McGraw-Hill Companies. Reproduced with permission of The McGraw-Hill Companies. **Figure 7.13** From John Santrock, *Life-Span Development* 9th ed. Copyright © 2003 by The McGraw-Hill Companies. Reproduced with permission of The McGraw-Hill Companies. **Figure 7.14** After Hasher, L., Chung, C., May, C. P., & Foong, N. (2001). Age, time of testing, and proactive interference. *Canadian Journal of Experimental Psychology,* 56, 200–207. **Figure 7.15** From John Santrock, *Child Development* 10th ed. Copyright © 2003 by The

McGraw-Hill Companies. Reproduced with permission of The McGraw-Hill Companies. **Figure 7.16** From John Santrock, *Child Development* 10th ed. Copyright © 2003 by The McGraw-Hill Companies. Reproduced with permission of The McGraw-Hill Companies. **Figure 7.17** After Wellman, Cross & Watson, "Meta-Analysis of Theory of Mind Development: The Truth About False Belief" in *Child Development,* 72, 655–684. ©2001 Society for Research in Child Development. Reprinted with permission.

Chapter 8

Figure 8.1 From John Santrock, *Children* 5th ed. Copyright © 1997 by The McGraw-Hill Companies. Reproduced with permission of The McGraw-Hill Companies. **Figure 8.3** From John Santrock, *Psychology* 7th ed. Copyright © 2003 by The McGraw-Hill Companies. Reproduced with permission of The McGraw-Hill Companies. **Figure 8.4** From "Correlation between intelligence test scores and twin status" *Handbook of Intelligence,* Robert J. Sternberg (ed.). Reprinted with the permission of Cambridge University Press. **Figure 8.5** "The Increase in IQ Scores from 1932 to 1997" by Dr. Ulric Neisser. Reprinted by permission. **Figure 8.6** From Raven's *Standard Progressive Matrices,* Item A5. Reprinted by permission of J. C. Raven Ltd. **Figure 8.7** From John Santrock, *Life-Span Development* 8th ed. Copyright © 2002 by The McGraw-Hill Companies. Reproduced with permission of The McGraw-Hill Companies. **Figure 8.8** From K. Schaie, 1994, "The Life Course of Adult Intellectual Abilities," *American Psychologist,* 49, 304–313. **Figure 8.9** From John Santrock, *Life-Span Development* 8th ed. Copyright © 2002 by The McGraw-Hill Companies. Reproduced with permission of The McGraw-Hill Companies. **Figure 8.10** From John Santrock, *Educational Psychology* 1st ed. Copyright © 2001 by The McGraw-Hill Companies. Reproduced with permission of The McGraw-Hill Companies. **Figure 8.11** From "Mental Retardation Based on Levels of Support". Copyright © 1994 by the American Association for Mental Retardation. All rights reserved. Reprinted by permission.

Chapter 9

Figure 9.3 From John Santrock, *Children* 7th ed. Copyright © 2002 by The McGraw-Hill Companies. Reproduced with permission of The McGraw-Hill Companies. **Figure 9.4** From John Santrock, *Children* 7th ed. Copyright © 2002 by The McGraw-Hill Companies. Reproduced with permission of The McGraw-Hill Companies. **Figure 9.5** From Jean Berko, 1958, "The Child's Learning of English Morphology" in *Word,* Vol. 14, p. 154. Reprinted by permission of the author. **Figure 9.6** From John Santrock, *Children* 7th ed. Copyright © 2002 by The McGraw-Hill Companies. Reproduced with permission of The McGraw-Hill Companies. **Figure 9.7** After Hart & Risley, 1995, *Meaningful Differences.* Baltimore: Paul H. Brookes Publishing Co. Reprinted by permission of Paul H. Brookes Publishing Co. and Betty Hart. **Figure 9.8** After Chall, J. S.

(1979), "The Great Debate: Ten years later, with a modest proposal for reading stages" in L. B. Resnick & P. A. Weaver (Eds.) *Theory and Practice of Early Reading*, Vol. 1, pp. 29–55. Reprinted by permission of Lawrence Erlbaum Associates, Inc. **Figure 9.9** Source: After National Assessment of Educational Progress (2000). **(art)** From Jean Berko Gleason, *The Development of Language*, 3rd ed., Figure 10.11, p. 336. Published by Allyn & Bacon, Boston, MA. Copyright © 1993 by Pearson Education. Reprinted by permission of the publisher. **Figure 9.8** After J. S. Chall, "The Great Debate: Ten years later, with a modest proposal for reading stages" in *Theory and Practice of Early Reading*, Vol 1, pp. 29–55, L. B. Resnick & P. A. Weaver (eds.). Copyright © 1979 Lawrence Erlbaum Associates. Reprinted by permission. **Figure 9.10** From John Santrock, *Child Development* 10th ed. Copyright © 2003 by The McGraw-Hill Companies. Reproduced with permission of The McGraw-Hill Companies. **Figure 9.11** From *Brain, Mind, and Behavior* by Floyd E. Bloom and Arlyne Lazerson. Copyright © 1985, 1988 by Educational Broadcasting Corporation. Used with permission of W. H. Freeman and Company.

Chapter 10

Figure 10.1 Adapted from J. Lewis, "Early emotional development" in *Infant Development*, A. Slater & M. Lewis (eds.). Copyright © 2002 by Oxford University Press Inc. Used by permission of Oxford University Press, Inc. **Figure 10.3** Reprinted by permission of the publisher from *Infancy: Its Place in Human Development* by Jerome Kaga, R. B. Kearsley, and P. R. Zelazo, p. 107. Cambridge, MA: Harvard University Press, Copyright ©1978 by the President and Fellows of Harvard College. **Figure 10.5** From John Santrock, *Children* 7th ed. Copyright © 2002 by The McGraw-Hill Companies. Reproduced with permission of The McGraw-Hill Companies. **Figure 10.7** From D. Mroczek and C. M. Kolarz, "The Effect of Age in Positive and Negative Affect" in *Journal of Personality and Social Psychology*, Vol. 75, Figure 1, p. 1339 and Figure 2, p. 1340. Copyright © 1998 by the American Psychological Association. Adapted with permission. **Figure 10.8** From L. Carstensen, et al., "The Social Context of Emotion" in the *Annual Review of Geriatrics and Gerontology* by Schaie/Lawton (eds.), 1997, Vol. 17, p. 331. Used by permission of Springer Publishing Company, New York 10012. **Figure 10.9** From T. D Wachs, "Fit, context and the transition between temperament and personality" in *The Developing Structure of Personality from Infancy to Adulthood*, pp. 209–222, C. Haverson, G. Kohnstamm, & R. Martin (eds.). Copyright © 1994 Lawrence Erlbaum Associates. Reprinted by permission. **Figure 10.10** From John Santrock, *Psychology* 7th ed. Copyright © 2003 by The McGraw-Hill Companies. Reproduced with permission of The McGraw-Hill Companies. **Figure 10.11** From M. D. S. Ainsworth and S. M. Bell, "Attachment, exploration, and separation: Illustrated by the behavior of one-year-olds in a strange situation" in *Child Development*, Vol. 41(1), pp. 49–67. Copyright © 1971 Society for Research in Child Development. Reprinted with permission. **Figure 10.12** From M. H. van Ijzendoorn and P. M. Kroonenberg, "Cross-Cultural patterns of attachment: A meta-analysis of the strange situation" in *Child Development*, 59, 147–156. Copyright © 1988 Society for Research in Child Development. Reprinted with permission. **Figure 10.13** From "Romantic development: Does age at which romantic involvement starts matter?" by Duane Buhrmester, April 2001. Paper presented at the meeting of the Society for Research in Child Development, Minneapolis, MN. Reprinted by permission of the author. **Figure 10.14** From "Age and Sex Differences in Satisfying Relationships across the Adult Life Span," from M. N. Reedy, J. E. Birren & K. W. Schaie, 1981, *Human Development*, 24, 52–66. Reprinted by permission of S. Karger AG, Basel, Switzerland. **Figure 10.15** From *The Triangle of Love* by Robert J. Sternberg. Copyright © 1988 by Basic Books Inc. Reprinted by permission of Basic Books, a division of HarperCollins Publishers, Inc.

Chapter 11

Figure 11.1 (graph only) The development of self-recognition in infancy. From John Santrock, *Life-Span Development* 4th ed. Copyright © 1999 by The McGraw-Hill Companies. Reproduced with permission of The McGraw-Hill Companies. **Figure 11.2** From Thomas E. Lickona (ed.), *Moral Development and Behavior*. Copyright © 1976. Used by permission of Thomas E. Lickona. **Figure 11.3** From Richard W. Robins, et al., "Global Self-Esteem Across the Life Span" in *Psychology and Aging*, 17, Figure 1, p. 428. Copyright © 2002 by the American Psychological Association. Adapted with permission. **Figure 11.4** From John Santrock, *Educational Psychology* 1st ed. Copyright © 2001 by The McGraw-Hill Companies. Reproduced with permission of The McGraw-Hill Companies. **Figure 11.5** From John Santrock, *Life-Span Development* 9th ed. Copyright © 2003 by The McGraw-Hill Companies. Reproduced with permission of The McGraw-Hill Companies. **Figure 11.6** From R. Schultz and J. Heckhausen, "A Life Span Model of Successful Aging" in *American Psychologist*, Vol. 51, Figure 2, p. 709. Copyright © 1996 by the American Psychological Association. Adapted with permission. **Figure 11.7** From Stewart, Osgrove, and Helson, "Middle aging in women: Patterns of personality change from the 30s to the 50s", Figure 3, in *Journal of Adult Development*, Vol. 8, pp. 23–37. Copyright © 2002 Kluwer Academic Publishers. Reprinted with permission. **Figure 11.8** From Stewart, Osgrove, and Helson, 2002, "Middle aging in women: Patterns of personality change from the 30s to the 50s", Figure 3, in *Journal of Adult Development*, Vol. 8, pp. 23–37. Reprinted with permission from Kluwer Academic Publishers. **Figure 11.9** From John Santrock, *Life-Span Development* 8th ed. Copyright © 2002 by The McGraw-Hill Companies. Reproduced with permission of The McGraw-Hill Companies. **Figure 11.10** From John Santrock, *Psychology* 6th ed. Copyright © 2000 by The McGraw-Hill Companies. Reproduced with permission of The McGraw-Hill Companies. **Figure 11.11** From John Santrock, *Life-Span Development* 9th ed. Copyright © 2003 by The McGraw-Hill Companies. Reproduced with permission of The McGraw-Hill Companies. **Figure 11.12** From John Santrock, *Life-Span Development* 9th ed. Copyright © 2003 by The McGraw-Hill Companies. Reproduced with permission of The McGraw-Hill Companies. **Figure 11.13** From Nansel, et al., 2001, "Bullying Behaviors Among U.S. Youth," *Journal of the American Medical Association*, Vol. 285, pp. 2094–2100. Reprinted by permission of American Medical Association. All rights reserved. **Figure 11.14** From John Santrock, *Life-Span Development* 9th ed. Copyright © 2003 by The McGraw-Hill Companies. Reproduced with permission of The McGraw-Hill Companies. **Figure 11.15** From Stewart, Osgrove, and Helson, "Middle aging in women: Patterns of personality change from the 30s to the 50s", Figure 3, in *Journal of Adult Development*, Vol. 8, pp. 23–37. Copyright © 2002 Kluwer Academic Publishers. Reprinted with permission. **Figure 11.16** From Stewart, Osgrove, and Helson, 2002, "Middle aging in women: Patterns of personality change from the 30s to the 50s", Figure 3, in *Journal of Adult Development*, Vol. 8, pp. 23–37. Copyright © 2002 Kluwer Academic Publishers. Reprinted with permission. **Figure 11.17** From Costa & McCrae in *Personality In Adulthood*, Figure 4, p. 91. Copyright ©2003 Guilford Publications, Inc. Reprinted by permission. **Figure 11.18** From John Santrock, *Life-Span Development* 9th ed. Copyright © 2003 by The McGraw-Hill Companies. Reproduced with permission of The McGraw-Hill Companies.

Chapter 12

Figure 12.1 From John Santrock, *Psychology* 7th ed. Copyright © 2003 by The McGraw-Hill Companies. Reproduced with permission of The McGraw-Hill Companies. **Figure 12.2** From John Santrock, *Psychology* 7th ed. Copyright © 2003 by The McGraw-Hill Companies. Reproduced with permission of The McGraw-Hill Companies. **Figure 12.4** From John Santrock, *Children* 7th ed. Copyright © 2002 by The McGraw-Hill Companies. Reproduced with permission of The McGraw-Hill Companies. **Figure 12.6** From John Santrock, *Psychology* 7th ed. Copyright © 2003 by The McGraw-Hill Companies. Reproduced with permission of The McGraw-Hill Companies. **Figure 12.8** From John Santrock, *Adolescence* 8th ed. Copyright © 2001 by The McGraw-Hill Companies. Reproduced with permission of The McGraw-Hill Companies. **Figure 12.9** Reproduced with the permission of The Alan Guttmacher Institute from J. E. Darroch et. al., *Teenage Sexual and Reproductive Behavior in Developed Countries: Can Progress Be Made?* Occasional Report, 2000, New York: The Alan Guttmacher Institute, No. 13. **Figure 12.10** From *Sex in America* by Robert Michael, et al. Copyright © by CSG Enterprises,

Inc., Edward O. Laumann, Robert Michael, and Gina Kolata. By permission of Little, Brown and Company, (Inc.).

Chapter 13

Figure 13.1 From John Santrock, *Psychology* 7th ed. Copyright © 2003 by The McGraw-Hill Companies. Reproduced with permission of The McGraw-Hill Companies. **Figure 13.2** From L. Kohlberg, "Stage and Sequence" in *Handbook of Socialization Theory and Research,* D. Goslin (ed.). Copyright ©1969 Rand McNally GBS. Reprinted with permission. **Figure 13.3** From Colby, et al., "A Longtudinal Study of Moral Judgment," *Monographs of the Society for Research in Child Development,* Serial No. 201. ©1983 Society for Research in Child Development. Reprinted with permission. **Figure 13.4** From John Santrock, *Adolescence* 9th ed. Copyright © 2002 by The McGraw-Hill Companies. Reproduced with permission of The McGraw-Hill Companies. **Figure 13.5** From John Santrock, *Adolescence* 9th ed. Copyright © 2002 by The McGraw-Hill Companies. Reproduced with permission of The McGraw-Hill Companies. **Figure 13.6** From John Santrock, *Adolescence* 8th ed. Copyright © 2001 by The McGraw-Hill Companies. Reproduced with permission of The McGraw-Hill Companies. **Figure 13.7** From John Santrock, *Adolescence* 8th ed. Copyright © 2001 by The McGraw-Hill Companies. Reproduced with permission of The McGraw-Hill Companies. **Figure 13.8** From P. Wink and M. Dillon, "Spiritual development over the adult life course: Findings from a longitudinal study", *Journal of Adult Development,* 9, 79–84. Copyright © 2002 Kluwer Academic Publishers. Reprinted with permission.

Chapter 14

Figure 14.1 From *The Changing Family Life Cycle,* 2nd ed., Betty Carter & Monica McGoldrick (eds.). Published by Allyn & Bacon, Boston, MA. Copyright © 1989 by Pearson Education. Reprinted by permission of the publisher. **Figure 14.2** From John Santrock, *Child Development* 10th ed. Copyright ©2003 by The McGraw-Hill Companies. Reproduced with permission of The McGraw-Hill Companies. **Figure 14.3** Source: U.S. Bureau of the Census, 2000. **Figure 14.4** Source: U.S. Bureau of the Census, 2000. **Figure 14.5** Source: U.S. Bureau of the Census, 2000. **Figure 14.6** Source: National Center for Health Statistics, 2000. **Figure 14.7** (text) From John Santrock, *Life-Span Development* 9th ed. Copyright © 2003 by The McGraw-Hill Companies. Reproduced with permission of The McGraw-Hill Companies. **Figure 14.8** From K. Curran, J. DuCette, J. Eisenstein, and I. A. Hyman, August 2001, "Statistical analysis of the cross-cultural data: The third year," paper presented at the meeting of the American Psychological Association, San Francisco, CA. Reprinted by permission of the author.

Chapter 15

Figure 15.1 Adapted from *Newsweek,* Health for Life, special section, Fall/Winter 2001. Copyright © 2001 Newsweek, Inc. All rights reserved. Reprinted by permission. **Figure 15.2** From Nansel, et al., 2001, "Bullying Behaviors Among U.S. Youth," *Journal of the American Medical Association,* Vol. 285, pp. 2094–2100. Reprinted by permission of American Medical Association. All rights reserved. **Figure 15.3** After Maccoby & Jacklin "Gender segregation in childhood" in *Advances in Child Development and Behavior,* Vol. 20, H.W. Reese (ed.). Copyright © 1987 Academic Press. With permission from Elsevier Science Ltd. **Figure 15.4** After T. Berndt, "Developmental Changes in Conformity to Peers and Parents" in *Developmental Psychology,* 15, Figure 1, p. 611. Copyright © 1979 by the American Psychological Association. Adapted with permission. **Figure 15.5** Source: National Center for Health Statistics, 2000. **Figure 15.6** From John Santrock, *Life-Span Development* 9th ed. Copyright © 2003 by The McGraw-Hill Companies. Reproduced with permission of The McGraw-Hill Companies. **Figure 15.7** Adapted from R. W. Larson, Table 1, "How U.S. children and adolescents spent time," *Current Directions in Psychological Science,* 10, 160–164. Copyright © 2001 American Psychological Society. Reprinted with permission. **Figure 15.8** From *Individualism & Collectivism* by H. C. Triandis. Copyright © 1995 by Westview Press. Reprinted by permission of Westview Press, a member of Perseus Books, L.L.C. **Figure 15.9** Adapted from Trafimow, et al., "The effects of language and priming on the relative accessibility of the private self and the collective self" in *Journal of Cross-Cultural Psychology,* 28, 107–123. Copyright ©1991 by Sage Publications, Inc. Reprinted by permission of Sage Publications, Inc. **Figure 15.10** From John Santrock, *Adolescence* 8th ed. Copyright © 2001 by The McGraw-Hill Companies. Reproduced with permission of The McGraw-Hill Companies. **Figure 15.11** Source: After data presented by the U.S. Census Bureau (2002) *National Population Projects I. Summary Files.* Washington DC: U.S. Bureau of the Census. **Figure 15.12** From Bradley, et al., "Home Environments of Infants by Ethnicity and Poverty Status," The Home Environments of Children in the United States, Part I, *Child Development,* 72, 1844–1867. Copyright © Society for Research in Child Development. Reprinted with permission.

Chapter 16

Figure 16.1 From *Learner-Centered Psychological Principles: A Framework for School Redesign and Reform,* 1997. Copyright ©1997 by the American Psychological Association. Reprinted with permission. **Figure 16.2** From *Young Children,* Vol. 41, pp. 23–27, September 1986. Reprinted with permission from the National Association for the Education of Young Children. **Figure 16.3** From John Santrock, *Child Development* 10th ed. Copyright © 2003 by The McGraw-Hill Companies. Reproduced with permission of The McGraw-Hill Companies. **Figure 16.4** From John Santrock, *Educational Psychology* 1st ed. Copyright © 2001 by The McGraw-Hill Companies. Reproduced with permission of The McGraw-Hill Companies. **Figure 16.5** From D. Stipek, *Motivation to Learn* 4th ed., Table 5.3. Published by Allyn & Bacon, Boston, MA. Copyright © 2002 by Pearson Education. Reprinted by permission of the publisher. **Figure 16.6** Reprinted with permissions from Stevenson, Lee and Stigler, 1986, Figure 6, "Mathematics Achievement of Chinese, Japanese and American Children," *Science,* Vol. 231, pp. 693–699. Copyright © 1986 American Association for the Advancement of Science. **Figure 16.7** Reproduced by special permission of the publisher, Psychological Assessment Resources, Inc. from Making Vocational Choices, Third Edition. Copyright © 1973, 1985, 1992, 1997 by Psychological Assessment Resources, Inc. Reprinted with permission. **Figure 16.8** Reprinted from R. Barnett, "Work-Family Balance" in *Encyclopedia of Woman and Gender: Sex Similarities and Differences and the Impact of Society on Gender,* Judith Worell (ed.). Copyright © 2001 Elsevier Science. Reproduced by permission from Elsevier Science Ltd.

Photo Credits

Section Openers

1: © Chuck Savage/The Stock Market/CORBIS; **2:** © Chuck Savage/The Stock Market/CORBIS; **3:** © Paul Barton/The Stock Market/CORBIS; **4:** © Julian Hirshowitz/The Stock Market/CORBIS; **5:** © Ariel Skelley/The Stock Market/CORBIS; **6:** © Dennis Stock/Magnum Photos

Chapter 1

Opener: © Charles Gupton/Stone/Getty Images; **p. 7:** © National Associate for the Education of Young Children, Robert Maust/Photo Agora; **p. 8:** © Renato Rotola/Liaison Agency/Getty Images News Service; **p. 14** (left to right): Courtesy of Landrum Shettles; John Santrock; © Joe Sohm/The Image Works; © CORBIS website; © James L. Shaffer; © Vol. 155/CORBIS; © CORBIS website; © CORBIS website **p. 19:** © Bettmann/CORBIS; **p. 20:** © Ted Streshinsky/ Bettmann/CORBIS; **p. 22:** © Yves de Braine/Stock Photo; **p. 23:** A.R. Lauria/Dr. Michael Cole, Laboratory of Human Cognition, University of California, San Diego; **p. 25:** Courtesy of Stanford University News Service; **p. 26:** Photo by Nina Leen/Timepix/Getty Images News Service; **p. 28:** Courtesy of Urie Bronfenbrenner; **p. 29:** © Nancy Agostini; **p. 33:** © Richard T. Nowitz/Photo Researchers; **p. 35:** © Bettmann/CORBIS; **p. 39:** © McGraw-Hill Higher Education, John Thoeming, photographer

Chapter 2

Opener: Photo Lennart Nilsson/Albert Bonniers Forlag AB, *A Child is Born,* Dell Publishing Company; **2.4:** © Sundstroem/Gamma; **2.5 (left & right):** © Custom Medical Stock Photo; **p. 59:** © 1989 Joel Gordon Photography; **p. 60:** © Andrew Eccles/Janet Botaish Group; **p. 68:** © Viviane Moos; **2.14 (top, middle, bottom):** Photo Lennart Nilsson/Albert Bonniers Forlag AB., *A Child is Born,* Dell Publishing Company; **p. 70:** © Jacques Pavlovsky/Sygma/CORBIS; **p. 73 (top):** Streissguth A.P., Clarren, S.K., & Jones, K.L. "Natural History of the Fetal Alcohol Syndrome: A 10-year follow-up of eleven patients" in *The Lancet, 2,* 85-91; **p. 73 (bottom):** © John Chiasson/Liaison Agency/Getty Images News Service; **p. 74:** © R.I.A./Gamma; **p. 76:** © Betty Press/Woodfin Camp & Associates; **p. 77:** © Alon Reininger/Contract Press Images; **p. 78:** © Charles Gupton/Stock Boston; **p. 80:** © SIU/Peter Arnold, Inc.; **p. 81:** © Marjorie Shostak/Anthro-Photo; **p. 84:** © Charles Gupton/Stock Boston; **p. 85:** Courtesy of Dr. Tiffany Field; **p. 87:** © Stephen Marks, Inc./The Image Bank/Getty Images

Chapter 3

Opener: © Lori Adamski Peek/Stone; **p. 95:** © Bob Daemmrich/The Image Works; **p. 102 (left):** © Bettmann/CORBIS; **p. 102 (right):** © Matthew Mendelsohn/CORBIS; **3.7:** © A. Glauberman/Photo Researchers; **3.11ab:** Courtesy of Dr. Harry T. Chugani, Children's Hospital of Michigan; **3.12a:** © David Grubin Productions, Inc. Reprinted by permission; **3.12b:** Image courtesy of Dana Boatman, Ph.D., Department of Neurology, John Hopkins University, reprinted with permission from *The Secret Life of the Brain,* Joseph Henry Press; **p. 108:** © 1999 Kenneth Jarecke/Contact Press Images; **3.16:** Courtesy of Dr. Fred Gage; **3.17:** From R. Cabeza, et al., "Age-related; differences in neural activity during memory encoding and retrieval: A positron emission tomography study" in *Journal of Neuroscience,* 17, 391-400, 1997; **3.18 (top & bottom):** © James Balog; **p. 118:** © Richard Hutchings/Photo Edit; **p. 120:** © AP/Wide World Photos; **p. 122:** © USA Today Library, Paul Wiseman, photographer. Reprinted with permission; **3.22:** Courtesy of Dr. Jerry Shay

Chapter 4

Opener: © Peter Correz/Stone/Getty Images; **p. 133 (top):** © George V. Mann, M.D.; **p. 133 (bottom):** © David Stoecklein/The Stock Market; **p. 135:** Courtesy of The Hawaii Family Support Center, Healthy Start Program; **4.3 (top & bottom):** © Alfred Pasieka/Science Photo Library/Photo Researchers; **p. 141:** Courtesy of Ellen Langer; **p. 143:** © Bruce McAllister/Image Works; **p. 144:** © Bob Dammrich/The Image Works; **p. 147:** © Tony Freeman/Photo Edit; **4.10:** Courtesy of Colin M. Bloor; **p. 153:** © PhotoDisc Vol. 70/Getty Images

Chapter 5

Opener: © Ariel Skelley/The Stock Market/CORBIS; **p. 167:** Courtesy of Esther Thelen; **5.2 (left & right):** © Dr. Karen Adolph, New York University; **p. 172 (left):** © Michael Greenlar/The Image Works; **p. 172 (right):** © Frank Baily Studios; **p. 175:** © Frederick Reglain/Liaison International/Gamma; **p. 177:** © Eyewire Vol. EP078 /Getty Images; **5.5:** © David Linton; **5.7:** Courtesy of Dr. Charles Nelson; **5.9:** © Enrico Ferorelli; **5.10:** © Dr. Bruce Hood, University of Bristol, England; **5.12 (left):** © Michael Siluk; **5.12 (right):** © Dr. Melanie Spence, University of Texas at Dallas; **5.14:** © Jean Guichard/Sygma/CORBIS; **5.15:** From D. Rosenstein and H. Oster "Differential Facial Responses to Four Basic Tastes in New-

borns," *Child Development,* Vol. 59, 1988. © Society for Research in Child Development, Inc.

Chapter 6

Opener: © Rick Gomez/The Stock Market/CORBIS; **p. 200:** © Archives Jean Piaget, Universite De Geneve, Switzerland; **6.3 (left & right):** © Doug Goodman/Photo Researchers; **6.7:** © Paul Fusco/Magnum Photos; **p. 212:** © Sean Sprague/Impact Visuals; **p. 215:** © Stewart Cohen/Stone/Getty Images; **p. 219 (left):** © James Wertsch/Washington University; **p. 219 (right):** © Elizabeth Crews/The Image Works; **p. 222:** Courtesy of Barbara Rogoff; **6.11 (left):** A. R. Lauria/Dr. Michael Cole, Laboratory of Human Cognition, University of California, San Diego; **6.11 (right):** © Bettmann/CORBIS; **p. 224:** © Jim Pickerell/Stock Boston

Chapter 7

Opener: © Don Mason/The Stock Market/CORBIS; **7.6:** Courtesy of Dr. Carolyn Rovee-Collier; **p. 244:** © 1999 James Kamp; **p. 258:** Courtesy of Judy DeLoache; **p. 259:** © Reuters Newmedia Inc/CORBIS; **p. 260:** Courtesy of Dr. Sherry Willis

Chapter 8

Opener: © Billy Hustace/Stone/Getty Images; **p. 271:** National Library of Medicine; **p. 276:** © Project Spectrum; **p. 288:** John Santrock; **p. 291:** © Elizabeth Crews; **p. 292:** © Jill Cannefax/EKM-Nepenthe/Coyote Crossings, Inc; **p. 293:** © Koichi Kamoshida/Newsmakers/Getty Images News Service; **p. 295 (left):** AP/Wide World Photos; **p. 295 (middle):** Courtesy Nina Holton; **p. 295 (right):** Courtesy of Jim Cox/The Salk Institute; **p. 296:** Courtesy Mihaly Csikszentmihalyi

Chapter 9

Opener: © Anne Rippy/The Image Bank/Getty Images; **9.2:** © 2003 University of Washington, Institute for Learning and Brain Sciences (I-LABS); **p. 309:** © ABPL Image Library/Animals Animals/Earth Scenes; **p. 319:** © Tim Davis/CORBIS; **p. 320:** © AFP/CORBIS; **p. 321:** From Curtis, *Genie: A Psycholinguistic Study of a Modern Day "Wild Child."* © 1977 Academic Press reproduced by permission of the publisher; **p. 322:** © John Carter/Photo Researchers

Chapter 10

Opener: © Latin Stock/The Stock Market/CORBIS; **10.2 (all):** © Michael Lewis, Institute for the Study of Child Development; **10.4:** © Michael Lewis, Institute for the Study of Child Development; **p. 345:** © Michel Tcherevkoff/The Image Bank/Getty Images; **p. 347:** © Judith Oddie/Photo Edit; **p. 349:** © Martin Rogers/Stock Boston; **10.11:** © Daniel Grogan; **p. 352:** © Penny Tweedie/Stone/Getty Images

Chapter 11

Opener: Artwork by Tom Stilitz, reprinted permission of the Decade of Behavior; **p. 369:** © Myrleen Ferguson Cate/Photo Edit; **11.5 (25 yrs.):** © Eyewire/Getty Images website; **11.5 (35 yrs.):** © PhotoDisc/Getty Images website;

11.5 (55 yrs.): © Corbis website; **11.5 (70 yrs.):** © PhotoDisc website; **11.5 (85 yrs.):** © Vol. 34/CORBIS; **p. 387:** © USA Today Library, Photo by Robert Duetsch. Reprinted with permission; **11.11 (top):** © CORBIS website; **11.11 (middle):** © Eyewire/Getty website; **11.11 (bottom):** © Vol. 67/PhotoDisc

Chapter 12

Opener: © Ranald Mackechnie/Stone/Getty Images; **p. 407:** © Digital Stock; **p. 410:** © Catherine Gehm; **p. 416:** © Shooting Star; **p. 417:** © G. Wayne Floyd/Unicorn Stock Photos; **p. 420:** © Barry O'Rourke/The Stock Market/CORBIS; **p. 428:** © Marilyn Humphries; **p. 429:** © Lawrence Migdale/Stock Boston; **p. 432:** © 1998 Frank Fournier

Chapter 13

Opener: © Nevada Wier/The Image Bank/Getty Images; **p. 448:** © David Frazier Photo Library, Inc.; **p. 449:** Courtesy of Carol Gilligan; **p. 457:** © Ronald Cortes; **p. 462:** © Mark Richards/Photo Edit; **p. 463:** © Charlie Neuman/SDUT/Zuma; **p. 465:** © Penny Tweedie/Stone/Getty Images; **p. 469:** © Paul Chesley/Stone/Getty Images; **p. 472:** © Bryan F. Peterson/The Stock Market/CORBIS

Chapter 14

Opener: © Ariel Skelley/The Stock Market/CORBIS; **p. 489 (top):** © Explorer/J.P. Nacivet/Photo Researchers; **p. 489 (bottom):** © Dean Press Images/Image Works; **p. 491:** © Ronald Mackechnic/Stone/Getty Images; **p. 495:** © S. Gazin/The Image Works; **14.7:** © Peter Correz/Stone/Getty Images; **14.9:** © Spencer Grant/Photo Edit; **p. 511:** © Christopher Arnesen/Stone/Getty Images; **p. 514:** © William Hubbell/Woodfin Camp & Associates

Chapter 15

Opener: © George Disanio/The Stock Market/CORBIS; **p. 530:** © Roy Morsch/The Stock Market/CORBIS; **p. 535:** © Richard Hutchings/Photo Edit; **p. 544:** © Marjorie Shostak/Anthro Photo; **p. 545:** © Suzi Moore-McGregor/Woodfin Camp & Associates; **p. 547:** © USA Today Library, photo by H. Darr Beiser. Reprinted with permission

Chapter 16

Opener: © Paul Barton/The Stock Market/CORBIS; **p. 565:** © Reggio Children; **p. 566:** © David DeLossy/The Image Bank/Getty Images; **p. 568:** © Mark Antman/The Image Works; **p. 570:** © H. Yamaguchi/Gamma; **571:** © Blair Seitz/Photo Researchers; **p. 575:** © Will McIntyre/Photo Researchers; **p. 577:** © John S. Abbott; **p. 591:** © Greg Sailor

Chapter 17

Opener: © Stan Honda/AP Wide World Photos; **p. 602:** © Herb Snitzer/Stock Boston; **p. 603:** © The Detroit News; **p. 606:** © Patrick Ward/Stock Boston; **17.3:** © Eastcott Momatinck/Image Works; **p. 616:** © Phyllis Picarci/Image State; **p. 618:** © Jennifer S. Altman; **p. 619:** © AP/Wide World Photos; **p. 620:** © Hermine Dreyfuss

Name Index

H

I

L

Subject Index

T